Guide to Canadian English Usage

Margery Fee and Janice McAlpine

Strathy Language Unit
Queen's University

Toronto   New York   Oxford
Oxford University Press
1997

To our families

Oxford University Press
70 Wynford Drive, Don Mills, Ontario M3C 1J9

Oxford   New York
Athens   Auckland   Bangkok   Mumbai
Calcutta   Cape Town   Dar es Salaam   Delhi
Florence   Hong Kong   Istanbul   Karachi
Kuala Lumpur   Chennai   Madrid   Melbourne
Mexico City   Nairobi   Paris   Singapore
Taipei   Tokyo   Toronto   Warsaw

and associated companies in
Berlin   Ibadan

Oxford is a trade mark of Oxford University Press

Canadian Cataloguing in Publication Data

Fee, Margery, 1948–
  Guide to Canadian English usage

Includes index.
ISBN 0-19-540841-1

1. English language – Canada – Usage.   2. Canadianisms
(English) – Dictionaries.*   3. English language –
Canada – Dictionaries.   I. McAlpine, Janice.   II. Title.

PE3235.F44 1997   428'.00971'03   C97-931121-7

Contents

Acknowledgements   iv
Introduction   v
Notes on Format   xvi
Sources   xvii
Works Consulted   xxiii

Usage Guide   1
Appendix I   534
Appendix II   535

Glossary   536
Index   542

Acknowledgements

A great many people and organizations provided funding, moral support, advice, and information—so many that we cannot name them all. We could not have accomplished such a large and varied project without them, however, and we are most grateful. The mistakes and inaccuracies that remain, which we hope are few, are ours.

We gratefully acknowledge the help of the following:
J.R. Strathy, whose generous bequest has funded the project since 1982 and will provide for regular revision;

The Department of English and the Faculty of Arts at Queen's University, many of whose members have devoted time and energy to the Strathy Language Unit, particularly George M. Logan; thanks are also due to Stella Gartland, Roberta Hamilton, Peter Sabor, Paul Stevens, and Laureen Snider;

The first director of the Strathy Language Unit, W.C. Lougheed, and Duncan Robertson, the late Helen MacDonald, and Phillip W. Rogers, for laying the foundations of the project;

The Social Sciences and Humanities Research Council of Canada, whose Major Research Grant supported much of the work on the guide, 1989–92;

The Advisory Committee of the Strathy Language Unit: J.K. Chambers (University of Toronto), Sandra Clarke (Memorial University of Newfoundland), the late A.M. Kinloch (University of New Brunswick), Leslie Monkman (Queen's University), T.K. Pratt (University of Prince Edward Island), D.O. Spettigue (Queen's University), and the late H.J. Warkentyne (University of Victoria);

Michael Morrow and E.S.C. Weiner (Oxford University Press, UK), and Katherine Barber (Oxford University Press Canada); Laurel Brinton (University of British Columbia), Pam Peters (Macquarie University, Australia), Lil Rodman (University of British Columbia), and Patricia A. Shaw (University of British Columbia) for advice on particular entries; and Charlotte Fee, for proof-reading;

All the authors and publishers who allowed their works to be copied into the Strathy Corpus of Canadian English; InfoGlobe and Dennis Ablett of Southam Electronic Publishing, who provided CD-ROMs for the project.

Production of the Guide and Corpus
Administration and copy coordination: Linda Garrison.

Research and writing: Carla Douglas, Sue Dreier, Susan Fisher, Peter Lapp, Heather McKend, Irwin Streight, Sandra Terry, Kathy Vanderlinden.

Assistance with scanning and editing corpus texts, checking quotations, proof-reading: Dorothy Adero, Anne Archer, Katie Baldwin, Jeffrey Bratt, Melanie Clare, Terri Gurnsey, Bonnie Hall, Robert Inkoom, Patricia Marois, Shuguang Qi, Tammy Reinhardt, Kurt Reinhardt, Jennifer Tinline.

We are also greatly indebted to Sally Livingston, whose editorial skills contributed immeasurably to the final form of the book.

Introduction

'Spelling flame' is a new term for an old phenomenon: outraged arguments about correct language usage. When someone criticizes the spelling or grammar, rather than the argument, of another participant in a discussion group on the Internet, the resulting torrent of acrimonious messages—the spelling flame—often derails the original discussion completely. One reason for the strong emotions that swirl around language use, even in the age of spell-checkers, is that people feel their identity is reflected in their language.

Lynn Johnston, whose cartoon strip *For Better or for Worse* is syndicated all over North America, has never pretended that the family she depicts lives south of the border: 'I refuse to spell *racquet* as *racket*. I want it to be Canadian' ('Michael Goes to Western'). In Margaret Laurence's novel *The Diviners*, Morag's daughter Piquette asks, 'Are there coyotes in these woods, Mum?' The answer is delivered 'with ludicrous pride and snappishness': '*We* say *kiy*-oot,' Morag replies, 'Only John Wayne says coy-*oh*-tee' (Laurence, 416). When Margaret Atwood received a medal recently in New York, Robert MacNeil (co-author of *The Story of English*), said as he introduced her: 'She makes me feel my Canadianness. . . . Her characters misbehave on chesterfields, not sofas.'[1] Here spelling, pronunciation, and word choice are all attached to national identity and seen as distinctively Canadian. Perhaps Canadians are particularly snappish about these issues because other people—even many Canadians—assume that their English is identical to American English.[2]

In fact, it is not: Canadian English is a variety of English in its own right. In the past, however, Canadians seeking information or advice on their language had to look to either British or American dictionaries and usage guides, neither of which reflected the distinctiveness of Canadian English. The *Guide to Canadian English Usage* differs from those other usage guides in two important ways: its comments and advice are based on evidence drawn from a corpus of 12 million words of contemporary Canadian writing, supplemented by some 650 million words of Canadian newspaper and magazine text,[3] and it is written from a Canadian perspective.

The idea of using evidence drawn from published writing is far from new in lexicography. Samuel Johnson used 114,000 quotations to support his definitions (Bryson, 154; see also Reddick). When James A.H. Murray was made editor of what was to become the *Oxford English Dictionary* (*OED*) in 1879, he inherited a huge pile of slips of paper, each bearing a quotation illustrating the use of an English word (Murray, 139), and the first edition of the *OED* contained 1,827,306 illustrative quotations (Willinsky, 50). Philip Gove, editor of *Merriam-Webster's Third New International Dictionary* (1961) inherited a collection of over one and a half million citation slips (Morton, 95), and his completed dictionary contained over 100,000 quotations, with an equal number of verbal illustrations (Morton, 101).

The principle that generalizations about the usage of words should be based on evidence was followed by H.W. Fowler and his brother F.G. Fowler in their first book on usage, *The King's English*, published in 1906. H.W. Fowler's name became synonymous with correct usage as his *Modern English Usage*, first published in 1926, went into printing after printing. Although certainly not above displays of arbitrary personal opinion (if the opinion of someone with such a formidable intellect can ever be described as arbitrary), Fowler frequently quoted examples gleaned from newspapers and supported his points with citations from the *OED*. Subsequent usage commentators have often been far more indebted to the *OED*, Fowler, and *Webster's Third* than they can bring themselves to reveal. Indeed, those without a collection of examples often purvey a set of prescriptions based on personal opinion cobbled together with ideas lifted from the works of their predecessors.

When J.R. Strathy left the Department of English at Queen's University an endowment to promote the use of correct English in Canada and to produce a usage guide for Canadians, the computer corpus was a fairly new research tool for language study. Strathy's generosity permitted W.C. Lougheed, who became the first director of the Strathy Language Unit in 1981, to invest in equipment and begin to compile the computer equivalent of Murray's millions of paper slips.[4] At that time the model for language corpora was the Brown Corpus, a one-million-word database compiled at Brown University by W. Nelson Francis and Henry Kučera. It consisted of 2000-word samples randomly selected from texts, all published in 1961, of different genres (fiction, history, literary criticism, science, etc.), different degrees of formality (popular magazines and books, newspapers, academic articles and books), and different styles. By the time collection for the Strathy Corpus began, advances in computer technology had made it possible to store much larger samples. The Strathy Corpus of Canadian English currently contains 12 million words of complete texts (rather than 2000-word samples) based on the categories used for the Brown Corpus but with the addition to its subject categories of feminism and computing. The use of the Brown Corpus as a model ensures a variety of genres, subject matter, contexts, styles, and degrees of formality.[5] The Strathy Corpus has been supplemented by CD-ROMs containing some 600 million words of newspaper text from across Canada and 50 million words of the newsmagazine *Maclean's* (March 1988–Dec. 1991). This corpus allowed us to check our initial list of usage problems, compiled from a wide range of usage guides, old and new, against actual usage. (In addition, a few examples were selected from sources not in the database: these sources are noted on pp. xvii–xxii.)

No clear definition of a 'usage problem' is possible, because usage problems are so various and because different usage guides cover different issues. We have excluded from this guide most of the issues that could be resolved by looking at a good desk dictionary, but many dictionaries are weak on matters of specifically Canadian interest; thus we have included a few 'dictionary' entries on items of this kind.[6] In addition we have included entries on a number of questions that might be answered by looking at a dictionary, because our evidence suggests that writers generally don't bother to look these particular items up. We have not included information that is more usefully found in an encyclopedia, except where it is necessary in explaining a usage issue. Nor do we address the many issues of written convention that are normally covered in book publishers' or newspaper style guides, although we do discuss such broad issues as capitalization and punctuation. Finally, like most usage guides, this one is designed for readers for whom English is either a first language or a language in which they have been educated: issues unlikely to trouble the fluent speaker are not discussed.

The pronunciations given here are mainly for rare words or those that are sometimes pronounced in ways stigmatized as non-standard, dialectal, or 'un-Canadian'. Here we must point out that the information available on the norms of Canadian pronunciation is limited. Only R.J. Gregg's sociolinguistic survey of 300 Vancouver English-speakers and H.B. Woods' survey of 100 Ottawa English-speakers can be called comprehensive, and we cannot assume that the pronunciations common in Vancouver and Ottawa are necessarily the most common ones across the country. Although we relied on Canadian sources where we could, sometimes our suggested pronunciations are based on less than solid evidence. We hope that in future revisions of this guide our ability to describe Canadian pronunciation will have improved.

In checking the usage problems discussed in other guides against our corpus, we discovered that some supposed problems in fact caused writers no trouble at all; these we usually dropped from our list. We also discovered some problems we hadn't expected to find; these were added. Sometimes we found that a well-known usage 'rule' was consistently 'broken' by most writers, including the famous and the well-educated, and these we retained for discussion. The words 'rule' and 'broken' are enclosed in quotation marks here because, although there are rules of grammar that are followed without difficulty by all adult native speakers, whatever their education, the reason that most of the issues addressed by usage guides have become topics is, in fact, that no clear 'rules' exist to deal with them: they are issues with which educated writers may have trouble or where usage is a matter of debate. Many questions arise in areas where change is occurring in speech; since writing is usually more public and more formal, the conventions surrounding it are far slower to shift.

That some usage distinctions are not followed, however, even by well-known writers, does not mean that those who believe strongly in them can simply be ignored. 'The CBC Language Guide' (a database that provides pronunciation advice for CBC radio and television announcers), *The Globe and Mail Style Book*, and *The Canadian Press Stylebook* all make it clear that listeners and readers frequently react so strongly to what they consider sloppy or incorrect use of language that they write, fax, e-mail, and phone their objections directly to the source. Debates about usage, often highly combative, are a staple of Letters to the Editor pages. In other words, beliefs about the 'correct' use of language do have a social reality. Most people who work with words, written or spoken, can remember motions overturned or proposals condemned because of disputes over usage. It is all very well to say that the 'rule' about split infinitives is nonsensical because it is based on a faulty analogy with the Latin infinitive, which can't be split because it is a single word. But if your employer or English professor believes that split infinitives are not acceptable, you may suffer the consequences. And even in less crucial circumstances, there is no point in distracting readers: they should be thinking about your argument rather than reacting against your usage. A writer who follows convention may be more persuasive, more credible, and more easily understood than one who flouts it. Yet as the entries in this guide reveal, there are few, if any, usage 'rules' that are consistently followed by professional writers. Usage conventions arise precisely in areas where choice is possible, and though usage guides are expected to approve one choice as 'correct' and the others as 'incorrect', sloppy, or vulgar, this guide—perhaps to the frustration of some readers—is more likely to lay out the possibilities and to discuss the contexts where different choices might be effective.

The history of canonical usage items, such as the split infinitive, is treated comprehensively by *Webster's Dictionary of English Usage*, which tracks down the origins of particular strictures in old guides and manuals and places them in the context of actual contemporary usage. The condemnation of the 'double negative', for example, began with the English grammarian Robert Lowth in 1762; the condemnation of *hopefully* as a sentence adverb (as in 'Hopefully, we will win') can be traced back only to 1964—because, apparently, it was rarely used in this way before the 1960s.

Sometimes, as in the case of *hopefully*, a usage is condemned simply because it is new. Although *hopefully* is only one of a large group of words used in much the same way (e.g. *curiously, admittedly, happily, mercifully*), it is the one that has been singled out for attention. Sidney Greenbaum, in *Good English and the Grammarian*, quotes several extremely negative comments about this use of *hopefully* from the *Harper Dictionary of Contemporary Usage* (e.g., 'It is barbaric, illiterate, offensive, damnable, and inexcusable') and remarks: 'most of us would agree that their vehemence is disproportionate to the offence' (11). The vehemence appears to originate in the fear that a whole set of values, including what is often called 'respect for the language', is in danger. Lapses in usage provide social commentators with what they see as symptoms of a wide range of moral failings.

This use of language as a moral barometer dates to the eighteenth century, when English was being standardized by grammars and dictionaries. In *From Old English to Standard English*, Dennis Freeborn notes that 'the contrasts between the *refined* language of the classically educated class and the *vulgar* language of the common people' were believed to mirror 'equal differences in intellectual capabilities, and also in virtue or morality' (191). Thus several petitions to Parliament, calling for electoral reform, were rejected on the grounds that their language was insufficiently 'decent and respectful' (191). Objections to language usage often camouflage judgments based on class, ethnicity, or political affiliation.

Every generation believes, it seems, that English is going downhill, that younger speakers and writers are careless with words, and that the result can only be bad. As Tony Crowley points out in *Standard English and the Politics of Language*, those who promote 'such reactionary nostalgia' do so in order to 'berate whatever it is at present that they find unpalatable' (272). James Sledd and Wilma R. Ebbitt, in *Dictionaries and That Dictionary*, collected a set of readings on the mixed reception of *Webster's Third New International Dictionary*, published in 1961. Most of the attacks on this dictionary were directed at the decision to reduce the number of usage labels, such as 'slang' and 'vulgar', and to use quotations from the speech of ordinary Americans to support its definitions. Herbert C. Morton's book on this controversy situates the battle in the Cold War polemics of the time. Philip B. Gove, the editor of *Webster's Third*, commented: 'There's no divine sanction in language. It's an instrument of the people who use it' (Sledd and Ebbitt, 57). Many reviewers and editorialists (including some in Canada) responded as if Gove had declared himself a godless Communist, ready to lead the masses into revolution against sacred traditions.

What these reviewers and editorialists didn't realize is that usage shifts in every generation, so that anyone reaching forty will likely notice that the following generation is using unfamiliar words and expressions, or using old ones in new ways. Many words and usages once condemned as unacceptable are now part of the general vocabulary, while other perfectly acceptable expressions have fallen out of use. Jean Aitchison concludes in *Language Change: Progress or Decay?* that although language changes all the time, 'there is no evidence that language is either progressing or decaying' (221).

Even Fowler (625) was well aware of the inevitability of language change:

> What grammarians say should be has perhaps less influence on what shall be than even the more modest of them realize; usage evolves itself undisturbed by their likes and dislikes. And yet the temptation to show how better use might have been made of the material to hand is sometimes irresistible.

These remarks come from Fowler's entry on 'that/which', where he admits he is making a distinction that (which?) many writers do not follow.

But this brings us to one of the most controversial questions raised by differences in usage. If even Fowler admits that usage produces conventions, not the other way around, who decides what is acceptable? If we find that a usage described by many commentators as unacceptable or even incorrect is widespread—and not just in the much-maligned sports pages, but in news, editorials, books, and magazines—and we describe it as acceptable, those who have been taught something different will simply see us as wrong. So we make it clear that no one need abandon a cherished distinction just because the majority has: what those who hold fast to such distinctions should not do, however, is berate others for sloppy usage and set themselves up as experts.

But, this group may reply, surely professional writers, English teachers, and other experts on language can provide the best guidance on how English should be used. And some dictionaries and guides do rely on the opinions of a 'usage panel' of professors and professional writers (for example, the *American Heritage Dictionary* and its companion usage guide, the *Harper Dictionary of Contemporary Usage*). However, as Thomas Creswell's *Usage in Dictionaries and Dictionaries of Usage* points out, dictionaries, usage guides, and usage panels rarely agree on how objectionable certain usages are, why certain usages are problematic, or even which usages constitute problems. Walter E. Meyers compared the usage glossaries of 50 American handbooks of freshman composition published from 1980 to 1990. He found that even the best of them were 'out-of-date, constricted by obsolete theories, and intensely derivative' (343); and almost half of all the items discussed in the 50 books appeared in only one glossary. This 'should warn us,' Meyers concludes, 'that glossaries of usage reflect mainly the personal quirks and crochets of the compilers' (342). If even the experts disagree, how useful are their opinions? The temptation is to define as expert those who agree on a specific set of 'correct' usages. But the studies done by Creswell and others show that in fact this definition would not identify the best educated, the most professional, or the most acclaimed writers. If a standard of correct usage excludes a large percentage of writers whose words appear before the public weekly, daily, and even hourly, whose books appear on bestseller lists or win prizes, what is the point of defining their usage as unacceptable? Unacceptable to whom? Only to a small group of self-constituted language experts. And we know that, as Fowler said, what becomes standard usage does not depend on what experts think, but on what becomes standard usage.

A favourite pastime of language experts is to catch their colleagues breaking their own 'rules': Bill Bryson, in *The Mother Tongue: English and How It Got that Way*, offers many examples of slips by such luminaries as Fowler, Robert Burchfield (editor of the supplements to the *OED* and *The New Fowler's Modern English Usage*), and Robert McCrum (one of the authors of *The Story of English*, which accompanied a popular

BBC-TV series on English). His point is that language changes and that the opinions of experts often bear little or no relation to actual contemporary usage—even their own. So experts on usage do not even practise what they preach, and many of their favourite strictures are simply rendered irrelevant by language change. Steven Pinker's comment on these experts is the vehement response of the linguist to the popular 'language experts' or what he calls, following William Safire, 'language mavens':

> Most of the prescriptive rules of the language mavens make no sense on any level. They are bits of folklore that originated for screwball reasons several hundred years ago and have perpetuated themselves ever since. For as long as they have existed, speakers have flouted them, spawning identical plaints about the imminent decline of the language century after century. All the best writers in English at all periods, including Shakespeare and most of the mavens themselves, have been among the flagrant flouters (373).

Well then. Does all this mean that anything goes? Absolutely not. There are language norms that can be discovered by looking at real language. Speakers and writers know that adhering to the language norms of particular social groups or genres of writing is important if their work is to be found acceptable by the audiences it is intended for. If, as Pinker suggests, usage 'rules' serve 'as shibboleths, differentiating the elite from the rabble' (374), those who wish to speak to the elite must take them into account. Usage guides in the computer age, however, will have to present more information than they did in the past. They will have to tell their readers not only what previous guides have said, but also what relation those commentaries bear to actual usage. The result is an attempt both to describe and to advise, in such a way as to make it clear to readers that both the description and the advice may well be quite different in the next edition of the guide. Now that computers permit us to tap into large quantities of language and catch it in the act of change—something that was impossible until the late 1980s—we cannot pretend that what usage guides often refer to as 'careful writers' all write alike, or that they all write the same way decade after decade. Thus we have decided that while a usage guide should provide advice (that's why people buy guides), it should also present enough information for readers to make up their own minds about particular issues.

What makes this guide Canadian? It is written from a Canadian perspective: it is not intended primarily for American or British readers, with a few Canadian entries tacked on. At times, of course, Canadian usage is quite like either American or British usage, or both. But this does not mean that Canadian usage is simply whatever can be clearly distinguished from the other two. Canadian usage includes all the ways in which English is used in Canada—it is not just a footnote to the ways English is used in other places. Much debate has taken place over whether Canadian English is a branch of American English or a branch of British English. This model, which parallels the model of imperial centre and colonial periphery, has recently been replaced by one that treats all varieties of English used at a national level as equal and therefore as producing their own standards, rather than deriving them from British English. Even regional varieties of English are seen as producing standards (see, for example, the entry on Quebec English). English, then, no longer 'belongs' to the English but, as Sidney Greenbaum points out in 'Whose English?', is now claimed as well by the much larger group of first-language English-speakers outside Great Britain.

However, this is not to say that one can ignore the strong influence of British and American English in Canada, often resulting from the way textbooks and dictionaries have been used in schools (which varies from province to province). Canadians inherit a strong British tradition, particularly in government, law, the military, education, and publishing, yet at the same time are heavily influenced by American media and American ideas in all fields of knowledge. In fact, Canadian usage is marked by its frequent retention of both 'British' and 'American' spellings, punctuation conventions, and diction, and therefore Canadians have a larger number of variants to argue about (is it *honour* or *honor*? do you protest something or protest *against* something? should you pronounce *hostile* to rhyme with *reptile* or *hostel*?)

A further complication arises if we imply that the Canadian writing in our database is Canadian in some definitive sense. Even though the texts in our primary database were published in Canada, and even though we have attempted to ensure that they were written by Canadians, what emerges at the end of the publication process does not necessarily reflect the writer's own usage. Publishers vary in their choice of style guides and dictionaries, and copy editors are not necessarily Canadian. Much of the material in newspapers comes from foreign wire services. Although we have tried to exclude material that is obviously *not* Canadian, we have no way of knowing where most of the writers in the database were born or educated: Canadian magazines, journals, and newspapers routinely publish work by writers from outside Canada. And even those who were educated in Canada read and hear English from outside Canada's borders every day of their lives. As I.W.V. Pringle points out, 'to include everything [as Canadian English] to which one has access in Canada is obviously too broad, but to restrict oneself to the English of Canadians born and bred is certainly too narrow' (27). If Canadians are concerned about the distinctiveness of things Canadian, including Canadian English, it is in part because approximately 20 million English-speaking Canadians live next door to some 275 million English-speaking Americans: hence the constant fear that Canadian English, along with the rest of English-Canadian culture, will disappear under the onslaught of American culture. Thus one often finds a particular spelling or pronunciation or usage touted as 'the' Canadian spelling, pronunciation, or usage, with the implication that those who don't adhere to it are disloyal sell-outs. Nevertheless, the feature that may be most distinctive about Canadian English writers and readers is their calm acceptance, even in the same sentence, of both American and British forms. *Editing Canadian English* (Burton et al.), a guide for Canadian book editors, points out that many Canadian writers and editors use both *-re* spellings (*centre, theatre, metre*, etc.) and -or spellings (*honor, glamor*, etc.), even though the former are classified as British and the latter as American. After recommending that editors not mix *within* a category (i.e., if you write *honour*, then you should also write *glamour*), they conclude: 'it seems that mixing *between* categories not only is acceptable, but may well constitute the "Canadian style"' (7). This conclusion may be deeply shocking to the many people who believe that, say, only British spellings are truly Canadian, or that the CBC's pronunciation of a word should set the Canadian standard. The idea that there is only one way to write or speak that can be called Canadian derives from a wider attitude that has been called the 'myth of uniform correctness'. This is the belief that where two or more ways of spelling, pronouncing, or using a word exist, only one can be correct. In fact, several variants, all quite acceptable, often coexist in standard Englishes.

The compilers of the Strathy Corpus took care to ensure variety both of style and of levels of formality by including published books, journals, magazines, and newspapers. Because the time and effort taken by writers and editors before publication vary greatly, with books usually receiving the most editorial attention and newspapers the least, the latter often serve as a good source of bad examples. Perhaps for this reason, or because of the informality of newspaper writing, usage writers routinely attack the English found in newspapers. However, it must be remembered that informal English is still standard English, and a writer who cannot vary his or her style from formal to informal cannot really be considered competent. Journalists work to extremely tight deadlines, and their writing receives little or no editing, so it is hardly surprising that newspapers provide countless examples of questionable usage. Yet many of the best writers in the country write for newspapers, and newspaper style guides are clear evidence of journalists' desire to find answers to their questions about language. James Murray used quotations from newspapers in the *OED*, even though his advisers at Oxford objected, because often he could not otherwise give an account of the history of a word. He told the Philological Society in 1884 that he found the criticism of newspaper writing 'by far the silliest that the Dictionary has elicited' and looked to a future 'when this criticism will be pointed out as a most remarkable instance of the inability of men to acknowledge contemporary facts and read the signs of the times' (Murray, 223). In this guide too, the only examples we could find for certain usage items came from newspapers. In part this reflects the preponderance of newspaper text available to us. In addition, however, newspapers and newspaper style guides are always at the forefront in suggesting alternatives when particular groups of readers find certain usages offensive. (Wheelchair users don't like being described as 'wheelchair-bound' and astronauts who are also women don't like being called 'lady astronauts'.) Newspaper readers are quick to react, and since newspapers depend on subscriptions for their survival, they are far more likely than book publishers to be up-to-date on what is acceptable to their readers.

This last set of usage items, where usages that offend particular groups are being replaced by more acceptable terms, is finally more important than many others. As David Crystal points out in *Who Cares about English Usage?* (116):

> If by magic everyone were to stop using split infinitives tomorrow, what actually would have been achieved? My argument is: nothing—and something might even have been lost....On the other hand, certain usage topics have brought to light real problems of a linguistic or social kind where unthinking language can lead to misunderstanding, disaccord, open hostility. These matters are certainly worth getting upset about, for they affect the way we live.

We hope, then, that this guide will help writers communicate in ways that avoid causing confusion, annoyance, or offence; we also hope that if we ourselves confuse, annoy, or offend, our readers will be kind enough to let us know so that we may improve subsequent editions.

Margery Fee
University of British Columbia
April 1997

Notes

1. I thank Jack Chambers for this example.
2. For more on Canadian English, see Bailey and Görlach, and 'Canadian English' and related entries in McArthur.
3. Two important usage guides quote examples and draw conclusions from a corpus. Pam Peters' *Cambridge Australian English Style Guide* (Cambridge: Cambridge University Press, 1995) uses the one-million word Australian Corpus of English; and *Collins COBUILD English Usage* (London: HarperCollins, 1992), aimed mainly at speakers of English as a second language, is based on the Collins Birmingham University International Language Database, nearly 200 million words of spoken and written English. Other important guides use citations to exemplify their points, including *Webster's Dictionary of English Usage* (Springield, Mass.: Merriam-Webster, 1989) and *The Oxford Guide to English Usage* (2nd ed.), E.S.C. Weiner and Andrew Delahunty (Oxford: Clarendon Press, 1993). Note that the term *corpus* is used in linguistics and lexicography to refer to a set of data that has been carefully selected to reveal certain aspects of language. The main Strathy Corpus is based on such a selection, but since we are not performing statistical analyses, we have not attempted to ensure that each category is represented by an equal number of words. Any generalizations we made across genres were based on the Corpus alone, and did not include the 650 million extra words of newspaper and magazine text that we found a useful source of examples.
4. See W.C. Lougheed, 'Towards a National Corpus on a Micro', *Literary and Linguistic Computing* 2.4 (1987): 207–12.
5. The International Corpus of English project, originated by Sidney Greenbaum at University College, London, is producing a set of parallel million-word corpora of over twenty national varieties of world English, including Canadian English. The Canadian corpus is being compiled by a team led by Nancy Belmore of Concordia University. It contains samples of spoken and written English based on different criteria from the Brown Corpus categories, including samples of unpublished writing such as personal and business letters and student essays and examinations. See Greenbaum, 'ICE'.
6. Several dictionaries do cover Canadian English well, including two that appeared too recently to be included in our reference list below: the recently published *ITP Nelson Canadian Dictionary of the English Language* (Toronto: Nelson, 1996) and the revised and expanded *Gage Canadian Dictionary* (Toronto: Gage, 1997). *The Canadian Oxford Dictionary* is forthcoming in 1998.

Works Cited

Aitchison, Jean. *Language Change: Progress or Decay?* 2nd ed. Cambridge: Cambridge University Press, 1991.

Bailey, Richard W., and M. Görlach, eds. 'The English Language in Canada'. *English as a World Language*. Ann Arbor: University of Michigan Press, 1982: 134–76.

Bryson, Bill. *The Mother Tongue: English and How It Got that Way*. New York: Morrow, 1990.

Buckley, Peter, ed. *CP Stylebook: A Guide for Writers and Editors*. Rev. ed. Toronto: Canadian Press, 1993.

Burton, Lydia, et al. *Editing Canadian English*. Prepared for the Freelance Editors' Association of Canada. Vancouver: Douglas and McIntyre, 1987.

'The CBC Language Guide'. CBC, 1995. (Not commercially available.)

Creswell, Thomas J. *Usage in Dictionaries and Dictionaries of Usage*. Publications of the American Dialect Society, nos. 63–64. April–Nov. 1975.

Crowley, Tony. *Standard English and the Politics of Language*. Urbana: University of Illinois Press, 1990.

Crystal, David. *Who Cares about English Usage?* Harmondsworth, UK: Penguin, 1984.

Fowler, H.W. *Fowler's Dictionary of Modern English Usage*. 2nd ed. Ed. Ernest Gowers. Oxford: Oxford University Press, 1965.

Francis, W. Nelson, and Henry Kučera. *Frequency Analysis of English Usage: Lexicon and Grammar*. Boston: Houghton Mifflin, 1982.

Freeborn, Dennis. *From Old English to Standard English*. Ottawa: University of Ottawa Press, 1992.

Greenbaum, Sidney. *Good English and the Grammarian*. London: Longman, 1988.

———. 'ICE: The International Corpus of English'. *English Today* 28 (1991): 3–7.

———. 'Whose English?'. *The State of the Language*. Ed. Christopher Ricks and Leonard Michaels. Berkeley: University of California Press, 1990.

Gregg, R.J. 'An Urban Dialect Survey of the English Spoken in Vancouver: Final Report to the Social Sciences and Humanities Research Council'. Unpublished ms. 1984.

Laurence, Margaret. *The Diviners*. Toronto: McClelland and Stewart, Bantam, 1975.

McArthur, Tom, ed. *The Oxford Companion to the English Language*. Oxford: Oxford University Press, 1992.

McCrum, Robert, William Cran, and Robert MacNeil. *The Story of English*. London: Faber, BBC Publications, 1986.

McFarlane, J.A., and Warren Clements. *The Globe and Mail Style Book*. Rev. ed. Toronto: Globe and Mail, 1993.

Meyers, Walter E. 'Usage Glossaries in Current College Handbooks'. *American Speech* 66.4 (1991): 341–58.

'Michael Goes to Western'. *University Affairs*. Aug.–Sept. 1996: 5.

Morton, Herbert C. *The Story of Webster's Third: Philip Gove's Controversial Dictionary and Its Critics*. Cambridge: Cambridge University Press, 1994.

Murray, K.M. Elisabeth. *Caught in the Web of Words: James Murray and the Oxford English Dictionary*. Oxford: Oxford University Press, 1979.

Pinker, Steven. 'The Language Mavens'. *The Language Instinct: How the Mind Creates Language*. New York: HarperPerennial, 1995: 370–403.

Pringle, I.W.V. 'The Complexity of the Concept of Standard'. *In Search of the Standard in Canadian English*. Ed. W.C. Lougheed. Occasional Paper Number 1. Strathy Language Unit, Queen's University. Kingston: Strathy Language Unit, 1986.

Reddick, Allen. *The Making of Johnson's Dictionary, 1746–1773*. Cambridge: Cambridge University Press, 1990.

Sledd, James, and Wilma R. Ebbitt, eds. *Dictionaries and That Dictionary: A Casebook on the Aims of Lexicographers and the Targets of Reviewers*. Chicago: Scott Foresman, 1962.

Weiner, E.S.C., and Andrew Delahunty. *The Oxford Guide to English Usage*. Oxford: Clarendon Press, 1993.

Willinsky, John. *Empire of Words: The Reign of the OED*. Princeton, NJ: Princeton University Press, 1994.

Woods, H.B. 'A Socio-dialectology Survey of the English Spoken in Ottawa: A Study of Sociological Variation in Canadian English'. Ph.D. dissertation. University of British Columbia, 1979.

Notes on Format

The entries are in alphabetical order, with cross-references to related entries. A glossary at the back briefly explains specialized and grammatical terms used in the entries. The index includes only those items that do not appear in the cross-references or as main entry headings. If you can't find what you are looking for in the body of the book, please check the index.

Examples Although we do not always provide examples of correct usage, we have tried to find evidence that the problems under discussion do occur in Canadian writing. In some cases we were unable to find a published example of a particular problem, but retained the entry because we have encountered it in student papers. All quotations have been checked for accuracy. However, most newspaper text was available to us only in CD-ROM versions; quotations from newspapers have not been checked against the published copy. Occasionally a quotation that beautifully illustrated the issue in question contained other usages (usually of punctuation, hyphenation, or capitalization) that did not conform to our recommendations in other entries; in these cases we have silently edited the quotation. That is, to avoid confusion, we have revised minor features of some quotations, but never the features under specific discussion in a particular entry. These features are always quoted accurately and, if they do not accord with our recommendations, the problems are noted in the comments directly after the quotation. The complete list of example sources can be found on p. xvii.

Newspapers Since newspapers rarely use accents or italics, we do not comment on the absence of these features in examples taken from newspapers, even though in other kinds of writing they might be recommended. Note also that, although levels of formality may vary widely even within a single newspaper, we usually regard newspaper style as informal, and comment accordingly.

Pronunciations Our decision to represent pronunciation by spelling out the sounds, rather than using the International Phonetic Alphabet, is inconsistent with the practice of major dictionaries. However, many people find using this alphabet difficult, particularly since stress is marked differently from dictionary to dictionary. We mark stress by using capital letters; for example, the pronunciation for *artiste* is given as *ar TEEST*.

Brackets Brackets around a word or phrase in a heading or cross-reference (e.g., [predominately]) indicate that it is non-standard.

Sources

The Strathy Corpus of Canadian English contains approximately 12 million words of published Canadian English. All the books, magazines, journals, and newspapers that make up the Corpus are listed below. Publications from which we have drawn examples but that are not part of the Corpus are marked with asterisks.

BOOKS

Atwood, Margaret. *Life Before Man*. Toronto: McClelland and Stewart, 1979.

———. *Second Words: Selected Critical Prose*. Toronto: Anansi, 1982.

*Ballstadt, Carl, ed. *The Search for English Canadian Literature*. Toronto: University of Toronto Press, 1975.

Batten, Jack. *Robinette: The Dean of Canadian Lawyers*. Toronto: Macmillan, 1984.

Bell, David V.J. *The Roots of Disunity: A Study of Canadian Political Culture*. Rev. ed. Toronto: Oxford University Press, 1992.

Beresford-Howe, Constance. *Night Studies*. Toronto: Macmillan, 1985.

Berton, Pierre. *The Promised Land: Settling the West, 1896–1914*. Toronto: McClelland and Stewart, 1984.

Bone, Robert M. *The Geography of the Canadian North*. Toronto: Oxford University Press, 1992.

Braithwaite, Max. *The Night We Stole the Mountie's Car*. Toronto: McClelland and Stewart, 1971.

Brodie, Janine, Shelley A.M. Gavigan, and Jane Jenson. *The Politics of Abortion*. Toronto: Oxford University Press, 1992.

Chambers, Jack. *Milestones I: The Music and Times of Miles Davis to 1960*. Toronto: University of Toronto Press, 1983.

Cheetham, Mark A., with Linda Hutcheon. *Remembering Postmodernism: Trends in Recent Canadian Art*. Toronto: Oxford University Press, 1991.

*Clarke, George Elliott. *Fire on the Water: An Anthology of Black Nova Scotian Writing*. Potter's Lane, NS: Pottersfield, 1991.

Clement, Wallace, and Glen Williams, eds. *The New Canadian Political Economy*. Kingston, ON: McGill-Queen's University Press, 1989. (One chapter.)

*Colombo, John Robert. *Dictionary of Canadian Quotations*. Don Mills, ON: Stoddart, 1991.

Cuneo, Carl J. *Pay Equity: The Labour-Feminist Challenge*. Toronto: Oxford University Press, 1990.

Davies, Richard, and Glen Kirkland, eds. *Dimensions*. Toronto: Gage, 1986. (Canadian selections.)

Davies, Robertson. *A Voice from the Attic*. Toronto: McClelland and Stewart, 1960.

———. *One Half of Robertson Davies*. New York: Penguin, 1978.

Davis, Ann. *Somewhere Waiting: The Life and Art of Christiane Pflug*. Toronto: Oxford University Press, 1991.

Dickinson, Terence. *Halley's Comet: A Mysterious Visitor from Outer Space*. Barrington, NJ: Edmund Scientific, 1985.

Dryden, Ken. *The Game*. Toronto: Macmillan, 1983.

Engel, Howard. *Murder Sees the Light*. New York: Penguin, 1984.

Forsey, Eugene. *A Life on the Fringe: The Memoirs of Eugene Forsey*. Toronto: Oxford University Press, 1990.

Frye, Northrop. *The Bush Garden: Essays on the Canadian Imagination*. Toronto: Anansi, 1971.

———. *The Educated Imagination*. Toronto: CBC, 1963.

———. *The Modern Century*. New ed. Toronto: Oxford University Press, 1990.

*Galbraith, John Kenneth. *The Scotch*. Baltimore, MD: Penguin, 1966.

Gawthrop, Daniel. *Affirmation: The AIDs Odyssey of Dr. Peter*. Vancouver: New Star, 1994.

Gibson, Frederick. *Queen's University, Volume II, 1917–1961: To Serve and Yet Be Free*. Kingston, ON: McGill-Queen's University Press, 1983.

Gunn, J.A.W. *Beyond Liberty and Property: The Process of Self-Recognition in Eighteenth-Century Political Thought*. Kingston, ON: McGill-Queen's University Press, 1983.

Heard, Andrew. *Canadian Constitutional Conventions: The Marriage of Law and Politics*. Toronto: Oxford University Press, 1991.

*Highway, Tomson. *The Rez Sisters*. Fifth House, 1988.

Hutcheon, Linda. *Splitting Images: Contemporary Canadian Ironies*. Toronto: Oxford University Press, 1991.

Ignatieff, George. *The Making of a Peacemonger*. Toronto: Penguin, 1987.

Jones, Jennifer. *Making the Links: A Book for Young Women about Sexual Violence, Drugs and Alcohol*. Kingston, ON: AWARE, 1992.

Keefer, Janice Kulyk. *Reading Mavis Gallant*. Toronto: Oxford University Press, 1989.

*Klinck, Carl F., gen. ed. *Literary History of Canada: Canadian Literature in English.* 2nd ed. 3 vols. Toronto: University of Toronto Press, 1976.

Kroetsch, Robert. *Badlands.* Toronto: General, 1975.

———. *The Words of My Roaring.* London: Macmillan, 1966.

*Laurence, Margaret. *The Diviners.* McClelland and Stewart, Bantam, 1975.

Lougheed, W.C., ed. *In Search of the Standard in Canadian English.* Occasional Paper Number 1. Kingston: Strathy Language Unit, 1986.

McKenna, Katherine M.J. *A Life of Propriety: Anne Murray Powell and Her Family, 1755–1849.* Montreal and Kingston: McGill-Queen's University Press, 1994.

Meyer, Bruce, and Brian O'Riordan, eds. *In Their Words: Interviews with Fourteen Canadian Writers.* Toronto: Anansi, 1984.

Neatby, Hilda. *Queen's University, Volume I, 1841–1917: And Not to Yield.* Montreal: McGill-Queen's University Press, 1978.

Nevitte, Neil, and Roger Gibbins. *New Elites in Old States: Ideologies in the Anglo-American Democracies.* Toronto: Oxford University Press, 1990.

Northey, Margot, and David B. Knight. *Making Sense in Geography and Environmental Studies: A Student's Guide to Research, Writing, and Style.* Toronto: Oxford University Press, 1992.

Norton, William. *Human Geography.* Toronto: Oxford University Press, 1992.

Pross, A. Paul. *Group Politics and Public Policy.* 2nd ed. Toronto: Oxford University Press, 1992.

Purdy, A.W., ed. *The New Romans: Candid Canadian Opinions of the United States.* Edmonton: Hurtig [1968].

Reynolds, Wendy, and Vera Madden. *Drug Wise: A Book for Older Women about Safe Drug Use.* Kingston, ON: AWARE, 1992.

Rosenthal, Henry M., and S. Cathy Berson, eds. *Canadian Jewish Outlook Anthology.* Vancouver: New Star, 1988.

Shek, Ben-Z. *French Canadian & Québécois Novels.* Toronto: Oxford University Press, 1991.

*Shields, Carol. *The Stone Diaries.* Toronto: Random House, 1993.

Silvera, Makeda. *Her Head a Village and Other Stories.* Vancouver: Press Gang, 1994.

Smyth, J.E., et al. *The Law and Business Administration in Canada.* Scarborough, ON: Prentice Hall, 1987.

*Story, G.M., W.J. Kirwin, and J.D.A. Widdowson, eds. *Dictionary of Newfoundland English.* 2nd. ed. Toronto: University of Toronto Press, 1990.

Sutherland, Fraser. *The Monthly Epic: A History of Canadian Magazines.* Toronto: Fitzhenry and Whiteside, 1989.

Taylor, Judith. *Women and Smoking*. Kingston, ON: AWARE, 1992.

Teatero, William. *John Anderson: Fugitive Slave*. Kingston, ON: Treasure Island Books, 1986.

Tucker, Alan, ed. *The Penguin Guide to Canada*. New York: Penguin, 1991.

Ursell, Geoffrey. *Perdue: And How the West Was Lost*. Toronto: Macmillan, 1984.

Waddington, Miriam. *Apartment Seven: Essays Selected and New*. Toronto: Oxford University Press, 1989.

Whitehorn, Alan. *Canadian Socialism: Essays on the CCF-NDP*. Toronto: Oxford University Press, 1992.

Williams, David. *Eye of the Father*. Toronto: Anansi, 1985.

*Willinsky, John. *Empire of Words: The Reign of the OED*. Princeton, NJ: Princeton University Press, 1994.

Wilson, Richard Albert. *The Birth of Language*. London: Dent, 1937.

*York, Geoffrey. *The Dispossessed: Life and Death in Native Canada*. Toronto: Lester and Orpen Dennys, 1989.

Zeitlin, Irving M., and Robert J. Brym. *The Social Condition of Humanity*. Toronto: Oxford University Press, 1991.

MAGAZINES

Arctic 41.1 (1988)
Atlantic Salmon Journal Summer 1990, Autumn 1990
Beautiful British Columbia Spring 1990
The Beaver Dec. 1989–Jan. 1990, Feb.–Mar. 1990
Bon Vivant Nov. 1981, Aug.–Sept. 1982, Feb.–Mar. 1983
Briarpatch December 1989, January 1990, April 1990
Business Journal June 1991
Canadian Architect March 1986, June 1986
Canadian Baptist January 1986, February 1986
Canadian Biker Magazine February 1990
Canadian Churchman April 1986, June–July 1986
Canadian Collector 21 (1986)
Canadian Consumer January 1985, January 1986, February 1986, March 1986
Canadian Fiction Magazine 63 (1988), 64 (1988)
Canadian Heritage Magazine Feb.–Mar. 1986, Aug.-Sept. 1986
Canadian Living 19 Apr. 1986, 17 May 1986
Canadian Rodeo News February 1990, March 1990
Canadian Thoroughbred January 1989, August 1989
Catholic Register 16 Aug. 1986, 23 Aug. 1986
Chatelaine April 1986, June 1986
City Magazine Spring 1988
Computer Dealer News 7 Mar. 1991, 21 Mar. 1991
Computing Canada 14 Feb. 1991, 1 Mar. 1991

Country Guide November 1986, December 1986
Dogs in Canada August 1986, Special Issue 1986
Engineering Dimensions May-June 1988, Mar.–Apr. 1988, July–Aug. 1988
Fuse Magazine 13.4 (1990)
Harrowsmith June–July 1985, Aug.–Sept. 1985, Oct.-Nov. 1985
Imperial Oil Review Spring 1988
Leisure Life May 1988
Maclean's 24 Feb. 1986, 31 Mar. 1986, 28 July 1986, 8 Sept. 1986
Mennonite Brethren Herald 7 Mar. 1986, 4 Apr. 1986
New West Review Oct.–Nov. 1989, Dec.-Jan. 1990, Feb.-Mar. 1990
Now Magazine (Toronto) 3–9 Nov. 1988
Our Times March 1990, April 1990
Performing Arts in Canada March 1988, July 1988, Spring 1990
Photo Life July–Aug. 1991, September 1991
Rites February 1990, March 1990
Saturday Night January 1986, February 1986, March 1986, April 1986, May 1986, July
    1986
Snow Goer October 1989, March 1990
Snowmobile Canada, 1991 Buyer's Guide
TLC...for plants Spring 1991, Summer 1991
Today's Skater 1991 ed.
Torch: University of Victoria Alumni Magazine Spring 1990, Autumn 1990
United Church Observer May 1986, June 1986
Uphere Jan.–Feb. 1990, Mar.-Apr. 1990
Vista 11.4. 12.2, 13.1, 15.3 (1983–87)
Western Grocer Magazine May-June 1990, Aug. 1990
Women and Environments 12.1 (1989–90), 12.2 (1990)

JOURNALS

Business Journal June 1991
Canadian Bar Review 66.3 (1987)
Canadian Geographer Spring 1989
Canadian Journal of Botany 67.4 (1989)
Canadian Journal of Earth Science 26 (1989)
Canadian Journal of History 14.1 (1989)
Canadian Journal of Philosophy 19 (1989)
Canadian Journal of Physics 67.1 (1989)
Canadian Journal of Psychology 44 (1990)
Canadian Journal of Sociology 14.2 (1989)
Canadian Journal of Zoology 67.4 (1989)
Education Canada Summer 1989
Perspectives: Profiles of Research at Queen's University 1986
Queen's Quarterly 92 (1985), 93 (1986), 94 (1987), 95 (1988), 96 (1989), 97 (1990), 98
    (1991), 101 (1994) (selections)
The Reader 1992
Room of One's Own March 1990, June 1990

NEWSPAPERS

Calgary Herald 14 Feb. 1988, 21 Feb. 1988
*Cape Breton Post (Sydney, NS) 27 June 1990
Chronicle-Herald (Halifax) 9 Apr. 1988; 6, 14 May 1988
Chronicle-Telegraph (Quebec City) 23, 30 Jan.; 6, 13, 20 Feb.; 6, 13, 20, 17 Mar.; 3, 10
    Apr.; 1, 8, 22 May; 5, 12 June; 3, 10, 17, 19, 24, 26, 31 July; 7, 14, 21 Aug., 1991
Daily Gleaner (Fredericton) 26 Apr. 1988
Edmonton Journal 8, 9, 10, 13, 14, 15, 16, 17, 18, 19, 20, 21, 22 Sept. 1992
Evening Telegram (St. John's) 20, 21, 23, 25, 26 May 1993
Gazette (Montreal) 29 June 1988: B2; 1–7 Mar. 1989
Globe and Mail (Toronto) 1 Nov. 1986: C5
Guardian (Charlottetown) 2 Nov. 1990, 7 Nov. 1990
Leader-Post (Regina) 13 Feb. 1988: A6; 27 Feb. 1988
London Free Press 6 May 1986: B6–7; 28 Apr. 1988
*Mirror (Montreal) 8 Jun. 1995
News North (Yellowknife)* 26 Feb. 1990, 19 Feb. 1990
*Queen's Gazette 28 Oct. 1991
Queen's Journal (Kingston) 2 Feb. 1993, 14 Sept. 1993, 8 Feb. 1994
*Times-Colonist (Victoria) 20 Jun. 1995
Vancouver Sun 14 Feb. 1990: A10; 17 Feb. 1990
Whig-Standard (Kingston) 29 Jun. 1985
Winnipeg Free Press 17 Nov. 1990
Yellowknifer (Yellowknife) 2 Mar. 1988

*TEXTS ON CD-ROM

(Approximately 650 million words; note that these are not part of the Corpus, but were
    used as sources of examples)

InfoGlobe. *Globe and Mail* (Toronto) 1985

The following are all produced by Infomart on CD, Southam Electronic Publishing and
    CEDROM-SNi Technologies:

Unity Disc: Canadian Confederation Issues and Opinions 1985–1991 (from Canadian
    news sources)
Canadian Newsdisc. Containing *Calgary Herald, Daily News* (Halifax), *Gazette* (Mon-
    treal), *Ottawa Citizen, Toronto Star, Vancouver Sun,* Jan.–Dec. 1993 (2 disks)
Canadian Newsdisc II. Containing *Canadian Speeches on Issues of the Day, Edmonton
    Journal, Financial Post, Province* (Vancouver), *Spectator* (Hamilton), *Toronto Sun,*
    Jan.–Dec. 1994.
Canadian Newsdisc. Containing *Calgary Herald, Daily News* (Halifax), *Gazette* (Mon-
    treal), *Ottawa Citizen, Toronto Star, Vancouver Sun,* CTV and CBC News, July–Dec.
    1994.
Gazette (Montreal), 1990–94
Maclean's, March 1988–91
Ottawa Citizen, 1985, 1986, 1989–94
Province (Vancouver), 1990
Vancouver Sun, 1990

Works Consulted

Following are the works we most frequently consulted in the course of writing the guide. Most citations of these works in the entries refer to the title (or a short form of it), with these exceptions: *OED* (*Oxford English Dictionary*), 2nd ed., 1989; Fowler (the original *Dictionary of Modern English Usage*, 1926); *Fowler's* (the second edition, 1965, revised by Sir Ernest Gowers); and 'Survey of Vancouver English' ('Final Report to the Social Sciences Research Council on An Urban Dialect Survey of Vancouver English'). Please note that more recent editions of these works may have appeared since the guide was completed: for example, *The New Fowler's Modern English Usage* (3rd ed.), edited by R. W. Burchfield (Oxford: Clarendon Press, 1996) and the recently revised *Gage Canadian Dictionary*, Gaelan Dodds de Wolff et al. (Toronto: Gage, 1997).

General Dictionaries

American Heritage Dictionary of the English Language. 3rd ed. Executive ed. Anne H. Soukhanov. Boston: Houghton Mifflin, 1992.

Collins COBUILD English Language Dictionary. Ed. in chief John Sinclair. London: Collins, 1987.

Concise Oxford Dictionary of Current English. 9th ed. Ed. Della Thompson. Oxford: Clarendon Press, 1995.

Dictionary of Canadianisms on Historical Principles. Ed. in chief Walter S. Avis. Toronto: Gage, 1967.

Funk and Wagnalls Canadian College Dictionary. Ed. Walter S. Avis. Toronto: Fitzhenry and Whiteside, 1989.

Gage Canadian Dictionary. Co-ordinating ed. Patrick D. Drysdale. Toronto: Gage, 1983.

Merriam-Webster's Collegiate Dictionary. 10th ed. Ed. in chief Frederick C. Mish. Markham, ON: Thomas Allen, 1993.

New Shorter Oxford English Dictionary. Ed. Lesley Brown. 2 vols. Oxford: Clarendon Press, 1993.

Oxford Encyclopedic English Dictionary. Ed. Joyce M. Hawkins and Robert Allen. Oxford: Clarendon Press, 1991.

Oxford English Dictionary. 2nd ed. Ed. J.A. Simpson and E.S.C. Weiner. 20 vols. Oxford: Clarendon Press, 1989. (Compact edition, one volume, 1991.)

Oxford English Dictionary Additions Series. Ed. John Simpson and Edmund Weiner. Oxford: Clarendon Press, 1993–.

Random House Webster's College Dictionary. Ed. in chief Robert B. Costello. New York: Random House, 1991.

Webster's New World Dictionary of American English. 3rd college ed. Ed. in chief Victoria Neufeldt. New York: Webster's New World, 1988.

Usage Guides, Style Guides, and Specialized Dictionaries

American Usage and Style: The Consensus. Roy Copperud. New York: Van Nostrand Reinhold, 1980.

Cambridge Australian English Style Guide. Pam Peters. Cambridge: Cambridge University Press, 1995.

Canadian Law Dictionary. 3rd ed. John A. Yogis. Happauge, NY: Barron's, 1995.

The CP Stylebook: A Guide for Writers and Editors. Rev. ed. Ed. Peter Buckley. Toronto: Canadian Press, 1993.

The Canadian Style: A Guide to Writing and Editing. Dept. of the Secretary of State. Toronto: Dundurn Press, 1985.

Chicago Manual of Style. 14th ed. Chicago: University of Chicago Press, 1993.

Columbia Guide to Standard American English. Kenneth G. Wilson. New York: Columbia University Press, 1993.

Dictionary of Canadian Law. Daphne A. Dukelow and Betsy Nuse. Scarborough, ON: Carswell, 1991.

Dictionary of Contemporary American Usage. Bergen Evans and Cornelia Evans. New York: Random House, 1957.

Dictionary of Modern English Usage. 1st ed. H.W. Fowler, 1926; 2nd ed. Rev. by Ernest Gowers. Oxford: Clarendon Press, 1965.

Dictionary of Modern Legal Usage. Bryan A. Garner. New York: Oxford University Press, 1987.

Editing Canadian English. Lydia Burton et al. Vancouver: Douglas and McIntyre, for the Freelance Editors' Association of Canada, 1987.

The Gazette Style. Rev. ed. Joseph N. Gelmon. Montreal: Gazette, 1995.

The Globe and Mail Style Book: A Guide to Language and Usage. Rev. ed. J.A. (Sandy) McFarlane and Warren Clements. Toronto: Penguin, 1995.

Good English Guide: English Usage in the 1990s. Geoffrey Howard. London: Pan Macmillan, 1993.

Harper Dictionary of Contemporary Usage. 2nd ed. William and Mary Morris. New York: Harper and Row, 1985.

The King's English. 3rd ed. Ed. H.W. Fowler and F.G. Fowler. Oxford: Clarendon Press, 1931.

Longman Guide to English Usage. Sidney Greenbaum and Janet Whitcut. Harlow, Essex: Longman, 1988.

Oxford Guide to English Usage. 2nd ed. E.S.C. Weiner and Andrew Delahunty. Oxford: Clarendon Press, 1993.

Reader's Digest Success with Words: A North American Guide to the English Language. New York: Reader's Digest, 1983.

Talking Gender: A Guide to Nonsexist Communication. Ruth King et al. Toronto: Copp Clark Pitman, 1991.

Webster's Dictionary of English Usage. New York: Merriam-Webster, 1989.

Databases

'The CBC Language Guide'. CBC, 1995. (Not commercially available.)

Surveys

The English Language as Used in Quebec: A Survey. Tom McArthur. Occasional Paper Number 3. Kingston, ON: Strathy Language Unit, 1989.

'Final Report to the Social Sciences and Humanities Research Council of Canada on An Urban Dialect Survey of the English Spoken in Vancouver'. R.J. Gregg. April 1984. (Ms.)

Modern Canadian English Usage: Linguistic Change and Reconstruction. M.H. Scargill. Toronto: McClelland and Stewart with the Canadian Council of Teachers of English, 1974.

'Socio-dialectology Survey of the English Spoken in Ottawa: A Study of Sociological Variation in Canadian English'. H.B. Woods. Ph.D. dissertation. University of British Columbia, 1979.

General Works on Canadian English and Usage in Canada

Focus on Canada. Varieties of English around the World, G11. Ed. Sandra Clarke. Amsterdam: John Benjamins, 1993.

In Defence of Plain English: The Decline and Fall of Literacy in Canada. Victoria Branden. Willowdale, ON: Hounslow, 1992.

In Search of the Standard in Canadian English. Ed. W.C. Lougheed. Occasional Paper Number 1. Kingston, ON: Strathy Language Unit, 1986.

Our Own Voice: Canadian English and How It Is Studied. R.E. McConnell. Toronto: Gage, 1979.

Social and Regional Factors in Canadian English: A Study of Phonological Variables and Grammatical Items in Ottawa and Vancouver. Gaelan Dodds de Wolf. Toronto: Canadian Scholar's Press, 1992.

Speaking Canadian English: An Informal Account of the English Language in Canada. Mark M. Orkin. New York: David McKay, 1970.

Words Fail Us: Good English and Other Lost Causes. Bob Blackburn. Toronto: McClelland and Stewart, 1993.

Writing on Canadian English 1792–1975: An Annotated Bibliography. Walter S. Avis and A.M. Kinloch. Toronto: Fitzhenry and Whiteside [1977].

Writings on Canadian English 1976–1987: A Selective, Annotated Bibliography. Occasional Paper Number N 2. W.C. Lougheed. Kingston, ON: Strathy Language Unit, 1988.

You Don't Say. Ed. George Rich. CBC office of Broadcast Language. Vols. 4.1–6.4, Dec. 1979–July 1981. (An in-house newsletter on usage and pronunciation for CBC announcers.)

Regional Dictionaries and Phrasebooks

Cold as a Bay Street Banker's Heart: The Ultimate Prairie Phrase Book. Chris Thain. Saskatoon: Western Producer, 1987.

Dictionary of Newfoundland English. 2nd ed. with supplement. Ed. G.M. Story, W.J. Kirwin, and J.D.A. Widdowson. Toronto: University of Toronto Press, 1990.

Dictionary of Prince Edward Island English. Ed. T.K. Pratt. Toronto: University of Toronto Press, 1988.

South Shore Phrase Book: A New, Revised and Expanded Nova Scotia Dictionary. Comp. Lewis J. Poteet. Hantsport, NS: Lancelot, 1988.

Wet Coast Words: A Dictionary of British Columbia Words and Phrases. Tom Parkin. Victoria: Orca, 1989.

Other

Cambridge Encyclopedia of Language. David Crystal. Cambridge: Cambridge University Press, 1987.

Canadian Encyclopedia. 2nd ed. Ed. in chief James H. Marsh. Edmonton: Hurtig, 1988. (Now available in an up-dated version on CD-ROM.)

Comprehensive Grammar of the English Language. Randolph Quirk et al. London: Longman, 1985.

Oxford Companion to the English Language. Ed. Tom McArthur. Oxford: Oxford University Press, 1992.

Pidgins and Creoles. 2nd ed. Loreto Todd. London: Routledge, 1991.

A

a, an *A* precedes words that begin with a conso-nant and *an* precedes those that begin with a vowel. This rule works by pronunciation rather than by spelling. The initial letters in the words *one, Euro-pean,* and *united* are the vowels *o, e,* and *u,* but the initial sounds are consonants (*w* or *y*). Thus these words are preceded by *a,* not *an*: 'a one-sided argu-ment', 'a European', 'a union'. When the consonant *h* is sounded at the beginning of a word, the word is preceded by *a*: 'a hutch', 'a house'. When it is silent, as in *heir, honour, hour,* and, for some speakers, *herb,* the word is preceded by *an.*

With the names of letters and abbreviations, the choice of *a* or *an* depends on how they would be read aloud: 'an *a*' but 'a *b*'; 'a Master's' but 'an M.A.'; 'a Hudson's Bay Company trading post' but 'an HBC clerk'. Similarly, figures are preceded by *a* or *an* according to how they are pronounced: 'a 3-speed bike' but 'an 11-kilogram cat'.

One oddity remains. Though Canadians pro-nounce the *h* in words such as *habitual, hallucina-tory, harmonious, historical, holistic,* and *hysterical,* they sometimes precede these words with *an* in formal writing. In British English in the past, the initial *h* was pronounced weakly or not at all in words with an unstressed first syllable, so *an* was generally used before these words. Canadians bor-rowed this practice, even when they pronounced the *h.* Now the British too are pronouncing the *h* in these words, and British usage guides are recom-mending against the unnecessary *an.* It is probably time for Canadians to let it go too.

> With more than 12,000 artifacts on display, the Huron County Pioneer Museum is truly an unique, educational and enjoyable place to visit.
> *Leisure Life* 1988: 97

(Here '*a* unique' would be correct; the writer followed the *an*-before-a-vowel rule without trying the phrase out loud.)

> [Marie-Claire] Blais made her literary debut ... with *La Belle Bête (Mad Shadows)*, an hallucinatory tale of jeal-ousy, hatred, mutilation and incest set in a lurid and only semi-real rural Quebec.
> Margaret Atwood *Second Words* 1982: 260

(Here '*a* hallucinatory' is recommended.)

> Two newer rocking chairs, made at an historic factory in Bass River, Nova Scotia, went from the sitting room and kitchen to bedrooms.
> *Harrowsmith* Aug.–Sept. 1985: 17

(Here '*a* historic' is recommended.)

See also HERB; THE, A, AN.

abbreviation, contraction, suspension, acronym, initialism Abbreviations are common and appropriate in scientific, technical, and business writing, and indeed in writing for any specialized audience familiar with a particular set of abbrevia-tions. Abbreviations are also acceptable in tables and lists where space is limited, as long as they are familiar or a key is provided. Anyone writing for a general audience, however, should be careful not to use an unfamiliar abbreviation without a full refer-ence or explanation. The most efficient way to introduce the abbreviation to the reader is to place it in parentheses after the first use of the full form and use the abbreviation thereafter: 'the Prime Minister's Office (PMO)'. Although usage guides often warn against the use of abbreviations in for-mal writing, it is unnecessary to avoid those that are never spelled out or are better known than their long forms; for example, *Ms., Mr., DNA, AIDS, BMW.* And even in formal writing it is better to use an abbreviation than to repeat a long title over and over again.

A true abbreviation is defined as a shortened form in which the first letter(s) of a word are used to stand for the whole; for example, *p.* for *page, co.* for *com-pany, Sept.* for *September.* Canadians normally use a period after such abbreviations.

A shortened form made by omitting letters in the middle of a word (as in the abbreviation for *man-ager, mgr.*) is usually called a suspension in North America and a contraction in Great Britain. Canadians normally use a period after suspensions too, with the notable exceptions of the French *Mlle* (for *Mademoiselle*) and *Mme* (for *Madame*). In British usage, suspensions (contractions) are not followed by periods, on the reasoning that the final letter of the complete word is included in the shortened form. *Editing Canadian English*, a guide for Canadian book editors, lays out the convention of using no periods after contractions and notes that it is often found in Canadian government publications. But this convention is far from widespread. Further, differentiating between contractions and true abbreviations leads to some odd-looking mixes: 'Asst Prof. Linda Wentzell'. In this guide we have chosen to use periods with both true abbreviations and suspensions.

An acronym is a pronounceable word formed from the first letter or letters of words in a phrase or name: for example, *CIDA* (*SEE da*), for Canadian International Development Agency; *NORAD* (*NOR ad*), for North American Aerospace Defence Command; *CUPE* (*KEWP ee*), for Canadian Union of Public Employees; and *CEGEP* (*SAY zhep*), for College d'enseignement général et professionel. A few acronyms have become full-fledged words, written in lower case, such as *radar* (radio detecting and ranging) and *scuba* (self contained underwater breathing apparatus). Generally, acronyms are written in capital letters without periods. Some widely used acronyms, such as *NATO*, *UNICEF*, and *AIDS*, are occasionally treated as proper nouns and appear with only initial capital letters: *Nato, Unicef, Aids*. Some acronyms are composed of capital and lower-case letters; thus the abbreviation for the Museum of Modern Art in New York may be written *MoMA*.

An initialism is formed from the first letters in a phrase or name, but—unlike acronyms—initialisms are usually pronounced letter by letter: *NHL* (*en aitch ell*); *RCMP* (*are see em pee*); *CBC* (*see bee see*). Some initialisms, however, although they look unpronounceable, are treated like acronyms: for example, *SSHRCC*, an initialism for Social Sciences and Humanities Research Council of Canada, is pronounced *SHIRK*. Like acronyms, initialisms are usually written in capital letters without periods. Punctuation of acronyms and initialisms with only two letters varies. Abbreviations of place names, such as *U.S.* and *B.C.*, and of academic degrees, such as *B.A.* and *M.A.*, tend to retain the periods even in publications where other two-letter initialisms, such as *UN* and *MP*, do not.

The *Chicago Manual of Style* (14th ed.), the principal guide for book editors in North America, admits that more and more writers are dropping the periods after abbreviations, but continues to use periods in its own examples. Dropping periods from abbreviations saves keystrokes and editorial fiddling, and many find the no-period style more attractive. Few style guides recommend dropping all periods, however.

Besides acronyms and initialisms, there are some categories of abbreviation that never take periods, no matter what style the editor or writer chooses:
• SI units (*kg*, *L*; see APPENDIX II)
• abbreviations for points of the compass: N, S, E, SSW (except with street addresses, where the period is usually retained)
• chemical symbols (*Fe*, *N*)
• post office abbreviations for the names of the provinces (*BC*, *ON*; see APPENDIX I)

Abbreviation, as well as referring to the forms discussed above, is the general term for any type of shortened form of a word or phrase. Forms such as *bike, hippo,* and *phone* are usually called clipped words. Forms where two words are made into one, such as *brunch* (breakfast and lunch), *Oxbridge* (Oxford and Cambridge), *permafrost* (permanent and frost), and *Socred* (Social Credit), are usually called blends or portmanteau words. As with all abbreviations, the question arises of whether these forms are appropriate in formal writing. The newer and more unfamiliar a clipped form or a blend is, the more likely it is to be condemned. For forms such as *didn't* and *can't* see CONTRACTIONS.

Following are some initialisms and acronyms that frequently appear in Canadian publications, or that are particular to Canadian English:

AARTC	Association des artistes de la radio-télévision canadienne
BQ	Bloc Québécois
CBC	Canadian Broadcasting Corporation
CEGEP	Collège d'enseignement général et professionel
CEO	chief executive officer
CFB	Canadian Forces Base
CIDA	Canadian International Development Agency
CN	Canadian National (Railway)
CNIB	Canadian National Institute for the Blind

CP	The Canadian Press/Canadian Pacific
CRTC	Canadian Radio-Television and Telecommunications Commission
CSA	Canadian Standards Association
CUPE	Canadian Union of Public Employees
EI	employment insurance
EST	Eastern Standard Time
GST	Goods and Services Tax
HMCS	Her Majesty's Canadian Ship
ISBN	International Standard Book Number
MLA	Member of the Legislative Assembly
MP	Member of Parliament
MPP	Member of Provincial Parliament (Ontario only)
NDP	New Democratic Party
NFB	National Film Board of Canada
NORAD	North American Aerospace Defence Command
OC	Officer of the Order of Canada
RSC	Royal Society of Canada
PCBs	polychlorinated biphenyls
PQ	Parti Québécois/Province of Quebec
PMO	Prime Minister's Office
PST	Pacific Standard Time/Provincial Sales Tax
RMC	Royal Military College of Canada
RRSP	Registered Retirement Savings Plan
SASE	self-addressed stamped envelope
SIN	social insurance number
TSE	Toronto Stock Exchange
UI	unemployment insurance
USC	Unitarian Service Committee of Canada
VON	Victorian Order of Nurses
VSE	Vancouver Stock Exchange
WCB	Workers' Compensation Board
WHO	World Health Organization

See also APPENDIX I; MISS, MR., MRS.; MS.; OXBRIDGE; SOCIAL CREDIT; STANDARD TIME.

abdicate see ABROGATE

abdomen see BELLY

abduct see KIDNAP

abide, abode *Abide* means tolerate; *abide by*, continue in accordance with. The past participle and past tense are *abided*: 'I've abided this situation too long'; 'They abided by the rules quite happily'.

Abode is an archaic past form associated with the archaic meaning of *abide*, to stay or reside: 'He abode among the tombs'. The noun *abode* means home or dwelling.

What only the water-bound portions of Canada realize is that politics can be abided only when it is fun.
Maclean's 29 Aug. 1988: A56

[His] numerous contributions throughout the *Companion* are first-rate; it is unfortunate that he abided by [the editor's] decision to have some publishers write necessarily biased self-commentary.
Queen's Quarterly 92 (1985): 404

abjure, adjure To *abjure* something is to renounce or reject it solemnly; to *adjure* someone to do something is to earnestly request him or her to do it. One could, for instance, adjure a friend to abjure the practice of drinking and driving. The Latin *jurare*, 'to swear', combines with the Latin prefix *ab*, 'away', or *ad*, 'to': thus to *abjure* means to swear off, while to *adjure* means (to ask someone) to swear to. Both words are rare.

Why not frankly abjure the use of nuclear weapons?
Globe and Mail (Toronto) 5 Jan. 1985: P9

In Bordeaux, producers of fine wine cultivate an image of old-fashioned rusticity, abjuring stainless steel when anyone is listening.
Globe and Mail (Toronto) 19 June 1985: SB11

And the means he adjures his readers . . . to embrace are perseverance and the strictest honesty.
Robertson Davies *A Voice from the Attic* 1960: 43

-able, (-at)able Verbs with two syllables ending in *-ate* are transformed into adjectives by dropping the final *e* and adding *-able*: for example, *debatable*, *dictatable*, *inflatable*, and *translatable*. Note, however, the exception of *placate/placable*.

Verbs with *more* than two syllables ending in *-ate* are transformed into adjectives by replacing *-ate* with *-able*: *allocate, allocable*; *calculate, calculable*; *communicate, communicable*; *demonstrate, demonstrable*; *educate, educable*; *imitate, imitable*; *manipulate, manipulable*. *Communicatable, demonstratable, educatable*, and so on, are non-standard.

See also -ABLE, (-E)ABLE; -ABLE, -IBLE.

-able, (-e)able A silent *e* following the letter *c* or *g* must be retained before the suffix *-able*: *changeable, faceable, manageable, peaceable, traceable*. But in other cases when *-able* is added to a word of one syllable, *e* may be dropped or retained. British writers tend to retain it and American writers to drop it. Canadians prefer *saleable* to *salable*, but usually drop the *e* in *livable* and *movable*; the pairs *likeable/likable* and *sizeable/sizable* are used with about equal frequency.

But how is that enforcable?
Vancouver Sun 10 June 1992: A16

(The silent *e* is retained after *c* or *g*: the correct spelling is *enforceable*.)

At first, Adam expands to the more-or-less managable height of 7 feet.
Toronto Star 17 July 1992: D2

(The correct spelling is *manageable*.)

See also -ABLE, (-AT)ABLE; -ABLE, -IBLE; -E.

-able, -ible   The suffix *-able/-ible* means 'capable of being'; thus someone lovable can be loved and something flexible can be flexed. It also can mean 'tending to': something perishable tends to rot and something profitable tends to lead to profit. There is no difference in meaning or pronunciation between the variants *-able* and *-ible*. They do, however, present a spelling challenge.

Newly coined words always end in *-able*: *microwavable*, *recyclable*. Generally, any word that can be negated with the prefix *un-* ends in *-able*: *uncomfortable*, *unpresentable*, *unreadable*, *unworkable*. Most words ending in *-ible* are negated with the Latin prefix *in-* (or its variants *il-*, *im-*, *ir-*) rather than *un-*: *inaccessible*, *incomprehensible*, *illegible*, *implausible*, *irresponsible*. Unfortunately, not all words negated with *in-* and its variants end in *-ible*; some end in *-able*: *ineducable*, *inexcusable*, *inimitable*, *irreparable*. When in doubt about *-ible* and *-able*, it is best to consult a dictionary.

The summit of Haleakala is accessable by car and is a popular tourist sight.
Vancouver Sun 24 April 1992: A17

(The correct spelling is *accessible*.)

Talk about an irresistable challenge.
Calgary Herald 16 May 1992: B9

(The correct spelling is *irresistible*).

See also -ABLE, (-AT)ABLE; -ABLE, (-E)ABLE.

able to be   Many stylists object to the construction *able to be*, as in 'The data will be able to be analysed more efficiently'. They argue that the adjective *able*, which suggests an active ability, should not be used to introduce a passive verb. The disputed structure can be avoided by using *can* or *could* or, in the future tense, an impersonal construction: 'The data can be analysed ...'; 'The data could be analysed ...'; 'It will be possible to analyse the data ...'.

... a period of separation is often required unless or until there are genuine changes evident in the relationship, until the victim is able to be assured of safety....
Mennonite Brethren Herald 7 March 1986: 6

(Here 'until the victim *can* be assured of safety' would be better.)

... this venture fell far short of being able to be considered a total success.
Computer Dealer News 21 March 1991: 47

(This sentence would be better rewritten: 'this venture *could by no means* be considered ...'.)

For while a goal goes up in lights, a permanent record ... a save is ephemeral, ... able to be wiped away, undone, with the next shot.
Ken Dryden *The Game* 1983: 117

(Here '*liable* to be wiped away' would be better.)

abode   see ABIDE

abolition, abolishment   *Abolition* is the more common word for putting an end to a custom or institution, but *abolishment* is also correct. A writer may choose one word over the other to avoid unintentional rhymes: for example, 'the abolition of Prohibition'.

Abolition is familiar because of its specific association with the abolitionist political movement, which ended slavery in Britain in 1833 and in the United States in 1865.

His mother has added the abolition of nuclear energy to her long list of crusades.
Margaret Atwood *Life Before Man* 1979: 116

Even more far-reaching ... was the abolishment of institutional mediation....
Canadian Journal of Sociology 14.2 (1989): 205

abominable snowman   see SASQUATCH

aboriginal, Aboriginal, Aborigine   From the Latin meaning 'from the beginning', *aboriginal* can refer to anything indigenous, including people. In Australia *Aboriginal* and *Aborigine* evolved to refer specifically to the Indigenous people of that country, and now are capitalized to indicate this use.

Most Australian authorities, including the Aborigines, prefer *Aborigine(s)* for the noun. *Aboriginal* is used as an adjective. More and more Aborigines are using terms derived from their own languages to describe themselves: for example, Nyoongah in Western Australia and Koori in New South Wales and Victoria.

In 1982 the Canadian Charter of Rights and Freedoms introduced the phrase 'the aboriginal peoples of Canada'. Until then the most common Canadian usage of *aboriginal* was in the Australian context, but now *aboriginal* (only as an adjective) is used to refer to Canadian Native people in phrases such as 'Aboriginal rights' and 'Aboriginal people'. When referring to Aboriginal peoples of either Australia or Canada, these words should be capitalized in accordance with the practice of capitalizing words that refer to other cultural or national groups.

I understand there was a school of Australian poets dedicated to putting as many aboriginal words into their poems as possible.
Northrop Frye *The Bush Garden* 1971: 176

(In order to be parallel with *Australian*, *Aboriginal* should be capitalized.)

When the aborigines sighted Captain Cook's ships, they ignored them because they knew such things could not exist.
Margaret Atwood *Life Before Man* 1979: 10

(Here *Aborigines* should be capitalized.)

Elijah Harper, the Manitoba native leader who ... became a symbol of ... aboriginal power and frustration, has been voted Canada's top newsmaker of 1990.
Ottawa Citizen 12 Dec. 1990: A8

(Both *Native* and *Aboriginal* should be capitalized.)

See also ABORIGINAL PEOPLE(S); NATIVE.

Aboriginal people(s), Native people(s), Indigenous people(s), Status Indian, Registered Indian, Treaty Indian, Non-Status Indian, First Nations, First Peoples, Amerindian As the political identity and constitutional status of Indians, Métis, and Inuit in Canada evolve, so do the terms that refer to them. The Canadian Constitution Act of 1982 discussed Indians, Métis, and Inuit under the general rubric *aboriginal peoples*. In 1994, the Government of Canada Terminology and Language Standardization Board (Public Works) made the following recommendations with respect to general references to Aboriginal people(s) in Canada. *Aboriginal* and *Native* should be capitalized to parallel other broad ethnic, linguistic, and geographic designations such as *Asian*, *Hispanic*, and *Nordic*. *Aboriginal* and *Native* should be used as adjectives only, as in 'Aboriginal peoples' and 'Native peoples' (*not* 'Aboriginals', 'Natives'). *Indigenous* should also be capitalized in the term *Indigenous peoples*, which is often used to refer to Aboriginal groups worldwide.

Since Aboriginal peoples are actively seeking self-government, it is recommended that phrases expressing geographical location rather than citizenship be used of them: 'Aboriginal people(s) in Canada', 'Native people(s) in Canada', 'Indigenous people(s) in Canada' (*not* 'Aboriginal Canadians', 'Native Canadians', 'Indigenous Canadians', or 'Canada's Native peoples', etc.). *People*, in these phrases, can mean either a group of individuals ('The Aboriginal people present at the meeting discussed the issue'), the entire body of Aboriginal persons ('Aboriginal people today are fully aware of their changing position with respect to the state'), or a particular group that shares ancestry, language, and sometimes geographical territory ('The Haida are an Aboriginal people'). *Peoples*, plural, always refers to a number of such groups, not a number of individuals.

According to the Indian Act of 1951, *Status Indians* (also called *Registered* or *Treaty Indians*) are those who belong to Indian bands that have treaties with the Canadian government. The many people of Aboriginal ancestry who do not fall into this category are called *Non-Status Indians*. These terms, which should all be capitalized, are rapidly being supplanted: Status Indians now often refer to themselves as *First Nations*, while *First Peoples*, as distinct from *First Nations*, is an umbrella term that covers Indians of whatever status, Métis, and Inuit. Another trend is for Aboriginal people to identify themselves by using the name of their particular Aboriginal group.

Many First Nations are abandoning the names given to them by Europeans and returning to their names for themselves in their heritage languages: e.g., Anishnabe (*a nish NAW bee*) instead of Ojibwa. Others are respelling their names to better represent pronunciations: e.g., Mi'kmaq instead of Micmac. Often these new names and spellings are unfamiliar to a general audience. Thus, for now, it will help the reader if both the old name and the new name are mentioned.

Generally, whether the name is old or new, it serves as an adjective ('Haida canoe'), a singular noun ('One Haida voted against the move'), and a plural ('The Haida are demonstrating against increased logging'). Exceptions include *Inuit* (adjective or plural noun; the singular is *Inuk*), and *Mi'kmaq* (adjective or plural noun; the singular is *Mi'kmaw*) and *Algonquin, Cree, Huron,* and *Mohawk,* which are usually pluralized with an *s*.

Although *Indian* may have declined in general use because it is thought to reflect Columbus's mistaken idea that he had landed in India in 1492, it is common in the usage of many Native people and embedded in legislation that is still in effect. Further, it is the only clear way to distinguish among the three most general categories of Aboriginal people: Indians, Métis, and Inuit.

The term *Amerindian* includes all the Aboriginal peoples of Canada as well as the rest of North America, Central America, and South America.

Aboriginal rights ... are included in the Constitution Act of 1982. Section 35 recognized the existing rights of the country's Indian, Inuit and Metis people.
Financial Post 22 Oct. 1990: 46

His specialty was native housing and he worked with the Native Council of Canada, now called the Congress of Aboriginal Peoples.
Ottawa Citizen 29 June 1994: B3

(Here *Native* should be capitalized.)

Taint the fish and fish-eating mammals with PCBs ... and you wipe out the traditional diet of native peoples across the North.
Vancouver Sun 23 June 1994: A8

(Here *Native* should be capitalized.)

He was a commissioned presenter for Indigenous peoples at Earth Summit 1992 in Rio de Janeiro.
Calgary Herald 7 May 1994: H8

The various legal capacities and cultures of status Indians, Inuit, non-status Indians and Prairie-based Metis were highlighted during the fruitless constitutional debate.
Toronto Star 2 April 1994: B2

(Both *Status* and *Non-Status* should be capitalized.)

Indian Affairs had 491,000 people on its registered Indian list at the time.
Ottawa Citizen 21 June 1994: A3

(Here *Registered* should be capitalized.)

The confederacy believes the [Assembly of First Nations] and Ottawa are trying to lump treaty Indians in with other aboriginal groups, failing to recognize the 'unique' rights of bands that signed treaties with Ottawa about 125 years ago.
Calgary Herald 3 Feb. 1994: B3

(Here both *Treaty* and *Aboriginal* should be capitalized.)

The first disc, covering music of the country's First Peoples and Canada's rich folk tradition, is in many ways the most astonishing.
Calgary Herald 17 Dec. 1995: D13

(The CD in question contains music by both Indian and Inuit performers.)

The Great Dying [from European diseases] reduced the population of Amerindians from 20% of the human species to just 3% in one century.
Toronto Sun 16 Oct. 1994: M6

See also ALGONQUIN; ATHABASCAN; BELLA COOLA; CARRIER; CHIPEWYAN; CREE; DENE; GITKSAN; INNU; INUIT; KOOTENAY; KWAKIUTL; LILLOOET; MÉTIS; MICMAC; NATIVE; NISHGA; NOOTKA; NUNAVUT; OJIBWA(Y); OTTAWA; RESERVE, RESERVATION; SARCEE; SHUSWAP; SLAVEY; THOMPSON.

abortion, pro-life, pro-choice, anti-abortion
In the debate over legal access to abortion, activists commonly call themselves *pro-life* (i.e., anti-abortion), or *pro-choice* (i.e., in favour of a woman's right to choose to have an abortion). Both sides dispute the other's choice of label. Pro-choice groups claim that pro-life groups' concern with life ends at birth, while pro-life groups claim that pro-choice groups' concern with choice excludes the unborn. Writers aiming for a balanced discussion should certainly avoid the negative and partisan terms *anti-choice* and *anti-life*. *Pro-abortion* should also be avoided, since many supporters of the pro-choice movement view abortion as always regrettable. The *Globe and Mail Style Book* (1995) recommends using *anti-abortion* and *pro-choice* as the most accurate and least offensive of these politically charged labels. The *Canadian Press Stylebook* (rev. ed. 1993) suggests using the term preferred by the person or organization concerned. Obviously, those involved in the debate will continue to use the terms they feel are most effective in promoting their cause.

The pro-choice/anti-abortion debate is a sensitive one.
Gazette (Montreal) 3 May 1992: D2

The women's and pro-choice movements will be concentrating serious efforts over the coming months to prevent the Tory anti-choice bill from passing.
Our Times March 1990: 20

(*Our Times* is a Canadian labour magazine; *anti-abortion* would be a less partisan choice.)

They did nothing to help the pro-life issue.
Catholic Register 16 Aug. 1986: 14

(Here *pro-life* is a partisan choice; *anti-abortion* would be more neutral.)

Too many women and too many doctors are too quick to follow today's anti-life trends.
Catholic Register 16 Aug. 1986: 5

(Here *pro-choice* would be less partisan.)

I would suspect that most people are neither 'pro-choice' nor 'pro-life' .... These phrases have been appropriated by the extremists in the two opposing views on the abortion issue, and we are not a society of extremists.
Globe and Mail (Toronto) 10 Jan. 1985: P7

abrogate, arrogate, abdicate   To *abrogate* something is to repeal, abolish, or do away with it. To *arrogate* something to (*or* unto) yourself, such as a privilege, power, or desirable characteristic, is to claim it for yourself without justification. To arrogate a characteristic, good or bad, to others is to ascribe it to them without reason.

To *abdicate* means to step down from the throne: 'Edward VIII abdicated in 1936'. It is also correct to say 'abdicate the throne' or 'abdicate from the throne'. To abdicate a responsibility is to evade it. To abdicate a right is to relinquish it.

'Unless we abrogate the free trade agreement there is no possible way that Canada can survive as a country.'
Vancouver Sun 14 April 1992: B8

... cultural or linguistic rights in ordinary legislation specifically protecting Quebec's interests would not be abrogated without ... consent of the province's senators.
Queen's Quarterly 95.3 (1988): 695

'I do not feel you should arrogate to yourself the right to determine the degree of impairment,' he wrote, 'in spite of a medical certificate furnished by a qualified doctor in which he recommends that a handicapped sticker be issued.'
Gazette (Montreal) 24 Nov. 1992: C6

... the security needs of a free and democratic society are, in a few basic essentials, much the same as those which totalitarian societies arrogate unto themselves.
London Free Press 28 April 1988: A6

Though the tsar had abdicated, the country did have a government....
George Ignatieff *The Making of a Peacemonger* 1987: 19

Mr. Long said managers abdicate their responsibility when they dump unclear research demands on their staffs at the last minute....
Globe and Mail (Toronto) 8 May 1985: B9

'We can't abdicate our rights because some people might be sensitive about what we say.'
Gazette (Montreal) 9 Feb. 1992: A5

absent   *Absent* has been used as a preposition meaning *in the absence of* or *without* since early in the twentieth century. From American legal writing it spread to Canadian legal writing and journalism. Canadian and American dictionaries accept the preposition as standard; British dictionaries do not list it. Many commentators consider the use a legalism, unsuitable for general formal writing.

Absent clear and compelling national security reasons, the state may commandeer them only with our explicit consent.
Toronto Star 30 Dec. 1992: A17

One recommendation narrows the defence of intoxication and provides that, absent fraud, duress, compulsion or reasonable mistake, someone performing the actus reus of a crime may be convicted of committing it 'while intoxicated' even though intoxication deprived him of mens rea.
Canadian Bar Review 66.3 (1987): 543

Absent a few details, we were the Cleavers.
Calgary Herald 26 Dec. 1992: G4

(Here the undisputed preposition *less* might be better.)

See also FUNCTIONAL SHIFT.

absolute adjectives   see COMPLETE; PERFECT; UNIQUE

absolute comparatives   When advertisers promise 'whiter washes', direct you to 'better bookstores', or offer 'higher interest rates', they are using absolute comparatives. An absolute comparative is a comparative construction (formed with either -*er* or *more*) not followed by *than*: that is, with no explicit basis of comparison. This structure annoys some language commentators who consider it intentionally imprecise. The claim of 'higher interest rates', for example, is so vague (higher than in 1962?) that it cannot be challenged. Commentators have also criticized particular absolute comparatives as snobbish ('better homes') or euphemistic ('older people' sounds less old than 'old people'). In spite of the criticism that absolute comparatives have drawn, they are not grammatically incorrect and cannot be avoided altogether. In fact, in everyday usage they are far more common than explicit comparisons: absolute comparatives that are not evasive or snobbish tend to go unnoticed.

In smaller schools, multigrade classes seem likely to increase....
Education Canada Summer 1989: 10

Shorter plants have higher rates of alternative pathway respiration.
Arctic 41.1 (1988): 1

[Hull] provides a welcome alternative to the prim correctness of some of the region's 'better' neighborhoods.
Ottawa Citizen 5 Dec. 1992: F2

(Here, as the quotation marks indicate, the absolute comparative did not go unnoticed.)

absorb, adsorb, absorption, adsorption   To *absorb* something is to take it in, to soak it up. The verb *adsorb* is a technical term meaning to draw molecules of liquid or gas to a surface and hold them there in a layer, not taking them in. The nouns *absorption* and *adsorption* are both spelled with a *p*.

Joshua's nimble mind absorbs melodies [the way] a sponge sucks up water.
Toronto Star 4 June 1992: SD1

Studies by Parkash and Brown (1976) showed that peat adsorbs titanium from aqueous solutions.
Canadian Journal of Earth Sciences 26 (1989): 212

Racquets are made from a variety of materials ... and have varying shock-absorbtion systems.
Ottawa Citizen 23 Aug. 1992: D10

(The correct spelling is *absorption*.)

academe, academia, academy, academic   *Academe, academia* and *the academy* are all used to refer to the world of scholarship and higher learning. Fowler objected to *academe* in this sense because in his view the word was a reference to Academus, a hero of Greek mythology. Plato founded his famous school near the olive grove sacred to Academus, and thus Plato's school became known as the *Academia*. The *Dictionary of Contemporary American Usage*, while accepting *academe* as an anglicized variant of *academia*, advises that it be used only in reference to Plato's Academy. Shakespeare, however, initiated a poetic tradition of using *academe* to mean a place of learning, and in this has proved more influential

than any language commentator: *academe* is now commonly used to mean the academic world. It is usually pronounced *a ka DEEM*.

Academe and *academia* (pronounced *a ka DEEM ya*) are often used facetiously or pejoratively. Likewise, the adjective *academic* has both a neutral meaning (having to do with scholarship or the university) and a pejorative one (of no practical import).

It is a story, in many ways, of failure—of women restricted by simple prejudice to the periphery of academe....
Queen's Quarterly 92.1 (1985): 20

Any conflict he had felt back in East St. Louis about where his musical future lay had been resolved by the head-to-head confrontation of the jazz clubs and academe.
Jack Chambers *Milestones* 1983: 33

I escaped from academia and bypassed journalism—which was the other career I considered....
Margaret Atwood *Second Words* 1982: 216

The university and its personnel are part of the dominant social order and the work that was produced and taught within the academy on the relations between men and women ... was deeply embedded in that assumed order.
Queen's Quarterly 92.1 (1985): 9

'The community has banquets to give out awards to athletes but we do nothing as a community for academic achievement.'
Toronto Star 28 Dec. 1992: A21

The debate between the advocates of a 'presidential' and 'parliamentary' system is therefore not just of academic interest to the West. It will probably determine whether the new Russia becomes more or less easy to live with.
Toronto Star 10 April 1992: A27

Acadia, Acadian, Cajun   *L'Acadie* or, in English, *Acadia* was the name given to the first permanent French settlement in North America. It ranged over the present-day provinces of New Brunswick, Nova Scotia, and Prince Edward Island, as well as the Magdalen Islands and parts of the Gaspé and Maine. Maritimers descended from these first French settlers are called *Acadians*. *Acadian* also refers to the dialect of French spoken in the Maritimes. The distinctive pronunciations and vocabulary of this dialect reveal that the original settlers came from south of the Loire River in France. (The majority of Quebec settlers came from north of the Loire.)

The British assumed control of Acadia in 1713 and in 1755 began to deport the Acadians, fearing their disloyalty in the ongoing wars between England and France. Many of the expelled Acadians settled in Louisiana, which was a French territory at the time. Some exiles later returned to Acadia and, together with fugitives who had escaped the British round-up, resettled the area. For generations, the Acadian community lacked both civil rights and French-language institutions.

By the mid-1800s the descendants of Acadians who had remained in Louisiana were known as *Cajuns*, an anglicized version of the French *Acadiens*. Though *Cajun* and *Acadian* are related terms, they are not synonymous. The two cultures diverged over the centuries. Cajun French was influenced by Spanish and the Creole French of the Caribbean. It is now a dialect in imminent danger of extinction. Cajun cuisine and music, on the other hand, are thriving.

'The older people didn't talk much about their life in Acadia because they saw the deportation as a humiliation.'
Gazette (Montreal) 5 Dec. 1992: B1

As in her earlier novels and plays, Maillet reveals the down-to-earth character of Acadian oral culture.
Ottawa Citizen 28 Nov. 1992: n.p.

Prime Minister Brian Mulroney's crack during the referendum campaign that Quebecers don't want to end up becoming Cajuns, dancing and playing banjos in Louisiana, didn't sit well with the Acadian community, which could mount a strong argument that Cajun musicians have generated more widespread awareness of the French fact in North America than all of Quebec's intellectuals and political poseurs combined.
Gazette (Montreal) 5 Dec. 1992: B1

See also BLACK; FRANCOPHONE; QUEBECKER.

accent, accentuate   The verbs *accent* and *accentuate* both mean to emphasize, but they have also developed some distinctive senses. Only *accent* means to stress a particular syllable in a word. *Accent* is the usual choice with reference to drawing attention to something by means of visual contrast ('accent the orange with a brick red'). Only *accentuate* means to intensify or aggravate a problem.

… suits with halter necks to accent the bust—reminiscent of 1940s glamor idols like Esther Williams—will also be in vogue.
Calgary Herald 22 Nov. 1994: B11

[They] are pleased with the changes Kirsch suggested to accentuate the suite's panoramic view.
Toronto Star 27 Aug. 1994: F1

Brilliant colors are very popular this year … with reds, burgundy and fuchsia topping color charts, shades often accented with emerald and turquoise.
Ottawa Citizen 20 Oct. 1994: E1

Those flimsy partitions and doors seemed, if anything, to accentuate the sound.
Max Braithwaite *The Night We Stole the Mountie's Car* 1971: 28

(Here *accent* is not possible.)

'… further polarization will tend to accentuate inequality in employment opportunities and earnings.'
Calgary Herald 7 Sept. 1994: B5

(Here *accent* is not possible.)

accent, dialect, variety   An *accent* is a way of pronouncing the language ('a foreign accent', 'a Southern accent', 'a South African accent'). Accents are relative: Canadians think Americans have accents, while Americans think Canadians do. Although there is no such thing as unaccented speech, sometimes speakers whose accent is the most widely accepted and prestigious will be described as having no accent.

A *dialect* is a regional or social variety of the language (Newfoundland English, working-class English) characterized by distinctive features of grammar and vocabulary. Because a dialect is often characterized as inferior to the standard language, the standard English of a particular nation (e.g., Australian English, Indian English, Nigerian English, British English) is usually referred to as a *variety* of English rather than a dialect. Indeed, any distinctive form of English may be referred to as a *variety* as a way of avoiding the often pejorative implications of the term *dialect*. A particular accent is usually linked to a particular dialect. Jamaicans speak Jamaican Creole English—a dialect of Jamaican English—with a Jamaican accent. However, the link is not a necessary one: Canadian or British English can be spoken with a Jamaican accent. The adjective form of *dialect* is *dialectal*.

See also LINGUA FRANCA; PIDGIN, CREOLE; STANDARD ENGLISH, STANDARD.

accent marks   see DIACRITICAL MARKS

accentuate   see ACCENT

accept *Accept* followed by an infinitive and used to mean agree ('Will they accept to come a day earlier?') is a non-standard usage, probably influenced by French.

In Standard English *accept* is occasionally followed by the *-ing* form of a verb. In this construction it means endorse or approve of: 'They don't accept eating meat'.

'That's why I accepted to come here. It was best for me.'
Gazette (Montreal) 13 Dec. 1993: D3

(The usual expression is 'agreed to come'.)

Is the Herald's policy to accept law-breaking?
Calgary Herald 2 July 1993: A6

access In the vocabulary of computing, to *access* means to gain access to or to retrieve data from. The use of *access* as a verb in contexts other than computing is still considered inappropriate by most commentators.

Immigration violations are now stored on a separate computer system that can't be accessed by police.
Gazette (Montreal) 2 July 1994: A15

(This use of *access* has been standard in computing since the early 1960s.)

[The] ecological reserve ... can be easily accessed by the lakeside Inkaneep campsite, another popular camping spot.
Beautiful British Columbia Spring 1990: 45

(Here *reached from* would be preferable.)

... it is important to know the steps to take to access professional help when they suspect their loved one has a mental health disorder.
Guardian (Charlottetown) 2 Nov. 1990: 8

(Here *find* would be preferable.)

See also FUNCTIONAL SHIFT.

accessary, accessory *Accessary* is an old spelling of the legal term for someone who incites or assists a criminal but does not actually commit the crime. Now *accessory* is the spelling used both for this sense and for the sense of something inessential or additional.

The first *c* in this word has a hard *k* sound.

Smith's reputation had not been seriously tarnished by the moral and financial support he had given to John Brown, even though he had been accused of being an accessory before the fact in the raid at Harper's Ferry....

William Teatero *John Anderson: Fugitive Slave* 1986: 122

Too many people keep a dog as an accessory rather than a friend.
Dogs in Canada Special Issue 1986: 56–7

accident, mishap An *accident* and a *mishap* are both unexpected or chance events, but an *accident* may be lucky or unlucky, while a *mishap* is always unlucky. Some style guides insist that *mishap* refers only to minor incidents. Many dictionaries do not qualify its meaning in this way, and in Canadian writing, usage is mixed.

... scientists close to evolutionary theory are beginning to believe that intelligence is an extraordinary accident, so fantastically improbable that it's quite likely it has happened only once so far in the whole universe.
Vancouver Sun 15 Dec. 1990: D21

The newspaper quoted nuclear experts saying such an accident could lead to a potentially catastrophic explosion with widespread nuclear fallout.
Calgary Herald 14 Feb. 1988: A3

I was told that the sign was an acknowledgement that I was harbouring ... dogs that would knowingly bite, thus setting myself up for a potential lawsuit should a mishap occur.
Dogs in Canada Aug. 1986: 10

The injury—a completely severed ligament—was a brutal mishap for a dancer.
Maclean's 20 Feb. 1989: A50

His body was pulled from Canoe Lake a week after his disappearance, ostensibly the victim of a fishing mishap—though whispers of a more sinister end persist today.
Gazette (Montreal) 16 July 1990: B9

accidentally, incidentally Because the *-al-* in *accidentally* and *incidentally* is seldom pronounced, these adverbs are often misspelled *accidently* and *incidently*. It may help to remember that adverbs are formed from adjectives; hence the adverb ending *-ly* is being added to the adjectives *accidental* and *incidental*, not the nouns *accident* and *incident*.

One dictionary, *Merriam-Webster's*, now lists *accidently* as a standard spelling variant. However, no other dictionary has followed suit, and usage guides uniformly recommend against this spelling.

Once domesticated, animals have often been moved from place to place, both deliberately and accidentally.
William Norton *Human Geography* 1992: 224

Anyone can accidently knock the gear-shift lever out of gear and disaster can soon follow.
Gazette (Montreal) 20 June 1992: H1

(The recommended spelling is *accidentally*.)

Loesser's book, incidentally, is not in it.
Queen's Quarterly 94 (1987): 62

Incidently, the gate receipts at the Skydome were $3,787,400....
Province (Vancouver) 12 Nov. 1990: 30

(The correct spelling is *incidentally*.)

acclamation, acclaim   In Canada, to be elected *by acclamation* or to *be acclaimed* means to win an election by default because no one else ran. These meanings of *acclamation* and *acclaim* are unique to Canadian English. In Britain and the United States the same expressions refer to winning in a vote decided by cheers and shouts rather than by ballots.

The noun *acclaim* means public approval. In British and American English, the loud and enthusiastic applause of a live audience is usually called *acclamation*. However, Canadians prefer to use *acclaim* in this context as well, reserving *acclamation* for its special political sense.

So it is appropriate to look at Sifton on the threshold of his federal career ... about to return triumphantly to his home town, where he knows he will shortly win his federal seat by acclamation.
Pierre Berton *The Promised Land* 1984: 8

Mayor Lorna Jackson is back for her fourth term on council. She was acclaimed when her only competitor ... dropped out of the race in early October.
Toronto Star 17 Oct. 1991: NY4

But it was the awesome performances by the American team that drew the acclaim of the full-house crowd of approximately 7,000.
Gazette (Montreal) 6 March 1989: C1

(Here *acclaim* means approval.)

acclimatize, acclimate, acclimatization, acclimation, adaptation   To *acclimatize* or *acclimate* (pronounced *AK li mate* or *a KLIME ut*) is to adjust to a new environment. Both words are acceptable. *Acclimatize* is more common. *Acclimate* is mainly restricted to Canada and the United States.

In biology the term *acclimatization* (or *acclimation*) is distinguished from *adaptation*: acclimatization is a short-term process that occurs within an individual's lifetime, whereas the adaptation of a species to its environment may span many generations.

[The sports exchange] will enable Canadian athletes to better acclimatize themselves to the surroundings for the 1988 Summer Games.
Globe and Mail (Toronto) 21 March 1985: M13

This process, known as 'hardening off,' gradually acclimates the plants to outdoor conditions.
Edmonton Journal 19 May 1994: C2

... he'll continue a major behavioral and molecular analysis of the spider, expected to reveal evolutionary secrets of the spider's adaptation to various environmental conditions.
Spectator (Hamilton) 10 March 1994: T1

See also ADAPTATION.

accommodate, accommodation   *Accommodate* and *accommodation* are frequently misspelled with one *m*. These words are related etymologically to *commodious*, 'roomy'—a point that may help with spelling.

But even now, when most women work outside the home, the tax system continues to best accomodate men.
Globe and Mail (Toronto) 6 April 1985: M10

(The correct spelling is *accommodate*.)

Residential accomodation—where the lease is for periods of one month or more—will not be subject to GST.
Financial Post 23 April 1990: 32

(The correct spelling is *accommodation*.)

accredit   *Accredited* does not mean acclaimed. To *accredit* means to lend credence to or endorse. Evidence that accredits a theory supports it. Professionals and organizations that are accredited are officially recognized or certified by a regulating body. Diplomats accredited to a certain country are official envoys to that country.

A second accepted meaning of *accredit* is to attribute. A quotation may be accredited to a source, or an effect to a cause.

The publisher's claim that the book was vetted by the Israeli military censor serves to simultaneously accredit the background data and explain the few stilted passages.
Toronto Star 8 Aug. 1992: K15

... all hospitals in the province must meet rigid standards, including infection control, in order to be accredited by the province.
Spectator (Hamilton) 16 Aug. 1994: T1

Canada will then accredit a Canadian representative to Eritrea who will work from the embassy in Addis Ababa.
Ottawa Citizen 21 April 1993: A2

This lateness has been a characteristic of the comet in its past seven revolutions. It is accredited to non-gravitational forces acting on it. . . .
Queen's Quarterly 92.2 (1985): 285

Twenty-two years later he produced Success Story, a highly accredited film about insect survival.
Spectator (Hamilton) 30 Sept. 1994: T3

(Here *acclaimed* or *regarded* should replace *accredited*.)

accused   see ALLEGED

ache   Words derived from *ache*, including *achy*, *achier*, and *aching*, are often misspelled.

Many of the originals have become 'too old, too bent and too achey' to turn out.
Calgary Herald 23 July 1992: N1

(The correct spelling is *achy*.)

achieve   *Achieve* and *achievement* are often misspelled with *-ei-* instead of *-ie-*.

The award recognizes outstanding lifetime acheivement in the intellectual life of Canada.
Edmonton Journal 15 March 1994: B5

(The correct spelling is *achievement*.)

Achilles' heel   An *Achilles' heel* is a point of vulnerability or a weakness. According to Greek mythology, when Achilles was an infant, his mother dipped him into the River Styx to make him invulnerable; however, since she held him by the heel, it did not go into the water and so remained unprotected. As Homer's *Iliad* recounts, Paris killed Achilles by shooting an arrow into his heel, after learning that it was his only vulnerable spot.
While dictionaries generally include the apostrophe following *Achilles*, some style guides do not, and usage is divided. *Achilles' heel* is more common in formal writing, but *Achilles heel* is also correct. The spelling to be avoided is *Achille's heel*: the *s* is part of Achilles' name.

You found my Achilles' heel.
Howard Engel *Murder Sees the Light* 1981: 65

Goaltending remains the Wings' Achilles heel in post-season.
Edmonton Journal 16 April 1994: F5

While the IOC has approved all of Quebec's other 63 event sites, choosing a site for the Olympic downhill race has proved an Achille's heel.
Calgary Herald 14 Nov. 1994: A2

(The apostrophe should follow the *s* in *Achilles*.)

See also POSSESSIVE.

acme   see EPITOME

acq-   see AQ-

acronym   see ABBREVIATION

activate, actuate   In technical contexts, *activate* and *actuate* are interchangeable: a machine can be either activated or actuated.
Some commentators object to the use of *activate* with reference to actions prompted by inner forces. They would prefer *actuate*: while external forces may activate people, inner promptings actuate them. In fact, *actuate* is formal and slightly old-fashioned in this use; *motivate* and *inspire* are more common choices today.

In communications laboratories, scientists are working furiously to produce viable voice-activated controls for television and other household technology.
Ottawa Citizen 26 June 1994: B1

When you select a memorized position, it actuates steering-wheel tilt and telescoping, door-mirror position and even rear-view-mirror setting.
Vancouver Sun 16 Feb. 1990: E1

Thorson denies that a Crown attorney 'whose conduct is actuated by malice cannot be considered to be engaged in the due enforcement of the criminal law.'
Globe and Mail (Toronto) 27 Sept. 1985: P117

If a love of Canada and a desire to preserve it are the aims that actuate the Newfoundland MLAs . . . then I don't doubt the outcome of the free vote.
Ottawa Citizen 14 June 1990: A15

But it is evident that neither the defenders nor the invaders of the settlement were activated by a 'territorial instinct'.
Irving M. Zeitlin and Robert J. Brym *The Social Condition of Humanity* 1991: 31

(Here some commentators would prefer *motivated* or *actuated*.)

'No doubt this experienced judge was activated by the best motives, but the interest of fairness requires a new trial. . . .
Vancouver Sun 27 Jan. 1990: A9

(Here some commentators would prefer *motivated* or *actuated*.)

actress   see JOB TITLES

actuate   see ACTIVATE

acute   see CHRONIC

ad   see ADVERTISEMENT

A.D., B.C., C.E., B.C.E., B.P.   *A.D.* is an abbreviation of the Latin phrase *anno Domini*, 'in the year of the (our) Lord'. It is used to distinguish years after the birth of Christ from years before, which are labelled *B.C.* ('Before Christ'). Most style guides recommend placing *B.C.* after the year ('55 B.C.') and *A.D.* before it ('A.D. 1511'), to conform to the complete phrase: '55 (years) before Christ'; 'the year of the (our) Lord 1511'. However, in informal writing *A.D.* is common in either position.

Some scholars have begun to use *C.E.* ('Common Era') and *B.C.E.* ('Before Common Era') instead of *A.D.* and *B.C.*. Although the dating system itself is not changed—the Common Era commences with the birth of Christ—the use of *C.E.* and *B.C.E.* removes the explicit Christian reference from the modern Western calendar. These alternative abbreviations are still uncommon enough to require an explanation.

Geologists and other scientists commonly use the international *B.P.* ('Before Present') dating system. An event is dated by subtracting years from the present (the present is defined by convention as 1950). Thus 3950 B.P. is the same as 2000 B.C.

Most publications (except newspapers) print all these abbreviations in small capital letters (A.D., B.C., etc.). The use of periods (A.D. *or* AD) is a matter of style.

Caesar Augustus issued decrees in 28 B.C. and 8 B.C., and again in 14 A.D.
Daily News (Halifax) 12 Dec. 1993: 42

(In formal writing, *A.D.* is usually placed before the year.)

Ratio data ... showed three lower and two higher-than-present timberline phases since 1600 BP, with timberline at its lowest elevation c. 500 BP.
The Canadian Geographer Spring 1989: 84

See also DATES.

adaptation, adaption   *Adaptation* and *adaption* are variants: either is acceptable in any sense. But *adaption* is used far less frequently, mostly in the context of creative writing: 'It was an original screenplay, not an adaption'.

After long adaptation to land conditions, slugs are unable to tolerate deep water and most species will drown if immersed in water.
Ottawa Citizen 3 Sept. 1994: J4

On the program that night was *The Devil's Mill*, an adaptation of a Czech folk tale which deals with human temptation.
George Ignatieff *The Making of a Peacemonger* 1987: 132

Nightwood's first work was an adaption of Sharon Riis's *The True Story of Ida Johnson*.
Fuse Magazine 13.4 (1990): 13

But he sees a more open market with Australia as a first step in the economy's adaption to competing successfully in world markets.
Globe and Mail (Toronto) 15 April 1985: IB3

(This use of *adaption* is uncommon.)

See also ACCLIMATIZE.

adapter, adaptor   Canadians use either *adapter* or *adaptor* to refer to a person who rewrites material for a different audience or medium, or to a gadget that makes equipment compatible. American and British dictionaries also list either spelling for either meaning. The *-er* spelling is more common in Canada and the United States, the *-or* spelling in Britain.

... Air Farce can be just as unsubtle in its humor as Voltaire [or] book adapter Hugh Wheeler. ...
Globe and Mail (Toronto) 21 Jan. 1985: S11

Harwood, the adaptor [of the script], has proudly declared himself culpable.
Globe and Mail (Toronto) 22 Oct. 1985: C1

The Puma Plus comes with power adapter, interface cables, utility software and set-up templates.
Computer Dealer News 21 March 1991: 69

To attach a flash gun to a tripod requires a special adaptor, available at any photo supply store.
Globe and Mail (Toronto) 9 Feb. 1985: E14

The company's Stericap system consists of an adapter, which fits over the bottle neck of injectable products, and a cap, containing a disinfectant in a small sponge, which fits into the adaptor.
Country Guide Nov. 1986: 32

(Although both spellings are correct, one or the other should be used consistently within a given text.)

See also -ER, -OR.

addresses   see COMMA

ad feminam   see AD HOMINEM

ad hoc   *Ad hoc* is a Latin phrase meaning 'for this'. An ad hoc committee is one that is set up for a special purpose, as opposed to an administrative committee set up to deal with recurrent issues.

The phrase *ad hoc* is sometimes used disparagingly to describe a style of management marked by lack of forethought, which consists entirely of reacting to crises. This style is also described by the noun *ad hockery* (sometimes hyphenated and sometimes spelled without the *k*). *Ad hockery* is a facetious coinage, as yet restricted to informal use.

> For many years judges have headed an array of ad hoc commissions of inquiry, ranging from the Gouzenko spy affair to the Dubin inquiry into drugs in sport.
> Andrew Heard *Canadian Constitutional Conventions* 1991: 134

> In the face of the rapid social and technological changes that were taking place it became apparent that our ad hoc approach to reforming and amending our Criminal Code was no longer adequate.
> *Canadian Bar Review* 66.3 (1987): 531

> The university has never earmarked much money for acquisitions, so curators have been largely dependent on what people have been persuaded to give them. Hence, the sense of high ad-hockery one gets while wandering through the various galleries.
> *Globe and Mail* (Toronto) 26 Oct. 1985: D13

> So when objections arose, or assumptions proved faulty, ad-hockery took over, with politicians making alternative plans with little regard for their rationality.
> *Ottawa Citizen* 4 Nov. 1991: A8

See also LATIN PHRASES.

ad hominem, ad feminam   *Ad hominem* is a Latin phrase meaning literally 'to the man'. It is used to label a type of fallacious argument that defames an opponent instead of addressing the points he or she is raising. In formal writing the phrase requires italics.

Ad hominem entered the English language in the sixteenth century, when the use of masculine pronouns and nouns as generic forms, referring to either men or women, was unquestioned. The phrase *ad feminam*, 'to the woman', is a humorous feminist coinage.

Many of the articles in the book have consisted mainly of ad hominem attacks on Cote himself that scarcely address the substance of what he's actually written.
Gazette (Montreal) 8 Dec. 1990: B3

Argumentum ad Hominem: 'John is a drunkard; therefore, he is wrong about disarmament.'
Globe and Mail (Toronto) 7 Sept. 1985: P6

See also LATIN PHRASES.

ad infinitum   *Ad infinitum* (pronounced *AD in fi NITE um*) is a Latin phrase meaning 'without limit' or 'endlessly'; it does not mean 'taken to an extreme'.

> At the opposite extreme is the belief that the miracles of modern science may be able to stave off every single thing that goes wrong with us, lengthening our lifespan ad infinitum.
> *Toronto Sun* 16 Feb. 1994: S10

> As has been repeated ad infinitum, the 27-year-old left-winger is going through the worst of his nine seasons as a pro.
> *Gazette* (Montreal) 21 March 1992: C2

> It's the modern, corporate, high-tech world ad infinitum. A world where people make lots of money and are plugged in, but have no time.
> *Canadian Speeches* April 1994: 34

(Here *ad infinitum* is inappropriate; 'taken to the extreme' would be better.)

> Women live longer than men, so Canada Pension Plan premiums should be higher for women if this argument is to be taken ad infinitum.
> *Toronto Star* 3 May 1993: A20

(Here *ad infinitum* is inappropriate; 'to the logical extreme' would be better.)

See also LATIN PHRASES.

adjectives and adverbs   Adjectives are words such as *green*, *calm*, *cultural*, and *defective*. They modify—that is, they describe or particularize—nouns: '*green* bananas', 'a *calm* day', 'a *cultural* pursuit', 'the *defective* switch'.

Adverbs—words such as *well*, *too*, *fairly*, and *remarkably*—serve many functions. They modify verbs ('He eats *well*'), adjectives ('*too* cold'), other adverbs ('*fairly* well'), and whole sentences ('*Remarkably*, he wasn't hurt'). For a discussion of adverbs that modify whole sentences—including *hopefully*—see SENTENCE ADVERBS.

The vast majority of adverbs are formed by adding -*ly* to an adjective: *brazen*, *brazenly*; *exceptional*, *exceptionally; merciful, mercifully.* Yet many of the most frequently used adverbs do not fit this pattern: *already, ever, here, late, often, together, very.* And not every word that ends in *-ly* is an adverb: a handful are adjectives, including *friendly, lovely, scholarly, stately,* and *ugly.* See FRIENDLY on the subject of turning this type of adjective into an adverb.

It is non-standard to use an adjective to modify a verb, as in 'He throws good'. For those who don't normally use adjectives adverbially, a sentence like 'They treat you decent' is linguistic slumming—a dialect shift for effect. However, concern for adhering to the standard can lead people to overcorrect their normal usage. This phenomenon is called hypercorrection. With respect to adverbs, there are two common forms of hypercorrection. The first consists in adding a superfluous *-ly* to common words that function as both adverbs and adjectives: 'Open widely'; 'Go easily on them'. In these contexts, *wide* and *easy* are correct.

The second type of hypercorrection consists in changing adjectives to adverbs because they follow verbs: 'I feel badly'; 'We all looked ridiculously in the new uniforms'. The modifier following a verb does not always have to be an adverb. It should be an adverb if it modifies the action of the verb: 'They sang dreadfully'. However, *be, become,* and *seem,* and in some cases other verbs such as *feel, look,* and *sound,* denote no action but instead describe the state of the subject of the sentence. Such verbs are correctly followed by adjectives.

They seem happy.

They play happily for hours.

We got wise.

We chose wisely.

He felt bad about the mix-up.

He dresses badly.

I feel good about the interview.

I wasn't feeling well.

Note that *well* is both an adverb ('They danced well') and an adjective meaning in good health, in good shape: 'I am well'; 'All is well'.

Whether—or when—it is acceptable to place an adverb between the function word *to* and a verb, as in 'to really understand', or 'to totally change', is a question that has vexed usage commentators for over two centuries. This issue is discussed under SPLIT INFINITIVE.

See also ABSOLUTE COMPARATIVES; ATTRIBUTIVE NOUNS; BAD, BADLY; COMPARISONS; HYPER-CORRECTION; MISPLACED MODIFIERS; REAL, REALLY; ZERO ADVERBS.

adjudication   see CONCILIATION

adjure   see ABJURE

admittance, admission   These words are sometimes interchangeable. However, *admittance* is more common in reference to physical entry; signs restricting access to an area say 'No Admittance'. *Admission* more often refers to (the price of) entrance to an entertainment (the phrase *no admission* usually means 'no entrance fee', not 'no entry'). Acceptance into a school or club is usually called *admission.* An acknowledgement of a failure, guilty secret, or problem is always an *admission,* never an *admittance.*

But two high-profile foes of NAFTA—Maude Barlow and Tony Clarke—were outside after being refused admittance.
Daily News (Halifax) 22 May 1993: 18

. . . the price of admission to these 'second-run' films at independent theatres is usually lower than to first-run offerings at the big chains.
Canadian Consumer Jan. 1985: 6

There's no admission and things get under way at 7 p.m.
Calgary Herald 14 Dec. 1993: A14

Basically each inn provides lectures for law students and examines candidates for admission to the bar [certification to practise law].
Globe and Mail (Toronto) 1 Nov. 1986: F5

Despite suggestions to the contrary, UTS is a public school in which any student who meets the entrance criteria can gain admittance.
Toronto Star 15 June 1993: A7

(In this context *admission* is more common.)

But there was no admission of mistakes by management.
Toronto Star 19 June 1993: B1

(Here *admittance* is not possible.)

ad nauseam   *Ad nauseam* is a Latin phrase meaning to a tedious extreme—literally, 'to the point of nausea'. It is often misspelled *ad nauseum.*

The boast 'we are strong' was repeated by the speaker ad nauseam.
Henry M. Rosenthal and S. Cathy Berson, eds. *Canadian Jewish Outlook Anthology* 1988: 37

The problem with this book is that it has all been said before—ad nauseum.
Vancouver Sun 18 July 1994: C4

(The correct spelling is *ad nauseam*.)

See also LATIN PHRASES.

adopted, adoptive Children are *adopted*; their new parents are *adoptive*. While it is considered wrong to substitute *adopted* for *adoptive*, as in 'adopted parents', it is acceptable to use *adoptive* to mean *adopted*, as in 'adoptive child' or 'adoptive country'. This latter usage is more common in British than Canadian English.

Adopted children, however happy they may be in their adoptive families, may yearn at some point to know more about their birth parents....
Globe and Mail (Toronto) 4 Dec. 1985: A6

The Ontario Society for the Prevention of Cruelty to Animals is looking for adoptive owners.
Toronto Star 30 June 1994: NY6

Before meeting his long-lost brother, Lussier met with his brother's adopted parents and they were stunned at the resemblance to their son.
Daily News (Halifax) 16 Oct. 1992: 40

(The word required here is *adoptive*.)

A West Vancouver couple re-mortgaged their home to pay the legal bills in their continuing fight to retain custody of their adoptive child....
Vancouver Sun 17 Sept. 1994: A4

His birth country boycotted the Olympics in 1984 and his adoptive country didn't rush through citizenship to get him on the team for Seoul four years later.
Gazette (Montreal) 28 July 1992: C3

adsorb, adsorption see ABSORB

ad valorem, value-added tax *Ad valorem* means 'according to the value'. It is used to describe taxes calculated by adding a percentage to the price of a taxable item: for example, a retail sales tax of 12 per cent. As a Latin phrase, *ad valorem* requires italics in formal writing.
A *value-added* tax is a particular type of *ad valorem* tax that is calculated only on the amount by which an article has increased in value at each stage of its production or distribution.

These two types of tax contrast with fixed or flat taxes, which are charged per unit: for example, a gasoline tax of ten cents per litre.
There is no hyphen in 'Value Added Tax' (European Economic Community), but the phrase *value-added tax* is almost always hyphenated in North American usage.

The original bill would have scrapped the existing ad valorem tax system—based on 20 per cent of the retail price of gasoline—and replaced it with a flat tax of 8.8 cents a litre.
Globe and Mail (Toronto) 4 Dec. 1985: A10

The ad valorem tax would have jumped 19 cents because it is based on the price of cigarets, which has risen significantly since the tax was frozen in July, 1984.
Globe and Mail (Toronto) 2 Nov. 1985: A5

Last year, Martin was frustrated in extensive talks with the provinces aimed at establishing a 12% value-added tax to replace both the GST and provincial retail levies.
Financial Post 10 June 1995: n.p.

See also LATIN PHRASES.

advance, advancement *Advance* is the more general word, referring to any type of movement forward or upward: 'The advance (*not* the advancement) of the snail was slow'. An improvement on a previous state of affairs is usually called an *advance* ('advances in eye surgery'); *advancement* is sometimes used in the same sense, but not all dictionaries list this meaning for it.
Advancement is generally reserved for two meanings: moving to a better position on the job or in society ('advancement through the ranks') or active promotion of a cause ('the advancement of women in sport').

The story recounts the relentless advance of raccoon rabies over the last two decades from Florida, then Virginia, and north until it now rages in raccoon populations only 20 kilometers from the Canadian border....
Ottawa Citizen 1 Sept. 1994: B1

If Gallo's results are validated in humans, it could represent a significant advance in treatment....
Gazette (Montreal) 9 Aug. 1994: A1

[Adult illiterates] work at low paying seasonal or service jobs where the opportunity for advancement and support from the employer is extremely limited....
Briarpatch April 1990: 5

FreeNet had argued that the network provided [for] the advancement of education and was a benefit of a charitable nature to the community.
Ottawa Citizen 14 Sept. 1994: E3

Not only the Eiffel Tower but also the most humble mud hut represented advancement when it was first created.
The Canadian Architect June 1986: 33

(Here 'an *advance*' would be better.)

'The new line is the most significant advancement in battery technology Sears has brought to its DieHard line in 27 years.'
Calgary Herald 30 Dec. 1994: E3

(Here *advance* would be better.)

adverbs see ADJECTIVES AND ADVERBS; SENTENCE ADVERBS; ZERO ADVERBS

adverse, averse *Adverse* means unfavourable, harmful, or opposed, as in 'adverse weather', 'adverse publicity', or 'an adverse decision'. To be *averse* to something means to dislike the idea of it; not to be averse to something means not to object to it, at least in principle. Usage commentators are divided over whether it is acceptable to say that someone is (or is not) *adverse* to something. Some commentators maintain that *adverse* is simply the wrong word in this context. Others claim that a distinction of sense can be made: someone averse to something dislikes it, while someone adverse to something is opposed to it. If such a fine distinction of sense is made in formal Canadian writing, we have not seen it: in formal writing, people are not described as adverse to things. In informal writing, therefore, it is most likely that the disputed use of *adverse* is simply a confusion with *averse*.

While not averse to expulsions as such, Serrati argued that the Comintern should leave it to the PSI to choose the moment to get rid of the reformists.
Canadian Journal of History 14.1 (1989): 31

But Sifton himself was not averse to hiring political rascals if they did the job.
Pierre Berton *The Promised Land* 1984: 12

Don't misunderstand. I'm not averse to glamor, to short skirts and lacy underthings.
Gazette (Montreal) 18 Nov. 1994: A3

For those who are well-heeled, or not adverse to carrying extra baggage, you could always take a small TV with you.
Toronto Star 17 Nov. 1994: G2

(Here *averse to* is recommended.)

The survey also found that people aren't adverse to a stronger regional government.
Vancouver Sun 13 Nov. 1990: B2

(Here *averse to* is recommended.)

advertisement, ad, advert *Advertisement* is the standard spelling in Canada, Britain, and the United States. *Advertizement* is an uncommon variant spelling even in North America, where -*ize* endings are generally preferred.

In Canada and the United States, *ad vur TIZE ment* is the predominant pronunciation, but *ad VUR tiss ment*—which is how the British say the word—is also common. It is likely this second pronunciation that leads to the fairly common misspelling *advertisment*.

The short form *ad* has become a standard word, but not a formal one: *advertisement* is still favoured in academic writing. In British English *advertisement* has two short forms: *ad* and *advert*. *Advert* is quite uncommon in Canada.

... groups often take out newspaper advertisements that urge like-minded citizens to send postcards, telegrams, and prepared coupons to MPs and Cabinet ministers.
A. Paul Pross *Group Politics and Public Policy* 2nd ed. 1992: 10

And he somehow missed advertisments and news stories warning voters to get on the list before the deadline.
Vancouver Sun 23 Oct. 1992: A10

(The correct spelling is *advertisements*.)

... she was advised to put a classified ad in the *Free Press*.
Pierre Berton *The Promised Land* 1984: 158

It's possible that Loach was trying to film a sensitive and gripping Marxist parable, but Riff Raff plays more like a feature-length advert for the Workmen's Compensation Board.
Toronto Star 27 March 1992: C7

See also -IZE, -ISE, -YZE, -YSE.

advice, advise The noun *advice*, as in 'good advice', is often misspelled *advise*. *Advise*, as in 'I advise caution', is the correct spelling for the verb.

I was honoured that he should even think of asking for my advice on such an important matter.
Queen's Quarterly 96.1 (1989): 52–3

'We want to advise people to go to other local hospitals in an emergency.'
Gazette (Montreal) 26 Nov. 1992: G1

'I'll sit down at Christmas and talk to some people and listen to their advise.'
Daily News (Halifax) 19 Nov. 1992: 67

(The noun is spelled with a *c*: *advice*.)

See also -CE, -SE.

adviser, advisor   Canadian writers use *adviser* more frequently than *advisor*. The newer *-or* ending has probably developed because it is close to the adjective form *advisory*, or perhaps by analogy with *supervisor*. Canadian, American, and British dictionaries and sundry usage guides all list both spellings.

See also -ER, -OR.

-ae-, -oe-, -e-   The two-letter combinations *ae* and *oe* are found in words derived from Latin or Greek, such as *aesthetic* and *oestrogen*. Both *ae* and *oe* are pronounced either as a long *e*, as in *weed*, or as a short *e*, as in *wed*. For many words either pronunciation is acceptable.

American spelling convention is generally to replace these two-letter forms with *e*, except in proper names such as Aeschylus and Oedipus. British convention is generally to retain them, and Canadian usage is somewhere in between.

Alternative spellings (Canadian preference*):

aegis*	egis
aeon	eon*
amoeba*	ameba
caesarean*	cesarean
diarrhoea	diarrhea*
encyclopaedia	encyclopedia*
faeces	feces*
foetid	fetid*
haemophilia	hemophilia*
haemorrhage	hemorrhage*
mediaeval	medieval*
oesophagus	esophagus*
oestrogen	estrogen*
palaeolithic	paleolithic*

Canadian journalists tend to follow American spelling conventions, using *fetus*, *esthetic*, and *anemia*, while the spellings most common in books and academic papers are *foetus*, *aesthetic*, and *anaemia*. Although some might feel that Canadians should be persuaded to aim for consistency in their treatment of these words and others like them, it is precisely this mix of British and American English that is the hallmark of Canadian English.

Formerly, *ae* and *oe* were printed as linked characters (*æ*, *œ*) called *ligatures*.

See also DIPHTHONG, DIGRAPH, LIGATURE; SPELLING, CANADIAN.

aegis, egis   In Greek mythology, *aegis* referred to the breastplate of Zeus or Athena and came to symbolize divine protection. In contemporary usage, *aegis* (pronounced *EE jiss*) usually means protection in the weaker sense of administration or sponsorship. *Aegis* is sometimes spelled *egis* in the United States.

... the system of feudalism was born primarily to give life a measure of security and normality under the aegis of a feudal landlord.
J.E. Smyth et al. *The Law and Business Administration in Canada* 1987: 9

He is one of the 22 volunteers from the Neighborhood Helpers Project operating under the aegis of the Downtown Eastside Seniors' Centre....
Vancouver Sun 27 June 1994: C4

Perhaps filing this one under the aegis of 'mistress' is unfair.
Gazette (Montreal) 5 June 1994: C3

(Here *aegis* has been confused with *heading* or *category*.)

See also -AE-, -OE-, -E-; AUSPICES.

aeroplane   see AIRPLANE

affect, effect   If something *affects* something, then it has an *effect* on it. Here *affect* is a verb meaning to have some influence on something or to modify it, and *effect* is a noun referring to the result of an action: 'Drinking affects your driving'; 'A slower reaction time is one effect of drinking'.

The verb *effect* means to bring about and can mean something quite different from the verb *affect*, so it is important not to confuse the spellings:

John's visit to the spa effected [brought about] his recovery. (Here he is cured.)

John's visit to the spa affected [helped or hindered] his recovery. (Here he may be better or worse.)

To *affect* may also mean to pretend to have or feel something: 'Some Canadians affect a British accent'. The noun *affect* is a psychological term meaning emotion or feeling.

'Pressure doesn't affect him.'
Toronto Star 30 June 1994: D1

Anxiety, tension, difficulty in sleeping ... can all be positively effected, for most of us, by the moderate use of wine.
Bon Vivant Nov. 1981: 13

(Here *affected* is required.)

The effect on Canadian democracy was deleterious.
A. Paul Pross *Group Politics and Public Policy* 2nd ed. 1992: 244

The search was expanded somewhat yesterday to account for the effects of wind and drifting.
Daily News (Halifax) 3 Jan. 1994: n.p.

Winter has arrived with an icy fury, bringing with it one of the season's worst dangers—the wind chill affect that can turn a cold day into a killer.
Province (Vancouver) 31 Dec. 1990: 45

(Here *effect* is required.)

The apparent futility of a time-consuming and expensive process is underlined by the fact that MPs themselves frequently bemoan their inability to effect real changes in legislation.
A. Paul Pross *Group Politics and Public Policy* 2nd ed. 1992: 77

She affects dramatic shifts of accent, posture, complexion and hair color, and her characters appear to be as much a triumph of alchemy as of acting.
Maclean's 28 July 1986: 36

Excuse my lack of affect, I'm male: In movies that featured human characters, the preponderance of males with plugged-up passions was impossible to ignore this year.
Calgary Herald 2 Jan. 1994: C1

affection, affectation *Affection* is genuine fondness for someone or something. Someone displaying an *affectation* is speaking or behaving in an artificial or unnatural way that is unlikely to win any friends.

Both men were smiling and their warm hug spoke volumes about the affection and respect they have for each other.
Spectator (Hamilton) 22 Dec. 1994: D4

William has produced his pipe, an affectation he by and large reserves for company.
Margaret Atwood *Life Before Man* 1979: 138

affidavit see EVIDENCE

affinity The choice of preposition to follow the noun *affinity* can sometimes cause problems: *for*, *to*, *with*, and *between* are all acceptable, but in Canadian English *for* and *to* are the most common choices.
Fowler disapproved of the use of *for* or *to* after *affinity*, arguing that the word *affinity* properly describes only a reciprocal relationship; thus the appropriate prepositions to use after *affinity* are *between* and *with*.

Most British usage guides still defer to Fowler on this point. However, American guides do not, for two reasons: first, particular prepositions are associated with certain words as much by convention as by logic; and, second, the meaning of the word *affinity* has broadened to include one-sided attractions. Certainly, in contemporary Canadian usage, *affinity* has a range of meanings: an instinctive rapport, an attraction, a similarity, an aptitude. Some of these meanings require the preposition *for* or *to*.

Even as an anglophone, I have discovered a strange affinity for these passionate French Quebecois people.
Gazette (Montreal) 13 Dec. 1994: B2

There is a spirit of place ... similar to the affinity that Rowell feels for his beloved Yosemite.
Vancouver Sun 31 Dec. 1994: D12

Even now, Canadians seem to feel an affinity to the steeply pitched roofs, picturesque buildings and sheer verticality of 19th-century Gothic.
Toronto Star 15 Oct. 1994: H8

Both mohair and angora have a special affinity for dyes, which means they reproduce colors with remarkable clarity....
Ottawa Citizen 20 Oct. 1994: E1

It is in *Brébeuf* particularly that Pratt shows his affinity to the oral poets in his respect for his sources.
Northrop Frye *The Bush Garden* 1971: 185

'I like running and building machines. I've always had a natural affinity for machines.'
Gazette (Montreal) 12 March 1994: B3

afflict, inflict *Afflict* is used with the prepositions *by* and *with*; *inflict* is followed by *on* or *upon*. *Inflict* is sometimes mistakenly substituted for *afflict*: 'She was inflicted with Lou Gehrig's disease'. Generally, things afflict people ('Sorrow afflicted the girl') while people inflict things on each other ('He inflicted a beating on the rebel').

Depression afflicts women roughly three times as often as men.
Globe and Mail (Toronto) 16 March 1985: M8

Gravelle ministers to those afflicted with AIDS and HIV.
Ottawa Citizen 23 Dec. 1994: A1

The commissioners were divided on whether the law should permit parents to inflict corporal punishment on children....
Globe and Mail (Toronto) 5 March 1985: P1

'I am very, very sensitive to the pain that has been inflicted on a great many people as a result of this company reducing its work force.'
Vancouver Sun 24 Nov. 1994: A16

No one deserves to be inflicted with such a deadly bacteria, not even someone who is trying to destroy my country.
Toronto Star 7 Dec. 1994: A28

(Here *afflicted* is the word required.)

affront, effrontery An *affront* is an open or intentional insult; to *affront* is to offend. *Effrontery* is shameless audacity or barefaced impudence. Because they sound alike and their meanings are similar, *affront* and *effrontery* are sometimes confused—and *effrontery* is often misspelled with an initial *a*.

This is a callous, insensitive affront to those who risked their lives defending our country.
Ottawa Citizen 30 March 1994: A10

They're offended, affronted, ticked off, vexed, irritated, galled and riled by the English they read and hear.
Vancouver Sun 9 April 1994: D9

As national chairman [of the CCF], Prof. Scott wrote a letter saying: 'You have barred your letter columns and your news columns to the CCF and now you have the effrontery to accuse it of silence which is an admission of guilt.'
Globe and Mail (Toronto) 1 Feb. 1985: M4

... worse than all of that is the affrontery of the secretary of defence, Mr. Weinberger, who takes it upon himself to tell us what kind of weapons should be placed on Canadian soil, while the presidential press secretary doesn't even know the name of the Canadian minister of defence.
Henry M. Rosenthal and S. Cathy Berson, eds.
Canadian Jewish Outlook Anthology 1988: 327

(The correct spelling is *effrontery*.)

What is most disturbing about both these incidents is the affrontery to my right to be on the street at the time of my choosing, and the fear that accompanies being approached by anyone in a threatening manner.
Ottawa Citizen 14 Nov. 1992: A11

(The word required here is *affront*.)

aforementioned, aforesaid, said *Aforementioned, aforesaid*, and *said* in general prose are criticized as hackneyed legalisms. Some critics object to their use even in legal and business writing. Usually a word such as *the, these*, or *those* followed by the noun is sufficient to alert the reader to a second mention of something that has already been specified.

Because they are strongly associated with the law, the words *aforementioned, aforesaid*, and *said* are often used to indicate mock seriousness and to generate humour. This type of humour is not, of course, to everyone's taste.

Gray, who is fluent in all the aforementioned languages, charges between $2,000 and $6,000 to subtitle a film.
Gazette (Montreal) 26 Aug. 1990: D3

(Here 'in all *these* languages' would be better.)

The aforesaid anchor sets a TV precedent when he uses a term for a male appendage usually frowned on in polite company (the term and the appendage).
Ottawa Citizen 12 May 1990: D6

If a prospective gun owner were required to present three adult Canadian residents who would sponsor him, by signing a contract assuming additional responsibility for that person's actions with said firearm, given his background would Marc Lepine have been able to carry out his nightmare?
Province (Vancouver) 23 Dec. 1990: 34

(No humour is intended; '*the* firearm' would be better.)

Discreetly test the relevant party's political savvy and affiliation.... [If] said party knows all 10 premiers, is fluent in the constitutional amending formula and can name most of the premier's political staff, it might be best to call for the check and call it a night.
Ottawa Citizen 20 Nov. 1992: A10

a fortiori *A fortiori* is a rarely used Latin expression meaning 'all the more'. In English prose it is a transitional phrase that introduces a conclusion. Its sense is 'If that is true, there is even less doubt of the following', or 'It follows even more strongly from this last argument that ...'.

The *a* in *a fortiori* can rhyme with either *say* or *saw*. *Fortiori* is pronounced in several ways: *FOR she OR eye, for she OR ee, FOR tee OR eye*, or *FOR tee OR ee*.

A fortiori, no changes appear between different full-sib families belonging to the same population.
Canadian Journal of Botany 67.4 (1989): 1259

See also LATIN PHRASES.

Africadian, African Canadian see BLACK

after see AFTERWARD(S)

aftermath *Aftermath* means either the consequences of an event or the period immediately following it. The word has acquired a connotation of unpleasantness, and is most often used in contexts of trauma such as wars, natural disasters, and economic upheavals.

In the aftermath of the Second World War, Germany lost considerable territory to Poland and the Soviet Union.
Vancouver Sun 14 Feb. 1990: A3

Like flies hovering over dead corpses, politicians of every stripe exploited the murders. The aftermath was almost as depressing as the event itself.
Fuse Magazine 13.4 (1990): 8

Engel belonged to the generation of writers who made their debut in the heady aftermath of Expo 67 and the nationalism generated by the country's centennial.
Globe and Mail (Toronto) 18 Feb. 1985: S13

(Here *afterglow* or *wake* might be better; in a positive context, *aftermath* suggests irony.)

afterward(s), after, afterword *Afterwards* is more common than *afterward* in Canadian writing. Both forms are used in Canada and the United States; *afterwards* is usual in Britain.

Some commentators consider the use of *after* as an adverb synonymous with *afterwards* to be informal unless a reference to time is made in the same sentence. Thus 'We went to the movie and walked home after' is viewed as informal, but 'We went to the movie and walked for hours after', or 'We went to the movie and walked home soon after', is considered appropriate for all levels of writing.

Occasionally *afterward* is confused with *afterword*, a commentary appended at the end of a book.

In the hospital, and afterwards in the institution, Caroline would not talk or even move.
Margaret Atwood *Life Before Man* 1979: 76

Soon afterward he came to see her mother.
Constance Beresford-Howe *Night Studies* 1985: 152

But the crack of thunder came after.
Robert Kroetsch *Badlands* 1975: 104

(This is the use of *after* considered inappropriate to formal writing.)

Shortly after, Malpeque received a sizable contingent of Scottish settlers, many of whom have descendants living in the area today.
Alan Tucker, ed. *The Penguin Guide to Canada* 1991: 121

(Here *after* is undisputed because it appears with a reference to time.)

See also -WARD(S).

age, aged   see -ED; MAJORITY; SENIOR CITIZEN

ageing   see AGING

agenda, agendum, hidden agenda   In Latin, *agenda* is a plural noun meaning 'things to do'. In English, it has long been treated as a singular noun referring to the list of things to be dealt with at a meeting. The plural is *agendas*. Use of the Latin singular *agendum* to mean an item on an agenda is obsolete: the usual phrase is *agenda item* or *item on the agenda*.

Since the 1950s, *agenda* has also referred to an underlying motivation or plan, which is sometimes veiled or unconscious: 'a political agenda', 'a hidden agenda'. Though not all dictionaries have yet recorded this recent meaning of *agenda*, some commentators already consider the phrase *hidden agenda* overworked.

The United Nations charter clearly says that the Security Council has to be ready to meet in an emergency at all times; an item on the agenda may be suspended only long enough to allow for consultation.
George Ignatieff *The Making of a Peacemonger* 1987: 97

Large foreign firms dominate the resource industry and therefore set the agenda for most resource development in the North.
Robert M. Bone *The Geography of the Canadian North* 1992: 140

... we pursue our own individual or neighborhood agendas at the expense of the larger public interest.
Vancouver Sun 17 Nov. 1990: B2

Smith's many detractors claim he has a hidden agenda to eventually force an amalgamation between the most successful CFL franchises and the NFL.
Toronto Star 5 June 1994: C12

See also PLURALS, REGULAR, IRREGULAR, FOREIGN.

aggravate, aggravation   To *aggravate* can mean either to make something worse or to exasperate someone. The first meaning is fully accepted. Although the second sense, to annoy, dates back to as early as 1611, it is still disputed by some language commentators. In Canadian writing, the verb *aggravate* usually means to make worse, while the noun and present participle, *aggravation* and *aggra-*

vating, usually mean annoyance and annoying respectively. There seems to be no reason to avoid the 'new' meaning of *aggravate* even in formal writing. What is more important for contemporary writers is to be aware of the older sense of the word: the legal term 'aggravated assault', for example, refers to a very serious assault, not to one where the victim has provoked or angered (i.e., 'aggravated') the assailant.

... a doctor who offers to give free aid to an injured person and negligently aggravates the person's injuries will be liable for damages.
J.E. Smyth et al. *The Law and Business Administration in Canada* 1987: 153

Anxiety was aggravated ... by current perceptions of undergraduate life. Exposés of 'flaming youth,' inflamed by booze, sex, and fast cars, appeared prominently in the popular magazines and on the Hollywood screen.
Frederick Gibson *Queen's University* 2 (1983): 74

Authorities at the prison fear the smell could aggravate prisoners and cause disturbances....
Vancouver Sun 21 Sept. 1990: A18

(Here *aggravate* means irritate.)

Another source of aggravation and personal embarrassment was the Canadian government's ambivalent attitude towards South Africa's policy of racial discrimination....
George Ignatieff *The Making of a Peacemonger* 1987: 239

(Here *aggravation* means annoyance or irritation.)

... it is most aggravating to anyone who cares about the English language that this country does not have a standard in spelling.
W.C. Lougheed, ed. *In Search of the Standard in Canadian English* 1986: 124

(Here *aggravating* means annoying.)

But children, though sometimes tedious and aggravating (to others: never to themselves) are also refreshing and delightful....
Margaret Atwood *Second Words* 1982: 82

(Here *aggravating* means annoying.)

See also ASSAULT, BATTERY.

aggressive, assertive *Aggressive* and *assertive* both mean forceful, but only *aggressive* suggests combativeness. Context determines whether the connotations of *aggressive* are negative or positive. Generally, *aggressive* is positive when it describes athletes, sports teams, or corporations, but decidedly negative when it describes children, countries, and animals. *Aggressive* is not usually applied favourably to women, either.

Aggressive is often misspelled with one *g*.

Scientists ... tested several groups of rats in a series of experiments and found the drug caused subordinate males to become more assertive although they did not become aggressive.
Daily News (Halifax) 4 Dec. 1994: 37

'When we played well this year, we played hard, aggressive and angry football.'
Globe and Mail (Toronto) 2 Jan. 1985: S3

Dr. Minde's team works on the theory that what is missing in overly aggressive children is the quality of empathy.
Globe and Mail (Toronto) 3 Jan. 1985: P17

Organizers have also tried to confine females to those sports believed to enhance traditional concepts of 'femininity,' such as swimming, tennis and gymnastics, and to devise 'girls' rules' to discourage the ambitious and aggressive play expected of boys and men.
Queen's Quarterly 94.1 (1987): 120

... Wal-Mart, an agressive discount chain founded in the 1960s by charismatic retail magnate Sam Walton, has had its eye on the Canadian market 'for some time.'
Edmonton Journal 15 Jan. 1994: C1

(The correct spelling is *aggressive*.)

aging, ageing Both spellings are accepted in Canada, Britain, and the United States. Canadians use *aging* far more frequently.

agnostic see ATHEIST

agreement, grammatical What is traditionally discussed under the rubric of *grammatical agreement* is number: that is, whether nouns, pronouns, and verbs should be singular or plural. 'He are right' violates number agreement because the subject of the sentence is singular while the verb is plural. But this is not a mistake a native speaker would make. This entry deals with types of subjects of sentences that native speakers sometimes have difficulty classifying as singular or plural. At the end of the entry many individual problem words and phrases are cross-referenced.

Compound subjects—subjects containing two or more elements linked by the word *and*—are plural and should be followed by plural verbs: 'Glazed paper and opaque glass are now collected'; 'A map and compass were issued'. There are a few exceptions to this rule, however.

When the two elements of a compound subject refer to the same person or thing, a singular verb is used: 'My coiffeuse and financial counsellor is getting out of mortgage funds'.

When the elements of a compound subject are to be considered serially, the verb is singular: 'Her writing speaks to us in the way Al Purdy's, Dennis Lee's, and Earle Birney's does'.

When two singular elements joined by *and* constitute a fixed expression, the verb is singular: 'A gin and tonic sounds great'.

Finally, when two singular elements of a compound subject are seen as a unit, the verb is singular: 'Your health and safety is our first concern'; 'The breadth and depth of the investigation was unprecedented'. However, the more idiosyncratic the notion is that the two elements of the subject are one, the more likely it is that this particular usage will be noticed and criticized. In formal contexts, if you aren't sure whether a compound subject constitutes one thing or two, it's better to use a plural verb.

Elements joined to the subject of the sentence by prepositions are not, strictly speaking, part of the subject, and do not affect the number of the verb: 'Robin and a partner are buying the Canadian rights', but 'Robin, with a partner, is buying the Canadian rights'. This issue is discussed further under TOGETHER WITH, AS WELL AS, IN ADDITION TO.

A subject consisting of singular elements joined by the word *or* takes a singular verb: 'A passbook or monthly statement is issued'; 'Soup or salad comes with the special'.

When *or* has little disjunctive force—that is, when *and* could be substituted for *or* without changing the meaning of the sentence—a plural verb is sometimes used: 'Chocolate or hazelnut are my favourite flavours'; 'Life or death were the same to him'. In formal contexts, however, this usage is questionable; it can be avoided either by changing *or* to *and* or by making the verb singular.

When *or* links singular and plural elements, the verb agrees in number with the nearest element: 'Both sides or only one side is finished'; 'One side or both sides are finished'. This issue is discussed further under EITHER and NEITHER.

The verb *to be* should agree in number with the subject that precedes it, not the complement that follows it: 'Committee reports are (*not* is) the next item of business'; 'The next item of business is (*not* are) committee reports'.

When phrases or clauses intervene between the bare subject of a sentence and the verb, errors of subject–verb agreement are fairly common. People lose sight of the true subject and make the verb agree with the immediately preceding noun. The following are correct: 'Parts of their story are (*not* is) true'; 'The literary merit of these works was (*not* were) never discussed'.

Plural measures of money, time, weight, etc., take a singular verb if they are considered as a unit:

'Sixty dollars was taken from the till.'

'Two weeks is not enough time.'

'Four metres of cloth make four skirts.' (Four individual metres.)

'Four metres of cloth is not enough.' (A total of four.)

In Canadian English, collective nouns are usually followed by singular verbs, but sometimes plural verbs are also possible: 'The crew is (*or* are) experienced'; 'Pat's family doesn't (or *don't*) get along'. See COLLECTIVE NOUNS.

Many usage problems involving number result from a tension in English grammar between formal and notional agreement. According to the principle of formal agreement, a noun or pronoun is inherently singular or plural and should be treated as such consistently. According to the principle of notional agreement, many nouns and pronouns are either singular or plural depending on the idea in the speaker's mind. For example, the word *family* may be singular or plural depending on whether the speaker is thinking of a unit or a group of individuals. These two contrary principles of agreement are at work in the sentence 'Everyone says they like it'. In form, the pronoun *everyone* is singular. And, in accordance with the principle of formal agreement, the verb *says* is singular. Notionally, however, *everyone* represents a group, and, in accordance with the principle of notional agreement, the personal pronoun that substitutes for *everyone—they*—is plural. A traditional grammarian would rewrite the sentence: 'Everyone says he likes it'. But to most English-speakers the corrected sentence would have an entirely different meaning. Adjusting the sentence using the principle of notional agreement yields no better result: 'Everyone say they like it' is consistently plural but certainly not English. What this discussion illustrates is that the principles of formal and notional agreement which operate in English cannot be used to solve usage problems, but only to clarify them. In many questions of number agreement, convention is the only arbiter.

Regarding the difficult question of which personal pronoun to use with *everyone, anyone,* and *someone,* see EVERYONE.

As the previous chapter demonstrates, the meaning and social construction of abortion has been subject to ongoing political struggle.
Janine Brodie, Shelley A.M. Gavigan, and Jane Jenson *The Politics of Abortion* 1992: 70

(Notional agreement overrides formal agreement in this sentence, and few readers would likely notice or quibble.)

Support and advice about coping with change is often much more helpful.
Wendy Reynolds and Vera Madden *Drug Wise* 1992: 16

(Here again notional agreement determines the number of the verb, but the singular verb in this sentence is more open to criticism because readers are more likely to regard 'support and advice about coping with change' as two separate things.)

No bone marrow or liver toxicity were observed.
Rites March 1990: 9

(Here *was* should replace *were*.)

I certainly do not think that government aid or subsidies is the answer.
Mennonite Brethren Herald 4 April 1986: 8

(Here, to agree with the plural 'subsidies', *is* should be replaced by *are*.)

Finally, Kagan's list of hopes that parents have for their children do not seem to jive with the literature or my own experience.
Ottawa Citizen 30 Sept. 1994: B4

(Since the subject of the sentence is 'Kagan's list', the verb should be the singular *does*. The plural *do* reflects the influence of the adjacent plural noun 'children'.)

See also ANY; ANYONE; BETWEEN; BUT ME; CASE; EACH; EVERY; MORE THAN ONE; NONE; ONE OF THE ... IF NOT THE; ONE OF THOSE THINGS; POSSESSIVE; POSSESSIVE WITH GERUND; THERE IS, THERE ARE.

a hold, ahold   see HOLD

ain't, aren't I   *Ain't* has a long and complicated history; it derives from *an't*, a contraction that appeared first in published writing in the late seventeenth century. The first citation for *ain't* is 1778; it was quickly singled out for criticism and since then has become almost a grammatical taboo. Though it is still common in rural and working-class dialects, educated speakers never use *ain't* unless they are sure that people will understand they know better.

Ain't may well have attracted negative notice because it serves as a sort of generic contraction, doing away with distinctions between different persons and even between *be* and *have*. That is, in nonstandard contemporary English *ain't* can replace *am not* ('I ain't done'); *aren't* ('You ain't invited'); *isn't* ('She ain't well'); and *hasn't* or *haven't* ('I ain't seen him').

Many commentators have noted with regret that the successful suppression of *ain't* created a gap in Standard English, which now has no fully accepted contraction of *am I not.* Although *amn't I* was used by speakers of Irish English, it was not adopted by speakers of Standard British English when *ain't I* fell from favour. *Aren't I* entered Canadian and American English from British English early in the twentieth century. In British English, since *r* is not pronounced after a vowel, *aren't* is merely a different way of spelling *an't* (an obsolete contraction of either *are not* or *am not*). In Canadian English, however, the *r* in *aren't* is pronounced. And, though *aren't I* is widely used in Canada, it is often uttered with misgivings about the patent incongruity of *I* and *are*. The alternative, the uncontracted *am I not*, often seems too stuffy for its context. Nevertheless, most Canadians use *am I not* in writing, and some prefer it to *aren't I* in speech.

We see that the economists who said there ain't no such thing as a free lunch, in the early 70's, were not wrong.
City Magazine 10.1 (Spring 1988): 39

(Here *ain't* is used in an expression of folk wisdom.)

'I ain't got that kinda money, you know that,' he said.
Canadian Fiction Magazine 64 (1988): 92

(Sometimes *ain't* is used to indicate the socio-economic status of fictional characters.)

'I could just see myself in Halifax today watching the Winter Olympics on TV, saying: "Why aren't I there?"'
Calgary Herald 14 Feb. 1988: OA6

Am I not misunderstanding the devotion to duty and the self-denying attitude which makes so many worthy people cut down on the time and energy they give to their private life, so that they may more vigorously serve mankind?
Robertson Davies *One Half of Robertson Davies* 1978: 71

At sixty-six Umberto asked her a last time. He must have someone, one person in the world, to be near as his own skin. 'Am I not?'
Canadian Fiction Magazine 63 (1988): 129

See also CONTRACTIONS.

air force   see CANADIAN ARMED FORCES

airplane, aeroplane   Canadians writers use *airplane*, as do Americans. *Aeroplane* is the usual British spelling, although *airplane* is also found in British writing. A minority of Canadians use the British pronunciation *AIR uh plane*, even though they spell the word *airplane*.

a.k.a., aka   see PSEUDONYM

à la   Originally French, *à la* means in the style or manner of. Writing 'sideburns *à la* Elvis' is more economical than 'sideburns in the style of Elvis' and avoids the complications of 'sideburns like Elvis's' or 'Elvis-style sideburns'.
À la is frequently used with reference to cookery, as in 'chicken *à la king*'. *À la mode* means fashionable or in style, unless it is preceded by the word *pie*: pie *à la mode* is served with ice cream.
À la is seldom found in formal writing, and in informal writing it often appears without an accent. Retaining the accent and using italics, however, make this brief foreign phrase more readable.

If you cannot stomach the *tripe à la parisienne*, veal kidneys in porto sauce, or sweetbreads in heavy cream and calvados, there is simpler fare....
Alan Tucker, ed. *The Penguin Guide to Canada* 1991: 549

Recommended Friday night is Picket Fences (CFRN), another quirky drama a la Northern Exposure....
Edmonton Journal 13 Sept. 1992: n.p.

He has embraced the concept of sustainable development and in the most recent throne speech presented himself, *a la* George Bush, as an environmentalist.
NeWest Review Oct.–Nov. 1989: 5

See also À LA CARTE.

à la carte, table d'hôte   These expressions are borrowed from French. When you dine *à la carte*, you select your meal from a menu on which each dish is priced separately. A *table d'hôte* meal is a fixed meal—usually limited choices are offered—at a fixed price. The expressions *table d'hôte* (pronounced *TA bluh DOTE*) and *à la carte* often lose their accents on restaurant menus. In formal writing, the accents are required.

Not so very long ago, restaurant critics would nearly always choose a la carte on a first visit in order to get the true measure of a restaurant's capabilities. The daily table d'hôte menu, there to satisfy economy-minded regulars, was usually unimaginative and a dumping ground for the regular menu's excesses.
Gazette (Montreal) 3 March 1989: C13

See also À LA.

albeit   *Albeit* means 'if only' or 'though admittedly'. Some guides describe it as antiquated or overly formal, but its common use in newspapers and popular magazines belies that criticism.

Parody and burlesque are, it seems to me, inherently cynical, albeit in a mild way.
Margaret Atwood *Second Words* 1982: 181

His secret was to combine a good product with a folksy, albeit aggressive, sales campaign.
Gazette (Montreal) 5 March 1989: C2

Calgary set designer Janice Blackie-Goodine is also featured on the project, albeit behind the scenes.
Calgary Herald 26 June 1993: C10

For half his first term, Harcourt did have the advantage of a Liberal opposition in disarray, albeit some complained he never sufficiently exploited that card.
Globe and Mail (Toronto) 16 March 1996: C8

Alberta   see APPENDIX I

alderman   see JOB TITLES

Algonquin, Algonkin, Algonquian, Algonkian
The Aboriginal communities along the Ottawa River between Ontario and Quebec are called *Algonquin* (pronounced *al GONE kwin*) or *Algonkin* (pronounced *al GONE kin*). The names of many Aboriginal peoples are already plural and should not be doubly pluralized by adding *s*; however, *Algonquins* is an exception (*Globe and Mail Style Book*). Algonquins also refer to themselves as Anissinapek or Anishinabeg.

Algonquin (or *Algonkin*) is also the language of the Algonquin nation (though not all Algonquins speak it). Algonquin is a dialect of Ojibway. Although their languages are related, the Algonquins and the Ojibwa (or Anishnabe) are separate Aboriginal nations.

Algonquian or *Algonkian* (pronounced *al GONE kee un* or *al GONE kwee un*) designates a large language family, which includes Algonquin and also Cree, Ojibway, and Mi'kmaq—the most widely-spoken Aboriginal languages in Canada. Algonquin-speakers form only a small subgroup of the many Algonquian-speakers across Canada from British Columbia to the Atlantic provinces, so it is important not to confuse the two words.

Three and a half years ago, Odjick was finishing his season as a Midget-aged player in the Desert River Band, an Algonquin reserve just outside Maniwaki, Que.
Province (Vancouver) 29 Nov. 1990: 83

At his gravesite, a young Algonkin lady sang a haunting song in honor of Don's life. . . .
Ottawa Citizen 11 Dec. 1993: A9

Giffin now believes this [number] has ballooned to include all Algonquins in Ontario, and perhaps Quebec, which could be as many as 15,000.
Ottawa Citizen 26 June 1994: D8

They called themselves the People of the Dawnland, the Abenaki in their distinct Algonquian language.
Gazette (Montreal) 19 Feb. 1993: A2

On a flat expanse of rock . . . are hundreds of carvings of symbolic shapes and figures which archeologists say were probably carved by Algonkian-speaking Indians between 500 and 1,000 years ago.
Gazette (Montreal) 2 June 1993: C2

The Algonkian Nation claims the site along with a much larger territory, including Parliament Hill, as ancestral land.
Ottawa Citizen 24 July 1990: A4

(Here it is not clear whether the reference is to the Algonquins or to a wider group.)

The natural world seemed full of mythological inspiration for the Algonkians who are said to have engraved [the petroglyphs].
Globe and Mail (Toronto) 27 July 1985: T2

(Here either *Algonquins* or *Algonquian-speaking people* would be clearer.)

See also OJIBWA(Y).

alias   see PSEUDONYM

alibi   In legal terms, an alibi is a plea or proof of having been elsewhere when a crime was committed. In fact, the Latin word *alibi* means 'elsewhere'. In general English, however, *alibi* refers more broadly to an excuse of any type, including a concocted one. Some commentators dispute this broader meaning, but it is common in informal usage.

If you want to know what I was doing between then and finding the body, I'm going to be hard-pressed to give you an alibi for the hours from eleven to eight in the morning.
Howard Engel *Murder Sees the Light* 1984: 61

He was in custody for seven hours, without shoes, and released after he and his wife gave matching alibi statements.
Daily News (Halifax) 23 June 1994: n.p.

Everton manager Howard Kendall didn't really want to use it as an alibi, but the grass at Varsity Stadium was too long for his team's tilt with Inex Canada last night.
Globe and Mail (Toronto) 1 Aug. 1985: P14

One ex-principal says it's not uncommon for the modern parent to immediately look for either an excuse or an alibi for his child's misbehavior.
Ottawa Citizen 13 Sept. 1994: B4

alight, alit   To *alight* means to climb down from a horse or vehicle or to touch down from the sky. To *alight on* means to come upon by chance or to happen to notice. *Alighted* is the usual past tense and past participle; *alit* is poetic.

Alight is also an adjective meaning lighted ('Every window was alight'), glowing ('Their faces were alight'), or on fire ('They poured gasoline on it and set it alight').

Occasionally people substitute *alit* for *alight* ('a single window alit') or use *alit* to mean *lit up* ('Her eyes alit with pleasure'). These uses are non-standard.

Fretful babies didn't cry, normally spirited children stood obediently by their parents, teenagers alighted from their bicycles and hung their heads. . . .
Toronto Star 23 June 1994: A6

There wasn't much I could say, so I sat there dumb as a stone, watching the bees alight on the blue chicory flowers beside the veranda. . . .
Miriam Waddington *Apartment Seven* 1989: 6

Then the eye looks deeper into the scene and alights on another of Montreal's unique views.

Alan Tucker, ed. *The Penguin Guide to Canada* 1991: 145

At dusk the sky will be alight with a pyrotechnic extravaganza, with each burst synchronized to music.
Toronto Star 30 June 1994: NY4

He set the next mound of chaff alight.
Geoffrey Ursell *Perdue: And How the West Was Lost* 1984: 70

. . . but his eyes alit when the Olympic flame came in and the cauldron was ignited. The message I saw in his eyes was that peace can ride on a hockey puck and bobsleds can carry dreams.
Calgary Herald 9 Feb. 1992: E9

(Either *lit up* or *came alight* is required here.)

See also LIGHT.

-alist   see -IST

alit   see ALIGHT

all around   see ALL ROUND

alleged, accused   The news media make liberal use of the words *alleged* and *accused* in crime reporting, partly in fairness to people wrongly accused, partly to avoid defamation suits. But many language commentators object to phrases such as 'alleged arsonist', 'accused murderer', and 'alleged drug dealer' because these phrases apply a criminal label to a person who has not been convicted of a crime.

Some commentators prefer *alleged* to *accused* in this context because they think that *alleged* lends a more tentative quality to the noun that follows. Other commentators find *alleged* a worse choice on grammatical grounds: you can accuse a person, but you can't allege a person. Therefore 'accused murderer' is possible, but 'alleged murderer' is ungrammatical. Most commentators agree that it is better to allege only actions: 'the alleged malpractice'; 'the youth alleged to have set the fire'. The disputed noun phrases, though fairly common in crime reporting, are not established in other types of writing, including more formal legal writing.

A final note: reporters are sometimes overzealous in applying the word *alleged*. Someone under investigation for a crime is a real suspect, not an 'alleged suspect'. A sexual assault may be described as an 'alleged assault' until it is proved, but there is no reason to refer to a break-in or a shooting as *alleged* if there is no doubt that it took place.

Accused murderer F——M—— is innocent, says a woman who says she is her sister.
Daily News (Halifax) 16 June 1994: n.p.

('F——M——, who has been accused of murder' would be better.)

Accused arsonist D——N—— has been released from jail into his parents' custody.
Daily News (Halifax) 13 May 1994: n.p.

('D——N——, accused of having set the fire' would be better.)

The alleged attacker had checked out of the hotel earlier in the day.
Ottawa Citizen 4 March 1994: B7

('The man alleged to have committed the attack' would be better.)

[He] told court he doesn't recall what happened the night of that alleged break-in because it was his brother's birthday and he had too much to drink.
Calgary Herald 13 July 1993: B1

(Here *alleged* should be omitted, since the break-in is unquestioned.)

See also SUSPECTED.

alleluia   see HALLELUJAH

allied   see ALLY

allophone   see FRANCOPHONE

all ready, already   *All ready* means either completely ready ('Your room is all ready') or each one ready ('Are you all ready, or is someone missing?'). *Already* is an adverb meaning before now ('It's already done') or as early as this ('Are they here already?').

all right, alright   *All right* is standard for all uses. The one-word spelling *alright* is considered incorrect by most commentators. However, it appears in print often enough that some dictionaries recognize it as a variant. Sometimes it seems to function as a visual cue indicating relaxed speech.

The government through lotteries is promoting the philosophy that it is all right not to work, if we can get out of it by living off the earnings of others.
Mennonite Brethren Herald 4 April 1986: 7

If a woman wants to do flower painting or crewel work or writing in her spare time, that's all right with us; you can do it at home, in between taking care of your family,

as long as it doesn't interfere with the serious business of life, which is your husband's.
Margaret Atwood *Second Words* 1982: 341

Oh, there's a narrator alright, always there though hardly omniscient—weaving past and present ... tragedies and family secrets, grandmas, sons, mothers and lovers, into one continuous, bluesy melodic line.
Globe and Mail (Toronto) 2 May 1992: n.p.

(The more widely accepted spelling is *all right*.)

'Alright, since you're so free, you be the one to lead us into the future.'
David Williams *Eye of the Father* 1985: 146

(The more widely accepted spelling is *all right*.)

all-round, all-around   Canadian writers use the adjective *all-round* ('best all-round player') slightly more often than *all-around*. Only *all-round* is standard in British English; *all-around* is the more common variant in American English. Either form should be hyphenated.

... for all-round, versatile usage, the claw hammer, able to both drive and remove nails, is by far the most popular.
Harrowsmith Oct.–Nov. 1985: 85

... I play [paintball] because of the exercise, adrenalin, excitement, humor and all-around good times the game offers.
Vancouver Sun 29 June 1990: A12

all together, altogether   *All together* means every one together, or in a group or whole: 'They were finally all together'. *Altogether* means on the whole or all told ('Altogether, we had a good time') or completely or entirely ('That is an altogether different story').

But the character which holds it all together and gives the book weight is Sponge himself....
Robertson Davies *A Voice from the Attic* 1960: 148

In fact, Riffs is a curious and not altogether satisfactory mixture of the two.
Toronto Star 13 Nov. 1993: J14

... it is said to have been committed under circumstances which either justified it altogether, or reduced the crime to manslaughter.
William Teatero *John Anderson: Fugitive Slave* 1986: 53

You might know there are all these people who are aware and sensitive who support you. But you don't see them altogether in one spot....
Vancouver Sun 22 Sept. 1990: C16

(Here *all together* is required.)

But when we're altogether we still sit down for loads and loads of food.
Gazette (Montreal) 22 Dec. 1993: F1

(Here *all together* is required.)

allude, elude, allusive, elusive   To *allude to* something is to make an indirect reference to it or to mention it in passing. To *elude* something is to keep out of its path; if something eludes you, it remains beyond your reach.

Writing that is *allusive* refers obliquely to other texts; if a piece of writing is described as *elusive*, its meaning is difficult to understand.

During his speech, [he] alluded to a few questionable operators promising potential franchise owners pie-in-the-sky.
Toronto Star 30 Oct. 1993: C2

The Black population of Brant and Norfolk counties sheltered him, and he eluded his pursuers for months.
William Teatero *John Anderson: Fugitive Slave* 1986: 24

... not infrequently they got the laughs that eluded the aspiring comedians.
Robertson Davies *One Half of Robertson Davies* 1978: 54

Gold's poems are allusive (references to Mayakovsky, Frank O'Hara and Charles Ives pepper the volume) and sophisticated, but their intelligence does not impair their sensuality....
Gazette (Montreal) 25 Sept. 1993: J2

The meaning of Ducharme's novels is elusive.
Ben-Z. Shek *French-Canadian & Québécois Novels* 1991: 75

ally, allied   *Ally* is both a noun and a verb. The noun is stressed on the first syllable (*AL eye*), the verb on the second (*a LIE*). When the adjective *allied* follows the verb *to be*, the second syllable is usually stressed: 'They were allied (*a LIED*) during the Second World War'. When it precedes a noun, the first syllable is usually stressed: 'Allied (*AL eyed*) Forces'. Both *allied to* and *allied with* are acceptable.

His own temperament was that of an artist, allied to a remarkable industry and the canniness of the English Midlands.
Robertson Davies *A Voice from the Attic* 1960: 44

This desire, sometimes allied with narrower economic interests, has been a basic force behind the creation and defence of a distinctive public enterprise culture in this country.
Gazette (Montreal) 10 Aug. 1991: B3

almost   see MOST; PRACTICALLY

alongside, alongside of   Canadian writers use *alongside* almost exclusively. *Alongside of*, the older form, is rare but acceptable, although some commentators find the *of* unnecessary.

> While leading the canoe alongside a wide ledge, I happened to glance at the rock below my feet.
> *Uphere* Jan.–Feb. 1990: 48

> There isn't much mystery about why Canada has recessions alongside the United States.
> *Vancouver Sun* 20 Nov. 1990: A7

a lot, lots [alot]   *A lot* and *lots* function both as adverbs ('We eat out a lot/lots') and as nouns ('A lot/Lots of us are going'). The question is often raised whether these uses are appropriate to formal writing. Certainly they are far less common in formal writing than in speech. However, most usage guides stop short of calling them inappropriate. Some writers prefer to use expressions with more serious connotations, such as *a great deal* or *a good number*, in formal writing. Others like the conversational tone of *a lot* and *lots*.

For many years now *a lot* has been appearing in unpublished writings as one word—*alot*—and this spelling is beginning to creep into newspapers. *Alot* may eventually become an accepted spelling, following the precedents of *amiss*, *apiece*, and *awhile*, which were all originally written as two words. But for now *alot* should be avoided. Dictionaries don't list it, and many people consider its use a mark of illiteracy.

> 'That's a lot of goals.'
> *Toronto Star* 1 Jan. 1994: F4

> You hear lots about the dangers of being overweight, but there's more to the story.
> *Toronto Star* 29 June 1994: B3

> Geller's 'Young Offenders in Conflict with the Law' summarizes a lot of fuzzy literature with the statement that the criminal justice system treats adolescent women's sexual behavior harshly while largely ignoring their criminal behavior, and does the reverse for adolescent males.
> *Canadian Journal of Sociology* 14.2 (1989): 255

> The Bible, of course, contains blasphemy, torture, rape, sodomy, orgies, murder, lying and lots of other unpleasant things. It also contains the Sermon on the Mount, which would mean a lot less without its setting.
> Margaret Atwood *Second Words* 1982: 354

> An easily accessible parking space makes alot of sense—but free? No way.
> *Gazette* (Montreal) 3 Oct. 1993: B3

(The correct spelling is *a lot*.)

> My mother used to make icebox cookies alot, often adding chopped walnuts to the dough....
> *Ottawa Citizen* 1 June 1994: F1

(The correct spelling is *a lot*.)

aloud, out loud   Some commentators consider *aloud* more acceptable than *out loud*. *Aloud* is the older and more common of these two expressions, but either is fine at any level of formality.

> In my day at Gage, and that is not so very long ago, when we proofread, we proofread aloud, and we proofread aloud to another person.
> W.C. Lougheed, ed. *In Search of the Standard in Canadian English* 1986: 133

> In the Middle Ages readers spoke aloud the words they read, and a temporary hoarseness or loss of voice was a sufficient reason for a scholar to suspend his studies.
> Robertson Davies *A Voice from the Attic* 1960: 15

> On this couch ... visiting poets and painters sat ... two or three abreast, listening to poetry being read out loud by one of them....
> Miriam Waddington *Apartment Seven* 1989: 4

alphabetical order   There are two systems for alphabetizing lists that contain both single words and phrases. Occasionally, this means that people don't find the heading they are looking for in an index or a reference work, because it is not where they expect it to be.

The first system is called 'word-by-word'. Alphabetization is interrupted by word breaks. Thus, in the example that follows, all the entries beginning with the word *black* alone precede those where *black*- is a combining form:

> black Loyalists
>
> black settlement
>
> Blackfoot
>
> blackrobes
>
> blacksmithing

In the second system, called 'letter-by-letter', word breaks are ignored. The same list of items looks like this:

> Blackfoot
>
> black Loyalists

blackrobes

black settlement

blacksmithing

Dictionaries and reference books are almost always compiled on the letter-by-letter principle, and this one is no exception. One very good reason for this is that readers may not know ahead of time whether there will be a word break in the item they are looking up. In the lists below, the usual letter-by-letter arrangement can be compared with word-by-word alphabetization:

letter-by-letter	*word-by-word*
bookend	book in
book in	book learning
booking	book value
book learning	bookend
bookstore	booking
book value	bookstore

The letter-by-letter system is the one now generally recommended by style books. In the letter-by-letter system, commas may or may not be ignored. That is, alphabetization may proceed across commas, or commas may serve as points of interruption, like word breaks in the word-by-word system. Interrupting alphabetization at commas is usually preferable. For example, in the list of headings below, it allows all the people named White to be grouped together. If the commas were disregarded, *white paper* and *White Pass* would appear in the middle of this list:

White, James

White, Nancy

White, Robert

White, Thomas

white paper

White Pass

A few other conventions of alphabetization follow. An initial *the*, *a*, or *an* is ignored in the alphabetization of titles. Titles beginning with the word *this*, however, are alphabetized under *this*. Names beginning with *St.* (e.g., 'St. Lawrence College') are often alphabetized as if the word *Saint* were spelled out. Acronyms are sometimes alphabetized as if written in full—a practice that is not recommended when the acronym is far better known than the words it stands for (*UNICEF*, *NATO*). Numbers may be alphabetized as if they were written in words: thus '24 Sussex Drive' would be listed under T (for 'twenty-four'). Alternatively, when there are many numbers in an alphabetical list—for example, when a listing of city streets contains many numbered streets—all the numbers may appear in numerical order before the *a*'s.

See also THE, A, AN.

Alpine   see SCANDINAVIAN

already   see ALL READY

alright   see ALL RIGHT

alter, altar   To *alter* means to change or modify something. A piece of clothing is altered or adjusted for a better fit. An *altar* is a raised place or table used in religious ceremonies.

> She was an active member of the alter guild in the All Saints Cathedral, Halifax. . . .
> *Daily News* (Halifax) 19 April 1994: 37

(The correct spelling here is *altar*.)

alter ego   *Alter ego* is a Latin phrase that means 'second self'. Cicero used the expression to refer to a close and trusted friend. In English that meaning is still possible today, but it is fairly uncommon. An alter ego is more likely to be the hidden side of someone's personality or a fictional character as brought to life by an author or an actor.

> Smart . . . was Sifton's alter ego. The two men were contemporaries—Smart was just a year older—and had grown up in Brandon politics together.
> Pierre Berton *The Promised Land* 1984: 11

(This is the older meaning of *alter ego*).

> He told officers that an alter ego called 'Eddie,' modelled on the demonic mascot of his favorite heavy-metal rock band, Iron Maiden, had influenced his actions.
> *Maclean's* 30 Jan. 1989: A43

> Over the course of a life, and some 470 books, Asimov came to regard [fictional character] Hari Seldon as his alter ego.
> *Calgary Herald* 29 May 1993: D11

> Kermit the Frog, the fuzzy green alter ego of the late muppeteer Jim Henson, will live on with a new voice.
> *Vancouver Sun* 14 Nov. 1990: A2

See also LATIN PHRASES.

alternate, alternative   An *alternate* is a back-up person, as for a delegate, a jury, or an Olympic team. An *alternative* is an option: 'What alternative did we have?'

The adjective *alternate* refers to every second one ('alternate Saturdays') or to two things that succeed each other by turns ('alternate sun and clouds'). The adjective *alternative* refers to something available as an option ('alternative route'), to something that can be substituted if necessary ('alternative telephone number'), or to something non-traditional ('alternative school', 'alternative medicine', 'alternative newspaper').

Three usage issues are associated with these two words. The first is whether there can be more than two alternatives. This question was raised in the last half of the nineteenth century because the Latin word *alter*, from which *alternative* is derived, means the other of two. Fortunately, this issue has been laid to rest. Contemporary commentators unanimously consider it pedantry to reject 'We have three alternatives'.

The second issue is whether the adjective *alternate* can be used as a synonym of *alternative*, as in 'alternate plan', 'alternate date', or 'alternate music'. This use of the adjective is obviously closely related to the meaning of the noun *alternate* and is well enough established to be recorded by all dictionaries. Nevertheless, since many commentators still consider it a mistake, it is not recommended in formal writing.

The third issue is whether, since the advent of the counterculture movement in the 1960s, the seemingly neutral word *alternative* has become politically charged. The answer is yes and no. The adjective *alternative* now often means opposed to the mainstream and left-leaning, but much more often it simply refers to an option. People don't seem to have trouble distinguishing the two meanings in context. However, people do sometimes have trouble decoding the latest vanguard meanings of *alternative*: that, for example, an 'alternative lifestyle' is gay and that 'alternative energy sources' include windmills and solar panels but not nuclear power plants.

Stephanie and Peter are designated team members, while Victoria is an alternate.
Calgary Herald 18 June 1994: B1

As governor general, he charmed Canadians with alternate displays of flawless decorum and engaging informality.
Maclean's 19 Aug. 1991: A17

On alternate weeks another doctor comes in from out of town.
Ottawa Citizen 28 Feb. 1993: A7

Iskandar said the town is studying several options to dispose of its snow, including using the St. Charles St. site, but he refused to describe the alternatives.
Gazette (Montreal) 30 June 1993: G1

(The use of *alternatives* to describe several options is common and acceptable.)

When they tried an alternative route, raging winds forced them to retreat to Alert.
Maclean's 11 Nov. 1991: A24

The Warehouse features alternative theater in a small house that seats 300 people on three sides of a floor-level stage, which brings the audience right into the play....
Alan Tucker, ed. *The Penguin Guide to Canada* 1991: 467

They are John Walke and Daniel Epstein—the double identity team behind Hombre, a new, alternative-to-the-alternative, more-or-less shocking, rough and ready fashion-and-style rag.
Gazette (Montreal) 28 June 1994: C5

All along this route car ferries cross the river to pastoral and historic peninsulas affording a variety of alternate routes back to Saint John.
Alan Tucker, ed. *The Penguin Guide to Canada* 1991: 96

(Here *alternative* would be better.)

Available on board the Golden Odyssey is an alternate menu for those on low-cholesterol or low-sodium diets.
Torch: University of Victoria Alumni Magazine Spring 1990: 16

(Here *alternative* would be better.)

Alternately, you can pay quarterly tax based on the previous year's tax.
Gazette (Montreal) 6 March 1989: B5

(Here *alternatively* would be better.)

although, though   *Although* and *though* are interchangeable as conjunctions: 'Although/though John is very conservative in his politics, his taste in clothes is quite radical'. Some usage guides suggest that *although* is more appropriate in formal writing. Canadian writers seem to be guided by other considerations. They use both words at all levels of formality, and often in the same piece of writing.

What a man considers indecent is an important clue to his character, and although there are exceptions, it has been my experience that book collectors have strange opinions on this subject, and few of them lack a book or two which they think they should conceal.
Robertson Davies *A Voice from the Attic* 1960: 264

They were not often needed for direct attendance upon the Royal Household, though the Bug Catcher once captured a single bedbug in the chamber of Princess Charlotte, with her fascinated assistance.
Robertson Davies *A Voice from the Attic* 1960: 126

P.K. Page's *The Metal and the Flower* ... got the Governor-General's Medal, and deserved it, although my opinion of the practice of giving a medal to any poet over the age of ten is not high.
Northrop Frye *The Bush Garden* 1972: 39

... and only Riel remains to haunt the later period of it, though he is a formidable figure enough, rather like what a combination of John Brown and Vanzetti would be in the American conscience.
Northrop Frye *The Bush Garden* 1972: 224

altogether   see ALL TOGETHER

alumnus, alumna, alumni, alumnae   These words referring to the graduates of a university are among the few Latin terms in popular use for which there are no regular English plurals. *Alumnus* is used of a male graduate, *alumna* of a female graduate, and the plurals are *alumni* and *alumnae* respectively. *Alumni* has long been established as the term for a mixed group, but that usage is now under fire from *alumnae* as sexist. *Alumnae and alumni*, *alumni/ae, former students*, and *graduates* are all recommended as non-sexist alternatives. *Alums* (pronounced *a LUMS*), an informal American plural, is not well known in Canada.

The term *alumni/-ae* is also often applied to former employees, former members of a group, former summer campers, etc. In literal translation, *alumni/-ae* are foster children.

The Latin plural endings *-ae* and *-i* can both be pronounced in English to rhyme with either *eye* or *see*. The more common pronunciations of *alumni* and *alumnae*, which serve to distinguish the two words, are *ah LUM nye* for the masculine plural and *ah LUM nee* for the feminine.

An alumnus of St. Pat's and St. Lawrence, Pierre is now studying at Glendon Campus of York University in Toronto.
Chronicle-Telegraph (Quebec) 14 Aug. 1991: 13

If you can read this story you're lucky. UVic alumna Linda Hackett works to help people who are not so fortunate.

Torch: University of Victoria Alumni Magazine Autumn (1990): 15

Young and two other alumni at *Maclean's*, Staff Writer Sherri Aikenhead and Ottawa Staff Correspondent Marc Clark, are evidence of that.
Maclean's 28 July 1986: 2

(Here *alumni* designates a pair of former students, one male, the other female.)

This, of course, has promoted an esprit de corps, one easily passed from generation to generation as students turned into alumni and alumnae, and as graduates sent their children down to Queen's.
Frederick Gibson *Queen's University* 2 (1983): 433

These Steinberg [Inc.] alumni certainly won't be the last executives to try merchant banking.
Financial Post 17 Nov. 1989: 48

See also PLURALS; SEXIST LANGUAGE.

a.m.   see TIME

a mari usque ad mare   *A Mari Usque Ad Mare*, the Latin motto affixed to the Canadian coat of arms, is a quotation from the Bible (Psalm 72: 8). It is officially translated 'From Sea to Sea' or 'D'un océan à l'autre'. 'From sea to shining sea', another phrase that Canadians often use, originates in the American song 'America the Beautiful'.

In formal writing, the Latin motto should be italicized; initial capitals are optional. Note the different spellings of *mari* and *mare*.

The essential element in the national sense of unity is the east-west feeling, developed historically along the St. Lawrence-Great Lakes axis, and expressed in the national motto, *a mari usque ad mare*.
Northrop Frye *The Bush Garden* 1971: iii

The name [Dominion of Canada] was chosen on the basis of a biblical text, 'He shall have dominion also from sea unto sea, and from the river unto the ends of the earth.'... The national motto, A mare usque ad mare, also comes from this text.
Toronto Star 1 July 1988: A18

(The first *mare* here should be spelled *mari*.)

amateur   In sports, an amateur athlete is differentiated from a professional one on the basis not of skill but of money: an amateur does not compete for money nor earn a livelihood from sports, whereas a professional does. In other contexts, *amateur* usually implies a lack of skill or seriousness; used in this way, the word may be synonymous with either *bungler* or *dilettante*.

Amateur is etymologically linked to the Latin for lover. An 'amateur of the arts', for example, can be someone with a cultivated appreciation of the arts. This usage, fairly common in the nineteenth century, is becoming rare—at least outside Quebec. There the English word *amateur* retains this older meaning because the most common meaning of the French word *amateur* is fan. (See QUEBEC ENGLISH.)

Pronunciations of *amateur* vary considerably. Most Canadians say *AM a cher*, but the last syllable may also be pronounced *ter*, *tour*, or *chure*.

> The Player agrees that during the term of this contract he ... will not play for or be directly or indirectly employed by or interested in any other amateur or professional hockey club.
> J.E. Smyth et al. *The Law and Business Administration in Canada* 1987: 185

> ... she dissents from the usual laudatory approach by claiming he was an incompetent observer, amateur in his laboratory techniques, a parochial philosopher, and a neurotic personality!
> *Queen's Quarterly* 92.2 (1985): 424

> The difference between the amateur autobiographer and the professional man of letters is that the former is concerned with self-approval, the latter with self-revelation.
> Robertson Davies *A Voice from the Attic* 1960: 298

> It is not for one who is an amateur of lexicography to offer authoritative pronouncements on the role of the dictionary in Canadian English.
> W.C. Lougheed, ed. *In Search of the Standard in Canadian English* 1986: 48

(Here *amateur* combines the senses of devotee and dilettante.)

> A keen amateur who has read and reread all 60 of the [Sherlock Holmes] adventures, de Freitas said he won't call them 'stories' because he maintains they are true.
> *Gazette* (Montreal) 10 June 1993: G5

(In Quebec English *amateur* often means fan.)

ambiguous, ambivalent, equivocal *Ambiguous* usually refers to external things, *ambivalent* to mental states. A sign, word, or expression that can be understood in two or more ways at the same time is *ambiguous*. A person who experiences opposing feelings or attitudes simultaneously is *ambivalent*.

Equivocal has several meanings. It can mean either ambiguous or ambivalent. A statement that reveals its author's ambivalence may be described as *equivocal*. Sometimes *equivocal* implies deception, contrived ambiguity, or pretended ambivalence. (The related verb to *equivocate* means to conceal the truth through ambiguity.) Occasionally *equivocal* means morally questionable or of dubious value.

> Some issues were dealt with explicitly, others were left vague and ambiguous, leaving room for various interpretations.
> *Queen's Quarterly* 94.3 (1987): 563

> The French, in their accounts of the period, display a marked ambivalence toward the Indians, depicting them as noble on the one hand and savage on the other—a stereotype that was unquestioningly accepted by later historians.
> *Saturday Night* July 1986: 50

> The government's ambivalent policy with regard to South Africa—condemning apartheid out of one corner of its mouth and encouraging improved trade relations out of the other—was a case in point.
> George Ignatieff *The Making of a Peacemonger* 1987: 245

(Normally a policy would be described as *ambiguous* rather than *ambivalent*. Because Ignatieff goes on to personify the policy by giving it a 'mouth', *ambivalent* works here.)

> Equivocal words are assigned the meaning that makes the contract enforceable, if at all possible.
> J.E. Smyth et al. *The Law and Business Administration in Canada* 1987: 268

(Here *equivocal* means ambiguous.)

> All females want to give feminists substantial promotions up the influence hierarchy. Male respondents are far more equivocal on that score.
> Neil Nevitte and Roger Gibbins *New Elites in Old States* 1990: 144

(Here *equivocal* means ambivalent.)

> Marriage, for instance (see 'Epithalamium,' one of the most equivocal poems in that genre I have ever read), introduces lovers to an Elysium which is the reflection of Eden, but full of serpents and bitter fruits.
> Northrop Frye *The Bush Garden* 1971: 78

> Whitehorn is equivocal. 'No one bore more responsibility,' he writes, 'but perhaps no one worked harder.'
> *Ottawa Citizen* 11 Sept. 1994: B3

> He said Mr. Miller has been vague and equivocal about the issue during the election campaign, apparently hoping to create the impression that he would consider changing the current policy.
> *Globe and Mail* (Toronto) May 2 1985: P8

(Here *equivocal* implies deliberate deceit.)

Other reasons listed as causes for censorship are: Ministers of religion in equivocal situations, blasphemous incidents, objectionable prison scenes, hospital incidents treated flippantly. . . .
Toronto Star 1 Sept. 1992: A10

(Here *equivocal* means morally questionable.)

The one sister in Terre Haute reappears to provide equivocal support in A Visit Home.
Gazette (Montreal) 20 Feb. 1993: K1

(Here *equivocal* means of dubious value.)

See also AMBIVALENCE, VACILLATION; LIE, EQUIV-OCATE; UNEQUIVOCAL.

ambivalence, vacillation   *Ambivalence*, a psycho-analytic term coined in the twentieth century, is the state of having simultaneous conflicting feelings, usually of attraction and repulsion, about something. *Vacillation* is the state of being unable to decide between two or more people, objects, or courses of action, and of repeatedly changing one's mind.

In concentrated form, it reflected the sharp anxiety of influence which some members of the Old Left felt toward their generational 'spokesman', their ambivalent urge both to embrace and break with him.
Canadian Journal of History 14.1 (1989): 6

One of the major problems plaguing Canadian English speakers is the prevalence of dual standards. Depending somewhat on context and locality, we vacillate between standards of American and British usage.
W.C. Lougheed, ed. *In Search of the Standard in Canadian English* 1986: 170

See also AMBIGUOUS, AMBIVALENT, EQUIVOCAL.

ameliorate   *Ameliorate* is related to the Latin *melior*, 'better'. Basing their argument on this relationship, some usage commentators have stated that *ameliorate* should be used only in contexts where *improve* or (*make*) *better* could be substituted. In this view, to *ameliorate* does not mean to reduce or relieve; one does not ameliorate hardship or pain, although one may alleviate or relieve it.

In this case, as in many, English usage has ignored Latin etymology, and the advice of these commentators can also be safely ignored. Today a negative complement, such as 'hardship' or 'pain', follows *ameliorate* far more often than not. A few recent dictionaries have made allowances for what is now the predominant usage by including both definitions: to improve and to make more tolerable, more bearable.

In the face of the mounting opposition of the common people, the oligarchy of nobles and rich merchants sometimes ameliorated the material lot of the people.
Irving M. Zeitlin and Robert J. Brym *The Social Condition of Humanity* 1991: 309

Clay soils can also be ameliorated with generous applications of organic matter such as compost, well-rotted manure or peat moss.
TLC . . . for plants Summer 1991: 26

We need not act to ameliorate animal suffering when it is caused by natural disasters rather than human depredation.
Queen's Quarterly 92.1 (1985): 203

(Some authorities dispute this usage.)

Enhanced legislative influence in the policy process ameliorates the tension between our spatial and sectoral systems of representation, but it does little to ensure that all interests in Canadian society have an equal opportunity to contribute to public decision-making.
A. Paul Pross *Group Politics and Public Policy* 2nd ed. 1992: 257

(Some authorities dispute this usage.)

Will an extra 5,000 peacekeepers ameliorate the danger?
Calgary Herald 12 Sept. 1992: A4

(Some authorities dispute this usage.)

We have a responsibility, not to ameliorate, but to eradicate poverty in this country by 2000.
Toronto Star 26 Sept. 1992: A8

(Some authorities dispute this usage.)

amenable   The word *amenable* is usually followed by *to*. The correct verb form after *amenable to* is the *-ing* form ('amenable to sharing'), not the infinitive ('amenable to share').

One of the most common meanings of *amenable* is willing to: 'They were amenable to sharing the cost of the freight'. Another common meaning is responsive: 'Most strains of tuberculosis are amenable to treatment'. In formal writing, *amenable to* sometimes means open to a particular type of testing or judgment.

When *amenable* is not followed by *to*, it means easily influenced or pliable. Increasingly, however, people are using the word to mean pleasing or congenial, probably because they associate *amena-*

ble with the unrelated word *amenity*, 'something that makes life more pleasant'. Note that 'pleasing' is not yet widely accepted as a sense of *amenable*.

The second syllable of *amenable* may be pronounced either *MEN* or *MEAN*.

'He seeks input and is very amenable to ideas and suggestions.'
Ottawa Citizen 23 March 1992: C1

Certainly today's reporters are less amenable to the notion that before, during and after military action it's somehow disloyal to question the interpretation of the facts by government and the armed forces.
Ottawa Citizen 24 June 1992: A10

... neurosurgeon James Drake similarly relies on a customized industrial robot for excising brain tumors in gravely ill children. Inner ears and prostates are also proving amenable to robotic assistance.
Ottawa Citizen 2 Aug. 1992: F1

Levin says they're amenable to passing on as much information as possible.
Ottawa Citizen 31 Oct. 1992: I1

Minnesota ... was understandably amenable to give it [their fifth-round draft choice] up this once for Mike McPhee.
Daily News (Halifax) 19 Aug. 1992: 42

(Here the *-ing* form of *give* is required: 'amenable to *giving* it up'.)

Eskenazi is more than amenable to shoot the breeze in the aisle and discourse on the Muppets and children's movies....
Gazette (Montreal) 10 Dec. 1992: F5

(Here again the *-ing* form is required: 'amenable to *shooting* the breeze ... and *discoursing*'.)

Freud found the tenacity with which religious beliefs are held to be psychologically remarkable. Though they are not amenable to rational or empirical proof, people cling to them anyway.
Irving M. Zeitlin and Robert J. Brym *The Social Condition of Humanity* 1991: 214

(Here *amenable* means open to a certain kind of testing.)

Comparisons and contrasts of this description are perhaps best housed in a casual essay, but some political relationships remain amenable and accessible to scholarly enquiry.
Canadian Journal of History 14.1 (1989): 114

(Here again *amenable* means open to a certain kind of testing or scrutiny.)

The problem for his patrons was that he turned out to be exactly what they said he was.... It remains to be seen whether his successor, Ali Kafi, will prove more amenable.
Calgary Herald 4 July 1992: B3

(Here *amenable* means manageable, easily influenced.)

Well that's my report for today. Now that it's done, I can return to more amenable surroundings, like the Ogilvy book shop.
Gazette (Montreal) 17 June 1992: A2

(Here *congenial* would be a better choice.)

While younger people usually relocate for economic advantage, seniors move for comfort, ... to a more amenable climate.
Vancouver Sun 24 March 1992: C1

(Here *pleasant* would be a better choice.)

Smith, who presented a detailed business plan for the league to the governors, said the concept of the cap is amenable to all teams.
Ottawa Citizen 30 April 1992: H6

(The word *amenable* means 'willing to accept', not 'acceptable'. Either 'the cap is acceptable to all teams' or 'all teams are amenable to the cap' would be better here.)

amend, emend, amendment, emendation Both *amend* and *emend* mean to revise, correct, or improve, but they are used in different contexts. *Amend* is appropriate in a broader range of contexts than *emend*; it is often used to refer to the revision of laws, motions, statutes, bills, or official documents. *Emend* is used more narrowly, referring most often to the scholarly editing of texts or the rewriting of musical scores. *Amendments* are made to laws, while *emendations* are made to texts and musical scores.

The Government introduced a bill yesterday to amend more than 50 federal statutes that the Justice Department believes are in clear violation of the Charter of Rights and Freedoms.
Globe and Mail (Toronto) 1 Feb. 1985: P1

It is hoped that the amnesty granted by the voluntary disclosure policy will prompt some remorseful taxpayers to file returns or amend incorrect returns.
Globe and Mail (Toronto) 7 Jan. 1985: B4

Amend soil with well-rotted compost or mushroom manure.
Vancouver Sun 31 Dec. 1994: E5

Unless your columnist has discovered emendations for very clear statements to the contrary in two of Cicero's letters to his good friend Atticus, he should more properly celebrate the great orator's nativity on Jan. 3....
Globe and Mail (Toronto) 25 June 1985: P6

Even in his own day, the noted British conductor (1879-1961) earned the scorn of scholars and purists for his free hand in reorchestrating and even occasionally rewriting Handel's music to make it palatable to contemporary listeners.... His emendations, anachronistic as they are, are never unmusical nor is the spirit of the music ever betrayed....
Calgary Herald 13 Jan. 1994: A18

American, America, the United States, the Americas

In Canada, *American* is used almost exclusively in reference to the United States and its citizens. Several American usage guides state that Canadians resent the appropriation of *American* by the United States. Whether or not this is so, many Canadians do resent being called *American*—something quite different—because they assume they are being mistaken for U.S. citizens. People who call Canadian travellers *American* may be using a short form for *North American*—a common usage in Britain and Europe—or they may be unable to distinguish Canadian and American accents.

Canadians seldom refer to the United States as *America*, although this usage is quite common around the world. Canadians say *the United States* or, informally, *the States*. The full name, 'the United States of America', and the long abbreviation, *U.S.A.*, are uncommon even in writing. But the short abbreviation *U.S.* is used frequently as an adjective in both formal and informal writing. *U.S.* usually refers to things associated with government ('U.S. Army', 'U.S. dollar') as opposed to culture ('American dream', 'American film industry'). Sometimes *U.S.* is used when *American* might have a broader, continental reference: 'the U.S. market'.

Political trends in the 1990s, such as the creation of world trading blocs and the international solidarity movement among Indigenous peoples, have raised Canadians' awareness of Canada as a country in the Americas. *The Americas* refers to the whole of North, Central, and South America, including the West Indies.

A city with clean subways, no graffiti and fans so polite that they didn't even boo the American national anthem even though the folks from the Big Apple had booed theirs after it was sung by a singer who couldn't remember the words.
Globe and Mail (Toronto) 19 Oct. 1985: E3

'A Canadian,' Arthur L. Phelps has said, 'is one who is increasingly aware of being American in the continental sense without being American in the national sense.'

Carl F. Klinck, ed. *Literary History of Canada* 1 (1976): 139

I am nonplussed for an answer, searching among the nebulosities of our national life, until I think of America, as we allow the citizens of the United States to name their fragments of the continent.
George Woodcock *The New Romans* Ed. A. W. Purdy 1968: 75

(This use of *America* is uncommon in Canada.)

Innis and the Latin American school were seen as legitimate because they were both outside the hegemony of U.S. scholarship....
Wallace Clement and Glen Williams, eds. *The New Canadian Political Economy* 1989: 122

'Mexico wants help to become the hub, the economic downtown of the Americas.'
Toronto Star 28 June 1994: D1

Ruptures is a literary quarterly published in Montreal by Edgard Gousse, an immigrant from Haiti with the vision of uniting in one magazine the four languages (English, French, Spanish and Portuguese) of the 'three Americas' (North, Central and South).
Gazette (Montreal) 25 June 1994: H3

Amerindian   see ABORIGINAL PEOPLE(S)

amid, amidst, among, amongst

Amid is used in Canadian writing far more often than *amidst*; either is correct. Although several guides have suggested that these words are bookish or quaint, both are quite common in Canada.

Some commentators suggest that *amid(st)* should be used with singular nouns ('amid the controversy'), while *among* should be used with plural nouns ('among the items'). This distinction is fanciful. The only real grammatical restriction is on *among*, which cannot be used with singular nouns ('among the controversy' would not be acceptable). However, *among* can be used with singular nouns that can be seen as notionally plural, such as *crowd* ('He walked among the crowd') or *grass* ('We found the beads among the grass'). *Among* is far more common than *amongst*. A few commentators call *amongst* old-fashioned, but that judgment is not borne out by Canadian usage.

... amid the nudges, winks, outrageous opinions and good humor is a foundation of useful information.
Province (Vancouver) 23 Dec. 1990: 71

The two men were led away amid a further exchange of invective, and business at the shop returned to normal.

J.E. Smyth et al. *The Law and Business Administration in Canada* 1987: 96

Symbolically, the romantic rendezvous between Denis and his girl-friend Lise takes place amidst the ruins of the old church building.
Ben.-Z. Shek *French-Canadian & Québécois Novels* 1991: 33

Amidst all the controversy his remarks caused, Berger resigned from the bench.
Andrew Heard *Canadian Constitutional Conventions* 1991: 131

'AIDS was first identified amongst homosexual males in large urban centres and subsequently amongst prostitutes and drug addicts.'
Daniel Gawthrop *Affirmation: The AIDS Odyssey of Dr. Peter* 1994: 63

See also AGREEMENT, GRAMMATICAL; BETWEEN, AMONG.

amok, amuck   *Amok* is the more common spelling. *Amuck* is a variant used more often in Britain than Canada or the United States. According to most dictionaries, to *run amok* means to run about in a homicidal rage or to go berserk. These are the meanings closest to the word's Malay origins, and, with allowances for figurative uses, the most common meanings in Canadian English. However, *run amok* and *go amok* are also used today to mean go too far or go wrong. Perhaps folk etymology is at work here: people may be associating *amuck* with *muck* and getting off the track. In any case, a few dictionaries have begun to list these newer, non-violent meanings.

Suffering from what the doctors called 'delusions of persecution and disease phobia', he'd run amok, jumped through a large window and run bleeding and screaming down the street.
Max Braithwaite *The Night We Stole the Mountie's Car* 1971: 159

The big question on everyone's mind was plain: will the killers, torturers and rapists who have run amok across the former Yugoslavia for the past year and a half really be brought to book?
Vancouver Sun 19 Nov. 1993: A13

But even benign addictions can run amok, as was the case with American collector Steven Blumberg.
Ottawa Citizen 16 Jan. 1994: C7

(Blumberg began to steal books.)

This is yet another example of an amateur sports bureaucracy run amok.
Gazette (Montreal) 12 Feb. 1994: C3

Crown attorney Michael Leshner professed to be 'appalled' by the idea and called it 'human rights gone amok.'
Daily News (Halifax) 17 Nov. 1994: 26

See also FOLK ETYMOLOGY.

among, amongst   see AMID; BETWEEN, AMONG

amoral   see IMMORAL

ampersand   An *ampersand* (pronounced *AM per sand*) is the symbol *&*. In published writing, the ampersand is not freely substituted for *and*. It is used as a space-saving device in tables, notes, and parenthetical documentation; it is used in business names (e.g., Fitzhenry & Whiteside), if that is the practice of the business; and it is used in certain abbreviations such as 'R & D' (research and development), 'R & B' (rhythm and blues), and 'B & B' (bed and breakfast). Note that the spaces are sometimes omitted in abbreviations containing an ampersand: 'R&B', 'B&B'. Either style is acceptable if used consistently.

Long before it was used in English, the ampersand stood for *et* (the Latin word 'and'); thus, until the twentieth century, the Latin abbreviation *etc.* was often written *&c*. Though the symbol *&* is centuries older, its name was not coined until the nineteenth century. *Ampersand* is a distortion of the phrase 'and *per se* and', which means '& by itself is and'. Perhaps this name distinguished the symbol *&* from *&c.*, 'etcetera'.

'This Philosophy both speculative & active is not only to be found in ye volume of nature but also in ye sacred scriptures, as in Genesis, Job, Psalms, Isaiah & others.'
Queen's Quarterly 95.1 (1988): 34

(In contemporary formal writing, *&* cannot be freely substituted for *and*.)

Familiarity is one of the fundamental bases of the recognition decision (Jacoby, Woloshyn, & Kelley, 1989; Mandler, 1980).
Canadian Journal of Psychology 44.3 (1990): 418

Montreal's seasonal events include the Benson & Hedges International Fireworks Competition....
Alan Tucker, ed. *The Penguin Guide to Canada* 1991: 174

Development areas received only 66 per cent of national average allocations of R & D expenditure.
The Canadian Geographer Spring 1989: 54

See also ETC.; PER SE.

amuck   see AMOK

an   see A

anachronism, anachronistic   An *anachronism* is a person, thing, event, or custom placed outside its proper historical period. A motorcycle, for example, would be anachronistic in a painting of the Red River uprising. It is acceptable to use *anachronism* to refer to something outdated or old-fashioned, but *anachronism* or *anachronistic* should not be used to describe something that is simply out of place or contradictory.

> ... what stands out is the anachronism that has Theudebert I, dead in 548, react to a Langobard invasion that occurred in 568.
> *Canadian Journal of History* 14.1 (1989): 94

> Our design of the school bus is an anachronism.
> *Gazette* (Montreal) 1 March 1989: B2

(Here *anachronism* means something belonging to a bygone era.)

> He has rejected allegations that [the United Nations] has become an expensive anachronism, too vulnerable to political opportunists to be of much further value.
> *Globe and Mail* (Toronto) 9 March 1985: P5

(Here again *anachronism* means something belonging to a bygone era.)

> The wider stuff, usually in silky, limp textures, is all over the place in long skirts cut in circles: take down the curtains, mother, I'm going out tonight. They look plain curious by day, but Italians love anachronisms in dress, so they make the point even clearer by adding a tough-looking biker's jacket in black leather....
> *Globe and Mail* (Toronto) 19 March 1985: F1

(A better word here would be *incongruities*.)

analog, analogue   Most Canadian writers use *analog* as a technical adjective meaning 'as opposed to digital' ('analog computer') and *analogue* as a general-purpose noun for something that is similar to or functions in the same way as something else. However, either spelling is acceptable for either use; both spellings are listed in British and American dictionaries.

> Instrument dials may look a bit like conventional analog units, but they are, in fact, all-digital, using a special screen.
> *Vancouver Sun* 21 Dec. 1990: E1

> Major drug companies are now racing to produce an orally active analogue, for at the present state of development the hormone can only be injected in acute situations in a hospital.
> *Perspectives: Profiles of Research at Queen's University* 1986: 25

> But once the present analogue cellular equipment is converted to digital equipment, a process scheduled to begin in 1992, the system's capacity will grow by 400 per cent.
> *Maclean's* 26 Sept. 1988: A34

(In technical contexts, as here, *analog* is more common.)

analogous, similar   Both *analogous* and *similar* are adjectives used to describe things that have a resemblance but are not identical. *Analogous* is usually found in technical and academic contexts and refers to things that work the same way or serve the same purpose, though they may differ in many respects. *Similar* is a more general word and, unlike *analogous*, can be modified by words such as *very*, *almost*, and *somewhat* to indicate the degree of resemblance. Where a preposition is needed, both words are followed by *to*.

The *g* in *analogous* is pronounced as in *go*.

> Logging is seen as a practice analogous to farming, from the 'harvesting of crops' to the creation of 'plantations.'
> *Vancouver Sun* 23 June 1990: B6

> Rather than being a 'colony of settlement' Canada might have been a 'colony of conquest' analogous to those of Asia and Africa.
> Wallace Clement and Glen Williams, eds. *The New Canadian Political Economy* 1989: 135

> There are three Holstein calves in one pen, all somewhat similar but not identical looking.
> *NeWest Review* Feb.–Mar. 1990: 13

> More, they were practical farmers with years of experience under conditions very similar to those on the northern plains.
> Pierre Berton *The Promised Land* 1984: 175–6

ancestor   see DESCENDANT

and   Despite school-day admonitions, there is nothing wrong with beginning a sentence with *and*. When *and* joins two clauses within a sentence, it is generally preceded by a comma, unless the clauses are quite short. A comma is optional before the *and* that precedes the last item in a list: 'hockey, basketball(,) and soccer' (see COMMA). When the subject of a sentence consists of two elements linked by *and*, a plural verb is required (see AGREEMENT, GRAMMATICAL).

> And who wants to take that risk?
> Ken Dryden *The Game* 1983: 230

And there was something else in his motive.
Jack Batten *Robinette* 1984: 82

And indeed, the content, if taken seriously, is disturbing, even frightening.
Miriam Waddington *Apartment Seven* 1989: 104

See also AMPERSAND; AND/OR.

and/or   Most commentators reject the combined form *and/or* except in business writing. For some, the reason is aesthetic: they don't like the virgule. Others find *and/or* clumsy in a sentence and argue that *and* or *or* alone usually suffices to carry the meaning: if greater precision is required, the phrase 'A or B or both' can be used. This phrase should be followed by a plural verb: 'Either a pickaxe or a shovel or both *are* required'.

And/or was first used in legal writing, but now even legal style guides recommend against it; too many court battles have been fought over the exact meaning of 'A, B, and/or C'.

Analysts of South African society, so often preoccupied with issues of race and/or class, have tended to take the state for granted as an agency of other social forces.
Queen's Quarterly 92.1 (1985): 226

(Here *or* is not needed; *and* alone would be preferable.)

It seems to me dangerous to talk about 'Canadian' patterns of sensibility in the work of people who entered and/or entered-and-left the country at a developmentally late stage of their lives.
Margaret Atwood *Second Words* 1982: 142

(Here *or* alone would be less confusing and would not alter the meaning.)

Where there is an unconditional contract for the sale of specific goods in a deliverable state, the property in the goods passes to the buyer when the contract is made, and it is immaterial whether the time of payment or the time of delivery or both is postponed.
J.E. Smyth et al. *The Law and Business Administration in Canada* 1987: 385

(Since *both* is plural, '*are* postponed' is required.)

anesthetist, anesthesiologist   An anesthetist (pronounced *a NEES thuh tist* or *a NES thuh tist*) is any medical person who administers anesthetics. An anesthesiologist is a doctor specializing in anesthesiology, which is the study of anesthetics, their effects, how to administer them, etc. Alternative, though uncommon, spellings of these words are *anaesthetist* and *anaesthesiologist*.

Anesthetists, nurses, technicians and surgeons from general surgery, plastic surgery, urology, and orthopedics took part in the operation.
Gazette (Montreal) 6 June 1994: A11

These thoughts only lingered for a few moments and I was put to sleep quickly by the anaesthetist.
Vancouver Sun 24 Jan. 1994: A3

On top of that, a surgeon would receive $1,310 and an anesthesiologist $455.
Calgary Herald 16 Jan. 1994: B2

See also -AE-, -OE-, -E-.

Anglo-Celtic   see CELT

anglophone   see FRANCOPHONE

Anglo-Saxon   see OLD ENGLISH

Anishnabe   see OJIBWA(Y)

anniversary   *Anniversary* is derived from the Latin for 'the year turned'; hence some commentators disapprove of expressions such as 'our six-month anniversary'. Most people are aware that an anniversary is supposed to come but once a year, and the first uses of the word to refer to shorter time periods were probably playful. However, the extended meaning is now established in newspaper writing in serious contexts. Eventually the new meaning may gain full acceptance because there is no other word for a recurrent date. But so far dictionaries don't list the meaning, nor is it used in formal writing.

Israeli authorities saw the Friday prayers as a serious test of Palestinians' mood on the one-week anniversary of the Hebron massacre.
Toronto Star 5 March 1994: A2

With her one-month anniversary as PM coming up tomorrow, Kim Campbell has not yet gone to New York....
Daily News (Halifax) 24 July 1993: 15

Annunciation   see ENUNCIATION

anoint   *Anoint* is frequently misspelled *annoint*.

After Parizeau appeared to annoint Bouchard as his successor when put on the spot in a newspaper interview, he made a point of saying that several members of the PQ would do just as well.
Ottawa Citizen 10 April 1991: A3

(The correct spelling is *anoint*.)

another, more Some commentators object to following the adjective *another* with a number, as in 'another fifty copies'. *Another*, they say, means *one more* or *a* different, and should be reserved for use with singular nouns: 'another round', 'another story'. *More*, the word generally used with plural nouns, is the appropriate word to use with a plural noun preceded by a number: 'fifty more copies', 'two more people to see'. However, this rule is breached continually, not only in speech but also in formal writing.

> When the doors were not opened for another 15 minutes, tempers flared and there was much pushing and shoving.
> William Teatero *John Anderson: Fugitive Slave* 1986: 76

> Another 10,000 or so people are found in the arctic lands located in Nouveau Québec and the five other census divisions containing tundra lands. . . .
> Robert M. Bone *The Geography of the Canadian North* 1992: 76

> She eventually signed a second contract to take another 35 hours of dancing lessons for $650.
> J.E. Smyth et al. *The Law and Business Administration in Canada* 1987: 239–40

> There were sixteen new appointments under Wallace by the end of his first academic session—some of them arranged before his arrival—another sixteen in 1937-38, and thirteen in the session 1938-39.
> Frederick Gibson *Queen's University* 2 (1983): 148

See also EACH OTHER, ONE ANOTHER.

antagonist, protagonist An *antagonist* is a rival, opponent, or opposing force, someone or something that acts against—*ant(i)*—another.

Some classically educated language commentators, including Fowler, could not abide the use of the plural *protagonists* to refer to the main characters in a play, film, or novel. Ancient Greek plays had only one leading actor, and he and he alone was referred to as the *protagonist*. However, as the *OED* points out in a usage note, restricting the number of protagonists to one makes sense only in reference to ancient Greek drama.

In the nineteenth century, the meaning of *protagonist* broadened to include a prominent figure in a real-life drama or a celebrated champion of a cause. By the 1920s this meaning had broadened once again so that *protagonist* could mean simply supporter, proponent, or advocate, as in 'My brother has become an ardent protagonist of animal rights'.

With this last shift, the whole notion of a protagonist as a leading figure is lost. Many commentators dispute this use because it is apparently based on the misconception that if antagonists are *against* something or someone, then protagonists must be *for* something or someone. In fact, the *pro-* in *protagonist* is not the Latin prefix meaning 'for'. *Protagonist* begins with the Greek prefix *prot(o)-*, meaning 'first' (also found in the English word *prototype*).

Some dictionaries list the disputed meaning, supporter or proponent, and some don't. In Canadian English, the disputed meaning is very rare, not used at all in formal writing, and probably best avoided. In British English, the disputed meaning has become the most common meaning, which has led some commentators to accept it, albeit with misgivings.

> Eventually Maude and Mavor became such bitter antagonists that in their respective books on the Doukhobor migration they scarcely mentioned one another.
> Pierre Berton *The Promised Land* 1984: 72

> He even formed a genial friendship with his antagonist across the aisle of the legislature, Premier William Davis, and to the amusement or chagrin of their caucus mates the two men expressed admiration for each other.
> *Saturday Night* May 1986: 40

> The narrative moves at a deliberate pace, taking time to look into the past that has shaped the present, and fill in the histories of the protagonists.
> *Canadian Churchman* Jun.–Jul. 1986: 20

(The use of *protagonists*, plural, is now accepted.)

> It ended with the heroine deciding whether or not to push the male protagonist off a roof, a conclusion that was well ahead of its time in 1963 and probably too indecisive now.
> Margaret Atwood *Second Words* 1982: 369–70

> 'If you share my view,' Fyfe wrote, 'I want you to be protagonist in the fight. At present the Campbell-Davis faction are shouting victory. I couldn't defeat them. Principals don't carry weight at Queen's.'
> Frederick Gibson *Queen's University* 2 (1983): 127

(Here *protagonist* means champion.)

> Even the most dedicated disarmament protagonist must have felt just the smallest twinge of Canadian pride watching on TV the early June visit of four Canadian warships to Vladivostok, Siberia.
> *Vancouver Sun* 27 July 1990: A11

(Here *proponent* would be a better choice.)

ante- see ANTI-

anthem   see O CANADA

anti-, ante-   *Anti-*, meaning against or opposed to, is an extremely prolific combining form. New compounds formed with the prefix are usually hyphenated, while established words rarely are, unless the first letter following the prefix is *i* (*anti-intellectual*) or a capital (*anti-American*).

Anti- also has a second meaning, which sometimes confuses people: 'false' or 'reversing conventional expectations', as in *anticlimax* or *antihero*. An anticlimax is no climax at all and an antihero is a very unheroic protagonist.

The prefix *ante-* means before or in front of. Most *ante-* words are well established and not hyphenated: *antebellum*, *antechamber*, *antedate*, *antenatal*, *anteroom*. New words tend to be formed with the prefix *pre-* rather than *ante-*: 'preseason', 'prepackaged'. One might expect *antipasto*, a pre-meal appetizer, to be spelled *ante-*, but the word and the spelling come directly from Italian.

Both *anti-* and *ante-* are usually pronounced *AN tee*. In American English *anti-* is sometimes pronounced *AN tie*, a pronunciation used occasionally in Canada.

Our foods are sources of natural antioxidants, the most common one being beta carotene, a plant form of Vitamins A, C, and E.
Toronto Star 6 May 1992: D11

The anti-intellectual pose is one of the unforeseen results of our great experiment in complete literacy.
Robertson Davies *A Voice from the Attic* 1960: 34

(The hyphen in *anti-intellectual* separates the two *i*'s).

... it is hardly consistent with the aims of the current government, which has shown itself to be heartless, anti-people, and pro-Big Business.
Toronto Star 1 July 1992: A12

(As a new coinage, *anti-people* is hyphenated.)

Using industrial materials like corrugated cardboard and aluminum beading, Harding constructs anti-art sculptures that walk a funny line between poignancy and banality.
Vancouver Sun 18 Dec. 1993: D7

(Here *anti-* means completely unconventional.)

There can be little doubt that Hailey ransacked Crawford's article in order to find some of the words that Davis speaks in the *Playboy* interview, rather than vice versa, not only because Crawford's article ante-dates Hailey's, but also because of textual evidence.
Jack Chambers *Milestones* 1983: ix

(The word *antedates* does not require a hyphen.)

anti-abortion   see ABORTION

anticipate   In Canadian English, the most common meaning of *anticipate* is expect or look forward to: 'We're anticipating a bumper crop this year'. This meaning has been disparaged in usage guides for over a century. According to *Fowler's* (1965), for example, it is a 'slipshod extension' of the true meaning of the word. Earlier meanings of *anticipate* involved not just contemplation of the future but action in relation to it. In other words, if you anticipated a raise, you spent it in advance; if you anticipated a problem, you forestalled it; and if you anticipated what someone else had to say, you said it first. The older senses of *anticipate* have not been superseded by the new, but today they are found mostly in formal and literary writing. The 'new' meaning of *anticipate*—now over two hundred years old—is established at all levels of Canadian writing. There seems to be no good reason to avoid it.

Roy [writing in the 1950s] thus anticipated the concerns of the younger writers of the 1960s and 1970s, and their preoccupation with language as a crystallization of the anxiety over cultural survival.
Ben-Z. Shek *French-Canadian & Québécois Novels* 1991: 37

'Much of my work is physically unstable or lacks a fixed presentation. This strategy anticipates and confounds any attempt to apply once and for all time a particular meaning to an individual painting.'
Mark A. Cheetham with Linda Hutcheon *Remembering Postmodernism* 1991: 18

It was anticipated that family participation scores would differ somewhat between the periods.
The Canadian Geographer Spring 1989: 40

(Some commentators would replace *anticipated* with *expected*.)

He had eagerly anticipated his involvement as a volunteer doctor for the swimming events, but now he could barely see the pylons he was stepping into at poolside.
Daniel Gawthrop *Affirmation: The Aids Odyssey of Dr. Peter* 1994: 48

(Some commentators would replace *anticipated* with *looked forward to*.)

'This is what I've known for the last 24 years and it was harder to walk away from it than I anticipated.'
Toronto Star 24 June 1994: E5

(Some commentators would replace *anticipated* with *expected*.)

antiseptic   see SEPSIS

antisocial, asocial, unsociable   The word *antisocial* usually describes destructive and violent behaviour. *Asocial* behaviour is not motivated by antagonism towards society or its members, but rather reveals an ignorance of or inattention to social conventions; however, *asocial* is commonly used as a synonym for *antisocial*. Although both words are used occasionally to describe shy or reserved behaviour, a more neutral alternative is *unsociable*.

Boys are especially vulnerable to antisocial acting out of problems when exposed to a violent father figure in the home....
Mennonite Brethren Herald 7 March 1986: 5

'... are you concerned that we are going to become asocial animals all sitting in front of our computers living completely on the Internet and not ever being able to relate to one another?'
CBC News [transcript] 20 Sept. 1994

Normally outgoing and active, [he] became withdrawn and unsociable....
Gazette (Montreal) 19 March 1992: A3

See also ANTI-, ANTE-.

antler, horn   Deer, reindeer, and moose have *antlers*, which are shed and regrown each year. Cattle, goats, sheep, and antelope have *horns*, which are not shed and which do not grow back if they are cut off. Antlers are branched, while horns usually are not. Antlers are found only on males in species of deer other than reindeer (both sexes of which carry antlers), whereas horns are borne by both males and females.

antonym   see SYNONYM

anxious, eager   The primary meaning of *anxious* is worried or uneasy. In addition, *anxious* is often used to mean eager or desirous. Some language commentators still condemn this use, even though it is common and can be traced back to as early as 1742. Since the 'eager' meaning of *anxious* is well established in formal Canadian writing, there is no need to avoid using it.

Dick was growing anxious that he'd be late for his four o'clock HSR shift.
Jack Batten *Robinette* 1984: 63

(Here *anxious* means worried.)

... there can never have been a time when people were so anxious as they now are to have emotional experiences, or sought them so consciously.
Robertson Davies *A Voice from the Attic* 1960: 12

(Here *anxious* means eager.)

Thus even the strongest partisans of the cause of civic virtue were less than anxious to solicit the presence or even the opinions of the bulk of the population.
J.A.W. Gunn *Beyond Liberty and Property* 1993: 267

(Here *anxious* means eager.)

any   The pronoun *any* is used with both singular and plural verbs: 'Was any found?'; 'Were any needed?'

The adverb *any* usually modifies adjectives or other adverbs: 'any hotter', 'any less'. In Canada and the United States, informal usage permits it to stand alone in sentences such as 'You're not helping any'. This usage is considered odd and questionable in Britain.

Sometimes the adjective *any* and a singular noun are used with the plural pronoun *their*: 'Any member can bring their friends'. This usage is long-established, and the fact that it is non-sexist recommends it. However, some authorities still regard it as a violation of grammatical agreement, and thus it is not completely acceptable in formal writing (see the full discussion of this issue in EVERYONE).

Is any of us so completely just, or merely so sober-sided, that he can take the name 'Samuel Smiles' quite seriously?
Robertson Davies *A Voice from the Attic* 1960: 42

'Are any of the opinions you express the result of adjudged cases?'
William Teatero *John Anderson: Fugitive Slave* 1986: 148

See also AGREEMENT, GRAMMATICAL.

anymore, any more   *Anymore* meaning any longer is usually written as one word: 'The falcons did not return anymore'. *Any more* as in 'I don't want any more, thank you' or 'Is that any more reasonable?' is written as two words.

Generally *anymore* is used in negative statements such as 'He doesn't live here anymore'. However, in some parts of Canada—Newfoundland, Prince Edward Island, and pockets of Ontario—a positive use of *anymore*, meaning nowadays, can be found in spoken English: 'Cod are scarce anymore'.

Not very many people know how to design a pysanka anymore.
Canadian Collector 21 (1986): 53

... a poet may talk forever about forests and prairies and snow and the Land of the North and not be any more Canadian than he will be Australian if he writes a sonnet on a kangaroo.
Northrop Frye *The Bush Garden* 1971: 131

The country we lived in was presented to us in our schools as colourless, dull and without much historical conflict to speak of, except for a few massacres, and nobody did *that* any more.
Margaret Atwood *Second Words* 1982: 378

(In this use, the recommended spelling is *anymore*.)

He said cabinet remains firm that the land is not free for development, and it does not intend to go through anymore hearing processes to battle the issue.
Guardian (Charlottetown) 2 Nov. 1990: 3

(When referring to quantity or extent, the correct form is *any more*.)

anyone, any one   The pronoun meaning any person is always written as one word: 'Anyone could have made that mistake'. If the word *single* can be inserted between *any* and *one* or can replace *one*, then the two-word spelling *any one* is correct: 'Any one of these candidates could do the job'; 'You can't blame any one person for that'.
Regarding the use of the plural pronoun *their* after *anyone*, see EVERYONE.

A month later, without telling anyone, he left for the United States.
The Beaver Feb.–Mar. 1990: 27

He asked the crowd if any one of them who had been in Anderson's position would have acted any differently.
William Teatero *John Anderson: Fugitive Slave* 1986: 102

From that perspective it is pointless to try to evaluate the influence of any one group in isolation.
Neil Nevitte and Roger Gibbins *New Elites in Old States* 1990: 134

anyplace   see -WHERE, -PLACE

any time, anytime   *Any time* should always be written as two words after *at*: 'He could be called in at any time'. Similarly, the two-word form is required when it means 'any amount of time': 'She never has any time for herself'. In fact, the two-word form is correct in all situations, and one way to avoid difficulty is simply to write *any time* every time. However, *anytime* is common and acceptable in informal contexts in both Canadian and American English when it is used as an adverb meaning at any time: 'Drop in anytime'. *Anytime* is also commonly used as a conjunction meaning whenever: 'Anytime there's trouble, the police are at our door'.

'On the reserve, I'm used to going into everybody's house anytime.'
Province (Vancouver) 29 Nov. 1990: 83

Think of fibre optics and the imminent demise of the postal system; think of satellite transmission, ready and able to beam anything anywhere any time.
Margaret Atwood *Second Words* 1982: 390

(Here *anytime* would also be correct.)

'Anytime they have trouble with our community they try to define and divide it.'
Gazette (Montreal) 29 Oct. 1990: A3

(The use of *anytime* as a conjunction meaning whenever is informal.)

It will apply to a vast array of goods and services never before taxed anywhere, at anytime, in Canada.
Ottawa Citizen 1 Dec. 1990: H4

(After *at*, the correct spelling is *any time*.)

At least two members—Gordy Mathews and Sue Leonard—haven't wasted anytime.
Province (Vancouver) 31 Oct. 1990: 56

(*Any time* is required here.)

anyway, anyways   *Anyway* is standard. Although *anyways* is common in informal speech, it is consistently labelled non-standard and should be avoided in writing.

Anyways, the McGillicuddys and all the folks of the village feel better once they've vented their spleen on the politicians every morning.
Vancouver Sun 8 Dec. 1990: B4

(Here, in a humour piece, the writer is imitating stereotypical rural speech.)

apartment   see SUITE

apex see EPITOME

apogee, zenith, perigee, nadir An *apogee* (pronounced *APP o jee*) is literally the farthest point from the earth in the orbit of a planet or satellite; the *zenith* (pronounced *ZEE nith* or *ZEN ith*) is the point in the heavens directly above an observer. Both terms are used figuratively to mean either the high point or the furthest reach.

A *perigee* (pronounced *PAIR i jee*) is the opposite of an apogee: it is the nearest point to the earth in the orbit of a planet or satellite. The word is seldom used figuratively.

The *nadir* (pronounced *NAY der* or *NAY deer*) is the opposite of the zenith; it's the part of the celestial sphere directly below an observer. *Nadir* is used figuratively to mean the low point.

Football reaches its apogee as the thermometer hits its nadir.
Calgary Herald 23 Feb. 1993: A5

The slap shot ... produced glamorous new stars, most especially Bobby Hull and Frank Mahovlich, and a glamorous new image. This was the league's competitive and commercial zenith.
Ken Dryden *The Game* 1983: 222

And when things are at their nadir and the reasons for which you wrote your book appear to have come completely unbuckled from the result ... you can always tell yourself that the pursuit of literature is a significant human activity.
Margaret Atwood *Second Words* 1982: 406

apology, apologia An *apology* is an expression of regret for having offended or hurt someone. An *apologia* (pronounced *app uh LOW jyuh*) is a statement defending and explaining a way of life, a system of belief, an institution, etc. An apologia may also be called an *apology*.

Chris Cobb's vacuous apologia for Alan King's execrable May 13 cartoon ... is probably one of the most twisted pieces of sophistry I have ever had the misfortune of attempting to decipher.
Ottawa Citizen 20 May 1993: A14

At the time of its release, the painstakingly researched document ... elicited much public comment and a contrite apologia from police administrators. Police Chief William McCormack vowed that the mistakes made in the handling of internal affairs complaints would not be repeated.
Toronto Star 15 Jan. 1993: A7

(An *apologia* is never an admission of guilt; *apology* is the word required here.)

Julius Grey's latest apology for the legal status quo [exacerbates] the apprehensions of the anglophone community.
Gazette (Montreal) 21 June 1994: B2

(Here *apology* means apologia.)

a posteriori *A posteriori* (pronounced *AY, or AH, po steer ee OR eye*) is a Latin phrase that means 'by inductive reasoning'. Inductive reasoning is reasoning from observable effects to probable causes, as in 'The stove is off, yet the burner is hot. A posteriori, the burner was on recently.'

It seems unfair to put *The Pegnitz Junction* and *Survival in Auschwitz* side by side: any memoir authored by a survivor is bound to have an authenticity and power that the fiction of an *a posteriori* observer cannot match.
Janice Kulyk Keefer *Reading Mavis Gallant* 1989: 177–8

See also A PRIORI; LATIN PHRASES.

apostrophe The *apostrophe* has two main uses: to mark a missing letter in a contraction (*ne'er, don't*) and to indicate the possessive case. Occasionally it is used to form plurals with odd lexical items, when the plural otherwise would be hard to read: 'I got five A's'; 'Dot your i's and cross your t's'; 'Mind your p's and q's'.

Note that the apostrophe is not the mark of an ordinary plural: 'No Dogs (*not* Dog's *or* Dogs') Allowed'.

The apostrophe was once commonly used with numbers ('the 1960's'), but now it is not required: 'the 1990s'.

The RT100 is a mid-size package of 97cc's, with styling from the YZ series.
Canadian Biker Magazine Feb. 1990: 16

One of the most fun motorcycle do's I attended in 1989 involved people who have never owned or ridden a motorcycle.
Canadian Biker Magazine Feb. 1990: 8

See also CONTRACTIONS; ITS, IT'S; POSSESSIVE.

apparent Some commentators dislike the expression 'died of an apparent heart attack', pointing out rather facetiously that only real heart attacks are fatal. Less controversial, if slightly longer, expressions that make the same point are 'The man died, apparently of a heart attack' and 'The man died from what appeared to be a heart attack'.

... a 68-year-old man lay dying of an apparent heart attack in a Montreal West park, waiting for an ambulance that neighbors say took too long to arrive despite repeated calls to 911.
Gazette (Montreal) 10 June 1994: A1

(Here 'dying of *what appeared to be* a heart attack' would avoid any criticism.)

appeal In law, to *appeal* is to ask that a case be referred to a higher court for review. The 'CBC Language Guide' states that one appeals a case; one does not appeal *against* a decision. General Canadian usage does not follow this distinction, however. People are described as appealing cases, rulings, convictions, and decisions and as appealing *against* convictions, rulings, and decisions with about equal frequency. 'Appeal against' is common in Great Britain (Garner, *Dictionary of Modern Legal Usage*), while 'appeal a decision, ruling (etc.)' is common in the United States.

Appeals are allowed or dismissed in Canada and Great Britain; in the United States they are affirmed or reversed (Garner).

Ultimately public opinion ... persuaded the firm to accept a much smaller sum and a commitment that the group would not appeal the case or pursue the issue farther.
A. Paul Press *Group Politics and Public Policy* 2nd ed. 1992: 182

... he plans to appeal both the conviction and the sentence, handed down late last week.
Edmonton Journal 28 Nov. 1994: A3

The town is currently waiting for a decision from an Ontario Municipal Board panel which heard an appeal against the current zoning bylaw by a master woodcarver who wants to continue making church monuments in a workshop behind his rural home.
Spectator (Hamilton) 15 Dec. 1994: C4

Three judges of the Nova Scotia Court of Appeal dismissed the appeal of [one man], but partly allowed the appeal of [another].
Daily News (Halifax) 3 May 1994: np

Rock said the government will also pay T——'s costs before the Supreme Court if the appeal is allowed.
Calgary Herald 19 May 1994: A13

appear *Appear* can mean either to become visible or to give a certain impression. When *appear* is followed by an infinitive ('He appeared to help'), its meaning is ambiguous. Substituting *arrive* or *seem* for *appear* will clarify the sense.

But the Montreal native appeared to help as Pittsburgh rebounded from a 7-2 humiliation in Hartford 24 hours earlier.
Calgary Herald 4 Jan. 1994: D4

(Here either or both senses of *appear* could be intended: the player in question *arrived* from the minor leagues and *seemed* to help his new team.)

appetizer see ENTRÉE

appraise, apprise, apprize *Appraise* means evaluate: 'Real estate agents appraise houses'. *Apprise* is a formal synonym of *inform*: 'I apprised her of her rights'. *Apprise* is often used in the passive: 'We were not apprised of all the facts when we made that decision'. Although some dictionaries equate 'to be apprised of' with 'to be aware of', there is a subtle difference in emphasis: if you say you are not apprised of all the relevant facts, you are placing the blame on others for not having told you.

Apprize is an obsolete synonym of *appraise* and *esteem* or a misspelling of *apprise*.

Elizabeth quickly appraises her clothes: jeans again.
Margaret Atwood *Life Before Man* 1979: 134

Nevertheless, the full Board of Trustees, meeting in April 1917 and by then apprised of the terms of Chancellor Douglas's proposed gift, decided that the question of the principalship must be settled as soon as possible.
Frederick Gibson *Queen's University* 2 (1983): 14

apprehend, comprehend Both words can mean understand, but their emphases differ: to *apprehend* something is to perceive or discern it, or to expect it with fear; to *comprehend* something is to have a thorough intellectual grasp of it.

Other freelancers will immediately apprehend tax difficulties with depreciable business-use property that also serves for decidedly non-business candle-lit dinners. Any accountants in the audience, please write.
Globe and Mail (Toronto) 2 March 1985: H4

(Here freelancers can *apprehend* problems that they need an accountant to help them *comprehend*.)

The judge said C—— lacked the capacity to comprehend what was happening, and give consent.
Calgary Herald 21 Dec. 1993: B4

apprise, apprize   see APPRAISE

approbation, opprobrium   *Approbation*, from the Latin *approbare*, 'to praise', is a formal word for praise, approval, or favourable opinion. *Opprobrium*, from the Latin *opprobare*, 'to reproach', is a state of public disgrace following some conduct considered shameful, or the contempt and criticism directed at someone in this state. Some writers mistakenly use *approbation* as if it were negative.

There are great numbers of people to whom the act of reading a book—any sort of book—is wondrous; they speak of the reader in the tone of warm approbation which they use otherwise when referring to pregnant women, or the newly dead.
Robertson Davies *A Voice from the Attic* 1960: 253

Yet, like Jackson, who left office shortly before his economic policies saddled his successor, Martin Van Buren, with a nasty economic depression following the Panic of 1837, Reagan seemed at every turn to escape major personal opprobrium.
Queen's Quarterly 95.4 (1988): 802

If intellectual ('uppity'?) women wish to pursue careers, they should pay considerable attention to their family roles.... In effect they should be superwomen. Those that fail 'naturally' incur public approbation. But recent social change has begun to alter this 'blame the victim' ideology and practice.
Canadian Journal of History 14.1 (1989): 153

(The word required here is *opprobrium*.)

With few exceptions, he has suffered the approbation of his peers and the loss of nearly all his friends.
Whig-Standard (Kingston) 18 July 1992: mag. 9

(The word required here is *opprobrium*.)

approve   A distinction is usually made between *approve of* and *approve*. To approve *of* something is to be pleased by it or satisfied with it, whereas to approve something ('Council approved the motion') is to ratify it.
Sometimes, especially in British English, *approve* followed by a direct object has the same meaning as *approve of*: 'This time my friends approved my choice'. However, British commentators advise against this usage.

A summary report by Acheson claimed that parents and teachers do not approve of multigrade classes.
Education Canada Summer 1989: 10–11

... the C.R.T.C. approved a renewal of the station's licence for only one year instead of the usual three years.

J.E. Smyth et al. *The Law and Business Administration in Canada* 1987: 282

'I feel a deep interest in this prisoner's case, because he is demanded as a criminal for doing what I must approve, holding as I do that to fight not to be a slave is noble.'
William Teatero *John Anderson: Fugitive Slave* 1986: 152

(Some commentators disapprove of this use of *approve*; this quotation dates from the mid-nineteenth century.)

April Fool's Day   see NEW YEAR'S DAY

a priori   *A priori* (pronounced *AY pry OR eye* or *AH pree OR ee*) is a Latin phrase that means 'by deductive reasoning'. Deductive reasoning proceeds from something known, or assumed, to a necessary conclusion: 'It's raining, and I forgot to bring in the clothes. They're going to be soaked.' Some a priori arguments are purely theoretical. Though they unfold logically, they start from an untested hypothesis. Thus *a priori* is sometimes used negatively to mean not based in real experience.

The United States, being founded on a revolution and a written constitution, has introduced a deductive or a priori pattern into its cultural life that tends to define an American way of life and mark it off from anti-American heresies.
Northrop Frye *The Bush Garden* 1971: 218

Hence Marx was trying to provide not a suprahistorical, a priori system but a historical-sociological method of inquiry.
Irving M. Zeitlin and Robert J. Brym *The Social Condition of Humanity* 1991: 91

Why must we accept, a priori, a definition of Canada and Canadianism supplied by people like Ford?
Calgary Herald 18 Oct. 1993: A5

See also A POSTERIORI; LATIN PHRASES.

apropos   The adjective *apropos* (pronounced *A pruh PO*) means pertinent, appropriate, or opportune. *Apropos of*—or, less commonly, *apropos* alone—is a preposition meaning with regard to or concerning: 'apropos of our discussion', 'apropos our discussion'.
Occasionally *apropos* is used as an adverb to introduce a sentence, in which case it means by the way or on that topic.
While *à propos* is two words in the original French, in English it is written as one word with no accent.

Written 1600 years ago, it has never been more apropos.
Catholic Register 16 Aug. 1986: 2

The Vancouver Symphony Orchestra was bashing away at Climb Every Mountain atop Whistler Mountain as part of its summer concerts series, and the backdrop was, yes, incredible. And apropos.
Province (Vancouver) 20 Aug. 1990: 41

Benjamin must have seen me looking at William, because he said, apropos of nothing that I could tell, 'It's hard to keep young ones on colony.'
Canadian Fiction Magazine 64 (1988): 130–1

Apropos of standards, the greatest fashions in the world are meaningless if not delivered on time.
Globe and Mail (Toronto) 22 Oct. 1985: E8

And apropos the rent we pay when abroad, what about reporting on our housing expenses, mortgage forfeiture or damage costs if we don't find the right tenants for our homes here?
Ottawa Citizen 12 May 1994: A10

(In this context *apropos of* is more common, but *apropos* alone is also correct.)

Apropos, having heard the Prime Minister on this subject several times, I am convinced there is no pride of authorship with regard to the accord.
Toronto Star 28 March 1990: A27

(Here *apropos* means by the way.)

Perhaps a 48-hour notice or a warning ticket for out-of-province license plates would be more a propos.
Gazette (Montreal) 11 Nov. 1990: B3

(The English spelling is *apropos*.)

apt   see LIABLE

aq-, acq-   Spelling mistakes are frequent in words beginning with *aq-* and *acq-*. Derivatives of the Latin word *aqua*, 'water', such as *aquamarine*, *aquarium*, *aquatic*, *aqueduct*, and *aqueous*, all begin with *aq-*, as does *aquiline*, meaning eagle-like. These are the only common words that begin with the letters *aq-*.
Acquaint, acquiesce, acquire, acquit, and all related words begin with *acq-*.

She enrols in school today and a week later leaves for the world acquatic championships in Rome.
Edmonton Journal 22 Aug. 1994: D4

(The correct spelling is *aquatic*.)

But he cautioned criminals will find other ways to aquire ammunition.
Vancouver Sun 24 June 1994: A9

(The correct spelling is *acquire*.)

There's a lot of friends and aquaintances that we've made over the years and I'm sure that there's going to be some things to be said.
Globe and Mail (Toronto) 17 June 1985: S5

(The correct spelling is *acquaintances*.)

aquiline nose, Grecian nose, Roman nose   An *aquiline* nose is hooked or curved like an eagle's beak (*aquila* is Latin for 'eagle').

A *Grecian* nose, also called a Grecian profile, lacks a hollow between the upper ridge of the nose and the forehead. A *Roman* nose does have this hollow, and is either straight or slightly aquiline.

Arabic, Arab, Arabian   *Arabic* is the language associated with Islam, a religion that originated in the Arabian peninsula (the southwest corner of Asia bounded by the Red Sea and the Persian Gulf) in the seventh century A.D. and spread through the Middle East and North Africa.

Arab is a loose term for the people who have in common the Arabic language and the Islamic tradition, including Arabic-speakers in Algeria, Egypt, Iraq, Jordan, Kuwait, Mauritania, Morocco, Oman, Palestine, Qatar, Saudi Arabia, Sudan, Syria, Tunisia, and the United Arab Emirates. Some people also consider Iranians 'Arab', though most Iranians speak Farsi (Persian). And some people would call Lebanon an Arab country, though much of the population is Christian.

For contemporary ethnic, political, or cultural references, the adjectives *Arabic* and *Arab* should be preferred to *Arabian*, which is obsolete in these contexts. In current English, *Arabian* is used either to evoke the exotic image of the East that captured the European imagination in the eighteenth century with the translation of *The Thousand and One Nights* or to refer to the Arabian Peninsula as a geographic region, as in 'Arabian deserts', 'Arabian fauna', 'Arabian horse'.

Fluent in English, French, Italian and Arabic, she graduated from the American University in Cairo. . . .
Gazette (Montreal) 7 March 1989: C1

Saudi Arabia's split with Tehran will heighten Iran's isolation in the Arab world and likely deepen U.S. involvement in the Persian Gulf region, Arab diplomats said Wednesday.
London Free Press 28 April 1988: 14

One of the best of many North African restaurants to open in recent years, Chez Fatma is decorated Arabian style complete with tented ceiling and Arabic music.
Gazette (Montreal) 4 March 1989: T4

See also ISLAM.

arbitration see CONCILIATION

arbitrator, arbiter According to most dictionaries, *arbitrator* and *arbiter* are synonyms for a person chosen to decide a dispute. In practice, *arbitrator* is generally reserved for a judge in legal disputes, such as labour disputes or child-custody battles, whereas *arbiter* refers to judges of other issues, especially matters of style and taste.

Both sides in the labor dispute that led to a work-to-rule campaign by Metro Toronto police met yesterday in an attempt to find a solution before an arbitrator is appointed.
Globe and Mail (Toronto) 21 Feb. 1985: M4

Despite the concerns and efforts, it is the viewer that remains the ultimate arbiter of Canadian and U.S. telecasting.
Globe and Mail (Toronto) 28 Aug. 1985: B5

... he associates value-judgements with class superiority—arguing that a critic who evaluates is an arbiter of taste....
Queen's Quarterly 92.2 (1985): 382

arc, arch Both words are used as verbs as well as nouns. To trace a curved path through the air is to *arc* or to *arch*. The past and present participles of *arc* are *arced* and *arcing*, rhyming with *barked* and *barking*.

Atlantis rose from its seaside pad at 9:56 a.m. and pierced a low deck of clouds as it arced over the Atlantic Ocean.
Gazette (Montreal) 1 Aug. 1992: A12

The ocean swirled against jagged rocks as a rainbow arced above the lighthouse.
Vancouver Sun 27 June 1992: E1

Rising atop a familiar column of fluffy, white vapor, it arched southeastward on a course that will keep it to the south of the United States on nearly all of its 111 orbits.
Toronto Star 1 Aug. 1992: A13

Swirls of turquoise water frothed against jagged rocks in the Gulf of St. Lawrence as a rainbow arched over the lighthouse.
Toronto Star 11 April 1992: G7

archaisms *Archaisms* are words and expressions, such as *quoth, runneth, 'twas, methinks, thee, whosoever*, and *verily*, that are no longer current and have a strong air of the past about them. But they have not been discarded. They are common in legal and liturgical language—where they make the weight of tradition felt—and they are used for humorous, poetic, and historical effects.

See also HITHER, THITHER, WHITHER; QUOTH; YE.

archetype, prototype, stereotype In the seventeenth century, an *archetype* was an ideal version of something or a standard pattern from which copies were made. Since the early twentieth century, however, *archetype* (pronounced *ARK e type*) has been closely associated with the theories of the psychoanalyst Carl Jung. Jung used the term *archetype* to refer to those ideas, images, and symbols that he believed to be pervasive in human experience, forming part of what he called the 'collective unconscious'. Northrop Frye adapted the term to literary criticism, where he used it to mean an image or symbol that recurs so often that it becomes conventional.

Prototype is close in meaning to the seventeenth-century meaning of *archetype*. In design and manufacturing, a trial model of a car, for example, is called a prototype. Another meaning of *prototype* is the most typical example of a category: thus a robin is a prototype of the bird, while the earth-bound ostrich is not.

A *stereotype* is a fixed, simplistic—usually negative—image of a group that is applied unthinkingly to individuals.

The usual adjective forms of these nouns are *archetypal* (pronounced *ark e TYPE ul*), *prototypical*, and *stereotypical*. None of these adjectives should be used to mean *typical*.

Rather than attempt a direct translation of Hearn's observations, Nakajima uses them as a springboard for her own exploration of mythical archetypes and rituals, helping them transcend their specific cultural roots to achieve a universal resonance.
Toronto Star 30 Oct. 1992: C14

Like the archetypal daisy pushing through asphalt, kids can refuse to be crushed by life.
Vancouver Sun 11 Dec. 1992: D6

Although the DCS 200 delivers good pictures, it has a number of quirks that give it the feel of a prototype model, rather than a fully developed camera system.
Toronto Star 12 Dec. 1992: G5

'But I do gravitate to forms and experiences that seem to be prototypical of their kind, that seem, somehow or other, to be imbued with an essence.'
Vancouver Sun 14 May 1995: D5

'Anybody who thinks we're promoting stereotypes is actually promoting a stereotype of uniformity—that we can ignore people's cultural differences.'
Vancouver Sun 28 Dec. 1992: A6

The stereotypical image of the Indian still exists within the business community, and contributes to the low number of natives in the workforce....
Calgary Herald 7 Dec. 1992: B1

... what is archetypal of political correctness among media sophisticates is a failure to appreciate [that] the aversion to homosexual practices is strong and deeply seated in Canada.
Toronto Sun 28 Oct. 1994: 11

(The word required here is *typical*.)

archives, archive   Large institutional collections of various types of records and documents valued for historical purposes are usually called *archives*, plural, as is the building in which the collection is housed. Either a singular or a plural verb is acceptable with *archives*: 'Where is (*or* are) the archives?'
Sometimes a collection of one specific type of material, or a small, personal collection, is called an *archive*, singular.

Some items that don't have sales value, such as photographs or memorabilia, might be welcomed by a local museum or archives....
Canadian Collector 21 (1986): 53

One of my wife's musical sources was in the church archive of a small town.
Ottawa Citizen 1 Oct. 1990: A11

His considerable literary archive constitutes a treasury of this phase of Jewish culture.
Henry M. Rosenthal and S. Cathy Berson, eds. *Canadian Jewish Outlook Anthology* 1988: 221

Arctic, arctic   The two common pronunciations of this word, *AR tik* and *ARK tik*, both reflect its etymology. *Arctic* is derived from the Greek word *arktikos*, 'bear', the name of the constellation of the northern sky (Ursa Major). In the 1400s, the English spelling of the word was *artic*, influenced by Old French *artique*. In the 1600s, however, Classical scholars became aware that the original Greek word contained an additional *c* or *k*, and they cor-

rected the spelling to *arctic*. Many Canadians say *AR tik*, especially in informal speech, but *ARK tik* is the recommended pronunciation.
Arctic is usually capitalized when it refers specifically to the region bounded by the Arctic Circle ('the Arctic', 'Arctic tundra') and uncapitalized when it refers to extreme cold.

The two ships, the Erebus and the Terror, reached the Canadian Arctic, only to be repeatedly trapped in ice.
Calgary Herald 30 June 1994: A8

MacInnis, a former member of the Canadian National Ski Team, was chosen for the journey for his wealth of experience in arctic survival techniques.
Toronto Star 2 April 1994: F7

Born north of the Artic Circle in Norway in 1909, young Lorntzsen took to the sea and travelled the world.
Vancouver Sun 3 Oct. 1994: C4

(The correct spelling is *Arctic*.)

aren't I   see AIN'T

Argentinian(s), Argentine(s)   *Argentinians* (pronounced *ar jen TIN ee uns*) is preferred to *Argentines* as the English name for the citizens of Argentina ('CBC Language Guide').
Either *Argentinian* or *Argentine* (pronounced *ar jen TINE* or *arj en TEEN*) is acceptable as the adjective form: 'Argentinian (*or* Argentine) beef'. Note that *Argentinian* ends in *-ian*, not *-ean*.

The circus was owned and operated by Argentines, and it was based in Mexico City.
Vancouver Sun 24 Feb. 1994: C6

(*Argentinians* is preferred to *Argentines*.)

[Matambre con ruso is] an Argentinean staple.
Mirror (Montreal) 8 June 1995: 31

(The correct spelling is *Argentinian*.)

argot   see COLLOQUIAL

armada, flotilla, raft   *Armada* (pronounced *arm AHD uh* or *ar MADE uh*) usually refers to a fleet of warships or armed ships. The term came into English from Spanish after the failed expedition of the Spanish Armada against England in 1588. *Armada* is capitalized in references to that historic Armada.
Flotilla (pronounced *flow TILL uh*), from the Spanish meaning 'little fleet', usually refers to a fleet either of few ships or of small ships and boats of any kind. Some people reserve *flotilla* for a small fleet of unarmed ships and boats, and would object to 'an

armada of fishing boats'. However, this distinction does not hold in the United States: in the U.S. Navy a *flotilla* is two or more squadrons of small warships, and *Merriam-Webster's Collegiate Dictionary* (10th ed.) gives as an example of *armada* 'a small armada of fishing boats'.

Flotilla and *armada* are also used to refer to groups of vehicles, objects, or people on land. Since these uses are metaphorical, their appropriateness must be judged case by case.

Sometimes *armada* and *flotilla* are used to mean simply 'a group of' or 'a lot of', perhaps by analogy to *raft*, which can bear the same sense. Dictionaries label this sense of *raft* informal, however, and the analogous use of *flotilla* or *armada* should probably be restricted to informal writing.

The Royal Canadian Navy contributed 110 ships, including two destroyers, and 10,000 sailors to the [D-day] armada.
Calgary Herald 5 June 1994: B1

It will be years before we see the ships of the Spanish Armada, even if the plan to raise the wrecks gets the go-ahead, said one expert.
Ottawa Citizen 17 June 1994: A9

And an armada of department stores and supermarkets continue to battle for business.
Ottawa Citizen 23 March 1994: F1

(Here *armada* fits with the extended metaphor of war.)

We know Montreal has the biggest snow-removal budget of any city except Sapporo, Japan, and the largest armada of equipment—68 snow blowers, 47 tractor-loaders, 123 sidewalk plows and 72 power graders....
Gazette (Montreal) 24 May 1994: A3

(Anyone who has seen these giant machines at work would agree to the aptness of *armada* here.)

Toronto harbour filled with the majesty of more than 25 tall ships last evening during a sailpast to kick off the international flotilla's six-day visit to Toronto.
Toronto Star 30 June 1994: A3

Behind him in the failing light sailed the rest of 31st Canadian Minesweeping Flotilla—six little minesweepers.
Vancouver Sun 4 June 1994: B3

There was a flotilla of British warships in Novorossiysk at the time, and the idea was that one of them would take us aboard and help us get out of Russia.
George Ignatieff *The Making of a Peacemonger* 1987: 25

(Some prefer *armada* to *flotilla* when the fleet is armed.)

... leaving a small flotilla of agents and assistants behind in New York, she flew alone to Sarajevo.
Ottawa Citizen 9 March 1994: B6

(This is an example of the informal sense.)

Strangway has no apologies for the raft of new facilities that are now completed, being built or on the drawing board.
Vancouver Sun 4 May 1994: B6

(This use of *raft* is informal.)

armed forces   see CANADIAN ARMED FORCES

armoury, armory, armo(u)ries   In Canadian and American English, *armoury* and *armory* are alternative spellings for a stockpile of weapons or a place where weapons are stored. *Armory* is the usual spelling in the United States; both spellings are common in Canada.

In Canadian English, the building where the militia trains is often referred to in the plural as the *armo(u)ries*. In American English, the local headquarters of the military reserve is the *armory*, singular.

In British English *armory* and *armoury* are two different words. *Armory* is a synonym of *heraldry*, the art of designing and assigning coats of arms, while an *armoury* is a stockpile of weapons or a place where weapons are kept.

And, on Saturday night, there will be period dances at the Lansdowne Park Coliseum and the armouries in Hull.
Ottawa Citizen 1 June 1994: B3

See also SPELLING, CANADIAN.

army   see CANADIAN ARMED FORCES

around, round   The use of *around* to mean approximately ('around fifty') is common in speech and informal writing. However, this expression is rare in formal writing.

In most contexts where Canadians and Americans say *around* ('around the corner', 'turn around'), British speakers are more likely to say *round*, but both variants are used on both sides of the Atlantic.

Around three percentage points were added to banks' prime loans, one-year mortgages and other short-term credits.
Toronto Star 30 March 1994: C2

See also ALL-ROUND, ALL-AROUND .

arrogate see ABROGATE

artful see ARTISTIC

article see THE, A, AN

artifact, artefact Both spellings are correct. Canadians and Americans usually write *artifact*. British dictionaries list *artefact* first.

artificial, synthetic Any product or situation that humans manufacture or contrive to resemble something natural can be called *artificial*: 'artificial flowers', 'an artificial island', 'an artificial scarcity'.

Synthetic has a narrower meaning. Synthetic products are specifically those created through the process of synthesis: that is, by combining chemical elements. Nylon and plastic, for example, are synthetic materials. By extension, any unnatural conglomeration can be called *synthetic*.

Both *artificial* and *synthetic* may refer to insincere or affected human behaviour, but *artificial* is far more common in this sense.

Synthetic does not have connotations of artificiality when it refers to a person's thinking; synthetic thinking is comprehensive, capable of linking and consolidating diverse ideas.

He had lost a leg in World War I, and though he managed remarkably well with an artificial leg, he always carried a spare in case of trouble.
George Ignatieff *The Making of a Peacemonger* 1987: 66

Today, it is difficult to think of a single facet of life which has not been affected, and probably improved, by the introduction of synthetic materials.
Perspectives: Profiles of Research at Queen's University 1986: 48

Haliburton seems to have believed that the ideal for Nova Scotia would be a combination of American energy and British social structure, but such a chimera, or synthetic monster, is hard to achieve in practice.
Northrop Frye *The Bush Garden* 1971: 218

In saying this, however, Sara is uncomfortable, and later she goes to artificial lengths to be courteous to Janet.
Canadian Journal of Philosophy 19 (1989): 250

... Müller had not the same comprehensive synthetic grasp of the whole field as Darwin had, so that his work had nothing like the rounded completeness of Darwin's,

which renders it capable of being easily held and visualized in a single view.
R.A. Wilson *The Birth of Language* 1937: 29

See also ERSATZ.

artillery see GUN

artist, artiste, artisan An *artist* is someone who creates or performs works of art in music, painting, sculpture, literature, drama, dance, etc. The word *artist* almost always has positive connotations, implying great creativity and skill. It is sometimes applied approvingly to people who have remarkable talent in a field not generally considered to be art, such as cooking, clothing design, or hairdressing.

Artiste (pronounced *ar TEEST*) the French variant of the word *artist*, can be applied to singers and dancers without insult. But in other contexts *artiste* is usually derogatory: it's applied to people whose artistic sensibility is difficult to bear, or to artists whose pretensions are thought to overshadow their talents.

An *artisan* is a skilled craftsperson such as a weaver, a potter, a woodcarver, or a cabinetmaker. Artisans produce useful objects, which is what generally distinguishes them from artists.

Unlike many great theatrical artists, she does not imprint her personality on her work.
Queen's Quarterly 98.1 (1991): 161

He was a great, creative jazz artist.
Jack Chambers *Milestones* 1983: 88

The road to success for the folk/roots artiste is much bumpier and longer than for rockers.
Vancouver Sun 4 May 1990: E7

The Toronto-based artiste is best known as a singer/songwriter who turns out quirky, diverse albums like last year's Bombazine, which earned her a Juno nomination for best new solo artist.
Ottawa Citizen 5 May 1994: C2

I'm very glad when I see artists of any kind getting involved in social action. It's too easy to say, 'I'm an artiste. I don't have anything to do with anything that isn't my ah-t.'
Vancouver Sun 22 April 1990: C5

(Here *artiste* has negative connotations.)

After one experience with a temperamental artiste who chased him from the kitchen, Mirvish says he brought his parking lot attendant into the restaurant and had him trained as a cook.
Financial Post 17 March 1989: 17

(Here *artiste* has negative connotations.)

If handmade bracelets, brooches, necklaces and earrings are on your Christmas list, it's probably worth a visit to see the work of Toronto artisan Donna Polichuk.
Ottawa Citizen 1 Dec. 1994: G4

Potters such as Tom Smith of St. Andrews and Peter Powning of Markhamville (near Sussex) have been accorded the status of artist rather than artisan.
Alan Tucker, ed. *The Penguin Guide to Canada* 1991: 83

See also ARTISTIC; ARTS.

artistic, artful, arty, artsy People who are *artistic* have a talent or affinity for art, while people who are *artful* are cunning, sometimes even deceitful. In reference to a creative endeavour, *artistic* means tasteful or successful, while *artful* means ingenious in design.

Arty and *artsy* are informal, sometimes disparaging adjectives. They always suggest a self-conscious connection to the arts, and sometimes they imply pretentiousness or triteness.

I don't know who I got it from; neither of my parents was artistic, yet even as a child of ten I was drawing.
Saturday Night March 1986: 34

By playing one off against the other, an artful minister might prevail over both.
J.A.W. Gunn *Beyond Liberty and Property* 1983: 282

[She] bought a pleated Issey Miyake 'because it was so sculptural and artistic looking.'
Calgary Herald 14 June 1994: B10

Green Water, Green Sky is composed of four self-contained sections linked by an artful fluidity of narrative line.
Janice Kulyk Keefer *Reading Mavis Gallant* 1989: 80

'Bands I hate the most are ones that put out those serious, black-and-white, arty press photos with shadows, where everyone's looking in a different direction, and they've all got perfect haircuts.'
Ottawa Citizen 19 Oct. 1990: D3

Unless you're really into heavy-handed symbolism and artsy pretension, this is one film to avoid.
Ottawa Citizen 10 Nov. 1990: G4

See also ARTIST; ARTS.

arts, visual arts, performing arts, performance art, fine arts, liberal arts *The arts* include drawing, painting, photography, cinema, sculpture, music, literature, drama, and dance. The *visual arts* are drawing, painting, and sculpture. The traditional *performing arts* are dance, music, and drama.

Performance art is an avant-garde mixture of drama and visual elements such as sculpture or video. The term *fine art(s)* is used to distinguish artistic work produced only to be contemplated from crafts and commercial art.

In a university setting, the creative arts are usually called *fine arts* to distinguish them from the humanities and social sciences (literature, languages, history, sociology, psychology, etc.), which are called *arts*. Canadians often use the terms *arts* and *liberal arts* as synonyms. In the United States, *liberal arts* has a slightly different meaning: it refers not only to arts but also to pure sciences, as opposed to professional studies such as engineering, medicine, and business.

The hair peeled away before the razor's advance like wool being sheared from a lamb. . . . It was all part of a performance art piece called Clearcut, one element of a wide-ranging, multi-media exhibit. . . .
Spectator (Hamilton) 17 Aug. 1994: B7

She . . . soon realized that her talents did not lie in fine art, and switched to fashion design.
Ann Davis *Somewhere Waiting* 1991: 4

He had studied painting at the University of Wisconsin at Madison and graduated with a degree in Fine Arts before joining the faculty of the Manitoba School of Art in 1973.
Queen's Quarterly 98.1 (1991): 11

The non-credit courses, covering a wide range of liberal arts and science subjects, are taught by resident faculty or local experts.
Calgary Herald 17 Sept. 1994: H4

(In Canadian usage, the term *liberal arts* doesn't usually include the sciences.)

Liberal arts refers to studies that impart general knowledge, rather than a vocation.
Edmonton Journal 31 May 1994: B8

(Here the speaker is an American university teacher.)

See also ARTIST; ARTISTIC.

artsy, arty   see ARTISTIC

as   The use of *as* instead of *that* as a conjunction or a relative pronoun is a regionalism, obsolete in Standard English: 'She says as she's your cousin'; 'Folks as went on the appointed day got tickets'.

See also AS, WHILE, BECAUSE; AS . . . AS, SO . . . AS; AS BEST; AS FAR AS; AS GOOD AS OR BETTER THAN; BEING AS; EQUALLY; LIKE, AS; SEEING AS; THAN; TOGETHER WITH, AS WELL AS, IN ADDITION TO.

as, while, because   *As* frequently means while or when: 'Please sign the register as you go out'. Much less often it means because or since: 'We stayed as we had no choice'. Some commentators object to the use of *as* to mean because, but all dictionaries recognize it as standard.

Generally, commentators who disapprove of the causal use of *as* think that it creates ambiguity. In the sentence 'She left as the speeches were about to begin', for example, *as* could refer to either the timing or the cause of her departure. Certainly in this sentence it would be better to replace *as* with *just as* or *because*. But this is a made-up and rather unlikely example. In actual usage, *as* often serves a useful purpose by combining the ideas of 'while' and 'because' in just those contexts where the two strands of meaning cannot be separated.

Janet comes into the kitchen as he's sliding the casserole dish into the oven.
Margaret Atwood *Life Before Man* 1979: 8

(Here *as* means while.)

... teachers need to be prepared to meet multi-level classes in a rural setting, as this is the norm.
Education Canada Summer 1989: 11

(Here *as* means because.)

Taking buses can be inconvenient, as the tourist sights are spread all over the city.
Alan Tucker, ed. *The Penguin Guide to Canada* 1991: 486

(Here *as* means because.)

As the reporter listened, nodding, writing, offering no argument in return, Larouche grew more and more sure of himself, and gradually more angry.
Ken Dryden *The Game* 1983: 144

(Here *as* means while—and possibly *because*.)

As news of the defeats of the Russian army filtered through the curtain of censorship, there was growing evidence of popular unrest....
George Ignatieff *The Making of a Peacemonger* 1987: 11

(Here *as* means both while and because.)

As government expanded and the role of the bureaucracy in policy formation became more pronounced, restrained behind-the-scenes lobbying became the norm.
A. Paul Press *Group Politics and Public Policy* 2nd ed. 1992: 82

(Here again *as* combines the notions of while and because.)

as ... as, so ... as   'Sarah is not *as* tall as Katie' and 'Sarah is not *so* tall as Katie' are both correct. In the past, some usage guides insisted on *so* in negative comparisons. *Not so ... as* was the usual construction until the twentieth century; now, however, it is much less common than *not as ... as*.

Clearly, young NDP members are not as consistently radical as many have assumed.
Alan Whitehorn *Canadian Socialism* 1992: 135

Professor Kaplan's achievement is all the more impressive because his subject is not as immediately sympathetic as theirs.
Queen's Quarterly 92.2 (1985): 409

It is not so easy as it seems.
Ken Dryden *The Game* 1983: 178

See also THAN.

as best, as well as [as best as]   The expressions 'I will manage as best I can' and 'I will manage as well as I can' are standard; 'I will manage as best as I can' is not. The last expression results from combining the preceding ones; it is comparable to the obviously non-standard 'I will run as fastest as I can'.

... the graceless, neglected Lucie gets through the weekend as best she can....
Janice Kulyk Keefer *Reading Mavis Gallant* 1989: 69

Is it any wonder then that the English literary community has finally taken it upon itself to nourish itself as well as it can?
Canadian Fiction Magazine 63 (1988): 5

'My job is managing the resources I have as best as possible.'
Gazette (Montreal) 2 March 1989: G5

(The standard phrasing is either 'as well as possible', or 'as best I can'.)

Serrati tried to defend the policies of the maximalists as best as he could.
Canadian Journal of History 14.1 (1989): 28

(The standard phrasing is either 'as best he could' or 'as well as he could'.)

He made small talk, joked with us, and I chatted as best as I could in my broken French.
Canadian Fiction Magazine 63 (1988): 116

(The standard phrasing is either 'as best I could' or 'as well as I could'.)

aseptic   see SEPSIS

as far as *As far as* is becoming established in spoken English as a preposition meaning 'with regard to'. In other words, people are using 'as far as his attitude' instead of 'as far as his attitude is concerned (*or* goes)' or 'as for his attitude'. At present this usage is limited to speech and informal writing, and most commentators disapprove of it in writing.

Christian Europeans indulged in a series of crusades, military invasions, to the Holy Land but the result, as far as geographic knowledge was concerned, was minimal.
William Norton *Human Geography* 1992: 14

'But as far as drawing the final picture, that's up to me.'
Gazette (Montreal) 11 June 1994: H5

(Here 'as far as drawing the final picture *goes*', or 'as *for* drawing…' would be more widely accepted.)

Canadian coach Currie Chapman said Percy still is in the thick of things as far as winning another medal.
Calgary Herald 21 Feb. 1988: OA6

(Here 'as far as winning … *is concerned*', or 'as far as winning … *goes*' would be more widely accepted.)

'It's not very promising and as far as thinking everything will be fine in two years, that's nonsense.'
Evening Telegram (St. John's) 23 May 1993: 1

(Here 'as *for*' would be more acceptable than 'as *far as*'.)

as good as or better than In speech, people quite often omit the second *as* in 'as good as or better than'. Some usage guides defend 'as good or better than' as idiomatic, but most criticize it as an example of faulty parallelism: that is, although the word *than* fits after *better*, 'as good than' is ungrammatical. In writing, it is probably safest to include the second *as* in 'as good as or better than', 'as bad as or worse than', 'as great as if not greater than', etc.

… but members of the classics department could hardly have sympathized entirely with the view that if one must study old languages the claims of Sanskrit were as good as or better than those of Greek or Latin.
Hilda Neatby *Queen's University* 1 (1978): 174

This album is as good if not better than her previous works.
Gazette (Montreal) 10 May 1992: F7

(The second *as* should be included: 'as good *as* if not better than'.)

'There's no doubt in my mind that Canada can be as successful because I believe our players are as good, and in some cases better, than those in the U.S.'
Vancouver Sun 23 May 1992: B8

(The second *as* should be included: 'as good *as*, and in some cases better *than*, those …'.)

See also EQUALLY; PARALLELISM.

as how see BEING AS; SEEING AS

Asia, South Asia, Southeast Asia, Far East Europe and Asia are considered separate continents, even though they form a continuous land mass. Tradition separates them in the north at the Ural mountains. To the south, the dividing line is the Caucasus mountains, between the Black and Caspian seas. Turkey and the countries of the Middle East are considered part of Asia, as is the island of Cyprus. At the eastern end of the continent, the large islands of Java, Borneo, and Sumatra and the smaller islands near them are considered part of Asia, while New Guinea is associated with Australia.
South Asia is a common term for the countries of the Indian subcontinent, separated from the north by the Himalayas, including India, Pakistan, Sri Lanka, Nepal, Bhutan, and Bangladesh. The peoples of this area can be referred to as South Asians.
Southeast Asia includes the countries of Burma, Cambodia, Thailand, Malaysia, Singapore, Vietnam, Laos, Indonesia, and the Philippines.
The *Far East* includes China, Japan, North and South Korea, and Taiwan.

See also INDIAN.

as me, as I see THAN

asocial see ANTISOCIAL

asphalt The first and often the only pronunciation given in dictionaries for *asphalt* is ASS fault. However, *ASH fault* is also widely heard. In fact, the 'Survey of Vancouver English' (1984) found it to be twice as common as *ASS fault*. Some people who say *ASH fault* may mistakenly think that ashes are an ingredient in this tarry paving material; others may simply be trying not to sound rude.

aspic see JELLO

as regards   see IN REGARD[S] TO

assault, battery   In general usage, the word *assault* suggests physical violence, unless it is clearly a figure of speech: 'His tie was an assault on good taste'. The legal meaning of *assault* is quite different. In criminal law, a charge of assault may be laid not only if an attack occurs, but also if the victim reasonably believes he or she is being *threatened* with physical harm.

Assault-related criminal charges include *aggravated assault*, in which the intention is to cause serious physical harm but not death; *common assault*, in which the physical harm—or the threat of physical harm—is less serious; *assault with a weapon*; and *sexual assault*, in which the intention is to violate a person's sexual integrity.

In civil law, which deals with legal actions between individuals, such as suits for damages, the offences of *assault* and *battery* are distinguished. These offences usually, but not invariably, occur together. *Assault* involves causing someone to fear that he or she will be harmed. Thus an assault can occur whether or not there was any physical contact and whether or not the defendant had any intention of carrying out the threats. Physically harming someone is *battery*. It is possible for one assault to incur both criminal charges and a civil action.

Police said they charged [one man] with assault because he admitted at the scene having beaten [another man].
Globe and Mail (Toronto) 1 Jan. 1985: P1

(Here *assault* is a criminal charge.)

The suit charges [him] with assault and battery, intentional shooting and intentional infliction of emotional pain....
Globe and Mail (Toronto) 30 Jan. 1985: P11

(Here *assault* and *battery* are offences named in a civil action.)

See also AGGRAVATE, AGGRAVATION.

assay, essay   The verbs *assay* and *essay* are usually pronounced with the stress on the second syllable: *a SAY, eh SAY*. Both verbs mean to try. Contemporary writers use *assay* to mean try in the sense of test or evaluate, and *essay* to mean try in the sense of attempt. *Assay* is used most often in scientific and medical writing. To *assay* a blood sample or a mineral ore is to determine the concentration of particular factors or ingredients. The verb *essay*, as in 'I

will essay to improve', is now uncommon enough in everyday language that most dictionaries label it formal or literary.

The company says it has extracted a 9,100-tonne bulk sample and assayed the ore.... Assay results are still preliminary.
Calgary Herald 15 Sept. 1994: E6

Like prospectors seeking the faintest glimmer of gold, they fanned out across the nation's heartland last week to assay the national soul.
Maclean's 18 Feb. 1991: A22

Sunday morning, having assayed delegate opinion overnight, the Campbell campaign believed it had 47 per cent of the delegates on its side.
Daily News (Halifax) 17 June 1993: 25

Fostering an exchange of ideas, presenting new perspectives, essaying new approaches to issues—these are defining qualities of documentary film-making.
Daily News (Halifax) 21 Nov. 1992: 15

The dark green space we enter in this work (the first time Bélanger has essayed the use of colour on this scale) is a technologically filtered and orchestrated reflection of a sacred space.
Mark A. Cheetham with Linda Hutcheon *Remembering Postmodernism* 1991: 64

... when the immortal Bjorn Borg assayed a comeback at Monte Carlo, some young players actually laughed when the racket Borg brought out was a wooden Donnay model he had won numerous Wimbledon and French Open titles with barely a decade ago.
Maclean's 3 June 1991: A57

(The 'attempted' sense is spelled *essayed*.)

assertive   see AGGRESSIVE

assure   see INSURE

asterisk   The star-shaped *asterisk* (*) is often used in short, informal texts to mark a footnote. Linguists use this symbol to mark a hypothetical, reconstructed form in an ancient language or a rule-breaking utterance in a contemporary language: for example, '*Run they'. A line of asterisks can mark a long omission in quoted material (although style guides now recommend a line of periods). In a work of fiction, a line of asterisks may signal an abrupt shift in the narrative.

Asterisk is sometimes misspelled *asterick* or *asterix*. The standard pronunciation is *ASS tuh risk*.

Countries followed by an asterix are estimated to be severely indebted.
Toronto Sun 4 Dec. 1994: 60

(The correct spelling is *asterisk*.)

as well as   see AS BEST; TOGETHER WITH

(-at)able   see -ABLE

Athabascan, Athapaskan, Athabaskan, Na-Dene
Athabascan is derived from the Cree word for the territory drained by the Athabasca River. *Athabasca(n)* is the spelling most common in place names. *Athapaskan* or, less commonly, *Athabaskan* is the name of a family of Aboriginal languages. There are about fifteen different Athapaskan languages, including Chipewyan and Dogrib. They are spoken by some 12,000 people in Canada in an area that runs from Alaska to the northern border of Manitoba and Ontario, but excludes coastal and southern British Columbia and the far north. Many speakers of Athapaskan languages identify themselves as belonging to the Dene Nation of the Mackenzie River Valley and the Barren Grounds in the Northwest Territories. Many linguists now refer to the Athapaskan language group as *Na-Dene*.

Mitsubishi is a controlling partner of the Alberta Pacific Forest Industries pulp mill near the northern Alberta community of Athabasca.
Calgary Herald 13 May 1993: A7

Ten major languages: Athapaskan (Yukon, northern and central British Columbia, eastern Northwest Territories, and northern Alberta, Saskatchewan and Manitoba). . . .
Ottawa Citizen 10 Nov. 1990: B2

As the most linguistically diverse area in Canada, B.C. is home to 31 languages in seven of the country's 11 linguistic groups: Salishan, Wakashan, Athabaskan, Tlingit, Tsimshian, Kutenai, and Haida.
Vancouver Sun 12 May 1990: R4

(*Athapaskan* is more common in this sense.)

Archaeological and linguistic evidence suggests that there were at least two later waves of migration from Asia—one about 12,000 years ago that brought Na-Dene-speaking peoples to the interior of Alaska and northern Canada and another wave about 7,000 years ago that brought Eskaleut-speaking people to the Arctic and coastal regions of Alaska, Canada and Greenland.
Ottawa Citizen 16 Sept. 1990: C5

(*Na-Dene* and *Athapaskan* are synonyms.)

See also CHIPEWYAN; DENE.

atheist, agnostic, heathen, pagan, infidel, gentile   An *atheist* does not believe in the existence of God, while an *agnostic* isn't sure. The Victorian scientist T. H. Huxley coined the term *agnostic* from the Greek *agnostos*, meaning unknowable.

Heathen is a word that monotheists (people who believe in one God, e.g., Christians, Muslims, and Jews) have applied to polytheistic peoples. The word *heathen* has fallen from favour in contemporary usage because it connotes backwardness and ignorance.

The Greeks and Romans of antiquity were never referred to as *heathens*, though they were polytheistic. They were and are called *pagans*. In contemporary usage, some orthodox Christians use *pagan* as a blanket term for non-Christians—a usage that many non-Christians find offensive. On the other hand, some people who have pointedly rejected the major established religions in favour of pre-Christian traditions, such as wicca, happily call themselves *pagans*.

Infidel means non-believer and is used to describe someone who does not follow the prevailing religion of the country. Historically, Christians have used the word to mean Muslims, while Muslims have used it to refer to Christians and Jews. Contemporary fundamentalist Muslims also use the word for Muslim critics of the religious state.

Gentile, often capitalized, is a biblical word meaning people of other nations, that is, non-Jews. In contemporary English it's also used by Muslims to mean non-Muslim, and by Mormons to mean non-Mormon.

She argues there are many areas of Canadian life where the atheistic perspective is slighted and the state weighs in with a religious, God-centred bias.
Calgary Herald 20 June 1992: B12

My personal choice of inscription will be 'A militant agnostic. Gone to the great perhaps.'
Toronto Sun 15 Sept. 1994: 12

Studies probing oral history now uncover reports from the few early missionaries to remote South Pacific islands who took time to listen and record 'heathen' tradition, before displacing it with the gospel.
Canadian Baptist Feb. 1986: 63

But that's where Valentine's Day has its roots—in ancient Rome and the pagan festival of Lupercalia.
Toronto Star 14 Feb. 1994: E1

Clearly, a distinction between pagan and Christian doctors, in terms of mindset and commitment, can be expected.
Mennonite Brethren Herald 1 April 1986: 11

As a teenager, Adler visited churches and synagogues but finally found the right religion for herself in 1971, joining the neo-pagan movement.
Calgary Herald 16 May 1992: E10

Thousands of Muslim fundamentalists, demanding [that] a feminist writer be put to death as a blaspheming infidel, clashed with opponents and police Thursday in the streets of Bangladesh's capital.
Gazette (Montreal) 2 July 1994: A12

This book tells the story of what may be called the major 'race riot' of Canadian history, in which hundreds if not thousands of Jewish and Gentile Torontonians fought on the streets of Toronto on the night of August 16, 1933.
Canadian Journal of Sociology 14.2 (1989): 239

athlete, athletics   Sometimes people insert an extra syllable in a word to make it easier to pronounce. *Athlete* is one of those words. The standard pronunciation has two syllables: *ATH leet*. The three-syllable pronunciation, *A thuh leet*, is common but often derided.

Athletics has two meanings in Canadian English. It can refer to sports and fitness activities in general or to track and field in particular. The former is the common American usage; the latter, the common British usage.

Athletics can be followed by either a singular or a plural verb: 'Athletics is (*or* are) important to her'.

Chris Newman, convener of athletics for the HIAC, said the high school hockey schedule is slated to begin in early December.
Spectator (Hamilton) 28 Sept. 1994: D3

(Here *athletics* refers to all sports.)

Tom McIllfaterick of the Canadian Sport Council said it appears single-sport federations, such as Athletics Canada and Basketball Canada, lost five to 10 percent of their budgets. . . .
Edmonton Journal 1 Oct. 1994: H8

(Here *athletics* means track and field.)

See also MISPRONUNCIATION AND PRONUNCIATION SHIFTS, EPENTHESIS, METATHESIS.

Atikamekw   see INNU

Atlantic provinces, Atlantic Canada, Maritime provinces, Maritimes, maritime   The Atlantic provinces are New Brunswick, Prince Edward Island, Nova Scotia, and Newfoundland; the whole region is called *Atlantic Canada*. The terms *Maritime provinces* and *Maritimes* refer only to New Brunswick, Prince Edward Island, and Nova Scotia.

This distinction is important to the people of eastern Canada. Culturally and economically, Newfoundland developed independently of the Maritime provinces because it was a colony of Britain until joining Canada in 1949. Newfoundlanders and Maritimers take pride in their distinctive histories.

Maritime(s) is capitalized when it designates the Canadian region, uncapitalized when it refers generally to the sea, seafaring, and coastal regions ('maritime law').

Pulling keepers off 35 lights in B.C., 32 in Newfoundland and three in the Maritimes may save $7 million a year.
Spectator (Hamilton) 14 July 1994: A8

Belle Isle . . . is rife with sultry political history, but it is the maritime lifestyle finely honed by centuries of just-being-French that eventually takes hold.
Toronto Sun 24 Dec. 1994: T8

at-sign   see E-MAIL ADDRESSES

attitude   *Attitude* meaning a bad, defiant, or hostile outlook is slang borrowed from African-American English. In formal English, the word *attitude* has neither positive nor negative connotations and requires a modifier of some kind.

Auntie Muriel's attitude towards Elizabeth was equivocal.
Margaret Atwood *Life Before Man* 1979: 122

Canada has a shy, silly attitude about hero-worship; a suspicious and puritanical fear about undue adulation.
The Beaver Feb.–Mar. 1990: 52

Cops say that if they have an attitude, there is a good reason.
Maclean's 15 April 1991: A11

(In formal writing a qualifier would be required: 'a *negative* attitude'.)

They eased the understanding [of the movie title

Arachnophobia] with the catchline 'Eight legs, two fangs and an attitude.'
Ottawa Citizen 15 July 1990: E1

(This catchline uses the slang meaning of *attitude*.)

attorney, attorney at law   see LAWYER

attributive nouns, false titles   Attributive nouns are nouns used in front of other nouns as modifiers: '*coffee* shop', '*football* coach', '*college* dictionary'. They are extremely common and generally unobjectionable. However, some commentators have taken exception to 'false titles': that is, strings of attributive nouns placed in front of people's names to identify them ('former world record holder Jim Ryun', 'jazz legend Oscar Peterson', 'Barriefield home owner Cynthia Harvey'). False titles (as opposed to genuine titles, such as '*Father* Boyle', '*Prime Minister* Campbell') are a hallmark of journalistic writing. They are useful because they convey information quickly and economically, and thus they're unlikely to disappear from reporting. But false titles are rarely found in other styles of writing. In literary, academic, and even conversational prose, the same information tends to be presented in a phrase or clause *following* the person's name: 'Jim Ryun, who held the world record . . .'.

A rare opportunity to hear Sexual Politics author Kate Millett occurs tonight when she gives a lecture in connection with her new book....
Toronto Star 31 March 1994: C13

(The phrasing 'Kate Millett, the author of *Sexual Politics*,' is recommended for non-reportorial prose.)

See also FUNCTIONAL SHIFT.

au   *Au*, which rhymes with *go*, occurs in phrases borrowed from French, such as *au courant*, 'up to date' or 'in the know', *au contraire*, 'on the contrary', *au naturel*, 'naked' or 'unadorned', and *au fond*, 'fundamentally'. These phrases are more common in breezy journalism than in formal prose, and some critics consider them pretentious.

Au is also frequently used in phrases describing styles of cooking: *au gratin* (topped with breadcrumbs or grated cheese), *au vin* (braised in wine), *au poivre* (coated with crushed peppercorns), etc.

'Our people are very much au courant,' Gentes-Ham said. 'They know that if the industry standard is a profit margin of 20 per cent and the taxpayer claims 10, then something is wrong.'
Ottawa Citizen 18 April 1994: A10

He doesn't toe the line, he doesn't pay homage to the establishment. Au contraire, Lagerfeld takes a perverse pleasure in persistently flouting protocol and thumbing his nose at tradition.
Globe and Mail (Toronto) 26 Nov. 1985: E14

Among desserts was a rich, dark, nutted chocolate mousse cake and good profiteroles au chocolat.
Gazette (Montreal) 26 Nov. 1994: T10

audience, spectators, congregation   *Audience* is derived from the Latin for 'hear', and until the mid-nineteenth century referred exclusively to listeners. Today, though, the word *audience* can refer to the people addressed by almost any form of art or entertainment: a speech, play, concert, book, radio or television program, record album, or painting.

Spectator is derived from the Latin for 'view', and although *audience* has become detached from its etymological connection with hearing, *spectator* retains its connection to seeing. It would seem odd, for example, to refer to the audience of a violin recital as spectators; rock concerts, however, with their emphasis on the visual, do have spectators. The people attending sports events are usually called spectators, while movies are viewed by spectators or audiences.

Congregation is used to describe those who assemble for a common and usually serious purpose: in particular, religious worship, but also political meetings, academic ceremonies, and so on.

This book is written with a broad audience in mind.
Neil Nevitte and Roger Gibbins *New Elites in Old States* 1990: ix

This is a North American phenomenon that has caused numerous problems for the art gallery audience and often in the art galleries themselves.
Queen's Quarterly 94 (1987): 561

The Puritans suppressed this sport, according to Macaulay, not because it gave pain to the bear but because it gave pleasure to the spectators.
Northrop Frye *The Educated Imagination* 1963: 41

'In a [television] series like Blanche, you know that 3 million people are glued to their television sets, but you still can't feel that special audience reaction the way you can by taking in your movie with 900 spectators.'
Gazette (Montreal) 10 Sept. 1994: C7

This is the first congregation of first ministers since Mr. Mulroney's Conservatives swept the Liberals out of office.
Globe and Mail (Toronto) 14 Feb. 1985: P7

auger, augur An *auger* is a tool for boring holes, or a spinning spiral channel inside a tube used to move grain, snow, etc. An *augur* was a Roman soothsayer. To *augur* means to bode and survives mainly in the phrases 'augur well' and 'augur ill'. The verb is often misspelled *auger*.

At the start, you'll need a post-hole digger—either a scissors or an auger type.
Vancouver Sun 8 May 1993: H8

As well, recent productivity gains augur well for job-creation prospects, even before the effects of nascent Tory efforts toward that end are felt.
Globe and Mail (Toronto) 1 March 1985: P6

This involvement from the youth augers well for the future of the association.
Daily News (Halifax) 30 Oct. 1993: 41

(The correct spelling is *augurs*.)

aught see NAUGHT

aunt Outside the Maritimes, most Canadians pronounce *aunt* the same as *ant*, but the majority of Maritimers rhyme *aunt* with *font* (*Modern Canadian English Usage*, 1974).

aura, aurora, aureole An *aura* is a distinctive air or quality that emanates from a person or thing. Until the 1700s *aurora* meant dawn, but now it always refers to a luminous electro-magnetic phenomenon in the sky, either *aurora borealis*, better known as the northern lights, or *aurora australis*, the parallel phenomenon in the southern hemisphere. An *aureole* is a halo or ring.

A special aura seemed to surround him at all times.
Queen's Quarterly 92.1 (1985): 100

With the aurora borealis, for instance, he observed quite rightly that, though not visible in the arctic summer, the northern lights were still present in the atmosphere.
Arctic 41.1 (1988): 41

[The Virgin of Bonsecours] is about 10 metres high with an aureole of stars above the head.
Gazette (Montreal) 2 Jan. 1993: H4

This confrontation between the forces of state authority and the aureoles of the nation was about exactly the same thing that whips ultra-conservatives into a lather.
Vancouver Sun 10 Aug. 1992: A11

(The confrontation referred to is a demonstration for women's right to shed their shirts in the heat, and the *aureoles* mentioned are those that surround nipples.)

auspice, auspices An *auspice* is a sign, usually a favourable one. This meaning is now rare, although it survives in the adjective *auspicious*, which describes something that promises future success. The plural noun *auspices* is used almost exclusively in the phrase 'under the auspices of', which means under the protection of or sponsored by.

This is the third feature movie project made under auspices of the Canadian Film Centre where Lynd studied.
Toronto Star 11 Nov. 1994: D3

.... family planning under the auspices of international organizations or individual countries in the developed sector runs counter to the best interests of people in the less developed world.
Queen's Quarterly 92.2 (1985): 254

See also AEGIS.

author The use of *author* as a verb, as in 'She authored two books', is often criticized by commentators who maintain that books are *written*, not *authored*. Dictionaries, however, consider the verb *author* standard, and it is certainly acceptable in contexts where the verb *write* doesn't fit well.

A much bleaker voice authored her poems.
Margaret Atwood *Second Words* 1982: 288

Allaire ... authored the ultra-nationalist platform the Quebec Liberal party rejected when it supported the Charlottetown constitutional accord last year.
Toronto Star 5 Nov. 1993: A1

Picking up a provincial bronze medal in the national final examinations authored by the Canadian Institute of Chartered Accountants of Canada was Carri Clark....
Calgary Herald 17 Dec. 1993: C6

Wilson has authored 11 books, including The Leaving, which won the 1991 Dartmouth Book Award for fiction.
Daily News (Halifax) 13 Nov. 1993: 22

(Here *written* is recommended.)

See also FUNCTIONAL SHIFT.

authoritarian, authoritative An *authoritarian* person is overbearing, domineering, or tyrannical, while an *authoritative* one acts decisively and commands respect. Thus people look for *authoritativeness*, not *authoritarianism*, in their leaders. An *authoritative* text is either an edition of a classic that scholars consider reliable or a widely respected contemporary treatment of a subject.

'They talk about democracy but it is a disguise for their authoritarian ambitions.'
Ottawa Citizen 26 March 1994: B2

Pratt recommends an 'authoritative style' of parenting that expects a great deal from the child but provides the warmth and support to make it possible for the child to meet these expectations.
Toronto Star 6 Jan. 1992: C1

Smart collectors of china don't buy so much as a bud vase before buying an authoritative reference on pottery and porcelain marks.
Vancouver Sun 25 June 1994: H6

Administrators should stop being authoritative and start seriously listening to the concerns of the student body.
Ottawa Citizen 10 June 1994: B4

(The word required here is *authoritarian*.)

autoroute   see ROAD

autumn, fall   In general, Canadian writers prefer *fall* to *autumn*, especially in the catalogue of seasons: spring, summer, fall, winter. *Autumn* is more common than *fall* in Canadian literary writing and in British English. Although the names of the seasons were once routinely capitalized, today they usually are not.

avant-garde, vanguard   *Avant-garde*, a term applied to jarring new styles in the arts and the innovative artists who introduce them, is often misspelled *avante-garde*. It may help to remember that the word before the hyphen is the French preposition *avant*, 'before'. *Avant-garde* is pronounced *A VON gard* or *A VONT gard*.

Interestingly, the expression *avant-garde* was borrowed twice from French. The first time, in the late fifteenth century, it was borrowed for its literal, military meaning (an advance guard or unit of soldiers that goes ahead of the main body of an army) and anglicized as *vanguard*. Today the expressions *vanguard* and *in the vanguard* are often used figuratively in political contexts.

The Fifth Generation is an avant-garde group of Chinese film-makers who use the increasing artistic freedom to tackle subjects long considered taboo, such as sexuality, pacifism and capitalism.
Ottawa Citizen 30 Dec. 1992: B10

It was done by avante-garde artist Mike Kelley, who also collected and photographed the stuffed animals that adorn the CD booklet.
Toronto Star 8 Oct. 1992: E3

(The correct spelling is *avant-garde*.)

The European Community is a strong proponent of global environmental reform with Holland, Denmark and Germany in the vanguard.
Calgary Herald 1 June 1992: A7

Sephardic Jews from Morocco were in the vanguard of those who pressured the Protestant School Board of Greater Montreal to establish a French-language branch in the 1960s and '70s.
Gazette (Montreal) 20 June 1992: B2

avenge, revenge   *Avenge* suggests seeing justice done, while *revenge* suggests getting even. To *avenge* usually means to seek retribution for an injustice done to someone else. The object of the verb can be either the person who has been wronged or the wrong itself: 'She avenged her sister' *or* 'She avenged her sister's murder'. To *revenge yourself* is to retaliate against someone who has harmed you.

However, not every act carried out on someone else's behalf seems impartial, and not every act carried out on one's own behalf seems base, which is probably why people also use the expressions *revenge someone else* and *avenge oneself*. Some commentators dislike these variants, but they are too common to be considered non-standard.

Yesterday, Kach officials issued a terse statement: 'The Lord will avenge his blood.'
Gazette (Montreal) 7 Nov. 1990: B2

Shiite militants have vowed to avenge the kidnapping.
Calgary Herald 25 May 1994: A5

In the film's most 'Disney' moment a bee revenges herself on a pair of meadowlarking, flower-squashing, lovers to the tune of Vivaldi's Concerto in C.
Province (Vancouver) 31 Dec. 1990: 34

There are also subplots as tangled as an Elizabethan maze—husbands spying on wives, servants revenging on masters, conspiring tavern owners....
Province (Vancouver) 24 June 1990: 82

(Here the idiom requires that *revenging* be followed by *themselves*.)

In Victor Hugo's play Le Roi S'Amuse it is the savage jester who, in his desire to avenge himself on an enemy, kills his own daughter—the only creature he loves.
Robertson Davies *One Half of Robertson Davies* 1978: 150

(Some commentators would recommend *revenge* here.)

There are two separate but linked stories—one about high society, the other about a journalist's quest to revenge his murdered daughter....
Ottawa Citizen 12 May 1990: D6

(Some commentators would recommend *avenge* here.)

average, mean, median   What in ordinary usage is called the *average* of a group of numbers is in mathematical usage called the *mean* or *arithmetic mean*. In a group of seven people aged 12, 20, 27, 30, 43, 55, and 65, the *average* or *mean* age is 36; the *average* or *mean* is obtained by dividing the sum of all the values in a group (here the sum of all ages, 252) by the number of values in a group (here, seven).

The *median*—which, confusingly, is sometimes also referred to as an *average*—is the middle value in a series of values arranged in order of size. In this example, with an odd number of ages, the median age is 30 because there are equal numbers of people above and below the age of 30. In an even-numbered series of values, the median is the mean, or average, of the middle two values: for example, in the series 3, 4, 6, 92, the median is 5 (the mean, or average, of 4 and 6).

> ... median incomes give a more accurate view of real earnings than average incomes because a welfare recipient or billionaire living in a community could wildly alter averages.
> *Calgary Herald* 23 July 1994: B1

(Here *average*, meaning 'mean', and *median* are contrasted.)

averse   see ADVERSE

avocation   see VOCATION

avow   see VOUCH

awful, awfully   The most common sense of *awful* today is extremely bad or unpleasant ('awful food', 'awful weather'). The adverb *awfully* is most often used as an informal equivalent of *very*: 'She's awfully helpful'. While these common uses have been criticized for straying from the seventeenth-century meaning of *awful*—inspiring fear or awe—they are firmly established.

Many adjectives and adverbs describing strong feelings have undergone the same kind of transformation as *awful(ly)*. For example, *dreadful, horrible, shocking*, and *terrible* can all be used to describe

handwriting, and a person can be called *dreadfully, horribly, shamefully, shockingly*, or *terribly* late. Nonetheless, these same words can still evoke a sense of powerful emotion in serious contexts: 'dreadful devastation', 'terrible anger', 'horribly disfigured'.

> When dinner came, the food was so awful he forgot one misery and replaced it with another.
> Pierre Berton *The Promised Land* 1984: 114

> In his defence, however, the original ticket, which he sent to us, is awfully hard to read.
> *Gazette* (Montreal) 17 June 1994: B4

> In this funny and terrifying sculpture, banality achieves an awful apotheosis.
> *Vancouver Sun* 18 June 1994: D15

(Here *awful* means awe-inspiring.)

> It was an awful scene guaranteed to stop the breath of any parent: at the side of a road moments after being rammed by a dumptruck, the battered school bus sat empty....
> *Gazette* (Montreal) 19 June 1994: B2

(Here *awful* means inspiring fear.)

awhile, a while   *Awhile* is an adverb. The one-word spelling is appropriate only where the phrase 'for a while' could be substituted: 'We chatted awhile'. The two-word spelling *a while* is appropriate for other uses: for example, after the prepositions *for, in*, or *after*, or before the word *ago*. This is the distinction that most usage guides uphold, although some accept *a while* as a variant spelling of the adverb.

> Hensall has an attractive downtown that offers a variety of shops. Stop and rest awhile.
> *Leisure Life* 1988: 36

> Leave it on the fire to boil awhile, then fill the mugs.
> *Uphere* Jan.–Feb. 1990: 73

> Mice and trackballs have, of course, been around for a while as standard issue for Apple Macs.
> *Computer Dealer News* 21 March 1991: 66

> 'After a while, the person you're influencing resents you, and you end up with his contempt.'
> *Chatelaine* April 1986: 28

> Then I thought about it for awhile and I realized I had been preparing myself for this the last couple of years.
> *Calgary Herald* 30 June 1994: C3

(Here *a while* is required.)

Every once in awhile, the 11 performers break out of character to sing a few Maritime favorites....
Daily News (Halifax) 19 June 1994: 36

(Here *a while* is required.)

AWOL *AWOL*, an acronym pronounced *AY WALL*, means absent without leave. It was coined during the First World War to describe an unauthorized absence from military duty. While still found in military contexts, *AWOL* has moved into casual speech and writing to describe anybody's unexplained absence. Occasionally, particularly in journalism, *AWOL* is used to refer to *things* that are sorely lacking. This use is very informal.

P——, known for his quick temper and a penchant for physical workouts, was reported AWOL from his unit on May 30.
Ottawa Citizen 5 March 1989: A1

They said many of the 27 boys at the group home were, and are, AWOL-prone.
Calgary Herald 11 Dec. 1993: B2

... the young quartet's sophomore effort ... adds an element of spunk 'n' funk that was AWOL the first time around.
Spectator (Hamilton) 8 Sept. 1994: n.p.

(Here *AWOL* means lacking.)

Their pass rush has been AWOL....
Vancouver Sun 3 Aug. 1990: D1

(Here *AWOL* means lacking.)

axe, ax *Axe* is the more common spelling in Canada, although *ax* is used occasionally. American writers prefer *ax*, but also use *axe*. The British use only the latter spelling.

B

baby bonus *Baby bonus*, like *pogey*, is a Canadianism. In 1945 the federal government established the Family Allowance, a national family subsidy that, in the late 1950s, was informally dubbed the *baby bonus*. The federal government stopped mailing out monthly cheques in 1993, replacing the Family Allowance with a program of tax credits. However, the term *baby bonus* is still used informally to refer to the federal Child Tax Credit as well as to the benefits that the Quebec government provides to families with children in that province.

Since Mikhail was born, his mother, Mary Anne, has been contributing his baby bonus cheques (now called the child tax benefit) to ... an 'informal in-trust account.'
Edmonton Journal 13 April 1994: C6

True, the more children you have in Quebec the higher your rewards from the baby bonus fund, much of which is supplied by Ottawa.
Financial Post 20 April 1994: 3

See also POGEY.

bachelor, ba(t)ch There is no *t* in *bachelor*, whether it refers to an unmarried man, a university degree, or a one-room apartment.

Batch with a *t* is an accepted spelling variant of the informal verb *bach*, meaning lead the life of a bachelor: 'Sean's baching (*or* batching) it while Melissa's away'.

back-formation Adding suffixes and prefixes to existing words is a common way of forming new words in English. *Revision*, for example, which dates from the early seventeenth century, is derived from *revise*, which dates from the mid-sixteenth century. *Back-formation* is the reverse of this common process of word creation: a new word is formed when a suffix or prefix—or what appears to be a suffix or prefix—is removed from an existing word. For example, *televise* (coined circa 1927) is a back-formation from *television* (1907).

While new words formed by adding suffixes and prefixes often enter the language unnoticed, back-formations tend to attract attention. Some back-formations are humorous coinages that never lose their note of jocularity: for example, *ept*, from *inept*, *couth*, from *uncouth*, and *gruntled*, from *disgruntled*. Some back-formations gain full acceptance fairly quickly: *automate*, from *automation*; *babysit*, from *babysitter*; *diagnose*, from *diagnosis*; and *escalate*, from *escalation*. But others continue to raise the hackles of commentators many years after they were coined. Still somewhat stigmatized are *emote* (c. 1917), from *emotion*; *enthuse* (c. 1827), from *enthusiasm*; *laze* (c. 1592), from *lazy*; *liaise* (c. 1928), from *liaison*; *sculpt* (c. 1864), from *sculptor*; and *surveil* (c. 1949), from *surveillance*.

A few back-formations have been formed by removing what only appeared to be a suffix. For example, the verbs *grovel* (1593) and *sidle* (1697) were created from *grovelling* and *sidling*, which people took to be the *-ing* forms of verbs. In fact, *grovelling* and *sidling* were directional adverbs (meaning 'face downwards' and 'sideways', respectively) with the *-ling* ending comparable to the *-long* ending in the adjectives *sidelong* and *oblong*. A contemporary example of the same phenomenon is the word *kudo*, a singular created by dropping the *-s* from *kudos*. But *kudos*, a Greek loan word meaning glory, is not in fact a plural. While *grovel* and *sidle* have long been accepted as standard words, *kudo* is not, because many people still recognize it as a back-formation based on a misconception.

> The rally, organized by Margaret Atwood and Erika Ritter, will bring together the beautiful people of the word to orate, recite, sing, incant ... against free trade.
> *Gazette* (Montreal) 14 Nov. 1987: B3

(Here the deliberate use of the back-formations *orate* and *incant* creates a humorously irreverent tone.)

See also BURGLE; COMMENTATE; EMOTE; ENTHUSE; KUDOS; LIAISON, LIAISE; ORATE; SCULPTURE, SCULPT.

backhanded compliment, left-handed compliment   A *backhanded* or, less commonly, a *left-handed* compliment is one of two things: a criticism that can be taken as a compliment, given its source, or a compliment that can also be viewed—and may have been intended—as an insult.

> Although I sympathize deeply with Laurence in her current plight, I think that ... it may be a back-handed compliment that the more reactionary elements of society find her work 'dirty and disgusting.'
> *Globe and Mail* (Toronto) 9 March 1985: M12

(Note that dictionaries spell *backhanded* without a hyphen.)

> Tifo amusedly brushed off the article during a recent interview. She knew that, coming from a theatre critic, the article was a back-handed compliment.
> *Gazette* (Montreal) 28 Feb. 1990: C2

> 'After the game, he said that I'd be the perfect quarterback for the CFL.... I thought it was a backhanded compliment.'
> *Gazette* (Montreal) 12 May 1994: E1

> While Canuck coach Bob McCammon called Nedved 'best of a bad lot' against the Canadiens, the backhanded compliment nevertheless was a boost to the youngster....
> *Vancouver Sun* 28 Dec. 1990: F1

See also COMPLIMENT, COMPLEMENT, SUPPLEMENT.

back of, in back of   In a survey of Canadian English-speakers (*Modern Canadian English Usage*, 1974), about one in six reported that they would say 'back of the house' or 'in back of the house' rather than 'behind the house'. But while the compound preposition *in front of* troubles no one, *in back of* and *back of* are contentious. British commentators tend to reject these expressions—or label them Americanisms—while American commentators staunchly defend them as standard. *Back of* and *in back of* are used by Canadian writers in informal contexts, especially sports writing, but not in formal prose.

> The Oilers beat Calgary 4-1 last night and are now just three points back of third-place Vancouver....
> *Province* (Vancouver) 28 Dec. 1990: 42

> Driving into Dornhoefer, Robinson hit him so hard that the Flyer's body dented a section of boards, leaving it an inch or so in back of where it had been just moments before.
> Ken Dryden *The Game* 1983: 95

(A more formal wording would be 'farther back than it had been'.)

backward(s)   see -WARD(S)

backwoods   see FOREST

bacterium, bacteria   *Bacterium* is the singular of *bacteria*. It's common only in scientific writing, where it refers either to a strain of bacteria or to a lone micro-organism.

Bacteria is the Latin plural form. In formal and scientific writing, it is always treated as plural and used with a plural verb: 'These bacteria are clearly visible when stained'.

In everyday English, *bacteria* is also used as a singular noun meaning a strain of bacteria: 'They said it was a bacteria, not a virus'. This singular use has generated a double plural: *bacterias*. *Bacterias*, meaning strains of bacteria, is fairly common in journalism, but not suitable for technical or formal writing.

Once a bacterium possessing the desired DNA segment—or gene—is located, it can be removed from the broth.
Queen's Quarterly 97.4 (1990): 606

(Here *bacterium* refers to one microbe.)

A naturally-occurring bacterium is still generating a toxic liquid which flows into Howe Sound.
Vancouver Sun 27 Nov. 1993: B4

(Here *bacterium* refers to a strain of bacteria.)

Though wine is a 'living thing', where bacteria thrive, only those bacteria harmless to humans seem to survive in wine.
Bon Vivant Nov. 1981: 12

(Here *bacteria* is treated as plural, as required in formal writing.)

Bt is a stomach poison, derived from a natural bacteria that kills the budworm after the poison has been eaten.
Globe and Mail (Toronto) 18 March 1985: M4

(In informal writing, *bacteria* is often treated as a singular.)

It quoted U.S. intelligence sources as saying the deadly viruses and bacterias include anthrax, typhoid and cholera.
Ottawa Citizen 12 April 1990: A1

(Here *bacterias* is acceptable, but *bacteria* would be better in formal writing.)

See also FLU; PLURALS, REGULAR, IRREGULAR, FOREIGN.

bad, badly   The verb *feel*, except when it means touch, is followed by adjectives, not adverbs: 'feel strong', 'feel hopeful', 'feel sad'. Thus commentators have disparaged the use of the adverb *badly* in the phrase 'feel badly'. Some commentators call it a hypercorrection; others, a genteelism acceptable in conversation. In any case, in writing, 'feel bad' is more widely accepted and far more common.

The adverb *badly* modifies action verbs and participles: 'play badly', 'behave badly', 'badly suited', 'badly made'. In informal speech, *bad* often replaces *badly*: 'He's hurt bad'; 'We didn't do bad'. However, *bad* is seldom used as an adverb in writing, and it is not accepted unless it is seen as a deliberately folksy touch.

Sexual violence can make you feel bad, dirty, ugly, crazy or different.
Jennifer Jones *Making the Links* 1992: 3

'I know that better than anyone else .... I feel badly about it.'
Gazette (Montreal) 19 June 1992: E1

(In writing, 'feel *bad*' is recommended.)

This time his face told us nothing, so we guessed he hadn't done too badly.
Queen's Quarterly 94.1 (1987): 55

Mine is badly done and incomplete.
Canadian Fiction Magazine 64 (1988): 25

'Sometimes you do well, sometimes you do bad, and here I have not done as well as I had hoped.'
Vancouver Sun 13 Jan. 1992: D4

(In writing, 'do *badly*' is recommended.)

'We wanted (the contract). If you want something bad enough, you'll pay for it.'
Calgary Herald 22 Jan. 1992: C5

(In writing, '*badly* enough' is recommended.)

See also ADJECTIVES AND ADVERBS; HYPER-CORRECTION; WORSE.

bail out, bale   In Canadian and American English, to *bail out* is to dip water out of a boat, to make an emergency exit from an aircraft, to assist someone in an emergency, or to guarantee security for the release of a person held in custody. To *bale* is to bundle and bind hay, cloth, etc.

In British English, *bale* means bundle and bind, but is also the preferred spelling for all the 'bail' meanings above except the last, to guarantee security for a person in custody.

Both have failed to clean out patronage, and both emerged red-faced from attempts to bail out financial institutions.
Saturday Night April 1986: 16

Newspapers, cardboard, etc. are each baled separately, ready for shipment.
Vancouver Sun 11 June 1994: A3

bait   see BATE

baklava, Balaklava, balaclava   *Baklava* (pronounced *BAK luh vuh* or *bak luh VAH*) is a rich Greek dessert. *Balaklava* (*ba luh KLA vah*) is a Crimean seaport and the site of the 1854 battle that inspired Tennyson's poem 'The Charge of the Light Brigade'. A *balaclava* is a woollen head and neck covering in the style of those worn by the Crimean soldiers.

The spellings *baclava*, *Balaclava* (with a *c*) and *balaklava* (with a *k*) are less common but also correct.

And don't miss the baklava, the Greek dessert made of flaky pastry, honey and nuts.
Globe and Mail (Toronto) 6 April 1985: T11

Librarians, office workers, and housewives formed groups to roll bandages and to knit balaclavas and mittens for the Red Cross.
Miriam Waddington *Apartment Seven* 1989: 18

bale   see BAIL OUT

baleful, baneful   *Baleful* and *baneful* both mean harmful, but *baleful* usually refers to looks or portents that threaten harm ('a baleful glance', 'a baleful indication'), while *baneful*, a less common word, refers to agents or results that actually are harmful ('a baneful role', 'baneful effects'). In some contexts either word is possible: 'a baleful (*or* baneful) influence'. Note that *baleful* does not mean woebegone.

Al, the Mad Hungarian, was as terrifying as his 99 m.p.h. fastballs. He wore a Fu Manchu mustache and a baleful glare.
Ottawa Citizen 5 Sept. 1993: C3

... cinematographer Robert Elswit catches the baleful grandeur of Montana's looming mountains, turning the jagged landscape into a silent conspirator.
Toronto Star 30 Sept. 1994: C6

Halley's appearance in 1910 was not without its own baleful associations, this time becoming mixed up with the death of King Edward VII, which had taken place on May 6, in the midst of Halley's visit.
Saturday Night Jan. 1986: 34

'Jean Chretien is playing in this fiscal matter the same baneful role he had in the constitutional debate, that of a destroyer disrespectful of democratic forms.'
Gazette (Montreal) 28 Sept. 1995: B3

Consumers following the news this week on trans-fatty acids heard one researcher say that they were probably worse than the baneful saturated fat in animal products such as butter.
Vancouver Sun 19 May 1994: A1

Political correctness is widely seen as a baleful American import.
Gazette (Montreal) 14 Nov. 1993: B4

(Here *baneful* could also be appropriate.)

... the Pavlovian response of turning to governments for solutions tends ... to lead to unanticipated baleful side effects.
Ottawa Citizen 19 June 1990: A13

(Here *baneful* would be better: the harm is already done and it was not foreseen.)

A harp seal stares at the camera with its baleful brown eyes; the seals are tame enough to pat.
Ottawa Citizen 21 Feb. 1987: G1

(Here *baleful* is inappropriate; perhaps *woeful* was intended.)

baloney   see BOLOGNA

baluster, banister, balustrade   A *baluster* is one of the upright posts supporting a handrail on a balcony or staircase. The banister is the handrail atop the balusters. The balustrade is the whole structure, posts and handrail. However, *banister* is occasionally used to mean *baluster*, and *banisters*, plural, to refer to the whole structure; these meanings are also accepted. *Bannister* is now a rare spelling.

Give the hand railing (the banister) and vertical elements (the balusters) a good sanding so that most imperfections and all the dirt and grime is gone.
Vancouver Sun 23 Nov. 1990: E10

Here is the bannister he slid down.
Vancouver Sun 21 April 1990: B1

(The usual spelling is *banister*.)

When the whole balustrade, including the handrail and newel post, feels loose, it indicates a breakdown of the joints between the steps and the outer stringer.
Vancouver Sun 16 April 1994: E14

David replaced the stairs and turned new banisters.
Ottawa Citizen 13 Oct. 1990: C1

(Strictly speaking, the posts referred to here are *balusters*, but *banisters* is also accepted.)

... the grand staircase is missing its great sweep of banisters.
Vancouver Sun 30 March 1994: B6

(Here *banisters* means the entire structure, the *balustrade*.)

baneful   see BALEFUL

banister   see BALUSTER

bank, credit union, caisse populaire, trust company   Canadians often use *bank* as a generic term to refer to a bank, credit union, caisse populaire, or trust company—in other words, any financial institution that receives deposits, provides chequing, and offers loans. In fact, though, Canada has only five chartered banks—the Bank of Montreal, the Canadian Imperial Bank of Commerce (CIBC), the Bank of Nova Scotia, the Royal Bank, and the Toronto Dominion Bank (TD Bank and Trust). Foreign-owned banks (e.g., the Hongkong Bank of Canada) are now allowed to operate in Canada, but the amount of business they can do in Canada is restricted by law. Banks are owned by stockholders to whom their profits accrue.

Credit unions differ from banks in being cooperatives, which means that their profits are shared equally and jointly by all depositors. Members (i.e., depositors) can also borrow from the assets of the credit union. Some credit unions are public; others are associated with trade unions or other employee groups.

Caisse populaire (pronounced *KESS pop yoo LAIR*) is the French term for credit union. In Quebec there is a strong province-wide network of community Caisses Populaires Desjardins—note the *s* at the end of *populaire* in the plural—named after their founder, Alphonse Desjardins.

The original purpose of *trust companies* was to manage assets placed in trust by judicial order or through the terms of a will. Now, however, banks are also allowed to act in this capacity, and trust companies, which originally could not provide chequing services, now offer chequing accounts. Thus banks and trust companies are becoming more and more alike from the point of view of the individual customer; however, large corporate accounts are still handled only by the chartered banks.

bar   see BEER PARLOUR

barbarian, barbaric, barbarous   *Barbarian* is derived from the Greek and Latin words for someone who doesn't speak the language, a foreigner. Eventually, in both Greek and Latin, the word acquired the pejorative sense of 'uncivilized outsider'. *Barbarian* passed into English in reference to the Germanic and Asian tribes that broke up the Roman Empire, and by extension it refers to a ruthless person, or one lacking culture and social graces.

The adjectives *barbaric* and *barbarous* overlap in meaning cruel or crude. However, *barbaric* can also describe something wildly beautiful.

It is, very briefly, about a German barbarian living in an early but vague period of history who is domesticated by a Grecian maiden called Parthenia.
Robertson Davies *A Voice from the Attic* 1960: 181

He finds these reactions of hers, not disappointing exactly, but surprising, as if only a barbarian or an illiterate could have the reactions she does.
Margaret Atwood *Life Before Man* 1979: 217

In response to Bishop John Sperry's conviction on sealing and trapping, I hope I am wrong in assuming the bishop tolerates creatures being skinned alive and left writhing in agony for days in some barbaric leg hold trap....
Canadian Churchman April 1986: 5

A river, they begin to move, the sun glinting off the metal of fifty thousand bikes ... moving like the magnificent barbaric horde of Attila crossing continents, ... one ever-flowing river of desolation ruled by divine cacophonous noise.
Canadian Fiction Magazine 63 (1988): 24–5

He quoted ... from advertisements for runaway slaves that depicted graphically the barbarous cruelties to which a runaway slave was subject—bloodhounds, heavy fetters, branding, flogging, and the ever-present threat of the 'dead-or-alive' reward offer.
William Teatero *John Anderson: Fugitive Slave* 1986: 148

barbarisms   In the past, some usage commentators educated in the Classics suggested that new English words should not mix Latin, Greek, and English elements. Words that fail this test include *television*, combining Greek *tele-*, 'far', and Latin *visio(n-)*; *speedometer*, combining English *speed* and Latin *metr-*; and *bureaucrat*, in which *-eau-* does double duty as the end of the word *bureau* and the beginning of the suffix *-ocrat*. Such supposedly malformed words were labelled *barbarisms*. Fowler, in the first edition of *Modern English Usage* (1926), went so far as to suggest that the 'barbarism' *electrocution* 'jars the unhappy latinist's nerves much more cruelly than the operation denoted jars those of the victim'. Perhaps predictably, the idea that English coinages should be subject to the rules of Latin and Greek word formation has not survived the de-emphasizing of the Classics in school curricula.

barbarous   see BARBARIAN

barbiturate   *Barbiturate* (a class of drugs derived from barbituric acid) is often misspelled without the second *r*—*barbituate*—and often mispronounced *bar BIT choo it*. The accepted pronunciations are *bar BIT chuh rit* and *BAR bi TYOO rit*.

> The Department of Defence would test armed forces employees for drugs such as marijuana, cocaine, heroin, morphine and barbituates.
> *Gazette* (Montreal) 13 June 1992: G7

(The correct spelling is *barbiturates*.)

barely   see EVER; HARDLY

baroque, rococo   Both *baroque* and *rococo* (often misspelled *rococco*) refer to artistic styles characterized by a rich profusion of details. In popular usage, *baroque* may suggest bewildering complexity, flamboyance, or a touch of the grotesque. *Rococo* (pronounced *ruh CO co* or, less often, *RO cuh CO*) suggests elaborate ornamentation.

Baroque and *Rococo* are often capitalized when they refer to specific historical periods, as opposed to styles loosely associated with them. *Baroque* designates a period in the seventeenth and early eighteenth centuries when European taste in art, architecture, music, and literature favoured an elaborate, decorous, and highly decorative style. In music during this period the orchestra and opera became established, and composers such as Bach, Handel, Scarlatti, Verdi, and Vivaldi flourished. *Rococo* is an even more ornamental style that developed near the end of the Baroque period, from approximately 1720 to 1780. In the visual arts it is characterized by curly decorative motifs such as scrolls and shells.

> Boyle has been compared with absurdist and experimental writers like John Barth and Thomas Pynchon, but these stories are not as formally inventive, baroque or convoluted as Barth's or Pynchon's more challenging work.
> *Gazette* (Montreal) 4 June 1994: 13

> U.S. soprano Jennifer Casey Cabot is a wonderful Donna Elvira, her voice generous, abundant, suitably rococo in its curves and gilt-on-cream colors.
> *Vancouver Sun* 21 March 1994: C3

UNSCOP ended up recommending a more clear-cut, surgical form of partition, without the rococo details of the Rand plan.
> *Globe and Mail* (Toronto) 21 Dec. 1985: D22

> Caccini's tender Baroque aria 'Amarilli' after intermission was only a token nod in the direction of better music. . . .
> *Queen's Quarterly* 94.2 (1987): 351

> The garden arrangement is mounted on a mirrored pink and gilded porcelain rococo stand that Chilton first noticed stashed away in a drawer at the ROM years ago.
> *Toronto Star* 13 Sept. 1992: E5

(Capitalizing *rococo* here would indicate that the porcelain piece actually dated from the Rococo period.)

barrage, fusillade, volley, salvo   In the military sense, a *barrage* is a defensive barrier of artillery fire so heavy that it prevents the enemy's advance or protects one's own troops when advancing or retreating. In non-military use, a *barrage* is a heavy onslaught or an overwhelming attack. This change from a defensive to an offensive meaning troubles some usage commentators, but the figurative use is well established in Canadian English.

Most authorities say that both *fusillade* (pronounced *FYOO zuh laid* or *FYOO zuh lod*) and *volley* refer to the continuous discharge of many firearms. Although there is some disagreement on how well planned or concerted this firing is, neither term should be used to refer to sporadic shooting.

Salvo (plural *salvos* or *salvoes*) is another military term for the simultaneous discharge of two or more weapons. A salvo from an aircraft is a whole load of bombs dropped at once. However, a salvo can also be a friendly gesture: at one time warships greeted friendly ships by discharging all their guns to prove that they were temporarily unarmed, and this practice has evolved into a formal military salute. *Salvo* and *salute* derive from the same Latin word meaning health.

All of these words are used figuratively more often than literally to describe an outpouring of criticism, cheers, applause, and so on.

> . . . the press was smarting under wounds inflicted by the veritable barrage of criticism that greeted its continuous coverage of the first trial. . . .
> *Queen's Quarterly* 95.4 (1988): 837

> We never knew where she was, except through a barrage of postcards from places she had already left, but at the end of the month she would always be in Rome.
> *Queen's Quarterly* 96.2 (1989): 236

By what means was the fatal shot fired, and synchronized with the fusillade of musket blanks?
Globe and Mail (Toronto) 11 May 1985: E17

During Mr. Chernenko's brief reign, a slow thaw in commercial and cultural intercourse was punctuated by occasional fusillades of editorial enmity.
Globe and Mail (Toronto) 13 March 1985: P11

A volley of whoops and hollers erupts and ricochets about the staid confines of a Toronto high school auditorium.
Performing Arts in Canada July 1988: 28

It has become my habit merely to duck slightly whenever another unctuous salvo from the religious right whistles overhead....
Toronto Star 3 March 1994: A22

Barrens, Barrenlands   see TUNDRA

barrio   *Barrio*, a word borrowed from Spanish into American English in the mid-nineteenth century, is now making its way into Canadian English. It means neighbourhood and in the U.S. often refers to the Spanish-speaking quarter of a city. Metaphorically, it is used like *ghetto*. *Barrio* is pronounced *BAHR ee oh*. The plural is *barrios*.

Today, except in the barrios of Latin America, in parts of Africa and Asia, 'street soccer' is dead, and ... with it has gone much of soccer's creative opportunity.
Ken Dryden *The Game* 1983: 133

Olmos—who also stars in the lead role as Santana, a man from the East Los Angeles barrio doomed, it seems, from birth to spend most of his life in prison—draws strong performances from a talented, mostly Hispanic cast and sets a tone that makes us see the story of one ruthless, brutalized criminal as part of the tragedy of a marginalized people.
Calgary Herald 13 March 1992: E9

And while the 1990s Whistler image is of deluxe condos, Bosco lives in the KOA [a family campground], Whistler's barrio.
Vancouver Sun 18 July 1992: C12

See also GHETTO.

barrister   see LAWYER

bases   *Bases* is the plural of both *base* ('round the bases') and *basis* ('the bases on which these decisions were made'). The plural of *basis* is pronounced *BAY seez*.

See also PLURALS, REGULAR, IRREGULAR, FOREIGN.

bass   *Bass* has two meanings and two pronunciations. When it refers to a fish, it is pronounced to rhyme with *pass*. When it refers to the lowest musical range ('He sings bass'; 'She plays the double bass'), it is pronounced like *base*.

Take the 14-pound, two-ounce largemouth bass reportedly caught in Stoney Lake in 1948....
Toronto Star 14 Oct. 1992: F8

By 2:15 the streets pulsate with the deep bass of car stereos cranked to the hilt.
Ottawa Citizen 4 Aug. 1992: A1

batch   see BACHELOR

bate, bait   In the phrase 'with bated breath' the adjective is often misspelled as *baited*. To *bate*, a variant form of *abate*, means to hold back or reduce. To wait with bated breath is to hold one's breath with interest or anxiety. The phrase is a cliché, now most often used humorously.

Bait comes from the Middle English and Old Norse for 'hunt'. To *bait* means to entice or lure, or to goad or torment.

Clearly, few Canadian establishments or consumers are awaiting GST with bated breath.
Financial Post 22 Oct. 1990: 38

While some Mac users are waiting with baited breath for its release, others ... are dreading the anticipated downtime that may result from bugs, incompatibilities and other problems.
Vancouver Sun 7 Feb. 1990: E1

(The correct spelling is *bated*.)

She refused to be baited during question period, instead challenging the executives and industry leaders to look beyond partisan politics towards her vision of a 'city of neighborhoods.'
Vancouver Sun 9 Nov. 1993: B3

Other Spanish fiestas are famous for throwing goats, bating bulls and decapitating geese.
Vancouver Sun 28 Aug. 1993: B3

(The correct spelling here is *baiting*.)

battery   see ASSAULT

bayman   see TOWNIE

B.C., B.C.E.   see A.D.

bear   see BORNE

bear, bearish   see BULL

bear, panda, koala   Though they look like bears, pandas and koalas do not belong to the bear family (Ursidae). In formal writing they should not be referred to as 'panda bears' or 'koala bears'.

See also GRISLY, GRIZZLY.

beat, beaten   The past tense of *beat* is *beat* and the usual past participle is *beaten*: 'The Sydenham team beat us last night, which means our team has been beaten twice so far this season'.

Beat is listed as a variant past participle in some dictionaries, but not all. It's very common in speech ('We've been beat fair and square') but some commentators consider this use uneducated. In writing, it is safer to use *beaten* unless you are aiming for a conversational tone.

> Party members who sat out the federal election in Ontario—every New Democratic MP was beaten—are prepared to sit out the next provincial vote, too.
> *Toronto Star* 26 Nov. 1993: A1

> 'I don't think we should hang our heads because we got beat. We should use this to try and get better as a team.'
> *Vancouver Sun* 26 Nov. 1990: C2

> (In writing, the usual past participle is *beaten*.)

beau, beaux, beaus, belle   *Beau*, from the French word meaning handsome, has been labelled old-fashioned when used to mean admirer, sweetheart, or boyfriend. However, it appears fairly often in Canadian writing. The French form is masculine and thus the word usually refers to men only; but a gender-neutral use of *beau* has also developed. The plural is usually the French form, *beaux*, but *beaus* is acceptable. Both plural forms are pronounced *BOZE* in English.

The feminine equivalent of *beau* in French is *belle*, which has also come into English as a noun; it means 'the woman most admired for beauty', as in 'She was the belle of the ball'.

> ... she married a couple of times (the first at 16, to a childhood beau) and has a 7-year-old daughter, Jessica.
> *Globe and Mail* (Toronto) 28 May 1985: F2

> Things get complicated when his jealous beau suspects the diplomatic mission might include an affair.
> *Vancouver Sun* 9 Oct. 1990: B10

> (Here the *beau* is a woman.)

> Be sure to take your best beau—the experience may just be enough to make you want to run off for a quickie wedding.
> *Vancouver Sun* 9 Aug. 1990: C2

> (Here gender is not specified.)

> A comedy about the manners and mores of Manhattan debutantes and their beaux may sound as relevant as learning how to mix the perfect dry martini....
> *Vancouver Sun* 5 Oct. 1990: C4

> The National Ballet of Canada played chaperone to a number of debutantes and their beaus who came out in style.
> *Globe and Mail* (Toronto) 28 Dec. 1985: D5

> She plunges right into her mother's most personal diaries and exposes the young Belle of Berlin's dalliances with an array of men and women.
> *Gazette* (Montreal) 4 Oct. 1993: C5

See also PLURALS, REGULAR, IRREGULAR, FOREIGN.

because   One of the most widely known maxims of prescriptive grammar is 'Never begin a sentence with *because*.' Yet grammatically there is nothing wrong with sentences beginning with *because*, and Canadian writers, including some noted stylists, don't avoid them. The 'rule' was probably devised in the classroom as a way to keep students from writing sentence fragments beginning with *because* when answering questions.

Some objections have been made to sentences in which a clause beginning with *because* is the subject of the sentence: 'Because they don't listen to classical music does not mean they are culturally impoverished'. This construction is informal, and though common in speech, it is much less common in writing. In formal writing, 'That they don't listen ...' or 'The fact that they don't listen ...' is recommended.

When *because* follows a negative clause, as in 'They didn't join the union because they feared for their safety', ambiguity results. In this example, either fear prevented them from joining the union or it was something other than safety issues that compelled them to join. Intonation disambiguates these two possible meanings in speech. In writing, however, it's best to rephrase: either 'Because they feared for their safety, they didn't join the union' or 'Fear for their safety was not the reason they joined ...'.

> Because I am a Canadian, my outlook may possess some novelty for readers in the United States, for my country

sees not only the greater part of the books produced in yours, but those published in Great Britain as well—not to speak of our own books.
Robertson Davies *A Voice from the Attic* 1960: 3

Because the United States is the most powerful centre of this civilization, we often say, when referring to its uniformity, that the world is becoming Americanized.
Northrop Frye *The Bush Garden* 1971: 247

'Just because someone's decided to get into sea kayaking doesn't mean that he or she is environmentally aware.'
Vancouver Sun 24 June 1994: B4

(In formal writing, 'That' alone or even 'The fact that . . .' would be preferable to 'Just because. . .'.)

See also AS, WHILE; FACT THAT; REASON IS BECAUSE.

beer parlour, beverage room, bar, pub *Beer parlour* and *beverage room* are Canadianisms for licensed establishments that serve primarily alcoholic beverages. *Bar* is now the usual term. *Pub* was originally a British abbreviation of *public house*. *Pub* is sometimes used in Canada for local establishments that make their own ale and beer and is often used interchangeably with *bar*, especially around universities. *Saloon* is not a common Canadian term, although it is sometimes used to create the atmosphere of the old American West. *Cocktail lounge* is a dated American expression that is not very common in Canada. The terms *taproom*, *lounge*, *club*, *café*, *roadhouse*, *tavern*, and *licensed premises* can also refer to businesses that are licensed to serve alcoholic drinks. During the Prohibition era in Canada in the 1920s, unlawful drinking places were known as *speakeasies* and *blind pigs*. Illegal after-hours bars today are often called *speaks*.

I also learned how to make a quick dash for the bush whenever the police raided the beer parlour in search of minors like myself. . . .
George Ignatieff *The Making of a Peacemonger* 1987: 45

You come into the beverage room here, in your blue pinstripe suit and suede overcoat, while I'm nursing a beer, minding my own business, and hand me your business card. . . .
Canadian Fiction Magazine 64 (1988): 106

Jazz musicians have been members of that subculture ever since their music was installed as a diversion in the bordellos of New Orleans, and they were charter members by the time jazz spread to the American heartland as an entertainment in Prohibition speakeasies.
Jack Chambers *Milestones* 1983: 80

begrudge   see ENVY

beg the question   An argument that *begs the question* is circular: that is, it's based on its own conclusion. For example: 'They have a big family. They must love children. People with big families love children.' The question begged (or avoided) is whether indeed all people with big families love children.

However, many people don't realize that *begging the question* refers to this logical fallacy. In fact, the expression leads a double life. It means one thing in formal writing and according to dictionaries, and quite another in popular use. In Canadian newspapers, *begs the question* almost always means raises the question or brings up the issue. Although this usage is very common, it should probably be avoided, because it is completely at odds with the formal meaning of the expression and consistently criticized by commentators.

'To say that a man is insane because he does not appreciate the insanity of his acts and is thus insane is to beg the question.'
Province (Vancouver) 7 March 1990: 6

The review was so unbalanced, so insensitive and so inaccurate it begs the question—did the reviewer actually see the show?
Ottawa Citizen 17 Dec. 1994: E4

(Here '*raises* the question' would be better.)

Prime Minister Chrétien said 'The Department of Justice will increase prosecutions and make full use of proceeds-of-crime legislation.' This begs the question—if the Department of Justice will now make full use of the proceeds-of-crime legislation, what was it doing before?
Ottawa Citizen 1 March 1994: A9

(Here '*raises* the question' would be better.)

See also VICIOUS CIRCLE.

behalf, on behalf of, on the part of, in behalf of
An action taken *on behalf of* a group is done for them. An action taken *on the part of* a group is done by them. *On behalf of* means as a representative of or in the interest of. *On the part of* means by or among. People often use *on behalf of* instead of *on the part of*: 'There seemed to be an unwillingness on behalf of the survivors to talk about the event'. This use is non-standard.

In behalf of is rare in Canadian English; it is used interchangeably with *on behalf of* in American English.

... I proposed a toast on behalf of the visiting Canadians to the Khrushchevs, 'our gracious hosts'.
George Ignatieff *The Making of a Peacemonger* 1987: 143

Running parallel to the concerted movement of women graduates for a women's residence was a growing interest on the part of men students in obtaining a social centre of their own.
Frederick Gibson *Queen's University* 2 (1983): 27

Although leaving is not necessarily the answer, a period of separation is often required ... until attitude change occurs on behalf of the abuser (usually only after extensive counselling).
Mennonite Brethren Herald 7 March 1986: 6

(Since it is the attitude of the abuser that must change, the expression required here is *on the part of*.)

On February 11, a rally organized by the Ontario Coalition for Abortion Clinics ... was marred by violence on the behalf of two unwanted elements: the vociferous and violent anti-choice minority and the Metro Toronto police.
Rites March 1990: 5

(The violence cited is directly attributed to the police and demonstrators. Thus the expression required here is *on the part of*.)

behest 'At the behest of Elizabeth' or 'at Elizabeth's behest' means because Elizabeth asked. A *behest* is an urgent prompting, something between a request and a command. The expression *at the behest of* is sometimes mistakenly used to mean subject to or under the control of.

The guilt or innocence of a criminal defendant cannot be made less by reason of the fact that the criminal act was done at the behest of another.
Gazette (Montreal) 5 March 1989: B3

Great plays ... demand the most expert work of the most gifted actors and directors to give them life on the stage; why expect them to leap into brilliance at the behest of [a reader's] unexercised imagination?
Robertson Davies *A Voice from the Attic* 1960: 163

In continuing to assume that judging art is entirely subjective, whimsical or at the behest of some community consensus, we do it a disservice.
Calgary Herald 4 June 1994: A6

(Here 'subject to' would be better.)

behoove, behooved, behove What *behooves* you is what it is necessary or fitting that you do. The most common construction begins with *it*: 'It

behooves the Senate to consult more widely'. *Behoove* rhymes with *move*; the past tense is *behooved*.
In Britain *behoove* is spelled *behove* and pronounced to rhyme with *rove*.

... the NBA wouldn't be coming here if it didn't think it could make money. So it behooves the league to make some concessions.
Toronto Star 20 Dec. 1993: A20

Despite the motion's failure, it behooved us to annul it at the following meeting so as to keep our record clean.
Gazette (Montreal) 21 Sept. 1994: B2

being as, being as how, being that, seeing as how These constructions are inappropriate except in writing that imitates very informal speech. *Because*, *since*, and *considering that* are more widely accepted substitutes. For example, 'Being as how he was going downtown, he offered to drive her' could be rephrased as 'Since he was going downtown ...'; 'I wanted to go to the beach, being that it was finally sunny' as 'Because it was finally sunny ...'; and 'Seeing as how we are friends ...' as 'Since we are friends ...'.

See also SEEING AS.

belabour, labour To go over and over the same point in a boring or ineffectual fashion is either to *belabour* or to *labour* it. Canadians favour *belabour* in this context. British commentators prefer *labour* because, in British English, *belabour* is still often used in the older sense, 'beat vigorously'.

Also, we are supposed to be talking about novels here, and, to belabour the obvious, a novel is not a scientific treatise....
Margaret Atwood *Second Words* 1982: 416

As far as sovereignty goes, he points out that everyone knows that the PQ is for it, so why belabor the point through advertising?
Toronto Star 19 Aug. 1994: D1

'I don't have to labor that point.'
Globe and Mail (Toronto) 7 March 1985: P18

See also -OUR, -OR.

belated, late *Belated* and *late* are synonyms in that both refer to something that happens after the usual or appropriate time. However, *belated* often adds the connotation of reproach or regret.

His was one of several wartime appointments made in a belated attempt to appease public opinion.
George Ignatieff *The Making of a Peacemonger* 1987: 11

... Sir William experienced a belated qualm of conscience.
Hilda Neatby *Queen's University* 1 (1978): 25

belie   The truth can *belie*, or give the lie to, a false impression. A false appearance can *belie*, or disguise, the truth. Hopes can be *belied*—that is, left unfulfilled—by the way things turn out. In each of these correct usages, *belie* implies a contradiction or reversal.

Occasionally *belie* is used like *betray* to mean simply show: 'His pallor belied his fear'. This usage should be avoided.

Face Off has been created to belie the notion that Canadian information telecasts are bland.
Gazette (Montreal) 18 Sept. 1994: F4

But Avvy Go's modest demeanor belies the powerful impact she's having in Toronto's legal and social justice circles.
Toronto Star 11 Dec. 1994: C1

'Trade! Trade! Find out where I'm going.' The remarks were in jest, but they belied a player's anxiety.
Calgary Herald 18 Aug. 1994: C4

(Here *betrayed* or *revealed* would be more appropriate.)

Bella Bella   see KWAKIUTL

Bella Coola, Nuxalk   The British Columbia Aboriginal people formerly called the *Bella Coola* now refer to themselves as the *Nuxalk* (singular and plural; pronounced *noo HALK*). Their language, Nuxalk, belongs to the Salishan language family.

The commercial gillnet fishermen who live in the Bella Coola Valley will be out of work ... the Nuxalk Indians who have caught salmon for thousands of years will lose a fundamental part of their culture.
Vancouver Sun 26 Nov. 1994: C8

belle   see BEAU

belly, abdomen, stomach, tummy, guts   *Belly* has been labelled too vulgar and *abdomen* (pronounced with the stress on either the first or the second syllable) too clinical for general use. Nevertheless, both words are used in serious non-medical Canadian prose for the part of the human body between the chest and the thighs, including the stomach, intestines, and internal reproductive organs. *Stomach*, the organ of digestion, is not a synonym for either term.

Most dictionaries describe *tummy* as a childish pronunciation of *stomach*, and many usage guides deplore its use by adults.

Guts meaning courage and determination is slang but very common in informal writing. *Guts* or *gut* can also mean intestines.

Martha punches him in the face, then begins kicking him in the shins. She's hampered by the long skirt of her dress, so she slugs him, aiming for the belly, hitting him in the rib cage.
Margaret Atwood *Life Before Man* 1979: 95

One man was shot in the left leg, another in the right arm and a third in the abdomen.
Gazette (Montreal) 9 Dec. 1994: A3

beloved   see -ED

benefactor, beneficiary   A *benefactor* is someone who gives help, especially financial help, to an organization or an individual, while a *beneficiary* is someone who benefits or will benefit from something. The people who receive a donation or who profit from a situation are sometimes mistakenly referred to as 'the benefactors'.

Queen's found a private benefactor in the person of James Douglas [who] endowed a chair in Canadian and colonial history....
Frederick Gibson *Queen's University* 2 (1983): 8

The main beneficiaries of the law will be small and medium companies, which often can't afford to go to court to get protection from their creditors....
Daily News (Halifax) 24 June 1992: 24

... the Argo offence was inept as usual and the Lions, 3-8, were the benefactors.
Edmonton Journal 20 Sept. 1992: B1

(The word required here is *beneficiaries*.)

The Easter Seal Society for crippled children is one of the main benefactors of the club's fundraising.
Ottawa Citizen 13 April 1992: B3

(The word required here is *beneficiaries*.)

You don't need a PhD to know intuitively that the real benefactors of a Sheppard subway will be commercial land owners and the cities of North York and Scarborough (through higher property taxes).
Toronto Star 9 April 1992: NY10

(The word required here is *beneficiaries*.)

Among the benefactors of the club's other good deeds is Emily Murphy House, a transition home for battered women.
Vancouver Sun 5 May 1992: B2

(The word required here is *beneficiaries*.)

beneficent, benevolent, benign, munificent
Beneficent means beneficial or, when used of a person, disposed to good deeds. *Benevolent* means kindly or full of good will. *Benign* means gentle or merely innocuous. *Munificent* (pronounced *myoo NIF i sunt*) means grandly generous and is applied to both people and things. Though these adjectives are not generally synonymous, in many contexts more than one of them may be appropriate.

... one of the most beneficent technological discoveries ever made [is] penicillin....
Queen's Quarterly 93.1 (1986): 92

In theory, that decision left room for an angel to come to the rescue, a beneficent someone who would resurrect the magazine as it was intended to be....
Vancouver Sun 26 June 1993: C4

Marx was little concerned with humanity in the mythical 'original state of nature'; yet he did assume that, once freed from the corrupting influence of a class society, people would be benevolent toward their fellows.
J.E. Smyth et al. *The Law and Business Administration in Canada* 1987: 10

His face was alert, yet there was a benign quality about him which reminded me of a medieval monk.
George Ignatieff *The Making of a Peacemonger* 1987: 130

We're approaching the stage now where the moderate consumption of wine is viewed as almost benign, that at least it won't hurt you.
Bon Vivant Nov. 1981: 12

So it is, too, with the munificent pensions that MPs enjoy after six years.
Gazette (Montreal) 3 Nov. 1993: B3

beneficiary see BENEFACTOR

benevolent, benign see BENEFICENT

bereaved, bereft The verb *bereave* has two past participles: *bereaved* and *bereft*. *Bereaved* is the form commonly used before a noun ('the bereaved parents') while *bereft* is used after a verb ('were bereft'). *Bereaved* almost always refers to the loss of a loved one; *bereft* commonly refers to other kinds of loss.

The bereaved young father stood at the graveside, clogged with grief, as the woman once so vibrant and

sensuous ... descended forever into the earth, cradling a stillborn baby the color of suet.
Margaret Atwood *Life Before Man* 1979: 148

He wants a new world ushered in by a second Jesus, feels honoured to be part of God's plan, and is genuinely bereft when the baby dies before birth.
NeWest Review Oct.–Nov. 1989: 53

As the film comes to a close, she finds herself bereft of her carefully nurtured illusion of romantic omnipotence....
Globe and Mail (Toronto) 18 March 1985: M7

See also -T, -ED.

Berkeley see DERBY

beseech, beseeched, besought The past tense and past participle of *beseech* may be either *beseeched* or *besought*: 'I beseeched *or* besought her to help me, just as she had beseeched *or* besought me earlier'. *Beseeched* is more common.

'Stop. Stop. Stop,' they beseeched in horror.
Vancouver Sun 15 Nov. 1990: B1

That's why they were invited—and repeatedly besought—to participate in multi-party talks on electoral and constitutional reforms.
Toronto Star 17 April 1994: C2

best see OPTIMUM

bestiality *Bestiality* is sometimes misspelled *beastiality*. This misspelling reflects a pronunciation, *BEESS tee al uh tee*, that is now well established in North America. However, many dictionaries don't include it. The older, more widely accepted pronunciation is *BESS tee al uh tee*.

A subscription to Playboy, or some similar non-electronic form of titillation, would probably prove more erotic than FreeNet discussions on spanking, beastiality and breasts.
Ottawa Citizen 7 Oct. 1994: A12

(The correct spelling is *bestiality*.)

bestow A gift, a talent, or an honour is bestowed *on* or *upon* a person. To say that a person is 'bestowed with' a thing is non-standard; one might say instead 'awarded' or 'provided with'.

It gives you information and, in subtle ways, information bestows confidence on the person who has it.
Daily News (Halifax) 21 Sept. 1992: 17

It was not long before his followers bestowed upon him the title der Fuehrer (the leader).
Irving M. Zeitlin and Robert J. Brym *The Social Condition of Humanity* 1991: 238

They gather, beginning at about 5:30 p.m., at a square in the city's financial district and are bestowed with an impressive array of literature and other goodies before the ride sets off.
Toronto Star 3 Dec. 1994: E6

(Here *provided with* would be better.)

bet, betted   *Bet* is the usual past tense and past participle of the verb to *bet*. *Betted* is a historically respectable variant, now rare and therefore probably best avoided in writing. However, *betted* may still have some currency in speech: several commentators suggest that some people use *betted* to refer to repeated past actions ('They betted compulsively') and *bet* to refer to a single event ('She bet ten dollars').

Birarda ... bet $1,000 US on the Canucks winning the Stanley Cup when he was in Las Vegas in April.
Vancouver Sun 11 June 1994: A1

By the time they got the horses loaded in the starting gate and closed the betting windows for the fourth, the public had bet it down to a 9-to-5 favorite.
Province (Vancouver) 19 Oct. 1990: 71

bête noire   A *bête noire*, from the French meaning black beast, is a thing or person feared or disliked intensely. *Bête noir* is a misspelling; *noire* always ends in *e* to agree with the feminine noun *bête*. The plural, *bêtes noires* (both words end in *s*), is pronounced the same as the singular: *BET NWAR*. In formal writing this phrase should be italicized and its accent should be retained.

We all have our betes noires. Mine was always mathematics.
Gazette (Montreal) 19 Dec. 1993: A3

(In formal writing *bêtes noires* would be italicized and would retain its accent.)

... some of their constituents are fearful that the project will mean expansion of the Ashbridges Bay treatment plant, the bete noir of their neighborhood.
Toronto Star 14 June 1994: A16

(*Noire* has a final *e*.)

better, had better   *Had better* is an idiom meaning ought to: 'You had better see for yourself'. In speech the word *had* is often dropped ('You better go'); in writing, however, *had* (or the contraction '*d*) should be included.

'We'd better go back inside.'
Calgary Herald 16 May 1994: A3

better stores everywhere   see ABSOLUTE COMPARATIVES

better than   Some usage guides recommend against the use of *better than* to mean more than, as in 'We spent better than three hours in bumper-to-bumper traffic'. More, as in this case, is not always better. However, the usage is idiomatic and widespread. Though uncommon in formal writing, it is accepted in informal contexts.

Skip Morris has been, for better than two decades, one of the top North American rod builders.
Atlantic Salmon Journal Autumn (1990): 17

Randy Johnson throws a fastball at better than 90 miles an hour....
Gazette (Montreal) 6 March 1989: C1

See also AS GOOD AS OR BETTER THAN.

between, among   Many writers believe that *between* must never be used in reference to relationships involving more than two things or people. However, *between* can be used with more than two items in some contexts. In a sentence describing a relationship or difference between each of the pairs in a group of three or more items, *between* is in fact the appropriate choice. For example, in 'They discussed the issue of trade between Canada, Mexico, and the U.S.', *among* would not work.
Among is the better word to use when discussing relationships that are general or collective: 'The organization aims to encourage equal distribution of food among nations'.
In some contexts either preposition is acceptable.

One of the things I've always admired about Shakespeare was that he distinguished between an African, an Ethiope and a Moor.
Toronto Star 1 Jan. 1994: F4

I have been a green card holder in California since 1966 but work between there, New York and Toronto.
Toronto Star 1 Jan. 1994: H8

(Here *among* would not be possible.)

... St. Laurent believed that most Canadians wanted their country to contribute to world peace and better understanding among nations.
George Ignatieff *The Making of a Peacemonger* 1987: 108

... Lipset is interested in his recent analyses in comparisons among the two Canadian cultures and American culture.
Canadian Journal of Sociology 14.2 (1989): 146

(Since a three-way comparison involves a sequential examination of pairs, *between* would also be possible here.)

... Station 7 at Parliament and Dundas Sts. had the most calls overall, split between three trucks.
Toronto Star 1 Jan. 1994: A4

(Here *among* is recommended.)

See also BETWEEN EACH.

between ... and *And* is the word normally used to link items after *between*. *Between ... or* (as in 'The choice is between you or me') and *between ... to* (as in 'Between five to ten per cent are flawed') are not accepted in formal writing.

... the Toronto *Globe* had daily, tri-weekly and weekly editions that together sold between 20,000 and 25,000 copies and were read religiously throughout the province.
William Teatero *John Anderson: Fugitive Slave* 1986: 47

Yet their albums sell between 10,000 to 20,000 copies.
Queen's Quarterly 95.2 (1988): 299

(Here either *between* should be deleted or *to* should be changed to *and*.)

... it might be desirable for public interest groups to have a choice between intervening as parties under Rule 13.01 or intervening as what are now described as non-party friends of the court under Rule 13.02.
Canadian Bar Review 66.3 (1987): 522

(Here *or* should be changed to *and*; or *between* could be deleted and *of* inserted: '... have *the* choice *of* intervening as parties ... or intervening as what are ...'.)

between each, between every Some commentators disapprove of *each* or *every* following *between*, as in 'Between each sentence, she paused', or 'Between every play-off game, he went through the same ritual'. They argue that *between* requires a plural or compound object ('between jobs', 'between a rock and a hard place'), while the noun that follows *each* or *every* ('between every meal') is singular. Commentators who accept the usage consider it idiomatic and note that the noun following

each or *every*, though grammatically singular, is notionally plural in meaning (see AGREEMENT, GRAMMATICAL).

Given how common *between each* is at all levels of writing—and how difficult it sometimes is to paraphrase—it seems quite defensible as an idiom. *Between every* is less common and seems to be avoided in formal writing.

Alcohol and pain threatened to obliterate his senses, but in the pause between each kick, he willed consciousness, desperate against the injustice. ...
Queen's Quarterly 94.2 (1987): 382

There are three knots between each bead.
Maclean's 2 Oct. 1989: A62

Still, a large number of those in the crowd applauded between every movement of both pieces.
Vancouver Sun 25 Aug. 1990: D4

(In formal writing '*after* every movement' would be better.)

... Meares Island is an example of the kind of deadlock that occurs when there is no discussion between every group with an interest in how lands are used.
Vancouver Sun 15 June 1990: A3

(In formal writing 'between *all* groups ...' would be better.)

See also BETWEEN, AMONG.

between Scylla and Charybdis see SCYLLA AND CHARYBDIS

between you and me *Between you and me* is correct, though *between you and I* is often heard. *I* is the subject form of the first-person pronoun; *me* is the object form. After a preposition (*between, about, after*, etc.), it is the object form that is required. No one is confused when only one pronoun follows a preposition: 'after me', *not* 'after I'.

People who say 'between you and I' probably learned as children not to use 'you and me' as the subject of a sentence and have overgeneralized the rule.

'I think (that is) the fundamental difference in philosophy between you and me.'
Vancouver Sun 10 Nov. 1989: A1

'Between you and I, a nitwit wouldn't propose something like that.'
Vancouver Sun 24 July 1990: D1

(The accepted form is *between you and me*.)

See also CASE; HYPERCORRECTION.

beverage room   see BEER PARLOUR

biannual, bimonthly, biweekly, biennial   *Biannual* means twice per year. *Bimonthly* and *biweekly* mean every two months and every two weeks. However, *biannual* is often used mistakenly to mean every two years, and twice per month and twice per week are secondary definitions of *bimonthly* and *biweekly*, according to most dictionaries. In short, there is so much confusion around these terms that it's best to avoid them altogether.

Biennial means occurring every two years. Plants with a two-year life cycle are called *biennials*.

> The CSA puts out a bimonthly magazine which reviews specific stocks and offers investment advice.
> *Toronto Star* 26 April 1992: H1

(Since *bimonthly* is ambiguous, it would be better to specify either 'twice a month' or 'six times a year'.)

> The backdrop was the New Democratic Party's biennial convention.
> *Toronto Star* 1 Dec. 1994: A31

(The convention is held every two years.)

Bible, bible   see SACRED WRITINGS

bid   When the verb *bid* means to make an offer, the past tense and past participle are *bid*. When it means to command, the past tense is usually *bade* and the past participle is usually *bid* or *bidden*. When *bid* is used with a greeting, as in 'She bade her friends farewell', the past tense and past participle are usually *bade*. *Bade* is usually pronounced like *bad*, or sometimes to rhyme with *made*.

Some authorities still object to the use of *bid* as a noun meaning attempt, as in 'The cat made a bid to occupy my chair'. This use of the word dates from the late 1800s, is recognized as standard by dictionaries, and is well established in all but quite formal writing. *Bid* is standard with reference to card games and auctions.

> ... when Barr put up a team of horses for sale, rival purchasers bid up the prices unnecessarily.
> Pierre Berton *The Promised Land* 1984: 124

> His company had bid to build only the second one, due for delivery in 1993.
> *Vancouver Sun* 8 Sept. 1990: H1

> The light bade him lift his eyes to the heavens, where the Big Dipper blazed in the sky above.
> *Queen's Quarterly* 95.1 (1988): 171

> Now Sigfrid goes as she is bid to her bedroom.
> David Williams *Eye of the Father* 1985: 118

> Brian Mulroney has sacrificed his personal credibility—and, in my opinion, honor—by failing to find the time to say 'Godspeed' to the people he has bidden to voyage to the gulf.
> *Gazette* (Montreal) 5 Sept. 1990: B2

> With a mournful blast of its whistle, The Canadian pulled out of Ottawa for the last time Sunday as about 300 protesters bade farewell to a victim of the VIA cuts.
> *Ottawa Citizen* 15 Jan. 1990: A4

> Parti Quebecois candidate Monique Simard was angry at having lost her bid for a National Assembly seat in the September provincial election.
> *Gazette* (Montreal) 31 Dec. 1994: B5

biennial   see BIANNUAL

bigfoot   see SASQUATCH

bilateral   see UNILATERAL

billion, trillion, milliard   In Canadian, American, and international scientific English, *billion* means a thousand million (1,000,000,000) and *trillion* means a million million (1,000,000,000,000). In British English *billion* was formerly used for a million million (what everyone else called a *trillion*) and *milliard* for a thousand million (what everyone else called a *billion*). Now, however, British usage is shifting to the international norm, and the word *milliard* is becoming obsolete.

bimonthly   see BIANNUAL

binomial   see SPECIES, GENUS

birth name   see MAIDEN NAME

bison, buffalo   In scientific terms, *buffalo* are large mammals indigenous to Africa and India, while *bison* are similar species indigenous to Europe and North America. In the past, North American bison were commonly called *buffalo*. Now the more precise term *bison* is more common in general use, but *buffalo* is still perfectly acceptable where confusion isn't likely to result. The *Dictionary of Canadianisms* lists nearly 70 historical compounds using *buffalo*, including 'buffalo robe' and 'buffalo wallow' (a pit made by wallowing buffalo). *Buffalo* has two plurals, *buffalo* and *buffaloes*; the plural of *bison* is always *bison*.

Occasionally *buffalo* is used informally as a verb meaning to baffle or intimidate.

As recently as two centuries ago, 60 million mangy wood and plains bison roamed the west.... So effective was the slaughter that by 1893 there were fewer than 500 wood bison left.
Globe and Mail (Toronto) 23 Nov. 1985: A8

At the Mountain Lake Bison Range near Owen Sound, visitors can watch the buffalo grazing in the pasture.
Globe and Mail (Toronto) 23 Oct. 1985: C6

In brief, don't be buffaloed by the stories about the federal government off-loading its debt problems on the doorsteps of the provinces.... The reports of provincial pain are ... without statistical support.
Ottawa Citizen 24 Feb. 1990: A3

bite, bit, bitten   The past tense of *bite* is *bit* and the usual past participle is *bitten* ('has bitten', 'were bitten', 'got bitten'). *Bit* is a variant past participle, rare in Canadian writing, though not uncommon in speech.

A 50-year-old Pointe Claire man was bitten by a mixed Labrador and German shepherd dog....
Gazette (Montreal) 15 Nov. 1990: I4

'I got bit by a poodle a while back and nobody wrote about how dangerous they are.'
Ottawa Citizen 3 July 1994: A8

(In formal writing *bitten* is recommended.)

biweekly   see BIANNUAL

black, coloured, Negro, white, African Canadian, Africadian   As a term for people of African descent, *black* is common and widely accepted in Canada. This term replaced the now obsolete *coloured* and *Negro* in the 1960s. Some writers capitalize it to designate an ethnic group with a shared culture and common goals. *Black* is always capitalized in expressions such as Black English, Black Power, and Black Muslim. The opposite term, *white*, is normally not capitalized, because it does not designate a particular cultural or ethnic group. If you choose to capitalize *black* and not *white*, you should probably explain the reasons for this decision to the reader, who may find the inconsistency puzzling or annoying.

In the United States, terms such as *African American* and *Afro-American* have recently come into use

as replacements for *black*. Parallel terms in Canada, such as *African Canadian*, are gaining popularity more slowly. Many Canadians of African ancestry are recent immigrants and prefer to use more specific terms, such as *Nigerian Canadian* or *Jamaican Canadian*. Since the black population in Canada is far more culturally heterogeneous than its counterpart in the United States, writers using *black* as a collective term should be aware that its use may obscure important cultural differences.

Africadian, from *African* and *Acadian*, is a term coined recently by the Canadian poet and critic George Elliott Clarke for those of African descent who live in the Atlantic provinces. Many Canadians are descended from the 3500 free blacks (escaped slaves and Loyalist soldiers) and the 2000 slaves belonging to Loyalists who came north to Nova Scotia and New Brunswick after the American Revolution.

George Clyke, a young Truro writer, says blacks in this town of 13,000 have not moved ahead over the years.
Chronicle-Herald (Halifax) 14 May 1988: 8

I use the term 'Africadian', a word I have minted from 'Africa' and 'Acadia' (the old name for Nova Scotia and New Brunswick), to denote the Black populations of the Maritimes and especially of Nova Scotia.
George Elliott Clarke *Fire on the Water* 1991: n.p.

See also CAPITAL LETTERS; RACE; VISIBLE MINORITY.

blatant, flagrant, patent   *Blatant* and *flagrant* are both adjectives commonly used to describe conspicuous transgressions. *Blatant* suggests that no attempt was made to conceal the offence, while *flagrant* suggests that the offence far exceeds the bounds of acceptable behaviour. In many contexts either word is appropriate.

Neither word should be used to mean simply obvious, as in 'a blatant cry for help'. In neutral contexts *patent* (pronounced *PAY tuhnt*), which means manifest or obvious, without the negative connotations, would be a fairly formal alternative. *Obvious* and *manifest* are also possible substitutes.

In one of the more blatant cases of corruption, a team of Chinese archeologists from Changsha, central China, recently opened their own antique shop and sold 5,000 pieces of porcelain and jade before being found out by tax auditors.
Toronto Star 20 Nov. 1994: A14

Supporters say the practice is a reasonable way for couples on a limited income to afford a high-tech baby. Critics say it's the blatant selling of human tissue.
CTV News [transcript] 12 Dec. 1994: n.p.

Players who commit two flagrant fouls in a game will be ejected.
Ottawa Citizen 1 Nov. 1994: C3

And why did he condone flagrant wrongdoing among the senior members of his department?
Pierre Berton *The Promised Land* 1984: 226

'[The referee] was out of position the whole night. He also took a goal away from us, which was a blatant goal. . . .'
Vancouver Sun 17 Feb. 1990: H3

(A better choice here would be *obvious*.)

blend   see ABBREVIATION

blessed   see -ED

bleu, rouge   *Bleu* is the equivalent in Canadian French of the English label *Tory* for a member of the Conservative Party, the traditional colour of which is blue. The radical reformers who opposed the Conservatives in Quebec during the 1850s and 1860s were known as the 'Parti rouge'; this party merged with the Liberals after Confederation. In present-day Quebec, a *rouge* is a member of the Liberal Party. In current English usage, *rouge* and *bleu* are not capitalized whether they are used as adjectives or as nouns. These terms should be italicized in formal writing.

He has always defined himself as a 'bleu' (Quebec's slang for conservatives)—but contrasts the 'bleu' tradition with the 'rouge' (liberal) tradition as the difference between a humanist approach and a technocratic approach.
Globe and Mail (Toronto) 27 Sept. 1985: P8

Once the Union Nationale expired in the early 1970s, the bleu vote in Quebec went in various directions—Liberal, PQ and Creditiste.
Globe and Mail (Toronto) 11 Dec. 1985: A6

The Liberals' present difficulties should not hide three enormous advantages: the historic rouge vote in Quebec, the ability to raise money from corporations and the non-ideological, brokerage nature of Canadian politics.
Globe and Mail (Toronto) 23 Jan. 1985: P6

See also CONSERVATIVE; GRIT.

bloc, block   A *bloc* is a group of people or regions sharing a common political, military, or economic interest. Sometimes the term refers to a formal alliance: 'the European trading bloc'. *Block* is the correct spelling for a cube ('building block'), an obstruction ('writer's block'), or a quantity of things regarded as a unit ('a block of theatre tickets').

The hard fact remains that the people who write books do not constitute a powerful voting bloc.
Ottawa Citizen 20 Dec. 1990: A15

The vast majority of part-time workers fall within provincial bounds, but the federal labor jurisdiction covers a large bloc of part-time workers in the banking field.
Globe and Mail (Toronto) 3 June 1985: B11

DiMonte's 'quarter-hour average' (defined by the BBM as the average number of listeners tuned to a 15-minute bloc of a radio program) is 57,100. . . .
Gazette (Montreal) 3 March 1989: C1

(The correct spelling in this context is *block*.)

See also POLITICAL PARTIES.

blond, blonde   In French, *blond* is the masculine form and *blonde* the feminine. In Canadian English, the adjective is spelled either way when it refers to a thing ('a blond *or* blonde wood finish'), but *blond* is more common in this context.

When people or their features are described, *blond* generally refers to men and boys and *blonde* to women and girls. Some usage guides consider *blonde* unacceptable in references to men, but none objects to *blond* for women because gender-neutral usage favours one unmarked spelling for both sexes.

The noun *blond* rarely refers to a man: 'There's a new blond in Sales'. It's probably best to avoid 'a blond(e)' in reference to women as well, since the expression often has demeaning connotations.

Bowen Island Brewery's Blonde Ale's the best new beer here in years.
Vancouver Sun 31 Dec. 1994: D6

(Here *blond* would also be acceptable.)

His accomplice is 6 feet tall, with short blonde spiked hair.
Toronto Star 22 Dec. 1994: OS6

(Here, in reference to a man, *blond* is recommended.)

And if you're a lone male the bellhop will still ask you, in the privacy of the elevator, if you'd like a blonde.
Toronto Star 19 Nov. 1994: L2

See also BRUNETTE; SEXIST LANGUAGE.

blue language   see PURPLE PROSE

Bluenose, herring choker   *Bluenose*, or sometimes *Bluenoser*, is a jocular label applied to Nova
Scotians. The origin of this nickname is obscure,
but it long precedes the naming of the famous
schooner pictured on the Canadian dime.

A *herring choker* is any Maritimer, but especially
one from New Brunswick.

Sobey was a hard-working, tough, shrewd Bluenose who
kept his ear to the ground, his shoulder to the wheel and
his eye on the main chance.
Globe and Mail (Toronto) 30 Aug. 1985: P101

Haliburton, for instance, was a Nova Scotian, a
Bluenose: the word 'Canadian' to him would have sum-
moned up the figure of someone who spoke mainly
French and whose enthusiasm for Haliburton's own
political ideals would have been extremely tepid.
Northrop Frye *The Bush Garden* 1971: 220

HERRING CHOKERS: ... Janice Seeley ... wants to hear
from former students, teachers and trustees of Waasis,
Bunkerville, Rusagonis, and South-West Rusagonis
schools [in New Brunswick].
Vancouver Sun 20 April 1992: B1

bluff   see FOREST

blush, flush, hot flash   To *blush* and to *flush* both
mean to become red in the face. While blushing is
always linked to embarrassment, flushing can have
various causes: anger, pride, exertion, sickness, and
so on.

Spells of feeling intensely hot experienced by
women at menopause are called *hot flashes* or, less
often, *hot flushes*. *Hot flush* is the more common
term in Britain.

I blushed at my confession, but I had begun and so I
went on.
Ottawa Citizen 17 Nov. 1992: C10

Birdie flushed with pleasure, then grimaced.
David Williams *Eye of the Father* 1985: 56

Once outside, she shivered in the chill, washed air, but it
cooled her flushed face and refreshed her.
Constance Beresford-Howe *Night Studies* 1985: 220

Many women are confused about the pros and cons of
taking estrogen to relieve menopausal symptoms, such
as hot flashes. ...
Chatelaine April 1986: 32

The 45-year-old University of Ottawa health economist
and author got hot flushes in airplanes.
Ottawa Citizen 4 Aug. 1992: E1

BNA Act   see CONSTITUTION

boat, ship   A *boat* is a small, usually open vessel
used on inland waterways or in coastal areas,
whereas a *ship* is a large sea-going vessel. Land-
lubbers frequently refer to ships as boats and are
unlikely to stop, although this may irritate those
familiar with nautical terminology. Submarines,
even the largest ones, are correctly referred to as
boats.

bog   see SWAMP

bologna, baloney   *Bologna*, the sandwich meat
with the poor reputation, is pronounced *buh LONE
ee* or *buh LONE uh*. The city in Italy that lent its
name to this sausage is pronounced *buh LONE yuh*.
Neither should be spelled *balogna*.

Baloney, or sometimes *boloney*, is both an informal
spelling of *bologna* and a mild expletive meaning
nonsense.

'I know people now that are feeding their family on a
slice of balogna and making do with home-made bread.'
Vancouver Sun 20 April 1994: A4

(The correct spelling is *bologna*.)

There's nothing very complicated about buying a house
in Toronto these days. There are three ways to do it: a)
win a lottery; b) inherit money from a rich uncle; or c)
eat baloney sandwiches for 25 years while paying off the
mortgage.
Gazette (Montreal) 4 March 1989: G1

That claim is 'total baloney,' Morrison said.
Daily News (Halifax) 10 March 1994: 26

bona fide, bona fides   *Bona fide* is usually pronounced *bone uh FIDE* (and sometimes misspelled
bonified). *Bona fides* is usually pronounced *bone uh
FIDE eez*. These Latin phrases were first used in law
to mean 'in good faith' and 'good faith', respectively: 'The offer was made bona fide (in good
faith)'; 'The bona fides (good faith) of the trustee
was in question.'

Over time, as these phrases came into general use,
they acquired new meanings. The adverb phrase
bona fide, 'in good faith', was re-interpreted as an
adjective meaning sincere ('a bona fide offer'), or
authentic, accredited ('a bona fide Chippendale', 'a

bona fide member'). This use is now both common and accepted. The use of *bona fide* as an adverb has become rare, even in formal writing.

The noun phrase *bona fides* was reinterpreted as a plural because it ends in *s*. *Bona fides* is now commonly used with a plural verb to mean 'credentials' or 'qualifications': 'Her bona fides were impeccable'. This use is disputed: some dictionaries list it but others don't. It's probably best to use only the older meaning of *bona fides*, 'sincerity' or 'good faith', in formal writing. Even in informal writing, use of *bona fides* with a plural verb may be criticized.

> The bride was presented as very much a child of her time, the mildly, even admirably rebellious offspring of a bona fide member of the old Liberal elite.
> *Vancouver Sun* 30 Oct. 1990: A6

> No one looked over the list of applicants for the all-British colony to see how many were bona fide farmers.
> Pierre Berton *The Promised Land* 1984: 106

> Patsy is that third element in the play that seems more like a vehicle for the exploration of Sydney's and Tawe's relationship ... than a truly bonified character.
> *Queen's Journal* (Kingston) 8 Feb. 1994: 23

(The correct spelling is *bona fide*; *truly* is redundant.)

> Revenue Canada stood by these letters ..., trusting the bona fides of the taxpayer requesting the ruling.
> *Financial Post* 9 Jan. 1991: 12

> A track record in politics, the Quebec civil service and private industry provides the 46-year-old executive with the bona fides to run an organization overseeing operations in 15 locally-managed ports across Canada.
> *Gazette* (Montreal) 17 Aug. 1985: 5

(Here *qualifications* would be better.)

> Those were the years when writers ran around establishing their blue-collar bona fides, and dustjackets were full of lumberjacks and dish-washers.
> *Globe and Mail* (Toronto) 16 Nov. 1985: E1

(Here *credentials* would be better.)

> 'As soon as our president's bona fides were established, we were able to operate like any other oil company'.
> *Ottawa Citizen* 2 Sept. 1990: B1

(Here either 'bona fides *was*' or 'credentials *were*' would be better.)

See also LATIN PHRASES.

bootless, footless   The most obvious meaning of *bootless* is without footwear. However, it also means profitless or unavailing, a sense derived from the

Old English *boot*, meaning profit, advantage, remedy, or satisfaction. This word survives in the expression *to boot*, which means as a bonus or besides.

Footless has three meanings in Canadian English. The most common meaning, and the only one shared with Standard British English, is without feet, as in 'footless tights'. Canadians and Americans occasionally use *footless* figuratively to mean baseless or insubstantial, as in 'footless plans'. North Americans have also borrowed an informal meaning from Scottish English: awkward or helpless, referring most often to an alcohol-induced state.

> If some uppity peasant complained that he never got to hear a cantata or sit for a portrait, a kindly aristocrat would explain that the bootless bumpkin couldn't possibly appreciate art, then have him flogged.
> *Province* (Vancouver) 26 March 1990: 6

> Now if only this kind of pragmatism could prevail in the UN General Assembly, where so many of the Third World states support unbalanced and counter-productive resolutions as if to compensate in bootless rhetoric for what they lack in economic and military clout.
> *Globe and Mail* (Toronto) 22 Oct. 1985: A6

> But let the economists and the politicians debate whether it's a recession, slowdown, downturn, depression, or whatever. The debate is bootless.
> *Vancouver Sun* 7 Aug. 1990: A9

> And in the late 18th and early 19th centuries, hard-bitten Scottish magnates of the fur trade drank themselves footless in Montreal at their Beaver Club dinners.
> *Financial Post* (Toronto) 1 Oct. 1990: 48

> But even now, with feature number one under his belt and a pocketful of good notices to boot, Hauka is still having a hard time making headway.
> *Vancouver Sun* 18 June 1993: C1

bore   see GUN

borne, born, bourn   The verb *bear* has two past participles, *borne* and *born*. *Borne* is used when *bear* means carry or withstand ('They've borne the brunt of it'), and also when it means give birth to ('She had borne him three sons'), unless the construction is passive. In passive constructions, the past participle is *born* ('He was born in 1917'), except when it's followed by *by* ('children borne by teenagers'). In other words, *born* is the past participle for an unattributed birth and *borne* for one in which the mother is given credit.

Bourn (or *bourne*) is an archaic word meaning goal or limit; Hamlet, in his famous soliloquy, refers to death as 'The undiscover'd country from whose bourn / No traveller returns'. This spelling may have affected some writers who intend *borne*.

The system benefits retailers and yet the cost of setting up the tracking system is borne by suppliers.
Gazette (Montreal) 6 Dec. 1994: C1

It can be transfused regardless of blood types and it won't harbour blood-born diseases like HIV and hepatitis.
CBC News [transcript] 23 Nov. 1994: n.p.

(Diseases carried in the blood are *blood-borne*.)

My wife has borne a child.
Gazette (Montreal) 22 Dec. 1994: C4

It so happened that Michelangelo died in the same year (1564) in which Shakespeare was born....
R. A. Wilson *The Birth of Language* 1937: 150

Babies can be borne by surrogate mothers....
Queen's Quarterly 92.2 (1985): 257

[Remittance men] were borne of primogeniture inheritance law, which left everything to the first-born....
Vancouver Sun 17 Dec. 1994: D15

(Before *of*, *to*, or any preposition except *by*, the correct spelling is *born*.)

Fears that the federal government wanted [a] rubber stamp for foreclosure-minded bankers have not been bourne out.
Country Guide Nov. 1986: 8

(The correct spelling is *borne*.)

-boro, borough   see -BURGH

borrow   The use of *borrow* to mean lend ('Could you borrow me yours?') is non-standard. The prepositions *off* and *off of* are commonly used after *borrow*: 'We borrowed it off of Joel's parents'. In speech this usage is disputed; in writing it should definitely be avoided. *From* is the preposition required.

The foreman seemed to like him. Borrowed smokes off him all the time, anyway.
NeWest Review Feb.–Mar. 1990: 30

(Here *borrowed ... off* is an imitation of casual speech; the standard expression is *borrowed ... from*.)

See also OFF, OFF OF, FROM.

Bosnia-Herzegovina, Bosnia-Hercegovina
Bosnia-Herzegovina is the name of the republic formed in 1992 out of part of Yugoslavia. *Bosnia-Hercegovina* is the Serbo-Croat version of the name. The second part of the name can be pronounced either *HEHR tseh GO vin ah* or *HEHR tseh go VEEN ah*. The CBC uses the former pronunciation.

bosom   see BREAST(S)

bottom line   Usage commentators have taken a distinct dislike to the expression *bottom line*, labelling it overworked business jargon; it is best avoided in formal writing. In informal contexts, however, the expression is quite defensible. Although it has developed several different uses, it has not become—as some critics suggest—a meaningless catch-all.

The top line of a financial statement is gross income. From this line costs are deducted, and on the bottom line net profit or loss is reported. Thus the literal meaning of *bottom line* is financial profit or loss. This meaning is still current.

The bottom line is the key consideration in business. Thus *bottom line* has also come to be used as a metaphor referring to the most important consideration in other types of endeavour. Extending this meaning, which first appeared in the 1970s, people began to use *bottom line* to refer to what they saw as the essential or relevant point in any situation. Thus the crux of a complex issue or the upshot of a chain of events may be called 'the bottom line'.

A less common and more recent meaning of *bottom line* is final bargaining position. This meaning is probably partly derived from the unrelated metaphor 'to draw the line'.

When hyphenated, *bottom-line* is an adjective meaning concerned only with profit or cost.

In an effort to improve the bottom line, companies are tempted to reduce promotional expenditures or, worse, completely suspend them.
Computer Dealer News 7 March 1991: 49

Socially and culturally, it remains to be seen whether the current narcissism has run its course and the possibility of a new, more inclusive public ethos might come about where the bottom line for community is something more than the dollar bill.
City Magazine Spring 1988: 40

'The bottom line is: what kind of agriculture are we going to have in Canada and who is going to control the production of food?'
Briarpatch Dec. 1989–Jan. 1990: 2

'The bottom line is that women are still the ones who raise the children and there is going to be an impact on the family if they have to be in Ottawa or Quebec five days a week.'
Toronto Star 31 Dec. 1992: B3

'Basically yes, I've gone as far as I can go,' the minister said.... 'It seemed to me that we were being reasonable all across the board, but their bottom line is that they just plain don't want this regulation.'
Toronto Star 14 Nov. 1992: A4

As business and government realize that they cannot push the arts any further along the road to bottom-line thinking, I believe that we will begin to see a return to—happy days—serious and more generous cultural subsidies.
Performing Arts in Canada Spring 1990: 46

[boughten], store-bought In some North American dialects, *boughten* is used as an adjective meaning purchased from a store rather than home-made. This usage is generally considered non-standard, though it is used in writing representing speech. *Store-bought* is an accepted alternative.

Storeboughten cookies are looked down upon.
Margaret Laurence *The Diviners* 1974: 29

(Here the dialectal *-en* captures the flavour of the speech of the novel's narrator, the young Morag Gunn.)

-bound The combining form *-bound* has two senses: constrained by and going in the direction of. In the first sense, familiar single-word compounds include *housebound*, *spellbound*, and *stormbound*. Hyphenated combinations include *desk-bound*, *duty-bound*, *honour-bound*, *muscle-bound*, and *root-bound*.

In the second sense, *eastbound*, *southbound*, *inbound*, and *outbound* are established as single words. Most other combinations take a hyphen: 'university-bound'. Proper names are always hyphenated when combined with *bound*: 'Alberta-bound'. Note that some combinations are ambiguous: *snowbound*, for example, could describe either avid skiers or frustrated travellers.

... the reigning doctrines are merely gender-bound and culture-bound parochial theories, with no grip on a reality common to all.
Queen's Quarterly 97.4 (1990): 616

He said he was reminded of a conversation he had overheard on a Toronto-bound train....
The Beaver Dec. 1989–Jan. 1990: 38

bourgeois, bourgeoisie, proletariat *Bourgeois* (pronounced *BOOR zhwah* or *boor ZHWAH*) is an adjective meaning middle-class and, occasionally, a noun meaning middle-class person. In Marxist theory the *bourgeoisie*, or middle class, are those who own the means of production, such as factories, and are thus able to exploit the lower social and economic class. The lower class, called the *proletariat*, survives by selling its labour.

Most people in contemporary Canadian society who would call themselves middle-class do not fit the Marxist definition of *bourgeois*. And few Canadian writers, other than historians and Marxist social critics, attempt to use the term as Marx defined it. Instead, *bourgeois* is often used with humour to describe people preoccupied with propriety and comfort.

The source of Plaskett's popularity is an unrepentantly bourgeois sensibility. His art is about home, hearth, comfort and security.
Ottawa Citizen 3 Oct. 1994: B6

... in all the capitalist democracies the industrial working class has become something other than the revolutionary proletariat that Marx anticipated.
Irving M. Zeitlin and Robert J. Brym *The Social Condition of Humanity* 1991: 133

bourn   see BORNE

B.P.   see A.D.

brace In informal English *brace*, like *bunch* or *slew*, is sometimes used to mean a considerable number. However, dictionaries have not yet recorded this use, probably because it conflicts with the standard definition of a brace as a pair.

The white, mild-tasting meat of a roasted brace of grouse ... is often preferred on the table over the dark breasts of waterfowl.
Ottawa Citizen 7 Oct. 1990: B6

(Here *brace* means pair.)

The latest head-turner is a brace of bodyguards. 'It's something different,' said Clayton Heffernan who celebrated his graduation Saturday with two hulking protectors at his side.
Toronto Star 23 June 1992: B1

(Here *brace* means pair.)

For spinsters with classical taste, there's a brace of Italians with smouldering eyes and chewy titles, among them Count Roffredo Gaetani-Lovatelli, ... and Count Ferdinando Brachetti-Peretti....
Ottawa Citizen 9 Sept. 1990: A10

(The use of *brace* to refer to more than two should be avoided.)

Both works have been recorded dozens of times since, and each new digital assault on the Matterhorn seems to get its brace of ecstatic reviews.
Gazette (Montreal) 17 Feb. 1990: H13

(The use of *brace* to refer to more than two should be avoided.)

bracket Some commentators dislike the use of *bracket* to mean group or level, and most Canadian writers avoid it in formal writing. However, phrases such as 'income bracket' and 'tax bracket' are so common in business writing that it seems clear they are acceptable in this context.

... the $151,000 he earns on the Supreme Court amounts to $75,000 in take-home pay because of his high tax bracket.
Gazette (Montreal) 2 March 1989: A15

See also PARENTHESES, BRACKETS.

brand names see TRADEMARKS

brand of In Canadian and American English, *brand of* is used figuratively in serious writing to mean kind or variety of. For example, one may have a brand of politics, religion, art, or even reality. Some British commentators consider this use appropriate only when humour is intended.

... Johnson's brand of Toryism might seem naturally unfriendly to political lessons from republicans....
J.A.W. Gunn *Beyond Liberty and Property* 1983: 30

He can hardly write Love without writing Death on the same page; his brand of immortality ... is reminiscent of Shelley's....
Margaret Atwood *Second Words* 1982: 98

breach, breech, breeches, britches *Breach* is a verb meaning break through ('breach enemy defences') and a noun meaning rupture or violation. The noun is most often used figuratively to refer to rifts, broken promises, and unfulfilled obligations: 'breach in their friendship', 'breach of etiquette', 'breach of trust'. The idiom 'to step into the breach' means to fill the gap or lend a hand where needed.

Breech is an obsolete word for buttocks that is still used in the expression 'breech birth'. *Breech* also refers to the back end of a gun barrel.

Breeches are tight pants fastened below the knee that are worn now only for some sports, like riding or fencing, or as part of uniforms or period costumes. *Britches* is a North American variant spelling that reflects the most common pronunciation of *breeches*, which also can be pronounced BREE chiz.

I have felt that it is well worth insulting the intelligence of some readers if one can do anything to breach the barriers of panic and prejudice in others.
Northrop Frye *The Bush Garden* 1971: 125

The languid Opposition of Leicester House and the Tories could take heart in the possibility that a breach between king and ministers might afford an alternative to the cultivation of the heir apparent as a road to power.
J.A.W. Gunn *Beyond Liberty and Property* 1983: 67

[Analysts] wonder whether yesterday's noisy split was a tactic, or a symptom of a breech too wide to mend.
Toronto Star 6 April 1994: A16

(Here the correct spelling is *breach*.)

The 10-member panel ... proposed that doctors reverse the current trend toward caesareans for breech births, where the baby is born buttocks-first.
Globe and Mail (Toronto) 28 Oct. 1985: A17

Amputated at either end, dull brown and black in color, its breach cracks open with a quick snap of the wrist to admit a single pellet shell.
Toronto Star 13 April 1994: A6

(Shells are inserted in the *breech*, not *breach*, of a gun.)

break and enter, breaking and entering see BURGLARY

breast(s), bust, bosom, chest The most common and least euphemistic name for a woman's mammary glands is *breasts*. *Bust* appears most often in descriptions of clothing and fashion. *Bosom* is euphemistic or literary. *Chest*, when applied to women, usually refers to the heart and lungs.

The upper front part of a male body is generally called the *chest*. *Breast* and *bosom* are poetic alternatives.

His splendid iron bosom, his mountainous biceps, his mouth-watering forearms, that proud tree-trunk neck, those shoulders set square; O, Stallone, what labors you have known!
Globe and Mail (Toronto) 23 May 1985: E3

breech, breeches see BREACH

bring, brought, [brung] *Brought* is the standard past tense and past participle of *bring*: 'I brought my lunch'; 'They have brought someone in from the outside'. *Brung* is non-standard.

> 'People all year have brung it up.'
> *Toronto Star* 23 Oct. 1992: B2

(The accepted past participle is *brought*.)

> What was Oscar Goldman's attitude towards the hero who brung 'em over the finish line a winner?
> *Ottawa Citizen* 20 Jan. 1990: F1

(Here *brung* is a deliberate folksy touch.)

bring, take Generally, *bring* indicates a motion towards the speaker or writer; *take*, a motion away from the speaker or writer: 'Please bring me a coffee'; 'Take this upstairs'. Native speakers of English don't often confuse these verbs. But a usage problem arises when the writer shifts his or her point of view without regard for where the reader is likely to be mentally situated, or fails to consider the position and movement of the people or things being described.

> Opposition critics howled indignantly, and South Cayuga residents immediately chartered buses to bring them to a mass demonstration before the Legislature.
> *Harrowsmith* Aug.–Sept. 1985: 32

(Here *bring* may well occur because the sentence starts in the legislature and thus the writer's perspective is situated there, rather than in South Cayuga. However, it would have made sense for the writer to use the residents' point of view: 'South Cayuga residents immediately chartered buses to *take* them to a mass demonstration'.)

> Mark your calendar, check your kids and bring your shopping list—Canada's largest wine festival is ready once more to educate, entertain and delight.
> *Bon Vivant* Aug.–Sept. 1982: 28

(Depending on the point of view, either *bring* or *take* could work here; *bring* implies that the speaker, at least in spirit, will be at the festival.)

Brit see BRITON

Britain, Great Britain, British Isles, United Kingdom *Britain* and *Great Britain* both refer to the island containing England, Scotland, and Wales. The *British Isles* comprise this island, Ireland, and several other islands, including the Isle of Man, the Isle of Wight, and the Channel Islands. The *United Kingdom* (formally, the United Kingdom of Great Britain and Northern Ireland; informally, the U.K.) is a political entity, comprising England, Scotland, Wales, and Northern Ireland, and excluding the Republic of Ireland. Canadian writers often don't distinguish among these terms.

See also BRITON, BRITISHER; IRELAND; SCOTTISH, SCOTS, SCOTCH.

britches see BREACH

British Columbia see APPENDIX I

British Isles see BRITAIN

British North America Act see CONSTITUTION

Briton, Britisher, Brit, Englishman, Englishwoman *Briton*, *Britisher*, and *Brit* are all used to refer to citizens of the United Kingdom. However, most British people prefer to be identified more specifically as English, Scottish, Welsh, or Northern Irish, or, where the noun is required, as Englishmen and Englishwomen, Scotsmen and Scotswomen, and so on.

> Another unheralded Briton, Michael Lankester, will be on the podium, in front of the commercially attractive Montreal Symphony Orchestra.
> *Gazette* (Montreal) 1 Sept. 1990: D7

> Britisher Wally Herbert, himself no slouch in Arctic exploration, presents a meticulous history of self-service gone berserk.
> *Ottawa Citizen* 6 Oct. 1990: J6

> Montrealer Alfred Baumgarten, who was born in Saxony, was the first non-Brit to serve as president of the Hunt Club.
> *Gazette* (Montreal) 14 Sept. 1990: D9

> He can rely on Northern Irish allies to bolster his slim majority of 14 seats.
> *Calgary Herald* 27 Nov. 1994: A10

> Our age has seen the utter decay of the funny Welshman, and the rise to a rivalry in eminence of the Witty Irishman and the Pawky Scot....
> Robertson Davies *A Voice from the Attic* 1960: 210

See also BRITAIN, GREAT BRITAIN, BRITISH ISLES, UNITED KINGDOM; IRELAND, EIRE, ULSTER, NORTHERN IRELAND; SCOTTISH, SCOTS, SCOTCH.

broach, brooch *Broach* is an uncommon noun meaning a skewer or spit. To *broach* something, like a cask, is to punch a hole in it to gain access to the contents; to *broach* a subject is to bring it up for discussion. A *brooch* is an ornamental pin. *Broach* rhymes with *coach*; *brooch* rhymes with *coach* or *pooch*.

He did not broach the politically sensitive question of reducing federal support for pensioners in order to help needy children.
Vancouver Sun 14 Oct. 1994: A19

There was also a little red Santa brooch.
Toronto Star 1 Jan. 1994: A2

A public relations fellow with flowing black curls wore a dashing red tunic, broach at the throat, with a gold chain drooping from the shoulder.
Globe and Mail (Toronto) 14 March 1985: M1

(The correct spelling is *brooch*.)

broke To be *broke* is to have no money. Some commentators label the expression slang, but in fact it is common in fairly formal writing. More formal synonyms such as *destitute* and *impoverished* suggest a more extensive loss of money, possessions, and social standing; being broke is usually only a temporary state, though often a recurrent one.

... O.M. Helgerson was so broke in 1908 he almost had to pawn his watch; but in seventeen months he had made $238,403.87.
Pierre Berton *The Promised Land* 1984: 327

As Wyrick and Owens have observed ... , black female offenders 'usually go to jail because they are broke and they often return to jail because they are still broke.'
Irving M. Zeitlin and Robert J. Brym *The Social Condition of Humanity* 1991: 271

Broke, unemployed, uncaring, I began loitering around magazine stands where I would surreptitiously rip advertising inserts from magazines.
Richard Davies and Glen Kirkland, eds. *Dimensions* 1986: 61

brooch see BROACH

brother-in-law see MOTHER-IN-LAW, IN-LAW

brought see BRING

brunch see DINNER

brunette, brunet *Brunette* is derived from French, which distinguishes between the masculine, *brunet*, and the feminine, *brunette*. Canadian dictionaries list both forms, but the use of *brunet* is largely an American phenomenon; Canadian writers use *brunette* almost exclusively.

Both men and women are called *blond*, but the term *brunette* is applied only to dark-haired white women.

In countless novels written fifty years ago the heroine, having discovered that her husband was deceiving her with the beautiful brunette, crept away to the nursery to weep over her beloved children.
Robertson Davies *One Half of Robertson Davies* 1978: 81

See also BLOND, BLONDE; SEXIST LANGUAGE.

[brung] see BRING

brusque, brusk *Brusque*, meaning abrupt and blunt in speech or manner, is pronounced to rhyme with *tusk* in Canada and the United States. British speakers are more likely to pronounce it with the vowel as in *put* or *boot*.
Brusk is an American spelling variant, rare in Canada and not listed in Canadian or British dictionaries.

Brusque and blunt, Ley was criticized in Hartford for his lack of sensitivity, especially his indelicate handling of the Ron Francis situation.
Vancouver Sun 19 March 1992: D10

buffalo see BISON

bug *Bug* has developed a number of meanings both as a noun and as a verb, some more acceptable than others in writing.
In North America, *bug* is widely used in informal writing to refer to insects, especially when the creatures are regarded as pests. In zoology, *bug* refers to a particular order of insects (Hemiptera), known as 'true bugs'. In Britain, the term is applied only to bedbugs (which are true bugs).
Any disease-causing micro-organism or unspecified virus may be referred to in informal writing as a *bug*: 'She's home from school with a bug'. When that meaning is extended to a newly developed enthusiasm ('He's caught the windsurfing bug') the usage is usually considered slang.
Some authorities have accepted *bug* meaning a defect, especially one in a mechanical device or in computer software, as appropriate to any context.

Bug meaning electronic listening device is considered appropriate to journalism, but not more formal writing. Some newspaper style guides distinguish between *tapping* a telephone and *bugging* a room. As a verb meaning to annoy or pester, *bug* generally is considered slang, more acceptable in casual speech than in writing.

A great admirer of the new mayor was George Brossard, the insect collector whose collection of butterflies and bugs is the basis of the city's Insectarium.
Gazette (Montreal) 26 Dec. 1994: A3

Doctors in Brantford are calling the virus ... a 'California A' bug, but Health Ministry officials say they don't know anything about a California A virus and doubt that one exists.
Globe and Mail (Toronto) 24 April 1985: M1

The bite of the gold bug drove me on.
Atlantic Salmon Journal (Autumn 1990): 27

Many bugs in software development emerge from trying to make one type of program work with other programs or new chips.
Ottawa Citizen 22 Dec. 1994: B5

Her home was bugged, her phone tapped.
Vancouver Sun 29 Jan. 1994: A15

'You're bugging Mrs. Harbison and that bothers me'.
Howard Engel *Murder Sees the Light* 1984: 164

bull, bear, bullish, bearish In the jargon of the stock market, a *bull* buys stocks, anticipating an increase in their value; a *bear* sells stocks, thinking their value may decrease. Thus a *bullish* market is rising and a *bearish* market is falling. Sometimes *bullish* and *bearish* are used more generally to mean optimistic and pessimistic.

[He] is bullish on Canadian stocks for 1995, with expectations of strong earnings growth and dividend increases leading to higher stock prices.
Gazette (Montreal) 31 Dec. 1994: C3

But the strength on the TSE this week isn't fooling ... the consistently bearish technical analyst. . . .
Toronto Star 16 Dec. 1994: E6

Far from conceding defeat, the man who will lead TVOntario into its 25th year is confident, even bullish, about the network's future.
Ottawa Citizen 27 Dec. 1994: C13

Same goes for his bearish buddy, Sheldon (Rob Reiner), an anti-establishment gasbag who prides himself on never having had one of his plays produced.
Toronto Star 4 Nov. 1994: D1

bum see BUTTOCKS

buoy, buoyant In Canada *buoy* is usually pronounced *BOY* (think of *buoyant*, *BOY ant*), although *BOO ee* (rhymes with *chewy*) is also used in some areas, particularly for the noun. American dictionaries list *BOO ee* as the usual pronunciation; British dictionaries give only the *BOY* pronunciation.
Buoy is sometimes misspelled *bouy*.

High Canadian interest rates are also continuing to bouy the dollar, he added.
Ottawa Citizen 9 Aug. 1990: A1

(The correct spelling is *buoy*.)

-burgh, -burg, -borough, -boro All these suffixes mean 'town'. In North American place names, *-burgh* is usually pronounced like *-burg*: *Pittsburgh*, *Newburgh*. The *-burgh* in *Edinburgh*, on the other hand, is pronounced like the *-borough* in *Scarborough* and *Peterborough*: *BUR rub*. The suffix *-boro*, as in *Peterboro Petes*, is an informal variant of *-borough*, mainly used in journalism as a space-saver.

burglary, break and enter, breaking and entering, theft, robbery, larceny Historically and in Canadian law, *burglary* is defined as the act of breaking into a dwelling, at night, with the intention of committing a serious crime, such as murder, rape, or theft. But in everyday usage *burglary* (often misspelled *burglery*) means breaking into a building with intent to steal (see also BURGLE).
Break and enter, as defined in Canadian law, is entry without lawful justification. The official name of the offence in the Canadian Criminal Code is *break and enter*; however, people commonly refer to the offence as *breaking and entering*. Forced entry is not a necessary component of this crime. The onus is on the accused to provide an innocent explanation for trespassing. The term in common use, *breaking and entering*, implies both forced entry and theft. The short form *B and E* is unfamiliar to many law-abiding citizens and should not be used without an explanation.
Theft is a very broad term for stealing that includes shoplifting, fraud, and misappropriation of real estate. A *robbery* is a face-to-face theft that involves intimidation or violence. People and places are *robbed*. Money and valuables are not *robbed* but *stolen* (see also ROB).
Larceny, which means theft of personal property, is a term used more in the United States than in

Canada or Britain, where it is not currently codified in law. Some American states distinguish between *petty* and *grand* larceny on the basis of the dollar value of the goods stolen.

... a visible, barking dog may serve as a deterrent to someone contemplating burglary in your absence, while a dog locked in a basement is no threat.
Dogs in Canada Special Issue 1986: 111

(Here *burglary* is used in the everyday sense.)

Burglery and thefts fell, however, except for car theft which increased 11.6 per cent.
Ottawa Citizen 2 April 1990: A6

(The correct spelling is *burglary*.)

Robbery includes the additional element that the taking must be by force or fear.
J.E. Smyth et al. *The Law and Business Administration in Canada* 1987: 428

Police are searching for leads after two men robbed a person making a bank deposit Monday.
Calgary Herald 28 Dec. 1994: B5

So far about 13,000 cars have been stolen in B.C. this year.... 'Some of these automobiles are worth $20,000 to $30,000 and in the U.S. it's treated as grand larceny.'
Vancouver Sun 22 Dec. 1994: B1

burgle, burglarize   The verbs *burgle* and *burglarize* are both in common use in Canada to mean break into a building to steal. *Burgle* is the more common term in Britain; in the United States *burglarize* is more common.

See also BACK-FORMATION; BURGLARY.

burst, bust   *Burst* is both the past tense and the past participle of *burst*; *bursted* is archaic.

Bust was originally a dialectal variant of *burst*, as *cuss* is of *curse*, but it has developed into a separate word with many meanings that *burst* does not share. For example, to *bust* means to break; *go bust* means go bankrupt; a *bust* is a failure, especially a financial failure. To *get busted* means to be arrested or to be demoted in the military. All these uses of *bust* are slang or informal: they are common in conversation and journalism, but avoided in more formal speech and writing.

... the doors burst open and Gerrit Smith strode into the hall amid tumultuous cheering.
William Teatero *John Anderson: Fugitive Slave* 1986: 122

He's got a busted leg, I said.
Canadian Fiction Magazine 64 (1988): 102

Way down south in Memphis, the 50th anniversary of Elvis Presley's birth on Tuesday turned out to be something of a bust.
Globe and Mail (Toronto) 11 Jan. 1985: E7

She was also famous for being regularly busted for running illegal drinking joints.
Province (Vancouver) 31 Oct. 1990: 2

bury, Sudbury   Rhyming *bury* with *hurry* is dialectal. In Standard Canadian English, *bury* rhymes with *hairy*.

Sudbury, the name of the Ontario city, is pronounced either *SUD BAIR ee* or *SUD buh ree*.

bus, omnibus   The plural of *bus* is either *buses* or *busses*. As a verb, to *bus* means to transport by bus or to set tables and clear dishes in a restaurant. The *-ed* form is *bused* or *bussed* and the *-ing* form *busing* or *bussing*. The *-ss-* spellings are all quite uncommon in Canada.

In the early nineteenth century, the Latin word *omnibus*, meaning 'for all', came into use in English to refer to vehicles that followed fixed routes and were open to everyone. *Omnibus* was soon shortened to *bus*, and today *omnibus* has only two common uses: an *omnibus bill* is a piece of legislation that covers several different items usually relating to one broad issue; an *omnibus* is a book containing several works by one author or on one subject. The plural is *omnibuses*.

'I hope the buses are still running'.
Canadian Fiction Magazine 63 (1988): 117

There are no busses, no taxis, no local trains.
Vancouver Sun 18 July 1992: B10

(The spelling *busses* is correct but uncommon.)

Last year, all the students were bused to school but this November the board said the busing would stop because the children live within the accepted walking distance of 1.6 kilometres.
Gazette (Montreal) 17 Dec. 1992: G1

The Liberal party of Nova Scotia will discuss at its general meeting in November the problems of bussing voters from one constituency to another to give a candidate additional support.
Daily News (Halifax) 21 Sept. 1992: 3

(The spelling *bussing* is correct but uncommon.)

He read Kant (Macmurray's favourite philosopher) when riding on an omnibus.
Eugene Forsey *A Life on the Fringe* 1990: 36

(The use of *omnibus* to mean bus is now rare.)

As Prime Minister Trudeau put it in the famous debate on the omnibus bill to reform the Criminal Code, 'the state has no business in the bedrooms of the nation.'
Janine Brodie, Shelley A.M. Gavigan, and Jane Jenson *The Politics of Abortion* 1992: 40–1

Mystery fans addicted to television series will delight in a huge new affordable anthology called The Television Detectives' Omnibus edited by Peter Haining.
Toronto Star 5 Dec. 1992: S1

bush   see FOREST

bust   see BREAST(S); BURST

but   It is not ungrammatical and is often stylistically effective to begin a sentence with *but*. But it shouldn't become a habit.

Armed with European weapons, tribal warfare became more bloody.... But the real killer in the post-contact period was disease brought to the New World by Europeans.
Robert M. Bone *The Geography of the Canadian North* 1992: 42

But while the choice of theme may have been easy, the theme itself is fantastically difficult.
Northrop Frye *The Bush Garden* 1971: 11

See also ONLY, BUT.

but me, but I   When *but* means 'except', it is normally followed by the object form of the pronoun: 'She asked everyone but me'. However, *but I* is also acceptable if a clause follows: 'Nobody but me will know' *or* 'Nobody but I will know'. Grammarians disagree about whether *but* functions as a preposition ('Nobody except me will know') or as a conjunction introducing an elliptical clause ('Nobody will know—but I will') in such sentences.

He 'has' her in his dreams—she 'has' everyone but him in hers.
Janice Kulyk Keefer *Reading Mavis Gallant* 1989: 124

See also CASE.

buttocks, bum, butt, fanny   The *buttocks* are rarely referred to as such except in the gym or the doctor's office. A host of synonyms substitute for the word in general conversation, including *seat*, *bottom*, *behind*, *backside*, *rear end*, *derrière*, and *keister* (*KEE ster*). In Canadian and British English the noun *bum* has two main senses: buttocks and someone who isn't earning his (usually) or her keep. Many Americans use the word only in the latter sense, and will be puzzled by the former. British English-speakers may well be puzzled by *butt*, North American slang for *buttocks*.

Canadians should also note that *fanny*, just another innocuous synonym for *buttocks* in North America, is rude slang for *female genitals* in Britain.

The first knocked her off her bike and mauled her head, while the other mauled her thighs, buttocks and chest.
Vancouver Sun 9 May 1994: A3

'One parent will mean a whack on the bum once in a while.'
Toronto Star 9 April 1994: J1

I got tired of feeling sorry for myself. I said, 'Come on, get off your butt. There are lots of people worse off than you.'
Toronto Star 6 June 1994: A6

The skirts will stop at any number of places on the leg, from just below the fanny to just below the knee.
Vancouver Sun 28 June 1994: C3

(A speaker of British English might be taken aback by this use of *fanny*.)

bylaw, by-law, byelaw   A *bylaw* is a municipal law or a regulation governing an organization; all these spellings of the term are correct. Canadians use *bylaw* and *by-law* with about equal frequency, but *byelaw* is rare. The prefix *by(e)* means 'town'.

See also ORDINANCE.

byzantine, labyrinthine   *Byzantine* is usually pronounced *BIZZ un teen* in Canada and the United States and *bi ZAN tine* in Britain. The term is capitalized when it refers to a highly decorated style of art and architecture that developed in fifth- and sixth-century Byzantium (present-day Istanbul). The political history of the Byzantine Empire (A.D. 476–1453) has been represented as rife with treachery and double-dealings; hence *byzantine*—usually without an initial capital—has developed the additional meanings of complex and underhanded. Sometimes *byzantine* merely means intricate or extremely complicated. But *labyrinthine* (pronounced *la buh RIN thine* or *la buh RIN theen*) may be a better choice to describe unfathomable complexity that doesn't involve deviousness. *Labyrinthine* is sometimes misspelled *labrynthine*.

> ... Baroque facades, Moorish domes and Byzantine mosaics are combined with strange but spectacular results.
> *Calgary Herald* 12 March 1994: D7

> Certainly Makarios was a wily, byzantine bishop in the tradition of nineteenth-century exarchs, who used the church to build themselves an impregnable power base and manipulate public opinion.
> George Ignatieff *The Making of a Peacemonger* 1987: 216–17

(Here *byzantine* suggests that the bishop was involved in devious political manoeuvring.)

> The Canada Council's granting system is a byzantine process of assessing about 20,000 applicants, only 3,700

of whom are awarded part of the $67-million annual grant fund.
> *Globe and Mail* (Toronto) 21 Sept. 1985: E3

(Here *labyrinthine* might be better.)

> One of them wanted to know how much all the labyrinthine financial calisthenics, stock issues, debenture issues, swaps and divestitures had cost in fees for lawyers, brokers, accountants and other professionals.
> *Gazette* (Montreal) 23 Sept. 1994: C1

> The floor around the bar was covered with dancers, as were the staircases, and the various landings that make up the labrynthine upstairs of the club.
> *Globe and Mail* (Toronto) 7 Sept. 1985: E13

(The correct spelling is *labyrinthine*.)

C

c., ca. see CIRCA

-c, -ck- Many but not all words that end in *-c* add *k* before adding the endings *-ed*, *-ing*, *-er*, and *-y*: *mimicked, frolicking, trafficking, picnickers, colicky*. This indicates that the *c* is pronouced as *k*. Note that in current English *k* is not added before *-al* (*economical, political*); *musickal* is an archaic spelling.

See also ARC; QUEBECKER, QUEBECER.

cacao see COCOA

cactus, cactuses, cacti Most dictionaries give three plural forms of *cactus*: *cactuses, cacti*, and *cactus*. The 'correct' form is a prickly issue for some cactus lovers, but there is no definitive answer. *Cactus* is a scholarly Latin term created in the seventeenth century from the Greek word *kaktos*. *Cacti* is its Latin plural; *cactuses* is the regularized English plural. *Cactus* is the scientific name of this genus of plants. All three forms are used in Canadian writing and all are accepted.

> Ledges along the front glass walls sport angled mirrors, birdcages, and cactuses.

> Alan Tucker, ed. *The Penguin Guide to Canada* 1991: 188

> Among the cacti and the rattlesnakes northeast of Calgary, paleontologists sift through the rocky debris where ancient rivers preserved bones in silt.
> *Maclean's* 5 Dec. 1988: A59

> Then you can wander outside to the garden, which features more than 350 species of cactus, succulents and desert plants.
> *Province* (Vancouver) 16 Sept. 1990: T2

> We headed west for our next vacation, to a land of cactus, jack rabbits, and of course, cowboys—every little boy's paradise.
> *Ottawa Citizen* 18 Aug 1990: H1

See also PLURALS, REGULAR, IRREGULAR, FOREIGN.

Caesar, Caesar salad *Caesar* (pronounced *SEE zur*) is frequently misspelled: note the *a* before the *e*, and the *-ar* ending. *Caesar salad* is apparently not named after Julius Caesar. There are several contenders for the honour; no etymology has been established conclusively.

Though Edison Bros. considered the machines a smash hit, Ceaser's [Palace] didn't.
Calgary Herald 22 Sept. 1994: B8

(The correct spelling is *Caesar's*.)

The scaloppini Tiberti is great, as are the mussels marinara, the Cesar and chef's salads.
Gazette (Montreal) 4 March 1989: T4

(The correct spelling is *Caesar*. Here the misspelling may have been influenced by the French *salade César*.)

See also CAESAREAN.

caesarean, caesarian, cesarean, C-section In the Canadian medical profession, the preferred spelling for the surgical delivery of a baby is *Caesarean* (after Julius Caesar, who is said to have been delivered this way). In general usage *caesarian* and *cesarean* (the form preferred in the United States) are alternative spellings, and the capitalization is unpredictable. Colloquially, and in medical shorthand, the operation is referred to as a *C-section* (the *C* is usually capitalized).

Some usage guides attempt to distinguish between *Caesarean* (or *cesarean*) for the operation and *Caesarian* for anything connected to Julius Caesar or the Caesars. Canadians, however, use both the -*ean* and -*ian* endings to refer to the surgical operation; the second sense of the word is rare.

A doctor orders a caesarean section for a pregnant woman because it's more convenient for her schedule.
Vancouver Sun 15 Sept. 1990: D15

The rate of Cesarean sections [has] been on the rise around the world since the early 1970s....
Gazette (Montreal) 27 Sept. 1994: A7

The number of caesarian sections in Canada is a matter of growing concern....
Globe and Mail (Toronto) 25 Oct. 1985: A18

C-sections are major surgery, and several women told the conference that the possibility of infection or hemorrhage, and the prolonged recovery time, make elective C-sections an unacceptable risk.
Globe and Mail (Toronto) 26 Oct. 1985: A21

See also CAPITAL LETTERS.

cahoots see COLLABORATION

caisse populaire see BANK

Cajun see ACADIA

caldron see CAULDRON

calendar, calender *Calendar*, meaning table of dates, is frequently misspelled *calender*. *Calender* is a separate word with two separate meanings: a machine with rollers used to give paper a glossy finish, or a member of a Sufic order of wandering dervishes.

Mark April 23 on your 1993 calender, because that's the day Quebec's trout-fishing season opens.
Gazette (Montreal) 27 Dec. 1992: D7

(The correct spelling is *calendar*.)

Political parties traditionally receive a large part of their income in the final month of the calender year for income tax reasons.
Daily News (Halifax) 15 Feb. 1992: 4

(The correct spelling is *calendar*.)

Calgary Calgarians usually pronounce the name of their city *KAL guh ree* or *KAL gree*. Other Canadians sometimes say *KAL GAIR ee*.

calibre see GUN

call see PHONE

callus, callous The noun referring to a thick, hardened area of skin can be spelled *callus* or *callous*. *Callous* is also an adjective meaning emotionally hardened or unfeeling. The -*ed* form, spelled *callused* or *calloused*, can refer to either hardened skin or hardened emotions. Some usage guides suggest that *callused* be reserved for the physical sense and *calloused* for the emotional one, but writers ignore this distinction.

Slender, with dark pop-star good looks, in a room of slab-muscled bodies, he looks immature and unused, like a hand without calluses.
Ken Dryden *The Game* 1983: 144

My ankles were like rubber and I developed callouses on them from ankle-walking.
Max Braithwaite *The Night We Stole the Mountie's Car* 1971: 81

Much bad art hides behind Christianity, for to criticize it on purely artistic grounds is to seem callous toward its inspiration....
Robertson Davies *A Voice from the Attic* 1960: 332

(This is the only correct spelling for the adjective *callous*.)

I know how easy it would be to dismiss this, callused as we are to things like drug overdoses.
Vancouver Sun 15 Sept. 1994: A3

He came from a family of peasants and artisans; two grandsons of his brother Jude ... were farmers with calloused hands who owned about twenty-five acres between them.
Queen's Quarterly 92.2 (1985): 342

Prof. Check cites a 1982 study ... showing that males who regularly view pornographic materials became 'calloused' or 'desensitized' in their perceptions of female sexuality.
Globe and Mail (Toronto) 9 March 1985: M7

Calvary, cavalry   *Calvary* is the hill near Jerusalem where Jesus was crucified; it is sometimes used figuratively to refer to a period of terrible suffering. The *cavalry* is the part of an army that fights mounted on horseback or, nowadays, from motorized vehicles.

He walked with a silver-handled cane and in such obvious discomfort that the Italian paper La Repubblicca referred to the visit as his Calvary.
Vancouver Sun 16 Sept. 1994: A14

Only 54 years ago American generals were arguing the merits of cavalry vs. tanks on the battlefield, while Hitler's modern machine of death rolled into Holland, Belgium and France.
Gazette (Montreal) 31 Dec. 1994: H3

It appears that a dashing former calvary officer claims he had a three year love affair with the Princess and that she contemplated leaving Prince Charles for him.
CTV News [transcript] 1 Oct. 1994: n.p.

(The word needed here is *cavalry*.)

He takes time out to rescue a woman ... who has been held up on her way to be with her husband, a Calvary Indian scout....
Ottawa Citizen 15 Oct. 1994: E6

(The word needed here is *cavalry*. *Cavalry* is usually capitalized only in reference to a specific organization. Here the reference to a cavalry unit of the U.S. army is not specific enough to require a capital letter.)

can   see MAY, CAN

Canada, Canadian   *Canada* functions as an adjective in some established names: for example, in familiar names of flora and fauna (*Canada goose, Canada jay, Canada lily, Canada thistle*), and in the names of some boards and corporations (*Canada Council, Canada Development Corporation, Canada*

Labour Relations, Canada Post). However, *Canadian* is the usual adjective form: *Canadian bacon, Canadian football, Canadian Shield*.

In order to make the names of federal government departments similar in both official languages, *Canada* is used as an adjective and placed after the noun: *Environment Canada/Environnement Canada; Revenue Canada/Revenu Canada; Statistics Canada/Statistique Canada*.

Canadian Armed Forces   In 1968 the Canadian Army, the Royal Canadian Navy, and the Royal Canadian Air Force were united under the official designation the *Canadian Armed Forces*. The terms *army, navy*, and *air force* are still used in unofficial contexts. The *Canadian Armed Forces* are also referred to as the *Canadian Forces* or the *Armed Forces*. Unification ensured a single pay and seniority system throughout the Armed Forces; however, some of the traditional naval ranks are still in use. The *Canadian Press Stylebook* contains a useful list of military titles and abbreviations.

Canadian Bill of Rights, Canadian Charter of Rights and Freedoms   The *Canadian Bill of Rights* and the *Canadian Charter of Rights and Freedoms* are both pieces of federal legislation designed to protect citizens against the state, and minorities against the legislative power of majorities. The Canadian Bill of Rights was enacted in 1960, during John Diefenbaker's tenure as prime minister. It applies to federal law only, because it was not ratified by the provinces, and it is not part of the Canadian Constitution.

The Canadian Charter of Rights and Freedoms was enacted in 1982 as part of the Constitution Act (at the time of the patriation of the Canadian Constitution). Strictly speaking, the constitutional Charter of Rights and Freedoms should not be referred to as the 'Canadian Bill of Rights'.

The Canadian Charter of Rights and Freedoms contains what is popularly known as the 'notwithstanding clause'. This clause allows Parliament or a provincial legislature to pass—for a limited period of time—legislation that contravenes the Charter; in other words, invoking this clause means that a federal or provincial statute may operate 'notwithstanding' (i.e., despite) a provision in the Charter. In 1988 Quebec invoked this clause to permit a French-only sign law, which contravened the Charter's guarantee of freedom of expression.

Stroud apparently does not know the Charter is part of our Constitution, and is legally superior to the Bill of Rights. At one point he even confuses the two.
Daily News (Halifax) 27 June 1993: 49

The government has legal advice indicating Quebec could restrict the use of English on signs without resorting to the use of the constitution's notwithstanding clause, the tool it used in 1988 to override the Charter of Rights and Freedoms and ban bilingual signs.
Gazette (Montreal) 25 April 1993: A1

See also CONSTITUTION.

Canadian Shield, Laurentian Shield, Precambrian Shield   All three names are correct for the rock formation that covers about forty per cent of Canada's area. Over time, this formation has been marked by the advance and retreat of glaciers. The Shield arcs around Hudson Bay from the Northwest Territories, through northern Saskatchewan and Manitoba and northern and central Ontario and Quebec, to Labrador and Baffin Island; the area is characterized by muskeg, thin soil, expanses of bare rock, and forest cover (in the south), and contains an abundance of lakes and rivers. The same Precambrian rock formation protrudes in Scandinavia, where it is known as the Baltic Shield.

In the heart of the Canadian Shield, a vast sweep of lakes and forest and mostly rock, it was an area largely unsettled until early this century when rich ore bodies were discovered—nickel and silver mainly to the south and west, gold to the west, iron, lead, zinc, and copper in and around Rouyn—and towns went up as if overnight.
Ken Dryden *The Game* 1983: 67

Hydro's transmission system is also weakened by its location on the Laurentian shield, whose rocky structure resists, rather than absorbs, the geomagnetic voltages.
Gazette (Montreal) 14 March 1990: A6

(*Shield* is usually capitalized.)

Even though most Canadians think the Precambrian shield is a birth control device, territorial integrity (holding on to our northern turf) remains our strongest sustaining myth.
Maclean's 21 Nov. 1988: A49

(*Shield* is usually capitalized.)

cancel out   Several commentators object to the phrase *cancel out* as a wordy synonym for *cancel*. However, *cancel out* conveys ideas not expressed by *cancel*. The phrase *cancel out* is generally used when each of two forces or things acts to offset or neutral-

ize the other. *Cancel out* is also used informally to mean withdraw, as in 'They cancelled out at the last minute'.

Canadians usually double the *-l-* (*cancelled, cancelling*), as do the British; however, Americans prefer single-*l* spellings (*canceled, canceling*).

Powell went on to a fine career in the Attorney-General's office, but when he looks back on the Ballard case, regret almost cancels out the satisfaction of having won.
Jack Batten *Robinette* 1984: 196

We all smiled in friendly fashion—notable because we all knew full well that our two votes were about to cancel out theirs. Or vice versa.
Ottawa Citizen 30 June 1991: F2

Actress Ann Jillian was originally scheduled to speak about breast cancer, but cancelled out for personal reasons....
Toronto Star 23 March 1993: A3

See also DOUBLING THE FINAL CONSONANT.

candelabrum, candelabra, menorah   The plural of *candelabrum* (a candle-holder with several branches) is either *candelabra* or *candelabrums*. In contemporary usage *candelabra* is also well established as the singular, yielding the plural *candelabras*. Dictionaries list all of these forms.

A *menorah* (pronounced *men OR ah*; plural *menorahs*) is a candelabrum—with seven to nine branches—that is a traditional symbol of Judaism.

Candles are lit in a special eight-branched candelabrum known as a menorah—one candle the first night of Hanukkah, two the second night and so on.
Gazette (Montreal) 12 Dec. 1990: A3

The most outrageous candelabra in this show were designed by Colleen Hussey.
Vancouver Sun 20 Dec. 1990: C15

(Here *candelabra* is plural.)

For the final touch, add a prop like a witch's broom, a candelabra for an opera phantom or a cave man's club.
Vancouver Sun 25 Oct. 1990: D3

(Here *candelabra* is singular.)

Greene offers a detailed description of how to make pretzel dough and form it into menorahs (candelabras), stars of David, and other shapes appropriate for Chanukah.
Globe and Mail (Toronto) 4 Dec. 1985: E9

(Here *candelabra* or *candelabrums* would also be accepted.)

See also PLURALS, REGULAR, IRREGULAR, FOREIGN.

cannot, can not Both *cannot* and *can not* are accepted. The single-word spelling is much more common.

> An important component of their argument was that a law which cannot be enforced is a bad law.
> Janine Brodie, Shelley A.M. Gavigan, and Jane Jenson *The Politics of Abortion* 1992: 40

> I would like to suggest that a person simply can not go around labeling groups of people.
> *Ottawa Citizen* 4 Jan. 1991: A10

(Here the word may have been split in order to make *not* more emphatic.)

cannot help, cannot but, cannot help but These three phrases are all used in Standard English to mean 'to be unable to do otherwise than'. Some commentators have criticized *cannot help but* as an illogical blend of *cannot help* and *cannot but*; logical or not, however, it has become an established idiom over the last fifty years, and is now quite common in formal writing.

> A review of a living poet cannot help being written with one eye on the poet: she will read it, whether it's a good review or not, and she will judge us.
> Margaret Atwood *Second Words* 1982: 307

> ... for the originals cannot last, and the copies cannot but lose of the life and truth.
> R. A. Wilson *The Birth of Language* 1937: 149

> Yet anyone who reads Gallant's work cannot help but come to the conclusion that for her there are two kinds of people: the free and the trapped.
> Janice Kulyk Keefer *Reading Mavis Gallant* 1989: 32

Cantonese see MANDARIN

Canuck, Johnny Canuck, Janey Canuck In contemporary usage, *Canuck* (stressed on the last syllable) is a nickname for Canadians generally. However, the term does have a history in Quebec and the northeastern United States of being used in a derogatory way to refer specifically to French Canadians. The origin of the term is obscure; it has been connected to the Iroquoian *kanuchsa*, 'hut'; to the Irish surname *Connaught*, which French Canadians used as a nickname for Irish Canadians; and to the Hawaiian word *kanaka* meaning 'man'. A simpler explanation connects it to the first syllable of *Canada*.

Canuck was first recorded in the mid-1800s. By the turn of the century *Johnny Canuck* was being used to personify Canada in the same way that *John Bull* personifies England and *Uncle Sam* the United States. And by 1901 Emily Murphy, a feminist and the first woman magistrate in the British Empire, had assumed *Janey Canuck* as her pen name. During the Second World War, Leo Bachle created the cartoon character *Johnny Canuck*, who fought the Nazis single-handedly. The major hockey team in Vancouver has been called the *Canucks* since 1946.

> In 1976, Canadian Toller Cranston won the short program and was second in the long but only fourth overall, because he had been fifth in figures. And without compulsories, Canuck Donald Jackson probably would have won the 1960 worlds. ...
> *Canadian Figure Skater* 1991: 30

(Here *Canuck* is simply a synonym for *Canadian*.)

> Martin O'Malley writes an interesting column on nomenclature, but I was disappointed that he did not include the Vancouver Canucks in his 10 worst list. Does he not realize that Canuck is an offensive term to many Canadians? That a Canadian team should bear the name Canucks is one of our lesser national disgraces.
> *Globe and Mail* (Toronto) 21 Jan. 1985: S8

(*Canuck* seems to be a nickname like *Yankee*: it is used both proudly and pejoratively.)

> With so much U.S. programming pouring across the border into Canada, it's about time U.S. viewers got a dose of Canuck culture.
> *Daily News* (Halifax) 2 June 1993: 25

> ... does anyone really think that Joe Canuck, whose care is being funded by the public hospital budget, will get the same care as Sam American, whose illness and care is bringing extra dollars into the hospital budget?
> *Toronto Star* 16 April 1993: A26

(Here *Johnny* has changed his name to *Joe*.)

See also YANKEE.

Canute According to legend, Canute the Great (995–1035), king of Denmark, Norway, and England, once commanded the tide to stop in order to show his sycophantic followers that in fact he was *not* all-powerful. In contemporary popular allusions to the story, Canute's motivation has been altered; he is depicted as a fool vainly trying to defy forces beyond his control. The reader must determine from the context whether an allusion to Canute connotes the wise king or the arrogant fool.

The two symbols come together in the fine opening poem, where the mist is the poet's mortality, like the waves that reminded Canute of the limits of his power.
Northrop Frye *The Bush Garden* 1971: 97

(Frye alludes to the original legend.)

For the court to try to prevent homosexual couples from being treated like conventional families is like King Canute trying to stop the tide.
Vancouver Sun 9 July 1990: A6

(Here the writer alludes to the popular notion that Canute thought he could hold back the tide.)

canvas, canvass   *Canvas* is the usual spelling for the heavy hemp or cotton material used for tents, sails, tote bags, etc. A *canvas* (plural *canvases*) is a piece of canvas prepared for a painting, especially in oils.

To *canvass* means to approach people systematically to solicit something from them, usually money for a charity, their vote in an election, or their opinion on an issue. A round of canvassing is called a *canvass*.

... I went to a boys' camp where we slept under canvas....
Richard Davies and Glen Kirkland, eds. *Dimensions* 1986: 116

Jackson Pollock painted canvases with tubes instead of brushes....
Jack Chambers *Milestones* 1983: 90

... Principal Snodgrass went up and down the country canvassing for endowment funds.
Frederick Gibson *Queen's University* 2 (1983): 3

Building a course entails clearcutting up to 121 hectares of forest near Cypress Provincial Park. Students in the youth alliance plan to canvass door-to-door against the project.
Vancouver Sun 30 Oct. 1990: A2

Clean canvass tents sit on the shore of a thawing fiord hemmed with mountains.
Ottawa Citizen 22 July 1988: C11

(Here the correct spelling is *canvas*.)

capital, Capitol   *Capital* is the spelling used for capital punishment, capital letters, capital cities, and accumulated money.

The *Capitol*, capitalized and spelled with an *o*, is the name of the massive domed building that houses Congress in Washington, D.C., and the elevation it is built on is called Capitol Hill. In some American states, the building that houses the legislature is also named the Capitol.

In antiquity, the Capitol was the Temple of Jupiter, built on the highest of the seven hills of Rome. Capitol Hill was the hub of Roman political life. Thus the name of the American house of government is an allusion to the government of Classical Rome.

The protected harbor was a perfect site for a provincial capital and Simcoe moved his headquarters from Niagara-on-the-Lake.
Toronto Star 1 Jan. 1993: A7

But the Clinton administration must also make sure not to alienate too many Republicans on Capitol Hill.
Ottawa Citizen 10 June 1993: F1

In Virden (oil capitol of Manitoba), it was the first movie in years to play the defunct Derrick Theatre....
Vancouver Sun 20 July 1990: D1

(The correct spelling is *capital*.)

Wisconsin Democrat William Proximire, known on Capital Hill as Senator Scrooge, is not on the American ballot this week.
Maclean's 14 Nov. 1988: A36

(The correct spelling is *Capitol Hill*.)

capital letters   What to capitalize? Style guides devote scores of pages to this question precisely because the answer is so often a matter of preference. In this entry, the established rules of capitalization are presented first; then some points are discussed where current usage is quite variable.

The first word of a sentence is capitalized unless the sentence is enclosed in dashes or parentheses and contained within another sentence:

Levi, on the other hand, writes not with detachment—how could that be possible for a survivor of Auschwitz?—but with a dispassionate lucidity that makes his observations all the more devastating.
Janice Kulyk Keefer *Reading Mavis Gallant* 1989: 178

The first word of a direct quotation is capitalized unless the quotation blends syntactically into the sentence in which it occurs:

Then the Mountie, shaking his head, remarked, 'And all we wanted was to get their names as the one thousandth car to cross the bridge.'
Max Braithwaite *The Night We Stole the Mountie's Car* 1971: 74

Are you telling me that English-speaking Canadians, almost exactly two hundred years later, 'still only grudgingly concede' the right of Claude Jodoin to go to Mass? Eugene Forsey *A Life on the Fringe* 1990: 85

When a reporting clause (e.g., 'Mary said') occurs in the middle of a quoted sentence, the second part of the quotation does not begin with a capital:

'It was awfully sketchy,' he says, 'and it didn't bring home to the jury the accused's side of the story.' Jack Batten *Robinette* 1984: 74

When two full sentences are linked by a colon, the second may or may not begin with a capital. Usually it does not:

The appeals worked: in 1957, the Conservatives came into federal power after twenty-two years as the official opposition. David V.J. Bell *The Roots of Disunity* 1992: 171

Only the first word of the complimentary close of a letter is capitalized: *Sincerely yours, Yours truly, Best regards, All the best*.

All proper nouns are capitalized, including the names of people, languages, religions, countries and their subdivisions, government departments, and organizations.

Noun–number combinations (things designated by number) begin with a capital letter: *Class 7B, Flight 104, Poll 54, Room 206*.

Popular names of geographic regions are usually capitalized: *the Barrens, the Canadian Shield, the Far North, the Gaspé, the Gaza Strip, the Gold Coast, the Maritimes, the Midwest, the Ottawa Valley, the Pacific Rim, the Panhandle, the Prairies, the Sunshine Coast, the West Coast*.

However, descriptions of geographic regions are not capitalized: *northern Alberta, the coast of Labrador*.

Names, scholarly or popular, given to time periods are capitalized: *the Gay Nineties, the Jurassic (period), the Me Decade, the Middle Ages, the Precambrian (era), the Quiet Revolution, the Renaissance*.

However, time periods without specific names are not capitalized: *the eighteenth century, the seventies*.

Names of months, days of the week, and holidays are capitalized. The names of the seasons used to be capitalized but are no longer.

The words *sun, moon*, and *earth* are not usually capitalized. However, they are capitalized, for consistency, when they appear with the names of other planets: 'Mars has two satellites and Earth has one'.

In binomial scientific names of plants and animals only the first term is capitalized: *Sequoia sempervirens* (redwood), *Parus atricapillus* (chickadee).

Common names of animals are not capitalized: *dachshund, gerbil, palomino, robin*. However, proper nouns in the names of species or breeds usually retain their capitals: *Canada goose, Holstein, Labrador retriever, Pekinese, Siamese cat*.

When words such as *company, department, group, unit*, and *university* form part of a name, they are capitalized: *Sales Department, Health Unit, Laurentian University, Ministry of Education*. Subsequent references to 'the department', 'the unit', 'the university', or 'the ministry' usually are not capitalized. The exception occurs in legal writing, where 'the Company', for example, is used throughout a document to designate a specific company named in the preamble.

In the titles of books and works of art, the first word and last word are capitalized, as are the first word and last word of the subtitle, if there is one. All internal words are also capitalized except for coordinating conjunctions (*and, but, nor, or*), articles (*a, an, the*), and prepositions of fewer than five letters: *A Man Called Intrepid: The Secret War; Memoirs of a Bird in a Gilded Cage; Life Before Man*.

Adjectives derived from proper nouns are capitalized when they refer to a specific person or thing: *Roman* (Rome's) *law, Shakespearean* (Shakespeare's) *comedies*.

When such adjectives begin to refer to a type of thing they usually lose their capitals: *quixotic impulses, roman* (vs. italic) *type, venetian blinds*.

But this rule is applied inconsistently. Adjectives of nationality often retain their capital letters, as do adjectives derived from proper nouns in medical terms: *Caesarean section, Dutch oven, Fallopian tubes, Irish coffee, Turkish bath*.

When in doubt about the capitalization of a particular term, you can always look in a dictionary. It's customary to follow the recommendations of one dictionary consistently in a single piece of writing.

Whether the names of people's positions should be capitalized is a matter of some uncertainty. In the past, the names of positions that were considered important were usually capitalized: 'our new Principal' but not 'our new Janitor'. Today the spirit of the times is more egalitarian. The incumbents of very prestigious posts are often referred to in small letters: 'the prime minister', 'the duke', 'the archbishop', 'the president', 'the chief of staff'. Names of high-ranking positions are capitalized consistently only when they are used as titles in front of a person's name:

> On most social and economic issues, Canadians know by now where Prime Minister Brian Mulroney stands.
> *Toronto Star* 2 Jan. 1992: A12

> He spent four years in Ottawa as an economic advisor to the prime minister and minister of finance.
> *Toronto Star* 2 Jan. 1992: A13

However, the Queen is an exception to this democratizing trend. The word *queen* is always capitalized when it refers to the Queen of England and Canada:

> The Rankin Family will be among the guests performing in the presence of the Queen today on Parliament Hill.
> *Daily News* (Halifax) 1 July 1992: 18

But note that the word *queen* is not necessarily capitalized when it refers to the monarch of a foreign country—here, the Queen of the Netherlands:

> Shortly before the queen and prime minister arrived, workers were being hoisted by a giant crane to search for bodies and survivors in apartments next to those plowed to bits by the plane.
> *Toronto Star* 5 Oct. 1992: A3

The variable treatment of *queen* illustrates the principle of relativity in capitalization. Names of positions and official bodies are more likely to be capitalized within their own domains. For example, Canadian newspapers refer to the Canadian *Armed Forces* but the U.S. *army*. Similarly, the in-house newsletter of a corporation or institution is likely to capitalize names of positions (*Vice-President, Personnel Director, Senior Analyst, Trustee*) that would not be capitalized by an outside publication.

Another area where capitalization varies is in the names of races and groups of people. *Black* and *white* usually are written without capitals. *Métis* and *Asian* are capitalized. *Native* and *Aboriginal* are capitalized in Canadian government documents (see ABORIGINAL PEOPLE[S]), though rarely in journalism. Politics can affect people's use of words that identify them. For example, *Black* may be capitalized as a point of pride (just as the word *Loyalist* is often capitalized in Canada), or to designate an ethnic group with a shared culture and common goals. And *Native people* is often capitalized when it parallels *Canadian people*, designating a political entity (see NATIVE).

When capitalization choices seem both arbitrary and sensitive, a writer should aim to be as impartial and consistent as possible. In other words, parallel terms should appear in parallel form in the same piece of writing: *not* 'Anglophone' and 'francophone', 'energy minister' and 'Minister of Finance', 'pope' and 'Dalai Lama', 'Nordic' and 'hispanic'.

See also BLACK; EAST, WEST, NORTH, SOUTH; NEW YEAR'S DAY; SACRED WRITINGS; THE, A, AN.

Capitol see CAPITAL

capitulate To *capitulate* used to mean to surrender only under specified conditions. However, the idea of conditions has disappeared from the current meaning, which is to yield completely.

> The public authorities reiterate their determination not to capitulate to blackmail/terrorism.
> *Calgary Herald* 18 March 1993: A5

> 'I'm hearing that the schools are capitulating to anti-choicers who don't want anything to do with Planned Parenthood.'
> *Calgary Herald* 28 April 1993: B3

capsulated, capsulize see ENCAPSULATE

captivate, capture To *captivate* means to fascinate or enthral ('The children were captivated by the puppet show') while to *capture* means to seize ('It captured their attention'). 'To captivate someone's interest', like 'to fascinate someone's interest', is redundant: *capture* is idiomatic when *attention, interest*, or *fancy* follows as an object.

> Each gesture threw another thread of a gossamer net of fascination around the men. Jack was particularly captivated.
> *Canadian Fiction Magazine* 64 (1988): 29

> The dancer's 30-minute routine captivates the crowd, including one 6-year-old boy who sits on the stage staring with his mouth open wide, hardly believing what his eyes are seeing.
> *Gazette* (Montreal) 5 March 1989: D2

> If a light-loving plant captures your fancy and you don't have enough natural sunlight to suit it, you can add artificial sunlight.
> *Canadian Consumer* Jan. 1986: 15

> This toy will captivate the interest of tots from 12 to 24 months with its simple sorting activity, working levers and peg people.
> *Vancouver Sun* 7 Dec. 1990: F2

(Here *capture* would be more idiomatic.)

carat, karat, caret   A *carat* is a unit of weight (200 milligrams) used for measuring precious stones. A *karat* (sometimes also spelled *carat*) is a measurement of the amount of gold in an object: a 24-karat gold ring is pure gold; an 18-karat gold ring is eighteen parts gold to six parts alloy; a 10-karat gold ring is ten parts gold and fourteen parts alloy, and so on.

A *caret* is a wedge-shaped mark used in copy editing to show where something is to be inserted into a text.

A shipwreck salvor says he has found a 964-carat emerald off the coast of Florida that he believes was once intended as a gift to Queen Isabella of Spain.
Vancouver Sun 5 April 1993: C8

The 22-karat $200 gold coin depicts a gymnast in full flight.
Ottawa Citizen 19 June 1993: J2

'I've seen 14-carat gold pacifiers worn by teenagers.'
Daily News (Halifax) 13 Feb. 1993: n.p.

(The more common spelling for the gold measure is *karat*.)

care   see COULDN'T CARE LESS

careen, career   People and vehicles that lurch from side to side, bounce, bob, or ricochet are said to *careen*; *careen* is also used figuratively to describe erratic thought and behaviour. To *career* means to move rapidly over a course, often out of control. Some commentators suggest that *careen*, unlike *career*, implies a swaying motion; but this distinction seems artificial, since fast-moving objects are quite likely to sway. In many contexts either word will do.

In British English the use of these two words is different. The usual British meaning of *careen* is lean or tip over: for example, a boat is careened for caulking or painting. The North American sense, to proceed erratically, is considered a confusion with *career*.

We can hear the bus coming long before it careens around the corner, reggae music blaring through the windows.
Torch: University of Victoria Alumni Magazine Spring 1990: 17

He careened from stage left to stage right, from front to back, bouncing around like a super-charged pinball.
Globe and Mail (Toronto) 24 Sept. 1985: E3

Gasps of joy turned to screams of terror yesterday as a Metro zoo monorail train lost power, careered backwards and slammed into another train, injuring 27 people.
Toronto Star 12 July 1994: A1

… an eastbound car went out of control, veered left and careered across the centre median.
Vancouver Sun 10 June 1994: B2

(Here *careened* would also be possible.)

carefree, careless   Generally, these two words are distinguished: *carefree* means untroubled, without a care, and *careless* means not vigilant enough, sloppy. In literary usage, however, *careless* is also used as a synonym for *carefree*.

I knew he meant our College quadrangle, for … it had been while he knew it a place of sunshine and of the laughter of the careless youths who play croquet there.
Robertson Davies *One Half of Robertson Davies* 1978: 114

(Here *careless* means free of cares.)

caret   see CARAT

Caribbean   see WEST INDIES

Cariboo, caribou   Historically, *cariboo* and *caribou* were spelling variants, but in this century they are clearly distinguished. *Cariboo* is the correct spelling for the region of the Cariboo Mountains in southern British Columbia, and for things associated with the gold rush of the 1860s, such as 'Cariboo fever' and the Cariboo Road.

Caribou is the correct spelling for the North American reindeer (plural *caribou* or, less often, *caribous*), which once ranged from coast to coast in Canada and as far south as Massachusetts; for the Caribou Inuit, who live west of Hudson Bay (so named because until recently they depended on caribou for food, clothing, and shelter); for the twin-engine airplane made by de Havilland; and for the names of several Canadian towns located outside B.C.

After spending several days touring the city, the more adventurous head to the Island (meaning Vancouver Island), the Southwest, the Cariboo, or the Okanagan.
Alan Tucker, ed. *The Penguin Guide to Canada* 1991: 570

Moose, wolves, and caribou populate the northern forests....
Alan Tucker, ed. *The Penguin Guide to Canada* 1991: 503–4

If after being raised domestically [wolves] are returned to the wild, they will observe caribous with only casual interest; even when they are hungry it never occurs to them that the caribous are potential prey.
Irving M. Zeitlin and Robert J. Brym *The Social Condition of Humanity* 1991: 28

(The more common plural is *caribou*.)

Councillor Ed McMaster of Caribou said he ... agreed the lobsters shouldn't be taken to New Brunswick for processing.
Chronicle-Herald (Halifax) 14 May 1988: 23

(This *Caribou* is in Nova Scotia.)

See also MOOSE.

cariole   see SLED

carnival, Carnaval   *Carnival* is the correct English spelling; *carnaval*, with three *a*'s, is French. The French spelling may be used in English to refer to the annual winter festival in Quebec City (*le Carnaval de Québec*), but only if the word is capitalized.

... Quebec City's winter carnival is the world's third largest outdoor bash, after Rio and New Orleans' Mardis Gras.
Calgary Herald 12 Nov. 1994: F6

We are reminded of this event, the Carnaval de Quebec, with a 14-cent stamp, issued in 1979.
Chronicle-Telegraph (Quebec City) 14 Aug. 1991: 10

But they won't upstage Bonhomme, Carnaval's cheerful mascot.
Gazette (Montreal) 21 Oct. 1994: A5

Caps have Carnaval against Nordiques: Capitals 12; Nordiques 2.
Gazette (Montreal) 7 Feb. 1990: D2

(The choice of *Carnaval* here may well have been a deliberate reference to the festival.)

carousel   see MERRY-GO-ROUND

Carrier, Nat'ooten, Wet'suwet'en, Dakelh, Sekani, Chilcotin, Tsilhqot'in   *Carrier* designates an Aboriginal group of the central interior of British Columbia. Now, although the name *Carrier* is still in use (e.g., the Carrier-Sekani Tribal Council in Prince George), some groups among the Carrier also use Aboriginal names: the *Nat'ooten*, the *Wet'suwet'en* (pronounced *weet SOOH wet an*; occasionally spelled Wit'suwit'en), and the southerly

Dakelh (*doll KEHL*). The languages of these peoples (one of which is called Carrier) belong to the Athapaskan family.

The *Sekani* (*SEK an ee*) are a related people who live to the north of the traditional territory of the Carrier but are associated with them politically.

The *Chilcotin*, now spelled *Tsilhqot'in* (*tsil KOAT in*), whose traditional territory is farther to the south, are closely associated with all these groups. Their language is also Athapaskan (Na-Dene).

Chief Jimmy Stillas was an admired leader of the 525 Carrier and Chilcotin Indians of the Ulkatcho reserve.
Vancouver Sun 9 Dec. 1992: A8

Carrier, spoken in north-central B.C., and Halkomelem, spoken in the Lower Mainland, are about as similar as English and Mandarin Chinese.
Vancouver Sun 12 May 1990: R4

Of 31 distinct indigenous languages still spoken in B.C., Carrier is in the best position [to survive], with 1,679 speakers.
Vancouver Sun 12 May 1990: R3

The Carrier-Sekani Tribal Council represents 12 central interior Indian bands.
Vancouver Sun 11 Aug. 1990: A13

The focus on land gained further strength in the court case launched by the Gitksan-Wet'suwet'en of the Smithers area in the early '80s.
Vancouver Sun 4 Oct. 1994: A13

The creation of Williston Lake to feed the turbines of the W.A.C. Bennett Dam in the late 1960s was the start of a 20-year search for a new way of life for the Sekanis, who hunted in the valleys between the Wolverine Mountains in the Omineca Range and the Rockies.
Toronto Star 18 Oct. 1992: B2

(The names of most Aboriginal groups are not made plural with *s*; *Sekani* would be better here.)

See also GITKSAN.

carryall   see SLED

case   In contemporary English, word order is critical to meaning: 'The man held the child' means something quite different from 'The child held the man'. In some languages, including Old English, endings added to *man* and *child* would distinguish between the actor and the acted upon in these sentences, and word order would not be crucial to the meaning. English nouns gradually lost all their case endings except for the possessive case, which is marked in writing with an *s* and an apostrophe or an apostrophe alone: 'John's book,'; 'the students' essays'. For pronouns three cases survive:

subjective	objective	possessive
I	me	my
you	you	your
he	him	his
she	her	her
it	it	its
we	us	our
they	them	their
who	whom	whose

Sometimes writers are unsure whether to use the subjective or the objective case. The subjective (sometimes called the nominative) case is used for the subject of the sentence ('I will'); the objective (sometimes called the accusative) case is used for the direct or indirect object of the sentence ('Try me'; 'Pass me that section') and after prepositions ('before us').

In speech and informal writing, the objective case is commonly used after the verb *be*: 'It's me'. In formal usage, however, the subjective case is called for because a pronoun that follows the verb *be* is a subject complement, not an object: 'It is I'; 'This is she'. To avoid sounding either ignorant or overly formal, many people respond with 'speaking' when someone asks for them on the telephone.

See also BETWEEN YOU AND ME; MYSELF, I, ME; POSSESSIVE; THAN; WHO, WHOM; WHO'S, WHOSE.

castrate   see NEUTER

catalogue, catalog   Canadian writers prefer the longer spelling. *Catalogue* is the more common spelling in Britain, *catalog* in the United States.

catalyst   In chemistry a *catalyst* is a substance that stimulates change in other substances, but that remains unchanged itself. *Catalyst* is also used metaphorically to refer to a person or thing that acts as a spur or precipitates change. The use of *catalyst* as a synonym for *reason* is disputed.

From last place to a Stanley Cup in four years, it could only happen because, as catalyst and driving force, Orr brought the Bruins along with him.
Ken Dryden *The Game* 1983: 104

Her novels and plays are at one and the same time a reflection of, a tribute to, and a catalyst for the Acadians' struggle to survive culturally against great odds.

Ben-Z. Shek *French-Canadian & Québécois Novels* 1991: 111

... Dormidontov hints getting rid of the Communist-era names was the catalyst for this week's decision to rename every street inside Moscow's Garden Ring, the moving traffic jam that encircles the city centre.
Gazette (Montreal) 13 June 1993: B5

(Here *catalyst* means reason—a use that is disputed.)

catastrophe, catastrophes   Usually, in English, a final *e* is silent, but there are several words borrowed from Greek in which a final *e* is pronounced *ee*, including *anemone, apostrophe, catastrophe, epitome, facsimile, simile,* and *strophe. Catastrophe* and its plural *catastrophes* are sometimes misspelled *catastrophy* and *catastrophies*.

The federal government must toughen standards for oil tankers before Canada's coasts are hit with an environmental catastrophy....
Ottawa Citizen 2 Nov. 1990: A5

(The correct spelling is *catastrophe*.)

We are vulnerable to such vicissitudes of nature as earthquakes, volcanic eruptions, and the like, but catastrophies caused by careless, greedy corporations are criminal and the perpetrators should be tried and convicted by the World Court.
Vancouver Sun 10 April 1989: A6

(The correct spelling is *catastrophes*.)

See also EPITOME.

catchup   see KETCHUP

cater-corner(ed)   see KITTY-CORNER

catholic, catholicity, Catholicism   Spelled with a small *c, catholic* means universal, or embracing all. The noun corresponding to this meaning is *catholicity*.

With a capital *c, Catholic* usually means Roman Catholic, though it can also refer to other Catholic churches, such as the Anglican, Eastern Orthodox, and Philippine Independent, in which an apostolic succession of bishops has been maintained, although the authority of the pope has been rejected. The noun form is *Catholicism*.

[The paper] is designed for people with catholic tastes 'who also watch TV and listen to the radio and may only have a half-hour to read the paper.'
Maclean's 28 March 1988: A61

But she has become a star of far more than the opera house—and one of the keys to that has been the deliberate catholicity of her film recording career (she has more than 65 recordings, films and videos on the market.)
Vancouver Sun 5 June 1993: C10

Protestant extremists retaliated yesterday by shooting and wounding a Catholic driver who was dropping off his child at school.
Financial Post 15 Nov. 1991: 2

Eling thinks he left St. Anne's—a parish that emphasizes the Catholic side of the Anglican tradition . . . in reasonably good shape.
Gazette (Montreal) 2 Jan. 1993: H8

He said he sees no conflict between his Catholicism and his biblical research.
Toronto Star 10 April 1993: A2

There's an evil genius behind this bill. The evil aspect is how it forces separate school systems to choose between a catholicity principle and a monetary interest.
Calgary Herald 21 April 1994: A3

(Here it is a principle of *Catholicism*, not *catholicity*, that is at stake if separate schools accept full public funding.)

catsup   see KETCHUP

catty-corner(ed)   see KITTY-CORNER

cauldron, caldron   Both spellings are correct. Canadian writers prefer *cauldron*. *Cauldron* is more common in Britain, *caldron* in the United States.

caulk   see KHAKI

cavalry   see CALVARY

cay   see QUAY

CCF   see NEW DEMOCRATIC PARTY

C.E.   see A.D.

-ce, -se   *Defence* is the usual choice for British and Canadian writers, especially in references to law or the military: 'The defence presented evidence'; 'Department of National Defence'. The American spelling *defense* is chosen less often, but is common in reference to sports: 'The team had a good defense'. The same pattern exists with *offence*: most Canadian and British writers use *c*; the American spelling is *offense*. Some Canadians may choose *s*, especially for references to sports, and *s* is the usual

choice in the phrase 'no offense taken'. Note that other forms, such as *defensible*, *defensive*, and *offensive*, are never spelled with a *c*.

Canadians spell the noun *licence* and the verb *license*, as do British writers; few use *s* for the noun, in the American fashion. Similarly, most Canadians spell the noun *practice* and the verb *practise*: 'She has a medical practice downtown'; 'He practises the tuba daily'. However, many Canadians spell the verb with a *c*, and this variant is recommended by some Canadian newspaper style guides. The American spelling is usually *practice* for all forms.

Pretence and *pretense* are both used by Canadians, while British writers prefer the *c* and American writers prefer the *s*.

See also ADVICE, ADVISE; SPELLING, CANADIAN; VICE, VISE.

-ceed, -cede, -sede   The endings of *proceed* and *precede* are often confused, with the result that either or both are misspelled. The correct spelling of the noun *procedure* probably reinforces the tendency to misspell *proceed*.

Only three English words end in *-ceed*: *exceed*, *proceed*, and *succeed*. The more common ending is *-cede*, as in *accede*, *concede*, *intercede*, *precede*, *recede*, and *secede*. All these words are derived from the Latin *cedere*, 'to go'.

Supersede is the only word that ends in *-sede*. *Supersede* is derived from the Latin words *sedere*, 'to sit', and *super*, 'on top of'.

If 1,000 employees don't leave voluntarily, then the company will procede with layoffs.
Vancouver Sun 1 Nov. 1990: C6

(The correct spelling is *proceed*.)

He learned how to count money and transact business in some of the many Black communities that had become so numerous in Upper Canada in the two decades preceeding the American Civil War.
William Teatero *John Anderson: Fugitive Slave* 1986: 16

(The correct spelling is *preceding*.)

Wrongly, Peterson allowed the interests of the Liberal party to supercede those of the province.
Ottawa Citizen 16 Sept. 1990: A11

(The correct spelling is *supersede*.)

CEGEP   see UNIVERSITY

celebrant, celebrator The original and still current meaning of *celebrant* is one who performs a religious rite, particularly the Christian Eucharist. Some object, therefore, to the use of the word to describe participants in less solemn celebrations. However, *celebrant* is widely used to describe people engaged in private festivities or public revelry. *Celebrator* is an accepted alternative for those objecting to the non-liturgical use of *celebrant*.

At noon, there is a sung eucharist in the ruined nave of the abbey. The celebrant and preacher will be the bishop of Ramsbury.
Canadian Churchman April 1986: 15

Irreverent poet emeritus, reverent celebrant of being alive, Purdy refuses to succumb to emotional or intellectual sclerosis....
Vancouver Sun 7 July 1990: D19

When several hundred celebrants took over Georgia Street, ... police quickly blocked off that portion of the street and rerouted the cars of more honking fans past the area.
Globe and Mail (Toronto) 25 Nov. 1985: C2

Provincial Culture Minister Karen Haslam stunned celebrators at an Art Gallery of Ontario open house last night by announcing a $2 million increase to the AGO's operating grant.
Toronto Star 22 Jan. 1993: A1

Celsius, centigrade, Fahrenheit The terms *Celsius* and *centigrade* refer to the same temperature scale, in which zero is the freezing point of water and 100 the point at which water boils. Since 1948, this scale has been officially called *Celsius*, after Anders Celsius (1701–44), its Swedish inventor. This is the scale of the international metric system, adopted by Canada in 1971.

Most Canadians are also familiar with Fahrenheit temperatures because they're still used in cooking, in measuring the temperature of the human body (at least outside the hospital setting), and in American weather reports. On the Fahrenheit scale, named after the German physicist Gabriel Fahrenheit (1686–1736), the freezing point of water is 32°F and its boiling point is 212°F.

The abbreviation for degrees Celsius is °C; for degrees Fahrenheit, °F. Newspapers omit the degree symbol (°), probably because it's not a character on the keyboard.

Mean July and January temperatures at Old Crow are 14.2 and -33.1°C, respectively, and mean annual temperature is -10.1°C.
Canadian Journal of Botany 67.4 (1989): 954

Bake at 350 F for 25 to 30 minutes.
Vancouver Sun 30 June 1992: C3

Celt, Celtic, Kelt, Keltic, Anglo-Celtic Both *Celt* and *Kelt* are correct, but *Celt* is far more common. The initial letter may be pronounced either *k* or *s*, although some object to the *s* pronunciation. The name of the Boston Celtics, an American basketball team, is always pronounced *SELL* tics.

The *Celts* were the first Indo-European people to inhabit Europe and the British Isles. In modern times the term refers to the Irish, Scottish, Welsh, and Cornish people of Britain, as opposed to the English, who are descended from a later group of Indo-European invaders, the Anglo-Saxons. Among the Celtic languages are Irish or Irish Gaelic (formerly referred to as Erse), Cornish, Welsh, and Scottish Gaelic.

In Canada, the umbrella term *Anglo-Celtic* often refers to Canadians of British descent, as opposed to those whose ancestors came from outside the British Isles.

It is often assumed that every region but Ontario has an authentic voice, just as it is assumed that every group but the Celts and Anglo-Saxons have loveable ethnic peculiarities and every city but Toronto has a soul.
Margaret Atwood *Second Words* 1982: 294

Every immigrant who arrived in the West was expected to accept as quickly as possible the Anglo-Celtic Protestant values of his Canadian neighbours.
Pierre Berton *The Promised Land* 1984: 59

A surprise in the Dictionary of Afro-American Slang is the variety of expressions for whiteys like me. Cracker, honkey, kelt, hayeater, paddy and pale all mean the same thing: a white person.
Gazette (Montreal) 10 March 1990: J2

See also WASP.

cement, mortar, concrete *Cement* is a fine grey powder made by burning limestone and clay. Mixed with sand and water, cement makes *mortar*, the paste used to hold bricks in place; when gravel is added to the mixture, the rock-hard substance it sets into is called *concrete*. Technically speaking, finished sidewalks and building foundations are not cement but concrete.

Cement also is used to refer to any paste- or glue-like substance used to fasten things together. It may be a verb as well as a noun, and is also used figuratively.

> The 105 were arrested after a blockade Feb. 7 at the clinic, a windowless cement building located in a quiet residential area.
> *Gazette* (Montreal) 1 March 1989: F12

(Strictly speaking, the building is *concrete*.)

> Starting a business isn't going to help cement a marriage.
> *Calgary Herald* 7 Nov. 1994: C1

censor, censorship, censorial, censorious, censure   To *censor* means to cut offending sections out of a play, film, letter, exhibition, or publication, etc., or to ban it entirely. The noun is *censorship*; those who exercise it are called *censors* and have *censorial* powers. People who constantly criticize others are described as *censorious*.

Censure is strong disapproval or harsh criticism; a book may be *censured* by critics without being *censored*.

> 'At one time, the pressures to censor were largely from fundamentalist sectors of the community. Now they are also coming from the feminist sector and minorities....'
> *Daily News* (Halifax) 28 Sept. 1994

> Many critics censured Sassafras, Cypress and Indigo for what they described as its deliberately alienating style.
> *Toronto Star* 24 Dec. 1994: G17

> He questioned whether school councils might be allowed to censure library books....
> *Calgary Herald* 4 Dec. 1994: B2

(The word required here is *censor*.)

> Eventually the activists made their point, helped by the threat of civil servants' censorious scissors snipping at advertising copy.
> *Globe and Mail* (Toronto) 25 Oct. 1985: n.p.

(Here *censorial* would be more appropriate.)

centigrade   see CELSIUS

centre, center   *Centre* is the British spelling and *center* the American. Generally, Canadian writers use *centre* when referring to a place, such as a shopping mall, a housing complex, or an entertainment or research facility. In the Prairie provinces, however, where spelling tends towards American

practice, *center* is more often found for places: for example, the Canadian Plains Research Center, in Regina.

For the meaning *midpoint*, Canadians use *center* or *centre* with equal frequency in all kinds of writing. The same is true of the verb, and all three possible spellings of the present participle are found in Canadian writing: *centering*, *centreing*, and *centring*.

> Raymond put the Redmen on the scoreboard 38 seconds into the second on a centering pass from defenceman Bryan Larkin.
> *Gazette* (Montreal) 2 March 1989: B4

> ... his soft centreing attempt hit Lindbergh's skates and slid in behind him.
> *Globe and Mail* (Toronto) 24 April 1985: S2

> Above the dinner tables floated clusters of blue and white balloons attached to a block of ice, centring the table....
> *Gazette* (Montreal) 6 March 1989: F3

See also -RE, -ER; SPELLING, CANADIAN.

centre around   *Centre around*, as in 'Discussion centred around job parity', is a widely used idiom. Nevertheless, some authorities have criticized the expression as illogical (because a centre is a point). To avoid criticism, in formal writing you may want to use *centre on*, or an expression such as 'focus on' or 'revolve around'.

> Most of these techniques centre around preparing the bird, physically and mentally, for a life in the wild....
> *Harrowsmith* Jun.–Jul. 1985: 58

(Here *revolve around* might be better.)

> The 1922 strike ... was clearly seen by management as centring around the general question of control at the point of production, rather than the narrower racial issue.
> *Queen's Quarterly* 92.1 (1985): 227

(Here *focusing on* might be better.)

centripetal, centrifugal   Forces tending towards the centre of a circle are *centripetal*. Forces tending outwards from the centre of a circle ('fugitive' from the centre) are *centrifugal*. Centripetal force pulls objects into the middle of a whirlpool. Centrifugal force makes it hard to stay on a curved highway ramp at high speeds. In both words the second syllable should be stressed: *sen TRIP it ul*; *sen TRIF yoo gul*.

> He describes the provinces as 'quasi-nations,' each struggling to hang on to its autonomy and way of life. As

economic forces push them toward integration, pride compels them to resist this centripetal pull.
Toronto Star 25 May 1993: A23

Tarah drops her gloves on the ice to get a better grasp on a friend's hands and they spin until the centrifugal force flings them in separate directions.
Ottawa Citizen 23 March 1993: C3

ceremonial, ceremonious Objects and occasions for ceremonies are *ceremonial. Ceremonious* means ritualistic, or formal and polite.

West Coast Indians were North America's greatest native artists, crafting totem poles, elaborate longhouses, carved dishes, ceremonial masks, drums, rattles, and household items.
Alan Tucker, ed. *The Penguin Guide to Canada* 1991: 537

In Provence, the Occitan dialect is no more than a folkloric prop, fetched from the cultural attic to furnish the odd ceremonial gathering with a few token phrases.
Gazette (Montreal) 27 June 1993: B1

In its early years, the business of the Royal Trust was conducted in formal and ceremonious ways.... Porters, in red uniforms, stood at its door.
Gazette (Montreal) 30 Jan. 1993: B4

It has a postmodern design, and a waiter named Hugo whose style is grave and ceremonious. Hugo serves me my $3 lunch with style, as though we were both at the Ritz in Madrid....
Gazette (Montreal) 15 April 1992: C1

The history books record no ceremonious flip of a switch, no speeches, no figurative smack on the bottom for the infant technology known as FM.
Province (Vancouver) 20 May 1990: 78

(Here *ceremonial* would be better.)

cesarean   see CAESAREAN

chaff, chafe, chafing dish   The noun *chaff* refers to the husks of seed or grain, or anything considered light and worthless. The verb to *chaff* means to tease good-humouredly.
The verb to *chafe* means to rub, often painfully, against skin, or to vex, or to grow irritated. A *chafing dish* is a dish in which food can be cooked or kept warm at table. This device is not new: *chafing dish* has been part of the vocabulary of English since the fifteenth century, when one of the meanings of to *chafe* (from Old French *chaufer*) was to warm.

There, several rings of men surrounded the wheat, and with flails beat the grain loose from the chaff.

Geoffrey Ursell *Perdue: And How the West Was Lost* 1984: 58

'A lot of it is junk,' admits Rayner of The Women's Bookstore—but a lot of it is anything but, she adds. You learn in time how to separate the wheat from the chaff.
Ottawa Citizen 27 June 1992: B3

Rub off the chafe of Freesia seeds and soak them 24 hours before sowing.
Daily News (Halifax) 8 March 1992: 37

(The word required here is *chaff.*)

As the Cowans made their book tour, they found that the men in television camera crews they worked with would chaff each other about such things as never learning how to operate the dishwasher.
Toronto Star 23 May 1992: J1

Most have a slightly higher crew neckband to conceal the collarbone and prevent chafing at the neck from the jacket.
Ottawa Citizen 19 March 1992: G2

He graduated to writing editorials and investigative features, but soon chafed at the constraints of a daily paper.
Saturday Night Feb. 1986: 10

The wool chaffing my legs made a rash of my pride.
Vancouver Sun 1 Feb. 1992: D4

(The word required here is *chafing.*)

Brides were inundated with chafing dishes, trays, bowls, pitchers and ice buckets....
Ottawa Citizen 2 May 1992: I16

chairman, chairwoman, chairperson, chair
Chairman is still commonly used to refer to a man or woman in charge of a meeting or organization, although many people object to this usage as sexist. *Chairwoman* is a better choice when a woman is in charge, but this term still links the job to the sex of the incumbent. *Chairperson* and *chair* are recommended and gaining popularity as gender-neutral designations. While *chairperson* dates from the 1970s, the use of *chair* to refer to someone in charge of a meeting dates from as early as 1658 (*OED*).

Steley is a wife and mother, co-acting chairman of the Canadian Craft Museum and an urban planner.
Vancouver Sun 20 Dec. 1990: F1

(A better choice would be *chair* or *chairperson.*)

Maryann Bird, chairwoman of council's race-relations committee, recommended that rental of all public buildings be reviewed.
Province (Vancouver) 2 May 1990: 10

A lawyer from the Canadian Environmental Law Association is studying the situation, said Michael Murphy, co-chairperson of the Gloucester Wetlands Action Committee.
Ottawa Citizen 13 June 1990: B4

Ruth Lotzkar, chair of the B.C.-based Environmentally Sound Packaging Coalition, supported green taxes for 'problem products' like tires and batteries....
Vancouver Sun 20 April 1990: B3

Until recently, he was a member of the board of directors and chair of the finance committee.
Rites Feb. 1990: 5

See also JOB TITLES; SEXIST LANGUAGE.

chaise longue, chaise lounge, lounge chair A chair you can stretch your legs out on—usually a piece of lawn furniture—is a *chaise longue* (plural *chaise longues* or *chaises longues*). The expression is borrowed from French and means 'long chair'. Since a long chair invites lounging, the French word *longue* was soon confused with the English word *lounge*, and many Canadians call this piece of furniture a *chaise lounge*. Both Canadian and American dictionaries list *chaise lounge* as a variant of *chaise longue*. British dictionaries do not. *Chaise longue* is the only form accepted in Britain, and there the term is most likely to refer to a piece of indoor furniture, a sofa with only one arm and a back along part of its length.

Happily, the whole issue of the correct form of this expression can be avoided by calling the object in question a *lounge chair*.

At the far end of her balcony Shier has created a restful nook for herself with a chaise longue hidden from the sight of rows of balconies that proliferate in her neighborhood.
Gazette (Montreal) 4 June 1992: C1

Her only concession to her growing health problem was a chaise lounge in her dressing room.
Daily News (Halifax) 28 March 1992: 18

Picture yourself stretched out on a lounge chair by a sparkling pool in a lush tropical setting and then tell me spring break is only for kids.
Gazette (Montreal) 27 Feb. 1992: G8

See also FOLK ETYMOLOGY.

challenged   see DISABILITIES

chamois, shammy A *chamois* (usually pronounced *SHAM ee*) is a very soft, supple piece of leather often used for polishing shoes, cars, or blackboards. The plural (*SHAM eez*) is spelled the same as the singular: *chamois*. *Shammy* is an informal spelling.

Originally, *chamois* were made only from the hide of a goat-like antelope of Europe and Western Asia called the *chamois*, though now they are also made from the skins of other animals and even from cotton. The name of the antelope, and occasionally the name of the leather, is pronounced *sham WAH*.

A recent tour of several Marks & Spencer stores turned up such fashion steals as a fabulous three-quarter-length, flange-shouldered wool jacket with chamois underlining....
Globe and Mail (Toronto) 20 Aug. 1985: F10

In a room filled with shammy vendors and encyclopedia salesmen, Starkey throws no pitch, wears no throat mike.
Province (Vancouver) 22 Aug. 1990: 16

champ at the bit   see CHOMP

character, personality, reputation   *Character* usually refers to distinctive moral and mental qualities ('a strong character'), *personality* to social relations ('a charming personality'), and *reputation* to society's perception of someone ('She has a reputation for efficiency'). Conceivably, someone with a sterling character might have a boring personality and an undeservedly bad reputation.

Despite objections from some usage commentators, *personality* is now fully established as a synonym for *celebrity*.

Character is informal when used to mean a person with an original or eccentric personality.

Former major league pitcher Rick Rhoden vaulted to the lead of the Chrysler Celebrity Classic yesterday at Emerald Hills Golf and Country Club and that's bad news for the other 67 sports and entertainment personalities in the field.
Toronto Star 26 June 1994: E6

'You just mention his name and they start talking about him.... Apparently, he was quite a character.'
Vancouver Sun 11 June 1992: A12

charades, charade   The guessing game involving pantomime is called *charades*. In the singular, the term is used figuratively to mean an obvious pretence or grotesque imitation. *Charade* is usually pronounced *sha RAID* in North America and *sha RAHD* in Britain.

New Democratic Party external affairs critic Pauline Jewett said her party believes the committee would be 'a charade, a mockery'....
Globe and Mail (Toronto) 16 May 1985: P4

Still, she doesn't feel like going through the charade of nodding and smiling; not right now.
Margaret Atwood *Life Before Man* 1979: 285

Charter of Rights and Freedoms   see CANA-DIAN BILL OF RIGHTS

Charybdis   see SCYLLA

chastise   *Chastise* is the standard spelling in Canada, the United States, and Britain. *Chastize* is an obsolete spelling variant that still occasionally finds its way into print.

Five years after the fact, a Federal Court judge has chastized the federal government for its footdragging in releasing studies on the impact of free trade with the United States.
Vancouver Sun 31 Aug. 1990: A15

(The usual spelling is *chastised*.)

Consequently, the educator needs to be publicly chastized for his failure to promote a high standard of language.
W.C. Lougheed, ed. *In Search of the Standard in Canadian English* 1986: 75

(The usual spelling is *chastised*.)

See also -IZE, -ISE.

chauvinism   see SEXISM

cheap, cheaply   *Cheap* is used in all kinds of Canadian writing to mean inexpensive or low-priced ('cheap parking', 'a cheap airline ticket'); these meanings do not have negative connotations. When applied to goods or accommodations, however, the word may also suggest shoddiness or inferiority. The context should make the connotation clear. Where it doesn't (as in 'They booked us into a cheap hotel') you may want to choose a different word.

Applied to people, *cheap* is both informal and derogatory, meaning ungenerous or stingy. *Cheap* is also very negative, suggesting unfairness, in the expressions 'cheap shot' and 'cheap trick'.

Cheap commonly precedes words like *price, cost, rate,* or *rent,* especially in informal writing. But this usage is also commonly criticized and best avoided in formal writing. Commentators argue that it is the item, service, or accommodation that is *cheap*; the cost, rate, or rent is *low*.

Cheap is also used as an adverb, most often in expressions such as 'come cheap', 'buy cheap', and 'get something cheap'. Some writers substitute the regular adverbs form, *cheaply*, in these contexts, but *cheap* is idiomatic and widely accepted.

Unlike most of his contemporaries, Wilson in particular, who had established the prewar plan in expectation of a short, cheap war, Kitchener believed in a long, costly conflict requiring mobilization of the resources of the British Empire.
Canadian Journal of History 14.1 (1989): 55

Try Vivaldi, which has reasonably satisfying Italian food and striking decor, or the Mazurka, a cheap and excellent Polish restaurant....
Alan Tucker, ed. *The Penguin Guide to Canada* 1991: 201

House parties tend to be a jumble of friends, relatives, neighbors and business associates who don't know each other scarfing bad canapes [and] cheap sparkling wine....
Gazette (Montreal) 30 Dec. 1990: A3

Eventually, nothing else mattered and the company began offering consumers a selection of cheap, shoddy products.
Gazette 8 Dec. 1990: D1

This sounds like a lot, but it's only 2.5 per cent of the government's annual payroll—a cheap price for fairness and justice.
Vancouver Sun 20 March 1990: A17

(In formal writing, *low price* would be better.)

The town bought the power at the cheap 1905 price and sold it to its citizen users at attractive prices that still yielded it a large profit.
J.E. Smyth et al. *The Law and Business Administration in Canada* 1987: 331

(Here some commentators would prefer *low*.)

But it's a thrill that doesn't come cheap.
Vancouver Sun 8 Oct. 1994: A21

Miracles don't come cheaply.
Spectator (Hamilton) 13 June 1994: B2

(Here *cheap* would also be acceptable.)

See also ZERO ADVERBS.

cheque, check, chequered, checkered   Canadian writers overwhelmingly prefer the spelling *cheque* for the bank draft, although they use *check* for all other senses of the noun ('a thorough check', 'check mark', 'the check for the meal') and verb ('Check it first').

Canadians prefer *checkered* ('a checkered table-cloth') over *chequered*, although both spellings are used.

The British also use *cheque* for a bank draft, but prefer *chequered* for the pattern. Americans rarely use the *-qu-* spellings, preferring *check* for all senses and the adjective *checkered*.

See also SPELLING, CANADIAN.

chest   see BREAST(S)

chesterfield, sofa, couch, davenport, divan, settee, settle   Canadians have several names for an upholstered piece of furniture with a back and armrests that seats more than two people, or on which one person can recline. *Chesterfield* is a Canadianism that emerged in the 1920s but has been declining in use since the 1970s. Of the 300 informants in the 'Survey of Vancouver English' (1984), 72 per cent gave *chesterfield* as one name for such an object and 30 per cent reported it as the only word they would use. However, age was an important factor in these results, since younger informants overwhelmingly preferred *sofa* or *couch*. Of these two terms, *couch* has connotations of serviceability and comfort, while *sofa* may suggest a more fashionable piece of furniture.

Davenport, divan, settee, and *settle* are also used by Canadians, but only rarely. A *settle*, strictly speaking, is a straight-backed wooden bench with armrests and a storage cupboard under the seat.

One by one, tiny babies were brought to the largest chesterfield in the house and plopped down in a row.
Vancouver Sun 23 June 1994: C10

Originally they had planned to create an interior design around their striped living-room sofa....
Gazette (Montreal) 26 May 1994: D1

Some say we should throw our remotes into the recycling bin and go back to the old days, when changing a channel involved walking from couch to set, twisting a knob, and returning, on foot, to couch.
Calgary Herald 26 June 1994: E8

See also CHAISE LONGUE.

Chicana, Chicano   see HISPANIC

Chilcotin   see CARRIER

childish, childlike, infantile, juvenile   The connotations of *childish* are usually negative, while those of *childlike* are usually positive: 'His childish fear of social encounters was the negative side of the

childlike simplicity everyone admired'. *Childish* can, of course, be neutral if the person being described is actually a child.

Infantile and *juvenile* are neutral when used of children, especially in scientific, legal, or sociological writing, but are often even more derogatory than *childish* when applied to adults.

Crankiness is an issue when working with child actors (and childish adults, but that's another story).
Gazette (Montreal) 15 May 1994: F1

He has worked for Holland America since 1986, travelling the world, collecting artifacts and satisfying a curiosity that is quite childlike in its intensity and innocence.
Vancouver Sun 8 July 1993: B5

I looked back to the two apple-cheeked girls in the doorway ... and I saw that their faces shone with a childish innocence, unabashed as they were by the attention they were provoking from the audience....
Canadian Fiction Magazine 64 (1988): 129

(In this description of children, *childish* is not derogatory.)

Some of them did a good deal to form my own infantile imagination, and I could well have fared worse.
Northrop Frye *The Bush Garden* 1971: 234

(Here *infantile* refers to an early stage of development.)

She also does a wonderful takeoff on a motherly Queen Elizabeth demanding the constitution back from some squabbling, infantile Canadian politicians.
Gazette (Montreal) 13 July 1990: F4

The works include two novels, two books of poetry, a juvenile novel and one book of photography.
Calgary Herald 11 June 1994: A17

(Here *juvenile* means 'written for children' and is neutral.)

We have all seen these juvenile dotards whose boast is that they are just as young as their sons or their grandsons; they do not realize what a pitiful boast that is.
Robertson Davies *One Half of Robertson Davies* 1978: 128

chimera, chimaera   A *chimera* (rarely, *chimaera*) is a Greek mythological monster with a lion's head, a goat's body, and a serpent's tail. By extension, it can be any horrid vision, mere illusion, or unrealizable fantasy. In this century biologists have appropriated the term for organisms containing genetically different tissues, formed by grafting or mutation. The *ch* in *chimera* is pronounced like a *k*, and the *i* can be either long or short: *kih MEAR uh* or *kye MEAR uh*.

Haliburton seems to have believed that the ideal for Nova Scotia would be a combination of American energy and British social structure, but such a chimera, or synthetic monster, is hard to achieve in practice.
Northrop Frye *The Bush Garden* 1971: 218

Down a concrete driveway, inside an open stall, is a chimera, a Friesen cow with Hereford markings.
NeWest Review Feb.–Mar. 1990: 10

See also -AE-, -OE-, -E-.

Chinese names When discussing Chinese names, the terms *first name* and *last name* inevitably lead to confusion. *Given name* and *family name* are preferable. In China a person's family name comes before his or her given name. For example, Mao Zedong's given name was Zedong; and if Eleanor Smith were a Chinese name, it would be written Smith Eleanor. (In fact, the practice of putting family names first is common in other countries where Chinese is spoken or Chinese characters are used in writing, such as Japan, Korea, and Vietnam.) Most, though not all, Chinese people living in Canada have reversed the order of their names to conform to the Western convention of putting the given name first. One way of indicating that the first name after the title is the family name is to capitalize it ('Mr. CHAN Siu Kan'). Women do not normally take their husbands' family names in China, but some Chinese-Canadian women do. Each woman's preference should be followed.

See also MANDARIN; PINYIN.

Chinese writing   see PINYIN; MANDARIN

Chipewyan, Chippewa The *Chipewyan* (pronounced *chip uh WYE un*) are an Aboriginal people whose traditional territories are in northern Manitoba, Saskatchewan, and Alberta and the southern Northwest Territories. *Chipewyan* is also the name of their language, which belongs to the Athapaskan (or Na-Dene) language group. Most of these people now also identify themselves as Dene or as members of the Dene Nation. (*Dene* is a word from their own language, while *Chipewyan* is the name the Cree called them).
Chipewyan can stand for both the singular and the plural noun, as with most terms for an Aboriginal group; *Chipewyans* is less common.
Chippewa (pronounced *CHIP uh waw*) and *Ojibwa* are two names for the same Aboriginal people. They speak Ojibway, an Algonquian language, and

their traditional territory is in Ontario around the shores of Lake Huron. Although most names designating Aboriginal groups do not need to be pluralized with *s*, *Chippewas* is accepted (*Globe and Mail Style Book*).

Matonabbee and his Chipewyans ranged a vast hunting territory, extending from Hudson Bay to the Arctic Ocean to Great Slave Lake.
Robert M. Bone *The Geography of the Canadian North* 1992: 53–4

(Some writers would avoid *Chipewyans* here by using a phrase like 'Chipewyan hunters'.)

The success of [Samuel Hearne's] amazing journey was due to Chipewyan knowledge of the land and animals.
Robert M. Bone *The Geography of the Canadian North* 1992: 53

This week, Consumer and Commercial Relations Minister Marilyn Churley announced that Orillia's Chippewa of Rama First Nation have been given a licence to build a casino.
Toronto Sun 8 Dec. 1994: 22

The band, members of the Chippewa Nation, have been fighting for 50 years for the return of 2,200 acres of their reserve, expropriated in 1942 for Camp Ipperwash.
Toronto Sun 24 Feb. 1994: 51

See also ATHABASCAN; DENE; OJIBWA(Y)

chomp, champ at the bit Canadians who *chomp* at the bit may slightly outnumber those who *champ* at it, but either word is correct in this idiom, which means to be impatient or eager to begin something. *Champ* and *chomp* are variants. *Champ* is the older word, dating from the sixteenth century. *Chomp* was a British dialect form that became predominant in Canada and the United States in the nineteenth century, and is now competing with *champ* in Standard British English. In Canada, the verb *champ* survives only in the idiom *champ at the bit*; indelicate chewing is always called *chomping*.

Unscrupulous car salespeople like nothing more than wide-eyed customers who chomp at the bit to buy a car.
Canadian Consumer March 1986: 5

People were champing at the bit to play the video gambling games.
Toronto Star 5 Jan. 1992: B1

See also STAMP, STOMP.

choose, chose Both the present tense and the infinitive form of *choose* are sometimes incorrectly spelled *chose*. This confusion may arise because the rhyming word *lose* is spelled with only one *o*. *Chose* is the past tense.

> Whatever path you choose to building a pension, start soon.
> *Canadian Consumer* Jan. 1985: 14

> Of the 11 players they chose Wednesday, the most promising may be Clark.
> *Calgary Herald* 30 June 1994: C2

> His 28-year-old wife, Nancy, said she and many of the other navy wives found it depressing trying to chose presents for their husbands.
> *Vancouver Sun* 20 Dec. 1990: A1

(The correct spelling is *choose*.)

> Pro-choice discourse advocates women's right to chose while pro-life advocates the primacy of the right to life of the foetus.
> Janine Brodie, Shelley A. M. Gavigan, and Jane Jenson *The Politics of Abortion* 1992: 70

(The correct spelling is *choose*.)

chord see CORD

Christian name see FIRST NAME

chronic, acute The word *chronic* characterizes the duration of an illness, not its severity. A *chronic* illness or problem persists over a long time. An *acute* illness is severe, sudden in onset, and resolved in the short term. Acute- and chronic-care medical facilities are those geared to short- and long-term stays respectively.

> 'They were ready to pay for John's immediate injury, right off the bat, but they won't pay for continuing pain and chronic problems.'
> *Toronto Star* 25 May 1992: A17

> … infants and young children infected with hepatitis-B virus rarely manifest an acute symptomatic illness, but commonly become chronically infected with the virus.
> *Gazette* (Montreal) 14 June 1994: B2

> Loyer predicted that more sick and frail elderly will be forced to fill expensive, acute-care hospital beds while they wait for a bed in a long-term care facility.
> *Ottawa Citizen* 2 June 1992: C2

> The committee objects to the fact that since March, veterans in chronic-care hospitals have had to pay for board and lodging.
> *Gazette* (Montreal) 10 Nov. 1990: A3

cigarette, cigaret *Cigarette* is the more common spelling, but *cigaret* is not incorrect. It's a chiefly American variant, seldom used by Canadian writers.

> If the effort to keep the College Militaire open should fail, the way the effort to keep cigaret taxes up failed, then proposals are being made to convert the site to some other use….
> *Ottawa Citizen* 10 March 1994: A13

circa, c., ca. *Circa* (pronounced *SIR ka*) the Latin word for 'around', is used in front of dates to mean approximately. It is usually abbreviated to *c.* or *ca.* (or *ca* if other contractions do not take periods).

> This is a study of private association in Venice c. 1297 to 1423; the author is interested in how Venetians of various classes interacted with one another.
> *Canadian Journal of History* 14.1 (1989): 97

See also LATIN PHRASES.

cite, sight, site To *cite* means to refer to a source or an example ('She cited four authorities'), or to single out either for praise ('She was cited for good work') or for blame ('He was cited for failing to obey orders').

To *sight* something is to see it. To *set your sights* on something is to aim for it.

A *site* is a location ('historic site', 'construction site'), unless it's a place that tourists must see, and then it may also be a *sight*. To *site* something is to put it in a particular location.

> The trusts have been so successful in the United States that three have been cited by the United Nations for special merit awards in 1987.
> *Vancouver Sun* 14 Nov. 1990: B2

> The environment ministry cited itself for its failure to clean up the contaminated soils on the former Expo site on False Creek.
> *Province* (Vancouver) 14 Dec. 1990: 42

cities see NAMES OF RESIDENTS

citizen, national, landed immigrant, subject, inhabitant, resident A *citizen* or *national* of a particular state has obligations to that state and in return receives rights and protection. Anyone born in Canada or to a Canadian citizen living abroad is a Canadian citizen. A *landed immigrant* is someone who has been admitted to Canada as a permanent resident, and is eligible to apply for citizenship after three years.

Nations, such as Britain, that have a monarch as head of state use the word *subject* as well as *citizen*. Because Canada recognizes the British monarch as the official head of state, Canadian citizens are

British subjects, though they are not British citizens. *Resident* and *inhabitant* are general words for people who live in a certain place, whether they are citizens or not.

See also CIVILIAN; EMIGRANT, IMMIGRANT.

civilian In war zones the term *civilian* refers to the general public as opposed to members of the armed forces. In peaceful settings *civilian* is also used to distinguish the public from police, fire-fighters, or any other uniformed group organized along military lines. Sometimes *civilian* refers to anyone outside a specified group, such as a sports team, band, or club, but this extended use is not suitable for formal writing. The phrase 'in civilian clothes' means in street clothes and may be applied to anyone who is out of uniform. Occasionally the term *civilian* is confused with *citizen*.

The fact is that the invention of the airplane destroyed the sanctuary of civilians beyond the range of surface weapons and changed the nature of warfare forever.
Ottawa Citizen 25 June 1994: B7

One person was killed and 20 civilians and 11 police officers were injured.
Gazette (Montreal) 3 March 1989: A3

(Here *civilians* are distinguished from police officers.)

Already dressed in civilian clothes, he was spotted nursing a beer in one of the Blue Jay training rooms.
Globe and Mail (Toronto) 17 Oct. 1985: C4

Kimberley civilians aren't buying this march-of-history angle, maybe because they think they can't afford it—and nobody's shown them a better way.
Canadian Heritage Magazine Feb.–Mar. 1986: 27

(The word required here is *citizens*.)

See also CITIZEN.

civil law see COMMON LAW

-ck- see -C

clad, clothed Some usage commentators have labelled *clad* (the irregular past participle of *clothe*) as archaic or obsolescent, suggesting *dressed* or the regular form (*clothed*) as alternatives. However, *clad* is used in perfectly ordinary contexts in many different kinds of writing and is quite acceptable. It is often found as part of a compound modifier: 'py-jama-clad', 'kilt-clad', 'fur-clad'.

Five youths clad in just T-shirts and sweat pants were in hospital yesterday after police found them running around in the snow in -20 C temperatures.
Province (Vancouver) 26 Nov. 1990: 6

… streetcars and buses were full of the kerchiefed heads and pants-clad legs of the country girls who flocked to the city to work in the munitions plants.
Miriam Waddington *Apartment Seven* 1989: 17–18

clandestine The basic meaning of *clandestine* is secret. Although the word strongly connotes illegality and underhandedness, it should not be used as a synonym of *illegal*.

Clandestine is usually pronounced *clan DES tin*; *CLAN dub stine* is a disputed pronunciaton.

Cocaine is prepared in clandestine labs and shipped from hidden airstrips dotting the tropical lowlands of eastern Bolivia near the Brazilian border.
Chronicle-Herald (Halifax) 14 May 1988: 5

He's part of the clandestine army of collaborators who help Israel keep the occupation running smoothly.
Toronto Star 20 Sept. 1992: F1

For some reason I can never find a flashlight even though I tend to attempt these things under the cover of darkness, for fear of being watched, perhaps, or out of some sense that I am engaging in clandestine activity.
Queen's Quarterly 96.2 (1989): 237–8

class see SPECIES

classic, classical, Classical In the seventeenth century the adjectives *classic* and *classical* were used interchangeably, and even today their uses are not completely differentiated. However, particular uses are commonly associated with each form, as follows.

Classic describes something of high quality and enduring interest, something that has become a benchmark by which similar efforts are judged: 'a classic study'. *Classic* also means absolutely typical: a 'classic case' exhibits all the features you would expect. In fashion and design, 'classic styles' are simple, tasteful, and as close to timeless as fashion gets.

'Classical music' is distinct from the popular music both of the present and of the past. 'Classical dance' is choreographed and performed in accordance with a codified tradition. A 'classical method', in any field, is standard or traditional as opposed to innovative. *Classical* also means having to do with ancient Greece and Rome—the language, literature, art, architecture, jurisprudence, and so on, of that era. In some contexts it isn't clear whether *classical* means ancient or merely traditional; thus it is a good idea to capitalize the adjective if it refers to ancient Greece and Rome.

In spite of the prairie dogma that every man was as good as the next, some were, in Orwell's classic phrase, more equal than others.
Pierre Berton *The Promised Land* 1984: 299

We need more, not fewer, of such dictionaries of usage, a good preparation for the compilation of which is still provided by Leonard Bloomfield's old, but still classical paper 'Secondary and Tertiary Responses to Language'.
W.C. Lougheed, ed. *In Search of the Standard in Canadian English* 1986: 49

(Here *classic* would be the usual choice.)

It was a classic scenario for a spinal injury.
Gazette (Montreal) 29 Dec. 1992: D1

The toolshed, which sometimes doubles as a garage, is a classic bluenose outbuilding and deserves to be immortalized by some magic-realist painter.
Harrowsmith Aug.–Sept. 1985: 14

'My fashions are wearable, classical, and we've already tested women's interest in the collection in Vancouver and it's been very good.'
Vancouver Sun 29 Dec. 1992: C3

(Here *classic* would be the usual choice.)

It is doubtful whether the market system ever worked in the automatic, self-regulating way in which the classical economists conceived of it.
Irving M. Zeitlin and Robert J. Brym *The Social Condition of Humanity* 1991: 77

To look at the range of Professor Kilpatrick's professional interests is to recognize both the vitality of the current renewal of interest in Classical studies and the breadth of vision that such study may yield.
Perspectives: Profiles of Research at Queen's 1986: 26

The book begins with the short chapter 'Aristotle and the Greeks,' then briefly covers the Roman and Late Classic Period.
Queen's Quarterly 94.3 (1987): 592

(The usual choice here would be *Classical*.)

clear see TRANSPARENT

cleave Two different words in Old English, with contrary meanings, have curiously evolved into one form in contemporary English: *cleave*. To *cleave*

means either to split or to cling. When it means split, the past tense is *clove*, *cleft*, or *cleaved*, and the past participle is *cleft* or *cloven* ('cleft palate', 'cloven hoof'). When it means cling, *cleave* is a regular verb with the past tense and past participle *cleaved*. Both verbs are literary or archaic, though the participles *cleft* and *cloven* are current.

There is some kind of maddening bond between them that I cannot seem to cleave.
Queen's Quarterly 96.2 (1989): 398

(Here to *cleave* means to split.)

Yet, though 'mate of the god of light,' she is also prepared (at least in the life of the mind) to renounce sexual passion, to cleave fully to her art.
Queen's Quarterly 92.2 (1985): 315

(Here *cleave* means cling to.)

Now Monette—hair thinner, frame fleshier though the famous cleft chin is as chiselled and classic as ever—is no longer acting.
Ottawa Citizen 24 July 1994: B1

See also -T, -ED.

clerk see DERBY

clever *Clever* suggests mental adroitness and the ability to find quick solutions to problems. *Clever* is not always a synonym for *intelligent*. It can be uncomplimentary, implying craftiness or a lack of deep thought.

At first I thought it was just a clever line and then it became more and more profound.
Bruce Meyer and Brian O'Riordan, eds. *In Their Words* 1984: 49

She believes that women should be clever, in a social sense, but that intellect in a woman is a dangerous thing. It threatens the male ego.
Queen's Quarterly 92.1 (1985): 54

cliché *Cliché* is derived from a French word meaning a printing-block; it almost always retains its acute accent. The adjective is usually *clichéd*, but *cliché'd* and *cliché*—as in French, where *cliché(e)* is both the past participle and the adjective—are also accepted.

The term *cliché* may be applied to ideas, images, or styles of almost any kind. Most often, however, a cliché is an expression that was once fresh but has become flat and trite through overuse. Examples include idioms ('good for nothing'), proverbs ('no smoke without fire'), stock metaphors ('tip of the iceberg'), well-known allusions ('sour grapes'), vogue terms ('boomers'), and fashionable jargon ('mission statement').

A curious problem with clichés is that, for all their familiarity, they are not always understood. To say that what someone is doing is like 'carrying coals to Newcastle' means that it is a waste of time, but this sense may be lost on someone who doesn't know that Newcastle (in the north of England) was a major coal-mining centre when the expression was coined. Similarly, people unfamiliar with the Bible may not understand the phrase 'manna from Heaven'; those unfamiliar with the Classics may not understand 'Achilles' heel'; and those unfamiliar with rural life may not understand why you shouldn't 'look a gift horse in the mouth'. (It's not because it might bite you, but because horses' teeth reveal their age. Thus to look a gift horse in the mouth is to scrutinize it as you would a used car, checking for defects.) To point out these problems is not to advocate the elimination of expressions that allude to the past or to unfamiliar cultures or places, but rather to encourage writers to think of their audiences.

Writing that is full of clichés seems devoid of original thinking. Yet clichés survive, and the reason is that they are useful. In speech, such expressions can improve the rhythm or sound of a sentence, or fill in a pause while the speaker thinks ahead. Thus phrases such as 'rack and ruin', 'each and every', and 'hard and fast' survive despite all criticism. Although clichés are both more common and more forgivable in speech than in writing, strenuously avoiding them in either form may lead to a style that is precious or strange. After all, stock expressions may sum up situations that are otherwise difficult to designate concisely ('sour grapes', 'brain drain'), or briefly allude to shared cultural experience ('stiff upper lip'), allowing the argument to go forward succinctly. Many excellent writers use clichés in their work when these expressions offer an efficient way of conveying ideas, images, and emotions.

Pointed hats are a cliché, it seems, and real witches often wear flowers in their hair.
Gazette (Montreal) 30 Oct. 1990: C1

When it is proposed to deface a city by, say, turning park lots into parking lots, the rationalization given is usually the cliché 'you can't stop progress'.
Northrop Frye *The Modern Century* 1990: 34

Their story starts off wobbly at first, like a toddler learning how to walk—the language is a bit awkward, sometimes clichéd. . . .
Province (Vancouver) 24 June 1990: 93

Just as musicals had their cliché situations, so too did war movies.
Gazette (Montreal) 18 Feb. 1990: D3

(This use of *cliché* as an adjective is accepted, though *clichéd* is more usual.)

See also DEAD METAPHOR; IDIOMS.

client   see CUSTOMER

climatic, climactic, climacteric   *Climatic* derives from *climate* and refers to prevailing weather conditions, while *climactic* and *climacteric* derive from *climax*. *Climactic* is an adjective relating to a high point or culmination. *Climacteric* (both a noun and an adjective) is now used mainly to refer to menopause, although it can be used more generally to refer to any major life change.

When we think of climate, we generally think of broad geographic bands, or climatic zones.
Harrowsmith Jun.–Jul. 1985: 24

You'd think a group from Iceland would have been prepared for the rigors of a North American winter, but the climatic changes of travelling from city to city have laid low the Sugarcubes' singer, Bjork Gudmundsdottir, in San Francisco with a hoarse throat.
Province (Vancouver) 23 Feb. 1990: P7

(The word required here is *climatic*.)

Wonderfully shot, with tons of fantastical apparitions and surreal backdrops (the climatic scene at the evil temple is a sight to behold), the film unveils unique and amazing special effects.
Vancouver Sun 14 Dec. 1990: E5

(The word required here is *climactic*.)

. . . . artists seem, if they are lucky, to approach and pass a climacteric in middle life which leaves them changed for the better.
Robertson Davies *A Voice from the Attic* 1960: 225

climax   see CLIMATIC; CRESCENDO

clipped words   see ABBREVIATION

clique, coterie   A small, exclusive group within a group (in society, in a school, in a workplace, etc.) is a *clique*. A *coterie* is a group of people united by common interests or pursuits. Although the term *coterie* may connote narrowness, it is not as negative as *clique*, which characterizes a group as snobbish, pretentious, selfish, or hostile to others.

Clique may be pronounced either *CLEEK* or *CLICK*; *CLEEK* is more common and more widely accepted in Canada.

The ruling clique makes self-righteous statements characterizing its critics as 'criminal elements, enemies of the state.'
J.E.Smyth et al. *The Law and Business Administration in Canada* 1987: 38

What about that clique of pretty-but-irritating high school girls who were forever sneering at the under-dressed and arguing about who among them were the best best friends?
Vancouver Sun 11 June 1994: D10

Painters and composers deal with arts capable of a higher degree of abstraction, but even they are likely to have their roots in some very restricted coterie in Paris or New York.
Northrop Frye *The Bush Garden* 1971: i

Still, it's building a reputation as an underground club with a coterie of regulars.
Gazette (Montreal) 2 June 1994: E6

clone   *Clone* originated as a biological term for a cell or individual that is genetically identical to another organism from which it has been asexually derived. Now *clone* is a popular metaphor for a nearly exact copy. In the marketplace, *clone* can be a neutral term, but in the arts, where slavish imitation is frowned upon, its tone is definitely disparaging.

Like many other prospective consumers, the Chings were looking at an IBM clone, the type found in 75 to 80 per cent of businesses and homes today.
Toronto Star 21 April 1994: G3

Obviously Gallant did not set out to write stories that would be clones of what *The New Yorker* was publishing in the late forties and early fifties.
Janice Kulyk Keefer *Reading Mavis Gallant* 1989: 34

close, shut, turn off, turn out   *Close* and *shut* are synonyms (a door or gate can be either closed or shut), but *close* is more often used metaphorically. Bank accounts, speeches, real estate deals, and parks are closed, never shut.

Generally, Canadians *turn off* or *shut off* their electrical appliances and *turn off* or *turn out* their lights, but speakers of English in Quebec may also

'close the lights'. This expression, influenced by similar expressions in French (*fermer la radio*, etc.), should be avoided in writing.

'We have noticed that when we close the lights in the room, the odor disappears.'
Gazette (Montreal) 3 June 1994: A4

('Close the lights' is a regional usage.)

clothed   see CLAD

coal oil   see KEROSENE

cocoa, cacao, coca, coco   *Cocoa*, a hot chocolate drink or the bitter powder from which it is made, is derived from the seeds of the *cacao* (pronounced *kuh KAY o* or *kuh KAH yo* or *kuh COW*) tree. These seeds are called either *cocoa beans* or *cacao beans*. *Coca* is a South American shrub from which cocaine is derived. A *coco* is a coconut palm tree or a coconut; the adjective *coco* describes things made of the fibres of husks of coconuts. *Cocoanut* is a variant spelling of *coconut*.

Maybe for a little treat she'd make herself a cup of cocoa, because for no reason that made any sense this early in the fall, she felt cold.
Constance Beresford-Howe *Night Studies* 1985: 114–15

Plantations produce such crops as coffee, tea, oil palm, cacao, coconuts, bananas, jute, sisal, hemp, rubber, tobacco, ground nuts, sugar cane, and cotton.
William Norton *Human Geography* 1992: 260

Democracy, unlike coca, does not have strong roots [in Peru].
Vancouver Sun 8 April 1992: A10

Coco and rubber mats are good for scraping off mud and large chunks of dirt, while mats made from carpeting will absorb moisture and attract smaller dirt particles.
Vancouver Sun 12 Sept. 1992: C14

He saw the frozen chocolate pie, the banana cream pie, and the cocoanut cream pie.
NeWest Review Feb.–Mar. 1990: 31

(The more common, and more widely accepted, spelling is *coconut*.)

He retired to his room with a cup of cacao and around midnight a footman found him reading in bed.
Ottawa Citizen 6 Feb. 1992: A11

(The word wanted here is *cocoa*.)

co-ed, coed   The term *co-educational* was coined in the late nineteenth century to describe what was then an innovation: educational programs and institutions open to both female and male students. In contemporary British usage, the informal abbreviation *co-ed* (or *coed*) refers to a co-educational school. In North America, by contrast, the noun *co-ed* refers to the female students (never the males) at mixed schools: 'undergraduates and co-eds'. This use, which is sexist and condescending, is now on the decline. In its latest use *co-ed* is a synonym for *mixed*, referring to activities and facilities open to both sexes, as in 'co-ed washrooms' or 'co-ed hockey'. Note that this use, which has nothing to do with education, is quite informal.

> Outside Victoria Hall, a former women's residence at Queen's University, there is a plaque which is signed 'Science 67' and which reads: 'She who is kissed by an engineer while standing by this plaque officially becomes a Queen's co-ed.'
> *Queen's Quarterly* 96.2 (1989): 237

(This use of the term is now discouraged as sexist.)

> A strong believer in the value of fitness, he works out three times a week in a co-ed aerobics class.
> *Catholic Register* 16 Aug. 1986: 21

> One regular highlight is the late afternoon volleyball game, usually pitting a rather erratic coed team of guests against a team of Fijian staffers. . . .
> *Globe and Mail* (Toronto) 26 Jan. 1985: T9

(Here *coed* is informal; *mixed* would be better in formal writing.)

See also SEXIST LANGUAGE.

coequal, co-equal   Official or political equals are sometimes described as *coequal* (or *co-equal*). While this word has sometimes been criticized as a redundancy for *equal*, it has been used in literary and formal contexts since the fourteenth century.

> The world over, that foundation assumption of political science—that all nation-states are sovereign and so are co-equal internationally—is being stood on its head, shaken and found wanting.
> *Toronto Star* 4 Sept. 1991: A21

> After 20 years of intensive effort, in which millions of English-Canadian children have studied French as a coequal official language, . . . Quebec's militant official assault on bilingualism is profoundly disillusioning.
> *Financial Post* 23 Feb. 1989: 14

cohort, crony, cronyism   *Cohort*, derived from the Latin word *cohors*, originally referred to the group of 600 soldiers making up one-tenth of a Roman legion. In the eighteenth century, the English used the word figuratively to refer to any group of people who supported a particular cause. Since *cohorts* meant troops, allies, or supporters of the cause, many people began to assume that a *cohort* was a single comrade-at-arms. Thus *cohort* has come to mean a comrade or companion. British critics tend to object to this last meaning, but *Webster's Dictionary of English Usage* (1989) remarks that it is too firmly established in North America 'to be eradicated by commentators demonstrating their knowledge of Roman military organization'. In sociology, a *cohort* is a group of people sharing similar demographic characteristics.

While a *cohort* is a comrade or colleague, a *crony* is a close friend. Recently *crony* has developed pejorative connotations of political friendship, and the term *cronyism*, meaning the practice of appointing unqualified friends to public office, has taken a firm hold in journalism.

> But I almost put the boots to my old friend and cohort, the redoubtable Pierre Berton, when he asked me on television why all the men in my recent book *Bodily Harm* were wimps.
> Margaret Atwood *Second Words* 1982: 424

(British commentators object to this usage.)

> Evidence showed that his job was to ward off other guards with a blunt-ended butter knife as his cohorts took hostages.
> *Globe and Mail* (Toronto) 25 May 1985: P4

> These later immigrants may have swelled the urban ghettos where, according to Akenson's argument, only a minority of the earlier cohorts had put down roots.
> *Canadian Journal of History* 14.1 (1989): 121

(This is the sociological sense.)

> Why doesn't a prime minister know that it is wrong to appoint his cronies to positions on the public payroll?
> *Vancouver Sun* 10 July 1990: A7

> With the appointment of Hartt, Mulroney . . . has reduced any small reliance he had on Wilson. 'It is,' says a former privy council staff member, 'the politics of cronyism.'
> *Saturday Night* March 1986: 28

coiffure, coiffeur   A *coiffure* (pronounced *kwa FYOOR*) is a hairstyle. A *coiffeur* (*kwa FUR*) is a hairdresser. Both terms are borrowed from French.

In French a female hairdresser is a *coiffeuse*, but in English *coiffeur* is acceptable for both sexes.

> Don King, the fight- and self-promoter with a coiffure like an abused Brillo pad, started his campaign through Givens and her mother, Ruth Roper.
> *Maclean's* 27 June 1988: A54

> Victoria Louise Flett is only twenty-two years old, a student at the University of Toronto, a tall stringbean of a woman with large hands and feet and straight blond unyielding hair that she bends carelessly behind her ears. So much for her coiffeur.
> Carol Shields *The Stone Diaries* 1993: 265

(A *coiffeur* is a hairdresser; the word needed here is *coiffure*, 'hairstyle').

> Having once made do with his sister's dolls, LeBlanc was given in Amadeus a coiffeur's tableau of epic proportions: more than 700 wigs were pressed into service to set the stage as eighteenth-century Vienna.
> *Globe and Mail* (Toronto) 22 March 1985: E1

coincident   see SYNCHRONOUS

coincidentally, incidentally   *Coincidentally* introduces a statement about two things happening at the same time—an occurrence that might seem to have been planned, but in fact was not: 'Coincidentally, my brother was driving on the same highway at the same time'. *Incidentally* indicates that a remark is a digression: 'Incidentally, we never got paid for that job'. People often use *coincidentally* where the idea of coincidence is weak or non-existent and the appropriate word is *incidentally*.

> Police say the alleged attacker was not stalking T——; he was seeing a friend off at the airport and coincidentally encountered [her].
> *Ottawa Citizen* 27 June 1992: B5

> Along narrow la rue Elle (a pun, incidentally, on *la ruelle*, or alley) are 12 up-market boutiques that specialize in European imports.
> Alan Tucker, ed. *The Penguin Guide to Canada* 1991: 209

> And you not only like it, but prefer it to our old size (which coincidentally you are now reading).
> *Toronto Star* 12 Dec. 1992: D2

(Here *incidentally* would be more appropriate.)

> Ottawa won its first game of the season, coincidentally against the Canadiens, and haven't won in 20 games since.
> *Gazette* (Montreal) 22 Nov. 1992: D3

(Here *incidentally* would be more appropriate, since no other mention is made of the Canadiens.)

COLA   In the domain of labour relations, a *COLA*, or *cola*, is a cost-of-living allowance or adjustment. In writing for a general audience, acronyms such as *COLA* should be explained. They are opaque to the uninitiated and seldom listed in dictionaries.

> Under the agreement, teachers will receive two per cent retroactive to Sept. 1 ... and 1.25 per cent plus a COLA on Feb. 1, 1994.
> *Ottawa Citizen* 24 April 1992: A1

See also ABBREVIATION, CONTRACTION, SUSPENSION, ACRONYM.

Coliseum   see COLOSSEUM

collaboration, collaborator, collaborationist, quisling, conspiracy, conspirator, co-conspirator, collusion, cahoots   *Collaboration* means either working with someone towards a common goal, usually artistic, scientific, or literary, or cooperating traitorously with an enemy. A *collaborator* is either a co-author or a traitor. The term *collaborationist*, coined in the twentieth century, invariably means traitor.

A synonym for *collaborationist* is *quisling*. Vidkun Quisling was a Norwegian politician who collaborated with the Nazis during the Second World War. The name *Quisling* probably would not have entered the English language as a generic label for traitors—it did not become part of French vocabulary—if it had not coincidentally echoed the English suffix *-ling*. Among the meanings of *-ling* are young, small (*duckling, gosling*) and inferior (*hireling, underling*), and in the latter sense it can sometimes have a pejorative connotation. Thus to English ears the name *Quisling* suggested something contemptible.

A *conspiracy* is a secret plan by a group to do something treacherous. In law, a *conspiracy* is an agreement between at least two people to commit a crime. A person involved in a conspiracy is a *conspirator*. The word *co-conspirator*, which seems redundant, is the standard legal term for defendants charged with the same conspiracy.

Collusion is illegal or immoral cooperation. Usually it is a secret agreement between people that allows them to perpetrate a fraud.

In cahoots means in partnership, usually to pursue questionable activities. This phrase, of uncertain origin, should not be used in formal writing.

Complaints that these Davis/Evans collaborations produced unrhythmic music were due to faulty hearing. . . .
Jack Chambers *Milestones* 1983: 261

More than 50 Israelis have died in the violence and about 300 Palestinians have been killed by fellow Arabs, most on suspicion of collaboration.
Vancouver Sun 6 Dec. 1990: A3

U.S. authorities did formally screen prospective refugees for Nazi connections, but it proved almost impossible to weed out those who hid their collaborationist past.
Globe and Mail (Toronto) 1 June 1985: E17

Despite Saddam Hussein's frenzied efforts to find a Kuwaiti to rule the country in his name, no quisling turned up.
Gazette (Montreal) 27 Aug. 1990: B3

'. . . the fact that a co-conspirator and co-accused is acquitted doesn't mean the same thing will happen to another co-accused.'
Gazette (Montreal) 15 Jan. 1994: A3

The historical reason for this special liability was to prevent the practice, once frequent in England, of collusion between carriers and highwaymen, whereby the highwayman would 'rob' the carrier of the shipper's goods and the carrier would plead that it was not his fault that the goods were taken.
J.E. Smyth et al. *The Law and Business Administration in Canada* 1987: 459

The slapstick is as broad as the Yellow River: two attendants in cahoots with a scheming mandarin are trying to get a father drunk so he will unwittingly sign away his daughter's hand in marriage.
Globe and Mail (Toronto) 22 Jan. 1985: P10

collective nouns   A collective noun is a noun that is singular in form even though it refers to a group of persons, objects, or acts: for example, 'a *committee* of concerned citizens', 'the *majority* of the student body', 'the provincial *government*', 'a *fleet* of fishing vessels', 'a *range* of musical styles', 'a *battery* of tests'.

A collective noun can be followed by either a singular or a plural verb depending on whether the writer regards the group as a unified whole or as a collection of individuals: 'The Canadian Olympic rowing team *is* favoured to win'; 'The Olympic rowing team *are* signing autographs'. The *team* is treated as a single unit in the first example and as a collection of individuals in the second.

While most Canadians would say 'The government *is* about to call an election', most speakers of British English would say 'The government *are* . . .'. Words such as *family, committee, council, board,* and *faculty* are more frequently used with plural verbs in British English than in Canadian or American English.

Once the choice has been made to regard a particular collective noun as singular (or plural) in a given context, it is important to be consistent in the use of verbs and pronouns. 'The company *is* planning to market the product soon. *They* will start a national advertising campaign next month': in these sentences, a plural pronoun (*they*) inconsistently follows a singular verb (*is*). Since the verb suggests that the company is being regarded as an entity, the pronoun should be *it*.

The word *number* is a special case. When preceded by *a* it is considered plural: 'A number of us *are* willing to help out'. When preceded by *the* it is considered singular: 'The number of participants *is* not as high as expected'. However, if a singular verb would sound awkward, *number* can always be made plural: 'The *numbers* of participants *are* increasing'.

The government is able to secure the passage of the bulk of its proposed bills. . . .
Andrew Heard *Canadian Constitutional Conventions* 1991: 78

(Here *government* is regarded as singular.)

When the federal government found out about the provincial complex they wanted one too.
Canadian Fiction Magazine 63 (1988): 100

(Here *government* is regarded as plural and followed by *they*.)

His committee were displeased with me, but as they were not paying me anything and I was writing simply out of political loyalty, I could afford to ignore their huffing and puffing.
Robertson Davies *One Half of Robertson Davies* 1978: 9–10

(Here the plural verb *were* is consistent with the pronoun that follows, *they*.)

If you are satisfied that the factoring company is thoroughly professional and that you can work with it, you will complete an application form for approval as one of their clients.
Computer Dealer News 7 March 1991: 56

(Here the writer has slipped, referring to the company first in the singular—*it*—and then in the plural: 'one of *their* clients'.)

See also AGREEMENT, GRAMMATICAL; TRIVIAL, TRIVIA.

college, collegiate   see UNIVERSITY

collide, collision   Many newspaper style guides state that a car cannot *collide* or be *in a collision* with a tree, because both objects in a collision must be moving. Contemporary usage, however, does not support this rule. The only restriction is that the subject of the verb *collide* must be in motion ('My toe collided with the coffee table', *not* 'The coffee table collided with my toe')—unless the speaker is intending to be funny. When the subject is compound, both elements must be in motion ('The canoe and the racing shell collided', but *not* 'The canoe and the dock collided'). What follows *collided with*, however, may be either stationary or moving. Thus 'The canoe collided with the shell' and 'The canoe collided with the dock' are both acceptable.

> The car, still chased by police, then collided with a sign on Queen St. near Airport Rd.…
> *Toronto Star* 25 June 1993: A7

> … he missed a curve and demolished the car in a collision with a rock-cut.
> J.E. Smyth et al. *The Law and Business Administration in Canada* 1987: 444

colloquial, informal, slang, jargon, argot   *Colloquial* English is the everyday spoken variety, as opposed to the English of formal writing or prepared speech. Dictionaries once used the label *colloq.* to indicate acceptable informal language, but many people interpreted this label to mean non-standard or slang. Many dictionaries and guides (including this one) now use *informal* to distinguish the casual usage of educated speakers from literary or formal language.

Slang is very casual language that is generally not acceptable in either formal or informal writing. Most slang is ephemeral. It develops as the 'in-language' of a specific group and functions as a code that distinguishes its members from the general population. Teenagers are well-known for coining slang—and discarding old expressions as soon as adults learn them. Some slang does become widely understood and widely used while retaining slang status: for example, *dud*, *big shot*, *bummer*. Other slang words, such as *piano* (a short form of *pianoforte*), *cheat*, and *jaywalk*, eventually become Standard English. Generally, slang should be avoided in writing; however, fiction writers often use it to represent speech or to set a particular tone.

Jargon usually refers to the language—the special terms and the phrasing—peculiar to a profession, occupation, or hobby: 'legal jargon', 'computer jargon', 'social-work jargon'. While initially jargon develops as a way of increasing precision in a field, ultimately it often has just the opposite effect, obscuring simple ideas. Specialist writers in any field need to make a continual effort to use jargon sparingly when writing for a non-specialist audience. Jargon is especially objectionable when used to impress or befuddle the reader.

Argot (pronounced *AR go* or *AR got*) originally referred to the coded language of French thieves. Now it's the general term in French for slang, and in English it's a synonym for *jargon*.

See also -ESE; FORMAL, INFORMAL WRITING; SCIENTIFIC ENGLISH; STANDARD, STANDARD ENGLISH; VERNACULAR.

collusion   see COLLABORATION

colon   The colon (:) is used to signal that an explanation, amplification, illustration, or list is to follow. It often serves a transitional function, replacing expressions such as *the reason being*, *that is*, *namely*, or *such as*:

> A small ad in a children's magazine set me going: it offered a free stamp.
> Richard Davies and Glen Kirkland, eds. *Dimensions* 1986: 60

> I also thought about me: a little wearied, a little worn, tormented by doubts and feelings and lifelong illusions I can no longer reconcile, yet still able to find joy in the game.
> Ken Dryden *The Game* 1983: 3

> Besides its logic and neutral spirit, his argument had exhibited one other quality: brevity.
> Jack Batten *Robinette* 1984: 17

> Ottawa is a small town that breaks easily into three basic chunks: Upper Town, Lower Town, and Sussex Drive.
> Alan Tucker, ed. *The Penguin Guide to Canada* 1991: 301

A list that is grammatically incorporated into a sentence (following *are* or *consists of*, for example) should not be preceded by a colon:

Cat food segments in order of national ranking are: luxury canned, dry, maintenance canned, semi-moist and cat treats.
Western Grocer Magazine Aug. 1990: 22

(Here the colon should be omitted.)

Occasionally a full sentence following a colon is capitalized, though it needn't be unless it is a quotation, a slogan, or the first in a series of parallel sentences ('The accident raises a number of questions: How did it happen? Who is responsible? How can such accidents be avoided in future?'):

A caution: Most Montreal drivers seem to have taken the New York cab drivers' training course.
Alan Tucker, ed. *The Penguin Guide to Canada* 1991: 15

The colon is also used to introduce quotations (especially if they are more than one sentence long); to separate a main title and subtitle (*When the Fat Lady Sings: Opera History as It Ought to Be Taught*); in biblical citations (Ruth 2: 1–4); in scholarly documentation (1993: 54); in time of day (6:55); in ratios (3:1); and in formal correspondence after the salutation ('Dear Sir or Madam:').

See also QUOTATION; TIME.

colonist, colonial, colonialist *Colonists* and *colonials* are people who live in a colony. *Colonists* also may refer more specifically to the people who first settled a colony; these people are also called settlers or pioneers. *Colonialists* usually refers to those who are advocates of colonialism or those in power in a colony.
The adjective *colonial* may be neutral, as when it refers to a period or style ('colonial architecture') or to the act of possessing colonies ('colonial powers'). It may also be negative, implying a lack of culture or sophistication in the colonies or referring to a sense of inferiority on the part of colonials.

Almost the entire francophone population of Quebec has therefore descended from about 10,000 original colonists who arrived between 1608 and 1760.
David V.J. Bell *The Roots of Disunity* 1992: 33.

British colonials adopted the style [jodhpurs] while playing polo in India.
Vancouver Sun 30 Aug. 1994: C1

Colonies breed something called 'the colonial mentality', and if you have the colonial mentality you believe that the great good place is always somewhere else.
Margaret Atwood *Second Words* 1982: 382

Colosseum, coliseum The *Colosseum* is the ancient amphitheatre built in the first century A.D. in Rome, while *coliseum* is a common name for a large building designed for public exhibitions, performances, and sports events in Canada and the United States. The British often use *colosseum* for this sense, although *coliseum* is also found.

Thanks to concrete, the Roman Colosseum still stands after almost 2,000 years.
Vancouver Sun 22 June 1990: H1

Once the season opens, sports-minded Quebeckers converge on the Coliseum ... to cheer the Nordiques on to higher National Hockey League heights.
Alan Tucker, ed. *The Penguin Guide to Canada* 1991: 291

The swimming pool, with surrounding walls made of bricks laid unevenly to emulate the Coliseum of Rome (Mr. Guccione's idea), glistens beneath electric simulated candles.
Globe and Mail (Toronto) 7 Nov. 1985: E11

(The correct spelling for the building in Rome is *Colosseum*.)

colour, spectrum, primary colour, secondary colour, hue, tint, shade, tone A gradation of wavelengths of light perceived as bands of *colour* is called a *spectrum*. In the atmosphere, this phenomenon is called a rainbow. Combining all the colours of the rainbow (red, orange, yellow, green, blue, indigo, and violet) produces white light.
Primary colours are colours that can be mixed to produce all the other colours of the spectrum. When mixing beams of light, the usual primaries are red, green, and blue; when mixing pigments, red, yellow, and blue. *Secondary colours* are colours produced by mixing two primaries. Orange, green, and violet are the secondary colours that result from mixing the primary pigments.
In popular use *hue* is a synonym for *colour*; in technical use it refers specifically to the wavelength of a colour. In popular use *tint*, *shade*, and *tone* all refer to nuances of colours, while in technical use a *tint* is a colour lightened by adding white; a *shade* is a colour darkened by adding black; and a *tone* is either a tint or a shade.

See also -OUR, -OR.

coloured see BLACK

colourless see TRANSPARENT

come The past tense is *came*. The use of *come*, as in 'Archie come home for Christmas last year', is dialectal. 'Come Sunday', as in 'Come Sunday, it'll all be over', is standard; this is an inverted subjunctive construction that exists in current English only in a handful of set expressions such as 'Be that as it may' and 'Perish the thought'.

> They were going to clap me in jail as soon as the baby come.
> David Williams *Eye of the Father* 1985: 11

(This use of *come* is dialectal; the standard word is *came*.)

See also SUBJUNCTIVE.

comic, comical *Comic* and *comical* both mean funny or amusing; *comic* is the more common, general word. *Comical* usually refers to something that is unintentionally or unexpectedly funny, but this is a tendency rather than a clear distinction of sense. Only *comic* can be used to refer to the genre of comedy: 'Comic conventions differ from tragic conventions'.

> As always, Bowes displays a comic flair.
> *Ottawa Citizen* 28 June 1993: B10

> In the comic context of this play, Len cares very little that in the end Leona runs off to California with brother Bill, since he gains the higher happiness of a lifetime of Mama's Peanut-Butter Roundup Cake and Cocoa-Vodka Puffs.
> *NeWest Review* Oct.–Nov. 1989: 52

> The sight of muscle-bound guards wearing huge chains loaded with keys swaggering in front of the women would be comical if it weren't so sad.
> *Toronto Star* 26 Nov. 1993: A23

(Here the humour is unintentional.)

> Often the narrative turns comical in its madcap non-sequiturs.
> *Toronto Star* 13 Nov. 1993: J15

(Here the humour is unintentional.)

comma The comma is the most often used and probably the most controversial of all punctuation marks. Although there are a few well-established rules governing comma usage, in many cases writers may use commas at their discretion to promote clarity and ease of reading.

The modern trend is to use a minimum of commas. If a sentence seems to require a thicket of commas, it probably needs rewriting.

The comma has so many possible uses that space does not permit listing them all. The following are some of the most common or troublesome constructions.

in compound sentences A comma separates two or more independent clauses joined by a coordinating conjunction—*and, but, or, nor, yet* (meaning *but*), *so* (meaning *therefore*), and *for* (meaning *because*)—unless the clauses are short and closely related:

> Tabitha took a flying leap at the catnip mouse intended for Cuddles, but she missed and landed in the magazine rack.

> The party was a bore and we left early.

Compound sentences are often confused with simple sentences in which a conjunction separates a compound predicate (two verbs with the same subject):

> Tabitha is a clumsy cat, but she has survived so far.
> (*Compound sentence.*)

> Tabitha is a clumsy cat but has survived so far.
> (*Compound predicate.*)

In the second example, *but* separates the two verbs *is* and *has survived*, which have the same subject, *Tabitha*; it does not introduce a clause and does not need a comma before it. However, some writers defend this use of the comma in long sentences as a means of breaking them up:

> Tabitha has frequently taken what can only be described as death-defying leaps of faith, but hasn't killed herself yet.

with introductory clauses and phrases A dependent clause (one that cannot stand alone) placed before the main clause is usually followed by a comma:

> If I tell you the truth, will you stay?

A comma may follow an introductory phrase but is often omitted, especially if the phrase is short:

> During the surprising summer of 1991, the world witnessed two Russian revolutions in quick succession.

> After suffering a series of blows, Sam came into a windfall.

> Running for the bus, Marina slipped and fell.

> In May she left home for good.

If an adverb phrase (one that modifies a verb) immediately precedes the verb, no comma is used:

Running along the ground was a fine wire.

In the kitchen stood a large china cupboard.

with adjective clauses or phrases following a noun An adjective clause or phrase following a noun is set off by commas if it is non-restrictive (if it adds information not essential to the meaning of the sentence). No commas are used if the clause or phrase is restrictive (if it limits the noun in a way that is necessary to the meaning of the sentence):

That book, which I will leave on the hall table for you, is one of my favourites.
(Non-restrictive, providing additional information.)

The book that is on the hall table is one of my favourites
(Restrictive, providing necessary information.)

My cat, lying curled up in the corner, seemed to be having an exciting dream.

The cat lying in the corner seems to be having an exciting dream.

with adverb phrases between subject and verb An adverb phrase occurring between the subject and verb is usually set off by commas:

Sam, after suffering a series of blows, came into a sudden windfall.

My cat, without any prompting, has learned to fetch.

Be careful not to put a comma between subject and verb, as in 'Learning how to fetch without prompting, is a sign of great intelligence in a cat'. This comma would seriously perplex the reader. If, on the other hand, you wrote 'Learning how to fetch, without prompting, is a sign of great intelligence in a cat', the punctuation would be acceptable because 'without prompting' would become a parenthetical comment. But note that the meaning of the sentence would shift: in this case, instead of first being taught to fetch with prompting and then figuring out how to fetch on its own, the cat would have learned the whole process—how to fetch—without any prompting.

It is also an error to put a comma between a verb and its complement or object: 'Cuddles ate, her food, Tabitha's food, and the salmon off the counter'.

in a series Commas separate words, phrases, or clauses in a series:

Mix in the dates, raisins, nuts, and seeds.

The cat stretched out, rolled over, and fell asleep.

It is a matter of debate whether to insert the final comma—called a series or serial comma—before the conjunction (as this guide does). Those in favour argue that the series comma prevents ambiguity, while those opposed contend that the conjunction makes it redundant. Both conventions are common, with the series comma somewhat more likely to be used in scholarly and more formal writing and less likely in newspapers and magazines.

Whichever style is chosen, it should be followed consistently within a given text. A decision not to use the series comma, however, does not preclude using it occasionally for greater clarity:

The boomers' future is likely to include nursing homes run like California spas, art and entertainment aimed at octogenarians, and service professionals of all kinds.

If a series is made up of long or complex phrases or clauses, especially if they include internal punctuation, it is usually best to separate them with semicolons. In this case, a final (series) semicolon is required:

I am getting a little tired of writing speeches that will be changed beyond recognition, on the spur of the moment, by ill-informed politicians; that will be deemed frivolous, libelous, or anti-family; or worse, that will be ignored altogether.

to enclose parenthetical elements Parenthetical terms such as *indeed, in fact, perhaps, though, nevertheless, of course, naturally, too,* and *oh* are usually set off by commas when they interrupt the flow of thought or call for a pause in reading:

In fact, I've seen it myself.

She told me, nevertheless, that there was no such thing.

There are two sides to everything, of course.

Oh, I hardly think so.

If such terms don't interrupt the flow of thought or call for a pause, they are usually not set off by commas:

She told me that the book in fact needs a chapter on constructing a home page.

Perhaps there have always been two sides.

He thinks so too.

Parenthetical phrases and clauses are also usually set off by commas:

Granola, no matter what you think, is not a healthful food.

In the morning, Mary decided, she would drive into town.

Be sure, though, that the element is in fact parenthetical. If it is essential to the meaning of the sentence, it should not be set off by commas:

In the morning Mary decided she would drive into town.

Here removing the commas changes the meaning of the sentence. Without commas, the sentence tells us when Mary decided; with them, we don't know when she made her decision, but we know when she will drive into town.

with nouns in apposition A word, phrase, or clause that is in apposition to a noun (a title, name, synonym, or definition that immediately follows the noun and has the same relation as the noun to the rest of the sentence) is set off by commas if it is non-restrictive but is not set off if it is restrictive:

His third novel, *No Respite*, caused a stir.

Asina Timbale won the coveted First Novel Award. Her novel, *Sinister Editors*, caused a stir.

Her novel *The Stone Diaries* won a Governor General's Literary Award.

In the first example the word *third* identifies which of the author's novels caused a stir, so the title is not essential to the meaning of the sentence; it is non-restrictive, so commas are used. Similarly, in the second example the context makes it clear that the author has written only one novel; thus the title is not essential and is set off by commas. In the third example, however, the title is essential: it restricts the comment to that particular novel, so no commas are used.

It is a common error to confuse restrictive and non-restrictive appositives. The distinction is important, however, since incorrect usage may convey the wrong meaning:

In Shakespeare's play, *Hamlet*, Ophelia goes mad.

(Here the punctuation implies that Shakespeare wrote only one play.)

Prime Minister Mulroney introduced his wife Mila.

(Here the lack of punctuation implies that Mr. Mulroney has more than one wife.)

The same rules apply with phrases and clauses:

In the adage 'Absence makes the heart grow fonder', we see the poignant hope of the estranged.

But the adage referred to earlier, 'Absence makes the heart grow fonder', is refuted by 'Out of sight, out of mind'.

In the second example, the words *referred to earlier* indicate that the adage has already been given, so repeating it is not essential but simply courteous; hence commas are used.

In some cases, nouns in apposition could be mistaken for a series:

Antony had three pets, two horses and a goat.

If Antony owns three animals, make that clear by replacing the comma with a colon or a dash. If he owns six animals, it would help to specify the pets (or use the series comma).

with parallel adjectives Use a comma to separate two or more adjectives that modify the same noun if they are parallel. The positions of parallel adjectives can be reversed with no ill effect: 'The happy, breathless children poured into the room' could also be written 'The breathless, happy children...'. *Happy* and *breathless* are parallel here, and a comma is needed to separate them. However, in 'The old wooden desk needs refinishing', *old* and *wooden* are not parallel; this sentence could not be written 'The wooden old desk ...', and so the adjectives are not separated by a comma.

Be careful not to put a comma between the last adjective and the noun or pronoun that follows, as in 'The breathless, happy, children poured into the room'. Over-punctuation of this kind will derail the reader.

with explanatory terms Commas usually set off definitions preceded by *or*:

The leaves were of a russet, or red, colour.

Sheba belonged to the *Felis*, or cat, family.

The commas in this case distinguish an explanation from a simple choice:

She hasn't decided whether to paint the walls russet or celadon.

with dates and addresses In month–day–year constructions a comma follows the day and the year. Be careful to include the comma following the year; it is often incorrectly omitted.

He met her on July 11, 1987, and never looked back.

In month–year constructions ('August 1991') usage is divided between those who insert a comma after the month and those who don't. The trend is towards omission.

In day–month–year constructions ('28 August 1991'), common in Europe and in some kinds of Canadian publications, no commas are used.

Commas are used to separate parts of an address. Note the comma following the final element ('Canada') when, as in this case, the sentence continues:

> She grew up in Medicine Hat, Alberta, Canada, and would often go on and on about it.

No comma separates province and postal code:

> His address was Suite 106, 16 Albert Square, Victoria, B.C. V8N 2L3.

to prevent misreading A comma is sometimes used to clarify meaning or ease reading even when no rule requires it:

> Whatever is, is good.

> To Ben, Nelson remained an enigma.

> She saw who came in, and gasped.

Be careful, however, not to use a comma to rescue a badly structured sentence, as in 'Those that fail, naturally incur public criticism'. Here *naturally* modifies the whole sentence; placed where it is, it may be read at first as modifying *fail*; then the desperate reader may try to attach it to *incur*. The writer has tried to use a comma to solve this problem, instead of restructuring the sentence: 'Naturally, those that fail incur public criticism'.

A comma occurring with parentheses is placed after, not before, them:

> Whatever she said (and I don't know what it was), she couldn't have meant it maliciously.

as the wrong punctuation choice Commas, which indicate the smallest pause or break in thought, are sometimes inadvisedly used where stronger breaks—dashes, colons, semicolons, parentheses, or even periods—are needed:

> She cleared the table and put away the food, she hardly knew what she was doing.
> *(Semicolon or period.)*

> I hope you can stand another example, many couldn't, because here it is.
> *(Dashes or parentheses.)*

A comma should not intrude between sentence elements connected by correlative conjunctions (*so. . .that, as. . .as, more. . .than, both. . .and, either. . . or, neither. . .nor*), as in 'In criminal law, a charge of assault may be laid, not only if an attack occurs, but also if the victim reasonably believes he or she is being threatened with physical harm'. Here the comma between *laid* and *not only* should be omitted.

See also DATES; NUMBERS, DECIMAL POINTS AND COMMAS WITH; QUOTATION, QUOTATION MARKS; SENTENCES, SENTENCE FRAGMENT, RUN-ON SENTENCE, COMMA SPLICE; WHICH, THAT.

comma fault, comma splice see SENTENCES

commentate *Commentate* is a back-formation from *commentator*. It has been criticized as a pretentious and unnecessary synonym for *comment*. Some recent usage guides have defended the word by pointing out that it is used differently from *comment*. While to *comment* means to make remarks, to *commentate* means to act as a commentator, to provide a running commentary on a live event for an audience. It may in fact be the rather vapid nature of much broadcast commentary that irks critics of the word *commentate*; whatever the reason, the word remains stigmatized. It is used occasionally in journalism, but is avoided in more formal writing.

> Tracy Wilson has left CTV Sports and is now working exclusively for CBS, who she commentated for at the Winter Olympics.
> *Toronto Star* 5 Sept. 1992: S3

> (In formal writing, 'for whom she *was a commentator*' or 'for whom she *provided commentary*' would be preferable.)

See also BACK-FORMATION.

commiserate One usually commiserates *with* someone *over* or *about* a problem. Because the Latin prefix *com-* means 'with', commentators used to deplore this usage, arguing that the verb was transitive: 'I commiserate you on your loss'. Usage has passed them by, however, and *commiserate* now often functions grammatically just as *sympathize* does. *Commiserate* may also be used without a preposition if it describes reciprocal action: 'They were disheartened; they commiserated'.

> Barnes commiserated with him, telling the youngster to put the experience out of his mind and go on with his life.
> *Vancouver Sun* 24 Nov. 1994: D3

They can share a contemptuous chuckle over the arrest of peace demonstrators and commiserate over the fiscal and political obstacles to rearmament.
Globe and Mail (Toronto) 14 Jan. 1985: P6

Inside the Allendale recreation centre dozens of homeless victims commiserated and asked newcomers for the latest news and weather reports.
Globe and Mail (Toronto) 1 June 1985: M4

Numbed by 20 hours of anxiety, I met Pound and the COA officials to commiserate at the hotel bar.
Ottawa Citizen 8 Dec. 1990: B2

commissionaire   see LEGION

committal, commitment   A *committal* is a burial, an involuntary admission to a mental hospital, or a court order sending someone to trial or to prison. A *commitment* is a pledge of one's time or money, a strong feeling of attachment to a vocation, cause, etc., or a sense of obligation or loyalty towards another person.

Note that *committal* (like *committed* and *committing*) is spelled with a double *t*, while *commitment* is not.

A funeral will be held at Lawrence Park Community Church today at 1:30 p.m. A committal service will be held later in Renfrew.
Globe and Mail (Toronto) 15 Jan. 1985: N11

He said the new program will ensure psychiatric patients are informed of their legal rights, including the right to a lawyer, a review of their comital by a regional board and the right to appeal the review decision.
Globe and Mail (Toronto) 19 Sept. 1985: P22

(The correct spelling is *committal*.)

But he never abandoned his commitment to writing, and continued to work on his novel until the day of his death in 1960, at the age of forty.
Miriam Waddington *Apartment Seven* 1989: 25

Ovide Mercredi, head of the Assembly of First Nations, has been briefed on the proposals by Clark and said the government's committment to self-government is still vague.
Gazette (Montreal) 10 Sept. 1991: A1

(The correct spelling is *commitment*.)

… Hugh Grant stars as Charles, a London bachelor beginning to sense the loneliness that his fear of committal may bring.
Ottawa Citizen 9 Sept. 1994: C2

(The word needed here is *commitment*.)

common   see MUTUAL

common law, civil law, common-law   In Canada, the *common law* is used everywhere except in Quebec, which instead uses the *civil law* derived from the Napoleonic Code and Roman law. The common law originated in England; it is based on the decisions of judges, called precedents, and on custom, rather than on comprehensive written statutes.

Common-law is usually hyphenated when it functions as an adjective, as in 'common-law marriage' or 'common-law spouse'. Canadian journalism guides recommend against the term *common-law spouse*, considering it too formal and legalistic, and prefer phrases such as 'the woman he lives with' or 'the man she lives with'. Use of *common-law* in Canadian journalism is largely restricted to contexts where it is important to clarify that two individuals cohabit as spouses but have not had a religious or civil marriage ceremony. When *common law* functions as an adverb ('They were living common law'), the phrase should not be hyphenated.

Nevertheless, even a strict interpretation of the Statute did not prevent it from thwarting a large number of contracts in the common law courts.
J.E. Smyth et al. *The Law and Business Administration in Canada* 1987: 254

He is still fighting that battle today, trying to get the same pension, health care and dental benefits for North as any common-law heterosexual couple would have.
Leader-Post (Regina) 27 Feb. 1988: A23

Under the law, individuals aged 60 to 64 who are married to or live common law with low-income pensioners can apply for the monthly supplement.
Toronto Star 5 Dec. 1991: A13

See also SPOUSE.

community college   see UNIVERSITY

comparable, comparative   Things that are *comparable* are similar enough to invite comparison; in colloquial terms, they're in the same league. Things that are *comparative* are either reckoned by comparison ('comparative worth') or systematically investigated through comparison ('comparative literature').

Comparable is usually pronounced with stress on the first syllable: *COM per a bull*. The pronunciation *com PAIR a bull* is criticized.

All are comparable in terms of quality and price.
Alan Tucker, ed. *The Penguin Guide to Canada* 1991: 494

Leitch was a respected Canadian company that had been active in mining in Northern Ontario for many years; Texas Gulf was a large and wealthy American corporation and a comparative Johnny-come-lately to Northern Ontario mining.
Jack Batten *Robinette* 1984: 145

Their successors have had occasional, but hardly comparative, success.
Vancouver Sun 16 Dec. 1992: D13

(The word required here is *comparable*.)

A week later, with no other comparative offers, here comes Wade Boggs for three years guaranteed.
Toronto Star 17 Dec. 1992: C4

(The word required here is *comparable*.)

comparatively   see RELATIVELY

compare to, compare with   Commentators have argued that *compare to* should be reserved for occasions when it could be replaced by *liken* or *see as comparable to*: 'They compared her behaviour to that of the suffragettes'; 'He compared Alfredo's to a three-star restaurant because the service is so good'. In references to the act of examining two things for the purpose of finding similarities and differences they recommend *compare with*: 'The reviewer compared the book with the movie and concluded that the director had not done the book justice'; 'They compared Toronto with Queen's to determine which was the better university'. However, Canadians do not appear to observe this distinction, even in formal writing.

Sometimes, of course, the context makes it difficult to decide which sense is intended: 'She compared him to his brother' could mean either that she saw the two as similar or that she undertook an analysis that distinguished them (in which case some commentators would prefer *with*). But without more context the sense is not clear.

comparisons   Few people have trouble making comparisons with adverbs or adjectives. Occasionally, though, mistakes are made when a writer uses both a comparative ending and either the compara-

tive form with *more* or *most* ('more better', 'most fastest') or a word that is already comparative on its own ('worser'). Although these 'double comparatives' were common in literary writing until the eighteenth century, they are now considered uneducated.

Adjectives and adverbs change form when they are used to make comparisons: 'She runs faster than John'; 'This plant has the greenest leaves of the three'. Adjectives and adverbs of one syllable produce the comparative with the ending *-er* (*faster, sweeter*) and the superlative form with the ending *-est* (*fastest, sweetest*).

Adjectives and adverbs with three or more syllables must make the comparative with *more* (*more beautiful, more generous, more gracefully*) and the superlative with *most* (*most beautiful, most generous, most gracefully*).

Two-syllable adjectives vary; some that are acceptable with either comparative endings or *more* and *most* are *clever, common, cruel, honest, pleasant,* and *polite*. Adjectives that end in *-le, -ow,* and *-y* usually make the comparative with endings: *abler, yellower, lovelier*.

Adverbs that end in *-ly* use *more* and *most*: *more slowly, most frequently*.

It is, of course, possible to use *more* and *most* to make comparisons with one- and two-syllable adjectives and adverbs for reasons of style or idiom: 'a more clear and convincing explanation'.

See also ABSOLUTE COMPARATIVES; COMPLETE; DIFFERENT FROM; LIKE, AS; PERFECT; THAN; UNIQUE; WORSE.

compass points   see EAST, WEST, NORTH, SOUTH

competence, competency   Both variants are acceptable in all senses, including the sense of enough money or property to live on: 'She inherited a competence *or* competency from her grandmother'. *Competence* is much more common, however. *Competency* is most often used in the contexts of education ('competency in Spanish') and the law ('ordered an assessment of his mental competency').

complaisant, complacent   *Complaisant* (usually pronounced *com PLAYS ent*) means deferential or obliging. *Complacent* (pronounced *com PLACE ent*) means smug, self-satisfied, or dangerously unconcerned.

Profumo (Ian McKellen) is not a figure of fun—an aging man dallying with a complaisant young woman—

but rather a bright, intense public figure who falls victim to an infatuation he cannot fight.
Financial Post 15 May 1989: 23

It also concluded that one reason for his dismissal was that Crowe was 'not sufficiently complaisant, not servile enough in thought and attitude to his administrative superiors.'
Toronto Star 18 July 1993: B1

Surely, we had become complacent and cocksure.
Maclean's 24 Feb. 1986: 13

compleat   Book publishers are largely responsible for reviving the seventeenth-century spelling of *complete*, currently in vogue in titles of handbooks and modelled on the title of Izaak Walton's classic *The Compleat Angler* (1653). *Compleat* is also used humorously in newspaper writing.

This curious blend of compleat outsider and middle-class manners is what lent Burroughs's work its unique qualities.
Gazette (Montreal) 4 March 1989: K11

But, we hear you ask in anxious chorus, can this jogger seriously consider himself compleat without the latest product of Puma Sportschuhfabriken KG of West Germany—a pair of jogging shoes with a built-in computer?
Globe and Mail (Toronto) 20 April 1985: P6

complement   see COMPLIMENT

complete   Some usage commentators object to the use of the comparative modifiers *more* and *most* with *complete* on the grounds that *complete* is an absolute adjective and therefore cannot be compared. The same objection is raised against using comparatives with *unique* and *perfect*. In the history of their use, however, these words have been freely modified.

There is little reason to use *more*, *less*, or *most* when *complete* means total or unequivocal, as in 'a complete surprise'; it's hard to imagine a partially complete surprise. But when *complete* is used to mean thorough or comprehensive, as in 'a complete investigation' or 'a complete collection', it is common and accepted at all levels of English to modify the word with the comparative terms *more* and *most*. A keen investigator is likely to do a more complete investigation than a lazy one, and a collector who finds a rare item now enjoys a more complete—or perhaps the most complete—collection.

A complete postglacial pollen profile is needed for a more complete understanding of Holocene paleo-climatic changes.
Canadian Journal of Earth Sciences 26 (1989): 263

Brébeuf is not only the greatest but the most complete Canadian narrative, and brings together into a single pattern all the themes we have been tracing.
Northrop Frye *The Bush Garden* 1971: 153

There is no admission charge at this museum, which holds the most complete collection of Canadian notes and coins in the world.
Alan Tucker, ed. *The Penguin Guide to Canada* 1991: 303–4

See also DESTROY; PERFECT; REPLETE; UNIQUE.

compliment, complement, supplement   To *compliment* someone is to praise him or her; a *compliment* is praise. *Complimentary* tickets are a gift.

Something that *complements* something else completes it or fits harmoniously with it. A *complement* is something that completes a set or pair, or the full number of people or things needed to perform some particular task.

To *supplement* means to add something to a whole, such as a vitamin supplement to a diet or an advertising supplement to a newspaper.

A parody is a compliment; nobody troubles to mock what nobody takes seriously.
Robertson Davies *One Half of Robertson Davies* 1978: 253

The city of Stratford has many other pleasures to complement and round out a visit to the famous Shakespeare Festival.
Leisure Life May 1988: 84

HMCS Huron, with a complement of 280 sailors, will sail Jan. 4 from Victoria. . . .
Vancouver Sun 20 Dec. 1990: A1

We encourage subscribers to use the full complement of safety features, such as hands-free speed dialling and voice activation.
Vancouver Sun 17 Oct. 1990: A12

Beaudoin said the proposed plane would compliment and not compete with Canadair's latest baby—its 50-seat Regional Jet. . . .
Gazette (Montreal) 27 June 1991: C1

(The correct spelling is *complement*.)

There are two complimentary but very different sections to the garden, referred to as 'the classical garden' and 'the park', and every detail in both seems to simulta-

neously contrast with and compliment some other, opposite detail.
Canadian Heritage Magazine Aug.–Sept. 1986: 37–8

(The correct spellings here are *complementary* and *complement*.)

See also BACKHANDED COMPLIMENT.

comprehend   see APPREHEND

comprehensible, comprehendible   Canadian writers use *comprehensible*. *Comprehendible* is listed as an alternative form of the adjective in American dictionaries.

Rabbior is president of the Canadian Foundation for Economic Education, a non-profit organization that tries to make economics comprehensible to the average person.
Toronto Star 21 Nov. 1994: A21

comprise   A whole comprises its parts. *Comprise* functions grammatically in the same way as the verb *include*. However, after *comprise* all the parts making up the whole are named, while after *include* only some need be mentioned: 'The set comprises twelve volumes'; 'The twelve-volume set includes an index'.
  The passive form, *be comprised of*, is disputed, often strenuously, although it is in common use. Usage guides tend to reject this form, probably because it is used with exactly the same meaning as the active form: 'The set is comprised of twelve volumes'. When *comprise* is used in the passive, it becomes analogous to *compose* rather than *include*.
  A second disputed usage reverses the subject and object of *comprise* so that the parts comprise the whole, or one part comprises a specified portion of the whole: 'Twelve volumes comprise the set'; 'Prince Edward Island comprises 0.1% of Canadian territory'. This usage is very common.
  To sum up, writers currently use the passive construction of *comprise* and the original active construction synonymously, and the original and the two disputed usages of *comprise* are all well established. Thus *comprise* is currently an anomalous and confusing verb. To avoid criticism, it is best to use *comprise* only in the active voice to mean 'consists of'. Where the passive voice seems more appropriate, *is made up of* or *is composed of* can be substituted for *is comprised of*. And where the parts making up a whole are the subject of the sentence, *constitute* or *make up* is a better choice than *comprise*.

The pot still process comprises four stages: malting, mashing, fermentation and distillation.
Bon Vivant Aug.–Sept. 1982: 13

The Quebec Furniture Conciliation Committee comprises one manufacturer and one retailer who are not involved in the dispute and two representatives of the Quebec Consumers' Association....
Canadian Consumer Jan. 1985: 7

Style is comprised of many elements, the major ones being diction, figurative language, sentences, and tone....
Richard Davies and Glen Kirkland, eds. *Dimensions* 1986: 181

(Here *comprises* or *is composed of* is recommended.)

The money was awarded to Target Downtown, a ten-member committee comprised of small business and local government representatives.
Canadian Heritage Feb.–Mar. 1986: 9

(Here *composed of* is recommended.)

The most sensitive or 'militant' group, who tend to be educated and affluent, comprised 17 percent.
Western Grocer Aug. 1990: 36

(Here the 'part', not the 'whole', is the subject: *constituted* is recommended.)

The various statutes comprising our companies and securities legislation now require a disclosure of information....
J.E. Smith et al. *The Law and Business Administration in Canada* 1987: 232

(Again the parts are the subject: *constituting* is recommended.)

comptroller, controller   A *comptroller* is the chief accounting officer of a business or institution. A *controller* is a person or device that directs or regulates something. The spelling *controller* may be substituted for *comptroller*—though the spelling choice of a company or institution should be respected—but the reverse is not true: there are no air traffic comptrollers. *Comptroller* is pronounced just like *controller*.
  Comptroller is a variant spelling of *controller* that was introduced around 1500 by scribes who mistakenly assumed that the word was related to the Latin *computare* and the French *compter*, 'to count'. In fact, the prefix in *controller* is derived from the French word *contre*, 'against'. The fourteenth-century controller was a person who kept contre- or counter-rolls, copies of household accounts, against which all expenditures were checked. Thus the

word *controller* referred to a financial officer before it had any broader application, and the variant spelling *comptroller* probably survived because it became entrenched as an institutional job title.

As construction of the third apartment building neared completion, the comptroller of Gilman pressed for payment in full of the account.
J.E. Smyth et al. *The Law and Business Administration in Canada* 1987: 329

He's been president of Richard de Boo Publishers, controller of Connaught Laboratories and vice-president of a trust company, among other things.
Business Journal June 1991: 33

compunction, compulsion   To feel no *compunction* about doing or saying something means to feel no shame or guilt about it. To feel no *compulsion* to do something means to feel unpressured or uncompelled to do it.

Goldman felt no compunction about comparing Jagger's influence on his audience with Nazism.
Queen's Quarterly 92.2 (1985): 273

Rarely can a salmon angler, when handed pen and paper, resist the compulsion to tell the world why and when, in his opinion, salmon take flies.
Atlantic Salmon Journal Summer (1990): 20

Another Christmas has come and gone, and myriads around the world have listened in their homes to records or radio, or have watched television performances, enjoying the glorious music of the Messiah without feeling the slightest compunction to jump to their feet to demonstrate a trance-like exaltation.
Globe and Mail (Toronto) 5 Jan. 1985: P7

(The word required here is *compulsion*).

computing   see E-MAIL ADDRESSES

concave, convex   *Concave* means hollowed (think of a cave). *Convex* means the opposite, bulging outward.

Climbing to the top of the castle, up stone steps worn concave over the centuries, takes time but is certainly worth it for the view.
Globe and Mail (Toronto) 2 Nov. 1985: F16

To smooth the caulk in place, try dipping an old spoon into a bowl of soapy water and then gently running the convex side along the bead.
Ottawa Citizen 6 Oct. 1990: C3

concerto   The second syllable of *concerto* is stressed and pronounced *CHAIR*. The plural is *concertos*, or sometimes, especially in historical references, *concerti* (*-ti* is pronounced *-tee*).

She has already played most of the major concertos for her instrument.
Calgary Herald 26 Sept. 1992: D14

Thibaudet is the soloist in ... the Liszt Concerti Nos. 1 & 2, Hungarian Fantasy and Totentanz. ...
Ottawa Citizen 4 July 1992: G2

See also -OS, -OES.

concession road   see ROAD

conciliation, mediation, arbitration, judicial determination, adjudication, judgment   These words have special legal meanings. In a labour dispute, if negotiations reach an impasse, *conciliation*, *mediation*, and *arbitration* are steps taken in the formal process of resolving the dispute. The first two facilitate negotiations without imposing a settlement; arbitration, however, is binding. The disputing parties can also decide to have a judge make the binding decision; this process is called *judicial determination*.

In law, *adjudication* generally follows a hearing, while *judgment* follows a trial.

Labour Minister Jean Corbeil ... wants the Canadian Union of Postal Workers back at the bargaining table for a second round of conciliation and not on the picket line after 15 months of often-troubled negotiations with Canada Post.
Province (Vancouver) 1 Nov. 1990: 16

The native concept of justice differs from the Canadian one; it focuses more on mediation and restitution than on retribution.
Gazette (Montreal) 12 Feb. 1990: B2

He must carry out his obligation, hearing the evidence to the end, before he makes his adjudication.
Province (Vancouver) 4 Jan. 1990: B1

concise, succinct, concision, conciseness   *Concise* implies that anything inessential has been removed or cut off. *Succinct* suggests compression, so that much is conveyed in few words. In general, however, these words are used synonymously.

Concision and *conciseness* both mean succinctness; either word is acceptable.

It was a commendable accomplishment; the entries are models of concision yet contain an impressive amount of information.
Globe and Mail (Toronto) 7 Sept. 1985: E1

Conciseness helps to win readers.
Financial Post 30 Jan. 1989: 9

concord   see AGREEMENT, GRAMMATICAL

concrete   see CEMENT; CONCRETIZE

concretize   To *concretize* means to make concrete and specific what was nebulous or abstract. Though the word has been criticized as business jargon, it is more often used in academic and essay writing.

Murray Favro's *Van Gogh's Room* (1973-74) is an installation piece that both concretizes and simulates (in Baudrillard's sense) a simulation—that is, a representation of a real thing.
Linda Hutcheon *Splitting Images* 1991: 24

Further, concretizing our 'free floating' fears of HIV—for example, in the form of visa restrictions—gives credibility to the unreasonable fears of many persons with respect to HIV.
Gazette (Montreal) 22 June 1990: B3

See also -IZE, -ISE; QUEBEC ENGLISH.

concurrent   see SYNCHRONOUS

condemn, contemn   To *condemn* is to express disapproval of, to find guilty, or to sentence to punishment. *Contemn* is a rare verb meaning to despise, scorn, or hold in contempt.

A long procession of clergymen came forward to condemn slavery and to sing the virtues of English liberty.
William Teatero *John Anderson: Fugitive Slave* 1986: 168

Oddly enough, self-made men generally yearn for acceptance from those they contemn, just as academics become misty-eyed in the presence of a bulging bank book.
Globe and Mail (Toronto) 19 June 1985: P6

conference, conferencing   The use of *conference* as a verb grew out of educational jargon and developed a second meaning in computer vocabulary. Both senses of this new verb are becoming more common. In its largely academic use, to *conference* means either to participate in a conference or to confer with someone. Advances in computer technology have made it possible for *conferencing* to refer to the conferring that people do when they are linked by computer, either through a local network or, more often, through the Internet. The terms for what happens when a video link is added, so that people can see and hear each other, are in flux: *video conferencing*, *teleconferencing*, or *video teleconferencing*.

Said one mother: 'Along with the three classes of gym a week, the field trips ... and teachers being pulled out of the classroom for pedagogical days, curriculum planning, special seminars and "conferencing," I can't see where there's enough time for serious study.'
Globe and Mail (Toronto) 16 May 1985: BL1

Relying largely on word-of-mouth advertising, a computer conferencing system at the University of Guelph ... has attracted more than 1,400 users in 29 countries.
Globe and Mail (Toronto) 12 July 1985: B13

Jardine ... took all her courses via television using the University of New Brunswick's teleconferencing network.
Chronicle-Herald (Halifax) 14 May 1986: 73

By 1995, for example, PCs that carry video images will appear on the market, says Steve O'Neil, manager of telecommunications systems for ... a Toronto-based distributor of video teleconferencing gear.
Computer Dealer News 21 March 1991: 32

confidant, confidante, confident   A *confidant* is a person who is respected and trusted with intimate information. A *confidant* can be either male or female. Sometimes, because *confidant* is borrowed from French, writers use *confidant* for men and *confidante* for women; *confidante* should be applied only to women. *Confidant* is usually pronounced *con fee DAUNT* or *CON fih DAUNT*.
Confident is the spelling of the adjective meaning self-assured.

Dunning, unlike Richardson, did not have a private fortune, but he was a trusted confidant of many who did.
Frederick Gibson *Queen's University* 2 (1983): 226

Sauvé has, after all, served as a constitutional confidant to her Prime Minister—in her case, three of them.
Toronto Star 28 Oct. 1990: B3

(Here *confidante* would also be acceptable.)

Again, the initial triangle becomes a second when husband exits and his best buddy becomes confidante to each of the women.
United Church Observer June 1986: 53

(The correct spelling here, in reference to a man, is *confidant*.)

confute   see REFUTE

congenial, genial   According to many usage guides, a *congenial* person is a person one gets along with, someone with similar interests and tastes, while a *genial* person is generally good-natured. This distinction is obsolete, however. In contemporary Canadian English, *congenial* and *genial* are used interchangeably to refer to people with a kind, friendly manner, while *congenial* is also used in more formal contexts to mean suited to a particular taste, purpose, mood, etc.

> He enjoyed drinking and had a few scrapes with the law, but overall [he] was considered a congenial person who often regaled friends with tales of his exploits around the world.
> *Gazette* (Montreal) 7 June 1992: A7

> He was a genial, easy-going man who enjoyed a drink, didn't take religion seriously, and was perfectly willing to let his wife take charge.
> Pierre Berton *The Promised Land* 1984: 280

> It would be hard to imagine a man more congenial to Grant in opinion and in temperament.
> Hilda Neatby *Queen's University* 1 (1978): 172

> Speech-making was very much in Fyfe's line, but the role of fund-raiser he found neither familiar nor congenial.
> Frederick Gibson *Queen's University* 2 (1983): 101

> In Britain and New Zealand, the Labour Party 'welfare leaders' found the redistributive consequences of Keynesianism to be particularly congenial to their social democratic goals.
> Neil Nevitte and Roger Gibbins *New Elites in Old States* 1990: 20

congenital, hereditary, genetic   A *congenital* disorder is one that dates from birth. It may be a problem caused during the birth process, such as a brain injury, or one that developed in the foetus before birth, such as a heart defect. Sometimes the word *congenital* is used figuratively to describe habits and attitudes so entrenched as to seem inborn.

A *hereditary* disorder is one that is passed genetically from generation to generation, such as hemophilia or Tay-Sachs disease. Not all hereditary problems can be called *congenital*, because they do not all appear at birth.

On the other hand, all hereditary problems are *genetic* because they have to do with genes—but not all genetic disorders are hereditary. For example, gene damage caused by radiation can result in sterility, which is obviously not a heritable condition.

> The baby was delivered by caesarean section ... with a number of congenital defects, the most serious being brain damage.
> *Vancouver Sun* 5 Dec. 1990: A1

> Alison, who is congenitally nervous of horses, was somewhat discomfited to find herself seated beside [the] Master of the Horse.
> George Ignatieff *The Making of a Peacemonger* 1987: 175

> Well, dogs can fall heir to a number of diseases, many of them hereditary. Some seem to occur in particular breeds or in certain types or sizes of canines.
> *Dogs in Canada* Special Issue 1986: 137

congratulate, congratulations   *Congratulate* and *congratulations* are often mispronounced, and occasionally misspelled, *congradulate* and *congradulations*. The association between graduations and congratulations may contribute to this error. The standard pronunciation of *congratulate* is *con GRACH yoo late*.

> Congradulations, Mary Humphries of North York. You're first.
> *Toronto Star* 10 Jan. 1994: A13

(This writer has misspelled *congratulations* on purpose to mimic the common mispronunciation.)

congregation   see AUDIENCE

conjugal, connubial   *Conjugal* (*CON jew gal*) and *connubial* (*con NUBE ee al*) are both formal words referring to the married state. *Conjugal* is far more common, perhaps because it occurs in the legal phrase 'conjugal rights': the rights of married partners to each other's company and affection, including physical intimacy. The word *connubial*, which is often found in the cliché 'connubial bliss', has connotations that are romantic rather than legal.

> Orton said courts have 'extended' benefits to disadvantaged groups before, ... allowing homosexual partners conjugal prison visits....
> *Vancouver Sun* 24 Feb. 1990: H14

> Roy says the courts should start giving stiffer penalties for conjugal violence.
> *Vancouver Sun* 4 Oct. 1990: A12

The trick had always been ... to behave well, or at least reasonably well, in exchange for parental or connubial love, a job, social position.
Gazette (Montreal) 8 Sept. 1990: K2

connive   Derived from the French for 'to close the eyes to' or 'to wink at', to *connive* in its historical sense means to pretend ignorance of wrongdoing. Thus a conniver doesn't actively participate in misbehaviour but condones it through silence and inaction. This meaning is still common in British English, but almost unknown in Canada and the United States.

Since the Second World War, in North America, *connive* has become a synonym for *conspire*: to actively participate with others in secret wrongdoing. This newer meaning has also become established in Britain. *Connive* in its older sense is followed by *at*: 'The secretary connived at the lawyer's misuse of funds'. When it is a synonym for *conspire*, *connive* is often used with *with*: 'The spy connived with the enemy'.

The opposition Labour Party called for the resignation of Defence Minister Michael Heseltine and a junior minister, John Stanley, saying they had connived to mislead Parliament.
Globe and Mail (Toronto) 12 Feb. 1985: P1

The Liberals connive at stopping the free-trade bill by lining up their Senate majority of faithful retainers against it—and have the gall to plead they are acting in the spirit of democracy.
Ottawa Citizen 21 July 1988: A8

The petition also said that the three trial judges connived with prosecutors to acquit the accused, saying that in one instance a judge allegedly passed a note to the defence.
Globe and Mail (Toronto) 20 Nov. 1985: A10

See also COLLABORATION, COLLABORATOR.

connoisseur   A *connoisseur* (pronounced *con uh SER*) is an expert in some particular matter of taste. This word was borrowed from Old French; in modern French it is spelled *connaisseur*. This modern French spelling sometimes leads to misspelling of the English word, especially in Quebec.

He did not consider himself a first-rate judge of plays, but he successfully asserted his claim to be regarded as a great connoisseur of acting, and his many books of collected criticism burn with a splendid and infectious enthusiasm.
Robertson Davies *A Voice from the Attic* 1960: 195

Connaisseurs and collectors tend to sniff at the choice and selection of the music offered by Discus....
Gazette (Montreal) 12 Nov. 1993: F1

(The correct English spelling is *connoisseurs*.)

connotation(s), denotation, connote, denote
The *connotations* of *thin* are fairly neutral; those of *lean*, *slender*, and *svelte*, usually positive; and of *skinny*, usually negative. Yet all these words have the same *denotation* or bald meaning: of less than average weight. *Connotations* are the indirect implications of words—the ideas and feelings habitually associated with them. *Denotation* is literal signification. Thesauruses may lead inexperienced writers astray because sometimes they list as synonyms words with the same basic denotation while ignoring their connotations. For example, *Roget's 21st Century Thesaurus* (1992) has after *thin* a long list of words with very different connotations, including *cadaverous, delicate, fragile, lanky, lean, skeletal, skinny, slim, small, spare,* and *spindly*.

The verbs *connote* and *denote* are used less technically and distinguished less carefully than the nouns *connotation* and *denotation*. *Connote* usually means imply or suggest. *Denote* has a range of meanings, including signify, represent, indicate, symbolize, and imply.

This literal definition, however, does not capture the rich web of associations and connotations that has developed around tabloid journalism.
Queens Quarterly 96.1 (1989): 94

There were few people in the Balkans who had not heard about the exploits of my diplomat grandfather ... so the Ignatieff name carried strong connotations in that part of the world.
George Ignatieff *The Making of a Peacemonger* 1987: 154

He also said the judge had used [a word] 'only in a descriptive and not in any other sense.' Yet linguists say that is impossible: words carry not only denotation, but connotation.
Vancouver Sun 20 Jan. 1990: B4

The design consists of a stylized open fan created to connote service and luxury.
Globe and Mail (Toronto) 20 Feb. 1985: B9

The suffix '-man' has lost its original masculine denotation and now connotes merely one-who-does-something.
Vancouver Sun 16 April 1990: A9

(Here *denotes* would also be possible.)

Alpenweiss translates, from the German, into 'Alps-white.' And that was fine as long as Alpenweiss denoted a white wine, but language experts were not pleased when the same name was applied to a sister red wine introduced subsequently.
Globe and Mail (Toronto) 30 Aug. 1985: P7

Barbers, in fact, were more responsible for caring for the wounded than doctors because they had the closest thing to sterile conditions. Hence the red and white barber's pole, denoting red blood and white bandages.
Globe and Mail (Toronto) 20 April 1985: P10

The plume of smoke that surrounded the face of many an author on the back of a dust-jacket was supposed to denote deep contemplation as well as exotic mystery.
Globe and Mail (Toronto) 12 Jan. 1985: E22

(Here *connote* would also be possible.)

See also SYNONYM, ANTONYM, THESAURUS.

connubial   see CONJUGAL

consensus   The common phrases *consensus of opinion* and *general consensus* are often criticized as redundant because *consensus* by itself means a general agreement: 'The board reached a consensus'. However, the disputed phrases are quite defensible as idioms referring to consensus in society, or in a broad group, as opposed to that reached by, say, a committee meeting in a boardroom. Note that *consensus* is frequently misspelled *concensus*.

It was the consensus of opinion that such a state cannot be a satellite of Israel and cannot be 'created by Israel' as a pseudo-solution to the refugee problem and the Arab-Israeli conflict.
Henry M. Rosenthal and S. Cathy Berson, eds. *Canadian Jewish Outlook Anthology* 1988: 161

The general consensus seemed to be that he acted out of compassion. Given this good motive, and their view that death should be a private matter, many Canadians expected [him] to be acquitted.
Toronto Star 22 Nov. 1994: A21

If Dartmouth MP Ron MacDonald was looking for concensus out of his first town hall meeting on social policy reform Tuesday, he didn't get it.
Daily News (Halifax) 8 Dec. 1994: D3

(The correct spelling is *consensus*.)

consequently, consequentially, consequential
Consequently and *consequentially* both mean therefore. *Consequently* usually implies a direct causal relationship, while *consequentially* suggests that what follows is an indirect result of what precedes.

In general English, *consequential* means important, significant. In Canadian law, the terms *consequential loss* and *consequential damage* refer to secondary damages, which are one stage removed from an initial breach of contract.

We found several instances of reviewers identifying an author as a 'housewife' and consequently dismissing anything she has produced (since, in our society, a 'housewife' is viewed as a relatively brainless and talentless creature).
Margaret Atwood *Second Words* 1982: 198

More than 30,000 [Loyalists] settled in Nova Scotia, tripling that colony's population and spilling into New Brunswick, which was consequentially established as a separate colony in 1784.
Neil Nevitte and Roger Gibbins *New Elites in Old States* 1990: 6

Mr. Caplan said the media now dominate the political process with their emphasis on personality politics, trivial and staged confrontation ... and their warped ethic of covering whatever is said as if it were consequential.
Globe and Mail (Toronto) 2 Feb. 1985: M5

For instance, failure to repair the heating system of a concert hall as promised in time for a performance in midwinter may lead to the cancellation of the program, making the heating contractor liable for the consequential losses due to cancellation, as well as for damage to the building by frozen pipes, since these were foreseeable harms.
J.E. Smyth *The Law and Business Administration in Canada* 1987: 352

Conservative, Progressive Conservative, Tory, Red Tory, Loyalist, United Empire Loyalists
Conservative and *Progressive Conservative* are used interchangeably for the political party in Canada, although *Progressive* has been part of its official name since 1941. The term *Tory* is well established as an informal name for members and supporters of this party. *Tory* has a long history in British politics; by 1689 it was associated with a new British political party that favoured conservatism. *Conservative* became the official name of that party in 1830, but *Tory* remains in use to refer to British Conservatives. A *Red Tory* is a member of the Conservative Party who has (or is said to have) liberal or populist leanings.

In American English, *Tory* refers to colonists who remained loyal to Britain and opposed independence at the time of the American Revolution. In

Canada, these people are called *Loyalists* or *United Empire Loyalists* (sometimes abbreviated *UEL*).

> But Beaulieu later rejected the Tory offer and decided to accept the Liberal nomination.
> *Maclean's* 8 Sept. 1986: 16

> To that end, the citizens of Riverview, a Moncton suburb, voted Liberal in last spring's by-election—the first time in thirty-seven years they failed to elect the Tory candidate.
> *Saturday Night* Jan. 1986: 29

> Only on a few social issues does he show any Red Tory instincts, any concern for the disadvantaged.
> *Saturday Night* March 1986: 24

consider *Consider* takes a direct object ('consider it') and sometimes a direct object and object complement ('Consider it *done*'; 'I consider them *the best*'). Some commentators have objected to the insertion of *as* between the object and the complement, preferring, for example, 'Consider me your friend' to 'Consider me as your friend'; although others argue that there is nothing wrong with this structure, the insertion of *as* does seem to imply an effort of the imagination: 'She considers the cockroaches as pets'.

> 'Writing is what I like to do, but I don't consider it a career.'
> Bruce Meyer and Brian O'Riordan, eds. *In Their Words* 1984: 154

> As a Nazi, Goetz refused to consider the thousands of German refugees driven from their homes and country by the Nazis as 'real Germans'.
> *Canadian Journal of History* 14.1 (1989): 74

consist *Consist* is usually followed by the preposition *of*. In formal writing, *consists in* is sometimes used, especially to describe the basis of an abstraction.

> Duress consists in actual or threatened violence or imprisonment as a means of coercing a party to enter into a contract.
> J.E. Smyth et al. *The Law and Business Administration in Canada* 1987: 237

consonants, doubling of see DOUBLING THE FINAL CONSONANT

conspiracy, conspirator, co-conspirator see COLLABORATION

Constitution, British North America Act, BNA Act, Constitution Act All the acts that make up the formal written part of the Canadian Constitution are called the Constitution Acts, 1867 to 1982. The Constitutional Act (1791) is only one of a series of earlier acts and proclamations, beginning with the Royal Proclamation of 1763, that established Canada as a legal entity. The Canadian Constitution is supplemented by laws having constitutional effect and by unwritten conventions. The British North America Act (abbreviated BNA Act) was passed in 1867 by the British parliament. It made a federation of the Province of Canada (Ontario and Quebec), New Brunswick, and Nova Scotia. Other provinces joined later. The Act remained a British statute, however, rather than a Canadian one. In 1982, as part of the move to bring the act under Canadian control, known as the patriation of the Canadian Constitution, the BNA Act was renamed the Constitution Act, 1867. The Canadian Charter of Rights and Freedoms is part of the Constitution Act, 1982.

See also CANADIAN BILL OF RIGHTS; PATRIATE, PATRIATION.

consul see COUNCIL

consummate The adjective, which means perfect, complete, unsurpassable, or, when describing a role, highly accomplished, is pronounced *CON sum it* or *con SUM it*. The verb, meaning complete or fulfil, is pronounced *CON sub MATE*. The verb refers to the first act of sexual intercourse in a marriage, which makes the marriage valid in canon law, or to the completion of a business deal or other transaction.

> Yet, ironically, Reagan was nothing during his eight years in office if not the consummate product of the consumer culture—and all its deficits, its emphasis upon style and personality, and its demand for instant gratification—that he claimed to abhor.
> *Queen's Quarterly* 95.4 (1988): 798

> Ford is a consummate politician with a set of ideas that could have been programmed by a pollster.
> *Ottawa Citizen* 1 Dec. 1994: C1

> She insisted on visiting her relatives for long periods and refused to consummate the marriage, not because of a physical complaint but because of a lack of desire.
> Jack Batten *Robinette* 1984: 41

> It is also likely that Quebec, the shunned partner, would not have been subject to a midnight deal consummated in a kitchen behind her back.
> *Queen's Quarterly* 95.3 (1988): 691

contact clauses   see THAT, OMISSION OF

contagious, infectious   *Contagious* and *infectious* are often used as synonyms in everyday speech and popular writing. In medical terms, however, these words don't mean exactly the same thing, and the distinction is worth maintaining in serious writing. All diseases caused by micro-organisms are infectious (e.g., colds, AIDS, scabies, malaria, and amoebic dysentery). But only those diseases transmitted directly from person to person are contagious. Of the diseases above, colds, AIDS, and scabies are contagious, transmitted by sneezing, sexual contact, and physical contact, but malaria, which is transmitted by a particular type of mosquito—never from human to human—is not contagious, and neither is amoebic dysentery, which is usually contracted by drinking contaminated water.

Both words are acceptable when used figuratively to describe something that spreads from one person to another: *contagious* is used more often than *infectious* when describing something unpleasant.

Now doctors are blaming bacteria for these painful craters in the stomach and upper intestine. Peptic ulcers an infectious disease? That's the controversial theory.
Ottawa Citizen 13 July 1994: B3

Victims catch [Legionnaires'] disease, which is not thought to be contagious, by inhaling minute water droplets in the air from contaminated cooling, air conditioning and hot water systems.
Globe and Mail (Toronto) 4 May 1985: P17

Paris terrorism is contagious.
Globe and Mail (Toronto) 25 June 1985: P7

Father Terry, who said he is basically a happy person, finds joy is infectious. 'If I'm bubbly and joyful it's contagious.'
Catholic Register 16 Aug. 1986: 21

contemn   see CONDEMN

contemporary, contemporaneous   Most dictionaries list 'existing at the same time' as the first meaning of *contemporary*, but since the 1940s its more common meaning has been modern or present-day. In some contexts it is difficult to decide which of these two meanings is intended. Some usage commentators suggest reserving *contemporary* to mean modern or up-to-date and using *contemporaneous* to mean existing at the same time. However, there are two problems with this advice: first, while *contemporaneous* is a useful and unambiguous term, it is quite formal and usually found only in academic writing; second, the word *contemporary* remains ambiguous to the reader, who still has to decide whether or not the writer is restricting it to one meaning. The best advice is to paraphrase *contemporary* in contexts where both meanings are plausible. For example, 'This production of *The Taming of the Shrew* is in contemporary costume' could mean that the actors are in Elizabethan costume—but it could also mean that they're in modern dress. Writing either 'modern costume' or 'Elizabethan costume' would remove any question.

One of the first projects that the Commission undertook was to carry out 'a deep philosophical probe' of Canada's criminal law, leading to the enactment of a comprehensive Criminal Code reflecting contemporary values.
Canadian Bar Review 66.3 (1987): 532

(Here *contemporary* means present-day.)

... once I have, so to speak, recovered myself as I used to be, I can look at the town, whose childhood was exactly contemporary with my own, with more understanding.
Richard Davies and Glen Kirkland, eds. *Dimensions* 1986: 139

(Here *contemporary* means existing at the same time.)

Coincidentally, the beginning of this European activity was roughly contemporaneous with a decline of both Chinese and Islamic exploratory activity.
William Norton *Human Geography* 1992: 16

The body itself is more realistically lifeless and blood-spattered than is usual in the idealized images of the Italian tradition.... The male angel on the right of the composition wears barely visible, transparent wings but sports a very contemporary short haircut.
Linda Hutcheon *Splitting Images* 1991: 123–4

(Given the way fashions in hairstyles change, it might be sensible to eliminate any possibility of confusion by writing either 'surprisingly modern-looking' or 'fashionable for the era'.)

contemptible, contemptuous   *Contemptible* means deserving of contempt; to be *contemptuous* is to feel contempt, to be scornful.

Real unity tolerates dissent and rejoices in variety of outlook and tradition, recognizes that it is man's destiny to unite and not divide, and understands that creating proletariats and scapegoats and second-class citizens is a mean and contemptible activity.
Northrop Frye *The Bush Garden* 1971: vi

A contemptuous Supreme Court of Ontario judge yesterday sent the kingpin of a massive marijuana importing operation to jail for 20 years....
Globe and Mail (Toronto) 11 June 1985: P1

continuance, continuation, continuity *Continuance* has two meanings. It may be a formal synonym for duration ('Its continuance was brief'); or it may refer simply to the fact that something continues ('Its continuance was taken for granted'). *Continuation* is also used in this second sense, but more often refers to an active addition to something, or a prolonging or renewal of it: 'It's a continuation of his previous novel'.

Continuity is the quality of connectedness between the parts in a whole or a series. In filmmaking, the person in charge of *continuity* ensures that there are no discrepancies in the details of scenes shot at different times. In radio and television programs, *continuity* is the music or commentary that introduces or links segments.

An environmental threat is one which endangers the continuance or permanence of living things.
Queen's Quarterly 92.1 (1985): 206

The green symbolized the continuance of life through the winter and meshed with the Christian belief of eternal life through Christ.
Toronto Star 27 Dec. 1994: A7

The continuation of the revolution depends on keeping the flame lit by Guevara alive.
Queen's Quarterly 92.2 (1985): 392

Sydney lies farther southeast on the highway's continuation around Sydney's Atlantic harbor.
Alan Tucker, ed. *The Penguin Guide to Canada* 1991: 64

To start fermentation, and also to ensure continuity of taste and character, must from a previous fermentation is added.
Bon Vivant Feb.–Mar. 1983: 9

continuous(ly), continual(ly) Something *continuous* goes on without a break: 'Their store is continuously monitored by video camera'. Something *continual* goes on and on but with breaks: 'Their store is continually being robbed'. Almost every usage guide presents this distinction, although many concede that it is widely ignored. In formal writing the distinction should be maintained. Occasionally, however, the choice is debatable: for example, does the population of a city grow continually or continuously?

Fully automatic weapons will fire continuously as long as the trigger is depressed; semi-automatics fire only once each time the trigger is pulled.
Gazette (Montreal) 3 March 1989: B1

With the weight of heavy packs, we continually sank to our knees in oozing, freezing black mud.
Uphere Jan.–Feb. 1990: 48

As an aside, the data presented clearly indicate that men, too, were greatly interested in finding an effective, safe way of avoiding continuous childbearing. . . .
Canadian Journal of Sociology 14.2 (1989): 247

(Here *continual* is recommended.)

contractions Contractions (*I'm, they're, don't, wouldn't, aren't,* and so on) are appropriate in reported speech, dialogue, personal letters, business letters, and light journalism. They are inappropriate in highly formal writing such as official documents. Commentators agree on this much. The grey area is formal writing such as essays, reports, serious journalism, and serious fiction. *Fowler's* (1965) deemed contractions too chatty—hence grating—in such contexts. However, some modern writing guides say that avoiding contractions altogether results in a stilted style. What is at issue is not just a typographical convention, but how writing 'sounds'. Writing without any contractions has an oratorical tone (*let us not, do not, is it not?*), while writing full of contractions (*there's, should've, we'd*) sounds conversational. In formal writing, what one wants is something between a pontifical and a chummy tone. Thus contractions can be used, but sparingly.

See also ABBREVIATION; AIN'T; [COULD OF]; ITS, IT'S; SHAN'T; THERE IS; YOUR.

contretemps Dictionaries define a *contretemps*— pronounced *CON truh tah(m)*—as an embarrassing incident or awkward mishap. Recently, though, the word has developed a new meaning: dispute, controversy, or altercation. Although this newer meaning now predominates in Canadian journalism, it's not fully accepted and should be avoided in formal writing.

The Prince, he assured his audience, had been in no way responsible for the 'unfortunate contretemps.'
William Teatero *John Anderson: Fugitive Slave* 1986: 44

(Here *contretemps* refers to a diplomatic blunder; this is an accepted use of the term.)

Weirdness of another kind erupted at the festival's advance-sales ticket booth last weekend, when two festival workers had a colorful contretemps in front of lined-up ticket buyers.
Vancouver Sun 12 Oct. 1990: C1

controller

(This use is disputed.)

Strand happily recalled the occasion when Basham physically defended him during a contretemps with some campus radicals.
Financial Post 21 Sept. 1990: 11

(This use is disputed.)

controller   see COMPTROLLER

conversant   To be *conversant* with (*or* in) something is to be familiar with it. The pronunciation is *con VER sunt* in Canada and Britain; *CON ver sunt* is a second accepted pronunciation in the United States.

While clearly conversant with the ways of the world, Sheila McCarthy tends to play innocents.
Globe and Mail (Toronto) 15 May 1985: SB8

Because these telemarketers are selling from a product line consisting of thousands of different items, they may not be completely conversant in every one of them.
Computer Dealer News 21 March 1991: 56

convex   see CONCAVE

convince, persuade   In current Canadian and American usage these two words are synonyms, but before the 1950s their meanings were more distinct (*Webster's Dictionary of English Usage*). *Convince* was then generally reserved for mental conviction alone, as in 'Joan was convinced of the justice of the feminist cause'. *Persuade* referred to mental conviction followed by action, as in 'Joan was persuaded to donate money to the cause'. Usage commentators sometimes object to the use of *convince* followed by an infinitive, but this structure is now firmly established and unobjectionable.

... in 1836 Robinson, now Chief Justice and retired from active politics, convinced Draper to enter politics as a means to an end—Draper's sole ambition was to secure a place on the bench, and politics was the preferred means of promoting that ambition.
William Teatero *John Anderson: Fugitive Slave* 1986: 140

(Here *convince* is directly linked to action.)

The ways of publishers are unfathomable, but I hope someone can convince New Press to bring Reaney's poems out in paperback soon....
Margaret Atwood *Second Words* 1982: 159

(Here *convince* is directly linked to action.)

Memories of what happened to the Wehrmacht in Yugoslavia in the Second World War should suffice to persuade foreigners that imposing solutions leads to even more problems in that proud, unforgiving, strong part of the world.
Financial Post 10 Oct. 1991: 15

(Here *persuade* refers solely to mental conviction.)

Coordinated Universal Time   see GREENWICH MEAN TIME

cop, cop out   In spoken English, police officers are usually referred to as *cops*. Yet the word *cop* is avoided in news writing and formal prose. At issue is not only the formality of the word, but whether it is respectful to officers of the law. Most newspaper style guides recommend against using *cop* in serious contexts, though it is certainly not a highly pejorative term: the police use it themselves.

Cop was used as an informal verb meaning capture or take by 1704; by 1844, to *cop* meant to arrest. Subsequently, the slang name for those who arrest became *copper*, which was later shortened to *cop* (*copper* is still common in Britain).

The slang expression to *cop out*, meaning to evade responsibility or back down from a promise, is related to *cop* meaning police. *Copping out* was first used in the 1920s to mean confessing to the police in exchange for leniency, a process that often involved implicating others. In other words, *copping out* first meant *copping a plea* or, in formal English, plea bargaining.

From the dock, where I went to take a fast swim, I couldn't see a cop car in the parking lot, only the regulars frying in the early sun.
Howard Engel *Murder Sees the Light* 1984: 188

(The word *cop* is often used in fiction where everyday speech is represented.)

Constable Joe Marshall of the Ontario Provincial Police would like to ask you to 'Adopt-A-Cop', especially him, to raise funds for Special Olympics.
Whig-Standard (Kingston) 10 May 1994: 13

(Here the police are calling themselves *cops*.)

The provincial police officer shot his killer twice before he was shot to death in Sudbury, Ont.
Ottawa Citizen 28 June 1994: A5

(In this context *cop* would be inappropriate.)

See also POLICE OFFICER.

copyright, copywriter *Copyright* is the legal right to copy a book, song, video, work of art, etc. *Copyright* is also an adjective meaning protected by copyright: 'a copyright production'. Note the spelling: *copyright*, not *copywrite*. A *copywriter* is someone who writes copy: that is, advertising or publicity material.

> The copyright UW Daily article was written by student Scott Reid, who was on the team in 1978, 1979 and 1981.
> *Globe and Mail* (Toronto) 3 May 1985: M10

> And few Canadian regulations apply to computer bulletin boards, which are covered by the federal Copywrite Act and Criminal Code.
> *Ottawa Citizen* 16 May 1992: F5

(The correct spelling is *copyright*.)

cord, chord A *cord* is a thick string or thin rope or cable. Cut wood is measured in units called *cords* because stacks of wood were once measured with a length of cord. *Cord* is also the name given the spinal *cord* and vocal *cords*. The spelling *chords* is often found after *vocal*; most North American authorities regard this as an error. British and Australian guides are more likely to see it as an acceptable variant.

Chord spelled with an *h* refers to music, emotional feeling, or geometry. A musical *chord* is a group of notes sounded together in harmony; to *strike a chord* in someone means to elicit empathy; a geometric *chord* is a straight line between two points on a curve.

> 'I thought I only had to do these things on Thursdays,' he says, forcing an enormous amount of disdain through those legendary vocal chords.
> *Ottawa Citizen* 18 Feb. 1993: E1

(The more common, and recommended, spelling is *vocal cords*.)

> 'I think we really struck a cord with women, particularly middle-aged women such as ourselves.'
> *Ottawa Citizen* 14 Jan. 1993: A12

(Here the correct spelling is *chord*.)

core, corps, corpse, corpus The *core* is the centre or essence of something. A *corps* (pronounced *CORE*) is a specialized military unit or a group of people engaged in a special activity: 'the diplomatic corps', 'the press corps', 'a dance corps'. A *corpse* is a dead body, usually a human body. A *corpus* is a complete collection of writings by a single author, or a collection of texts or recordings having to do with a particular subject of study, usually literary or linguistic. The plural of *corpus* is *corpuses* or *corpora* (pronounced *CORP or uh*).

> Having been a member of the cadet corps ... I was convinced that I was destined to serve the Allied cause as an infantry soldier.
> George Ignatieff *The Making of a Peacemonger* 1987: 56

> ... our regular editorial staff ... will be assisted by a corps of freelance writers with special interests and expertise.
> *Bon Vivant* Nov. 1981: 3

> The reader is convinced that the model aptly represents the designated category, but is left unsure as to the place of the work in the evolving corpus of black dramatic literature.
> *Queen's Quarterly* 92.1 (1985): 171

> Louis Bruce in geology and J.A. Gray in physics, holders of the university's two research chairs, made valuable contributions of their own and trained a corpus of young scientists.
> Frederick Gibson *Queen's University* 2 (1983): 322

(In reference to a group of people, the word required is *corps*.)

cork   see KHAKI

corporal, corporeal The adjectives *corporal* (pronounced *CORP er ul*) and *corporeal* (pronounced *cor POR ee ul*) both mean bodily. *Corporal* is found almost exclusively in the phrase 'corporal punishment'. *Corporeal* is used mainly to indicate that something is physical, substantial, or material in nature, as opposed to spiritual or immaterial.

> The new policy will prohibit foster families from using corporal punishment—spanking, hitting, punching or shoving—as a means of discipline....
> *Globe and Mail* (Toronto) 18 Jan. 1985: P1

> The dancers ... appear to enjoy giving the dissonance of the music a corporeal form.
> *Globe and Mail* (Toronto) 10 Jan. 1985: E3

> The whole idea of virtuosity is that the mental component is there as well, and the mental ideas are made corporeal through technique.
> *Globe and Mail* (Toronto) 23 April 1985: M11

corporation   see FIRM

corps, corpse, corpus   see CORE

cost, costed, cost out When to *cost* means to have as a price, the past tense and past participle are *cost*: 'That is twice what it cost last week'; 'It had cost him a fortune'. When to *cost* means to calculate or estimate the cost of something, the past tense and past participle are *costed*: 'She costed the print run at $1500'. In Canada and the United States, *cost out* is a common variant of *cost* meaning to calculate the cost of.

> ... they couldn't be costed in the regular way ... because of the unprecedented nature of the roof. Only two major cities have tried a retractable dome.
> *Globe and Mail* (Toronto) 22 June 1985: E15

> The candidates said the scheme had not been costed out, but there would be a return for the city from long leases on the land.
> *Vancouver Sun* 12 Nov. 1993: C1

coterie see CLIQUE

couch see CHESTERFIELD

couldn't care less, could care less Both phrases mean the same thing: the speaker does not care at all. The far more widely used and approved form is *couldn't care less*. How the reversal *could care less* came to mean the same thing has puzzled word historians. Some speculate that it may have to do with the rhythm of the phrase: dropping the negative particle shifts the emphasis from the grammatical word *couldn't* to the content word *care*, which allows for a more lingeringly sarcastic delivery of the phrase. *Could care less* is often criticized as illogical, and both versions of the phrase are informal.

> Above all, I loved the experience of proving myself, of being accepted as one of the boys by teammates who couldn't care less who I was or where I came from.
> George Ignatieff *The Making of a Peacemonger* 1987: 46

> Rick would have to fight his own battles. And if he got beat up in the process, Harley could care less.
> *Canadian Fiction Magazine* 64 (1988): 66

[could of], [would of], [should of], [might of], eye dialect *Could of, might of, should of,* and *would of* are non-standard spellings of contractions with *have*: *could've, might've, should've,* and *would've*. In normal speech, *could of* and *could've* sound the same, which is what leads people to make this error. These *of* spellings rarely find their way into print except in fiction, where they may be used to set a certain tone

or to suggest laxness of speech. This literary effect is called *eye dialect*, since its impact is not on the ear—there's no real divergence from the standard pronunciation—but on the eye.

> Mind you, father Adrian tried his best to turn things around and to make Ben the boss. And Ben would of let him. But I wasn't having any of that ... !
> *Canadian Fiction Magazine* 64 (1989): 88

> 'I should of blasted out the nearest exit.'
> *Canadian Fiction Magazine* 63 (1988): 134

coulee see SWAMP

council, councillor, counsel, counsellor, consul A *council* is a group of elected representatives of a city, town, village, township, or county, and members of council are called *councillors* (or, rarely, *councilors*). Any advisory or deliberative body, or assembly of such a body, may be called a *council*.

The noun *counsel* means advice; to *counsel* means to give advice. A *counsellor* (or sometimes *counselor*) is a therapist, an adviser, or a supervisor at a children's camp. Lawyers in Canadian court proceedings are occasionally referred to as *counsellors*; more often they are called *counsel* (singular and plural): 'Defence counsel objected'. As in this example, the word is normally used without an article: 'Did he have counsel?' (that is, did he have a lawyer?).

A *consul* is an official appointed by a country to look after its business interests and its citizens in a foreign city.

> The case was seen as a key test of refugee law so the United Nations High Commission for Refugees and the Canadian Council for Refugees were allowed to present legal arguments.
> *Gazette* (Montreal) 2 July 1993: B1

> 'I said I wouldn't come,' said Bonnie McKinnon, a newly elected counsellor from the Surrey Electors Team (SET).
> *Vancouver Sun* 29 Nov. 1993: B1

> (The correct spelling for a member of a council is *councillor*.)

> It is hard to think of someone more likely to give good counsel than Mitchell Sharp.
> *Gazette* (Montreal) 5 Nov. 1993: B2

> An employment counsellor based in Courtenay, O'Hara repeatedly saw clients stressed from too much work and others stressed from not having any.
> *Vancouver Sun* 16 Dec. 1993: B6

Neil Reeder, consul at the Canadian Commission here, said the mission offers special advice to Chinese Canadians who use Hong Kong as a base for business with China.
Calgary Herald 25 Nov. 1994: C6

See also LAWYER; SPELLING, CANADIAN.

coup de grâce, pièce de résistance   Occasionally people confuse these French expressions. Translated literally, *coup de grâce* means 'mercy blow': the stroke that puts an end to the suffering of an opponent or a wounded animal. In contemporary English usage, however, the expression rarely connotes mercy: a *coup de grâce* is a death blow.

The *pièce de résistance* is the best part or feature of something: the most delicious dish of a meal, the high point in a concert, the best room in a house, and so on. Originally, the *pièce de résistance* was the most substantial dish in a meal, but now the term refers to quality, not quantity.

Coup de grâce is pronounced *coo duh GRASS*; the plural is *coups de grâce*. *Pièce de résistance* is pronounced *pee ESS duh RAY zee stahnce*; the plural is *pièces de résistance*. The plural *s* is not pronounced. Though newspapers don't put these expressions in italics, in formal writing they should be italicized and should retain their accents.

It might have been the *coup de grâce*; it proved instead to be the beginning of a fresh start for Queen's.
Hilda Neatby *Queen's University* 1 (1978): 113

If France today rejects the Maastricht Treaty it will deal the coup de grace to swift European unification, a process already badly shaken by this week's monetary crisis.
Calgary Herald 20 Sept. 1992: A6

The piece de resistance, however, was the ... salad ($3.95) we also ordered.
Ottawa Citizen 20 Feb. 1992: C5

The piece de resistance of the Canada pavilion is the front courtyard, which extends under the building like a huge cavern and brings a feel of the icy north to a place where summer temperatures can reach 50 degrees Celsius.
Vancouver Sun 18 April 1992: A1

Wedgewood's coup de grace is two-fold: an open-concept kitchen/breakfast combo overlooking the sunken family room, separated by a solid oak railing.
Toronto Star 1 Feb. 1992: E12

(The expression required here is *pièce de résistance*.)

Even with a career that includes four feature films to date, Burnett's undisputed coup de grace will likely forever be The Carol Burnett Show, which ran for 11 highly successful seasons on CBS.
Calgary Herald 29 June 1992: A14

(The expression required here is *pièce de résistance*.)

coureur de bois, voyageur   The terms *coureur de bois* (plural *coureurs de bois*) and *voyageur*, borrowed from Canadian French into English in the eighteenth century, both refer to the European and Métis fur-traders and adventurers who operated across much of the region that is now Canada and the northern United States.

Coureurs de bois (*cuh RER duh BWAH*), 'runners of the woods', was the term in general use until 1680, when the fur trade in New France was licensed. At that time select coureurs de bois were hired by Montreal merchants and were given the title *voyageur* (*voy a ZHUR*), 'traveller'. These voyageurs travelled the continent in freight canoes, establishing and maintaining trade with Native trappers. *Coureurs de bois* then became the designation for independent, unlicensed traders.

cousin   In the sixteenth century *cousin* was a general term for relatives outside the immediate family. Nieces and nephews, for example, were often called cousins. In contemporary usage the term is more restricted. Your *cousin*, or *first cousin*, is the son or daughter of your aunt or uncle. Your *second cousin* is the son or daughter of your mother's or father's first cousin. Children of second cousins are *third cousins* to each other. First cousins have the same grandparents, second cousins the same great-grandparents, third cousins the same great-great-grandparents, and so on.

Cousins who are *removed* are of different generations. You and the child of your first cousin are *first cousins once removed*. You and the grandchild of your first cousin are *first cousins twice removed*. To the children of your second cousin, you are a *second cousin once removed*.

Cousin is often used figuratively in current English for things in the same general category and for people related by race or culture.

We found routers with such expensive gadgets as dust vacuums and electronic controls perform no better than their less expensive cousins....
Canadian Consumer Feb. 1986: 32

His compatriots ... would never forget the way their cousins across the Atlantic had come to their assistance during the darkest days of World War II.
George Ignatieff *The Making of a Peacemonger* 1987: 108

covet see ENVY

coyote In North America *coyote* has two pronunciations, one with two syllables (*KYE oat*) and one with three (*kye OH tee*). The CBC recommends the two-syllable pronunciation to its announcers. Some Canadians believe that the two-syllable pronunciation is particularly 'Canadian', but it is also found in the United States. Other names for the coyote—which is smaller than the wolf, but closely related to it—are brush wolf and prairie wolf.

crass *Crass* is notoriously difficult to define. However, it is certainly pejorative, and it covers a range of senses that includes indelicate, insensitive, vulgar, stupid, materialistic, and contemptible.

Mid-Depression America was crass, materialistic, and shallow.
Canadian Journal of History 14.1 (1989): 70

Despite the explicit nature of her actions, she never seemed crass, but maintained a proud, noble manner.
Queen's Quarterly 98.1 (1991): 166

I wonder, too, how some doctors could have been so crassly unfeeling, whereas others were both skillful and sensitive.
Chatelaine April 1986: 135

credence, credibility To give something *credence* (pronounced *CREE dense*) is to believe it, whereas to give or lend something *credibility* is to make it more believable and convincing, or at least to make it appear more reputable.

A *letter of credence* is an official or confidential recommendation or a letter of introduction. A *credibility gap* is a discrepancy between what is presented as truth and what is accepted as true.

Any organization can be discredited if one chooses to give credence to the fringe elements within it.
Globe and Mail (Toronto) 30 Jan. 1985: P7

An audit can give an organization credibility because it shows that its money is properly and professionally handled.
Canadian Baptist Jan. 1986: 55

Because such international events invariably involve 'official' relations with the supplying countries (and provide representatives of those nations with valuable windows for public relations), they confer upon the Festival a degree of credence.
Queen's Quarterly 95 (1988): 819

(The word required here is *credibility*.)

Presenting my letters of credence turned out to be an even more interesting experience than I had expected.
George Ignatieff *The Making of a Peacemonger* 1987: 153

See also CREDIBLE.

credible, incredible, credulous, incredulous, creditable, discreditable *Credible* means believable. A credible story rings true, and a credible witness seems reliable. *Incredible* can simply mean not credible, not believable, but it usually means far beyond belief ('an incredible tale') or, in informal use, wonderful or great ('an incredible party', 'an incredible amount').

Credulous means gullible or overly disposed to believe ('credulous investors'); *incredulous* means skeptical or shocked and unable to believe something.

Creditable and *discreditable* are applied to actions rather than people. *Creditable* acts are praiseworthy, and *creditable* performances are reasonably good; *discreditable* actions are blameworthy, bringing disrepute.

Of all the surveys done by pollsters, the least credible is the one claiming to establish that 40 per cent of adults are shy.
Vancouver Sun 26 Nov. 1990: A8

The stories of four women who accuse their brothers of sexually abusing them for 15 years are so horrific and incredible they can't be true, a lawyer said. ...
Toronto Star 8 Dec. 1993: A14

The sky is an incredible clear blue smudged with white clouds.
Vancouver Sun 15 Dec. 1990: B1

But many weak-minded, inexperienced and credulous would-be speculators are caught, for the land speculation fever spreads very easily once it gets a footing.
Gazette (Montreal) 2 Jan. 1994: B3

'I honestly can't believe they have sunk that low,' he said. 'I am incredulous.'
Daily News (Halifax) 12 May 1994: n.p.

He clicks his tongue and shakes his head the way Montrealers do when they hear something incredulous.
Canadian Fiction Magazine 63 (1988): 115

(The word required here is *incredible* or *unbelievable*.)

Actor and vocal coach Trish Allen does a creditable job in her debut as a director.
Vancouver Sun 26 March 1994: EA17

'There are other people, equally creditable, who say, "This is death, don't touch it."'
Vancouver Sun 31 March 1994: D1

(Here *credible* is required.)

See also CREDENCE, CREDIBILITY.

Créditiste   see SOCIAL CREDIT

credit union   see BANK

credulous   see CREDIBLE

Cree   The Cree, one of the most numerous and widespread of the First Nations, generally refer to themselves by names that specify local groups: for example, Ermineskin, Lubicon, Star Blanket, Sunchild. They are also divided into regional groups marked by dialectal and cultural differences: Plains Cree (Alberta and Saskatchewan), Woodlands Cree (Saskatchewan and Manitoba), and Swampy Cree (Manitoba, Ontario, and Quebec). *Cree* is the name of the language of all of these groups; the six Cree dialects are East, Moose, Northern, Plains, Swampy, and Woods. Although most names designating Aboriginal groups are not pluralized by adding *s* ('two Inuit' *not* 'Inuits'), either *Cree* or *Crees* is acceptable (*Globe and Mail Style Book*).

The Cree, one of the largest Indian nations on the continent, live from Northern Quebec west to British Columbia and south to the northern United States.
Gazette (Montreal) 13 June 1994: A8

Singing Wolf, a Plains Cree Indian ... is a volunteer teacher of the program's native crafts and culture.
Ottawa Citizen 21 June 1994: B3

The Crees of James Bay have a provocative proposal: If separatists win a referendum on secession, aboriginal territory will simply remain in Canada as a province with Nemaska replacing Quebec City as the capital.
Ottawa Citizen 31 May 1994: A1

creole   see PIDGIN

crescendo, climax   *Crescendo* (pronounced *kruh SHEN doe*) is an Italian word meaning 'growing'. It was first used in English as a musical term to de-scribe a gradual increase in loudness. The plural is *crescendos* or *crescendi*.

Figuratively, a *crescendo* is a progression towards a *climax* or peak. Increasingly, however, the word is used to refer to the climax itself: 'Tensions reached a crescendo'. This use is criticized and in formal writing it is best avoided.

... the island of Illyria is ultimately a never-never land ... where the castaway Viola can disguise herself as a boy and enter the court of Duke Orsino where she sets off a crescendo of romantic love and sexual confusion.
Ottawa Citizen 31 May 1994: B6

Taylor predicts that demands for a September federal mini-budget, or at least an economic statement from Finance Minister Michael Wilson, will soon reach a crescendo.
Vancouver Sun 24 Aug. 1990: A1

(This use is disputed; *climax* would be better.)

With no [tachometer], you shift when the noise from the ever-whirring cooling fan reaches a crescendo.
Financial Post 11 Oct. 1991: 38

(This use is disputed; *climax* would be better.)

criminologist, criminalist   A *criminologist* is a sociologist specializing in the study of crime and penal systems. *Criminalist* is a chiefly American term for a technician who collects and tests physical evidence from the scene of a crime.

Andre Normandeau, a criminologist at the University of Montreal, said abuse of power by police has decreased during the past decade.
Toronto Star 30 Dec. 1994: A19

A police criminalist said three tests show a blood spot leading from the murder scene could not have come from the two victims.
CTV News [transcript] 8 July 1994: n.p.

crippled   see DISABILITIES

criterion, criteria   *Criterion* is the singular and *criteria* is the plural: 'Should academic ability be the only criterion for admission?'; 'Each submission is judged on five criteria'.

'Seniors have said we must examine programs where the only criterion (to qualify) is age ... we must have criteria other than age.'
Calgary Herald 30 Sept. 1993: B2

For another school the results of the Canadian Test of Basic Skills were used as a criteria for comparison purposes.
Education Canada Summer 1989: 12

(The singular *criterion* is required here.)

The author suffers a serious credibility loss by first basing her comparisons on an outdated study, and then brazenly adding criterion as she goes along.
Vancouver Sun 17 June 1990: 93

(The plural *criteria* is required here.)

See also PLURALS, REGULAR, IRREGULAR, FOREIGN.

criticize, critique To *criticize* a literary work or artistic performance is to judge its merits as well as its faults. In ordinary use, however, someone who criticizes something is pointing out its faults. The disparaging overtones of *criticize* may have prompted the recent revival of *critique* as a neutral verb meaning to judge. Some commentators have criticized the verb to *critique* as faddish, but since the *OED* cites its use as early as 1751, and it serves a useful purpose, it will probably gain full acceptance.

The Giraffe Project has also created an array of educational and motivational programs.... One of the programs, called Standing Tall, is currently being critiqued by several Vancouver teachers.
Vancouver Sun 25 March 1994: B2

When you critique the Vancouver Canucks, it's tough to make a case for the defence.
Vancouver Sun 21 Feb. 1990: B6

See also FUNCTIONAL SHIFT.

crony see COHORT

cum *Cum* (pronounced *COOM* or *CUM*) is a Latin preposition meaning 'with'. To graduate *cum laude* is to graduate 'with distinction'. *Cum* is often used in journalism to form compound titles (usually hyphenated) for people or things that function in more than one capacity: 'teacher-cum-coach', 'studio-cum-laundry room'. This use, often facetious, is always informal.

On May 26, 1954, the retired athlete-cum-politician was up to bat in a charity softball game against members of the press on the lawn of Parliament Hill.
Toronto Star 26 May 1994: E1

Playing an insurance investigator cum gentleman rancher cum doting daddy, Wagner wears his high-class duds and his low key manner with equal aplomb.
Globe and Mail (Toronto) 24 Sept. 1985: E1

At Cut Offs 'n' Jeans, a hair-salon-cum-jean-emporium, Pamela Mannix decorates worn-but-loved jeans in all the right places.
Calgary Herald 8 Feb. 1994: B8

See also LATIN PHRASES.

curb, kerb Canadians use *curb* for all senses, as do Americans. British writers use *kerb* to refer to the edging at the side of a road, and *curb* for all other senses of both the noun and the verb.

curriculum vitae Literally, this Latin phrase means 'the course of a life', but in English usage a *curriculum vitae* is an account of one's qualifications, education, and previous experience that is submitted with applications for professional or academic positions, grants, or scholarships. In most situations the abbreviation *cv* can be used, and thus the plural is not a problem: *cv's*. However, the abbreviation looks a little odd in very formal contexts. The Latin plural of the unabbreviated phrase varies: *curricula vitae*, if you are referring to several versions of one person's *curriculum vitae*; or *curricula vitarum* if you are referring to those of more than one person: 'Please forward curricula vitarum for all four applicants'.

See also RÉSUMÉ.

customer, client, patient, patron Generally *customers* buys *things*, while *clients* purchase *professional services*, such as those of a lawyer, accountant, architect, or hair stylist. However, *client* is sometimes used as a snobbish synonym for *customer*. Someone receiving medical services is a *patient*, but *client* is often used for people seeing a counsellor or psychotherapist. *Patron* is a common synonym for *customer* in the context of theatres, restaurants, and accommodation. A 'patron of the arts' is someone who financially supports arts organizations or buys works of art.

His father owned a car dealership and during the hockey season gave away hockey sticks to his customers as a promotion.
Ken Dryden *The Game* 1983: 57

Depression doctors and lawyers went unpaid, and joined many of their patients and clients in common poverty.
Canadian Journal of Sociology 14.2 (1989): 252

The program offers individual counselling and group activities for its clients, most of whom range from 65 to 75.
Calgary Herald 26 May 1994: B7

In one club where he was opening for blues legend Muddy Waters, he was knocked cold by a patron swinging a ketchup bottle.
Globe and Mail (Toronto) 18 Jan 1985: E4

customs   see TAX

cutter   see SLED

cyclone, hurricane, typhoon, tornado, twister, funnel cloud, waterspout   *Cyclone* is the most general term for a weather system in which winds circle an area of low pressure. A *cyclone* can blow over huge areas with relatively little effect, but if the system is compressed over land, the winds rushing towards the central low-pressure area can literally lift houses.

East of the International Date Line, the most severe cyclonic storms, with winds reaching 120 to 460 kilometres per hour, are called *hurricanes*. Similar storms originating west of the date line are called *typhoons*.

The centre of such a storm is called *the eye*. This centre is quite calm; hence references to 'the eye of the hurricane' should not imply that the eye itself is stormy, even though it is circled by high winds.

Although *tornado* and *cyclone* are sometimes used as if they were synonyms, *tornado* is best reserved for a funnel-shaped column of rotating air that touches the ground in a narrow but very destructive path. A *twister* is small tornado whose damage is limited to 100 metres. Several tornados may be attached to one cyclone, and several twisters to one tornado. If the column of rotating wind does not touch the ground it is called a *funnel cloud*, and if it touches down over water it is called a *water spout*. *Tornado* can be made plural by adding either -*s* or -*es*.

When a wide band of 11 tornadoes swept across southern Ontario last May 31, one of the deadliest ripped through the city of Barrie....
Maclean's 10 Feb. 1986: 9

Due to hurricane winds, however, the largest fish caught was only 305 pounds.
Bon Vivant Nov. 1981: 11

Gale force winds had spawned nine screaming cyclones, which twisted their way over 100 kilometres, shattering glass, etching metal and sucking up whole sections of earth....
Canadian Heritage Magazine Feb.–Mar. 1986: 15

D

dais, rostrum, podium, lectern   A *dais*, *rostrum*, or *podium* is a platform for speakers. Often a *dais* (pronounced *DAY iss* or *DIE iss*) is a raised surface or low stage at the front of a classroom or hall. A *podium* is sometimes a small platform for one person, such as a musical conductor. A *lectern* is a stand with a slanted top to hold a speaker's notes. The word *podium* is commonly used to mean lectern, and a few dictionaries now list this meaning; however, some authorities consider this use a mistake.

Rostrum and *podium* each have two plurals: *rostrums* and *rostra*, *podiums* and *podia*.

The dons took their place at High Table ... [which] stood on a raised dais above the rest of us.
Toronto Star 23 Oct. 1994: A11

Moroccan Prime Minister Mohammed Karim Lamrani announces from the rostrum that his country has agreed to a unilateral cease-fire in its battle with insurgents in the Western Sahara.
Globe and Mail (Toronto) 26 Oct. 1985: A6

A respectful hush ripples through the audience at Montreal's Tudor Hall as Alexander Brott approaches the podium. The maestro raises his baton.
Performing Arts in Canada March 1988: 26

With each word he pounded his lectern, sounding for all the world like an old-time fire and brimstone preacher.
Toronto Star 8 April 1991: A9

At one point during his speech, Juneau began pounding the podium as he lashed out at what he called an obsession with the distribution aspect of the film and broadcasting industry.
Globe and Mail (Toronto) 13 April 1985: E12

(Strictly speaking, he is pounding the *lectern*.)

See also PLURALS, REGULAR, IRREGULAR, FOREIGN.

Dakelh   see CARRIER

dangling modifiers   Sometimes part of a sentence, usually an introductory element, does not actually modify any word or clause in the sentence. The detached element of the sentence is called a *dangling modifier*. In some contexts dangling modifiers are barely noticeable; in others they seriously disrupt the sense of the sentence. What follows are some examples of dangling modifiers that should be rewritten, and then a discussion of those contexts where language commentators consider 'dangling' modifiers allowable.

> Hard-working volunteer and full-time paramedic, the rewards had been a long time coming.
> (*Rewritten*: For Jane Johnson, hard-working volunteer and full-time paramedic, the rewards had been a long time coming.)

> Driving through the pass, our muffler fell off.
> (*Rewritten*: While we were driving through the pass, our muffler fell off.)

> Once taken to pieces, you should carefully clean the rust off the parts.
> (*Rewritten*: Once you have taken the mechanism to pieces, carefully clean the rust off the parts.)

> At age three, his family moved to the Yukon.
> (*Rewritten*: When he was three, his family moved to the Yukon.)

Some contexts permit dangling modifiers. In instructions, for example, the subject of the main clause is not stated, but is commonly understood to be *you*:

> To prepare for an audit, [you should] locate all the accounting records, any supporting invoices, payroll records, deposit slips, contracts and other related documents.
> *Canadian Baptist* Jan. 1986: 55

Technically, phrases such as 'taking this into consideration', 'to begin with', 'to sum up', and 'assuming that' all introduce dangling modifiers. But they are used in all kinds of writing and refer implicitly to either the writer or the reader.

> Assuming Trixie has all the qualifications of a carefree traveller, there are still certain types of vacations on which Trixie's presence would be a burden, rather than a pleasure.
> *Dogs in Canada* Special Issue 1986: 12

> To look back to an earlier precedent, while the European invention of moveable type in the fifteenth century supported the replacement of Latin as the language of literacy, it did so through a strong standardization of Europe's vernacular languages.
> W.C. Lougheed, ed. *In Search of the Standard in Canadian English* 1986: 106

> To assess the influence of Montesquieu's distinction it may be useful to compare complaints about the state of liberty before and after the appearance of his book.
> J.A.W. Gunn *Beyond Liberty and Property* 1983: 240

(This could be rewritten 'To assess the influence of Montesquieu's distinction one may find it useful ...', but Canadian writers rarely use *one* as a pronoun, even in formal contexts.)

In scientific experimentation, the individual experimenter's identity is downplayed, since it should be irrelevant to the result. Hence the common use of the passive in scientific writing and the frequency of structures such as the following, where the human agent who is the clearly implied subject of the modifier does not appear in the sentence:

> To further define the phenomenon, the fate of the virus populations in whole plants derived from the disk cultures was studied.
> *Canadian Journal of Botany* 67.4 (1989): 985

Legal writers also tend to avoid explicitly stating the human subject in their sentences, either because the identity of this subject remains to be proven or because it is unimportant:

> To bring a substituted agreement into existence, a major alteration of the original agreement must be made with the consent of all parties.
> J.E. Smyth et al. *The Law and Business Administration in Canada* 1987: 310

See also MISPLACED MODIFIERS.

dash   A *dash* (—) marks an abrupt break in a sentence; it's often used where a colon is also possible:

> The standard joke now referred to George Brown's reversible coat—orange on one side and green on the other.
> William Teatero *John Anderson: Fugitive Slave* 1986: 21

He was generous, and was constantly buying John clothes—once he returned from a trip with three button-down, Oxford cloth shirts.
Daniel Gawthrop *Affirmation* 1994: 19

A pair of dashes, like a pair of commas or parentheses, may be used to set off an aside:

However, I declined to state—or attempt to state—the racial origin of either my wife or myself.
Richard Davies and Glen Kirkland, eds. *Dimensions* 1986: 122

An exclamation mark or question mark may be retained inside the second of a pair of dashes:

The examiner who rebuked him was an old man, who explained courteously and patiently—but oh, the courtesy and patience of Oxford can burn like a refiner's fire!—that the word had no respectable ancestry....
Robertson Davies *One Half of Robertson Davies* 1978: 12

A dash is often used in front of the name of the person to whom a quotation is attributed:

The real utopia is a world not to see but to see by.
—NORTHROP FRYE

Dashes should be used judiciously in formal writing, since too many dashes can make a writer's style seem breathless or choppy.

Because most keyboards do not have a dash, two hyphens, with no space before or after, are generally used to make a dash.

See also COLON; COMMA; PARENTHESES.

data   In scientific and academic writing, and even in journalism, *data* is used both as a plural noun with a plural verb ('These data are misleading') and as an uncountable singular noun, like *information*, that takes a singular verb ('This data is misleading'). Most commentators accept both usages. The plural construction is more formal. For consistency, when *data* is treated as a plural noun, subsequent references should be to *they*, not *it*. Like the uncountable noun *information*, *data* is never preceded by a number: one speaks of 'twenty-five pieces of data' rather than 'twenty-five data'. *Datum*, the Latin noun meaning 'thing given' and the singular form of *data*, is very rare even in scientific writing. *Data* is pronounced either *DATT uh* or *DATE uh*.

This means that when you book a flight to, say, Winnipeg, your data is zapped through a mainframe in Tulsa, Okla.
Toronto Star 31 Dec. 1994: D1

Salinity and temperature data used in the calculations of the freshwater content of James Bay were obtained during early March and August 1976.
Arctic 41.1 (1988): 8

(Here the verb *were* indicates that *data* is being treated as a plural.)

Data come from a Statistics Canada survey of about 40,000 Canadian households.
Gazette (Montreal) 21 Dec. 1990: B1

(Here the plural verb *come* indicates that *data* is being treated as a plural.)

The PN phase showed a reasonable fit to the standard curve, but too little data were derived for the PG and SN phases for one to make a conclusive judgement on these phases.
Canadian Journal of Earth Sciences 26 (1989): 379

(Here *data* is treated as singular and plural simultaneously. The sentence should read either 'too *few* data *were*...' or 'too *little* data *was*...'.)

See also PLURALS, REGULAR, IRREGULAR, FOREIGN.

dates   Two styles of dates are currently used in business correspondence and published writing:

July 1, 1962, was the first day of the strike.
The strike began 1 July 1962.

In the first style, commas precede and follow the year. Many writers omit the second comma, but style guides insist on it. The second style, originally British and now becoming more popular in Canada and the United States, requires no commas. One style should be used consistently throughout one piece of writing.

When we say dates aloud, we use ordinal numbers: 'March 15th', 'December 1st', 'November 2nd'. However, in formal writing, even when the year is not given, dates are usually written as cardinal numbers: 'March 15' *or* '15 March'. An ordinal number may be used in formal writing if it is written as a word: 'The fifteenth of March passed uneventfully'.

The traditional short form for dates ('3/9/96') is ambiguous. In Britain 3/9/96 means 3 September 1996; in the United States it means 9 March 1996. In Canada it could mean either. Fortunately, this short form is being supplanted by an unambiguous computer-style date. In the computer style, two digits are devoted to the year, the month, and the day in that order (YY/MM/DD). Thus 9 March 1996 is rendered 96/03/09.

Decades, in formal writing, may be referred to either in words or in figures: *the sixties, the thirties, the '50s, the 1930s, the 1860s, the 1780s.* (In an older style, now seldom used, an apostrophe separated the letter *s* from a numeral: *1930's.*) The first and second decades of a century are best referred to as such and not as, for example, 'the teens'.

> The redistribution of the sediment provided by the June 28, 1984, event contributed to these changes.
> *Canadian Journal of Earth Sciences* 26 (1989): 336

> Tenders must be submitted on or before 3:00 p.m., 4 July 1982.
> J.E. Smyth et al. *The Law and Business Administration in Canada* 1987: 225

> On January 31, 1991 a tie vote in the Senate of Canada defeated Bill C-43, An Act Respecting Abortion.
> Janine Brodie, Shelley A.M. Gavigan, and Jane Jenson *The Politics of Abortion* 1992: 4

(The year should be followed by a comma.)

> Burke's speech of 14 June made the same point, with some typical embellishments, when he pointed to the ominous aspect of appealing to the sense of the people.
> J.A.W. Gunn *Beyond Liberty and Property* 1983: 282

> On December 30th the Winnipeg Art Gallery was opening a show of her work, including her Paris and Tunis pieces....
> Ann Davis *Somewhere Waiting* 1991: 227

('December 30', or '30 December', is preferable in formal writing.)

> Its success ... owed something as well to new developments in criticism during the twenties and thirties.
> *Queen's Quarterly* 95.3 (1988): 563

> Indeed from the 1920s to the 1950s there was an on-going battle between the controlling body of the Law Society—the Benchers—and the university-minded academics....
> *Queen's Quarterly* 96.3 (1989): 590

> As early as the second decade of the nineteenth century, the economist Sismondi in his *Nouveaux Principes d'Economie Politique* (1819) demonstrated that the poor suffer most from economic crises....
> Irving M. Zeitlin and Robert J. Brym *The Social Condition of Humanity* 1991: 77

See also A.D., B.C.; NEXT, THIS.

davenport   see CHESTERFIELD

daylight time, daylight saving(s) time   see STANDARD TIME

de-, dis-   These prefixes are used before both verbs and nouns to mean undo, do the opposite of, or remove, as in *declassification, delouse, desegregate,* and *disassemble, disillusionment.* Words formed with the *de-* prefix in particular tend to proliferate in the jargon of technology and government: *decriminalize, de-energize, dehire.* When an established expression exists, such as *legalize, unplug,* or *lay off,* it should be chosen over a newer *de-* coinage. When the *de-* prefix is added to a noun or verb beginning with a vowel ('de-emphasize', 'de-ink'), it's usually followed by a hyphen.

> It takes an average of 11 man-hours to destuff a container, compared with only 2.8 hours to process it intact, shipping officials have estimated.
> *Globe and Mail* (Toronto) 25 March 1985: IB5

(Here *unpack* would be better.)

dead metaphor   The dial of a clock is its *face,* and a chair stands on *legs*; a potato has *eyes,* a shoe a *tongue,* and an airplane a *nose.* These implied comparisons with parts of the human body no longer strike us as figures of speech. Some metaphors have been in use for so long that they have become *dead metaphors.*

A *dead metaphor* is different from a *live metaphor* in that it no longer evokes a literal image in the reader's or listener's mind. For instance, in the sentence 'They worked hard to build support for the campaign', the metaphor of building does not call to mind a group of workers equipped with hammers and saws. *Build* is merely a synonym for *increase,* and thus a dead metaphor. On the other hand, in the sentence 'Snow blanketed the region', the idea of a blanket may well come to mind, which means that *blanket* is still a live metaphor. We tend to use live metaphors consciously and dead metaphors unconsciously. Occasionally a problem arises when a writer unwittingly uses a dead metaphor along with another figure of speech. The second metaphor may bring the defunct metaphor back to life, resulting in incongruity or unintentional humour: 'They went overboard and we were left high and dry'; 'I offered to give him a hand, though he didn't have a leg to stand on'. To avoid unintentionally resuscitating dead metaphors, it's a good idea to check figurative language carefully.

See also CLICHÉ; MIXED METAPHOR.

deal   The past tense of *deal* is always *dealt*, never *dealed*, except in the expression *wheeled and dealed*.

'Every two or three years he shuffled these cards [themes] and dealt himself a hand that became his next film.'
Vancouver Sun 12 Feb. 1994: D16

The accused, an Ontario man who wheeled and dealed on both sides of the world's longest undefended border, applied to the court to be released on bail.
Calgary Herald 7 June 1992: B5

debacle   A *debacle* is a fiasco or a disaster. Usually the word is spelled without its French accents, but in formal writing it may retain them: *débâcle*. The usual pronunciation is a modified French one: either *dih BAHK le* or *day BAHK le*. The anglicized pronunciation *DEB i kul* is criticized. Although this disputed pronunciation follows the stress pattern of other French loan words such as *miracle* and *spectacle*, these were borrowed early, in the twelfth century, while *debacle* was borrowed much later, in the nineteenth century.

The loan debacle pushed Royal Trust's parent, Royal Trustco Ltd., to the brink of bankruptcy.
Gazette (Montreal) 21 June 1993: C2

… Hu Yaobang was dismissed in 1987 for failing to control pro-democracy demonstrations, and Zhao Ziyang fell in 1989 after the debacle on Tiananmen Square.
Gazette (Montreal) 26 May 1993: B3

debar, disbar   To *debar* someone from doing something is to officially prohibit him or her from doing it. Circumstances may also debar, or preclude, someone from doing something, and a person may be debarred (banned) from a place.

Disbar is used only in a particular legal sense. To be disbarred is to be deprived of the right to practise law.

Speaking of staff appointments in his installation address, he said that a man 'may debar himself by his beliefs.'
Frederick Gibson *Queen's University* 2 (1983): 343

A lawyer in those years might borrow twenty-five dollars from his clients' accounts to pay the rent and take food home. He'd be caught and disbarred.
Jack Batten *Robinette* 1984: 34

debark   see EMBARK

debate   see DISCUSS

debus   see EMBARK

début   see PREMIÈRE

decades   see DATES

deceitful, deceptive   People are *deceitful* when they intentionally hide the truth to gain advantage. People are *deceptive* when—intentionally or unintentionally—they create a misleading impression. Appearances and things can also be deceptive: 'The way it looks from the outside is deceptive; inside it's huge'.

Justice Douglas Cunningham called [the defendant] clever, deceitful and fraudulent for duping investors out of $400,000 in two aborted condo developments….
Gazette (Montreal) 1 Oct. 1993: B12

The process that the Liberals are using to reform the social safety net is also very deceptive. While a great deal of effort has been put into making the process seem open, fair and consultative, the real agenda for the reform has been set privately, behind closed doors.
Ottawa Citizen 18 Oct. 1994: A9

She had the manner of a conventional lady bountiful, but that manner was deceptive.
Miriam Waddington *Apartment Seven* 1989: 19

decided, decisive   A *decided* victory is clear, not likely to be mistaken for defeat, while a *decisive* victory is conclusive, turning the balance in the series or finally settling the score. A *decided* person is resolute or firm, while a *decisive* person is capable of making decisions quickly. To some extent, the senses of these words overlap.

We have to face the fact that many students go into engineering with a decided bias against literature, history and philosophy.
Engineering Dimensions May–Jun. 1988: 24

Mr. Attorney General Macdonald has expressed a decided opinion against the fugitive.
William Teatero *John Anderson: Fugitive Slave* 1986: 61

The error led to a 2-on-1 break for the Blues and the decisive goal in a 3-2 Chicago loss.
Gazette (Montreal) 28 Dec. 1993: D3

Chretien won last month's election because he is honest, hard-working, decisive and capable of bringing out the best in people.
Toronto Star 13 Nov. 1993: B1

decimal points   see NUMBERS, DECIMAL POINTS AND COMMAS WITH

decimate   Decimation was a Roman punishment for mutinous military units: one-tenth of an offending unit's members were chosen by lot and executed. Originally, then, to *decimate* meant to kill one in every ten. In current English it means to all but destroy, and it doesn't always suggest intentional destruction: disease or famine can decimate a population.

Decimate has been used to mean massacre or drastically reduce since as early as 1663 (*OED*). This use has been criticized because it doesn't match the original Latin meaning of the word, but as *Webster's Dictionary of English Usage* remarks, 'Most recent usage books recognize that the Latin etymology does not rule the English word.' Anyone who does use *decimate* to mean reduce by one-tenth certainly risks being misunderstood.

Student numbers were not decimated by the depression, but the areas of decline are revealing.
Frederick Gibson *Queen's University* 2 (1983): 102–3

(Here *decimated* means radically reduced.)

The words describe the American General Sherman's plan to decimate the buffalo stocks in order to cripple the native population.
Mark. A. Cheetham with Linda Hutcheon *Remembering Postmodernism* 1991: 81

(Here *decimated* means greatly reduced.)

Today, abandoned villages and brooding mortuary poles ... stand in mute testimony to the extent of the culture which flourished for thousands of years throughout the islands, before the Haida were decimated by smallpox a century ago.
Canadian Heritage Magazine Aug.–Sept. 1986: 25

(Here *decimated* means greatly reduced.)

See also MASSACRE.

decision   The most common idiom is *make a decision*, although we also *come to a decision* or *reach a decision*. Several Canadian style guides warn against *take a decision*, claiming that the expression is a recent import from French (*prendre une décision*).

This notion appears to be unfounded, since *take a decision* is used more in Britain, where French exerts little influence, than in Canada. British and American guides do not mention *take a decision* as a problem, and the idiom is listed without comment in several British dictionaries. In Canada it appears most often in newspaper writing and reported speech.

External Affairs Minister Joe Clark ... urged U.S. Secretary of State James Baker 'to weigh fully the impact the Mack amendment will have on U.S.-owned enterprises in Canada as well as our bilateral relationship before a decision is taken to sign this bill into law.'
Vancouver Sun 3 Nov. 1990: B12

decisive   see DECIDED

deck   see PORCH

declaim   see DECRY

decline   *Decline* should not be used as a synonym for *refuse* or *reject*, as in 'He declined an interview' or 'My application was declined'. When *decline* takes a direct object, it means to politely reject something that has been offered, as in 'She declined the invitation' or 'We declined the offer'. *Decline* followed by an infinitive means to refuse, again politely, a request to do something, as in 'He declined to elaborate' or 'She declined to wait'. 'Declined comment' is an idiom that has become almost a cliché in newspaper writing. Some commentators object to it as a euphemism for 'refused to comment'.

She declined Templeton's invitation to view the vessel, reminding him that she had already seen it when she accompanied her son Stanley.
J.E. Smyth et al. *The Law and Business Administration in Canada* 1987: 420–1

Calgary West Reformer Stephen Harper declined to participate because he felt his French wasn't up to par.
Calgary Herald 22 Oct. 1993: A11

Sather, reached in Winnipeg where the Oilers played the Jets last night, declined comment.
Gazette (Montreal) 4 March 1989: C2

In fact, without adequate funds in a customer's account, transactions will be declined by the system.
Maclean's 25 Nov. 1991: A53

(Here *refused* or *rejected* would be better, since nothing has been offered that the system could politely turn down.)

decry, descry, declaim, disclaim To *decry* is to speak out strongly against. To *descry* (pronounced *dis CRY*) is to barely discern or catch sight of. To *declaim* is to speak or recite in a theatrical manner. To *disclaim* is to renounce a legal claim to something, or to disown, disavow, or deny something.

They are quick to decry the garbage going into our atmosphere and the pollution of large corporations, yet they throw away their newspapers, popcorn and soft-drink containers and, worst of all, cigarette butts are jettisoned from car windows when the ashtray is right at hand.
Province (Vancouver) 1 June 1990: 48

That the leopard's spots were not changed overnight is indicated ... by a casual remark in the *Journal* as many as eleven years later that at last 'the law of equal rights' is 'dimly descried'.
Hilda Neatby *Queen's University* 1 (1978): 196

But reviewing a dead poet pressures the reviewer into declaiming like Brutus over Caesar's corpse.
Margaret Atwood *Second Words* 1982: 307

If [Quebec] intends to preserve its credit rating, it surely is not about to disclaim its fair share of Canada's debt.
Toronto Star 20 Nov. 1990: A20

deduction, induction In ordinary speech and writing a *deduction* is a conclusion or conjecture inferred from known facts. In logic *deduction* and *induction* refer to opposite types of reasoning. The process of *deduction* starts with a general principle that is used to predict particular cases. The process of *induction* involves examining specific cases in order to reach a general rule or principle that accounts for all of them.

He saw nothing and made the incorrect deduction that there was nothing to see.
Ottawa Citizen 24 March 1993: A11

(Here *deduction* means inference.)

Deductive reasoning depends upon the acceptance of the initial generalizations as the assumed truth.
Margot Northey and David B. Knight *Making Sense in Geography and Environmental Studies* 1992: 16

The quality of knowledge arrived at through inductive reasoning depends upon the representativeness of the specific cases used as the bases for generalization.
Margot Northey and David B. Knight *Making Sense in Geography and Environmental Studies* 1992: 16

See also A POSTERIORI; A PRIORI.

deem To *deem* something (to be) true is to believe it to be true. *Deem* is a formal synonym for *consider* or *judge*.

As the result of a court ruling Friday, customs officers no longer have the power to seize material which they deem to be 'immoral or indecent.'
Globe and Mail (Toronto) 19 March 1985: M4

... Peled recognized that every state (Israel or a Palestinian state) has the right to organize whatever contingency programs they deem necessary within their borders....
Henry M. Rosenthal and S. Cathy Berson, eds. *Canadian Jewish Outlook Anthology* 1988: 194

deer, red see MOOSE

defective, deficient *Defective* means faulty or flawed. *Deficient* means insufficient or lacking in some particular way. In cases where these two meanings overlap, either word is correct.

The only sound was a faint rasping buzz from a defective fluorescent tube overhead.
Constance Beresford-Howe *Night Studies* 1985: 132

Compost and wood ashes will certainly work, but if the soil is severely depleted or deficient in nutrients, I believe the gardener should follow the recommendations given with the soil analysis.
Harrowsmith Jun.–Jul. 1985: 112

The clerk, not wanting to pass up a bargain on items they need anyway, purchases a large quantity of deficient, shoddy goods.
Calgary Herald 17 June 1993: B8

(Here *defective* would also be possible.)

defer, defray To *defer* an expense is to delay it; to *defray* an expense is to offset it or provide for its payment.

Blencoe said senior citizens, widowed spouses and homeowners with physical disabilities can defer their taxes until they die or sell their homes.
Vancouver Sun 3 April 1992: C11

A federal grant from Unity Minister Joe Clark's office of about $80,000 helped to defray travel and lodging expenses.
Toronto Star 12 April 1992: G4

Admission is free, or pay-what-you-can to help defer costs involved.
Toronto Star 7 Dec. 1992: B6

(The word required here is *defray*.)

deficient   see DEFECTIVE

definite, definitive   *Definite* means unambiguous, clearly defined, or certain. *Definitive* conveys a sense of finality and means authoritative or decisive. A *definite* plan—one with all its details worked out—might not be the *definitive* plan: that is, the final choice. In some contexts either word is appropriate.

> The answer is a definite 'no', for although no action may be brought on the contract itself, it may affect the legal relations between the parties in several ways.
> J.E. Smyth et al. *The Law and Business Administration in Canada* 1987: 251–2

(Here *definite* means unambiguous.)

> He indicated in a interview Friday that his plans are definite and he will formally announce his plans this upcoming week.
> *Leader-Post* (Regina) 27 Feb. 1988: A4

(Here *definite* means certain.)

> Earlier this month, the bank signed a definitive agreement with Gentra Inc. ... to buy its international and Canadian operations.
> *Calgary Herald* 30 June 1993: D3

(Here *definitive* means final.)

> Setting definitive standards for hearing damage is difficult, says Whitehead, because sound tolerance varies between individuals.
> *Daily News* (Halifax) 27 June 1993: 34

(Here *definitive* means authoritative, but *definite*, meaning precisely defined, would also be appropriate.)

> I, for one, would appreciate a definitive public statement from the Anglican Church of Canada on Canadian military policy....
> *Canadian Churchman* April 1986: 5

(Here *definitive* means authoritative, but *definite*, meaning unambiguous, would also be appropriate.)

definite article   see THE, A, AN.

defray   see DEFER

defuse   see DIFFUSE

déjà vu   *Déjà vu* was borrowed from French at the end of the nineteenth century as a psychological term denoting the illusion of having previously experienced something that is actually being encountered for the first time. In psychology *déjà vu* always refers to an illusory impression. In general usage the expression is sometimes used humorously to imply that a supposedly new experience is in fact tediously predictable. Occasionally *déjà vu* is mistakenly used to mean premonition or expectation.

Déjà vu should retain its two accents, especially in formal writing, but it no longer needs to be italicized as a foreign phrase.

> Checking in with the wilderness volunteer was like deja vu—Jennifer's twin sister, Jeanine, worked this entrance.
> *Toronto Star* 3 Dec. 1994: F20

(Here *deja vu* refers to an illusion. Note that *déjà* requires accents in formal writing.)

> A Commons committee has suggested a 'temporary tax' to help pay down the deficit.... Déjà vu—income tax was introduced as a 'temporary measure' in 1917.
> *Vancouver Sun* 14 Dec. 1994: A14

(Here *déjà vu* is used humorously.)

> Hilda Gregory, who heads the diocese of New Westminster's 127 Society, has feelings of deja vu about the evictions. 'This is what we knew would happen,' she says.
> *Canadian Churchman* April 1986: 7

(Here something has been foreseen: thus '*expected* the evictions' would be better.)

deke   see FEIGN

delimit   see LIMIT

deliverance, delivery   *Deliverance* means release or rescue from evil or oppression. *Delivery* refers to getting something to its destination, or to childbirth, or to the style of making a speech. Both nouns are related to the verb *deliver*, but *deliverance* is used only of things that we are delivered *from*.

> It was a hard heart that wasn't lifted with the weekend drama of Nelson Mandela's deliverance.
> *Vancouver Sun* 12 Feb. 1990: A8

> Whether the free trade pact offers Canadians betrayal or deliverance, the authors of the three books agree on one thing: free trade marked a radical shift in Canada's political and economic direction.
> *Maclean's* 9 Dec. 1991: A62

> The wealthier *Canadien* merchants consequently returned to France; their less prosperous colleagues stayed, but were allowed neither to take delivery of

goods from France nor to establish ties with British trading firms.
Irving M. Zeitlin and Robert J. Brym *The Social Condition of Humanity* 1991: 166

The audience was impressed with the delivery but not many were buying the contents of Quebec Premier Jacques Parizeau's speech yesterday.
Toronto Star 23 Nov. 1994: A32

demean   *Demean* is two distinct verbs. The older one—related to the noun *demeanour*—means to behave: 'Always strive to demean yourself in a manner befitting your calling'. This meaning is nearly obsolete. Today writers are more likely to choose a verb such as *behave*, or *conduct*, or *comport*.

The newer verb—related to the adjective *mean*, meaning inferior—dates from the seventeenth century: to *demean oneself* is to lower oneself; to *demean someone* is to disparage him or her; to *demean something* is to debase it. This 'new' verb was criticized as a confusion throughout the eighteenth and nineteenth centuries and labelled uneducated by Fowler. Nevertheless, today it predominates, and it is considered standard by commentators.

Although Parker ... was notorious for singling out his young idolators and treating them with cruel condescension—making them carry his saxophone case, hold doors for him, run trifling errands, and otherwise demean themselves—nothing we know about Davis suggests that he would play that role.
Jack Chambers *Milestones* 1983: 25

demi-   see SEMI-

demur, demure   To *demur* is to hesitate or object because one has doubts. *Demure* is an adjective meaning modest or dainty. *Demur* rhymes with *fur*, *demure* with *pure*.

As the name of Sir John A. Macdonald had been suggested for the chancellorship, Cook had demurred a little at accepting the honour.
Hilda Neatby *Queen's University* 1 (1978): 125

At first, she demurred, but then she too said, 'Why not?'
Henry M. Rosenthal and S. Cathy Berson, eds. *Canadian Jewish Outlook Anthology* 1988: 287

Deborah Kerr, the demure English rose of British and American movies of the 1940s, shed her goody-two-shoes image in From Here to Eternity, the 1953 film in which she and Burt Lancaster had a steamy love scene on the beach at Honolulu.
Toronto Star 13 Dec. 1992: D5

'It's just another form of motivation,' said Pape, demur on dry land.
Gazette (Montreal) 28 March 1992: C1

(Pape is the forceful female coxswain of a men's rowing team; the context requires *demure*.)

But he demures. He talks about priorities and family.
Vancouver Sun 7 Aug. 1992: D1

(The context requires *demurs*.)

Dene, Na-Dene   *Dene* (pronounced *DEN ay*) an Athapaskan word meaning 'the people', refers to those Aboriginal peoples of the Barren Grounds and the Mackenzie Valley of the Northwest Territories who have been politically represented since 1978 by the Dene Nation (formerly known as the Indian Brotherhood of the Northwest Territories). Strictly speaking, it is redundant to refer to the 'Dene people', since *Dene* already means people. *Dene* is used for both singular and plural.

The Dene call their traditional territories Denendeh (*DEN en DAY*), meaning 'home of the people'. Most members of the Dene Nation come from groups whose traditional languages are Athapaskan; some, however, come from groups whose traditional language is Cree. The Dene Nation has been negotiating with the federal government for a self-governing territory in the western Arctic, which would be a counterpart to a self-governing Inuit territory in the central and eastern Arctic (see NUNAVUT).

Mr. Erasmus later said he was optimistic the Queen would meet with him, adding he was prepared to travel to Britain to press his case for Denendeh, as the Dene call the land they claim.
Spectator (Hamilton) 22 Aug. 1994: A2

House, 20, plays the rebellious teenager Teevee Tenya on the popular show *North of Sixty*, which depicts a fictional Dene settlement called Lynx River.
Daily News (Halifax) 27 July 1994: 29

Stung, the federal government said it would now negotiate land claim settlements separately with any groups who wished to do so, thereby fracturing the Dene Nation as a political entity that spoke for all the Indians of the Mackenzie Valley.
Toronto Star 31 July 1994: E1

While the Inuit make up about 80 per cent of the Eastern Arctic's population, the West is a mix of several Dene nations, Metis, the Inuvialuit of the Beaufort Sea area and non-native people.
Ottawa Citizen 5 May 1992: A3

See also CHIPEWYAN; SLAVEY.

Dene-Tha(h)   see SLAVEY

denizen   A *denizen* is an inhabitant. Although the word is applied figuratively to people who inhabit or frequent a certain place, it should not be used simply to refer to a fan or devotee.

> As a denizen of one of the most wintery cities in North America, I have great difficulty accepting that Washington, D.C., where the cherries blossom, is a Winter City....
> *City Magazine* Spring 1988: 47

> Earle's words, and those of the other authors, are accompanied by stunning photos of the weird, beautiful denizens of the deep [i.e., fish].
> *Toronto Star* 31 Oct. 1992: H18

> At both weekend concerts the long-suffering denizen of Place des Arts could only marvel anew at how much greater an orchestra the MSO [Montreal Symphony Orchestra] seems in Carnegie Hall....
> *Gazette* (Montreal) 19 Oct. 1992: A11

> Having been a denizen of Parliament Hill for nearly 40 years, I have few illusions about the place.
> *Ottawa Citizen* 25 Nov. 1994: A12

> 'What's going on in the sports world worth writing about?' asked a disgruntled denizen of the games people play.
> *Daily News* (Halifax) 15 March 1992: 67

(Here *fan* would be appropriate.)

> An announced crowd of 8,761 dizzy-headed denizens filed through the turnstiles to claim a piece of the action as the Halifax Windjammers nipped the upstart expansionist Hamilton Skyhawks 111-105....
> *Daily News* (Halifax) 3 May 1992: 75

(Here *fans* would be appropriate.)

denotation, denote   see CONNOTATION

dependent, dependant, independent   *Dependent* is an adjective: 'The children are dependent on her for food'; 'dependent family members'. *Dependant* is a noun: 'Her child is her dependant'. Canadian and British writers generally follow this distinction; American writers use *dependent* for both the adjective and the noun.

Some Canadian newspapers follow the American style; style guides for the Montreal *Gazette* and the Toronto *Globe and Mail*, for example, recommend the *-ent* form in all senses. The *Canadian Press Stylebook*, however, recommends the *-ent/-ant* distinction.

Independent is spelled the same whether it is used as an adjective ('an independent act') or as a noun meaning a politician not affiliated with any particular party ('She sits in Parliament as an independent').

> Because the dog sled is their only means of winter transport, they are still in part dependent on subsistence hunting.
> *Arctic* 41.1 (1988): 53

> ... you can only claim medical expenses for the child if your child is also claimed as a dependant.
> *Financial Post* 25 Nov. 1991: 14

> The extra attention provided to the utterly dependant newborns at the hospital's 28-bed special care nursery reinforces attention from parents and the unit's round-the-clock staff of 10 nurses.
> *Vancouver Sun* 19 Aug. 1990: 83

(The adjective is usually spelled *dependent*.)

See also DESCENDANT, DESCENDENT.

deplane   see EMBARK

depreciate, deprecate, self-deprecating, self-depreciating   With respect to financial matters, to *depreciate* means to decrease or reduce in value. It also means to undervalue or speak disparagingly of. To *deprecate* means to censure or deplore. *Self-deprecating* and *self-depreciating* both mean self-belittling. Some commentators think that *self-depreciating* is the more apt term for this activity, but *self-deprecating* has far more currency in Canadian English. Either word is acceptable.

> Unlike new furniture that depreciates in value from the moment it's unpacked in your living room, antiques increase in value through the years.
> *Vancouver Sun* 13 Nov. 1993: E7

> Certainly a large number of them are members of the educated middle class, conditioned through many years of schooling to depreciate things Canadian.
> Margaret Atwood *Second Words* 1982: 189

> Islam glorified the holy war against unbelievers, but strongly deprecated war between fellow Muslims.
> *Toronto Star* 4 Dec. 1993: H15

> Comedian David Broadfoot ... warmed up the audience with his own brand of self-deprecating Canadian humor. How many Canadians does it take to change a lightbulb? None. We accept them the way they are.
> *Ottawa Citizen* 30 Nov. 1990: D3

Self-depreciating humor: It is hard to lose with these jokes. You can poke fun at your own weight and the eccentricities of your ethnic group.
Ottawa Citizen 20 Sept. 1994: B6

deputy speaker   see SPEAKER

derby, clerk, Berkeley   Most Canadians and Americans pronounce the *er* in *derby* and *clerk* like the *ur* in *lurk*. Most British speakers, on the other hand, rhyme *derby* with *Barbie* and *clerk* with *lark*.

The first syllable of *Berkeley*, the American city, rhymes with *lurk*; the first syllable of *Berkeley*, the eighteenth-century British philosopher, rhymes with *lark*.

Other words containing *er*, such as *jerk* and *perk*, rhyme with *lurk* on both sides of the Atlantic.

de rigueur   *De rigueur* (pronounced *duh ree GUR*) is borrowed from French and means 'proper' or 'currently considered indispensable'. *De rigueur* is often misspelled without the first *u*, perhaps because several familiar borrowings from French (*auteur, hauteur, provocateur*) end in a consonant followed by *-eur*.

Alarming revelations are de rigueur in biographies now, it seems.
Vancouver Sun 22 Oct. 1994: D17

So tans became de rigeur for the leisured classes, a signal that their owners could pursue lives of sailing, golf and lying about on the beach at Corfu.
Vancouver Sun 25 July 1994: A9

(The correct spelling is *de rigueur*.)

derisive, derisory   A hundred years ago *derisive* and *derisory* were used interchangeably to mean either expressing derision (mocking) or deserving ridicule (trifling). Today both words are used in the first sense ('derisive *or* derisory laughter'), but only *derisory* is used in the second ('a derisory sum of money').

When she's at a distance from Auntie Muriel she can think of derisive and vulgar things to say to her, but in her presence she knows she would be mute.
Margaret Atwood *Life Before Man* 1979: 163

It's no wonder that the survey was greeted by derisory hoots.
Toronto Star 31 Dec. 1988: M3

'Given the very long absence of five years, this argument is diluted to the point of seeming derisory,' Judge Duranleau ruled.
Globe and Mail (Toronto) 12 June 1985: P3

descendant, ancestor, descendent   Our descendants will live in the future, after us; our ancestors lived in the past. *Descendants* and *ancestors* usually refer to relatives whose lifetimes do not overlap with ours, rather than our children and grandchildren or parents and grandparents. Most Canadian and British usage guides echo an eighteenth-century pronouncement by Samuel Johnson that *descendant* is a noun and *descendent* an adjective. Thus a *descendant* is a person born of a particular family or a thing derived from an earlier model, while *descendent* means moving downward, as in 'a diagonal descendent from left to right'. In reality this distinction may never have been as firmly established as Johnson hoped it would become. The adjective is so rare a word that its correct spelling is debatable. The predominant spelling of the noun in contemporary Canadian English is *descendant*, but *descendent* is common enough that it should be considered an acceptable variant—which is how it is listed in American dictionaries and now also in the *New Shorter Oxford English Dictionary*.

It shows the State Department was mindful that separatist sentiment in Quebec and New Brunswick might spread to descendants of Acadians living in the U.S. northeast.
Toronto Star 30 Dec. 1992: D19

Recording contracts are the direct descendants of film contracts from the 1930s and '40s, which tied an actor or director to a studio indefinitely.
Toronto Star 30 Nov. 1992: B4

In it, the settlers or their descendents would 'come to terms with' their 'own real past' and so live with fewer delusions in less destructive ways.
NeWest Review Feb.–Mar. 1990: 34

Amenartas fled from Africa and gave birth to a son, through whom her story has passed along a line of descendents to Leo Vincey, an Englishman who decides to explore the mystery....
Margaret Atwood *Second Words* 1982: 39

See also DEPENDENT, DEPENDANT.

descry   see DECRY

desert   see DESSERT

despatch   see DISPATCH

despite, in spite of, notwithstanding   These three prepositions all mean the same thing. *Despite* is by far the most common. *Notwithstanding* is used mainly in formal academic writing and is sometimes positioned after its object: 'notwithstanding this rebuke' *or* 'this rebuke notwithstanding'.

All three prepositions may be combined with the phrase 'the fact that' to introduce a clause. In most contexts, however, this construction is wordy, and *although* or *even though* is preferable.

> Notwithstanding these criticisms, the work should be of interest to the specialist in British military or European diplomatic history as a source for the study of the occupation.
> *Canadian Journal of History* 14.1 (1989): 144

> Hall had been trying 'about 20 years' to have a baby and, colic notwithstanding, she's thrilled with motherhood.
> *Toronto Star* 20 Dec. 1993: B11

> Despite the fact that the plaintiff was a widow 78 years of age who had just broken her glasses, the court found her careless in signing a deed she had been unable to read, and thus bound by subsequent dealings in the property transferred in the document.
> J.E. Smyth et al. *The Law and Business Administration in Canada* 1987: 221

> In spite of the fact that most Canadians assess American English to be inferior, most ESL texts in Canada are American.
> W.C. Lougheed, ed. *In Search of the Standard in Canadian English* 1986: 141

See also CANADIAN BILL OF RIGHTS.

dessert, desert, just deserts   The name for a sweet last course of a meal is spelled with a double *s*: *dessert* (*di ZERT*). The name for a sometimes sandy region with very low rainfall is spelled with one *s*: *desert* (*DEZ ert*). *Desert* is also used as an adjective to describe a barren, desolate, or uninhabited area that may not necessarily be a desert in the technical sense: for example, a 'desert island'. Figuratively, a desert is an uninteresting period, subject, or area, as in 'a cultural desert'. The verb *desert* (*di ZERT*) means to abandon or leave.

The plural noun *deserts* (*di ZERTS*) means what is deserved and survives mainly in the expression *just deserts*: 'Voters know he abused their trust and he'll get his just deserts at the polls'. Because the pronun-

ciation of this word is the same as that of *desserts*, the expression 'just desserts' occasionally appears as a pun on menus, as the name of a restaurant, or in other references to food.

> The First Week is gloomy: it envisages sin and its just deserts, death and damnation.
> *Canadian Journal of Philosophy* 19 (1989): 197

> ... if he believes so strongly in the so-called exceptional athlete getting his just desserts, why doesn't he suggest they be paid on a strict 'merit' basis instead of their absurdly high long-term contracts?
> *Financial Post* 23 Feb. 1990: 8

(Here the correct spelling is *deserts*.)

> It was a bake sale designed to give the Tories their just desserts.
> *Vancouver Sun* 9 March 1990: 3

(Here *just desserts* is an intentional play on words.)

destroy   To *destroy* a thing is to render it useless or to end its existence; to *destroy* a person is to ruin him or her financially, professionally, or in some other way. Some usage experts criticize 'completely destroyed' as redundant and 'partly destroyed' as a contradiction in terms, but most find no fault with these expressions. Parts of a whole can be destroyed: if a building survives a fire with some rooms ruined and others intact, it could be described as 'partly destroyed', whereas a building razed by fire could be called 'completely destroyed'.

> If the goods are only partly destroyed, the contract is not discharged completely; instead the carrier is absolved from liability to the extent that the damage was caused to the goods by an act of God and must deliver them as they are.
> J.E. Smyth et al. *The Law and Business Administration in Canada* 1987: 314

> Some paintings, including Death of Adonis by Sebastiano del Piombo, a follower of Michelangelo, were completely destroyed. Several statues had their arms and legs chopped off by flying glass.
> *Calgary Herald* 28 May 1993: D9

See also COMPLETE.

detract   see DISTRACT

detrain   see EMBARK

deus ex machina   *Deus ex machina* (usually pronounced *DAY us ex MAK in uh*) is a Latin phrase used in literary criticism. It describes a character or event introduced suddenly and implausibly to resolve a difficulty in the plot. The literal translation of *deus ex machina* is 'god from a machine'. This phrase is a reference to ancient Greek drama, in which the gods (played by actors suspended from pulleys above the stage) would descend at the end of the play to resolve conflict.

Deus ex machina should be italicized in formal writing.

Shields herself used the term 'deus ex machina' to describe an unlikely scene inserted towards the book's end.
Gazette (Montreal) 28 March 1992: K1

Obstacles arise haphazardly and are often resolved by a convenient deus ex machina. The plot has neither real suspense nor any continuity.
Ottawa Citizen 25 March 1990: E3

The ending hinges on an historical event that takes place outside the created world of the novel. It impinges, changing everything: deus ex machina without the deus.
Calgary Herald 26 Sept. 1992: D7

(Here the writer plays on the literal meaning of *deus ex machina*.)

See also LATIN PHRASES.

develop, developed, development *Developed* is often misspelled with a double *p*, and *development* is often misspelled with an *e* after the *p*. In Canada these misspellings may be influenced by the French words *développer* and *développement*.

Although still in its first year, the students already seem to have developped a sense of identity.
Gazette (Montreal) 16 Dec. 1993: G8

(The correct spelling is *developed*.)

The home could be moved flush to the corner to maintain some heritage character while creating infill space for developement.
Vancouver Sun 20 Aug. 1994: D14

(The correct spelling is *development*).

devil's advocate Originally, the devil's advocate was a Roman Catholic official appointed to present a case against the proposed canonization of a saint, thus ensuring that the case for canonization would be properly tested. By extension, a devil's advocate is anyone who introduces an unpopular or contradictory view to test—and possibly strengthen—the original view. A devil's advocate does not necessarily believe in the view she or he is defending, although those who play the devil's advocate risk having their arguments mistaken for their true beliefs. A devil's advocate is not simply someone who holds an unpopular view.

Mowat's friends presumably were convinced that there could be no better appointment, but there is no evidence that any one on the board felt the serious obligation at least to play the part of the devil's advocate for any one of the other candidates.
Hilda Neatby *Queen's University* 1 (1978): 68

(Here the role of the *devil's advocate* would be to promote one of the other candidates, making the board look less partial and presumably strengthening the case for Mowat's appointment.)

... [Ball] warned Kennedy privately that it would be a tragic blunder to commit U.S. troops to Vietnam. 'Within five years, we'll have 300,000 men in the paddies and jungles and never find them,' Ball recalled saying.... During Lyndon Johnson's presidency, Ball was often called the 'Devil's advocate' on Vietnam....
Gazette (Montreal) 28 May 1994: G16

(Ball was not, strictly speaking, a *devil's advocate* because he sincerely believed that U.S. involvement in the war was a mistake.)

diacritical marks, diacritics, diaeresis, accent marks *Diacritical marks*, *diacritics*, or *accent marks* are added to letters to indicate variations in pronunciation. English uses very few of these, and writers often drop them even in borrowed words that have them in the original language. For example, while in French *élite* is written with an accent, in English Canadians usually drop it: *elite*. Often the difficulty is technical: many typewriters, word processing progams, and printers lack the capacity to produce diacritical marks.

A *diaeresis* or *dieresis* (the former spelling is favoured in Britain, the latter in the U.S.) consists of two points set over a vowel; in German this mark is called an *umlaut*. In English it indicates that the vowel so marked is to be pronounced separately rather than run in with another vowel or left silent. Among the few words that are still found with a diaeresis are the proper names *Brontë*, *Noël*, and *Zoë*, and *naïve* and its derivatives. Even these, however, appear without the mark in many publications.

An *accent mark* is sometimes similarly used to indicate that a syllable that is normally not stressed should be pronounced separately (generally in poetry or songs). For example, in the phrase 'my piercèd side, O Thomas see', *pierced* is pronounced with two syllables (*PEER sed*) rather than the usual one (*PEERST*). This accent may be written in two ways ('piercèd' or 'piercéd').

See also -ED; NAIVE.

diagnose   *Diagnose* is derived from a Greek word meaning recognize or discern. Many usage writers object to wording that makes the patient, rather than the disease, the object of *diagnose*. In formal writing, 'Bob was diagnosed as having pneumonia' should be rewritten 'Bob's illness was diagnosed as pneumonia', since the doctor diagnosed (recognized) not Bob, but Bob's disease. However, in speech and informal writing patients are often said to be diagnosed.

> In the interests of public safety, a trend toward the public at large using home tests to diagnose their own conditions should be arrested at once.
> *Maclean's* 31 March 1986: 4

> Most patients are diagnosed in their 70s, but it can strike men in their 40s.
> *Gazette* (Montreal) 2 March 1989: B1

> (In formal writing this sentence should be reworded: 'The condition is usually diagnosed when patients are in their 70s ...'.)

See also BACK-FORMATION.

diagonal   see SLASH

dialect   see ACCENT

dialect, eye   see [COULD OF]

dialectic(s), dialectical, dialectal   A very general meaning of *dialectic(s)* is discussion and logical analysis. But the term can also refer specifically to one of several philosophical approaches and schools of thought to which it has been applied throughout history, including Socratic dialectics, Hegelian dialectics, and the dialectical materialism of Marx and Engels—the official Communist Party philosophy. What all these philosophies have in common is the resolution of opposites. Thus a *dialectic* is often simply something that encompasses two opposing elements or forces. *Dialectics*, with an *s*, usually refers to the process of examining and discussing contradictory forces with the aim of finding a resolution.

The adjective form of *dialectic* is *dialectical* or, less often, *dialectic*. *Dialectal* is the adjective associated with *dialect*, meaning regional or class variety of speech.

> There are manifold contradictions here, but without dialectic, just the pervasive co-existence of opposites indifferently clashing without combustion or progression.
> *Queen's Quarterly* 96.1 (1989): 107

> Generating great excitement is charismatic Toby Stephens, 25, as Coriolanus in Shakespeare's fierce dialectic about dictatorship and the power of the masses.
> *Toronto Star* 19 Nov. 1994: J9

> In fact, this is the great dialectical moment of today's history: economics versus ecology. Suzuki is able to show that the synthesis of an ecologically oriented economy is the wave of the present.
> *Calgary Herald* 16 April 1994: B10

> This settlement pattern, with the populace mainly located along the coast-line, raises basic problems not simply logistical for the conduct of dialectal research in Newfoundland....
> G.M. Story, W.J. Kirwin, and J.D.A. Widdowson, eds. *Dictionary of Newfoundland English* 2nd ed. 1990: xviii

> What can this chap know about the dialectical distinctions between west Texas and east Texas?
> *Ottawa Citizen* 23 June 1994: H12

> (The chap referred to is a speech coach; the word required here is *dialectal*.)

dialogue, dialog   In the early 1960s, *dialogue* came to mean an exchange of ideas and opinions, as in the 'East–West dialogue' that dominated the global politics of that era. Usage commentators called this meaning of *dialogue* faddish, but it has since become established, and *dialogue* is now widely used in Canadian writing to refer to any discussion or exchange of information between parties.

The verb to *dialogue* is not new. The *OED* records it in the works of Shakespeare and also in literary works of the eighteenth and nineteenth centuries. Perhaps the current censure of the verb can be attributed to its overuse by bureaucrats. Although the verb is listed in major American and Canadian dictionaries, usage commentators generally despise it and Canadian writers generally avoid it.

Dialogue is the more common spelling in Canadian, British, and American English. *Dialog* is a variant that is used infrequently in Canada.

> If we are to have a serious dialogue about the vital issue of peace between East and West, NATO and the Warsaw Pact must address the fundamental question 'Who is the enemy?'
> George Ignatieff *The Making of a Peacemonger* 1987: xi

To speed up this process, the centre has established a dialogue with Quebec software producers and recently met with 40 companies to discuss their needs.
Computing Canada 14 Feb. 1991: 30

'I think it's been encouraging,' he says, and then slips into bureaucratese to describe the organizing process: 'We're dialoguing in a non-confrontational way with clients.'
Globe and Mail (Toronto) 11 March 1985: M1

diaspora, Diaspora, Dispersion   A *diaspora* (pronounced *dye ASP uh ruh*) is a dispersion, usually forced, of a people from their homeland; *diaspora* may also refer to the people themselves who are living outside their ancestral homeland. The term was first used to refer to the dispersion of the Jews from Palestine, beginning in the eighth century B.C. For this meaning it is usually capitalized; in other references no capital is required, though one is sometimes used. The English translation of *diaspora, dispersion*, also refers to the Jewish Diaspora when it is capitalized: *Dispersion*.

A perpetual diaspora of all peoples is the book's thematic underpinning: Individuals wander about the globe, full of longing and sadness, seeking ancestors and cultural roots.
Toronto Star 1 Oct. 1995: H18

The sacrifice is reminiscent of the Jewish Diaspora, whose investment in children and education helped the Jewish faith to flourish in exile over nearly two millennia.
Ottawa Citizen 16 July 1994: A6

(Here *Diaspora* refers to the people themselves.)

This is the first official homecoming for the Acadian diaspora and has attracted people from France, Belgium, Texas, Louisiana, New England, California and from across Canada, where there are more than 1.5 million people of Acadian descent.
Daily News (Halifax) 17 Aug. 1994: n.p.

When the state of Israel was established in 1948, it became necessary to find a language that was common to all Jews, despite their many centuries of dispersion....
Gazette (Montreal) 24 Dec. 1994: G2

(In this sense, *dispersion* is often capitalized.)

dice   see DIE

diction, enunciation   *Diction* may refer either to a writer's choice of words or to the clarity of a speaker's word production. *Enunciation* in this con-

text refers solely to the clarity of the production of words in speech (but see ENUNCIATION, ANNUNCIATION). Usage experts, especially in the United States, have often recommended confining *diction* to the sense of word choice in order to completely differentiate these two words. However, *diction* was used to refer to clarity of speech as early as the mideighteenth century (*OED*), and in contemporary English this meaning is both common and accepted.

The forbidding landscape is not relieved by his fondness for the imagery of dry bones and dead trees, nor by dense tangled diction that all too often makes the reader stop and wonder what the hell he is talking about.
Northrop Frye *The Bush Garden* 1971: 17

(Here *diction* refers to word choice.)

Her diction was excellent, though much of what she sang was in Old French and was not entirely intelligible to the likes of me.
Ottawa Citizen 4 Dec. 1994: C7

(Here *diction* means clarity of word production.)

Genius he may be, but there's a tendency for Van Morrison in live performance to sing as if he has a large wad of cotton batting in his mouth ... through all the syllables there's that familiar Marlon-Brando-as-Don-Corleone wuff-wuff in the enunciation.
Globe and Mail (Toronto) 29 Aug. 1985: E5

die, dice   In the past, gamblers rolled one *die* but two or more *dice*. Increasingly, however, *dice* is used for both the singular and the plural. Most authorities now accept 'one dice' in informal use. The more formal singular *die* survives in the expression 'The die is cast'.

... piece movement is determined by the roll of a die.
Ottawa Citizen 30 July 1994: J2

(Here the formal singular *die* is used.)

We're willing to bet our financial futures on the roll of a dice.
Vancouver Sun 8 Dec. 1994: D1

(This use of *dice* as singular is informal.)

'I'm afraid there are people who have come to the conclusion that the dice are loaded against the poor in the Axworthy reform program.'
Gazette (Montreal) 7 Dec. 1994: A1

die of, die from   *Die of* and *die from* are both acceptable. *Die of* is more common, and preferred in formal writing. If the cause of death is indirect, however, *from* must be used: 'The child died from lack of attention'.

Terry Fox died of osteosarcoma, a form of bone cancer.
Queen's Quarterly 97.2 (1990): 256

All the others died of natural causes.
Alan Tucker, ed. *The Penguin Guide to Canada* 1991: 8

differ *Differ from* indicates dissimilarity, while *differ with* indicates disagreement.

How does the role of an appeal court differ from that of a trial court?
J.E. Smyth et al. *The Law and Business Administration in Canada* 1987: 42

As a professional actress who has often worked on thrust stages, I differ with Mr. Godfrey in his opinion that thrust stages are 'a rare breed … so difficult to work on.'
Globe and Mail (Toronto) 10 Jan. 1985: P6

Tolerance and truth—we want to hold firmly to those great cardinal truths … yet at the same time be tolerant and charitable in the way we treat those who differ with us.
Mennonite Brethren Herald 7 March 1986: 24

(Here *differ from* would be more appropriate: the context implies that we should be tolerant of those who are not like us, not simply of those who disagree with us.)

different from, different than, different to *Different from* is common in sentences such as 'Your book is different from mine' or 'Ravens are different from crows'. Here a noun follows *from*. Some usage guides suggest that *from* should follow *different* in all cases. However, *different than* is frequently used by Canadian writers in sentences like those above. It is even more common, and more widely accepted, in comparisons where a clause (rather than a noun) follows *than*: 'What happened was different than (what) we had expected'; 'He looks different than he did last week'; 'Hilda is a very different person than she was last year'. To rewrite this last sentence 'Hilda is a very different person from the person she was last year' is no real improvement, since *person* must be repeated.

Different to is a British form regarded as informal (at best) by British commentators; this form is uncommon in Canadian English.

Whether you are using *from* or *than*, it is important to make sure that readers know what is being compared with what.

Liberals will sound very different from Tories by the time the next election rolls around.
Saturday Night March 1986: 17

Thus, no share of a given class can be given a different voting power from other shares of the same class.
J.E. Smyth et al. *The Law and Business Administration in Canada* 1987: 708

'A bishop occupies a different role than a priest,' he stressed.
Canadian Churchman April 1986: 6

Against this background moral reasons take on a different appearance than Larmore gives them.
Canadian Journal of Philosophy 19 (1989): 323

See also VARIOUS DIFFERENT.

differentiate, distinguish, discriminate All three words mean to recognize or separate on the basis of difference. *Differentiate* is commonly used with the prepositions *from* and *between*. *Distinguish* and *discriminate* are used with *between*, *from*, and *among*.

Discriminate can have either positive or negative connotations. In the positive sense, to *discriminate* is to distinguish subtle differences between similar things: people with this knack, such as connoisseurs of wine, art, food, and fashion, are called *discriminating*. When *discriminate* is used negatively, as in 'This study discriminates against women', it is always followed by *against*, and the related adjective is *discriminatory*.

It seeks to differentiate between long-term, structural unemployment, often related to simultaneously declining and expanding industries or technological change, and short-term unemployment, attributable, say, to insufficient aggregate demand.
Canadian Journal of Sociology 14.2 (1989): 261

For it does not enable us to distinguish among the various kinds of social groups we all know about—families, friendship groups, residential communities, formal and complex organizations, etc.—all of which may be regarded, according to the definition, as 'social systems.'
Irving M. Zeitlin and Robert J. Brym *The Social Condition of Humanity* 1991: 84

'And in Alan Wilde we see an effort to discriminate its modes: "mediate irony", "disjunctive irony", and "postmodern" or "suspensive irony" with its yet more radical vision of multiplicity, randomness, contingency, and even absurdity.'
Linda Hutcheon *Splitting Images* 1991: 90

(Here, to *discriminate* means to categorize on the basis of subtle distinctions.)

... [Aboriginal peoples] were largely forced to give up their old ways and are unable to enter the Canadian mainstream because white Canadians discriminate against them.
Irving M. Zeitlin and Robert J. Brym *The Social Condition of Humanity* 1991: 161

diffuse, defuse To *diffuse* means to spread or scatter in all directions. A *diffuse* argument is rambling and unfocused. The verb is pronounced with a final *z* sound: *di FYOOZ*. The adjective has a final *s* sound: *di FYOOSS*.

To *defuse* (pronounced *dee FYOOZ*) means literally to remove a fuse, rendering an explosive or other device harmless. Figuratively, to *defuse* means to counteract a potentially harmful or tense situation. Sometimes the way to defuse a confrontation is to diffuse anger or tension.

> Choose one of the cushion fabrics as side drapes for the window and use creamy white sheers to help diffuse the strong sunlight.
> *Ottawa Citizen* 3 Dec. 1994: I4

> Negotiations were under way in October 1956 to defuse the situation when Britain, France, and Israel decided to take matters into their own hands and invaded Egypt.
> George Ignatieff *The Making of a Peacemonger* 1987: 122

(Only *defuse* is appropriate here.)

> A strong economy helps defuse tensions and much of the economic boom has been spearheaded by entrepreneurial Russians.
> *Ottawa Citizen* 28 Dec. 1994: F6

(Here *defuse* means make less dangerous; *diffuse*, meaning disperse, would also be possible.)

> Harcourt said the kids-at-risk projects will diffuse the potentially explosive situations many students face and are aimed at helping reduce the drop-out rate.
> *Vancouver Sun* 2 Dec. 1994: B3

('Explosive situations' can't be dispersed; the word required here is *defuse*.)

digraph see DIPHTHONG

dilemma A *dilemma* is a choice between two undesirable alternatives (sometimes called the 'horns of the dilemma'). Often the only thing that makes these alternatives undesirable is their exclusivity: choosing one rules out the other. Now, especially in informal writing, *dilemma* is also used to mean difficulty, problem, or predicament, with no suggestion of choice. Many usage guides still resist this extended sense, however, and it is best avoided in academic and formal writing.

> The government faced a dilemma: it could not allow the demise of close to nineteen hundred souls; neither could it be seen to thwart the religious aspirations of a devout and inoffensive religious sect.
> Pierre Berton *The Promised Land* 1984: 87

> He may find himself in the dilemma that if he does not interfere, the business may fail completely; yet if he chooses to exercise some control in order to save the business, he will incur unlimited liability.
> J.E. Smyth et al. *The Law and Business Administration in Canada* 1987: 665

> A lottery winner's dilemma. Is losing privacy worth 39 million dollars?
> *CTV News* [transcript] 14 Dec. 1994: n.p.

> With this emphasis upon their geographical identity, historians were faced with the dilemma of how to deal with residents of Quebec who were not of French origins.
> *Queen's Quarterly* 92.1 (1985): 88

(This use of *dilemma* is informal; in this academic article, *problem* would be a better choice.)

> Finding a unique gift for a special person is a chore that accompanies the otherwise delightful Christmas season. But Canada's antique shops, auctions and shows offer an easy solution to the dilemma....
> *Canadian Collector* 21 (1986): 1

(This use of *dilemma* is informal.)

See also HOBSON'S CHOICE; SCYLLA AND CHARYBDIS.

dilettante *Dilettante* is derived from the Italian word for 'delight', and in the eighteenth century it was used positively to refer to an admirer or devotee of the fine arts. Now the word is almost always used negatively to describe someone who dabbles in arts or letters in a superficial and unfocused way.

Canadians and Americans usually say *DILL uh taunt*, while the British prefer the Italianate pronunciation *di li TAN tee*. The plural is *dilettantes* or, less commonly, *dilettanti*. A dilettante is *dilettantish* and engages in *dilettantism* or *dilettanteism*.

> It's possible to go to the other extreme, to be a dilettante so bemused by possibilities that one has no convictions or power to act at all.
> Northrop Frye *The Educated Imagination* 1963: 32

The 1980 election saw resurrected Liberals determined to disprove obituaries that painted the Trudeau years as dilettantish and uninspired.
Globe and Mail (Toronto) March 30 1985: P6

My generalism (please do not confuse this with dilettantism because they are not the same) clearly led me to seek the editorship because of the scope it allows for putting this predilection into practice.
Queen's Quarterly 92.2 (1985): 442

dinner, supper, lunch, luncheon, tea, brunch
In the past, especially in rural settings, Canadians ate up to four meals a day: breakfast, dinner (a large meal at noon), supper (a lighter meal in the evening), and lunch (a light snack late in the evening). The main meal was served at noon to sustain farm workers for an afternoon of heavy labour. Urbanization changed this pattern of cooking and eating. Today, when many people do not go home for a midday meal, the large meal is served in the evening and is called *dinner* or *supper*. The 'Survey of Vancouver English' (1984) indicated that *dinner* is preferred to *supper*, although many informants used either word. Those who do distinguish these words as terms for the evening meal use *dinner* for a hot, substantial meal and *supper* for a quicker cold meal. *Lunch* is now the name of the midday meal, although in Atlantic Canada and the Prairie provinces *lunch* may also refer to a late-night snack.

At one time *luncheon*, not *lunch*, was the usual term for the midday meal. *Lunch* is now established as the preferred form, and *luncheon* usually refers to a formal meal for a group of people gathered for a meeting or entertainment.

Tea in Canada is often an afternoon social event to which guests are invited. In Britain and Australia, especially among working-class speakers, *tea* is the everyday word for dinner.

The term *brunch*, a blend of *breakfast* and *lunch*, was coined by students at Oxford at the end of the nineteenth century and is now fully established in North America.

diphthong, digraph, ligature *Diphthong* is a linguistic term for a vowel sound that is actually two vowels run together. For example, the vowel sounds in *boy*, *loud*, and *tide* are diphthongs: *oi*, *au*, and *ai* respectively. Traditionally, the *ph* in *diphthong* has been pronounced as in *phone*: DIF thong. While this pronunciation is recommended, many dictionaries and usage guides now also list the pronunciation *DIP thong*.

A *digraph* is two letters pronounced as one sound: for example, *ph*, *ch*, *th*, the *ea* in *bead*, or the *ps* in *psychology*.

Ligature is a printer's term for two letters joined together: for example, *æ* in *æsthete* or *œ* in *fœtus*. Ligatures occur in English borrowings from Greek. Sometimes ligatures are mistakenly called diphthongs, probably because in the original Greek they represented diphthongs, though in English pronunciation they do not.

See also -AE-, -OE-, -E.

directions   see EAST, WEST, NORTH, SOUTH

dis-   see DE-

disabilities   People with disabilities have recently begun to challenge demeaning traditional labels that equate them with their disabilities, as in 'a diabetic', 'an epileptic', 'a Down's child', 'a cripple', 'a mental case', 'an MS-victim', and so on. The Secretary of State supports this point of view and recommends to Canadian editors that they abandon noun labels, such as those above, in favour of descriptive phrases such as 'who has epilepsy', 'who has Down's syndrome', 'whose mobility is impaired by arthritis', 'who uses a wheelchair', 'who has mental health problems', 'who is intellectually impaired', and so on. In the Secretary of State's recommended usage, a person is always mentioned before his or her disability; a disability is mentioned only if it is relevant to the context; and it is described in neutral terms. Expressions that are disrespectful or pitying ('crazy', 'crippled', 'victim of', 'devastated by', 'stricken with') should be avoided.

Most deaf people are not, in fact, mute, so phrases such as 'deaf-mute' and 'deaf and dumb' are inaccurate. In addition, the contemporary connotations of *dumb* render the latter phrase insulting. Instead of saying that someone is unable to speak, indicate how they do communicate: for example, by signing, with a voice synthesizer, with the help of a computer.

'Blind people' is preferred to 'the blind', though 'the deaf' is accepted because those deaf people who sign constitute a language community.

The term *challenged*, as in 'intellectually challenged' or 'physically challenged', is a euphemism that has spawned jokes such as 'vertically challenged' for short people, and 'sartorially challenged' for sloppy dressers; it's not recommended for serious use.

> Booth, 33, is a student in the social services program at Fraser Valley Community College in Abbotsford. He has had multiple sclerosis since 1982 and has been nearly blind for three years.
> *Province* (Vancouver) 29 Oct. 1990: 50

> But it's no toy. MS sufferer Richard Beecroft, of Ottawa, will be riding a custom-built, three-wheeled bicycle like the one he rode on a three-year trek around the world to raise awareness about MS.
> *Province* (Vancouver) 7 Aug. 1990: 53

(Here 'who has multiple sclerosis' would be preferable to 'MS sufferer'.)

> Finley, an epileptic who can't work, lost 50 pounds during the period.
> *Gazette* (Montreal) 7 July 1990: A14

(Here 'who has epilepsy' would be preferable.)

> I take issue with your description of Percy Wickman as 'wheelchair bound' and 'confined to a wheelchair'.... You might as well describe everyone else as 'car-bound' or 'confined to shoes'.
> *Maclean's* 24 April 1989: A6

(Here 'who uses a wheelchair' would have been preferable.)

See also DOWN'S SYNDROME.

disaffected, unaffected   *Disaffected* people are unhappy either with society in general or with some particular thing they were once committed to, such as their work, a relationship, an ideal, or an organization. People who are *unaffected* either don't put on airs or don't feel the impact of a change.

> Amerindians could become a permanently disaffected group, as happened with the Irish in Great Britain.
> *Toronto Star* 29 Aug. 1992: G10

> By introducing anti-refugee provisions the government is hoping to win back support from disaffected Tories who have joined the Reform party.
> *Toronto Star* 19 Aug. 1992: A19

> When I entered his office, I was greeted by an unaffected charming man with an impish glint in his eyes and a shock of red hair.
> *Chatelaine* April 1986: 139

> MacEachern said the children were assessed by a school psychologist and a Health Department official, who found them generally unaffected.
> *Gazette* (Montreal) 19 Nov. 1994: A26

(Here the context disambiguates *unaffected*: the children aren't disarmingly sincere; they are untouched by a bad experience.)

disassemble   see DISSEMBLE

disassociate   see DISSOCIATE

disastrous, wondrous, thunderous   All three words are commonly misspelled. Note that the *e* is dropped from *disaster* and *wonder* to form the adjectives *disastrous* and *wondrous*, while in *thunderous* the *e* is retained.

> One result of the Tory changes was the disasterous drop in Saskatchewan's share of the Indian market, from 50 percent to 8 percent.
> *Briarpatch* Dec. 1989–Jan. 1990: 12

(The correct spelling is *disastrous*.)

> A red glow casts the downtown core in wonderous orange and golden shimmering waves of light.
> *Toronto Star* 24 March 1994: C5

(The correct spelling is *wondrous*.)

> She received a thundrous ovation for her hilarious turn as a dizzy diva who sang several well-known arias with a comic touch.
> *Gazette* (Montreal) 14 Feb. 1994: A14

(The correct spelling is *thunderous*.)

disbar   see DEBAR

disburse   see DISPERSE

disbursement   see DISPERSION

disc, disk   *Disc* and *disk* are spelling variants. In the recording industry, *disc* is the usual spelling: *disc jockey, disco, discography, compact disc. Disk* is preferred internationally for disks used in computers (apart from compact discs): *high-density disk, hard disk*. In other contexts *disc* is the more common spelling in Canada and Britain ('slipped a disc', 'an enormous red disc', 'disc-shaped'), while *disk* is preferred in the United States.

disclaim   see DECRY

discomfit, discomfiture, discomfort *Discomfit* is a verb meaning to disconcert or embarrass; the related noun is *discomfiture*. *Discomfort* is usually used as a noun meaning physical or mental unease, but it can also be used as a verb meaning to make uncomfortable. *Discomfit* refers only to mental or emotional states, while *discomfort*, although it covers both mental and physical states, is more commonly used of the latter.

Trying to produce small talk when isolated with Trudeau at a stand-up cocktail reception has proved discomfiting for the most accomplished social lioness.
Maclean's 31 March 1986: 15

It is a protest against the dehumanization of society made by women on behalf of everyone, because it is women who are most discomforted by the gap between who they are and what they are supposed to be.
Queen's Quarterly 92.2 (1985): 428

To add to my discomforture and embarrassment I have noticed a letter in your paper, Feb. 7, from my daughter....
Globe and Mail (Toronto) 21 Feb. 1985: M11

(Either *discomfiture* or *discomfort* would be appropriate here.)

discreditable see CREDIBLE

discreet, discrete *Discreet* is often misspelled *discrete*. *Discreet* means tactful, prudent, and circumspect; the related nouns are *discretion* and *discreetness*. *Discrete* means distinct, separate, or discontinuous, and the related noun is *discreteness*.

Though Arafat insists on the PLO's right to attack Israeli military targets, his discreet efforts to stop the raids reflect worry that the U.S. might call off talks with the PLO.
Gazette (Montreal) 3 March 1989: A7

He tackles the unity question not as a discrete problem but within the broader issue of enhancing Canadian justice and international peace.
Toronto Star 26 Feb. 1994: J13

Finally, I treated the complete picture with what's called a facet filter, a filter that separates a photographic image into discrete patches of color that resemble dabs of paint on a canvas.
Gazette (Montreal) 15 Oct. 1994: J2

The seventh-inning stretch takes on a new meaning as a less than discrete couple in the SkyDome Hotel are caught copulating by fans that originally thought the

entertainment was on the field between the Seattle Mariners and Toronto Blue Jays.
Ottawa Citizen 29 Dec. 1990: C3

(The word intended here is *discreet*.)

discriminate see DIFFERENTIATE

discuss, debate *Discuss about* is non-standard: 'We discussed schools', *not* 'We discussed about schools'. *Discuss* without an object is also non-standard: 'Last night we had a discussion', but *not* 'Last night we discussed'.

Debate is sometimes followed by a preposition, either *about* or *over*: 'They debated about moving again'. Usually, though, it takes a direct object: 'They debated children's rights'. Some authorities dislike *debate about* and *debate over*, but the prepositions serve the purpose of emphasizing indecision.

The sessions enabled composers to discuss their common problems, especially of attracting audiences for contemporary concert music.
Queen's Quarterly 94.1 (1987): 177

'We're not saying it's perfect but it's saying natives will have autonomy and First Nations will discuss nation to nation [with Quebec].'
Gazette (Montreal) 3 Dec. 1990: A5

(*Discuss* requires a direct object: 'First Nations will *discuss issues* nation to nation.')

At Montreal's Jewish General Hospital, the 12-member ethics committee ... debated for 90 minutes last month over whether to discharge a 48-year-old schizophrenic who wanted to go back to living on the city streets.
Maclean's 1 May 1989: A56

Both were highly regarded on The Street a few years earlier, and listeners inevitably debated their relative merits....
Jack Chambers *Milestones* 1983: 141

disembark see EMBARK

disenfranchise, disfranchise To deprive people of their rights, particularly voting rights, is to *disenfranchise* or *disfranchise* them. Both are correct. Most usage guides recommend the shorter form, *disfranchise*, but Canadian writers overwhelmingly prefer *disenfranchise*.

Instead, shareholders overwhelmingly approved an amendment under which they may have disenfranchised themselves....
Globe and Mail (Toronto) 7 March 1985: B1

Speaking to a subdued crowd of about 100, congress chairman Bernard Finestone said he did not think the Quebec government went out of its way to disfranchise members of Montreal's ethnic communities.
Gazette (Montreal) 17 June 1985: A4

dishevelled, disheveled *Dishevelled* (pronounced *di SHEV uld*) means untidy. It refers to wayward hair (the root of the word is the Old French word *chevel*, 'hair') or now, more commonly, a generally rumpled personal appearance. Occasionally things in disarray are called dishevelled. *Disheveled* is an alternative spelling, preferred in the United States.

Her hair was terribly sparse and what there was of it was dishevelled.
Canadian Fiction Magazine 63 (1988): 87

The roly-poly Klein, who always looks slightly dishevelled—with his tie askew, his shirttail sticking out and his hair mussed up—shrugged off suggestions he doesn't look much like a premier.
Vancouver Sun 28 Dec. 1992: A4

Yet it could not even put up a decent byelection fight against the Civic Party, a disheveled assemblage with no real leader, program or philosophy of government.
Gazette (Montreal) 4 Nov. 1992: B2

See also DOUBLING THE FINAL CONSONANT.

disingenuous see INGENIOUS

disinterested, uninterested, disinterest *Disinterested* means impartial, without selfish motives or not standing to gain, while *uninterested* means not interested: that is, bored by or incurious about something. A good referee is disinterested but never uninterested in the game.

Disinterested is also used to mean uninterested. All dictionaries list this meaning, but most commentators object strongly to it, fearing that the special sense of *disinterested* will be obscured or lost. Canadian usage provides no grounds for this fear. *Disinterested* is rarely ambiguous in context, and, at least in writing, it is still used far more often to mean impartial than bored. Those who use *disinterested* to mean bored or indifferent are not likely to be misunderstood, but they do run a substantial risk of being criticized; it is best to avoid the disputed usage in formal writing.

Note that the noun *disinterest* can mean either impartiality or lack of interest. Both meanings are accepted.

Uninterested in school, she had begun smoking grass, taking LSD, and hanging around the hippie district of Yorkville.
Ann Davis *Somewhere Waiting* 1991: 249

Since the mediator is disinterested, he can adopt an objective attitude toward the conflict.
Irving M. Zeitlin and Robert J. Brym *The Social Condition of Humanity* 1991: 62

I am no disinterested reviewer of *Still Barred From Prison*. The author is one of my favorite persons.
Henry M. Rosenthal and S. Cathy Berson, eds. *Canadian Jewish Outlook Anthology* 1988: 338

At times, the 120 attending the hour-long question-and-answer luncheon seemed completely disinterested. In fact, at one point there was a lull in the action as no one had a question at the three microphones.
Winnipeg Free Press 17 Nov. 1990: 10

(This use of *disinterested* is disputed.)

The particular culprits in this regard are the wholesalers who seem disinterested in searching out and offering a Canadian manufacturer or Canadian alternatives for foreign goods that they have represented over the years.
Vista 11.4 (May 1983): 1

(This use of *disinterested* is disputed.)

That is to say, they conceive of participation in the elective process as a vestigial duty, rather like going to church.... Apathy or disinterest of this sort is one of the great privileges of the tiny fraction of the world which calls itself democratic.
Queen's Quarterly 94.4 (1987): 973

(Here *disinterest* means lack of interest.)

disk see DISC

disorganized, unorganized *Disorganized* and *unorganized* are synonyms meaning lacking system and order. *Unorganized* also has a specialized sense, referring to workers who do not belong to a labour union.

Our impressions of human life are picked up one by one, and remain for most of us loose and disorganized.
Northrop Frye *The Educated Imagination* 1963: 24

... Kanata was once a stable, planned suburban community. He says it's now in a period of unorganized growth and intense real-estate speculation.
Ottawa Citizen 12 July 1994: A1

dispassionate, impassive, impassable *Dispassionate* means either unswayed by emotions, and thus unbiased and fair, or, sometimes, cold and aloof. *Impassive* means unflinching, not roused to emotion, or not betraying emotion. *Impassable* means impossible to travel over or through.

> But more than his formal qualifications, it was his capacity for dispassionate, objective analysis that I found so impressive.
> George Ignatieff *The Making of a Peacemonger* 1987: 79

> But 'neath the lovely minimalist jazz-pop exterior, her delivery is cold and dispassionate.
> *Vancouver Sun* 17 Feb. 1990: D2

> Mr. Justice Eugene Ewaschuk, describing the crime as 'particularly cruel and odious,' sentenced an impassive H—— to life in prison with no opportunity for parole for 14 years.
> *London Free Press* 28 April 1988: B5

> It was the dead of winter, school finally closed till spring, with roads impassable for all but poker players.
> David Williams *Eye of the Father* 1985: 98

dispatch, despatch Dictionaries list both spellings. *Dispatch* is far more common; *despatch* first appeared in Johnson's *Dictionary* (1755) and may have been a typographical error, since Johnson used *dispatch* in his own writings.

The verb *dispatch* means to send with haste, or to dispose of some work, or to kill someone. The noun means speed and efficiency (this is an element of all meanings of the noun and the verb) or a report of some kind (e.g., a military report or a news report filed by a correspondent).

> By then Secretary General Dag Hammarskjold had become convinced that the only hope of bringing the situation under control was to dispatch an international peace-keeping force to the Congo.
> George Ignatieff *The Making of a Peacemonger* 1987: 192

> Now they require him to snatch and despatch a KGB executioner in East Germany as a reprisal for breaching the unwritten code of espionage forbidding violence against one another's agents on their home ground.
> *Globe and Mail* (Toronto) 23 Feb. 1985: E15

(Here *despatch* means kill.)

> Our diplomats are responsible for the way in which we analyze changing realities in the world, but the Government is accountable for the dispatch with which we respond to those changes.
> *Globe and Mail* (Toronto) 19 Feb. 1985: P9

(Here *dispatch* means speed and efficency.)

> The confidential dispatch from Prime Minister Brian Mulroney to the premiers last week included both a request and a warning.
> *Maclean's* 28 July 1986: 12

dispel *Dispel* is occasionally misspelled *dispell*, probably because similar words, such as *appal*, *enrol*, and *expel*, are correctly spelled with either a single or a double *l* in Canadian English. Note, however, that the past tense and present participle, *dispelled* and *dispelling*, are spelled with a double *l*.

> It dispells an erroneous view of them as being tolerant cultural relativists and, instead, portrays them as human beings of their own times, and with their own cultural and personal biases and illusions.
> *Arctic* 41.1 (1988): 86

(The correct spelling is *dispel*.)

See also DOUBLING THE FINAL CONSONANT; SPELLING, CANADIAN.

dispersal see DISPERSION

disperse, disburse Unruly crowds are *dispersed* or broken up by police; sums of money are *disbursed* or paid out. To *disperse* also means to spread over a wide area, as in 'The wind dispersed the seeds' or 'The centre disperses information'.

> In addition, many Arctic plants depend on the wind to disperse their seeds in winter, when the seed heads are mature and well dried.
> *Uphere* Mar.–Apr. 1990: 42

> Where do you get the wisdom you disperse?
> Robertson Davies *One Half of Robertson Davies* 1978: 73

> He said no money has been disbursed by the fund, but organizers expect to get the first hundred cheques out next week.
> *Globe and Mail* (Toronto) 1 Aug. 1985: M5

> Social workers and volunteers make sure rent and food are paid for, and disperse spending money.
> *Canadian Churchman* April 1986: 12

(The word required here is *disburse*.)

See also DISPERSION.

dispersion, dispersal, disbursement, [dispersement] *Dispersion* and *dispersal* are both accepted nouns derived from *disperse* (to scatter or disseminate). *Disbursement* is derived from *disburse* (to pay out funds). *Dispersement* is an unacceptable hybrid patterned on *disbursement*.

... Petro-Canada has agreed to build a new 100-metre stack within two years that will improve the dispersion of pollutants and reduce odor and emissions.
Globe and Mail (Toronto) 5 Dec. 1985: C5

With wind dispersal of seeds, the group has also invaded the islands of Madagascar, Sri Lanka and the Canaries.
TLC ... for plants Spring 1991: 8

Once the money is collected, no agency will receive less than it has in the past and an audited statement showing the disbursement of funds will now be published in July.
Calgary Herald 6 Feb. 1993: E9

... the only way to prevent the displacement and disbursement of destructive minnow species to waters where they could prove harmful to native fish is to completely ban the sale, use and transportation of live minnows province-wide.
Gazette (Montreal) 1 March 1994: D12

(The word required here is either *dispersal* or *dispersion*.)

The exhibition charts the dispersement of the Metis throughout the West, and their inability to find acceptance at conventional employment through a mix of racial intolerance and poor education.
Globe and Mail (Toronto) 24 July 1985: S7

(Either *dispersion* or *dispersal* is required here.)

See also DIASPORA; DISPERSE.

dispute   see REFUTE

disrespect   *Disrespect* is a noun meaning lack of respect, or discourtesy. In Standard American English it is also a verb meaning to feel or exhibit a lack of respect for. The verb *disrespect* is archaic in British English and informal in Canadian English, where it occurs almost invariably in quoted speech.

'I know how to make a living on the street,' she says, 'and I never hated or disrespected myself for knowing how to.'
Gazette (Montreal) 25 June 1992: C7

Cory, a Grade 11 student at Ernest Manning senior high, chipped in: 'It makes you feel disrespected.'
Calgary Herald 18 June 1992: B1

'There was a point when I wanted to return to Ottawa, but that was before they began disrespecting me as a football player and person,' Allen said, his smile quickly replaced by a very serious look.
Ottawa Citizen 17 June 1992: E2

He accused the ministry of 'creating a welfare program with natural resources' and said a government cull

'disrespects the rights of hunters to exercise abilities and duties.'
Toronto Star 11 Jan. 1992: B7

dissatisfied   see UNSATISFIED

dissemble, disassemble   To *dissemble* is to conceal the truth or hide one's real intentions or feelings. To *disassemble* something is to take it apart in an orderly fashion.

The Australian army may be dissembling when it claims that the 541,000 condoms it bought are for waterproofing guns.
Globe and Mail (Toronto) 23 Oct. 1985: A7

To get to the wheel you may have to disassemble the machine.
Canadian Consumer Jan. 1985: 38

dissociate, disassociate   Both forms are accepted, and both date from the seventeenth century. Some style guides insist on the shorter and more common *dissociate*, perhaps because it has a Latin antecedent (*dissociare*).

dissolvable   see SOLUBLE

distinct, distinctive   *Distinct* means separate, different, or clear: 'There are two distinct bacteria on this slide'. *Distinctive* means characteristic or distinguishing: 'His crazy laugh is his most distinctive feature'. In some contexts the senses overlap.

In recent Canadian history, the attempt to produce a constitutional accord to which the Quebec government would agree has led to frequent use of the phrase 'distinct society'. One meaning of *distinct*, in both English and French, is separate. Yet the whole point of constitutional negotiations is to allow Quebec to remain in Canada while preserving its cultural difference or *distinctiveness*. Some regard this ambiguity positively; others find it troublesome.

Under the deal, the Ouje-Bougoumou will be recognized as a distinct band. Until now, they had been lumped with the Mistassini Cree, a different group, as a bureaucratic convenience.
Gazette (Montreal) 28 Dec. 1992: B2

(Here *distinct* means separate.)

Kindly note that Dominica and the Dominican Republic are two separate and distinct countries.
Gazette (Montreal) 4 Dec. 1990: B2

The venerable and once mighty International Typographical Union is on its way out as a separate and distinct labor institution after more than 132 years.
Globe and Mail (Toronto) 21 Jan. 1985: B7

Friesen does an excellent job of explaining the political differences of the three Prairie provinces. Like brothers, each has its own distinct personality.
Globe and Mail (Toronto) 5 Jan. 1985: E15

(Here either *distinct* or *distinctive* would work.)

Also because the child actors are always bundled up in snowsuits and tuques, they needed to have distinctive faces so viewers could tell them apart.
Globe and Mail (Toronto) 5 Feb. 1985: P16

(Obviously the children have different or distinct faces; here *distinctive* is the only choice possible, meaning that they have faces that will allow the viewers to distinguish them clearly from one another.)

Can we carve out a truly distinctive society, living under the (often patronizing) gaze of a superpower neighbour?
City Magazine 1988: 11

(Canada is *distinct*—that is, politically separate—from the United States. What is at issue is whether its society is culturally *distinctive*.)

When supporters of Meech Lake assert that 'of course Quebec is a distinct society; we can all see that,' what they really mean is that Quebec is a distinctive society, which it certainly is.
Financial Post 14 Nov. 1989: 14

'Those in favor of accepting the accord claim that Quebec already exists as a distinct society, by which they seem to mean "different", and those opposed fear the word because it already means to them "separate".'
Gazette (Montreal) 19 March 1990: B2

The distinctive society clause [of the now-defunct Meech Lake Accord] affects only Quebec.
Vancouver Sun 11 April 1990: D4

(The word required here is *distinct*.)

distinguish   see DIFFERENTIATE

distract, detract   To *distract* someone is to draw his or her attention away from something: 'His partner distracted the security guard'. To *detract from* something is to take away from it or diminish it: 'The squalling detracted from the ceremony'. The phrases 'distract attention' and 'detract attention' have both been used for centuries to mean

divert attention, but the latter is less common and is likely to be considered a mistake.

They are going to determine if car phones distract motorists.
Daily News (Halifax) 28 June 1994: n.p.

Members of the church also shun publicity. There's a feeling that earthly gratitude might somehow detract from the final reward for service to your fellow man.
Canadian Heritage Feb.–Mar. 1986: 22

The political fallout over the closing of the St. Jean college has detracted attention from the fact that Canada, before this week's budget, already had as many military colleges as the United States.
Gazette (Montreal) 26 Feb. 1994: B1

(The usual expression is '*distracted* attention'.)

distrust, mistrust   *Distrust* and *mistrust* can be used interchangeably. *Distrust* is more common, both as a noun and as a verb.

Distrust is mutual.
Vancouver Sun 24 June 1994: B1

'I distrust all labels, ideologies and all ideologues.'
Bruce Meyer and Brian O'Riordan, eds. *In Their Words* 1984: 22

There is resentment and mistrust on both sides.
Ottawa Citizen 22 June 1994: B1

Personally, I mistrust the notion of thinking on one's feet; I have known many speakers who prided themselves on that ability, and I am sorry to say that many of them were blatherers; they did not know when to stop.
Robertson Davies *One Half of Robertson Davies* 1978: 9

Ditidaht   see NOOTKA

divan   see CHESTERFIELD

dived, dove   *Dived* and *dove* are both accepted in Canadian English as the past tense of *dive*. *Dived* is more common in writing; *dove* is more common in speech, but is also found in all types of writing.
Dove is rare as a past participle: 'has dived' is recommended. *Dove* is in common use as the past tense form in Canada, the northern United States, and some parts of Britain, but is not used in Standard British English.

Early in the war, when nerves were particularly on edge, an F-16 landed in the middle of an air-attack alert at Canada Dry One and the troops dived for cover.
Maclean's 4 March 1991: A34

Now, unemployment in the Toronto area has dived to 3.2 per cent, while a building boom has created intense demand for skilled labor.
Maclean's 23 May 1988: A26

I folded a towel on the end of the dock and dove into Big Crummock Lake.
Howard Engel *Murder Sees the Light* 1984: 159

The CCB's board and management, the auditors, the government, and the regulators all dove for cover.
Saturday Night July 1986: 47

divide   see WATERSHED

division   see SPECIES

do   The plural of the noun *do* is either *do's* or *dos*: 'Do's and Don'ts for Visitors'; 'The food is always wonderful at their dos'. The former is less likely to puzzle the reader.

One of the most fun motorcycle do's I attended in 1989 involved people who have never owned or ridden a motorcycle.
Canadian Biker Feb. 1990: 8

The insurance bureau has pamphlets spelling out the Dos and Don'ts of moving.
Gazette (Montreal) 30 June 1994: A4

See also DON'T, DONE.

doctor, Dr.   The honorific *Dr.* is used for medical doctors and people who hold academic doctorates. If the degree M.D. or Ph.D. (or D.Litt., D.Ed., Th.D., etc.) is listed after the name, the honorific is not used before the name: *Joan Treverton, M.D.* or *Dr. Joan Treverton*, but not *Dr. Joan Treverton, M.D.*
Psychologists and psychiatrists are doctors of two different types: a psychologist has a Ph.D. in psychology and a psychiatrist is a medical specialist. In Canada, licensed practitioners of osteopathy, chiropractic, podiatry, optometry, dentistry, and veterinary medicine may also use the title *Dr.*
Outside academic circles it is often assumed that anyone referred to as *Dr. So-and-so* is a medical doctor. Thus, in writing for a general audience, the use of *Dr.* as an academic title should be accompanied by a gloss: '*Dr. So-and-so*, a professor of sociology at Queen's University'.
In Britain, the abbreviation is written *Dr*, without a period at the end. This is the general rule there for abbreviations where the last letter of the abbreviation is the last letter of the full word. This style is becoming more popular in Canada. It is recommended by the authors of *Editing Canadian English*

and is now used in Canadian government documents, but *Dr.* with a period is still the usage favoured by the Canadian Press and the *Globe and Mail*. Both styles are accepted.

See also ABBREVIATION, CONTRACTION, SUSPENSION; JOB TITLES.

-dom   A *kingdom* is a king's realm; *freedom* is the state of being free; *x-dom*, in contemporary English, is 'the state of being an *x*' or 'the land of the *x*'s—where the *x*'s reign'. New words formed with *-dom* are usually humorous and always informal: *jockdom, moviedom, officialdom, wifedom, yuppiedom*.

She came into my life as I was becoming bored with jockdom and ready to stretch my intellectual wings.
Vancouver Sun 28 May 1994: D13

If they were too short, you were banished to geekdom, your 'highwaters' flapping in the wind.
Toronto Star 25 Feb. 1993: F8

The discovery of oil in commercial quantities the previous summer had set in motion the forces of officialdom.
Uphere Jan.–Feb. 1990: 70

Downing, the last great champion of dogdom, was sold for $150,000.
Globe and Mail (Toronto) 11 March 1985: S1

domineer, dominate   Both *domineer* and *dominate* mean to exercise control over, but their connotations differ. *Domineer*—which most frequently appears as an adjective, *domineering*—is always negative. People who are *domineering* are overbearing and tyrannical in their attempts to control, whereas people who *dominate* sometimes do so without arrogance or self-assertion; they are merely conspicuously successful in a particular setting.

She had a domineering father who stunted her and wouldn't let her go to college because college was for boys.
Margaret Atwood *Life Before Man* 1979: 105–6

In many western settlements, they dominated the first white-collar class: they were the doctors, teachers, bankers and merchants in agricultural communities where the producers were Britons, Irishmen, Germans, French Canadians and, of course, other Ontarians.
W.C. Lougheed, ed. *In Search of the Standard in Canadian English* 1986: 12

don't, done   In some American regional dialects, *doesn't* doesn't exist and *don't* is used in its place: 'She don't drive'; 'It don't seem right'. This usage is obsolete in Britain and considered uneducated in Canada.

The use of *done* instead of *did* as the past tense of *do* ('They done it again') is a non-standard, chiefly North American usage.

The use of *done* with the verb *be* to mean 'finished', as in 'The casting is done', or 'Yes, I'm done, thanks', was criticized in the past; 'I have finished' was considered more genteel. But *be done* is certainly standard in Canadian English today. It is a construction that is mainly used in speech.

See also DO; DON'T THINK.

don't think 'I don't think I'll be finished in time' usually means 'I think I won't be finished in time'. The other possible interpretation, which requires a heavy stress on *think*, is 'I don't *think* [i.e., I *know*] I'll be finished in time'. Many language commentators have called the more common interpretation of this sentence illogical because the verb *think* is negated even though the negation actually applies to the clause that follows. However, logical or not, sentences like the first one above are perfectly good English.

Linguists call the rule by which negation is shifted from the reported clause ('I won't be finished in time') to the reporting clause ('I think') 'negative-raising'. Other verbs that allow negative-raising include *believe, seem, expect*, and *suppose*; for example, 'We didn't expect you before three' means 'We expected you, but not before three'. Note that all such verbs report interior states or perceptions. Verbs that describe interactions between people are not amenable to negative-raising: 'I didn't tell them I was coming' means something quite different from 'I told them I wasn't coming'. Though some commentators would restrict negative-raising to informal writing, it is fairly common in formal prose.

W.J. White, then Acting Superintendent of Immigration, didn't think Barr would be successful.
Pierre Berton *The Promised Land* 1984: 109

I don't believe audiences have the same spontaneous and genuine interest in her playing as in the Labèque Sisters'....
Queen's Quarterly 94.3 (1987): 644

Some women's groups don't feel we've been giving them the kind of material they would like to have.
Canadian Baptist Feb. 1986: 47

Income from student fees could not be expected to cover more than a fraction of the educational costs; actually in the 1920s it covered less than one third.
Frederick Gibson *Queen's University* 2 (1983): 29

dot see E-MAIL

double entendre A *double entendre* is a pun, especially a bawdy one. *Double entendre* is standard contemporary English but archaic French (the current French phrase for an ambiguous expression is *phrase à double entente*). *Double entendre* is pronounced either *DUB ul on TAWN druh* or *DOO blon TAWN druh*.

The message is a double entendre on sex and condom use: 'You'd be crazy to do without it.'
Province (Vancouver) 18 Oct. 1990: 59

(Here *it* is a condom or sex or both.)

See also PUN.

double negative A *double negative* is a construction, such as 'I didn't do nothing', that contains two negative words—here, *didn't* and *nothing*. This sentence has two possible interpretations: either 'I did nothing at all' or 'I chose to act'. In the first interpretation, *didn't* and *nothing* together reinforce the idea of negation. This construction is called the emphatic double negative, and it is strongly disapproved of by teachers and language commentators. In the second interpretation, the two negatives create an understated positive: 'I did something; I *didn't do nothing*'. This construction, called the rhetorical double negative, is standard. When sentences such as 'I didn't do nothing' are spoken, they are never ambiguous: stress and intonation always make the meaning clear.

The traditional explanation for the rejection of the *emphatic* double negative is that it is not logical: logically, two negatives in one sentence cancel each other out, making a positive meaning. If this were actually the way the language worked, then three negatives would make a sentence revert to a negative meaning, and 'We never did nobody no harm' would pass muster as Standard English. Of course it does not, for the basis of the censure of the emphatic double (and triple) negative in English is not logic but convention. The rule that two negatives make a positive was invented by eighteenth-century English grammarians. It is not a rule that exists in French or German, where multiple negatives are standard, nor did it exist in English before the eighteenth century, nor does it exist in many present-day dialects of English. However, in Standard English the rule has been so successfully propagated that, justified or not, it cannot be ignored. The prejudice against the emphatic double negative is very real, and people who use it are perceived as uneducated or ignorant.

Less conspicuous than sentences of the 'didn't do nothing' variety but still non-standard are sentences that combine a negative adverb, such as *scarcely* or *hardly*, and a negated verb ('We didn't hardly have time to start when he stopped us') and sentences where the negation of one clause is repeated in the next ('I wouldn't be surprised if she didn't walk right through that door'). Although some commentators have defended these structures as idiomatic, all agree that they are inappropriate in writing. The accepted versions of these sentences are 'We hardly had time to start when he stopped us' and 'I wouldn't be surprised if she walked right through that door'.

'I wouldn't drink nothin' my pa had a hand in making.'
Queen's Quarterly 93.3 (1986): 477

(The standard form would be 'I wouldn't drink *anything*'. In fictional dialogue, here and in the examples below, the emphatic double negative is used to indicate that the speaker is uneducated or not concerned with social niceties.)

She stood up, turned towards me, giving me a full front-on view and, I'll tell you, that pink negligee didn't conceal nothing.
Canadian Fiction Magazine 64 (1988): 102

(The standard form would be 'didn't conceal *anything*'.)

'You don't have to take that shit from nobody.'
Robert Kroetsch *Badlands* 1975: 85

(The standard form would be 'from *anybody*'.)

'My ma's the bravest, lookit her, don't nothing faze my ma'....
Queen's Quarterly 94.1 (1987): 91

(The standard form would be 'nothing *fazes* my ma'.)

See also HARDLY; REGARDLESS.

double possessive   Sometimes the possessive is marked by both an *of* phrase and an apostrophe: 'a sweater of Linda's'. This construction is called the double possessive and usually occurs when the 'possessor' is human and has more than one of the 'possessions' in question: for example, 'I borrowed an old hat of my father's'; 'Greed is a fault of John's'.

The double possessive is sometimes used to avoid confusion: 'a student of Northrop Frye's' once took a course from him, while 'a student of Northrop Frye' is studying Frye's life, thought, and writing. 'I took my mother's picture' could mean either 'I took a picture of my mother's' or 'I took a picture of my mother'. Although the double possessive has been criticized as inelegant, it is idiomatic and often useful.

Let us say it is an opera of Benjamin Britten's—*The Turn of the Screw*.
Robertson Davies *A Voice from the Attic* 1960: 10

See also POSSESSIVE.

doubling the final consonant   When adding an ending to a word that ends in a consonant, sometimes the consonant is doubled and sometimes it is not. There are general rules for when to double and when not to double.

Most one-syllable words that end in a single consonant double it when an ending that begins with a vowel or *y* is added to the word: *big, bigger, biggest*; *quit, quitter, quitting*; *sad, sadder, saddest, saddened*; *stub, stubby*; *wed, wedded, wedding*.

If the vowel sound of the one-syllable word is written as two letters, the final consonant is not doubled: *boat, boating*; *green, greener, greenest*; *soak, soaked, soaking*; *treat, treated, treating*.

If the word has more than one syllable, the rules become more complicated. If the final syllable has a single vowel, then you must determine which syllable bears the stress. The final consonant is doubled only if the stress falls on the final syllable, as in *admit (admitted, admittance, admitting), begin (beginning, beginner)*, and *occur (occurred, occurring, occurrence)*. If the stress falls on the first syllable, the final consonant stays single: *bias (biased, biasing)*, *differ (differed, difference), focus (focused, focusing)*, *offer (offered, offering)*. However, some people double the final *s* in *bias* and *focus* before endings (*biassed, focussing*), and this is accepted.

Note that, for some words, the spelling shifts as the stress shifts: *confer (conferring, conference), defer (deferring, deference), prefer (preferring, preference), refer (referring, reference)*. Thus the rules still hold: double consonants when the stress falls on the second syllable, single when it falls on the first.

There is a general exception to this rule. If the final syllable of a multisyllable word can stand alone as a single word, then the rule that applies to this single word applies to the longer one: *kidnap (kid-*

napped, kidnapper) and *worship* (*worshipped, worshipper*). A few other words that follow this rule are *eavesdrop, handicap, leapfrog, nonplus, program,* and *zigzag*. About a third of Canadian writers would add *benefit* to this list, writing *benefitted* and *benefitting*, but most use the single-*t* forms.

If the vowel of the second syllable is written with two letters, the final consonant is not doubled: *bemoan, bemoaned, bemoaning; repeat, repeated, repeatable*.

The final consonants *h, w, x,* and *y* are never doubled.

Words that end in *l* are handled differently in the United States and Britain. The American spelling convention follows the rules above for doubling the final consonant. The British tradition favours doubling the *l* before all endings except *-ize*, as in *totalize*. Most Canadians follow the British convention: *dispel, dispelled, dispelling; equal, equalled, equalling; model, modelling; signal, signalled, signalling; total, totalled, totalling; travel, travelled, travelling*.

See also -C, -CK-; FULFIL; -L-, -LL-; SPELLING, CANADIAN.

doubtful   see DUBIOUS

doubt if   see DOUBT WHETHER

doubtless   *Doubtless* is an adverb: 'Doubtless this was not the first time'. While dictionaries also list *doubtlessly*, the *-ly* form is much less common and is criticized by commentators.

> Haitians, Bosnians and Somalis would doubtless make the same observation.
> *Gazette* (Montreal) 31 Dec. 1993: B1

> It doubtlessly helped that after Larkin moved to Belfast, they always lived in different cities.
> *Calgary Herald* 30 Oct. 1993: C10

(This form is criticized; *doubtless* is recommended.)

doubt whether, doubt if, doubt that   A clause following the verb *doubt* may be introduced by *whether, if, that,* or no conjunction at all: 'I doubt he'll come'. All these constructions are accepted in Canadian English. Some commentators suggest that the conjunction *that* is appropriate only after a negative statement of doubt ('I don't doubt that ...'; 'We never doubted that ...'), but Canadian writers do not restrict its use in this way.

But he doubted whether Imogen Hughes had ever shed a tear in her life.
Constance Beresford-Howe *Night Studies* 1985: 10

I now have so much work lined up that I doubt if I would have time to visit your showings. . . .
J.E. Smyth et al. *The Law and Business Administration in Canada* 1987: 149

Yet his mother never doubted that both her boys were stolen from her, Wayne as much as Charles, by the curse of her father's life.
David Williams *Eye of the Father* 1985: 158

There was nothing in the UN charter to provide for such a peacekeeping force, and Secretary General Dag Hammarskjold at first doubted that it could be made to work, particularly with the western powers so bitterly divided.
George Ignatieff *The Making of a Peacemonger* 1987: 123

(Here *that* is used after a positive statement of doubt.)

Few doubt that the Meech Lake constitutional paralysis and the post-Meech malaise have adversely affected Canadian federalism.
Alan Whitehorn *Canadian Socialism* 1992: 244

I doubt it is there.
Arctic 41.1 (1988): 77

dove   see DIVED; PIGEON

downfall   *Downfall* usually refers to a sudden fall from prosperity, eminence, or success. It can also refer to the cause of this fall: 'Their downfall was a failure to plan for inflation'. *Downfall* should not, however, be used to refer to a minor drawback or shortcoming that does not lead to failure.

In business writing *downfall* has taken on a new sense synonymous with *downturn*: that is, a sudden drop in value or loss in earnings.

> Walesa said the downfall of communism in eastern Europe last fall actually began in August 1980, when he and a government representative signed the Gdansk Accords.
> *Gazette* (Montreal) 1 Sept. 1990: A8

> Her downfall was her reluctance to become a Canadian. Quebec Culture Minister Marie Malavoy resigned Friday after admitting she had voted in several elections before obtaining her citizenship.
> *Calgary Herald* 26 Nov. 1994: A8

> Free-Net's greatest downfall parallels [that of] the busy bar—you have to line up to get in, and that turns a lot of people off.
> *Ottawa Citizen* 7 Dec. 1994: D3

(Here *shortcoming* would be better.)

downplay, play down For reasons unknown, usage commentators are especially reluctant to approve of new compound words that begin with adverbs. *Ongoing, upcoming,* and *downplay* have all been disparaged by commentators. The *Globe and Mail Style Book* (1994) goes so far as to call *downplay* 'a non-word'. Other usage guides call it 'journalese'; all commentators recommend *play down* instead. However, *downplay*—which dates from the 1950s— is as widely used in Canadian academic prose as it is in newspaper and magazine writing; *play down* is used far less frequently.

A persisting tendency to downplay the division between usage and convention, as well as the pervasive trend to ignore distinctions among conventions, greatly weakens our understanding of the informal rules shaping the Canadian constitution.
Andrew Heard *Canadian Constitutional Conventions* 1991: 141–2

By ignoring or downplaying questions of domestic labour and the double day of labour, feminist groups seem to have fallen into the 'passive revolutionary' trap of being enticed by the state agenda much more readily than either neo-conservative or anti-feminist groups.
Carl J. Cuneo *Pay Equity* 1990: 150

The maximalist party leadership, downplaying the gravity of the disagreement, appointed a three-man commission. . . .
Canadian Journal of History 14.1 (1989): 24

Because the authority they possessed in the twentieth-century university would, it seemed, be exercised in the classroom, the growing tendency of research-minded scholars to play down the importance of the teaching role was anathema to them.
Queen's Quarterly 95.3 (1988): 556

Down's syndrome, Down syndrome Either *Down's syndrome* or *Down syndrome* may be used to refer to the medical condition named after an English physician, J.L.H. Down. (It is caused by a chromosomal abnormality and distinguished by varying degrees of mental disability and a characteristic physical appearance.) The spelling *Down syndrome*, as in the Canadian Down Syndrome Society, avoids the problem of inserting the apostrophe correctly. *Mongolism*, a term once applied to this condition, is now considered offensive.

When I was five years old we didn't know what DNA did, how many chromosomes humans have, what causes the differences in males and females, or the cause of Down's syndrome.
Queen's Quarterly 93.1 (1986): 86–7

I . . . think the show is a great learning experience, as it has made me more aware of the abilities of people with Down Syndrome.
Vancouver Sun 9 March 1990: TV3

Over the years identification of other genetic disorders will surely follow—hemophilia perhaps, or Downs syndrome, or phenylketonuria, or diabetes mellitus.
Gazette (Montreal) 20 April 1990: B2

(Either *Down's* or *Down* would be correct.)

See also DISABILITIES.

downward(s) see -WARD(S)

Dr. see DOCTOR

draft, draught Both spellings are pronounced the same way. *Draft* is the more common spelling in Canadian writing for a current of air, beer on tap, or the depth of water needed to float a boat; *draught*, the usual British spelling, is an accepted alternative.
Draft is the only spelling for a rough version of a document, a written order for payment of funds by a bank, or military conscription.

See also DRAFTSMAN.

draftsman, draughtsman, technical illustrator Someone who is employed to do technical drawings by hand is called a *draftsman* in Canada and the United States and a *draughtsman* in Britain. *Draftsman* in British English refers to someone who drafts legal or other documents.
Nowadays, mechanical and architectural drawings are usually done on a computer, and the skills of the person operating the drawing program may range from engineering to desktop publishing. For those whose primary work is drawing plans on a computer, current job titles include *technical illustrator* and *design technician*; unlike *draftsman*, these terms have the virtue of being non-sexist.

See also DRAFT, DRAUGHT.

drama Canadians and Americans pronounce *drama* either *DRA muh* or *DRAW muh*; the British say *DRAW muh*.

drank   see DRINK

draught   see DRAFT

drink, drank, drunk, drunken   In Standard English, the past tense of *drink* is *drank* and the past participle (the form used after *have*) is *drunk*. Thus 'I drunk too much last night' and 'I have drank too much again' are non-standard. Some commentators accept *have drank* in informal speech, but many people consider the usage uneducated.

Normally, *drunken* is used as the adjective preceding a noun ('drunken revellers'), while *drunk* is the predicate adjective form (the form used after a verb): 'They were drunk again'. However, *drunk* is commonly used preceding the noun in references to driving: 'drunk driving', 'drunk driver'.

> For one thing, Descartes assures us, his altered state was not the result of inebriation: he had not drunk wine for three months before.
> *Canadian Journal of Philosophy* 19 (1989): 214

> When the lights went up, Minty left the table where he and his two buddies had drank the night away and sauntered over....
> *Canadian Fiction Magazine* 64 (1988): 98

(Here a fictional speaker says *had drank*; the standard form would be *had drunk*.)

> Heath said if not for a water-borne bacterium that brings on an ailment known as 'beaver fever', he might have drank some water from side creeks during the first few days of the expedition.
> *Vancouver Sun* 14 Sept. 1990: B1

(The standard past participle is *drunk*.)

> An insane or drunk person is liable for a reasonable price for the necessary goods.
> J.E. Smyth et al. *The Law and Business Administration in Canada* 1987: 178

> 'The Collector of Customs at Winnipeg is a drunken reprobate.'
> Pierre Berton *The Promised Land* 1984: 28

(Here *drunken* means habitually intoxicated.)

drought, drouth   A *drought* is a dry spell or, figuratively, a prolonged lack of anything. *Drouth* is an alternative spelling, rare in Canada.

> Deliveries to Vancouver are running only slightly ahead of last year, when drought cut grain exports by 30 per cent.
> *Vancouver Sun* 14 Feb. 1990: D10

> Skywatchers then suffered a comet drought until 1947, when a fairly impressive celestial visitor navigated the postwar skies.
> Terence Dickinson *Halley's Comet* 1985: 36

drunk, drunken   see DRINK

dubious, doubtful   Someone can be either *dubious* or *doubtful* about future prospects. Something can be of *dubious* or *doubtful* value. Both words mean uncertain, skeptical, or questionable, and in these contexts there is little to choose between them. However, 'a *doubtful* starter' inspires uncertainty, while 'a *dubious* character' arouses suspicion and unease. When *dubious* is used attributively (directly before a noun) it often means shady or suspect, a meaning not shared by *doubtful*.

> Newspaper editors were plainly dubious about the new comet, having been burned by heavily promoting Kohoutek as 'The Comet of the Century,' then watching as it barely gained naked-eye visibility.
> Terence Dickinson *Halley's Comet* 1985: 38

> It is doubtful whether the market system ever worked in the automatic, self-regulating way in which the classical economists conceived of it.
> Irving M. Zeitlin and Robert J. Brym *The Social Condition of Humanity* 1991: 77

> Racial statistics, so-called, have proven to be of little or doubtful significance and value to sociologists.
> Richard Davies and Glen Kirkland, eds. *Dimensions* 1986: 123

> But driving it [the rate of inflation] to zero has dubious value and enormous economic and human costs.
> *Gazette* (Montreal) 24 July 1993: B5

> The dubious bookshops of London offer the strangest assortment, to suit as many tastes as possible.
> Robertson Davies *A Voice from the Attic* 1960: 277

> In 1804, he struck out on his own, leaving Lennox and Maitland and becoming mixed up in some dubious business concerns.
> Katherine M.J. McKenna *A Life of Propriety* 1994: 137

due to   According to *Webster's Dictionary of English Usage*, '*Due to* has entered the folklore of usage.' At issue is whether *due to* is a compound preposition like *because of* and *on account of*, and thus whether it is acceptable in sentences such as 'Due to bad weather, the road was closed'. Certainly this is just how the phrase is often used by educated Canadian,

American, and British writers. Nevertheless, this use is criticized, which leaves many writers under a vague pall of unease about the phrase.

Commentators who criticize the prepositional use of *due to* claim that *due* is an adjective, meaning 'attributable', and *to* is the preposition. According to this view, *due to* should not be used in any sentence where 'attributable to' wouldn't also be possible. Thus 'Due to [attributable to] bad weather, the road was closed' is unacceptable, while 'The closure of the road was due to [attributable to] bad weather' is acceptable. The traditional advice is that *due to* is acceptable after a copula verb (*is, seems, appears to be,* etc.), which links *due* to a particular noun (here, 'closure'), but not acceptable at the beginning of a sentence where it functions as a preposition heading an adverb phrase that modifies the whole sentence.

Of course it is always possible to substitute *because of* or *on account of* for the disputed prepositional use of *due to*. On the other hand, you may well feel justified in ignoring a prescription that is clearly at odds with contemporary educated usage.

His hero's plight is due to the ways of the world, which, Leacock implies, nothing can ever change.
Miriam Waddington *Apartment Seven* 1989: 68

(The use of *due to* after the verb *to be* is undisputed.)

Due to the uncertain distance of that close approach, the gravitational influence on Halley's orbit is impossible to pin down, making it difficult to determine its precise orbit before 1404 B.C.
Terence Dickinson *Halley's Comet* 1985: 8

(Some commentators disapprove of this prepositional use of *due to*.)

On 24 February, at the end of a meeting of the Arab Cooperation Council, Iraq's president predicted that, due to the decline of Soviet power, the US would exercise hegemonic power in the Middle East for five years.
Queen's Quarterly 97 (1990): 532

(Some commentators disapprove of this prepositional use of *due to*.)

dumb   see DISABLED

durum, Durham   *Durum* as the name for a kind of wheat is often misspelled *Durham*. This wheat was not named after Lord Durham, who was briefly governor general of Canada, but comes from the Latin word *durus*, 'hard'. Durum is a hard wheat typically used to make pasta.

Returns on amber durum will rise by 9 per cent to $204 a tonne and feed oats will rise by 7 per cent to $107 a tonne.
Globe and Mail (Toronto) 12 Jan. 1985: B4

He has learned his Durham from his barley and can tread conversationally into the realms of swathing, quotas and fertilizers.
Globe and Mail (Toronto) 26 Aug. 1985: P4

(The correct spelling is *durum*.)

duty   see TAX

dye, dyed, dyeing   The past and present participles of the verb *dye*, meaning to colour or stain, are *dyed* and *dyeing*. *Dyeing* is often misspelled *dying*—which is the present participle of the verb to *die*. And *dyed* is often misspelled *died* in the expression *dyed-in-the-wool*.

If the leather is contemporary, it will not crack or peel as the old leather did because the new dyeing process is much better.
Daily News (Halifax) 7 June 1992: 62

Singer Emmylou Harris says she has no intention of dying her grey hair.
Daily News (Halifax) 17 Feb. 1992: 18

(The correct spelling is *dyeing*.)

It is important to know that she considers herself a dyed-in-the-wool feminist.
Ottawa Citizen 26 Jan. 1992: B3

If you're a died-in-the-wool baseball fan, you can, if you work hard enough, see a game in a different park in a different area of Florida every day.
Gazette (Montreal) 8 Feb. 1992: I5

(The correct spelling is *dyed-in-the-wool*.)

E

-e   Usually words that end with a silent *e* drop it when endings beginning with a vowel or *y* are added (*craze, crazy; extreme, extremism; note, notable*) and retain it when endings beginning with a consonant are added: *amazement, extremely, whiteness.* Exceptions:
- keep the *e*: *acreage, mileage*
- drop the *e*: *argument, awful, duly, ninth, truly, wholly*
- Sometimes the *e* is retained to avoid confusion with other words: *dyeing* (to colour, as opposed to *dying*), *lineage* (line of descent, one's family tree, as opposed to *linage*, number of lines), and *singeing* (scorching, as opposed to *singing*).
- Words ending in *-ce* and *-ge* retain the *e* before endings beginning with *a* and *o* to indicate that the consonants are 'soft' (pronounced like *s* and *j*): *peaceable, courageous.*
- If the word ends in *-oe*, the *e* is kept before *-ing*: *canoeing, hoeing, shoeing.*
- If the word ends in *-dge*, Canadian writers vary in their decision to drop the *e*; most drop it (as do Americans) in *judgment* but keep it in *acknowledgement.* Usage with *abridg(e)ment* is mixed.
- In words where Canadians and Americans tend to drop the silent *e* (*aging, livable, lovable*), the British tend to retain it (*ageing, liveable, loveable*). Canadians are evenly divided on keeping the *e* in *likeable/likable.*

See also -ABLE, -(E)ABLE; DYE.

(-e)able   see -ABLE

each   When *each* is the subject of the sentence, it is followed by a singular verb: 'Each is sure she is right'. When *each* acts as an adjective modifying a singular noun subject, the singular verb form is also used: 'Each woman is sure she is right'. Most grammarians insist that when *each* is followed by a phrase beginning with *of*, the verb should remain singular; 'Each of the women is (*not* are) responsible for setting up her own computer'.

Though grammatically *each* is singular, the sense it conveys is often plural, which leads writers to use the plural forms *they* and *their* after it: 'Each brings a lunch and they share'; 'Each has their own strengths'. This usage is very common, but some commentators consider it informal. For more discussion of this point, see EVERYONE.

When *each* acts as an adjective modifying a plural subject, a plural verb always follows: 'They each have their own clientele'. Once disputed, this usage is no longer contentious.

> Each of the three women in *Dawn* has a 'philosophy,' and Angela's is a pure belief in individual immortality.
> Margaret Atwood *Second Words* 1982: 42

(Here the subject *each* correctly takes the singular verb *has* even though a plural noun phrase, *three women*, intervenes.)

See also AGREEMENT, GRAMMATICAL; BETWEEN EACH; EACH AND EVERY; EACH OTHER; EVERYONE.

each and every   Many language commentators have warned that *each and every* is both redundant and a cliché. Even so, many good writers use the phrase to focus a sentence, improve its rhythm, or add emphasis.

> We could go into considerable detail tracking the fortunes of each and every group.
> Neil Nevitte and Roger Gibbins *New Elites in Old States* 1990: 141

(Here *each and every* emphasizes the difficulty of the task.)

> Language, then, is the vehicle by which the accumulated wisdom and experience of numerous generations is transmitted to each and every one of us.
> William Norton *Human Geography* 1992: 14

> We learned later that John McAllister was always loaded, since he drank about a half gallon of home-brew each and every day.
> Max Braithwaite *The Night We Stole the Mountie's Car* 1971: 55

each other, one another   An old rule states that *each other* refers only to two people, while *one another* refers to three or more. There seems to be little historical precedent or support in modern usage for this rule; writers use either phrase for any number of people.

The possessive form is *each other's*, not *each others'*: 'They read each other's books'.

Several guides warn against using either phrase as the subject of an embedded clause: 'We know what each other likes in a work of art'. This should be rephrased as 'We each know what the other likes in a work of art'.

eager   see ANXIOUS

Early Modern English   see OLD ENGLISH

early on   The phrase *early on* has been criticized as redundant. Although *early* alone can sometimes be substituted for it, *early on* usually conveys a different meaning: at an early stage. Canadian writers use the phrase freely in all kinds of writing.

Early on became common in Britain after the First World War and was criticized mainly by American authorities, but it is now fully established in Canada, Britain, and the United States.

Early on, when President Kennedy had asked the Canadian leader's advice, Pearson had answered that the right American policy would be to get out [of Vietnam] if they could, but to do it while saving face.
Queen's Quarterly 95.1 (1985): 111

(Here *early* could not be substituted for *early on*.)

That was early on, when they were having a good time.
Margaret Atwood *Life Before Man* 1979: 26

(Here too, *early* could not be substituted for *early on*.)

He [B.H. Haggin] had discovered early on that much of the writing about music, performance and events differed from what he heard for himself or discovered by investigation.
Queen's Quarterly 94.3 (1987): 654

(Here *early on* conveys the sense that Haggin was at an early stage in his research.)

earth, planets   *Earth* may be capitalized when it refers to our planet, but the uncapitalized spelling is more common. The other eight planets in our solar system are named after Roman gods, and their names are always capitalized: *Mercury, Venus, Mars, Jupiter, Saturn, Uranus, Neptune*, and *Pluto. Earth*

should be capitalized for consistency when it appears with any of these names. Although some critics claim that it is unidiomatic and potentially ambiguous to drop *the* before the name of the planet, it is often done ('heaven on earth', 'where on earth'). The context makes it clear whether the reference is to the planet or to soil.

'You train constantly for months and suddenly you're up there above the Earth, seeing the most privileged, most exalted view any human being could hope for.'
Leader-Post (Regina) 27 Feb. 1988: B16

This time around, Halley will be greeted by five spacecraft sent from Earth to view the spectacle close up.
Terence Dickinson *Halley's Comet* 1985: 2

... it is hard to imagine any country on earth investing so much of its per capita wealth and energy on the business of governance.
Calgary Herald 29 Dec. 1993: A4

earthen, earthy, earthly   *Earthen* means made of earth or baked clay. *Earthy* describes anything with the characteristics of earth, such as its colour or smell. *Earthy* also describes people, attitudes, etc., that are unpretentious, down to earth, sensuous, or coarse. *Earthly* is the opposite of *other-worldly*; it describes the material or worldly aspects of the human condition. *Earthly* also means 'possible' in some idiomatic expressions: 'Of what earthly good is that?'

... the Peninsula People came here to bury their dead in earthen mounds which can still be seen today; one serpentine mound and eight oval ones.
Globe and Mail (Toronto) 24 Aug. 1985: T2

In appearance, the cows' impenetrable blotches of black on a sharply contrasting white background differed markedly from the solid, earthy colours of such well-established breeds as Guernseys and Jerseys.
Harrowsmith Oct.–Nov. 1985: 38

'I write very much from a vulnerable point of view,' says McLachlan, whose earthy humor ... is so unlike the celestial waif imagery of her songs.
Toronto Star 25 Nov. 1993: WO10

It was good to take the focus away from the earthly pressures for a while and have time to reflect on spiritual values.
Mennonite Brethren Herald 4 April 1986: 9

earth tremor   see TREMOR

east, west, north, south   Generally, the names of the compass points (*east*, *west*, *north*, *south*), and their derivative adjectives (*northern*, *northward*, *northerly*, *northwest*, etc.), are not capitalized: 'a garden to the east of the house', 'a southern exposure'. They are, however, capitalized in place names, including the informal names of districts: 'the South Shore', 'the Eastern Townships', 'the West End'. They should not be capitalized in mere descriptions of geographic areas: 'fisheries off the south shore', 'species found in eastern North America'. Quite often it is a moot point whether an area is named or merely described, and in these cases capitalization varies.

> Known for her abrasive manner and sharp tongue, she got into vicious battles with the Cree of Northern Quebec over the James Bay hydroelectric projects.
> *Ottawa Citizen* 15 Dec. 1993: A12

> She got into battles with the Cree of northern Quebec over the James Bay hydroelectric projects.
> *Vancouver Sun* 15 Dec. 1993: A8

> The North Toronto couple said they are not aware of any payments made to Morgan's natural mother.
> *Toronto Star* 9 Dec. 1993: A1

> Workers also demonstrated outside Hydro's north Toronto service centre on MacPherson Ave.
> *Toronto Star* 5 Nov. 1993: A2

Canadians usually capitalize '(down) East', '(out) West', and '(up) North', as regions of the country. To western Canadians *east* and *eastern* refer to anything east of the border of Manitoba, but to inhabitants of Ontario and Quebec *east* and *eastern* refer only to the provinces east of Quebec. Unlike the United States, Canada has no region that is routinely called 'the South'. The majority of Canadians live on the southern border of the country, but they do not think of themselves as living in the south because the stereotype of Canada subsumes all of it into the 'True North'. However, those who live in northern Canada refer to the more populated southern regions of the country as 'the South'.

The authors of *Editing Canadian English* recommends capitalizing *Eastern* and *Western* when *Canadian* is omitted, as in 'Eastern fisheries' and 'the Western provinces', while the *Canadian Press Stylebook* recommends *eastern* and *western*. Both styles are common and accepted.

See also CAPITAL LETTERS; NORTHERLY.

East Indian   see INDIAN

eatable   see EDIBLE

echelon   *Echelon* (pronounced *ESH uh lawn*) is a French loan word meaning 'a rung on a ladder'. It was adopted by the English military in the eighteenth century to describe step-like formations of troops, ships, and so on. During the First World War its sense was extended to describe levels in the chain of military command, and since then the meaning has again been extended to describe the ranks or levels within any type of organization or society. The 'civilian' use of *echelon* has been criticized in the past, but it is now predominant and unquestionably standard.

> As Chief of the General Staff and later chairman of the Chiefs of Staff Committee, he did a job nobody else in the top echelon of the Canadian military could have done.
> *Globe and Mail* (Toronto) 2 Nov. 1985: D20

> 'Corruption has penetrated into the top echelons of power, and if the situation remains unchanged, the state itself will become criminal.'
> *Toronto Star* 24 Aug. 1993: A14

> There was nothing easy about the gardening life in the lower echelons of the gardening ranks.
> *The Beaver* Dec. 1989–Jan. 1990: 12

eclectic   *Eclectic*, which means derived from various sources, can have negative, neutral, or positive connotations. It can mean haphazard, diverse, or carefully selected, depending on the context.

> Hawks players used to laugh when they saw Hasek walking around the Stadium dressing room in black socks and white tennis shoes. Eclectic outfits of this nature made the Czech a more amazing sight off the ice than on during his years in Chicago.
> *Toronto Star* 20 Dec. 1993: D2

(Here *eclectic* has negative connotations.)

> From glitz to funk, Queen Street West (University to Bathurst, and slowly spreading) is an eclectic blend of artists, literati, and progressive music clubs.
> Alan Tucker, ed. *The Penguin Guide to Canada* 1991: 365

(Here *eclectic* is neutral.)

> His eclectic evolutionary approach draws widely on his scientific expertise in biology, anthropology, craniotomy, paleontology, and field research.
> *Queen's Quarterly* 92.2 (1985): 423

(Here *eclectic* is positive.)

Because his approach to this question has been thoroughly eclectic, his vision is far wider than others in this group.
Wallace Clement and Glen Williams, eds. *The New Canadian Political Economy* 1989: 127

(Here *eclectic* is positive.)

ecology, environment *Ecology* is a scientific word, coined in the 1870s, that refers to the study of the relationships among living organisms and between those organisms and their physical surroundings. *Environment* means surroundings; often it refers to the whole earth from the point of view of its capacity to sustain life. Some writers use *ecology* where *environment* would make more sense, as in 'damage to the ecology'.

An *environmentalist* is a person concerned about the state of the *environment*; an *ecologist* is a scientist who studies *ecology*.

Environment is often misspelled *enviroment*.

More detailed studies of the breeding biology and ecology of arctic populations are less common and, with the exception of Cade (1960), have concentrated mainly on the late incubation and nestling phases of the nesting cycle.
Arctic 41.1 (1988): 18

In the mind of the consumers, then, packaging is detrimental to the environment.
Western Grocer June 1990: 95

Hydrocarbons occur naturally and, while many hydrocarbons could ultimately damage the environment, they are more easily dispersed than CFCs.
Western Grocer Aug. 1990: 48

Dozens of species of trees, flowers and other plant life also contribute to the wonderfully varied ecology of Point Pelee—a living museum of natural history.
Leisure Life 1988: 6

(It is the *environment* of Point Pelee that is varied.)

Prime Minister Brian Mulroney is to blame for the federal government's failure to protect the country's troubled ecology, a coalition of major environmental groups said yesterday.
Province (Vancouver) 19 Oct. 1990: 12

(The word required here is *environment*.)

He was a member of a committee set up in 1987 by the B.C. enviroment ministry to draft commercial rafting regulations.
Vancouver Sun 14 July 1993: B8

(The correct spelling is *environment*.)

See also GREEN.

economic, economical Generally *economic* means having to do with the economy, or economics, or viability in business terms, while *economical* means thrifty, not wasteful.

The *e* in *economic(al)* is pronounced as in either *bet* or *beet*.

It is stifling economic growth with too much regulation, he said.
Daily News (Halifax) 1 July 1993: 14

'We've got new technology like 3-D seismic and horizontal drilling that's made the Western Sedimentary Basin economic again.'
Calgary Herald 26 Dec. 1993: C14

It's easier and more economical to perfect one recipe and make multiple batches than it is to prepare half a dozen different items.
Calgary Herald 10 Nov. 1993: B8

'Audio-visual documents have a social, political, economical, cultural and artistic value'.
Gazette (Montreal) 21 Dec. 1993: A4

(Here *economic* is required.)

-ed *Aged, beloved, blessed, cursed, dogged,* and *learned* each have two spoken variants; unfortunately, there is no general rule governing which variant is used in which situation.

The adjective *aged* is pronounced with two syllables when it modifies a human subject: 'an ag*ed* man'. When it is used to refer to something subjected to aging, such as cheese or brandy, it is pronounced as one syllable. The past participle and past tense of the verb are also monosyllabic: 'only for those *aged* 65 and over'; 'It *aged* him'.

The adjective *learned* has two syllables when it refers to someone or something distinguished by or associated with learning: 'a learn*ed* judge'; 'a learn*ed* journal'. When it means simply that something has been learned, it is pronounced with one syllable: 'a *learned* habit'.

Dogged is pronounced with two syllables when an adjective ('dogg*ed* determination'), and with one when a verb ('*dogged* by reporters').

Blessed and *cursed* are usually pronounced as two syllables before a noun ('the bless*ed* martyrs', 'curs*ed* luck'), and as one syllable after a linking verb ('She was *blessed*'; 'They were *cursed*'), but this is by no means a rule. The pronunciations of *blessed* and *cursed* are quite variable. The pronunciation of *beloved* is similar: it usually has three syllables before a noun and two after a linking verb.

Sometimes in poetry an accent is used to ensure that an *-ed* is pronounced as a separate syllable: 'O curséd (*or* cursèd) spite'.

See also DIACRITICAL MARKS, DIAERESIS; -T, -ED.

edible, eatable The adjectives *edible* and *eatable* are interchangeable, although several commentators have tried to distinguish them. They claim that *eatable* refers to food that is reasonably tasty and not spoiled, while *edible* distinguishes something that is not poisonous from something that is. Canadians use *edible* in all senses and *eatable* only rarely. The antonyms are *inedible* and *uneatable*.

The food was meagre and barely edible; better fare was available in the commissary but 'for prices that New York night clubs would be ashamed to ask'. . . .
Pierre Berton *The Promised Land* 1984: 53

Is there any way of telling if the fish are edible by examining them?
Canadian Consumer Jan. 1985: 8

edifice A building fittingly described as an *edifice* is grand and imposing in size or design. Used figuratively, *edifice* refers to a large organizational or conceptual structure.

Donated by the province, the Dominion Building is a wonderfully decorated, pseudo-classical stone edifice surmounted by a dome and a remarkable statue of Britannia seated with lions at her feet.
Canadian Collector 21 (1986): 56

Descartes, notoriously, views his system of beliefs as an edifice.
Canadian Journal of Philosophy 19.2 (1989): 202

educationist, educationalist, educator An *educationist* or *educationalist* is a specialist in the theory and methods of education.

An *educator* is a teacher, an administrator in the field of education, or an educationist. Sometimes those trained to work with very young children are called 'early childhood educators'.

Other recipients [of the Saskatchewan Award of Merit] are . . . Frederick Gathercole, a retired educationist and community leader. . . .
Globe and Mail (Toronto) 21 Nov. 1985: A3

Gerald Graham . . . hailed the advent of a principal 'who is not only an administrator but a superb scholar—who is incapable of talking the jargon of the educationalist'. . . .
Frederick Gibson *Queen's University* 2 (1983): 306

The number of educators—teachers and administrative staff—rose by almost 20 per cent over that period to about 333,000. . . .
Calgary Herald 20 Dec. 1994: A3

The course was developed by Donna Wood, an early childhood educator with years of experience working in nursery schools.
Globe and Mail (Toronto) 4 April 1985: CL4

effect see AFFECT

effete *Effete* was first used in the seventeenth century to mean physically depleted and incapable of reproducing, usually in reference to domestic animals. By the beginning of nineteenth century the word was also being applied to people and systems that were intellectually or morally spent. More recently the word has taken on connotations of weakness, decadence, effeminacy, and affectation, and the original meaning of exhaustion has all but disappeared. Although several commentators have objected to this 'semantic drift', the new meaning is firmly established in Canadian usage and is now listed in most dictionaries.

The image of the Bushman . . . lawless, unwashed and above all virile, composing four-line ballad verses with irrepressible gusto, is set up against a pale straw-man of a nail-gnawing Canadian intellectual, smothered in Englishness, bleating and effete.
Margaret Atwood *Second Words* 1982: 31

It set the Prime Minister apart from the effete Easterners who had no conception of pioneer prairie life.
Pierre Berton *The Promised Land* 1984: 259

While effete Vancouverites lounge around their upscale billiard-and-cappuccino clubs decadently discussing the works of Euripides, Polyclitus and Kim Campbell, we in the rest of the country spend the winter months engaging in less affected discourse.
Vancouver Sun 5 Feb. 1994: D3

effrontery see AFFRONT

e.g. see I.E.

egis see AEGIS

egotist, egoist, ego(t)ism, egocentric, egomaniac The traditional distinction characterizes an *egotist* as conceited and boastful and an *egoist* as self-centred but not necessarily attention-seeking. In Canadian usage, *egoism* and its variants are quite uncommon, and *egotism* often refers to self-interest rather than boastfulness. *Egocentric* means egotistic or self-centred. An *egomaniac* is extremely self-centred and boastful.

> Aw, America, smarten up. You are a world-class egotist. You almost seem to savor slighting your neighbors....
> *Toronto Star* 5 Nov. 1987: A29

> 'I'm the classic egoist, I do this for myself.... My motivation has always been self-imposed.'
> *Ottawa Citizen* 27 Nov. 1991: E7

> Blondie, said McLuhan, 'is efficiently masculine, purposive, egotistical and hard, just as Dagwood is ineffectually feminine, altruistic and sensitive.'
> *Vancouver Sun* 12 April 1994: A11

(Blondie is not given to bragging; here *egotistical* is used as a synonym of *egoistic*.)

> We are the egocentric species. We spend most of our time thinking about ourselves—one generation of time, that's all.
> *Vancouver Sun* 7 April 1994: A15

> She was a great medical reformer, an excellent surgeon and something of a rebel, but no egomaniac.
> *Globe and Mail* (Toronto) 2 Nov. 1985: A7

egregious   In the sixteenth and seventeenth centuries, *egregious* (pronounced *eh GREE juss*) often meant prominent or outstanding. Now, however, the word invariably means outrageous or outstanding in a bad way: 'egregious blunder', 'egregious liar'.

> What do Canadians expect from a major change of government? The correction of outstanding abuses, no doubt, such as the total indulgence of patronage and the egregious waste of taxpayers' money on failing public projects.
> *Globe and Mail* (Toronto) 4 Sept. 1985: P6

> Lunch at the National Arts Centre consisted of egregious sandwiches.
> *Globe and Mail* (Toronto) 28 March 1985: CL2

(They were remarkably bad.)

eh?   The informal question word *eh* ('You're back Wednesday, eh?') is not unique to Canadian English, but Canadians seem to use it more widely and more often than other English-speakers. *Eh?* can be the equivalent of 'What did you say?', 'Isn't that so?', or 'Are you with me so far?'.

> It was intriguing that many tourists who understand formal English will be completely thrown by an English-speaking Canadian's expression. Thus, Rule 1 be-

came: 'Speak slowly and do not use idioms. It is also well to avoid the Canadian "eh?"'
Vancouver Sun 22 Dec. 1994: A17

> At the metaphorical border of Customs and Immigration at Toronto International Airport I was startled to hear an immigration official say, upon checking my passport, 'Vindicated at last, eh?' (The up-turned 'eh' is a species of linguistic dim-witticism to which Canadians are addicted.)
> Quentin Crisp and John Hofsess *Manners from Heaven: A Divine Guide to Good Behaviour* 1984: n.p.

-ei-   see -IE-

Eire   see IRELAND

either ... or, neither ... nor   The first vowel in *either* is pronounced like the vowel in *eel* by most Canadians, but like *eye* by a sizeable minority; many use both pronunciations. The former is more common in the United States, the latter in Great Britain.

Either can be an adjective ('either way', 'either system'), a pronoun ('either will do'), or, in combination with *or*, a conjunction ('Either I'll come myself or I'll send someone else.') When there are more than two alternatives, the adjective or pronoun form of *either* changes to *any*: 'Either of the older two children could help; in fact, any of the kids could do it'. This has led to the argument that *either* should never be used in situations where there are more than two alternatives. However, when *either ... or* is used as a conjunction, there are often more than two alternatives: 'Either John, Martha, or David will come to the meeting'. Here changing *either* to *any* also changes the meaning: 'Any of John, Martha, or David will come ...'. This sentence, unlike the previous one, permits the possibility that one, two, or all three of those named could turn up at the meeting. The previous sentence indicates that only one person will come. Thus the use of *either ... or* with more than two alternatives is defensible.

In formal writing, care should be taken to observe the rules of grammatical agreement with *either*. The pronoun *either* is singular and takes a singular verb: 'Either is fine with me'. When *of* and a plural noun follow *either*, a plural verb is often used: 'Are either of the applicants here yet?' Nonetheless, in writing *either* should be treated as singular: 'Is either of the applicants here yet?'

Either ... or is a disjunctive conjunction, which means that the elements it links are considered separately. The formal convention for verb agreement with subjects linked by *either ... or* is that the verb should agree in person and number with the nearer subject: 'Either several or just one is chosen' *or* 'Either just one or several are chosen'. Since these grammatically correct constructions can sound quite stilted, you may want to avoid them altogether by splitting such sentences into two clauses: 'Either Elizabeth is coming tonight or I am'.

As a point of style in written English, the elements that follow *either* and *or* should be grammatically parallel: for example, 'Put it either on the desk or on the chair' or 'Put it on either the desk or the chair', but *not* 'Put it either on the desk or the chair'.

All the comments made with respect to *either ... or* also apply to *neither ... nor*.

> Furthermore, the independence of the judiciary has to be protected from attempts by either the legislature, the executive, or private parties to direct the outcome of the case.
> Andrew Heard *Canadian Constitutional Conventions* 1991: 120

(This is an example of the accepted use of *either* to introduce three alternatives.)

> They were interviewed either in person, through focus groups or by telephone.
> *Rites* March 1990: 5

(This is an example of the accepted use of *either* to introduce three alternatives.)

> Either additional time to compute the relationship between the principal axis and the XYZ axes or additional time to identify a foreshortened principal axis are plausible accounts of the effect we obtained in Experiment 2.
> *Canadian Journal of Psychology* 44 (1990): 382

(For all their complexity, the two subjects linked by *either ... or* are both singular. To agree with the nearer subject ('time to identify...'), the verb *are* should be replaced by the singular *is*, followed by 'a plausible *account*'.)

> Since your car is still running, you can shop around for the best price and either have a rebuilt or used transmission installed.
> *Gazette* (Montreal) 4 March 1989: F1

(Since *either* precedes a verb in the original sentence, one is led to expect another verb after *or*. Placing *either* after *have* and adding a second article ('a used ...') makes the second alternative grammatically parallel to the first: 'have *either* a rebuilt or *a* used transmission installed'.)

> The NBA has mandatory counselling for players either convicted of drug offences or players who voluntarily come forward to seek treatment.
> *Gazette* (Montreal) 4 March 1989: C2

(Stylistically, it would be better to place *either* before *players*: 'for *either* players convicted of drug offences or players who ...'. Alternatively, the second *players* could be omitted.)

See also AGREEMENT, GRAMMATICAL; NEITHER; PARALLELISM.

elder, eldest, older, oldest   The use of the adjectives *elder* and *eldest* is now largely restricted to ranking the birth order of family members. *Elder* is used when speaking of the first-born of two children and *eldest* for the first-born of three or more children. Some usage commentators recommend *eldest* rather than *oldest* to refer to the first-born of three or more children, but Canadians use either word.

Older and *oldest* may be used of both people and things. *Older* and *younger* are ambiguous when applied to siblings: 'my older brother' may be older than me or older than another brother. *Elder* is never used to make comparisons with *than*, though it may be used with *of*: 'She is older than her brother'; 'She is the elder of two children'.

The noun *elders* refers to older people generally, to particular older people held in high esteem in a community, or to the lay officers of certain churches.

> The Jiraneks' eldest of two sons, Martin, was selected by the Washington Capitals in the National Hockey League supplemental draft....
> *Today's Skater* 1991: 63

(The comparative adjective *elder* is used when referring to one of two children.)

> Joan Sadleir, the oldest, born in 1932 and the best student among the three daughters ... recalls: 'I was the only person who was allowed to go into the library at night.'
> Jack Batten *Robinette* 1984: 153

> Only the elders, traditional leaders of Chechen society, are holding them back from an all-against-all struggle with the Russians, they said.
> *Toronto Star* 31 Dec. 1994: A2

elderly   see SENIOR CITIZEN

else

elect To *elect* meaning simply to choose, rather than to choose by voting, is most often found in formal writing, especially legal writing. It is seldom used in newspaper and magazine writing, where *choose* is more common.

A *president-elect*, *governor-elect*, etc., is an official who has been elected but has not yet officially assumed duties.

> Perhaps not surprisingly, the defendant elected to keep the lease, as amended by the court, and to return to the plaintiff the portion over the store.
> J.E. Smyth et al. *The Law and Business Administration in Canada* 1987: 210

> Since I considered [military] intelligence on horseback somewhat obsolete, not to say conspicuous, I elected to wait.
> George Ignatieff *The Making of a Peacemonger* 1987: 56

electronic mail see E-MAIL

elegy, eulogy An *elegy* is an expression of mourning for a person, a group, or a way of life that has passed; traditionally, it takes the form of a poem. A *eulogy* is a speech praising a person or action. A funeral oration, however sorrowful, is called a *eulogy* because it praises the deceased. *Eulogy* (pronounced *YOO luh jee*) is preceded by *a*, not *an*.

> [The song] 'Men At The Cafe,' on Memory To Steel, is an elegy for the men killed in the Scotia Tower accident of 1987.
> *Toronto Star* 13 Nov. 1994: C3

> The final section [of the dance] is a lament, an elegy for people dead of AIDS.
> *Vancouver Sun* 17 Nov. 1994: C1

> Auntie Muriel had not composed her own eulogy, which laid heavy stress on the words dedication and generosity.
> Margaret Atwood *Life Before Man* 1979: 275

> 'His is the temperament of the pioneer,' Sifton's own newspaper wrote in April, 1905, in a eulogy of the new minister.
> Pierre Berton *The Promised Land* 1984: 206

(Here the *eulogy* is in praise of a living man.)

elemental, elementary Both words describe something fundamental: 'elemental *or* elementary foods', 'elemental *or* elementary rights'. However, only *elemental* suggests the uncontrollable power of nature: 'unleashing elemental forces'. Only *elementary* suggests simplicity, or self-evidence: 'elementary precautions'.

> We used our first cold frame ... to provide a transitional home for flat-grown seedlings on the way from the warm and windless environment of our kitchen to the elemental uncertainties of the open garden.
> *Harrowsmith* Aug.–Sept. 1985: 86

> In short, the way to counteract the claims of those like Zundel who deny what appear to most to be elementary truths about the Holocaust is not to prevent them from publishing their views but to refute them in argument.
> *Queen's Quarterly* 95.4 (1988): 853

elicit, extract, extort To *elicit* means to draw forth or bring out; to elicit information from someone implies questioning but no use of force. To *extract* a confession suggests that it was obtained with difficulty, perhaps through accusation, or interrogation, or even torture. To *extort* information or a response from someone implies the use of some form of threat.

> The physiology lecturer drew extensively on a repertory of 'anecdotes' apparently designed deliberately to elicit laughter and applause from the back benches of the men and to draw undue attention to the presence of the women.
> Hilda Neatby *Queen's University* 1 (1978): 214

> Drapeau extracted an on-air promise from Gaucher that the cost of building the structure would not exceed the money being put up by the province of Quebec.
> *Globe and Mail* (Toronto) 2 Feb. 1985: E6

> Hope is Jean-Bertrand Aristide returning to Haiti with the consent of the military—albeit a consent extorted by the United States, which threatened invasion.
> *Gazette* (Montreal) 30 Dec. 1994: B3

elk see MOOSE

ellipsis points see QUOTATION, QUOTATION MARKS

else When the expressions *nobody else's*, *somebody else's*, and *who else's* came into common use in the middle of the nineteenth century, they were flatly rejected by usage commentators. The latter defended the older forms *nobody's else*, *somebody's else*, and *whose else*, arguing that *else* functions as an adjective or an adverb, but is certainly never a noun or a pronoun and should not take the possessive ending.

In fact, however, *else* does not behave at all like a typical adverb or adjective. Although it is used with indefinite pronouns and adverbs (*anybody*, *where*), it is never used with nouns: 'Will anybody else be late?' but *not* 'Will a student else be late?'. Also, when *else* is used with an indefinite pronoun, the two words cannot be separated: one never says 'Nobody will come else now'. Phrases such as *anybody else* and *nobody else* function as if they were single words, which is why the possessive ending has shifted to the end of the phrase.

> This is a sensible decision since there is little to be said for attempting to resolve one's own legal dispute in the procedural context of someone else's lawsuit.
> *Canadian Bar Review* 66.3 (1987): 499

> So it could certainly be said that I used the power that I was given, the power of procreation, for my own purposes, and that I empowered myself at somebody else's expense.
> *Queen's Quarterly* 96.2 (1989): 233

> I became a specialist in American art to 1917. After that date it became somebody else's field.
> *Queen's Quarterly* 93.1 (1986): 68

elude, elusive   see ALLUDE

e-mail addresses   *E-mail* stands for 'electronic mail': mail that is sent through phone lines from computer to computer. An e-mail address is broken up into sections, usually by an at-sign (@) and one or more dots (.); some addresses also include an underbar (_). Thus 'Ken_Morris@mid.ca' would be read 'Ken_Morris at em eye dee dot see ay'. The last letters in an e-mail address are either a country code ('ca.' is Canada's country code) or a descriptive zone name, such as 'com.' for commercial organizations or 'edu.' for eductional institutions. These addresses are regulated in Canada by the Canadian Association of Internet Providers (CAIP).

embark, debark, disembark, emplane, deplane, entrain, detrain, embus, debus   To *embark*, from the French *embarquer*, originally meant to get on board a boat. Nowadays one can also *embark* on a train, plane, or bus. To *embark* also means to begin a voyage, literal or figurative; thus one can embark for Auckland or embark on a program of fiscal responsibility. The verb *embark* may also be used transitively to mean load or take on: 'The stevedores embarked the cargo'; 'The ship embarked passengers'.

Disembark and *debark* are synonyms, meaning to get off a ship or other public conveyance; *disembark* is more common.

In addition to the generic terms *embark* and *disembark*, parallel terms have arisen to refer to particular modes of transportation. Air travellers are offered assistance 'emplaning' and 'deplaning'. To *emplane* is to board or load a plane. *Entrain* and *detrain* were familiar words during the Second World War, when troops were transported by train. *Embus* and *debus* are in common use in Britain but not in Canada or the United States.

> Having established myself in my job and in my home, it was now time to embark on the grand plan.
> Max Braithwaite *The Night We Stole the Mountie's Car* 1971: 46

> The station is deserted as the train from which he has just disembarked vanishes in the distance.
> *Canadian Fiction Magazine* 63 (1988): 15

> But once I'd deplaned from the 'Red Eye,' I was able to head straight for the room Trophy Lodge had booked for me in one of Edmonton's finest hotels.
> *Uphere* Jan.–Feb. 1990: 54

> By the time the Doukhobors entrained, the commissary cars were loaded with 1,700 two-pound loaves of bread, 1,700 pounds of baked beans . . . and 50 pounds of coffee.
> Pierre Berton *The Promised Land* 1984: 76

emcee   see HOST

emend, emendation   see AMEND

emigrant, immigrant, in-migrate, out-migrate, migrate, migrant   An *emigrant* and an *immigrant* can be the same person, depending on the perspective from which he or she is viewed: an *emigrant* is leaving one country and moving permanently to another; an *immigrant* is arriving (as the Latin prefixes *e-*, 'out of', and *im-*, 'in', indicate). Usually people are said to *emigrate from* and *immigrate to*, but this generalization is far from absolute. It is also possible to say that someone who left France for Canada emigrated *to* Canada or immigrated *from* France.

The verbs *in-migrate* and *out-migrate* describe movement from one area to another within the same country; these words are often used by demographers.

The verb *migrate* means to move from one place to another permanently or temporarily, and is often used to refer to the seasonal movements of animals.

The noun *migrant* often refers to people who move for economic reasons. In the United States, where many migrant agricultural workers are illegal immigrants, the term can have negative connotations. In Australia, however, *migrant* is a neutral word meaning immigrant.

In the early 1950s, the family had emigrated from Iran to start a carpet importation business in Montreal.
Saturday Night May 1986: 51

He emigrated to England in the sixties and shed his Marxist beliefs.
Canadian Journal of Sociology 14.2 (1989): 264

Before she married her banker suitor and immigrated to Canada, she was one of the first women graduates of Trinity College, Dublin. . . .
Saturday Night Jan. 1986: 24

Cosentino's parents immigrated from Italy and settled in Hamilton. . . .
Globe and Mail (Toronto) 30 Nov. 1985: C1

An influx of new residents and a slowing of out-migration has increased Manitoba's population by 22,000 to about 1,050,000 in the past two years.
Globe and Mail (Toronto) 25 Jan. 1985: R5

But migrants who enter countries illegally to find work get no such special treatment.
Gazette (Montreal) 19 Nov. 1994: B3

See also ÉMIGRÉ.

émigré, exile, refugee, expatriate   These words all refer to someone who has left his or her native land. *Émigré* often refers to a person who is forced to emigrate because of political activity; it is spelled with an accent over each *e*. The French feminine form *émigrée* is rarely found in English; it should be used only in references to women. An *exile* is someone who has been banished from or has felt compelled to leave his or her native land. A *refugee* is someone who takes refuge, usually in a foreign country, to escape danger or persecution. The words *émigré* and *exile* have literary, diplomatic, and class (aristocratic) connotations that are not shared by the neutral term *refugee*.

An *expatriate*—derived from the Latin *ex-*, meaning 'out of', and *patria*, 'native country'—is someone who willingly lives in a foreign country without giving up his or her original citizenship.

Ex-patriot, which would correctly refer to someone whose nationalist fervour has abated, is a fairly common misspelling of *expatriate*.

The latter is a work published pseudonymously in Paris (by a Russian émigré living in Istanbul). . . .
Globe and Mail (Toronto) 30 Nov. 1985: E2

And it weaves through the collection of characters 'dreamed' by a troubled Chilean emigree in Janet Hinton's . . . new play.
Edmonton Journal 11 Feb. 1995: F5

(In formal writing, *émigrée* should be written with accents.)

An exile from his native land, an escapee from a Siberian cell, expelled from Switzerland, imprisoned in France, this one-time royal aide and army officer had an international reputation. . . .
Pierre Berton *The Promised Land* 1984: 66

There is no electricity and little food, and the refugees of war are on the run.
CBC News [transcript] 30 Dec. 1994: n.p.

Duncan is an expatriate Scot who came to Canada for Expo 67 and never went home.
Gazette (Montreal) 20 Dec. 1994: D7

'It's a very nationalistic market, even when we sell [Canadian art] abroad, it's usually to a Canadian ex-patriot.'
Toronto Star 23 May 1993: G3

(The word required here is *expatriate*.)

See also CITIZEN; EMIGRANT.

eminent   see IMMANENT

emote   *Emote* is an early twentieth-century back-formation from the noun *emotion*; it means to show emotion, especially in acting or as in acting. Commentators warn that this word should not be used in formal prose, but its facetious connotations make such use unlikely.

Now, actors love to show off with hysterics, especially actors like Ellen Burstyn and Marsha Mason (the respective moms), who emote buckets all over their squeaky-clean living rooms.
Globe and Mail (Toronto) 9 Feb. 1985: E3

It would seem that having actors emote furiously behind frozen expressions just doesn't have the resonance it once did.
Toronto Star 2 July 1993: E10

See also BACK-FORMATION.

emotional, emotive   *Emotional* means having to do with the emotions ('emotional problems'), showing or arousing emotion ('an emotional scene'), or susceptible to emotion ('an emotional person'). *Emotive* is a more technical and less common adjective used to describe something that elicits or generates strong emotion: 'emotive language', 'an emotive issue'.

Here the student of Greek will be impressed by Shankman's analysis of the emotive power of Pope's translation, and the student of the eighteenth century may be amazed by the obvious modernity of Pope's technique of psychological portraiture.
Queen's Quarterly 92.2 (1985): 407

According to a poll of senior executives carried out for Report on Business Magazine, the issue of closer Canada-U.S. relations is not the vexed or emotive one it once was.
Globe and Mail (Toronto) 1 March 1985: 120

'I know we are going to have to deal with a huge emotional issue out there,' said the MLA who ... will lead her team of five Tories through five weeks of public meetings across the province on the youth crime problem.
Calgary Herald 19 June 1994: A5

(Here *emotive* would also be appropriate.)

'We are supposed to be the emotive, irrational founding nation. English Canada is supposed to be the rational one,' says David Cliche, a member of the Parti Quebecois.
Calgary Herald 8 June 1994: A5

(A better choice here would be *emotional*: Quebeckers are supposed to feel, rather than elicit, emotion.)

empathy, sympathy, empathetic, empathic In general usage, *empathy* is the capacity to enter imaginatively into another person's experience, while *sympathy* is a feeling of compassion or like-mindedness.

Empathy was coined early in the twentieth century as a translation of the German word *Einfühlung* (a technical term in aesthetics). In this now rare sense, *empathy* is the ability to project oneself emotionally into a work of art in order to discover its meaning.

The original adjective form of *empathy* was *empathic*, but now *empathetic*, which parallels *sympathetic*, is far more common. Both forms are accepted.

'I implore parents and teachers to teach ethnic and racial tolerance,' he said. 'Empathy needs to be cultivated.'
Daily News (Halifax) 29 June 1994: 31

There is intimacy and a keen empathy among officers when one of their own comes in harm's way.
Toronto Star 20 June 1994: A7

You cannot, no matter how much sympathy you have for the parties, condone the taking of a life.
CTV News [transcript] 24 Dec. 1994: n.p.

Anyway, in the last few days there's been a subtle but perceptible shift in public sympathy toward the owners and away from the players, regardless of the sport.
Toronto Star 26 Sept. 1994: E1

One hopes 'the black experimentress' will turn her attention to other subjects and leave the biography of Canadian poets to more empathetic hands.
Ottawa Citizen 23 Oct. 1994: B3

Sister Cecilia, forthright and yet empathic, considers her home visits to the isolated and lonely in the neighborhood a vital part of her calling.
Globe and Mail (Toronto) 18 April 1985: CL1

Evernden's response is to advocate the cultivation of a more modest and empathic relationship with nature.
Globe and Mail (Toronto) 21 Sept. 1985: E22

emphasis Stylistically speaking, a sentence should lead its reader towards the main point. To make a point effectively in a long or complex sentence, put the most important idea at the end. When concessions or qualifications are added after the main point, the effect is anticlimactic.

Although the split-level dining room is always full, it never seems crowded.
Alan Tucker, ed. *The Penguin Guide to Canada* 1991: 287

(In this sentence, the emphasis is on the diner's comfort. If the clauses were in reverse order, the emphasis would fall on the popularity of the place.)

From last place to a Stanley Cup in four years; it could only happen because, as catalyst and driving force, Orr brought the Bruins along with him.
Ken Dryden *The Game* 1983: 104

(In this sentence, the amazing improvement in the record of the Bruins could easily overshadow the point that credit is due to Orr. Therefore the writer has put his main point in the position of emphasis at the end.)

To apply the term 'sister Church' to a non-Catholic body is also unfortunate (even though the Pope has used the term).
Catholic Register 16 Aug. 1986: 4

(Ending the sentence with a parenthetical comment undercuts the writer's point.)

emplane see EMBARK

emulate In current English, to *emulate* usually means to imitate zealously, to hold up as a model for oneself. But an earlier meaning of the word is still used by some writers: to imitate in order to equal or outdo.

In computer jargon, software or hardware designed to accommodate or reproduce the action or function of a competitor's product is said to *emulate* it.

The same goes for trainees in the martial arts, who observe the master, then emulate him until they achieve technical perfection.
Ottawa Citizen 29 May 1994: B1

The White Paper's other main cost savings are of a sort that the whole government should emulate—reducing administrative positions in headquarters to increase the number of soldiers in the field.
Vancouver Sun 3 Dec. 1994: A16

For all his intellectual powers and inexhaustible curiosity, Coleridge realized that he did not possess the literary gifts of Wordsworth or Percy Bysshe Shelley....
[Coleridge's] inability to emulate the best of the Romantic poets pained him until his death in 1834.
Maclean's 16 April 1990: A58

(Here *emulate* means rival or outdo.)

The lack of software specifically written for RISC-Unix workstations shouldn't be a problem for business users, he says. Most RISC units can easily emulate PCs that use the popular 80386 chip, for which there's a wide selection of software.
Financial Post 13 Dec. 1991: 15

The situation is particularly poignant for Amiga users ...because the computer once was the leader in the multimedia technology now being emulated by Apple and by makers of IBM-compatible computers.
Calgary Herald 10 Nov. 1994: C10

encapsulate, capsulize, capsulated To *encapsulate* and to *capsulize* are synonymous in the sense of to summarize, to condense. *Encapsulate* is clearly the preferred choice of Canadian writers; *capsulize* is rare in formal prose.

Though *capsulate* is not used as a verb, *capsulated* is a standard adjective synonymous with *encapsulated* and *capsulized*.

His dream of encapsulating 'in a single canvas ... the entire object, the entire subject; everything that he was: all his experience, all his love, and thus attain infinite hope ...' was never realized.
Ben-Z. Shek *French-Canadian & Québécois Novels* 1991: 76–7

The surprise, here, is that each of these efforts is so easy to take. In fact, they play like capsulized versions of those damnably 'relevant' made-for-TV movies.
Globe and Mail (Toronto) 21 Feb. 1985: E4

Surtitles are capsulated English translations projected on to a screen above the stage.
Globe and Mail (Toronto) 3 Jan. 1985: E5

endemic, epidemic, pandemic All three terms are both adjectives and nouns describing patterns of disease occurrence. All are also used metaphorically to describe non-medical problems, and it is in these uses that they are often confused.

Epidemic and *endemic* both refer to the occurrence of something in a particular area or among a particular group of people: something *epidemic* is widespread or prevalent there at a particular time, whereas something *endemic* is a constant problem. *Pandemic*, a less common word, refers to something that affects a broad population over a very wide area. Thus a 'world-wide epidemic' would be a *pandemic*.

Something *endemic* is a persistent but not necessarily common problem in a particular area or group. Sometimes non-scientific writers use the word as if it were the adjective form of *epidemic*. This confusion may have arisen because *epidemic* usually appears as a noun and *endemic* as an adjective.

'Rabies is endemic to Southern Ontario and goes in cycles of outbreaks among wildlife, so you might have an epidemic in certain areas at certain times.'
Globe and Mail (Toronto) 16 Dec. 1985: A13

I also revelled in the psychological warfare that is endemic to sports, and loved to probe a competitor's personality....
Queen's Quarterly 94.1 (1987): 125

Academic observers of South African politics say the violence today is unique because of its length ... and its endemic spread throughout the country.
Globe and Mail (Toronto) 25 July 1985: P1

(The word required here is *epidemic*.)

Since the collapse of the Soviet Union in 1991, theft of lucrative military equipment has become endemic.
Ottawa Citizen 1 June 1994: A6

(The word required here is *epidemic*.)

enervate The verb *enervate* is often mistakenly used as a synonym for *energize*. In fact, to *enervate* something is to sap it of its strength, to weaken it physically or morally.

Traffic jams are a way of life for motoring suburbanites. Commuting to work or the cottage, drivers curse the

inevitable, enervating snarl, the perpetual post-ponement.
Toronto Star 2 Oct. 1994: F11

... we Canadians are no longer victim to that enervating sense of uncertainty that derives from self-perceived 'colonial' status....
Ottawa Citizen 17 Sept. 1985: A9

Bob Rae, leader of the Ontario NDP, said 'It's entirely natural for Canadians to be debating their relationship with the United States. It's been enervating to see people talking about free trade on the streetcars.'
Toronto Star 21 Nov. 1988: A1

(Here *energizing* would make more sense.)

The nationalist fervor of their parents may be ebbing, but passions are still lively here. These CEGEP-level students at College Jean de Brébeuf are the children of the Parti Québécois: [Raised] on an enervating potion of Quebec nationalism, they have never developed an appetite for their country [Canada].
Toronto Star 12 Oct. 1991: B6

(These young Quebeckers are not less fervently nationalistic than their parents, but more so: the word required here is *energizing*.)

English see OLD ENGLISH, ANGLO-SAXON, MIDDLE ENGLISH, EARLY MODERN ENGLISH, MODERN ENGLISH; QUEBEC ENGLISH; SCIENTIFIC ENGLISH; STANDARD ENGLISH, STANDARD

Englishman, Englishwoman see BRITON

enjoin, injunction To *enjoin* is to command or urge. The usual construction is *enjoin* someone *to* do something, as in 'Sarah enjoined the caucus to re-examine its goals'.

However, *enjoin* may also mean prohibit. This meaning is the usual one in a legal context. If the court *enjoins* a company *from* selling a product, then it issues an *injunction* freezing sales.

Because of its two different meanings, *enjoin* is highly ambiguous when it takes a direct object. For example, if the board of trustees enjoins the sale of a school, has it ordered the sale or prohibited it? To avoid confusion it is best to choose another word altogether, such as *orders* or *vetoes*, in such contexts.

None of them enjoined their followers to act upon the world, for the highest good was a contemplative flight from it.
Irving M. Zeitlin and Robert J. Brym The Social Condition of Humanity *1991: 222*

To get well, especially when in the hospital, Jews, particularly children and the old, are permitted, indeed enjoined, to eat what they are served....

Henry M. Rosenthal and S. Cathy Berson, eds. Canadian Jewish Outlook Anthology *1988: 54*

Today we learned that CTV has been enjoined from showing an interview with Margaret Trudeau until after her book *Beyond Reason* is published.
Ken Dryden The Game *1983: 20*

This was in keeping with Korean funeral rites, which enjoin public wailing by bereaved relatives.
Ottawa Citizen 20 July 1994: A9

(Here, without context, *enjoin* is ambiguous; either *require* or *forbid* would be clearer.)

enormity, enormousness Both words are derived from the Latin *enormis*, meaning irregular, unusual, or immense. *Enormity* was originally used to mean extraordinary wickedness, while *enormousness* meant extraordinary size. Since the late 1700s, *enormity* has also been used to mean great size with no implication of evil. Yet to this day usage experts disagree on whether this substitution of *enormity* for *enormousness* is acceptable. In Canadian writing *enormousness* is not a common word. Canadians use *enormity* to mean either great size or extreme wickedness, or a combination of both.

Undaunted by the enormity of the task before him, he began to select participants from a wide variety of musicians he'd met over many years of professional travel.
Performing Arts in Canada March 1988: 22

(Here *enormity* carries no connotation of evil.)

Similarly, a painting of a mountain must have empty space around it so you can appreciate the enormity of the mountain.
Ottawa Citizen 4 March 1990: A3

There is great interest in the case because of the enormity of the crime, adds Travers, and the curiosity is highlighted by the publication ban on evidence.
Ottawa Citizen 27 Nov. 1994: A8

(Here *enormity* connotes both magnitude and evil.)

The country's enormousness infused the saga of the construction of the Canadian Pacific Railway, its bright silver rails forging across the continent to stitch together a nation.
Toronto Star 23 Dec. 1991: A18

See also -NESS.

enquire, enquiry see INQUIRE

en route Major dictionaries list only *en route* (two words), from the French meaning 'on the way'. Although *enroute* is beginning to appear in published prose, until this single-word spelling becomes established, it's best to use the standard form.

VIA Train 66 was en route from Toronto to Montreal on Nov. 20 when it struck a piece of rail lying across a track at Brighton.
Toronto Star 21 Dec. 1994: A12

Longing for Jennifer often surfaced during a working day when Julie, enroute to one of her frequent meetings outside her office, would catch sight of a baby in a stroller.
Chatelaine April 1986: 128

(The accepted spelling is *en route*.)

ensure   see INSURE

enthuse   The verb *enthuse* is a back-formation from the noun *enthusiasm*. It is very common in current journalism, but hovers just beyond the pale of full respectability. Recently published dictionaries still label it 'informal' or 'colloquial': in other words, unsuitable for formal prose. The continuing resistance to *enthuse* has two likely causes. One is that the word has been commented upon unfavourably since 1870—long enough for it to become a shibboleth. The second is that the participial form *enthused*, as in 'Lee was enthused about the opportunity', duplicates the sense of the longer-established adjective *enthusiastic*.

Such a speech could not enthuse an intelligent audience.
Henry M. Rosenthal and S. Cathy Berson, eds.
Canadian Jewish Outlook Anthology 1988: 38

(A different word, such as *inspire*, would forestall criticism.)

'Now it can provide the collection with the kind of home it deserves...,' enthused Mr. Breede.
Leisure Life May 1988: 67

(In formal writing, *said enthusiastically* would be better.)

But not all are as enthused about the Liberals' approach.
Ottawa Citizen 17 Dec. 1994: A1

(In formal writing, *enthusiastic* is recommended.)

See also BACK-FORMATION.

entitle, title   Either word may introduce a title: 'a book entitled *or* titled *Elimination Dance*'. Some people mistakenly assume that *entitled* can mean only 'justified in claiming', as in 'Everyone is entitled to a share'.

entomology   see ETYMOLOGY

entrain   see EMBARK

entrée, appetizer   The French word *entrée* was used in English in the eighteenth century to mean a light dish served after the first course of fish and before the main meat dish. It was called an entrée because it marked the entry into the main meal. Over the centuries eating habits have changed and so has the meaning of *entrée*. The *entrée* is often still the second course of a meal, but now it is the main course—at least in most of Canada. Speakers of English in Quebec tend to follow the French usage, in which the *entrée* is the first course, or what most English Canadians call the *appetizer*.
Entrée usually retains its accent in formal writing.

For appetizers, we had one winner (delicious garlic prawns at $6.95) and one loser.... My entree was the superbly seasoned ... rack of lamb....
Vancouver Sun 23 Nov. 1990: P9

The man next to me was still raving about an entree of melted goat cheese in puff pastry with a cumin sauce when his poussin façon Wantzenau, a little golden-roasted Rock Cornish game hen, arrived.
Gazette (Montreal) 4 March 1989: K6

(Here *entrée* is used in the sense of appetizer common in Quebec English.)

The eggplant parmigiana entree might well serve as a main dish and is very good.
Gazette (Montreal) 27 Oct. 1990: T4

(Here *entrée* is used in the sense of appetizer common in Quebec English.)

See also HORS D'OEUVRE.

enunciation, Annunciation   An *enunciation* is a detailed statement of rules or principles or a public declaration. *Enunciation* also means manner of articulation (see DICTION, ENUNCIATION). The term *Annunciation* refers to the angel Gabriel's announcement to the Virgin Mary that she would give birth to Christ (Luke 1: 26–38). Occasionally *annunciation* is also used to refer to any formal announcement.

Discussion of the variety and utility of the approaches taken is warranted, for the clear enunciation of methodology is a crucial issue facing interpretive social science.
The Canadian Geographer Spring 1989: 94

... doubts about this should have been dispelled in 1968, following the Soviet invasion of Czechoslovakia, by the enunciation of the Brezhnev Doctrine, which proclaims the right of the Soviet Union to intervene in

any 'socialist' country whose government deviates from the Marxist-Leninist path.
Globe and Mail (Toronto) 8 June 1985: E17

One of the angels of Jewish, Christian and Muslim tradition, [Gabriel] is the second of the archangels, angel of the Annunciation, and messenger of God.
Globe and Mail (Toronto) 23 March 1985: M2

See also IMMACULATE CONCEPTION, VIRGIN BIRTH.

envelop, envelope   The verb *envelop*, meaning to surround or cover, is spelled with no final *e* and pronounced with the stress on the second syllable: *en VEL up*.

The noun *envelope* is stressed on the initial syllable, which may be pronounced either *EN* or *ON*. The *ON vuh lope* pronunciation is sometimes criticized as affected or pseudo-French; however, it's very common and comes naturally to many English-speakers.

envious, enviable   *Envious* means feeling or showing envy, while *enviable* means evoking or apt to evoke envy.

Others who have cast envious glances at the Carlton St. cashbox say it's worth more.
Toronto Star 11 April 1994: B1

He has the rare and enviable knack of making complexities clear, of speaking engagingly without ever talking down.
Vancouver Sun 7 May 1994: D9

Certainly he had an envious vantage point for watching the story unfold.
Globe and Mail (Toronto) 18 Dec. 1993: C8

(The word required here is *enviable*.)

'Without greater economic growth, Canada's envious quality of life will be endangered.'
Toronto Star 3 May 1994: A18

(The word required here is *enviable*.)

See also ENVY.

environment   see ECOLOGY; GREEN

envision, envisage   Both these verbs mean to form a mental picture of something, often in the future. Canadian writers use both words equally in all styles of writing. British writers prefer *envisage*, Americans *envision*. Some commentators attempt to distinguish between these terms, but in current usage all distinctions have vanished. *Envisage* once meant to face squarely or confront, but this sense is now rare.

Canadians may finally get the museums the Massey Commission envisioned over thirty-five years ago in spite of twenty years of administrative and bureaucratic obstacles.
Queen's Quarterly 94.3 (1987): 568

Obviously the kind of settlement Pearson envisaged could not be negotiated quickly or under the pressure of constant border clashes.
George Ignatieff *The Making of a Peacemonger* 1987: 122

envy, jealousy, covet, begrudge   The connotations of *envy* range from mild feelings of rivalry to bitter resentment of another's advantages, possessions, or achievements. *Jealousy* usually implies fairly strong feelings of envy. Its meaning extends beyond that of *envy* in that one can be jealous not only of something someone else owns, controls, or has achieved, but also of one's own relationships, privileges, possessions, etc. In other words, *envy* refers to the perception of oneself as lacking or deprived in relation to someone else, while *jealousy* may refer either to this perception *or* to the feeling that one is likely to suffer a loss at someone else's hands. For example, a jealous husband fears losing the affections of his wife to someone else. *Jealous* and *zealous* are related etymologically; this connection is clear in phrases such as 'a jealously guarded secret', where the senses of *zeal* and *jealousy* combine.

To *covet* means to desire something belonging to someone else, and often suggests a longing that is morally or legally wrong. Sports reporters—playing on these dire connotations—often use *covet* with reference to athletic rivalries. To *begrudge* means to resent another person's good fortune. The noun forms are *covetousness* and *begrudgement*.

Now it goes without saying that people envy the life of scholars—the long summer vacations, the excursions to distant lands.
Canadian Fiction Magazine 63 (1988): 72

What a woman writer is often unprepared for is the unexpected personal attack on her by a jealous male writer. The motivation is envy and covetousness, but the form is often sexual put-down.
Margaret Atwood *Second Words* 1982: 202

As one would expect, a prime source of employment in a critically depressed area is guarded jealously by the people.
Daily Gleaner (Fredericton) 26 April 1988: 4

It is a fact that all ethnic, racial, and social groups, including the very rich, contain individuals who covet and unlawfully take the property of others.
Irving M. Zeitlin and Robert J. Brym *The Social Condition of Humanity* 1991: 274

Of course, the grandpa of them all was Cy Young, for whom the award all pitchers covet was named.
Globe and Mail (Toronto) 23 April 1985: S1

The scheme has also aroused resentment among workers who don't work so hard and begrudge the growing disparity between their earnings and those of their gung ho work mates.
Globe and Mail (Toronto) 16 Feb. 1985: P1

See also ENVIOUS, ENVIABLE.

epenthesis   see MISPRONUNCIATION AND PRONUNCIATION SHIFTS

epic   An *epic* is a long narrative poem that celebrates the achievements of a hero. It is written in a formal style and often expresses the ideals of a nation. *Beowulf*, Homer's *Iliad*, Virgil's *Aeneid*, and Milton's *Paradise Lost* are all epic poems. *Epic* is also used as an adjective to describe long, usually historical movies and novels, or achievements and events unusual in their magnitude and importance. Critics have disparaged these extended uses of *epic*, but they are widely used and accepted. In literary criticism, where *epic* is used as a technical term, the extended meanings should be avoided.

Epic is often used humorously to mean *huge* or *grandiose*. This usage is always informal.

This synthesis takes place most notably in 'The Pride,' an almost epic long poem which traces the history of western Canada through the defeat and dispersal of the Indians and ends by seeing the current inhabitants—'we' or 'us'—as their metaphorical descendants.
Margaret Atwood *Second Words* 1982: 126

(Here *epic* is a technical term.)

Clark's new epic novel about the life of Freydis, daughter of Erik the Red and sister of Leif the Lucky, reads like a cross between a bodice-ripper and a living-history textbook.
Ottawa Citizen 19 June 1994: B3

... Pearson ended up laying his wreath on a ridge which had changed hands many times during the epic World War II struggle for Stalingrad, and where 36,000 identifiable bodies were found when the battle was over.
George Ignatieff *The Making of a Peacemonger* 1987: 140

Forget Paul Henderson's jump for joy after scoring the winning goal of the 1972 Summit Series.... The World Cup is here. And that means post-goal celebrations of epic proportions.
Toronto Star 17 June 1994: B9

(This use of *epic* is informal.)

Examples span from the country's first trans-continental railway in the 1880s ... to the now notorious and epic Dome Petroleum fiasco of the 1980s....
Queen's Quarterly 94.4 (1987): 939

(This use of *epic* is informal.)

See also ODYSSEY.

epicurean, epicure, Epicurean   An *epicurean* is especially fond of eating, drinking, and sensual pleasure. An *epicure*—like a gourmet—has refined tastes in food and wine. To some extent these two terms are used interchangeably, but this is the distinction of sense presented in most dictionaries.

When capitalized, *Epicurean* refers to *Epicurus*, the Greek philosopher who taught that pleasure is the highest goal. Epicurus defined pleasure not as sensualism—that interpretation distorts his teachings—but as freedom from anguish, which he associated with a life of moderation and simplicity.

D—— is Ontario's soon-to-be-former deputy health minister ... and, it seems, enthusiastic epicurean.... according to expense claims released this week by the opposition, [he has] claimed $11,238.94 in meals.
Ottawa Citizen 18 Nov. 1993: A14

Our epicure prides himself on exotic chow from India, Italy, France, Mexico and Thailand.... 'Something about the perfumes and flavors,' muses Comeau....
Gazette (Montreal) 7 May 1994: D1

See also GOURMET, GOURMAND.

epidemic   see ENDEMIC

epigram, epigraph, epitaph, epilogue, epithet   An *epigram* is a short, pointed statement in prose or verse. Epigrams are satiric and witty. Frequently, as in this verse by B.K. Sandwell (editor of *Saturday Night*, 1932–51), they are of topical and local, rather than universal, interest:

Toronto has no social classes.
Only the Masseys and the masses.

An *epigraph* is an engraved inscription on a building or monument, or a short statement, usually a quotation at the beginning of a book or part of a book. The statue of Sir George-Étienne Cartier in Jeanne-Mance Park, Montreal, includes a carved scroll with the epigraph 'Above Everything, We Are Canadian'. An epigraph may well appear on a tomb, although the usual term for such inscriptions is *epitaph*.

An *epitaph* is a short composition written in memory of a dead person, often engraved on a tombstone. Reginald Fessenden, a pioneer of Canadian radio-communications, is buried in St. Mark's Church, Bermuda. His epitaph reads:

By His Genius
Distant Lands Converse
And Men Sail
Unafraid Upon the Deep.

An *epilogue* is the final speech of a play or the concluding section of a novel or poem; it is the opposite of a *prologue*.

Finally, an *epithet* is a descriptive expression or phrase attached to someone's name; it is usually an adjective, as in 'Ivan the Terrible' or 'Ethelred the Unready'. Sometimes *epithet* means a term of abuse: 'They hurled racist epithets'. Some usage commentators object to this use of the word, but it is well established in Canadian writing.

What they had discovered were gardens known as lazy beds, a term derived from 'lazy root,' an English epithet for the potato.
Harrowsmith Jun.–Jul. 1985: 125

A Jewish resident in the surgical clinic ... at a famous Berlin hospital is making his rounds in the wards when a brutal Nazi patient begins to shout anti-Semitic epithets at him.
Queen's Quarterly 92.1 (1985): 133

epileptic   see DISABILITIES

epilogue   see EPIGRAM

epiphany   *Epiphany* is capitalized when it refers to the Christian festival held on 6 January. At Epiphany some churches celebrate the manifestation of Christ's divinity at his baptism; other churches celebrate the manifestation of Christ to the Magi. An

epiphany (not capitalized) is an appearance by a deity, or an important revelation, or, in current extended usage, a sudden insight.

In Rome the storm coincided with the traditional arrival of Befana, the old woman who brings Italian children presents for the feast of Epiphany.
Globe and Mail (Toronto) 7 Jan. 1985: P10

But Page holds back before releasing her joyful tears, and the film achieves a magnificent epiphany.
Maclean's 24 Feb. 1986: 65

This remarkable epiphany [the realization that you can see what the weather is like by looking out the window] is the reason that, when Bert Adkins is on the air, you never drive through a rainstorm and listen to a radio report that tells you it's clear out.
Ottawa Citizen 30 Dec. 1993: A1

(Here *epiphany* is ironic.)

epitaph, epithet   see EPIGRAM

epitome, exemplar, acme, apex, pinnacle, paragon, ne plus ultra   An *epitome* (pronounced *eh PIT uh mee*) is a prime example. A person or thing perfectly embodying or representing a quality is said to be 'the epitome' of it. An *exemplar* is someone or something that serves well as an example or model. Thus an inn that is the *epitome* of comfort might also be described as *exemplary* with respect to comfort. *Epitome* and *exemplar* can both refer to negative as well as positive things: 'the epitome of selfishness'; 'an exemplar of the neglected child'. Because *epitome* does not mean highest point or peak, some critics object to the expression 'to reach the epitome'. *Acme*, *apex*, and *pinnacle*, which all mean highest point, are better choices in this context, although *acme* is rarely used in Canadian writing except as part of a company name ('Acme Glass Ltd.', for example). A *paragon* is a model of excellence or perfection (and *paragon* is the name of a perfect diamond of 100 carats or more). The Latin expression *ne plus ultra* refers to the highest or farthest point. Meaning literally 'nothing more beyond', *ne plus ultra* is said to have been inscribed on rocks at the western gate of the Mediterranean as a warning to sailors. This phrase should be italicized in formal writing.

With chocolate cheesecake brownies, brownies with milk chocolate icing and caramel fudge pecan brownies, she seems to have reached the epitome of this particular craft.
Globe and Mail (Toronto) 11 Dec. 1985: E8

(Here *apex* or *pinnacle* would be a better choice.)

'He has all the physical characteristics to play in the CFL,' Hargreaves said. 'But playing in the NFL is the epitome for young athletes.'
Globe and Mail (Toronto) 5 Dec. 1985: D12

(Here *ultimate achievement* would be more appropriate.)

To me, this was not surprising because generally, I have not found mourning doves to be the epitomy of intelligence.
Gazette (Montreal) 2 June 1990: L3

(The correct spelling is *epitome*.)

For the time being this may mean quick-fix loans and perhaps exemplary punishment for culpable former politicians.
Globe and Mail (Toronto) 11 Sept. 1985: P7

(Here *exemplary* describes something unpleasant that is meant to serve as an example.)

See also APOGEE; CATASTROPHE; LATIN PHRASES; SINE QUA NON.

epoch The older meaning of *epoch* (pronounced either *EE pock* or *EH puck*) is a turning-point in history or the beginning of an era. This sense is now rare. Most writers now use *epoch* as a synonym for *era*: a period of time that is distinct in some way. Most dictionaries list the new meaning; however, some commentators still disparage it.

The older meaning is recalled by the adjective *epoch-making*, which describes highly significant events or achievements, and means literally 'marking the beginning of a new era'. Commentators caution against trivializing this word.

Simple though these words may sound, the movement represented a historic epoch in the saga of the Jewish people.
Henry M. Rosenthal and S. Cathy Berson, eds. *Canadian Jewish Outlook Anthology* 1988: 74

(Here *epoch* is used in the older sense of turning-point.)

It was the best of times, it was the worst of times, it was the age of wisdom, it was the age of foolishness, it was the epoch of belief, it was the epoch of incredulity—in short, it was the beginning of the Autumn Term, and the year was 1969.
Robertson Davies *One Half of Robertson Davies* 1978: 107

(Here *epoch* means era.)

In that epoch humans first emerged as food gatherers.

Irving M. Zeitlin and Robert J. Brym *The Social Condition of Humanity* 1991: 92

(Here *epoch* means era.)

In 1859 Charles Darwin published his theory of biological evolution in an epoch-making book called *On the Origin of Species by Means of Natural Selection*.
Irving M. Zeitlin and Robert J. Brym *The Social Condition of Humanity* 1991: 1

(Here *epoch-making* refers to a scientific discovery that in fact marked the beginning of a new era.)

eponym, eponymous An *eponym* is a person's name that has been given to something else, such as a place, institution, discovery, object, invention, or work of literature. For example, the sandwich is named after the fourth Earl of Sandwich, who, according to the legend, demanded a snack that was easy to eat so that he would not have to leave the card table; similarly, the stetson was named after the American hat-maker J.B. Stetson. *Bombardier* is the name given an early snowmobile, after its Canadian inventor, Armand Bombardier of Valcourt, Quebec.

Titles of works of fiction often bear the name of their main character, as in *Anna Karenina*. In such cases the title character and the title are said to be *eponymous*. A title should not be referred to as *eponymous* if it simply describes rather than names the main character, as in *The Egoist*.

Formerly the host of Variety Tonight, she now has a new show, eponymously called Gabereau.
Globe and Mail (Toronto) 6 July 1985: E1

(The 'she' is CBC radio host Vicki Gabereau.)

What children are to the eponymous heroine of 'Irina'—darling zeros—Linnet's husband is to her, and one is not too sure that the darling part was ever applicable.
Janice Kulyk Keefer *Reading Mavis Gallant* 1989: 131

(The heroine of the story 'Irina' is named Irina.)

... more sympathetic portraits are to be found in Grete Toeppler of 'The Latehomecomer' or the eponymous heroine of 'His Mother'....
Janice Kulyk Keefer *Reading Mavis Gallant* 1989: 106

(The heroine of 'His Mother' should not be called *eponymous*, since 'his mother' is not her name.)

For the next two hours, Geraldine Page turns the Countess Aurelia, the eponymous heroine of Jean Giraudoux's 1945 farce The Madwoman of Chaillot, ... into a theatrical banquet....
Globe and Mail (Toronto) 26 Feb. 1985: M7

(The heroine of *The Madwoman of Chaillot* is not properly called *eponymous*.)

equable, equatable, equitable   Something *equable* is unvarying or steady. The word is most frequently used to describe climatic conditions. Things that are *equatable* (*ee KWAIT uh bul*) can be considered equivalent. *Equitable* (pronounced *ECK wit uh bul*) means fair: an equitable solution or arrangement is one in which all parties are treated justly.

Its equable climate, the country's balmiest, draws retirees from across Canada, giving Victoria its dichotomous character, the genteel-among-the-great-outdoors aspect.
Alan Tucker, ed. *The Penguin Guide to Canada* 1991: 562

In England, where the word [serviette] is used less in any case, it is more or less equatable with a napkin, cloth or paper.
W.C. Lougheed, ed. *In Search of the Standard in Canadian English* 1986: 59

The report also suggests that the unions should address non-traditional issues of collective bargaining, such as equitable pay for women, greater worker participation in decision-making, and health and safety issues.
Globe and Mail (Toronto) 27 Feb. 1985: P12

equally   Phrases such as 'equally as hard' and 'equally as good' are criticized because *equally as* is redundant. Either *equally* or *as* can stand alone in a comparison: 'Her new play and her previous ones are equally good' *or* 'Her new play is as good as her previous ones'.

In addition, she would compel male academics to take early retirement at age 60, while allowing women to work to age 65—a proposal equally as offensive as the reverse requirement once in place at the university.
London Free Press 6 May 1988: B6

(Here *equally* could be omitted; if emphasis is required, *just* or *every bit* could precede *as*.)

Robinette was almost equally as effective in making points with his cross-examination of a variety of other crown witnesses.
Jack Batten *Robinette* 1984: 86

(Here 'almost *as* effective' or 'almost *equally* effective' would be better.)

For anglers on a tighter budget, there are less costly—but in my opinion equally as enjoyable—ways to visit and fish Ireland....
Atlantic Salmon Journal Summer 1990: 23

(Here the *as* should be dropped.)

See also AS GOOD AS.

equatable   see EQUABLE

equinox, solstice   The *equinox* is the day of the year when day and night are of equal length (occurring twice per year, around 22 September and 20 March). The *solstice* is the longest or shortest day of the year (around 22 June and 22 December).

equitable   see EQUABLE

equivocal   see AMBIGUOUS

equivocate   see LIE

-er, -or   Both *-er* and *-or*, when added to a word, can signify something or someone that performs a function: *baker, computer, investigator, radiator*. Today only *-er* is used to form new words. There is no difference in the meaning or pronunciation of the two endings, but they do present a spelling challenge. Some words can be spelled either way: for example, *adviser, advisor* (the former is more common) and *conveyer, conveyor* (the latter is more common for the mechanical device; in reference to people, usage is mixed).
   If the same word can refer to either a person or an object, the *-er* ending is often used for the form designating a person and the *-or* ending for the one designating an object, as in *resister* (someone who resists) and *resistor* (a device that has electrical resistance). However, in legal language the *-or* ending is strongly favoured for words referring to people (e.g., *grantor, mortgagor, executor*).

See also ADVISER, ADVISOR.

err   Most Canadians pronounce *err* like *air*, but the British usually pronounce it to rhyme with *her*.

ersatz   *Ersatz* (pronounced *UR zats* or *AIR zats*) means artificial or imitation, and its connotations are negative. German manufacturers developed many products during the two world wars to replace food and commodities that were in short supply, and the German word for these substitutes was borrowed by the English.

Once, a Bruce woman had doubtless thought these pieces were elegant, but they were not antiques, and they were not cheerful. They were ersatz Victorian, decidedly lumpy and vaguely funereal.
Harrowsmith Aug.–Sept. 1985: 16

See also ARTIFICIAL.

escalation An *escalation* is a step-by-step increase that seems self-propelled. The phrases 'escalation of international good will' and 'sudden escalation of happiness' sound peculiar, perhaps because *escalation* is almost always linked to worrisome things such as costs, violence, and hostilities. From such negative contexts some writers have wrongly inferred that *escalation* means worsening or deterioration.

> One presidential candidate warned that an escalation of tension between Aristide and Lafontant could lead to civil war.
> *Gazette* (Montreal) 16 Dec. 1990: B1

> 'I am nevertheless distressed about this exorbitant escalation of rent for downtown office space,' Mr. Johnston wrote.
> *Globe and Mail* (Toronto) 29 Jan. 1985: P5

> In one article, a professor at the University of Calgary blamed women for the decline of family stability and the escalation of ethics in North America.
> *Queen's Journal* (Kingston) 2 Feb. 1993: 3

> (Here, unless ethics are viewed as a social scourge, *escalation* is used wrongly to mean deterioration.)

> The shooting represents a significant escalation in [Israeli] settlers' tactics against Arabs....
> *Toronto Star* 11 Dec. 1993: A11

> (Here *escalation* is wrongly used to mean worsening rather than increase; 'escalation in the violence of ... tactics' would be more appropriate.)

-ese The suffix *-ese* has two functions. It is used to form adjectives referring to a place or its residents (*Chinese, Maltese, Portuguese, Viennese, Vietnamese*) and to create nouns specifying distinctive manners of speaking or writing (*Brooklynese, bureaucratese, journalese*). This second *-ese* is often used in the popular media to produce ad hoc words to describe the jargon of a particular group: for example, *legalese* and *computerese*. Some of the more inventive creations of Canadian writers follow.

> This is indeed a welcome relief to his impeccably written double-starched Doctoralese.
> *Queen's Quarterly* 92.1 (1985): 218

> You didn't know I could talk Architectese, did you? I have always been a good linguist and can pick up a smattering of any language quite quickly.
> Robertson Davies *One Half of Robertson Davies* 1978: 77

> In a world of complexity and ambiguity, Reagan reduced everything to 3 x 5 note cards, single-page briefings, or ghost-written telepromptese.
> *Queen's Quarterly* 95.4 (1988): 802

See also COLLOQUIAL, INFORMAL, SLANG, JARGON.

Eskimo see INUIT

esoteric see EXOTIC

especial(ly) see SPECIAL

espresso, expresso The Italian coffee is properly called *espresso* (ess PRESS o). Dictionaries accept the variant spelling *expresso*, which reflects a common pronunciation, but some commentators still condemn it. Meaning 'pressed out' in Italian, *espresso* refers to the process of making the strong, concentrated coffee: steam under pressure is forced through finely ground beans. The plural is *espressos*.

> His mother had prepared hot bread rolls with orange jam and tiny cups of espresso.
> *Queen's Quarterly* 96.2 (1989): 354

> You get the pleasantly odd feeling that it's an extraordinarily permanent set built by a Hollywood movie company for High Noon, and Gary Cooper should be happily swilling expresso on one of its many outdoor restaurant terraces.
> *Globe and Mail* (Toronto) 18 June 1985: S2

> (This spelling is quite uncommon in Canada.)

Esquire, Esq. *Esquire* most often appears as *Esq.* after a man's name in a mailing address. It should not be combined with *Mr.*; either 'Mr. Richard Harris' or 'Richard Harris, Esq.' is correct. In Canada *Esq.* is used as an honorific for lawyers (non-sexist usage guides recommend using it for women lawyers too); in any other context some consider it very stuffy. In Britain it is used more widely, particularly on formal occasions when titles are de rigueur. In the medieval period, an esquire was an aspirant knight and a sort of knight's assistant. Later an esquire was part of the landed gentry, ranked just below a knight in the British social hierarchy. Now *Esq.* is appropriate for any man without another title.

> ... his grandfather, the late J.J. McGill, Esq., sat on the MGH Board of Management from 1919 to 1939.
> *Gazette* (Montreal) 6 Dec. 1990: F4

> G. Ross Davis, Esquire, for appellant.
> *Globe and Mail* (Toronto) 17 Oct. 1985: B11

(This quotation is from the Osgoode Hall court reports.)

essay see ASSAY

et al. This phrase is an abbreviation of *et alia*, Latin for 'and others'. Since only the second word is an abbreviation, only one period is required, after *al. Et al.* is most often used in citing a publication that has three or more authors. For example, a 1991 article written by Smith, Jones, and Brown can be referred to as 'Smith et al. 1991'. (Note that both names are always given when a source has only two authors.)

Although etymologically justified, the use of *et al.* to mean 'and other things' has been criticized, as has its use in expository prose. Such uses are often facetious, playing on the scholarly connotations of *et al.* When no humour is intended, *etc.* can be substituted.

> On the broader scale, Hannah grapples with the usual [Woody] Allen issues—love, death, the perfect pastrami sandwich et al.
> *Gazette* (Montreal) 4 March 1989: T3

(Here *et al.* is used facetiously.)

See also ETC.; LATIN PHRASES.

etc. *Etc.* (pronounced *et SET er ab*) is an abbreviation of the Latin phrase *et cetera*, which means 'and other things'. It is wholly integrated into English, where its meanings include 'and so on', 'and the rest', 'and the like'. *Etc.* generally occurs at the end of a list where the next items are obvious; it allows the writer to avoid boring the reader with too much detail. One valuable point stressed by many guides is that readers should have no trouble deciding what *etc.* is intended to stand for: it should not be used evasively to avoid giving necessary information.

Strunk and White, in their influential guide *The Elements of Style*, summarize the opinion of many commentators: 'In formal writing, *etc.* is a misfit.' But in fact *etc.* is used far more often in academic prose than in magazines and newspapers; there is no need to avoid it in formal writing.

Because the Latin phrase refers to things, not people, some commentators suggest that it should not be used at the end of a list of people, where they prefer 'and others' or even *et al.* However, Canadian writers treat *etc.* as an English word and cannot be expected to use it only in its Latin sense.

In the past, some major style guides have insisted that *etc.* be preceded by a comma and, if the sentence continues, followed by one too. Generally, Canadian writers do put commas around *etc.*, although sometimes the second one is omitted. In any case, some style guides have dropped this rule, following a trend to less punctuation generally.

The practice of using an ampersand to replace *et* ('and')—*&c*—has all but disappeared. *Etc.* need not be italicized.

> The Corporation was to provide and to manage the common services (finance, personnel, security, etc.) of all the museums; the four museum directors were to direct the museum functions (collection, conservation, documentation, exhibition, etc.) in their respective museums.
> *Queen's Quarterly* 94.3 (1987): 556

> Have you had a recent or chronic or major ailment, especially rheumatoid arthritis, anemia, emotional stress that required medications etc.?
> *Globe and Mail* (Toronto) 5 Feb. 1985: F5

(Here *etc.* is ambiguous; depending on which meaning is intended, 'or other treatment' should follow *stress* or 'or other treatment' should follow *medications*.)

> He assumes another Canadian tradition, which he thinks of as the other 'half' and which he sees as consisting of people like Richardson, Leacock, MacLennan, Lampman, Livesay, Marriott, Mitchell, Haliburton, Callaghan, etc.
> Margaret Atwood *Second Words* 1982: 146

(Here Atwood uses *etc.* at the end of a list of people.)

See also AMPERSAND; ET AL.

ethics, ethical *Ethics* meaning the study and philosophy of moral conduct takes a singular verb: 'Ethics is taught to business students'. *Ethics* as a personal or professional code of conduct takes a plural verb: 'Her professional ethics were impeccable'. *Ethic* also may appear as a singular noun, as in the phrase 'Protestant work ethic'. The established form of the adjective is *ethical*, not *ethic*.

etymology, entomology *Etymology* is the study of word origins and derivations; *entomology* is the study of insects.

Many arguments about the 'correct' meaning and use of disputed words and expressions are based on etymology. The arguments about words derived from Classical Greek and Latin have been particularly bitter. Since knowledge of these languages was until recently the sign of an educated gentleman, in the past the appeal to etymology often succeeded—at least until the gap between the 'original' sense of the word and established English usage became too large. Now English is spoken and written mostly by people who have never studied the Classical languages, and these arguments cannot be expected to prevail over the actual usage of educated people. For more about these arguments, see ALTER EGO; ANTAGONIST, PROTAGONIST; COMMISERATE; DECIMATE; ET AL.; ETC.; INTERNECINE; KUDOS; SUPERIOR, SENIOR, INFERIOR, JUNIOR, MAJOR, MINOR.

> Jeanne d'Arc's monicker, La Pucelle, bears no relationship to a flea, either etymologically or entomologically, so his flea-bitten argument about fumigation doesn't wash.
> *Globe and Mail* (Toronto) 10 July 1985: P7

> The latest version [of the Oxford English Dictionary] took 31 years to update and will include 290,500 main words, their etymologies and about 2.4 million quotations illustrating shades of meaning and differing usage.
> *Maclean's* 20 Feb. 1989: A9

See also BACK-FORMATION; FOLK ETYMOLOGY.

eulogy   see ELEGY

euphemism   A *euphemism* is a polite or socially acceptable way of saying something that might be disagreeable or offensive if stated directly. Not surprisingly, English-speakers have developed roundabout or more palatable terms for many things felt to be taboo, terrifying, or disgusting, especially in matters of sex, death, and bodily functions. Euphemisms range from the tactful to the dishonest. An abiding Victorian concern for propriety remains in such terms as *washroom, bathroom*, and *comfort station*, euphemisms for *toilet* (itself originally a euphemism). Euphemisms for all manner of sexual matters abound: *making love, having a good time, swinging, cruising*. The common euphemism for *die* is *pass away*.

Most insidious are those euphemisms that attempt to obscure or deny the reality they pretend to describe. Government, military, and business are the greatest offenders, producing such euphemisms as *strategic misrepresentation* for lying; *destabilize* for wage war against; *collateral damage* for civilian deaths in an act of war; *net profits revenue deficiency* for a business loss; and *adult books/movies* for pornography.

The extent to which a particular euphemism is employed is more a matter of taste or ethics than usage. In general, however, honest and responsible writers will use euphemisms only to avoid unnecessarily blunt terms.

> High-density suburb is a euphemism for the dusty, boxhouse, all-black townships skirting the formerly all-white residential preserves—the low-density suburbs—of the lush, gardened inner city.
> *Globe and Mail* (Toronto) 14 Jan. 1985: B12

> Managed trade is a euphemism for a system in which open, competitive trading arrangements are replaced by agreements between governments to restrict and confine trade flows.
> *Globe and Mail* (Toronto) 3 May 1985: B2

> They are summoned to sessions of political 're-education.' Sometimes they are beaten, sometimes imprisoned. Sometimes they disappear.
> *Gazette* (Montreal) 5 March 1989: B5

> (Here the quotation marks around 're-education' mark it as a euphemism for mental and physical harassment and torture.)

evacuate   To *evacuate* a building, area, cavity, or bodily organ is to empty it. *Evacuate* also means remove, as in 'Evacuate the gases from the flask'. The most recent meaning of *evacuate* is to remove people to safety, as in 'Dozens of residents were evacuated from the area'. Wags who resisted the introduction of this newer meaning suggested that evacuating (i.e., emptying) people would be a very messy business. However, moving people to safety has been a standard meaning since the Second World War.

> Unfortunately the drainage system is just under the roofing membrane and there is no way to evacuate water which accumulates underneath or is absorbed by the insulation.
> *Gazette* (Montreal) 2 March 1989: F2

> A Soviet official said last year Chernobyl could cause an additional 1,000-2,000 deaths from cancer among the over 100,000 citizens evacuated from near the station.
> *Chronicle-Herald* (Halifax) 14 May 1988: 28-C

ever   The use of *ever* is sometimes criticized as redundant in phrases such as *barely ever, hardly ever, rarely ever*, and *seldom ever*. True, 'They rarely ever arrive on time' means the same as 'They rarely arrive on time'. But the use of *ever* for emphasis in expressions of frequency has been solidly established over hundreds of years of English usage. Canadian writers use it this way in all kinds of writing.

> The truth of the matter is that there is a very ample storehouse of integrity with the business that barely ever rates a media mention.
> *Financial Post* 18 May 1990: 19

> Another reason, of course, is that our English departments rarely teach much about modern English and hardly ever require their students to know anything about it.
> W.C. Lougheed, ed. *In Search of the Standard in Canadian English* 1986: 153

> 'So he was doing what Robinette rarely ever had to do.'
> Jack Batten *Robinette* 1984: 147

See also RARELY EVER; SELDOM EVER.

every   The adjective *every* precedes a singular noun and is used with a singular verb: 'Every dog has its day'. The use of a plural verb, as in 'Every one of her pay cheques go straight into the bank', is considered non-standard by most commentators. Regarding the use of *every* with the plural pronoun *their*, see EVERYONE.

See also AGREEMENT, GRAMMATICAL; BETWEEN EACH, BETWEEN EVERY; EACH AND EVERY; EVERYONE.

everybody   see EVERYONE

everyday, every day   *Everyday* is an adjective meaning typical, ordinary, or daily, as in 'everyday events' or 'everyday clothing'. In the phrase *every day*, *every* can be replaced by *each*: 'She visited him every (each) day'; 'Every (each) day he waited for her to arrive'. Where *each* does not make sense, as in 'Their meetings became an each day occurrence', the single-word spelling, *everyday*, should be used.

> There's a third set of dishes for everyday [use], which her parents bought themselves, oven-to-table stoneware.
> Margaret Atwood *Life Before Man* 1979: 175

> Breakfasts could include everyday fare such as instant oatmeal, individually-boxed cereal and pancakes from pre-made batter.
> *Leisure Life* May 1988: 62

> Students are curious about the language they hear every day.
> W.C. Lougheed, ed. *In Search of the Standard in Canadian English* 1986: 83

> If you look at newspaper headlines every day for a month, or carefully watch the various reports in the national television news, you will very quickly learn what Canadians perceive to be their major priorities.
> *Queen's Quarterly* 93 (1986): 86

> In fact violence against women is taking place everyday in this way.
> *Fuse Magazine* 13.4 (1990): 24

(Here the two-word form *every day* is called for.)

> Here in Yellowknife for another meeting with the chiefs, we go over to Dettah village everyday by bus to meet.
> *News North* (Yellowknife) 26 Feb. 1990: A7

(Here again, *every day* is required.)

> The Nomad is not one of your average, every day wading jackets, which normally rely on either wax (as in Barbour garments) or a microporous film (such as Goretex) to protect the wearer against rain.
> *Atlantic Salmon Journal* Autumn 1990: 35

(The adjective *everyday* is needed here.)

everyone, everybody   *They* and *their* are the pronouns most commonly used with the indefinite pronouns *everyone*, *everybody*, *anyone*, *anybody*, *someone*, *somebody*, and *no one*, *nobody* ('Everyone does just what they like'; 'Everybody has their problems'), as well as singular nouns modified by adjectives such as *any*, *each*, *every*, and *no* ('Every listener has their favourite show'). Although the following comments focus on *everyone*, they apply to all constructions of this kind.

Everyone...they constructions can be found as early as 1530. However, eighteenth-century grammarians decided that it was incorrect. *Everyone*, they said, is a singular pronoun. The verb that follows it is always singular (*does* and *has*, not *do* and *have*, in the examples above), and any pronoun replacing it should be singular. Thus *they* and *their* were rejected and *he* and *his* approved for use with *everyone*: 'Everyone does just what he likes'; 'Everybody has his problems'. Though *he* and *his* are masculine pronouns, they were to be understood to refer to women as well. This usage became standard in formal writing.

For the most part, however, people went on using *they* and *their*. One reason is that *everybody* and *everyone*, though grammatically singular (as evidenced by the singular verbs they take), are notionally plural: that is, these words do not refer to one person, but to people in general. As the *Dictionary of Contemporary American Usage* points out, it is often impossible to use the approved pronoun *he* with *everyone* when the two words are in separate clauses. 'Everyone was at risk, as I tried to tell him' means something quite different from 'Everyone was at risk, as I tried to tell them'.

Another reason *everyone* continued to be used with *they* and *their* is that *they* is gender-neutral, applying equally to men and women. The notion that 'Everyone . . . he' could refer to women always seemed artificial to some people, and today many would label the usage sexist. For this reason most contemporary usage guides approve of the use of *they* and *their* with *everyone*, at least in speech and informal writing. However, they evade the question of what to do in formal writing. There are many people who still consider the use of *their* with *everyone* unsuitable in formal writing. While it is possible to replace 'everyone . . . his' with 'everyone . . . his or her' (*or* 'his/her'), even handbooks of non-sexist usage generally note that this solution is awkward. Thus they suggest rephrasing the sentence. Often *their* can be omitted with little damage to the sense: 'Everyone has problems' instead of 'Everyone has their problems'. Alternatively, it may be possible to replace *everyone* with a plural noun or pronoun: 'We all have our problems'; 'Students do just what they like'. Eventually, one hopes, 'everyone . . . their' will regain its good standing in all levels of writing, and evasive tactics such as these will be unnecessary.

Interestingly, Robertson Davies uses the *everyone . . . they* construction when the notion expressed by *everyone* is plural, and *everyone . . . he* when it is singular (see examples below). Perhaps the example of an eminent writer will convert those who feel that *everyone . . . they* has no place in formal writing.

St. Vincent's School would like to thank everyone for their work, interest and presence at the fair.
Chronicle-Telegraph (Quebec City) 22 May 1991: 9

(In speech and informal writing, *everyone . . . their* is accepted.)

That is the ingenious premise for *Hook*, director Steven Spielberg's $79-million attempt to give everybody everything they have always wanted for Christmas: magic.
Maclean's 16 Dec. 1991: A64

'You haven't spoken and treated everybody in such a manner as to convince them that you are now going to do the job.'
Financial Post 9 Dec. 1991: 1

The pragmatic socialism of Turati had produced nothing and everyone was in a position to judge for himself whether the man in Moscow or the man in Milan had contributed more in terms of socialist literature and revolutionary theory.
Canadian Journal of History 14.1 (1989): 28

(Though once approved, the use of *him* or, as here, *himself* with *everyone* is now criticized as sexist.)

Teach everybody to read, and they will read what appeals to them, what accords with their experience and ideal of life.
Robertson Davies *A Voice from the Attic* 1960: 24

(Here the notion expressed by *everybody* is plural. Since the emphasis is on what will happen when many people learn to read, Davies uses *they*.)

I struggled, as must everyone who concerns himself with this matter, with the question of nomenclature.
Robertson Davies *A Voice from the Attic* 1960: 274

(Here the notion expressed by *everyone* is singular. Imagining people struggling with this question one by one, Davies uses *himself*.)

See also AGREEMENT, GRAMMATICAL; ANY; EACH; SEXIST LANGUAGE.

everyplace, everywhere   see -WHERE, -PLACE

evidence, testimony, affidavit, proof   *Evidence* is the general term for anything that points towards the truth or falsity of something. In a court of law, testimony, test results, and objects could all be presented in evidence.

In general use, *testimony* is anything said or done that demonstrates something: 'It was (a) testimony to his good nature'. In law, *testimony* is a written or oral statement made by a witness.

An *affidavit* is a sworn document that may be used as testimony in court if the testifier cannot appear in person; affidavits are used, for example, to attest to a defendant's alibi or good character.

Proof is evidence that leaves no room for doubt. Legally, it is what permits a judgment 'beyond a reasonable doubt' in criminal cases, and 'on a balance of probabilities' in civil cases.

In disputes before the courts, written evidence of a contract will aid the judge in determining what the terms are and in resolving a conflict of testimony by the parties, each with a different recollection of the contract.
J.E. Smyth et al. *The Law and Business Administration in Canada* 1987: 245

In his written complaint, Mr. Cornblum noted contradictions between Mr. Greenberg's testimony and information contained in building records.
Globe and Mail (Toronto) 4 Jan. 1985: M6

... scientific proof of the creation of the universe out of nothingness faces some formidable problems—not the least of which being that no one knows what to look for to test the theory. ...
Globe and Mail (Toronto) 21 Jan. 1985: P12

If the creditors present convincing proof of the insolvency of their debtor, the court adjudges him bankrupt and appoints a licensed trustee to take charge of his property.
J.E. Smyth et al. *The Law and Business Administration in Canada* 1987: 300

evoke, invoke, evince   To *evoke* is to call forth something, such as an emotion, a memory, or a response, while to *invoke* is to call upon something, usually a higher power or authority. Thus anger or nostalgia is evoked; God or a law is invoked. To *evince* something is to reveal or demonstrate it: 'Her performance evinced an ability to deal with conflict'.

Even though the first criticisms ... evoked anger, the novel [*Maria Chapdelaine*] had many imitators. ...
Ben-Z. Shek *French-Canadian & Québécois Novels* 1991: 19

Cooke invoked rules the NDP wrote to limit debate on government laws.
Toronto Sun 26 Oct. 1992: 42

He ... then plunged into an argument that centred on the 'constitutional convention' which the provinces had evoked.
Jack Batten *Robinette* 1984: 235

(The word required here, in the context of appealing to a legal precedent or other authority, is *invoke*.)

It has been asserted by solemn scholars that the unappeasable appetite for puns which the Victorians evinced ... was the dawn of a literary theater, the pun being essentially a literary device.
Robertson Davies *A Voice from the Attic* 1960: 180

The quick costume change is an old theatre trick. Nevertheless, it evinced gasps and applause from the capacity audience.
Globe and Mail (Toronto) 21 Feb. 1985: E3

(The word required here is *evoked*, meaning called forth.)

Iranian officials have begun talking of establishing a terminal outside the Strait of Hormuz. ... Thus far, the idea has yet to evince much enthusiasm in the marine insurance community.
Globe and Mail (Toronto) 4 Feb. 1985: B13

(The word required here is *evoke* or *inspire*.)

ex-   see EXH-

exacerbate   The historical meaning of *exacerbate* is to embitter. Although several critics still decry the more general sense, 'to make worse', it is now common in all varieties of writing and attested in most dictionaries.

As the tensions within the quintet grew, they were exacerbated by Parker's erratic behavior, which caused all the members grief.
Jack Chambers *Milestones* 1983: 83

The Canada Council's actions have exacerbated the shortage of talented curators in the institutions.
Queen's Quarterly 94.2 (1987): 557

(Here *exacerbated* means made worse.)

exacting, exact   An *exacting* task requires considerable effort and attention to details; an *exacting* employer is demanding and hard to please; and an *exact* measurement is accurate. The emphasis in the adjective *exacting* is on the demands made and the effort required; *exact* simply means correct and precise. To *exact* something from someone is to demand and obtain it.

Any surgeon may attempt cosmetic surgery but only plastic surgeons are trained in the technically exacting operations.
Globe and Mail (Toronto) 26 July 1985: P74

He could not provide exact numbers.
Calgary Herald 21 Dec. 1993: D6

... the day he found Evelyn slumped over the peonies she was planting in the front yard ... [was] a day he could describe in exacting detail right down to the interior colors of the ambulance. ...
Ottawa Citizen 24 Dec. 1990: A14

(The word required here is *exact*.)

Sequential releasing was formerly worked out on exacting charts, timing the availability of films from the first-run theatre showings to airline use, small-town distribution, 16mm rental to schools, free television and so on.
Globe and Mail (Toronto) 9 Sept. 1985: S12

(Here 'worked out *exactly* on charts' would make better sense.)

[The military] exacted a price in regimentation, but it offered ... the promise of advancement, a secure job and a decent living wage, even for the lower ranks.
Vancouver Sun 11 Feb. 1995: A1

The ordeal has exacted a toll from [his] family.
Calgary Herald 14 Jan. 1995: A1

See also EXACT SAME.

exact same   Many usage guides note that *exact* is not an adverb and thus should not be used to modify the adjective *same* in the phrase *exact same*. However, *exact same* is idiomatic and accepted in conversation and informal writing. In formal writing *exactly the same* should be used.

It is sometimes unnerving, though, that my father and I are in almost the exact same field, and there is this slight, subliminal competition going on as to whether people will think of me as David Helwig's daughter, or him as Maggie Helwig's father.
Ottawa Citizen 20 Oct. 1990: B7

My gripe is city transit buses that pull out at the exact same time as they signal—regardless of whether or not there are cars in the lane beside them.
Province (Vancouver) 30 Dec. 1990: 17

Two winters ago, a saw-whet owl used this exact same perch daily for several months.
Vancouver Sun 17 Feb. 1990: A13

See also EXACTING, EXACT.

exalt, exalted, exaltation   see EXULT

exceptionable   see UNEXCEPTIONABLE

excise   To *excise* is to cut out. *Excise* or *excise tax* is a tax or duty levied on goods produced within the country. Sometimes these words are misspelled *exise*.

In her will, however, she stipulated that this reference be excised in all subsequent printings, and this was done.
Ben-Z. Shek *French-Canadian & Québécois Novels* 1991: 31

In the case of gasoline and beer, for instance, existing excise taxes will be removed, leaving consumer prices unaffected.
Vancouver Sun 14 Dec. 1990: D6

The current 13.5 per cent federal sales tax on Canadian manufactured goods is matched by customs and exise taxes on imports.
Vancouver Sun 26 Sept. 1990: C2

(The correct spelling is *excise*.)

See also TAX.

exclamation mark   The exclamation mark (called an exclamation point in the United States) should be used sparingly in serious writing. An exclamation mark cannot bolster a weak argument or add force to a sentence that lacks it. This is the usual advice given in writing guides.

For some writers, however, overuse is not the problem. For fear of seeming unsophisticated, they have banished the exclamation mark from their writing, with the result that their readers may be puzzled by the tone of an utterance such as 'How the responsibility weighed on him'. Unless this is part of a title ('How the Responsibility Weighed on Him and Led to his Premature Demise'), it requires an exclamation mark: 'How the responsibility weighed on him!' Sentences that begin with *how*, *what*, or *why* and are not questions are always exclamations: 'How tall you've grown!'; 'Why there you are!'; 'What a mistake that was!' Occasionally, sentences in question form may also be exclamations; when 'What did you say?' is an expression of astonishment or a threat, it should be punctuated with an exclamation mark: 'What did you say!' Interjections, such as *hey*, *hi*, *oh*, or *oops*, should be followed by an exclamation mark if they are said in excitement ('Hey! Get out of there!), by a comma ('Oh, soon, I think') if they are not. Though exclamations are often incomplete sentences, they are not considered ungrammatical: 'If only I'd known!'; 'To think that you were there the whole time!'; 'If it isn't Rob!'

True exclamations can be recognized by their tone. In informal writing, the exclamation mark often tags the content of a non-exclamatory sentence as notable or interesting: 'Bob will be sending Melinda in his place!'; 'One of them was issued in 1944!' This use of the exclamation mark as a graphic equivalent of 'Interesting, eh?' is not suitable for formal writing. It is probably this use that writing guides are trying to forestall when they advise using the exclamation mark sparingly.

Double exclamation marks, strings of exclamation marks, and exclamation marks combined with question marks are found in journalism but never used in formal writing.

The disquietude has even begun to awaken moral philosophers from the dogmatic slumbers of our moral anthropocentrism. A good thing that!
Queen's Quarterly 92.1 (1985): 209

(An exclamation mark is the appropriate punctuation here and should not be avoided because the context is formal.)

'What a prodigious task!'
W.C. Lougheed, ed. *In Search of the Standard in Canadian English* 1986: 66

Just the other day I was looking through a box of old souvenirs from my childhood and I spotted some old hockey card wrappers from the mid-1970s and noticed in those days packs sold for 15 cents!
Evening Telegram (St. John's) 25 May 1993: 13

(This use of the exclamation mark is informal.)

Your television can now remind you of important dates, watch the baby in another room, and deliver programs in two languages at once!
Canadian Consumer Jan. 1986: 27

(This use of the exclamation mark is informal.)

See you all there!!!
Chronicle-Telegraph (Quebec City) 6 June 1991: 3

(Using more than one exclamation mark is informal.)

What do you mean it probably will happen to my daughter!?
Evening Telegram (St. John's) 23 May 1993: 15

(Combining a question mark and an exclamation mark is informal.)

See also QUOTATION, QUOTATION MARKS.

exemplar   see EPITOME

exh-, ex-   When the letter *h* follows the prefix *ex-* it is silent. *Exhibition, exhilarating,* and *exhort* are often misspelled without *h*, while *exorbitant, exonerate,* and *exuberant* are often misspelled with an *h* after the prefix *ex-*.
   Related words may be helpful in remembering which of these words contain *h*. Spelled with an *h* are *exhibition,* like *inhibition*; *exhilarating,* like *hilarious*; and *exhort,* like *hortatory*. Spelled without an *h* are *exorbitant,* like *orbit*; *exonerate,* like *onerous*; and *exuberant,* which is related to the Latin word *uber,* 'fruitful', and the English word *udder.*

Galerie Old Chelsea ... March 6-14, Solo exibition by gallery member.
Ottawa Citizen 29 Aug. 1992: L18

(The correct spelling is *exhibition.*)

[Their] exilerating music can be described as sea-shanty style traditionals with a contemporary, often jazzy spin.
Province (Vancouver) 5 Nov. 1990: 2

(The correct spelling is *exhilarating.*)

Shannon, attracted by Cruise's too perfect and sculpted exterior, arrives at his window via a ladder to exort him to accompany her to America.
Calgary Herald 22 May 1992: E2

(The correct spelling is *exhort.*)

Network ratings are dwindling and TV executives are re-examining the boomtime priorities that convinced them to pay exhorbitant sums for sports programming.
Vancouver Sun 15 Dec. 1992: D7

(The correct spelling is *exorbitant.*)

'Our position has been very clear from the beginning and we're sure that in due time we'll be exhonerated and justice will be done.'
Vancouver Sun 17 May 1990: A10

(The correct spelling is *exonerated.*)

'I don't think anyone expected me to do that, including myself,' an exhuberant Wallach said afterwards.
Calgary Herald 9 July 1992: F4

(The correct spelling is *exuberant.*)

exhaustive, exhausting   *Exhaustive,* which means comprehensive or very thorough, is often confused with *exhausting,* which means very tiring.

'The body remained unidentified for 19 years despite an exhaustive investigation.'
Vancouver Sun 18 Dec. 1993: B6

'We're gonna get cured of all our ills,' Graham Parker promised the faithful about 100 minutes into Tuesday night's exhausting rock 'n' roll marathon.
Gazette (Montreal) 22 March 1990: D13

Add in a demented Pole named Wojtek Dmochowski doing exhaustive calisthenics to the songs and you've got your full concert experience.
Gazette (Montreal) 15 Nov. 1990: C1

(Here *exhausting* would be a better choice.)

Although the officials with the B.C. Coroner's Service declined to comment at the finale of the Cindy James inquest, privately they have stated the case was the most bizarre and exhaustive they have encountered.
Vancouver Sun 29 May 1990: B3

(If the sense intended was that the case was very taxing, the correct word would be *exhausting.*)

exhibition, exhilarating, exhort   see EXH-, EX-

exile   see ÉMIGRÉ

exist see SUBSIST

exonerate, exorbitant see EXH-, EX-

exotic, esoteric, exoteric *Exotic* once meant simply foreign, not native. Today, in botany and zoology, *exotic* still means simply not indigenous, but in general use it means strange or unusual, often in a fascinating or beautiful way. *Exotic dancer* is usually a euphemism for stripper.

Esoteric and *exoteric* were originally used to refer to disciples in the Greco-Roman world. The master shared his deepest thoughts with the 'inner circle' of *esoteric* disciples. The *exoteric* disciples were the large group who were given only general knowledge. *Exoteric*, meaning capable of being understood by a general audience, is now rare, but *esoteric*, meaning comprehensible only to those with special knowledge, is fairly common.

More exotic plant species were relegated to conservatories and botanical exhibits.
Canadian Consumer Jan. 1986: 13

A reference work of this kind is meant to be used selectively. Some entries require thorough study, others should be read for the factual information they provide, and a few will prove to be too esoteric for the general reader's interest.
Queen's Quarterly 92.2 (1985): 403

But another Hechler contribution to today's collections is the quantity of elaborate and attractive envelopes he prepared in his flowing handwriting. These covers, to and from many esoteric destinations, now grace some of the best collections.
Globe and Mail (Toronto) 26 Jan. 1985: CL16

(The word required here is *exotic*.)

expatriate see ÉMIGRÉ

expect The use of *expect* to mean suppose or guess, as in 'I expect I will', is labelled informal in most dictionaries. Yet it's common in fairly formal Canadian writing. Perhaps it could be more accurately described as having a conversational tone.

When they cut Mary Webster down the next day, she was, to everyone's surprise, not dead. . . . I expect that if everyone thought she had occult powers before the hanging, they were even more convinced of it afterwards.
Margaret Atwood *Second Words* 1982: 331

'I expect you'd like some breakfast too.' She didn't wait for an answer.
David Williams *Eye of the Father* 1985: 43

I expect you are all familiar with the real significance of the symbol of Aquarius.
Robertson Davies *One Half of Robertson Davies* 1978: 59

See also ANTICIPATE.

expedient see EXPEDITIOUS

expedite, [expediate] To *expedite* means to hasten or streamline a process; this word is often used with reference to bureaucratic or legal procedures. *Expediate* is a non-standard variant, probably influenced by *expedient*. The *OED* records *expediate* as a persistent error; current dictionaries do not list it at all. Though it is not accepted as a word, *expediate* does appear in print occasionally.

Accordingly, once the war was over, Principal Wallace did everything he could, by way of negotiation and pressure, to expedite the discharge of Queen's staff members from the armed services. . . .
Frederick Gibson *Queen's University* 2 (1983): 244

Terrace reveals Plan B, a possible OMB hearing swap with another party to expediate rezoning farmland for an arena.
Ottawa Citizen 7 Dec. 1990: C4

(The correct spelling is *expedite*.)

See also EXPEDITIOUS, EXPEDIENT.

expeditious, expedient An *expeditious* manner of proceeding is speedy and efficient. An *expedient* course of action serves the purpose well, though it may be morally questionable.

'Funding considerations are not a legitimate reason for [court] cases not being dealt with in an expeditious fashion,' Hall said.
Calgary Herald 5 Nov. 1994: A9

But the darker side of the North, the bureaucratic decisions made in the 1950s to transport Inuit from their homelands farther north as an expedient way of claiming territory for Canada, isn't mentioned.
Ottawa Citizen 31 Oct. 1993: C6

More important it is a party that has lost the confidence of the Canadian people—and not even the judicious, politically expeditious removal of former leader Kim Campbell will restore that confidence.
Calgary Herald 19 Dec. 1993: A6

(The expression *politically expeditious*—politically speedy—doesn't make sense. If the author did mean to emphasize speed, *expeditious* by itself would be better; otherwise the word required is *expedient*.)

See also EXPEDITE.

explicit   see IMPLICIT

exploitive, exploitative   These variants are equally acceptable and about equally popular in Canadian English.

ex post facto   *Ex post facto* is a Latin phrase meaning 'after the fact'. An '*ex post facto* analysis' benefits from hindsight; Canadian criminal laws are not enforced *ex post facto*—that is, retroactively. This phrase requires italics in formal writing.

See also LATIN PHRASES.

expresso   see ESPRESSO

expressway   see ROAD

extemporaneous, impromptu   Both words mean without preparation. An unrehearsed comment or performance may be called either *extemporaneous* or *impromptu*. A spontaneous action is usually *impromptu*: 'an impromptu visit'. In the context of formal public speaking, an *extemporaneous* speech has received some preparatory attention but is delivered without notes and has not been memorized. An *impromptu* speech is spontaneous, completely unpremeditated.

Davis ... and Hank Jones, a superior accompanist who plays beautifully throughout this session, fashion a long, apparently extemporaneous movement at the end of *Autumn Leaves*....
Jack Chambers *Milestones* 1983: 275–6

... Esposito is remembered for his remarkable all-round play, for being the emotional heart of his team, the man who made a poignant impromptu speech to the nation on TV after the crushing fourth-game defeat in Vancouver.
Ken Dryden *The Game* 1983: 103

See also EXTEMPORIZE.

extemporize, temporize   To *extemporize* is to speak off the cuff, to improvise; to *temporize* is to stall or delay purposely.

'Julia Duffy comes in every day with the script totally memorized.... And so does David—of course David is more apt to extemporize, or improvise.'
Vancouver Sun 23 July 1994: A13

Their temporizing and backsliding have disappointed many of their supporters....
Toronto Star 4 June 1994: B4

See also EXTEMPORANEOUS.

extort, extract   see ELICIT

exuberant   see EXH-, EX-

exult, exultant, exalt, exalted, exultation, exaltation   To *exult* is to rejoice (you feel *exultant*). To *exalt* is to raise someone in status (so that he or she enjoys an *exalted* rank) or to fill someone with joy (then he or she is, or feels, *exalted*.) *Exultation* and *exaltation* both suggest rejoicing and elation, but only *exaltation* refers to spiritual uplifting or an elevation of status.

'With one second left, we got a goal,' exulted Ray Diabo.
Gazette (Montreal) 22 Nov. 1992: D1

But beneath the tumbling quiff of hair and behind the guarded amused eyes, [k.d.] Lang is exultant.
Calgary Herald 19 June 1993: D5

... we remain a society which exalts lawyers and looks down on the people who know how to run your basic laser-powered widget buster.
Gazette (Montreal) 16 March 1993: A3

Yet until recently, the exalted critical status of [Bruno Bettelheim's] The Uses of Enchantment had gone virtually unchallenged.
Gazette (Montreal) 6 June 1992: J1

'He said he would be back, he said he would play again and he said he would get drafted,' exalted Jackie Marshall.... 'And he's done it!'
Daily News (Halifax) 21 June 1992: 64

(The word required here is *exulted*.)

Hamilton coach Don Sutherin wasn't going to ruin his feelings of exultation by pondering Hamilton's tenuous playoff situation.
Edmonton Journal 17 Oct. 1994: D2

Delacroix's Liberty Leading the People shows us the exaltation of righteous struggle.
Gazette (Montreal) 30 April 1994: A1

Hollywood, in David Gurr's eyes, is the exultation of the average.
Calgary Herald 16 April 1994: B11

(The word required here is *exaltation*, meaning glorification.)

eye dialect   see [COULD OF]

F

-f, -v- A small group of nouns that end with *f* or with *f* followed by a silent *e* (e.g., *knife*) form their plurals in *-ves*: *calf, calves; elf, elves; half, halves; knife, knives; leaf, leaves; life, lives; loaf, loaves; self, selves; sheaf, sheaves; shelf, shelves; thief, thieves; wife, wives; wolf, wolves.* However, many similar words are pluralized in the regular way, simply by adding *s*: *beliefs, carafes, chiefs, handkerchiefs, proofs, roofs, safes, skiffs, staffs.* For a few words, either an *-s* or a *-ves* plural is accepted: *cloverleaf* (the highway junction), *dwarf, hoof, scarf, wharf.*

Generally, new coinages and compounds are pluralized regularly: for example, *low-lifes.* Paintings of flowers and fruit are called *still lifes.* And Toronto's National Hockey League team is called the *Maple Leafs,* which may account for Canadian writers' tendency to use the unacceptable plural *leafs* for the parts of a plant or the pages in a book.

Once you get a puzzle piece, bring it to the office tower atrium at Harbor Centre, where one of Santa's friendly elfs will fit your puzzle piece into a gigantic jigsaw puzzle.
Province (Vancouver) 7 Dec. 1990: 16

(The accepted plural is *elves*.)

But don't think that just because your cereal box shows sheafs of grain and a wholesome farm-family background, what's in it is healthy.
Ottawa Citizen 14 Feb. 1990: C1

(The accepted plural is *sheaves*.)

Torontonians Valdine MacLeod and her husband Norman lugged two plastic shopping bags filled with Canadian first editions to the reading, hoping the writers would find time to lay their John Hancocks ... on the front leafs.
Globe and Mail (Toronto) 8 May 1985: P19

(The accepted plural is *leaves*.)

In more remote regions we sit under thatched roofs and eat off banana leafs with our fingers.
Globe and Mail (Toronto) 6 March 1985: SB1

(Perhaps the presence of the regular plural *roofs* here influenced the writer; the only accepted plural for this sense of *leaf* is *leaves*.)

See also MAPLE LEAF; -SELF, -SELVES.

facile *Facile* usually has negative connotations: a facile remark is glib, a facile argument superficial, and a facile emotion shallow. Occasionally *facile* is used in the positive sense of smooth or easy. The pronunciation is *FASS ill.*

Yet this is not to say that Gallant is a dishonest writer, a superficial or facile spinner of verbal webs.
Janice Kulyk Keefer *Reading Mavis Gallant* 1989: 58

Lawren Harris makes it clear that what drove him and his colleagues out to the northern part of Canada was their distrust of the 'picturesque,' that is, the pictorial subject which suggests a facile or conventional pictorial response.
Northrop Frye *The Bush Garden* 1971: 209

... Davis was asleep on the floor, completely unaware of Gillespie's facile manipulation of the trumpet part that had stumped him.
Jack Chambers *Milestones* 1983: 41

(Here *facile* is used in a positive sense.)

facilitate, facilitator To *facilitate* means to help or ease. Several commentators note that things and actions, not people, are facilitated: 'The work of the cook was facilitated by the new microwave oven', *not* 'The cook was facilitated by the new microwave oven'.

In the jargon of social work, a *facilitator* is a person who chairs a meeting or leads a group through a workshop. The Quebec English equivalent is *animator.* Thus the verb *facilitate* has developed a new meaning: to lead a group through a meeting.

facility *Facilities* are premises, equipment, or services tailored to a particular purpose: 'conference facilities', 'storage facilities'. Some usage guides object to the use of the word *facility* where a more common or precise word exists: for example, 'educational facility' instead of 'school', or 'correctional facility' instead of 'prison'. While *facility* is sometimes used euphemistically or to exaggerate the importance of a structure, it is also used appropriately when there is no common word for what is being described.

> Like the first, most of which was shot at Toronto's former Queen Street mental health facility, it will be filmed in Toronto.
> *Globe and Mail* (Toronto) 11 Jan. 1985: E7

(Here *mental health facility* is a euphemism for *psychiatric hospital*.)

> He said if he ever had a few million dollars to spare he'd love to build an indoor facility with 12 basketball courts.
> *Globe and Mail* (Toronto) 15 Nov. 1985: D20

(Although the proposed *indoor facility* is a *gym*, the word *gym* would not have suggested the intended size.)

facsimile   see FAX

fact   see FACT THAT; TRUE FACTS

factious, fractious, factitious   Someone who is *factious* (pronounced *FACK shuss*) causes strife by showing loyalty to a faction: a small group within a larger group. Groups with factious members are faction-ridden and frequently engage in factional disputes. *Fractious* (pronounced *FRACK shuss*) means unruly or irritable; since those who are *factious* are often *fractious* as well, these terms are sometimes confused.

The adjective *factitious* (pronounced *fack TISH us*) refers to something that is artificial or contrived.

> Supporting the Americans against Lord North, he still reflected that opposition to the war came from factious politicians.
> J.A.W. Gunn *Beyond Liberty and Property* 1983: 207

> The ever-popular Something True, a French filly with an attitude problem, was fractious at the gate and delayed the start of the race....
> *Canadian Thoroughbred* Jan. 1989: 29

> ... it may seem to some readers that I have raked over a handful of forgotten, or almost forgotten, books of the past century, attributing to them a factitious significance by reading into them what is not there.
> Robertson Davies *A Voice from the Attic* 1960: 152

> Giving a report on a conference working group on the mutual development of the East Coast's fisheries, Mr. MacLean said the industry is fractious and 'there are four serious splinter groups in New England.'
> *Globe and Mail* (Toronto) 19 June 1985: P5

(The word required here is *factious*.)

> As Western Europe continues to integrate, large chunks of Eastern Europe are rapidly disintegrating. Yugoslavia remains mired in a bloody civil war and the former Soviet Union is dissolving into fractious republics.
> *Financial Post* 30 Dec. 1991: 36

(The contrast with an integrating Europe suggest that *factious* is meant here, although either word is possible.)

See also FICTIVE, FICTIONAL, FICTITIOUS.

fact that, the   Phrases containing *the fact that* are almost universally condemned by usage experts on the grounds of wordiness. They recommend replacing 'in spite of the fact that' with *although*; 'in view of the fact that' with *because* or *considering that*; and 'due to the fact that' with *because*. Despite the experts' advice, 'in spite of the fact that' and 'in view of the fact that' are quite common, especially in academic writing. Since eliminating *the fact that* is usually easy and almost always results in improvement, writers should try to cut it. However, there are cases where it is difficult to avoid (for example, where a fact is the focus of attention), and in these cases *the fact that* is defensible.

> Wodehouse is a popular writer, and the fact that he is a popular writer has a lot to do with his use of stock plots.
> Northrop Frye *The Educated Imagination* 1963: 15

(Here '*the fact that* he is a popular writer' could be replaced by two words: 'his popularity'. Frye may well have deliberately chosen this structure to emphasize the phrase 'a popular writer'.)

> .... he has somewhat modified this conclusion because of the fact that he did not then take into consideration sufficiently that the war had provoked a temporary speeding-up of the rhythm of economic phenomena....
> *Queen's Quarterly* 96.3 (1989): 616

(Using *of the fact that* after *because* is redundant.)

> It is estimated that 24,000 cancer deaths could result.... The gravity of this should not be understated, especially in view of the fact that the [Chernobyl] accident was far from unavoidable.
> *Queen's Quarterly* 95.2 (1988): 313–4

(Here *in view of the fact that* could be replaced with *since*.)

> This is probably due to the fact that he views ... religion (or culture) and social structure as distinct ontological entities.
> *Canadian Journal of Sociology* 14.2 (1989): 213

(Here *because* would be a better choice.)

Much was made of the fact that he bought up all the oats in town for 40 cents a bushel and sold them for a dollar when the going rate was only 23 1/2 cents.
Pierre Berton *The Promised Land* 1984: 124

(Here a fact is the focus of attention).

Meanwhile I was agonizing over the fact that I'd spent the summer trying to read *The Waste Land* and hadn't understood a word of it.
Margaret Atwood *Second Words* 1982: 399

(Here a fact is the focus of attention).

faculty   see UNIVERSITY

fag, faggot   In Britain *fag* is slang for a cigarette, a tedious chore, or a public-school boy who waits on a senior boy, and a *faggot* (also spelled *fagot*) is a bundle of sticks used for making a fire. However, Canadians would be unlikely to use these words in these senses. In North America *fag* and *faggot* are highly derogatory terms for a gay man.

Indeed, on Oct. 1, 1985, Cockburn took part in a taping for CBC television and accidentally saw program notes describing him as a 'Commie fag sympathizer'.
Maclean's 8 Sept. 1986: 68

See also GAY, LESBIAN, HOMOSEXUAL.

Fahrenheit   see CELSIUS

fail to   *Fail to* usually has overtones of recrimination: 'He failed to complete the assignment'. Using this expression with a non-human subject may create an unintentionally humorous effect: 'The new carpet failed to cheer him up'.
Some usage guides recommend using *fail to* only in contexts where there is an unsuccessful attempt to do something ('I failed to convince her') or where there is negligence ('They failed to warn the passengers of the additional risk'). But this advice is too restrictive. While it would prevent unintentional humour in sentences such as 'The fire failed to burn down the whole house', it would also rule out the idiomatic use of *fail to* to express a departure from what was expected or hoped for: 'Over a fifteen-year period, the wage gap had failed to narrow'; 'Our tests fail to replicate Hennessy's results'.

Machiavelli, so often now hailed as a great realist, failed to impress Horsley, who was armed with a new standard for judging insight.
J.A.W. Gunn *Beyond Liberty and Property* 1983: 37

Only one tissue, a basidioma of Hebeloma crustuliniforme, failed to yield DNA....We suspect that contaminants present in the tissue coprecipitated with the DNA, preventing rehydration of the DNA in the final solution.
Canadian Journal of Botany 67.4 (1989): 1237

(This use of *failed to* with a non-human subject is idiomatic in the sciences.)

During the past decade, few issues of the Book Review Index have failed to list at least one of Akenson's works....
Canadian Journal of History 14.1 (1989): 120

(Some critics would object to *fail to* here, since the 'few issues' omitting Akenson cannot be faulted.)

fain   see FEIGN

fair, fare   The adjective *fair* means pleasing, or pretty good, or just and equitable, or light in skin or hair colour. The noun *fair* means exhibition.
The noun *fare* means food or entertainment offered to the public, or the amount one pays to ride a public conveyance. The verb *fare* means to get along or succeed. It is the verb that is most often misspelled.

The victim was ... treated for a gunshot wound and is in fair condition.
Toronto Star 2 July 1992: A5

Taxi fares are based on time or distance travelled, said Phillip Seymour of the Calgary taxi commission.
Calgary Herald 20 Dec. 1992: A4

There's a good selection of light fare for noontime and a few more substantial dishes....
Ottawa Citizen 24 Dec. 1992: C5

When her mother caught sight of her, she called out, 'Well, my daughter, how did you fare?'
Ottawa Citizen 13 Dec. 1992: F3

The other Nova Scotia team did not fair as well.
Daily News (Halifax) 7 Nov. 1992: 41

(The correct spelling is *fare*.)

In contrast, countries such as Scotland, which integrated the subject across the curriculum, faired poorly.
Globe and Mail (Toronto) 23 Oct. 1992: n.p.

(The correct spelling is *fared*.)

fall   see AUTUMN

fallacy, fallacious   In logic, a *fallacy* is a statement that appears to be sound but is actually faulty. (Two logical fallacies described in this guide are *begging the question* and *ad hominem* argument.)

In ordinary usage, a *fallacy* is a mistaken belief or faulty concept. The adjective *fallacious* usually means deceptive or misguided, and some critics maintain that it should not be used simply to mean erroneous. Most Canadian writers appear to observe this distinction.

It's a critical fallacy of our times, derived perhaps from psychology or optimistic self-help books, that a writer should 'grow,' 'change,' or 'develop.'
Margaret Atwood *Second Words* 1982: 621

However, the fallacy of pegging investment to anticipated leaps in petroleum prices was illustrated all too clearly in the early 1980s.
London Free Press 6 May 1986: B6

(Here *fallacy* means erroneousness.)

Thus if someone argues that wars accomplish a kind of 'natural selection' among humans, it is easy to see why the argument is fallacious.
Irving M. Zeitlin and Robert J. Brym *The Social Condition of Humanity* 1991: 27

'Such imaginative accounting serves only to produce a most fallacious bottom line.'
Gazette (Montreal) 10 Oct. 1990: A1

(Here, although the bottom line is indeed wrong, the point is that this is not just an inadvertent error, but one intended to mislead.)

falsehood, falsity, falseness   A *falsehood* is an untrue statement. *Falsity*, *falsehood*, and *falseness* all refer to the quality of being untrue. Applied to a statement or belief, these words do not suggest any intent to deceive; applied to a person, however, that is exactly what they imply. *Falsehood* in a person is the habit of lying. *Falsity* once commonly meant a lover's infidelity, but now this use sounds a little quaint. *Falseness* in a person is insincerity.

As a result, even intentional and malicious falsehoods uttered in Parliament are completely immune from action in the courts.
J.E. Smyth et al. *The Law and Business Administration in Canada* 1987: 92–3

Consequently he's judged by the truth or falsehood of what he says—either there was such a battle or there wasn't, and if there was he's got the date either right or wrong.
Northrop Frye *The Educated Imagination* 1963: 24

It is the duty of one who has innocently made a misstatement and who later learns of its falsity to inform the

other party of the true situation if it is not already too late to avoid injury.
J.E. Smyth et al. *The Law and Business Administration in Canada* 1987: 227

false titles   see ATTRIBUTIVE NOUNS

falsity   see FALSEHOOD

family   see SPECIES

fanny   see BUTTOCKS

fantasy, phantasy   *Fantasy* is the usual Canadian spelling for all meanings of the word; *phantasy* is literary or archaic. In British English, however, *phantasy* still has some currency as a medical term for delusions.

The 'melodrama of the American Dream' involves a fantasy of social mobility doomed to failure.
Queen's Quarterly 97 (1990): 95

Schoenberg was represented first by his Phantasy for Violin and Piano, Op. 47, with David Zafer, violin, and Sharon Krause, piano.
Globe and Mail (Toronto) 19 Jan. 1985: E10

far away, faraway, far-away   *Far away* is two words except when it's an adjective used directly before a noun. Then the spelling is *faraway* or, less commonly, *far-away*.

From far away a deep voice rumbled at me.
Room of One's Own June 1990: 80

He seemed very far away.
Geoffrey Ursell *Perdue: And How the West Was Lost* 1984: 144

He headed Canadian delegations to Africa and other faraway places.
Globe and Mail (Toronto) 23 Jan. 1985: P1

Russia was not about to expend large sums on a build-up in the distant Pacific or get involved in some far-away adventure of dubious outcome.
Queen's Quarterly 92.1 (1985): 182

fare   see FAIR

Far East   see ASIA

far-sighted   see NEAR-SIGHTED

farther, further In the past *farther* and *further* were used interchangeably both as adverbs ('He went farther *or* further') and as adjectives ('further *or* farther research'). Now *farther* is most often used when literal or figurative distance is implied ('We slid farther'), while *further* is most often used to mean additional ('no further help'). In British English *further* is common in all senses.

The analyses of 22 relatively unaltered samples reported in Store *et al.* (1984) and a further 18 that were analysed recently ... are considered here.
Canadian Journal of Earth Sciences 26 (1989): 408

St. Hubert MP Pierrette Venne herself suggested that [the proposal] be referred to the party's executive for farther study....
Gazette (Montreal) 1990: A1

(Here *further* is recommended.)

fascist The Fascists (*Fascisti* in Italian) were an Italian political party that set up a dictatorship under Benito Mussolini in 1922 and joined forces with the Nazis. Fascist policy was racist and ultranationalist. Now the adjective *fascist* is applied to anything or anyone considered dictatorial or undemocratic. Although the term is historically connected to the right, today it is often applied to left-wing groups.

The *sc* in the middle of *fascist* is pronounced *sh*. The word should be capitalized only when referring to the political party.

Sun writers have attacked the Ontario Human Rights Commission for what they see as potentially fascist tendencies. *Sun* writers have argued that non-whites in Canada are, perversely, favoured over whites; and they have condemned organized multiculturalism.
Saturday Night April 1986: 6

It is this breakdown of what Krizanc calls the Fascism of theater that is at the play's heart.
Performing Arts in Canada Spring 1990: 14

(*Fascism* should not be capitalized here.)

fatal, fateful A *fatal* event results in death or disaster. A *fateful* event is highly significant, marking a turn of fortune for better or worse. Though both words may be applicable in some contexts, they are not synonyms in current usage.

The most fatal disease of friendship is gradual decay.... Richard Davies and Glen Kirkland, eds. *Dimensions* 1986: 22–3

History will regard this as the fateful day in the life of the Meech Lake Accord.
Ottawa Citizen 22 June 1990: A1

Nineteen forty-five was a fateful year in the history of humankind. It was the year of defeat for Hitler's fascism and its Japanese militaristic variant. It was the year of victory for a coalition of Western capitalist democracies and the world's only socialist state—the USSR.
Henry M. Rosenthal and S. Cathy Berson, eds. *Canadian Jewish Outlook Anthology* 1988: 153

(Here both the positive and the negative senses of *fateful* are illustrated.)

A sustained determination to make the best possible appointments to the academic staff is one means of avoiding a fateful descent into the cosy and second-rate, but it was only one weapon in the armory of Principal Grant.
Frederick Gibson *Queen's University* 2 (1978): 435

(The use of *fateful* to mean disastrous or ruinous is uncommon; *fatal* would be a better choice.)

father-in-law see MOTHER-IN-LAW

faucet see TAP

fauna see FLORA

faux pas *Faux pas* (pronounced *FO PAW*) is an expression borrowed from French. It translates literally as 'false step' and refers to a blunder, especially a social one. The plural is *faux pas* (pronounced *FO PAWS* or, as in French, *FO PAW*). *Faux pas* is sometimes hyphenated, though it shouldn't be.

Suddenly realizing his faux pas, he quickly added: 'Ah! Poor woman.'
Terence Dickinson *Halley's Comet* 1985: 26

Those fortunate people got their kicks by pointing out the fashion faux pas of others.
Ottawa Citizen 3 June 1992: C4

Was she supposed to tell Shireen of these plans, or would this be committing an enormous cultural faux-pas?
Ottawa Citizen 8 March 1992: B4

(The hyphen should be deleted.)

fax, facsimile A document or graphic image sent or received through the public telecommunications system is usually called a *fax*. What emerges from the machine receiving such a message is not the sender's copy but a *facsimile* of it: the word *fax* is a shortened (and respelled) version of *facsimile*. Some writers avoid *fax* because it sounds like slang; however, in using *facsimile* they risk being misunderstood, since many people don't make the connection between the two words. Even in the most formal contexts *fax* will probably supplant *facsimile* eventually, for it is now in wide use as a verb—'They faxed us back immediately'—and, while *facsimile* can also be used as a verb, its parts (*facsimiled, facsimileing*) are daunting.

Occasionally *fax* is used as a tongue-in-cheek (and very informal) spelling of *facts*.

After checking the results, he said he faxed them to Mellow the same day.
Ottawa Citizen 11 July 1990: B2

FAX OF LOVE: Italian porn star-politician Ilona (Cicciolina) Staller and American sculptor Jeff Koons have fallen in love by fax and plan to marry on Valentine's Day.
Vancouver Sun 5 Dec. 1990: A2

(The headline in this example is a pun.)

Technology engulfs him: A powerful personal computer sits before him, a facsimile machine on one side, laser printer and copier behind.
Business Journal June 1991: 29

faze see PHASE

feasible *Feasible* is used to mean both possible and probable. Because it is derived from the French verb *faire*, 'to do' or 'to make', Fowler suggested restricting its meaning to the sphere of practical accomplishment. In other words, he approved of using *feasible* as a synonym of *doable, achievable, makable,* or *suitable* ('a feasible plan'), but disapproved of using it to mean *probable, reasonable,* or *likely* ('It's feasible it will rain'; 'a feasible explanation'). Many writers observe this distinction of sense; some dictionaries include *probable* as a standard sense and others don't.

The opposite of *feasible* is usually *unfeasible; infeasible,* used in Britain, is far less common in Canadian English.

Any lingering illusion that the route was feasible for a canal had vanished.
Queen's Quarterly 92.2 (1985): 360

You may be shocked to know that existing legislation concerning the responsibilities of drink servers makes it feasible for private party throwers to be sued by drunk drivers and their victims.
Province (Vancouver) 24 Dec. 1990: 31

(Here *feasible* sounds odd because it is used in a passive construction. A better choice would be *possible*; or the construction could be rewritten: 'makes it feasible for drunk drivers and their victims to sue private party throwers'.)

Psychoanalysis and Nazism—is there another relationship feasible between the two than mutual enmity?
Henry M. Rosenthal and S. Cathy Berson, eds. *Canadian Jewish Outlook Anthology* 1988: 125

(Here *conceivable* would be better.)

February Although teachers encourage their pupils to pronounce both the *r*'s in *February* (FEB *rew air ee*), many—perhaps most—educated Canadians say FEB *yew air ee*, which is analogous to *January* and easier to articulate. Most Canadian, American, and British dictionaries now list both pronunciations without comment.

See also LIBRARY.

feel good, feel bad see ADJECTIVES AND ADVERBS; BAD, BADLY

feet see FOOT

feign, feint, deke, fain *Feign* is a verb meaning pretend, as in 'feign illness'. A *feint* is a pretend blow or delusive move intended to draw an opponent out of position; today this sense is most common in the context of sports. *Feint* is also used as a verb meaning to execute a feint. *Deke* is a slang synonym of *feint*; the word originated in hockey, but is now used more widely.

Fain is an archaic word that functions as both an adjective and an adverb. The adverb means gladly or rather, as in 'I would fain retreat'. The adjective means happy, willing, or compelled, as in 'We were fain to rest'.

'You have a point, Toma,' said Workun, feigning joviality.
NeWest Review Feb.–Mar. 1990: 23

Like a big stallion, feinting with fluid crossing strides, he prances languorously right, then left, swinging his body to shield the puck, easing by them.
Ken Dryden *The Game* 1983: 192

Four helicopters fly to his appointments, deking here and there to confuse assassins.
Globe and Mail (Toronto) 24 Sept. 1985: P14

'At first we walked with tolerable speed over the broken rocks, and through the intersecting gullies; but the kind of ladder exercise which this imposed taxed the muscles so severely, that the strongest was fain to slacken his pace, as the same interruptions and impediments multiplied upon us,' he wrote.
Uphere Jan.–Feb. 1990: 71

(This quotation dates from the 1830s.)

fell swoop   In Shakespeare's play *Macbeth*, Mac-Duff uses the phrase 'at one fell swoop' to describe how his whole family has been murdered by Macbeth. Here *fell* is used in the now rare sense of cruel or savage; the image recalls a bird of prey suddenly attacking a helpless victim. In contemporary use the phrase retains only the sense of events occurring all at once, without the original connection to ruthlessness and disaster. Canadian writers most often begin the phrase with *in*, but *at* is still common. The expression appears mostly in journalism. Some critics consider it a cliché, and it is best used sparingly.

The firm has developed a water filtration system that siphons off a variety of contaminants in one fell swoop, without the need for several filters or heavy doses of chlorine.
Province (Vancouver) 29 April 1990: 44

felony   see INDICTABLE OFFENCE

fever   see TEMPERATURE

fewer, less   According to most usage guides and writing handbooks, *fewer* refers to a smaller number, while *less* refers to a smaller amount. In other words, *fewer* should be used of things that can be counted ('fewer books', 'fewer students', 'fewer votes') and *less* of things that are regarded as wholes ('less flour', 'less crime', 'less money'). Phrases like *less people* or *less books* are widely regarded as incorrect and should definitely be avoided both in speech and in writing.

In idiomatic structures, however, *less* often occurs with numbers and quantities. For example, the phrase *or less*, rather than the technically correct *or fewer*, often follows countable nouns: '100 words or less', 'two children or less'. The very common phrase *more or less* reinforces this usage to the point that *or fewer* may well sound odd to some people.

Less than is commonly used with quantities of time, money, distance, etc., that, although they are countable, are usually regarded as wholes: 'less than ten dollars', 'less than 40 per cent', 'less than two months', 'less than 400 km'. Note that these quantities are often treated as singular in other ways: 'Ten dollars is enough'; 'Four hundred kilometres is not very far'. In addition, countable nouns often follow the expression *no less than*: 'They had been to Europe no less than five times in two years'.

These structures are idiomatic and very common in all kinds of Canadian writing. It would be pedantic to insist on *fewer* in these structures, although *fewer* is certainly correct.

Other store owners say it's not that there are fewer customers—they're just buying less.
Gazette (Montreal) 18 Dec. 1990: A3

'Obviously, the broader you are the less restrictions you put on them and the better the trustees can do.'
Edmonton Journal 8 Sept. 1992: n.p.

(Here, directly preceding a countable noun, *fewer* would be a better choice.)

Job ranking is feasible in small organizations or businesses with roughly a hundred jobs or fewer.
Carl J. Cuneo *Pay Equity* 1990: 97

(Although this sentence follows the rule, the phrase *or fewer* is rare in Canadian writing.)

In most jurisdictions, short-term leases, usually for three years or less, need not be registered or even in writing. . . .
J.E. Smyth et al. *The Law and Business Administration in Canada* 1987: 589

The remaining 52 percent of all forested land in the province is held by private individuals in parcels of 200 acres or less.
Harrowsmith Jun.–Jul. 1986: 123

All you had to do was state in fifteen words or less why you liked Cleanso Soap.
Max Braithwaite *The Night We Stole the Mountie's Car* 1971: 207

Artisanal families were small nuclear units with two children or less.
Canadian Journal of History 14.1 (1989): 97

Wayne Gretzky became the first player in NHL history to score 50 goals in fewer than 50 games.
Gazette (Montreal) 30 Dec. 1990: D5

(Although this sentence follows the rule, often Canadian writers use *less than* before numbers.)

[Moore] points out that the records cite less than twenty offences, mostly minor in nature, for a detachment of 212 men over four years of rigorous service.
Canadian Journal of History 14.1 (1989): 108

In the twenty-seven months from its debut in Baltimore until it became a sextet, the great quintet was disbanded no less than four times. . . .
Jack Chambers *Milestones* 1983: 216

The Newtonian theory which seemed so entrenched proved within less than 250 years to be false, strictly speaking.
Queen's Quarterly 95 (1988): 25

While on average each woman must have 2.1 children in order to insure that the population size does not fall, women are now having fewer than 1.7 children on average.
Irving M. Zeitlin and Robert J. Brym *The Social Condition of Humanity* 1991: 181

fictive, fictional, fictitious　All three words have to do with the invented or imaginary, and all three have a secondary meaning: not true, not genuine. In current English, however, they often have distinct applications. *Fictive* refers to the capacity to create stories: 'the fictive imagination'. *Fictional* refers to invented stories and the literary techniques used to write them, while *fictitious* has come to mean false, counterfeit, or feigned (see also FACTIOUS, FRACTIOUS, FACTITIOUS).

As long ago as 1981, New Yorker writer Kennedy Fraser took note of a 'salacious new public interest in the fashion world' and of how this world . . . has been fodder for the fictive mind.
Globe and Mail (Toronto) 16 July 1985: E1

. . . Oliva concentrates exclusively and superficially on the content of the book, with no consideration of Ellis's fictional techniques.
Ottawa Citizen 15 Oct. 1994: E12

He did his business at the Tower Bank, where from time to time he filed statements of largely fictitious assets as a basis for increasing loans.
J.E. Smyth et al. *The Law and Business Administration in Canada* 1987: 242

fiddle, violin　*Fiddle* and *violin* may be used as synonyms, although generally *violin* suggests classical music, symphony orchestras, and string quartets, while *fiddle* suggests barn dances and bluegrass.

Sometimes the instruments used in these different milieux have actual physical differences. The instrument used for classical music tends to be unamplified, strung with three strings made of gut (or a modern substitute) and a single steel string, and fitted with friction tuning pegs. The instrument used in bluegrass, country, and traditional music is strung with five steel strings and can be amplified. The amplified instrument, though usually called a fiddle, may also be called an electric violin. Jazz musicians who use this instrument play 'jazz violin'.

In Newfoundland English a *fiddler* is the musician who plays the music for a dance, no matter what instrument is played; it may be a fiddle but it's often an accordion.

fifth estate　see FOURTH ESTATE

fight with　*Fight with* is ambiguous, meaning either fight alongside or fight against: 'The Serbs fought with the Croats during the Second World War'. Where the context leaves any doubt as to which meaning is intended, it's best to avoid the phrase.

figuratively　see LITERALLY

figurehead　A *figurehead* on a ship is a carved figure on the prow. By metaphorical extension, a *figurehead* is a leader in name only, without real authority or responsibility. The connotations of this term are pejorative or at least dismissive. The term shouldn't be used when the context is positive.

They dismiss the current press lord as 'Young Ken,' an immature figurehead whose main accomplishment was to be his father's only son.
Maclean's 14 Oct. 1991: A44

But Mulroney himself is certain to be the leading government spokesman in the constitutional struggles that lie ahead, and that might discourage him from consigning Clark to what could easily become a frustrating role as a mere figurehead minister.
Maclean's 14 Jan. 1991: A18

Prime ministers take more care in choosing Supreme Court justices than they do in picking the governor-general, perhaps because they feel the former are important while the latter is merely a symbol, a figurehead.
Vancouver Sun 23 Oct. 1990: A13

People who love fine things know that Kenneth Donald McLeish has long been a figurehead among Canada's hardy breed of antique dealers.
Canadian Collector 21 (1986): 12

(Here *leader* would be a better choice.)

While breakaway Parti Quebecois members are talking of setting up an active new independence group in Quebec, a traditional figurehead of Quebec nationalism, the Societe St-Jean Baptiste, is privately struggling to maintain its influence in the nationalist debate.
Globe and Mail (Toronto) 3 April 1985: P7

(The Société St-Jean Baptiste would be better described as 'a traditional *leader* in promoting Quebec nationalism'.)

filet, fillet   *Filet* and *fillet* are spelling variants, and both the French pronunciation (*fi LAY*) and the British (*FILL it*) are acceptable for either spelling. A *filet* or *fillet* is a narrow band or thin slice of anything. To *fillet*—the verb is usually spelled with a double *l*—means to debone a fish or cut meat into thin strips. *Filet mignon*, a particular cut of beef, is always spelled with a single *l* and usually pronounced *FI lay MEE nyaw(n)*. *Filet* (pronounced *fi LAY*) also refers to lace of a particular weave.

Filet of Sole ... is a busy concourse at lunch and between 6:00 PM and curtain time.
Alan Tucker, ed. *The Penguin Guide to Canada* 1991: 354

Fillets of sage are placed about their heads, ankles, and wrists; a whistle is suspended about the neck; their bodies are rubbed with white clay.
Pierre Berton *The Promised Land* 1984: 215

Lloyd had caught me filleting the pickerel and right away knew what kind of fisherman I was.
Howard Engel *Murder Sees the Light* 1984: 25

finalize   Many commentators have scorned *finalize* since it came into general use in the 1920s. It has been called gobbledygook and an unnecessary synonym for *complete*. In fact, though, *finalize* has a special meaning: to put in final form or give final approval to. Deals, plans, and agreements are all commonly said to be finalized. The frequent occurrence of *finalize* in bureaucratic prose may have contributed to its poor reputation. But there seems to be no good reason to avoid the word in any context where it expresses the desired meaning.

In the fall of 1976, more than a year after Cameron's arrival, the adoption still hadn't been finalized.
Saturday Night April 1986: 32

After NATO foreign ministers had finalized the wording of the communiqué, some members of the alliance sought credit for the wording that made the agreement possible.
Maclean's 12 June 1989: A24

Soon the children will finalize their costumes and come upstairs to display themselves, which is the point of the whole game.
Margaret Atwood *Life Before Man* 1979: 262

See also -IZE, -ISE.

fine arts   see ARTS

fiord   see FJORD

firearm   see GUN

fireman, firefighter   see JOB TITLES

firm, corporation   Sometimes *firm* is used loosely to refer to any type of business; properly speaking, however, a *firm* is a commercial partnership of two or more people. Legal, accounting, and consulting partnerships are often firms: 'The firm of Smith and Doe prepared the report'. *Firm*, like other collective nouns, may take a plural verb in British usage, but in North American writing it usually takes a singular verb.

A *corporation* is a business or organization that is recognized as a legal person: that is, a legal entity distinct from its owners and employees.

The large corporation has replaced the small family firm as the decisive unit of the economy, and government consultation with big business forms a major basis for the formulation of economic policy.
Irving M. Zeitlin and Robert J. Brym *The Social Condition of Humanity* 1991: 124

His reputation as a brilliant young lawyer had already been established, and his successful Toronto firm frequently acted as agents for Crown business.
William Teatero *John Anderson: Fugitive Slave* 1986: 171–2

It is available only to firms which use the carrier for business travel.
Globe and Mail (Toronto) 5 Jan. 1985: T10

(Some object to the general use of *firm* for any company or business.)

firstly   Although dictionaries list *firstly* as an adverb used in enumerated lists of items, usage commentators do not necessarily approve of it. Some consider it a pretentious or ridiculous substitute for *first*. For others the issue is consistency: *either* 'first', 'second', 'third' *or* 'firstly', 'secondly', 'thirdly'. To steer clear of the shoals of criticism, the safest choice is 'first, second, third'.

first name, given name, Christian name, forename *First name* and *given name* are the terms commonly used in Canada for the personal name before the surname. *Given name* is less likely to cause confusion (see CHINESE NAMES). The term *Christian name*, which technically applies to the name given at a Christian baptism, is also sometimes used interchangeably with *first name* or *given name*. The British term *forename* is uncommon in this country.

First names were rare and reserved for close relatives.
Miriam Waddington *Apartment Seven* 1989: 2

Jordan, whose given names were Irving Sydney but who was known only as Duke to musicians and fans alike, came from Brooklyn....
Jack Chambers *Milestones* 1983: 59

A few months earlier it would have been inconceivable for her to call my father by his Christian name.
George Ignatieff *The Making of a Peacemonger* 1987: 31

First Nations, First Peoples see ABORIGINAL PEOPLE(S)

First World War, World War I, Second World War, World War II *First World War* and *World War I* are both correct, as are *Second World War* and *World War II*. Many Canadian style guides stipulate one form or the other, but there is no clear Canadian preference. You should use one form or the other throughout a single piece of writing for consistency.

first-year student, freshman, frosh A Canadian university student in first year is called a *first-year student*, one in second year is called a *second-year student*, and so on. In the United States, students in successive years of any four-year program—high school, college, or university—are called *freshmen*, *sophomores*, *juniors*, and *seniors*. *Freshman* is also used in Canada, but the other American terms are not. *Freshman* is used of either sex, but the fact that it is not gender-neutral may have boosted the popularity of the slang variant *frosh*—used of men and women alike in both the singular and the plural.

Freshman is widely used in newspaper writing to describe male newcomers to sports and politics.

First-year students did Latin, Greek, and mathematics, second-year students more of the same, and in the third year logic, moral philosophy, and natural philosophy were added.
Hilda Neatby *Queen's University* 1 (1978): 58

At the time the proposed shutdown was announced, a majority of third-year and fourth-year students, backed by many teachers, were boycotting the most crucial aspect of their design studies....
Saturday Night May 1986: 14

Two freshmen, Jennifer Williams, 19, of Mississauga, Ont., and Mike Morse, 19, of Thornhill, Ont., were injured.
Globe and Mail (Toronto) 7 Sept. 1985: P14

I was a 'frosh,' a freshman at university.
Gazette (Montreal) 4 Oct. 1990: A2

... the university came up with a frosh orientation program that included discussions on campus violence, date rape, sexism, peer pressure and virginity.
Gazette (Montreal) 10 Sept. 1990: B4

See also CO-ED; GRADUATE, POSTGRADUATE, POSTDOCTORAL.

fish, fishes *Fish* and, less commonly, *fishes* are both accepted plural forms of *fish*. Some usage guides suggest using *fishes* for more than one species of fish: 'The piranha is one of the few freshwater fishes that eat flesh'.

Fish absorb pollutants from the water and their daily diet, storing metals and chemicals in their body tissue, and some fish species are more susceptible to contamination than others.
Canadian Consumer Jan. 1985: 8

Two pale blue barrettes, shaped like fishes, held back Leah's hair at her temples.
Canadian Fiction Magazine 63 (1988): 44

In vertebrates, almost all major length variation and heteroplasmy was seen in the fishes, reptiles, and amphibians.
Canadian Journal of Zoology 67.4 (1989): 899

(Here *fishes* refers to various species.)

fix see NEUTER

fjord, fiord Both spellings are correct, and Canadians do not show a marked preference for one or the other. British dictionaries list *fiord* first; American dictionaries, *fjord*. But in Britain and the United States, as in Canada, both spellings are common.

flack, hack A *flack* is a press agent or public-relations person. The word is often used in the same contexts as *hack*, which is a light-hearted or derogatory slang term for journalist. *Hack* can also be used pejoratively to refer to a mediocre or mercenary writer. Someone who gains a position through influence or political connections rather than merit may also be called a *hack*.

> Although he fundamentally disagrees with nearly everything [environmentalists] say, he is willing to debate the issue, instead of hiding behind a public relations flack.
> *Maclean's* 22 April 1991: A41

> But it also is silent on 'spin doctor,' the current term in both countries for a business or government 'communicator' (otherwise known as a 'flack') who tries to get journalists to twist the story toward a client's interest.
> *Ottawa Citizen* 6 April 1990: F8

> But the paper's dotty proprietor mistakenly sends a meek, innocent gardening correspondent named Boot to get the story instead of a seasoned hack.
> *Vancouver Sun* 28 Dec. 1990: TJ24

> The New Democrats charged that the law permitted the cabinet to appoint a political hack as acting commissioner without consulting anybody.
> *Vancouver Sun* 2 Oct. 1990: A8

See also FLAK.

flagrant see BLATANT

flair, flare These two homophones are sometimes confused. *Flare*, meaning a blaze of light or a widening (usually in trouser legs or skirts), is used where *flair*, meaning aptitude, talent, or knack, is meant.

> Smillie tells his history with the flare of a good adventure writer.
> *Canadian Churchman* April 1986: 16

(The word required here is *flair*.)

> To provide those guidelines, Goldsmith chooses musicians for her concert series who have a flare for discussing their work.
> *Vancouver Sun* 5 Sept. 1990: C4

(The word required here is *flair*.)

flak, flack During the Second World War, German anti-aircraft fire came to be called *flak*, an acronym for the air defence weapon called the *Fliegerabwehrkanone* in German. In the early 1960s, a figurative use of *flak*, meaning harsh criticism, arose in American slang. The term was frequently spelled *flack*, which is now an accepted variant spelling for this sense. Canadians prefer *flak*. Like its literal counterpart, figurative *flak* is often 'run into', 'encountered', 'caught', or 'taken'.

> He told an audience of about 200 ... that some UN agencies deserve criticism, but not all should catch flak.
> *Globe and Mail* (Toronto) 19 March 1985: P5

See also FLACK, HACK.

flamingo, flamenco A flamingo is a long-legged pink or scarlet wading bird with a penchant for standing on one leg. The plural is *flamingos* or, less often, *flamingoes*. *Flamenco* (pronounced *fluh MENG ko*) is a vigorous Spanish style of music and dance, involving stamping heels and clicking castanets; the plural is *flamencos*. The word *flamingo* was borrowed from Portuguese, *flamenco* from Spanish. Both words are closely related to the Provençal word *flamenc*, 'flaming' or 'fiery', which aptly describes both the colour of the bird and the spirit of the dance.

> Visitors stroll along 16 kilometres (10 miles) of pathways, passing pools where pink flamingos look pallid compared with the flowers around them.
> *Toronto Star* 25 April 1992: G21

> For dancer Nuria Casanovas-Tamayo, flamenco is more than a style of dance—it's also a means of conveying a passion.
> *Gazette* (Montreal) 20 Aug. 1992: G6

> And the *Monitor*, the student newspaper at King's College, of which I am the titular publisher, ran ... a cutline under a picture that pretended to portray José and Miranda, famed flamingo dancers....
> W.C. Lougheed, ed. *In Search of the Standard in Canadian English* 1986: 90

(The word required was *flamenco*.)

flammable, inflammable, non-flammable, non-inflammable, inflammatory *Flammable* and *inflammable* are synonyms; both words describe things that catch fire easily. *Inflammable* is derived from the Latin *inflammare*, 'to set on fire'. However, with the development of highly combustible synthetic materials, fire officials and insurance underwriters came to fear that people would think the *in-* prefix indicated a negative (i.e., '*not* likely to catch fire'); thus they promoted *flammable* for use on warning labels. Things that won't burn easily or ignite are labelled *non-flammable* or, rarely, *non-inflammable*.

Literally, *inflammatory* means causing fire. The word is often used figuratively to mean the opposite of *conciliatory*.

flare   see FLAIR

flat   see SUITE

flaunt, flout   To *flaunt* something is to show it off: 'If you've got it, flaunt it!' To *flout* is to treat laws, rules, or conventions with contemptuous disregard: 'He doesn't just break the rules, he flouts them'. These words not only look and sound alike but also have similar negative connotations of display and disregard for convention. *Flaunt* is frequently used where *flout* is meant ('She flaunts convention'), though the converse is rare. This confusion is a favourite target of usage commentators.

These are not fashions for the timid—you must be the flaunt-it type. See-through lace jeans and blouses, body-hugging stirrup pants, lambada skirts and camisoles, skin-tight leathers (black, naturally), and show-off accessories are the rule.
Alan Tucker, ed. *The Penguin Guide to Canada* 1991: 208

The girls liked to flout convention. Marriage and children were not their calling; art was.
Globe and Mail (Toronto) 26 Oct. 1985: H4

The transnational power of these large companies means they can flaunt environmental and health safeguards at the national and regional levels, all in the name of being compelled by international market forces.
Briarpatch Dec. 1989–Jan. 1990: 31

(The word required here is *flout*.)

... to this day no one has forgotten King George III's illustrious son Prince Edward, who flaunted local propriety with his French mistress, Julie St. Laurent.
Alan Tucker, ed. *The Penguin Guide to Canada* 1991: 35

(The word required here is *flout*.)

'[He] has purposely flaunted a court order to achieve the purpose of profit,' Justice Daniel Chilcott said in his judgment.
Ottawa Citizen 25 Feb. 1990: A7

(The word required here is *flouted*.)

flee   Both the past tense and the past participle (the form used after *have*) are *fled*. *Fleed* is non-standard.

The armed robber fled with an undisclosed amount of money.
Gazette (Montreal) 30 Dec. 1990: A3

... Employment and Immigration Canada won't consider an application for refugee status unless the applicant has fled his host country.
Ottawa Citizen 14 July 1990: A12

fleur-de-lis   Since 1948 the official flag of Quebec has borne an emblem called the *fleur-de-lis* (literally, 'flower of the lily'), a stylized iris that was part of the royal arms of France before the Revolution. *Fleur-de-lis*, rather than the variant *fleur-de-lys*, is the preferred spelling in Quebec, and the name of the flag, 'the Fleur-de-lis', should be capitalized. In French the phrase is pronounced *flur duh LEECE*, but in English the final *s* sound is often dropped. The plural, *fleurs-de-lis*, may be pronounced *flur duh LEE* or with a *z* sound (*flur duh LEEZ*).

flier   see FLYER

floor   see STORY

flora, fauna   *Flora* refers to the plants and *fauna* to the animals of a certain region or period. The rarely used plural forms are *floras* or *florae* and *faunas* or *faunae*. The plural forms are most likely to be used when comparing 'the floras' or 'the faunas' of two different environments. A *flora* is also a systematic description of all the plants of an area.

Each island has unique varieties of flora and fauna that have evolved to meet a particular set of climatic and geological conditions.
Vancouver Sun 12 Feb. 1994: C1

florescence   see FLUORINE

flotilla   see ARMADA

flounder, founder   To *flounder* is to struggle clumsily, while to *founder* is to fail utterly or sink. Something or someone who flounders is still functioning. Drunkards flounder; ships founder. This distinction is useful, but in some cases either word can be appropriate.

A risk attendant on this type of home ownership, however, is that the whole co-operative venture may flounder because of bad management and insolvency: all members are affected equally by the failure....
J.E. Smyth et al. *The Law and Business Administration in Canada* 1987: 578

(In this example the venture fails; thus *founder* would be better.)

... those willing to go further than the flawed surfaces of his prose in search of significant archetypes may well founder in a morass of half-grasped symbols. ...
Margaret Atwood *Second Words* 1981: 35–6

(Here *flounder* could also work.)

The commercial real estate market has also been foundering. Some markets, like Toronto's office rental market, face an oversupply of new construction.
Vancouver Sun 27 July 1990: D9

(Here *floundering* would be better, since complete failure is not yet evident.)

Now, these Socred insiders are foundering in a state my source describes as 'shaken.'
Province (Vancouver) 18 Sept. 1990: 6

(The word required here is *floundering*.)

flout   see FLAUNT

flu, virus, bacteria, germ   *Flu* is a shortened form of *influenza* and, strictly speaking, refers to a disease caused by the influenza virus. However, people often use *flu* generally to refer to a cold or any short-lived illness involving fatigue, sore muscles, or nausea. Although a virus is the agent of such ailments, the ailment itself is sometimes called a *virus*: 'She was in bed with a virus'. These extended meanings of *flu* and *virus* are informal, but not likely to cause confusion.

Not all noxious microbes are viruses. Some are *bacteria*: 'Antibiotics can kill bacteria but not viruses'. *Germ* is the general term used to cover both types of micro-organism.

Marianne habitually has lunch with Trish, who's off with the flu.
Margaret Atwood *Life Before Man* 1979: 79

The package of disposable diapers instructs parents to rinse the diapers before placing them in the garbage, but since most parents don't take the time to do this, ... raw sewage, containing many viruses, [is] sent to landfill sites instead of the sewage treatment plant.
Western Grocer Aug. 1990: 48

(Bacteria are much more likely than viruses to be a problem in sewage; the general term *germs* would be a better choice here.)

See also BACTERIUM, BACTERIA.

fluid, liquid   In scientific terms, a *fluid* is a substance that changes shape readily: that is, either a liquid or a gas. A *liquid* changes shape readily but, unlike a gas, cannot be compressed. In general writing, however, both words are used to refer to liquids and, figuratively, to describe things that flow freely or are not fixed.

... convective heat transfer [is] a method of cooling in which energy is transferred from a hot surface to a fluid (either a gas or a liquid) that flows over it.
Perspectives: Profile of Research at Queen's University Dec. 1986: 32

It was a comparable insight that led champions of influence to conclude that government was a fluid process of mutual accommodation, not a static balance of stalemated forces.
J.A.W. Gunn *Beyond Liberty and Property* 1983: 203

In theory, if bonds and shares are to serve the purposes of a capital market they should be readily transferable (that is, 'liquid'). ...
J.E. Smyth et al. *The Law and Business Administration in Canada* 1987: 687

fluorine, fluoride, fluorescent, florescence   The words *fluorine*, *fluoride*, and *fluorescent* (emitting light in the presence of certain types of light or radiation) are often misspelled with *flour-* at the beginning instead of *fluor-*. *Fluor-* is derived from the Latin verb *fluere*, 'to be in a state of flux'.
Flour- (as in *flourish*) and *flor-* (as in *floral*) have to do with flowers. *Florescence* means period of flowering.

The element has been best known for its use in flourescent lighting. ...
Globe and Mail (Toronto) 1 Oct. 1985: B6

(The correct spelling is *fluorescent*.)

'[This] toothpaste not only removes stubborn smoking plaque effectively and gently, it also gives long-lasting fresh breath and hardens the teeth with flouride.'
Globe and Mail (Toronto) 27 Feb. 1985: B7

(The correct spelling is *fluoride*.)

... light intensity [was] 90 mol: m-2.5-1 from combined florescent and incandescent lamps.
Canadian Journal of Botany 67.4 (1989): 991

(The adjective *florescent* means flowering. The word required here is *fluorescent*.)

flush   see BLUSH

flyer, flier Either *flyer* or *flier* is correct for any sense, including flying machines, the people in them, pilots, some insects, most birds, fast passenger trains, and advertising circulars. Canadians prefer *flyer* for all meanings.

The invitation to the party was among the pile of letters, cards, and flyers inside his door.
Queen's Quarterly 96.2 (1989): 356

Last year offered white-knuckle flyers good reason to grip their armrests more tightly.
Canadian Consumer Feb. 1986: 29

Hudson Bay Co. of Winnipeg puts out a twice-yearly fashion flier called Applause, described . . . as following a 'news magazine format'.
Globe and Mail (Toronto) 16 Jan. 1985: B6

Edwards . . . served as a sailor and then as a flier in the First World War.
Gazette (Montreal) 11 Feb. 1990: D5

folk, folks *Folk* used to designate traditional art forms or ways—folk art, folk dances, folklore, folk music, folk singers, folk songs, folktales, folkways—is acceptable in all forms of writing.

Folk or *folks* meaning people has warm connotations. Someone who speaks of country folk, old folk, or prairie folk, for instance, is usually thinking of the common characteristics that unite the designated group, and may also be conveying a sense of affection for its members. Where these connotations are not appropriate, it's better to use the neutral word *people*.

Folks is also an informal word for parents or close family.

Among Church of Scotland folk in Canada there was much disgust at the spread of this controversy to a country where the rights of patronage did not exist and where there was no real equivalent to the Scottish state church.
Hilda Neatby *Queen's University* 1 (1978): 45

(Here *folk* is used to underline the unpretentious character of these members of the Church of Scotland.)

It's motorhomes and fishing tackle that are bringing folks into the Regina Sportsmen's Show.
Leader-Post (Regina) 27 Feb. 1988: A3

(This use of *folks* suits the breezy, informal style of the event itself.)

folk etymology *Folk etymology* is the process by which the speakers of a language alter the spelling or pronunciation of an unfamiliar word or phrase so that it makes sense to them. For example, in Cree the Canadian jay is called *weskuchanis*. English-speakers borrowed this name, but soon altered it to accord with familiar English words, calling the bird *whisky-john* and *whisky jack*. Similarly, the French borrowing *chaise longue*, 'long chair', was altered to *chaise lounge*—a chair for lounging. Such alterations are likely to be criticized by those aware of the 'true' etymology of the word. Nevertheless, the altered words often become standard over time.

Or *angishore*, also *angashore*, *angyshore*, an Irish Gaelic borrowing for 'a weak, sickly or unfortunate person deserving pity,' which since an aspirate (h) is frequently pronounced initially in words beginning with vowels, is often pronounced and spelled *hangashore*, and this is turn has been re-interpreted by folk etymology as 'a man regarded as too lazy to fish.'
W.C. Lougheed, ed. *In Search of the Standard in Canadian English* 1986: 47–8

See also AMOK; CHAISE LONGUE; ETYMOLOGY; FREE REIN; HELPMATE; PARTING SHOT; SLED; SPITTING IMAGE; TACK, TACT; TOE THE LINE; WHET THE APPETITE.

foot, feet The plural of *foot* is *feet*, whether the foot is an extremity or a unit of measurement: 'He always lands on his feet'; 'Your subject should be at least three feet from the camera'.

However, when a measurement in feet functions as an adjective, directly before a noun, the plural *feet* becomes *foot*: 'They built an eight-foot fence'. A hyphen usually appears between the number and the word *foot*. After the verb *be*, either *feet* or *foot* is correct and there is no hyphen: 'The fence was eight foot *or* eight feet'.

When describing a person's height in feet and inches it is customary to say either 'Mary is five feet four inches tall' or 'Mary is five foot four'.

When one is four feet high, ten-foot willows are a sufficient cover, and ten acres are a wilderness.
Richard Davies and Glen Kirkland, eds. *Dimensions* 1986: 135

A 40-foot ketch accompanied it to facilitate the shoot.
Photo Life Jul.–Aug. 1991: 13

The mystery merchants . . . are getting nice new signs: ED'S HARDWARE in two-feet-red, and, maybe, *quincaillerie* in six-inch-black at the top left corner, maybe even as big as the phone number.
Canadian Fiction Magazine 63 (1988): 110

(This use of *feet* is not idiomatic: 'two-*foot*-red' would be better.)

There is that 6,000 feet difference from port to peak.
Bon Vivant Nov. 1981: 32

(Here again, the idiom requires *foot*.)

football see SOCCER

footless see BOOTLESS

for see LIKE FOR, WANT FOR, SAY FOR

forbear, forbears see FOREBEARS

forbid The past tense of *forbid* is *forbade* (usually pronounced *for BAD*) or *forbid*. Only *forbade* is seen in published writing. The past participle is *forbidden* or, rarely, *forbid*.

The construction 'to *forbid* someone *from doing* something' (as in 'I forbid you from taking part') is recorded by the *OED* in citations from as early as 1526 and is quite common in writing at all levels of formality. Nonetheless, it is widely condemned in usage guides and should be avoided by writers with a low tolerance for criticism. The approved constructions are 'to *forbid* someone *to do* something' and 'to *forbid* the *doing of* something'.

'My father, Miles the first, was born six years after the Emancipation and forbade me to play music because the only place a Negro could play then was in barrel houses.'
Jack Chambers *Milestones* 1983: ix–x

... workers were forbidden to organize and bargain collectively with factory owners about rates of pay and other working conditions.
J.E. Smyth et al. *The Law and Business Administration in Canada* 1987: 10

China has issued new rules on its technology imports that forbid foreign companies from putting restrictive articles into contracts. ...
Globe and Mail (Toronto) 7 June 1985: B20

(This is the disputed construction.)

... in the capacity of an employer in his own right he was forbidden by the Labour Relations Act of British Columbia from participating in union activities.
J.E. Smyth et al. *The Law and Business Administration in Canada* 1987: 519

(This is the disputed construction.)

After two notices, a B.C. dog owner can be forbidden from having a dog for up to a year.
Dogs in Canada Special Issue 1986: 19

(This is the disputed construction.)

... [He] was declared guilty, when serving as Nova Scotia's Minister of Social Services, of a breach of the Nova Scotia Information Act, which forbids any department official from releasing confidential information about an individual.
Andrew Heard *Canadian Constitutional Conventions* 1991: 166

(This is the disputed construction.)

forceful, forcible In Canadian usage, *forceful* is preferred for a figurative use of force ('She presented a forceful argument'), while *forcible* implies the use of physical force ('forcible confinement'). The connotations of *forceful* are often favourable, while those of *forcible* are usually unfavourable. In British English, however, *forcible* is used favourably (and figuratively) in phrases such as 'a forcible reminder', 'a forcible argument', and 'a forcible expression of opinion'. The figurative use of *forcible* may create unintentional humour for Canadian readers.

Direct and simple language always has some force behind it, and the writers of gobbledegook don't want to be forceful; they want to be soothing and reassuring.
Northrop Frye *The Educated Imagination* 1963: 61

Since 1960 3 million black South Africans have been forcibly moved off their land or from their homes in the cities onto the 13 percent of land left for non-white use.
Briarpatch Dec. 1989–Jan. 1990: 24

His professors ... spoke in warm terms of his 'modest and manly character,' his devotion to philosophic study, his special gift of a clear and forcible English style, and his logical vigour and metaphysical insight.
Hilda Neatby *Queen's University* 1 (1978): 136

(This figurative use of *forcible* is uncommon in Canadian prose.)

In the fall of 1910, Miss Ella Constance Sykes, a high-born English woman of redoubtable energy and enterprise, was struck forcibly by a letter to *The Times*, which reminded her of the hard future faced by so many of the million surplus women in the United Kingdom.
Pierre Berton *The Promised Land* 1984: 156

(This figurative use of *forcible* is uncommon in Canadian prose.)

forebears, forbears, forbear *Forebears* (the noun is almost always plural) are ancestors, those who have come before. *Forbears* is an uncommon spelling variant. *Forebearers* is an error.

To *forbear* is to hold back, to keep oneself from saying or doing something.

About one-third of the valley's 2,000 residents are Bella Coola Indians. Their forebears met explorer Alexander Mackenzie in 1793, that wily Scot who discovered this overland path to the Pacific....
Harrowsmith Jun.–Jul. 1985: 42

Many of us were baptized and married here, and likely will be buried from here as well—as were our forebears, in some cases three, four, five generations back.
Chronicle Telegraph (Quebec) 3 July 1991: 10

Not that all our forbears were deluded.
Robertson Davies *A Voice from the Attic* 1960: 101

(This spelling is the less usual one.)

The chapter on origin and history is full of references to old drawings and articles on poodles plus some charming pictures of our poodles' forebearers.
Dogs in Canada Aug. 1986: 64

(The correct spelling is *forebears*.)

I cannot forbear from commenting on his rather patronizing remark....
Gazette (Montreal) 21 March 1993: D2

forego   see FORGO

foreign phrases   see LATIN PHRASES; FRENCH WORDS; GERMAN WORDS

forename   see FIRST NAME

forensic   *Forensic* is derived from the Latin *forum*, the place where court cases were argued, and means legal or having to do with a court of law. It is often used in combination with other words to indicate a legal specialization within a field: 'forensic accounting', 'forensic anthropology', 'forensic chemistry'. *Forensic medicine* is the use of medical knowledge to establish guilt or innocence. *Forensic* is so often used with reference to medical evidence that several dictionaries now list 'pertaining to medical evidence' as one of its senses.

An older meaning of *forensic*, related to the debates held in the Roman Forum, is 'rhetorical' or 'suited to debate'.

He used the services of a team of forensic accountants from the firm of Touche Ross & Co. to analyze every piece of Maple Leaf Gardens paper.
Jack Batten *Robinette* 1984: 193

A forensic toxicologist was of the opinion the chemicals could be dangerous taken in large quantities....
London Free Press 28 April 1988: A2

Forensic evidence presented at the trial indicated that the blood was consistent with Christine's....
Winnipeg Free Press 17 Nov. 1990: 8

(This is the new sense of *forensic* meaning medical.)

By the time John Robinette arrived in the courtroom, the forensic approach to litigation was giving way to a less showy and more measured style.
Jack Batten *Robinette* 1984: 36

(Here *forensic* means rhetorical.)

foreseeable future   This phrase is often condemned as trite. However, it does serve to distinguish the future about which it may be thought possible to make sensible predictions from the future in general. Note that *foreseeable* is often misspelled without its first *e*, as *forseeable*.

Dental anesthetic, delivered by the dreaded needle, will be around for the forseeable future despite a universal longing for alternatives.
Province (Vancouver) 26 Nov. 1990: 43

(The correct spelling is *foreseeable*.)

forest, woods, wood, grove, bluff, stand, backwoods, bush   A large, heavily treed area is usually called a *forest*. *Woods* are less dense or wild than forests. In Britain a grove of trees is called a *wood*, but in Canada this usage is rare (usually literary).

In the 1970s, a survey (*Modern Canadian English Usage*, 1974) asked Canadians what they would call a group of trees. Given a choice of *copse*, *grove*, *bluff*, *clump*, and *spinney*, most respondents chose *grove* (44 per cent), with *clump* a close second (38 per cent). However, Albertans preferred *clump*, while in Manitoba and Saskatchewan *bluff* was more common than either *clump* or *grove* among adults, although schoolchildren in these two provinces favoured *grove*. It is likely that a group of trees is called a *bluff* on the prairies because from a distance it appears as a sudden rise in the flat landscape. A *stand* is a thick standing growth of trees or other plants, primarily of one type, covering a small area.

The bush and *the backwoods* are common expressions for an unpopulated or sparsely populated area: 'He had just come out of the bush, where he had lived for six months'. These terms occasionally carry derogatory connotations; to describe people as 'from the backwoods' may imply that they lack refinement. In Canadian English to *be bushed* means to be tired, or, in bush country, to show signs of mental confusion as a result of isolation.

Two nights before, shivering in a cottonwood bluff, they had slept in six inches of snow.
Pierre Berton *The Promised Land* 1984: 91

The Cheyenne is the perfect choice for someone who lives or works in the backwoods, where the snowmobile is essential to the transportation of goods and passengers to and from the chalet.
Snowmobile Canada 1991 Buyers Guide: 44

It was the sort of house rich people sometimes have off in the bush where they can go to rough it.
Max Braithwaite *The Night We Stole the Mountie's Car* 1971: 117

foreword, preface Both are introductory statements in a book. A *foreword* is literally something before the main text. The word *preface* is derived from the Latin for 'say before'. Most dictionaries make the distinction that a *preface* is written by the book's author, while a *foreword* is written by someone else (thus it is possible for a book to have both a foreword and a preface), but these words are often used interchangeably.

Foreword is spelled with an *e* and two *o*'s. Occasionally it is misspelled *forward*.

... White decided to put some of his disparate short pieces together. The result is an entrancing medley of poems, stories and oral histories garnished with photographs, sketches, maps and a foreword by Barry Broadfoot.
Vancouver Sun 17 Nov. 1990: D19

(Here someone other than the author wrote the foreword.)

Although Clark wrote only a new foreword for *Beyond the Fall of Night*, the book is a roadsign to his past.
Vancouver Sun 13 Oct. 1990: D18

(Here the author himself wrote the foreword.)

for free Some commentators consider the informal expression *for free* childish, and maintain that *free* by itself will always do: 'The movie was free (*not* for free)'. There are many contexts, however, in which *for free* is idiomatic ('He'll play for free') and *free* alone is not ('He'll play free'). In formal writing it's best to substitute 'at no cost' or 'without payment' or 'free of charge' for the disputed phrase.

You could get warm for free there.
Constance Beresford-Howe *Night Studies* 1985: 4

For 75 cents ... buy Sunday's Province and I'll tell you or your nagged ones how to stop smoking. The rest of the paper you can have for free.
Province (Vancouver) 27 Dec. 1990: 14

Boris Becker refused to play in the $6 million US Grand Slam Cup tournament because he objected to the obscenely high prize money, but he'll play for free.... the German star won't charge for playing in an Adelaide charity event to benefit children with cancer.
Vancouver Sun 28 Dec. 1990: F2

forget, forgot, forgotten 'He had forgot about his ticket' and 'He had forgotten about his ticket' are both acceptable in Canadian English. In British English *forgot* is archaic as a past participle.

And he winked at Alf who had forgot all about his camel humps.
David Williams *Eye of the Father* 1985: 73

forgo, forego The word meaning to do without or relinquish is spelled either *forgo* or *forego*. The word meaning precede is always spelled with the *e*: 'the foregoing remarks'.

The past tense and past participle of both verbs are patterned on the root verb *go*: *for(e)went, for(e)gone*. In the phrase 'a foregone conclusion', *foregone* means predictable or inevitable.

But the police should have thought about the consequences of credit cards before advising people to forgo cash for plastic.
Gazette (Montreal) 25 Oct. 1990: G2

Several hundred loggers from across Vancouver Island are expected to forego a day's wages to attend a solidarity rally Monday at the Nanaimo courthouse.
Vancouver Sun 3 Nov. 1990: A6

In the light of what has been considered in the foregoing pages, that comment may not seem an overstatement.
Canadian Bar Review 66.3 (1987): 613

Oscar de la Renta forewent his party-boy reputation and offered several muted suits with only velvet trim by way of fanciness.
Globe and Mail (Toronto) 14 May 1985: F1

formal, informal writing In this book, reference is made to formal and informal writing when a usage is considered generally more appropriate to one level of formality than another; this is not to say that a usage labelled 'informal' should be avoided altogether. There is no firm boundary between formal and informal writing, and some writers will always write more formally than others in similar circumstances. Broadly speaking, however, formal writing is the style found in academic journals, judicial opinions, legal documents, government reports, civic announcements, speeches for ceremonial occasions, submissions or reports to authorities, literary journalism, and letters to people one has never met. It tends to be serious, precise, and impersonal.

Writing in most magazines and newspapers is informal. Informal writing is closer to everyday speech: it does not make use of elevated vocabulary or studied syntax, and it may take a familiar tone with its readers. Friendly correspondence is often more informal still. It may contain slang, abbreviations, vague references, ellipses, sentence fragments, and syntactic U-turns. These features, which would mar formal writing, add warmth and immediacy to a personal letter.

See also COLLOQUIAL; STANDARD, STANDARD ENGLISH; VERNACULAR.

former name   see MAIDEN NAME

formidable   The standard pronunciation of *formidable*, which means inspiring awe or fear, is *FOR mi duh bul*. The alternative pronunciation *for MID uh bul* is accepted in Canada and the United States, but disputed in Britain.

forte   *Forte*, meaning a person's strong point, is almost always pronounced *FOR tay* or *for TAY* in North America. Some commentators have recommended the pronunciation *FORT* because the word is not derived from Italian, in which it would be pronounced with two syllables, but from French. Although this one-syllable pronunciation is found in British English, it has not caught on in North America. The most common pronunciation in the Canadian musical world is *FOR tay*.

fortuitous, fortunate   *Fortuitous* and *fortunate* are both derived from the Latin *fors*, 'chance' or 'luck'. Most dictionaries distinguish between *fortunate*, meaning lucky or privileged, and *fortuitous*, meaning accidental or by chance, and most usage guides warn against confusing them: a fortuitous event may well have an unfortunate result. However, many writers use *fortuitous* only in the sense of 'by lucky chance'. Some dictionaries record this sense, and it can't really be faulted since it falls within the scope of the approved meaning. What should be avoided is the use of *fortuitous* to refer to a state of prosperity rather than a lucky accident.

It is fortuitous and to a large extent arbitrary which persons are detected as being HIV antibody-positive and refused entry [to the country].
Gazette (Montreal) 22 June 1990: B3

(Here *fortuitous* means by chance and is connected to an unfortunate event.)

Hennessy's involvement with the musical was fortuitous rather than planned.
Gazette (Montreal) 26 July 1990: D10

... rich provinces like Alberta and B.C. have a duty to share the wealth they acquired not by their inherent genius but by fortuitous circumstance.
Vancouver Sun 28 May 1990: A7

It has been a fortuitous Year of the Horse for the Hongkong Bank of Canada. The nation's largest foreign bank racked up a 38.9-per-cent increase in profits....
Province (Vancouver) 19 Dec. 1990: 36

(The word required here is *fortunate*.)

forty, four, fourth, fourteen   *Forty* is the only variant of *four* that omits the *u*; it is sometimes misspelled *fourty*. *Fourth* is sometimes misspelled *forth*.

Fourty-three of 46 coureurs de bois earned gold medals or gold bars, going the distance after camping outdoors overnight.
Gazette (Montreal) 12 Feb. 1990: D7

(The correct spelling is *forty*.)

forty-ninth parallel   The *forty-ninth parallel* divides Canada and the United States from Lake of the Woods on the border of Manitoba and Ontario to just south of Vancouver on the mainland of British Columbia. Although the southern tip of Vancouver Island and most of the populated areas of Eastern Canada are south of the forty-ninth parallel, the term is used loosely to describe the Canada–U.S. border. The phrase is perfectly comprehensible to Canadians, but is best avoided when writing for a wider audience.

The expansion of *Harrowsmith* demonstrates that, in certain ways, the forty-ninth parallel is irrelevant.
Saturday Night Feb. 1986: 12

Californian speech is probably even closer to Canadian than the General American heard immediately south of the forty-ninth parallel, and the pronunciation presented by Newman as 'correct' is the pronunciation you would hear almost anywhere in Canada.
Saturday Night March 1986: 50

francophone

founder   see FLOUNDER

four, fourth, fourteen   see FORTY

fourth estate, fifth estate   In pre-industrial Europe, society was divided into three 'estates': the nobility, the clergy, and the common people. The press established itself as the *fourth estate* (a fourth political force) when it began to report on parliamentary debates and decisions in the late eighteenth century. In current usage the term *fifth estate* refers to the electronic media of television and radio. This term is familiar to many Canadians as the name of a CBC public affairs show.

> ... modern historians continue to date the rise of the press as the fourth estate from the effective acknowledgment after 1772 of the press's right to publish parliamentary debates.
> J.A.W. Gunn *Beyond Liberty and Property* 1983: 90

> Demers is a skilled manipulator of the media, Murray suggested, and now that Demers is a member of the fifth estate he has concocted a piece of folklore to make himself look good.
> *Vancouver Sun* 23 Oct. 1990: C2

fractions   see HYPHENATION

fractious   see FACTIOUS

francization, francize   *Francization* (pronounced *fran si ZAY shun*) is the process of assimilating or converting things into French. French-speakers have always *francized* words borrowed from other languages (English *budgetary* became French *budgétaire*), just as English-speakers have anglicized foreign borrowings. However, in the province of Quebec today, francization is not just a spontaneous linguistic process but a legislated policy. The provincial Office de la langue française oversees the creation of technical terms to parallel terminology developing in English and other languages. The Office also oversees the francization of business in Quebec: all large and medium-sized companies operating in the province must use French as their working language and must be certified to that effect. The word *francization* is used as well in reference to policies and programs designed to assimilate immigrants to the province's francophone rather than anglophone population.

The legislated promotion of the French language is a new Canadian sense of *francization*. In earlier British usage the word meant conferral of French national status or acculturation to France.

Francize and *francization* are anglicized spellings of the French words *franciser* and *francisation*. Occasionally the noun is spelled with an *s* instead of a *z* in Canadian English.

> 'The young anglophones that I am in touch with are functionally and operationally bilingual,' said Guilotte, who develops francization programs for large companies in Montreal.
> *Gazette* (Montreal) 8 March 1990: A6

> 'But it is only by fostering access to all immigrants to adequate francization services that Quebec will maximize the spinoffs from immigration.'
> *Gazette* (Montreal) 14 Dec. 1990: B3

> The trouble with francization is that it makes it more difficult to remain in blissful ignorance of the mindset of francophone Quebecers....
> *Gazette* (Montreal) 2 May 91: B3

> ... the Centre de linguistique de l'entreprise, which helps Quebec businesses 'francize' their operations, or increase the use of French, [reported] that some businesses have to give their francophone employees basic courses in their mother tongue.
> *Gazette* (Montreal) 18 Mar. 1992: B3

See also FRANCOPHONE.

Franco-   see FRANCOPHONE; QUEBECKER.

francophone, anglophone, allophone   A *francophone* is a French-speaker—in Canada, usually someone whose first language is French. The adjective *francophone* means French-speaking, or French-language, or having to do with the French-speaking population. An *anglophone* is an English-speaker. An *allophone* (from the Greek for 'other sound') is an immigrant to Quebec whose first language is neither French nor English.

Francophone, anglophone, and *allophone* have all been absorbed into Canadian English from Canadian French over the last few decades. Normally, words with the prefixes *Anglo-* and *Franco-*, such as *Anglo-Irish, Anglophile,* or *Franco-Prussian*, are capitalized in English, but in the case of *francophone* and *anglophone* the French convention of writing these words without capitals has been adopted.

Allophone in the sense outlined above is a Canadianism, because it takes its meaning from a particu-

219

larly Canadian linguistic and political situation. However, *allophone* is also used around the world as a technical term in linguistics.

> That may be why ... young francophones are now about as likely as young anglophones to complete university.
> Irving M. Zeitlin and Robert J. Brym *The Social Condition of Humanity* 1991: 165

> At least one francophone country artist, Gilles Goddard, a bilingual songwriter and performer from Cornwall, Ontario, has received recognition from the Quebec music industry.
> *Queen's Quarterly* 95 (1988): 297

> This distinction is important to many of the 47 member countries of the francophone summit.
> *Gazette* (Montreal) 9 June 1992: B6

> But that job went to Montreal broadcaster and former anglophone rights activist Royal Orr.
> *Vancouver Sun* 16 Dec. 1992: C5

> But Constas said he does not consider himself an allophone. 'I speak French to my two children,' he said. 'The only thing that isn't French about me is my name.'
> *Gazette* (Montreal) 14 June 1992: A3

> By 2000, the percentage of allophone Montrealers will rise to 26 per cent from the current 19 per cent.
> *Gazette* (Montreal) 7 April 1992: A3

See also ACADIA; FRANCIZATION; QUEBECKER.

Frankenstein   In Mary Wollstonecraft Shelley's novel *Frankenstein, or The Modern Prometheus* (1818), Frankenstein is the scientist who constructs a man-like monster and eventually perishes in a desperate effort to regain control over the creature. Shelley did not give a name to Frankenstein's creation, but generations of movie-goers believe that Frankenstein is the name of the monster. Those familiar with the book are likely to refer to 'Frankenstein's monster' or 'a Frankenstein monster'; however, the use of *Frankenstein* to mean monster is standard according to the dictionaries.

> It's a Chinaman, a Frankenstein monster and a child in a rat suit [a halloween scene].
> Margaret Atwood *Life Before Man* 1979: 44

> Perhaps, Dyer and the National Film Board think all these things are bogeymen like Frankenstein on late-night movies.
> *Maclean's* 31 March 1986: 9

Fransaskois   see QUEBECKER

free   see FOR FREE

freedom fighter   see GUERRILLA

freelance, freelancer, free-lance, free lance   In Canadian usage, the most common spelling of the verb is *freelance*. *Freelancer* and *freelance* are alternative forms of the noun. The adjective is spelled *free-lance* or, less commonly, *freelance*.
 In the Middle Ages, a *free lance* was a mercenary soldier.

> After graduation he took his one and only salaried job as a department-store window designer before going on to freelance as a commercial artist for 10 years.
> *Vancouver Sun* 28 Dec. 1990: 17

> Such lucrative projects enabled Brittain—who has worked as a freelancer since 1968—to spend time on painstaking, low-budget documentaries for the NFB and the CBC.
> *Maclean's* 28 March 1988: A42

> The Hampstead headmaster's son, born in 1882, began his writing career as a freelance for Punch.
> *Vancouver Sun* 22 Dec. 1990: D20

> The chilling effect would be all the more noticeable for free-lance and academic researchers who do not have the resources of a corporation behind them.
> *Ottawa Citizen* 1 Nov. 1990: A4

> Now he's back as a freelance drummer working with the best B.C. bands and creating a solo recording career.
> *Vancouver Sun* 10 Aug. 1990: 25

free rein   *Free rein* is a figurative application of the expression for loosening one's grip on a horse's reins, allowing it to go wherever it pleases. Since *rein* and *reign* sound alike, the expression is often misconstrued as *free reign* or anarchy.

> Callers yesterday to a Kahnawake open-line radio show said Chateauguay police are not enforcing the law at the highway barricade, but giving free reign to rabble-rousing town residents who are burning effigies on municipal lamp-posts.
> *Gazette* (Montreal) 18 July 1990: A4

> (The usual expression is *free rein*.)

> Both Chisholme and Christie made it quite clear in their reviews that they regarded literature in which the fancy was given free reign as being inappropriate to a new country.
> Carl Ballstadt, ed. *The Search for English Canadian Literature* 1978: xvii

(The usual expression is *free rein*.)

See also FOLK ETYMOLOGY.

freeway see ROAD

French Canadian, French-Canadian see QUEBECKER

French words, pronunciation of What follows is a brief guide intended to help with the pronunciation of French words and phrases commonly used in English. Generally, consonants at the ends of words are not pronounced (e.g., *esprit de corps* is pronounced *ess PREE duh CORE*); a single *m* or *n* at the end of a word (and often in the middle) is barely pronounced itself, but affects the sound of the vowel that precedes it. Thus *temps* is pronounced (roughly) *TAH(m)*; *sans*, *SAH(n)*; and *mont*, *MOH(n)*. A number of these pronunciations are only approximate, since some French vowel sounds are not found in English.

French	English	
à	a (bad)	à la (*A LA*)
â	a (bad)	château (*sha TOE*), grâce (*GRASS*)
as	aw (law)	pas (*PAW*)
au(x)	o (so)	faux (*FOE*)
é(e)	ay (say)	cliché (*klee SHAY*), née (*NAY*)
è	e (bed)	pièce (*pee ESS*)
ê	e (bed)	bête (*BET*)
eau(x)	o (so)	beau(x) (*BO*)
et	ay (say)	gourmet (*goor MAY*)
eu	uh	bleu (*BLUH*)
ç	s	garçon (*gar SOH[n]*)
g (before *e*, *i*, or *y*)		
	zh	rouge (*ROOZH*), gendarme (*zhah[n] DARM*)
j	zh	joual (*zhoo AL*)
o, ô	o (so)	table d'hôte (*TA bluh DOTE*)
oeu	uh	hors d'oeuvre (*or DUH vre*)
oi(s)	wah	noir (*NWAR*), bourgeois (*BOOR ZHWAH*), coiffure (*kwa FYOOR*)
qu	k	clique (*KLEEK*)

See also À LA; À LA CARTE; TABLE D'HÔTE; AU; BEAU, BEAUX; BÊTE NOIRE; BLEU, ROUGE; BLOC; CLICHÉ; CLIQUE; COIFFURE, COIFFEUR; CONNOIS-SEUR; CONTRETEMPS; COUP DE GRÂCE, PIÈCE DE RÉSISTANCE; COUREUR DE BOIS, VOYAGEUR; DE-BACLE; DÉJÀ VU; DOUBLE ENTENDRE; ÉMIGRÉ; ENTRÉE; FAUX PAS; FLEUR-DE-LIS; FRANCO-PHONE; GARAGE; GENDARME; GOURMET; HORS D'OEUVRE(S); JOUAL; LARGESSE; MACABRE; MANQUÉ; MÉTIS; NAIVE; PASTICHE; PÉQUISTE; PREMIÈRE, DÉBUT; QUEBECKER; RECONNAIS-SANCE, RECONNOITRE; REPERTOIRE; RÉSUMÉ; SANS; SAULT; TUQUE; VIS-À-VIS.

freshman see FIRST-YEAR STUDENT

friendly, friendlily Though *friendly* is listed in dictionaries as both an adjective and an adverb, the adverb use is so rare in contemporary English that it sounds ungrammatical: 'They greeted us friendly'. *Friendlily* first appeared in the seventeenth century as an alternative adverb, but it too is rare, probably because the double ending sounds awkward. The most common way around this difficulty is to recast the sentence to allow the use of the adjective: 'She gave us a friendly smile'; 'They insulted each other in a friendly fashion'.

Friendly is one of several words that entered English before the seventeenth century, at a time when the *-ly* ending was used to create adjectives as well as adverbs. Others include *courtly*, *homely*, *kindly*, *princely*, *rascally*, and *scholarly*.

> They went on hikes with their little picks and kits, and chipped samples off cliffs; then they ate jelly sandwiches and copulated in a friendly way behind clumps of gold-enrod and thistles.
> Margaret Atwood *Life Before Man* 1979: 111

> But even Mrs. Thatcher's Conservative diehards are now beginning to look at the American military presence in a less friendly light.
> *Canadian Churchman* Jun.–Jul. 1986: 9

See also ADJECTIVES AND ADVERBS.

from see BORROW; OFF, OFF OF; FROM

front-runner The term *front-runner* was coined early in the twentieth century to refer to a contestant who likes to take the lead at the beginning of a race and force the pace, as opposed to one who likes to come from behind. The idea that the front-runner was in a strategic position was lost when the term began to be used metaphorically. *Front-runner* now usually means leading contender or favourite. Though criticized as a debasement, this meaning is too well established to be considered wrong. In fact, the older meaning of *front-runner* is virtually unknown outside horse-racing circles. Although most dictionaries hyphenate *front-runner*, one- and two-word spellings are not uncommon.

'There's no clear frontrunner,' said one Tory constituency president.
Calgary Herald 11 Sept. 1992: A12

(Here *frontrunner* means leader.)

It was no disgrace to find himself behind such perennial stars as Dizzy Gillespie (second), Roy Eldridge (fourth), and Louis Armstrong (sixth), or even the swing trumpeter Harry James (third), but the other front-runners were about the same age as Davis and had been learning their scales or sitting anonymously in band sections when he was already making innovations.
Jack Chambers *Milestones* 1983: 175

(Here the *front-runners* are leaders.)

Emily MacLennan of C.P. Allen, national champion in the under-15 1500m, is the front runner in the intermediate girls category.
Daily News (Halifax) 6 Nov. 1992: 62

(Here *front runner* means favourite.)

No front-runner has ever won the Mile, and Gulfstream's tight course doesn't favor early speed.
Toronto Star 11 Oct. 1992: G10

(The older meaning of *front-runner* is intended here, in the context of horse racing.)

frosh   see FIRST-YEAR STUDENT

froze, frozen   The use of *froze* as an adjective ('I was half froze') or as a past participle ('We could have froze') is non-standard. *Frozen* is correct.

'I am frozen with an insane fear that keeps me cowering in the bottom of the trench.'
The Beaver Dec. 1989–Jan. 1990: 58

'I realized I would have frozen to death'.
Edmonton Journal 21 Sept. 1992: n.p.

Michael kept watching the homeless and thinking about ... how he had read in the newspaper that a street person in Seattle had froze to death in the surprising cold.
Province (Vancouver) 28 Dec. 1990: 14

(Here *frozen* is required.)

fruition, fructification   *Fruition* and *fruit* come from the same Latin root, *fruor*, 'enjoy'. According to *Fowler's* (1965), *fruition* properly refers to the enjoyment that comes from eating or possessing

real or figurative fruits, and should be distinguished from *fructification*, the bearing of fruit. While 'enjoyment' is the oldest meaning of *fruition*, it's not the current one. Few usage guides uphold the distinction pointed out by *Fowler's*. *Fruition* is now commonly used to mean the bearing of fruit, either literal or figurative, while *fructification* is found only in scientific writing.

His mature style blossomed during his months in Davis's sextet and came to full fruition almost immediately after he left it.
Jack Chambers *Milestones* 1983: 300

Some had managed to clear a small patch and to bring a few vines and fruit trees to fruition.
Irving M. Zeitlin and Robert J. Brym *The Social Condition of Humanity* 1991: 307

The use of sex hormones to induce species to spawn in captivity is coming to a literal fruition.
Globe and Mail (Toronto) 18 March 1985: P11

fuchsia   *Fuchsia* (pronounced *FEW shuh*) is the name of a flower and a colour—an intense purplish red or purplish pink. The word is commonly misspelled *fuschia*. The plant was named after the German botanist Leonhard Fuchs; remembering this may help with the spelling.

Hovering below a fuschia, a hummingbird sips nectar from the red flowers it prefers.
Province (Vancouver) 6 Sept. 1990: 28

(The correct spelling is *fuchsia*).

-ful, cupful, spoonful, teaspoonful   The plural of words ending in *-ful*—*cupful, spoonful, teaspoonful, carful*, etc.—is usually formed by adding a final *s*: *cupfuls, spoonfuls, teaspoonfuls, carfuls*. The variants *cupsful, spoonsful, teaspoonsful* and *carsful* are much less common, and are criticized by some authorities.

With spoonfuls of buffalo stew half-way to their mouths, she and Perdue paused, turned to the kitchen window.
Geoffrey Ursell *Perdue: And How the West Was Lost* 1984: 106

In this country, almost daily, a generous providence provides the weary scribe with large drams of paradox and heaping spoonfuls of irony.
Vancouver Sun 30 Jan. 1990: B1

'I take just two spoonsful of the mixture every day.'
Gazette (Montreal) 23 Sept. 1990: D3

(This usage is less common and less widely accepted.)

I recently learned that a glass of apple juice—with no added sweetener—can contain six teaspoonsful of fruit sugar.
Gazette (Montreal) 11 April 1990: E5

(This usage is less common and less widely accepted.)

See also PLURALS.

fulfil, fulfilment, fulfill, fulfillment Canadian spelling is about evenly divided between *fulfil* and *fulfill*. The Canadian Press recommends *fulfil*, so this spelling is dominant in newspapers and in the many magazines that follow the Canadian Press guidelines. The *Globe and Mail Style Book* recommends *fulfill*. It also, rather inconsistently, recommends *fulfilment* rather than *fulfillment* for the noun. Canadians use both these spellings about equally, but for consistency it makes sense to use either *fulfil* and *fulfilment* or *fulfill* and *fulfillment*. The *l* must be doubled in two forms of the verb: *fulfilling, fulfilled*.

Fulfil presents other traps for the unwary. The first *l* is frequently doubled—*fullfil*—and occasionally, perhaps because this first *l* is not enunciated by many speakers, it is sometimes dropped: *fufil*.

To Heavysege, a man who, like Jephthah, worships a God who demands fulfilment of a rash vow of sacrifice even if it involves his own daughter, is really a man in the state of nature....
Northrop Frye *The Bush Garden* 1971: 151

For [Jane] Foster, passing the [fighter-pilot] course was the fulfillment of a life-long dream.
Ottawa Citizen 11 June 1989: A1

... the horse was supposed to run in the July 14 Ascot Sophomore at 1 1/8 miles; but because of an oversight his connections did not fullfil all nomination obligations.
Province (Vancouver) 12 Aug. 1990: 99

(The first *l* is always single: either *fulfil* or *fulfill* would be correct.)

'Canadian companies have good products and good marketing. They fufill their commitments.'
Financial Post 11 Sept. 1989: 11

(The correct spelling is *fulfil* or *fulfill*.)

See also DOUBLING THE FINAL CONSONANT.

fulsome Often found in the phrase 'fulsome praise', *fulsome* has long meant insincere or excessive. Sometimes, however, it is also used to mean abundant, enthusiastic, or comprehensive, and this usage can cause confusion.

As party president Gerry St. Germain noted in a fulsome letter, 'you and Mrs. Mulroney have been the glue that has preserved the unity of our party and the focus and effectiveness of our caucus.'
Calgary Herald 26 Feb. 1993: A4

(Here the writer suggests that the letter was excessive in its praise.)

With a net income of $2.22 per common share, the bank was the most profitable in the country. Analysts and competitors were fulsome in their praise.
Saturday Night July 1986: 41

(Here, since the praise was likely genuine and not excessive, *enthusiastic* would be better.)

'I put it to you that as this case progressed, your allegations became more fulsome and complete because you are fabricating them,' Kaplan told the woman.
Vancouver Sun 27 May 1993: A3

(Here *full* or *detailed* is intended.)

fun Most dictionaries consider the use of *fun* as an adjective ('We had a fun time') colloquial. This usage is common in conversation and in the popular media; however, it should be avoided in formal writing. *Fun-filled, enjoyable*, and *entertaining* can all serve as substitutes.

It is common to complain of the brutality of some of our ancestors' fun, though if we think about the jokes of our own time, we may find them equally harsh.
Robertson Davies *A Voice from the Attic* 1960: 205

(In formal writing, *fun* is used only as a noun.)

Next week, the cubs and scouts will be going to Mont St-Sacrement for their winter camp. We have planned a fun weekend of different winter activities....
Chronicle Telegraph (Quebec City) 27 March 1991: 2

(This use of *fun* is informal.)

See also FUNCTIONAL SHIFT.

functional shift In language, a functional shift occurs when a word that has commonly been used as one part of speech starts also to be used as another. The most common shift is from a noun to a verb. Recent examples of such shifts are *access, format, parent*, and *impact*, nouns of long standing that are increasingly used as verbs too.

Though this tendency is disparaged by language purists, many English words have made successful functional shifts. Verbs that have shifted to nouns include *streak* and *spiral*. Verb phrases now used as compound nouns include *flashback, handoff, takeover*, and *wind-up*. Nouns that are now undisputed as verbs include *audit*, *bypass*, *contact*, and *index*. Adjectives now also used as nouns include *local* (a local person or thing), *natural* (someone with seemingly innate skills), and *temporary* (an office worker hired for a short time). The Gulf War introduced the military use of *unfriendly* as a noun (*an unfriendly*, *unfriendlies*) for the enemy. Adjective-to-verb shifts are relatively uncommon, though *short* is now used as a verb meaning to cheat and *green* is used to mean address (or appear to address) environmental issues.

While the English language has considerable tolerance and precedent for such functional shifts, they usually provoke strong opposition for some time before gaining wide acceptance.

With their new upgrading of Information Access software and hardware this broker looks forward to networking with other customers.
Western Grocer Aug. 1990: 27

(The use of *network* as a verb is still criticized.)

... the major emotions that accompany mating and parenting no longer have to occur within rigid legal and traditional boundaries.
Chatelaine April 1986: 48

(The use of *parent* as a verb was initially scorned.)

The 'Greening' of the grocery store must continue—for the sake of our planet's future.
Western Grocer Aug. 1990: 34

funnel cloud   see CYCLONE

funny, funnily   Usage guides still occasionally warn against the use of *funny* to mean strange, perplexing, or odd. Yet the word is used in these senses almost as often as it is to mean amusing. This usage is perfectly acceptable, except perhaps in the most stodgy prose. On the other hand, the use of *funny* as an adverb meaning oddly, as in 'dress funny' or 'talk funny', is quite informal and not recommended for writing that isn't meant to imitate speech. *Funnily* is the accepted adverb; it means either oddly or amusingly.

In a gutsy, very funny and completely bilingual opening set, Massicotte trashed Ladas ('the only cars on the market that are biodegradable')....
Gazette (Montreal) 18 Nov. 1990: F5

I happened to glance at the rock below my feet. Funny little lines aroused my curiosity and I bent down for a closer look.
Uphere Jan.–Feb. 1990: 49

It's funny how so many of those old wives' tales are resurrected as modern medical science.
Bon Vivant Nov. 1981: 12

For they too were strangers; they too were 'different': they dressed funny and they talked funny and, like so many others who came to the West in those years, they refused to reject the roots of the culture in which they had been nurtured.
Pierre Berton *The Promised Land* 1984: 145

(This adverbial use of *funny* suggests informal speech.)

Satire lacerates, but, funnily enough, it also endears politicians to the public and makes them more human than their speeches or TV news sound bites.
Toronto Star 22 Feb. 1993: C5

Goldman shows us—rapidly, funnily—that those images are real, but that there's a lot more going on behind the scenes.
Province (Vancouver) 6 May 1990: 91

funny money   see SOCIAL CREDIT

further   see FARTHER

fusillade   see BARRAGE

futile   see HOSTILE

future   see FORESEEABLE

G

G7 see GROUP OF SEVEN

gaff, gaffe A *gaff* is a pole with a hook on the end used for landing big fish. *Gaff* is also the name of a spar on a sailboat. The verbal, social, or diplomatic blunder is spelled *gaffe*. A gaffe is almost always embarrassing.

> But, besides that embarrassing gaffe, the dance proceeded relatively unblemished.
> *Globe and Mail* (Toronto) 22 June 1985: E8

> Instead, O'Brien's listing appears on page 1085 in the spot occupied last year by Miroslav Zzub. Bell officials were unable to explain the alphabetical gaff.
> *Ottawa Citizen* 22 Jan. 1990: A2

(The correct spelling is *gaffe*.)

gage see GAUGE

galore *Galore* means in abundance, and is placed after the noun it modifies: 'kittens galore'. It conveys a light-hearted tone inappropriate to very serious or melancholy topics or formal prose.

> Complete with television coverage, international recognition and goals galore, the first world championship got under way in the city that claims to be the birthplace of women's ice hockey.
> *Province* (Vancouver) 21 March 1990: 70

gambit, gamut see GAUNTLET

gaol see JAIL

garage Two hundred and forty Vancouverites were interviewed for the 'Survey of Vancouver English' (1984), and among them they produced twenty discernibly different pronunciations of *garage*. The most common Canadian pronunciation is *guh RAHZH*, rhyming with *mirage*. This is also the most popular American pronunciation. The second and third most common Canadian pronunciations are *guh RAJ*, rhyming with *badge*, and *guh RAZH*, in which the vowel sound in *badge* precedes *zh*. These

two pronunciations are distinctly Canadian. Americans are more likely to rhyme *garage* with *lodge*. None of these pronunciations is popular in Britain, where the stress falls on the first syllable: *GA rahzh*, *GA rahj*, or *GA rij*, rhyming with *carriage*.

The pronunciation of *garage* is so variable because it was borrowed from French only at the beginning of this century. The British have anglicized the stress pattern so that it matches the pattern of Middle English borrowings such as *courage* and *passage*. North Americans have preserved the French stress pattern, which is also retained in similar words borrowed from French, such as *mirage* and *ménage*. Since *zh* is not a native English sound, there is confusion on both sides of the Atlantic about how to pronounce the final *g* of *garage*, and Canadians specifically have not settled on how to pronounce the *a* that precedes it.

garnish, garnishment, garnishee To *garnish* something, especially food, is to decorate it; the decorative items, such as sprigs of parsley or slivers of pimento, are *garnishes* or, rarely, *garnishment*.

In law, *garnishment* is the legal seizure of a portion of someone's salary or property in payment of a debt. The verb is either to *garnish* or to *garnishee*; *garnishee* (pronounced *GAR ni SHEE*) is more common in Canada. In the United States *garnish* is the more common form of the verb because there the debtor who is subject to the process is called 'the garnishee'. *Garnishee* is often mispronounced as if it were spelled *garinshee*.

> They garnish the church with final harvest products such as corn stalks and pumpkins....
> *Globe and Mail* (Toronto) 14 Oct. 1985: A14

> Another man faced garnishment because he stopped paying support to his ex-spouse....
> *Ottawa Citizen* 19 Nov. 1990: E1

> If the usual series of written notices and telephone calls proves fruitless, the final recourse is taking a debtor to

court. In most cases, an order to garnish the debtor's wages is sought.
Ottawa Citizen 29 Nov. 1990: B1

... unless he eventually receives a discharge from the courts in bankruptcy proceedings, any property he acquires for many years to come may also be seized, and judgment creditors may garnishee his salary or wages.
J.E. Smyth et al. *The Law and Business Administration in Canada* 1987: 717

gauge, gage   *Gauge* and *gage* are variants. Both spellings rhyme with *cage*; *gauge* is far more common. To *gauge* something is to measure or estimate it. A *gauge* is a measuring device, or a means of roughly measuring something, or a standard of measure, as in '12-gauge shotgun' or 'narrow-gauge railway'.

It is in caucus that the Cabinet is able to gauge the level of backbenchers' support for a policy.
Andrew Heard *Canadian Constitutional Conventions* 1991: 83

Many of your plants will respond to these changes; it's up to you to gage their response and attend to your plants accordingly.
TLC ... for plants Summer 1991: 9

See also GUN.

gauntlet, gamut, gambit   A *gauntlet* is a type of glove that covers the wrist and may extend up the forearm. Gauntlets were originally part of a knight's armour; throwing one to the ground was a formal way of issuing a challenge. The expressions 'throw down the gauntlet', meaning to challenge someone, and 'pick up the gauntlet', meaning to accept the challenge, have their origins in this medieval custom.

The unrelated expression 'to run the gauntlet' comes from a form of military punishment in which a prisoner was forced to walk between two rows of men armed with clubs and other weapons. This punishment, known in Swedish as *gatlopp*, came to be called *gauntlet* in English through a common process whereby a familiar word is substituted for a foreign one. (See FOLK ETYMOLOGY.) *Gantlet* is a chiefly American spelling variant.

A *gamut*, derived from the medieval Latin word for a musical scale, is a range of something. To 'run the gamut' means to move through a range of things, usually from one extreme to another: 'The courses offered ran the gamut from Art to Zoology'.

A *gambit* is an opening move in chess in which a player sacrifices a piece in the hope of gaining an advantage later on. By extension, *gambit* is used to mean tactic. This calculated move may or may not involve sacrifice. A gambit can also be an opening remark intended to start a conversation. *Gambit* is sometimes mistakenly substituted for *gamut*.

A pair of gauntlet gloves completed the uniform.
Max Braithwaite *The Night We Stole the Mountie's Car* 1971: 124

... recommendations on arms control and disarmament which were being drafted before I left for Geneva in February 1969 reached me in June, presumably after running the gauntlet of interdepartmental brickbats.
George Ignatieff *The Making of a Peacemonger* 1987: 245

... the views on public interest intervention expressed by these courts run the gamut from enthusiastic endorsement to grave suspicion.
Canadian Bar Review 66.3 (1987): 504

When Williams persisted in wanting to see the one displayed, the sales agent replied that it was not actually for sale, but was being used as an advertising gambit.
J.E. Smyth et al. *The Law and Business Administration in Canada* 1987: 145

As an opening gambit he informed me that the Canadian smoked oysters, which were being served as hors-d'oeuvres, tasted like cod liver oil and felt like rubber.
George Ignatieff *The Making of a Peacemonger* 1987: 137

Another type of pain, that from cancer, is regarded as a separate kind, even though cancer covers a whole gambit of diseases which cripple the immune system and leave it vulnerable to other infections, too.
Globe and Mail (Toronto) 27 May 1985: P13

(The word required here is *gamut*.)

gay, lesbian, homosexual   *Gay*, *lesbian*, and *homosexual* are all used as both nouns and adjectives. The words *gay* and *homosexual* may refer to both men and women who prefer same-sex relationships, but sometimes they refer only to men, so it is best to use an inclusive phrase ('lesbians and gays', or 'gay men and lesbians') when reference to both sexes is intended.

The adjective *homosexual* has more clinical connotations than *gay*; *gay* is preferred by gays and lesbians themselves. In the seventeenth century, 'gay' men were rakes and 'gay' women were prostitutes. Even then, *gay* may also have referred to same-sex relationships: historically, in English, several slang words for *prostitute*, such as *queen* and *molly*, have been applied to, and subsequently adopted by, gay men. Nonetheless, it was not until the twentieth century that the 'homosexual' meaning of *gay* was documented in dictionaries.

Recently the words *dyke*, an insulting synonym for *lesbian*, and *queer*, a slur that encompasses lesbians, gay men, and bisexuals, have been adopted intentionally by writers and activists who refuse to accept the stigmatization of non-heterosexual identities.

> Never before have we heard a leader of a national party speak about equality for lesbians and gay men to a national television audience.
> *Rites* Feb. 1990: 10

> 'While it was happening, police officers made offensive remarks to the women, saying "You're all a bunch of dykes."'
> *Rites* March 1990: 5

> I have been out as a dyke since 1976....
> *Rites* Feb. 1990: 4

(Here *dyke* is used in a positive way by a lesbian speaker.)

See also FAG, FAGGOT; SEXUAL MINORITIES.

gendarme, gendarmerie *Gendarme* is borrowed from French and derived from 'gens d'armes', meaning men-at-arms. In France, *gendarmes* are military police officers, members of one branch of the armed forces, whose duties include internal defence and law enforcement in rural areas. *Gendarmerie* refers either to a corps of police officers (as in the French name of the Royal Canadian Mounted Police, la Gendarmerie royale du Canada) or to the headquarters of the force.

Since gendarmes are not municipal police, some usage commentators disapprove of English-speaking writers who use the term generally for any French-speaking police officer. But Canadian writers do use the term in this way, especially in humorous contexts. The loose English use of *gendarme* is not a problem unless the context requires a precise term.

> At that time, the French Government sent in an emergency gendarme corps from Paris to restore order.
> *Globe and Mail* (Toronto) 28 Feb. 1985: P11

> It can be found in U.S. overall strategy for the Middle East, which casts Israel in the role of *gendarme* enforcing 'stability' on the area and its oil supplies.
> Henry M. Rosenthal and S. Cathy Berson, eds. *Canadian Jewish Outlook Anthology* 1988: 169

> City-operated and private parking lots are jammed throughout the tourist season [in Quebec City] ... and the local gendarmerie takes a dim view of violators in no-parking zones.
> Alan Tucker, ed. *The Penguin Guide to Canada* 1991: 280

gender, sex In some languages nouns are grouped into *genders*: categories labelled masculine, feminine, and sometimes neuter. Gender may determine word endings and agreement with other words. Gender is not necessarily tied to sex: for example, in German the word for 'girl' is neuter, while inanimate objects may be feminine or masculine. In English, with a few exceptions, nouns are not gendered, and the gender of English pronouns (*he*, *she*, *it*, etc.) corresponds to biological sex, or the lack of it. There is a convention of using feminine pronouns to refer to ships and cars in English, but that practice has been labelled sexist and may be on the wane.

Some commentators condemn the use of *gender* except as a grammatical term. However, many people today use *gender* as a synonym for *sex*. And these two terms are distinguished by many academic writers who use *gender* to refer to the roles and characteristics associated with men and women by society and *sex* to refer to characteristics that can be classified as anatomical, genetic, or biological; this distinction can be a useful one.

> In their daily speech they abandoned some basic rules of Old English grammar, giving us our wonderfully simple adjectives, with no inflectional endings, and our natural, gender-free nouns.
> *Saturday Night* March 1986: 43

> Most respondents view sex pre-selection—tests used to select the gender of a child—as the technology with the strongest potential for abuse.
> *Ottawa Citizen* 19 Sept. 1990: A14

(Here *sex* and *gender* are used as synonyms.)

> Authorities on women were usually men. They were assumed to possess that knowledge, like all other knowledge, by virtue of gender.
> Margaret Atwood *Second Words* 1982: 216

> Each partner must feel that they are giving and receiving equally in the relationship, whether or not more traditional gender roles prevail.
> *Women and Environment* 12.2 (1990): 29

(Here *gender* refers to cultural expectations linked to sex.)

gender-neutral   see JOB TITLES; SEXIST LANGUAGE

generation   How long is a generation? According to most dictionaries, the average age difference between parents and children defines the length of a generation, and that is usually reckoned at thirty years. However, the word *generation* is also commonly used to describe a set of people born about the same time, who share childhood memories and youthful experiences and who reach adulthood in the same social and economic climate. In this sense, a generation spans about a decade.

First-generation is used to refer both to the first generation to arrive in Canada ('first-generation immigrant') and to the first generation to be born in Canada. This makes expressions such as 'second-generation Canadian' ambiguous unless they are qualified somehow.

> After eleven generations am I still a Frenchman, rather than a North American? Are my children, who are half-Scottish, to be listed as French because three hundred years ago one of my ancestors was Huguenot?
> Richard Davies and Glen Kirkland, eds. *Dimensions* 1986: 123–4

> The new darlings of advertising and Network Row are people in their 20s—the group that advertisers have dubbed the baby-bust generation....
> *Gazette* (Montreal) 28 June 1992: F2

> Residents and nonresidents alike were part of a generation of students with certain distinctive qualities which set them apart from those who came immediately before and after—both from those competent veterans of the late 1940s and from their self-confident and critical successors of the 1960s.
> Frederick Gibson *Queen's University* 2 (1983): 408

> ... the values of the first-generation immigrants make them even more difficult to break away from than your average Canadian-born, out-of-it parents.
> *Spectator* (Hamilton) 6 Oct. 1995: C6

> 'I'm [a] first generation Canadian of parents who were liberated by Canadian solders.'
> *CBC News* [transcript] 11 May 1995: n.p.

> I am a third generation Canadian and very much a product of my culture.
> *Vancouver Sun* 1 April 1995: D3

> (Here 'third generation' may mean either the third generation to be born in Canada or the second.)

genetic   see CONGENITAL

genial   see CONGENIAL

genie, Genie, genius   A *genie* (plural *genii* or *genies*) is a magical spirit. A *Genie* (plural *Genies*) is an award presented by the Academy of Canadian Cinema and Television. A *genius* (plural *geniuses*) is a person whose intellectual or creative gifts are considered extraordinary.

Sometimes a spirit is called a *genius*, as in 'the genius of the place'; the plural is *genii*. Occasionally, *genius* in the sense of gifted person is pluralized *genii*.

> When the boards were torn from the doors and windows of New Westminster's Paramount Theatre in 1988, a century of entertainment ghosts rose up from the dust, the dirt, the shame, and the shadows over Columbia Street, like genies released from a lamp.
> *Province* (Vancouver) 19 Oct. 1990: 32

> In the beginning, the Soviet president probably didn't know that the genii he released would take on lives of their own outside his control.
> *Ottawa Citizen* 16 Oct. 1990: A10

> Excitement surrounding the film culminated last March at the Genies, when *My American Cousin* walked away with six awards, including best picture, director and screenplay.
> *Chatelaine* June 1986: 98

> The great mathematical geniuses often do their best work in early life, like most of the great lyrical poets.
> Northrop Frye *The Educated Imagination* 1963: 54

genitive   see POSSESSIVE

genius   see GENIE

genocide   see HOLOCAUST

gent   While *gentleman* is a neutral or respectful term, its short form, *gent*, is usually humorous and often refers to a dandy.

> When you add a Scotland Yard gent or two and a local aristocrat-turned-sleuth you have the ingredients for some of the most popular reading of the past century.
> *Globe and Mail* (Toronto) 21 Dec. 1985: D21

> The City gent with his bowler hat and rolled umbrella may be no more than an unkind caricature, but even the City's admirers would acknowledge that this square mile in east London has shown itself peculiarly resistant to change.
> *Globe and Mail* (Toronto) 4 May 1985: R2

gentile   see ATHEIST

genuine   The British and the Americans pronounce *genuine* the same way: *JEN yoo in*. The pronunciation *JEN yoo wine*—very common and unstigmatized in Canada—is considered a vulgarism in both the United States and Britain.

genus   see SPECIES

geriatrics, gerontology, geriatric   *Geriatrics* is a branch of medicine that deals with the diseases of the aged and aging, while *gerontology* is the study of the processes and problems of aging. *Geriatrics*, like *obstetrics* and *ethics*, is treated as a singular.

  The adjective *geriatric* means relating to the elderly. *Geriatric* is sometimes used facetiously to describe anything decrepit or run-down; some may find this use insensitive.

> ... take your dog in for a geriatric check-up (heart, kidneys, etc.) while he's still 'middle-aged' and there's time to make changes in diet or treatment which will ease and extend the later years.
> *Dogs in Canada* Special Issue 1986: 66

> But David MacDonald, Canada's African aid co-ordinator, described the UN as an 'infant' rather than the 'geriatric institution' it is often thought to be.
> *Globe and Mail* (Toronto) 7 March 1985: P1

germ   see FLU

German words, pronunciation of   German words—unlike English words—tend to be pronounced exactly as they are spelled. But the relationships between letter combinations and sounds are not always the same in English and German. The following chart may aid in the pronunciation of German loan words and names.

German	English	
au	ow (how)	Frau, Bauhaus
äu, eu	oy (boy)	Fräulein, Freud, Deutschmark
ch	ck*	dachshund
ee	ay (pay)	Beethoven
ei	I	Heinz, stein, Reich
ie	ee (see)	diesel, Diefenbaker
j	y	Johann, jaeger
sch	sh	Schiller, schnapps, schnitzel
tsch	ch	kitsch, Deutschmark
w	v	Wagner, Weltanschauung
z	ts	Mozart, Nazi

*-ch- in words borrowed from German is often pronounced as if it were spelled *ck*. But for words such as *Bach* and *Mach*, were -ch appears at the end of the word, a more German pronunciation results if the -ch is pronounced as an exaggerated version of the English initial *h*, as in *help, hurt*, etc.

gerontology   see GERIATRICS

gerund   see POSSESSIVE BEFORE GERUND

gesture, gesticulation   A *gesture* is a movement, especially of the hands, used to express or amplify one's meaning. *Gesture* (noun and verb) can also refer to any action undertaken to indicate one's intentions or to show politeness. *Gesticulation* is the use of physical gestures, usually in an excited, energetic, or theatrical way. *Gesticulation* is used both as an uncountable noun ('a lot of gesticulation') and in the plural ('wild gesticulations'). The *g* sound in all these words is soft, that is, pronounced like *j*.

> He extends one hand toward the door handle and reaches his other hand out ... in a grand, biblical gesture to the eight school trustees ranged around him.
> *Province* (Vancouver) 6 Dec. 1990: 14

> Restaurant staff borrowed the Quebec flag and raised it Tuesday beside the Canadian flag as a friendly gesture to their guests....
> *Province* (Vancouver) 29 June 1990: 54

> Carving out his thoughts with constant gesticulation, he speaks with the strength and confidence of a stage actor.
> *Maclean's* 21 Oct. 1991: A34

> One girl did a sort of half-knee bob while her left hand made wild gesticulations around the upper half of her body.
> *Catholic Register* 23 Aug. 1986: E4

get   Sometimes *get* is used in place of *be* in passive constructions: for example, 'They got hurt' rather than 'They were hurt'. Some language commentators have called this construction ugly and unnecessary. However, the *OED* includes citations of the passive use of *get* from as early as 1652, and the structure has its special uses.

  First, the *be* structure sometimes leaves it unclear whether an ongoing state or a single event is being described. For example, 'Most of their stock was stolen' could mean either that they routinely offered stolen goods for sale or that they had had a break-in. The *get* passive unambiguously describes an event: 'Most of their stock got stolen'. Second, only the *get* passive can be combined with the emphatic *do*: 'Merchandise does get stolen!'

The *get* passive is quite legitimate but generally informal. In academic writing it is used only when the regular passive would be stilted or ambiguous.

Just because we get elected doesn't mean we get up the next day with any special wisdom.
Saturday Night Feb. 1986: 23

I know people are going to get killed.
Saturday Night July 1986: 14

Sometimes, of course, metaphors got mixed, for it cannot have been easy to proclaim a faith fashioned for rulers from the modest station of an insecure subject.
J.A.W. Gunn *Beyond Liberty and Property* 1983: 163

Sukhomlin also got involved in a furious polemic with the Menshevik Georgii Plekhanov....
Canadian Journal of History 14.1 (1989): 19

See also GOT, GOTTEN.

ghetto, ghettoize In sixteenth-century Venice, the *ghetto* was the area where Jewish people were forced to live. Confining the Jews to a certain quarter was common practice in European cities at the time, and was justified on the grounds that their religion would contaminate the Christian faith. Since the 1900s, any area to which a minority group is restricted by official policy, by poverty, or by racism has been termed a *ghetto*. More recently, *ghetto* has been used figuratively to stress limitations or restrictions on economic and social forms of mobility, as in 'job ghetto' or 'ghetto mentality'. And, more recently still, it has been used without negative connotations to describe voluntarily formed communities: 'student ghetto', 'gay ghetto'.

Although some desk dictionaries do not list the verb *ghettoize*, meaning restrict to a (literal or figurative) ghetto, this verb is perfectly acceptable and current in Canadian writing. Interestingly, the *OED's* earliest quotations for *ghettoization* and *ghettoize* come from Canadian sources: the *Jewish Standard* (Toronto, 1939) and the *Canadian Jewish Chronicle* (1939).

Ghettos is the more common plural of the noun, but *ghettoes* is also accepted.

It is therefore clear that crime in the ghetto is rooted in blocked economic opportunities and in racial discrimination.
Irving M. Zeitlin and Robert J. Brym *The Social Condition of Humanity* 1991: 271

He criticizes them for knee-jerk reactions, overblown rhetoric, and a ghetto mentality which suggests that all those who are not for them are against them.
The Beaver Feb.–Mar. 1990: 59

I began to get worried about the possibility of a new ghetto: women's books reviewed only by women, men's books reviewed only by men, with a corresponding split in the readership.
Margaret Atwood *Second Words* 1982: 106

Likewise several inner city neighbourhoods in Toronto and Vancouver have become identifiable singles ... and gay ghettoes ... with a fully developed commercial infrastructure to serve them.
City Magazine Spring 1988: 36

Rue St-Denis is Montreal's boulevard St Michel, the *quartier Latin*, a Francophone student ghetto of bookstores, cafes, boutiques, restaurants, smoky jazz clubs, cinemas, and theaters.
Alan Tucker, ed. *The Penguin Guide to Canada* 1991: 165

The people at the society have done much to break the old stigma of jazz, seen for so long as an art form ghettoized to late-night hours in smoky clubs in neighborhoods decent folks are afraid to enter.
Vancouver Sun 21 June 1990: F16

And while more women are in the workforce, many are still in low-paying female job ghettos.
Vancouver Sun 19 Oct. 1990: D11

Although there are more women than ever in the work force today, they are still concentrated in the same pink-collar ghettoes as their mothers before them, she said— in jobs with precarious futures, poor salaries and the absence of union protection.
Gazette (Montreal) 20 Feb. 1989: D3

See also BARRIO.

gibe see JIBE

gipsy see GYPSY

Gitksan This Aboriginal group's traditional territory is along the Skeena River and in the Bulkley Valley in northwestern British Columbia. They rose to public attention in a land-claims case, concluded in 1991, that they undertook with their Wetsuwet'en (Carrier) neighbours.

Gitksan (GIT ksan) is sometimes misspelled *Gitskan*; the name of their reconstructed traditional village near Hazelton is Ksan, which should help with the spelling. Their language, Nass-Gitksan, belongs to the Tsimshian family. *Gitksan* is used for both singular and plural.

> In the Gitskan-Wet'suwet'en case, Chief Justice Allan McEachern reject[ed] present-day aboriginal title and the right to self-government.
> *Vancouver Sun* 15 Dec. 1994: SR1

(The correct spelling is *Gitksan*.)

See also CARRIER.

give   The past tense is *gave*. The use of *give* as the past tense, as in 'She give me this puzzle and helped me put it together', is dialectal.

> He give me a blank look. His cheekbones were sharp enough to puncture my lies.
> David Williams *Eye of the Father* 1985: 37

(This use of *give* as the past tense indicates the narrator's lack of education.)

given name   see FIRST NAME

gladiolus, gladiola   Some writers, botanists, and gardeners cringe when a *gladiolus* is called a *gladiola*. The form *gladiola* for a single flower appeared because people, hearing *gladiolus* as *gladiolas*, thought it was a regular English plural and dropped the *s* to form a singular. Thus *gladiolus* is the technically correct singular form, but *gladiola* is acceptable in informal, non-technical contexts.

The preferred plural in formal and technical writing is *gladioli*. However, in everyday speech Canadians tend to avoid pluralizing the word, either by saying 'gladiolus plants' or by using the informal short form *glads*. Canadians also use *gladiolus* as a collective noun: 'I planted gladiolus'. The regularized plural *gladioluses*, though acceptable, is seldom used.

> But women still baked pies, boiled jam and steamed bread for the cooking contests and competed to see who could grow the tallest gladiola.
> *Gazette* (Montreal) 1 Sept. 1990: 15

(In informal writing *gladiola* is acceptable.)

> Larger gladioli are attractive cutting flowers, but I particularly like the butterfly gladiolus.
> *Vancouver Sun* 5 May 1990: C8

> Late-blooming tubers such as dahlias, gladiolas and canna lilies … will also provide some interest in late September and early October.
> *Gazette* (Montreal) 13 Sept. 1990: D3

(Here, in a gardening column, *gladioli* would be more appropriate.)

> Glads can be planted as soon as the digging is good.
> *Ottawa Citizen* 17 May 1990: G7

> Gladiolus plants can be left in the garden until after the first light frosts.
> *Province* (Vancouver) 23 Oct. 1990: 73

> Ferncliff Gardens [offers a] massive selection of dahlias, gladiolus, irises, and peonies.
> *Province* (Vancouver) 8 Nov. 1990: 103

(Here *gladiolus* is used as a collective noun.)

> When can gladioli bulbs be planted and how deep should they be?
> *Ottawa Citizen* 17 May 1990: G7

(The correct form here, where the noun is being used as an adjective, is *gladiolus*; saying *gladioli bulbs* is like saying *tulips bulbs*.)

See also PLURALS, REGULAR, IRREGULAR, FOREIGN.

glance, glimpse   To *glance* at something is to look at it purposely but briefly. To *glimpse* something is to catch sight of it, to see it briefly or partially. With *glance* the emphasis is on the person looking and the action; with *glimpse* the emphasis is on the thing seen.

> When I glanced back again, only her face was visible.
> *Queen's Quarterly* 94.1 (1987): 52

> At last I saw a clearing forming in the distance, and when I got there I could glimpse water spread out ahead through the trees.
> Howard Engel *Murder Sees the Light* 1984: 116

Gloucester, Worcester, Worcestershire, shire   *Gloucester* and *Worcester* are pronounced with only two syllables. *Gloucester* rhymes with *roster*. Some people rhyme *Worcester* with *rooster—WOO ster*. More commonly, though, the first vowel is pronounced like the *oo* in *wood*.

Worcestershire is the name of an English county and of a spicy steak sauce. The *-shire* in *Worcestershire* (and the other shires) is usually rhymed with *hear* or *sure*, not *sire*. However, the word *shire* by itself does rhyme with *sire*.

glutton   see GOURMET

go   see GO, SAY; GO, WENT; GO AND; GOES WITHOUT SAYING; GO MISSING; GONNA

go, say   The substitution of *go* for *say* in recounting conversations is slang ('I go, "Can I come in?" and he goes, "No problem"'). In Standard English, these descriptions of conversations would use *say* in the past tense ('I said, "Can I come in?" and he said, "No problem"'). This usage is currently popular among teenagers and young adults and reviled by many older people. It was first noticed by language commentators in the 1970s. The *OED* connects the new slang meaning to one of the standard meanings of *go*, to emit a characteristic sound, as in 'The sheep goes baaa'. It may also be related to the standard meaning 'be written', as in 'The words go like this'. In print, the substitution of *go* for *say* is still quite self-conscious.

Many young people use 'go' instead: 'So I go, "Where's the restaurant?" And he goes, 'Find it yourself"'.
Ottawa Citizen 23 Dec. 1990: F3

Two weeks later you overhear her whining to a friend. 'So, then he goes, "We're o-ver."'
Ottawa Citizen 2 Sept. 1990: F5

go, went, gone   In Standard English the past tense of *go* is *went*: 'She went'. The past participle is *gone*: 'She has gone'. In some dialects these parts of the verbs are reversed: 'She gone'; 'She has went'.

go and   The phrase 'to *go and do* something' (where *do* can be replaced by any verb) may mean to blunder or make a mistake: 'Now you've gone and done it'; 'He's gone and bought a pet pig'. *Go*, with or without *and*, is also sometimes used to intensify the verb that follows it: 'Go jump in the lake'. These expressions are informal.

'And what kind of a mess have you gone and made this time?' Dora snapped at Nadia.
Canadian Fiction Magazine 63 (1988): 82

She's gone and saved the lucky bastard.
Robert Kroetsch *Badlands* 1975: 69

gobbledygook, gobbledegook   *Gobbledygook* is the original spelling, but *gobbledegook* is also standard for unintelligible speech, writing, or ideas. An American Congressman named Maury Maverick coined the term in 1944 to refer specifically to governmental and bureaucratic reports, which often use complex grammar, indirect phrasing, and inflated vocabulary. As some politicians know, the effect of gobbledygook is to leave people confused. *Bafflegab* is a synonym.

A plethora of benumbing gobbledygook and grandiloquence has been said and written on the subject, mostly by self-professed experts.
Toronto Star 2 June 1990: D3

Ten years ago, aboriginal rights—let alone self-government—was considered a loony idea propounded by a small group of native radicals. When the Dene Assembly of the Northwest Territories asserted its nationhood within Canada in 1975, a senior federal minister dismissed the idea as 'gobbledegook.'
Globe and Mail (Toronto) 4 April 1985: P6

Some ministers stumbled, while others showed they had taken a remarkably firm grip on government gobbledegook. Here, for instance, is how the chairman of Management Board, Elinor Caplan, replied to a question on reviewing programs announced by the Miller cabinet: 'Let me assure the leader of the Opposition that this Government is reviewing carefully and with a sense of sensitivity the commitments made to ensure that the review will be undertaken in a co-ordinated and efficient manner and that we will be proceeding clearly in the immediate future to determine which, if any, of the commitments we will be undertaking.'
Globe and Mail (Toronto) 11 July 1985: P7

See also COLLOQUIAL, INFORMAL, SLANG, JARGON.

God, god   *God* is capitalized when the word refers to the supreme being of any monotheistic religion. This practice usually, though not always, extends to expletives: 'Good God, when did he get back?' References to deities in religions that have more than one god are not capitalized: 'the gods of the ancient Greeks'.

Capitalized pronouns and adjectives relating to the Christian God are beginning to disappear, although their use is still accepted and they are preferable in religious writing.

I prayed to God that if I died in Toronto He would be good enough to take care that this last event in my life should happen on a Saturday to save me from one Toronto Sunday.
Henry M. Rosenthal and S. Cathy Berson, eds.
Canadian Jewish Outlook Anthology 1988: 345

'For god's sake, look at yourself, Karen.'
David Williams *Eye of the Father* 1985: 149

See also HINDU, HINDUISM; ISLAM; RELIGION; SACRED WRITINGS; SIKH.

God Save the Queen   see O CANADA

goes without saying, needless to say Some argue that both these phrases are illogical, since if something goes without saying, it literally is needless to say. Both phrases, however, are idiomatic and common. Like the adverbs *obviously* and *naturally*, they function to suggest without lengthy explanation that a statement is (or should be) self-evident. Writers should avoid overusing these phrases, but they are considered unobjectionable by most commentators.

> It goes without saying that there is considerable variation in the degree to which different men exercise control over different women.
> Carl J. Cuneo *Pay Equity* 1990: 196

> This fact, needless to say, poses a serious challenge to our conclusions.
> *Canadian Journal of Philosophy* 19 (1989): 220

See also OF COURSE.

Goldwynism see MALAPROPISM

go missing To *go missing*, meaning to disappear, is informal. Although the expression is common in speech and in the popular press, in formal writing the verb *disappear* is preferable.

> Indeed, a spokesman for Lloyd's of London noted that in 1984 insurance companies had paid out $385 million to the owners of satellites which had gone missing in space or malfunctioned after being launched.
> *Maclean's* 10 Feb. 1986: 30

> The 33-year-old speech therapist and mother of two went missing on Dec. 17, 1988, after a domestic dispute with her husband.
> *Winnipeg Free Press* 17 Nov. 1990: 1

gone see GO, WENT

gonna *Gonna* is a slang contraction of the phrase 'going to'. The construction is generally used to express an intention or expectation: 'She's gonna work hard all summer'; 'He's gonna be sorry'. *Gonna* is never used for 'going to' in the sense of moving towards a destination: 'I'm going to (*not* gonna) Toronto'. When *gonna* appears in Canadian journalism and fiction, it is meant to imitate very casual speech. It is inappropriate in other contexts and should be used sparingly; most dictionaries do not list it.

> 'I told his secretary, "Look, I'm gonna be there tomorrow morning and if I have to, I'm going to sit down on his doorstep until he talks to us".'
> *Globe and Mail* (Toronto) 4 March 1985: P13

> I was gonna carry on about the mess our country is in, about Quebec's demands, about Brian's idiocy and stuff like that.
> *Province* (Vancouver) 8 Dec. 1991: A55

> The policeman stepped closer and said, 'Are you goin' peaceful, or am I gonna put handcuffs on you?'
> Jack Chambers *Milestones* 1983: 314

> When I decided I was gonna marry that man I knew what I had to do.
> *Canadian Fiction Magazine* 64 (1988): 87

good see ADJECTIVES AND ADVERBS; AS GOOD AS OR BETTER THAN

goodbye, good-bye, goodby, good-by All these spellings are standard, but Canadian writers overwhelmingly prefer *goodbye*.

gormandize see GOURMET

got, gotten Canadians use both *got* and *gotten* as the past participle of *get*: 'I had got *or* gotten a lot done by then'. Both past participles are also used in the United States, while in British dictionaries only *got* is listed. Before 1800, both *got* and *gotten* were in common use in Britain, but after that date *gotten* became obsolete; *Fowler's* (1965) called *gotten* archaic and affected. In North America *gotten* has never become obsolete and certainly could not be condemned on the grounds of affectation. Nonetheless, some North American usage guides, influenced by British ones, have also condemned it. Canadians in general have ignored the unwarranted censure of *gotten*, but academics have taken it to heart. Although common in every other type of writing, *gotten* is rare in academic prose.

> The difference may be that had I been a husband and failed, I might have got away with it.
> *Queen's Quarterly* 96.2 (1989): 232

> Soon, I had gotten as much line out as I was going to, which wasn't a lot.
> *Atlantic Salmon Journal* Autumn 1990: 43

> Mostly we have gotten what we wanted.
> Ken Dryden *The Game* 1983: 110

See also GET; HAVE GOT, HAVE GOTTEN; HAVE GOT TO.

gourmet, gourmand, glutton, gormandize Many commentators maintain that a *gourmet* is a connoisseur of fine food and wine, while a *gourmand*, though appreciative of quality, is more interested in quantity. However, *gourmand* is often used interchangeably with *gourmet*. Unlike *gourmand*, *glutton* always has pejorative connotations of greed and excess.

Gourmet is used more often as an adjective than as a noun, describing such things as menus, restaurants, or specialty food shops. To *gormandize* is to eat either voraciously or discerningly.

> Gourmets from across the globe trek to John Tovey's Miller Howe Hotel here as if it were mecca.
> *Bon Vivant* Aug.–Sept. 1982: 7

> First off, no self-respecting Japanese gourmand would even set foot in a new sushi bar without being taken there by a regular and formally introduced to the head chef.
> *Globe and Mail* (Toronto) 6 April 1985: M8

> (Some commentators would insist on *gourmet* here.)

> What a gourmand for love and punishment he was....
> *Canadian Fiction Magazine* 64 (1988): 80

> (Here *gourmand* replaces *glutton* in a play on the idiomatic expression 'glutton for punishment'.)

> In this atmosphere, gourmandizing does not easily thrive. When was the last time you ate haute with The Beach Boys on tap?
> *Globe and Mail* (Toronto) 5 Sept. 1985: S6

> (The correct spelling is *gormandize*.)

See also EPICUREAN.

government *Government* is often incorrectly spelled without the first *n*. Correctly spelled, *government* contains the word *govern*.

> It has reached the point that all statements of intent on the issue from the goverment are suspect.
> *Financial Post* 9 March 1990: 12

> (The correct spelling is *government*.)

governor general see HEAD OF STATE

graduate, be graduated, graduand From one perspective, a university or other institution graduates students: 'Queen's graduated a record number of students in English this year'. This perspective produces 'Mary Smith was graduated from Queen's', which sounds slightly old-fashioned but is still fairly common. From another perspective, however, students graduate *from* a university. This perspective produces 'Mary Smith graduated from Queen's', which is more common nowadays. Both of these forms are accepted. However, the construction 'Mary Smith graduated Queen's' is both rare and disputed.

Those who are about to receive a degree in a graduation ceremony or convocation are sometimes referred to as *graduands*; once the degree is conferred, they become *graduates*.

> He refers to Mr. Miller as a used-car salesman. Mr. Miller was graduated from McGill University with a science degree in chemical engineering.
> *Globe and Mail* (Toronto) 22 Feb. 1985: P7

> Joe Zuken graduated with distinction from the Winnipeg Peretz Shule.
> Henry M. Rosenthal and S. Cathy Berson, eds. *Canadian Jewish Outlook Anthology* 1988: 375

> I have often heard an honorary graduand, whose achievements had been amply rehearsed in the speech in which he was presented to the Chancellor, go over the whole of that ground again, explaining in detail how he took every step in his distinguished, and wearisomely long, career.
> Robertson Davies *One Half of Robertson Davies* 1978: 54

See also GRADUATE, POSTGRADUATE, POSTDOCTORAL.

graduate, postgraduate, postdoctoral In Canada *graduate* is more often used than *postgraduate* to refer to students who have completed a first university degree and are pursuing a program of study leading to an advanced degree. British and Australian writers use *postgraduate* more often in this context. American dictionaries note that in the United States *postgraduate* may refer to studies following high school as well as university, while *graduate* refers mainly to studies beyond the first university degree.

Postdoctoral refers to research and study beyond a doctoral degree (e.g., a Ph.D.). Many Canadians write *post-doctoral* and *post-graduate*, though major dictionaries do not hyphenate these words.

> He emphasized the importance of liberal and humane studies, rather than science; the importance of undergraduate education, as opposed to graduate studies....
> Frederick Gibson *Queen's University* 2 (1983): 428

> After four years of undergraduate and three years of postgraduate study, my husband entered a four-year medical program at the University of B.C.
> *Vancouver Sun* 5 Nov. 1990: A7

> (In Canada *graduate* is more common than *postgraduate* in reference to studies carried out after completion of an undergraduate degree.)

> The new research ... will require a systems analyst, a good computer and a post-doctoral fellow with expertise in mineral deposits.

Torch: University of Victoria Alumni Magazine Spring 1990: 11

See also GRADUATE, BE GRADUATED, GRADUAND.

grammatical agreement see AGREEMENT, GRAMMATICAL

grand, grandiose Sometimes the adjective *grand* hints at pretension, but often it conveys a very positive impression. *Grandiose* always describes something overambitious, inflated, or pretentious.

He does not appear to be interested in the big conceptual effect or the grand gesture.
Globe and Mail (Toronto) 3 Jan. 1985: E4

In an era when professional historians lament the difficulty the lay public faces in engaging with much that contemporary historians write, Ambrose's work is a refreshingly accessible narrative, written in the grand style....
Queen's Quarterly 95.4 (1988): 808

Even as the boom collapsed several Western cities were still contemplating grandiose schemes designed to enhance their prestige.
Pierre Berton *The Promised Land* 1984: 343

The urge to erect grandiose, egotistical monuments has long been a French characteristic. Louis XIV's immense seventeenth century palace at Versailles is one obvious example, as is the Eiffel Tower, built in 1889 to commemorate the centenary of the French Revolution.
Globe and Mail (Toronto) 16 Oct. 1985: A7

grapple The verb *grapple*, meaning to take hold of, or grip, or wrestle, is used both literally and figuratively. In literal use *grapple* sometimes takes a direct object. When used figuratively, however, *grapple* almost always takes a preposition: usually *with*, but occasionally *for* or *over*.

Muscular linemen grapple ferociously, the ball dips gracefully to earth and the pass connects.
Globe and Mail (Toronto) 17 Oct. 1985: E1

Travel agents must grapple with mountains of ever-changing information.
Canadian Consumer Jan. 1986: 34

... of all the civil servants grappling for job tenure in the department only a minute percentage are of native ancestry.
Globe and Mail (Toronto) 8 May 1985: P6

Any author who attempts to grapple this subject is threatened by engulfment, as if by a giant amoeba, and Dr Matthews is to be congratulated on the degree to

which he imposes form on such a sprawling mass of tenuously related data.
Margaret Atwood *Second Words* 1982: 30

(This figurative use of *grapple* without a preposition is unusual.)

grateful, gratified Usually one is *grateful to* benefactors *for* their help; one is *gratified by* an event or experience, or *gratified that* something has happened.

So, with unintentional sexual messages rampant even in the least likely places, I, for one, am grateful to those who vigilantly expose them.
Harrowsmith Oct.–Nov. 1985: 18

Ray Goldman, one of 15 Canadian fish dealers who tested Dallas as a market, was gratified by the interest Texans showed in some traditionally underutilized varieties.
Globe and Mail (Toronto) 6 April 1985: P6

He was gratified that the CBC purchased the script for a series on Canadian history and gave it a first-class production.
Globe and Mail (Toronto) 31 Oct. 1985: E13

gratuitous, gratuitously *Gratuitous* usually means unnecessary, unwarranted, unsolicited, or unjustified. It can also mean free, but this older meaning is rare. *Gratuitously*, the adverb, is used commonly to mean either 'unnecessarily' or 'without charge'. From the common phrase 'gratuitous violence' some people have mistakenly inferred that *gratuitous* means explicit or graphic.

In Canada, parents, players, teachers, and government leaders have contributed to the effort to eliminate the gratuitous violence of ice hockey.
Queen's Quarterly 94.1 (1987): 127

Saving people from drowning was not Joe Vincent's job, but he did it anyway. It was a voluntary, gratuitous service.
Gazette (Montreal) 16 June 1990: B2

(This usage may be influenced by the French *gratuit*, 'free' or 'without charge'.)

In the meantime, it was agreed that all available facilities should be given to the medical faculty gratuitously.
Hilda Neatby *Queen's University* 1 (1978): 73

(Her *gratuitously* means without charge.)

Even the doctor in the white lab coat delivers her graphic message that there are only three ways to con-

tract AIDS in a way that is easily understood without being gratuitous.
Vancouver Sun 4 April 1990: A11

(Here *gratuitous* is mistakenly used to mean explicit or graphic.)

gray   see GREY

Great Britain   see BRITAIN

Grecian   see HELLENIC

Grecian nose   see AQUILINE NOSE

Greek   see HELLENIC

Green, green   The Green Party, a political party formed in Germany that focuses on environmental issues, and Greenpeace, an environmental activist group formed in Canada, both originated in the 1970s. Members of the Green Party, which has spread to other countries from Germany, are called *Greens* (capitalized). Since the 1970s, *green* (uncapitalized) has been used to describe anything or anyone that protects the environment, or claims to do so. *Green* is also used as a verb in the same contexts.

... institutions such as the Green Party have achieved for the social and political reformer and visionary a more established and politically influential status.
Queen's Quarterly 94.1 (1987): 10

This is the politics of personal awareness and commitment which McConkey espouses, and is increasingly reflected in the emerging paradigm of 'green consciousness', which seems to be taking root and beginning to thrive on a global scale.
City Magazine 10.1 (1988): 41

Naturally, retailers are eager to obtain information on how well green products are selling, particularly with industry surveys indicating that consumers will not only pay more for green products but also switch to a supermarket that provides them.
Western Grocer Aug. 1990: 34

The Australia New Zealand Bank has been 'greened' and is seen as a model of corporate environmental responsibility.
Ottawa Citizen 29 April 1990: C6

The more I ponder, the more I feel that better use of our existing infrastructure could go a long way toward greening up our rush-hour traffic blues.
Vancouver Sun 17 May 1990: A17

See also ECOLOGY, ENVIRONMENT; FUNCTIONAL SHIFT.

green paper, white paper   A *green paper* is a preliminary report prepared by the government to promote debate on an issue in the House of Commons before legislation is drafted. A *white paper* outlines proposed legislation in what the government hopes is its near-final form. These terms are also used in the United Kingdom. Several newspaper style guides recommend capitalizing these names only in the formal title of a document, but most journalists capitalize them in all uses; this is probably a good policy to follow when writing for an audience not familiar with the terms.

Instead of creating the socialist Swedish model, the NDP's recently published Green Paper on Rent Controls will lead to a New York-style rent control system.
Financial Post 12 April 1991: 10

Ten days ago, Mr. Parizeau's successor, Yves Duhaime, released the white paper, a 380-page document entitled White Paper on the Personal Tax and Transfer Systems.
Globe and Mail (Toronto) 19 Jan. 1985: P8

A White Paper produced by the federal government in 1969 proposed eliminating the special legal status of Indians.
Queen's Quarterly 94.3 (1987): 674

(Since readers of this journal are likely familiar with the term, *white paper* need not be capitalized here.)

Greenwich Mean Time, Coordinated Universal Time, UTC   In 1985 the task of operating the atomic clocks that keep the world's time passed from the Royal Observatory near Greenwich, England, to the International Bureau of Weights and Measures in Paris. Since then, *Greenwich* (pronounced *GREN itch*) *Mean Time* has also been known as *Coordinated Universal Time*, abbreviated internationally as *UTC*.

The Globe reports each day the temperatures in various cities around the larger globe. It is curious and tantalizing that these temperatures are taken at noon, Greenwich Mean Time. One would think that the maximum temperature of the day, or the temperature at noon local time, would be of more general interest.
Globe and Mail (Toronto) 2 Jan. 1985: P6

See also STANDARD TIME.

grey, gray   Canadian writers spell this word *grey* more often than *gray*. *Grey* is also the most common British spelling; the American spelling is *gray*.

However you spell the colour, you have no choice with certain proper names:

grey	gray
Grey Cup	Gray's Anatomy
Grey Nuns	Gray's 'Elegy Written in
Greyhound bus	a Country Churchyard'
Earl Grey tea	Gray's Inn (the English
Grey Owl (the	law society)

Englishman, Archibald Belaney, who lived and wrote as a part-Apache)

grievance, grievous, grieve Both *grievance* and *grievous* are often misspelled with the *e* before the *i*. *Grievous* is pronounced *GREE vus*. Sometimes it is mispronounced with an extra syllable, which leads to the misspelling *grievious*.

To *grieve* is to feel grief. Recently the verb has developed a new meaning: to lodge a formal complaint in the workplace.

What's consistent in all these accounts is the sense of grievance, defensiveness and fear among both blacks and whites.
Toronto Star 30 May 1992: J12

Yet, as the players have found out, it's difficult selling your greivances to a Canadian hockey public that has its own selfish agenda.
Vancouver Sun 7 April 1992: D8

(The correct spelling is *grievances*.)

... the court convicted Col. Yehuda Meir of causing greivous bodily harm and behaving in a manner inappropriate for an officer.
Financial Post 24 April 1991: 2

(The correct spelling is *grievous*.)

Since there is no collective agreement in effect, such an employee cannot grieve a discharge.
Toronto Star 3 Aug. 1992: C1

Chief Justice Frank Callaghan ... said the case was before the courts only because the government doesn't have its own process allowing employees to grieve disciplinary actions.
Toronto Star 1 Oct. 1992: A9

grisly, grizzly *Grisly* means horrible or disgusting. *Grizzly* means grey or grey-haired. The 'grizzly bear' gets its name from the appearance of its fur, which ranges from black to brown to blond, but which is always grizzled—flecked with white or grey—on the flanks, back, and shoulders. Although some dictionaries list *grizzly* as a variant of *grisly*, most do not. This distinction is worth keeping.

And this is a book that gives us a clear if grisly view of the various forms of class terror practiced by masters against slaves—progressive mutilation, dismemberment, beheadings, starvation in cages....
Queen's Quarterly 92.1 (1985): 195

Our conversation, in spite of its grizzly subject matter [instruments of torture], was integrating Des and his friend into the group....
Howard Engel Murder Sees the Light 1984: 82

(The standard spelling is *grisly*.)

When painted on a large scale, the same subjects tend to be as intimidatingly theatrical as the grizzly scene of David holding Goliath's head painted by Giambattista Tiepolo.
Ottawa Citizen 10 March 1990: C4

(The standard spelling is *grisly*.)

Grit, Whig, Liberal Members of the Liberal Party of Canada and its provincial counterparts are informally referred to as *Grits*. The name dates from the 1840s, when a radical reform party in Upper Canada was called the *Clear Grits*. In 1870 this party joined with reformers from Quebec to form the Liberal Party.

Since *grit* is abrasive, some feel the nickname is derogatory. However *clear grit* (meaning pure grit) was an expression of praise in the 1840s, acknowledging tenacity. The term is now used neutrally.

Whig is an old British term for members of the political party that favoured political reform and opposed conservatism. The Whigs changed their name to *Liberals* in the mid-1800s. *Whig* is not used as a nickname for the Liberals in Canadian politics, although the term survives in the name of the Kingston, Ontario, newspaper, the *Whig-Standard*.

His parents were Conservative farmers and doctrinaire Methodists. But a single speech by the great Liberal orator Edward Blake turned Dafoe into a Grit....
Pierre Berton The Promised Land 1984: 34

In the past, Raina has run provincially for the Liberals in his native eastern Ontario and has been involved in other Grit campaigns.
Now Magazine 3–9 Nov. 1986: 13

See also CONSERVATIVE.

grizzly see GRISLY

Group of Seven, G7 The *Group of Seven* was a group of Canadian artists whose work challenged the nineteenth-century values that still dominated the Canadian art world in the first decades of the twentieth century. The seven original members, based in Toronto, were Franklin Carmichael, Lawren Harris, A.Y. Jackson, Frank Johnston (who later changed his first name to Franz), Arthur Lismer, J.E.H. MacDonald, and F.H. Varley. A.J. Casson replaced Frank Johnston in 1926. In an attempt to broaden the national perspective of the group, Edwin Holgate of Montreal was invited to join in 1930, and a Winnipegger, L.L. Fitzgerald, joined in 1932. The group existed officially between 1920 and 1933. Tom Thomson painted with several members of the group but died in 1917, three years before it was formally established.

The term *Group of Seven* is also used for the seven leading industrialized countries: the United States, Japan, Germany, the United Kingdom, France, Italy, and Canada. This name is often shortened to G7.

grove   see FOREST

grow   Some commentators have objected to phrases such as 'grow smaller', 'grow thinner', and 'grow narrower', because *grow* suggests adding to or increasing in size. This argument ignores the commonly accepted use of *grow* to mean become, which is found in all types of writing.

The past tense is *grew* and the past participle is *grown*. Sometimes the incorrect past tense *growed* is used for humorous effect. 'I 'spect I just growed' is an allusion to Harriet Beecher Stowe's novel *Uncle Tom's Cabin*; it's the answer the character Topsy gives when she's asked where she came from.

> Looking in through the reflections, it's tempting to contemplate a world which grows smaller and more dangerous as we feed our illusions.
> *Vancouver Sun* 19 Sept. 1990: A13

> But the window for deep interest-rate reductions is rapidly growing narrower.
> *Ottawa Citizen* 14 Sept. 1990: A1

> Like Topsy, the phenomenon just growed.
> *Gazette* (Montreal) 16 Nov. 1990: B7

guarantee, guaranty, warranty   Canadian writers use the spelling *guarantee* for both the noun and the verb, despite the traditional recommendation in style guides that *guarantee* be used as the verb form and *guaranty* as the noun. In Canada, *guaranty* is most commonly seen in the names of various financial or insurance companies.

An assurance by a seller to a buyer that goods or services will be satisfactory is a *guarantee* or a *warranty*. Both words are thought to derive from the same Germanic word meaning guarantor; however, they were borrowed at different times, *guaranty* from Old French and *warranty* from Old Norman French, which accounts for the different spellings. In current writing, Canadians prefer *warranty* for this sense, as in 'The toaster is under warranty for one year'.

> That the process involved federal-provincial negotiation was itself almost enough to guarantee failure.
> *Queen's Quarterly* 94.3 (1987): 667

> A guarantee is a promise to pay only if the debtor defaults: 'If he does not pay you, I will.'
> J.E. Smyth et al. *The Law and Business Administration in Canada* 1987: 246

> Mr. Johnson said Quebec supports Article 23 in the Constitution, which guarantees access to education in either official language wherever numbers warrant, but he added that Article 23 alone is not a sufficient guaranty of minority rights.
> *Globe and Mail* (Toronto) 27 May 1985: P5

(This writer makes the traditional distinction in spelling, using *-ee* for the verb and *-y* for the noun.)

> He said artificial trees, which range from $99 to $199, come with a 10-year guaranty....
> *Financial Post* 19 Dec. 1989: 4

(Here *guaranty* is not incorrect, but *warranty* is the more common term.)

> Car companies will have to double the warranty on emission-control equipment and make available to California as many as one million cars that run on alternative fuels.
> *Ottawa Citizen* 16 Nov. 1990: A7

guerrilla, guerilla, freedom fighter, terrorist   Canadian writers use *guerrilla* (pronounced like *gorilla*) far more often than *guerilla*, but both spellings are accepted. The word, taken from the Spanish for 'little war', dates from the Napoleonic Wars. Guerrilla warfare is usually carried out by irregular, independent forces acting against superior forces, and involves hit-and-run attacks or ambushes rather than large-scale confrontation.

Freedom fighter has been in common use since the Second World War, when it referred to regular or irregular forces that used guerrilla tactics to resist Nazi occupation.

Guerrilla is a fairly neutral term. Those who support the political aims of a particular group of guerrillas, and who view their violence as justified, might well describe them as *freedom fighters*. Those who disagree with their their aims might well call them *terrorists* (a term that dates from the post-revolutionary Reign of Terror in France), especially if their tactics involve harming civilians.

> The peace plan calls for the gradual removal of all foreign military advisers and bases in Central America, an end to support of guerrilla armies, and respect for self-determination and territorial sovereignty.
> *Maclean's* 24 Feb. 1986: 44

> Actually, the October Crisis doesn't really mean all that much today, except to the family of the man who died at the hands of a few tragically inept, muddle-headed romantics playing at urban guerrilla.
> *Gazette* (Montreal) 6 Oct. 1990: B3

> Ignored as well are U.S. President Ronald Reagan's 'freedom fighters,' whose terrorist activities in Nicaragua have resulted in the deaths of more than 5,000 civilians, and who have been condemned as the 'worst human rights violators in Latin America'....
> *Globe and Mail* (Toronto) 13 Feb. 1985: P6

(Here the quotation marks around *freedom fighters* indicate that the writer does not agree with the application of the term to this group.)

> Meanwhile, in Italy the interior ministry ordered increased security measures, citing evidence that Italian Red Brigade guerrillas may have formed an alliance with other European terrorist groups.
> *Maclean's* 28 July 1986: 19

(Here *guerrilla* and *terrorist* are equated.)

guest   see INVITED GUEST

guide dog, Seeing Eye Dog, seeing-eye dog
Guide dog is the general term for a dog trained to assist people with disabilities. *Seeing Eye Dog* is the registered trademark of an American company in New Jersey that trains dogs specifically to lead people who are blind. Although *seeing-eye dog* is sometimes used generically, the non-proprietary term *guide dog* is preferable. *Guide dog* may also be used to refer to a dog trained to help people whose hearing or mobility is impaired.

> A blind woman denied entry to a Saskatoon restaurant because she was accompanied by a guide dog has been awarded $500 compensation in a human rights settlement agreement.
> *Vancouver Sun* 8 Nov. 1990: C8

> Manon Dube gets around outside by using a white cane, because she 'doesn't have time' for a seeing-eye dog.
> *Province* (Vancouver) 1 March 1990: 20

guilty, not guilty   see PLEAD GUILTY

gun, small arms, firearm, artillery, shot, calibre, bore, gauge   *Gun* is a broad term, covering everything from handguns to cannons. *Small arms*, or *firearms*, can be carried by one person; these are guns with a calibre (the internal diameter of the barrel) of less than 20 mm. *Artillery* includes both guns and missiles; this is a useful general term for large-calibre weapons.

The *calibre* of rifles and pistols (which both fire bullets) may be expressed in millimetres: 'a 9 mm rifle'. But traditionally it is expressed as decimals of inches: 'a .22-calibre rifle' or 'a .45-calibre pistol'. In references to shotguns (which fire pellets or *shot*), *calibre* is usually called *bore*: 'a .410 bore shotgun'. Shotguns are also measured by *gauge*. The gauge of shotgun pellets indicates the number of them that amount to a pound. Thus shot for a 12-gauge shotgun (12 pellets to a pound) is bigger than shot for a 20-gauge shotgun (20 pellets to a pound), as are the shotguns themselves.

See also GAUGE; ORDINANCE, ORDNANCE.

gunwale, gunnel   Either spelling of this word, meaning the top edge of the side of a boat, is correct. Canadians use *gunwale* far more frequently. Both are pronounced to rhyme with *tunnel*.

> And now I was up to the gunwales in Big Crummock Lake.
> Howard Engel *Murder Sees the Light* 1984: 137

guts   see BELLY

guttural   *Guttural* is sometimes misspelled with *-er-* instead of *-ur-*. The term is derived from the Latin *guttur*, 'gullet' or 'throat'. A guttural sound comes from the throat, not the gutter.

> Dropping my lower E string to a D gave me that bizarre, gutteral sound.
> *Ottawa Citizen* 29 June 1990: D3

(The correct spelling is *guttural*.)

gybe   see JIBE

gym, gymnasium   *Gym*, the shortened version of *gymnasium*, is labelled informal by some dictionaries. However, *gym* is used far more frequently than *gymnasium* in all but quite formal Canadian writing.

Occasionally *gymnasium* refers not to a room for sports but to a German secondary school. For this meaning only, the pronunciation is *gim NAW zee um*, with a hard *g*, as in *get*.

After the lecture and a short warm-up in the gym, we move out to the track.
Imperial Oil Review Spring 1988: 15

The house is a converted Russian Orthodox church, with four storeys and a gymnasium in the basement.
Jack Chambers *Milestones* 1983: 298

Their children were grown and had graduated from a gymnasium and the boys prepared to enter their father's business.
Henry M. Rosenthal and S. Cathy Berson, eds. *Canadian Jewish Outlook Anthology* 1988: 62

gym shoes   see RUNNING SHOES

gypsy, gipsy, Gypsy   Canadian, British, and American dictionaries all list the spelling *gypsy* first. *Gipsy* is an uncommon variant. *Gypsy* should be capitalized in reference to the ethnic group whose language is Romany.

Every evening, groups gather at candle-lit tables to the sound of a gypsy violinist.
Vancouver Sun 29 Dec. 1990: A3

H

h-   Canadians, like Americans, pronounce *herb* either *URB* or *HURB* and *human* either *HYOO mun* or *YOO mun*. In Standard British English both words are always pronounced with an initial *h* sound. *Heir, honest, honourable, hour,* and related words are pronounced without an initial *h* sound by English-speakers everywhere.

Canadians generally pronounce the *h* in *historical,* but often write 'an historical' (see A, AN).

Because of the heavy stress on the first syllable of the words *vehicle* and *vehement,* the *h* that follows is not pronounced. However, the *h* is pronounced in the adjective *vehicular* because the main stress is on the second syllable: *vee HICK yoo ler.*

See also HERB.

hack   see FLACK

had better   see BETTER

[had have], would have   'If I had been there' and 'Had I been there' are standard constructions. 'If I had have been there' and 'If I would have been there' are non-standard.

Sentences that deal with what will or might happen under certain circumstances are called conditional sentences. Conditional sentences present facts ('If I am there, that won't happen'), possibilities ('If I were there, that wouldn't happen'), or counter-factual possibilities in the past ('If I had been there, that wouldn't have happened'). The tenses in clauses such as 'If I had have been there' and 'If I would have been there', intended to describe counter-factual conditions in the past, are non-standard. Note that *had have* is always unacceptable—grammarians call this spurious tense the 'plupluperfect'—while *would have* is correct in the clause that follows the *if*-clause. It is non-standard only when it is inserted into the *if*-clause as well.

The non-standard constructions are common in informal speech, where they often go unnoticed because the verbs are contracted. People often say 'If I had've been there' or 'If I had've known'. When they are used in writing, however, these constructions are condemned. Doubly stigmatized in writing are the clauses 'If I had of been there' and 'If I would of been there', where *'ve*, the contraction of the spurious *have*, is rendered by *of*—a word that sounds the same.

The non-standard *had have* construction is certainly not an innovation; there is evidence that it existed as early as the fifteenth century. All in all, it may be more accurate to describe these aberrant tenses as colloquial usages of long standing that have never been accepted in writing or formal speech.

> 'If a strong stand had of been made when the cuts were first announced perhaps they might have been able to do something.'
> *Chronicle-Herald* (Halifax) 12 Jan. 1990: B1

(Here *of* should be omitted: 'If a strong stand *had been* made' is the standard construction.)

See also COLLOQUIAL; [COULD OF]; IF I WERE YOU; SUBJUNCTIVE.

Haida The *Haida* (singular and plural) are a group of Native people who live on the Queen Charlotte Islands, off the coast of British Columbia. Their distinct language is also called *Haida*. Their traditional territory is called *Haida Gwai*, and they are renowned for their wood carvings (canoes, totem poles, longhouses) and paintings.

hail see HALE

hairbrained see HAREBRAINED

Haisla see KWAKIUTL

halcyon, halcyon days *Halcyon* (pronounced *HAL see un*) is an adjective meaning calm or peaceful; today it is also used to describe any period of happiness and prosperity. The word comes from Greek mythology: after Alcyone and her husband were turned into sea birds called *halcyons*, her father, the god of wind, decreed that the seas would be calm for two weeks each year around the winter solstice, so that the halcyons could breed in their floating nest. These fourteen days of calm and happiness were called the *halcyon days*.

In contexts where achievement is being emphasized rather than happiness, *heyday* is a more appropriate expression than *halcyon days*.

> Back in the halcyon days of the Toronto Maple Leafs, when Punch Imlach's teams were winning Stanley Cups, the team practised every day during the playoffs.
> *Globe and Mail* (Toronto) 9 May 1985: M11

(Here *heyday* would be more appropriate.)

See also HEYDAY, SALAD DAYS.

hale, hail *Hale* means robust or healthy, and is most often used in the phrase 'hale and hearty'. The verb *hale*, meaning to haul or compel ('He was haled into court'), is nearly obsolete.

All other senses of the word are spelled *hail*: 'She hailed a taxi'; 'rain turning to hail'; 'a hail of bullets'. The expression 'hail fellow well met' describes someone friendly and easy to get along with.

> The hale Michener is honorary 'master' of The Masters Games for mature athletes....
> *Globe and Mail* (Toronto) 23 April 1985: M9

half, half- To 'cut something *in half*' is idiomatic even though logically two *halves* result.

'A half dozen' and 'half a dozen' are both acceptable, but 'a half a dozen' should not be used in writing.

When *half* is used as the subject of a sentence, the verb that follows may be singular or plural, depending on the sense (see COLLECTIVE NOUNS): 'Half (of) the delegates is not enough'; 'Half (of) the delegates are undecided'.

With a *half-brother* or *half-sister* you share one biological parent (see STEP-, HALF-).

See also AGREEMENT, GRAMMATICAL.

half-breed see MÉTIS

half-mast, half-staff Some usage commentators argue that a flag partly lowered to honour the dead should be said to be at *half-mast* only when it is on a ship, and at *half-staff* when it is on land. However, while *half-mast* is the usual expression for such a flag on a ship, *half-mast* and *half-staff* are both in common use for flags on land, and both terms are perfectly acceptable. The two-word spellings *half mast* and *half staff* are fairly common, but most dictionaries hyphenate these terms.

> Quebec, which had greeted the new Constitution five years earlier with flags at half-mast, was triumphant.
> *Financial Post* 24 April 1989: 1

> Earlier, with the flag atop Parliament fluttering at half-staff, the Prime Minister had asked a hushed House of Commons: 'Why such violence in a society that considers itself civilized and compassionate?'
> *Maclean's* 18 Dec. 1989: A14

Haligonian see NAMES OF RESIDENTS

hallelujah, alleluia *Hallelujah* and *alleluia* are the most common spellings used to render in English the Hebrew word meaning 'Praise the Lord'. The word is used in Christian liturgy and songs, and sometimes as a spontaneous exclamation of joy or gratitude.

There are plenty of songs, frequent cries of 'hallelujah' and 'praise the Lord,' hand-wavings and stern admonitions to follow the scriptural words of Jesus.
Globe and Mail (Toronto) 31 Aug. 1985: P13

Sing hallelujah, because color, glorious color, is simply everywhere.
Globe and Mail (Toronto) 26 March 1985: F6

'Alleluia,' responds Louise. 'Let's give him a load of hand-clapping.'
Calgary Herald 28 May 1994: C6

Halley's comet The British astronomer after whom this comet is named was Edmund Halley (1656–1742); *Halley* is pronounced with an *a* as in either *hall* or *hat*. Halley did not discover this comet, which has been on record since 239 B.C., but was the first to accurately predict its return.

Halley's comet is often misspelled or mispronounced *Hailey's comet*, an error that has probably been reinforced by the name of a popular rock and roll band of the 1950s: Bill Hailey and the Comets.

Halley's comet is practically the only one whose name is not that of its discoverer.
Queen's Quarterly 92.2 (1985): 284

hangar see HANGER

hanged, hung *Hanged* is standard as both the past tense and the past participle of *hang* in the sense of execution: 'They hanged him'; 'He was hanged'. *Hung* is the past tense and past participle of *hang* in all other senses: 'Is the wash hung out?' Canadians still make this traditional distinction in writing, although *hung* in the sense of executed is very common in speech. Some commentators will accept this usage in informal contexts, but it is best avoided in writing.

Canada's last executions took place in 1962, when two men were hanged in Toronto.
Globe and Mail (Toronto) 4 Feb. 1985: S13

They were the last of 700 to be hanged in Canada.... 'We have lots of inquiries about where they are buried,' says [the] manager of Prospect Cemetery. 'I guess it's because they were the last two men hung.'
Globe and Mail (Toronto) 21 Jan. 1985: P17

(This example includes both the standard written and the common spoken usage.)

hanger, hangar Clothes hang on *hangers*; airplanes are kept in *hangars*.

But the ballroom is as big as an airplane hangar....
Saturday Night April 1986: 60

The test is being conducted at the airline's maintenance hanger at Vancouver International Airport.
Province (Vancouver) 10 Dec. 1990: 34

(The correct spelling is *hangar*.)

hara-kiri, seppuku *Hara-kiri* is the correct spelling for the Japanese ritual suicide by disembowelment, practised by Samurai warriors in disgrace. It is correctly pronounced *hah rah KEER ee*, though often, especially in facetious use, it is misspelled and mispronounced *hari-kari* (*HAIR ee KAIR ee*). In fact, *hara-kiri* is Japanese slang that literally means 'belly-cutting'; the Japanese themselves prefer the term *seppuku* for the ritual. Since *hara-kiri* has a venerable history in Japanese culture, facetious figurative use of the term may give offence.

... it is a complex movie made in Japan in Japanese by an American director about a novelist who killed himself by committing seppuku (hara-kiri) at the age of 45.
Globe and Mail (Toronto) 16 May 1985: E1

The palate, weary of comparing Chateau Jolys' sweet Jurancon with Inniskillin's Vidal beerenauslese, could commit hara-kiri with innumerable gourmet salad dressings, dusty crackers and chocolate dainties.
Globe and Mail (Toronto) 23 Oct. 1985: F2

(This is the facetious use.)

harass, harassment, sexual harassment *Harass* is spelled with only one *r*—unlike *embarrass*, which is spelled with two. Some Canadians pronounce *harass* and *harassment* with stress on the second syllable, while others stress the first. Either is correct; commentators are divided in their recommendations. Many British commentators recommend that the stress be placed on the first syllable, so that *harass* sounds like the surname *Harris*; nonetheless, in Britain as in North America, younger, educated speakers are more likely to say *huh RASS*. To *harass* means to annoy, wear down, or attack someone persistently. *Sexual harassment* is one particular type of harassment; it consists of persistent unwelcome sexual advances or ongoing disparagement of a person's sex or appearance.

Collection agencies—accused from time to time of using high pressure tactics and harassment to collect outstanding debts—are also subject to similar registration requirements.

J.E. Smyth et al. *The Law and Business Administration in Canada* 1987: 414

Gretzky ... didn't even get a shot on goal as Tikkanen hooked, tripped, hounded and harrassed him.
Province (Vancouver) 19 April 1990: 72

(The correct spelling is *harassed*.)

harbinger In the twelfth century a *harbinger* was a person who provided lodging for an army; later the term came to refer to a person who went ahead of the army to find lodging. Now a harbinger is anything that announces or indicates the arrival of something else. The *g* is soft, pronounced as in *passenger*.

Groundhog Day ... is an adaptation of the old German view of the spiny-coated hedgehog as a harbinger of spring.
Globe and Mail (Toronto) 4 Feb. 1985: S14

hardly, barely, scarcely *Hardly*, *barely*, and *scarcely* all mean by a small margin or with difficulty. Critics argue that when these words are used in conjunction with other negative words, such as *not* or *without*, they form a double negative. Constructions like 'I can't hardly walk' and 'She didn't scarcely try' may be found in speech, but Canadian writers generally avoid them, preferring 'I can hardly walk' and 'She scarcely tried'.

A few commentators state that these words, when used in the sense of 'only just', may be followed by *when* or *before*, but not by *than*. For example, 'I had scarcely made it to my seat when the movie started' and 'I had scarcely made it to my seat before the movie started' are acceptable, but 'I had scarcely made it to my seat than the movie started' is not. These disparaged constructions in which *hardly*, *barely*, and *scarcely* are followed by *than* may be influenced by the expression *no sooner ... than*, in which *than* is standard and *when* is criticized. See NO SOONER.

When a sentence begins with one of these adverbs, the subject and verb that follow it change positions: 'Scarcely had I opened the letter when the doorbell rang'.

The 1950s had scarcely opened before educational authorities in the United States were predicting ... an explosion in American university enrolments [in the 1960s].
Frederick Gibson *Queen's University* 2 (1983): 313

Scarcely were our words committed to print than McDonald's Canada announced that it would indeed switch from foam containers to cardboard.
Vancouver Sun 5 Nov. 1990: A6

(Replacing *than* with *when* or *before* would forestall any criticism.)

See also DOUBLE NEGATIVE; EVER.

hardy, hearty *Hardy* and *hearty* can both be used as synonyms for *healthy* or *robust*. However, they cannot be used interchangeably in the sense of resistant to hardship, which is the primary definition of *hardy*, or to mean nourishing, which is one sense of *hearty*. Thus a *hardy* plant is one that can withstand harsh conditions and a *hearty* meal is a nutritious and plentiful one. The similar pronunciations of these words may explain their occasional misuse.

Now my mother may be slender, but she has a hardy constitution, got from climbing over fences with an easel on her back....
Queen's Quarterly 96 (1989): 399

Fritz's beef, as it turned out, was hardy fare, piquantly seasoned....
Gazette (Montreal) 18 April 1990: D1

(The word required here is *hearty*.)

... more than 24,000 hearty souls braved Boston's inclement winter weather to attend NetWorld last month.
Computer Dealer News 7 March 1991: 1

(A *hearty soul* is a person full of good cheer; a *hardy soul* is someone able to withstand harsh conditions, such as Boston's 'inclement winter weather'.)

harebrained [hairbrained] The accepted spelling is *harebrained*, referring to a foolish, flighty person who has no more sense than a hare. *Hairbrained* is an alternative spelling that dates from the sixteenth century but is listed in only one major current dictionary. Most dictionaries do not hyphenate *harebrained*, although it often appears that way in print.

When it comes to harebrained schemes, those who want to save Canada are just as guilty as those who want to destroy it.
Maclean's 22 April 1991: A11

These are gloomy reflections, and hard-headed readers may think them hare-brained.
Robertson Davies *A Voice From the Attic* 1960: 350

hark, harken, heark, hearken, hark(en) back, heark(en) back *Hark* and *heark*, *harken* and *hearken* all mean listen carefully, as in 'Hark! The herald angels sing'.

To *hark back*—and, increasingly, to *harken* (or *hearken*) *back*—is to revert to a topic or to suggest an earlier time. *Hark back* was originally used as a call to hunting hounds telling them to retrace their steps.

> Looking toward the future, I would like to hark back to the suggestions I have already made for new research plans.
> W.C. Lougheed ed. *In Search of the Standard in Canadian English* 1986: 167

> The idea of individuals walking in a city on a mission carrying a candle harkens back to medieval times.
> *Globe and Mail* (Toronto) 1 Jan. 1985: M1

> … the parents who had come of age during the Depression hearkened back to the stern rigors of that childhood.
> *Globe and Mail* (Toronto) 26 April 1985: P6

have got, have gotten Most Canadians and Americans make a distinction of sense: 'She's got a laptop' means she owns one, while 'She's gotten a laptop' means she's just acquired one. This distinction of sense can't be made in Standard British English, where the past participle *gotten* is archaic.

See also GOT, GOTTEN; HAVE GOT TO.

have got to Commentators have condemned the use of *have got to* meaning be compelled to, recommending *must* or *have to* instead: that is, 'I must (or have to) go' rather than 'I have got to go'. However, *Webster's Dictionary of English Usage* notes that Otto Jesperson collected many examples of *have got to* from a range of important British writers, among them Dickens, Trollope, and Shaw, and its authors add a list of their own that includes William Faulkner and several American presidents. In other words, it is not necessary to avoid *have got to*.

See also GOT; HAVE GOT.

he, him, his see CASE; EVERYONE; GENDER

head of state, governor general, lieutenant-governor In Canada the prime minister is the head of government, but the Queen is the head of state. When the Queen is not on Canadian soil, the head of state is the governor general. The lieutenant-governors, appointed by the governor general on the advice of the prime minister, represent the Crown in each province.

Canadians in general show no sign of establishing a clear preference regarding hyphenation of the terms *governor general* and *lieutenant-governor*. However, the Department of the Secretary of State recommends hyphenating only *lieutenant-governor*. *Governor* is the main noun in both of these titles, and thus it is the word pluralized: *governors general, lieutenant-governors*.

Both *Governor General* and *Lieutenant-Governor* should be capitalized when they are used directly in front of an incumbent's name: 'Lieutenant-Governor Garde Gardom'. References to 'the governor general' or 'past Lieutenant-Governors' are sometimes capitalized, sometimes not, according to the editorial policy of individual publications.

> The sweeping legal powers of the Governor General are transferred by convention to the Cabinet.
> Andrew Heard *Canadian Constitutional Conventions* 1991: 1–2

> Yeltsin and his wife stayed at the governor-general's residence.
> *Gazette* (Montreal) 20 June 1992: B1

> (Government publications do not hyphenate *governor general*.)

> When the provincial environment minister visited the Daily Bread Food Bank yesterday, she heard five would-be lieutenants-governor give their versions of the Throne Speech to the Legislature.
> *Toronto Star* 21 April 1992: A6

> (The correct plural is *lieutenant-governors*.)

See also CAPITAL LETTERS; HONOURABLE; LIEUTENANT.

headquarters, headquarter *Headquarters*, the noun meaning an administrative centre for business or military operations, is both the singular and the plural form: 'One headquarters is enough; two headquarters are too many'. *Headquarters* meaning management is usually treated as a singular: 'Headquarters is sending out conflicting statements'.

Some usage guides classify the verb *headquarter*, meaning either to have headquarters or to establish headquarters, as jargon. It is used extensively in business and financial contexts, but is not yet found in other types of writing.

Nortel's transmission group world headquarters is situated in Edmonton.
Globe and Mail (Toronto) 29 March 1985: P42

The headquarters for many of Washington's leading lobbyists are located in the modern office buildings lining K Street, a few blocks north of the White House.
Maclean's 24 Feb. 1986: 19

... Shamian Island [was once] headquarter for the opium trade....
Vancouver Sun 1 June 1990: G1

(The noun always ends in *s*: *headquarters*.)

... headquartered in Montreal, the firm is growing rapidly.
Western Grocer May–June 1990: 84

Current clientele ranges from V-P Dan Quayle to leading Saudi families who headquarter here for their shopping sprees.
Financial Post 1 May 1991: 62

See also FUNCTIONAL SHIFT.

healthful, healthy   *Healthful* has one meaning: conducive to good health ('a healthful climate'). *Healthy* has two: possessing good health ('a healthy person') and conducive to good health ('a healthy breakfast'). Although the use of *healthy* in the second sense has been criticized, most authorities now accept it.

Fruit and vegetables all qualify as healthful, but a few merit 'super' status because of their larger amounts of vitamins and minerals.
Gazette (Montreal) 1 March 1989: C1

Geared for children aged seven to 12, Pam's Kitchen features instructions ranging from how to fix a quick, healthy breakfast to embellishing celery sticks and yogurt in a multitude of ways.
Province (Vancouver) 24 June 1990: 83

Grocery store owners are getting this confused message from consumers who say they want healthy food but continue to eat out and buy snack food.
Province (Vancouver) 13 June 1990: 48

heark, hearken, heark(en) back   see HARK

heart-rending   To *rend* means to tear or break; something *heart-rending* arouses deep distress and figuratively rends the heart. Some dictionaries omit the hyphen: *heartrending*. *Heart-rendering* is a mistaken (sometimes humorous) form, influenced by the more familiar verb *render*.

Everybody loves a story about horses and kids, and there's no finer story around than the classic sentimental tale of a Victorian girl's heartrending search for her missing colt.
Gazette (Montreal) 1 Sept. 1990: T48

Bishop Matthews not only ministered to the condemned man, but also to his mother, and referred to the experience as the most 'horrible, heart-rending time you can imagine.'
Canadian Churchman Jun.–Jul. 1986: 17

Canadian peacekeepers who have served in Croatia are bringing home memories of war both horrific and heart-rendering.
Edmonton Journal 11 Sept. 1995: A2

(The *-er-* should be dropped.)

hearty   see HARDY

heathen   see ATHEIST

heave, heaved, hove   The past tense of *heave* is *heaved*. The nautical expressions *hove into sight* ('came into view') and *hove to* ('came or brought to a stop') retain the otherwise archaic past tense *hove*; these expressions are sometimes used figuratively.

And much to her surprise, friends heaved a huge sigh of relief, glad to have the old Nancy back.
Vancouver Sun 15 Sept. 1990: C1

In school, we sat up straight and stopped flicking inkballs as soon as 'sir' hove into sight.
Vancouver Sun 20 Oct. 1990: B5

Hebrew   see JEW

hegemony   *Hegemony* is domination, especially the domination of one political state over another; the word is often used figuratively. Pronunciation varies, but the *g* is usually pronounced like a *j*. The stress may fall on the second syllable (*heh JEH muh nee*) or on the first (*HEDGE eh moh nee*).

... the British and French ... would presumably oppose any border settlement that threatened their naval hegemony in the Pacific.
George Ignatieff *The Making of a Peacemonger* 1987: 5

' ... education for women poses a threat to male hegemony in the family; a threat to male dominance that few male egos can withstand.'
Briarpatch April 1990: 7

Heiltsuk   see KWAKIUTL

heir, heir apparent, heir presumptive Technically, in law, an *heir* is not an heir until inheritance takes place.

Heir apparent and *heir persumptive* are technical terms arising from the British system of primogeniture, whereby estates and titles pass to the closest male relative (usually the eldest son). In this system, an *heir apparent* is someone who will definitely inherit as long as he survives the relevant relative (usually his father). Some mistakenly think that the *heir apparent* is only 'apparently' the heir, but the word *apparent* here carries an older sense: manifest or unquestionable. An *heir presumptive*, however, will inherit only as long as no one else is born who is more closely related to the title-holder.

Heir and *heir apparent* are both used figuratively. An *heir apparent* is cultivated as a successor; an 'apparent heir' is the person most likely to take over.

As heirs to a family fortune valued at about $435 million, Paul Desmarais Jr., 31, and his brother Andre, 29, are among Canada's wealthiest businessmen.
Maclean's 24 Feb. 1986: 46

As heir apparent, this Prince of Wales sees confidential cabinet papers and he is well informed about day-to-day political issues.
Maclean's 14 Nov. 1988: A40

The still-youthful premier has no apparent heir and thus leaves a political vacuum that Quebec's separatists ... hope to fill.
Daily News (Halifax) 19 Sept. 1993: 19

Marois said Bloc Quebecois Leader Lucien Bouchard, heir apparent to retiring Premier Jacques Parizeau, knows about the proposal....
Calgary Herald 13 Dec. 1995: A15

See also PRESUMPTIVE.

Hellenic, Hellene, Hellenist, Hellenistic, Grecian, Greek *Hellenic* is an adjective formed from the Greek word for Greece, *Hellas*; it's applied to both ancient and modern Greece. A *Hellene* is either a modern or an ancient Greek. A *Hellenist* is an expert on Greek language or culture, or, in ancient history, a non-Greek, especially a Jew, who adopted the Greek language and customs. *Hellenistic* refers to the period between the death of Alexander the Great and the reign of Augustus (the fourth to the first century B.C.).

Grecian usually describes something in the style of or pertaining to ancient Greece as opposed to something from Greece today: 'a Grecian pillar', but 'a Greek wine'.

The recent visit of former Defence Minister Robert Coates to Turkey was observed with great interest by the entire Hellenic community of Canada.
Globe and Mail (Toronto) 20 Feb. 1985: P6

Rexroth, invoking the shade of Walter Pater, declares: 'H.D.'s Greece was a land that never was' and, more recently, David Perkins suggests that 'her "Greece" was typically Romantic and literary, a Hellenic world distilled from Shelley, Keats, Byron, Arnold....'
Queen's Quarterly 92.2 (1985): 312

It includes Late Minoan III tomb artifacts, Hellenistic sculpture, Roman glass and ancient coins dating back to Ptolemy.
Globe and Mail (Toronto) 19 Oct. 1985: G17

It is, very briefly, about a German barbarian living in an early but vague period of history who is domesticated by a Grecian maiden called Parthenia.
Robertson Davies *A Voice from the Attic* 1960: 181

'You stand on a terrace flanked by a row of unreal Grecian columns.'
Margaret Atwood *Second Words* 1982: 241

helpmate, helpmeet *Helpmate* derives from the older and now rarer word *helpmeet*. *Helpmeet* first arose in seventeenth-century writing from an aural misinterpretation of a passage from the King James Bible, in which God considers the creation of 'an help meet for' Adam (Genesis 2: 18). The *help* in the reference was Eve; *meet* was an adjective meaning suitable, but it became part of a new noun, *helpmeet*, meaning wife or partner. By the eighteenth century the term coexisted with *helpmate*, which became the standard form in the nineteenth century. No one is sure why the *-mate* form developed. The most common explanation is that it is a product of folk etymology: the meaning of *meet* was lost and the substitution of *mate* made more sense.

Today *helpmate* refers to any helpful companion, but especially to a wife or husband. Wives are more likely to be called *helpmates* and cast in the supporting role. For this reason, guides to non-sexist language suggest avoiding the word unless it is applied equally to men.

Carole Longpre, the pair's trainer and foster mother, is preparing the monkeys for use as companions and helpmates to severely disabled people.
Ottawa Citizen 4 March 1990: A5

Liberal Leader John Turner and his anti-free trade helpmates on the left, the NDP, behaved as though the Marines had just stormed the border at Buffalo.
Ottawa Citizen 10 April 1987: A2

There is no stinting, however, when it comes to the great love of his life and helpmate in every way, Nancy.
Vancouver Sun 8 Dec. 1990: D20

(This is the use that non-sexist language guides are wary of. Is 'he' also Nancy's helpmate?)

See also FOLK ETYMOLOGY.

hemi- see SEMI-

he or she see SEXIST LANGUAGE

her see CASE; EVERYONE; GENDER

herb Canadians pronounce *herb* URB or *HURB*, with or without an audible *h*. Written Canadian English reflects this practice: both 'a herb' and 'an herb' are used. Most Americans do not pronounce the *h*. In Standard British English, the *h* in *herb* is always pronounced. Because *herb* was derived from the Old French word *erbe*, the *h* was initially not pronounced, nor was it written except by Latinists. However, nineteenth-century British usage writers, aware of the word's Latin antecedent, *herba*, recommended pronouncing the *h*.

A neighbour of ours, Doreen Kapala, tends a gem of a lakeside garden, that features ... a herb bed around a sundial....
Harrowsmith Aug.–Sept. 1985: 86

It is not easy to decide how important an herb garden would have been in a town the size of Kingston.
The Beaver Dec. 1989–Jan. 1990: 15

See also H-.

hereditary see CONGENITAL

heroism, heroics Most usage guides and dictionaries distinguish between the noun *heroism*, which suggests courage and nobility, and the noun *heroics* (always plural), which is used pejoratively to mean flamboyant behaviour or language, or unnecessary gallantry.

We read about the heroism of Grace Darling in saving shipwrecked mariners off the coast of Scotland....
Robertson Davies *One Half of Robertson Davies* 1978: 282

Professor Barton Bernstein, one of a Stanford, Calif., team studying medical ethics, voiced concern about the 'bravado, foolhardiness and heroics' associated with heart surgery.
Globe and Mail (Toronto) 14 March 1985: P7

The two occupants managed to escape from the cockpit just before the explosion and one witness said only the pilot's heroics prevented death.
Province (Vancouver) 13 Nov. 1990: 20

(The word required here is *heroism*.)

herring choker   see BLUENOSE

hers   see ITS

herstory, history In the 1970s, American feminists coined the word *herstory* to refer to past events recounted by women rather than by men or from a female rather than a male perspective. A writer of herstory is sometimes called a *herstorian*. Although *history* is not etymologically derived from 'his story', as the formation of *herstory* implies, it does come from Greek *histor*, 'a wise or learned man', and *herstory* effectively draws attention to the traditionally male-dominated viewpoint of history.

It is as if, in Patricia Smart's words, writing 'son histoire à elle' (herstory)—as opposed to 'son histoire à lui' (his(s)tory)—will offset the pessimism encoded there.
Ben-Z. Shek *French-Canadian & Québécois Novels* 1991: 92

heyday, salad days *Heyday* means the period of greatest success, fame, or prosperity. It is sometimes misspelled *heydey*.

The expression *salad days* suggests youth, enthusiasm, and inexperience. It comes from a speech in Shakespeare's *Antony and Cleopatra*, in which Cleopatra refers to 'My salad days, when I was green in judgement' (1.5.73). Although the expression has been condemned by usage guides as a cliché, overuse has not made the meaning transparent. It is often used in contexts where *heyday* would be more appropriate.

Mildred certainly qualifies as a donor—in her heyday as a 4-year-old, she produced almost 23,000 pounds of milk in a 305-day lactation period....
Harrowsmith Oct.–Nov. 1985: 36

Politicians in southwest Montreal, a district whose industrial heydey was 60 years ago and centred around the Lachine Canal, are long on promises and plans to raise their community out from under a chronic depression.
Gazette (Montreal) 31 Oct. 1990: A4

(The correct spelling is *heyday*.)

So we find, as we begin at last to face the facts of life, that serious thought is a harder exercise than we expected in our salad days of innocence.
Vancouver Sun 2 March 1991: B4

In his salad days, Foreman was one of boxing's most powerful punchers.
Financial Post 12 Jan. 1990: 39

(From the context, it appears that the writer is reflecting on a time when the famous boxer was in his prime, not on a period of inexperience or 'greenness' in the profession; in this case, *heyday* is the word required.)

The Ritz, in its salad days, didn't have Vanderbilt and Gould, but it did have Brian Mulroney and Mordecai Richler in the Maritime Bar.
Maclean's 22 April 1991: A68

(The columnist has been comparing the glory days of two of Montreal's most distinguished hotels; *heyday* would make more sense here.)

See also HALCYON, HALCYON DAYS.

hiccup, hiccough   The spelling *hiccup* is preferred over the rare variant *hiccough*, although both are found in dictionaries. Both versions are pronounced to rhyme with *pickup*. Some dictionaries and usage guides insist on the spellings *hiccuped* and *hiccuping* for the inflected forms; others insist on *hiccupped* and *hiccupping*; and still others recognize both spellings.

A final despairing hiccup from the car's engine and a deep, velvety silence closes in as we sit in the car with the damp orchard all around.
Globe and Mail (Toronto) 20 July 1985: T4

Stock markets around the world hiccuped today following the second-largest plunge ever of the Tokyo Stock Exchange's key index.
Vancouver Sun 2 April 1990: C1

Buses are the cheapest and most popular form of transportation around the city and the sight of these heaving, hiccoughing monsters has even become something of a tourist attraction.
Globe and Mail (Toronto) 23 Feb. 1985: T15

See also DOUBLING THE FINAL CONSONANT.

hidden agenda   see AGENDA

highway   see ROAD

hike   The use of *hike* to mean increase, whether as a noun ('a price hike') or as a verb ('taxes were hiked') is regarded as informal by some. It is common in Canadian journalism, but should be avoided in more formal writing.

In the United States, the freeze and subsequent price hike ... meant increased sales for instant breakfast drinks.
Western Grocer May–Jun. 1990: 25

For, where Lock tends to hike up the volume for his stereophonic dancing, Laurin opts for a more subdued approach.
Globe and Mail (Toronto) 27 March 1985: M7

hindrance   see OBSTACLE

Hindu, Hinduism, Hindi, Urdu, Hindustan, Hindustani   A *Hindu* follows the traditions of *Hinduism*, the religion of the majority of the people of India and Sri Lanka. In the past *Hindu* was used to refer to any native of India. However, since many Indians are Muslim, Sikh, Buddhist, Christian, etc., this usage should be avoided. *Hindi* is one of the most widely spoken languages of India and one of the country's official languages. *Urdu* is one of the official languages of Pakistan. Urdu and Hindi are mutually intelligible, but are distinguished on sociopolitical grounds.
Hindustan refers to the northern section of India; a *Hindustani* is someone from that area. *Hindustani* is also the related adjective and the name of a language of northern India closely related to both Hindi and Urdu.

We notice that 'Canadian' in this poem means French Canadian habitant: O'Grady no more thinks of himself as Canadian than an Anglo-Indian colonel would think of himself as Hindu.
Northrop Frye *The Bush Garden* 1971: 165

(Frye used *Hindu* to mean *Indian* in this piece published in 1956. This usage is now dated.)

See also GOD, GODS; INDIAN; SACRED WRITINGS.

Hispanic, Latin American, Latino, Latina, Chicano, Chicana, Mexican American, Tex-Mex   *Hispanic* means 'Spanish-speaking' and is the broadest term available to describe Spanish-speaking peoples and cultures in both Europe and the Americas. In American usage it often refers specifically to those of Spanish-language background within the United States: for example, the communities of Cuban immigrants in Miami,

Puerto Ricans in New York City, and Mexicans and descendants of early Spanish settlers in California and the American Southwest. Occasionally *Hispanic* is mistakenly applied to those with language backgrounds other than Spanish, such as Portuguese-speakers in Brazil and speakers of Indigenous languages in Central and South America.

The term *Latin American* applies to all Central and South American speakers of Romance languages and thus includes Portuguese-speakers from Brazil and French-speakers from French Guiana. *Latinos* are Latin Americans or people of Latin American descent living in the United States. The singular *Latino* can be used of both men and women, although *Latina* is also used to refer to women.

Chicano (plural *Chicanos*) is an altered, shortened form of the Mexican Spanish word for Mexican, *Mexicano*. In the early twentieth century, American-born Hispanics used the term sometimes insultingly to refer to more recent immigrants from Mexico. *Chicano* later came to be used pejoratively by those outside the community to describe all Mexican Americans. However, during the American civil-rights movement of the 1960s, *Chicano* was reclaimed by politicized Mexican Americans and used with pride to designate their Spanish, Mexican, and American cultural heritages. The feminine form *Chicana* came into popular use in English around 1960. Today some dislike the word *Chicano* because of its political flavour and prefer *Mexican American*.

In use since the 1940s, *Tex-Mex* is a slang reference to language and cultural traditions that combine Texan and Mexican influences. In Canada *Tex-Mex* is used mostly to describe a style of cooking.

> For example, the Hispanic community in the United States now stands at some 20 million—six times the entire population of New Zealand—and in such states as Florida and California efforts have been made to legislate English as the official language.
> Neil Nevitte and Roger Gibbins *New Elites in Old States* 1990: 17

> It appears to be the slice-of-life story of a 37-year-old Chicana welfare recipient named Consuelo, whose past history we are given in the first few pages of the book.
> Margaret Atwood *Second Words* 1982: 272

[hisself], [theirselves]   *Himself* and *themselves* are standard. *Hisself* and *theirselves* are highly stigmatized dialect forms. Presumably the non-standard forms persist because they follow the pattern of the other reflexive pronouns (*myself, yourself, ourselves*)

in adding *-self* or *-selves* to a possessive adjective (*my-, your-, our-*). Standard forms are not always products of logic.

> Instead, Sullivan contented himself with a sensible address to the jury.
> Jack Batten *Robinette* 1984: 72

> Most Western cities found themselves in the same predicament.
> Pierre Berton *The Promised Land* 1984: 340

> 'Man needs somethin' to keep his mind off of hisself,' he said, peeking out from under his flattop hat minutes before Lyle fired the opening pitch.
> *Toronto Star* 11 May 1992: C4

(Here *hisself* has been preserved to illustrate the speaker's rural dialect.)

> The music stops abruptly ... and one of them says, 'Man, the cat's cutting hisself.'
> Jack Chambers *Milestones* 1983: 192

(Here *hisself* is dialectal.)

> And like teachers, serious and gentle-voiced, the marshals (what they called theirselves) was slipping, sliding up and down the row, lighting candles here and there.
> *Queen's Quarterly* 94.1 (1987): 95

(Here *theirselves* is dialectal.)

See also -SELF, -SELVES.

historical, historic   The adjective *historical* means having to do with the past ('historical novel') or the study of the past ('historical approach'). The adjective *historic* is used to describe events that are significant for a whole society ('historic breakthrough') and places that are better known for past than present glories ('historic Milltown').

Interchanging these adjectives was perfectly acceptable in the nineteenth century and is still fairly common today. However, it makes sense to follow the contemporary trend towards distinguishing them.

> In this tame historical romance about French Canada in 1661, Bishop Laval was portrayed as a bigot.
> Fraser Sutherland *The Monthly Epic* 1992: 146

> There is only one aspect which I find particularly lacking within the organized snowmobile community, and that is a sense of historical perspective.
> *Snowmobile Canada Buyer's Guide* 1991: 4

> The Baptist Union of South Africa took historic action at its annual assembly in October when it urged South

African President Botha to lead in abolishing evil apartheid.
Canadian Baptist Feb. 1986: 53

The Downtown Development Corporation ... of St. John's and Main Street Canada have signed a three-year, $185,000 agreement aimed at breathing new life into the Newfoundland capital's downtown, particularly the historic Water Street area.
Canadian Heritage Magazine Feb.–Mar. 1986: 10

When he came to realize the deep flaws in the historic record of Indian activities, Trigger ... scoured all contemporary accounts for the names of individual Hurons....
Saturday Night July 1986: 50

(Here *historical* is recommended.)

An innocent comment opened the door for Prime Minister Brian Mulroney to turn on his legendary Irish charm and break the ice at Sunday's historical meeting with aboriginal leaders.
Ottawa Citizen 29 June 1992: A3

(Here *historic* is recommended.)

See also A, AN; PRESENT TENSE, LITERARY PRESENT.

history   see HERSTORY; PAST HISTORY

hither, thither, whither   *Hither, thither,* and *whither* are old-fashioned words now used for comic or rhetorical effect. *Hither* means to this place; *thither* means to that place; *whither* means to which place, to whatever place, or to what end. In other words, *hither, thither,* and *whither* mean here, there, and where, respectively, with the emphasis on movement to or towards. *Whither* is sometimes misspelled *wither.*

Some days, say Spruce Lake oldtimers, you can hardly hear yourself think for the float planes buzzing hither and yon.
Vancouver Sun 20 Feb. 1992: D6

Thither I repaired one afternoon when school was out, and came home lugging a four-pound gong of the kind they used to place on the outside of school walls to ring in the children from recess.
Richard Davies and Glen Kirkland, eds. *Dimensions* 1986: 118

Whither go the flowers, so goes mankind.
Ottawa Citizen 12 April 1992: B2

A poster in the halls announced that he was giving a talk on 'Whether the United Nations Now.'... it should

have been 'whither,' but Sulzner had got it wrong over the phone from New York.
Saturday Night May 1986: 36–7

Wither no man knoweth.
Toronto Star 13 May 1992: A7

(The correct spelling is *whither*.)

See also ARCHAISMS; HITHERTO.

hitherto   *Hitherto* means up to this time, or until now. Some usage guides warn against using *hitherto* in reference to past events because, they claim, it does not mean until then or previously. But this advice seems pedantic. *Hitherto* is used far more often in reference to a past moment than to the present. *Thitherto,* expressly meaning 'until then', is obsolete.

Perhaps the most significant finding of our 1983–86 field work was the discovery of Nearctic species not hitherto recorded in the Thule district, namely, the sandhill crane and the Canada goose.
Arctic 41.1 (1988): 57

... a hitherto unpublished essay by Roger North (d. 1734), arguing for the supremacy of the Crown, also appeared in that year.
J.A.W. Gunn *Beyond Liberty and Property* 1983: 174

'He was continually discovering new, hitherto unknown, properties of natural objects.'
Irving M. Zeitlin and Robert J. Brym *The Social Condition of Humanity* 1991: 9

See also HITHER, THITHER, WHITHER.

hoard   see HORDE

Hobson's choice   This expression, although it seems to imply a choice, actually means no choice at all; modern equivalents are 'my way or the highway' and 'take it or leave it'. Thomas Hobson (d. 1631) rented out horses in Cambridge. So that each horse would get regular exercise, he required that his customers take the most rested one. Students at Cambridge University, including John Milton, immortalized him in various comic verses, and so his name entered the language. Language commentators often make a point of distinguishing between 'Hobson's choice' and 'a dilemma'—the need to make a choice between unpalatable alternatives. However, Hobson's customers might also be said to have faced a dilemma: take a horse they didn't like, or walk.

... Mr. Bourassa represents Hobson's choice for many anglophone voters—they do not want Mr. Bourassa again, but they do not want the PQ.
Globe and Mail (Toronto) 9 Nov. 1985: A4

Even the Quebecois who want nothing to do with separation ... will vote PQ if they want a change in government. It is a Hobson's choice: Take what is offered, or get nothing at all.
Calgary Herald 11 Sept 1994: A6

Apple was faced with a Hobson's choice. Either leap to a new chip or be left behind by more powerful processors from competing hardware manufacturers.
Daily News (Halifax) 19 Dec. 1994: 19

See also DILEMMA; SCYLLA AND CHARYBDIS.

hoi polloi Literally translated from the Classical Greek, *hoi polloi* means 'the many', that is, the common people as opposed to the elite. In English usage the phrase is the equivalent of 'the masses'; it is often used in humorous contexts.

Some people mistakenly use *hoi polloi* to refer to the people at the top rather than the bottom of the social ladder. Perhaps this confusion stems from the similar sound of the expressions *hoi polloi* and *hoity-toity*, which means condescending or haughty.

Because *hoi* is the Greek definite article, some usage experts have argued that to say 'the hoi polloi' is the equivalent of saying 'the the many'. While some writers do omit the English *the*, it is neither necessary nor idiomatic to do so.

Maybe the silliest article in the new Fame is by Countess Donina Cicogna, who pines for the old days on the French Riviera, back in the '60s, when the beau monde reigned supreme and before the hoi polloi invaded Antibes and St. Tropez.
Vancouver Sun 16 June 1990: D7

On a trip to the Soviet Union one of the flight attendants heard from a pal of his in first class that the richest man in the U.S. was on her plane. She went back into tourist to spread the news to the hoi polloi.
Financial Post 4 Oct. 1991: 11

It was interested in taxation and the maximization of revenue, not in the social security of hoi polloi.
Canadian Journal of History 24.1 (1989): 90

(Here the writer has dropped the English article.)

Every label has been given a chance to show off, whether in a free-standing boutique all its own (Gucci) or spotlit areas in the menswear department (Armani, Klein). But while the names may be distinctly hoi polloi, the displays are not forbidding.
Globe and Mail (Toronto) 20 Dec. 1985: D14

(The writer has mistakenly used *hoi polloi* to refer to the elite of the fashion world.)

hold, a hold, ahold The phrase 'get hold of' is acceptable in writing as well as in speech. But the variant 'get *a* hold of', though often heard in speech, is inappropriate in formal writing. Some consider the fused spelling *ahold* (which parallels *aside*, *ahead*, etc.) even less acceptable than *a hold*.

As a result I was dispatched to 10 Downing Street with instructions to get hold of the highest placed person possible and make sure the Canadian division received appropriate mention.
George Ignatieff *The Making of a Peacemonger* 1987: 72

Sigfrid looks up through her tears, struggling to get hold of herself.
David Williams *Eye of the Father* 1985: 112

'I found that these documents were very difficult to get a hold of. ...'
Globe and Mail (Toronto) 5 Jan. 1985: M4

(This example is reported speech; especially in writing, *get hold of* would be preferable.)

'The other side of the lawsuit might get ahold of it. ...'
Vancouver Sun 23 Aug. 1990: A10

(Here *ahold* appears in reported speech.)

holiday, vacation, holidays A one-day break from work is *a holiday* in Canada, the United States, and Britain. Such days may be called 'public', 'civic', 'general', or 'statutory' holidays. When the reference is to a longer break, *vacation* and *holiday(s)* are used differently in Britain and North America.

Canadians and Americans use *vacation*, *holiday*, or *holidays* to refer to any extended break from school, work, or regular routine. However, *vacation* is more often used to refer to the summer break, while *the holidays* is more often used of the week or so that many people take off between Christmas and New Year's. Similarly, the *vacation season* usually means summer, while the *holiday season* usually means the Christmas season. In the context of labour law, *holidays* are statutory one-day breaks, while a *vacation* is an employee's annual break, usually of two weeks or more.

In Britain, the term *vacation* is generally reserved for periods when institutions such as Parliament, universities and schools, or the law courts are officially not in session. Otherwise a break from work or the usual routine is called a *holiday* or *holidays*.

... compared with production workers, the 'new working class' enjoys a number of significant advantages: more paid holidays, more frequent and longer paid vacations. ...
Irving M. Zeitlin and Robert J. Brym *The Social Condition of Humanity* 1991: 131

But some of them could also work for others, and they were prepared for long hours, few holidays, and no vacations.
Pierre Berton *The Promised Land* 1984: 165

... spending the holidays without your mother or father, husband or wife is still daunting.
Province (Vancouver) 29 Dec. 1990: B2

(Here *holidays* refers to the Christmas season.)

... university students are eager for holiday jobs, and few of them seem to know that in the beginning, university vacations were made long so that students could spend them in reading which would augment their formal studies.
Robertson Davies *A Voice from the Attic* 1960: 34

See also NEW YEAR'S DAY.

holocaust, genocide *Holocaust* is derived from a Greek word for burnt sacrifice and now usually means a great destruction of life, especially when fire is involved. 'The Holocaust', usually capitalized, refers to the systematic execution of millions of Jews by the Nazis in the Second World War.

Genocide is a twentieth-century term for the planned extermination of a cultural or racial group. The Holocaust was an attempted genocide of the Jewish people.

This rooting for the home team by Canadian film writers—an admitted relief after the holocaust of the tax shelter—is not provincialism.
Performing Arts in Canada July 1988: 16

(Using *holocaust* facetiously may give offence; *disaster* would be preferable here.)

Modern genocide, in contrast, is mass murder in 'cold blood,' involving a centrally planned and co-ordinated attempt at the total annihilation of a racial, religious, ethnic, or political group.
Queen's Quarterly 92.1 (1985): 134

He likened the placement of Indian and Métis children in white homes outside Manitoba to 'cultural genocide.'
Saturday Night April 1986: 35

See also DECIMATE.

home in on, hone in on The standard expression for finding a target is *home in on*, as in 'homing pigeon', not *hone in on*. Since to *hone* means to sharpen, *honing in*, sharpening the focus, is an understandable reinterpretation of the phrase (see FOLK ETYMOLOGY).

One project homed in on Revenue Canada employees who were claiming rental losses on their own returns.
Financial Post 25 March 1991: 13

Once in the soil, the nematodes seek out targets by homing in on their heat and carbon dioxide emissions.
Gazette (Montreal) 28 June 1990: F4

In one method, the broth is laced with radioactivated RNA molecules which hone in on the desired DNA strip and mark it.
Queen's Quarterly 97.4 (1990): 606

(The standard expression is *home in on*.)

Colorado potato beetles dote on my potatoes; cucumber beetles consume my cucumbers; squash beetles ravage my squash; and tomato hornworms hone in on my tomatoes, all with the unerring instinct of compass needles swinging in tune to the Earth's unseen forces.
Harrowsmith Jun.–Jul. 1985: 70

(The standard expression is *home in on*.)

Finally, the Toronto group's development of a genetically engineered probe—a monoclonal antibody—that specifically hones in on drug resistance holds out the promise of a drug-delivery system that pinpoints the hard-to-kill cells for attack.
Globe and Mail (Toronto) 21 Oct. 1985: A12

(The standard expression is *home in on*.)

homophone, homograph, homonym *Homophones* are words that sound the same but have different meanings: for example, *pair* and *pear*. *Homographs* are words that are spelled the same but have unrelated meanings: for example, *rest* (repose) and *rest* (remainder). *Homonym* is the general term for words that are pronounced or spelled the same.

homosexual see GAY

hone in on see HOME IN ON

honourable, honorable Canadian spelling of *honourable* is mixed. *Honourable* is more common in books, magazines, and journals, while *honorable* (recommended by the Canadian Press) is more common in newspapers (except for the *Globe and Mail*, which has used *-our* endings since 1990).

Though members of Parliament and the provincial legislatures are often referred to as 'honourable' members (note that the spelling for this sense normally requires the *u*), this honorific is not an official designation. Officially, in Canada, cabinet ministers, senators, the Speaker of the House, Supreme and Federal Court judges, and the lieutenant-governors of the provinces are called *the Honourable* for life. Provincial cabinet ministers, Speakers of the provincial legislatures, and provincial court judges above the level of district judge are also called *the Honourable*, but only during their terms of office. Governors general, prime ministers, and chief justices of Canada are called *the Right Honourable* for life.

The abbreviated forms *the Hon.* and *the Right Hon.* are also correct and quite common, even in formal writing, but they should appear only before a person's name. *Right* may be abbreviated to *Rt.* in informal writing.

... after the trustees' meeting Principal Mackintosh addressed himself to the Hon. W.M. Nickle, Kingston's representative in the provincial legislature....
Frederick Gibson *Queen's University* 2 (1983): 382

The federal government's immediate response was to appoint a high-ranking judge (the Honourable Willard Estey of the Supreme Court) to investigate the bank failures....
Queen's Quarterly 94.4 (1987): 935–6

But not a Canadian among them—not even the Rt. Hon. Pierre Trudeau, who is usually considered to have achieved emeritus status in the 'most eligible' category in North America.
Ottawa Citizen 9 Sept. 1990: A10

Many of the honorable senators in the Red Chamber wear their title with pride and a touch of pomposity.
Ottawa Citizen 16 Dec. 1990: A1

(Since *honorable* here is the honorific, it should be spelled *honourable*.)

Another Hon. Senator glared at his Conservative adversaries across the aisle, drew a mighty breath, and expressed his displeasure at the parliamentary process by blowing on a kazoo.
Ottawa Citizen 6 Oct. 1990: A1

(The capital letters and abbreviation are appropriate only before a person's name: the form required here is *honourable senator*.)

See also -OUR, -OR.

hopefully   see SENTENCE ADVERBS

horde, hoard   A *horde* is a swarm or a gang, or a nomadic clan; a *hoard* is a quantity of treasure, food, or other valuables. To *hoard* something is to gather and store a hoard of it.

'They were troubled by the hordes of mosquitoes.'
Geoffrey Ursell *Perdue: And How the West Was Lost* 1984: 37

Facing more than a dozen TV cameras, a thicket of microphones, and a horde of reporters, [he] was grilled on whether police had checked the room where the body was found.
Province (Vancouver) 25 Oct. 1990: 46

It is a fascinating treasure hoard, displayed with taste and clarity.
Globe and Mail (Toronto) 15 May 1985: P15

But if Spector was irritated, I was pugnacious—a primitive Canadian, I told him, one of those nationalists who still believes that we should hoard our resources.
Saturday Night May 1986: 30

Smith says souvenir sales are already more than $200,000 above the expected horde of $750,000.
Vancouver Sun 27 July 1990: D3

(The correct spelling for this sense is *hoard*. However, *take* or *income* might work better here, since *hoard* implies something saved up and stored away.)

horn   see ANTLER

hors d'oeuvre, hors d'oeuvres   *Hors d'oeuvre* are finger foods or small appetizers served before a meal or at a cocktail party. The word comes from the French phrase meaning outside the meal (literally, 'outside the work'). In French *hors d'oeuvre* is both the singular and the plural form, but English-speakers sometimes add an *s* to form the plural: *hors d'oeuvres*. Both spellings are accepted. The phrase is pronounced *or DUH vre* or sometimes *or DURV(Z)*.

The hors d'oeuvre were a mixture of Canadian and Chinese.
Globe and Mail (Toronto) 18 Jan. 1985: M6

The seminar will be followed by cocktails and hors d'oeuvres....
Computer Dealer News 7 March 1991: 8

host, emcee   Non-sexist usage guides suggest using the noun *host* for men or women and avoiding the gender-marked *hostess*.

Some usage guides object to the use of *host* as a verb, as in 'host a party' or 'host an event', preferring the verbs *give* or *hold*. However, according to dictionaries the use of *host* as a verb is standard, and when the reference is to a radio or television show only *host* will do.

The verb *emcee*, from the abbreviation for 'master of ceremonies' (*M.C.* or *MC*), is still labelled slang by many dictionaries.

Early in 1972, I was invited to appear on a late-night talk show called Appelez-moi Lise. It was hosted by a bright, dynamic woman named Lise Payette, at the time the most popular TV personality in Quebec....
Ken Dryden *The Game* 1983: 26

Hank Snow, a Nova Scotian who began performing professionally in 1929 and by the mid-30s hosted a Halifax radio show, is usually cited as our first major country star.
Queen's Quarterly 95.2 (1988): 295

The evening will be emceed by radio announcer Robert Gillet.
Chronicle Telegraph (Quebec City) 5 June 1991: 6

(To avoid using *emceed*, this sentence could be rewritten: 'Radio announcer Robert Gillet *will be the master of ceremonies* for the evening.')

See also FUNCTIONAL SHIFT; SEXIST LANGUAGE.

hostile, futile   Many Canadians rhyme *hostile* and *futile* with *reptile*. Most Americans, on the other hand, pronounce *hostile* like *hostel* and rhyme *futile* with *brutal*. In the past, Canadian border guards used words like these in a test to distinguish Canadian and American citizens. Today such a test would be less useful because increasing numbers of Canadians are adopting the American pronunciations.

hot flash   see BLUSH

hove   see HEAVE

how come   *How come* meaning 'why' occurs in speech and written dialogue, but it is too casual for formal writing.

'How come my contract says I'm so rich and this check says I'm not?' he wonders, knowing the answer.
Ken Dryden *The Game* 1983: 152

When someone asks you, live, on air, how come you're such a pessimist and why you don't have happier endings, you can think to yourself, 'Because I'm writing in the ironic mode, thickhead.'
Margaret Atwood *Second Words* 1982: 406

How come, one boy said after a wistful silence, we're so backward here in North Dakota?
David Williams *Eye of the Father* 1985: 74

If Wayne Gretzky is so great, how come he can't keep his hockey sweater on right?
Vancouver Sun 17 Feb. 1990: D2

Hudson Bay, Hudson's Bay   The large body of water and the small Saskatchewan town are both spelled *Hudson Bay*. The *Hudson's* Bay Company, established in 1670, is Canada's oldest incorporated company. These spellings are frequently confused.

At hand, for the creative process, they had the assembled resources of the Hudson's Bay Company Archives: the historic portraits, maps and documents, the drawings of James Isham, the water-colours of William Richards—the mixed-blood Company servants whose work gave life to the day-to-day journals of events at the forts on Hudson Bay in the 1770s.
The Beaver Feb.–Mar. 1990: 50

(In this example both spellings are correct.)

Throughout the 40's, the disease spread south on both sides of Hudson's Bay, and in the early 50's raced across Alberta and the prairies in the coyote population.
Perspectives: Profiles of Research at Queen's University 1986: 8

(The correct spelling here is *Hudson Bay*.)

In the late 1800s the Hudson Bay Company had begun weaving imitation sashes on looms.
Canadian Collector 21.4 (1986): 33

(The spelling of the company's name is *Hudson's Bay*.)

hue   see COLOUR

human, humane, inhumane, inhuman, non-human, unhuman   A long tradition in usage maintains that *human* is an adjective, as in 'the human touch', and not a noun, as in 'The ability to speak distinguishes humans from animals'. Canadian writers use *human* as a noun in all kinds of writing, however, and this usage is perfectly acceptable.

Human, when not simply a descriptive term, as in 'human tissue', means characterized by typically human sympathies and foibles: 'It's only human to long for company'. *Human* can also have the negative connotations of 'human error'. *Humane*, on the other hand, is invariably positive: a humane person shows compassion for the suffering of others, human or animal. 'Humane killing' is the killing of animals in a way that minimizes suffering.

Inhumane is the opposite of compassionate; *inhuman* is a more negative synonym meaning unfeeling or cruel and brutal. However, *inhuman* can also mean lacking human qualities: 'He displayed an inhuman perfection'. Even in phrases like this one, where cruelty and brutality are not implied, *inhuman* usually has negative connotations. *Non-human* usually means not human in the biological sense only. *Unhuman*, meaning inhuman, superhuman, or non-human, is very rare in Canadian English.

... it's especially hard to write about communication between cats and humans in any way that isn't whimsical.
Margaret Atwood *Second Words* 1982: 275

Suitable cats are placed for adoption while those that 'display aggressive behavior' or 'illness' are euthanized 'by approved humane methods.'
Daily News (Halifax) 8 Dec. 1993: n.p.

Some are subjected to particularly inhumane treatment, imprisoned for years in cells reserved for those sentenced to death.
Fuse Magazine 13.4 1990: 40

Of course slavery was nowhere regarded in the ancient Greek world as fundamentally immoral or inhuman.
Irving M. Zeitlin and Robert J. Brym *The Social Condition of Humanity* 1991: 310

In *Maria Chapdelaine* the forest is constantly seen as a threat, described always in sombre, hostile, inhuman terms, while high value is placed on its reduction and clearing.
Ben-Z. Shek *French-Canadian & Québécois Novels* 1991: 22–3

I, on the other hand, consider a bed made as long as there's nothing non-human living in it.
Toronto Star 11 Sept. 1993: J1

Most of the rest [of the 22 million vertebrate animals killed annually for research and education] are dogs, cats and non-human primates.
Daily News (Halifax) 1 Aug. 1993: 21

humanitarian, humanitarianism, humanist, humanism, humanities A *humanitarian* is someone who is concerned with the welfare of humanity; the beliefs or practices of such a person are called *humanitarianism*. Usually these words imply a practical involvement in helping others through such humanitarian activities as social work or philanthropy. The senses of *humanitarian* and *humanitarianism* overlap with the meanings of the terms *humanist* and *humanism*, but these latter words have a much wider range of senses.

Humanism frequently refers to a philosophical stance that stresses the importance of the human over the supernatural or the divine. It may refer to the belief that human problems can be solved through reason. Often a *humanist* is contrasted with a religious believer: a secular humanist may believe that Christ was an exceptional human being, but does not accept his divinity. The movement among scholars and artists during the Renaissance from a purely Christian focus to an interest in Latin and Greek culture is called *Humanism*; its founders and exponents are called *Humanists*. Both words are capitalized because they refer to a particular historical movement and a specific group of people. In academic contexts, *humanist* is occasionally used to refer to the study of the *humanities*: that is, the branches of learning associated with human culture, such as art history, history, literature, languages, and philosophy (see also ARTS).

In the international community, Canada is being recognized for its peace-keeping and humanitarianism and for its immigration and refugee policies.
Vancouver Sun 6 Nov. 1993: A3

Meanwhile, a Canadian Forces crew made Canada's one-thousandth humanitarian relief flight into Sarajevo early Wednesday....
Vancouver Sun 30 Dec. 1993: A4

The Victorian humanists who called for a lessening of the harshness of prison life made the point that the infliction of unnecessary suffering debases and brutalizes the society that condones it.
Richard Davies and Glen Kirkland, eds. *Dimensions* 1986: 67

He aroused all our liberal, humanist, do-gooder, middle-class guilt.
Gazette (Montreal) 16 Dec. 1993: A2

Chenevert's humanism is restricted to abstract beings suffering in distant parts of the world—he finds it difficult to relate to people around him.
Ben-Z. Shek *French-Canadian & Québécois Novels* 1991: 38

In postmodern art today, it might be said that the humanist interest in 'the moral' has been transcoded into an interest in 'the political'.
Linda Hutcheon *Splitting Images* 1991: 152

'True-blue' humanists, on the other hand, reject the authority of God and believe that they are sufficient in themselves.
Canadian Baptist Feb. 1986: 14

'The material I am writing tries to show that humanists can live a life that is fully moral without following a special dogma or tenets of a specific religion.'
Toronto Star 24 July 1993: H14

hung   see HANGED

hurdle, hurl   see HURTLE

hurricane   see CYCLONE

hurtle, hurl, hurdle   To *hurtle* is to move with great speed. To *hurl* is to fling violently or throw down. Insults and invective are figuratively hurled, and a speeding train hurtles along. To *hurdle* means to leap or overcome a barrier.

An ICBM is a three-part rocket that can hurtle across the world in half an hour or less.
Saturday Night Jan. 1986: 14

'She started hurtling insults at me.'
Globe and Mail (Toronto) 4 May 1985: M1

(The word required here is *hurling*.)

The searing heat of the detonation scorched the shirt of a farmer standing on his porch 40 miles away. Seconds later a deafening shock wave hurled him to the ground, knocking him unconscious.
Terence Dickinson *Halley's Comet* 1985: 61

He sat beside the constable and across from the jailer, and he watched the flat white fields hurling past the window.
William Teatero *John Anderson: Fugitive Slave* 1986: 144

(The word required here is *hurtling*.)

He vaults the low iron railing of the cement porch, hurdles the short hedge onto the neighbors' lawn.
Margaret Atwood *Life Before Man* 1979: 265

husk, shuck   The husks of grain crops are removed by *husking*. Corn is either *husked* or *shucked* (or, in some dialects, *chucked*); shellfish are *shucked*. The informal expression 'to *shuck* something *off*' means to discard it.

If oysters in the shell aren't available, look for them shucked and packed in plastic tubs.
Gazette (Montreal) 21 Dec. 194: E4

It's just recently that McCurdy the potter shucked off her cocoon to become McCurdy the ceramic artist.
Daily News (Halifax) 12 Jan. 1994: 21

hyper-, hypo-, hyper   The prefix *hyper-* means above, beyond, or excessively; the prefix *hypo-* means below, under, or insufficiently. Thus someone with a high fever is *hyperthermic*, whereas someone suffering from exposure to severe cold is *hypothermic*.

Since the 1970s, *hyper* has come into common use among North Americans as an adjective describing tense or excessively active people. *Hyper* in this sense is probably an abbreviation of *hyperactive*. It is listed in some North American dictionaries, always as slang; in formal writing *excitable* or *nervous* would be a better choice.

Hence hyperrealism: that which is more realistic than the realistic.
Queen's Quarterly 96.1 (1989): 105

'At night [the temperature] really drops and you can get hypothermic.'
Ottawa Citizen 2 Sept. 1990: B7

Most of the time Curtis is hyper, grabbing at the air with her hands when she talks, as if reaching for the centre of attention.
Province (Vancouver) 16 March 1990: P4

hyperbole, hyperbola, hyperbolic   *Hyperbole* (pronounced *high PER buh lee*) is a figure of speech, the use of exaggeration for emphasis and rhetorical effect: 'He invested a fortune in lottery tickets'. A *hyperbola* is a geometric curve. *Hyperbolic*, the adjective for both nouns, is pronounced *high per BAWL ic*.

hypercorrection   This is the name for the 'over-correct' pronunciations and grammatical structures that result when someone whose normal usage is not standard tries to produce a standard ('correct') form and goes too far. The Cockney, for example, who typically does not pronounce the *h* at the beginning of words (saying *'art* for *heart*), when attempting to produce Standard English often adds an *h* even to words that don't have one (saying *harm* for *arm*). In the American comedy *All in the Family*, Archie Bunker's pronunciation of *toilet* as *terlet* reflects an attempt to correct a particularly stigmatized pronunciation associated with Brooklyn, which produces, for example, *toity-toid* instead of *thirty-third*. Archie's attempt to correct this non-standard pronunciation (by substituting *er* for *oi* wherever it occurs) takes the correction too far. In grammar, the most common example of hyper-correction is probably the use of *between you and I* when *between you and me* is correct.

See also ADJECTIVES AND ADVERBS; BAD, BADLY; BETWEEN YOU AND ME; WHO, WHOM.

hyphenation Hyphens have two major functions. The first is to indicate that a word has been divided at the end of a line. The general principle to follow is to insert the hyphen where it will least distract the reader, usually at a syllable break (which can be checked in a dictionary).

The second use of hyphens is to combine discrete verbal elements into a single unit of meaning. For example, in the sentence 'I went to a few more-highly-recommended restaurants' the hyphens indicate that the speaker visited some less-highly-recommended restaurants before moving on to the better establishments. Without the hyphens this sentence would suggest that the speaker visited *only* highly recommended places. Generally speaking, hyphens are inserted to prevent ambiguity or make reading easier.

Hyphens often follow prefixes in new words (*'non-stick* cookware') or words coined for an occasion ('my *pre-trip* checklist'). The more familiar a word becomes, the less likely it is to be spelled with a hyphen. Canadian and American writers are quicker to drop these hyphens (e.g., in words such as *nonprofit* and *predate*) than the British (*non-profit, pre-date*). Canadians are also less likely than the British to spell compound words with a hyphen, often preferring an open compound (such as *bear hug, slave driver*) or a solid word (*northeast, newlywed*) to a hyphenated British spelling (*bear-hug, slave-driver, north-east, newly-wed*). Given that hyphens are more common in British than in North American writing, Canadians who routinely use a British dictionary may want to shift to one that reflects North American practice for hyphenation.

It is not always possible to use a dictionary to settle a hyphenation problem. Some words are too new to be in the dictionary, and some combinations, such as 'more-highly-recommended restaurants' in the example above, will never appear in a dictionary because they are linked to a particular context. Editors and usage guides have developed some useful general guidelines for cases where dictionaries fail. Hyphens are normally used in the following contexts:

- after a prefix preceding a numeral ('mid-1900') or a capital letter ('un-Canadian')
- where dropping the hyphen would produce a word with another meaning (*'co-op* housing', not *'coop* housing'; *'re-cover* the footstool' not *'recover* the footstool')
- in a compound consisting of multiple elements ('non-German-speaking visitor', 'mid-twentieth-century scholarship')
- in a phrase describing age, length, etc. ('six-year-old child', '12-foot-high fence')
- between double vowels (*anti-intellectual, re-examine, multi-entry, pre-issue*) or identical consonants (*non-national*); however, note that many familiar words with double vowels or consonants (these will be found in a dictionary) do not require a hyphen (e.g., *cooperate, coordinate, bookkeeping, cutthroat, nighttime*)
- after paired prefixes where the first stands alone, as in 'nineteenth- and twentieth-century scholarship' or 'pre- and post-operative care'
- in spelled-out fractions ('three-quarter length', 'one-fifth reduction', 'four and one-quarter'), unless the denominator already contains a hyphen ('one thirty-second'); note that when fractions are written as numerals, a slash, not a hyphen, is used to separate the numerator and denominator (3/4).

Many multi-word modifiers that are not hyphenated when they follow a verb *are* hyphenated if they directly precede a noun:

He is completely burned out. / He's a burned-out executive.

This schedule is out of date. / An out-of-date schedule is useless.

Similarly, noun phrases that are not normally hyphenated often *are* hyphenated when used attributively (i.e., in front of another noun):

My son is in day care. / He goes to a day-care centre.

They support law and order. / They ran on a law-and-order platform.

Nouns designating ethnicity, such as *French Canadian* or *African American* (as in 'His mother was a French Canadian, his father an African American') are hyphenated when they are used as adjectives: 'French-Canadian literature', 'African-American history'.

They are several contexts where writers are tempted to insert unnecessary hyphens. Hyphens are *not* required in the following contexts:

• in an adjectival phrase consisting of a foreign phrase ('ad hoc decision', 'in camera meeting')—unless the foreign phrase is hyphenated in the original language ('laissez-faire policy')

• after an -*ly* adverb modifying a past participle ('politically charged situation', 'newly coined words'); it is only irregular adverbs that might be mistaken for adjectives that are joined to past participles by hyphens ('the best-known case', 'much-used material').

Phrasal verbs should not be hyphenated or written as one word unless they are being used as adjectives or nouns (see PHRASAL VERBS):

They turn out to every game.

They expected a better turnout.

He sugars off when the weather is right.

Sugaring-off season brings visitors.

See also DASH; PREFIX, SUFFIX; RE-; SEMI-; SLASH.

hypo-   see HYPER-

hypocrisy, idiosyncrasy   Both these words end in -*sy*, not -*cy*.

It began early with the British accusing other Commonwealth countries of hypocricy on the sanctions question and quoting statistics purporting to show Canadian trade with South Africa unchanged....
Toronto Star 18 Oct. 1987: B4

(The correct spelling is *hypocrisy*.)

I've a downtown friend whose neighbors are not totally pleased with one of his idiosyncracies.
Toronto Star 24 July 1994: F6

(The correct spelling is *idiosyncrasies*.)

I

I   see CASE; MYSELF; PRESENT WRITER

-(i)ana   The suffix -*(i)ana* is used to form a collective noun meaning 'things associated with' the place, person, pastime, or period in the root word. It usually refers to books or memorabilia. *Canadiana* is a familiar example. In addition, the *OED* includes *Walpoliana*, *Churchilliana*, *Africana*, *cricketana*, *Victoriana*, and *Shakespeariana* (also spelled *Shakespeareana*).

ibid., op. cit.   *Ibid.* is an abbreviation of *ibidem*, Latin for 'in the same place', and *op. cit.* is an abbreviation of *opere citato*, Latin for 'in the work cited'. Both these abbreviations were designed to reduce the length of footnotes, which helped typesetters save both time and page space. Now many modern scholarly publishers have turned to endnotes rather than footnotes, a practice that permits longer notes and reduces the need for abbreviations. Most disciplines have one or more recognized styles for articles published in scholarly journals. The *Chicago Manual of Style* (14th ed.) is the style guide used by most scholarly book editors.

Instead of *ibid.* and *op. cit.*, many of these style guides recommend putting references in the text itself, enclosed in parentheses, and reserving footnotes or endnotes for comments of some substance. This system gives the page number in parentheses directly after the quotation; if the text does not make it clear who is being quoted, the page number is preceded by the last name of the author(s); if more than one work by the same author(s) is cited, the date of publication or a short version of the title in question is included to identify it.

See also LATIN PHRASES.

-ible   see -ABLE

-ic, -ical   Many -*ic/-ical* adjective pairs are essentially interchangeable, including *botanic/botanical*, *electric/electrical*, *fanatic/fanatical*, *geographic/geographical*, *ironic/ironical*, *mythic/mythical*. Other pairs are partially or completely differentiated (see CLASSIC, CLASSICAL; COMIC, COMICAL; ECONOMIC, ECONOMICAL; HISTORIC, HISTORICAL; POLITIC, POLITICAL).

-ic, -ically   see PUBLICLY

ice cream, ice water, iced tea, ice   Canadians write *ice cream* and *ice water*, but *iced tea*. Originally, the dessert and water were also termed *iced*, since these products are not made of ice; rather, ice is used to cool them. The *-ed* ending began to disappear in the eighteenth century. Canadians and Americans do not usually hyphenate *ice cream* or *ice water* unless they are modifying a noun, as in 'ice-cream cone'.

In Britain if you ask for 'an ice' you will be offered iced sweets such as ice cream, sherbet, or frozen fruit juice.

> We've told them a million times that it's not ice cream, it's iced cream.
> W.C. Lougheed, ed. *In Search of the Standard in Canadian English* 1986: 78

> One of the few buildings not destroyed was an ice-cream booth; firefighters, their eyes smarting from the smoke, gained relief by slathering their faces with chocolate and strawberry-flavored ice cream.
> *Globe and Mail* (Toronto) 24 May 1985: P7

> ... many chickens are cooled using iced water.
> *Western Grocer* Aug. 1990: 56

(The more common expression is *ice water*.)

> Iced tea is synonymous with warm summer months and tea companies have worked hard to cash in on the traditional image of someone drinking a tall, frosted glass of lemon-flavoured iced tea on a sweltering July day.
> *Western Grocer* May–Jun. 1990: 29

> We took our first swim and iced-tea break at the lake formed behind the grist mill dam.
> *Globe and Mail* (Toronto) 30 March 1985: T9

See also SKIM MILK, SKIMMED MILK, WHIP CREAM, WHIPPED CREAM.

ideology, ideological, ideologue   *Ideology* is frequently used to refer to a set of political beliefs that determines the actions of a particular party or group. Although the term can be used neutrally or positively, it is generally applied to beliefs that, in the speaker's view, are held dogmatically or distort reality. Supporters of both the left and the right have accused their opponents of adhering to ideology in the negative sense.

Marxist theory holds that widespread systems of beliefs—ideologies—are designed to justify and preserve the power of a dominant class, and that they serve that end by representing social structures as natural and inevitable.

Ideologue, like *demagogue*, is almost always a negative term. An *ideologue* is a person who promotes a particular—implicitly false—ideology.

> Rogin argues that cultural historians must take film seriously, both because political groups use the medium as an instrument of control and change, and because cinema can reveal important clues to the mind-set and ideology of these groups.
> *Queen's Quarterly* 95.4 (1988): 807

> Schickel is obviously concerned with the obvious—with image, appearance and style—and that is precisely his point, that ideology is irrelevant to the American electorate, the headless body that embraced Reagan because he was 'the genial host of the great American talk show....'
> *Globe and Mail* (Toronto) 27 April 1985: E19

(Here *ideology* is used positively to mean political principles.)

> Above all, our evaluation should move beyond ideology to a concrete, pragmatic and enlightened assessment of our interest.
> *Globe and Mail* (Toronto) 28 May 1991: P7

(Here *ideology* is used negatively.)

> Yet, when a Canadian journalist reports the purges, repressions and doubletalk, well, he or she becomes a fascist right-wing ideologue.
> *Maclean's* 19 Sept. 1988: A9

idioms   An *idiom* is a phrase, such as 'have the heart to' or 'be on top of', that can't be interpreted literally. English, like all languages, has many idioms. Though generally they pose no special problem for the native speaker, they often mystify the second-language learner.

The meaning of an idiom is a metaphorical extension of its literal, or word-for-word, meaning. When we learn the meaning of an unfamiliar idiom we file it away just as we would that of a new word. Because they are items of vocabulary, idioms are inflexible. With even a slight change of wording, an idiom devolves into literal speech. 'He's spreading me with butter' does not mean the same thing as 'He's buttering me up'. Nor does 'Don't take your shirt off' have the same meaning as 'Keep your shirt on'.

Phrasal verbs form a special class of idiom in English. These are verbs with prepositional particles attached to them that alter their meaning.

'Look out', for example, is a phrasal verb in 'Look out for the car!' while it is two independent words in 'Look out over the water'. 'Look up' is a phrasal verb in 'Look up their phone number', but not in 'Look up, so I can take your picture'. Other examples of phrasal verbs are *carry on, carry out, fill in, get by, go on about, put up with*, and *take off*. Phrasal verbs are so common in English that native speakers may not realize how much trouble they can pose for non-native speakers.

Idioms, including phrasal verbs, need not (indeed cannot) be avoided. However, if you are writing for an audience that may have trouble comprehending idioms, it's a good idea to repeat your central points in several different ways.

See also CLICHÉ; PHRASAL VERBS.

idiosyncrasy   see HYPOCRISY

idiot savant   see SAVANT

i.e., e.g.   An abbreviation of the Latin phrase *id est*, *i.e.* means 'that is'; *e.g.* is an abbreviation of *exempli gratia*, meaning 'for example'. The meanings of these two abbreviations are different: *i.e.* introduces a paraphrase or further explanation, while *e.g.* introduces an example.

Although *Fowler's* (1965) suggested that these abbreviations should appear only in notes, and The *Chicago Manual of Style* confines them to notes and parenthetical comments, they appear increasingly in running text in works of all kinds. Most guides recommend that *i.e.* and *e.g.* be preceded and followed by commas. They need not be italicized.

> The feminist and pro-choice movement's call for reproductive rights rests on the fundamental liberal principles of 'bodily integrity' (i.e., citizens have a right to make decisions about their own bodies free from state interference) and 'individual conscience' (i.e., women are autonomous, rational, and moral agents capable of exercising choice).
> Janine Brodie, Shelley A.M. Gavigan, and Jane Jenson *The Politics of Abortion* 1992: 72

> Between 15 and 18 January, i.e., between the first and fourth day of the congress, Paul Levi ... attempted another compromise with Serrati.
> *Canadian Journal of History* 14.1 (1989): 39

> Motorists entering Canada should ... note that some provinces (e.g., Ontario) do not allow studded tires. ...
> Alan Tucker, ed. *The Penguin Guide to Canada* 1991: 13

> If industrial production is stopped (e.g., by a strike) every member of society feels the consequences.

> Irving M. Zeitlin and Robert J. Brym *The Social Condition of Humanity* 1991: 149

> ... Carsten lacked those silly misconceptions [held] by some travellers (i.e., all Canadians live in igloos, all Aussies wrestle alligators in their spare time).
> *Calgary Herald* 21 July 1995: B4

(Here *i.e.* should be replaced by *e.g.*)

See also LATIN PHRASES.

-ie-, -ei-   Most writers know the rule: *i* before *e* (*achieve, believe, chief, relieve*) except after *c* (*ceiling, conceit, receive*), but there are exceptions: *caffeine, codeine, either, leisure, neither, protein, seize, sheik, weird*. And there are many instances where the rule does not apply.

First, the rule does not apply if the *i* and the *e* are pronounced separately, as in *science*, or if the *c* is sounded like *sh*, as in *conscience, species*, and *sufficient*.

Second, the rule does not apply if the sound is a long *a*. A long *a* sound is spelled *ei*: *feign, freight, inveigle, neighbour, rein, reign, veil, vein, weigh*. In fact, any vowel sound other than the long *e* sound (as in *achieve, believe*, etc.) is usually spelled *ei*: *height; counterfeit, forfeit* (but *mischief*); *heir, their; foreign, sovereign* (but *friend*—because a *friend* is a friend to the *end*).

See also WEIRD.

-ies   see -Y

if, whether   The most common meaning of *if* is 'in the case that': 'If you see them, say hello'. *If* also means 'whether': 'Ask if I can come'. Sentences in which *if* could have either meaning ('Let us know if you are coming') should be avoided. Depending on which meaning is intended, this sentence should be rephrased: either 'If you are coming, let us know' or 'Let us know whether you are coming'.

When either *if* or *whether* is possible, the usual choice in formal writing is *whether*.

When *if* means 'whether', it should not be followed by the subjunctive: 'He asked if I was (*not* were) aware of the implications'.

> And when they ask if you want a medium hot salsa or the 'dangerous stuff' they're not kidding about the latter.
> Alan Tucker, ed. *The Penguin Guide to Canada* 1991: 190

(This use of *if* meaning 'whether' is common in speech and informal writing.)

It remains to be seen whether this abnormal biochemistry is a cause of Alzheimer's, or an effect....
Queen's Quarterly 92.1 (1985): 155

See also IF I WERE YOU; SUBJUNCTIVE.

if I were you   Sometimes *were* displaces the usual past tense in a clause introduced by *if*:

If I made all the arrangements, would you come? / If I were to make all the arrangements, would you come?

If she was eligible, she would apply. / If she were eligible, she would apply.

The use of *were* indicates that the condition named in the *if*-clause is purely hypothetical, or at least highly unlikely. The clause containing *were* is said to be in the subjunctive mood. Note that the subjunctive *were* is a stylistic option, not a grammatical necessity—with one exception: in formal writing and speech, Canadians never use the phrase 'If I was you'. The subjunctive 'If I were you' is the norm. In British English 'If I was you' is viewed more tolerantly.

See also SUBJUNCTIVE.

ignoramus   An *ignoramus* is an ignorant or stupid person. The word derives from a Latin verb form meaning 'we do not know'. Because it is derived from a verb, it does not form a normal Latin plural; the accepted plural is not *ignorami* but *ignoramuses*. *Ignoramus* was popularized as a term of derision in the early seventeenth century, when the playwright George Ruggle used it as the name of a lawyer in his play *Ignoramus* (1615).

A person who knows nothing about literature may be an ignoramus, but many people don't mind being that.
Northrop Frye *The Educated Imagination* 1963: 2

ignorant   see ILLITERATE

-ile   see HOSTILE

ilk   'Of that ilk' now means 'of that sort or type'. In Scotland an older meaning—'of the same place, estate, or name'—has been retained, mainly in the names of landed families. Thus 'Moffatt of that ilk' means someone named Moffatt whose lands are in a place called Moffatt. Some commentators would restrict *ilk* meaning sort or kind to informal contexts, but Canadian writers use the expression in all kinds of writing.

Peregrine will be known as the Moncreiffe of That Ilk, a ... title in which the word Ilk means 'the same.' The title means Moncreiffe of Moncreiffe.
Globe and Mail (Toronto) 28 Feb. 1985: P16

Kristin and Tay John are both figures of this sort, demigods, with unusual births and strange attributes; like satyrs and their ilk, they are bridges joining the human world, the natural world and the supranatural world.
Margaret Atwood *Second Words* 1982: 240

... teachers who love to see young people learn and mature will see to it that their pupils do. How many of us remember with great fondness teachers of that ilk ... ?
Province (Vancouver) 16 March 1990: 56

ill   see SICK

illegal, unlawful, illicit   *Illegal, unlawful,* and *illicit* are all used to mean contrary to law. *Illegal* is most common in general writing that describes acts contravening the law of the land. However, the Canadian Criminal Code uses *lawful* and *unlawful* almost exclusively; thus this word occurs frequently in the press in such fixed phrases as 'unlawful confinement', 'unlawful assembly', and 'unlawful possession'.

Illicit usually describes things or activities that are illegal under certain circumstances ('illicit drugs', 'illicit trade') or are not approved of under certain circumstances ('illicit sex').

Burglary, as a criminal offence, consists in the unlawful entry of premises with or without force....
J.E. Smyth et al. *The Law and Business Administration in Canada* 1987: 428

The illicit arms trade is a major concern for Canadian officials.
Maclean's 28 July 1986: 8

Watching *Home Alone* is as boring as babysitting a child you don't like, in a house with an empty fridge, no TV, not even a medical book or dirty magazine for a few illicit adolescent thrills.
Vancouver Sun 16 Nov. 1990: D4

illegible   see UNREADABLE

illicit   see ILLEGAL

illiterate, computer(-)illiterate, illiteracy, innumerate, ignorant   An *illiterate* person does not know how to read or write. Someone who is 'functionally illiterate' cannot read or write well enough to cope with everyday tasks such as reading directions, looking up telephone numbers, or filling out application forms. By extension, *illiterate* can be used to describe a person who does not possess the rudiments of a specified subject. For example, someone who is unable to use a computer may be termed 'computer-illiterate'. (This is the adjective form, as in 'Computer-illiterate students are at a disadvantage'. The noun form does not take a hyphen: 'He is a computer illiterate'; 'Computer illiterates are no longer common in the department'.)

Usage guides may use the term *illiteracy* to label a usage that they condemn. Often, however, their examples are culled from newspapers, and the perpetrators of these offensive usages not only are literate but make their living by writing. The terms *illiteracy* and *illiterate* can both be used as insults rather than descriptive terms; they should be applied with caution.

Innumerate is the term for those lacking adequate skills in arithmetic or knowledge of mathematics and science.

Ignorant means lacking in knowledge either generally or in a particular subject area. Although to be called ignorant is insulting, to be deemed ignorant of some specific area of knowledge is not necessarily an insult: 'He is ignorant of cell phones, having spent the last three years in the Amazon basin'; 'I claimed ignorance of the missing chocolate'.

Informally, *ignorant* has come to mean rude and obnoxious.

He was illiterate, and 'his principal object in marrying was to have a wife who was able to read his parts to him'; he must have been a quick study and she must have been a good wife, for he occasionally acted two brand-new parts on two successive days.
Robertson Davies *A Voice from the Attic* 1960: 208

He finds these reactions of hers, not disappointing exactly, but surprising, as if only a barbarian or an illiterate could have the reactions she does.
Margaret Atwood *Life Before Man* 1979: 217

If you're illiterate or innumerate in a society where the fastest growing group in the workforce is the technical and professional class, you're in big trouble.
Ottawa Citizen 24 Oct. 1990: A11

Naturally, you don't have to buy educational CD-ROMs for home use ... if you don't mind consigning your child to the computer-illiterate slagheap of the 21st century.
Province (Vancouver) 23 Aug. 1995: A22

Our children probably never pined for home versions of video-arcade games, nor did we worry that our children

were becoming computer illiterates, space-age versions of the village idiot.
Canadian Consumer Jan. 1986: 11

I'm sure that the dictionary definition of 'ignorant' gives you license to use the word in your Feb. 22 headline, 'Finding 12 ignorant jurors for North was a trial in itself,' but surely colloquial usage would give you pause. 'Finding 12 jurors ignorant of North ...' would have been a lot better.
Gazette (Montreal) 1 March 1989: B2

imaginary, imaginative Something *imaginary* exists only in the mind, while something *imaginative* demonstrates the creative powers of the mind. Thus a child's 'imaginary friend' is not real, while an 'imaginative friend' is one full of fanciful and intriguing ideas. Both words are applied to works of art: an imaginative (creative) work may evoke an imaginary world. The term *imaginative literature* is sometimes used to distinguish literary writing from other kinds of writing that are also referred to as literature. For example, social scientists use *literature* to refer to all the published material on a particular topic ('a review of the literature on drug abuse'), and groups attempting to attract support use it to refer to their promotional material ('We have some literature you might like to read').

Here society is seen as controlled by certain anxieties, real or imaginary, which are designed to repress or sublimate human impulses toward a greater freedom.
Northrop Frye *The Bush Garden* 1971: 230

The terms physicists have ascribed to elementary particles of matter—leptons, bosons, weakons, quarks—seem like names invented by lonely children with imaginary friends.
Canadian Fiction Magazine 63 (1988): 36

The books I read as a child transformed me, gave meaning and perspective to my experiences and helped to mould whatever imaginative, intellectual or creative strengths I can lay claim to now.
Canadian Living 19 April 1986: 62

The idea of possessing the means and the milieu for a life devoted entirely to imaginative creation is extremely attractive, especially to the story-telling sort of talent.
Robertson Davies *A Voice from the Attic* 1960: 304

The aim of propaganda is to convince, and to spur people to action; the aim of writing is to create a plausible and moving imaginative world, and to create it from words.
Margaret Atwood *Second Words* 1982: 204

(Here Atwood may have chosen *imaginative* to avoid the fairy-tale connotations of *imaginary*; normally, one would expect *imaginary* here.)

The Romantic poets ... elevated *imaginative* literature to a status far above other kinds of writing....
Queen's Quarterly 95 (1988): 557

imbue, instil, infuse, inculcate These near-synonyms are now most often used figuratively. But because of their different literal senses, they are followed by different prepositions, and this is where the usage difficulties arise. *Imbue*, literally to soak or dye, is usually followed by *with*; *instil*, literally to introduce drop by drop, is usually followed by *in* or *into*; *infuse*, literally to steep in or pour into, may be followed by *with* or *into*. *Inculcate*, originally meaning to press in with the heel, may be followed by *in*, *into*, or *upon*. Objections have been raised to *imbue into*, *instil with*, and *inculcate with*. As the literal meanings fade from use, these objections will doubtless fade as well, but until then it is safest to use the prepositions that are conventionally found with each word.

Instill is the common spelling in the United States and Canada; *instil* is usual in Britain. *Instilled* and *instilling* always have two *l*'s.

The Seabird band is one of about 100 B.C. bands in charge of its own education. That means the band can imbue its young with a respect for their heritage....
Vancouver Sun 8 Sept. 1990: A7

These are the largest and oldest trees in the world, and their age and size imbue this forest with a solemnity so deep it seems to many visitors spiritual.
Vancouver Sun 16 June 1990: A1

Contrary to the industrious image of overseas Chinese, the work ethic does not seem necessarily imbued into modern mainland China—as it is ... in modern Japan.
Globe and Mail (Toronto) 26 Dec. 1985: A7

(The sentence could be rewritten: '... modern mainland China does not necessarily seem *imbued with* the work ethic—as modern Japan is'; or '... the work ethic does not necessarily seem to have been *instilled into* [or *inculcated in*] modern mainland China...'.)

'Munich has never really become a big city,' says August Everding, a 'Prussian' who for two decades has instilled his ebullient spirit into the city's opera and theatre.
Globe and Mail (Toronto) 9 Feb. 1985: T12

Even when the dance catapults into the ridiculous, she manages to instil the whole thing with some moments of calm—a difficult feat considering the bustling variety of dance styles in the play.
Globe and Mail (Toronto) 30 Jan. 1985: M9

(Since the 'moments of calm' are intermittent, a more appropriate verb might be *introduce*: '... she manages to introduce some moments of calm...').

In his new role as chairman of the Metro Toronto Board of Police Commissioners, he talks wistfully of infusing fresh talent into the corporation.
Globe and Mail (Toronto) 4 May 1985: M1

Children generally don't have much money, but bankers want to inculcate a savings ethic in them early.
Globe and Mail (Toronto) 30 Dec. 1985: B1

immaculate see IMMACULATE CONCEPTION; IMPECCABLE

Immaculate Conception, virgin birth *Immaculate* means pure, without spot or stain. The term *Immaculate Conception* (usually capitalized because it is the official name of a dogma) does not, as is popularly thought, refer to the special circumstances of Jesus Christ's conception (i.e., that he was fathered by the Holy Spirit). Rather, it refers to a Roman Catholic dogma, dating from 1854, according to which Mary, in preparation for her role as the Mother of God, was born without original sin.

The expression *virgin birth* is the popular name of the doctrine that Christ was born of a mother who was a virgin; because it is not an official term, it is not capitalized.

See also ENUNCIATION, ANNUNCIATION.

immanent, imminent, eminent, pre-eminent *Immanent* means inherent or existing within and is usually found in theological, philosophical, and psychological writing. *Imminent* means impending or likely to happen in the very near future. *Eminent* means outstanding or prominent. *Pre-eminent* and *eminent* are sometimes used interchangeably, although *pre-eminent* carries the sense of most distinguished, and excelling above all others: an eminent lawyer is not necessarily the pre-eminent, or most distinguished, lawyer in town.

At the root of the problem, writes Sennett, was a 19th-century secularism 'based on the code of the immanent, rather than the transcendent. Immediate sensation, immediate fact, immediate feeling, were no longer to be

fitted into a pre-existent [religious] scheme in order to be understood.'
Ottawa Citizen 26 Nov. 1994: B6

My stay in Bulgaria came to an abrupt end when I was informed by the British legation in Sofia that war was imminent and that, with my name, I would be well advised to leave the country as quickly as possible.
George Ignatieff *The Making of a Peacemonger* 1987: 53

From the deer and fish in Isabella Crawford's 'The Canoe' to the frogs and toads in Layton, from the white narcissus of Knister to the night-blooming cereus of Reaney, everything that is central in Canadian writing seems to be marked by the imminence of the natural world.
Northrop Frye *The Bush Garden* 1971: 247

(Frye appears to mean *immanence* here: that is, the pervasiveness of the natural world, rather than its imminence.)

Philip said talk of an immanent deal was premature. 'I do not see it completed in two days', said Philip.
Financial Post 31 Oct. 1991: 3

(The correct spelling is *imminent*.)

Eminent ancestors make one's causes and programs respectable; disreputable ancestors taint and disgrace.
Canadian Journal of History 14.1 1989: 10

... given the claim that the king was pre-eminent within British government, it seems probable that he was the supreme power who was to be obeyed....
J.A.W. Gunn *Beyond Liberty and Property* 1983: 182

immigrant   see EMIGRANT

immigrant, landed   see CITIZEN

imminent   see IMMANENT

immoral, amoral, non-moral, unmoral   Many usage guides caution readers to distinguish between *immoral*, meaning contravening accepted standards of morality, and *amoral*, meaning lying beyond the sphere in which moral judgments apply. This distinction reserves *immoral* for those capable of understanding morality—that is, responsible adult human beings, as opposed to children, other animals, or forces of nature.

In practice, however, *immoral* tends to be used specifically of behaviour that violates sexual conventions, while *amoral* often refers to other kinds of moral transgressions—the kinds of things that in a more religious age might have been called *evil*. *Amoral* is often used with the implication that the

people in question are acting as if they were beyond the range of moral judgment or had no concept of the prevailing standards of morality. These uses seem acceptable for most audiences.

Because of the ambiguity that may attach to the use of *amoral*, some people writing on ethics or philosophy use *non-moral* or *unmoral* to refer to those matters outside the scope of moral judgment.

Peter De Vries in *The Tunnel of Love* has brilliantly caricatured an editor who sets out on an adulterous path for which he has no talent and small appetite, in order to show that he can be as immoral as any of the creative men with whom his work associates him.
Robertson Davies *A Voice from the Attic* 1960: 315

'We consider it is amoral to use the hostages for political ends,' he told the joint news conference....
Ottawa Citizen 29 Oct. 1990: A1

(The speaker thinks that the behaviour of the hostage-takers is evil; thus most usage guides would recommend *immoral* here.)

He believes American individualism is an amoral creed leading to a selfish, Hobbesian state of nature, and that our sense of collective rights and of shared social responsibilities makes a better model for the future.
Saturday Night July 1986: 51

(Here many usage guides would recommend *immoral*.)

The Beats, according to their journalistic image, were amoral, apolitical bohemians who celebrated their freedom in quick sexual liaisons and spontaneous art works.
Jack Chambers *Milestones* 1983: 247

(Here many usage guides would recommend *immoral*.)

The mini-series audience seems absolutely fascinated with repellent, amoral and self-centred characters—provided they're real. We can't hear enough about real people who break all the bounds of decency that restrain the rest of us....
Ottawa Citizen 3 Feb. 1990: C8

(Here many usage guides would recommend *immoral*.)

It's called 'realpolitik'. That's the term for a hard-nosed, amoral attitude toward the rest of the world.
Province (Vancouver) 20 March 1990: 31

It casts moral values as obligations and makes them overriding. Its effect is to leave no room for non-moral considerations.
Canadian Journal of Philosophy 19 (1989): 298

immunization, vaccination, inoculation   In current medical usage, *immunization* and *vaccination* are synonymous and are preferred to *inoculation*, which is considered an outmoded term. However, *inoculation* is still the word most likely to be used in a figurative sense.

The frequent misspelling *innoculate* is probably influenced by the double *n* in the similar but etymologically unrelated word *innocuous*.

> The students also learn how immunization with vaccines has helped prevent a wide range of human diseases around the world.
> *Toronto Star* 20 Jan. 1994: NY2

> I am afraid we were never able to innoculate him with the Queen's spirit.
> Frederick Gibson *Queen's University* 2 (1983): 131

(The accepted spelling is *inoculate*.)

impact   The verb to *impact* is by no means new. It's been used for centuries in its literal sense, to hit or compress; this use, however, is relatively rare except in dentistry: 'impacted wisdom tooth'. The figurative use of *impact* to mean affect or influence became popular in business writing in the 1980s: 'Our earnings were negatively impacted by the recession'. Some commentators consider this use jargon, and you may want to avoid it in general writing.

> The Berkeley team announced their findings as evidence that an asteroid had impacted the Earth 65 million years ago, causing the extinction holocaust.
> Terence Dickinson *Halley's Comet* 1985: 64

> Fortunately the errors would not impact greatly upon ice seamanship.
> *Arctic* 41.1 (1988): 85

(This sentence could be rewritten: '. . . would not greatly *affect* ice seamanship'.)

See also FUNCTIONAL SHIFT.

impassable, impassive   see DISPASSIONATE

impeach, impeachment   *Impeach* has two main senses: to censure or criticize someone for wrongdoing and to remove someone from office for misconduct. Although some commentators insist that only the first sense is acceptable, it is less common than the second.

> But when you consider that NBC puts Gumbel out there every morning as someone viewers can trust to conduct serious and sober interviews with political leaders and other important national figures, then perhaps viewers do have a right to know what type of person he is, how he forms his judgments and if he is to be trusted. It should be noted that the memo does not necessarily impeach Gumbel on those points. . . .
> *Gazette* (Montreal) 6 March 1989: F4

(Here Gumbel has been criticized rather than removed from office.)

> 'I wouldn't want to say I'd stand again. Who knows, I could be challenged and voted out. Or I might be impeached before the two years is up, who knows?'
> *Canadian Rodeo News* March 1990: 15

(Here *impeach* means remove from office.)

> Impeachment would no doubt have served as a means of punishing individual ministers, but that procedure fell into disuse.
> J.A.W. Gunn *Beyond Liberty and Property* 1983: 65

> 'I don't recall Mulroney speaking forcefully against Quebec's sign law here. I don't want to impeach his motives, but given the strong nationalist feelings in his own Quebec caucus, he probably doesn't dare to.'
> *Ottawa Citizen* 10 Feb. 1990: B7

(Here *impeach* means criticize.)

> 'If there was any way to impeach this government before then [the next election] I wish we would.'
> *Maclean's* 17 Dec. 1990: A18

(Here *impeach* means remove from office.)

> What Canadians are telling them, time and time again, over the phone and face to face, is that the prime minister must go. If he cannot be impeached, and he cannot, then he must resign. . . .
> *Ottawa Citizen* 13 Feb. 1991: A2

(Here *impeach* means remove from office.)

> It is also the time to develop an impeachment process to recall and depose legally a government that acts illegally.
> *Ottawa Citizen* 27 Sept. 1990: A14

(Here *impeachment* refers to removal from office.)

impeccable, immaculate   *Impeccable* is derived from the Latin meaning 'not sinning'; *peccadillo*, 'a trifling sin', is derived from the same root. Some usage guides would restrict *impeccable* to descriptions of people or their behaviour, presumably because only people or their behaviour can be described as sinless. Even these guides accept that *impeccable* may be used in the sense 'exemplary' or 'flawless', as in 'Gertrude spoke impeccable French'.

Impeccable is also, however, quite commonly used as a synonym for *immaculate* with reference to clothes, decor, design, and so on, and it is unlikely that appeals to etymology will stop this trend. *Impeccable* can now be applied to anything that might be described as flawless or spotless.

Nevertheless, British authorities went on placing unquestioning faith in traitors such as Philby, Maclean, and Blunt whose impeccable family and school credentials provided a perfect camouflage for their subversive activities.
George Ignatieff *The Making of a Peacemonger* 1987: 64–5

Her sound was clear, her articulation impeccable, her approach to the lead part of Mozart's Quartet for Flute and Strings, K. 285 irresistibly fresh and sunny.
Globe and Mail (Toronto) 4 March 1985: S14

Ferre is an acknowledged perfectionist. Every seam, every stitch, every belt, shoe or bracelet is impeccable, precise and original.
Globe and Mail (Toronto) 19 Feb. 1985: F6

As the Act I curtain falls, she is giving birth while the fussy civil servant dashes around his impeccable apartment uttering tiny whoops of consternation.
Globe and Mail (Toronto) 20 Aug. 1985: S8

See also IMMACULATE CONCEPTION; PRISTINE.

impediment   see OBSTACLE

impinge, infringe   Both *impinge* and *infringe* can be used to mean encroach on, but they are generally distinguished in usage. *Impinge* is most often used to mean have an effect on someone or something; this effect may be neutral or negative. *Infringe* denotes a transgression of some kind, a violation of a boundary, a law, an oath, or personal freedom. Although *infringe* is sometimes used without a preposition ('to infringe copyright law'), both words usually take a preposition: either *upon* or, much more commonly, *on*.

Speakers of Canadian English cannot avoid being aware of two other existing standards which impinge on them, namely the British and the American....
W.C. Lougheed, ed. *In Search of the Standard in Canadian English* 1986: 163

But the judge said the inquiry provides adequate opportunities for examination to the defence and does not infringe on Mr. B——'s rights.
Globe and Mail (Toronto) 3 April 1985: M3

Now the laws passed by parliament are subject to review by non-elected courts, which have the power to strike down any laws they believe infringe the rights and freedoms contained in the charter.
Catholic Register 16 Aug. 1986: 7

The court held that this impinged freedom of speech, and this was such an unreasonable decision as to be outside of the board's jurisdiction.
Globe and Mail (Toronto) 24 June 1985: B11

(The verb *impinge* is normally followed by *on* or *upon*. However, in this case the verb itself might be better changed: in the context of a violation of rights, *infringe* is the usual choice.)

implicit, explicit   *Implicit* means inherent or contained within: 'a flaw implicit in the design'. It often refers to a message indirectly expressed by (i.e., contained within) another message: 'The implicit message was that we were to do nothing'.

Explicit means clear or open to view. In this sense it may refer specifically, and somewhat euphemistically, to nudity or sex: 'explicit photos'. *Explicit* also means directly and unambiguously stated: 'I had explicit instructions'.

Implicit in the decision to open the centres is the belief that industry and government can work together.
Globe and Mail (Toronto) 1 March 1985: R4

Since South African law forbids the advocacy of economic boycotts, Bishop Tutu's carefully chosen words amount to implicit encouragement of Canadian trade unions and church activists who call for disinvestment.
Globe and Mail (Toronto) 18 Jan. 1985: P7

Police said a man was arrested after a woman in suburban Etobicoke complained that sexually explicit scenes suddenly appeared on her television set....
Calgary Herald 30 Dec. 1994: B7

Many Nova Scotians have 'living wills' with explicit health-care instructions in case a time comes when they can't make their own decisions.
Daily News (Halifax) 28 Dec. 1994: n.p.

imply, infer   To *imply* something is to hint at it without stating it directly. To *infer* something is to gather it or deduce it from what one hears or observes. *Imply* refers to the transmitting of an idea, *infer* to the receiving of one. Some writers use *infer* to mean *imply*, and some dictionaries record this usage; however, it is not generally accepted.

'... people have tried to identify me with a certain period, particularly some hostile critics who imply that my work is obsolete.'
Now Magazine (Toronto) Nov. 1988: 25

To make things worse ... people were returning to New York full of news about young trumpeters coming along for whom Davis, they implied, was no match.
Jack Chambers *Milestones* 1983: 165

Cadieux was wrong when he said I had 'implied' lack of coordination. I had spelled it out to the best of my ability. . . .
George Ignatieff *The Making of a Peacemonger* 1987: 245

Today astronomers only infer the nature of the heart of a comet. No one knows for sure precisely what it is.
Terence Dickinson *Halley's Comet* 1985: 3

. . . the political success of one party or another gives only a slender basis for inferring the state of the public mind.
J.A.W. Gunn *Beyond Liberty and Property* 1983: 122

Senior prosecutor James Jardine contends the nine items, if taken as a whole, infer R—— had access to the main components from which the bomb was made.
Vancouver Sun 6 Dec. 1990: D1

(The word required here is *imply*.)

See also IMPLY, INSINUATE.

imply, insinuate   To *imply* or *insinuate* something is to suggest it indirectly, without coming right out and saying it. What is *implied* may be positive or negative; however, only negative things are *insinuated*. A second meaning of *insinuate* is to move something, often oneself, gradually and stealthily into a desirable position: 'He insinuated himself into the front row'. When *insinuate* is used figuratively in this sense, it overlaps with *ingratiate*: 'She insinuated herself into their affections' or 'She ingratiated herself with them'. An insinuating person is deviously self-promoting; an insinuating remark hints at something improper or negative.

Insinuate must take a direct object. In other words, one cannot say 'Robin is insinuating again'. Whatever the intended meaning—hinting at improprieties or slithering into place—Robin must be insinuating *something*. Moreover, in contemporary English *insinuate* in the sense of suggest requires a human agent: only people, not objects or circumstances, can insinuate things. The sentence 'The flag on his balcony insinuates his politics' would have been perfectly acceptable in the eighteenth century. Today, however, the use of *insinuate* to mean signify is obsolete.

I've implied that the writer functions in his or her society as a kind of soothsayer, a truth teller; that writing is not mere self-expression but a view of society and the world at large, and that the novel is a moral instrument.
Margaret Atwood *Second Words* 1982: 353

In a number of famous recent cases, judges insinuated that women who stayed out late, dated more than one

man or separated from husbands without prior consent had somehow 'provoked' their own rape, murder or beating.
Briarpatch Dec. 1989–Jan. 1990: 23

But what I take exception to is the government's continuous attempt to test our level of intelligence by insinuating that the country is soundly managed.
Ottawa Citizen 14 Feb. 1990: A9

(The picture the government is painting is positive, not negative; thus *implying* would be more appropriate here.)

Robert Stanfield warned of the dangers to democracy when otherwise legitimate lobby groups are able to insinuate themselves directly into the political process.
Vancouver Sun 17 Dec. 1990: A11

He was insinuating and over-familiar.
Vancouver Sun 17 April 1990: A11

The loss of historical specificity results in an ill-defined, almost generic sense of the period: virginal heroines exuding dewy beauty; rakes whose every pose insinuates their sexual prowess; fops who mince across the stage, lisping their lines. . . .
Queen's Quarterly 97.1 (1990): 144

(Here *insinuates* is used in an obsolete construction, but one that is appropriate in the context of an academic article about an eighteenth-century play.)

See also IMPLY, INFER; INGRATIATE.

important   see MORE IMPORTANTLY

impractical, impracticable, unpractical   A suggestion that is *impractical*, meaning not practical or useful, may also be *impracticable*, meaning impossible to put into practice. But an impracticable suggestion need not be impractical: it may well offer a practical solution to a problem, even though this solution cannot be carried out with the means at hand. Understandably, *impractical* and *impracticable*, a less common word, are sometimes confused, but they are generally well distinguished in usage. Although the form *unpractical* is given in some dictionaries, it is rarely used and is considered archaic.

The commission also recommends an exception to prior authorization in circumstances where obtaining it is highly impracticable because the evidence is destructible.
Globe and Mail (Toronto) 13 June 1985: P1

Cream is great in coffee, but for today's smaller families and single-person households, the 250 mL carton can be

impracticable. Some of the cream in an opened carton may spoil before it gets used.
Country Guide Nov. 1986: 27

(The context makes clear that the word required is *impractical*, here meaning something like 'not sensible'.)

There were many dead ends ... in our search for the fireweed nectar that summer. Sometimes, patches of fireweed would add up to only a handful of plants, or the roads were steep and bridges washed out so that further travel was impractical.
Harrowsmith Oct.–Nov. 1985: 51

(When a bridge is missing, travelling further on a road is not just *impractical*, not sensible, but *impracticable*, not possible.)

With a 20-game schedule for each team, travelling to each club for games would be unpractical, so the conference plays its schedule by way of four tournaments between early January and March....
Globe and Mail (Toronto) 7 Jan. 1985: S5

(Though it can be found in some dictionaries, *unpractical* is almost never used; the preferred negative form is *impractical*.)

See also FEASIBLE.

impromptu   see EXTEMPORANEOUS

impugn, impute   To *impugn* (pronounced *im PYOON*) something is to challenge or discredit it; to *impute* (*im PYOOT*) something to someone is to ascribe a quality (usually negative) to him or her. To *impugn* Stan's motives is to challenge them; to *impute* selfish motives to Stan is to accuse him of selfishness.

At Rafferty-Alameda, environmentalists managed to impugn provincial jurisdiction on division-of-powers grounds.
NeWest Review Dec. 1989–Jan. 1990: 6

He began to impugn and attack the character of the prime minister and the integrity of the government.
Ottawa Citizen 12 Dec. 1985: A9

Can such words, imputing sin and guilt, be justified?
Globe and Mail (Toronto) 16 April 1985: P7

All of the judges were careful not to impute blame to the child, to say that her behavior did not excuse L——'s, and to uphold his conviction.
Province (Vancouver) 30 Jan. 1990: 25

impunity   *Impunity* is freedom from punishment or reprisal; 'with impunity' means without punishment. The slang equivalent of doing something with impunity is 'getting away with' it.

Inscribed around the edge of the coin is the motto of the Order of the Thistle, Nemo Me Impune Lacessit (no one provokes me with impunity).
Toronto Star 5 Nov. 1994: K2

impute   see IMPUGN

in, into   The primary function of the preposition *in* is to indicate location ('Your socks are in the laundry basket') or state or condition ('He is in good spirits'). A secondary use of *in* is with verbs indicating motion, and it is this use that sometimes meets with objections. While there is no difference of meaning in the sentences 'I went in the house' and 'I went into the house', some usage commentators argue that *into* is preferable because it more strongly suggests the idea of entering something. In addition, because *in* can also indicate location, there are contexts with verbs suggesting motion in which *into* must be used in order to avoid confusion: 'The furniture was moved out of her room into the garage'. However, to make a rule that only *into* should be used with verbs of motion would be pedantic and would mean ignoring the idiomatic uses of *in* in such expressions as 'Go jump in a lake' or 'Throw it in the garbage'. In brief, *into* is usually used with verbs of motion, but it is not considered a serious infraction to use *in* instead when there is no possibility of ambiguity. Most writers seem to choose the one that best fits the rhythm of the sentence.

'Just Do It' has been credited with everything from pulling couch potatoes into the gym to giving women the courage to leave abusive husbands.
Ottawa Citizen 7 Aug. 1994: B4

The eight-year-old tried to jump and fell in the water.
Ottawa Citizen 17 March 1990: A21

It's an effective way to beat the dilemma of 'whether to watch television or go in the whirlpool.'
Edmonton Journal 19 Sept. 1992: n.p.

See also INTO, IN TO.

in absentia   *In absentia* is a Latin expression that means in someone's absence. It is generally used in formal circumstances: at university convocations, where degrees are conferred *in absentia* on members of the graduating class who are not present; and in courts of law, where rulings are made *in absentia* if the defendant is not present. *In absentia* should be italicized in formal writing.

> He was convicted in absentia by a Dutch court after he fled the country.
> *Financial Post* 23 Oct. 1991: 2

(In formal writing *in absentia* requires italics, but newspapers rarely use them.)

> He returned to Canada on a brief visit in 1894, and the following April Queen's was the first university anywhere to award him an honorary degree, a doctorate of laws conferred *in absentia*.
> *Queen's Quarterly* 92 (1985): 224

See also LATIN PHRASES.

in addition to   see TOGETHER WITH

inasmuch as   see INSOFAR AS

in back of   see BACK OF

in behalf of   see BEHALF

in camera   This Latin phrase entered legal English in the late nineteenth century with the meaning 'in the judge's chambers' as opposed to 'in open court'. Now, both in law and more widely, *in camera* refers to legal proceedings or formal meetings held behind closed doors. The usual justification for in camera proceedings is that they deal with prejudicial or confidential matters. *In camera* need not be italicized, nor should it be hyphenated even when it is used as an adjective, as in 'an in camera hearing'.

> In June, after weeks of investigation in camera, the royal commission submitted its report, a document of more than 600 pages containing information so damaging that the commissioners recommended it not be published.
> Frederick Gibson *Queen's University* 2 (1983): 275–7

> No date has been set for the appeal of the in camera ruling, which Blanchard has argued violates freedom of the press guarantees in the Canadian Charter of Rights and Freedoms.
> *Gazette* (Montreal) 12 Jan. 1990: A4

> … he wanted an in-camera hearing with the public banned.
> *Vancouver Sun* 21 Dec. 1990: A8

(Latin phrases such as *in camera* do not take hyphens.)

See also LATIN PHRASES.

inchoate   The use of *inchoate* to mean 'in chaos' is well-established, even in formal writing, although *chaos* and *inchoate* are unrelated etymologically. *Chaos*, which means 'total confusion', was the ancient Greek word for the infinite void that preceded the creation of the ordered universe, the *cosmos*. *Inchoate* (pronounced *in KO ate*, *in KO it*, or *IN ko it*) means just beginning, early, or undeveloped and is derived from the Latin *incohare*, 'to begin'. This original meaning of *inchoate* is uncommon but still in use, especially in legal contexts.

Some dictionaries present the new meaning as a logical extension of the old—i.e., something 'formless' is 'not yet fully developed'—but it is more likely that the shift in meaning occurred as a result of the resemblance between the words *inchoate* and *chaos*. Whenever a language development appears to be based on a misconception—in this case, a faulty derivation—usage-guide writers rush in. In this instance, however, the new meaning was well entrenched before the attack was even mounted.

> But he does believe he is tapping into an inchoate feeling that something has gone wrong in the land.
> *Toronto Star* 10 Oct. 1994: A13

(Here *inchoate* means not yet fully formed.)

> … learning Mandarin was easy for a person who had spent years at the agonizing task of memorizing material that presented itself as an inchoate jumble of characters.
> *Globe and Mail* (Toronto) 2 Nov. 1985: B1

(Here *inchoate* means *chaotic*.)

> This equates inner-city blight and unemployment with inchoate anger and mindless violence.
> *Globe and Mail* (Toronto) 8 June 1985: S1

(Here *inchoate* means formless.)

incidence   see INCIDENTS

incidentally   see ACCIDENTALLY; COINCIDENTALLY

incidents, incidence   *Incidents* is the plural of *incident*: 'We hope to prevent any more incidents of that nature'. *Incidence* is the rate at which something occurs, or the fact or scope of its occurrence: 'The incidence of HIV infection among street children is appalling'.

> It's normal procedure for an outside force to investigate incidents in another police force, such as shootings and serious complaints from the public.
> *Ottawa Citizen* 28 Dec. 1992: B2

Although the characters and incidents in the two-part series were fictitious, the story was inspired by recent events in Newfoundland.
Daily News (Halifax) 30 Dec. 1992: 8

Large doses of vitamin C don't seem to decrease the incidence of the common cold, but they may have an effect on symptoms and severity.
Ottawa Citizen 30 Dec. 1992: A16

Yet the incidence of hamburger disease does not result in the shut-down of all the fast-food restaurants.
Calgary Herald 19 Nov. 1992: A4

Obviously we should ... provide more services for women who are victims of violence, but this will not reduce the incidents of violence against women.
Gazette (Montreal) 28 Dec. 1992: B3

(The word required here is *incidence*.)

He was part of the Police Association of Nova Scotia's critical incidence stress debriefing team that helps firefighters, police officers, health care workers and draegermen.
Daily News (Halifax): 25 Nov. 1992: 1

(The word required here is *incidents*.)

See also PRECEDENCE, PRECEDENTS.

incredible, incredulous   see CREDIBLE

inculcate   see IMBUE

incumbent, present incumbent, incumbent on (upon)   The term *the incumbent* usually refers to the person who currently holds an office. However, an incumbent is simply someone who holds or has held office, whether in the present or in the past. Thus the usual prescription against *present incumbent* as a tautology is unfounded.

When *incumbent* is used as an adjective, it is usually in a phrase implying that something is someone's duty or responsibility and is followed by either *on* or *upon*: 'It is incumbent on (*or* upon) her to respond'.

One more appointment was that of Adam Shortt, one of the most famous of Queen's early professors and the first incumbent of the Sir John A. Macdonald Chair of Political and Economic Science founded in 1899.
Hilda Neatby *Queen's University* 1 (1978): 180

(Here *first incumbent* means the first one to hold the office.)

The larger the corporation, the more difficult it is to dislodge an incumbent board of directors, but there have been a number of instances of dissatisfied shareholders' turning out the entire board of directors....

J.E. Smyth et al. *The Law and Business Administration in Canada* 1987: 708

(Here *incumbent* is used as an adjective meaning existing or currently acting.)

St. Gregory the Illuminator was elected as the first Supreme Patriarch and Catholicos of the Armenian Church, thus establishing the long and continuous line of Catholicoi up to the present incumbent, His Holiness Vazken I. ...
Globe and Mail (Toronto) 2 Nov. 1985: F19

At some stage, therefore, it will be incumbent on the Supreme Court to settle such outstanding questions.
Canadian Bar Review 66.3 (1987): 613

The various decisions make it clear that it is not incumbent upon an accused to bring himself to trial.
Globe and Mail (Toronto) 3 June 1985: P7

independantiste, independentist   see SEPARATIST

indecipherable   see UNREADABLE

independent   see DEPENDENT

Indian, East Indian, Indo-Canadian, South Asian, West Indian   *Indian* is the name given to citizens of the Republic of India or to those whose ancestors came from India. Although the term *East Indian* is sometimes used by Canadians, it echoes the name of the British East India Company (which colonized India) and is sometimes disliked by contemporary Indians. Canadians whose ancestors came from India often refer to themselves as *Indo-Canadian*. Since *Indian Canadian* may be confused with *Canadian Indian*, writers should ensure that there is no possibility of confusion; however, now that *Indian* is declining as a term for Native people, confusion is becoming less likely.

Those from the Indian subcontinent who are not citizens of India should not be referred to as Indian, but as Sri Lankan, Bangladeshi, Nepalese, Pakistani, or Bhutanese. If a general term for people from the Indian subcontinent is needed, *South Asian* is now preferred.

It is said that when Christopher Columbus touched land on his westward voyage from Spain in 1492, he thought he had reached India and thus gave the name *Indian* to the Indigenous inhabitants of the Caribbean (also known as Caribs). The term was subsequently extended to the Indigenous peoples of North, Central, and South America. The use of *Indian* has lately declined in Canada as a label for Indigenous people (see ABORIGINAL PEOPLE[S]).

However, *Indian* is still the only simple term to distinguish this group of people from the other two main Aboriginal groups: the Métis and the Inuit.

West Indian is the general term for people who come from the West Indies, of whatever ancestry. Most of the indigenous Caribs were killed, died of disease, or fled to mainland South or Central America shortly after contact with Europeans, although a few of their descendants now live in Dominica and St. Vincent. In the West Indies, therefore, the term *Indian* usually refers to someone whose ancestors came from India. After the emancipation of the slaves in the West Indies in 1838, many Indians were brought from India to the West Indies as indentured labourers, and their descendants, concentrated in Guyana and Trinidad and Tobago, form a large proportion of the population today. They refer to themselves as *Indo-Caribbean* or *East Indian* when it is necessary to distinguish themselves from the majority of West Indians, who are of African descent.

And in Calgary's Riley Park, East Indians and Pakistanis dressed in whites play cricket on weekend afternoons.
Maclean's 11 July 1988: A8

(This sentence could be rewritten in two ways: either *East* could be omitted, or *South Asians* could replace the entire phrase 'East Indians and Pakistanis'.)

Attempts by governments, churches and the general population to change Indians, Metis and Inuit into just another ethnic group in the multicultural mosaic have failed.
The Beaver Feb.–Mar. 1990: 58

The Carnival parade is only one feature of this year's Caribana, an 11-day celebration of all things West Indian.
Globe and Mail (Toronto) 1 Aug. 1985: M7

See also ASIA, SOUTH ASIA, SOUTHEAST ASIA; VISIBLE MINORITY; WEST INDIES.

indict, indite   Both *indict* and *indite* rhyme with *incite*. To *indict* means to charge with a crime or to publicly censure. To *indite* means to write or compose something such as a letter or poem; *indite* is now rare.

Both ... later admitted their guilt and were indicted for murder....
Gazette (Montreal) 31 Aug. 1992: A3

That about summarizes the book; it indicts the entire securities industry as a parasite in a three-piece suit.
Vancouver Sun 26 Oct. 1992: D9

indictable offence, felony, summary offence, misdemeanor   In Canadian law, *indictable offence* is the term for a serious crime, such as murder or armed robbery. The comparable American term is *felony*. A less serious crime is called a *summary offence* or *summary conviction offence* in Canada; in American law the equivalent term is *misdemeanor*.

indigenous   *Indigenous* means original or belonging to a particular place. For example, the maple tree is indigenous to Canada; the lilac bush, which was brought over by European settlers, is not. The term can be applied not only to plants, animals, and landforms but also to people, practices, and institutions. Confusion may arise when *indigenous* is applied to people, since it can refer to the Aboriginal peoples of a nation as well as to the descendants of those who arrived after European contact. In Canada, *Native* and *Aboriginal* are the general terms most often used when referring to Inuit, Indian, and Métis people; however, *Indigenous* is frequently used in reference to the Aboriginal populations of other countries. It is now recommended that *Indigenous* be capitalized when it refers to Aboriginal people; this practice also reduces the possibility of ambiguity.

Point Pelee is one of the four national parks in Ontario. This spectacular haven provides an ideal environment for hundreds of migrating and indigenous species of birds.
Leisure Life 1988: 6

Their region was said to need more indigenous banking services which would be more attentive to local interests.
Queen's Quarterly 94.4 1987: 940

(Here *indigenous* means local.)

In Canada Sotheby's was hardest hit in the early 1980s when the bottom fell out of the indigenous art market....
Canadian Collector 21.2 (1986): 13

A government policy of accepting refugees, immigrants, etc., does not guarantee acceptance by the indigenous population.
Globe and Mail (Toronto) 18 Jan. 1985: P6

(Here *indigenous* refers to all long-term residents.)

'Responsible trapping as it contributes to the survival of Canada's indigenous culture is acceptable and welcome.'
United Church Observer June 1986: 19

(Here the reference is to Aboriginal people; the recommended spelling is *Indigenous*.)

See ABORIGINAL; ABORIGINAL PEOPLE(S); NATIVE.

indirect speech see QUOTATION; WONDER

indiscriminate, undiscriminating *Indiscriminate* means not selective ('an indiscriminate reader'), or haphazard ('an indiscriminate collection'), or random ('indiscriminate attacks'). *Undiscriminating* suggests a lack of good taste or good judgment. *Indiscriminating* is an uncommon American variant of *undiscriminating*.

Yet necrotizing fasciitis, commonly known as the flesh-eating disease, is a swift, indiscriminate killer, capable of destroying skin, fat and muscle so fast that antibiotics don't stand a chance.
Vancouver Sun 3 Dec. 1994: A12

Then apparently responding to public pressure, Yeltsin called on the army to stop indiscriminate bombing of the Chechen capital.
CBC News [transcript] 27 Dec. 1994: n.p.

Of all the American culture that slops over the border and is soaked up by undiscriminating Canadians, gun love is perhaps the most noisome.
Vancouver Sun 31 Aug. 1994: A18

indite see INDICT

Indo-Canadian see INDIAN

induction see DEDUCTION

infamous see NOTORIOUS

infantile see CHILDISH

infectious see CONTAGIOUS

infer see IMPLY

inferior to, superior to Several usage guides point out that the standard preposition with these words is not *than* but *to*: 'A's work is superior to B's'. It is difficult to argue with this observation; *inferior than* and *superior than* are very rare.

See also SUPERIOR, SENIOR.

infidel see ATHEIST

infinitive see SPLIT INFINITIVE

inflammable, inflammatory see FLAMMABLE

inflict see AFFLICT

informal see COLLOQUIAL; FORMAL, INFORMAL WRITING

informer, informant, source Both *informer* and *informant* mean someone who provides information. *Informer* has negative connotations and is the usual choice when describing someone who gives information to police or other officials in exchange for money or favours. *Informant* is either neutral or positive in its connotations; for example, it is the usual term for someone who provides information to a researcher. Journalists usually call their informants *sources*.

... an RCMP informer told of threats he had overheard to kidnap Canadiens players, somehow interpreted as Lafleur and me.
Ken Dryden *The Game* 1983: 138

An informant in Arkansas writes to say that the loons and geese wintering in that southern state have gathered their belongings and even now are flying north....
Globe and Mail (Toronto) 14 March 1985: M10

infrastructure *Infrastructure* was first used in 1927 in reference to the Maginot Line, the defensive fortification built between 1929 and 1934 to defend France's northeastern boundary against German invasion. Although many language critics have criticized *infrastructure* as jargon or gobbledygook, it is now used in all types of writing to mean structural supporting elements. Some critics are wary of this word because of its broad application to everything from social structures to sewers; where *infrastructure* is vague, you may want to choose a more precise term.

It [job searching] can be one of the loneliest activities on earth unless there is emotional support as well as the infrastructure of an office, telephone answering service and secretarial facilities, etc.
Queen's Quarterly 94.4 (1987): 864

In addition to a large part of the population, the economic infrastructure was almost totally destroyed. Trains, buses, cars, banks, factories, post offices, power plants and a hydroelectric dam were dynamited, as well as schools, hospitals, market buildings, mosques, churches, pagodas, about one million houses and libraries.
Henry M. Rosenthal and S. Cathy Berson, eds. *Canadian Jewish Outlook Anthology* 1988: 140

Feminist writers, who began to create their own institutional infrastructures, treated the feminine condition openly....
Ben-Z. Shek *French-Canadian & Québécois Novels* 1991: 87

The mixed-farm economy gave rise to a socioeconomic infrastructure that is notably similar across much of North America, and remarkably enduring.
The Canadian Geographer Spring 1989: 33

infringe see IMPINGE

infuse see IMBUE

ingenious, ingenuous, ingénue, disingenuous
Someone with the ability to find original solutions to problems is *ingenious*; such solutions themselves are also called *ingenious. Ingenuous* (pronounced *in JEN yoo us*) means frank or innocent, usually to the point of naivete. The noun *ingénue* (usually pronounced *ahn zhay NOO* or *AN jen NOO*) can refer to an innocent young woman, or an actress playing such a character, or the part itself. Dictionaries list the word both with and without the accent; it need not be italicized. There is no male equivalent for this term.
Disingenuous, the opposite of *ingenuous*, is applied to people, actions, or statements that seem sincere but are in fact insincere or devious.

And he proudly produced a tiny pocket flashlight set into a plastic heart and attached to a key-ring by some ingenious manufacturer in Taiwan.
Constance Beresford-Howe *Night Studies* 1985: 165

Dictionaries of music contain amusing accounts of ingenious machines which were designed to enable people who were not composers to write music.
Robertson Davies *A Voice from the Attic* 1960: 316

Its surprises come from its frank and ingenuous stating of things that everybody knows but rarely says.
Globe and Mail (Toronto) 5 Oct. 1985: D14

In faded jeans and with a student book-bag slung over her shoulder, she still suggests the all-Canadian ingenue.
Spectator (Hamilton) 22 Dec. 1995: E4

Such a fault of character was duly noted by Hoadly, along with the High-Tory tendency to employ terms such as 'hereditary right' in disingenuous ways.
J.A.W. Gunn *Beyond Liberty and Property* 1983: 139-140

... Subaru's disingenuous tribute to Volvo turns on the conceit that Subaru's brakes make it unnecessary for you to crash into concrete walls. The sly suggestion is that Volvo's sturdy frame is necessitated by a shoddy braking system.
Vancouver Sun 24 Nov. 1990: C2

ingratiate *Ingratiate* is a reflexive verb: in other words, it is always used with a reflexive pronoun (*myself, himself,* etc.) To *ingratiate* oneself means to bring oneself into favour with someone or something else. Other people or things cannot be ingratiated. Thus 'He tried to ingratiate himself with his in-laws by cutting their grass' is idiomatic, but 'He tried to ingratiate his in-laws by cutting their grass', or 'He tried to ingratiate his dog with his in-laws', is not.

Maria Monk was a girl who appeared in New York in 1835 and ingratiated herself with two clergymen who published a paper called The Protestant Vindicator....
Robertson Davies *A Voice from the Attic* 1960: 279

Now free to express their views, Whigs were still at times confined by strategic considerations, wishing to ingratiate the new order with as many fellow citizens as possible.
J.A.W. Gunn *Beyond Liberty and Property* 1983: 147

(This use of *ingratiate* is not idiomatic: 'make the new order appeal to' would be better.)

inhabitant see CITIZEN

inhuman, inhumane see HUMAN

inimical, inimitable, [inimicable] *Inimical* means unfriendly. Something inimical to something else is unfavourable or injurious to it. *Inimitable* means defying or surpassing imitation. Although some usage guides accept *inimicable* as a rare but standard variant of *inimical*, contemporary dictionaries do not list this spelling, and it is best avoided.

'Everything from the shameful wages of day-care workers to the isolation of the at-home mother is evidence of how ... our culture remains inimical to children and to the people raising them.'
Ottawa Citizen 9 Nov. 1992: C1

There is also no doubt that, despite all reassurances to the contrary, such a [treatment] facility would be inimical to the community in which it is situated.
Harrowsmith Aug.–Sept. 1985: 31

One's own distinctive, inimitable style, she suggests, is 'the distillation of a lifetime of reading and listening, of selection and rejection'.
Janice Kulyk Keefer *Reading Mavis Gallant* 1989: 28

Set during World War II in French-ruled Morocco, Casablanca is the story of Rick (the inimitable, genre-defining Humphrey Bogart)....
Gazette (Montreal) 9 July 1992: E4

Buthelezi envisages the limitation of federal powers to the extent that they are inimicable to state laws, local control of taxation and a regional police force.
Gazette (Montreal) 10 Dec. 1992: B6

(The accepted spelling is *inimical*.)

initialism   see ABBREVIATION

injunction   see ENJOIN

in-law   see MOTHER-IN-LAW

in-migrate   see EMIGRANT

innocent   see PLEAD GUILTY

Innu, Montagnais, Naskapi, Atikamekw   These people have traditionally called themselves *Innu* (more recently, the *Innu Nation*). In Quebec they are usually called *Montagnais-Naskapi* (the Montagnais live south of the Naskapi); in Labrador, *Innu*. *Atikamekw* (sometimes spelled Attikameg) is another name used by some Innu. They are Indian, not Inuit, and live in northeastern Quebec and northern Labrador. Their traditional language, Montagnais-Naskapi, belongs to the Algonquian family.

The Naskapi-Montagnais Innu Association had asked the court to issue an injunction forcing the defence department to stop the controversial flights....
Vancouver Sun 14 April 1990: A16

The Atikamekw and Montagnais claim 550,000 square kilometres of northeastern Quebec and another 150,000 square kilometres in Labrador....
Gazette (Montreal) 22 Oct. 1992: A6

Labrador Innu have staged numerous protests at the base in recent years to express opposition to military training flights by NATO jets.
Calgary Herald 2 Dec. 1992: A6

... the Montagnais, who number about 11,000 in Quebec and are known as the Innu in Labrador, are running out of patience.
Toronto Star 24 Nov. 1992: A14

... Kashtin, the Quebec Montagnais duo who sing contemporary songs in the Innu language.
Ottawa Citizen 27 June 1991: D5

(Linguists refer to the language of the Innu as Montagnais-Naskapi.)

Flanked by a representative of Quebec's Grand Council of the Cree and the Conseil Atikamekw-Montagnais, [Konrad] Sioui said the forum isn't enough.
Gazette (Montreal) 8 Nov. 1990: A7

See also INUIT.

innumerate   see ILLITERATE

inoculation   see IMMUNIZATION

input   Many commentators object to the verb *input*—a technical term borrowed from computing, electronics, and economics—meaning to enter data into a computer. Canadian writers rarely use it outside these contexts.

Some also object to the use of the noun *input* to mean opinions or recommendations. This use is well established in the press, but rare in more formal writing.

He added pollution is not a 'left-wing or right-wing issue', but must have input from all sectors.
Guardian (Charlottetown) 2 Nov. 1990: 2

(It is decision-makers, not pollution, that must have *input*; 'be commented upon by all sectors' might be better.)

inquire, enquire, inquiry, enquiry   The preferred Canadian and American spelling is *inquire*, though *enquire* is occasionally used for all senses of the word. *Inquire* is widely used in Canada as a slightly formal synonym for *ask*.

British usage once distinguished the verbs *enquire* (merely seek information) and *inquire* (conduct a formal investigation). This distinction is not upheld by North American dictionaries or usage. However, Canadian writers do tend to distinguish the nouns *inquiry* and *enquiry*, preferring the former for legal or formal investigation and the latter for scholarly research or intellectual work.

I felt there was something about this trip I didn't know and should but, when I obliquely inquired, I was put off with more laughter and leers.
Max Braithwaite *The Night We Stole the Mountie's Car* 1971: 154

... when she enquired about her package, a customs agent told her the book was being held to determine whether it was 'suitable' for entry into Canada.
Vancouver Sun 27 Dec. 1990: B1

The inquiry by a Royal Commission in Nova Scotia into the wrongful conviction of Donald Marshall Jr for murder raised the broader question of whether judges can be required to explain their reasons for particular decisions.
Andrew Heard *Canadian Constitutional Conventions* 1991: 126

Until quite recently musical aesthetics has been a monistic field of intellectual enquiry.
Queen's Quarterly 92.1 (1985): 218

in regard[s] to, with regard[s] to, as regards, regarding Usage commentators are unanimous in their objection to the phrases *in regards to* and *with regards to*, considering them blends of the acceptable phrases *as regards* and *in* or *with regard to*. The disputed phrases occur most frequently in newspapers and magazines in quoted speech and letters to the editor. *With regards to* with an *s* is perfectly acceptable when it means 'with best wishes to'. Some critics consider both *in* and *with regard to* wordy and suggest using *regarding* instead.

'I don't think the committee was as well informed in regard to the recent violations of human rights in the Mohawk issue....'
Gazette (Montreal) 25 Oct. 1990: A1

In regards to Betty Olson's Aug. 28 letter to the editor, I was under the impression that lottery profits were originally meant for hospitals and schools.
Province (Vancouver) 14 Sept. 1990: 56

(The standard expression is 'in regard to'.)

The forest industry as a whole has fumbled these issues. With regard to environmental concerns particularly, they were caught napping.
Vancouver Sun 15 Dec. 1990: E3

... the only matter science seems to agree on, with regards to global warming, is that the evidence is inconclusive.
Atlantic Salmon Journal Summer (1990): 5

(The standard expression is 'with regard to'.)

insanitary see UNSANITARY

insidious, invidious Something is *insidious* if its slow or subtle progress makes it seem less harmful than it actually is. Something *invidious* is likely to cause ill will because it is, or seems to be, unjust.

Meanwhile poverty, that insidious hired gunman of the state, stalks women daily.
Fuse Magazine 13.4 (1990): 9

Meanwhile, that colourless, invisible bacterial plaque continues to develop and work its way insidiously into the gumline.
Canadian Consumer Feb. 1986: 26

In 1861 William Ireland ... was engaged to relieve the professors of an invidious task by collecting all fees from the students for a commission of five per cent.
Hilda Neatby *Queen's University* 1 (1978): 78

... the authors have lapsed into invidious role stereotyping by identifying a particular workplace with a particular sex.
Canadian Bar Review 66.3 (1987): 670

'The only explanation I can give,' Skelton added, 'is that after the wrecking of the English Department it has been felt that it would be invidious not to wreck the Economics Department also.'
Frederick Gibson *Queen's University* 2 (1983): 57

insinuate see IMPLY

in situ *In situ*, 'in place', is a Latin borrowing. It is usually synonymous with *on site* in English, but it also has a special medical meaning: a cancer that has not spread from its original location to other parts of the body is said to be *in situ*. The phrase should be italicized in formal writing. Used as an adjective before a noun, *in situ*, like other Latin phrases, is not hyphenated.

Once there, Galileo will deploy a probe into Jupiter's liquid and gas atmosphere to make in situ measurements of the chemical and physical forces at work.
Vancouver Sun 4 Aug. 1990: B6

Results from transplant studies are often more convincing than in situ studies because they are the product of an experimental rather than an observational approach.
Canadian Journal of Zoology 67.4 (1989): 855

... fewer than 100 cases of carcinoma in situ (considered a non-invasive cervical cancer) were reported to the registry.
Globe and Mail (Toronto) 22 Jan. 1985: M2

See also LATIN PHRASES.

insofar as, inasmuch as, [insomuch as] *Insofar* and *inasmuch* are written as one word. *Insofar as* means to the extent that and is more common than *inasmuch as*, which usually means since or because, but may also mean to the extent that. *Insomuch as* is an archaic variant of both expressions.

Success, insofar as it appears in modern fiction, is given a wry turn.
Robertson Davies *A Voice from the Attic* 1960: 71

Once developed, a learning system provides student-friendliness inasmuch as it outlines the scope of programs and courses they will undertake and the criteria by which they will be evaluated. . . .
Education Canada Summer (1989): 33–5

insoluble   see SOLUBLE

[insomuch as]   see INSOFAR AS

in spite of   see DESPITE

instil   see IMBUE

insure, ensure, assure   If you *insure* something, such as a house or a car, you take out an insurance policy on it so that you will be compensated in the event of loss, damage, or liability. If you *ensure* something, you verify that it is so, or you take steps to make certain that it will happen: 'I ensured that the company was reputable'; 'Our lawyer will ensure that our rights are not violated'. In the past, *insure* and *ensure* were mere spelling variants, but in contemporary Canadian and British English the two spellings usually have these distinct meanings. Many American writers use the spelling *insure* for all senses, but *ensure* is current there too.

One thing can *assure* another thing, meaning make it inevitable: 'Her wealth assured her welcome'. More commonly, *assure* is used with both a personal subject and a personal object: someone *assures* someone of something, meaning someone tells someone that something is certain: 'They assured us of jobs'; 'They assured us that the barking would stop'. A few usage guides treat *ensure* and *assure* as interchangeable. While there are contexts in which either word is correct, there is always a slight difference in meaning between the two. *Ensure* emphasizes action, taking steps, while *assure* emphasizes inevitability, removing doubt.

When one insures his life, he enters into a contract of insurance with an insurance company.
J.E. Smyth et al. *The Law and Business Administration in Canada* 1987: 290

He asked Mr. Timbrell what he would do, as premier, to ensure that 'all people are treated equally' and no one has special rights.
Globe and Mail (Toronto) 16 Jan. 1985: P5

'Quotas in school admissions and job hiring should be used to insure black representation.'
Neil Nevitte and Roger Gibbins *New Elites in Old States* 1990: 110

(The usual Canadian spelling is *ensure*. This sentence is quoted from an American source.)

The recent election of Abraham Lincoln to the presidency seemed to assure the break-up of the American union.
William Teatero *John Anderson: Fugitive Slave* 1986: 75

For one thing, Descartes assures us, his altered state was not the result of inebriation: he had not drunk wine for three months before.
Canadian Journal of Philosophy 19 (1989): 214

intelligent, intellectual, intelligentsia, IQ   An *intelligent* person is quick of mind; an *intellectual* person, in addition to being intelligent, enjoys exercising his or her mental abilities. The noun *intellectual* sometimes carries a derogatory connotation of self-conscious superiority and lack of practicality.

The collective noun *intelligentsia* was coined in mid-nineteenth century Russia, where it referred to a reform-minded class of society consisting of educated thinkers. In English it now refers, often derisively, to any group of highly educated people in a society. *Intelligentsia* is pronounced *in tel i JENT see uh* or occasionally *in tel i GENT see uh*, with a hard *g* as in *get*.

IQ (Intelligence Quotient) is a number used as a measure of intelligence and calculated from the score obtained on standard tests that are intended to measure innate intelligence rather than acquired knowledge. Though designed to be universally applicable, IQ tests have been criticized as skewed in favour of those from the dominant social and cultural groups.

Part of that price has been the resignation of literary taste, by the intelligent reading public, into the hands of professionals, of experts, of an intelligentsia.
Robertson Davies *A Voice from the Attic* 1960: 34

intense, intensive   Something may be *intense* (strong, acute, extreme, forceful) without being *intensive* (highly concentrated or focused). Normally, *intense* modifies such things as feelings, colours, and sensations: 'intense anger', 'intense red', 'intense heat'. *Intensive* often modifies processes or regimens: 'intensive farming', 'intensive training', 'intensive study'. In phrases such as 'labour-intensive' and 'capital-intensive' *intensive* means requiring a great deal of.

So intense were the flames that the workmen did not bother to use the doors; they got out through the windows.

J.E. Smyth et al. *The Law and Business Administration in Canada* 1987: 430

His flushed complexion and twitching nose, I was soon to discover, were tell-tale signs of intense annoyance.
George Ignatieff *The Making of a Peacemonger* 1987: 172

The latter got the most cursory once-over; the former—especially the Blacks—were subjected to intensive medical examinations, which in some cases were fraudulent.
Pierre Berton *The Promised Land* 1984: 183

Following this period of intensive mergers, more clearly defined corporate identities distinguished themselves.
Western Grocer Aug. 1990: 69

The psychophysiological effects of wine are increasingly the object of intensive scientific scrutiny—with some mildly startling discoveries.
Bon Vivant Nov. 1981: 13

(Here either word would make sense.)

intents and purposes, to (for) all   The phrase *to* (or *for*) *all intents and purposes* has been criticized as longwinded. *In effect* is more succinct. Occasionally people write 'to all intensive purposes', an error that indicates they have probably heard this cliché more often than they have read it.

For all intents and purposes, a majority government rules with the authority of a dictatorship for up to five years.
Vancouver Sun 19 Oct. 1990: A17

(Here *in effect* could be substituted)

... a peacekeeping force had become more or less a permanent fixture, and the armistice line had evolved, to all intents and purposes, into an international frontier.
George Ignatieff *The Making of a Peacemonger* 1987: 238

(Here 'had *in effect* evolved' or 'had evolved into a *de facto* international frontier' might be better.)

inter   see INTERN

inter-, intra-   The prefix *inter-* means between; *intra-* means within. For example, *intercontinental* trade occurs between different continents, whereas *intracontinental* trade occurs within one continent.

'The intramural athletic competitions,' reported the director of physical education in 1943, 'have, during the past season, attracted more competitors than ever before.' A year later Principal Wallace noted the same phenomenon: 'There has been a very great increase in the active interest that the individual student has taken

in sport during the years when intercollegiate athletics has not been possible.'
Frederick Gibson *Queen's University* 2 (1983): 187

(The term *intramural* means within the walls of a single institution; *intercollegiate* means between colleges or universities.)

See also HYPHENATION.

interface   An *interface* is the surface that forms the boundary between and connects two regions. The word, which dates from the late 1800s, is now often used figuratively. It is also used as a technical term in computing to refer to a device or software that allows information to be passed from one system or program to another. Some object to its appearance as a verb outside the context of computing. Most occurrences of *interface* as a verb in published Canadian texts are in quotations of speech; although *interface* is a perfectly reputable noun, use of the same word as a verb is still disputed.

[Pheasants] are creatures of the edges, of the interface between woods and meadow, birds that feed in the open spaces but take refuge in the undergrowth of thick brush.
Harrowsmith Jun.–Jul. 1985: 53

Shah and Parikh represent the new generation of South Asian dancers who perform at the interface of east and west—tradition and innovation.
Vancouver Sun 16 May 1994: C1

Members also approved a motion to set up a task force to 'make recommendation to the Board of Governors regarding the interface and relationship' between the foundation and its local membership.
Canadian Heritage Magazine Feb.–Mar. 1986: 8

The product can interface with any type of computer including PCs, laptops and handheld data collectors, printing on whatever surface.
Computing Canada 1 March 1991: 41

Mr. Mulroney's aide Fred Doucet called Miss MacDonald one of several staff members who 'interface with the children'.
Globe and Mail (Toronto) 20 March 1985: P4

He was astounded to learn that another man is paid in excess of $200,000 a year to actually run the railroad, with Mr. Smith expected to keep order at the board meetings and 'interface' with the federal government.
Vancouver Sun 2 Jan. 1990: B1

See also FUNCTIONAL SHIFT.

intern, inter   To *intern* is to place in detention. To *inter* is to bury.

> By the time the RCMP's two-day sweep of Montreal's Little Italy district was over, 2,400 Italian males—some no older than 16—had been rounded up and 236 of them were interned.
> *Gazette* (Montreal) 10 June 1994: A4

(The reference is to the internment of 'enemy aliens' during the Second World War.)

> John Montagu's life disproves the adage that the evil men do lives after them while the good is oft interred with their bones.
> *Toronto Star* 18 June 1994: L7

> Michiko Ayukawa, a 65-year-old women's historian and PhD candidate who was interred with the rest of her Japanese family in the Second World War, says she spent four decades assimilating, being anglo, living in the suburbs.
> *Times-Colonist* (Victoria) 20 June 1995: C6

(The word required here is *interned*.)

internecine   The adjective *internecine* (pronounced *in tur NEE sign* or *seen*) is used to describe destructive conflict between people one would expect to be allies. Interestingly, this standard current use of the word is at odds with its etymological roots. The word is derived from the Latin verb *internecare*, 'to exterminate or slaughter'. Here *inter-* does not have the usual meaning of between or among; it is a separate prefix used in a number of Latin verbs to denote destruction. Originally, in English, *internecine* was used in its Latin sense to describe murderous, bloody conflict. However, in his *Dictionary of the English Language* (1755) Samuel Johnson defined the word as meaning 'mutually destructive'. Johnson's definition soon gained ground. As Fowler points out, English has many synonyms for *slaughter*, but no word with this particular meaning. Here is a rare instance in which language commentators have given more authority to custom than to etymology.

> The Zulus had abandoned the south and were occupied in internecine wars (in what is now Zimbabwe) which left 1.1 million dead at the hands of their brothers.
> *Globe and Mail* (Toronto) 23 March 1985: P7

> The best thing that could happen out of all the internecine squabbling between standardbred and thoroughbred horsemen over post times would be that the harness people carry out their threat to split from the Ontario Jockey Club.
> *Globe and Mail* (Toronto) 24 Jan. 1985: P22

> Such integration was ordered by the U.S. Securities and Exchange Commission to put an end to the internecine rivalries between regional exchanges—rivalries which have been all too frequent in Canada.
> *Gazette* (Montreal) 3 March 1989: D6

See also INTER-, INTRA-.

interpretive, interpretative   Both adjectives are accepted, although many critics prefer *interpretative*, arguing that it follows the Latin formation of the word. Canadian writers use the briefer *interpretive* more often.

> Today the restored defense site is a small park, marked with interpretive signs and open free of charge every day from May through mid-October.
> Alan Tucker, ed. *The Penguin Guide to Canada* 1991: 276

> Reading is my theme, and reading is a private, interpretative art.
> Robertson Davies *A Voice from the Attic* 1960: 8

into, in to   To turn a lost handbag *in to* a police officer is a virtuous act; to turn a lost handbag *into* a police officer would require supernatural powers. In the first phrase, the *in* is part of a phrasal verb, *turn in* (meaning to hand over), and *to* is a preposition whose object is *police officer*. In the second phrase, *into* belongs to the phrasal verb *turn into* (meaning to transform). Writers seldom have any difficulty with expressions such as these. However, if you are suddenly seized by doubt, you can simply look the base verb up in a dictionary. Phrasal verbs are usually listed at the end of the definitions.

See also IN, INTO; PHRASAL VERBS.

intra-   see INTER-

intrude, obtrude   To *intrude* means to thrust in and to *obtrude* means to stick out, but these two verbs are now synonymous in the sense of imposing oneself without warrant or welcome. A distinction of sense is maintained in the adjectives: something *intrusive* is invasive or unwelcome, while something *obtrusive* is noticeable enough to be bothersome.

> An estimated 300 donkeys roam the smallest of the three main U.S. Virgin Islands. They knock over garbage cans, chew up gardens, wake people in the night, intrude on campers....
> *Gazette* (Montreal) 4 March 1989: I14

Long before TV or the telephone, the privacy of the home in Poe's day was being obtruded upon by the public street light....
Globe and Mail (Toronto) 20 Feb. 1985: P7

The Tory retreat from a more intrusive government has been dictated in large measure by the harsh imperative of the deficit and the debt, and by the need to keep business competitive.
Financial Post 4 March 1991: 11

Most of the time the motor is relatively unobtrusive.
Financial Post 7 June 1991: 42

Inuit, Inuk, Inuktitut, Inuvialuit, Eskimo, Inupiat, Inupiaq   The Indigenous people of the Canadian Arctic prefer to be called *Inuit* (singular *Inuk*), the word meaning 'the people' in their language, *Inuktitut*. The Inuit Circumpolar Conference formally established the use of *Inuit* in 1977, although Inuit political organizations, such as the Inuit Tapirisat (*TAP ir EET sat*), had used the term earlier. The Inuit of the Mackenzie Delta in the western Arctic call themselves the *Inuvialuit*. The Inuit and Inuvialuit were formerly called *Eskimos*, a word that is thought to be derived from an expression in an Algonquian language meaning 'eaters of raw meat'. The word *Eskimo* is still used in historical references; *Eskimo* is also used to refer to one breed of the large northern sled dog popularly known as the husky.

Inuit is sometimes spelled with two *n*'s. The singular form *Inuk*, which refers to one person, is rarely used by non-Inuit writers. Instead, *Inuit* is often used as an adjective: 'an Inuit person'. This adjectival use of *Inuit* is acceptable, but note that neither *Inuk* nor *Inuit* should be pluralized with an *s*.

The term *Inuit* is not completely accepted in Alaska, where *Eskimo* is still current. Only one of the four linguistic groups in Alaska identifies with the label *Inuit*. This one group may be called *Inupiat* (singular *Inupiaq*; also the name of their language) as well as Inuit. (The three other groups are Central Yupik, Alvtiiq, and Siberian Yupik.)

In general the Inuit are known for their engaging sense of humour, their sharing....
Arctic 41.1 (1988): 76

But Robert Aknavigak, an Inuk from Cambridge Bay on the Arctic Ocean, said he was for the Hamilton Tiger Cats because 'I like cheering for the underdog.'
Globe and Mail (Toronto) 25 Nov. 1985: C3

Of the council's 27 regional members, there are only three women—a black, an Inuit and a Metis—who step

outside the usual mold of women and men appointed by the government to the CACSW.
Gazette (Montreal) 28 Dec. 1990: B5

(The accepted singular form is *Inuk*.)

And yesterday marked the day when George Erasmus, national chief of the Assembly of First Nations, launched his own uphill battle in London to educate West Europeans about the claims of the anti-fur campaign and how it threatens the single most important source of independent income for the majority of Indians, Inuits and Metis in Canada, Alaska and Greenland.
Globe and Mail (Toronto) 4 Oct. 1985: A9

(The preferred plural is *Inuit*.)

Eva Deer does not buy the stereotype of the downtrodden Inuk female.
Vancouver Sun 21 June 1990: 36

(The accepted adjectival form is *Inuit*.)

The fisheries department will change regulations to permit the harvest of bowhead whales, if the hunters are Inuvialuit, the waters Canadian, and the total catch within limits set by the International Whaling Commission for aboriginal subsistence use.
Ottawa Citizen 29 Dec. 1990: A5

The 37 pieces of 'early' Inuit sculpture at the embassy date from the middle of this century, when James Houston and the Canadian Handicrafts Guild began to promote traditional Eskimo carvings.
Ottawa Citizen 29 Aug. 1992: H9

In some parts of Newfoundland, Eskimo dogs—even cross-breeds—are forbidden.
Dogs in Canada 1986: 19

Animal names, previously rendered by phrases such as 'something for doing the act dogs do when pulling a sled' to describe a horse, are now translated by their Inuktitut equivalents.
Ottawa Citizen 7 April 1990: J7

See ABORIGINAL PEOPLE(S); INNU; NUNAVUT.

invalid   As an adjective meaning not valid, *invalid* is pronounced *in VAL id*. As a noun meaning a weak, sickly person, the pronunciation is *IN va lid*. But see also DISABILITIES.

inveigle, inveigh   To *inveigle* someone is to lure him or her by deception or flattery *into* something. To *inveigh* is to protest or complain bitterly *against* something or someone. *Inveigle* is pronounced *in VAY gul* or *in VEE gul*. *Inveigh* rhymes with *weigh*. These terms are seldom confused, though they are occasionally misused.

She was just strange and impulsive enough to order Dick killed out of pique, and she was unquestionably persuasive enough to inveigle B—— and her father into the plot.
Jack Batten *Robinette* 1984: 66

Abandoning vocal finesse, they mumble those opening dirges of boredom, emptiness and crushed dreams that inveigle so many directors (and, we briefly fear, this one too).
Globe and Mail (Toronto) 23 Feb. 1985: M8

(The verb *inveigle* is always followed by *into* or *to*; perhaps the writer meant *seduce*.)

More surprisingly, the government press in these years inveighed against the 'rabble'....
J.A.W. Gunn *Beyond Liberty and Property* 1983: 102

invidious   see INSIDIOUS

invite   Usage commentators are unanimous in viewing the noun *invite*, the clipped form of *invitation*, as slang or informal, even though the *OED* reveals that it has been in use for over three centuries. Some words remain informal no matter how long they have been in use; the noun *invite* is largely restricted to breezy journalism.

> Whereas one short year ago, buyers and press would cheerfully have killed for an invite, last season's attendance was merely lacklustre....
> *Globe and Mail* (Toronto) 22 Jan. 1985: F6

> To add to the confusion, the invite says 'Black Tie Optional or Period Costume.'
> *Province* (Vancouver) 6 Sept. 1990: F23

invited guest   Commentators have criticized the phrase *invited guest* as redundant. However, judging from the mail to Dear Abby, many people see themselves as the reluctant hosts of uninvited guests. Thus the expression may be useful in distinguishing between solicited and unsolicited visitors. It's also appropriate in descriptions of events where the general public is welcome or at least permitted, but where some people have received personal invitations.

> But Paul George, an invited guest at the ceremony and the founder of the Western Canada Wilderness Committee, was skeptical....
> *Calgary Herald* 5 Dec. 1992: B10

(Paul George received a special invitation to a public ceremony.)

On a given night some hundreds of invited guests assembled in Convocation Hall at eight o'clock.
Hilda Neatby *Queen's University* 1 (1978): 145

(Here the qualifier *invited* indicates that invitations were issued.)

The great thing about a prom is the fact that ... all the invited guests know each other well and are of approximately the same age.
Ottawa Citizen 5 May 1994: E1

(Here *invited* could well be omitted.)

in vitro, in vivo   *In vitro* and *in vivo* are Latin expressions commonly used in scientific writing to describe the conditions under which an experiment is conducted. Literally, *in vitro* means 'in glass'; *in vivo* means 'in life'. An *in vitro* experiment is carried out in simulated conditions in a laboratory, whereas an *in vivo* test or experiment takes place in a living system, such as an animal or a natural ecosystem. The term 'in vitro fertilization' has become common recently in press reports about reproductive technologies. In this procedure, an egg cell is removed from a woman's body and fertilized in a glass dish in which the necessary chemical and physical conditions are provided to sustain it temporarily until it can be implanted in the uterus. Both terms should be italicized in formal writing.

> Today, from the IUD and the pill to artificial insemination and in vitro fertilization, women have better, if not perfect, means of controlling their own fertility.
> *Chatelaine* April 1986: 48

> ... the responsible selective mechanism might be directly associated with the changes that occur during the rapid development of plant tissues and organs both in vitro and in vivo.
> *Canadian Journal of Botany* 67.4 (1989): 985

See also LATIN PHRASES.

invoke   see EVOKE

IQ   see INTELLIGENT

Ireland, Northern Ireland, Ulster, Irish Republic, Eire, Irish Free State   The island of Ireland has been divided into two political entities since 1920. *Ireland* usually refers to the whole, although it may sometimes refer to one of the two states.
The smaller, northern section, officially known as *Northern Ireland*, has a Protestant majority and is a part of the United Kingdom. This region is some-

times referred to as *Ulster*, especially by those who favour maintaining links with Britain rather than uniting with the Republic of Ireland to the south. Note that *Northern Ireland* is a more neutral term, and that some Canadian readers may require an explanation of the name *Ulster*. *Ulster* is also the name of one of the four provinces of the Republic of Ireland.

The larger, southern section of the island, with a Roman Catholic majority, officially became the *Republic of Ireland* in 1949, when it withdrew from the British Commonwealth. Less formally it is known as the *Irish Republic*, and sometimes it is still called *Eire*, which was its official name from 1937 to 1949. *Eire* (pronounced *AIR ah* or *IRE ah*) is the Gaelic word for Ireland. This name may be chosen to distinguish the Republic from the north, or for its Gaelic flavour, but writers should note that its significance may be lost on Canadian readers.

When the southern region was first given the status of a dominion, in 1921, it was called the *Irish Free State*; this name is no longer in use.

When the famine in Ireland drove thousands of farmers to Canada, a typhus epidemic broke out.
Chronicle-Telegraph (Quebec) 7 Oct. 1991: 11

But he personified the aspirations of his compatriots, and somehow he succeeded in preventing Cyprus from becoming another Ireland.
George Ignatieff *The Making of a Peacemonger* 1987: 216

Three members of the Ulster Resistance Movement, a right-wing loyalist paramilitary organization in Northern Ireland, were arrested in Paris for attempting to exchange a surface-to-air missile for South African weapons.
Briarpatch Dec. 1989–Jan. 1990: 26

But the danger of prolonging a rebel siege beyond reasonable time can surely be seen in Ulster, where many die while no one wins.
Vancouver Sun 12 Sept. 1990: B1

Northern Ireland remains part of the British Empire, while southern Ireland, or Eire, is independent, a self-governing nation that divorced itself completely from the Crown in 1949.
Atlantic Salmon Journal Summer 1990: 22

In pleasant rolling countryside, in a tranquil corner of County Monaghan, Republic of Ireland, the man [Tyrone Guthrie] who gave so much to theatre in Canada and the United States found his home and family, and the continual renewal of his energies and inspiration.
Globe and Mail (Toronto) 12 Jan. 1985: T7

To date, the hangup has been not how to arrange self rule, but getting the North's nationalists (Catholics) and unionists (Protestants) to agree to sit down with each other and representatives of the Irish Republic and the British government.
Vancouver Sun 8 Dec. 1990: B8

In Eire there is no real line between church and state.
Province (Vancouver) 12 March 1990: 6

After all the threats and mumbles from the villagers of Slane in the Republic of Eire, Bruce Springsteen will play at Dublin Castle on June 1 after all.
Globe and Mail (Toronto) 3 May 1985: E7

See also BRITAIN.

iridescent   *Iridescent*, meaning luminous and rainbow-like, is often misspelled with two *r*'s. It is derived from the Latin word *iris*, 'rainbow'.

Lilly Kreise, a sales clerk in the coat department of The Bay downtown, says the newest all-weather coats ... are made in irridescent polyester with zip-out linings.
Vancouver Sun 4 Oct. 1990: C1

(The correct spelling is *iridescent*.)

Irish bull   see MALAPROPISM

Irish Free State, Irish Republic   see IRELAND

Iroquois, Six Nations, Iroquoian   *Iroquois* originated as the name of a confederacy of tribes living in what is now northern New York State; the Iroquois Confederacy was also called the Five Nations (Seneca, Cayuga, Oneida, Onondaga, and Mohawk). When the Tuscarora joined in the early eighteenth century, the Iroquois Confederacy became known as the *Six Nations*. The Six Nations, with the exception of the Oneida, supported the British during the American War of Independence, and after that war many moved north to Canada. Members of the Six Nations may be called Iroquois, although they also identify themselves as Mohawk, Tuscarora, etc.

Iroquoian is the name of a language family: the six different languages of the Six Nations are all Iroquoian. It is estimated that only 500 people still speak these languages in Canada. *Iroquoian* is also used as an adjective to refer to members of the Six Nations or their ancestors.

The Six Nations Confederacy negotiators, who have been a moderating force, flatly rejected proposals Thursday by the federal and provincial governments

and allied themselves ... with the Mohawks trapped in Kanesatake.
Vancouver Sun 7 Sept. 1990: A8

The spokesman said the Mohawks' Six Nations Iroquois Confederacy passports were accepted by most West European countries.
Province (Vancouver) 25 Oct. 1990: 42

There is a large variety of native languages, including the major families of Algonkian (Cree, Ojibway), Athapaskan (Dene), Inuktitut (Eskimo), Iroquoian, and others.
Queen's Quarterly 94.3 (1987): 668

Iroquoian cultural ambassadors promise to add some excitement to the annual Shondecti, or rendezvous, at Midland's living history site, Sainte-Marie-among-the-Hurons.
Globe and Mail (Toronto) 13 July 1985: T3

[irregardless]   see REGARDLESS

irreparable   see REPAIRABLE

irrespective   see REGARDLESS

-ise   see -IZE

Islam, Muslim, Moslem, Muhammed, Koran, Qur'an, [Mohammedan], Mecca   *Islam*, which means 'surrender to God' in Arabic, is the name of one of the world religions. Its adherents, called *Muslims*, worship Allah and revere Muhammed, his prophet. Their holy book is the *Koran*.

Moslem is an older variant of *Muslim*; the latter is now preferred. *Muhammed* is preferred to *Mohammed* in the United States and Britain, although *Mohammed* is retained in the names of historical figures. Canadians still use *Mohammed* about as often as *Muhammed*. Although *Qur'an*, a variant spelling for *Koran*, is closer to the Arabic, it has not replaced *Koran*.

Mohammedan is a term sometimes used for Muslims; however, since it incorrectly implies that they worship Muhammed, not Allah, it is considered inappropriate.

Muslim and *Islamic* are both used as adjectives, *Islamic* most often in reference to religious law.

Mecca, in Saudi Arabia, is the birthplace of Muhammed and the site of religious pilgrimages. Muslims face Mecca (which is not necessarily to the east) when they pray. Some usage guides point out that to use the word *mecca* to refer to sites of more secular pilgrimage—as in 'Las Vegas is a mecca for gamblers'—trivializes Islam.

Najmuddin Shaikh, ambassador from Pakistan and spokesman for the Islamic nations with representatives in Canada, said there is a general feeling among Muslims that Rushdie's book has made a joke of Islam and created contempt and hatred in the West for followers of the Prophet Mohammed.
Gazette (Montreal) 2 March 1989: B1

See also ARABIC; GOD; SACRED WRITINGS.

-ism   The suffix *-ism* has a number of established uses. It identifies an action or practice (*fetishism, snobbism, cannibalism*), a state or condition (*alcoholism, dwarfism, optimism*), a doctrine or belief (*monotheism, Judaism, Darwinism*), or a specific linguistic usage (*Canadianism, euphemism, witticism*).

Recently, a number of new *-isms* have established themselves, modelled on words, such as *racism* and *sexism*, that name a basis of discrimination. These include *able-bodyism* (discrimination against people who are physically disabled), *agism* or *ageism* (discrimination based on age), *lookism* (discrimination on the basis of physical appearance), *heterosexism* (discrimination in favour of heterosexuals, and implicitly against homosexuals), and *speciesism* (discrimination against certain species, usually a reference to human exploitation of animals). This new use of the *-ism* suffix is prolific and appears well-established in informal North American English.

When an *-ism* word is formed from a proper name it retains the initial capital: for example, *Marxism, Mormonism, Platonism, Thatcherism*.

Several *-isms* appear frequently in academic and media commentaries on Canadian culture and politics: *biculturalism, bilingualism, federalism, multiculturalism, regionalism*.

Atwood had risen to speak when everyone else had addressed the meeting sitting down. 'I suffer from heightism,' Atwood explained.
Chatelaine June 1986: 100

So we've developed laws against such things as racism and sexism. But now we must deal with a new form of discrimination: 'agism.'
Richard Davies and Glen Kirkland, eds. *Dimensions* 1986: 76

... racism, sexism, homophobia, able-bodyism, ageism—they are all about invasion.
Room of One's Own June 1990: 45

What Singer has done singularly is to give a name—speciesism—to the flawed intellectual reasoning that sanctions the slaughter of an estimated 10 million animals a day for food and several million a year by experimenters. Speciesism joins two other scourge isms of the 20th century—racism and sexism—as unresolved torments imposed by the powerful on the weak.
Vancouver Sun 9 June 1990: B5

See also -IST, -ALIST.

Israeli, Israelite   see JEW

Issei, Nisei, Sansei, Yonsei   These words, borrowed from Japanese, are plural nouns referring to different generations of people of Japanese descent in North America. The first wave of Japanese immigrants to Canada and the United States in the late nineteenth and early twentieth centuries are referred to as *Issei* (pronounced *EE say*), meaning first-generation. Children born of Issei are known as *Nisei* (*NEE say*). A third generation of Japanese Canadians, born mostly in the 1950s and 1960s of Nisei parents, are called *Sansei* (*SAN say*). Although, according to statistics, more than 90 per cent of the Sansei have married outside the Japanese community, the children of both mixed and unmixed Sansei marriages are called *Yonsei* (*YON say*), fourth-generation. These Japanese words are always capitalized in Canadian writing; they are understood most widely in areas where many Japanese Canadians live, such as British Columbia.

Included in this wholesale confiscation was the property of Issei, naturalized Japanese-Canadian veterans of the First World War, 54 of whose names can be found on the Vimy Ridge Memorial and scattered Canadian graves in France as well as the memorial in Stanley Park, Vancouver.
Globe and Mail (Toronto) 20 April 1985: P7

Every spring, the ranks of San Francisco's 12,500 residents of Japanese descent are swelled by thousands of Nisei, Sansei and Yonsei from all over northern California.
Globe and Mail (Toronto) 13 April 1985: T9

'We Issei first-generation Canadians couldn't do the work of the young people, the Nisei second-generation and Sansei third-generation.'
Vancouver Sun 22 March 1990: A15

See also GENERATION.

-ist, -alist   An adherent to an *-ism* can usually be identified by changing the *-ism* to *-ist*: someone who believes in transcendentalism is a transcendentalist; a person who practises Buddhism is a Buddhist; a proponent of federalism is a federalist. The *-ist* suffix is also used to identify a person with particular qualities or beliefs (*conformist, conventionalist, idealist*), to name someone working in a particular artistic style, area of interest, or discipline (*impressionist, philatelist, physicist*), and to designate someone who is proficient on a musical instrument (*cellist, guitarist, violinist*). Recently the *-ist* ending has come to designate someone who practises a certain type of discrimination, as in *sexist* or *racist*. Note that any final vowel is dropped when combined with *-ist*: *futurist, pianist, propagandist*.

Some words can be formed with either the *-ist* or the *-alist* ending: for example, *agricultur(al)ist, education(al)ist, horticultur(al)ist*. Which form to use in such cases is largely a matter of preference. But see NATURALIST, NATURIST.

Thus the defeat of Menaud following the death of his son ... becomes a harsh blow to nature in favour of culture, in this case the agriculturalist, right-wing nationalist ideology.
Ben-Z. Shek *French-Canadian & Québécois Novels* 1991: 23

District agriculturist Bill Smith said yesterday it appears average yield losses in the country could be between $123 and $247 a hectare.
Globe and Mail (Toronto) 24 July 1985: P8

Funds continue to come in ... and will be used to create an Amelia Hall award for educationists in the festival's Young Company program.
Globe and Mail (Toronto) 8 May 1985: P19

Gerald Graham ... hailed the advent of a principal 'who is not only an administrator but a superb scholar—who is incapable of talking the jargon of the educationalist'. ...
Frederick Gibson *Queen's University* 2 (1983): 306

Expert horticulturalist Trevor Cole recommends that imported plants ... have excess fertilizers flushed out of their soil.
Canadian Consumer Jan. 1986: 14

Mr. Sherk, a horticulturist, is also the president of the new Trillium chapter of The Beer Can Collectors of America. ...
Globe and Mail (Toronto) 4 May 1985: A3

Sexists violate the principle of equality by favoring the interests of their own sex. Similarly, speciesists allow the

interests of their own species to override the greater interests of members of other species.
Vancouver Sun 9 June 1990: B5

See also -ISM.

is when, is where   Many usage experts describe definitions containing *is when* or *is where* as immature and unsophisticated. The grammatical objection is to following the verb *to be* with an adverb clause rather than a noun phrase or noun clause. In writing, constructions such as 'A strike is when people refuse to work' should not be used except to represent speech. The disputed usage can be avoided by replacing the verb *to be* with *to occur* ('A strike occurs when . . .'), by inserting a noun in front of the adverb clause ('A strike is an occasion when . . .') or, better yet, by reframing the definition around a different verb ('In a strike people refuse to work'). The disputed construction 'An example of this *is when* . . .' can simply be replaced by 'for example'.

'Haute Wasp is when you have this tatty carpet that looks like hell but cost a million bucks, and only a few people know it.'
Margaret Atwood *Life Before Man* 1979: 85

(Here *is when* occurs in a fictional conversation.)

A paradigm opportunity is when we meet someone for the first time and can deliberately try to shape our response to that person along different lines than our immediate inclination.
Queen's Quarterly 94.1 (1988): 9

(This sentence could be rewritten by replacing *is* with *arises* or by rewording entirely: 'We are presented with a paradigm opportunity when we meet someone. . . .')

'Proper maintenance is when the operator knows what to do and does it correctly.'
Gazette (Montreal) 5 March 1989: A1

(This sentence, referring to airplanes, could be reworded: 'They can be properly maintained if the operator knows what to do and does it correctly.')

italics and quotation marks   Italics and quotation marks are both means of highlighting certain words in a text. Their different uses are governed by convention.

Italics are used to indicate:

• words that require especially strong emphasis in a sentence:

The Court received exhaustive evidence about the inferior quality of education black children were *in fact* receiving under the purported equality of the dual education system in many states.

J.E. Smyth et al. *The Law and Business Administration in Canada* 1987: 26

• words and letters referred to as such:

Doubling of consonants (especially *l*, as in *marvellous* or in *signalled*) created general confusion.
W.C. Lougheed, ed. *In Search of the Standard in Canadian English* 1986: 128

• foreign words or phrases that have not been fully assimilated into English (*fin de siècle*, *Weltanschauung*):

They agreed that the only sensible solution was to sell the farm, and father was presented more or less with a *fait accompli*.
George Ignatieff *The Making of a Peacemonger* 1987: 39

• Latin scientific names of genera and species (see SPECIES, GENUS):

The deer mouse *Peromyscus maniculatus* occurs throughout North America in a variety of habitats.
Canadian Journal of Zoology 67.4 (1989): 789

• publications, including books, newspapers, magazines, journals, pamphlets, long poems, and long musical works as well as titles of films, plays, and radio or television programs. However, note that the names of sacred books, such as the Koran, the Bible, and the Talmud, and the names of musical works identified only by form and number, such as Beethoven's Symphony no. 7 in A, are *not* italicized:

Dualism has rarely had such a thorough and successful presentation as in *The Strange Case of Dr. Jekyll and Mr. Hyde*, written by Robert Louis Stevenson in 1886.
Robertson Davies *One Half of Robertson Davies* 1978: 236

The Bible and the world were God's revelations and man should have freedom to search both.
Hilda Neatby *Queen's University* 1 (1978): 232

(*Exception*: names of sacred books are not italicized.)

Joyce expects the reader to know, or to have the pleasure of finding out, as does Eliot in the shot-gunning plethora of allusions in *The Waste Land*.
Queen's Quarterly 94.2 (1987): 298

And Bruce Hutchison, while editor of the *Vancouver Sun* and Winnipeg *Free Press*, actually wrote speeches for Lester B. Pearson.
Pierre Berton *The Promised Land* 1984: 39

Such films as *My Beautiful Laundrette*, *El Norte*, and *Smooth Talk*, originally produced for broadcast, . . . can earn added revenues through theatrical release.
Queen's Quarterly 95.2 (1988): 323

Music I Like was an afternoon show in 1976, to which non-musician guests brought along their favourite records (*My Fair Lady*, the *Moonlight Sonata*) and chatted about why they liked them—just ordinary folks like you and me.
Queen's Quarterly 92.1 (1985): 28

However, readers of Mr Schonberg's book will find no mention of Gould's achievements and no warning against his excesses, of which his disfiguration of Beethoven's sonata op. III on records was a good example at the time.
Queen's Quarterly 94 (1987): 67

(*Exception*: musical works named by form and number are not italicized.)

• titles of paintings and sculptures:

The cross itself is reminiscent of her own earlier and more overtly emotional abstract paintings like *Constellation of the Great Owl* and *Cross by the Sea* of 1985.
Mark A. Cheetham with Linda Hutcheon *Remembering Postmodernism* 1991: 30

• names of ships and spacecraft:

His father ... went down with the *Titanic* in 1912.
Pierre Berton *The Promised Land* 1984: 289

When writing by hand or using a word processing system that will not print italics, you may underline. By convention, italics and underlining are considered equivalent.

Quotation marks are conventionally used to indicate:

• words quoted exactly:

Then on July 29, 1976, a reporter from *The Gazette* called me a 'veteran goalie'.
Ken Dryden *The Game* 1983: 13

• the first mention of an unfamiliar word:

Not that domestic service was necessarily hard, for even in a modest household two or three servants might be kept—a nurse, a cook, a housemaid, and possibly also a 'rough girl'....
Robertson Davies *A Voice from the Attic* 1960: 137

• the translation of a foreign word or phrase:

Trompe l'oeil, which is French for 'deceive the eye,' is an eye-fooling painting on a wall, ceiling or floor.
Vancouver Sun 20 Nov. 1993: F3

• titles within publications—that is, titles of chapters, stories, articles, poems, songs, etc., within books, journals, magazines, newspapers, compact discs:

'Goodmorning and Goodbye', published by *Preview* in 1944, has as its only character or centre of consciousness a Jewish refugee living with a Canadian family.
Janice Kulyk Keefer *Reading Mavis Gallant* 1989: 71–2

• words used ironically:

There are a couple of 'good' Indians, too; Pontiac is noble-looking, as befits a chief; Oucanasta and her brother both get points for helping the British.
Margaret Atwood *Second Words* 1982: 139

On signboards and in advertisements, quotation marks are sometimes used for straight emphasis: '"fresh" coffee'. In any other context the quotation marks would signal irony—that the coffee was actually less than fresh. This use of quotation marks for emphasis is strongly disparaged by usage commentators, who recommend using more accepted markers of emphasis such as bolding, italicization, or underlining.

Neither italics nor quotation marks are used to highlight names of legal documents or legislative acts:

However, we now have a new, extensive Charter of Rights in the Constitution Act proclaimed April 17, 1982.
J.E. Smyth et al. *The Law and Business Administration in Canada* 1987: 21

In formal writing and in books, these guidelines are followed fairly strictly. Omitting italics or quotation marks is considered a stylistic flaw. Newspapers are less stringent; titles and foreign words are rarely highlighted, although journalists do take care to indicate direct quotations:

Kline would much rather portray Shakespeare's Hamlet, which he's done twice, or the nutty fascist crook in A Fish Called Wanda, which won him an Academy Award, or the lusty Pirate King in the hit Broadway production of The Pirates of Penzance.
Calgary Herald 2 Jan. 1992: B9

(Newspapers rarely use italics. In formal writing, both the film title *A Fish Called Wanda* and the play title *The Pirates of Penzance* would be italicized.)

See also LATIN PHRASES; QUOTATION, QUOTATION MARKS; SACRED WRITINGS; THE, A, AN.

iterate   see REITERATE

it is I, it's me   see CASE

its, it's   *Its* is both a possessive adjective (like *my, your, his, her, our, their*) and, rarely, a possessive pronoun (like *mine, yours, his, hers, ours, theirs*). Although the apostrophe is normally used to mark possession, it is not used with these words: 'The dog has its bone'; 'We have our amusements; it has its'. People often incorrectly insert an apostrophe: 'This is *it's* collar'. In moments of confusion it may be helpful to remember that *its* is exactly parallel to *his*: if *his* would fit where *its* is being used, no apostrophe is required.

It's with the apostrophe is a contraction of *it is*. If *it is* fits where *its* is being used, an apostrophe is needed.

Sometimes the form *its'* is found; this is never correct.

The money will allow the Banff Centre to revive its arts journalism program, which was dropped due to budget cuts in 1985.
Calgary Herald 21 Feb. 1988: B6

Threading it's way through the animations is a concern for our planet's disappearing natural wonders.
Province (Vancouver) 31 Dec. 1990: 34

(The possessive adjective is *its*.)

Bench-bound Expos take heart: relief is on it's way.
Gazette (Montreal) 17 May 1990: E1

(The possessive adjective is *its*.)

One of her favorite cheeses is ricotta, even though it's not the lowest in fat.
Gazette (Montreal) 3 March 1989: C3

(Here *it's*, meaning *it is*, is correct.)

See also POSSESSIVE.

-ize, -ise, -yze, -yse   Where there is a choice between *-ize* and *-ise* endings, or between *-yze* and *-yse*, Canadian writers, like Americans, tend to choose the endings with z. Note, however, that Canadian, American, and British writers all use *-ise* for *advertise, supervise,* and *surprise*. All prefer *-ize* for *recognize, civilize* and *civilization, organize* and *organization, realize* and *realization,* and *specialize* and *specialization,* though some Canadian and British dictionaries offer *-ise* as an alternative form. In Canadian usage, if *organisation* is chosen, it is most often for a proper name.

Canadians prefer the American spellings *catalyze* and *paralyze* to the British *catalyse* and *paralyse*. Canadian usage of *analyse* and *analyze* is almost equal, with more newspaper journalists using *-yze*.

The *-ize* ending is often used to coin new words, and dictionaries list a wide range of meanings for it. Words with this ending have been annoying readers and hearers since as early as 1591, when Thomas Nashe, cited in the *OED*, commented on having been reprehended for making up new words with this ending. Most recently, *finalize* and *prioritize* have been singled out for criticism, even though no one today objects to *demoralize, economize,* or *terrorize*.

See also ADVERTISEMENT; FINALIZE; PRIORITIZE; SPELLING, CANADIAN.

J

jail, gaol   *Jail* and *prison* can be used interchangeably, but in Canada and the United States *jail* usually refers to a place of short-term detention and *prison* to a place where long sentences are served. *Gaol* is a British spelling variant of *jail* with exactly the same pronunciation and meaning. Unless the reference is to a historic place, such as the Reading Gaol (made famous by Oscar Wilde's 'Ballad of Reading Gaol'), *jail* is now the more common spelling even in Britain. *Gaol* survives in some legal references in Canada. It is sometimes misspelled *goal*.

In the mornings, he breathes the antiseptic smell of jails, the smell of coops, caged flesh, sour air breathed in and out too many times; the smell of boredom and hatred.
Margaret Atwood Life Before Man *1979: 251*

Motion by the plaintiff for an order directing that the ... defendant ... be committed to the common gaol for

contempt of the Judgment of the Honourable Mr. Justice Henry dated September 4, 1984.
Globe and Mail (Toronto) 18 Jan. 1985: B4

The claimed perpetrator of the AIDs [computer] virus disk is sitting in an Ohio gaol awaiting extradition to England, where he faces charges of blackmail and extortion.
Province (Vancouver) 21 Feb. 1990: 41

(The British spelling *gaol* is unusual in this context.)

jamb   Windows, fireplaces, and doors have jambs, that is, vertical sidepieces. Because the *b* is silent, the word is sometimes misspelled *jam*. *Jamb* is derived from the French *jambe*, meaning 'leg'; remembering this may prevent writers from dropping the final *b*.

Dead bolts for doors, reinforced door jams, locks for sliding glass doors, screws to join top and bottom sashes of double-hung windows; all can present a time-consuming obstacle to burglars.
Vancouver Sun 9 Nov. 1990: E15

(The correct spelling is *jambs*.)

Janey Canuck   see CANUCK

jargon   see COLLOQUIAL

jealousy   see ENVY

jeer   In British English *jeer* is used with the preposition *at*: 'The boys jeer at him'. Canadian and American writers also have the option of using *jeer* without a preposition: 'The boys jeered him'. This transitive use of *jeer*, which makes it parallel to its rhyming antonym *cheer*, is more common in journalism than in formal writing.

I am not the man to jeer at it, because it moved me profoundly when I read it as a schoolboy....
Robertson Davies *One Half of Robertson Davies* 1978: 252

... it was believed that the principal had encouraged Queen's students to jeer at temperance lecturers in Kingston.
Hilda Neatby *Queen's University* 1 (1978): 236

[Gorbachev's] reception in Canada was generally warm, but protesters jeered him yesterday on Parliament Hill.
Province (Vancouver) 31 May 1990: 13

... I allowed four goals in a first period against Vancouver, then was jeered by Forum fans the rest of the game.
Ken Dryden *The Game* 1983: 43

Kiniski, 61, retired from the mat two years ago, his days as world heavyweight champion a faint memory even to those who once jeered him as Mean Gene and cheered him as Gentleman Gene.
Province (Vancouver) 3 April 1990: 42

jello, Jell-O, jelly, aspic   In North America *jello* (originally a trade name, *Jell-O*) refers to the wobbly dessert known in Britain as *jelly*. On either side of the Atlantic a savoury gelatinous salad made with tomato juice or meat stock is usually called an *aspic*. In Canada, the term *jelly* is reserved for the clear thickened fruit mixture used as a condiment or like jam.

Chicken-flavoured rice, green beans, hot rolls, jello made this morning—yes, that would please the computer expert.
Room of One's Own June 1990: 59

She picks highbush cranberries for juice and wild raspberries and black currants for jam and jelly....
Harrowsmith Aug.–Sept. 1985: 78

Jew, Jewish, [Jewess], Israeli, Israelite, Hebrew, Yiddish   *Jew* and *Jewish* refer to those who, however nominally, adhere to Judaism, or more generally to those of Jewish ancestry who identify with the Jewish people, history, and culture. *Jewess*, like many other feminine forms, is no longer accepted usage.

Israeli refers to all citizens of the state of Israel, who are of various religious and cultural backgrounds. The term *Israeli Jew* distinguishes members of the Jewish majority from other groups. *Israelite* designates the historical ancestors of the Jews.

Classical *Hebrew* is the sacred language of Judaism; modern *Hebrew* is the official language of Israel. *Hebrew* is no longer used as an ethnic designation.

Yiddish is a Germanic language that originated in Eastern Europe in the ninth century. It is written in Hebrew characters, and about fifteen per cent of its vocabulary is Hebrew. Jewish immigrants brought Yiddish to North America, where many of its expressions—such as *kibitz* and *klutz*—have moved into English.

... in the 1950s discriminatory quotas prevented many Jewish students from entering the McGill University medical school. So some Jews left Quebec and went to Swiss medical schools, or they chose rewarding careers in other fields, such as business and law.

Irving M. Zeitlin and Robert J. Brym *The Social Condition of Humanity* 1991: 172

In the northern port city of Haifa, about 4,000 Jews and Israeli Arabs marched in the streets holding signs and shouting slogans demanding Israeli withdrawal from the West Bank of the Jordan River and Gaza Strip. . . . *Calgary Herald* 14 Feb. 1988: B6

jewellery, jewelry, jeweller, jeweler Canadian writers use the spellings *jewellery* (the common form in Britain), and *jewelry* (the common form in the United States) with about equal frequency. Canadian retailers strongly prefer *jeweller* to *jeweler* (the usual American spelling).

For women who are always the first with the latest, streamlined gold jewellery with modern geometric edges is a perfect 'thank you.' *Province* (Vancouver) 7 Jan. 1990: B11

The good life for some women also means the ability to buy their own fur coats, jewelry and trips around the world. *Bon Vivant* Feb.–Mar. 1983: 16

See also SPELLING, CANADIAN.

jibe, gibe, gybe, jib, jive Except for *jib* and *jive*, these words are pronounced the same: *JIBE*. The difficulty with them is deciding which spellings to use for which senses. To *jibe* or *gibe* means to tease or taunt; *jibes* or *gibes* are insults. Some usage guides recommend *gibe* for this sense, but Canadian writers use *jibe* about twice as often as *gibe* in every type of writing. *Jive* is also found in this sense in informal contexts.

Jibe and *gybe* also are used in a nautical sense: the *jib* is the foresail of a sailing boat, and to *jib*, *jibe*, or *gybe* is to change course so that the sails *jibe* or swing around suddenly from one side to the other. The magazine *Canadian Yachting* uses the spelling *gybe* for this manoeuvre, as do most British writers, while American writers use *jibe*. Canadian writers and sailors use both.

Jibe has another common sense, to be in accord with: 'That story doesn't jibe with my experience'. This use is regarded as informal by some critics. However, it is found in serious journalism and historical writing, and there seems to be no reason to avoid it.

Sometimes *jive* is also used to mean accord with: this usage should probably be reserved for informal contexts.

He pricked balloons, jeered at the newly rich, attacked the bluestockings, poked fun at boosterism, jibed at humbug and bombast. Pierre Berton *The Promised Land* 1984: 265

'I've got a long memory when it comes time to appoint Cabinet ministers,' Mr. Turner reportedly gibed. . . . *Globe and Mail* (Toronto) 23 Sept. 1985: P5

Clark far outranks Brian Mulroney or any other national figure jibe for jibe on the two programs. *Toronto Star* 22 Feb. 1993: C5

He was superb at reducing her to weepy incoherence, even though his gibes were repetitive and came by rote. *Room of One's Own* June 1990: 4

'I distinctly remember playing hockey with other kids and being jived about wearing a kilt and blowing into a bagpipe.' *Calgary Herald* 18 July 1994: B4

(Here, in informal speech, *jived* means teased.)

But Thomson is not in Montreal to jive and joust with folks. *Ottawa Citizen* 6 Dec. 1994: F4

(Here too *jive* means tease or taunt, again in an informal context.)

When True North One hits the water, it will have its own computer on board that will analyze and record every tack, gybe and mark rounding during a 24-mile race. *Globe and Mail* (Toronto) 21 Feb. 1985: M8

We . . . learned how to jibe in open seas. *Vancouver Sun* 7 Nov. 1992: E10

That many historical facts of 'Old Hickory's' life did not jibe with the legend did not always matter. *Queen's Quarterly* 95.4 (1988): 800

That statement . . . jibes perfectly with everything we know about Davis's disdain for rehearsals and multiple takes. Jack Chambers *Milestones* 1983: 310

'We just happened to have personalities that gibe, I guess.' *Dogs in Canada* Special Issue 1986: 88

(The accepted spelling for this sense is *jibe*.)

job titles The sentence 'He is a male nurse' is redundant: the sex of the nurse is identified twice, in the pronoun *he* and in the adjective *male*. Yet the sentence does not seem redundant, because for many people *nurse* is gender-marked 'female'. One goal of non-sexist language reform in English has been to dissociate gender from job titles.

Interestingly, in Quebec French the opposite tack has been taken. The Office de la langue française has overseen the creation of feminine versions of the titles of all traditionally masculine occupations and vice versa. In both cases, the intent of the reform is the same: to promote the idea that every type of work is open to either sex, and to facilitate compliance with the law that forbids discrimination on the basis of sex in job hiring. Though detractors of non-sexist language consider gender-neutral job titles silly, in public or official communications they are now de rigueur. Following is a sample of traditional and non-sexist titles. (Prospective employers and others can obtain more information on this topic from various government publications.)

traditional	preferred
actress	actor
advance man	advance agent
alderman	councillor
anchorman	anchor
chairman	chair
cleaning lady	housecleaner, cleaner
fireman	firefighter or (for someone tending a furnace) stationary engineer
mailman, postman	mail carrier, letter carrier
male nurse	nurse
paperboy	carrier
policeman	police officer
salesgirl, saleslady	clerk, sales representative
waitress, waiter	server
weatherman, weather-girl	weather reporter or (for someone compiling reports) meteorologist
woman doctor, lady doctor	doctor
workman	worker

See also CHAIRMAN; SEXIST LANGUAGE; WAITER.

jodhpurs   This word is often misspelled *jodphurs* and mispronounced *JAWD furs*; the correct pronunciation is *JAWD purs*. The British borrowed the design of these riding breeches, cut loose above the knee and tight on the calf, from Jodhpur, India.

At end of a long day in court, lawyer Susan Mackey can't wait to trade her briefcase for a hard hat and jodphurs.
Ottawa Citizen 8 July 1990: B7

(The correct spelling is *jodhpurs.*)

Johnny Canuck   see CANUCK

joual   *Joual* (pronounced *zhoo AL*) is a non-standard dialect of Quebec French. First found in print in the 1930s, the word is supposed to represent a rural pronunciation of *cheval* ('horse'). *Joual* has been disparaged by some educated Quebeckers because it contains many words borrowed from English and because its speakers (usually rural or working-class) are regarded as ignorant of grammar and sloppy in their pronunciation. However, the term is not always used disparagingly. Since the 1970s many Quebec writers, including the playwright Michel Tremblay, have participated in *le mouvement joual-isant*: by choosing to write literature in relaxed Quebec French, they have given legitimacy to *joual* and to the ways in which Quebec French differs from Parisian French.

Joual should be italicized in formal writing.

What had begun as a complaint by Dr. Fabrikant about the instructor smoking … degenerated into vitriolic criticism of the teacher's methods and accent, which Dr. Fabrikant characterized as 'joual.'
Gazette (Montreal) 1 June 1994: A8

Beau Dommage gained popularity for songs sung in joual that captured the spirit of Montreal.
Gazette (Montreal) 12 Nov. 1994: C1

jubilant   The accepted pronunciation of *jubilant* is *JEW bi lunt*. The quite common pronunciation *JEW byew lunt* is not recorded in dictionaries. *Jubilant* is often misspelled *jubiliant*.

'It was for an 8-pound, 2-ounce little girl at home,' said a jubiliant Galley of his gamewinner at 3:42 of overtime.
Ottawa Citizen 22 April 1990: B1

(The correct spelling is *jubilant.*)

Is Montreal the jubiliant crowds who cram the streets during the jazz festival each summer, or the lone pilgrim mounting the steps of St Joseph's Oratory on her knees?
Gazette (Montreal) 26 May 1990: K4

(The correct spelling is *jubilant.*)

judgment, judgement   Both spellings are found in Canadian writing, but *judgment* (also preferred in the United States) is far more common in all types of writing, including academic, than *judgement* (the spelling preferred in Britain).

It's a judgment call, but one based on the highest sense of professionalism, not on prurient curiosity intended to titillate.

Richard Davies and Glen Kirkland, eds. *Dimensions* 1986: 147

The most dangerous physical condition that wind chill causes is hypothermia, the rapid lowering of body temperature that inhibits judgment and reasoning.
Province (Vancouver) 31 Dec. 1990: 45

His documentation is thorough, his overall treatment and judgements generally comprehensive and balanced, and his workmanlike style clear.
Canadian Journal of History 14.1 (1989): 124

See also CONCILIATION; SPELLING, CANADIAN.

judicial, judicious *Judicial* usually refers to judgments in law, but it can also be applied to moral or aesthetic judgments. *Judicious* means showing good judgment, in the sense of choosing sensibly.

There are doubtless self-defined limitations on judicial law-making power....
Canadian Bar Review 66.3 (1987): 505

The *Journal* attempted a judicial comment on the incident, rebuking both parties.
Hilda Neatby *Queen's University* 1 (1978): 197

The other large division of critics may be called judicial, and their best writing is usually about what they have not liked.
Robertson Davies *A Voice from the Attic* 1960: 195

While supposedly accountable for the judicious use of funds, BILD 'did not request nor did it receive from ministries any information about the economy, efficiency, or effectiveness of [the] program or projects funded.'
Globe and Mail (Toronto) 9 Dec. 1985: A6

Not infrequently verbose and repetitive, [this book] could have benefited from judicious editing.
Canadian Journal of History 14.1 (1989): 122

judicial determination   see CONCILIATION

juncture, junction   A *juncture* is a point in time; a *junction* is a literal or figurative place of meeting. Sometimes *junction* is mistakenly substituted for *juncture* in the expression 'at this juncture'. Although a juncture need not be a particularly critical or crucial time or state of affairs, some object to the phrase 'at this juncture' if it is merely a circumlocution for 'now'.

At this critical juncture in relations between the two countries a stalemate ... led to a situation in which by 1931 relations between Germany and France were char-

acterized by confrontation, rather than a willingness to compromise on important issues.
Canadian Journal of History 14.1 (1989): 145

At this juncture, however, it is also useful to recall that respondents were asked two sets of questions about influence....
Neil Nevitte and Roger Gibbins *New Elites in Old States* 1990: 139

It would be prudent, however, to sound a note of caution at this junction.
Queen's Quarterly 95.1 (1988): 21

(A train sounds a note of caution at a *junction*; a point in an argument is a *juncture*.)

Canada's capital, *Ottawa*, in Ontario at the juncture of the Ottawa River and the Rideau Canal, has a small-town feel, a Parliament to watch, museums to visit, and in winter a canal skating rink that runs for miles.
Alan Tucker, ed. *The Penguin Guide to Canada* 1991: 10

(The confluence of two rivers or water systems is a *junction*.)

junior   see SUPERIOR

junta   *Junta* is a Spanish word meaning 'government council' or 'committee'. In contemporary English it refers to the group that takes power after a revolution or coup. The CBC has long directed its announcers to pronounce the word *JUN ta* (so that the first syllable rhymes with *bun*) on the grounds that it was added to our English vocabulary hundreds of years ago. Today, however, the Spanish pronunciation *HOON ta* may actually be the more common one in Canada.

juror, jurist   A *juror* is a member of a jury. A *jurist* is an expert in the field of law. In Canadian and British English, a *jurist* is a noted legal scholar. In American English, judges and lawyers are also commonly called *jurists*.

Custom appears to have overcome law, or have been considered as being law in this instance—an absorbing matter for consideration by jurists, even if not for contract lawyers.
Canadian Bar Review 6.3 (1987): 613

Last February no less a jurist than Justice Bertha Wilson of the Supreme Court of Canada told an audience at Osgoode Hall that some aspects of criminal law 'cry out for change....'
Ottawa Citizen 8 Nov. 1990: A13

(Here Wilson is being singled out for her knowledge of the law.)

just deserts   see DESSERT

juvenile   see CHILDISH

juvenilia   Usually *juvenilia* refers to the works that a writer, artist, or composer produced while still a child or adolescent. Occasionally it is used to refer to artistic productions aimed at young people. *Juvenilia* takes a plural verb and is usually pronounced *jew vuh NILL yuh*. The common misspelling *juvenalia* (perhaps influenced by the word *marginalia*, referring to things written in the margins of texts) and the corresponding mispronunciation *jew vuh NAIL yuh* can be avoided by remembering that juvenilia is produced by juveniles.

Walker's Zastrozzi is supposed to have got its loose

inspiration from an obscure piece of juvenilia by the poet Shelley.
Calgary Herald 31 Oct. 1992: D16

The program is an unusual mix of juvenilia and such grandly scaled masterpieces as the Polonaise-Fantasy, Op. 61 and the Allegro de Concert.
Calgary Herald 12 Nov. 1992: D1

And that's the heart of the cynical film industry: juvenilia and genitalia.
Vancouver Sun 2 April 1992: A 15

(Here *juvenilia* refers to productions aimed at young people.)

Early literary works, called 'juvenalia' in the rare-book world, are valuable not only because they are rare and often bear a celebrity's signature, but also because they can give scholars insights into how the author's style developed....
Toronto Star 24 July 1992: C11

(The correct spelling is *juvenilia*.)

K

karat   see CARAT

Kelt, Keltic   see CELT

kerb   see CURB

kerosene, kerosine, coal oil, paraffin   These are all terms for the same oil, which is used to fuel lamps, stoves, heaters, etc. *Kerosene* is a Canadianism coined by the Nova Scotian who invented the distillation process for producing the oil, Dr. Abraham Gesner (1797–1864). *Kerosine*, formed by analogy with *gasoline*, is an accepted but uncommon spelling variant. *Coal oil* is another term used by some Canadians and Americans. *Paraffin* has two meanings: in Britain it is the name of the oil itself, and in Canada it refers to the oil in solid form—a wax used for making candles and sealing jars.

> The place was wired for electricity, and two or three dirty bulbs were burning over the grease pit, but kerosene lanterns were hanging from beams nearby, just in case.
> Howard Engel *Murder Sees the Light* 1984: 53

All those long, lone nights in a dingy room, probably working by the light of a coal-oil lamp, he sat and wrote and re-wrote and re-wrote.
Max Braithwaite *The Night We Stole the Mountie's Car* 1971: 159

Cover with a very thin layer of melted paraffin. Let stand until wax is set and cold.
Vancouver Sun 8 Aug. 1990: C3

ketchup, catsup, catchup   All three spellings are standard. The origin of the word is uncertain, though it may be related to the Cantonese word for 'tomato juice'. Canadian and British writers strongly prefer *ketchup*; Americans prefer *ketchup* but also use *catsup* and *catchup*.

key   see QUAY

khaki, caulk, cork   *Khaki*, the name given to the colour of British military uniforms, derives from the Hindi word meaning 'dust-coloured'. In the United States and Britain it is pronounced either *KAK ee* or *KAH kee*. Many Canadians, however, particularly those who served in either of the world wars, favour the pronunciation *KAR kee*. Because the English do not generally pronounce *r* before a consonant (for example, they pronounce *farm FAHM*), Canadian soldiers assumed that when the British referred to *KAH kee*, they were simply not pronouncing an *r*.

The same phenomenon occurs in the name of the boots worn by loggers, *caulk(ed) boots* (i.e., boots with spikes or caulks). *Caulk(ed) boots* are often referred to in Canada as 'cork boots'.

kibitz, kibitzer, kibbutz *Kibitz* was borrowed from Yiddish in the 1920s to describe the act of looking on at a card game and offering unwanted advice. By extention a *kibitzer* is a busybody or meddler. In recent usage to *kibitz* means to speak or behave in a joking manner. Both the noun and the verb are colloquial.

A *kibbutz* is a communal settlement, especially a farming settlement in modern Israel.

A good kibitzer should be able to see the cards at least from a slightly bent position.
Max Braithwaite *The Night We Stole the Mountie's Car* 1971: 176

'I think it was really important for him all those years to be able to get away from politics and have a chance to laugh and kibitz.'
Leader-Post (Regina) 27 Feb. 1988: A4

At a yuppie restaurant in Granville Island, the venerable poet holds court, kibitzing with the waitress, telling stories in a loud voice....
Vancouver Sun 15 Dec. 1990: D17

During the late 1960s when ideas of the so-called 'new left' were in fashion, there were two popular ways for young people to demonstrate their commitment to the ideals of socialism. One was to spend time living and working on a kibbutz in Israel; the other was to volunteer to work cutting sugar cane in Cuba.
Calgary Herald 26 Aug. 1994: A5

kickoff, kick off *Kickoff*, a word borrowed from football, is considered standard but informal when used to refer to the start of a public event. Some dictionaries and usage guides still consider it slang, although it is common in Canadian journalism. When it is used as a noun or an adjective, *kickoff* is sometimes hyphenated: 'A kick-off dinner will be held'. *Kick off* (two words) is a verb: 'A dinner will kick off the festival'.

'And it's obviously the unofficial kickoff to the next election campaign.'
Ottawa Citizen 18 Nov. 1994: A4

After the kick-off news conference here, Copps flies to Hamilton for a rally....
Province (Vancouver) 12 Jan. 1990: 74

The train was part of a campaign to kick off ... a marketing promotion.
Western Grocer Magazine June 1990: 20

See also HYPHENATION; PHRASAL VERBS.

kidnap, abduct Both words mean to forcibly carry someone away. When a person is kidnapped, however, a ransom of some kind is usually demanded, which is not necessarily the case with abduction. A parent, therefore, *abducts* rather than *kidnaps* his or her own child, since usually no ransom is demanded in such cases. According to Canadian law, it is possible to be charged with the abduction of a child under 14 simply for harbouring him or her with the intent of depriving a parent or guardian of the child. In other words, in legal contexts, forcible carrying-off is not always part of the definition of *abduct*.

Canadian and British writers double the *p* (*kidnapped, kidnapping, kidnappers, kidnappee*). A person who kidnaps is a *kidnapper*; someone who abducts is an *abductor* (sometimes misspelled with an *-er* ending).

Parental abduction, the unlawful taking of a child by a parent without permission of the other parent or caregiver, made up the second largest number of missing child cases.
Ottawa Citizen 17 Oct. 1990: A5

When they did not find the boy ... she and her ex-husband had to face the fact that he had probably been abducted. And because no one demanded a ransom, they feared that he was being exploited for sexual purposes.
Maclean's 10 Dec. 1990: A54

Because kidnapping one's own child is not an offence in the U.S., A—— was arrested only because of the Canadian warrant.
Province (Vancouver) 10 Dec. 1990: 16

(Here *abducting* would be more accurate.)

A child with magical powers ... is kidnaped, and for uncertain reasons, only Murphy can save him.
Ottawa Citizen 15 Sept. 1990: TT4

(The *p* is almost always doubled in Canadian spelling.)

The teenager was dragged into a van while a woman trying to rescue her was punched by the abducter.
Ottawa Citizen 10 Dec. 1990: A5

(The correct spelling is *abductor*.)

See also DOUBLING THE FINAL CONSONANT.

kind of, sort of   The phrases *kind of* and *sort of* are similar not only in the ways they are used but in the disputes they have occasioned; the recommendations that follow apply to both.

Expressions such as 'these kind of things' and 'those sort of people' have been under attack for two hundred years because the plural determiner, *these* or *those*, does not agree with the singular noun that it modifies, *kind* or *sort*. Nevertheless, such expressions are idiomatic and have a long literary pedigree; *Webster's Dictionary of English Usage* cites examples from the writings of Sidney, Shakespeare, Milton, Dryden, Pope, Austen, and Dickens. In Canada the idiom makes its way into print only in quotations or representations of speech. In other published writing, the determiner and the noun *kind* are either both singular (*this kind* or *that kind*) or both plural (*these kinds* or *those kinds*).

In Canadian English, when *kind* is made plural before *of*, the noun that follows *of* is usually made plural too (unless the noun is uncountable, like *bread* or *gasoline*): 'What kinds of players is he planning to draft this year?' In British English, the noun that follows *of* is often left singular: 'What kinds of player is he planning to draft this year?'

Some language commentators have objected to *a* or *an* in phrases such as 'this kind of an account'. Their argument is that *account* is being used to describe a category or genre rather than a specific account, so that the particularizing *an* is illogical. While in formal writing the construction without *a* or *an* ('this kind of account') is more common, the construction that includes the indefinite article is also found. As the *Longman Guide to English Usage* points out, the presence of the article can be significant. 'What kind of job is that?' ('How would you categorize your work?') means something quite different from the insulting rhetorical question 'What kind of a job is that?'

As an adverb, *kind of* means fairly or rather: 'kind of silly'. This use is informal and should be avoided in writing except in representations of speech.

> Since that time, Christie has learned to deal with these kinds of situations.
> *Canadian Living* 17 May 1986: O8

> I'll go to the postwar years, when I began to have a memory, and trace for you my own progress from wild

> colonial girl to the person who gives these kinds of speeches. . . .
> Margaret Atwood *Second Words* 1982: 376

> No, I'm damn careful now about booze. Some kinds of painkiller just aren't worth it.
> Constance Beresford-Howe *Night Studies* 1985: 95

> 'Those kind of horses are subject to those things happening.'
> *Canadian Thoroughbred* Jan. 1989: 29

(This sentence is a direct quotation of speech; in formal writing, *those kinds* is recommended.)

> 'I think perhaps that maybe a bit more time needs to elapse before those kind of decisions are made.'
> *Gazette* (Montreal) 4 March 1989: F7

(In formal writing, *those kinds* is recommended.)

> 'And what kind of a mess have you gone and made this time?' Dora snapped at Nadia.
> *Canadian Fiction Magazine* 63 (1988): 82

> Treslan described her number as 'kind of wild,' adding it's 'tiring, but a lot of fun.'
> *Today's Skater* 1991: 70

(Here the adverbial *kind of* is part of a direct quotation of speech.)

kingdom   see SPECIES

kitty-corner, cater-corner, catty-corner   Canadians prefer *kitty-corner* to describe something obliquely opposite. The equivalent terms *cater-corner(ed)* and *catty-corner(ed)* are more common in British and American English. All these terms derive from the obsolete English word *cater* (from the French *quatre*), meaning four.

> Phoenicia Foods, kitty-corner to Gus's Grill on Agricola Street at North in Halifax, sells the chestnuts for $4.95 a pound.
> *Daily News* (Halifax) 5 Dec. 1994: n.p.

See also FOLK ETYMOLOGY.

knowledge, knowledgeable   *Knowledge* and *knowledgeable* are frequently misspelled. First, the *d* is often left out of both words. Second, the final *e* of *knowledge* in *knowledgeable* is often omitted. It is necessary, however, to signal the soft *g* sound, as in *changeable* and *manageable*.

> Without this knowlege, wine producers are powerless to reduce the amounts of the substance. . . .
> *Globe and Mail* (Toronto) 11 Dec. 1985: A1

(The correct spelling is *knowledge*.)

MacDonald said the group was highly knowledgable about AIDS ... yet did not act to protect themselves from the disease.
Ottawa Citizen 17 Sept. 1990: A5

(The correct spelling is *knowledgeable*.)

See also -ABLE, -(E)ABLE.

koala see BEAR

Kootenay, Kutenai, Ktunaxa-Kinbasket The *Kootenay* (or *Kutenai*) are an Aboriginal people whose traditional territories are mainly in southeastern British Columbia, Alberta, and the United States, between the Selkirk Mountains and the Rockies. They are represented by the Ktunaxa-Kinbasket Tribal Council in Cranbrook, B.C. Their language, also called *Kootenay* or *Kutenai*, is an isolate—the only member of its language family. *Kootenay* is pronounced *KOO tin ay*; *Ktunaxa-Kinbasket* is pronounced *ktoo NA ha* (with an exaggerated *h* sound) *KIN bas ket*.

Two companies battled for the lucrative fur trade with the Kootenay Indians who travelled in the foothills of Alberta.
Calgary Herald 10 July 1993: D3

The town [Creston, B.C.] also boasts a fine museum (home to one of the few remaining Kutenai canoes)....
Calgary Herald 21 May 1994: C7

Sophie Pierre, an elected chief of the St. Mary's band of the Ktunaxa Nation in the Kootenays, said aboriginal women face some unique hurdles in becoming leaders.
Gazette (Montreal) 4 May 1993: B4

Koran see ISLAM; SACRED WRITINGS

Ktunaxa-Kinbasket see KOOTENAY

kudos *Kudos*, a Greek word meaning glory or renown, looks like an English plural. People who don't realize that *kudos* has no plural (it is an uncountable noun, like *pathos* or *prestige*) occasionally use *kudo* as a singular noun meaning an accolade. *Kudos* is more common in journalism than in formal writing. It is properly pronounced either *KOO doss* or *KYOO doss*, but *KOO doze* is also often heard.

British Columbians won kudos yesterday as the United Nations honored individuals and groups at the forefront of environmental activism.
Province (Vancouver) 5 June 1990: 13

But the media did get a kudo from Chief Justice Charles Dubin, who complimented them for 'acting responsibly' in respecting the gag order....
Toronto Star 3 Feb. 1994: A2

(The singular construction *a kudo* is non-standard; 'a word of praise' would be better here.)

See also BACK-FORMATION

Kutenai see KOOTENAY

Kwakiutl, Haisla, Heiltsuk, Bella Bella, Oweekeno, Kwakwaka'wakw, Kwagiulth The traditional Kwakiutl territories lie both on the mainland of British Columbia and on northeast Vancouver Island. *Kwakiutl* ((*kwa kee OOTL*) is still used with reference to the past and to shared cultural practices, but subgroups of the Kwakiutl are now generally referred to in more specific terms. The *Haisla* (*HY sla*) are the northern group on the mainland. The people formerly described as the southern branch of the mainland Kwakiutl are the *Heiltsuk* (*HALE tsuk*), some of whom were formerly called *Bella Bella*, and the *Oweekeno* (*oh WEE kee no*). The southernmost Kwakiutl group on the mainland is now called the *Kwakwaka'wakw* (*kwa KWA ka WA kw*). Their languages—Haisla, Heiltsuk, Oweekeno, and Kwakwala—all belong to the Wakashan family. The Kwakiutl on Vancouver Island call themselves *Kwagiulth* (*kwa GYOOLTH*); they also speak Kwakwala. None of these names should be pluralized with *s*.

Despite this opposition, the Kwakiutl clung to the potlatch, refusing to give it up, knowing it was essential to their social fabric.
Ottawa Citizen 6 Dec. 1994: F1

... following a Haisla decision not to hunt bear in the newly protected Kitlope wilderness, the B.C. government put a moratorium on grizzly hunting in the area.
Vancouver Sun 18 Nov. 1994: A27

'I think people forget quite quickly the grievances of the past,' said David Gladstone, an artist, historian, and hereditary chief from the Heiltsuk ... band in Bella Bella.
Calgary Herald 19 Aug. 1994: A1

Tribal differences between Haida, Kwakwaka'wawkw, Gitksan, Salish and Nuu-chah-nulth are at least as sharp as those that separate the French from the Germans.
Gazette (Montreal) 24 Aug. 1994: C1

Representatives of ... the Coast Salish, the Nuu-chah-nulth and the Kwagiulth ... offered athletes, dignitaries and spectators a traditional chanted welcome....
Ottawa Citizen 19 Aug. 1994: D1

L

-l, -ll The spellings of several words ending in *l* vary in Britain, Canada, and the United States. The British usually end the following words with a single *l*: *appal, distil, enrol, enthral, fulfil, instil*. Most Americans spell the same words with two *l*'s (*appall, distill*, etc.) and retain both of them when adding endings (*-ed, -ing, -ment*). Those who use the single-*l* spelling do double the *l* before endings beginning with a vowel: *appalling, enthralled*. Before endings beginning with a consonant, however, they leave the *l* single: *enrolment, fulfilment*.

Canadians, as usual, vary their practice, but generally follow the British spellings.

See also DOUBLING THE FINAL CONSONANT; FULFIL; SPELLING, CANADIAN.

laborious see -OUR, -OR

labour see BELABOUR

labyrinthine see BYZANTINE

lackadaisical A *lackadaisical* person is lazy or lacking in enthusiasm. The word derives from *lac-kaday*, an alteration of 'Alack the day!'—an archaic exclamation of regret. This word is commonly mispronounced *laxadaisical*.

lack for Some usage guides condemn *lack for* outright on the grounds that it means the same as *lack*. *Lack for* is almost always used in negative constructions ('They do not lack for money'). This idiom is used in Canadian writing at all levels of formality. Those who continue to condemn such widespread usages are doomed to futility.

> The writer, in his traffic with that realm in which dream, and myth, and fairy-tale become mingled with the most ordinary circumstances of life, does not lack for rewards and very great rewards.
> Robertson Davies *One Half of Robertson Davies* 1978: 133

> With 100,000 bachelors on the prairies, most of them young and virile, the bawdy houses did not lack for customers.
> Pierre Berton *The Promised Land* 1984: 296

laconic *Laconic* does *not* mean lethargic—at least according to dictionaries. Yet this usage has become very common. *Laconic* is derived from the Greek word for 'Spartan'. In the ancient world the Spartans were noted for not wasting words. Thus a laconic person is one who uses few words. A concise utterance or style of writing may also be called laconic. The word is pronounced *la KON ik*.

> It turns out David, usually so reserved and laconic he makes Presbyterians seem garrulous and forthcoming, becomes Chatty Carl when he laces on the shoes.
> *Financial Post* 9 July 1991: 11

> Like Whitman, Piercy must be read in chunks, not sips, and appreciated for her courage, gut energy and verbal fecundity, not for laconic polish.
> Margaret Atwood *Second Words* 1982: 278

> Environmental pollution has been known to cause hyperactivity and laconic behavior in children, he said.
> *Globe and Mail* (Toronto) 8 Feb. 1985: M3

(Here *lethargic* may be the word intended.)

> His Wonder Dog, Mighty Manfred, was a laconic pooch who tended to fall asleep.
> *Vancouver Sun* 17 March 1990: D2

(Here *lethargic* is almost certainly the word intended.)

> Interest rate-sensitive sectors, including the banks, also came under selling pressure amid mounting investor frustration with the laconic pace of U.S. interest rate declines.
> *Financial Post* 12 Dec. 1989: 24

(Here *slow* is intended.)

> Ron Guidry, sitting at a locker marked 'Gater's Corner' held court for a crowd of reporters, answering questions in his laconic Louisiana drawl.
> *Globe and Mail* (Toronto) 13 Sept. 1985: S1

(A drawl cannot be described as *laconic*, and Guidry does not seem to be at a loss for words. The word intended is probably *slow*.)

While both are laconic off the ice, the CH [team crest] on their chests might as well be an S [for Superman] when they play.
Gazette (Montreal) 14 April 1990: G1

(Here *easy-going* seems to be intended.)

Mulroney is the opposite, as furiously ambitious as Trudeau was laconic.
Financial Post 9 July 1991: 11

(Here *detached* seems to be intended.)

lactovegetarian   see VEGETARIAN

lam, on the lam   *On the lam* is an informal expression meaning on the run from the law. Occasionally people write *lamb* for *lam*, perhaps thinking that the expression has something to do with stealing young sheep. In fact, the expression derives from a Standard British English verb that is rare in Canadian English: *lam*, meaning beat or hit. *Lam it* is a British slang expression meaning to go away or run for it, analogous to the North American *beat it*.

He abducts his grandmother, Armen, from the unsavoury home for the aged where his father has put her and goes on the lam.
Queen's Quarterly 95.2 (1988): 410

I advised her to go on the lam, up to the mountains.
Canadian Fiction Magazine 64 (1988): 73

Harrison Ford stars in this re-make of the TV classic about a doctor on the lamb for a crime he didn't commit.
Whig-Standard (Kingston) 28 Aug. 1993: C2

(The correct spelling is *lam*.)

landed immigrant   see CITIZEN

larceny   see BURGLARY

largesse, largess   *Largesse* means gifts or money, usually bestowed by someone in a high position on people with less standing; it is often used ironically. Canadian writers most often use the *-esse* spelling, but *largess* is also accepted. Pronunciation varies, but the *g* is always soft, pronounced either as in *jest* or as in the French *je*.

Under the New Deal, the Fair Deal, the New Frontier and the Great Society, it was the hand of government that bestowed largesse on the people.
Globe and Mail (Toronto) 1 March 1985: P51

Not all of this potential largesse will simply flow to the baby-boom generation, for many seniors may opt instead to invest in their grandchildren.
Vancouver Sun 2 July 1990: A8

… Red Wing owner Mike Ilitch spent more than $7-million on free agents and is expecting to see something more than a large number in the loss column to justify his largess.
Globe and Mail (Toronto) 19 Oct. 1985: C6

last   see LATEST

last post, taps   (*The*) *last post* is a bugle call played in the Canadian and British armed forces at the end of the day, at military funerals, and on Remembrance Day. The American equivalent is *taps*.

Flags flew at half-mast as the band played the Last Post and a list of 24 lost warships and nine merchant ships was read aloud.
Daily News (Halifax) 3 May 1993: n.p.

(Though newspapers often capitalize *last post*, dictionaries do not.)

Twirling one end of the hose [an improvised musical instrument], he played taps.
Province (Vancouver) 19 Feb. 1990: 11

late   see BELATED; LATE, THE

late, the   Literally, *the late* before someone's name means 'the recently living'. The expression is used as a sign of respect for someone who has died. Some usage guides say it is appropriate to use *the late* only for ten or fifteen years after a person's death, but others maintain that the honorific is appropriate as long as the deceased person is in living memory. 'Widow (or widower) of the late So-and-so' is redundant. *Late* should not be used with job titles ('late Head of the History Department') since it's unclear whether the incumbent has died or has simply changed jobs.

… many famous works of art, such as the late Michelangelo's statue of David getting ready to fight Goliath, are not wearing a stitch of clothing.
Province (Vancouver) 27 Dec. 1990: 44

(Here *the late* is inappropriate, since the sculptor died over 400 years ago.)

Neither, understandably, were the late Pablo Picasso, or the long-dead Rembrandt, also represented in the new fifth-floor gallery in Simpson's downtown Toronto department store.
Vancouver Sun 22 Dec. 1990: D16

(Here the author distinguishes between the *late* Picasso, who is still in living memory, and the *long-dead* Rembrandt.)

... it was he, along with Maurice Smith, late sports editor of the *Winnipeg Free Press*, who paved the way for a national schoolboys' championship....
The Beaver Dec. 1989–Jan. 1990: 51–2

(Here it would be clearer to say either '*the late* Maurice Smith, *then* sports editor' or 'Maurice Smith, *former* sports editor'.)

latest, last Both *latest* and *last* are superlatives of *late*. Thus both *latest* and *last* can mean most recent. *Last* also means final. Occasionally *last* is ambiguous: 'the last issue of the magazine' could be the most recent or the final issue. For this reason, a few language commentators have advised that *last* be used only to mean final. Following this rule, however, would produce quite unidiomatic English. *Latter*, meaning second-mentioned (of two things) or last-mentioned (of three or more), can be a useful substitute for *last* if one is needed to avoid ambiguity.

Allow me to elaborate on this last [his own previous] statement.
W.C. Lougheed, ed. *In Search of the Standard in Canadian English* 1986: 66

(Here *latest* could not be substituted for *last*, even though *last* clearly does not mean final.)

lath, lathe *Lath* rhymes with *bath*. Laths are strips of wood fastened across the studs in a wall, over which plaster is applied. *Lath* can be used either as a countable noun ('He used some laths to make a trellis') or as a collective noun ('The plaster is crumbling, but the lath is fine').

Lathe rhymes with *bathe*. A lathe is a machine that shapes wood or metal by turning it against a fixed cutting tool.

Then the crews for plaster and lath moved in.
Geoffrey Ursell *Perdue: And How the West Was Lost* 1984: 48

The day may soon come at the Fisheries Museum of the Atlantic at Lunenburg, N.S., when, next to the living display of a retired fisherman planing planks for a traditional dory, there'll be another nailing lathes on to the spruce-bough frame of a wooden lobster pot.
Vancouver Sun 17 June 1992: A9

(The word required here is *laths*.)

The profusion and similarity of rope-twist table legs ... also indicates some form of screw-thread lathe, capable of producing at least rough turned rope-twist table legs in quantity.
Canadian Collector 21.2 (1986): 35

See also COLLECTIVE NOUNS.

Latina, Latin American, Latino see HISPANIC

Latin phrases, foreign phrases Expressions taken from other languages can cause difficulties for readers.

Most Latin in use in English today has been passed down through the professional ranks, from one generation of doctors, lawyers, scientists, academics, or priests to the next. For this reason, some people regard the use of Latin as elitist. Others condemn such disapproval as philistine. A very good argument against using Latin phrases, or any other foreign expressions, especially in non-technical writing, is that they are often not understood. On the other hand, there are occasions when the advantages of using a Latin phrase are unmistakable. For example, a phrase such as *tempus fugit*, 'time flies', a thousand years older than our mother tongue, appeals to our sense of history, reminding us that certain aspects of human life have not changed. Like all borrowings from foreign languages, however, Latin phrases should be used judiciously. While a Latin tag such as *caveat emptor*, 'buyer beware', would be highly inappropriate, even dangerous, in a public safety announcement, it would not be out of place in something written for readers who have the time and inclination to consult a dictionary.

Even today it is possible for a Latin phrase to gain currency with a new audience. The Latin phrase *quid pro quo*, for example, which means 'something for something', was not widely known outside the field of law until recently. However, lawyers and women's rights advocates began to use the phrase as a label for that particular variety of sexual harassment in which an employer or supervisor bargains for something, in this case sexual favours, by offering an employee something in return, such as a promotion or more hours of work. When cases of sexual harassment became headline news, the media introduced *quid pro quo* to the general public.

The more familiar a foreign phrase is, the less likely it is to be italicized. Latinisms such as *status quo*, 'the current state of things', *per diem*, '(a payment made) on a daily basis', and *ad hoc*, 'to this (immediate end)' are so much a part of some people's everyday vocabulary that they are no longer perceived as foreign, nor are they marked as such. For less familiar phrases, however, italics are still required, at least in formal contexts. In this book, individual entries recommend italicization in formal writing only where two of three dictionaries (*Concise Oxford*, *Webster's New World*, and *Random House Webster's College*) use italics. (Note that not all dictionaries indicate which foreign words should be italicized.) If an entry on a foreign phrase does not recommend using italics, it can be assumed that they are not necessary.

The pronunciation of Latin in English is muddled because different systems are used. In one system the words are pronounced in a manner approximating the speech of the ancient Romans (closer to modern Italian than to English). In another tradition the words are pronounced just as if they were written in English. The most common pronunciations of the most widely used Latin expressions are hybrids of these two systems. When in doubt, check a dictionary for typical pronunciations.

> In each [lesson], Diana talks about some aspect of [sexual harrassment]—for example, the two types of harrassment: 'quid pro quo' and 'hostile environment.'
> *Toronto Star* 4 May 1995: J4.

See also FRENCH WORDS; GERMAN WORDS; PLURALS, REGULAR, IRREGULAR, FOREIGN.

laudable, laudatory *Laudable* means worthy of praise and usually refers to people or actions. *Laudatory* means full of praise or commendatory; it usually refers to comments, remarks, speeches, reports, and so on.

> The integration of forest and wildlife management on Canadian public lands is a laudable goal, but one which governments have not pursued with any rigour.
> *Queen's Quarterly* 94.3 (1987): 618

> In her book she dissents from the usual laudatory approach by claiming he was an incompetent observer, amateur in his laboratory techniques, a parochial philosopher, and a neurotic personality!
> *Queen's Quarterly* 92.2 (1985): 424

Laurentian Shield   see CANADIAN SHIELD

lawyer, counsel(lor), barrister, solicitor, notary public, attorney, power of attorney, attorney at law   *Lawyer* is the general term for a person trained in the law, especially one who advises clients on legal matters or acts for them in court. *Counsel* and *counsellor* are also used to refer to lawyers in Canadian court proceedings. A lawyer retained by a city or an organization is often called a *solicitor*. In the Canadian system, outside Quebec, all lawyers are granted the titles *barrister* and *solicitor*, and all lawyers called to the bar are also sworn in as *notaries public*. Notaries public draw up deeds, contracts, and other documents and take affadavits.

In Quebec, notaries (*notaires*) and lawyers (*avocats*) perform different functions: notaries perform the functions of notaries public elsewhere, and lawyers act in legal disputes.

In the British legal system, and in some former British colonies, there is an important distinction between solicitors and barristers. Solicitors deal directly with clients and prepare cases for barristers to take to court. Only barristers can plead cases before superior courts.

Attorney is a synonym for *lawyer* in the United States. In Canada, however, the term is usually restricted to compound titles. The federal minister of justice in Canada is called the *attorney general* (plural *attorneys general*). He or she oversees all prosecutions on behalf of the Crown. Each province also has an attorney general. The federal *solicitor general* oversees the Canadian Correctional Service and the RCMP. The lawyers who prosecute for the Crown are called *Crown attorneys*. The American equivalent is *district attorneys*.

A *power of attorney* is a document by which someone grants another person the right to conduct his or her business. And, by law, any person who has the legal authority to act on someone else's behalf is an attorney; strictly speaking, a lawyer is an *attorney at law*.

See also COUNCIL.

lay   see LIE, LAY

lead, led   *Led*, not *lead*, is the past tense and past participle of the verb *lead*. The confusion may arise because *lead*, the metal, is pronounced the same way as *led*, the past tense, and because both the past and the present tense of the verb *read* are spelled *read*.

He led a string of young children, playing his bejewelled trumpet.
Toronto Star 1 July 1992: A1

Silver ... had been around New York for almost four years, playing in bands lead by Stan Getz and Lester Young, among others....
Jack Chambers *Milestones* 1983: 182

(The correct spelling is *led*.)

leading question, loaded question A *leading question* is one phrased so that it contains its own answer, or strongly suggests a particular answer. In a court of law, a lawyer must not ask a leading question of his or her own witness because that would amount to coaching the witness. Such questions are permitted only in cross-examination of uncooperative witnesses.

A *loaded question* is one that is risky to answer because it is subtly incriminating, or emotionally charged, or highly controversial.

After a few days in court, I began to calm down and look at him as just another lawyer in the sense that he, too, had faults. One of them was that he showed a great penchant for asking leading questions of witnesses.
Jack Batten *Robinette* 1984: 217

'Can one really distinguish between the mass media as instruments of information and entertainment, and as agents of manipulation and indoctrination?'—Herbert Marcuse.... Marcuse's loaded question requires a loaded answer.
Globe and Mail (Toronto) 31 Aug. 1985: E1

lectern see DAIS

led see LEAD

leer, leery A *leer* is a lascivious or predatory look; to *leer* is to cast such a look. The original meaning of *leer*, derived from the Old English *hleor*, 'cheek', was a sidelong look; now even a direct stare is often referred to as a leer.

Leery means wary. To be *leery of* something is to be suspicious of it. In British English *leery* is slang, but in North America it is standard.

... he sidled up to you, his sharp, pinched face in an obsequious leer.... He never actually faced anyone....
Max Braithwaite *The Night We Stole the Mountie's Car* 1971: 64

(Here Braithwaite is using the original sense.)

... she has straddled him, as he still sits there on the bench. Her mouth hungrily searches his.... 'Excuse

me,' he says to the woman on top of him.... But the leering hag doesn't budge.
Canadian Fiction Magazine 63 (1988): 16–17

(This *leer* is definitely not sidelong.)

... he was willing to allow a certain amount of Jewish colonization there, but the British were leery of repercussions in the Arab world.
Canadian Journal of History 14.1 (1989): 139

left-handed compliment see BACKHANDED COMPLIMENT

legion, legionnaire, legionary, Legionnaires' disease, commissionaire *Legion* should be capitalized when it refers to a particular group: the Royal Canadian Legion, the American Legion, the Royal British Legion, etc. Members of these associations are called *legionnaires*. *Legionnaire* may also refer to a member of the French Foreign Legion, which consists of soldiers who are not French citizens. *Legionary* most commonly refers to soldiers in ancient Rome.

The name of the strain of pneumonia identified in 1976 at a convention of the American Legion is usually capitalized: *Legionnaires' disease*.

In Canada a *commissionaire* is a member of the Corps of Commissionaires, a group of retired servicemen employed as security guards. Note that *commissionaire* has only one *n*, while *legionnaire* has two.

... among educated urbanites the 'corny' country songs emanating from the lounges, Legion halls, and car radios of Canada are all too often associated with rural backwardness, social and political conservatism, or even worse, American mass culture.
Queen's Quarterly 95.2 (1988): 292

Legionnaire Alfred Bowden, 74, said members of Branch 24-106 don't dwell on their wartime experiences.
Gazette (Montreal) 3 June 1990: A3

Retrospective studies have demonstrated cases of Legionnaires' disease as far back as 1943, and 23 species of the bacteria have been found—only a few of which are dangerous to humans.
Vancouver Sun 2 June 1990: F6

Legionnaire's disease is caused by bacteria that often thrive in cool, standing water.
Province (Vancouver) 12 Jan. 1990: 28

(Dictionaries place the apostrophe after the *s*: *Legionnaires'*.)

Visitors to the building had to get a pass from the commissionaire's desk.
Daily News 31 Dec. 1994: n.p.

legislatures   see APPENDIX I

legitimate, legitimize, legitimatize   All three forms are accepted as verbs.

... regardless of legal determinations, politicians will read the section as legitimating unilingualist political drives.
Queen's Quarterly 94.4 (1987): 799

... the basis of psychoanalysis is materialistic; it strives after truth, disregarding 'authority' that is not legitimized by reason, rejecting mysticism and metaphysics.
Henry M. Rosenthal and S. Cathy Berson, eds. *Canadian Jewish Outlook Anthology* 1988: 127

We hope that when our wonderful work comes out, some of the confusion may be resolved; editors will feel less guilty about making their own choices; we will be able to legitimize our choices.
W.C. Lougheed *In Search of the Standard in Canadian English* 1986: 137

Argueta says the old code, even though accepted by the industry, really legitimatized censorship, and that the same thing could happen again.
Toronto Star 12 Feb. 1992: B3

leisure   Note the correct spelling: *-ei-*, not *-ie-*. Two-thirds of the Canadians surveyed in 1972 (*Modern Canadian English Usage*, 1974) reported that they pronounced *leisure* to rhyme with *seizure*—the usual American pronunciation. But 55 per cent of the Vancouverites surveyed in 1979–80 ('Survey of Vancouver English', 1984) pronounced *leisure* to rhyme with *pleasure*—the British pronunciation. Thus it's difficult to say which pronunciation is currently more common in Canada. Certainly either is standard, and many Canadians use both.

To serve the liesure class, and to travel from place to place, numerous boats were built....
Gazette (Montreal) 23 May 1992: J4

(The correct spelling is *leisure*.)

See also -IE-, -EI-.

lend   see LOAN

lengthy, long   Several usage guides, including *Fowler's* (1965), suggest that *lengthy* means overly long and implies tediousness, and should not be used as a simple synonym of *long*. This recommendation is at odds with Canadian usage, in which *lengthy* sometimes implies comprehensiveness or thoroughness.

By contrast, a secured creditor need not invoke the rather lengthy judicial machinery required to obtain an execution....
J.E. Smyth et al. *The Law and Business Administration in Canada* 1987: 735

(Here the words 'rather' and 'judicial machinery' suggest that the process is indeed tedious.)

Goetz took special care with this lengthy novel, wishing to make 'every sentence and every picture genuine.'
Canadian Journal of History 14.1 (1989): 75

(Here *lengthy* means long, but not tedious.)

Closed on an off-and-on basis since 1989 for a lengthy expansion and development project, the museum officially reopens this year....
Alan Tucker, ed. *The Penguin Guide to Canada* 1991: 278

(Here *lengthy* means long, but not necessarily tedious.)

lesbian   see GAY

less   see COMPLETE; FEWER; TIMES LESS

lessor, lessee, mortgagor, mortgagee   The *lessor*, the landlord, lets a house to the *lessee*, the occupant. The *mortgagor*, the impecunious housebuyer, mortgages (i.e., pledges) his or her house to a *mortgagee*, usually a bank or trust company. If the mortgagor fails to make loan payments, then the ownership of the house is transferred to the mortgagee. In short, the people who make the monthly payments are the lessee and the mortgagor.
Mortgager is an uncommon spelling variant of *mortgagor*.

This insurance protects the lender (mortgagee) rather than the borrower (mortgagor).
Globe and Mail (Toronto) 20 April 1985: H4

... sellers and lessors of computer products no longer would be able to place disclaimers on warranties limiting their responsibility for product performance.
Globe and Mail (Toronto) 16 Oct. 1985: B6

The relationship between Public Works, which is the largest lessor of office space in Ottawa, and Campeau, the largest renter of space, was questioned by Mr. St. Germain.... In his report, Mr. Dye charged that the government ended up signing a 10-year lease for $155-

million, $43 million more than Campeau was originally willing to take.
Globe and Mail (Toronto) 30 Jan. 1985: P5

(Here *lessor* is used incorrectly for *lessee*. Since Public Works is leasing space owned by Mr. Campeau, Public Works is the lessee.)

See also -ER, -OR.

lest The conjunction *lest* is fairly common in Canadian prose in spite of its oratorical ring. It means 'in order that . . . not' or 'for fear that'. *Lest* is followed by *should* or by a verb in the subjunctive mood. In the latter case, the verb following *lest* takes the form of the bare infinitive: 'Lest he perish (*not* perishes)'.
In British English *lest* is commonly followed by *should*: 'Lest he should perish'.

When you are a senior, your options are closed, your [financial] situation is fixed and you can only guard it carefully lest it erode further.
United Church Observer May 1986: 33

The writer in more popular pages has only to pity, and reject, and readers who have no firm opinions of their own will acquiesce, lest their own sophistication and modernity be called in question.
Robertson Davies A Voice from the Attic 1960: 33

See also SUBJUNCTIVE.

liable, likely, apt *Liable* meaning responsible, especially fiscally responsible, is followed by *for*: 'They were liable for damages'. *Liable* meaning vulnerable is followed by *to*: 'They were liable to increased infection after surgery'.
The traditional distinctions between *liable, likely,* and *apt* are that *liable* indicates exposure to the risk of something undesirable ('liable to be robbed'), *likely* indicates probability ('likely to come back'), and *apt* indicates a tendency, habit, or inclination ('apt to bolt'). Some commentators add that *liable* and *apt* should be applied only to people. On the whole, however, Canadian usage is not so discriminating. For those who would still like to observe some distinction, it may be useful to remember that *likely* is the most widely applicable and least controversial of these three words.

Children as young as seven years old were liable to imprisonment in a penitentiary with hardened criminals.
Vancouver Sun 10 Dec. 1990: A2

There is in Canada, too, a traditional opposition to the two defects to which a revolutionary tradition is liable, a contempt for history and an impatience with law.
Northrop Frye The Bush Garden 1971: 14

A hard-hitting piece of writing by a man is liable to be thought of as merely realistic; an equivalent piece by a woman is much more likely to be labelled 'cruel' or 'tough.'
Margaret Atwood Second Words 1982: 197

(Here Atwood uses *liable* and *likely* as synonyms.)

Organic pollutants like PCBs are stored in fatty tissue, so high-fat species like trout, salmon, arctic char, smelt and perch are likely to have higher levels of PCBs than are other species.
Canadian Consumer Jan. 1985: 8

When these folks aren't whining about their personal misfortunes, they're apt to be yapping on about the larger adversities around them.
Vancouver Sun 23 June 1990: D22

Out of the basic research is apt to emerge the next batch of miracle drugs or an industrial breakthrough.
Vancouver Sun 28 July 1990: B6

(Here some would substitute *likely*.)

Pneumonia is more apt to occur during the fall and spring months, he explains.
Country Guide Nov. 1986: H22

(Here some would substitute *likely*.)

liaison, liaise The word *liaison* has long referred to communications within the military and to secret sexual relations. Now it also commonly refers to the job of fostering connections between groups. Although this use has been criticized, it's well established.
The verb *liaise*—a back-formation from *liaison*—still raises the hackles of many usage commentators. It is rare in formal Canadian writing, but common in journalism.
The most common pronunciations of *liaison* are *lee AY zun* and *LEE ay ZON*. Occasionally these words are misspelled without the second *i*.

. . . I spent a year at the Imperial Defence College in London before taking up my new duties as chief of the defence liaison division in the Department of External Affairs.
George Ignatieff The Making of a Peacemonger 1987: 120–1

. . . the nameless narrator relates his liaison with the former mistress of a pro-revolutionary colleague. . . .

Ben-Z. Shek *French-Canadian & Québécois Novels* 1991: 50

... the committee decided not to make a decision on forming a minority liaison committee until it has heard from its new community liason officer.
Daily News (Halifax) 26 Jan. 1993

(Here *liaison* is spelled first correctly and then incorrectly.)

When selecting workers, both for immigration and for work permits, visa officers liaise with the department of employment, which provides them with updated lists of occupations in Canada for which there is more demand than supply.
Vancouver Sun 7 Aug. 1990: A9

See also BACK-FORMATION.

Liberal   see GRIT

liberal arts   see ARTS

libertine, libertarian   Today a *libertine* is a sexually licentious person, usually a man. Historically, however, a *libertine* was a freedman, a man released from slavery in ancient Rome. A *libertarian* is either a believer in free will or a proponent of civil liberties such as freedom of the press, or the right to vote and assemble. Libertarians in this sense are often wary of government—in particular, of what they see as its encroachment on the privacy, freedom of belief, or right to expression of the individual, in the name of the public good.

In the President's resentful mind Trudeau possessed the cardinal sins of intellectual arrogance, a libertine lifestyle, and a liberal inclination that bred softness on defence and in relations with the East.
Queen's Quarterly 92.1 (1985): 115

[He] poses as a sexual libertine, but with his double standards and outdated attitudes he is simply old-fashioned.
Maclean's 24 Feb. 1986: O4

Thus, although ideological evolution in Quebec is generally seen as positive ... there is also the emergence of a Left, which, in the narrator's view, began by being libertarian then became authoritarian.
Ben-Z. Shek *French-Canadian & Québécois Novels* 1991: 94

Despite the libertarian and anti-etatist [anti-state] principles of much nineteenth-century statecraft, bourgeois society created the modern interventionist state....
Queen's Quarterly 94.4 (1987): 976

library   Both *r*'s in *library* should be pronounced; *LIE berry* is considered uneducated.

See also FEBRUARY.

licensed premises   see BEER PARLOUR

lichen   *Lichen*, the plant, and *liken*, the verb, are pronounced the same way. In British English *lichen* may also be pronounced to rhyme with *kitchen*.

lie, equivocate, waffle, prevaricate, misspeak oneself   *Lie* is the bluntest and most negative of these verbs. *Equivocate, waffle,* and *prevaricate* are less harsh because they admit a grey area between truth and untruth, though people who are not inclined to accept grey areas would call these words euphemisms. *Equivocate* has two meanings. The first is to use ambiguity to create the wrong impression; the second is to speak in such a vague or contradictory way that one cannot be held to account. *Waffle* is the slang word for this practice. *Prevaricate* means to speak or act evasively; it suggests either weakness or immorality. To *misspeak oneself* is to lie accidentally by saying the wrong thing without noticing; the expression was used as early as 1894 in the United States.

Sales staff who will do anything to make a sale—who will blatantly lie or mislead a customer—are not an asset to their employers.
Globe and Mail (Toronto) 8 Jan. 1985: F9

Five per cent of five hundred million dollars ... was enough to make any witness equivocate on his testimony.
Jack Batten *Robinette* 1984: 148

While such questions were at the centre of attention in Latvia, Lithuania and Estonia, most of Georgia's radical leaders waffle on the big questions.
Ottawa Citizen 13 Oct. 1990: B4

If William Vander Zalm is shown to be a clownish prevaricator (that's liar in English), then who wants to support the development of a strong provincial government?
Vancouver Sun 16 May 1991: A17

There is no margin of error, no time for reflection and certainly no possibility of pulling a Ronald Reagan and declaring afterwards you misspoke yourself.
Ottawa Citizen 1 Sept. 1990: B5

See also AMBIGUOUS, AMBIVALENT, EQUIVOCAL.

lie, lay *Lie* and *lay* cause trouble because their principal forms overlap.

	past tense	past participle
lie (make false statements)	lied	(has) lied
lie (recline)	lay	(has) lain
lay (place, set down)	laid	(has) laid

In casual speech and in some dialects the forms of *lay* are often used where standard speech and writing require *lie*.

In Standard English *lay* requires an object. You have to lay *something*: 'Lay your coat over the end of the bed'; 'I laid the table'; 'She laid great emphasis on training'; 'The media has laid seige to her house for days'. The only exception to this rule is that hens can be said simply to lay. (Presumably no object is needed because it is widely known *what* they lay.)

Lie never takes an object: 'She lies in bed for hours'; 'Since his accident, he can neither sit nor lie'; 'The fault lies with the manufacturer'; 'When she was here, she lay on the rug to watch television'; 'He had lain down to sleep, when he remembered the stove was still on'.

accepted form	non-standard or dialectal form
Let it lie.	Let it lay.
I went in to lie down.	I went in to lay down.
He lies around all day.	He lays around all day.
I lay on the couch yesterday.	I laid on the couch yesterday.

Some speakers have become so wary of using *lay* where *lie* is called for that they do just the opposite, inappropriately substituting *lie* for *lay*: 'Lie the folder on the desk'; 'Tell me where you have lain the keys'. This error is known as hypercorrection. The accepted versions are 'Lay the folder on my desk' and 'Tell me where you have laid the keys'.

See also HYPERCORRECTION.

lieutenant Canadians are more likely to pronounce the first syllable of this word *loo-* than *lef-*. (*Modern Canadian English Usage*, 1974; 'Survey of Vancouver English', 1984). Americans use only the former pronunciation, and the British use only the latter. Some Canadians feel that only *lef TEN ant* is acceptable. The 1979 'Socio-dialectology Survey' of English spoken in the Ottawa region revealed that, in general, the frequency of the *lef-* pronunciation rose with the speaker's socio-economic status; however, there was a strong shift towards *loo-* in younger speakers from all socio-economic groups.

lieutenant-governor see HEAD OF STATE; LIEUTENANT

ligature see DIPHTHONG

light, lighted, lit The forms *lighted* and *lit* can both serve as either the past tense or the past participle of the verb *light*. Either form may also be used before a noun.

He lighted a cigarette and grinned at Harley.
Canadian Fiction Magazine 64 (1988): 61

We lit fires in what is now Sunnybrook Park, roasted hot dogs, and boiled cans of water for our tea.
Miriam Waddington *Apartment Seven* 1989: 29

Changes in lighting at the airstrip will enable a medical helicopter to land there at night instead of at a lighted playing field in town.
Vancouver Sun 27 July 1990: B7

The toothbrush foamed whitely at the front of my mouth while a lit cigarette hung from the left corner of my lips, curling yellow smoke through my teeth.
Province (Vancouver) 27 Dec. 1990: 14

See also ALIGHT, ALIT.

lightning, lightening *Lightning* is accompanied by thunder. A *lightening* is a lessening of darkness or weight. *Lightning* is often misspelled *lightening*.

Occasionally a blink of lightning cut the darkness.
Constance Beresford-Howe *Night Studies* 1985: 137

His face changed, lightening unmistakably with enthusiasm.
Robertson Davies *One Half of Robertson Davies* 1978: 108

Chatham is a very small town and word travels at lightening speed on the street.
Globe and Mail (Toronto) 12 June 1985: P7

(The correct spelling is *lightning*.)

light-year In scientific usage a light-year is a measurement of distance, not time. It is the distance that light travels in one earth year in the vacuum of space (about 9,460,500,000,000 km). *Light-year* is often used figuratively to refer to cultural or social distance. In scientific contexts the common use of *light-year* to refer to a very great length of time should be avoided.

The nearest star, Alpha Centauri, is 4.3 light-years away, or about 25 trillion miles.
Terence Dickinson *Halley's Comet* 1985: 43

(In this example *light-years* is a measure of distance.)

This bastion of Montreal's English-speaking establishment was light-years removed from the home life I led with my mother and my brother Leonid.
George Ignatieff *The Making of a Peacemonger* 1987: 42

(Here *light-years* is used figuratively to refer to cultural difference.)

The worksheet is from a home economics course taught at John Oliver in 1960. That's 1960s, as in 34 light years ago.
Vancouver Sun 11 May 1994: A13

(Here *light-years* refers to the enormous cultural distance between the 1960s and the 1990s.)

like, as *Like* preceding a noun, noun phrase, or pronoun is accepted: 'He laughs like a hyena'; 'Karen looks like her father when he was a baby'; 'We can't all write like him'. In these examples, *like* is being used as a preposition.

However, many usage guides strongly object when *like* is used as a conjunction. Subordinate conjunctions, such as *because*, *since*, and *although*, precede more than just a noun or noun equivalent: they precede a clause with a *verb* in it ('because I *know* him'; 'since they *came*'; 'although she *dances* well'). Objections are raised when *like* is used as a subordinate conjunction meaning *as* ('Are you going to treat me like you treated him?'), *as if* ('It looks like he's in trouble again'), *(in) the way (that)* ('Put your hands on your hips like she does'), or *such as* ('She was wearing a hat like you used to see on matrons at lunch'). In each of these examples, *like* should be replaced by the italicized phrase preceding the parentheses. The problem with this hard distinction between preposition and conjunction is that several words can be either: *after*, for example, can be a preposition ('He went out after the dog') or a subordinate conjunction ('She went out after Harry started to tell jokes'). The *OED* lists citations for *like* as a conjunction from the 1500s on, and this usage appears to be increasing.

That said, it is true that most of the examples we have found of *like* used as a conjunction come from quoted speech, fiction, or fairly informal prose. Thus it makes sense to avoid this construction in more formal writing.

'I tell Peggy that she's like a rock star in Canada.'
Chatelaine June 1986: 100

Nothing promotes an appreciation of peace like losing.
Saturday Night March 1986: 5

The arts in Canada are not flourishing as they should be.
Saturday Night March 1986: 8

'At first it looked like I was going to win by acclamation....'
Saturday Night March 1986: 30

(Here *like* is used as a conjunction in speech; in writing it should be replaced with *as if* and *was* should be changed to *were*.)

What if we waited a year like we promised and they still didn't want us to marry, then what?
Chatelaine April 1986: 153

(In a more formal context, this *like* should be replaced with *as*.)

They are thick and wet, not drawn and white like they used to be.
David Williams *Eye of the Father* 1985: 177

(In non-fiction, an editor would probably change this *like* to *the way*.)

See also LIKE, SUCH AS.

like, such as According to some conservative editors, the word *like* should be reserved for resemblance: 'Sally, like Mary Meigs, took up writing late in life'. In their view, an actual example of something should be introduced by *such as*, and never by *like*: 'Antibiotics, such as penicillin and tetracycline, are ineffective against a cold'. Many writers try to observe this rule, especially in formal writing, but many others, including some language commentators, reject it as niggling.

Since language commentators can so rarely resist a nice distinction, their balking at this one bears closer attention. What seems to make the difference is that this rule does not take into account the idiomatic use of *like* to introduce an actual example intended to suggest a type, not merely to illustrate one: 'I'm so glad to have a friend like Paul'. The speaker is happy not just to have a friend resembling Paul but to have Paul as a friend: Paul is an example defining a type. *Such as* would not be idiomatic in this context. Even in formal writing, *like* is preferable to introduce examples that suggest rather than merely illustrate a category.

Privacy, like individualism, is a historical product; it emerges only when there is a public domain, that is, in relation to the state.
Queen's Quarterly 96.2 (1989): 303

(Here *like* indicates resemblance.)

The primary focus of Edelson's book is on the attacks made in the last decade and a half by philosophers of science such as Ernest Nagel, Karl Popper and Adolf Grünbaum.
Queen's Quarterly 92.2 (1985): 416

One way of getting around this problem is by comparing units of analysis smaller than countries, such as provinces or states.
Canadian Journal of Sociology 14.2 (1989): 167–8

Movement heroes like Noam Chomsky and Norman Mailer also praised Orwell.
Canadian Journal of History 14.1 (1989): 8

(Some conservative editors would substitute *such as* for *like* here.)

Certainly it is unwise to start with something like *The Unnamable*.
Queen's Quarterly 94.2 (1987): 294

('*The Unnamable*' is an example that defines a category; *like* is idiomatic.)

But why use terms like 'racial origin' at all when they are so inexact?
Richard Davies and Glen Kirkland, eds. *Dimensions* 1986: 123

('Racial origin' is an example that suggests a category; *like* is idiomatic.)

And, since the world that Wallace draws from is woman-centred, her poems have a female perspective—in strong contrast to the male-centred viewpoint of a Purdy poem like 'At the Quinte Hotel' or even of a Lee poem like 'The Death of Harold Ladoo'.
Queen's Quarterly 98.1 (1991): 59

(The poems mentioned suggest types; *like* is idiomatic.)

The theory enables us to do things such as fly around the world in a heavy bulk of metal.
Queen's Quarterly 97.4 (1990): 622

(Here *like* would be preferable because the example suggests a category.)

See also LIKE, AS.

like for, want for, say for *Like for* ('We'd like for you to come') is heard in the speech of the Ottawa Valley and the American South. The usage is considered dialectal. *Want for* ('He wants for us to stay

in school') is rare in writing and considered non-standard. Standard Canadian English omits the *for* in both instances.

British commentators also object to *say for* meaning tell ('She said for me to wait'). Although this construction may not appear in formal Canadian writing, it is certainly unobjectionable in speech.

> Just once I'd like for a game to stop. For a referee to say, 'Take your time, Ken. Ready when you are,' and with everyone fading to the side, to look up at the crowd....
> Ken Dryden *The Game* 1983: 199

likely see LIABLE.

like(s) of *The likes of* is most often used either to praise or to disparage. Usually it precedes a famous name or a list of famous names, but it can also be used slightingly: 'I wouldn't be caught dead with the likes of him'. Some commentators have taken a distinct dislike to this expression, calling it non-literary and even non-standard. However, the phrase has been Standard English for over 200 years and is used in all kinds of Canadian writing. *The like of* is a rare variant. Some commentators suggest that it is preferable to *likes* before a single name, but writers do not make this distinction.

> Overall it was judged the eighth best city—ahead of any other Canadian city and up there with the likes of Florence, Paris, and San Francisco.
> *Beautiful British Columbia* Spring 1990: 6

> I yearned for a place at the round table in the Algonquin..., parrying witticisms with the likes of Robert Benchley, James Thurber, Harold Ross, Franklin Pierce Adams and the rest.
> Max Braithwaite *The Night We Stole the Mountie's Car* 1971: 11

> Not only did he consider himself ... several notches above the likes of me; he also made it clear that he found my remarks offensive and inappropriate.
> George Ignatieff *The Making of a Peacemonger* 1987: 172

Lillooet, Stl'atl'imx The Aboriginal people formerly called *Lillooet* now prefer to be known by different names, depending on the location of their traditional territories. Those whose traditional lands are around Lillooet, British Columbia, are the *Stl'atl'imx* (*STLA tlimh*); their language is *Stl'atl'imxec* (*STLA tlim hutch*). Those whose traditional lands are around Mount Currie, B.C., are the *Lil'wat* (*LILL wat*).

Mr. Wolfman is a descendant of the B.C. Lillooet band and has been selected as one of the six chefs to represent Canada at the 1992 World Culinary Olympics. . . .
Ottawa Citizen 7 Oct. 1992: F2

Williams, 43, is a non-status Stl'atl'imx Indian raised in Lillooet and knows a thing or two about rednecks.
Daily News (Halifax) 12 July 1992: 15

He has been working full-time with the Stl'atl'imx Nation Tribal Police since January.
Vancouver Sun 18 Nov. 1994: A2

. . . land claims have been made on the Stein by the Nlaka'pamux (Lytton) and the Lil'wat (Mt. Currie) peoples.
Vancouver Sun 15 July 1994: B4

limit, delimit   To *limit* something is to allow it go to a certain point and no further. To *delimit* something is not to hold it within bounds, but to define or determine its bounds. When something is delimited by an inanimate object, that inanimate object forms its natural boundary: 'The northern boundary is delimited by a creek'.

The Elmwood expects to limit its membership to 1,500 members.
Bon Vivant 1981: 18

The thrust of these works . . . is not to delimit the borders of the novel but rather to break down established boundaries [between the novel, biography, travel writing, etc.].
Queen's Quarterly Spring 1985: 198

limpid   see TURGID

lingua franca   The phrase *lingua franca* is Italian for 'Frankish tongue'. In the seventeenth century it referred to the working language of eastern Mediterranean sea ports, a hybrid of Italian, French, Spanish, Greek, Arabic, and Turkish. Now a *lingua franca* (plural *lingua francas*) is any common or hybrid language used by people who do not share a native tongue. For example, Spanish is the lingua franca of diverse Indian peoples of Central America and English is a lingua franca in India. Metaphorically, anything that allows people of different backgrounds to understand each other is a lingua franca. A lingua franca may be a fully developed language (e.g., Latin in the Middle Ages) or a pidgin (e.g., Nigerian Pidgin in the multilingual Nigeria).

'Between the last vestiges of empire remaining to England and the global domination of America,' Urdang told his audience, 'the English language has become established as the lingua franca.'
Gazette (Montreal) 19 May 1990: K2

It was developed back in the '70s by a publishing industry group as a lingua franca for data base operators and typesetters.
Business Journal June 1991: 18

'Violence is a lingua franca (in prisons). I'm just surprised there isn't more of it,' said Mr. Graham, an 11-year veteran of the correctional service.
Globe and Mail (Toronto) 30 March 1985: M5

'Even white wine has fallen into disuse; the lingua franca of the lunch set is iced tea with Sweet'n Low.'
Globe and Mail (Toronto) 25 Oct. 1985: D4

(This is a dubious use of *lingua franca*, since the communicative power of tea is limited.)

See also PIDGIN, CREOLE.

lion's share   The expression *lion's share* comes from Aesop's fable in which a lion and several smaller animals go hunting. The lion first divides the kill and then claims everything for himself. Some commentators argue that the *lion's share* of something should mean all of it, because the lion in the fable took all of the kill. However, in English usage the *lion's share* means the largest portion, and this meaning is widely accepted.

Almost all of the $60,000 donated has been spent so far. The lion's share—including $40,000 in postage—has been used to produce and distribute the more than one million posters in circulation.
Maclean's 23 Sept. 1991: A14

The lion's share, more than 95 per cent, leaves the country, and the chief beneficiaries are the Hollywood majors.
Vancouver Sun 27 Nov. 1990: B11

liquid   see FLUID

lit   see LIGHT

litany   A *litany* is a type of prayer in which the officiant recites or chants verses, and the congregation chants formulaic responses. *Litany* is also used figuratively to refer to any repetitive, monotonous recital or account. Some people, however, use *litany* simply to indicate a large number. This extended use is not recommended.

Plamondon recited a litany of historical 'humiliations' endured by Quebecers and speculated that a new party could be formed to work for sovereignty-association.
Vancouver Sun 26 June 1990: A1

Irving also seems to know his CanLit: at one point, Wheelwright offers a litany of praise for Canadian authors ... that reads more like a book list than a scene from a novel.
Maclean's 3 April 1989: A63

Among the litany of great songs to follow ... were several from the band's latest album, Word of Mouth.
Globe and Mail (Toronto) 21 March 1985: E4

(This writer probably did not mean to imply that the songs were boring; 'the *host* of', or simply 'the *many*', would be better here.)

It presented a 'grim litany on the growing problem of Jewish unemployment and the plight of the Jewish poor.'
Henry M. Rosenthal and S. Cathy Berson, eds. *Canadian Jewish Outlook Anthology* 1988: 311

(The meaning of *litany* in this context is unclear; the author may have meant *commentary*.)

literally, figuratively

Literally is derived from the Latin word for 'letter'. To use words literally means to use them without metaphorical or allegorical intent, adhering strictly to the 'letter'. In different contexts, 'That car is hot' can mean (literally) that the engine has overheated or the passenger area is hot, or (figuratively) that it is either stolen or trendy.

Often, however, *literally* is used loosely to mean 'almost' or 'virtually', as in 'We were literally climbing the walls'. The speaker of this sentence would not expect to be asked how they did it. In fact, *literally* here overlaps in meaning with its opposite, *figuratively*. Although this extended use of *literally* is common in speech, it is criticized and should be avoided in writing.

The ground staff at O'Hare Airport pulled out all the stops—literally stopping Flight 831 after it left the terminal to get the surgeon aboard for the flight to Winnipeg.
Vancouver Sun 29 June 1994: B1

This type of mousse ... not only keeps stray strands in place, but can also keep hair literally standing on end.
Globe and Mail (Toronto) 22 Jan. 1985: F8

(Here, because 'to have one's hair standing on end' is usually a figurative expression denoting terror, the writer has used *literally* to qualify it.)

That situation ... assured that the Athenian political stew would be boiling over—literally.
Globe and Mail (Toronto) 29 May 1985: P1

(Here *literally* should be omitted.)

Just 15 years earlier he had been, literally, king of the jazz world.
Globe and Mail (Toronto) 11 May 1985: E8

(Here *unquestionably* would be a better choice.)

See also VERITABLE.

literary present   see PRESENT TENSE

loaded question   see LEADING QUESTION

loan, lend

In spoken English and in financial circles, *loan* is often used as a verb: 'Loan me your coat'; 'They loaned her 4 million dollars'. In fact, *loan* has been used as a verb since at least the sixteenth century. However, it fell out of use in England after the seventeenth century, and although it has continued to be used as a verb in North America, many North American commentators disapprove of the usage. The more common verb, especially in writing, is *lend* (past tense *lent*): 'I lent her my coat last night'. To avoid criticism it's best to use *loan* only as a noun ('The picture is on loan') in general formal writing.

They undertook to ... to lend it $75,000 at 6 per cent for nine years, and to make a second loan of the balance for fourteen years with no interest for the first nine.
Frederick Gibson *Queen's University* 2 (1983): 65

The board loaned him $1-million (U.S.), at three per cent interest, to purchase a house.
Saturday Night July 1986: 42

(In the context of banking, the verb *loan* is not disputed.)

... I remembered the camera somebody had loaned me for the trip, which I hadn't even used once.
Canadian Fiction Magazine 63 (1988): 51

(Some commentators strongly prefer *lent*.)

loath, loth, loathe, loathsome

The adjective meaning reluctant is usually spelled *loath*; the older form, *loth*, is becoming obsolete. Both spellings are pronounced to rhyme with *both*.

The verb *loathe*, which means to detest, always has a final *e*. The adjective *loathsome* (sometimes misspelled *loathesome*) means repulsive. The *th* sound in these two words is like that in *breathe*.

As the fate of the Meech accord continues to hang precariously, most of the key players in the original negotiations are more loath than ever to talk on the record about their historic closed-door sessions back in 1987.
Gazette (Montreal) 14 April 1990: B1

We are probably loathe to interfere with a system [the justice system] that has such tradition behind it.
Ottawa Citizen 9 Dec. 1990: A10

(The correct spelling here is *loath*.)

Those who like the new car like it a lot; those who hate it loathe it—there's no middle ground.
Ottawa Citizen 28 July 1990: A25

This night he tells a story about Beowulf; how the Saxon lord crosses the sea to Denmark to rid the Danes of Grendel, a loathsome monster.
Vancouver Sun 23 July 1990: B4

Greg Kramer's Petruchio is a fairly loathesome, swaggering brute, a bellowing presence with an ugly demeanor and an underlying sickliness.
Ottawa Citizen 16 July 1994: F5

(The correct spelling is *loathsome*.)

lode, lodestar, lodestone A *lode* is a vein of metal ore. A *lodestar* is a star, such as the North Star, that shows the way; *lodestar* is used figuratively to mean a guiding principle or leading light. *Lodestone* is a naturally magnetic rock; the word is used figuratively to mean a strongly attractive person or thing.

The bite of the gold bug drove me on. Even after the Chilcoot Pass in '98, my one burning dream was to find the mother lode in the lost mine of the Sierra.
Atlantic Salmon Journal Autumn 1990: 27

The last significant group of artists nurtured in Sugar Hill were the young jazz musicians who emerged in the wake of the bebop revolution, and among them Sonny Rollins was the lodestar.
Jack Chambers *Milestones* 1983: 123

Besides there's a wee stumbling block; I get lost. A lot. Without the conveniently named North Shore mountains as my lodestar, I'd never get home.
Province (Vancouver) 4 March 1990: 85

... already she's contemplating a further trip back to Newfoundland. It has become her lodestone, her private magnet.
Gazette (Montreal) 6 June 1994: C3

Conflict of interest is not a strong suit in the Vander Zalm understanding of life. Because of the public impression that he was using his office to enhance the worth of what became known as Schlock City, the theme park became the lodestone for demonstrators.
Financial Post 11 Sept. 1990: 13

-log, -logue see ANALOG; CATALOGUE; DIALOGUE

long see LENGTHY

long-sighted see NEAR-SIGHTED

lookout, overlook Canadians use *lookout* as a noun meaning a place that affords a good view of a scene below. Americans use *overlook* as a noun for this sense.

... [we] hiked to a lookout atop Flapper Hill to watch the morning sun brighten forested islands, strewn like stepping stones across the bay.
Globe and Mail (Toronto) 4 May 1985: T11

You're a hop and a skip, then, to the top of the dam. There are scenic overlooks worth stopping at en route.
Globe and Mail (Toronto) 2 Feb. 1985: T20

(This example comes from an article about Nevada written by an American.)

loonie, toonie The informal, popular name for what the Canadian Mint calls the one-dollar coin is the *loonie* (plural *loonies*). The two-dollar coin has been dubbed, by analogy, the *toonie* (plural *toonies*). The loonie was introduced in 1987, the toonie in 1996. The spelling of both words, now stabilized, varied for a while: *looney, loony, twonie,* and *twoonie* were all briefly tried but rejected.

In financial news, *loonie* is sometimes used as a synonym for *Canadian dollar*.

Interestingly, the loonie would have had a different name if the original design, depicting a voyageur, had not been lost, forcing the substitution of the second-choice design, a loon.

[He] will be hanging around outside the Vancouver Art Gallery this weekend, crooning for loonies and gyrating for passers-by.
Vancouver Sun 25 Aug. 1994: D1

The loonie has been drifting lower for some time, setting eight-year lows this week. However, it is still above the all-time low of 69.20 cents US....
Calgary Herald 30 Dec. 1994: C7

lose, loose *Lose* (misplace) is sometimes misspelled *loose* (not tight)—perhaps because *lose* rhymes with *choose*. This mistake is rare in published writing.

See also CHOOSE, CHOSE.

lot, lots   see A LOT

loth   see LOATH

lounge chair   see CHAISE LONGUE

Loyalist   see CONSERVATIVE

luck into, luck in, luck out   To *luck into* something is to have the good luck to encounter or acquire it. To *luck in*, as in 'I really lucked in when I met Martha', means to get lucky. To *luck out* is to be lucky. These two expressions mean almost the same thing, but many people think *luck out* means just the opposite. There is, in fact, some evidence that during the Second World War *luck out* meant run out of luck, but in the 1950s the positive meaning became established. *Luck into*, *luck in*, and *luck out* are all informal.

It was 10 years ago that McCaffrey basically lucked into the sport.
Calgary Herald 27 June 1992: C4

There's a quiche featured most days, and I hope they're all as successful as the broccoli one I lucked into.
Ottawa Citizen 29 Oct. 1992: H5

Dillon lucked out: he got the role of Tyler, one of the Denim Blues nice guys.
Ottawa Citizen 17 June 1992: C9

Harry and Muriel O'Reilly lucked out. They had proof that their grandchildren really belonged to them when they faced a Canada Customs officer at the Canada-U.S. border....
Vancouver Sun 26 May 1992: A3

'We've lucked out the last couple of years, losing to both John Base in Medicine Hat and Al Edwards from the U.S. in Cornwall.'
Globe and Mail (Toronto) 14 March 1985: M9

(Here *luck out* refers to bad luck.)

lumber   see TIMBER

luminous   see TRANSPARENT

lunch, luncheon   see DINNER

luxuriant, luxurious   *Luxuriant* means lush, prolific, or fertile; it usually refers to vegetation, or to a head of hair or a beard. *Luxurious* means extremely comfortable, even opulent, and often has connotations of self-indulgence.

In Brazil's portion of the luxuriant Amazon River basin alone, at least 20 per cent of the region's rain forest—covering 9.8 million acres—has already disappeared as settlers clear land for agriculture and cattle-grazing.
Maclean's 5 Sept. 1988: A38

Many a weak chin was concealed behind a luxuriant growth of hair.
Gazette (Montreal) 26 Aug. 1990: D3

As you enter the luxurious lobby try to determine which are the new pillars and which are the restored 85-year-old originals.
Alan Tucker, ed. *The Penguin Guide to Canada* 1991: 344

For those aching to play the elegant sophisticate with traces of Grace Kelly minimalism, there is a luxuriant balmacaan-style coat in cashmere.
Globe and Mail (Toronto) 27 Aug. 1985: F3

(Balmacaan coats are usually made of tweed, which is not really hairy enough to be described as *luxuriant*; perhaps *luxurious* was intended.)

The vignettes in The Wall Street Journal Book of Chief Executive Style show vividly that the combination of luxuriant lifestyle and the distance most CEOs keep from subordinates has created a new class in North American society.
Financial Post 18 Dec. 1989: 12

(Lifestyles are *luxurious*.)

M

ma'am, madam, madame *Ma'am* is an oral form that is written down only in representations of speech. *Ma'am* and *madam* are sometimes used by sales clerks, restaurant staff, and people on the street to address women they don't know by name. This usage now strikes some women as overly deferential. *Ma'am* remains an appropriate way to address the Queen in speech.

A letter to a woman whose name is not known may begin 'Dear Madam'. *Madam* is also used as a formal title, preceding the name of a woman's rank or office: 'Madam Prime Minister', 'Madam Chair', 'Madam Justice'. A *madam* (plural *madams*) is the keeper of a brothel.

Madame, abbreviated *Mme*, without a period (plural *Mesdames*, abbreviated *Mmes*), is French for *Mrs.* or *Ms.*: in French all adult females are addressed as *Madame*, regardless of their marital status. *Madame* is sometimes used by English-speakers to refer to the wives of foreign dignitaries: 'Madame Chiang-kai-shek'. Professional women in the performing arts sometimes take the title *Madame* as well.

See also MISS, MR., MRS.; MS.

macabre, macaber Some American dictionaries list *macaber* as an alternative spelling, but Canadian writers prefer the older spelling, *macabre*. The *-er* spelling probably developed to match the pronunciation used by English-speakers unaccustomed to French: *ma CAW ber*. The more common pronunciations are closer to the original French: *ma CAW bruh* and *ma CAWB*.

See also -RE, -ER.

Machiavellian Niccolò Machiavelli (1469–1527) was an Italian statesman and political theorist whose name has become synonymous with unscrupulous political manipulation. His best-known work, *Il Principe* (*The Prince*), is remembered for the assertion that, although a ruler is morally obligated to his subjects, all means and actions are justified in order to maintain power.

The *ch* is pronounced as if it were *k* and the main stress is on *vell*. Most writers and dictionaries capitalize the adjective: *Machiavellian*.

> Macdonald—previously relatively unknown to the British public—became infamous now as a Machiavellian, cunning politician conniving for profit and prejudice with slavers and manstealers.
> William Teatero *John Anderson: Fugitive Slave* 1986: 114

> What makes the difference is luck … because no organization, however sophisticated or Machiavellian, can fully anticipate or manipulate the public agenda….
> A. Paul Pross *Group Politics and Public Policy* 2nd ed. 1992: 102

macho, machismo Borrowed from Spanish in the 1960s, these words commonly describe an exaggerated, aggressive brand of masculinity; both are generally used disapprovingly. The adjective *macho* is also sometimes used as a noun (plural *machos*) meaning a macho man.

Macho is pronounced *MAH cho*. In Spanish the noun *machismo* is pronounced with the *ch* of *church* and the *i* is sounded as a long *e*: *mah CHEEZ mo*. Some dictionaries give only this pronunciation, but the anglicized pronunciation, with the *ch* sounded as in *mechanic* and followed by a short *i* sound, is also accepted: *mah KIZ mo*.

> Asked what they would change about men, women said men should express their feelings more, be more understanding of women's needs, be more sensitive and less macho.
> *Vancouver Sun* 30 Oct. 1990: B6

> He's also extremely macho, drinks too much scotch, inadvertently says cruel things to people, has a warped sense of humor and generally leads a meaningless life.
> *Vancouver Sun* 17 Nov. 1990: D18

> Machos with reform on their minds can do well by following the example of broadcaster Jim Robson, who

has maintained a sunny attitude despite two decades of watching hockey's hapless Canuckleheads.
Province (Vancouver) 11 March 1990: 75

The Calgary Police Department, which has the most restrictive chase policies in Canada, has regulations aimed at attacking the traditional machismo of such pursuits.
Globe and Mail (Toronto) 3 Jan. 1985: P1

mad, madding In conversation and informal writing *mad* means angry, while in formal and literary contexts it means insane.

Madding is an uncommon word meaning frenzied. 'The madding crowd' is an allusion to Thomas Gray's poem *Elegy Written in a Country Churchyard* (1751) and Thomas Hardy's novel *Far from the Madding Crowd* (1874). Now writers often use *madding* as a synonym for *maddening*, or even substitute *maddening* for it in the phrase 'the madding crowd'.

'I hope you're not mad at me for going through your wallet?'
Howard Engel *Murder Sees the Light* 1984: 181

... nobody could visit the patients in these places except the persons who had committed them; thus, once in a country asylum, a man or woman was lost to the world, and those who were not mad already quickly became so.
Robertson Davies *A Voice from the Attic* 1960: 118

'I'm downtown, but because I'm on Rene Levesque [a street in Montreal], I'm not in the middle of the madding crowd.'
Gazette (Montreal) 16 June 1994: D3

In expressing the pain of gay-bashing they experience, Cadell sings poetically about 'what a lovely day on the beach it will be' when the maddening crowd 'swooshes out to sea, leaving all of the different ones, shining and free.'
Toronto Star 11 Sept. 1993: F14

Madam, Madame   see MA'AM

Magdalen(e), magdalen(e), maudlin   *Magdalene* and *Magdalen* are variant spellings. The name of the former prostitute in the New Testament is usually spelled Mary *Magdalene*. The *Magdalen* Islands are a group of twelve islands in the Gulf of St. Lawrence. A *magdalen(e)* is a reformed prostitute or a shelter or reformatory for prostitutes. *Magdalen(e)* is pronounced *MAG da leen* or *MAG da lin*.

The names of *Magdalen* College at Oxford and *Magdalene* College at Cambridge are pronounced *MOD lin*, preserving a former British pronunciation of *Magdalene*. The adjective *maudlin* (*MOD lin*) means overly emotional or tearfully sentimental (Mary Magdalene is usually shown weeping dramatically in paintings of the Crucifixion).

Luke tells us that Jesus was accompanied on an extensive preaching tour by 'the 12' and by many women, including Mary Magdalene, Joanna and Susanna, 'who provided for them out of their means.'
United Church Observer June 1986: 16

Swimming, bicycling, wind-surfing, seafood, and scenery draw thousands of visitors to the *Magdalen Islands* each year.
Alan Tucker, ed. *The Penguin Guide to Canada* 1991: 118

He remembers with great pride hearing Oxford University's Magdalene College Chapel Choir sing one of his compositions. . . .
Performing Arts in Canada Spring 1990: 32

(The Oxford college is spelled *Magdalen*.)

Magna Carta, Magna Charta   *Magna Carta*, the 'Great Charter', was signed by King John at the demand of the English barons at Runnymede on 15 June 1215. It guaranteed personal and political liberties and limited the power of the monarch. The term is now also used figuratively to refer to any constitution or document that guarantees civil and political rights. Canadians prefer the spelling *Magna Carta* to the alternative *Magna Charta* for both literal and figurative uses.

Magna Carta does not take the definite article *the* when it refers to the historical document.

It took me ... from reading Magna Carta in the British Museum Library to a Headless Valley soccer match between weary firefighters. . . .
Vancouver Sun 14 Feb. 1990: A11

... the Act itself may be regarded as the Magna Carta of a large number of Her Majesty's subjects in Upper Canada.
William Teatero *John Anderson: Fugitive Slave* 1986: 37

maiden name, birth name, former name, née, né   *Maiden name* refers to the original surname of a woman who takes her husband's name at marriage. Non-sexist usage guides recommend *birth name* or *former name* as gender-neutral alternatives. These terms are broader than *maiden name*, since they can refer to anyone's original or previous name; names are also changed for professional reasons (taking a pen name or stage name) or on adoption or ennoblement.

Né and *née*, the masculine and feminine adjectives meaning 'born' in French, are also used to indicate a person's birth name. *Né*, the masculine form, is rare. Most often *née* is used in English to specify a married woman's surname at birth. Some commentators point out that since only the surname changes with marriage, *née* should apply to it alone: 'Elizabeth Myers, née Smith', not 'Elizabeth Myers, née Elizabeth Smith'. The accent on *née* is often omitted in newspapers. However, it is useful in indicating the accepted pronunciation, which is *NAY*; some dictionaries also list the anglicized pronunciation *NEE*. Since *né(e)* is another term marked by gender, some non-sexist guides suggest substituting *formerly*, which can be used for both men and women.

Sometimes *né* or *née* is used in journalism to indicate the former name of an object or place, or to introduce the real person or place behind a fictional depiction. Dictionaries do not mention these uses, and they should be avoided in formal writing.

His wife, Bernadette, is a French immersion teacher, and he changed his name from Strom to Morin-Strom—Morin being her maiden name—to reflect their three daughters' francophone culture.
Ottawa Citizen 24 July 1990: B5

As in other Hébert works, the heroine has several names—her stage name, Flora Fontanges, her birth name, and the name that had been given her by the disagreeable Upper Town family she was adopted by to erase her Lower Town origins.
Ben-Z. Shek *French-Canadian & Québécois Novels* 1991: 104

This week we got a letter from Mrs. J.W. Rose (nee Constance Nicholl) of Dawlish Avenue, Toronto.
Globe and Mail (Toronto) 16 May 1985: E3

(Here *née* is followed by the full name before marriage, because Mrs. Rose is using her husband's initials.)

... the gown designed by Montreal-born designer Arnold Scaasi (ne Isaacs, which is Scaasi spelled backwards) was available at Holt Renfrew.
Gazette (Montreal) 3 Aug. 1992: C7

(The use of *né* to refer to a man's birth name is uncommon.)

... [he] was a mainstay at Calgary's Skyline Hotel (nee Four Seasons) for more than a decade.
Calgary Herald 7 Oct. 1994: D1

(Here *née* is used because it is the common form.)

The 'high, fast living' is regarded by the young men with genuine horror ... and is intended as a clear, effective antidote to the 'quaintness' of the old town of Salterton (nee Kingston).
Gazette (Montreal) 20 Oct. 1994: B2

(Robertson Davies' fictional town of Salterton is based on the real Kingston, Ontario.)

But Isadora (nee Erica) is now 50, and the titillation of *Fear of Flying* has been replaced by prurient shlock.
Calgary Herald 27 Aug. 1994: A16

(Isadora, the heroine of Erica Jong's novel *Fear of Flying*, bears some resemblance to Erica Jong herself.)

mailman   see JOB TITLES

major   see SUPERIOR

majority, minority, plurality, age of majority
Majority means more than half or, in reference to more than two things, the greatest number. It should be avoided in references to uncountable things, such as weather, time, or work; in these contexts *most* or *most of* is better.

Majority can take a singular or a plural verb depending on whether it is considered to refer to a single unit or a group of individuals. The plural verb form is the more common choice.

In reference to voting, when there are more than two candidates, the winner is often—loosely—described as having a majority of the votes even though he or she may not have won more than half the votes cast. Strictly speaking, a candidate who wins by a *majority* receives more than half the total number of votes cast. To make it perfectly clear, this is often called an 'absolute majority'. A *plurality* is a winning number of votes that is still less than half the total number of votes cast. If, out of 22 votes cast, Potvin received 12, Levy 7, and Smith 3, Potvin would win 'by a majority' of 2 votes. If, on the other hand, Potvin received 9 votes, Levy received 8, and Smith received 5, Potvin would win 'by a plurality' of one vote. A 'majority government' is one with more seats than all opposition seats combined; a 'minority government' has the most seats of all parties, but fewer than half the total seats.

In Canada the *age of majority* is the age of full legal responsibility, at which one may vote and enter into contracts. By common-law tradition, this age is twenty-one, but it has been lowered to eighteen or nineteen in several provinces and territories.

The majority of the growth over the forecast period will stem from an acceleration in upgrades and expansion of

the telecommunications infrastructure by the major telephone companies.
Computer Dealer News 21 March 1991: 16

(Here 'Most growth' would be more appropriate and less wordy.)

Quebec is also the only province where Chretien does not have an absolute majority of support among those who expressed support for a new Liberal leader.
Gazette (Montreal) 5 March 1990: A2

At least part of that alienation can be traced to our practice of electing MPs from single-member constituencies in which the candidate with the plurality wins.
Ottawa Citizen 11 Dec. 1991: A 11

However, a plurality of French-speaking Quebeckers— 47 per cent to 41 per cent—said they'd reject a constitutional deal if Canada's rights charter took precedence. Twelve percent were unsure.
Ottawa Citizen 2 June 1991: A4

Minority governments have not worked badly in our history.
Vancouver Sun 3 April 1991: A16

'He didn't say how it broke down, but the majority sees things your way.'
Howard Engel *Murder Sees the Light* 1984: 205

(Note the singular verb form.)

The majority of the netsmen are tenants, and do not own the fishing rights.
Atlantic Salmon Journal Summer 1990: 35

(Note the plural verb form.)

See also COLLECTIVE NOUNS.

malapropism, Goldwynism, Irish bull A *malapropism* is a misuse of words, especially by someone trying to sound sophisticated, resulting from a confusion between words that are similar in sound and appearance. The term derives from the name of a character in Richard Brinsley Sheridan's play *The Rivals* (1775): Mrs. Malaprop. Fowler calls Mrs. Malaprop 'the matron saint of all those who go wordfowling with a blunderbuss'. Though the accidental misuse of words had been used humorously in literature by Shakespeare and others before Sheridan, the speeches of Mrs. Malaprop (from the French *mal à propos*, 'unsuitable', 'out of place') constitute classic examples: 'Sure, if I *reprehend* anything in this world, it is the use of my *oracular* tongue, and a nice *derangement* of *epitaphs*' (read *comprehend*, *vernacular*, *arrangement*, and *epithets*, respectively).

A *Goldwynism* is a verbal blooper resulting from an illogical word choice—often a word that is the opposite of what would make sense. It takes its name from Samuel Goldwyn, the movie mogul and founder of Metro-Goldwyn-Mayer (MGM), who is said to have uttered such gems as 'Include me out' and 'You've improved it worse!' *Goldwynisms* are similar to what the British call *Irish bulls*—ludicrous, self-contradictory statements. Classic examples of Irish bulls are 'The next time I take you anywhere you'll stay home' and 'It was hereditary in his family to have no children'. The origin of the term *Irish bull* is uncertain, but it is not likely to have been the Irish who coined it.

Although his name may not become a permanent part of the language, Roger Bacon (Premier of Nova Scotia 1990–91) is famous for bloopers that have been called 'Bacon bits'. Bacon has called life a 'three-way street', and once summed up the problem of unemployment by noting, 'If those people weren't unemployed, they'd be working today' (*Maclean's* 22 Oct. 1990: 16–17):

Addressing an international meeting of tugboat operators in Halifax last month, Bacon welcomed the visitors who had come, he said, 'from all the countries across Canada.'
Macleans's 22 Oct. 1990: 17

John Robert Colombo's *Dictionary of Canadian Quotations* (1991: 318) lists a couple of Canadian malapropisms:

After nine rounds of a slam-bang boxing match at Maple Leaf Gardens, radio commentator Chuck Murphy expected a strong finish: 'Believe me, folks,' he told his audience, 'this is one close fight—a real cliff-dweller.'

Kierans: Of course I have my own ox to grind here.

See also SLIPS OF THE TONGUE.

malinger To *malinger* is to pretend to be sick. The use of *malingering* as a synonym for *remaining* or *lingering*—with negative connotations suggested by the prefix *mal*—is something new, and as yet non-standard.

But Krutov's advisers decided it was time to clear the air and answer charges that he was overweight, malingering and has lost his desire to play the game.
Vancouver Sun 18 Sept. 1990: C6

There are still a few malingering ZZ Top fans who figure the band blew its credibility when it bear-hugged the MTV ethic five years ago with the Eliminator album.
Gazette (Montreal) 14 Oct. 1990: F5

(Here *remaining* would be a better choice.)

The restoration of old street names ... is also a demonstration of the complaint of some of Moscow's new insurgent leaders that the malingering Communist system has left them with little more than cosmetic powers.
Ottawa Citizen 6 Nov. 1990: A10

(Here *lingering* would be a better choice.)

man   see SEXIST LANGUAGE

mandarin, Mandarin, Cantonese   The nine highest ranks of educated officials of the Chinese Empire were called *mandarins* (not capitalized) by Portuguese explorers in the sixteenth century. In English *mandarin* now refers to a high-ranking civil servant, or any influential person, and is suggestive of closed ranks and conservative behaviour. A *mandarin* (sometimes spelled *mandarine*) is also a small orange.

Mandarin (capitalized) is the official language of mainland China; it's the dialect of Chinese taught in school, used in government, and now used as a lingua franca throughout the country. The Chinese spoken in Hong Kong is Cantonese.

He took postings in Ottawa, London, and Paris, and lived the life of a government mandarin.
Vancouver Sun 31 May 1990: A10

'Does a finance minister really run things, or is he just a captive of the mandarins?'
Saturday Night March 1986: 28

Yeung, who speaks fluent Mandarin and Cantonese and can understand several other dialects of the Chinese language, said there are numerous benefits to having ethnic minorities in positions of power.
Vancouver Sun 27 April 1994: B4

See also CHINESE NAMES; PINYIN.

maneuver   see MANOEUVRE

mania   see PHOBIA

manikin   see MANNEQUIN

Manitoba   see APPENDIX I

manitou   In the Algonquian family of languages *manitou* means mysterious being or spirit. The supreme deity is called *Gitchi Manitou*, 'Great Spirit'.

The Ojibwa named the place Manitou Land after the great god, Gitchi Manitou.
Globe and Mail (Toronto) 17 May 1985: P4

mankind   see SEXIST LANGUAGE

mannequin, manikin, mannikin   *Mannequin*, *manikin*, and *mannikin* are variant spellings of the same word. *Manikin*, 'little man', was borrowed from Dutch around 1600 and used literally to describe people of very short stature; figuratively, it was an epithet of contempt. These meanings are obsolete. However, *manikin* was also used very early to refer to models of the human body, such as those used by artists, tailors, and doctors-in-training, and this meaning has survived.

Around 1900, the same word was borrowed into English again, this time via French. The French spelling, *mannequin*, is the one usual in fashion writing and recommended by most Canadian style books. Nevertheless, some writers prefer the anglicized *mannikin*.

In French and in British English, a *mannequin* is usually a person: a living, breathing fashion model. This meaning may come as a surprise to Canadians for whom a *mannequin* is a dummy.

The headphones were tested using an 'average' ear from the head of a special dummy called a Knowles Electronics Manikin for Acoustic Research. . . .
Canadian Consumer Jan. 1985: 21

In passing, Lesje glances into the windows of dress shops, department stores, appraising the cadaverous mannequins who stand with their pelvises thrust forward, hands angular on hips, legs apart, one knee bent.
Margaret Atwood *Life Before Man* 1979: 18

As she stood stone still in the window of a fashion store called Workshop, it was difficult to tell whether she was real or a mannequin.
Saturday Night May 1986: 55

In his very first collection, he startled the audience with the languorous pace of his presentation, to the sound of Bach, a speed dictated by the fact that he could afford only six mannikins.
Globe and Mail (Toronto) 5 Feb. 1985: F8

(Here the *mannikins* are live models; this spelling is unusual in this context.)

manner (manor) born, to the   'To the manner born' is the original quotation; it comes from Shakespeare (*Hamlet* 1.4.15) and it means accustomed from birth to a certain way of life. 'To the manor born', meaning accustomed to the high life, is a witty corruption; it's widely used, but regarded by some as an error.

> As if to the manner born, Quebec Liberals accept their place at the nerve centre of the party.
> *Gazette* (Montreal) 5 May 1988: B3

> She swished the kettle to see that it was nearly full, then lit the gas as though to the manner born.
> Howard Engel *Murder Sees the Light* 1984: 167

> Aristocratic 'Poppy' Bush of Andover and Yale may have been to the manor born, but he's going to run a Main St., down-home presidency.
> *Financial Post* 18 Jan. 1989: 13

(Here *to the manor born* means accustomed from birth to a high position.)

mannikin   see MANNEQUIN

manoeuvre, maneuver   *Manoeuvre* and *maneuver* are alternative spellings. *Manoeuvre* is favoured in Canada and Britain, *maneuver* in the United States. *Manoeuvre* and its derivatives are misspelled almost as often as they are spelled correctly. Note that in the correct spellings there is no *e* between the *v* and the *r: manoeuvred, manoeuvring, manoeuvrability, manoeuvrer*. However, most Canadians pronounce *manoeuvring* as four syllables, not three, and this is probably what leads people to insert the extra *e*.
Manoeuvre is a French borrowing, and in the past the *o* and the *e* were typeset, as in French, as a ligature, *œ*. In current Canadian English the ligature is not used.

> The electorate, however, was unsympathetic to this manoeuvre and Coutts lost the election.
> *Queen's Quarterly* 95.3 (1988): 664

> Precision skating is a team skating sport where up to 30 girls are required to perform complicated maneuvers in unison.
> *Today's Skater* 1991: 59

(In Canadian English *maneuver* is much less common than *manoeuvre*.)

> 'Nickle is certainly manoeuvering to make a place for himself,' Richardson wrote to Macdonnell in March....
> Frederick Gibson *Queen's University* 2 (1983): 86

(The correct spelling is *manoeuvring*.)

> ... there are six different products being offered, all with light-weight tubular steel shafts that are cranked or angled near the top to give easy manoeuverability without extra effort.
> *TLC ... for plants* Summer 1991: 44

(The correct spelling is *manoeuvrability*.)

See also DIPHTHONG, DIGRAPH, LIGATURE.

manor born, to the   see MANNER BORN

manqué   *Manqué* is an adjective borrowed from French; it follows the noun it modifies and indicates a frustrated or unfulfilled vocation: 'He's a successful lawyer but a poet manqué'. In formal writing the accent should be retained. The feminine form *manquée* is not used.

> ... Miss Feinstein, a policewoman manqué ... listens constantly to the police radio from her mayoral limousine.
> *Globe and Mail* (Toronto) 23 Feb. 1985: P9

> Blaikie denied that he and his colleagues were actors manque. 'No. We all want to be directors.'
> *Gazette* (Montreal) 28 Nov. 1992: E15

manse, parsonage, rectory, vicarage   The name of the house traditionally built beside a church to house the incumbent minister varies by denomination. Presbyterian ministers live in a *manse*, as do some ministers of the United Church (depending on the denomination of the congregation before 1925, when the United Church was formed). Other United Church ministers, like their Methodist forerunners, live in a *parsonage*, while Roman Catholic or Anglican priests usually live in a *rectory*. In the Anglican Church, a vicar served a parish whose tithes did not pass to him (as they did to a rector); a vicar lived in a *vicarage*.

> His father was a Presbyterian minister, and Law's childhood home was in a manse close to the broad Richibucto River....
> *Globe and Mail* (Toronto) 15 June 1985: T3

> The [Anglican] church was built by its members in the late 1800s, says Les, and its rectory may have been the first mission house in the area.
> *Canadian Heritage* Feb.–Mar. 1986: 18–19

See also RECTOR, VICAR; UNITED CHURCH.

mantel, mantle   Originally these were variant spellings of the same term, but most dictionaries and commentators now distinguish them. In contemporary use a mantel is a shelf above a fireplace; a mantle is a cloak or cover. *Mantle* often means cloak in a figurative sense: 'In becoming a politician she chose to wear her father's mantle'; 'He wore the mantle of secrecy'.

In the dining room, the mantel is swagged with pine cones, holly and fruits.
Toronto Star 2 Dec. 1989: H14

Pierre Elliott Trudeau inherited the mantle, the issues and the conflicts of Wilfrid Laurier.
Maclean's 31 March 1986: 13

'In a brilliant public relations stroke, Michael Wilson has stolen the mantel of earlier tax reforms, but left behind their substance.'
City Magazine Spring 1988: 8

(Here the context requires *mantle*.)

A friend of mine had hand-cut and sanded and worked the mantle with a jacknife.
Canadian Heritage Feb.–Mar. 1986: 20

(Here the context requires *mantel*.)

Maple Leaf, Maple Leaves, Maple Leafs   *Maple Leaf* is usually capitalized when it refers to Canada's national emblem. The official name of the flag is the National Flag of Canada, but it is often unofficially called the Maple Leaf. The Royal Canadian Mint produces a gold coin called the Maple Leaf.

Since the standard plural of *leaf* is *leaves*, using *Maple Leaves* as the plural for the emblem, flag, or coin is probably best. However, traditional usage at the mint favours *Maple Leafs* for the coins, and *Maple Leafs* is the correct name for Toronto's National Hockey League team.

Twenty-five years ago, on a cold, damp Ottawa morning, Canada's new red-and-white Maple Leaf flag unfurled from Parliament's Peace Tower.
Province (Vancouver) 15 Feb. 1990: 14

They wrapped their leader's shaky personal credibility in giant Maple Leafs and American-style rah-rah.
Gazette (Montreal) 19 Nov. 1988: B5

(Referring to the flag, *Maple Leaves* would be more widely accepted.)

A spokesman for the Royal Canadian Mint in Ottawa said sales of Maple Leafs in the U.S. market are up by almost a third from last year's pace.
Globe and Mail (Toronto) 7 June 1985: B1

(Either *Maple Leafs* or *Maple Leaves* is acceptable for the coins.)

When this gleaming memorial [a mural, Hockey Knights in Canada] to the famous rivalry between the Maple Leafs and Canadiens was unveiled last Sunday, [artist Charles] Pachter welcomed the crowd on the subway platform to the 'Sistine basement.'
Globe and Mail (Toronto) 18 April 1985: E7

(*Maple Leafs* is the name of the hockey team.)

An hour of picking our way along the trail ... brought us to a 100-foot-deep rocky valley with a small stream splashing down into a dark pool with red and orange maple leafs adrift on its surface.
Financial Post 18 Oct. 1991: 46

(When a maple leaf is foliage, the standard plural is *leaves*.)

See also -F-, -V-.

maritime, Maritimes, Maritime provinces   see ATLANTIC PROVINCES

marsh   see SWAMP

marshal   *Marshal* is the recommended spelling for both the noun ('field marshal') and the verb ('marshal your forces'). Among major dictionaries only *Merriam-Webster's* lists *marshall* as an acceptable alternative. The final *l* of *marshal* is usually doubled before -*ed* or -*ing*.

Richard McConomy will be the grand marshal of the parade.
Gazette (Montreal) 12 Feb. 1992: F6

In his ability to absorb and marshal facts, especially the strengths and vulnerabilities of fellow politicians, Nixon rivalled Lyndon Johnson.
Queen's Quarterly 95.4 (1988): 809

... the rationality of a belief appears to be normally a matter of factors in which it is grounded, and of how they enable the agent to respond to relevant considerations, not of [a person's] ability to marshall such factors in defending it.
Canadian Journal of Philosophy 19 (1989): 263

(The recommended spelling is *marshal*.)

Are [pressure] groups adept at marshalling public opinion?
A. Paul Pross *Group Politics and Public Policy* 2nd ed. 1992: 92

But while Sherry quickly marshaled her resources against the physical attack of AIDS, finding the emotional strength to fight was harder.
Calgary Herald 9 Aug. 1992: A9

(The single *l* before -*ed* is quite uncommon, but not unacceptable.)

See also DOUBLING THE FINAL CONSONANT.

massacre, slaughter   *Massacre* and *slaughter* can both refer to the deliberate slaying of a large number of people, but only *slaughter* can properly be applied to one person. However, in informal speech and writing, these terms are often used with reference to defeat at games and sports; thus it is possible for one person to be figuratively massacred at, say, chess.

> The move comes in the wake of the massacre of 14 Montreal-area women at a university campus by Marc Lepine, who used a semi-automatic assault rifle.
> *Vancouver Sun* 14 Feb. 1990: B2

> And if Dennis could hear the tepid revelations provoked by his death, he might've had second thoughts about self-slaughter.
> *Calgary Herald* 29 June 1994: D9

See also DECIMATE; HOLOCAUST, GENOCIDE.

masterful, masterly *Masterful* can mean skilful, powerful, domineering, or authoritative, whereas *masterly* almost always means skilful. In many contexts either word is appropriate.

The adverb form of *masterly* poses some problems. No one seems to use the awkward form *masterlily*, and though *masterly* can be used as an adverb, it's confusing; *masterfully* and *in a masterly manner* are less troublesome alternatives.

Guides to gender-neutral usage suggest avoiding both words in favour of synonyms, such as *skilful*, *authoritative*, and *accomplished*, that do not imply that skill and authority are primarily male ('the master's') qualities.

> Scotch is such a masterful liquor that it does not take kindly to mixing with inferior potations.
> *Bon Vivant* Aug.–Sept. 1982: 13

(Here *masterful* means powerful.)

> It is a masterful piece of drumming, probably Roach's best showing until the two takes of *Ko Ko*....
> Jack Chambers *Milestones* 1983: 38

(Here either word is appropriate.)

> The style is masterly, for it is unceasingly witty without blinding the reader by a display of fireworks—candlelight on fine silver is rather the effect.
> Robertson Davies *A Voice from the Attic* 1960: 238

(Here either word is appropriate.)

> Her fictions are masterfully constructed, and critics are correct in drawing our attention ... to the intricate texture and surface polish of her narratives.
> Janice Kulyk Keefer *Reading Mavis Gallant* 1989: 36

(The adverb *masterfully* means skilfully or authoritatively, or both.)

See also SEXIST LANGUAGE.

materialist, materialistic, material A *materialist* prizes the pleasures that money can buy over spiritual or intellectual ones. The adjective form is *materialist* or *materialistic*. These words generally describe people or attitudes, and their connotations are always unfavourable. *Material* simply means concrete, physical, or real, and is neutral in its connotations. Sometimes writers use *materialist* or *materialistic* where *material* would make more sense.

> [In the drama] my grandfather emerges as a materialistic, naive, rather shallow person, more interested in accumulating fame and wealth than in taking care of the Dionnes.
> *Daily News* (Halifax) 30 Nov. 1994: 21

> 'No matter what happens—whether we have a negotiated settlement or an imposition—there will be a transition period and that means there won't be a material effect for 1995.'
> *Gazette* (Montreal) 22 Nov. 1994: C8

> The truth is that, besides all his materialistic contributions, such as helping Hydro Quebec, Levesque is largely responsible for the incredible advancement of Canada's second-largest province.
> *Toronto Star* 1 Nov. 1987: D3

(The word required here is *material*.)

See also MATÉRIEL.

materialize Some critics, Fowler among them, have recommended restricting the use of *materialize* to its literal meaning, 'to give or take material form'. However, the metaphorical meanings 'to appear suddenly', 'to become fact', and 'to be borne out' have become so well established at all levels of writing in contemporary English that they cannot be considered either pretentious or incorrect.

> Yet his presence never left me; years later, when I was nursing my second child, I would wake at 3 A.M., and in the quiet of that hour George would suddenly materialize to talk about art and to entertain me with his anecdotes.
> Miriam Waddington *Apartment Seven* 1989: 21–2

> There are really two contracts in contemplation: first, the option agreement itself and second, the actual sale which will materialize if the option is exercised.
> J.E. Smyth et al. *The Law and Business Administration in Canada* 1987: 134

> This myth is pernicious because it leaves many women feeling inadequate, baffled or even evil if the promised happiness and fulfillment fail to materialize.
> Margaret Atwood *Second Words* 1982: 255

matériel *Matériel*, spelled with an accent over the first *e*, is a military term for equipment and supplies; it should not be confused with *material*. *Matériel* is usually pronounced *ma teer ee ELL*; the accent is sometimes dropped in informal writing.

They also shipped vast amounts of war materiel to Iraq.
Maclean's 13 Aug. 1990: A20

maudlin see MAGDALEN(E)

maunder, meander To *maunder* means to express oneself in a dreamy or rambling, often incoherent, manner. The connotation is strongly negative, the implication being that the speaker is not thinking clearly. To *meander* means to follow a winding course or to wander aimlessly. A river might meander through the countryside, or a walker through a neighbourhood. *Meander* is also used in reference to speech and writing. Here the connotation is usually negative—readers tend to grow impatient with a writer who will not get to the point—but it is not necessarily so: a writer's digressions may be stimulating and enjoyable.

His own arguments for Meech Lake have been maundering sentimentalism, spiked with historical falsehoods.
Ottawa Citizen 4 March 1990: A10

Answers are so heavily edited and condensed to eliminate any mis-statements and general maundering that they often bear practically no resemblance to the transcript of the tape.
Financial Post 1 Aug. 1989: 9

(Here the context seems to indicate that the tapes have been edited to eliminate *meandering*.)

Lewis could have been forgiven if he had meandered easily through a lazy little talk.
Saturday Night May 1986: 38

But [the playwright's] meandering journey to this climactic encounter is refreshingly witty and inventive.
Gazette (Montreal) 28 May 1994: C7

may, can The traditional distinction between these two words is that *may* is associated with permission, *can* with ability. Children are frequently taught to use *may* when asking permission, and are told that expressions like 'Can I go now?' are rude. The may/can distinction is a traditional feature of elementary-school education, rather like the use of 'Sir' in the military. In writing the distinction is rarely required except when the writer is representing speech. In adult speech, in the few cases where adults must ask permission to do something, *can* with an appropriate politeness marker such as *please* ('Can I leave this here for now, please?') is certainly acceptable, as, of course, is *may*.

See also MAY, MIGHT.

may, might In some contexts, *might* acts as the past tense of *may*. For example, if someone says 'That may be true', we report it to someone else this way: 'He said that it might be true'. Often, however, the two words are used similarly to express a possibility ('I may be able to help you'; 'I might be able to help you'). Although *might* is felt by some speakers to express a more tentative possibility than *may* in sentences like these, others perceive little difference between them. This perception may explain the occasional production of puzzling sentences that use *may* where only *might* is appropriate: 'More careful drug testing may have averted the tragedy'. Here 'the tragedy' did in fact occur: the possibility of averting it existed only in the past, and so *might* is required.

U.N. Secretary-General Boutros Boutros-Ghali also told CBC ... that quick intervention may have prevented the wave of brutal killings that followed the death of Rwandan president Juvenal Habyarimana in an April attack.
Toronto Star 30 Nov. 1994: A21

(Here, since the killings have taken place, *might* is required.)

See also MAY, CAN.

me see MYSELF; PRESENT WRITER

mea culpa *Mea culpa* is a Latin phrase meaning 'through my fault' or 'my mistake'. In English a *mea culpa* is a formal apology, or an acknowledgement that one has done something blameworthy. *Mea culpa* is also used facetiously to mean something like 'Go ahead and blame me'. The popularity of the humorous use of *mea culpa* in journalism may account for the rarity of the phrase in academic writing.

Mulroney's mea culpa came when he emerged from the meeting: 'What we have done so far leaves much to be desired.'
Vancouver Sun 24 Nov. 1990: B2

One outcome of the prolonged, public dispute may be the extraction of something approaching a mea culpa from Moscow for 1956, similar to the apology given to

Czechoslovakia late last year for the Soviet-led invasion of 1968.
Ottawa Citizen 4 July 1990: F9

Mea culpa, mea culpa. I went home to wash out my mouth with soap.
Gazette (Montreal) 22 Sept. 1990: J2

See also LATIN PHRASES.

mean   see AVERAGE

meander   see MAUNDER

meantime, meanwhile   *Meantime* is commonly used as a noun, in the phrase 'in the meantime', whereas *meanwhile* usually appears alone in a sentence, as an adverb ('Meanwhile, back at the ranch ...'). However, one does occasionally find 'in the meanwhile' or 'meantime, back at the ranch'.

In the meantime, the Elizabeth Fry Society and other advocacy groups continue their work to address the particular problems faced by women in conflict with the law.
Briarpatch April 1990: 11

The working of their mill was thereby delayed, and the plaintiffs meanwhile lost profits of several hundred pounds.
J.E. Smyth et al. *The Law and Business Administration in Canada* 1987: 365

Meantime, the number of Massey dealerships in big-tractor country continues to fall slowly.
Country Guide Nov. 1986: 9

(As an adverb *meantime* is less common than *meanwhile*.)

In the meanwhile ... Toman readily admits that the company has 'lots of work to do.'
Whig-Standard (Kingston) 29 June 1985: n.p.

(As a noun *meanwhile* is less common than *meantime*.)

measurement   see APPENDIX II; MILE

Mecca   see ISLAM

media   see MEDIUM

median   see AVERAGE

mediation   see CONCILIATION

medicine   The fourth letter in *medicine*, as in *medical*, is *i*. The word is often misspelled *medecine*. For some people, the confusion probably arises from the French spellings *médecine*, 'medicine', and *médecin*, 'doctor'.

The 12-member commission, headed by Laval University dean of medecine Jean Rochon, will have 30 months to report to the provincial Government....
Globe and Mail (Toronto) 20 June 1985: P3

(The correct spelling is *medicine*.)

medieval, mediaeval   The usual spelling is *medieval*. Its pronunciation varies: *meh DEE vul, meh dee EE vul*, and *mee dee EE vul* are all quite common.

See also -AE-, -OE-, -E-.

mediocre   *Mediocre* means middling, average, neither good nor bad. However, this adjective appears to be on a downhill slide; more and more it is used to mean inferior or poor. Because of this second sense, now recorded in most dictionaries, *mediocre* can be ambiguous. Context should be provided to make its meaning clear.

'You get 30, 35 starts a year. Ten times you have great stuff, 10 times it's mediocre and 10 times you have poor. Tonight, I'd have to rate my stuff as poor.'
London Free Press 28 April 1988: C1

(Here *mediocre* clearly means neither good nor bad.)

'Staying focused is what separates the good teams from the great teams and great men from mediocre men.'
Winnipeg Free Press 17 Nov. 1990: 53

(Here *mediocre* means average.)

The rankings—from one star for mediocre to five stars for excellent—are purely subjective.
Ottawa Citizen 29 Oct. 1994: L2

They maintain that the United States, in addition to boasting many excellent universities, also has a large number of mediocre institutions providing students with an inferior grade of education.
Maclean's 21 Oct. 1991: A28

(Here *mediocre* is used pejoratively to mean below standard.)

medium, media   A *medium* is a means by which something is conveyed or through which something acts: for example, a medium of communication or an art medium. The plural is *media* or *mediums*. A psychic *medium* is a person through whom the deceased purportedly speak; the plural for this type of *medium* is always *mediums*.

The media usually refers to the news media (radio, television, newspapers, and magazines) or to the journalists who work in this field. In this sense *media* has become a collective noun like *committee* or *team*. It can correctly be followed by either a singular or plural verb, depending on whether the media are being considered as a collection of individuals or a unit.

Occasionally *media* is mistakenly used for *medium*, as in 'That's one media we haven't tried'.

And a key point here is that the language of the world at large is the medium of poets, and is always in advance of and more alive than the language of institutions.
Queen's Quarterly 92.2 (1985): 377

Movies and music are other media through which language develops specific patterns that are soon adopted by youthful minds.
W.C. Lougheed, ed. *In Search of the Standard in Canadian English* 1986: 69

The novel's structure is also determined by its perception of that most fluid of all mediums, time.
Janice Kulyk Keefer *Reading Mavis Gallant* 1989: 80

The media is responsible for so many problems with language and written expression that I have ceased to be frustrated by daily blunders.
W.C. Lougheed, ed. *In Search of the Standard in Canadian English* 1986: 66

(Here *media* is a singular collective noun.)

The media hold a mirror up to society, but do so selectively.
Richard Davies and Glen Kirkland, eds. *Dimensions* 1986: 147

(Here *media* is a plural collective noun.)

... in one scene, while queuing up at the cinema, the Allen character overhears a highbrow conversation about some esoteric aspects of the film media....
City Magazine Spring 1988: 20

(Here the singular form '*medium* of film' would be more appropriate.)

See also COLLECTIVE NOUNS; PLURALS, REGULAR, IRREGULAR, FOREIGN.

meld This blend of *melt* and *weld* means to blend or merge; it appeared in American English around 1935. At first it was criticized as a misuse of the card-playing term *meld*, which means to show your cards and add up your points, especially in canasta.

But *meld* meaning blend is in fact a separate word, now used and accepted in all types of writing as both a verb and a noun.

Its shimmering blue waters stretch along the southern end of B.C.'s Okanagan Valley, where the Monashee Mountains roll down from the east and meld with the Thompson Plateau.
Beautiful British Columbia Spring 1990: 38–40

The *Bank of Canada*, nearby on the south side of Wellington, is an architecturally interesting meld of two worlds: Modern glass towers flank the original bank building....
Alan Tucker, ed. *The Penguin Guide to Canada* 1991: 303

memento, [momento] A *memento* is something concrete that brings back a memory; often it's a souvenir, or a gift to mark an occasion. The first three letters in *memento* are the same as in the related word *memory*. The common—but unrelated—word *moment* has had such a strong influence on the spelling and pronunciation of *memento* that *momento* is now listed as a variant spelling in some dictionaries. However, style guides unanimously recommend *memento*. The plural is *mementos* or *mementoes*.

The booklet is valuable when visiting the exhibition and a good memento when it ends.
Ottawa Citizen 21 Feb. 1993: C2

Terry O'Reilly ... has asked for the penalty box from the Boston Garden as a personal momento of his National Hockey League playing days.
Calgary Herald 8 Oct. 1994: C1

(The usual—and more widely accepted—spelling is *memento*.)

See also -OS, -OES.

memorandum, memoranda, memorandums, memo, memos *Memorandum* is the singular form and *memoranda* the traditional Latin plural. *Memoranda* is occasionally misused as the singular. *Memorandums*, the anglicized plural, now appears frequently in Canadian newspapers and magazines, but *memoranda* is still preferred in formal and academic writing. The short form *memo* (plural *memos*) is informal.

In early January, Macdonald had drafted a careful memorandum on Anderson's case and dispatched it to Governor General Head....
William Teatero *John Anderson: Fugitive Slave* 1986: 115

In addition there are 280 technical memoranda on different facets of the tax which are written primarily for accountants and tax lawyers.
Ottawa Citizen 21 June 1990: E2

Over the past five years, there have been studies, reports, interdepartmental memorandums....
Vancouver Sun 27 April 1990: A1

As well, Andre Bissonnette, federal Minister of State for Small Business, signed a memoranda of understanding with most provinces and the territories....
Globe and Mail (Toronto) 11 Oct. 1985: B8

(The word *memoranda* is plural; Bissonnette either 'signed a *memorandum*' or 'signed *memoranda*'.)

See also PLURALS, REGULAR, IRREGULAR, FOREIGN.

mendacity, mendacious, mendicancy, mendicity, mendicant *Mendacity* is the habit of lying. *Mendacious* means prone to lying. *Mendicancy* or *mendicity* is the state of being a beggar, or the action of begging. *Mendicant* can be either an adjective ('begging') or a noun ('beggar').

Milli Vanilli was a scandal fuelled, like most scandals, by ambition, greed and mendacity.
Gazette (Montreal) 22 Nov. 1990: E1

At his worst, he has been by turns mendacious, blinkered and spiteful....
Globe and Mail (Toronto) 22 June 1985: P6

I am ashamed of my whining, cringing, mendicant contemporaries. Canadian seniors have never had it so good.
Globe and Mail (Toronto) 27 June 1985: P6

menorah   see CANDELABRUM

mentality, mindset *Mentality* generally refers to mental character, attitude, or stance, as in Northrop Frye's description of the typically Canadian 'garrison mentality'. Phrases such as 'colonial mentality', 'siege mentality', 'herd mentality', 'bottom-line mentality', and 'ghetto mentality' are common in journalism and academic writing. *Mindset*, a recent import into general speech and writing from psychology, is fairly close in meaning to *mentality*. Some object to *mindset* as jargon, and it is far less common in formal writing than *mentality*.

The Hollywood blockbuster mentality, which decrees that a movie is either Indiana Jones and the Temple of

Doom or nothing, has rendered the modestly scaled independent film an endangered species.
Globe and Mail (Toronto) 5 April 1985: E1

The play—like the film—was a dark and scathing indictment of the burgeoning Nazi mindset in Germany.
Gazette (Montreal) 12 Nov. 1994: D7

meow, miaow, mew   In Canada and the United States cats *meow*; in Britain they *miaow*. Cats on both sides of the Atlantic *mew*.

According to a cat expert with the British Museum, cats never use meows when addressing each other, only when addressing humans.
Globe and Mail (Toronto) 10 Oct. 1985: P6

See also ONOMATOPOEIA.

meritorious, meretricious *Meritorious* means having merit or deserving praise. *Meretricious* means flashy and deceptively attractive, but lacking in real merit or substance. In the seventeenth century *meretricious*, derived from the Latin for 'harlot', meant befitting a prostitute: this meaning is now rare, though it may sometimes colour the current use of the word.

The government has gone to some lengths in arguing the case in favor of the goods and services tax to point out that the uniform taxation is meritorious because it eliminates some of the distortionary effects which creep in otherwise.
Financial Post 27 June 1990: 12

That they're travelling in a luxurious motor home, complete with a microwave that browns, somehow sets the stage for their experience of the wilderness: the vulgar and meretricious beauty of Las Vegas and a view of Hoover Dam.
Globe and Mail (Toronto) 27 April 1985: M8

'The Other Paris' roots the distinction between what is meretriciously accurate and what is true deep within the world of traditional female experience.
Janice Kulyk Keefer *Reading Mavis Gallant* 1989: 140

(Here *meretriciously* means superficially.)

The new tower, while initially seductive in a meretricious sort of way, is, on closer examination, deficient in the intellectual rigor, subtle detailing, powerful presence and historical resonance of the building it is planned to replace.
Vancouver Sun 8 Dec. 1990: D16

(Here there may be a metaphoric connection with prostitution.)

merry-go-round, carousel   The fairground ride consisting of painted wooden horses, or other animals, revolving to music is usually called a *merry-go-round* in Canadian and British English. The common American name is *carousel*, which some Canadians think of as a fancy word for a merry-go-round, or a term for a particularly elaborate merry-go-round.

Carousel has taken on extended literal meanings: circular slide trays and revolving luggage platforms in airports are called *carousels*. *Merry-go-round* is far more common than *carousel* in figurative uses.

> Visitors to the PNE's Playland may get their last chance this year to ride the 73-year-old Vancouver carousel, which is slated for the auction block. Unless $350,000 is raised to purchase the 36-horse merry-go-round ... it will be dismantled and sold....
> *Vancouver Sun* 24 Aug. 1990: B5

> After years of self-hatred and denial, I came to the conclusion that I had been riding on that particular merry-go-round for too long and I wanted off.
> *Vancouver Sun* 14 May 1993: A2

metal, mettle   *Metal*, meaning the hard, shiny substance that conducts heat and electricity, should not be confused with *mettle*, meaning spirit or courage. The past tense of the verb *metal*, meaning to cover in metal, is spelled *metalled* in Britain and *metaled* in the United States. Canadian dictionaries list both spellings. In the context of roads, *metalled* is a chiefly British synonym for *gravelled*.

> The promised sleek International Express, 'all first class, with air conditioned berths that are modern, metalled and well appointed,' turned out to be, at least this time, six second-class cars, four with berths and none air conditioned....
> *Globe and Mail* (Toronto) 16 Feb. 1985: T20

> 'It doesn't look all that bad but don't let appearances fool you,' said resident Alex Kennedy as he wheeled a maroon sedan around the reserve's winding metalled roads.
> *Maclean's* 3 July 1989: A40

> The Second World War was a time when the Royal family truly showed their mettle.
> *Canadian Churchman* Jun.–Jul. 1986: 21

See also DOUBLING THE FINAL CONSONANT.

metaphor   see DEAD METAPHOR; METONYMY, SYNECDOCHE; MIXED METAPHOR

metathesis   see MISPRONUNCIATION AND PRONUNCIATION SHIFTS

methodology, method, methods   A *methodology* is a systematic procedure of inquiry used in a particular discipline, or any system of methods with a philosophical basis. In reference to everyday activities, *methodology* is usually overblown: *method* or *methods* will do the job ('a method for making an omelette', 'indoor training methods').

> ... it is not clear that we know enough about how English Canadian society is stratified to be confident that the methodology used in European and U.S. sociolinguistic studies is the right methodology for Canada.
> W.C. Lougheed, ed. *In Search of the Standard in Canadian English* 1986: 24

> Very often, the articles in this magazine attempt to reveal the similarities of motivation and methodology that unite researchers in widely divergent fields.
> *Perspectives: Profiles of Research at Queen's University* 1986: 30

> Other methods of timing fireworks to music are primitive, Jim says.
> *Calgary Herald* 29 June 1992: C1

> Churches, synagogues, mosques and temples are playing important roles individually and collectively [in creating a harmonious society]. The methodology and tactics may differ, but there is no doubt about our goals....
> *Province* (Vancouver) 21 March 1990: 29

(This is the overblown use.)

meticulous, scrupulous, punctilious, punctual   All these words mean painstakingly exact, but they have different connotations and applications. In the sixteenth and seventeenth centuries *meticulous* meant fearful, and in the early nineteenth century it was used disparagingly to mean timidly over-fussy. It is now used as a compliment meaning extremely careful and attentive to detail.

Scrupulous suggests a careful attention to detail so as to ensure that what is done is morally and ethically correct.

Punctilious means carefully observant of laws, rules, ceremony, and conduct and usually has negative connotations. *Punctual* means on time.

> Indeed, it was the meticulous attention to detail that was the most striking feature of McNeill's economies.
> Frederick Gibson *Queen's University* 2 (1983): 99

> And in their puppy-dog eagerness to spur development the donors were often none too scrupulous about how they did business. They must carry their share of re-

sponsibility for the climate of corruption that now covers Africa.
Ottawa Citizen 17 April 1993: B4

All was done with a punctilious attention to legality, with the law employed as an instrument of policy to be promulgated as needed and interpreted by obliging judges.
Queen's Quarterly 92.1 (1985): 135–6

The next evening, a punctual bus and subway connection delivered Tyler to work early, as he'd hoped it might, without expecting that it would.
Constance Beresford-Howe *Night Studies* 1985: 59

Métis, half-breed   During the fur-trading era in the region that is now Manitoba and northern Ontario, the term *Métis* (from the French for 'mixed') was used to describe anyone with both Aboriginal and European ancestry; there were both anglophone and francophone Métis. The Aboriginal ancestry was usually Cree, the European usually French or Scottish. The specific application of the term *Métis* to French-speakers reflects the cultural solidarity of francophone Métis in the regions that became Manitoba and Saskatchewan, who resisted the appropriation of their lands by the Canadian government and incoming settlers in the two uprisings led by Louis Riel (Red River, 1869–70; North-West, 1885).

In 1982 the Constitution Act granted the Métis and anyone of mixed ancestry, whether associated with this particular western Canadian group or not, the same constitutional protection as other Aboriginal peoples. Since then the term has once again come to be used to refer to anyone of mixed Aboriginal and European ancestry. Some English-speaking people of mixed ancestry call themselves *half-breeds*, a term that is derogatory if used by non-Natives.

Métis is pronounced *MAY tee*, although some people in the Prairie provinces say *MEH tis*, as if the word were English, and some Métis and Aboriginal people say *MET chif*. *Métis* is both the adjective and the noun form, singular and plural. The accent should be retained in formal writing.

Attempts by governments, churches and the general population to change Indians, Metis and Inuit into just another ethnic group in the multicultural mosaic have failed.
The Beaver Feb.–Mar. 1990: 58

The term Métis originally applied to people of French and Indian descent, but now applies to any mixed-blood Native people who identify themselves as Métis.

Geoffrey York *The Dispossessed: Life and Death in Native Canada* 1990: 58

One of [Theytus Press's] finest books, The Native Creative Process, is an extended dialogue between Metis architect Douglas Cardinal and Indian poet Jeannette Armstrong.
Ottawa Citizen 28 Nov. 1992: n.p.

See also ABORIGINAL PEOPLE(S); INDIAN.

metonymy, synecdoche   *Metonymy* (pronounced *meh TAWN uh mee*) is a figure of speech in which an object closely associated with something is used to name it: 'the bottle', 'the press'. 'The pen is mightier than the sword' means that rhetoric is more effective than violence.

Synecdoche (pronounced *si NEK duh kee*) is a figure in which a part stands for a whole ('All hands on deck'; 'private eye'; 'new wheels'); a whole stands for a part ('Canada [the team] brings home the gold'; 'She was family [a relative]'); or an example stands for a class ('He was no Einstein').

metric   see APPENDIX II

Metro, subway   The underground railway in Paris is *le métro* ('the Metro'), short for *chemin de fer métropolitain*, 'urban railway'. Montreal borrowed this term. In Toronto and Edmonton the underground rapid transit is the *subway*. In British English a *subway* is an underground walkway; the London underground train system is simply called 'the underground' or, informally, 'the tube'.

Metro (often capitalized) is an abbreviation of 'metropolitan area', which refers to a large urban centre and the areas immediately adjacent to it. *Metro* and *Toronto* are often used interchangeably by Torontonians, who should take note that among Haligonians *metro* means the greater Halifax area.

Police are warning people who take the Metro to be extra cautious after more than 12 people were robbed during the past two weeks.
Gazette (Montreal) 13 Oct. 1994: F4

. . . I worked for a demolition company tearing down houses to create a narrow above-ground strip for the latest extension to the Toronto subway.
Ken Dryden *The Game* 1983: 60

Metro's future is on the line but information shortfall and politicians' lack of vision are threatening to turn what should be Metro's most momentous election into a political travesty.
Now Magazine 3–9 Nov. 1988: 10

(Here *Metro* means the Toronto area.)

Peggy's Cove, the famous protected seacoast village, is also in metro's domain, on St. Margaret's Bay, 40 minutes southwest of Halifax over winding two-lane roads.
Alan Tucker, ed. *The Penguin Guide to Canada* 1991: 43

(Here *metro* means the Halifax area.)

mettle   see METAL

mew, miaow   see MEOW

Mexican American   see HISPANIC

Micmac, Mi'kmaw, Mi'kmaq   The Aboriginal people formerly called *Micmac* now spell their name *Mi'kmaw* (singular; pronounced *MIK MAW*) and *Mi'kmaq* (plural; *MIK MAK*). The Union of Nova Scotia Indians and the Mi'kmaq Grand Council have adopted these forms and request that others follow their practice. (Outside the Maritimes, you will need to explain the change of name.) The new spellings more closely reflect the Mi'kmaq language (a member of the Algonquian group). The original Mi'kmaq territory was coastal Gaspé and the Maritime provinces east of the Saint John River. Now communities of Mi'kmaq are also found in Cape Breton, Newfoundland, and New England, particularly Boston.

In Drumbeat, officials and chiefs of several First Nations—the Innu of Ungava, the Mi'kmaq, the Mohawks of Akwesasne ... describe the real story of relations between Native peoples and white settlers.
Ottawa Citizen 17 March 1990: J11

An illegal hunt controversy was avoided in the fall of 1989 because the two sides sat down and struck a deal to give the province's Micmacs freedom to hunt.
Financial Post 29 March 1990: 12

(The plural form *Mi'kmaq* is preferred by the people themselves.)

Marshall, a Micmac Indian, was wrongly convicted of murdering a companion, Sandy Seale, in a Sydney park in 1971.
Vancouver Sun 12 Oct. 1990: A10

(Here *Mi'kmaw* could replace *Micmac Indian*.)

Middle English   see OLD ENGLISH

midnight   see TIME

[might of]   see [COULD OF]

mighty   The use of *mighty* to mean 'very' has a long, respectable tradition; in fact, it appears in literary writing from the fourteenth century. Exactly when it began to be considered informal or even slang is not clear, but most commentators now associate it with down-home American speech. It is considered inappropriate for formal writing.

It was the first time I'd seen my name in print and it looked mighty good.
Max Braithwaite *The Night We Stole the Mountie's Car* 1971: 217

Like a gun-slinger, a trial lawyer must be mighty fast on the draw.
Business Journal June 1991: 25

migrant, migrate   see EMIGRANT

Mi'kmaq, Mi'kmaw   see MICMAC

mile   Although distances in Canada are now usually recorded in metric units (SI), the *mile* is still current in some contexts. The land or statute mile, used to express the limits of territorial waters, is 5280 feet (1.609 km); the air mile and the traditional nautical mile are both 6080.2 feet, or one-sixtieth of a degree of longitude measured at the equator (1.853 km). The new internationally recognized nautical mile is 6076.1 feet (1.851 km).

See also APPENDIX II.

militate, mitigate   A factor that *militates against* something reduces the likelihood that it will occur, succeed, be borne out, etc. (It might help to remember that *militate* comes from the same root as *military* and *militant*: something that militates against something else threatens to defeat it.) To *mitigate* means to soften the effect of, to alleviate, or to assuage. *Mitigate against* is often mistakenly used for *militate against*.

Also, [potential female politicians] hesitate to leave their families for the extended periods of federal parliamentary sessions: Canada's very vastness militates against mass female participation.
Gazette (Montreal) 19 Nov. 1994: I3

Such a pedigree [of 'celebrating Hollywood puffery'] ought to militate against his writing an interesting novel set at the world's most prestigious film festival—yet *Cannes* is surprisingly readable.
Vancouver Sun 7 July 1990: D19

Living closer together does not mean that we will be cramped as long as new communities are designed to mitigate the effects of high density living.
Vancouver Sun 14 Nov. 1990: B2

An air of judicial calm must prevail, particularly on the part of the judge, who can often mitigate the explosive situation with diplomatic intervention.
Province (Vancouver) 6 Dec. 1990: 50

In Quebec, where the language difference mitigates against U.S. imports, magazine publishers still depend on the newsstand to compete for readers.
Ottawa Citizen 16 Jan. 1993: F4

(The expression wanted here is *militates against*.)

millennium, millenarian, millenary, millinery
A *millennium* is a period of one thousand years. According to the calendar in use in most of the world (the Gregorian calendar), we are now in the second millennium A.D. and approaching the third. The word *millennium* also refers to a thousandth anniversary or the turning year of a millennium. 'The millennium', in the belief of some Christian sects, is a thousand-year period during which Christ will reign on earth and good will triumph over evil. The term is used figuratively to mean a long period of prosperity and happiness when good will prevail.

Millenarians, people with *millenarian* beliefs, believe literally in the doctrine of Christ's thousand-year reign. Sometimes the term *millenarian* is also applied to those who believe in the possibility of perfecting human society. Millenarians occasionally predict the end of the world and gather large numbers of followers, particularly around significant dates such as A.D. 1000 or 2000. Technically, because there is no year zero, the new millennium begins at the end, not the beginning, of the year 2000.

It is easy to misspell either *millennium* or *millenarian* because only the former has a double *n*. The inconsistency is attributable to different etymologies. *Millennium* derives from the Latin *mille*, 'thousand', and *annus*, 'year', while *millenarian* derives from the Latin adjective *millenarius*, 'consisting of a thousand'. The plural of *millennium* is *millenniums* or *millennia*.

Millenary (noun and adjective) is a synonym of both *millennium* and *millenarian*. *Millinery* is the designing or selling of women's hats.

Persian Iran has been a traditional foe of the Arab world for a millennium.
Ottawa Citizen 15 Aug. 1990: A1

... such unknowledgeable merrymakers will do their special celebrations on the night of Dec. 31, 1999–Jan. 1, 2,000—one year before the end of the decade, the century and the second millennium.
Ottawa Citizen 14 Oct. 1990: C7

We are approaching a millennium; the year 2000 draws on apace.
Robertson Davies *A Voice from the Attic* 1960: 350

(Some would argue that Davies should have written 'the year 2001 draws on'.)

Communism-Marxism may be dead and buried (good riddance) but its millenarian ideals, borrowed heavily from Judeo-Christian egalitarian fantasies, remain intact, resurrected in various guises as social democracy, social(ist) justice and its newest reincarnation, the Greens who are merely Reds in camouflage.
Financial Post 13 Oct. 1989: 10

After completing fashion design and millinery courses in Vancouver, Crowe packed up her hat boxes and moved to London, England.
Vancouver Sun 2 Aug. 1994: C1

milliard   see BILLION

millinery   see MILLENNIUM

-minded   *Career-minded, closed-minded, health-minded, high-minded, right-minded, single-minded*, and a host of other *-minded* combinations are evidence of the current popularity of *-minded* as combining form. These expressions are usually hyphenated. In long-established forms, the first element tends to be an adjective, such as *fair* or *simple*, characterizing a person's mind. New combinations usually begin with a noun, such as *budget* or *outdoors*, describing a person's preoccupation or focus.

In Britain, where lack of representation was a more serious problem, the cause of political liberty underwent no decline in popularity among those who were reform-minded....
J.A.W. Gunn *Beyond Liberty and Property* 1983: 257

Research and graduate studies advanced together. It was not merely that research-minded professors attracted advanced students; such students, by acting as research assistants and teaching assistants, facilitated research.
Frederick Gibson *Queen's University* 2 (1983): 321

mindset   see MENTALITY

minimal   Several usage guides maintain that the adjective *minimal* has only one meaning: the smallest or the least possible ('the minimal effective dose'). Dictionary definitions sometimes support this view, but in practice *minimal* has a much wider range of meanings. It's used in all types of writing to mean very small or insignificant.

> Maybe he had a minimal cult then, a tiny number of people starting to really love his music.
> Jack Chambers *Milestones* 1983: 289

(Here *minimal* means very small.)

> In 1950–51, after two decades of minimal growth, [the professoriate] was top-heavy: nearly 77 per cent occupied positions in the two senior ranks of professor and associate professor.
> Frederick Gibson *Queen's University* 2 (1983): 343

(Here *minimal* means very small.)

> Club fees are low and earnings from most recordings are minimal.
> *Queen's Quarterly* 95.2 (1988): 299

(Here *minimal* means insignificant.)

minor   see SUPERIOR

minority   see MAJORITY; SEXUAL MINORITIES; VISIBLE MINORITY

minuscule   *Minuscule* is spelled *miniscule* so frequently that many dictionaries list *miniscule* if only to note that it is an error. Some critics argue that it should be considered a standard variant. *Minuscule* was formerly used to refer to some medieval writing styles and to uncapitalized letters; the first documented use in the current sense, very small, dates from 1893.

> The Canadian markets ended a disappointing week with miniscule gains.
> *Gazette* (Montreal) 21 July 1990: H5

(The correct spelling is *minuscule*.)

> The problem is that the funds available for such deals are miniscule in relation to developing country debt.
> *Financial Post* 17 May 1990: 10

(The correct spelling is *minuscule*.)

> My copy now contains hundreds of corrections, most of them on miniscule details....
> Jack Chambers *Milestones* 1983: x

(The correct spelling is *minuscule*.)

misandry, misanthrope, misanthropy   see MISOGYNY

miscellany   A *miscellany* is collection of various writings or things. The word may be pronounced *MISS uh lain ee* or *miss SELL uh nee*. The latter pronunciation is particularly British.

West Edmonton Mall is eight city blocks long and three blocks wide, a two-level, yellow-brick structure that houses a miscellany of modern recreation.
Saturday Night May 1986: 49

mischievous   The standard pronunciation of *mischievous* is MIS chuh vus. The widespread, long-standing, but still unacceptable pronunciation *mis CHEE vee us* accounts for the common misspellings *mischevious* and *mischievious*.

> As in the preceding example, the effect is more than mischievious....
> *Arctic* 41.1 (1988): 77

(The correct spelling is *mischievous*.)

> Sure, we get a glimpse of Lennon the mischevious troubadour, artist and social thinker....
> *Gazette* (Montreal) 5 March 1989: T65

(The correct spelling is *mischievous*.)

misdemeanor   see INDICTABLE OFFENCE

mishap   see ACCIDENT

misogyny, misogynist, misanthropy, misanthrope, misandry   *Misogyny* (pronounced *mi SAH jin ee*) is hatred of women. A person who hates or disdains women is called a *misogynist*. *Misanthropy* (*mi SAN throp ee*) is hatred or distrust of the whole human species, and a person so inclined is called a *misanthrope* (*MEE zan thrope*); the word is borrowed from French. *Misanthropist*, a fairly common anglicized variant of *misanthrope*, is considered non-standard by many authorities.

Misandry is a little-used word meaning hatred of men.

misplaced modifiers   Modifiers may be adjectives, adverbs, phrases, or clauses; misplaced modifiers make a sentence ambiguous or unintentionally funny. The normal cure is to shift the modifier closer to what it modifies, or, if that doesn't work, to rewrite the sentence. Some usage guides make no allowance for readers' common sense, and criticize what they consider the 'misplacement' of modifiers that in fact would cause no reader any confusion. Thus they would rewrite 'She watched the children swimming from the cliff' as 'From the cliff, she watched the children swimming', even though few would find the first sentence confusing. However, 'She watched the children swimming from the dock' doesn't make it clear whether she was watching from the dock, or the children were swimming from the dock. Here either 'From the dock, she watched the children swimming' or 'She watched the children, who were swimming from the dock' would make things clearer. Some readers take a great deal of malicious pleasure in discovering sentences such as 'His mother remarried at the age of six and he went to live with his grandparents' or 'Jones hit the first pitch off Carmichael's leg, which was fielded and thrown to first by Riley'.

The difference in the placement of adverb modifiers (such as *only*, *just*, *almost*, and *even*) in formal and informal styles is discussed under ONLY.

See also DANGLING MODIFIERS.

mispronunciation and pronunciation shifts, metathesis, epenthesis, prothesis *Metathesis* (pronounced *meh TA thuh sis*) is a grammatical term for the unintentional transposition of letters, sounds, or syllables within a word. This linguistic phenomenon, which occurs in both spoken and written English, has accounted for the creation of some common Standard English words. For instance, the Old Norse word for excrement, *drit*, was borrowed into Middle English and metathesized as *dirt*. *Brid* was the original Old English spelling for *bird*. And the Dutch verb *crul* and noun *cruller* became *curl* and *curler* in English.

Sometimes words are metathesized to produce an easier sound sequence: *curl* is easier to say in English than *crul*, and children often pronounce *spaghetti* as *puh SKET ee*. Sometimes it is the sound pattern in other words that leads to mispronunciations; for example, people often pronounce *integral* as if it were spelled *intregal*, presumably influenced by the *intr-* form of words as *intricate* and *introduce*.

The introduction of a sound into the middle of a word is termed *epenthesis* (*e PEN thuh sis*). Epenthesis occurs in the common pronunciation of *sherbet* as *sherbert*. What linguists call the epenthetic schwa accounts for the disputed two-syllable pronunciation of *film* (*FILL um*) or the three-syllable pronunciation of *athlete* (*ATH uh leet*).

The addition of an extra sound at the beginning of a word is known as *prothesis*. This phenomenon is more common in the Romance languages than in English. For example, the Latin *schola*, from which English derived *school*, became *école* in French and *escuela* in Spanish.

A fine athelete, he was a college football hero. . . .
Financial Post 9 Jan. 1990: 11

(Here the misspelling of *athlete* reflects the epenthetic pronunciation.)

See also CALVARY, CAVALRY; HYPERCORRECTION; MALAPROPISM; SLIPS OF THE TONGUE; SPOONERISMS.

Miss, Mr., Mrs., Messrs., Mmes. *Mr.* and *Mrs.* are never unabbreviated before a name. The long form *mister* sometimes appears as a term of direct address ('Mister, could you move your car?'), but the connection between *Mrs.* and its original long form, *mistress*, has been lost. 'The missus', a slang synonym for wife, reflects the current pronunciation of *Mrs.*

In British English *Mr* and *Mrs* are spelled without periods. The British convention (which some North American editors follow) is that an abbreviation that ends with the same letter as the full word takes no period.

The plural of *Miss* is *Misses*. The plural of *Mr.* is *Messrs.* (from the French *messieurs*): 'Dear Messrs. Harmond and Lyle'. The plural of *Mrs.* is *Mmes.* (from French *mesdames*).

Regarding the choice between *Ms.*, *Mrs.*, and *Miss*, see MS.

See also MA'AM, MADAM, MADAME.

missing   see GO MISSING

misspeak oneself   see LIE

misspell   The word *misspell* is often misspelled as *mispell*—an error that can be quite embarrassing to the writer intent on pointing out someone else's mistakes.

Misspelt is less common than *misspelled*, but either form is correct as the past tense or the past participle.

Lomas, who mispelled Richthofen, wrote: 'Met 24 Triplanes and Albertros Scouts with 14 (Sopwith) Camels.'
Gazette (Montreal) 5 Sept. 1990: A10

(The correct spelling is *misspelled*.)

Adding insult to injury, her first name was misspelt.
Province (Vancouver) 5 Feb. 1990: 15

Brasserie Creek was also misspelled in the story.
Ottawa Citizen 27 April 1990: A2

mistrust   see DISTRUST

mitigate see MILITATE

mixed metaphor A mixed metaphor is a sequence of distractingly incongruous figures of speech that may produce a ludicrous image in the reader's mind: 'If I were in the driver's seat, we wouldn't be barking up the wrong tree'; 'The human eye had never before set foot in such a place'.

See also DEAD METAPHOR.

Modern English see OLD ENGLISH

modifiers see DANGLING MODIFIERS; MISPLACED MODIFIERS

modus operandi, modus vivendi *Modus operandi* is a Latin phrase meaning manner or method of operating. In police jargon it is often abbreviated to *m.o.* or *M.O.*, and refers to the characteristic way a criminal proceeds. The plural is *modi operandi*.
Modus vivendi means way of living. It refers far less often to a chosen lifestyle than to a way of coping or of getting along despite differences or disagreements. *Modus vivendi* should be italicized in formal English; its plural is *modi vivendi*.

When writing fiction, Findley's modus operandi is to find his voice first, his characters second.
Vancouver Sun 24 Nov. 1990: C17

'But I've never seen this kind of M.O. (modus operandi or operating technique) in 27 years of police work.'
Ottawa Citizen 4 Dec. 1990: A12

'We had a large series of break and enters with very similar modus operandis.'
Ottawa Citizen 17 May 1990: A16

(The accepted plural, which would be required in formal writing, is *modi operandi*. In this informal context 'with *a* very similar *modus operandi*' might be less awkward.)

Her awareness of the *modus vivendi* forced on city children is neither sentimental nor censorious....
Janice Kulyk Keefer *Reading Mavis Gallant* 1989: 199

The unease has spread as members of Canada's two dominant language groups look for a new modus vivendi after 21 years of official bilingualism.
Ottawa Citizen 24 March 1990: B4

No amount of inept negotiating by Oka or provincial governments, or bungled enforcement by Quebec police, can justify the Warriors' modus vivendi....
Financial Post 6 Aug. 1990: 7

(Here *modus operandi* would make more sense.)

See also LATIN PHRASES.

Mohammed see ISLAM

mold see MOULD

momentarily *Momentarily* means briefly, for a moment, or for the moment. It is often used in speech and newspapers to mean imminently or in a moment—a usage strongly disparaged by most usage guides. The disputed sense is not commonly found in Canadian books or academic journals, and should be restricted to informal writing.

[The airplane] recovered momentarily as it lifted up again, then finally crashed into the dirt.
Vancouver Sun 22 May 1990: A13

Luc Besson's first film, *Le Dernier Combat*, was never released in Canada, though his second picture, *Subway* ... should be in the theatres momentarily.
Globe and Mail (Toronto) 6 Sept. 1985: E9

(Here *very soon* would be a better choice.)

See also PRESENTLY.

[momento] see MEMENTO

money, monies, moneys Both *monies* and *moneys* are listed as standard plural forms in current dictionaries. Canadian writers prefer the *-ies* plural. In most uses *money* needs no plural, but the plural form is frequently used to refer to currencies from different countries or, in business contexts, as a synonym for *funds*. In other contexts the plural is either pretentious or humorous: 'I've depleted my monies'.

Whether or not the provincial government was set to seize $7.4 million in unspent public school board monies is now beside the point.
Calgary Herald 2 Dec. 1994: A4

Montagnais see INNU

moose, caribou, reindeer, elk, wapiti, red deer Some confusion is possible because the popular names for three species of large deer found in Canada are used differently in North America and Britain. What we call *moose* (Latin name, *Alces alces*) the British usually call *elk*. What we call *caribou* (*Rangifer tarandus*) they call *reindeer*. And what we call *elk*, *North American elk*, or *wapiti* (*Cervus canadensis*) they call *red deer* (*Cervus elaphus*). North

American elk and European red deer are so similar that some biologists consider them the same species.

The antlers of the male moose have hand-shaped ends, and both male and female have the distinctive roman noses, wattles, knobby knees, and large hooves that make them easy to distinguish from elk and caribou. The head of a caribou is depicted on the Canadian 25-cent piece. Caribou are slightly smaller than elk, but their antlers are heavier.

> The program has dramatically improved the survival rate of calves born to such big game animals as moose, elk, and caribou.
> *Globe and Mail* (Toronto) 27 March 1985: P8

moot   One long-established sense of the adjective *moot* is 'debatable', and this is the usual meaning of the word in the phrases 'a moot point' and 'a moot question'. In legal parlance a 'moot court' is a practice court where law students debate hypothetical cases. Another sense has arisen from an American legal usage in which *moot* refers to an issue that has already been decided; this sense of *moot* has moved into general usage, where it means 'academic' or 'of no practical importance'. Some dictionaries and usage commentators are reluctant to acknowledge this new meaning; however, Canadian writers use the adjective *moot* in both senses. Context should be provided to make the intended sense clear.

> Whether the point has been carried far enough, and whether their forms should have been more clearly articulated in view of the civic buildings to follow later is a moot point.
> *Canadian Architect* June 1986: 34

(Here the point is debatable.)

> Rudyard Kipling would hate me for this, but it's now a moot point whether the English, the Americans, etc., can keep order in their own countries, let alone those inhabited by his 'lesser breeds without the Law.'
> *Globe and Mail* (Toronto) 17 July 1985: P6

(Here the point is debatable.)

> … the table may not accurately reflect the true grades of some hogs. It's perhaps a moot point for producers, since a revised table probably wouldn't change how much they receive.
> *Country Guide* Nov. 1986: 33

(Here, as the context makes clear, the *moot point* is one of no practical significance.)

> Whether or not King is a believer is a moot point. If this were a tragic representation of human sufferings in a

war, he would not have drawn a cartoon and you would not have printed it.
> *Ottawa Citizen* 8 June 1994: A12

(Here the *moot point* is one of no import, irrelevant.)

moral, morals, morale, moral support   The adjective *moral* means ethical and upright, or having to do with *morals*. *Morals* meaning ethics or a standard of conduct is always plural. A *moral* is a lesson conveyed by a story.

Morale (pronounced *mor AL*) means state of mind or level of enthusiasm. *Moral support* improves morale (rather than morals). People offer it through their physical presence or their expressions of encouragement; moral support is often contrasted with financial support.

> … the most effective restraint on Canadian military action may not be any moral qualms among political leaders, but the weakness of Canada's depleted armed forces.
> *Maclean's* 23 Dec. 1991: A12

> The moral of the story? 'Police officers are victims like anybody else,' said Bildfell.
> *Calgary Herald* 3 Feb. 1994: A1

> Managers strive to introduce robots in physically demanding and monotonous jobs because they recognize that workers' morale is higher when they work at more pleasant and challenging tasks requiring more thought and skill.
> Irving M. Zeitlin and Robert J. Brym *The Social Condition of Humanity* 1991: 360

> Although she said agency brass consider the camp 'a great idea' and offer moral support, they have no money to contribute to the project.
> *Gazette* (Montreal) 19 July 1990: G1

more   see ANOTHER; COMPARISONS; COMPLETE; TIMES LESS, TIMES MORE

more importantly, more important   Many commentators dislike the adverb phrase *more importantly* and prefer *more important*, which they view as the legitimate contraction of the original expression *what is more important*. However, it is the adverb form of this sentence modifier that Canadians favour; *more importantly* is far more common in all varieties of writing.

> More importantly, if he is properly prepared to accept students as students, he will certainly recognize the complexity of English.

W.C. Lougheed, ed. *In Search of the Standard in Canadian English* 1986: 73

But we *are* all in this together, not just as citizens of our respective nation states but more importantly as inhabitants of this quickly shrinking and increasingly threatened earth.
Margaret Atwood *Second Words* 1982: 392

They still have an office at a convenient ground-level location in the city and, more importantly, they know where Wales is.
Gazette (Montreal) 10 June 1992: E1

More important, the modern religious poet is apt to confuse inspiration with a state of grace....
Northrop Frye *The Bush Garden* 1971: 79–80

See also SENTENCE ADVERBS.

more perfect   see PERFECT

more so   In the phrase *more so, so* stands for—and makes it unnecessary to repeat—part of the preceding sentence or clause: ' His first novel was marred by poorly delineated characters; his next one was even more so'. Sometimes writers use *more so* when *more* alone will do: 'Jack does it more so than Phil'. In informal writing *more so* often begins a sentence fragment ('They are popular here. More so in Toronto'). In formal writing, the period should be replaced by *and*.
Occasionally writers mistakenly spell *more so* as one word.

I replied that I understood perfectly, all the more so since my brother was overseas with the Calgary Highlanders....
George Ignatieff *The Making of a Peacemonger* 1987: 78

'All our analyses show that Quebecois remain open-minded about immigration, perhaps even more so than other Canadians.'
Gazette (Montreal) 29 June 1994: A7

Perhaps more so than any previous Rider coach, Rita separates work from play.
Ottawa Citizen 23 June 1994: E1

(Here the *so* is unnecessary.)

But the Portland game could turn out to be the most interesting of all, moreso off the ice than on, especially with Gretzky on the sidelines.
Financial Post 19 Sept. 1991: 51

(The correct spelling is *more so*.)

Well, you've got to admit that it catches the eye. Moreso perhaps than the picture offered Canadian movie goers—a young boy and a young girl at piano practice, holding hands....
Ottawa Citizen 7 July 1990: G3

(Here the period after *eye* should be changed to a comma, *moreso* replaced by *more*, and *perhaps* shifted to precede *more*.)

See also SENTENCES, SENTENCE FRAGMENT.

more than one   Logically, *more than one* is plural, but by grammatical convention it is treated as singular: 'More than one head is going to roll'. Occasionally, notional agreement motivates a plural verb after *more than one*: 'When more than one of them *are* in the same class, they cause trouble'. Some commentators label this usage non-standard.

'... in each instance more than one male was involved.'
Toronto Star 30 Dec. 1992: A8

More than one man Sadie knew was drowned doing things like this.
Richard Davies and Glen Kirkland, eds. *Dimensions* 1986: 118

'What the hell was that?' more than one of us asks.
Ken Dryden *The Game* 1983: 31

See also AGREEMENT, GRAMMATICAL.

mortar   see CEMENT

mortgagee, mortgagor   see LESSOR

Moslem   see ISLAM

most   see COMPARISONS; COMPLETE

most, almost   *Most* meaning 'almost' is accepted when it modifies indefinite adjectives and pronouns, such as *all, any, anybody, anyone, everybody*, and *anything*, but is considered dialectal, quaint, or facetious in other contexts: for example, 'I most laughed out loud'; 'It's most empty'.

The chapter could comfortably fit in most any book on social theory.
Canadian Journal of Sociology 14.2 (1989): 267

'Most of them can do most anything.'
Queen's Quarterly 96.2 (1989): 306

Most everyone agrees that from the start people in need of quick cash would go, usually with discretion, to the small side room of her elegant colonial home.
Canadian Fiction Magazine 63 (1988): 119

However, the important point in all this was now grasped by most everyone.
Henry M. Rosenthal and S. Cathy Berson, eds. *Canadian Jewish Outlook Anthology* 1988: 317

most perfect   see PERFECT

mother-in-law, in-law   The plural of *mother-in-law* is *mothers-in-law*, not *mother-in-laws*. The same is true for *brothers-*, *sisters-*, and *fathers-in-law*.

In-laws is standard as a generic term meaning relatives by marriage.

> ... mothers-in-law drew high marks along with moms who apparently are conjuring up everything from perogies and quiche to Black Forest cake....
> *Vancouver Sun* 24 Oct. 1990: C1

> 'Sometimes you walk into offices on a sales call, and it's like walking into the Pick N Save of mother-in-laws. Everybody has a daughter, a friend's daughter, a neighbor they want to set you up with.'
> *Calgary Herald* 3 Jan. 1992: A2

(The desirable bachelor quoted here should have used *mothers-in-law*).

> They must build harmonious family relationships (which often centre on good relations with in-laws), do a heavy stint of housework, support their husbands' careers, and raise fine and talented children.
> *Canadian Journal of History* 14.1 (1989): 153

Mother Nature   Non-sexist usage guides suggest laying *Mother Nature* to rest. Traditionally *Mother Nature* has been used to describe both the creative and nurturing force that brings spring flowers and the malevolent and unpredictable force that causes storms. One example of this association of nature and the feminine was that hurricanes and tropical storms were given feminine names. Now, in response to protests, they are given feminine and masculine names alternately. To avoid stereotyping women and excluding men, some guides recommend calling *Mother Nature* simply *nature*. However, the impulse to personify nature is so strong that *Mother Nature* is not likely to disappear soon.

> As several hundred New Glasgow residents waited anxiously ... for a plane to fly by and 1,500 miniature balls to fall from above, Mother Nature ruined the day....
> *Chronicle-Herald* (Halifax) 14 May 1988: 1

> Mother Nature decreed the north end of the island to be a driftwood beach and winds and tides have obeyed her.
> *Chronicle-Herald* (Halifax) 14 May 1988: 9

> Mother Nature played havoc with the snow sculptures entered in the national competition, many of them melting or falling apart on Sunday, judging day.
> *Chronicle-Telegraph* (Quebec City) 6 Feb. 1991: 1

See also SEXIST LANGUAGE.

motorway   see ROAD

mould, mold   Either spelling is appropriate for all senses, including the noun meaning fungal growth and the verb meaning shape. In Canadian texts *mould* is found more often than *mold* for all senses. *Mould* is the more common British spelling; Americans prefer *mold*.

moustache, mustache   Canadian writers prefer *moustache*, although *mustache* is occasionally found. In Britain the usual spelling is *moustache*; in the United States, *mustache*.

mow, mowed, mown   The past tense is *mowed*: 'She mowed the lawn'. The past participle is *mowed* or, less commonly, *mown*: 'She has mowed (*or* mown) the lawn'. *Mowed* and *mown* are both used as adjectives, but here *mown* is more common: 'mown (*or* mowed) fields'.

A *hay mow* is a storage loft in a barn. In this sense only, *mow* rhymes with *cow*.

> My sense of superiority was not totally out of control as I thought of the trainloads of weeds I had pulled, the miles of lawn I had mowed ... in my previous life as a garden-enslaved fool.
> *Vancouver Sun* 11 May 1990: 35

> 'And they talk. "Oh, the parson hasn't had his lawn mown. How horrible...."'
> *Gazette* (Montreal) 4 Nov. 1990: D1

> [The wind] carries the sweet scent of freshly mown alfalfa from the river bottoms below.
> *Vancouver Sun* 29 Oct. 1990: A11

> A polo field, a huge expanse of closely mowed turf, measures 274 metres by 137 metres—roughly the size of nine football fields.
> *Gazette* (Montreal) 19 July 1990: H1

> Inside the barn there were roomy stalls for the horses and cows, a hay mow, a loft where oats and barley were stored, and nooks and crannies where chickens made their nests.
> *Gazette* (Montreal) 31 July 1994: C1

Mr., Mrs.   see MISS

Ms.   *Ms.* (pronounced *MIZ*) was first suggested in the early 1950s as a convenient way of addressing business mail to a woman whose marital status was unknown. Like *Miss* and *Mrs.*, *Ms.* is an abbreviation of *Mistress*. However, *Ms.* did not become popular until the 1970s, when the women's movement recognized its usefulness as an honorific that paralleled the male honorific *Mr.* in not indicating marital status. *Ms.* is now fully established, although it has not replaced *Miss* and *Mrs.*, which some women prefer. It is only polite to address a woman using the honorific of her choice, when it is known.

In North America *Ms.* is generally spelled with a period, while *Ms* is the usual spelling in British English. The British convention (which some North American editors follow) is to omit the period when the abbreviation ends with the same letter as the complete word.

'Spirit of Community' is the subject of the presentation to be given by Ms. Von Tscharner and her husband Friday morning....
Guardian (Charlottetown) 2 Nov. 1990: 9

When a camera crew said it had missed their greeting, Mr. Gromyko shook Mr. Clark's hand again while Mrs. Gromyko welcomed Ms McTeer a second time.
Globe and Mail (Toronto) 3 April 1985: 1

(Note the spelling of *Ms* without a period. *Mr.*, *Mrs.*, and *Ms.* should be spelled consistently—either all with a period or all without.)

See also MA'AM, MADAM; MISS, MR., MRS.

much   see VERY

mucus, mucous   *Mucus* is the noun. *Mucous* is the adjective. These words, which usually appear in a medical context, are often confused when they are used in other types of writing.

A raspy hack that clears mucous from your respiratory system is doing an important job.
Canadian Consumer Jan. 1985: 17

(The noun should be spelled *mucus*.)

The candida grows and then invades the mucus membranes, becoming less friendly, increasing allergic reactions.
Globe and Mail (Toronto) 21 Feb. 1985: CL3

(The adjective should be spelled *mucous*).

Muhammed   see ISLAM

multilateral   see UNILATERAL

munificent   see BENEFICENT

muskeg   see SWAMP

Muslim   see ISLAM

mustache   see MOUSTACHE

mutual, common, reciprocal   Some usage commentators distinguish between *mutual* and *(in) common*. They restrict *mutual* to contexts where there is reciprocity or exchange: 'The feeling is mutual'. Where no exchange is involved, they insist on *common* or *in common*: 'They had interests in common (*or* common interests)'.

The expression 'mutual friend' has often been excepted from the distinction because of fears that 'common friend' might be misunderstood to mean vulgar friend. Today *common* is rarely used to mean vulgar, but the expression 'mutual friend' has a long lineage (dating from the mid-1600s) and is considered idiomatic even by purists. 'Mutual fund' is another established expression in which *common* would fit the prescribed usage better than *mutual*. Although some usage commentators consider the distinction between *mutual* and *common* to be one entirely contrived by the experts, phrases such as 'mutual goals', 'mutual problems', or 'their mutual high regard for Robert' are still liable to be criticized.

Mutual and *reciprocal* are often synonyms. However, *reciprocal* can be used in situations where something is not yet mutual but is hoped or expected to become so: 'We hope that our generous gesture will elicit a reciprocal generosity from our opponents'.

[Diaries] can reveal a great deal about European-native cultures and their mutual transformation in the Canadian West.
The Beaver Feb.–Mar. 1990: 551

Two, [a novel] by Isaac Bashevis Singer, describes a pair of married men living in pre-war Poland who admit their mutual attraction and run away.
Gazette (Montreal) 18 June 1994: I3

Last week, their mutual mudslinging reached an ugly crescendo that may ultimately prove costly to both.
Maclean's 7 Nov. 1988: A30

... the two reveal several mutual neuroses. Both Florence and Glen had unhappy childhoods.
NeWest Review Feb.–Mar. 1990: 43

(Here some critics would insist on *common* or *shared*, because the neuroses are not reciprocal.)

When Henry returned to Canada, he and his uncle discovered their mutual interest and started serious work.
Toronto Star 30 June 1994: E1

(Here too some critics would insist on *common* or *shared*.)

Like Grant ... he had accompanied their mutual friend the chancellor, Sandford Fleming, on a transcontinental journey before the building of the railway....
Hilda Neatby *Queen's University* 1 (1978): 247–9

(The phrase *mutual friend* is accepted, though it is at odds with the rule.)

Consumers will notice the feelings are reciprocal; the company donates a portion of its profits to local SPCA shelters.
Gazette (Montreal) 25 Nov. 1990: B7

myriad Originally *myriad* was a noun meaning ten thousand. It is now used as both a noun and an adjective and means a vast number, or innumerable.

There are a myriad of wines from France to seek out, to taste and to enjoy.
Queen's Quarterly 94.3 (1987): 605

Modern nails come in myriad types and sizes—North American manufacturers make more than 300 kinds....
Harrowsmith Oct.–Nov. 1985: 85

See also COLLECTIVE NOUNS.

myself, I, me Many usage guides object to the substitution of *myself* for *I* or *me*. They argue that *myself* has only two acceptable uses: for emphasis ('I myself don't like Yorkshire pudding, although I make it often') and as a reflexive pronoun ('I dressed myself warmly').

However, the substitution of *myself* for *I* or *me* often occurs in compound sentence subjects and objects: 'Marco, Mikhail, and myself finished our group project at midnight'; 'Jack and Julia invited my mother, my father, and myself to the opera'. These substitutions may have originated in the desire to avoid writing *I* where *me* is correct, or vice versa (see CASE), or in the feeling that saying *I* and *me* too often is vulgar. These substitutions are widespread in speech; they are less common in formal writing, although this may be partly attributable to the tendency in such writing to avoid using the first person.

Myself is also quite often found instead of *me* as the object of a preposition (*for, including, to*, etc.),

even in formal writing. *Myself* is particularly likely to appear after *than* or *as*. Which form of the pronoun should be used after these two words has generated considerable debate. And in structures like 'She is bigger than I/me' and 'She reads just as well as I/me', many speakers and writers evade the dilemma by substituting *myself*. *Myself* commonly replaces *me* after the preposition *like*: 'She looks just like myself'; 'Workaholics like myself can only dream of holidays'. Perhaps the reason is that *like* is a verb as well as a preposition, and the beginning of a sentence such as 'You like me have lost interest' could be misread.

It seems perfectly acceptable to use *myself* for *I* or *me* in all these contexts in speech and informal writing. In more formal contexts, however, it's probably best to avoid using *myself* where *I* or *me* is possible, especially as part of a compound sentence subject or object.

Becky, Linda and I met at 7 pm sharp at the Keele subway station.
Women and Environments 12.1 1990: 9

'The poems that Irving Layton, Louis Dudek and myself were writing at the time weren't all that fashionable with the general readership of the period.'
Bruce Meyer and Brian O'Riordan, eds. *In Their Words* 1984: 89

(This is a transcription of speech.)

'The Haig and myself played a few times and we shared the same liquid refreshment afterwards,' Sutherland once said.
Vancouver Sun 29 Dec. 1990: C3

(This is a transcription of speech.)

'All these men and many more, including myself, were drawn to nuclear physics as a result of our undergraduate contact with Gray.'
Frederick Gibson *Queen's University* 2: 1983: 122

It is many months since I was invited to speak to you, and in the interval several letters have passed between your club and myself.
Robertson Davies *One Half of Robertson Davies* 1978: 14

... an axe fight with an Irishman as hot-tempered as myself might well have killed either one of us.
George Ignatieff *The Making of a Peacemonger* 1987: 45

If I'm correct in my estimation, Br. Quiring must be younger than myself.
Mennonite Brethren Herald 4 April 1986: 8

Even in the life of one person like myself, living in a raw provincial city like Winnipeg, you can find the presence of duality and paradox that is so characteristic of Canadian life.
Miriam Waddington *Apartment Seven* 1989: 38

Canadian authors were invisible to the general public... and considered oxymorons by snobbish young would-be writers like myself, who thought we had to run away to

England in order to let our genius fully flower.
Margaret Atwood *Second Words* 1982: 402

It makes it impossible for historians like W.J. Baker and myself to continue to regret that the field of Victorian women's sports remains an historiographical desert.
Canadian Journal of History 14.1 (1989): 126

See also LIKE, AS; PRESENT WRITER; -SELF, -SELVES; THAN.

N

Na-Dene   see ATHABASCAN; DENE

nadir   see APOGEE

naive, naif, naivete, naivety   *Naive* is the French feminine form and *naif* the French masculine form of the same word. In English, whatever the gender of the subject, *naive* is generally used as the adjective: 'He was a naive man'. *Naif*, which is less common, appears only as a noun meaning naive person: 'She was such a naif'. In Canada the noun is usually spelled *naivete*. *Naivety* is a predominantly British spelling.

Any of these words may appear, as in French, with a diaeresis (two points) above the *i*, which indicate that it is pronounced separately; *naïveté* may also have an acute accent over the final *e*. These markings appear less often in contemporary usage, perhaps because most writing nowadays is done not by hand but on keyboards without accents.

Naive is pronounced *nye EVE*. *Naif* is pronounced *nah EEF*; and *naivete* is pronounced *nye EVE tay* or *nye EVE TAY*.

Children sometimes demand to know who invents jokes, and often their elders think this question naïve.
Robertson Davies *A Voice From the Attic* 1960: 214

In Canada ... there appears every year a fair quantity of naive or primitive verse, to use terms more familiar in the criticism of painting.
Northrop Frye *The Bush Garden* 1971: 3

Probing interviews reveal Dutilleux as a scam artist and Sting as at best a naif, at worst a fool.
Gazette (Montreal) 22 April 1990: F2

Throughout the film, demonstrations against the Marcos Government cross the paths of uncomprehending characters, political naifs who fail to realize their complaints are being addressed by the demonstrators, whose cause they neither share nor understand.
Globe and Mail (Toronto) 13 July 1985: E8

In my naivete, I was not prepared for petty office politics and hysterical, demanding clients.
Vancouver Sun 16 June 1990: C1

Through our naivety, we aid these companies by telling them whether we're working or retired, the ages of our children and how much money we make.
Vancouver Sun 27 June 1990: C2

(This spelling is uncommon in Canada.)

See also DIACRITICAL MARKS.

naked, nude   When used of people, *naked* and *nude* both mean unclothed. However, *naked* often conveys an additional sense of vulnerability, of being stripped bare or left unprotected. *Naked* is also more likely than *nude* to be used figuratively for non-human subjects. *Nude*, sometimes called a euphemism for *naked*, most often suggests deliberate or artistic nakedness. It is the usual choice when referring to art, or activities in which people choose to go without clothing ('nude dancing'), or the places where they do so ('nude beaches').

Later that night he set fire to the bed in his hotel room and was arrested wandering around naked; he was eventually confined to Camarillo State Hospital in a rehabilitation program.
Jack Chambers *Milestones* 1983: 50

They reach a grubby factory, lead their man down a set of dark, slippery stairs and into an airless basement where naked light bulbs hang from smoky ceilings.
Pierre Berton *The Promised Land* 1984: 307

The third work in the series, *The Studio Group* (1957), has as its theme students working from a nude model.
Queen's Quarterly 95.1 (1988): 152

names   see CHINESE NAMES; FIRST NAME; MAIDEN NAME, BIRTH NAME; NAMES OF RESIDENTS

names of residents of cities and provinces
There is no commonly accepted general term for the proper nouns that name the residents of a place, such as *Calgarian* for a person from Calgary. A term that has been suggested is *demonym*, from the Greek roots *demos*, 'people', and *-nym*, 'name'. Although there are phonological rules for forming these terms (they are based on the last syllables in the place name), it is usually the residents of a particular city, province, state, or country who have the last word about what they are called.

In Canadian usage the residents of some provinces are known by more than one name. Both *Saskatchewanian* and *Saskatchewaner* are in use, as are *New Brunswickian* and *New Brunswicker*. *Quebecker* was the English spelling preferred by René Lévesque for a resident of the province of Quebec; however, *Quebecer* is also widely used. The term *Québécois(e)* is usually reserved for francophone Quebeckers. Although, informally, residents of British Columbia are sometimes called *BCers*, in written English the term is *British Columbians*.

Other established names for residents of Canadian provinces are *Albertan, Manitoban, Nova Scotian, Newfoundlander, Ontarian*, and *Prince Edward Islander* (or simply *Islander*). *Yukoner* and *Labradorian* are in use, but there is no common term for a resident of the Northwest Territories.

The most distinctive name for a resident of a Canadian city is *Haligonian* for a native of Halifax, Nova Scotia. How and why this name was chosen remains a mystery. *Hambletonians* is sometimes used humorously for residents of Hamilton, Ontario (who are *Hamiltonians* in serious contexts). A person from Saint John, New Brunswick, is called a *Saint Johner*, while someone from St. John's, Newfoundland, is a *St. Johnsian*. In the English-language press all citizens of Montreal are *Mont-*

realers. In French-language publications a citizen of Montreal is either *un Montréalais* (male) or *une Montréalaise* (female).

Other established names for citizens of Canadian cities include *Vancouverite, Edmontonian, Moose Jawanian* (or *Moose Javian*), *Winnipegger, Torontonian, Ottawan*, and *Monctonian*. A resident of Medicine Hat, Alberta, is sometimes called a *Hatter*, a resident of Winnipeg, Manitoba, a *Pegger*.

In the 1930s, according to Prairie fiscal legend, a Saskatchewanian with a million-dollar income would have paid 105 per cent of it in federal and provincial income tax.
Vancouver Sun 31 July 1990: C1

Don't think we dusty, denim-clad, straw-chewin' Saskatchewaners don't appreciate The Globe's semi-annual forays out here into the land of Ma and Pa Kettle to fill in the rest of the country on two-month-old news stories.
Globe and Mail (Toronto) 7 Sept. 1985: P7

I told Crosbie that a prominent businessman in Vancouver, a bilingual New Brunswicker, had called me earlier in the week to tell me he was more afraid than ever for the future of his country.
Vancouver Sun 28 Feb. 1990: 29

'She was a true Québécoise, a born Montrealer.'
Canadian Fiction Magazine 63 (1988): 115

A contrasting figure is Stompin' Tom Connors, a Prince Edward Islander who arrived on the scene in the late sixties....
Queen's Quarterly 95.2 (1988): 303

Yukoners have an exuberant sense of fun, which is a good thing in February, when winter's darkest and cabin fever runs high.
Uphere Jan.–Feb. 1990: 11

Henry Beckman, a Haligonian who left Nova Scotia for New York City in 1946, has been around the block a few times.
Vancouver Sun 6 May 1990: D88

Come the rainy season, many Vancouverites turn to their favorite comfort food, clam chowder.
Vancouver Sun 5 Dec. 1990: F3

One doesn't need to travel to Toronto to find it; indeed Torontonians find it in Montreal, and Montrealais in Paris, and (these days) Parisiens in New York.
Globe and Mail (Toronto) 16 Feb. 1985: E3

Former Winnipegger Tim Lee, who lives in Toronto, will act as master of ceremonies....
Globe and Mail (Toronto) 12 Oct. 1985: A22

See also QUEBECKER; SAINT JOHN, ST. JOHN'S.

napkin, serviette A synonym for *napkin*, *serviette* is the less common term in Canada and is almost unknown in the United States. Its use in Canada may be influenced either by British usage or by the fact that *serviette* is the French term and appears on Canadian packages. For Canadians a *serviette* is usually a paper napkin, while a *napkin* is generally made of cloth.

> An American painter of this school played a joke on his bitchy wife by painting one of her best napkins so expertly that she grabbed at the canvas trying to pull it off.
> Northrop Frye *The Educated Imagination* 1963: 40

> And cloth can replace paper towels and serviettes, even facial tissue if you don't mind doing extra laundry.
> *Vancouver Sun* 13 July 1990: D10

> He'd carry a little pad in his pocket, or draw on serviettes at the Arts and Letters Club.
> *Saturday Night* March 1986: 37

Naskapi see INNU

national see CITIZEN

national anthem see O CANADA

National Assembly, nationalist The National Assembly is the legislature of Quebec. In Quebec English the word *nationalist* means sovereignist, not federalist.

> [Johnson's] uncompromising federalist stand renewed criticism that he isn't nationalist enough to run Quebec.
> *Toronto Star* 11 Sept. 1994: A10

See also SEPARATIST.

native, Native *Native* is etymologically connected to the Latin word for birth. Thus a native plant is one that is indigenous to an area: it originated there, and was not introduced from somewhere else. A native of Toronto is someone who was born there, though not necessarily a resident (someone who lives there now).

Native is also used to refer to the Aboriginal people of Canada. The Secretary of State's Terminology and Language Standardization Board recommends that this word be used as an adjective only—*Native people(s)*, not *Natives*—and that it be capitalized in references to Aboriginal peoples.

> Sanipas, a native of Big Cove, N.B., scored twice in Sunday's game.
> *Globe and Mail* (Toronto) 2 Jan. 1985: S2

> A native lawyer from Merritt is taking legal action to get her children registered as status Indians.
> *Province* (Vancouver) 23 Dec. 1990: 26

(*Native* and *status* should be capitalized.)

> Alberta also has all-native emergency firefighting crews.
> *Calgary Herald* 7 Aug. 1994: B2

(*Native* should be capitalized.)

See also ABORIGINAL PEOPLE(S).

Nat'ooten see CARRIER

naturalist, naturist A *naturalist* is a nature lover or a professional botanist or zoologist. A *naturist* is a nudist.

> Throughout Canada ... growing numbers of amateur naturalist groups are popping up, no doubt tied to society's recent ecological awakening.
> *Vancouver Sun* 31 May 1990: E18

> Nature walks are conducted by a resident professional naturalist, who is eager to share the wonders of this timeless land.
> *Vancouver Sun* 6 Oct. 1990: E7

> 'There's a lot of fear and misunderstanding out there,' says David Horton, a longtime nudist and a B.C. director of the Federation of Canadian Naturists.
> *Province* (Vancouver) 31 Oct. 1990: 3

naught, nought, aught *Naught* (rhymes with *knot*) and *nought* (rhymes with *ought*) are archaic words meaning zero, or nothing. They survive in phrases such as 'to bring to naught', 'to set at naught', 'to come to naught' and 'it was all for naught'. Both spellings are accepted, although *naught* is more common, particularly in academic writing.

Aught is the now-archaic opposite of *naught* and means all or anything; it survives, barely, in the jocular or dialectal 'for aught I know', meaning 'for all I know'.

> We can set management goals and establish preserves in Canada for our forest birds, but this will be for naught if tropical forests vanish.
> *Queen's Quarterly* 94.3 (1987): 618

> And if Cineplex fails, all the agony of the last year will be for nought.
> *Gazette* (Montreal) 6 Jan. 1990: D1

nauseous, nauseating, nauseated, sick In general usage, *nauseous* most often means *nauseated* or *sick*. However, several guides disapprove of this usage; they argue that *nauseous* is a synonym for *nauseating* or *sickening*, and many people agree with them. To avoid criticism, it's best not to use *nauseous* to mean *sick*.

> They make the whole idea of reading nauseous to thousands of decent people.
> Robertson Davies *A Voice from the Attic* 1960: 37

> Elizabeth can still see herself ... nauseated with pain.
> Margaret Atwood *Life Before Man* 1979: 106

> Not everyone drank the arrack but those who did became dizzy and nauseous on Christmas Eve.
> *Gazette* (Montreal) 29 Dec. 1990: A7

(Here *nauseated* or *sick* would be better.)

See also SICK.

naval, navel *Naval* describes anything related to the navy. The noun *navel*, referring to the place where the umbilical cord was once attached, is often applied figuratively.

> He then reviews naval and military bases and discusses political, economic, strategic and environmental factors that led to the selection of many colonial capitals.
> *The Canadian Geographer* Spring (1989): 93

> [The cultural tastes of the baby-boom generation] looked really self-indulgent, especially with navel-gazing soaps like Thirtysomething blazing the trail, dinosaur rock bands recycling themselves indefinitely and old-gold rock stations playing Hey Jude forever, like a loop from hell.
> *Province* (Vancouver) 27 May 1990: 89

navy see CANADIAN ARMED FORCES

NDP see NEW DEMOCRATIC PARTY

né, née see MAIDEN NAME

near, nearly *Near* is standard in combinations with nouns and adjectives: 'near-miss', 'near-disaster', 'near-perfect score'. 'Nowhere near', as in 'I'm nowhere near finished', is considered informal by some commentators.

Sentences in which *near* is substituted for *nearly* before a verb, as in 'I near fainted', sound dialectal or old-fashioned. This construction should be avoided in writing except in representations of speech.

> The selection of delegates to the leadership convention in Calgary next June is nowhere near complete but already it has made a mockery of fair play and party loyalty.
> *Vancouver Sun* 19 March 1990: 48

> I damn near bawled to think I could have asked him to tag along.
> David Williams *Eye of the Father* 1985: 13

near-sighted, far-sighted, short-sighted, long-sighted In Canada and the United States *near-sighted* refers to someone who sees nearby objects better than distant ones; *far-sighted* is the opposite. *Short-sighted* is most often used figuratively to describe someone who lacks foresight. *Far-sighted* is used figuratively to describe someone with good judgment about the future. Hyphenation of these words varies.

In British English *short-sighted* and *long-sighted* are the terms commonly used in reference to physical vision.

> 'Many of the children were so near-sighted that it was difficult for them to see clearly beyond a couple of feet.'
> *Vancouver Sun* 12 Dec. 1994: B5

> It's like being farsighted, the distant lake and its beaches and smooth-backed basking sauropods clear-edged in the moonlight, her own hand a blur.
> Margaret Atwood *Life Before Man* 1979: 142

> Short-sighted since childhood, he had to sit in the front of the class to see the blackboard.
> *Leader-Post* (Regina) 27 Feb. 1988: C1

> Ten storeys of stone facade on this early concrete framed building culminate in a flourish of Greek ornamental detail that you've got to be long-sighted, or have binoculars, to properly see.
> *Vancouver Sun* 29 Dec. 1990: D16

née see MAIDEN NAME

needless to say see GOES WITHOUT SAYING

negative see DON'T THINK; DOUBLE NEGATIVE

negative-raising see DON'T THINK

Negro see BLACK

neither In formal English the pronoun *neither* always takes a singular verb: 'Neither of them is (*not* are) adequate'. The conjunction *neither* should be paired with *nor*, not *or*.

Regarding agreement of the verb after a 'neither ... nor' construction, pronunciation, and whether *neither* should be used to introduce more than two items, see EITHER.

See also AGREEMENT, GRAMMATICAL.

ne plus ultra   see EPITOME; SINE QUA NON

nepotism   Although *nepotism* is similar in meaning to *favouritism* and *patronage*, it refers specifically to the favouring of family members.

News item: Two Tory MPs from Ontario and one from Quebec are investigated for allegedly circumventing anti-nepotism rules by hiring one another's sons and daughters.
Vancouver Sun 23 Feb. 1990: A13

It would have been acceptable if the Conservatives stuck to the Canadian tradition of political patronage, former Liberal solicitor-general Robert Kaplan says, but they strayed into the taboo territory of nepotism.
Globe and Mail (Toronto) 8 June 1985: P5

Lynn Patrick was 22 and he had only one year of senior hockey experience in Montreal when he was signed by the New York Rangers.... His father, coach Lester Patrick, immediately was accused of nepotism by the New York media.
Province (Vancouver) 24 Dec. 1990: 150

Magna [International] indulged in nepotism.... Having the only rising talent in an organization come from one group ruins morale.
Financial Post 26 March 1990: 2

(Since the 'group' referred to isn't a family, *favouritism* would be preferable here.)

Is there a form of regional nepotism going on? Six of the top executives of the Royal are from Saskatchewan, three of the top Imperial bosses.
Maclean's 21 Oct. 1991: A108

(Here too *favouritism* would be preferable.)

-ness   Although the words *certainness, clearness, deepness, difficultness, graveness, intenseness, loyalness, sincereness,* and *warmness* can all be found in dictionaries, they almost never appear in published writing. Their preferred synonyms are *certainty, clarity, depth, difficulty, gravity, intensity, loyalty, sincerity,* and *warmth.* The suffix *-ness* is freely added to adjectives to create nouns. The noun means the state or quality of being whatever the adjective denotes. Many writers and editors object

to new words ending in *-ness* that mean the same thing as established words containing the older noun suffixes *-ty* and *-th.*

See also ENORMITY, ENORMOUSNESS.

neuter, sterilize, castrate, spay, fix   A number of verbs refer to the surgical sterilization of animals. Both male and female animals can be *neutered* or *sterilized.* Male farm animals are *castrated*; but for male house pets more euphemistic terms are often preferred (*neuter, sterilize*). Female animals are *spayed* (sometimes this word is misspelled *spade*). *Fix* is slang for *neuter* or *sterilize.*

Most importantly, male dogs that are neutered run a significantly reduced risk of medical problems later on in life.
Ottawa Citizen 6 Jan. 1990: F7

Unless you've decided to enter your dog in conformation or obedience events, or have made a conscious decision to be a dog breeder ... you should have your dog spayed or neutered.
Dogs in Canada Special Issue 1986: 66

Pigs are usually castrated within the first few weeks of life. This pig was heading helter-skelter into puberty, uncastrated and obviously happy with his self-image.
Harrowsmith Oct.–Nov. 1985: 16

New Brunswick   see APPENDIX I

New Democratic Party, NDP   The New Democratic Party was founded in 1961, an amalgamation of the Co-operative Commonwealth Federation (CCF), affiliated unions of the Canadian Labour Congress (CLC), and New Party clubs. It is a democratic socialist party. The abbreviation *NDP* is much more common than the full name of the party in Canadian news reporting. Members may be called *NDP members, New Democrats,* or less formally, *NDPers.* The adjective is *New Democratic, New Democrat,* or *NDP,* as in 'an NDP policy'.

The classic cure for the Grits would be to move left and attempt to supplant the NDP in the hearts and minds of the voters by co-opting the New Democrat policies.
Ottawa Citizen 13 Dec. 1990: A3

It's been New Democratic policy for years to protect farmland....
Ottawa Citizen 13 Nov. 1990: A2

... some wonder ... whether a proposed regional garbage incinerator could be trashed by NDPers who see it as an environmental hazard.
Ottawa Citizen 8 Sept. 1990: A13

Newfoundland   see APPENDIX I

New Year's Day, April Fool's Day, Thanksgiving Day, St. Jean Baptiste Day   There is an apostrophe before the *s* in *New Year's Day*. References to the *new year*, meaning the year about to begin, should be capitalized only in a holiday greeting: 'Happy New Year'. Canadians and Americans often shorten *New Year's Day* or *New Year's Eve* to *New Year's*, a usage that sounds odd (or wrong) to speakers of British English.

April Fool's Day and *April Fools' Day* are both correct, with the former preferred in Canada. The victim of an April Fool's Day joke is an *April fool. April fool!* is the shout of the gleeful perpetrator.

Thanksgiving Day is celebrated on the second Monday in October in Canada, and on the fourth Thursday in November in the United States.

St. Jean Baptiste Day, 24 June, is the national holiday of Quebec. *St-Jean-Baptiste* is the French spelling, with no period after *St* and two hyphens. Both spellings, French and English, are in common use, as are hybrid variants (which should be avoided).

> CP Forest can now run the mill on New Years Day, Easter and Labor Day.
> *Ottawa Citizen* 21 Dec. 1990: C7

(An apostrophe should precede the *s*: *Year's*.)

> One game was scheduled for New Year's day.
> *Saturday Night* March 1986: 23

(*Day* should be capitalized.)

> As we begin a New Year, we look both back and forward, and our attitude will make all the difference.
> *Canadian Baptist* Jan. 1986: 17

(In references to the year rather than the day, *new year* is not usually capitalized.)

> During most of these years Montgomery gave Cavendish a large turkey for New Year's ....
> J.E. Smyth et al. *The Law and Business Administration in Canada* 1987: 592

> Children are welcome and Hessel, whose book about family life is a change from his local histories, promises to make an April Fool of himself.
> *Ottawa Citizen* 31 March 1990: K2

(*Fool* is not usually capitalized except in references to *April Fool's Day*.)

> In an unrelated matter, the PQ announced that it will hold a separate parade after the St.-Jean Baptiste parade in Montreal this Sunday.
> *Vancouver Sun* 21 June 1990: A10

(Either all-French or all-English spelling would be preferable: *St. Jean Baptiste* or *St-Jean-Baptiste*.)

See also HOLIDAY.

next, this   The expression *next Friday* is used in two ways. Sometimes it refers to the coming Friday, in which case it is synonymous with 'this Friday'; and sometimes it means Friday of next week. In other words, if on Monday you tell people about a party *next Friday*, some people will think it is happening in four days, others in eleven. *Collins COBUILD English Usage* says *next* should not be used to refer to a day in the same week, but in fact it often is. Given the potential for confusion, it's best not to use *next* with a day of the week unless you are also specifying the date. The expressions 'this Friday' and 'a week from Friday' are unambiguous alternatives to *next Friday*.

> This Saturday it's shopping. Next Saturday it'll be a mom-and-daughter pottery class....
> *Vancouver Sun* 18 Feb. 1992: C1

> Blue Jay first baseman John Olerud, Argonaut lineman Jim Kardash, and Maple Leaf centre Doug Gilmour will be the big wheels next Friday in the Bike Helmet Festival.... The festival runs from noon to 2 p.m. on June 12 and will feature events for both adults and children.
> *Toronto Star* 7 June 1992: E2

(Here *next Friday* means this Friday; this would have been confusing had the date not been given as well.)

> Later in the week, The Gazette has put together a series of lectures by specialists in many fields of financial planning, during the four-day Savings & Investment Marketplace, to be held in Place Bonaventure from next Friday, Jan. 31, through Feb. 3.
> *Gazette* (Montreal) 27 Jan. 1992: TWIB5

(Here again *next Friday* means this Friday, which would not have been evident if the date had not been given.)

nice, nicety   Almost anything that is not offensive can be described as *nice*, which leads some usage experts to complain that this adjective is greatly overworked. Although there is nothing grammatically incorrect about using *nice* as an all-encompassing adjective of approval, substitution of a more precise adjective, explaining why the person, object, or situation is considered 'nice', tends to produce a more interesting statement.

When it first appeared in English, in the 1300s, *nice* (from the Latin *nescius*, 'ignorant') meant foolish or ignorant. Since then its meaning has evolved through timid, fussy, fastidious, dainty, extravagant, precise, exact, and careful to the most commonly used current senses: agreeable or delightful, first recorded in 1769, and kind or thoughtful, first recorded in 1830. An older meaning of *nice* is reflected in expressions such as 'a nice distinction' (fine or subtle), as well as in the noun *nicety*, which means subtlety rather than niceness.

> It is a nice prairie, covered with beautiful grass, and dotted here and there with little poplar forests which gives the whole a very romantic appearance.
> *NeWest Review* Oct.–Nov. 1989: 13

> This operation required a nice balancing of two gauges on the switchboard and the tripping of a switch.
> *Imperial Oil Review* Spring (1988): 28

(Here *nice* means delicate or careful.)

> As a working musician, Davis showed no interest in the theoretical niceties of his innovation except as a means of relieving his music of the predictable chord progressions, creating an aural effect of lightness, and challenging his melodic ingenuity.
> Jack Chambers *Milestones* 1983: 309

nickel, the nickel belt, Nickel Belt   *Nickel* is the correct spelling for both the metal and the five-cent coin. *Nickle* is a common misspelling. The nickel belt (not capitalized) is the geographic area around Sudbury, Ontario, where much of the world's nickel is mined. Nickel Belt (capitalized) is the name of an electoral riding in the area.

> I'd never even seen a beaver, except on the back of a nickel.
> Howard Engel *Murder Sees the Light* 1984: 57

> Now, as health minister, his fate is to nickle-and-dime the provinces to death over health costs.
> *Ottawa Citizen* 19 Aug. 1990: A6

(The correct spelling is *nickel*.)

> Married, with three children, he became MPP for Nickel Belt in 1971 and has been re-elected six times.
> *Maclean's* 26 Aug. 1991: A16

> With McLaughlin's encouragement, Barrett teamed up with the similarly aggressive Nickle Belt MP John Rodriguez to form what caucus members call 'the nasty boys.'
> *Maclean's* 13 Aug. 1990: A12

(The correct spelling is *Nickel*.)

Nisei   see ISSEI

Nishga, Niska, Nisga'a   Formerly called *Nishga* (or *Niska*), this First Nation in British Columbia now goes under the name *Nisga'a* (singular and plural), pronounced *NIS gaah*. The Nisga'a language belongs to the Tsimshian family.

> Leaders representing the 6,000 Nisga'a people from the Nass Valley near the B.C.-Alaska border are trying to negotiate a treaty with Victoria and Ottawa to define their land and other aboriginal rights.
> *Vancouver Sun* 23 Sept. 1994: B2

Nlaka'pamux   see THOMPSON

nohow   *Nohow* means 'in no manner'. It is most frequently used in double negatives ('I couldn't start the car nohow'), which are condemned by grammarians. It is standard in constructions without a second negative ('She could nohow write the test'), but this usage is extremely rare in Canada.

> He too is nervous but his nerves are in a state that does no good for nobody no-how.
> *Canadian Fiction Magazine* 63 (1988): 137

(The author is using non-standard dialect.)

> ... He feels he's in a personal slugfest with Brian Mulroney, and he isn't going to back down nohow.
> *Gazette* (Montreal) 20 Jan. 1990: B3

(Here again the non-standard use is intentional.)

See also DOUBLE NEGATIVE.

noisome   *Noisome* is sometimes mistakenly used to mean noisy. It derives from the same Middle English word that gave us *annoy*. It means harmful, offensive, or disgusting, and often implies a foul smell.

> Most caddies have nicknames, including one known as Downwind Vic, a caddie everyone tries to keep ahead of due to a noxious and noisome anatomical defect....
> *Globe and Mail* (Toronto) 26 Aug. 1985: S2

> Of all the American culture that slops over the border and is soaked up by undiscriminating Canadians, gun love is perhaps the most noisome.
> *Vancouver Sun* 31 Aug. 1994: A18

nom de guerre, nom de plume   see PSEUDONYM

nonchalant   see NONPLUSSED

none *None is* and *none are* are both correct. Generally, *none* can be followed by either a singular or a plural verb: 'None of them has a car'; 'None of them have jobs'. *None* requires a singular verb only when it means 'no part of a mass or whole': 'None of it makes (*not* make) any sense'.

> As for the writers Mathews mentions, none of them has the above combination.
> Margaret Atwood *Second Words* 1982: 141

> I find it of interest, too, that of all the ones he mentions, none are of his own generation or younger.
> Margaret Atwood *Second Words* 1982: 148

> Of thirty-five undersecretaries-general, none is a woman.
> *Saturday Night* May 1986: 43

> Above all, however, we hope you share our dream of a world where all dogs are loved—where none are killed because no one wants them....
> *Dogs in Canada* Special Issue 1986: 4

> None of this emerges.
> *Edmonton Journal* 13 Sept. 1992: n.p.

(Here *none* means no part and the plural verb *emerge* is not possible.)

See also AGREEMENT, GRAMMATICAL.

non-flammable see FLAMMABLE

non-human see HUMAN

non-inflammable see FLAMMABLE

non-moral see IMMORAL

nonplussed, nonchalant *Nonplussed* means puzzled or at a loss as to what to say or do. The word comes from the Latin *non plus*, meaning literally 'no further', and suggests a state in which nothing more is forthcoming. The *non-* prefix, however, appears to indicate that the word means *not* something. *Nonplussed* is so often used to mean unconcerned, indifferent, or unruffled that it seems clear people are confusing it with *nonchalant*.

Canadian writers prefer the British double-*s* spelling; *nonplused* is a chiefly American variant.

> She seems nonplussed at the idea that she might have chosen a different career. 'Art is what holds me,' she says.
> *Torch: University of Victoria Alumni Magazine* Spring (1990): 15

It's also so unrealistic in the assumptions it makes about the rest of Canada that you're nonplussed as to how someone as astute as Bourassa ... could be so totally disconnected from the mood of the land mass immediately to the east and west of the Quebec border.
> *Toronto Star* 14 Aug. 1990: A13

> The reporter was momentarily nonplussed: How could the small Satomi caddy for four players? Answer: Japanese technology.
> *Vancouver Sun* 25 Jan. 1990: F9

> 'Hey Shutty,' Lapointe taunts, 'there's your meal ticket.' Shutt, who has made a career feasting off his linemate's rebounds, is typically nonplussed. 'Ah, that's the way I like to see him,' he says, 'ready, but not too ready. There'll be rebounds tonight.'
> Ken Dryden *The Game* 1983: 174–175

(Steve Shutt is characterized in Dryden's memoir as one who always has a quick retort and is typically calm. Here *nonplussed* is used incorrectly to mean something like *unruffled* or *nonchalant*.)

> [James Murray] cast it in linguistic terms, pointing out with a nonplused ethnocentrism that for those possessing 'the language of a civilized nation', the empire offered no less than 'the subject matter of new ideas, and the theme of new discourse'.
> John Willinsky *The Empire of Words: The Reform of the OED* 1994: 202

(Here too *nonplused* seems to mean *unruffled*, *nonchalant*, or even *unselfconscious*.)

non-standard see STANDARD ENGLISH, STANDARD

Non-Status Indian see ABORIGINAL PEOPLE(S)

non-white see VISIBLE MINORITY

noon see TIME

no one, no-one, [noone] *No one* is the form commonly used by writers and listed in dictionaries. *No-one* is rarer, but is recognized by a few authorities. *Noone* appears occasionally, but is considered an error.

> When he asked how improvements could be made noone could provide any answers.
> *Financial Post* 20 March 1989: 5

(The accepted spelling is *no one*.)

See also EVERYONE.

Nootka, Nuu-chah-nulth, Ditidaht The First Nation formerly called *Nootka*, whose traditional territories are on western Vancouver Island in British Columbia, are now referred to as *Nuu-chah-nulth* (pronounced *NOO CHAH NOOHL*) and, in the southeastern quarter of this territory, *Ditidaht* (*DIH dih dat*). Their traditional language belongs to the Wakashan family. In *Nuu-chah-nulth*, *chah* and *nulth* are usually not capitalized. *Nuu-chah-nulth* and *Ditidaht* are used for both singular and plural.

Cook landed at the Nuu-chah-nulth village of Yuquot, home of the powerful Chief Maquinna, setting off the fur trade, colonization and the spread of European diseases that nearly wiped out the Native people.
Vancouver Sun 15 Dec. 1994: SR1

A major Madrid museum is sending a famous hat worn by Nuu-Chah-Nulth Chief Maquinna to the exhibit. Woven and adorned with a whale hunt motif, the hat was collected by Perez at Nootka Sound.
Province (Vancouver) 14 Dec. 1990: 56

(Normally only the first letter is capitalized: *Nuu-chah-nulth*.)

The Ditidaht Indian band opened a $500,000 visitors centre on Tuesday to serve the West Coast Trail.
Calgary Herald 30 July 1992: A11

nor see NEITHER

Nordic see SCANDINAVIAN

normality, normalcy According to some commentators, *normality* is the only standard noun form of *normal*. Warren G. Harding used *normalcy* during the 1920 campaign for the presidency of the United States. His opponents derided him; his supporters pointed out that this form had been used before in Great Britain. Fowler called it a 'spurious hybrid', presumably because the *-cy* suffix is typically used to form a noun only from an adjective ending in *t* or *te* (*pregnant, pregnancy; accurate, accuracy*). However, the word gained currency and now, long after the Harding dispute has been forgotten, *normalcy* and *normality* are both listed in dictionaries. One is used just about as often as the other in Canadian English.

Durkin's *The Magpie* depicts the post World-War-I struggle between those who strive for a return to prewar normality and those who want to bring in changes.
Miriam Waddington *Apartment Seven* 1989: 101

For all the normalcy of the situation, the tension is oppressive, almost unbearable, because we know—as they cannot—that the world's first nuclear bomb is about to explode and reduce Hiroshima to ashes.
Gazette (Montreal) 20 May 1990: F3

north see EAST, WEST, NORTH, SOUTH

northerly Generally, *northerly* means situated to the north. A northerly wind blows *from* the north.

It is not the end of passenger rail service between Halifax and Montreal: the Ocean, a longer, more northerly route, will continue. But Saint John and other southern communities will no longer have rail service.
Daily News (Halifax) 17 Dec. 1994: n.p.

The game-time temperature was 1 C with a northerly wind at 29 m.p.h. and a wind chill of zero.
Ottawa Citizen 6 April 1994: C2

See also EAST, WEST, NORTH, SOUTH.

Northern Ireland see IRELAND

Northwest Territories Though *Northwest* is written as one word (not *North West*), the traditional abbreviation contains three periods: *N.W.T.* The postal service uses *NT*. Residents prefer 'Northwest Territories' to '*the* Northwest Territories'. The preferred usage parallels usage for the names of provinces; that is, one doesn't say 'the Alberta'.

See also APPENDIX I.

no sooner The construction *no sooner ... than* is standard: 'No sooner had he signed the agreement than he wanted to make changes'. However, many critics have noticed and disapproved of the variant construction *no sooner ... when*: 'No sooner had my neighbour stopped practising her tuba when the radiators started to bang'. In fact, *no sooner ... when* is often used, as in the example above, when the connection between two consecutive events is random rather than logical. Although it can be argued that this is a legitimate distinction, the fact remains that *no sooner ... when* has been tainted by criticism: in formal writing it's probably best avoided.

But no sooner had the report been tabled in the House of Commons than Quebec Premier Robert Bourassa smelled a rat.
Vancouver Sun 19 May 1990: B2

No sooner did the evidence appear in the press than Pedley was forced to resign.
Pierre Berton *The Promised Land* 1984: 248

He no sooner arrived in the village than he was requested to leave....
William Teatero *John Anderson: Fugitive Slave* 1986: 15

He was no sooner free of them when he met up with a
tall, thin, middle-aged farmer named Seneca F.P.
Digges.
William Teatero *John Anderson: Fugitive Slave* 1986: 13

(Some editors would change *when* to *than*.)

No sooner had emergency crews fixed one problem
when another would occur.
Province (Vancouver) 28 Dec. 1990: 5

(Some editors would change *when* to *than*.)

No sooner had the author landed at Tel Aviv's Ben
Gurion airport when an incident occurred that illus-
trated the country's difficult and disputatious nature.
Maclean's 14 Nov. 1988: N3

(Some editors would change *when* to *than*.)

notable   see NOTICEABLE

notary public   see LAWYER

noticeable, notable, noted   Not everything *noticeable* is necessarily *notable*: noticeable things are
those that can be noticed, no matter how mundane;
only notable things are worth noticing. Notable
people or places are *noted* for their beauty, character, charm, skill, etc.

... he walked with a noticeable limp, couldn't skate, and
was forced to watch practice from the stands.
Gazette (Montreal) 18 Dec. 1995: F3

While [this year] there was no single breakthrough ...
there were more notable [musical] releases than ever.
Daily News (Halifax) 30 Dec. 1995: 27

Tremolo was not, of course, nearly as well known as
Rigoletto, but a noted music critic has recently observed
that he was quite as good.
J.E. Smyth et al. *The Law and Business Administration in
Canada* 1987: 304

notional agreement   see AGREEMENT, GRAM-
MATICAL

notorious, infamous   *Notorious* means 'of ill re-
pute'; that is, well-known for something negative:
'notorious criminal', 'notorious for not returning
borrowed books'. If a cook is notorious for her
cookies, they are quite likely inedible.

In very formal usage *notorious* sometimes means
simply well-known. However, this meaning is possible only in reference to facts.

Infamous means widely known as evil or troublesome, and may apply to people or things. *Infamous*
is pronounced *IN fuh muss*, not *in FAY muss*.

In the past, major league baseball players were notorious
for reporting to spring training overweight and out of
shape.
Canadian Living 19 April 1986: 113

The mood was certainly upbeat, with the notorious
Ottawa Fire Department Marching Band at centre-
stage.
Ottawa Citizen 12 Dec. 1990: D3

(Either *well-known* is intended here or the reference is
humorous.)

A further element of adverse possession is that it must be
open and notorious—a person who furtively creeps into
a deserted house each night and sleeps there for a period
equal to the limitation period would not thereby extin-
guish the title of the owner.
J.E. Smyth et al. *The Law and Business Administration in
Canada* 1987: 585

(In this highly formal use, *notorious* simply means well-
known.)

During the 1914 war, the country had produced no
weapons apart from the infamous Ross rifle and war
production had been largely confined to the manufacture of shells for the always hungry guns in France.
The Beaver Dec. 1989–Jan. 1990: 59

not too, too   The use of *not too* meaning 'not very'
is well established in both formal and informal
Canadian writing, though some usage commentators still object to it. Their objections are founded
on the possible confusion with *not too* meaning 'not
excessively', as in 'not too hot to cook the crepes'.
This is rarely a problem, since the context usually
makes clear which sense is intended. *Not too* is a
useful device for making an understatement.

My principal objection is that the author is really not too
informative about pressure ridges.
Arctic 41.1 (1988): 85

What children are to the eponymous heroine of
'Irina'—darling zeros—Linnet's husband is to her, and
one is not too sure that the darling part was ever
applicable.
Janice Kulyk Keefer *Reading Mavis Gallant* 1989: 131

But an understanding of collective unconscious is not
too different from an understanding of tradition.
Miriam Waddington *Apartment Seven* 1989: 91

Here the ideal society is associated with a not too remote future.
Northrop Frye *The Modern Century* 1990: 33

notwithstanding   see CANADIAN BILL OF RIGHTS; DESPITE

nought   see NAUGHT

nouns as adjectives   see ATTRIBUTIVE NOUNS

Nova Scotia   see APPENDIX I

nth   In mathematics n is used to indicate an indefinite number. Because n could be any number, large or small, Fowler objected to the figurative use of 'the nth degree' to mean utmost, but this sense is now fully established.

Each and every actor plays his or her character to the nth degree of detail.
Rites March 1990: 16

... Orleans is still in every way Joan of Arc's town; and that blunt assertion is reinforced to the nth degree during the May festival, which has been going on for more than five centuries.
Globe and Mail (Toronto) 5 Jan. 1985: T13

nuclear   *Nuclear* is frequently mispronounced as if it were spelled *nucular*, even by some scientists who might be expected to connect it with the noun form *nucleus* and therefore pronounce it correctly. CBC radio receives more calls about the pronunciation of this word than almost any other ('You Don't Say', the CBC's in-house language advisory guide). The disputed pronunciation occurs because people find the arrangement of consonants in *nuclear* difficult to pronounce, or have a tendency to produce the more familiar sound of words such as *muscular* and *circular*. Thus the mispronunciation is well entrenched. However, because it is also strongly stigmatized, the standard pronunciation, *NUKE lee er*, is recommended.

See also MISPRONUNCIATION AND PRONUNCIATION SHIFTS.

nude   see NAKED

number of   see COLLECTIVE NOUNS

numbers   Publishers' style guides give varying answers to the question of when numbers should be written out as words and when figures are appropriate in text. A good rule of thumb is to use words for numbers up to and including ten and figures for larger numbers. However, when they are associated with figures in a sentence, numbers to ten should also be written as figures: 'Only 3 of the 357 respondents mentioned this'. Figures are always acceptable in dates and times.

See also AGREEMENT, GRAMMATICAL; ALPHABETICAL ORDER; AVERAGE; DATES; HYPHENATION; NUMBERS, DECIMAL POINTS AND COMMAS WITH; TIME.

numbers, decimal points and commas with   Canadian practice is affected by the use in this country of both French and English conventions. In the former, the decimal marker is the comma, not the period, which instead is used to separate figures of more than three digits into smaller groups. Thus what is written 1,500,428 in the English convention is written 1.500.428 in the French, whereas what is written 1.38 in the English convention is written 1,38 in the French. In the latter case, Legal Metrology (formerly the Metric Commission Canada), the division responsible for weights and measures, recommends retaining the traditional decimal point in English-language documents, but for figures of more than four digits it splits from both conventions, English and French: instead of either commas or periods it recommends using a space: '1 500 428'. However, the government of Canada continues to use the comma in these figures in its financial documents (*The Canadian Style*). Four-digit figures may be written without the space if they are isolated examples; if they are in a context that contains other figures of four digits or more, however, the space should be retained. The figures representing years never take a space: '1997'.

A figure should never begin or end with a decimal point ('0.5', *not* '.5') except in references to the calibre of guns ('.22-calibre'), the purity of gold ('.999 fine gold'), or stock quotations (where both '.07' and '0.07' are accepted).

See also NUMBERS.

Nunavut, Denendeh   *Nunavut*, meaning 'our land' in Inuktitut, is the name selected by the Inuit of the eastern Arctic for the part of the Northwest Territories ceded to them by the government of

Canada in 1992. The new name will not appear on maps until 1999, when the residents of this area assume self-government.

Denendeh (pronounced *DEN en DAY*) means 'home of the people'. It was the name proposed for a self-governing territory in the western Arctic that would result from land-claims negotiations between Canada and the Dene Nation, representing all the Aboriginal groups of the Mackenzie Valley. However, agreement on this claim was not reached, and subsequently several Aboriginal groups within the Dene Nation negotiated separate claims. Thus it is not clear whether *Denendeh* will ever appear on the map.

Denendeh is sometimes misspelled *Denedeh*.

Even after Nunavut is created by federal law in 1999, the transfer of jurisdiction is to be phased in gradually so that vital health and other services are not jeopardized.
Ottawa Citizen 7 May 1992: A12

The complex land-claim deal that would create Nuna-vut—which will be double the size of B.C. but contain only 20,000 people—must be ratified this November by the Inuit.
Vancouver Sun 29 July 1992: A4

The Dene—who generally live in the sub-Arctic and speak five languages—still have to work out their own way to achieve self-government, perhaps in a new territory called Denendeh.
Vancouver Sun 29 July 1992: A4

If equality in a reformed Senate is worth ripping apart the country to achieve, why should Yukon, Nunavut and Denendeh (if that's what they call the N.W.T. Part Two) put up with only 25 per cent of the seats that Alberta gets?
Vancouver Sun 19 June 1992: A19

See also DENE; INUIT.

Nuu-chah-nulth   see NOOTKA

Nuxalk   see BELLA COOLA

O

object, objective   *Object* has been used to mean aim or goal since the sixteenth century, and *objective* has been used as a noun with the same meaning since the late nineteenth century. *Objective* is a shortened version of the military phrase 'objective point', meaning the position that a particular manoeuvre was intended to capture. Commentators try to distinguish between *object* and *objective* in various ways: for example, by having *object* refer to an ultimate goal or aim and reserving *objective* for a strategic step towards that goal. However, such distinctions are not widely maintained. Some commentators recommend *object* as the shorter, less pretentious word, but you may choose freely—both words are standard.

But the correctional technique remained punitive: its object was to make life so miserable for the convict that he would never consider committing another crime.
Richard Davies and Glen Kirkland, eds. *Dimensions* 1986: 67

... unlike the land companies and the railways, the government was not in the real estate business for profit; its only object was an orderly development of the West.
Pierre Berton *The Promised Land* 1984: 181

Clark's main objective, as department head and later as dean, was to foster a research atmosphere at Queen's.
Frederick Gibson *Queen's University* 2 (1983): 21

Instead of aiming at radical change, he [Hume] strove for moderation in party politics as his major political objective.
Queen's Quarterly 95 (1988): 600

When Participaction began in 1972, its sole objective was to get Canadians moving—literally.
Canadian Living 19 April 1986: 96

See also CASE.

oblige, obligate   Both these words are used by Canadian writers when referring to a person, group, or organization that is, or feels, compelled to do something by social, legal, or moral forces.

Some commentators would limit *oblige* to contexts where the sense of compulsion is internal (a moral obligation) and *obligate* to situations where the compulsion is external (a legal obligation). However, Canadian writers do not make this distinction. *Oblige* is more commonly used for both senses in all contexts except legal writing, where *obligate* is more common.

One of the tasks of the Canadian writer is to show Canada to itself. He is not obliged to do this, but it is one of his options.
Robertson Davies *One Half of Robertson Davies* 1978: 281

Instead of accepting established moral dogma, he felt obliged to study and weigh positions intellectually.
City Magazine Spring 1988: 3

As in the United States, Canadian vehicle dealers are not obligated to stick to suggested retail prices.
Canadian Consumer Jan. 1986: 9

Once the offeree has performed the act, he is not obligated to do anything more.
J.E. Smyth et al. *The Law and Business Administration in Canada* 1987: 141

(In legal usage *obligate* is the preferred term.)

Newton, who was born in London but lived in Zambia until she was five, felt obligated to do the roles because it gave her an opportunity to speak about the issues they raise.
Ottawa Citizen 16 Sept. 1995: F4

(Here *obligated* is used even though the sense of obligation is internal.)

He felt obligated to offer me the choice in spite of his total lack of funds.
Henry M. Rosenthal and S. Cathy Berson, eds. *Canadian Jewish Outlook Anthology* 1988: 280

(Here *obligated* is used even though the sense of compulsion is internal.)

obliquity, obliqueness   Several usage guides suggest that the noun form *obliquity* (pronounced *oh BLICK wi tee*) should be used when referring to indirection in speech or conduct, while *obliqueness* should be used in descriptions of lines, angles, and so on. However, this distinction does not stand up to scrutiny. Either noun is used whether the meaning is figurative or literal; *obliqueness* is used more frequently.

Stottlemyre's problem ... was muscular in nature and partially caused by a hip misalignment. 'Pelvic obliquity' was the way trainer Tommy Craig put it.
Toronto Star 25 July 1994: B4

Egoyan is a master burlesque artist himself; he pretends to reveal big things about love, sex, and alienation but forever obscures them behind his trademark obliqueness....
Province (Vancouver) 14 Oct. 1994: B6

Authorial impersonality and the obliqueness it engenders are crucial to the very project of her fiction.
Janice Kulyk Keefer *Reading Mavis Gallant* 1989: 45

oblivious   *Oblivious* once meant forgetful; now it means unaware, unnoticing, or unperturbed. It is usually followed by a prepositional phrase beginning with *to* or *of*, though sometimes it stands alone.

People just stood there in silence while the band onstage, oblivious of this terrible news, kept on wailing.
Jack Chambers *Milestones* 1983: 198

Many reformers, not entirely oblivious to the attractions of fashion, nevertheless tried to wean women from superficial criteria of beauty and to promote health and exercise through more comfortable forms of dress.
Queen's Quarterly 92.2 (1985): 426

The child slept on, oblivious.
Geoffrey Ursell *Perdue: And How the West was Lost* 1984: 180

obloquy   An *obloquy* (pronounced *OB luh kwee*) is a strong condemnatory utterance. The plural is *obloquies*. As an uncountable noun, *obloquy* refers to abusive language generally, or to a state of disrepute.

... the defendants were seen on the evening television news, their heads hung low in the airstream of the judge's obloquy.
Globe and Mail (Toronto) 20 June 1985: P18

Such poetry acquired illegitimate virtues twenty years ago from the masochism of bourgeois intellectuals; it acquires illegitimate obloquy now that the masochism has turned in a different direction.
Northrop Frye *The Bush Garden* 1971: 31

... you may condemn their scurrile and malicious obloquies, flouts, and calumnies, and scorn them as railers and detractors.
Robertson Davies *One Half of Robertson Davies* 1978: 168

observation, observance The verb *observe* has two main meanings: to watch ('observe how it's done') and to remember and respect ('observe the law', 'observe a holiday'). The noun *observation* is related to the first meaning, the noun *observance* to the second. Thus *observation* involves looking and taking notice, while *observance* refers to maintaining customs, performing religious rites, marking holidays, and so on.

In contemporary English, substituting one of these nouns for the other is usually regarded as a mistake. However, many dictionaries list both meanings for both words because, from the sixteenth century through the nineteenth, the words were used more or less interchangeably, with one exception: *an observation* in the sense of a remark or comment has never been called *an observance*.

'There are times I'm not sure what's happening at practices or what's being said before games,' he says. 'But you learn just by observation.'
Vancouver Sun 23 June 1992: D9

Dr. Smol counters that *all* sciences, in their early phases, are more concerned with observation than with experimentation....
Perspectives: Profiles of Research at Queen's University 1986: 20

With the exception of London, major European markets were closed in observance of a religious holiday.
Toronto Star 9 June 1992: B6

A towering classic of the French theatre, it is renowned for its precise, rigid structure, and strict observance of the neoclassical rules of unity and decorum.
Queen's Quarterly 97.4 (1990): 641

The story revolves around the family's observance of and interaction with a wag-about-town and self-appointed protector of their favorite cafe.
Toronto Star 30 May 1992: J15

(This use of *observance* is disputed; *observation* is preferable.)

And when all the classes gather together to go through the Oneg Shabbat—the religious observation that marks the beginning of the Sabbath—staff members lead them through the ritual with patience and love.
Toronto Star 5 July 1992: A6

(This use of *observation* is disputed; *observance* is preferable.)

Finance Minister Glen Clark's observation that a new tax on non-residential parking spaces in Greater Vancouver will not be a popular move has to be the understatement of the week.
Vancouver Sun 17 June 1992: A14

obsolete, obsolescent *Obsolete* means no longer in use, or outdated. *Obsolescent* describes something that is becoming obsolete. 'Planned obsolescence' refers to the practice of designing and building objects so they wear out and need to be replaced.

We assume, of course, that dictionaries and other usage guides will not become obsolete tools but will enter the new era by becoming computerized themselves.
W.C. Lougheed, ed. *In Search of the Standard in Canadian English* 1986: 159

Scores of obsolete, polluting factories will have to be torn down, and no one knows what to do about some 15,000 dumps of hazardous toxic waste.
Irving M. Zeitlin and Robert J. Brym *The Social Condition of Humanity* 1991: 371

Canada's obsolescent railway service stands in sharp contrast to the rejuvenation of the European and Japanese systems.
Vancouver Sun 13 Jan. 1990: B4

obstacle, obstruction, impediment, hindrance An *obstacle* is any object or condition that holds back progress, either literally or figuratively. An *obstruction* completely blocks a passage or progress. An *impediment* retards or interferes with regular activity: for example, a 'speech impediment' interferes with the flow of speech. *Hindrance* can be a synonym for any of these words; it is often used to refer to something that might be expected to be a help, but in fact is a liability.

The Madawaska River is now an esteemed white water canoeing river, and the rapids which were difficult obstacles to Thompson are sources of delight to modern canoeists.
Queen's Quarterly 92.2 (1985): 348

More people understand the necessity to preserve our heritage and preservation is no longer seen as an obstacle to progress or an attack on property rights.
Canadian Heritage Magazine Aug.–Sept. 1986: 7

The bumper rail is installed along the edge of the door and activates a stop or reverse switch if a door closing encounters any obstruction.
Country Guide Nov. 1986: H-3

Other statements in the ... judgement, however, place several impediments in the way of legislators who dare the attempt.
Canadian Bar Review 66.3 (1987): 644

In those days the world wanted to read about Canada; no author needed to conceal his origins or hedge her locale; a Canadian setting was an asset, not a hindrance.
Pierre Berton *The Promised Land* 1984: 304

obtrude   see INTRUDE

obtuse   A new use of *obtuse* to mean unclear or difficult to understand is drawing criticism from language commentators. *Obtuse* has been used figuratively in English to mean dull, stupid, or insensitive for over five hundred years. This figurative use is an extension of the literal meaning of the word in geometry, where an obtuse angle is one of between 90 and 180 degrees, while an acute, or sharp, angle is one of less than 90 degrees. Someone who is obtuse, therefore, is not acute.

The new use of *obtuse* could result from confusion with *obscure* and *abstruse*, or it could be a deliberate extension of the figurative sense. In any case, using *obtuse* to mean unclear is still considered non-standard and should be avoided.

> With increasing American dependence upon coal-fired power plants, even the environmentally obtuse Reagan administration has backed research into cleaner coal-burning technology.
> *Queen's Quarterly* 95.2 (1988): 313

(This is a standard use of *obtuse*).

> Streamlining a system with so many vested interests concealed in the most obtuse legal verbiage will not be accomplished easily.
> *Globe and Mail* (Toronto) 21 Oct. 1985: A7

(Here *obscure* would be better.)

> If you manage to figure out the obtuse on-screen directions for moving the cursor down and getting on-line help, you will be presented with some even more obtuse help messages.
> *Gazette* (Montreal) 22 Dec. 1990: L2

(Here *incomprehensible* would be better.)

O Canada, God Save the Queen   'O Canada' was approved as Canada's national anthem in 1967; lyrics in both official languages were officially proclaimed by Parliament in 1980. 'God Save the Queen', the former national anthem, is now designated the *royal anthem*.

'O Canada' was originally written in French in 1880. The English version sung today was written in 1908 and revised in 1980. The first verse is as follows:

> O Canada! Our home and native land!
> True patriot love in all thy sons command.
> With glowing hearts we see thee rise,

> The True North strong and free!
> From far and wide, O Canada,
> We stand on guard for thee.
> God keep our land glorious and free!
> O Canada, we stand on guard for thee.
> O Canada, we stand on guard for thee.

> My wife and I were among the thousands of Canadians who welcomed the Queen with spirited applause and the singing of God Save the Queen in addition to our own national anthem ... in both French and English.
> *Ottawa Citizen* 11 July 1992: A9

occasion   *Occasion* and *occasional* are correctly spelled with two *c*'s and one *s*.

> They wore white T-shirts made for the occassion.
> *Ottawa Citizen* 2 Aug. 1990: B1

(The correct spelling is *occasion*.)

> Also among the 170 exhibitors at the psychic corral are astrologers, crystal-ball gazers, palm readers, mediums and the ocasional rare gem.
> *Gazette* (Montreal) 20 Oct. 1990: H10

(The correct spelling is *occasional*.)

occurrence   *Occurrence* is often misspelled with only one *r*, or with an *a* instead of an *e*. *Occurred* and *occurring* are spelled with two *r*'s.

> From the number of stories I heard in the building Friday, I figured that these run-ins must be a regular occurence.
> *Gazette* (Montreal) 22 Oct. 1990: A3

(The correct spelling is *occurrence*.)

> Actually, what Browning forecast was that there is a good chance of cataclysmic occurrance....
> *Vancouver Sun* 29 Oct. 1990: A4

(The correct spelling is *occurrence*.)

See also DOUBLING THE FINAL CONSONANT.

octopus, octopuses   The usual and most widely accepted plural of *octopus* is *octopuses*. The Latin plural *octopi* is also fairly common and listed by many dictionaries. It is best avoided in formal writing, however, because several authorities consider it an error. In the first edition of *Modern English Usage* (1926) Fowler argued that only a Latin word from the classical period would have a regular Latin plural. Since *octopus* is late scholars' Latin, based on a Greek word, even in Latin it would have retained a Greek plural: *octopodes*. Many dictionaries list this Greco-Latin plural. But it cannot be recommended, since it seems to exist only in dictionaries and usage guides. In fact, by the 1960s even *Fowler's* (1965) recommended *octopuses*.

Most octopuses are about the size of a grapefruit, and many are closer to the size of a golf ball.
Calgary Herald 9 Feb. 1992: B8

If there were rebounds, they were usually cleared easily by the octopi disguised as Petes defencemen, all six over six feet.
Ottawa Citizen 28 March 1992: F3

(In formal writing, *octopi* should be avoided.)

See also PLURALS, REGULAR, IRREGULAR, FOREIGN.

oculist   see OPHTHALMOLOGIST

Odawa   see OTTAWA

odyssey   An *odyssey* (pronounced *ODD uh see*) is a long, adventurous journey or an intellectual or spiritual quest. The *Odyssey*, always capitalized, is Homer's epic telling of the ten years of travel undertaken by the Greek king Odysseus (also known as Ulysses) following the sacking of Troy. An odyssey is not a long story of heroic deeds; that is an *epic*.

It was Terry Fox who inspired wheelchair athlete Rick Hanson to undertake his two-year 'Man in Motion' odyssey around the world.
Alan Tucker, ed. *The Penguin Guide to Canada* 1991: 447

This approach seems a useful one for charting the intellectual odyssey of the High-Tories.
J.A.W. Gunn *Beyond Liberty and Property* 1983: 192

Although a quick peek at the guide might have solved the mystery—Robert Kennedy And His Times, a three-night odyssey starting tomorrow at 8 on CTV and CBS—a discerning eye would have known all along.
Globe and Mail (Toronto) 26 Jan. 1985: E1

(The word intended here is *epic*.)

See also EPIC.

-oe-   see -AE-

-oes   see -OS

of course   *Of course* is frequently used when what is being stated is considered to be common knowledge or self-evident. In these contexts the use of *of course* signals that the writer is aware that most readers are probably informed of a certain fact, but feels it needs to be mentioned in order to maintain the flow of the discussion or to draw a conclusion. When it introduces a fact that is widely known, *of course* is a courteous way of acknowledging the reader's intelligence.

However, there are two contexts in which *of course* raises the hackles of commentators: first, where it introduces an abstruse bit of information (and sounds snobbish) and, second, where it is used to prop up a premise or conclusion that is far from self-evident. Context and intended readership are important considerations when determining whether *of course* is appropriate. Because it is overused at all levels of writing, a good rule of thumb is to consider eliminating it.

The main difference between sherry and its colleagues, port and Madeira, is that the wine is allowed to ferment out fully before fortification with grape spirit. Port, of course, undergoes an arrested fermentation while Madeira [is] a cross between the two.
Bon Vivant Nov. 1981: 24

(Here the writer assumes that discriminating wine and food lovers, at whom this magazine is aimed, know the difference between sherry and port, if not between port and Madeira.)

The problem of how to deal with colours, sounds, heat and the like, given Descartes's geometicized conception of matter, is, of course, one which Descartes inherits from Galileo, and he grapples with it throughout his scientific work.
Canadian Journal of Philosophy 19 (1989): 183

(Philosophers, the writer assumes, would be aware of Descartes's debt to Galileo.)

Of course, early V-6s were literally hacked-down versions of 90-degree V-8s.
Edmonton Journal 18 Sept. 1992: n.p.

(Here *of course* might be better deleted or replaced by *in fact*, since the average newspaper reader is not likely to know this.)

See also GOES WITHOUT SAYING.

off, off of, from   Following the verbs *buy*, *beg*, *borrow*, *take*, or *steal*, the use of *off* (*of*) plus a noun or pronoun referring to a person is regarded as uneducated in speech and is rarely found in writing. In sentences such as 'I bought the cabinet off (of) a second-hand dealer' or 'She borrowed a dollar off (of) him', Standard English requires *from* rather than *off* or *off of*.

Generally, the two-word preposition *off of* is considered informal. It is accepted in speech ('Take that hat off of your head'), but not in writing, where the single word *off* is preferred. Note, however, the danger of mechanically cutting all occurrences of *off of* from your writing. The two words are legitimately adjacent when the preposition *of* follows a verbal noun ending in *off*, as in 'the rounding off of figures'.

> The foreman seemed to like him. Borrowed smokes off him all the time, anyway.
> *NeWest Review* Feb.-Mar. 1990: 30

(In this example from fiction, *off* indicates casual or uneducated speech.)

> Cut a four-inch-wide strip off of [the] fabric....
> *Vancouver Sun* 27 Dec. 1990: C3

(The *of* is unnecessary.)

> Today we need to reacquaint ourselves with the value of small talk among strangers in taking the cold edge off of mass society.
> *City Magazine* Spring 1988: 16

(The *of* is unnecessary.)

> A sense of a lonely pessimism, of the shutting off of communication, of the inevitable victories of winter and darkness, gives the poems a plaintively muted quality....
> Northrop Frye *The Bush Garden* 1971: 56

(Here *of* is a simple preposition following the verbal noun *shutting off*.)

See also BORROW.

offence   see -CE, -SE

offence, indictable   see INDICTABLE OFFENCE

officious, official   *Officious* is not a synonym for *official*; it means generally meddlesome, or domineering and petty in exercising authority. The original meaning of *officious*, ready to serve, is now obsolete.

> In the title story, a middle-aged woman ... finds herself admitting to a priest and to herself that she hates her arrogant, officious husband.
> *Vancouver Sun* 28 July 1990: D20

> As William Faulkner says, the writer has supreme vanity. He does not want to be influenced or taken apart; he does not want the officious help of people who cannot, as he knows intuitively, be anything but nuisances to him.
> Robertson Davies *A Voice from the Attic* 1960: 309

> 'My government will manage our province's finances in the responsible and officious manner that the public has demanded for so long.'
> *Ottawa Citizen* 27 May 1994: A12

(In this otherwise positive context, *officious* appears to be the wrong word; perhaps the speaker meant something like *professional*.)

offspring   Children, real or figurative, are *offspring*, not *offsprings*.

> The new generation of Quebec entrepreneurs has remarkable tools at its disposal, tools which amount to a vibrant, if not unique, model of economic development in North America: Hydro-Quebec, and its offsprings Lavalin and SNC.
> *Financial Post* 28 Feb. 1990: 12

(Here either *offspring* or *offshoots* would be better.)

of which   see WHO'S, WHOSE

oh   see ZERO

Ojibwa(y), Anishnabe   Terms referring to this First Nation are in flux. The *Globe and Mail Style Book* recommends *Ojibwa* for the people (both singular and plural) and *Ojibway* for their Algonquian language. It makes an exception to this rule for the Ojibways of Onegaming First Nation. However, general usage shows that *Ojibwa* and *Ojibway* are used with almost equal frequency for both the people and their language, and that both these words are often pluralized with *s*. Ojibway, a member of the Algonquian language family, has six dialects, which have the same names as the six groups within this nation: Algonquin, Chippewa, Mississauga, Ottawa, and Saulteaux. Note that many Ottawa now call themselves Odawa.

Some members of this nation are adapting the name *Anishnabe* (*a nish NAW bee*) as in the 'Anishnawbe Health Centre' in Toronto. The spelling of this name varies.

> The Ojibwas of Nawash and of Saugeen filed the claim in Ontario Court ... earlier this month and announced it yesterday in Owen Sound.
> *Toronto Star* 15 June 1994: A12

> Nowadays, no self-respecting supporter of the cultural rebirth uses the term Ojibway. Most Ojibways prefer to be known as the Annishnawbe.
> *Globe and Mail* (Toronto) 1 June 1993: A24

'Anishnabe is our word for "people". Ojibwa is the European name for us.'
Toronto Star 6 May 1993: W04

See also ALGONQUIN; CHIPEWYAN, CHIPPEWA; OTTAWA, ODAWA.

okay, OK, O.K. *Okay* is an American slang expression now used around the world. In writing, it most often appears in quotations or representations of speech. Canadians use the spelling *okay* far more than *OK* or *O.K.* Writing the expression out as *okay* permits it to be treated as a regular noun or verb: *okays, okayed,* instead of *OK's, OK'd,* or *O.K.'s, O.K.'d.*

Fascinating but inconclusive debate rages about the origins of this expression. Allan Walker Read, cited in the *OED* under 'O.K.', argues that it derives from a club called the O.K. Club, founded in 1840 by the supporters of the Democratic president Martin Van Buren. His nickname, based on his birthplace, Kinderhook, N.Y., was Old Kinderhook, or O.K. for short. In *Pidgins and Creoles,* however, Loreto Todd notes that similar forms meaning *yes* are found in a variety of West African languages, and that the expression 'oh ki' for *yes* had been recorded from Jamaica before 1839, the date of the first American citation (*OED*).

My Mother blew Lizzie a kiss, 'Okay, sweetheart.'
Room of One's Own March 1990: 36

The 45-year-old former social worker refused to give his name. 'Just call me Jack, OK?'
Gazette (Montreal) 6 March 1989: B4

'I'm leaving, and I need your help,' Tom said. We were stone still. 'O.K.' I said.
Queen's Quarterly 93.4 (1986): 856

... seven applications for statutory holidays opening in York Region have been okayed, although this won't include Christmas Day.
Toronto Star 8 Dec. 1995: NY2

'I ended up okaying the repairs (I need my car for work), but [the dealer] won't cover the job under my warranty.'
Gazette (Montreal) 5 Jul. 1995: A2

Old English, Middle English, Early Modern English, Late Modern English, Modern English, Anglo-Saxon Those who are not English Literature students are tempted to refer to any form of English that looks archaic as 'old'. However, English has a long history. Scholars use the label *Old English* for a Germanic language brought to England by invaders starting around 450 A.D.; Old English displaced the local Celtic languages and can be regarded as the ancestor of the English spoken today.

Conventionally, the history of the English language is divided into three main periods: the Old English period (450–1150), the Middle English period (1150–1500), and the Modern English period (1500–present). Some divide the Modern English period into two: from 1500 to 1700 (Early Modern English) and from 1700 to the present (Late or Later Modern English).

Old English is sometimes called Anglo-Saxon, after the names of two of the Germanic tribes that colonized Britain in the fifth century and whose language is the basis of English. The most important literary work from this period is an anonymous epic poem, *Beowulf* (c. A.D. 1000). Chaucer (c. 1342–1400) wrote his *Canterbury Tales* in Middle English. Early Modern English is familiar to us from the works of Shakespeare (1564–1616) and the King James Bible (1611). The Late Modern English period is characterized by the rise of Standard English—that is, the English taught in schools and used in most published writing—and the development of a wide range of varieties of English, more or less distinct from British English, in former colonies of Britain. Increasingly, English is becoming a world language, used widely in international trade, commerce, and transport.

See also STANDARD, STANDARD ENGLISH.

older, oldest see ELDER

oldster see SENIOR CITIZEN

omelette, omelet Canadian writers prefer the French spelling, *omelette,* but *omelet* is not uncommon. British dictionaries list *omelette* first, American dictionaries *omelet.*

omnibus see BUS

on see ON TO, ONTO

on account of *On account of* meaning 'because *of*' (as in 'He stayed indoors on account of the cold weather') is standard. However, *on account of* meaning simply 'because' (as in 'I walked on account of my car broke down') is stigmatized and rare in writing.

Few modern writers discuss the propriety of a governor's dismissing a government on account of some scandal.
Andrew Heard *Canadian Constitutional Conventions* 1991: 29

on behalf of, on the part of   see BEHALF

one   see YOU

one another   see EACH OTHER

one of the ... if not the ...   Use of the construction *one of the ... if not the ...* leads to faulty parallelism: 'She is one of the best, if not the best, dancer in the company'. The plural *dancers* is required after 'one of the', while 'if not the' must be followed by a singular noun, *dancer*. The sentence can be corrected in several ways: 'She is one of the best, if not the best, of the dancers in the company'; 'She is one of the best dancers in the company, if not the best'. It may be better yet to avoid the whole structure: 'She is possibly the best dancer in the company'.

Undoubtedly, language is one of the most, if not the most, important factor promoting unity or disunity.
William Norton *Human Geography* 1992: 166

('Undoubtedly, language is one of the most important factors promoting unity or disunity; indeed, it may be the most important factor.')

See also PARALLELISM.

one of those things, one of those who   The problem with these phrases is deciding whether the verb that follows should be singular, to agree with *one*, or plural, to agree with *those*. Does the phrase refer to the *one* thing or person in question, or to something characteristic of *those* many things or people of which the subject is but one example? In quoted speech the verb is often singular: 'It's just one of those things that happens'. In edited prose the more widespread practice is to make the verb plural to agree with *those*. This seems logical because statements beginning with *one of those* usually proceed to describe something common to a particular group of people or set of circumstances. However, there is no hard and fast rule about this usage. In formal contexts it's best to use a plural verb, but elsewhere either plural or singular is accepted.

Freelance journalist and film-maker Brian McKenna is one of those who remember.
Maclean's 7 Nov. 1988: A66

(Here the plural form of the verb is used following *one of those*.)

Browning is certainly one of those who has made Edmonton the City of Champions.
Edmonton Journal 16 Sept. 1992: n.p.

(Here the writer has chosen to use a singular verb following *one of those*.)

See also AGREEMENT, GRAMMATICAL; COLLECTIVE NOUNS.

ongoing   *Ongoing* is well established; however, some disparage it as a vogue word, preferring *continuing* or *unresolved* instead. The clichéd phrases 'ongoing situation' and 'ongoing process' have been singled out as particularly objectionable.

Just the same, there is an ongoing argument among journalists, as there is among academics and others, about the standard, even if we don't use the phrase.
W.C. Lougheed, ed. *In Search of the Standard in Canadian English* 1986: 90

The underlying issue, which has been ongoing for nearly a decade, was the definition of the term 'Product of Canada' in a manner more consistent with international standards, consumer expectations and industry requirements.
Canadian Consumer Jan. 1985: 48–9

In fact, I see justice reform as an ongoing process, responding in a deliberate and well-reasoned way to the changing needs of British Columbians.
Vancouver Sun 1 Feb. 1990: A11

(Although criticized as a cliché, *ongoing process* is appropriate in this example.)

See also DOWNPLAY.

only   For over two hundred years language commentators have been stating that *only* should always be placed directly before the element it modifies. In fact, though, this is not a rule of grammar: it is simply a question of style. The precise placement of *only* characterizes a formal or academic style. In conversation and in literary prose that mimics conversational rhythms, *only* is usually placed between the subject and the verb, no matter which element of the sentence it modifies.

Thus, while some commentators would say that 'Experienced servers only need apply' means every applicant with experience will be hired on the spot, most English-speakers would be highly unlikely to interpret the sentence in this way. Similarly, 'Rob only wanted five dollars' is not likely to mean he was too shy to verbalize his desire. The typical position of *only* in conversational English is between the subject and the verb: context and sentence intonation indicate what *only* modifies. In formal writing—where a precise style is valued—and whenever there is a real risk of misunderstanding, *only* should be placed directly in front of the element it modifies: 'Only experienced servers need apply'; 'The board requested only five thousand dollars'.

When you come from the city, you can only take outdoors in small doses.
Howard Engel *Murder Sees the Light* 1984: 117

(In formal writing *only* would come later: 'only in small doses'.)

He was only interested in the money.
Constance Beresford-Howe *Night Studies* 1985: 136

(In formal writing *only* would come later: 'interested only in the money'.)

... there is substantial support for the notion that the governors should intrude into the democratic process only to the minimum extent absolutely required for the basic functioning of parliamentary government.
Andrew Heard *Canadian Constitutional Conventions* 1991: 47

By 1941, the Native population likely comprised only one-quarter of the total population.
Robert M. Bone *The Geography of the Canadian North* 1992: 79

See also ONLY, BUT.

only, but   The use of *only* to mean 'but' ('I wanted to, only I couldn't') is standard but informal. In Canadian writing it appears most often in fiction.

Their mother used to do this too, go blind, and deaf, only she did it over crossword puzzles and a cigarette.
Queen's Quarterly 95.3 (1988): 612

Oh yes, a true painting there somewhere, only how to paint it?
David Williams *Eye of the Father* 1985: 79

See also ONLY.

onomatopoeia, onomatopoeic, onomatopoetic
Onomatopoeia (pronounced *on oh MAT uh PEE uh*) is a technical term for a word that imitates a sound; these words are also called *echoic* or *imitative*. There are hundreds of such words in English, including *hush, murmur, plop, sizzle, squish, whisper, whizz,*

and *zoom.* Of the two adjective forms, *onomatopoeic* (sometimes misspelled *onomatopoeiac*) is preferred to *onomatopoetic.*

Ontario   see APPENDIX I

on the lam   see LAM

on the part of   see BEHALF

on to, onto   Some guides recommend against the use of *onto,* preferring *on to,* and certainly *on to* is acceptable in all contexts. The two-word form is the more common one in Canadian academic writing and in British writing generally.

However, most American writers and many Canadian writers use *on to* to mean 'on as far as' and *onto* to mean 'to a position on'. This distinction is both useful and acceptable: it differentiates 'We walked on to the bridge', meaning we walked that far, from 'We walked onto the bridge', meaning we stepped on the bridge itself.

Canadian writers use *onto* and *on to* with about equal frequency in the idiomatic expression 'to be onto something': 'We're onto (*or* on to) your tricks'.

While employees ... were getting the buses ready for loading at dockside in Vancouver, a mast supporting the tackle equipment broke. A bus fell from a great height on to the dock and was demolished.
J.E. Smyth et al. *The Law and Business Administration in Canada* 1987: 448

(Here *onto* would also be possible.)

The fluid lapped at his shoes, dripped down from his hands on to his suit.
Geoffrey Ursell *Perdue: And How the West Was Lost* 1984: 157

(Here *onto* would also be possible.)

Convinced he was onto something, Reibling ... began easing his 183 acres back into crop rotation.
Harrowsmith Jun.–Jul. 1985: 37

Perhaps Elizabeth Wood, the woman who remained apprehensive about John Logie Baird's experiments, was on to something after all.
Queen's Quarterly 95 (1988): 325

opaque   see TRANSPARENT

op. cit.   see IBID.

ophthalmologist, oculist, optometrist, optician
An *ophthalmologist*—the word is pronounced *off thal MAW luh jist* and often misspelled without the first *h* or *l*—is a medical doctor specializing in diseases and defects of the eye, who may perform eye surgery. *Oculist* means the same thing, but this term has fallen out of favour within the profession. An *optometrist* is licensed to test eyesight and prescribe lenses. An *optician* makes or sells optical goods, such as prescription glasses and telescopes.

The word *optometrist* is rare in Britain. There *ophthalmic opticians* test eyesight while *dispensing opticians* make lenses or fill prescriptions.

> Devine's health minister, Graham Taylor, invoked that provision last August when four of Regina's five opthalmologists opted out.
> *Saturday Night* April 1986: 12

(The correct spelling is *ophthalmologist*, with two *h*'s.)

> The New Westminster ophthamologist is no stranger to civil war.
> *Vancouver Sun* 12 April 1994: A9

(The correct spelling is *ophthalmologist*.)

> [MDs'] resistance to other legally licensed health-care practitioners, notably chiropractors and in British Columbia optometrists, has had the style of a self-interested cartel. . . .
> *Saturday Night* July 1986: 6

> Singing is the first love of Paul Lorieau, an Edmonton optician who performs the national anthem before hockey games at the Northlands Coliseum.
> *Maclean's* 24 Feb. 1986: 26

opine To *opine* is to express an opinion. This verb, in use since the fifteenth century, is not common in Canadian writing. As usage critics note, *opine* now seems overly formal or stilted, except where the intended effect is humorous. Today it is most often used by writers who want to indicate, in a droll manner, their disagreement with others' opinions. The suggestion is that the person who 'opines' opines wrong.

> When asked, most of us would opine that ulcers are caused by stress and improper lifestyle, especially a poor diet.
> *Province* (Vancouver) 5 Nov. 1990: 49

> Mr. Berry opined the Senate was fulfilling its proper role in performing a check on the elected government.
> *Financial Post* 18 Oct. 1990: 12

> Parti Québécois leader Jacques Parizeau was opining the other day, speaking as another spectator to the

present marchpast of history, that just about any geographic and social collectivity can claim sovereignty and set up shop as a nation.
> *Toronto Star* 4 Sept. 1991: A19

opprobrium   see APPROBATION

optician   see OPHTHALMOLOGIST

optimum, optimal, best   The *optimum* is the perfect amount or degree of something. *Optimal* conditions are those most conducive to something's happening. Although *optimal* is the adjective form, *optimum* is frequently used as an adjective as well. These terms were first used in biology to describe the conditions most favourable to growth and reproduction in living organisms. They should not be used simply to mean biggest or best.

> . . . under optimal growing conditions . . . an acre of fireweed bloom could yield as much as 450 pounds of honey.
> *Harrowsmith* Oct.–Nov. 1985: 51

> If conditions are not optimum, they may grow but not multiply.
> *Harrowsmith* Aug.–Sept. 1985: 68

> Selecting the optimum observation post begins by scouting the countryside within a reasonable driving distance of your home.
> Terence Dickinson *Halley's Comet* 1985: 111

> 'Borders appears to be at his optimum right now.'
> *Globe and Mail* (Toronto) 2 Oct. 1991: C12

(Here *best* would be better.)

optometrist   see OPHTHALMOLOGIST

-or   see -ER; -OUR

oral   see VERBAL

orate   *Orate*, a verb formed from the noun *oration*, is often used in a humorous way to describe pompous speech-making or inflated rhetoric. It's best not to use this word where no irony is intended.

> Thomas D'Arcy McGee could orate about building a 'great new northern nation' which would not be French-Canadian or British-Canadian, but just Canadian.
> *Ottawa Citizen* 24 May 1989: A8

> The highlight of the movie for me was the continual street scene which shows inner London in perpetual

disorder ... with voice-over accompaniment by Margaret Thatcher orating on new prosperity.
City Magazine (Spring 1988): 42

... the convention seemed to pay not the slightest attention to the person orating from the platform.
Queen's Quarterly 97.3 (1990): 464

See also BACK-FORMATION.

orchestrate   The figurative sense of *orchestrate*—to organize or coordinate various elements to achieve a desired effect—has been established since the 1880s. This use has aroused some negative comment but is widely found in all kinds of writing.

Thus both the king's puppet-like performance and the response to it were orchestrated by the ministers.
J.A.W. Gunn *Beyond Liberty and Property* 1983: 65

Instead, as deputy government whip, he helps formulate answers and orchestrate the government response to opposition queries.
Ottawa Citizen 11 April 1994: B1

order   see SPECIES

ordinance, ordnance   An *ordinance* is an authoritative decree, a religious rite, or a bylaw passed by a local authority. *Ordnance* means artillery, but also refers more generally to weapons and military equipment and the military division responsible for them. The maps that Canadians refer to as large-scale maps or detailed topographical maps are known in Britain as Ordnance Survey maps because they were originally produced for military purposes.

[He said] that Kamloops had not passed any ordinance or bylaw banning the use of cedar shingles....
Province (Vancouver) 8 June 1990: 47

A junior ordnance officer in 1944, he was included in the plot because ... he had a thorough knowledge of the building where the bomb was to be set off.
Globe and Mail (Toronto) 8 May 1985: 1

Sturdy hikers clutching their ordinance survey maps will find it.
Globe and Mail (Toronto) 6 July 1985: T8

(The correct spelling here is *ordnance*.)

See also BYLAW; GUN.

organic   With the recent proliferation of terms such as 'organic farming' and 'organic foods', *organic* has come to be seen as the opposite of *synthetic*, and as a synonym for *natural* or *healthful*. In chemistry, however, all substances are classified as either organic (meaning that they contain carbon) or inorganic (meaning that they do not contain carbon). All organic (i.e., living) matter is made of chemicals that contain carbon; it does not follow that anything organic is harmless. Many pesticides shunned by 'organic' farmers are in fact organic chemicals, and hundreds of natural organic substances found in plants and animals are extremely poisonous. Thus the adjective *organic* should not be relied on as an indicator of harmlessness.

Many inorganic and organic chemicals can be removed from drinking water by a process known as reverse osmosis.
Country Guide Dec. 1986: 15

Klein said the key reason for delaying the mill was the panel's concern over the level of chlorinated organic pollutants and the effect they would have on the fish downstream....
Vancouver Sun 3 March 1990: B1

orient, orientate   Canadian and American writers prefer the verb *orient*, while British writers more commonly use *orientate*. The figurative meaning of *orient(ate)* is to adjust to one's surroundings or to a new situation. Originally to *orient* meant to place something so that it faced east; over time this meaning was extended to refer to any direction.

So when a service comes along that makes it easier for... travellers to get oriented when they hit the ground, you know it's a good thing.
Gazette (Montreal) 29 April 1994: D3

The display suite is oriented so the kitchen and breakfast nook look out to the central courtyard....
Vancouver Sun 12 Oct. 1990: E8

They are orientated on the triangular lot to both maximize views to the south over the river and provide view corridors for the surrounding residential properties.
Vancouver Sun 27 Jan. 1990: E5

See also -ORIENTED.

-oriented   Compounds formed with *-oriented* are widely used, especially in journalism and academic writing, to indicate a particular emphasis, interest, or bias: for example, 'career-oriented' or 'customer-oriented'. Some commentators consider this prolific combining form overused, and often the meaning of the new compounds is vague. Where an established adjective could convey the same meaning, it is probably better to use it.

This is to be expected, he argues, because Canadians are more collectivity-oriented.
Canadian Journal of Sociology 14.2 (1989): 144

He prepared an excellent ... resumé and was in a good position to provide succinct, accomplishment-oriented written material.
Queen's Quarterly 94.4 (1987): 860

(Here the meaning of *accomplishment-oriented* is unclear.)

... acid rain is a problem which results from our industrialized, leisure-oriented life-style.
Queen's Quarterly 94.3 (1987): 614

I have kept in mind, however, other more exclusively text-oriented critical methods....
Ben-Z. Shek *French-Canadian & Québécois Novels* 1991: viii

See also ORIENT, ORIENTATE.

-os, -oes Most words that end in *o* are pluralized in the regular way by adding *s*: *altos, cellos, hippos, infernos, kangaroos, photos, radios*. However, some fairly common words in which a final *o* is preceded by a consonant are pluralized by adding *es*: *buffaloes, echoes, embargoes, heroes, noes, potatoes, tomatoes, torpedoes, vetoes, volcanoes*.

Note that an *e* never precedes the *s* if the word is a short form (*hippos, photos*) or a proper name (*Filipinos*), or if a vowel precedes the *o* (*cameos, ratios*).

Some words can be pluralized either way: *bravo, cargo, domino, ghetto, mango, memento, mosquito, salvo, tornado, zero*.

Residents in Alberta contended with clouds of mosquitoes that swirled over the prairies like tornados.
Vancouver Sun 4 Aug. 1990: B7

(Although both *mosquito* and *tornado* can be pluralized with *s* alone or with *es*, some editors would insist on consistency here: either *mosquitoes* and *tornadoes* or *mosquitos* and *tornados*.)

The board game [Trivial Pursuit] has made its inventors, Chris Haney and Scott Abbott, national heros and multi-millionaires.
Province (Vancouver) 5 Jan 1990: 52

(Only *heroes* is accepted.)

ostentatiously, ostensibly When people do something *ostentatiously*, they do it in a showy manner, to attract attention. When people do something *ostensibly* for a certain reason, this reason is the one they are making public, although it may conceal their real motivation. Occasionally writers use *ostentatiously* where *ostensibly* is required: 'Ostentatiously, he only wanted to help'.

In court last week S——, ostentatiously carrying a Bible, explained that she had found God after leaving W——, and wasn't in this for the money, not at all.
Gazette (Montreal) 25 Nov. 1992: C3

I formed the habit of bringing out my hearing aid rather ostentatiously; Andrew, catching sight of it, would raise his voice to what for most people would have been normal.
Eugene Forsey *A Life on the Fringe* 1990: 141

Ostensibly, the dinner is being held in honor of the paper's 80th anniversary. In fact, its main purpose is to raise money to pay off Le Devoir's accumulated $1.5-million debt.
Gazette (Montreal) 16 Nov. 1990: A1

Now Hydro is seeking an annual three-per-cent increase in its rates for the next few years, ostensibly to promote conservation and protect the environment. As the saying goes, if you believe that, have I got some real estate for you in Florida.
Province (Vancouver) 22 Feb. 1990: 38

Military involvement of any kind, however ostentatiously peaceful in its intentions, bestows influence as well as power upon the foreign nations participating in the operation.
Ottawa Citizen 22 Dec. 1992: A6

(The word required here is *ostensibly*.)

Saddam wants ... ostentatiously, linkage to Israel, but to humiliate the U.S. more than out of any concern for the plight of Palestinians....
Vancouver Sun 19 Dec. 1990: A3

(The word required here is *ostensibly*.)

Ottawa, Odawa The Algonquian-speaking people who were named the *Ottawa* by Europeans now prefer the name *Odawa* (singular and plural), pronounced *oh DAW wa*. Closely related to both the Ojibwa/Anishnabe and the Potawatomi, many Odawa settled on Manitoulin Island after the War of 1812. Now many of their descendants continue to live there; other groups are found throughout Ontario, and in Michigan, Wisconsin, and Oklahoma.

Sir Francis Bond Head, lieutenant-governor of Upper Canada, signed a treaty with the Ojibway and Odawa in 1836 that was an attempt to relocate all the native peoples of Upper Canada on Manitoulin Island.
Toronto Star 5 Aug. 1994: D11

See also OJIBWA(Y).

-our, -or For some Canadians, the choice of *-our* spellings is a marker of Canadian writing, since American writers by far prefer *-or*. In fact, however, preferences vary across Canada, with Ontario, British Columbia, and English-speaking Quebec leaning towards *-our* and the rest of the country leaning towards *-or*. Furthermore, preferences are not consistent across the whole set of *-our/-or* words. In Canadian writing generally, for example, *colour* and *behaviour* are more common than *color* and *behavior*, but *odor* and *favorite* are more common than *odour* and *favourite*. Newspapers have traditionally used the shorter *-or* forms, but in 1990 the *Globe and Mail* adopted *-our* spellings. The federal government also uses *-our*.

Note that words with root forms that can be spelled either *-or* or *-our* drop the *u*, even in British English, when the endings *-ation*, *-iferous*, *-ific*, *-ize*, and *-ous* are added (*Oxford Dictionary of English Usage*). The following are among the words that are often misspelled by over-zealous *-our* fans: *coloration*, *glamorous*, *honorarium*, *honorary*, *honorific*, *humorist*, *humorous*, *laborious*, *odoriferous*, *rigorous*, *valorize*, *valorous*, *vigorous*.

> One is left labouriously reading field notes from someone else's study....
> *Canadian Journal of Sociology* 14.2 (1989): 238

(The correct spelling is *laboriously*.)

> ... the only purpose that he could have had was to make his letter either humourous or provocative.
> *Canadian Baptist* Jan. 1986: 38

(The correct spelling is *humorous*.)

See also SPELLING, CANADIAN.

ours *Ours* is a possessive pronoun like *mine* or *theirs* or *his*: 'That's ours'. Correctly spelled, it has no apostrophe. It is sometimes misspelled *our's* because the apostrophe is associated with possession.

> 'If they won't allow us into their market, we'll have to keep them out of ours.'
> *Gazette* (Montreal) 3 March 1989: A4

> 'Tonight, our's didn't do too much.'
> *Ottawa Citizen* 24 Nov. 1990: E5

(The correct spelling is *ours*.)

See also POSSESSIVE.

ourself, ourselves see -SELF, -SELVES

outfit, outfitter The noun *outfit* originally referred to clothing and other equipment required for a particular activity. Later it came to be used as a collective noun identifying a group of people engaged in the same task, such as a military unit, a business organization, or a sports team. This use is informal.

An *outfitter* provides guiding services and supplies for activities such as camping, fishing, hunting, and exploring in wilderness areas.

In historical Canadian usage, an *outfit* was the annual shipment of supplies from the Hudson's Bay Company to fur-trading posts; by extension, the term came to be used for the fiscal year of the HBC.

The verb to *outfit*, meaning to provide with clothing or gear, doubles its final *t* in the forms *outfitted* and *outfitting*.

> The memo ... does not say, however, whether Canadian seamen will be put back into bell bottoms and round sailor caps, an outfit commonly known as square rig.
> *Globe and Mail* (Toronto) 4 Jan. 1985: P4

> Trophies ... were won by Arizona Audio at competitions in Quebec and Ontario. The outfit has more than 30 awards to its credit.
> *Gazette* (Montreal) 24 March 1994: B1

(This use of *outfit* is informal.)

> Canoeing the legendary Nahanni River ... is a two-week trip offered by Black Feather tour outfitters and instructors....
> *Globe and Mail* (Toronto) 11 May 1985: T11

> Sec. 57 [of the Wildlife Act] further states that an outfitter can be licensed for only one guiding area.
> *Vancouver Sun* 26 Nov. 1990: B1

> When Defence Minister Sam Hughes decided that Canadian troops should be armed with an all-Canadian weapon, soldiers were outfitted with a rifle designed by his friend Sir Charles Ross.
> *Globe and Mail* (Toronto) 26 Jan. 1985: T6

out loud see ALOUD

out-migrate see EMIGRANT

overlook see LOOKOUT

overweening *Overweening* means arrogant, presumptuous, or excessive, and is derived from the Old English words *wenan*, 'to presume', and *ofer-*, 'too much'. It is not related to the verb *wean* and is not spelled *overweaning*.

> There is also the Big Brother factor—the tendency of overweaning officials to burrow into every nook and cranny of citizens' lives.
> *Gazette* (Montreal) 6 Jan. 1994: B3

> (The correct spelling is *overweening*.)

ovolactovegetarian see VEGETARIAN

Oweekeno see KWAKIUTL

Oxbridge *Oxbridge* is not a real place but a blend of the words *Oxford* and *Cambridge*. This expression refers collectively to the two oldest and most prestigious universities in Britain, distinguishing them from the 'red-brick' and 'new' universities established in the late nineteenth century and after the Second World War. The word is normally used as an adjective; the tone of Canadian use tends to be irreverent.

> Real power is exercised, informally, by a clique of businessmen and bureaucrats dominated by graduates of the University of Tokyo and its law school—a far more powerful and tightly knit Old Boys' network than even the Oxbridge elite in England.
> *Maclean's* 11 Sept. 1989: T8

> 'She was being interviewed by one of the Oxbridge BBC interviewers, with slicked blonde hair and an exquisite suit.'
> *Gazette* (Montreal) 4 April 1990: C1

> Her interchangeable characters are Oxbridge types, who may be exquisitely educated but who live in the world of make-believe in their attempts to solve the problems of their friends and to construct elaborate justifications for the selfishness of their own behavior.
> *Ottawa Citizen* 20 Jan. 1990: 17

See also ABBREVIATION.

oxymoron An *oxymoron* is a rhetorical or literary device in which two contradictory terms are placed together: 'burning cold'. Phrases such as 'civil service', 'military intelligence', 'industrial park', and 'Toronto life' are jokingly called *oxymorons*. The plural is either *oxymora* or, more commonly, *oxymorons*.

> I can't write as an ordinary woman because such a thing does not exist: it is an oxymoron, a contradiction in terms. We all know that in our species the ordinary, the norm, is constituted by the male ... against whom the female stands out as extra-ordinary, beyond the ordinary, or ordinary plus.
> *Queen's Quarterly* 96.2 (1989): 229

> If '"oxymoron" is a paradoxical utterance combining two terms that in ordinary usage are contraries' ... then what are the 'Progressive Conservatives'?
> *Globe and Mail* (Toronto) 16 April 1985: P7

P

pablum, pap, pabulum Literally, *pablum* and *pap* mean baby food; figuratively, these words describe something lacking intellectual substance or artistic quality. *Pablum* is in fact a trade name for the first vitamin-enriched, prepared baby food, which was developed at Toronto's Hospital for Sick Children around 1930 and patented in the United States. However, *pablum* is rarely found with a capital letter, and in Canadian English this trade name has almost completely supplanted the non-proprietary word from which it is derived: *pabulum*. *Pabulum*, from the Latin for 'food', now usually means insipid intellectual fare, but in the past it had positive connotations and meant food for thought as well as nourishment for the body.

> You're anti-this or anti-that unless you homogenize your opinions into a creamy concoction of useless pablum.
> *Province* (Vancouver) 23 Aug. 1990: 43

> That a woman who is offended by the word 'arts' should be in a position to mutilate the only programming on the dial that isn't musical pablum ... is incredible.
> *Globe and Mail* (Toronto) 24 July 1985: P6

The Liberals' vaunted social policy review, touted for months as radical, turns out to be yet another serving of bureaucratic pabulum.
Calgary Herald 6 Oct. 1994: B1

pace This Latin expression (derived from *pax*, 'peace') typically appears in academic or literary prose. It means 'with all due respect to' and precedes a proper name. *Pace* signals that the opinion being expressed is contrary to the views of the person named: for example, '*pace* Marx' means 'despite Marx's opinion to the contrary'. Because many people are unfamiliar with this construction—and some people think it means just the opposite ('according to Marx')—it is probably best to avoid *pace* altogether. If you do use the word, note that it requires italicization as a foreign expression. The usual pronunciation is *PAH chay*, although *PAY see* is also accepted.

Their book—among others—reveals that Canada has turned out, *pace* McGregor, a lot of able and effective satire....
Linda Hutcheon *Splitting Images* 1991: 14

(Gaile McGregor has argued that Canadian writers have not produced effective satire.)

Dr. Jekyll is a misspelling (*pace* Robert Louis Stevenson) of Jackie McLean's title, Dr. Jackle.
Jack Chambers *Milestones* 1983: 276

See also LATIN PHRASES.

pachyderm A *pachyderm* (pronounced *PACK ee DERM*) is a large, thick-skinned, hoofed animal that does not chew cud, such as an elephant, rhinoceros, or hippopotamus. In the press, *pachyderm* is most often used as a jocular synonym for *elephant*.

One of the keepers had a young elephant out for a stroll and just dropped by for a visit. Thank goodness. The runs may be spacious but a pachyderm is pushing things a bit.
Dogs in Canada Aug. 1976: 84

The style is epigrammatic, and in epigram the poet throws harpoons while the reader amiably pretends to be a pachyderm and tests them for sharpness.
Northrop Frye *The Bush Garden* 1971: 29

(Here Frye invokes the pachyderm for its thick skin rather than its elephantine size.)

paean, pean, peon A *paean* (*PEE un*) is an outpouring of praise or thanksgiving; *pean*, the spelling used by many American writers, is very uncommon in Canada. A *peon* (*PEE on*) is a Latin American farm labourer; in the past, the term was also used in British colonial society, in India, Sri Lanka, and Malaysia, to refer to orderlies, messengers, and soldiers. Now *peon* can be used figuratively to refer to anyone from a less exalted walk of life.

Sometimes *paean* is misspelled *paeon*; less often *peon* is misspelled the same way.

I guess if you've tried only the bottled variety, you're baffled by this paean of praise to horseradish's fiery benison.
Toronto Star 24 April 1992: C18

One had to see and hear Murley's incredible, passionate soloing on Bad Back Blues, a heartfelt paeon from Elmes' pen, to believe the commitment, drive and sheer joy these musicians take in their art....
Spectator (Hamilton) 16 Feb. 1994: D9

(The word intended here is *paean*, although it seems odd that anyone would write a paean to a bad back.)

The peons ridicule the mighty.
Toronto Star 7 Sept. 1992: B1

'We tend to provide low pay to the person in the information booth or the clerk. They're treated like paeons.'
Spectator (Hamilton) 21 May 1994: A7

(They're treated like *peons*.)

See also -AE-; DIPHTHONG, DIGRAPH, LIGATURE.

pagan see ATHEIST

paid, payed *Paid* is both the past tense of *pay* ('He paid no attention') and the past participle ('They have all been paid'). *Payed* is an obsolete spelling, accepted only when *pay* means to let out a rope or cable.

... the tethered satellite will be payed out slowly, unreeled from a drum by an electric motor [to rise] 20 kilometres above the shuttle's orbit of 298 kilometres.
Vancouver Sun 29 July 1992: A10

(Here *payed* is correct.)

Mullin had already payed Cowie $6,000, so the balance of the award is $43,500.
Daily News (Halifax) 10 April 1992: 7

(The correct spelling is *paid*.)

Until recently, manufacturers of industrial safety shoes payed about as much attention to the styling of their products as fashion observers did to workwear in general.
Vancouver Sun 25 June 1992: C3

(The correct spelling is *paid*.)

pajamas   see PYJAMAS

palate, palette, pallet   The *palate* is the roof of the mouth and, by extension, the sense of taste. A *palette* is the board on which an artist mixes colours for painting. *Palette* is also used figuratively to refer to a range of colour, sounds, or materials. A *pallet* is straw mattress or a wooden frame on which goods are stacked in a warehouse.

paleo-, palaeo-   This prefix means ancient or pre-historic. Canadians and Americans usually spell it *paleo-*, as in *paleontology*, the study of extinct plants and animals through fossils. The British spell it *palaeo-*.

See also -AE-, -OE-, -E-.

palette   see PALATE

palimpsest, pentimento   During the Middle Ages, parchment and vellum were so expensive that old texts were often scraped off to make way for new ones. Literally, a *palimpsest* (pronounced *PAL imp sest*) is a piece of reused writing material. Sometimes, however, the old texts were still visible enough to be recovered; many Classical texts were recovered in this way from under layers of more recent writings. Thus *palimpsest* is often used figuratively to describe layers of text or meaning.

Similarly, canvases were reused by artists. *Pentimento* is the effect created when parts of an earlier painting show through one painted over it.

> There are times when the second piece shimmers like a palimpsest, a parchment scroll where the original writing is not yet completely worn away beneath a newer text.
> *Vancouver Sun* 18 May 1990: C6

> 'From such a post-modern perspective landscape seems less like a palimpsest whose "real" or "authentic" meanings can somehow be recovered with the correct techniques, theories or ideologies, than a flickering text displayed on the word-processor screen whose meaning can be created, extended, altered, elaborated and finally obliterated by the merest touch of a button.'
> *The Canadian Geographer* Spring 1989: 95

> Beam's *The North American Iceberg* (1986; Plate 20) is a pentimento-like collage displaying the 'tip' of many layers of native history....
> Mark A. Cheetham with Linda Hutcheon *Remembering Postmodernism* 1991: 81

pallet   see PALATE

palpable   Literally, *palpable* means touchable. Figuratively, however, the word is often used to describe something intangible that is so obvious or inescapable as to seem physically present: 'palpable fear'. Some critics consider this figurative use a bit stale; certainly it is now far more common than the literal meaning.

> A palpable demoralization had set in.
> Henry M. Rosenthal and S. Cathy Berson, eds. *Canadian Jewish Outlook Anthology* 1988: 163

> The feeling of revitalization is palpable in Dr. Kilpatrick's enthusiastic endorsement of several recent developments in curriculum....
> *Perspectives: Profiles of Research at Queen's University* 1986: 26

> It is difficult for us to imagine a life in which the fight to keep alive is so intense, in which the will to live is as constant and palpable as the heartbeat.
> Northrop Frye *The Bush Garden* 1971: 122

(Here the literal and figurative meanings of *palpable* overlap, revitalizing the 'stale' metaphor.)

See also LITERALLY, FIGURATIVELY.

panacea   A *panacea* (pronounced *pan uh SEE uh*) is something that cures all ailments or, figuratively, solves all problems. Although a simple remedy for a single complex problem is often called a panacea ('a panacea for inflation') as well, this use is disputed and should be avoided in formal writing. In Classical mythology, Panacea (from Greek *pan*, 'all', and *akeistha*, 'to heal') was the daughter of Aesculapius, the god of medicine.

> Nor is enhancing the status of women a panacea for all our problems.
> *Province* (Vancouver) 2 March 1990: 41

> We've heard an awful lot about clear-cutting. We've heard reasons for and reasons against and we've heard the solution of selective logging held up as the panacea.
> *Vancouver Sun* 19 May 1990: A12

(Here the meaning of *panacea* is closer to 'perfect solution' than 'cure-all'; this extended meaning should be avoided in formal writing.)

panda   see BEAR

pandemic   see ENDEMIC

pander, panderer To *pander to* once meant to pimp for, but now it means to cater to. Someone who panders is a *pander* or, more commonly in Canada and the United States today, a *panderer*. *Pander* came into English from the name of a character in Chaucer's *Troilus and Criseyde*, Pandare, who acts as a go-between for the two lovers.

> We pander to the ideal of Work as few Victorians did. . . .
> Robertson Davies *A Voice from the Attic* 1960: 34

> It makes him sound like a writer who's deliberately pandering to some kind of cheesy popular taste, though in reality nothing could be further from the truth.
> Margaret Atwood *Second Words* 1982: 320

> But Clinton is no panderer to the powerful.
> *Financial Post* 27 Dec. 1991: 36

> Mulroney also described Liberal Leader Jean Chretien as a flip-flopper and Reform Leader Preston Manning as a panderer of regional resentment.
> *Toronto Star* 29 Nov. 1991: A1

(Here *panderer* should be followed by *to*, not *of*. However, it is also possible that *promulgator* was meant; if so, 'promulgator of' is the accepted phrase.)

> His 'human' feelings are a sham, and director Robert Rooney makes this numbingly clear by having Ted Dykstra play him in extravagant style, bounding from tier to tier of the Coliseum-like set, sloppily kissing his whore, and exchanging conspiratorial glances with his pander, Amor.
> *Globe and Mail* (Toronto) 27 Sept. 1985: E5

(The noun *pander* is uncommon in Canadian English; here it literally means *pimp*.)

pants *Pants* are outerwear in Canada and the United States, underwear in Britain. What North Americans call *pants* the British call *trousers*. What the British call *pants* North Americans call *underpants*.

> I took off my shoes and socks and rolled up my pants.
> Howard Engel *Murder Sees the Light* 1984: 57

pap see PABLUM

paparazzo, paparazzi *Paparazzi* has been recently borrowed from Italian as a name for the photographers who stalk celebrities in hopes of snapping a candid shot. The singular *paparazzo* is seldom seen; *paparazzi*, the plural form, appears frequently in newspaper and magazine writing. The pronunciations are *pah pih ROT so* and *pah pih ROT see*.

> But it's just part of the job, explains Roger Karnbad, a 10-year paparazzo who's packing twin Nikons for this shoot.
> *Gazette* (Montreal) 18 Aug. 1990: H8

> The camera bugs reminded me of paparazzi from the gutter tabloids in pursuit of some unlucky movie celebrity.
> *Vancouver Sun* 13 Jul. 1990: A13

> 'It's simple, really,' says paparazi Mike Erickson, 'People enjoy looking at photographs of other people.'
> *Province* (Vancouver) 24 May 1990: P11

(A single camera-wielding celebrity hound is a *paparazzo*. The word is misspelled as well: the *z* should be doubled.)

paperboy see JOB TITLES

para- The prefix *para-* has three meanings. In the words *paramedic*, *paramilitary*, and *paranormal*, *para-* is derived from a Greek preposition meaning 'beside', 'beyond', or 'outside'. The second meaning of *para-* is 'guarding against', derived from the Latin verb *parare*, 'to prepare': thus a *parachute* guards against a fall and a *parasol* guards against the sun. Finally, *para-* is a clipped form of *parachute* in such words as *paratrooper*, *paraglider*, and *parasailing*. *Para-* compounds normally do not take a hyphen.

> Hence, Alberta and British Columbia now provide paralegal services to aboriginals who have to face the court.
> Irving M. Zeitlin and Robert J. Brym *The Social Condition of Humanity* 1991: 277

> Three members of the Ulster Resistance Movement, a right-wing loyalist paramilitary organization in Northern Ireland, were arrested in Paris for attempting to exchange a surface-to-air missile for South African weapons.
> *Briarpatch* Dec. 1989–Jan. 1990: 26

> . . . parasailing, wind surfing, snorkelling, scuba diving, deep sea fishing all vie for your attention and your pesos.
> *Leader-Post* (Regina) 27 Feb. 1988: B18

See also HYPHENATION.

paradigm *Paradigm* means pattern or example. Since the seventeenth century *paradigm* has been used by grammarians to describe the inflected forms of nouns, verbs, and pronouns. In scholarly writing it often refers to a model, theoretical framework, or structural pattern. Several commentators consider the word overused and pretentious and suggest alternatives such as *model, example*, or *framework*. However, sometimes *paradigm* is particularly apt because it blends the meanings of these alternatives.

> Canadians elsewhere have always watched Saskatchewan closely because the province has been both a harbinger and a paradigm for the rest of the country.
> *Saturday Night* April 1986: 10

> As he laboured up to street level, it occurred to him that this procedure in all its details and circumstances was a paradigm of his whole life, and his long face broke into a crooked grin.
> Constance Beresford-Howe *Night Studies* 1985: 1

paraffin   see KEROSENE

paragon   see EPITOME

paragraph   A paragraph is a block of text that is distinguished typographically, by indenting the first line or by leaving an extra line space above and below, or by both means. Composition books generally describe the paragraph as a subsection of an argument in which one main idea is discussed. However, paragraphing varies in newspapers, academic books and journals, magazines, reference works, advertising copy, etc. A paragraph can be as short as a single sentence or many sentences in length. Both the look of the text on the page and the reading habits of the intended audience influence paragraph length.

parallelism   Parellelism (the repetition of a particular grammatical structure or part of speech) can be an effective rhetorical device: 'I came, I saw, I conquered'; 'short and sweet'; 'what's hot and what's not'. Once a parallel series has been set up, however, the writer must ensure that all the elements in it have the same form. For example, 'The puppy likes to sleep, to eat, and to play' is fine. But 'The puppy likes to sleep, eating, and to play' won't do, since 'eating' is not parallel to the other forms, which begin with 'to'. Similarly, in 'He came for the food, the drink, and because he is such a social animal', the first two elements are nouns, while the third is a clause and therefore not parallel. This could be rewritten in various ways: for example, 'He came because he likes good food, good drink, and good company'.

In a series of more than two elements, it is possible either to repeat the prepositions (*on, at*, etc.), the *to*

in infinitives (as in *to eat*), or the articles (*a, an, the*) each time, or to drop them after the first use: 'The puppy likes to sleep, (to) eat, and (to) play'; 'We brought a stereo, (a) picnic lunch, and (a) beach umbrella'. In a series with only two elements, however, dropping these words for the second element creates an unbalanced effect, and many usage guides warn against it. Such problems usually occur with the following correlative conjunctions: *both ... and; not only ... but also; either ... or; neither ... nor*. What follows the second element in these constructions should be parallel with what follows the first: 'The book is either on the bed or on the chair' (*either* and *or* followed by a prepositional phrase) and 'The book is on either the bed or the chair' (*either* and *or* followed by a noun) are both acceptable, but 'The book is either on the bed or the chair' is not. A similar problem arises in sentences like 'Calcium is not only found in milk but also in vegetables'; this should be rewritten 'Calcium is found not only in milk but also in vegetables'.

Another form of faulty parallelism occurs with possessives. A structure such as 'the great physicist Albert Einstein's insights' makes 'the great physicist' (a common noun phrase) parallel to 'Albert Einstein's' (a possessive noun phrase). The solution is to rewrite: 'the insights of the great physicist Albert Einstein'.

Finally, items treated as parallel in a list should be at roughly the same level of generality: for example, 'We visited Newfoundland, Nova Scotia, and New Brunswick' or 'We visited St. John's, Dartmouth, and Moncton', but not 'We visited Newfoundland, Dartmouth, and New Brunswick'.

parameters, perimeter   A *parameter* is a measurable feature or property that determines the character or outcome of something. For example, temperature, barometric pressure, and wind speed are parameters of weather. In business and politics *parameter* is a vogue word used more loosely to mean factor, element, or guideline, or sometimes, in the plural, scope or limit. Some commentators strongly object to these newer uses of *parameter* as ambiguous. Nevertheless, they are common both in formal writing and in educated speech.

Some usage commentators caution against the confusion of *parameter* with *perimeter*—the outer edge or boundary of something. In Canadian writing *perimeter* is used to describe literal boundaries ('The perimeter of the field is fenced'), while *pa-*

rameter is used to denote a figurative limit. Rarely are the established literal and figurative uses of the terms confused.

Using a supercomputer, the materials science technology division has modelled the process, taking into account several dozen parameters including temperature of the mold and metal.
Globe and Mail (Toronto) 26 July 1985: B14

... it takes no account of the extremely complex, patterned covariation which always seems to exist in society's use of language between linguistic parameters and such other parameters as socioeconomic status, sex, race, age, situation and content.
W.C. Lougheed ed. *In Search of the Standard in Canadian English* 1986: 36

For the past few months a joint working committee has been developing the project parameters.
Western Grocer Magazine May–Jun. 1990: 51

As the parameters of the modern welfare state expanded beyond the narrow domain of the 'night watchman' to embrace a broader range of social and economic issues, they expanded into the traditional domain of women.
Neil Nevitte and Roger Gibbins *New Elites in Old States* 1990: 75

The coffeepot-shaped province is tucked into Quebec along its northern perimeter and joined to Maine all along its western boundary; a narrow neck of land on the east connects New Brunswick to Nova Scotia.
Alan Tucker, ed. *The Penguin Guide to Canada* 1991: 82

Each cow had its own door, and the doors, equidistant around the perimeter of the circle, were worked by a central pulley.
Margaret Atwood *Second Words* 1982: 336

... the bleachers, portable washrooms and concessions would be erected entirely within the existing parameters of the stadium and would not infringe on park territory.
Vancouver Sun 6 April 1990: D2

(Since the sense here is literal, *perimeter* is required.)

'There are still some minor negotiations going on concerning the perimeters of the terms.'
Globe and Mail (Toronto) 11 Oct. 1985: C2

(This figurative use of *perimeters* is unusual; the word intended was probably *parameters*.)

paramount, tantamount *Paramount* means most important or supreme. *Tantamount to* means equal or equivalent to.

Leisure activities have always been of paramount importance to the Inuit, who are very social in nature.
Arctic 41.1 (1988): 76

Accent is of paramount importance; generally, the more 'correct' the accent and manners the less funny the individual is held to be.
Margaret Atwood *Second Words* 1982: 178

For some people, the idea of reimbursing hospitals for the expenses they incur in organ retrieval may seem tantamount to paying a bounty for organs.
Gazette (Montreal) 12 May 1994: B2

'Sending the children back to Chernobyl is tantamount to sending them back to a Nazi gas chamber.'
Gazette (Montreal) 22 Feb. 1994: A3

paraphernalia *Paraphernalia* is derived from a plural Latin noun referring to a woman's personal belongings, separate from her dowry. In modern English it means trivial odds and ends or equipment, and is used with either a singular or a plural verb. Note the spelling; sometimes the second *r*, which is usually not pronounced, is left out in writing.

Parenthetical hints and tips, reverse chronology, asides and footnotes, all the paraphernalia of post-modernist ambiguity is here in controlled profusion.
Globe and Mail (Toronto) 16 Feb. 1985: E17

(In this example the noun *paraphernalia* takes a singular verb, *is*.)

Official paraphernalia, including Blue Jays caps, pennants, buttons and 'No. 1 fingers'—giant gloves with the index finger raised—were being sold faster than vendors could replenish the stock.
Globe and Mail (Toronto) 7 Oct. 1985: A12

(In this example *paraphernalia* takes a plural verb, *were*.)

Its collection includes not only the expected paraphernalia of conflict—torpedoes, tanks, and cannons—but more than 7,000 artworks that describe war through the eyes of artists from several countries.
Alan Tucker, ed. *The Penguin Guide to Canada* 1991: 309

Many fans wore outlandish costumes while others waved signs and other paraphenalia.
Vancouver Sun 3 Dec. 1990: D9

(The correct spelling is *paraphernalia*.)

See also AGREEMENT, GRAMMATICAL; COLLECTIVE NOUNS.

parentheses, brackets Printers and editors usually differentiate between *parentheses* and *brackets*, using the former term for round brackets ( ) and the latter for square [ ]. However, *brackets* is also a generic term for round brackets, square brackets, or braces { }.

The singular of *parentheses* (pronounced *puh REN thuh seez*) is *parenthesis*. A parenthesis is a parenthetical remark—that is, an interjection or aside—or one half of a pair of parentheses: 'You forgot the closing parenthesis'.

Parentheses enclose matter that interrupts the flow of a sentence or paragraph. For example:

• digressions:

> The two election pamphlets, 'A Fair Deal for Canada' and 'Meeting the Challenge' (neither of which was widely distributed), took a similar approach.
> Alan Whitehorn *Canadian Socialism* 1992: 220

• particularizations:

> The majority of the judges (5 of 7) had decided that Section 251 violated Canadian women's constitutional rights to the security of the person.
> Janine Brodie, Shelley A. M. Gavigan, and Jane Jenson *The Politics of Abortion* 1992: 59

• examples:

> ... a province may exempt itself from the effect of an amendment derogating from its legislative powers or proprietary rights (e.g., in natural resources), by resolution of the legislature.
> *Queen's Quarterly* 94.4 (1987): 786

• translations:

> In the long run he decides to ... offer his manuscript to the city and the world, including the *vendus* (sellouts) who have betrayed him.
> Ben-Z. Shek *French-Canadian & Québécois Novels* 1991: 52

• optional elements:

> 1/2 cup cocoa
> (1/2 cup chopped walnuts)

• alternative phrasings:

> If three or more units out of 500 fail the test(s), the lot is sent back, explained Wong.
> *Computer Dealer News* 21 March 1991: 26

• documentation of sources:

> However, recent work has identified several dense and productive populations (Alliston and Patterson, 1978; Calef and Heard, 1979; Bromley, in press).
> *Arctic* 41.1 (1988): 18

In some contexts it is possible to replace parentheses with paired commas or dashes. Parentheses usually signal a stronger disruption of syntax than paired commas, but a less dramatic break in the sentence than dashes.

Newspapers often use parentheses to enclose explanatory information inserted in a quotation:

> 'We hope that this (Black Sea) incident will not hinder the process of bettering Soviet-American relations.'
> *Calgary Herald* 14 Feb. 1988: A2

In books and academic writing, the convention is different: anything added to or altered in a quotation is enclosed in square brackets. Parentheses are reserved for material that was in parentheses in the original:

> 'The Reichsfuhrer [Himmler] has summoned me to take up a special assignment in Russia.'
> *Canadian Journal of History* 14.1 (1989): 77

> One claims that the lyric is 'by and large, [the] least ironical' of all the literary forms.
> Linda Hutcheon *Splitting Images* 1991: 25

> 'I want to tell you myself before you hear from any other source,' he wrote to Chancellor Richardson, 'that George V (whiskers and all) has been graciously pleased to offer me the principalship of Aberdeen University and that I have been graciously pleased to accept.'
> Frederick W. Gibson *Queen's University* 2 (1983): 128

> (Here the parenthetical element was added by the letter-writer, not the quoting author.)

The Latin word *sic* in square brackets is used to flag mistakes or peculiarities in quoted matter. *Sic* means 'thus' (i.e., 'It was thus in the original'). The use of [*sic*] prevents readers from thinking that the quoting writer has introduced a mistake into a quotation, or failed to notice something amiss. However, the device should be used judiciously. It can seem priggish and condescending, and sometimes merely reveals the ignorance of the quoting writer. *Sic* should be italicized:

> Ross, an early Canadian modernist, noted that Canada has 'quite a number of poems about diving, whereas they are lacking in US and english [*sic*] writers.'
> *Queen's Quarterly* 97.3 (1990): 426

> With the stress on dependency, it becomes startling to suddenly read of the 'mutual interdependence [*sic*] of trader and Indian'....
> *Arctic* 41.1 (1988): 77

The conventions for combining parentheses with other types of punctuation are as follows. When a sentence in parentheses stands alone, its final punctuation mark goes inside the closing parenthesis:

(The present decade began, too, with the failure of the Meech Lake Accord, and the Mohawk crisis, both of which have affected Quebec deeply.)
Ben-Z. Shek *French-Canadian & Québécois Novels* 1991: 46

A parenthetical sentence contained within another sentence has no initial capital or final period. It may, however, end in a question mark or exclamation mark:

My generalism (please do not confuse this with dilettantism because they are not the same) clearly led me to seek the editorship because of the scope it allows for putting this predilection into practice.
Queen's Quarterly 92.2 (1985): 442

A society-page roster of a recent Hunt Club soirée at the Ritz (what could be more anglo?) reads like a *Who's Who* of francophone high society, with a sprinkling of WASPs for old time's sake.
Alan Tucker, ed. *The Penguin Guide to Canada* 1991: 144

I was surprised at first and a little angry, for it seemed he hadn't understood at all (then I realized he was only doing his general manager's job).
Ken Dryden *The Game* 1983: 15

(Note the position of the period here—outside the final parenthesis.)

A comma is never placed in front of an opening parenthesis. If a parenthetical remark occurs at a point in a sentence where a comma is normally required—for example, between a subordinate clause and a main clause—the comma is placed after the closing parenthesis:

If she were to discover a country which had never been discovered before (and she fully intended to do this sometime), she would of course name it after herself.
Margaret Atwood *Life Before Man* 1979: 80

One final remark on style: most writing guides caution against the overuse of parenthetical remarks in discursive writing. While conversation is full of asides and derailments, it is usually considered better form in an essay to plan the sequence of ideas and to stay on topic. Short parenthetical remarks may be helpful, but long ones should be scrutinized. They can often be transformed into notes or dropped altogether.

parkway   see ROAD

parlay, parley   *Parlay* (pronounced *PAR LAY* or *PAR lee*) has a long-standing meaning among American gamblers: to stake all the winnings from one bet on another wager. (The British term is *double up*.) The extended definition of *parlay* is to build upon a small advantage or piece of good fortune. In the extended use the element of risk is de-emphasized. The usual construction is 'to parlay *x* into *y*', *y* being something much better.

Historically, a *parley* (pronounced *PAR lee*), from the French verb *parler*, 'to speak', is an informal conference between enemies, usually to discuss terms of surrender or points of disagreement. In popular usage, however, *parley* can refer to any kind of informal discussion.

In 10 years, he had parlayed his navy training as a supply officer into the position of general manager of Refinery Engineering Ltd....
Globe and Mail (Toronto) 3 Jan. 1985: E4

It has taken the basic product of electrical wire and parlayed it into a successful diversified business with such products as lawn mowers and snow blowers.
Globe and Mail (Toronto) 21 June 1985: P106

It required a Shultz-Gromyko parley in January to launch the arms talks.
Globe and Mail (Toronto) 15 March 1985: P6

Canada's native Indians in parley are apparently not as exciting as South African slums, although some reserves suffer impoverished conditions equal to anything in the Third World.
Vancouver Sun 12 March 1990: A7

(Here *parley* means discussion.)

... the United Steelworkers are having a big parley later this week to discuss different strategies for dealing with Cominco's changed management style.
Vancouver Sun 6 Feb. 1990: C1

(Here *parley* means conference or meeting.)

When wages went down, they parleyed a student business loan into their own one-truck outfit ...
CBC News [transcript] 22 May 1995

(The word needed here is *parlayed*.)

parlous   *Parlous* (pronounced *PAR lus*) is an archaic variant of *perilous*. It usually appears in stock phrases such as 'parlous conditions' and 'parlous times'. Critics warn against its use unless a writer deliberately wants to create an arch tone.

A mother-fixation resulted from these parlous years, later expressing itself in Wagner's inordinate fondness for soft fabrics and well-upholstered women.
Queen's Quarterly 92 (1985): 215

We live in parlous times when the only political leaders speaking up for a strong and united Canada are those who failed to deliver when the chips were down.
Vancouver Sun 15 Aug. 1990: A12

parsonage   see MANSE

part   see BEHALF

Parthian shot   see PARTING SHOT

parties, political   see POLITICAL PARTIES

parting shot, Parthian shot   A cutting remark made just as one is leaving (or retreating) is sometimes called a *parting shot*. This expression appears to have been derived from *Parthian shot* (see FOLK ETYMOLOGY). *Parthian shot* alludes to the horsemen of ancient Parthia who, even while turned in flight, were able to devastate an enemy with their arrows. The unfamiliar expression *Parthian shot* developed the more transparent alternative form *parting shot*, which appears to have completely supplanted the original in Canadian English.

[She] can't resist a few parting shots at the professions of architecture and architectural criticism. Even to the innocent eye, the feisty text is bound to appear motivated ... by revenge....
Globe and Mail (Toronto) 25 May 1985: E11

A will should be your last statement of caring to those you hold dear. Unfortunately, Johnston says, many people choose to use it as their parting shot.
Vancouver Sun 26 March 1994: C7

partner   see SPOUSE

passive voice   see WORDINESS

past history   The phrase *past history* is idiomatic and used by many established writers, even though the word *past* is, strictly speaking, redundant. *Past history* can suggest water under the bridge, or history that is not relevant to present considerations; or *past* may balance the adjective *future* in another phrase in the same sentence. In other words, there are contexts where this idiom, a favourite target of language commentators, is quite defensible.

The three covered their tracks so well that no whisper of scandal leaked out until a royal commission ... brought down its report in 1915. By then it was past history.
Pierre Berton *The Promised Land* 1984: 245

Past history is no guarantee of future performance, but it can tell you a lot about management ability....
Ottawa Citizen 17 Dec. 1990: F1

The effect of such words is to give the impression that all past history was a kind of bad dream, which in these enlightened days we've shaken off.
Northrop Frye *The Educated Imagination* 1963: 62

pastiche   *Pastiche* (pronounced *pass TEESH*) usually means a mixture of different, often incongruous, things. A specialized sense found in academic writing refers to any piece of art, music, literature, or architecture that imitates an earlier style, or combines several styles. Both of these senses can be pejorative, but they are not always so.

The video is a pastiche of interviews with teachers, parents, school officials and students. It emphasizes the quality of curriculum, range of special education programs, discipline and accountability of the public school system.
Globe and Mail (Toronto) 10 Jan. 1985: M5

(Here *pastiche* is clearly descriptive and is not used pejoratively.)

Palmer's effort looks like a pastiche of footage from a dozen different directors, none willing to see an inch of his sacrosanct celluloid trimmed for the sake of the whole.
Globe and Mail (Toronto) 21 May 1985: M11

(The use of *pastiche* here is obviously pejorative.)

But as a counterbalance to this haunting vignette we have a pastiche of Kafka, as Christine looks absently out the train window to observe a family party climbing a hill to what they have been assured is a museum-castle.
Janice Kulyk Keefer *Reading Mavis Gallant* 1989: 175

Art-historical citation, then, can move beyond the superficial pastiche described by Jameson to a profound ... engagement with the notions of pastness and history in general.
Mark A. Cheetham with Linda Hutcheon *Remembering Postmodernism* 1991: 7

patent   see BLATANT

patient   see CUSTOMER

patio   see PORCH

payed   see PAID

patriate, patriation   The verb *patriate* is a recent Canadianism referring to the process of giving full control of the Canadian Constitution to Canadians. Until 1982, all amendments to Canada's Constitution had to be passed by the British parliament. As early as the 1960s, people talked about *repatriating* the Constitution; but, since *repatriate* means to bring someone or something back home, the word was inappropriate for the Constitution, which had never resided in Canada. The new coinage *patriate* is now fully established and means to bring legislation under the constitutional authority of an autonomous country (*OED*). By extension of this meaning, *patriate* is now sometimes used of strategies for bringing or keeping wealth in a country.

> The Canadian government and nine provinces reached an agreement on a plan to patriate the British North America Act and entrench a Charter of Rights four years ago today.
> *Globe and Mail* (Toronto) 5 Nov. 1985: A14

> 'I got enthused, I got emotionally involved in what I was doing,' he says, pointing to his considerable efforts in support of former Prime Minister Pierre Trudeau's campaign to repatriate the Constitution.
> *Globe and Mail* (Toronto) 12 Oct. 1985: A10

> (Here *patriate* would be more accurate.)

> The use of the word 'repatriate' in reference to Quebec is both historically inaccurate and insulting to the intelligence of all Canadians. Neither the people of Quebec nor its government had seceded from Confederation.
> *Gazette* (Montreal) 5 March 1989: B2

> (The writer is objecting to *repatriate* because it means to bring 'back' to the country, and Quebec has not seceded.)

> The plan was to bring on gold options to help patriate some of the futures trading directed to U.S. exchanges and capture new business developing in Canada in precious metals.
> *Globe and Mail* (Toronto) 31 Jan. 1985: B3

> 'British Columbia's decision to patriate its entitlement to the downstream benefits is key to long-term power planning on both sides of the 49th parallel.'
> *Vancouver Sun* 12 Jan. 1990: A1

See also CONSTITUTION.

patron   see CUSTOMER

patronage   see NEPOTISM

peaceful, peaceable   The usual distinction between these words is that *peaceful* means characterized by peace, and thus can describe either a person or a place, while *peaceable* means fond or desirous of peace and usually describes only people.

A people's desire for peace is extended to their nation in Northrop Frye's well-known characterization of Canada as a country on a quest for 'the peaceable kingdom' (*Literary History of Canada*, 1965). Frye took the phrase from the title of a painting (c. 1830) by the American Edward Hicks, which shows William Penn working out a treaty with some Native people, while in the foreground a child sits with a group of animals including lions, tigers, and bears (an allusion to Isaiah 11: 6).

Both *peacefully* and *peaceably* are used to mean in a peaceful manner.

> Although our country is one of the most peaceful and prosperous on earth, although we do not shoot artists here, although we do not execute political opponents and although this is one of the few remaining countries in which we can have a gathering like this without expecting to be arrested or blown up, we should not overlook the fact that Canada's record on civil rights issues is less than pristine.
> Margaret Atwood *Second Words* 1982: 395

> Outside, a sturdy shelter belt of poplars and spruce encircles the house protectively; the winter fields are peaceful and deserted.
> *Chatelaine* April 1986: 190

> In Europe you can go from one city to another, from village to village, with hardly an open field between.... In Canada that space is a given, if a luxury; it is why we are the peaceable nation.
> *Chronicle-Telegraph* (Quebec City) 14 Aug. 1991: 12

> Although strikers are entitled to picket at or near the place of the employer's business, they must do so peaceably and only for the purpose of obtaining or communicating information.
> J.E. Smyth et al. *The Law and Business Administration in Canada* 1987: 516

peak, peek, pique   Writers occasionally use *peak* (high point) when they mean *peek* (glance).

The verb *pique* means stimulate: 'My curiosity was piqued by the flashing lights'. Since interest can both *peak* (reach a peak) and *be piqued*, *peak* and *pique* are also occasionally confused.

With participant interest now at its peak, it was time to announce the winning hands.
Canadian Biker Magazine Feb. 1990: 20

And four delirious young girls from New Jersey do their darndest to sneak a peak at the Fab Four....
Gazette (Montreal) 5 March 1989: T65

(The correct spelling here is *peek*.)

Over the years a favorite way to deal with hockey intermissions has been to switch channels. Occasionally a between-periods interview can pique interest....
Globe and Mail (Toronto) 12 Oct. 1985: P12

The officers' curiosity peaked even more when a computer check of the papers the motorist gave them indicated he wasn't who he alleged to be.
Gazette (Montreal) 26 May 1990: A3

(Although curiosity can be said to *peak*, it cannot peak 'even more'. The sense here requires the passive verb *was piqued*.)

pean   see PAEAN

pedagogue, pedant   These words do not mean the same thing. A *pedagogue* is a teacher. A *pedant* is someone more concerned with correcting others than teaching them, and more interested in the mastery of minutiae than the broad implications of learning. When a pedagogue is also a pedant, the context must make it clear: *pedagogue* in itself is not pejorative.
   The spelling *pedagog* is an alternative in the United States but is not used by Canadian writers.

Both musicians have graduated in organ performance ... and are now continuing their studies with the internationally renowned concert organist and pedagogue Antoine Bouchard.
Chronicle-Telegraph (Quebec City) 24 July 1991: 4

Tyler stuffed his books and papers into the shabby briefcase whose clasp rarely closed properly, and set off, one shoulder slightly higher than the other, for his next class.... It was harder than usual tonight, for some reason, to feel much confidence in pedagogy ... or in himself as a pedagogue.
Constance Beresford-Howe *Night Studies* 1985: 90

How many times were we corrected on these two phrases alone, and how often do we say 'It is I' or 'I took only one cookie' because we suspect some pedagogue's hammer is still hovering above our cerebellum?
W.C. Lougheed, ed. *In Search of the Standard in Canadian English* 1986: 80

(Here the *pedagogue* is also a *pedant*.)

[The play] sharpens and clarifies complex issues which are deliberately obscured by legal pedants, political cynics, blustering bureaucrats, and ... the mealy-mouthed rhetoric of grasping business interests.
Vancouver Sun 13 Jun. 1990: A13

pedal, peddle, pedlar, peddler   *Pedal* comes from the Latin *pedalis*, meaning 'of the foot'. A *pedal* is a lever operated by the foot, and to *pedal* is to operate a machine by pushing its pedals. Canadian writers are divided on whether to use a single or a double *l* before the endings -*ed*, -*ing*, and -*er*. British dictionaries double the final consonant; American dictionaries do not.
   To *peddle* is to sell something, especially in small quantities, or to promote an idea or way of life. Canadian writers favour the noun *peddler* (the American spelling) but also use the older variant *pedlar*. In Britain the usual spelling is *pedlar*, although *peddler* is used in Britain for someone who sells drugs.

When I peddled past 25 miles an hour, the bicycle actually took off and flew. You could steer through the air by leaning to one side or the other....
Vancouver Sun 5 Sept. 1990: D1

(The correct spelling is *pedalled* or *pedaled*.)

The provincial capitals are monstrosities of iron and concrete, representatives of a Soviet subspecies of urban planning inhabited by joyless pedallers bent over the handlebars of their identical lives.
Globe and Mail (Toronto) 24 Aug. 1985: 1

Far from developing and nurturing a sturdy sense of self-reliance, he has been a peddler of pipe-dreams.
Financial Post 17 Sept. 1990: 12

He was a prosperous pedlar of gents' natty garments and ladies' whalebone corsets.
Vancouver Sun 3 Feb. 1990: B4

See also DOUBLING THE FINAL CONSONANT.

pedant   see PEDAGOGUE

peddle, peddler   see PEDAL

pedigree   see PUREBRED

pedlar   see PEDAL

peek   see PEAK

peer, peerless A *peer* is equal to someone else, being in the same age or social group, or having the same level of ability. *Peerless* describes something with no equal. *Peer* is also used to refer to a member of the British nobility.

By the time Davis ... left the Charlie Parker Quintet in December 1948, he had already laid the foundation that would make him Parker's peer in the development of jazz.
Jack Chambers *Milestones* 1983: 89

Everybody loves a winner, and the Canadiens were without peer.
Globe and Mail (Toronto) 20 April 1985: S3

(In other words, they were *peerless*.)

It was a day when normally peerless Zurbriggen had to concede he had made an error.
Globe and Mail (Toronto) 8 Feb. 1985: P14

The idea of a British peer dictating to Canadians ... did not sit easily in a region where, in principle at least, every man was considered the equal of every other if he was willing to work.
Pierre Berton *The Promised Land* 1984: 192

pellucid see TURGID

pen name see PSEUDONYM

pensioner see SENIOR CITIZEN

pentimento see PALIMPSEST

penultimate, ultimate *Penultimate* means the 'last but one' or 'next to last'. Sometimes *penultimate* is mistakenly used as a synonym for *ultimate*, which means last, best possible, or unsurpassable.

Scoresby's survey of the Greenland coast was his penultimate voyage to the Arctic. His last was in 1823.
Arctic 41.1 (1988): 46

Once a week when the Liberals ran Ottawa, about 30 of the town's deputy ministers—the princes of the public service—would gather ... for the insiders' penultimate plum, a high-level briefing on what had happened that week in the meetings of the Cabinet and its most important committees.
Globe and Mail (Toronto) 29 Nov. 1985: P32

(Here *penultimate* is incorrectly used to mean *ultimate*.)

Her tireless networking ... led inexorably to that penultimate phone call July 6, 1987, from Tory eminence grise Dalton Camp, her ace-in-the-hole link to the prime minister.
Province (Vancouver) 24 June 1990: 92

(Here *penultimate* is incorrectly used to mean *ultimate*.)

peon see PAEAN

people, peoples see PERSONS

people of colour see VISIBLE MINORITY

Péquiste A *Péquiste* (pronounced *PAY KEEST*) is a member or supporter of the Parti Québécois (or PQ), the provincial political party seeking the independence of Quebec. The word *Péquiste* was formed by adding the suffix *-iste* to the party initials *PQ*. Because it is derived from a proper name, the term is not italicized in English: 'He supports the Péquistes'. When the noun is used as an adjective, capitalization is optional: 'péquiste candidate'. In formal writing the acute accent over the first *e* is required, though it seldom appears in English newspapers.

But this secured for the Péquistes only 6% of the seats in the National Assembly.
David V.J. Bell *The Roots of Disunity* 1992: 112

Too bad the 'youth executive' of the Liberal and Pequiste parties didn't resign a couple of decades ago!
Gazette (Montreal) 30 July 1992: B2

(In formal writing *Péquiste* would retain its accent.)

'My parents are pequistes (members of the Parti Quebecois), so I will vote No.'
Vancouver Sun 23 Oct. 1992: A1

(The noun *Péquiste* should be capitalized.)

Guitard, a former pequiste activist, draws her support from all parties.
Ottawa Citizen 5 Dec. 1992: F2

(Capitalization of the adjective is optional.)

per cent, percent Canadian newspapers overwhelmingly use two words: *per cent*. The single-word spelling *percent* is sometimes found in other types of Canadian writing. British dictionaries list *per cent* first, American dictionaries *percent*.

Per cent is followed by either a single or a plural verb form, depending on the noun concerned: 'Fifteen per cent of the total is added to the bill for service' or 'Only twenty per cent of the students are going to pass the test'.

The per cent symbol (%) is used only with figures: '8%'.

See also NUMBERS.

perfect, more perfect, most perfect Some usage experts consider perfection an absolute condition; hence they argue that the adjective *perfect* should not be used in comparisons, and they object to the phrases *more* (or *less*) *perfect* and *most* (or *least*) *perfect*. However, *more perfect* and *most perfect* have long been used to suggest the varying degrees to which perfection may be approximated. *Perfect* belongs to a set of adjectives—including *complete, excellent, extreme*, and *unique*—that denote superlative qualities without being considered grammatically superlative terms. *More perfect* is enshrined in the American Constitution, which aims for 'a more perfect union' of the United States. Though some may object, the consensus is that *perfect* can be compared.

Thus by the end of the 1950s the universities of Canada were seen not merely as the means for achieving a more perfect social justice, but also as holding the keys to economic prosperity and even national survival.
Frederick Gibson *Queen's University 2* (1983): 357

The Great Cross in the churchyard is one of the world's most perfect specimens....
Canadian Churchman April 1986: 11

See also COMPLETE; UNIQUE.

performance art, performing arts   see ARTS

perigee   see APOGEE

perimeter   see PARAMETERS

period of time, time period A number of usage commentators criticize the phrases *period of time* and *time period* as redundant, arguing that either *period* or *time* should be used, but not both together. However, these phrases are idiomatic, and in fact there are many contexts in which *period* or *time* alone will not do: 'What period of time should we reserve?' Both *period of time* and *time period* appear in the work of well-known Canadian writers.

Each essay treats the development of an idea or a set of ideas over a period of time.
J.A.W. Gunn *Beyond Liberty and Property* 1983: 1

When ... performance is spread over a period of time and is to be paid for on completion, a frustration of the contract before its completion may cause serious hardship for the performer or his estate.
J.E. Smyth et al. *The Law and Business Administration in Canada* 1987: 319

... tradition is a body of practice in a certain area, accumulated over a certain period of time, that for one reason or another is considered meaningful enough to be passed on from one generation to the next.
Miriam Waddington *Apartment Seven* 1989: 84

But brain-fever was generally invoked by novelists when they wanted to get a character out of the way for an unspecified period of time.
Robertson Davies *One Half of Robertson Davies* 1978: 164

The book's point of departure is the time period after the crash, after Millett has been 'trashed' by the media, the women's movement, and various friends and lovers who could not deal with her success.
Margaret Atwood *Second Words* 1982: 210

perk, perquisite, prerequisite A *perk* is a special privilege on top of a salary or wage, such as the right to use a company car. *Perk* is actually a short form, and most dictionaries label it informal. In formal writing the long form *perquisite* should be used.

Commentators caution writers not to confuse *perquisite* with *prerequisite*. A *prerequisite* is a requirement that must be fulfilled before something else can happen.

The discounters can afford to take those cuts by eliminating the perks offered by the large firms—plush offices, sophisticated sales teams and highly trained analysts who evaluate stocks and advise customers.
Maclean's 24 Feb. 1986: 48

It isn't the praise, or the generous perks of celebrity; it is the implicit, unstated respect it gives.
Ken Dryden *The Game* 1983: 13

These 'new people' ... did not know that gentlefolk had new candles in every stick every day, and objected to the lively trade in long candle ends which was part of cook's perquisites.
Robertson Davies *A Voice from the Attic* 1960: 138

An ethical society is not a prerequisite of scientific advancement. Neither is respect for ethical values a prerequisite for scientific insight and achievement.
Canadian Journal of Philosophy 19 (1989): 294

... the craft unceremoniously dumped us out.... Even though we were both experienced flat-water canoeists, lessons and supervision with qualified white-water instructors should have been a prerequisite.
Gazette (Montreal) 20 May 1994: D4

pernickety   see PERSNICKETY

perogy, pyrohy   The word for a Ukrainian dumpling filled with potato, cheese, or meat is spelled in various ways. In western Canada *pyrohy* is popular, but *perogy* is probably the most common Canadian spelling. The usual pronunciation is *puh ROH gee*.

perpetrate, perpetuate   To *perpetrate* a crime or evil act is to commit it. To *perpetuate* something is to ensure that it continues.

> ... I could see with my own eyes the horrors that were being perpetrated in the name of supposedly just causes.
> George Ignatieff *The Making of a Peacemonger* 1987: 23

> When they mark their ballots, the delegates will be voting not for a mere leader but for a man they judge able to perpetuate the dynasty for another decade.
> *Globe and Mail* (Toronto) 19 Jan. 1985: P1

> Abuses are still being perpetuated upon our environment, and our generation will probably go down in history with a record our children and grandchildren will not be proud of.
> *Vancouver Sun* 29 Dec. 1990: G4

(The word required here is *perpetrated*.)

> Many men and some women have insisted his act represents but a single horrific incident perpetuated by a madman.
> *Province* (Vancouver) 5 Jan. 1990: 34

(The word required here is *perpetrated*.)

> Wolf 'kills' make good headlines, but I think your article missed a crucial opportunity to enlighten the public at large, rather than perpetrate polarization on an issue for which solutions must be found.
> *Province* (Vancouver) 25 May 1990: 48

(The word required here is *perpetuate*.)

perquisite   see PERK

per se   *Per se* (pronounced *per SAY* or, especially in legal circles, *per SEE*) is a Latin expression that means 'in or of itself', 'intrinsically', or 'as such': 'This drug is not a poison *per se*, but, if you drink alcohol while you are taking it, you become very sick'.

According to dictionaries, *per se* does *not* mean 'strictly speaking' or 'in the narrow sense of the word', as in 'We're not making a promise *per se*, but we're fairly confident of being able to deliver a dividend soon'. However, this sense of *per se* is very common in speech and journalism.

Some writers condemn any use of *per se* as affected and pedantic.

> Some traditionalists counter that rising divorce rates actually have little to do with changing economic circumstances.... Instead, they contend, it is the liberalization of divorce laws per se that has caused divorce rates to soar.
> Irving M. Zeitlin and Robert J. Brym *The Social Condition of Humanity* 1991: 194

> It is not guns per se that are the problem. The problem has several aspects, including cultural conditions and a lack of application of existing law.
> *Vancouver Sun* 2 Aug. 1990: A10

> He had no commitment to freedom and democracy per se, but realized they were necessary to revitalize the economy.
> *Financial Post* 29 Aug. 1991: 7

> It's not a matter of the Optima being a bad car, per se, but more of it not being a good one.
> *Province* (Vancouver) 21 Sept. 1990: 103

(Here *per se* is misused to mean exactly.)

> 'It wasn't a spill per se.'
> *Vancouver Sun* 22 Nov. 1990: E7

(Here *per se* is misused to mean strictly speaking.)

> 'We don't believe there is a policy per se.'
> *Financial Post* 14 Sept. 1990: 13

(Here *per se* is misused to mean strictly speaking or officially.)

See also LATIN PHRASES.

persnickety, pernickety   *Persnickety* and *pernickety* are both informal words meaning fussy or punctilious. Both forms are used in North America, but *persnickety* is more common. *Pernickety* is the only form used in Britain.

> The Canadian Auto Workers seem awfully persnickety about swapping Canadian holidays for U.S. dates. A day's a day, isn't it?
> *Province* (Vancouver) 13 June 1990: 24

> Trudeau campaigned with vigor, but without notes. Here was the gunslinger in dramatic contrast to fumbling, yet persnickety, Joe Clark.
> *Toronto Star* 22 Sept. 1986: A14

> No, my concern is that of a writer, and on occasion a formal speaker, who wants to be as careful and even pernickety about meanings as he can.
> Robertson Davies *One Half of Robertson Davies* 1978: 13

> The curse of all architects, it seems, is the meddling politician. Right after him come the cost-cutting accountant, the nit-picking bureaucrat, the pernickety lawyer....
> *Ottawa Citizen* 8 April 1990: E3

persona   In Latin a *persona* is an actor's mask, and this meaning is preserved in the modern English use of *persona* for an actor's stage personality or a fictional voice assumed by a writer. Another meaning became popular at the beginning of the century when the writings of the psychoanalyst Carl Jung were translated into English. Jung used *persona* to mean the externalized outer self that we use in our social dealings, as opposed to our private inner self or soul. Thus any person's public personality or façade may now also be called a *persona*. The plural is either *personae* or *personas*.

> The unnamed 74-year-old nurse recounts to the main persona crucial and extraordinary, yet believable, incidents of tragic womanhood....
> Ben-Z. Shek *French-Canadian & Québécois Novels* 1991: 94

(Here the *persona* is a fictional character.)

> On this particular trip, he played the peasant rather than worker and his persona allowed him to gather extensive information on the individuals and settlements he visited.
> *Canadian Journal of History* 14.1 (1989): 68

(Here *persona* refers to a façade or assumed role.)

> He still talks constantly of inflation and interest rates, but the edge in his voice has gone, as if he does so now only because the team expects it of him, as part of his team persona.
> Ken Dryden *The Game* 1983: 69

> Now she's trying to find an adjective to describe her on-air persona, having already rejected descriptions like bubbly, quirky and boisterous.
> *Globe and Mail* (Toronto) 15 May 1985: S10

> Her breezy writing style and public persona concealed a melancholy outlook on life.
> *Women and Environments* 12.2 (1990): 12

See also PERSONA NON GRATA.

personal, personally   *Personal* is often called redundant when used in combinations such as 'personal opinion' or 'personal friend', since opinions and friends are assumed to be personal. Constructions such as 'I personally think ...' are criticized on similar grounds. However, *personal* and *personally* are not necessarily empty words in these phrases. Sometimes a distinction is being made between private and public life, and sometimes first-hand involvement is being emphasized, as in 'I personally took your order'.

> Whatever personal opinions the sovereign may hold or may have expressed to her Government, she is bound to accept and act on the advice of her ministers....

> Andrew Heard *Canadian Constitutional Conventions* 1991: 43

(Here *personal opinions* are private beliefs as opposed to public policy.)

> For Milwaukee speed skater Marty Pierce there was a moving personal memory when it was all over.
> *Calgary Herald* 14 Feb. 1988: 19

(Here *personal* indicates that the memory was important in a private way.)

> Burroughs's personal reputation, like his professional status, was open to interpretation.
> *Gazette* (Montreal) 4 March 1989: K11

(Here *personal* is used to parallel *professional*.)

> He won a solid majority in the 1986 provincial election, largely on the basis of his personal charisma.
> *Chronicle-Herald* (Halifax) 9 April 1988: 6

(Here *personal* is indeed redundant, since charisma can only be personal.)

personality   see CHARACTER

persona non grata, persona grata   *Persona non grata* is a term used to describe a person who is not welcome or wanted; *persona grata* describes one who is welcome. These Latin phrases were first used in diplomacy. A foreign representative whom a country was willing to accept was *persona grata*, while one deemed unacceptable was *persona non grata*. Of course, a chilling in the relations between two countries might quickly cause *persona grata* to become *non grata*.

   The plural of *persona non grata* is *personae non gratae*, but in journalism *persona non grata* is often used as a plural. Some language commentators recommend this usage on the grounds that *persona non grata* is now being used like an adjective in English (equivalent to 'unwelcome'), and thus should be invariable. However, word plays such as 'male persona non grata' (in reference to a man barred from a mother–infant group) and 'pachydermata non grata' (in reference to elephants on the rampage) demonstrate that at least some writers still construe *persona non grata* as a modified noun rather than a phrasal adjective. Thus the plural form of the phrase should be preserved, if not in newspaper writing, at least in formal usage.

   In formal writing *persona non grata* should be italicized as a foreign phrase. *Persona* is spelled with only one *n*. Note that these expressions are used without an article.

Morel is likely persona non grata in Calgary after his call in overtime of Game 6 of the Flames Smythe Division semifinal against Los Angeles....
Ottawa Citizen 18 April 1990: C3

A tiny force of 15 Native policemen, trained by Quebec and Ontario police, have some control of the Canadian side, but are persona non grata on the American side.
Province (Vancouver) 4 May 1990: 20

(In journalism, though not in formal writing, *persona non grata* may be used with a plural antecedent.)

... he was disqualified ... as one who still maintained friendly if not cordial relations with those *personae non gratae* George Lawson and George Weir.
Hilda Neatby *Queen's University* 1 (1978): 109

Those expelled did not include 11 Iraqi diplomats declared personae non grata by French President Francois Mitterrand.
Ottawa Citizen 17 Sept. 1990: A6

(Formal writing would require *gratae* here.)

The Lions have also added veteran defensive end Rick Klassen, ... a man who was personna non grata for a time, to the roster.
Vancouver Sun 4 Sept. 1990: D2

(The correct spelling is *persona*.)

See also LATIN PHRASES.

personnel *Personnel* (*per sun ELL*) means staff. It is treated as singular when considered as a unit ('Personnel is our main concern') and as a plural when considered as a collection of individuals ('All personnel are expected to attend the meeting'). Many critics object when *personnel* is used with a number ('fifteen personnel') on the grounds that *personnel* is a collective noun. However, the use of *personnel* as a countable noun is also well established.

Sometimes *personnel* is misspelled *personel*.

Personnel were dropped, agencies reorganized, salaries reduced.
Pierre Berton *The Promised Land* 1984: 211

Canada has about 1,700 military personnel in the Persian Gulf.
Winnipeg Free Press 17 Nov. 1990: 52

It's also a popular area for military and RCMP personel.
Ottawa Citizen 21 May 1994: E1

(The correct spelling is *personnel*.)

See also COLLECTIVE NOUNS.

persons, people, peoples Some usage guides state that *persons* rather than *people* should be preferred as the plural of *person* ('We had five persons over for dinner'); these guides would reserve *people* for collective uses ('the people of India'). In Canadian writing, however, *persons* is most commonly found in legal and bureaucratic contexts, and the usual plural for *person* in general contexts is *people*. *Persons* would probably strike most readers as affected.

When *people* refers collectively to an ethnic group or nationality, its plural is *peoples*: 'The peoples of the two countries are at war'.

... the cooperation of two persons can accomplish considerably more than can two individuals working alone.
Irving M. Zeitlin and Robert J. Brym *The Social Condition of Humanity* 1991: 62

The funnel uprooted trees, destroyed farms and houses and left eight people dead, 269 injured and 600 homeless.
Maclean's 10 Feb. 1986: 5

Caribou, musk-ox and buffalo have become integral parts of the diets of Canada's northern peoples....
Vancouver Sun 18 Dec. 1990: B5

perspicacious, perspicuous, perspicacity, perspicuity Someone who is *perspicacious* (*per spi KAY shus*) is discerning and perceptive; prose that is *perspicuous* (*per SPICK yoo us*) is clear and lucid. *Perspicacity* is superior discernment, a quality attributed to people, while *perspicuity*, clarity of expression, is a quality usually attributed to a style of writing, an argument, etc.

The words *perspicuous* and *perspicuity* are seldom used by Canadian writers, which may be why *perspicuity* tends to be confused with *perspicacity*.

Presumably an experienced lawyer perspicacious and prudent enough to qualify as a judge should not need a 'code of conduct to regulate behavior on and off the bench'.
Gazette (Montreal) 26 Oct. 1994: B2

With the perspicacity that hindsight bestows, however, I can now see how the elements of Tory success were present in that committee room.
Globe and Mail (Toronto) 19 June 1985: P7

U.S. forward Tony Granato took a hooking penalty in front of the net and then questioned the perspicacity of referee Mark Faucette.
Globe and Mail (Toronto) 30 April 1985: S3

(In other words, Granato questioned the referee's powers of observation, doubtless to little avail.)

Looking into the future takes perspicuity but so does looking into the past and human nature.
Vancouver Sun 27 Nov. 1993: C6

(The word required here is *perspicacity*.)

Hidden in cellars and barns for 60 years or more, many of these works of art might have been lost had it not been for the extraordinary tenacity and perspicuity of a clerk employed at the Canadian Embassy from 1946 to 1978.
Ottawa Citizen 27 Nov. 1994: B3

(The word required here is *perspicacity*.)

persuade   see CONVINCE

persuasion   In the nineteenth century the word *persuasion* was widely used to refer to a set of religious convictions or to the group of people holding these beliefs ('the Jewish persuasion', 'the Episcopal persuasion', 'the Catholic persuasion'), or to political parties and their followers (e.g., 'the Tory persuasion'). By the mid-nineteenth century this usage was being mocked by writers who began to use *persuasion* facetiously as a synonym for *race*, *sex*, *nationality*, and so on: in other words, to describe any category of person, whether united by conviction or by mere happenstance ('the female persuasion', 'the Irish persuasion', 'the haircutting persuasion'). Eventually, *persuasion* became a general synonym for *kind* or *sort*, applied to things as well as to people. However, this extended sense has always retained a facetious air, making it unsuitable where a comic effect is not desired.

The market area abounds in restaurants of every persuasion.
Alan Tucker, ed. *The Penguin Guide to Canada* 1991: 307

Nor will a cabbage culture suffice for us, however many persuasive political and literary people of the truck-garden and green-grocer persuasion may appear among us.
Robertson Davies *One Half of Robertson Davies* 1978: 284

True, there are a couple of fillies in there but the vast majority is of the male persuasion.
Province (Vancouver) 31 July 1990: 58

peruse, perusal   To *peruse* is to read or study, but there are two conflicting uses of the verb in current English: to go over thoroughly and to skim quickly. Dictionaries have been slow to acknowledge the second, newer sense, which is widely used in informal writing and in speech. However, writers should be aware of the word's potential ambiguity. In formal Canadian usage *peruse* almost always means to read through carefully or study in detail. The related noun is *perusal*.

... I had wisely invested the time required to peruse it from cover to cover.
Canadian Journal of Sociology 14.2 (1989): 230

[They] submitted two documents for the cabinet's perusal: Kennedy's judgment and a written argument from Robinette. The cabinet took five months to make up its mind.
Jack Batten *Robinette* 1984: 206

Having briefly perused your letters to the editor, I was both alarmed and outraged by the comments of one writer.
Vancouver Sun 7 July 1990: D23

(In newspaper writing *peruse* is often used in its more recent sense, to look through quickly.)

The book is arranged in two-page spreads, with drawings on one side and text on the other. Readers can plow from cover to cover or peruse randomly.
Vancouver Sun 17 Nov. 1990: D17

(Here to *peruse* means to skim.)

phantasy   see FANTASY

pharisee   The *Pharisees* were members of an ancient Jewish sect characterized as very strict and hostile to the early Christian church. Since the 1500s *pharisee* has been used to refer to any self-righteous or hypocritical person. The adjective form is *pharisaic(al)*. *Pharisee* should be capitalized when referring to the ancient sect and uncapitalized in its figurative sense.

That religious practices could become harmful addictions might initially strike one as paradoxical. Yet the lives of the Pharisees quickly come to mind as graphic examples. ...
Mennonite Brethren Herald 7 March 1986: 29

In the mid-nineteenth century, the use of anesthetics in childbirth was denounced as impious. The then head of the Anglican Church [Queen Victoria], a forthright and fecund woman, accepted anesthesia in her deliveries and the Pharisees were routed.
Globe and Mail (Toronto) 8 March 1985: P7

(Here *pharisees*, uncapitalized, would be preferable.)

Political pharisees in Victoria and Ottawa still wrestle with the 'morality' of attempting to address street kids and prostitutes in their own earthy language and imag-

ery—a decision that gave Jesus Christ no second thoughts.
Vancouver Sun 3 Jan. 1990: A11

phase, faze A *phase* is a stage. Things can be *phased in*, meaning introduced by stages, or *phased out*, meaning withdrawn or taken out of production in stages.

If you are *fazed* by something, you are daunted or perturbed by it. *Faze* is an informal variant of the obsolete word *feeze*, meaning put to flight. Because the word *phase* is more common, *faze* is sometimes misspelled *phase*.

His medical-missionary phase began at the age of 30, when he abandoned a successful career as a musicologist and religious educator to study medicine.
Globe and Mail (Toronto) 14 Jan. 1985: P16

Montreal has been chosen as the home of a new United Nations organization that will help developing countries phase out ozone-depleting substances.
Gazette (Montreal) 22 Sept. 1990: A3

The sudden glimmer of personalized contact fazed the attacker and he left the girl alive.
Gazette (Montreal) 6 Oct. 1994: A9

Occasional power failures in the seniors' building where [she] lives don't faze her, but they're inconvenient if she wants to get down from her 17th-floor apartment.
Gazette (Montreal) 13 Dec. 1990: D9

'Like many hopeful people, Gilbert isn't phased by bad news.'
Canadian Fiction Magazine 63 (1988): 38

(The correct spelling here is *fazed*.)

phenomenon, phenomena, phenomenons The singular is *phenomenon*, the plural *phenomena*. However, the *OED* cites uses of *phenomena* as a singular noun as far back as 1576. In speech *phenomena* is often used as a singular ('a strange phenomena'), and it can occasionally be found in edited prose. However, unlike *agenda* and *candelabra*—formal Latin plurals whose use as singular nouns is now accepted—*phenomena* is not yet recognized as a singular. *Phenomenons* is sometimes used as the plural, especially in reference to exceptional or remarkable people, but *phenomena* is more widely accepted.

It would be hard to improve upon the clear logical image which Shakespeare has given us here of the unique character of language as a phenomenon among other phenomena of the world....
R. A. Wilson *The Birth of Language* 1937: 152

The unchallenged ethos of this new phenomena was dedication and loyalty to the organization in work and personal life.
City Magazine Spring 1988: 31

('This' indicates the singular; thus *phenomenon* would be the standard usage here.)

As space shuttle photography has made clear, political boundaries are unnatural phenomenons.
Financial Post 21 June 1989: 1

(In formal writing the recommended plural is *phenomena*.)

See also AGENDA; CANDELABRUM; CRITERION.

phial see VIAL

philistine The *Philistines* were a tribe in ancient Palestine characterized as barbaric by their enemies the Israelites. In figurative use a *philistine* is any person who disdains cultural pursuits, who is materialistic and smug. *Philistine* is also used as an adjective. Both the adjective and the noun should be capitalized only in references to the ancient Philistines.

These people are traditionally known as philistines and the only thing they collect is interest on their money.
Globe and Mail (Toronto) 4 May 1985: A1

If he is revolutionary, the poet in him may have to argue with a Philistine materialist also in him who does not really see the point of poetry at all.
Northrop Frye *The Bush Garden* 1971: 133

(Here *philistine*, uncapitalized, would be preferable.)

People who don't know about art but know what they like make philistine cheap shots that pass in some circles as wit but which are really profound revelations of ignorance.
Vancouver Sun 24 March 1990: A13

phobia, mania In medical terms, a *phobia* is a morbid, incapacitating fear and a *mania* is an excited madness. In common use, however, these meanings are somewhat attenuated: a *phobia* is an irrational fear and a *mania* is a craze or desire for something. The plurals are *phobias* and *manias*.

Fear of motherhood. You don't have to be single to be susceptible to the new phobias surrounding dependence and commitment.
Chatelaine June 1986: 107

What with the puritan mania for health and exercise driving all before it, the smokers' style is beginning to look corny, definitely out of the past.
Globe and Mail (Toronto) 12 Jan. 1985: E22

phone, call, ring *Phone* is the accepted clipped form of *telephone* and does not need to be spelled with an apostrophe (*'phone*); *telephone* is more suitable than *phone* in formal writing. Canadians usually talk *on the phone*; *over the phone* is less common. *By phone* is used mainly when referring to a procedure carried out using the telephone: 'I ordered the tickets by phone'. Canadians refer to the action of contacting a person by telephone as *phoning*, *calling*, or occasionally, in speech, *giving someone a ring*, but they rarely use the British and Australian expressions *ring* and *ring up*. Unlike Canadians, the British do not use the verb *call* to mean *telephone*.

phony, phoney Canadian writers use these two spellings about equally. Though some dictionaries and usage guides label *phon(e)y* informal or slang, its use in formal and academic prose is incontestable. If you prefer the *phony* spelling, the plural is *phonies*; if you choose *phoney*, the plural can be either *phonies* or *phoneys*.

> But this was the phony war.
> William Teatero *John Anderson: Fugitive Slave* 1986: 47

> If our experience is limited, we can be roused to enthusiasm ... by something that we can later see to have been second-rate or even phoney.
> Northrop Frye *The Educated Imagination* 1963: 44

> Gretzky and the entire Edmonton Oiler team ... were called phonies and undeserving of their vaunted status.
> *Globe and Mail* (Toronto) 24 May 1985: M7

> Immigration officials say that's because phoneys have stopped applying for refugee status.
> *Gazette* (Montreal) 6 May 1989: B1

phrasal verbs A phrasal verb consists of a verb combined with one or two prepositions, which in this context are often called particles. The phrase functions as a single word with a sense distinct from the literal meaning of each word on its own. For example, the sense of *go out* is different in 'She went out the door with Sam' and 'She went out with Sam for two years'. In the second sentence, *went out (with)* is a phrasal verb meaning dated.

Occasionally writers will hyphenate phrasal verbs, presumably because they have seen the noun and adjective forms of these verbs hyphenated. Note that 'They break up often' needs no hyphen, but in 'Their break-up (*or* breakup) was final' the two words must be hyphenated or joined; similarly, 'He backs up his players', but 'The back-up group is great'.

Modifiers formed from phrasal verbs are almost always hyphenated ('I think the calibre of play is better in *play-off* season'), while nouns formed from phrasal verbs are either hyphenated or solid ('I watch the NHL play-offs/playoffs'). A noun compound should be written with a hyphen if its form might be confusing without one. Compounds formed with *-in* are almost always hyphenated: *break-in*, *cave-in*, *shut-in*. And noun compounds with *-on* are usually hyphenated: *carry-on*, *slip-on*, *turn-on*, *walk-on*. Perhaps this is because *-in* and *-on* are common word endings. Compounds formed with *-out*, on the other hand, are usually written as one word: *burnout*, *handout*, *takeout*. And nouns formed with *-over*, *-off*, and *-up* are quite often written without a hyphen: *carryover*, *makeover*, *pushoff*, *takeoff*, *breakup*, *setup*. A hyphen is recommended when the first word in the compound has more than one syllable: *cover-up*, *follow-through*.

> They line-up 40 strong at the try-outs hoping to run laps if Andy doesn't like the way they threw a ball or dogged it on the way to first after popping up.
> *Province* (Vancouver) 19 Aug. 1990: 63

(The phrasal verb is two words, *line up*; *line-up* is the noun form.)

> Subsidies ... cause overproduction of food in certain places, rip-off consumers and taxpayers, and drive farmers off the land.
> *Financial Post* 10 April 1989: 16

(The slang phrasal verb required here is two separate words, *rip off*; *rip-off* or *ripoff* is the noun form.)

> ... jot down a list of extra activities that need to be done—not make-work projects, but important operational challenges for your organization such as ... technical back up for a quality circle team or improved liaison between production and design.
> *Engineering Dimensions* Mar.–Apr. 1988: 15

(The noun form required here is usually treated as a solid compound: *backup*.)

> He was appointed deputy director of the CIA in 1972, just a few weeks before the breakin at the Watergate Hotel that was to bring down Mr. Nixon's presidency.
> *Globe and Mail* (Toronto) 1 April 1985: P11

(The usual form is *break-in*.)

Members ... that could have done the translation were no doubt suffering from burn-out already.
Fuse Magazine 13.4 (1990): 11

(The usual noun form is a solid compound, *burnout*.)

When followthrough cannot be guaranteed, it is better to do more than promised rather than less than expected.
Globe and Mail (Toronto) 18 Nov. 1985: B12

(The recommended spelling is *follow-through*.)

See also IDIOMS.

phylum   see SPECIES

pidgin, creole   A *pidgin*, sometimes misspelled *pigeon*, is a simple language used for communication by two or more groups who do not share a language. For example, Chinook Jargon was a pidgin spoken on the Pacific coast of North America, from California to Alaska, from the 1830s until the early twentieth century. A mixture of two Aboriginal languages, Nootka and Chinook, with English and French, it was used by the various groups involved in the sea otter hunt, in logging, in trade, and in the gold rush. Some of its expressions have passed into English, including *muckety-muck* (also *muckymuck*, *muck-a-muck*), 'important person', and *saltchuck*, 'ocean'.

Children who grow up hearing mainly pidgin learn it as their first language. A pidgin that becomes the first language of a generation of native speakers is called a *creole*. A creole rapidly develops additional vocabulary, more complex grammatical structures, and greater stylistic flexibility. An example is Jamaican Creole English. The West Africans brought to Jamaica as slaves spoke a variety of languages and were forced to develop a pidgin to communicate with their masters and with each other. Their children transformed this pidgin language into a creole.

The speakers of a creole are often subjected to social pressure to 'decreolize', or make their language conform more closely to the standard version of the colonial language. But sometimes the speakers of a creole assert their pride in their culture by accentuating the differences between their language and the dominant one. This tendency is called 'hypercreolization'; the lyrics of rap music are an example of the hypercreolization of Black English in the United States.

And so, as the sun sinks slowly into the saltchuck, we bid farewell to Maggie Tefler, friend of fallen womanhood.
Margaret Laurence *The Diviners* 1974: 307

See also ACCENT, DIALECT; LINGUA FRANCA.

pièce de résistance   see COUP DE GRÂCE

pigeon, dove   Pigeons and doves belong to the same family, Columbidae. The common names of individual species may contain either *pigeon* or *dove*: 'band-tailed pigeon', 'mourning dove'. *Pigeon* is the word generally chosen to describe the sometimes annoying birds that flock in public squares and roost in gables. *Dove* is the more poetic word, connoting peace and, in Christian belief, symbolizing the Holy Spirit.

Now, St. Mark's Square is flooded about 100 times each winter, forcing the pigeons to the filigreed stone of the cathedral's spires....
Bon Vivant Feb.–Mar. 1983: 11

The dove designates the pavilion as a place of peace.
United Church Observer May 1986: 18

See also PIDGIN, CREOLE.

pinch-hit, pinch-hitter   In baseball, someone who *pinch-hits* goes to bat for another player. A *pinch-hitter* is a better batter than the player who is replaced. In figurative use, however, a person who pinch-hits for someone else is brought in as a substitute in an emergency. Some language commentators and baseball fans complain that the figurative use ignores the idea of the pinch-hitter's superiority. Nonetheless, the figurative sense is popular, common, and recognized by dictionaries.

Pitch-hitter is sometimes mistakenly used for *pinch-hitter*; a *pinch-hitter* goes in to bat in a *pinch*.

I was sent to Paris in January 1962 to pinch-hit for Jules while he was convalescing in southern France....
George Ignatieff *The Making of a Peacemonger* 1987: 199

At the last minute, he was asked ... to pinch-hit a speech for Vernon Walters, the Reagan Administration's nominee as ambassador to the world body.
Globe and Mail (Toronto) 30 April 1985: P16

In June, 1974, Prime Minister Trudeau could not attend a NATO heads of government meeting in Brussels because of the election campaign, so he asked me to pinch-hit.
Globe and Mail (Toronto) 23 Nov. 1985: A10

With the bases loaded, Richmond sent pitch-hitter Luis Lopez and his .355 to the plate.
Ottawa Citizen 26 April 1994: F2

(The usual expression is *pinch-hitter*.)

pinnacle   see EPITOME

pinyin, Wade-Giles, Chinese writing   Several attempts have been made to convert Chinese writing into the Roman alphabet. The most recent and most widely used conversion is called *pinyin* (sometimes *Pinyin*). This system was officially adopted by the Chinese government in 1958 and uses 58 symbols combining roman letters and accents (which are usually dropped in English texts). Pinyin represents the sounds of *putonghua* (Beijing Mandarin), the language that the Chinese government is attempting to make standard across China. Pinyin differs from the earlier widespread system of Chinese translation, the Wade-Giles (W-G) system. For example, 'Peking' is a Wade-Giles conversion, whereas 'Beijing' is pinyin; 'Mao Tse-tung' is a Wade-Giles conversion, whereas 'Mao Zedong' is pinyin. Today pinyin is generally preferred to Wade-Giles, but if for some reason the older system is chosen it should be used consistently throughout a piece of writing.

See also CHINESE NAMES; MANDARIN.

pique   see PEAK

pistol   see GUN

pitiful, pitiable, piteous   All three words can mean evoking pity. In addition, *pitiful* and *pitiable* are sometimes applied to people or things that arouse a mixture of pity and contempt. These two words also mean meagre or negligible; this last sense is related to the previous ones, because something meagre or inadequate may arouse either pity or contempt. The word *piteous* is less common; it often describes sounds such as cries or sobbing, and rarely expresses disdain.

The first thing that occurs to you as you enter the camp is that the walls and the watchtowers are lower than you had imagined—a pitiful reminder of how powerless the inmates were.
Globe and Mail (Toronto) 29 April 1985: P7

[The Tories] had become, at least last autumn, a kind of national joke, somehow transformed from triumphant conquerors into rather pitiful incompetents.
Saturday Night Feb. 1986: 5–6

According to Martin Kenny, an agricultural researcher at Cornell University who has been studying the impact of the new reproductive technologies on Third World countries, the benefits go to a pitiful few.
Harrowsmith Oct.-Nov. 1985: 46

(Here *pitiful* means meagre.)

Here Holtby and his family came upon a pitiable sight: a horse had struggled to the top only to drop dead of exhaustion, the ants and hawks already transforming the cadaver into a skeleton.
Pierre Berton *The Promised Land* 1984: 131

Nothing could persuade him to look at his speech before going on the air, and ... every now and then he would gag over something—a subordinate clause, or a crumb of unfamiliar punctuation—and reveal himself in all his pitiable insufficiency.
Robertson Davies *One Half of Robertson Davies* 1978: 9

The colonialists imposed foreign religions and taxes on the natives, brought diseases with them, introduced forced labor at pitiable wages and destroyed family units with alcohol in one hand and the Bible in the other.
Vancouver Sun 13 Aug. 1990: A7

(Here *pitiable* means meagre.)

When no human audience ventured within earshot [of my recorder playing], I entertained dogs on the beach at David Bay, oblivious to their piteous howls.
Vancouver Sun 30 Aug. 1993: A3

Ever eager for visual drama, some Western editors are pressing their correspondents for images of famine, piteous children with swollen bellies.
Vancouver Sun 17 Dec. 1990: A3

-place   see -WHERE

place names   The Canadian Permanent Committee on Geographical Names regulates place names and standardizes their spelling. It issues the *Gazetteer of Canada* series, published by the Canada Communication Group. These gazetteers are the authoritative source for the spellings of Canadian place names.

See also ASIA; ATLANTIC PROVINCES; BOSNIA-HERZEGOVINA; BRITAIN; BURY, SUDBURY; CALGARY; CAPITAL LETTERS; CARIBOO; GLOUCESTER, WORCESTER; HUDSON BAY; IRELAND; NORTHWEST TERRITORIES; NUNAVUT; QUEBEC; SAHARA;

SAINT JOHN, ST. JOHN'S; SAULT, THE SOO; SCANDI-NAVIAN; ST., STE.; UKRAINE; WEST INDIES, CARIB-BEAN.

plaid   see TARTAN

planets   see EARTH

platonic   The adjective that refers to the philosopher Plato and his teachings is capitalized: *Platonic*. Uncapitalized, *platonic* is usually part of a phrase such as 'platonic friendship' or 'platonic relationship', where it means purely spiritual, non-sexual. Occasionally *platonic* is used more generally to mean idealistic or visionary but impractical.

'Plato is a classic ... but who nowadays wants society to follow the Platonic view of life?'
Vancouver Sun 12 March 1990: A1

Sceptics had previously criticized Platonic claims to know entities that lie beyond the world of sense experience....
Queen's Quarterly 95.3 (1988): 595

Ackroyd parts company with previous Dickens biographers who conjecture that this was a decidedly un-Victorian sexual relationship, arguing theirs was a platonic, though no doubt, passionate, affair.
Vancouver Sun 22 Dec. 1990: D19

For the next few months, she and I became 'friends' in what, for me, was a painfully platonic relationship.
Chatelaine April 1986: 150

play down   see DOWNPLAY

playwright, playwriting   A person who writes plays is a *playwright*, not a *playwrite*. A *wright*, as in *wheelwright* or *shipwright*, is someone who designs or builds things; the term is now obsolete except in combinations.
   Though *playwrite* is never used as a finite verb ('She playwrites'), the *-ing* form *playwriting* is common, functioning as an adjective or a noun.

This warm and moving story won the 1988 Alberta Culture playwriting award.
Leisure Life 1988: 58

... PWM, widely recognized as Canada's premier play development centre, is now celebrating its 25th year in the business of encouraging and promoting Canadian playwriting.
Gazette (Montreal) 4 March 1988: H4

See also COPYRIGHT.

plead, pleaded, pled, plead   In Canadian English the past tense and past participle of *plead* are usually *pleaded* and occasionally *pled* or *plead* (pronounced *PLED*). *Pleaded* is the safest choice for formal use, since some commentators label *pled* dialectal and many dictionaries do not even list the *plead* spelling for the past tense or participle.

The Nova Scotia Judicial Council clearly stated in 1989 that Judge ——, who pleaded guilty to an assault on his wife, could not deal impartially with similar cases in his court.
Andrew Heard *Canadian Constitutional Conventions* 1991: 124

He pled the pup's case with every possible airline....
Edmonton Journal 23 July 1994: D4

He plead not guilty at a July appearance and a trial date was set for the fall.
Ottawa Citizen 27 Oct. 1990: I6

See also PLEAD GUILTY.

plead guilty, plead not guilty, plead innocent   The established phrases in Canadian courts are *plead guilty* and *plead not guilty* or *enter a not-guilty plea*. The popular expression *plead innocent*, criticized by some usage guides, is rarely found in Canadian writing, whether legal or journalistic.

He had earlier confessed to the crimes but pleaded not guilty.
Mennonite Brethren Herald 7 March 1986: 27

Michael O'Shaughnessy said his client ... will plead innocent to a first-degree murder charge when he appears in provincial court in Brockville Friday.
Ottawa Citizen 21 March 1990: B2

(The technically correct expression *plead not guilty* is preferable in court reporting.)

See also PLEAD, PLEADED, PLED, PLEAD.

pled   see PLEAD

plenitude   *Plenitude* means abundance. *Plentitude* is a rare variant that, although sometimes found in print, is considered an error by most authorities. *Plenitude* is labelled literary or formal by some dictionaries and guides, but it is found fairly often in Canadian journalism.

One thing they do take advantage of is Quebec City's plenitude of eateries.
Financial Post 1 Nov. 1990: 94

The road ahead figures to be painful some nights, joyous on others while the Canucks work in a plentitude of unpredictable young talent.
Vancouver Sun 24 Oct. 1990: F1

(The usual spelling is *plenitude*.)

pleonasm   see WORDINESS

plethora   In the 1500s *plethora* (pronounced *PLETH or uh*) was a medical term for an excess of body fluid; by 1700 *plethora* referred to any excessive fullness. Dictionaries still consistently define a *plethora* as a superfluity or overabundance, but Canadians commonly use the word to mean simply a lot, or a wealth, and they use it as often with positive connotations as with negative ones.

When the phrase 'a plethora of' is followed by a plural noun ('a plethora of examples'), the verb that follows may be singular or plural, depending on whether the writer views the 'plethora' as a unit or as a collection of individual items.

In addition to many useful maps and a chronology of events, it contains a plethora of primary source material both in the text and in a very useful 104 pages of appendices....
Canadian Journal of History 14.1 (1989): 144

(Here *plethora* means wealth and has a positive connotation.)

The plethora of different rules and exemptions have ... resulted in double taxation and excessive compliance costs at all levels of business.
Financial Post 28 Nov. 1990: 17

(Here the connotations of *plethora* are negative. Also note the plural verb *have*; *has* would also be correct.)

See also AGREEMENT, GRAMMATICAL; COLLECTIVE NOUNS.

plow, plough   *Plow* is the usual spelling of both the noun and the verb in Canadian newspapers, but *plough* is common in other types of writing. *Plow* is almost non-existent in British English, and *plough* is almost non-existent in modern U.S. English.

... now the plow cuts below the topsoil to expose the rocks that prevent a more luxuriant growth.
Vancouver Sun 2 June 1990: D20

Readers can plow from cover to cover or peruse randomly.
Vancouver Sun 17 Nov. 1990: D17

The chilled steel plough was ideal for turning the tough sod of the Canadian prairie.
Pierre Berton *The Promised Land* 1984: 13

... I ploughed on through the rest of the paper without a second thought.
NeWest Review Oct.–Nov. 1989: 20

plurality   see MAJORITY

plurals, regular, irregular, foreign   The regular English plural simply adds *-s* to the singular noun: *apple, apples*. However, there are several general categories of exception to the rule.

If the singular form ends in *-s* (or *-x*, *-sh*, or *-ch*), *e* is added before the *s*: *buses, the Joneses, successes; foxes; lashes; benches*. But note *stomachs*: when *-ch* is pronounced as *k*, no *e* is added.

If the singular ends in *-y* preceded by a consonant, the *y* becomes *i* and *-es* is added to make the plural: *pony, ponies; spy, spies*. Proper names are exceptions to this rule: 'the three Marys', 'the Hornbys'. Words ending in a vowel plus *-y* form regular plurals: *days, pulleys*.

If the singular ends in *-f* or *-fe*, the plural ending is sometimes *-ves*: *loaf, loaves; knife, knives*. See -F, -V-.

Three nouns add *-(r)en* to form the plural: *brethren, children, oxen*.

Many nouns referring to animals and fish have the same form in the singular and plural, including *cod, deer, moose, salmon, sheep*.

Some nouns change the vowel to make the plural: *foot, feet; goose, geese; man, men; tooth, teeth; woman, women*.

If the singular ends in *-o*, usually the plural is formed by adding *-s* (*banjos*), but some words require *-es* (*heroes*). See -OS, -OES.

compound nouns Compound nouns generally form the plural in the usual way by adding *-s* at the end: *babysitters, mail carriers, has-beens*. However, if a noun referring to a person forms the first element of a compound, it is usually pluralized: *passers-by, daughters-in-law, governors general, poets laureate*.

The lists below contain common words borrowed from foreign languages that often, especially in formal or technical writing, form their plurals as they would in the source language.

Latin plurals Most English words derived from Latin form their plurals in the regular way, by adding *-s* or *-es*, and this is the safest choice if you are in doubt (see also -US). However, there are some Latin borrowings that still form their plurals according to the rules of Latin, at least in formal contexts:

- singular ends in *-a*, plural in *-ae*: *alumna, alumnae; formula, formulae; larva, larvae*
- singular ends in *-ex* or *-ix*, plural in *-ices*: *appendix, appendices; cortex, cortices; index, indices; matrix, matrices*
- singular ends in *-um*, plural in *-a*: *addendum, addenda; bacterium, bacteria; compendium, compendia; cranium, crania; crematorium, crematoria; curriculum, curricula; datum, data; medium, media; memorandum, memoranda; quantum, quanta; spectrum, spectra; stratum, strata*
- singular ends in *-us*, plural in *-i*: *alumnus, alumni; bacillus, bacilli; cactus, cacti; crocus, croci; focus, foci; fungus, fungi; gladiolus, gladioli; narcissus, narcissi; nucleus, nuclei; papyrus, papyri; radius, radii; stimulus, stimuli; streptococcus, streptococci; stylus, styli; syllabus, syllabi; terminus, termini; uterus, uteri*
- singular ends in *-us*, plural in a vowel plus *-ra*: *corpus, corpora; genus, genera, opus, opera*

Greek plurals - singular ends in *-sis* (pronounced *-siss*), plural in *-ses* (pronounced *-seez*): *antithesis, antitheses; axis, axes; basis, bases; crisis, crises; ellipsis, ellipses; hypothesis, hypotheses; metamorphosis, metamorphoses; oasis, oases; parenthesis, parentheses; synopsis, synopses; thesis, theses*
- singular ends in *-a*, plural in *-ata*: *lemma, lemmata; schema, schemata; stigma, stigmata*
- singular ends in *-on*, plural in *-a*: *criterion, criteria; phenomenon, phenomena*

French plurals - singular ends in *-eau, -eu, -iau*, plural adds *-x*: *beau, beaux; bureau, bureaux; château, châteaux; fabliau, fabliaux; milieu, milieux; plateau, plateaux; tableau, tableaux*
- singular ends in *-s*, plural is unchanged: *chamois, chassis, corps, faux pas, patois*

Italian plurals - singular ends in *-o*, plural in *-i*: *concerto grosso, concerti grossi; graffito, graffiti; maestro, maestri; paparazzo, paparazzi; virtuoso, virtuosi*

See also ALUMNUS, ALUMNA, ALUMNI, ALUMNAE; APOSTROPHE; BACTERIUM; BASES; BEAU; BÊTE NOIRE; BUS; CACTUS; CANDELABRUM; CARIBOO, CARIBOU; CATASTROPHE; CRITERION; CURRICULUM VITAE; DAIS; DATA; -F, -V-; -FUL; GLADIOLUS; GENIUS; HORS D'OEUVRE; LOONIE; MAPLE LEAF; MEDIUM; MEMORANDUM; MONEY; OCTOPUS; -OS, -OES; PAPARAZZO, -I; POSSESSIVE; REFERENDUM; RHINOCEROS; STRATUM; -Y, -IES.

plus Some commentators condemn *plus* in any context other than the arithmetical. However, *plus* is standard when it means 'as well as' or 'in addition to'. Note that this usage does not affect the number of the verb: 'The rent from the basement apartment plus her pension is (*not* are) what she lives on'.

There are two common disputed usages. One is to equate *plus* with *and* and use it to join two clauses: 'She goes to school plus she has kids'. The other is the use of *plus* to mean *besides* or *besides which*: 'I don't want to invite him because his ex-girlfriend will be here; plus I just don't like him.' These two uses of *plus* are informal and should be avoided in all but the most breezy writing.

Plus is also used as a noun meaning advantage ('Experience is a plus'); *pluses* is the usual plural.

... our games reduce almost to formula: physical readiness plus emotional readiness equals victory.
Ken Dryden *The Game* 1983: 183

This is how the photo of the woman, plus the photographer and his equipment, has physically been made possible.
Linda Hutcheon *Splitting Images* 1991: 18–19

Forty-eight hourly and staff employees, plus a number of exploration geologists, have been laid off at Timmins.
Province (Vancouver) 13 Dec. 1990: 86

(The plural subject, *employees*, determines the plural verb, *have*.)

The master bedroom, with en suite bathroom, plus a third bedroom are located on the third floor.
Vancouver Sun 30 Nov. 1990: E5

(Since the main subject, 'master bedroom', is singular, the verb should also be singular: '*is* located'. Alternatively, *and* could be substituted for *plus*, and then the plural verb would be correct.)

... this one offers discount deals at retail establishments, and sells for only $10, plus it's easy to find everywhere.
Province (Vancouver) 18 Dec. 1990: 40

(The use of *plus* to join clauses is criticized; *and* would be better here.)

'It's much easier to pack and travel once, plus you don't have to pay high mileage charges,' she said.
Calgary Herald 2 July 1994: E1

(This use of *plus* to mean *besides* is informal.)

See also AGREEMENT, GRAMMATICAL; TOGETHER WITH.

p.m.   see TIME

podium   see DAIS

pogey, unemployment insurance, UI, UIC, employment insurance, EI   *Pogey* is a Canadian slang expression referring to welfare payments or insurance benefits for the unemployed. *Pogey* was originally used to refer to the hostels and relief centres set up for the unemployed during the Great Depression, as well as the food, clothing, shelter, or payments doled out to the needy. Unemployment benefits are also referred to by the initialism *UI* (or *UIC*, after the Unemployment Insurance Commission). However, in 1996 the official name of the program was changed to *employment insurance* (*EI*).

Cape Bretoners are a proud people, [and] social programs like pogey and welfare are the last resort.
United Church Observer May 1986: 38

Still, Montreal has more people on pogey than any other reporting area, closely followed by Toronto.
Financial Post 2 Dec. 1991: 3

'Francois and I had a little money from other small projects ... but we were all on UIC.'
Globe and Mail (Toronto) 15 June 1985: E7

See also BABY BONUS.

poison, toxin, toxic   A *poison* is any substance that can cause death or injury to the living organism into which it is introduced, whereas a *toxin* is a poisonous substance produced by a living organism. Certain bacteria, plants, insects, shellfish, and other organisms produce toxins. For example, salmonella bacteria synthesize a toxin responsible for food poisoning in humans. The adjective *toxic* can refer to either poisons or toxins; thus 'toxic chemicals' are always poisonous but are not necessarily toxins. Few general readers will find the use of *toxin* to mean *poison* disturbing; however, the distinction is worth maintaining in scientific contexts.

The Saguenay River is so highly polluted—partly by heavy metals and other toxins ... —that whales and other marine life have been poisoned.
Gazette (Montreal) 6 March 1989: A4

(Since heavy metals are not produced by living organisms, it would be is more accurate to refer to them as 'toxic substances'.)

The leak of toxins from an abandoned gold mine into a river that supplies drinking water ... rivals the Valdez oil spill off the coast of Alaska, the area's MP says.
Province (Vancouver) 25 Oct. 1990: 31

(Here 'toxic substances' would be more accurate.)

police officer, cop, policeman, policewoman   Police forces in Canada do not make the military distinction between officers and the ranks; thus any member of a police force is a *police officer* and may be addressed as *officer*. Terms for the various ranks—constable, patrol officer, detective, sergeant, inspector, superintendent, etc.—vary from force to force. *Cop* is informal, but not generally considered offensive. *Police officer* is preferred to *policeman* or *policewoman* as non-sexist usage.

A cop who turned criminologist believes the key to university security is more students patrolling their own campuses.
Vancouver Sun 4 Dec. 1990: A2

The turning point, says Joly, came in 1974 when the Ontario Police Commission abolished the rank of 'policewoman' and required all forces to give women the same starting rank as men—constable.
Ottawa Citizen 15 Aug. 1990: D3

(In Ontario before 1974, *policewoman* designated not only the gender of the police officer, but her particular—low—rank.)

Ottawa's policemen are fitter than their counterparts in the Ontario Provincial Police, the Quebec Police Force and the RCMP.
Ottawa Citizen 15 July 1990: A10

(This statement could suggest to some readers either that there are no women officers on the Ottawa force or that the women officers were not part of the fitness study; *police officers* would be better here.)

A Toronto policewoman, Const. Cindy Grant, was recently praised by her colleagues for helping nab a suspected bank robber by chasing his vehicle on foot.
Ottawa Citizen 15 July 1990: A10

(Substituting *police officer* for *policewoman* would de-emphasize the constable's sex; here, however, this was likely just what the writer wanted to stress.)

See also COP; JOB TITLES.

politic, political, polity, politics   In modern English the adjective *politic* means shrewd or prudent when applied to people, and judicious or expedient when applied to actions. *Politic* meant *political* until the eighteenth century; this sense is now found only in the phrase *body politic*, meaning nation or state. The noun *polity* refers to a political organization or government.

When *politics* means political beliefs or sympathies, it usually takes a plural verb ('His politics are different from mine'), but when it means the business of government or public life, it usually takes a singular verb ('Politics is consuming his life').

The Mick Jagger of music magazine interviews is canny and politic, yet impatient with superficial or silly questions.
Queen's Quarterly 92.2 (1985): 268

Many ... consider it more politic to quietly fire an employee ... than admit publicly that they have been conned, risking loss of customer confidence or even stockholder liability.
Globe and Mail (Toronto) 26 July 1985: P82

Many subsequent political theorists agreed that moderate property and economic independence are a precondition for a stable polity.
Irving M. Zeitlin and Robert J. Brym *The Social Condition of Humanity* 1991: 100

Wieland's politics in the early 1970s were clearly as nationalist as they were feminist; they were also ecological.
Linda Hutcheon *Splitting Images* 1989: 103

Even politics, although taken seriously by the inhabitants, is a laughing matter for Leacock: Smith the con-man rigs the election by circulating the rumour that he has won, and Mariposa, ever sensitive to majority opinion, votes for him en bloc.
Margaret Atwood *Second Words* 1982: 187

political parties   The most recently formed federal political parties are the Bloc Québécois, espousing a sovereign Quebec (members are called 'Bloquistes'), and the Reform Party of Canada (members are informally referred to as 'Reformers').

See also BLEU; CONSERVATIVE; GRIT; NEW DEMOCRATIC PARTY; PÉQUISTE; SOCIAL CREDIT PARTY.

politics   see POLITIC

polyglot   *Polyglot*, derived from the Greek for 'many-tongued', is most often used to mean 'of many languages': a city or a text may be described as polyglot. An extension of this meaning to include 'culturally or ethnically mixed' is becoming common. Some dictionaries list this sense, which seems unobjectionable. However, the indiscriminate use of *polyglot* to mean mixture or mishmash is not accepted.

Mr. Vito-Finzi, described as an entrepreneurial polyglot, was born on a British ship off Australia of diplomatic Italian and Russian parents.
Globe and Mail (Toronto) 2 Feb. 1985: S12

A note of panic crept into the press reports when the United States was mentioned: with its polyglot immigrant masses, it was seen as a mongrel nation.
Pierre Berton *The Promised Land* 1984: 139

The third in a family of 12 children, Mass was born on Rachel Street in Montreal, in the modest, polyglot neighborhood made famous by novelist Mordecai Richler.
Ottawa Citizen 13 Nov. 1993: B5

When Dolores Chew came to Canada from India at age 20, she said it wasn't as much of a culture shock because she is 'kind of a polyglot,' a mix of Indian, Chinese, Irish and French blood.
Gazette (Montreal) 22 Nov. 1993: F1

(Here the emphasis is on cultural rather than linguistic diversity.)

... the volumes of the new building are purer, larger, and less broken up than the existing abbey, itself an unusual polyglot of architectural styles.
Gazette (Montreal) 18 Sept. 1993: J3

(Here *polyglot* is used to mean a mixture; *pastiche* would be an acceptable substitute.)

pom-pom, pompon   Canadians prefer the spelling *pom-pom* (or *pompom*) although *pompon*, ending in *n*, is the older form. The *Globe and Mail Style Book* recommends *pompon* for the small tufts on tams and sombreros, clown suits, and honeymoon cars, and *pom-pom* for the larger balls waved by cheerleaders, but Canadian writers in general wave these distinctions aside.

Pom-pom is the only accepted spelling for the anti-aircraft gun.

Among the honored was Vancouver promoter Murray Pezim, who donned a tartan tam with a pom-pom.
Financial Post 9 March 1989: 3

Her pom-pom bow ... can be used to decorate everything from garlands and wreaths to gifts and napkin holders.
Gazette (Montreal) 6 Dec. 1990: I4

There is a drum-beating, beer-throwing, pompon-tossing argument in progress south of the border about the origin of 'the wave.'
Vancouver Sun 20 Oct. 1990: D6

pond   Canadians who visit Walden Pond in Massachusetts are often surprised at how big it is. While most Canadians think of a *pond* as a rather small body of still water, in New England and Newfoundland dialects a pond is a lake.

pop   see SOFT DRINK

porch, veranda(h), stoop, patio, deck   A *porch* can be large or small, covered or uncovered. Thus the term *porch* can be applied to the structures that some people call either *verandas* or *stoops*. *Veranda* (less often, *verandah*) usually labels a structure that is quite grand, attached to a large, elegant house. A *stoop* is always a very simple, small structure, usually without a roof, belonging to a modest dwelling. *Patio* and *deck* are newer terms describing more recent additions to domestic architecture. Unlike porches, they are generally attached to a back or side entrance; neither is normally roofed. A *patio* is usually stone or cement, while a *deck* is made of wood; both are large enough to allow several people to sit in a group.

I turned to her, thinking she'd gone mad and brought us to a haunted house, for ... the gabled porch running around all four sides sagged. ...
Queen's Quarterly 96.2 (Summer 1989): 393

And then it assailed him again, those smells, [from] a house whose leaning front porch looked as though it was being allowed to rot slowly into the ground.
Canadian Fiction Magazine 63 (1988): 60

Most Canadians can recall evenings around a pot-bellied stove, or on a screened veranda with a favorite uncle picking a tune on a battered guitar. ...
Vancouver Sun 31 May 1990: E58

And the sweep of verandah around two or three sides of the house gave architects the opportunity to exaggerate the contrasts of dark and light on the facade, and to unite the house with its garden.
Canadian Collector 21 (1986): 46

A pot of tea simmers on his wood stove, replenished occasionally with ice water dipped from the lake, 20 metres from his door stoop.
Globe and Mail (Toronto) 6 March 1985: P1

pore, pour   To *pore* over something is to study it or be absorbed in it. This verb is often misspelled *pour*.

Hundreds of auditors would pore over as many as 10,000 randomly selected tax returns.
Ottawa Citizen 29 May 1990: B8

The illustrations are to be poured over and the language is so rich and colourful that it will keep even the adult returning for another look.
The Reader 11.4 (1992): 17

(The correct spelling is *pored*.)

port, starboard   *Port* is the left side of a boat or aircraft if one is on board and facing forward; *starboard* is the right. *Starboard* is from the Old English *steorbord*, meaning steering side. Old English boats were always steered by a paddle on the right side, and therefore were moored with the left side of the vessel facing the shore or *port*.

It was a three-storey structure made of wood siding and had a distinct list to starboard.
Max Braithwaite *The Night We Stole the Mountie's Car* 1971: 25

(These nautical terms are not applied only to ships; here *starboard* forms part of an extended ship metaphor.)

portend, portent, portentous   *Portend* is a verb, usually applied to circumstances rather than people, meaning to presage or foreshadow. *Portent* is a noun referring to an omen or a sign of things to come. *Portentous* is an adjective describing something significant with respect to the future, or something gravely important or ponderous. Occasionally it is used to mean self-important, and it is often misspelled *portentious*—perhaps because of confusion with *pretentious*.

In Winnipeg ... the continued marginalization of the city in the national urban hierarchy does not portend a good future for the new middle class and therefore the renewal of the inner city.
City Magazine Spring 1988: 39

Police and prosecutors say there is no evidence of the childhood abuse that typically portends such adult violence.
Toronto Star 2 July 1994: K6

Recalling a portent of success, Martin tells of wandering down a Dublin street in 1982. He was confronted by a ragtag youngster who promised luck for a penny.
Vancouver Sun 17 Jan. 1990: A8

Is there cause for optimism? Ahead on the highway is as strong a portend as any, a sign marking the conclusion of our journey: The town of Hope.
Vancouver Sun 13 Aug. 1994: C1

(The word required here is the noun *portent*.)

Samuel Black Freeman, defender of Anderson, the man with the portentous name [he defended a slave who had escaped to Canada], the victorious counsel in a legal battle of immense significance, nearly evaporates from the pages of history.
William Teatero *John Anderson: Fugitive Slave* 1986: 170

The commission on Quebec's future began its public hearings yesterday on a grave, even portentous note.
Gazette (Montreal) 7 Nov. 1990: B3

And the portentous manner of the message's delivery—including allusions to Romeo and Juliet ... gives the whole enterprise the feel of an epic-by-rote.
Toronto Star 27 Nov. 1993: J3

portmanteau word   see ABBREVIATION

possessive   The possessive case is marked either by an apostrophe or by an *of* phrase: *Brian's book, the days of the week*. The possessive case (also called the genitive case) is associated with possession in rather a loose sense; in fact, it is used to indicate a wide range of relationships, including description (*a summer's day*) and association (*a writers' club*).

An apostrophe followed by *s* forms the possessive of singular nouns and some pronouns: *the university's administrators, Martha's hat, everyone's answer, Canada's climate, one dollar's worth, a day's income, a year's results, no one's responsibility*.

Traditionally, Classical names ending in *s* are marked possessive with an apostrophe only: *Mars' anger, Herodotus' narrative, Socrates' wisdom*. Similarly, other names that end with an *iz* sound often take only an apostrophe: *Moses' tablets, Jesus' teachings, Bridges' poetry*. However, it is also always acceptable to add *'s* to a name that ends in *s*: *Charles's role, Keats's poetry, Descartes's theory* (in French names such as this, the *s* ending the name is not pronounced).

The possessive of regular plural nouns is formed by adding an apostrophe after the *s* marking the plural: *their parents' lives, the students' vote, the Browns' dog*.

The few English plurals that do not end in *s* add *'s* to indicate the possessive: *the children's party, the men's lockers, the women's room, people's needs*.

Where possession is joint, only the last noun in a series of two or more nouns needs to be marked possessive: *Gilbert and Sullivan's operas* (they wrote them jointly); *John and Mary's children* (they have the same children). Where possession is separate, each noun should be marked possessive, at least in formal writing: 'He is playing a selection of Beethoven's and Mozart's concerti'; 'John's and Mary's children are coming' (they have different children). In speech and informal writing this nicety is seldom observed.

Difficulties sometimes arise with family names, which are pluralized just like other nouns. Thus Mr. Brown, Mrs. Brown, and the Brown children are the Browns. When we visit them, we go to the Browns' house—or just to the Browns'. When the family name ends with *s*, things get a little more complicated. We try to keep up with the Joneses; if we are lucky enough to be invited there, we go to the Joneses'. Some proprietary names ending in *s* contain an apostrophe (*Bollum's Books, McDonald's*) and others don't (*Zellers*). Here the style of the company should be followed. Canadian companies with operations in Quebec dropped the English possessive form from their names in that province to comply with the Charter of the French Language (Bill 101, passed in 1977), which required that public signs be in French only; thus *Eaton's* is *Eaton* in Quebec.

Sometimes, particularly in phrases that express affiliation, such as *citizens' band, teachers' college*, or *veterans' club*, the apostrophe is dropped after a plural noun. The plural noun is treated as an adjective (see ATTRIBUTIVE NOUNS) rather than a possessive. Usage guides are divided on whether this trend should be encouraged. Newspaper style books support omitting the apostrophe here (and in expressions such as *five weeks' work*). More conservative authorities recommend retaining the apostrophe. The official names of organizations reflect the current lack of consensus on this point: *Ontario Secondary School Teachers' Federation, Nova Scotia Music Educators Association*.

In speech it is common and acceptable to add a possessive marker to the end of a clause: *the man who lives next door's dog*. In writing, this construction should be avoided by using an *of* phrase: *the dog of the man who lives next door*.

Although the possessive is traditionally used with inanimate nouns, especially nouns of place and nouns closely associated with people and their work (*Mercury's orbit, Vancouver's architecture, the hospital's budget*), an *of* phrase is usually preferable in formal writing; for example: *the erosion of the bluff* rather than *the bluff's erosion*; *the mysteries of economics* rather than *economics' mysteries*.

> Beaune [is] a tasters' dream: any day you can wander into the cellars at a dozen establishments....
> *Bon Vivant* Aug.–Sept. 1982: 10

(The singular *taster's* is required here.)

> Most Canadian's perception of the quality of European wines is nonsense.
> *Bon Vivant* Nov. 1981: 38

(The plural *Canadians'* is required here.)

> Some womens' groups don't feel we've been giving them the kind of material they would like to have.
> *Canadian Baptist* Feb. 1986: 47

(The correct spelling is *women's*.)

> A Saskatchewan library exhibit about Palestinian and South African childrens' art was condemned....
> *Briarpatch* April 1990: 3

(The correct spelling is *children's*.)

> 'When Eaton's, Ogilvy's and Steinberg's and the rest were asked to shed their apostrophes'—one form of Francization stipulated in the bill—'why didn't they just stand together, denounce the law as lunatic, and refuse to comply?'
> *Toronto Star* 26 Sept. 1991: A29

See also APOSTROPHE; CASE; DOUBLE POSSESSIVE; ELSE; ITS, IT'S; PARALLELISM; POSSESSIVE BEFORE GERUND; PRONOUN WITH POSSESSIVE ANTECEDENT; OURS; THEIRS; WHO'S, WHOSE; WORTH; YOUR, YOU'RE, YOURS.

possessive before gerund   When the *-ing* form of the verb is used as a noun, it is usually called a gerund or verbal noun (e.g., '*Running* is his life'). A major usage debate centres on the use of the possessive with the gerund. Some commentators (notably Fowler, 1926 and 1965) argue that the possessive is the only correct possibility (as in 'I worry about *his* running so much on pavement'; '*Jane's* being on the committee has improved matters'). Others have no difficulty with object pronouns and common nouns preceding gerunds ('I worry about *him* running so

much on pavement'; '*Jane* being on the committee has improved matters'). In these latter examples, the *-ing* forms are treated as if they were participles, like those in the somewhat clumsier sentences 'Running so much on pavement, he has made me worry' and 'Being on the committee, Jane has improved matters'.

In formal writing, Canadian writers do tend to use possessive pronouns before gerunds. And even in informal writing and speech, the possessive form of pronouns is more likely at the beginning of a sentence. Consider the difference between 'My talking to his sister made him nervous' and 'Me talking to his sister made him nervous'. The latter sentence seems odd, even ungrammatical or uneducated. When nouns precede gerunds, however, emphasis plays a part in the decision whether to use the possessive form. In 'The committee disapproved of the researcher's collecting rare specimens', the focus is on the collecting; in 'The committee disapproved of the researcher collecting rare specimens', the focus is on the researcher (and the sentence implies that the committee might not object to a different researcher). Long noun phrases before the gerund are rarely made possessive: 'The emergency brake release sticking was the last straw'.

It appears that writers have always varied their use of the possessive with the gerund according to considerations of formality, emphasis, and sound without much self-torment (unless they have read Fowler) and we suggest they continue to do so.

> I think for them my being gay was more difficult to deal with than my being potentially terminally ill.
> Daniel Gawthrop *Affirmation* 1984: 68

> I do not relish our becoming the turkey dinner on the table of the Americans.
> *Now Magazine* (Toronto) 3–9 Nov. 1988: 8

> They seemed not to find anything odd in Christiane's being in bed and Karen and Heinz's anxious hovering.
> Ann Davis *Somewhere Waiting* 1991: 59

> Much of her fiction portrays the awfulness of children's being subjected to their parents' whims.
> Janice Kulyk Keefer *Reading Mavis Gallant* 1989: 17

> Plainly there was no chance of the union's getting all it wanted, as there was no chance of the general manager's being able to get away with conceding nothing.
> Eugene Forsey *A Life on the Fringe* 1990: 74

> This rubbish about the British North America Act's being 'foreign' and 'imposed' still keeps cropping up.
> Eugene Forsey *A Life on the Fringe* 1990: 156

(Forsey—or his editor—has been particular to insert the possessive here; few people would notice if it were dropped.)

I never heard of him going near there.
Howard Engel *Murder Sees the Light* 1984: 102

Robinette said it was okay, he'd admit whatever it was Smythe was going to testify to without him going in the box.
Jack Batten *Robinette* 1984: 195

I'd like to see them taking a much larger part in public life....
Maclean's 10 Feb. 1986: 8

But when did we last hear of a picture being burned?
Robertson Davies *A Voice from the Attic* 1960: 264

I remember him being sent sprawling by a cow he was trying to milk....
George Ignatieff *The Making of a Peacemonger* 1987: 34

postdoctoral, postgraduate   see GRADUATE

posthumous   *Posthumous* means occurring after death. Thus a book published posthumously is published after the death of the author, and a posthumous child is one born after the father has died. The word is pronounced *PAWST yoo muss*.

John Heath's *Aphrodite* ... is a posthumous collection of poems by a writer who was killed in Korea at the age of thirty-four.
Northrop Frye *The Bush Garden* 1971: 104

postman   see JOB TITLES

pothole   see SWAMP

pour   see PORE

power of attorney   see LAWYER

practically, almost   Some usage guides say that *practically* should not be used as a synonym for *almost*, but should be reserved for the sense 'in a practical way', the opposite of 'theoretically'. However, the *OED* records that *practically* was being used to mean *almost* by the mid-1700s. Certainly this is its most common meaning in various types of Canadian writing, including journalism, literary essays, autobiography, biography, and history, as well as in fictional dialogue.

Practically every match was a mismatch.
Globe and Mail (Toronto) 17 Jan. 1985: M10

Practically everybody who habitually reads poetry habitually writes it as well.
Northrop Frye *The Bush Garden* 1971: 56–7

(Here Frye uses *practically* to mean *almost*.)

The simultaneous influence of two larger nations speaking the same language has been practically beneficial to English Canada, but theoretically confusing.
Northrop Frye *The Bush Garden* 1971: 218

(Here, where Frye uses *practically* to mean 'in a practical way', it stands in contrast to *theoretically*.)

practice, practise   see -CE, -SE

prairie, Prairie provinces   The word *prairie* should not be capitalized when it refers to any flat grassland: 'The sky dominates the prairie landscape'. *Prairie* is capitalized, however, when it refers to a specific region: 'The Prairie electorate sent a clear message to Ottawa'. The term *Prairie provinces* refers to Manitoba, Saskatchewan, and Alberta.

When I was growing up in the prairies in the mid-twenties and early thirties, we were taught in school that the sunsets of Manitoba were the most spectacular in the world, and we believed it.
Miriam Waddington *Apartment Seven* 1989: 36

(Here *prairies* means a specific region of Canada and therefore should be capitalized. Waddington says she grew up 'in' the prairies, just as one would say 'in' the Prairie provinces.)

[Separation from the rest of Canada] would leave the prairie Provinces without an outlet to the Western Sea, but that could be a boost for beleaguered Churchill, Manitoba....
Ottawa Citizen 30 June 1994: A9

(Here *Prairie provinces* is recommended.)

Precambrian Shield   see CANADIAN SHIELD

precede   see -CEED, -CEDE, -SEDE

precedence, precedents   *Precedence* means priority, the fact of preceding something else in time, space, or rank. A *precedent* is an earlier occurrence or case that is used as a guide or justification in subsequent cases. *Precedents*, the plural of *precedent*, is sometimes confused with *precedence* because the two words are pronounced the same way.

The reason is based on precedence: that is, a writer has to write something before a critic can criticize it.
Margaret Atwood *Second Words* 1982: 11

Devine's government persuaded Ottawa to make good all Pioneer deposits, not just those below the legal ceiling of $60,000—a costly precedent for the later, larger failures in western banking.
Saturday Night April 1984: 12

This first panel, however, did establish some precedence for use in the future.
Financial Post 23 Oct. 1989: 3

(The required word here is *precedents*.)

See also INCIDENTS, INCIDENCE.

precipitous, precipitate *Precipitous* is related to *precipice*; thus 'a precipitous bluff' is a very steep one; 'a precipitous drop in interest rates' is a sharp decline; and 'a precipitous road' is at the edge of a steep drop-off.

The adjective *precipitate* (pronounced *pruh SIP i tut*; the noun and verb are *pruh SIP i TATE*) means sudden or hasty and often implies recklessness. Because a steep decline often occurs suddenly, there is some overlap in the senses of these two words. However, *precipitous* emphasizes steepness and should not be used of anything that cannot be thought of metaphorically as dropping off like a cliff-face; *precipitate* emphasizes suddenness and should not be used of material things. Confusion is widespread: *precipitous* is often misused to mean rash.

Later the same day we drove along a winding and sometimes precipitous coastal road to Mishkor....
George Ignatieff *The Making of a Peacemonger* 1987: 140

(Here *precipitous* means that the road was on the edge of a cliff.)

... the Prangnell era turned out to be a time of precipitous decline.
Saturday Night May 1986: 13

(Here *precipitous* is used figuratively.)

He had ... shocked the Canadian government into precipitate action, and bamboozled everybody into taking part in an adventure whose outcome was uncertain and, for some, would be horrific.
Pierre Berton *The Promised Land* 1984: 114

(Here *precipitate* means hasty or rash.)

The introduction ... of experimental procedures for investigating association formation resulted in a precipi-

tous shift in the subject matter of animal development studies.
Canadian Journal of Psychology 11 (1990): 314

(The word required here is *precipitate*, meaning sudden.)

Thus, although we find compelling both the notion of a fixed maximum life span of 115 years and the notion that the onset of infirmity due to chronic disease can be delayed, we realize that to accept either at the moment may prove to have been precipitous.
Queen's Quarterly 97.1 (1990): 13–14

(Here *precipitate*, 'rash', would make more sense.)

precondition *Precondition*, coined in 1825 by Samuel Taylor Coleridge, has become a popular word, especially in the fields of social science and politics. Several usage guides declare the word redundant, arguing that *condition* means the same thing. However, it is not always clear whether a condition is something required before something else can happen or whether it is a necessary coexistent factor. The word *precondition* resolves this ambiguity.

In the tumultuous days of the English civil war, Hobbes produced his Leviathan (1651), a classic study of power as a precondition of social peace.
Irving M. Zeitlin and Robert J. Brym *The Social Condition of Humanity* 1991: 74

(Here *condition* would be ambiguous.)

... he argues that a background which is structured by image schemata is an important part of an utterance's meaning, not just a precondition of the utterance's having meaning.
Canadian Journal of Philosophy 19 (1989): 302

predecessor, successor A *predecessor* precedes you; a *successor* takes your place or succeeds you.

By means of language we are also given the opportunity to acquire the socially inherited knowledge and experience of our predecessors—without having to repeat their trials and errors.
Irving M. Zeitlin and Robert J. Brym *The Social Condition of Humanity* 1991: 14

Its membership and income had both dropped, and it had to contend with finding an adequate successor to the dynamic René Lévesque.
Alan Whitehorn *Canadian Socialism* 1992: 213

'Of course, in five years it's possible that my predecessor will say that we can't afford noble sentiments such as these.'
Queen's Journal (Kingston) 14 Sept. 1993

(Here *successor* is the word required.)

predominant, predominate *Predominant* is the adjective that corresponds to the verb *predominate*, just as *dominant* corresponds to *dominate*. However, a surprising number of writers use *predominate* as the adjective, and have done so for at least four centuries, according to the *OED*. *Predominate* is listed as a variant form of *predominant*—and the adverb *predominately* of *predominantly*—in some dictionaries.

Although *predominate* and *predominately* can be found in Canadian writing, the much more common *predominant* and *predominantly* are recommended.

> Nova Scotia, predominant producer of yuletide lobster, ships about 360 tonnes each December to France....
> *Spectator* (Hamilton) 23 Dec. 1994: C11

> In Ontario, two grapes predominate in ice wine production: vidal and Riesling.
> *Spectator* (Hamilton) 19 Nov. 1994: 21

(Here *predominate* is used correctly as a verb.)

> The predominate fuel source of the proposals is natural gas....
> *Ottawa Citizen* 1 March 1990: E12

(Here *predominant* is recommended.)

> From a varietal perspective, red wines aged in wood and made predominately from cabernet sauvignon, pinot noir or syrah/shiraz are good bets.
> *Vancouver Sun* 28 March 1990: C5

(Here *predominantly* is recommended.)

pre-eminent see IMMANENT

preface see FOREWORD

prejudice, prejudiced Strictly speaking, a *prejudice* can be either a favourable or an unfavourable opinion, but in actual usage a prejudice is usually negative. A 'negative prejudice' is a prejudice *against* something; a 'positive prejudice' is one *for* or *in favour of*. The word is often misspelled *predjudice*, with a *d* before the *j*.

Occasionally the adjective *prejudiced* is also misspelled without its final *d*, perhaps because it is not clearly audible in speech: 'He's prejudice' instead of 'He's prejudiced'.

> The protesters had gathered ... for a rally organized by the Canadian Centre on Racism and Predjudice.
> *Gazette* (Montreal) 10 Nov. 1992: A3

(The correct spelling is *prejudice*.)

première, début A *première* is the first public performance or the opening of a play, film, work of music, etc. A *début* (pronounced *DAY byoo* or *day BYOO*) is the first public appearance of a performer or the formal entrance into society of a young woman. Normally, only people make débuts. The verb *première*, meaning to open or perform for the first time, is standard. Although in journalism *début* is used as a verb meaning to make a début, this use is considered unacceptable in more formal contexts, probably because the English verb forms look awkward, cause spelling difficulties, and lead to pronunciations that are far from the original French: *débuts, débuted, débuting* (which—if you must say them—are pronounced *day byoos, day byood*, and *day byoo ing*.) Both words often appear without accents, and some dictionaries list the accentless forms first, indicating that they are the most common.

> The Toronto Symphony subsequently premiered Alexina Louie's *The Eternal Earth*....
> *Queen's Quarterly* 94.1 (1987): 179

> Now the resident ingenue at The Variety Dinner Theatre in Toronto, Shilton debuted in Variety's 1983 smash hit Pump Boys and Dinettes.
> *Maclean's* 10 Feb. 1986: 44

(Here 'made her début' or 'made her first appearance' would be more formal.)

> Témoin de mon amour by Fridda Boccara debuted in the Top 10 at No. 8 after four weeks of release.
> *Gazette* (Montreal) 2 March 1989: E2

(Here neither *début*, which should be used of people, nor *première*, which should be used of first performances, is really satisfactory. The following would be acceptable: 'Témoin de mon amour ... first appeared in the Top 10....')

See also FUNCTIONAL SHIFT.

premise, premises, premiss A *premise* (plural *premises*) is a statement, assumed to be true, that is taken as the starting point of an argument or line of reasoning. *Premiss* (plural *premisses*) is a British spelling variant used occasionally in Canadian scholarly writing. *Premises* is a plural noun referring to a building and grounds. Because *premises* looks like a plural, some people incorrectly assume that there is a singular form, *premise*, for this sense.

The Nemaiah Chilcotins filed suit in B.C. Supreme Court a year ago to stop clearcut logging on the premise that it would destroy their traplines.
Vancouver Sun 18 Dec. 1990: B2

He believes a novel demands acceptance of the writer's premises, 'so I often read the first page of a book many times.'
Vancouver Sun 26 Oct. 1990: P35

Given Descartes' distinction between intuition and deduction ... and his claim ... that at least in some cases conclusions can be drawn from premises in a single 'unclouded' glance, I do not want to press the notion of proof very hard.
Canadian Journal of Philosophy 19 (1989): 227

At Fifty-Six Gallery ... the refurbished premises have opened with a group show....
Vancouver Sun 27 Oct. 1990: D10

... Rose's production of Krizanc's play ... [was] staged by Necessary Angel in the Canadian Stage Company's Berkeley Street premise.
Queen's Quarterly 97.3 (1990): 376

(The word required here is *premises*.)

preposition at end   The English poet and dramatist John Dryden (1631–1700) is to be blamed for propagating the notion that a sentence should never end with a preposition. Dryden probably got the idea from Latin, where a preposition cannot be the last word in a sentence. Critics of the structure in English call it 'inelegant'. In some cases it is just that. In other cases, however, trying to avoid a final preposition results in noticeable inelegance.

Sometimes a preposition functions as part of a phrasal verb: 'look out', 'move on', 'break up'. In sentences where a phrasal verb ends a sentence, there is no avoiding a preposition at the end: 'We're done for'; 'Come on in'; 'It must be seen to'. Questions such as 'What are you waiting for?' and 'Who is that story by?' can be rephrased as 'For what are you waiting?' and 'By whom was that story written?'; but these alternative constructions sound stilted in all but the most formal contexts.

Prepositions appeared at the end of written English sentences in Old English, and examples can be found in the works of Chaucer, Shakespeare, Milton, Swift, and other famous writers. Although Fowler called the supposed rule a 'cherished superstition', and current usage guides unanimously agree with him that a sentence ending with a preposition is good English, the usage still has its op-

ponents. However, those who oppose this usage on the grounds that good writers have characteristically avoided it haven't a leg to stand on.

We have, then, at least three possible concepts of *standard* to deal with.
W.C. Lougheed ed. *In Search of the Standard in Canadian English* 1986: 34

The court assumes that a minor living at home is provided for.
J.E. Smyth et al. *The Law and Business Administration in Canada* 1987: 175

These are qualities which the more self-advertising poems give little hint of.
Northrop Frye *The Bush Garden* 1971: 69

Of course, we should not forget the millions of our tax dollars that are spent on telling us what a finer-than-frog-fur place this Ontari-ario is in which to live.
Harrowsmith Jun.–Jul. 1985: 4

(It would be more consistent with the rhythm and tone of this sentence to end with 'is to *live in*' than to avoid the final preposition with the *in which* clause.)

In the old theatres they had smelly kennels in which to change their clothes.... Gentlemen, I appeal to you with all the force of which I am capable: give us back a theatre which it is a pleasure to be in!
Robertson Davies *One Half of Robertson Davies* 1978: 80

(This example shows Davies using both constructions.)

See also PHRASAL VERBS.

prepositions after verbs   see PHRASAL VERBS

prerequisite   see PERK

prescribe, proscribe   To *prescribe* means to order or direct, or to lay down a rule; to *proscribe* means to condemn, forbid, or outlaw. Laws can both prescribe and proscribe things; this is where confusion may arise.

Zoning by-laws prescribe the use and type of buildings that may be erected in various districts of a municipality....
J.E. Smyth et al. *The Law and Business Administration in Canada* 1987: 570

It was not just the Sun Dance that was proscribed. The more severe and committed Protestant sects on the frontier were opposed to all dancing.
Pierre Berton *The Promised Land* 1984: 216

Ontario natural resources officials, who are conducting the proscribed fire as part of a regular program to clear

budworm-destroyed trees, said the burn is tentatively set for next Sunday....
Globe and Mail (Toronto) 16 July 1985: P4

(A fire that is deliberately set by forestry officials must have been *prescribed*.)

War crimes are common law offences, the study said, because they are internationally prescribed offences and 'there is a duty imposed on individuals by international law not to commit war crimes.'
Globe and Mail (Toronto) 12 Feb. 1985: P1

(The word required here is *proscribed*, 'outlawed'.)

presentation   see PRESENTIMENT

presentiment, presentment, presentation   A *presentiment* is a premonition, a feeling that something is about to happen, particularly something evil. *Presentment*, rare in general usage, has several specialized senses in law and business. It is occasionally found as a formal synonym for the far more common *presentation*.

It is not a rational feeling; it is a mood, a presentiment, an aura.
Miriam Waddington *Apartment Seven* 1989: 131

present incumbent   see INCUMBENT

presently   Some usage specialists maintain that the only acceptable contemporary meaning of *presently* is soon; others, that *presently* can also be used to mean at present, or now. The first group argue that accepting the second meaning may lead to ambiguity—yet all agree that 'now' was the original meaning of the word; the sense 'soon' appeared in the sixteenth century. The *OED* states that *presently* meaning at present has been obsolete in literary English since the seventeenth century, but that it has remained in use in British dialects and has been revived in the United States in the twentieth century.

Canadian newspaper style guides list 'soon' as the only correct sense, but North American dictionaries list 'at present' as a second meaning. In Canadian usage both senses are found: the more common one is actually 'at present'. Canadian writers need not hesitate to use either sense, but should ensure that the context prevents any ambiguity.

That is a point to which we shall presently return.
Irving M. Zeitlin and Robert J. Brym *The Social Condition of Humanity* 1991: 61

And this selection is, finally, only half the show it should be, but more of that presently.
Globe and Mail (Toronto) 19 Oct. 1985: D13

The presently accepted doctrine of parliamentary privilege ... appears to be a necessary policy to pursue.
Andrew Heard *Canadian Constitutional Conventions* 1991: 99

In fact, the tone of the book seems more contemporary now than it did in, say, 1971, when it was believed that society could change itself a good deal faster than presently appears likely.
Margaret Atwood *Second Words* 1982: 370

See also MOMENTARILY.

present tense, literary present   The present tense is often used in English to refer to events in the near future: 'I leave Friday'; 'When is your appointment?'

In both formal and informal English, the present tense is sometimes used to make the recounting of past events seem vivid and immediate: 'The fog is closing in. The children are playing in the water, oblivious. We call to them....'

A convention in literary criticism, sometimes referred to as the *literary present*, is to use the present tense to discuss the action of a story, film, or play, or to refer to writers who are no longer living. The reasoning is that the story is not over and done with, but may continually be experienced by readers or viewers. Similarly, a dead writer's words will speak to us in the present: 'Rupert Brooke speaks of the "unseizable virginity" of the Canadian landscape' (Northrop Frye, *The Bush Garden*, 1971: 220).

present writer, this writer   Some writers refer to themselves as 'the present writer/author/reviewer' or 'this writer/author/reviewer' in an effort to avoid *I*, *me*, and *my*. Many commentators find such constructions old-fashioned, falsely modest, and overly formal. 'The present writer' and similar phrases are likely to bewilder or alienate readers and are therefore best replaced by the more direct *I* or *me*.

The present reviewer does not share the surprise, if it is there, but he fully concurs in the admiration.
Northrop Frye *The Bush Garden* 1971: 48

(This sentence sounds quite formal by today's standards, and few readers would object if Frye referred to himself as *I* rather than *the present reviewer* and *he*.)

Although this story ... and many of my other stories about salmon fishing contain interactions between poachers and law officials, it is in no way the intention of

this writer to glorify poachers or the act of breaking the law.
Atlantic Salmon Journal Summer 1990: 45

(Since the author has written 'my other stories', there is no reason not to continue in the first person by writing '*my* intention'.)

prestigious, prestige   In the seventeenth century both *prestige* (pronounced *press TEEZH* or *press TEEDZ*) and *prestigious* (pronounced *press TIZ yus*) referred to deception and conjuring. In the nineteenth century the meaning of *prestige* shifted and the word came to refer to respect based on a good reputation. *Prestigious* followed a similar transformation, but was not so readily accepted by the critics. Even in the 1980s, some authorities insisted that *prestigious* implied deception and should not be used to mean having a solid reputation or imparting prestige. However, no dictionary supports this antiquated view, and *prestigious* is used with positive connotations in all types of contemporary writing.

To me 'prestigious' means, and always will mean, juggling tricks, because it derives from *praestigiae*, and when it is used in the modern way I feel as though a rusty sword had been thrust into my—well, not perhaps into my heart, but into some sensitive part of my body.
Robertson Davies *One Half of Robertson Davies* 1978: 12–13

... we can imagine [most societies] as pyramids: hierarchies of strata with the wealthiest, most powerful and most prestigious at the top, and the impoverished, weak and despised at the bottom.
Irving M. Zeitlin and Robert J. Brym *The Social Condition of Humanity* 1991: 112

Two Vancouver writers are in the running for a prestigious national writing award.
Province (Vancouver) 18 Nov. 1990: 78

presumptive, presumptuous   *Presumptive* is almost exclusively a legal or technical term, meaning based on likelihood or reasonably presumed. For example, a 'presumptive diagnosis' is one that is based on a reasoned consideration of the available evidence.

The derogatory term *presumptuous* describes behaviour that is unduly bold or overly familiar—behaviour that presumes too much. *Presumptious* is an archaic spelling, now considered an error.

'The presumptive diagnosis is a viral diarrhea outbreak,' said Dr. Douglas Pudden....
Globe and Mail (Toronto) 16 Oct. 1985: A19

Both Steiniger's and Leroy's ... observations provide presumptive evidence of an important role of social learning....
Canadian Journal of Psychology 44 (1990): 316

Because of her Algerian background, she realized it would be wrong to expect these women to change their ways abruptly, and presumptuous to interfere with their customs.
Saturday Night Feb. 1986: 66

'The problem has to be solved in Canada, by Canadians.... We are not being so presumptive as to tell you what to do.'
Vancouver Sun 1 Dec. 1990: B7

(The word required here is *presumptuous*.)

'It is presumptious of the commission to proceed as they are doing,' board chairman John Tolton told reporters after the hearing.
Globe and Mail (Toronto) 9 Feb. 1985: P15

(The correct spelling is *presumptuous*.)

See also HEIR.

pretense, pretence, pretension, pretentious   Canadians use the spelling *pretense* (favoured in the United States) slightly more often than *pretence* (the British spelling).
Note that *pretension* is spelled *-sion*, while *pretentious* is spelled with a *t*.

Less skilled passers ... made no pretense of passing, instead shooting the puck ahead of them to the corners, and chasing after it.
Ken Dryden *The Game* 1983: 217

Few people have illusions that all Third World countries can pay their debts, or even service them, but many people insist on the pretence.
Globe and Mail (Toronto) 30 July 1985: P6

Murray, the quintessential Canadian pop singer, doesn't have a whiff of glitz or pretension about her.
Gazette (Montreal) 19 June 1994: F1

A pretention alarm goes off when I hear writers being elevated to the rank of hermit-like martyrs....
Ottawa Citizen 19 June 1994: B6

(The correct spelling is *pretension*.)

See also -CE, -SE.

pretty   *Pretty* used as an adverb (meaning fairly or somewhat) is found in all kinds of writing. Although some critics have tried to restrict its use to informal or colloquial contexts, they have had little success.

Social man is pretty well tamed by what we call civilization, until a war or a disaster shatters the cellophane wrapping.
Robertson Davies *A Voice from the Attic* 1960: 110

These policy recommendations were ... more economic than political, since he had concluded that the political arrangements were, on the whole, pretty good.
Queen's Quarterly 95.3 (1988): 598

By and large, anglophone Canadians look pretty much like all Canadian respondents; little if any movement towards the British norm can be detected.
Neil Nevitte and Roger Gibbins *New Elites in Old States* 1990: 129

... some insects make pretty fair architects, and beavers know quite a lot about engineering.
Northrop Frye *The Educated Imagination* 1963: 5

prevaricate   see LIE

preventive, preventative   Most usage guides suggest that both *preventive* and *preventative* are correct; however, some note that *preventive* is more common, and a few call it preferable. While Canadian writers use *preventive* far more commonly, either word is correct as an adjective or a noun.

Fries argues ... that it is possible to postpone the onset of the common chronic diseases by a variety of measures, mostly preventive and mostly involving aspects of life-style....
Queen's Quarterly 97.1 (1990): 7

Motorists ... reported an average cost of $661 a year for mechanical auto repairs and preventative maintenance.
Calgary Herald 11 Feb. 1994: E2

If the daily administration of a preventative is interrupted for any reason, the blood must be checked before resuming.
Dogs in Canada Special Issue 1986: 66

(Here *preventative* is used as a noun.)

primary colour   see COLOUR

primitive, primeval, primordial   *Primitive, primeval,* and *primordial* all refer to the earliest times or the earliest stages of something. *Primitive* is the most commonly used word; it usually suggests something rudimentary and undeveloped. In the past *primitive* was often used by English colonists to describe Indigenous cultures, but this usage—unless carefully qualified—is now seen as Eurocentric or racist.

Primeval (also spelled *primaeval*) and *primordial* are less common words, meaning existing from the beginning or prehistoric, and often suggesting something mysterious or unspoiled: 'primeval cave paintings', 'primordial forests'. Since *primordial* in French means essential, it occasionally appears in Quebec English with this sense.

The barn has two working toilets, few lights, and primitive cooking and washing facilities.
Vancouver Sun 28 June 1994: A3

Where townsfolk are swilling beer and swatting flies, Lindsay's independent women are draped in shimmering gauze and straw hats, swimming in primeval waters and getting in touch with their innermost physical selves.
Gazette (Montreal) 15 April 1994: C1

Before Shoemaker-Levy [a comet that shattered], most astronomers thought comets were single pieces of primordial ice left over from the formation of the solar system.
Toronto Star 29 May 1994: E7

'Our first principle is to respect the primordial mission of Belanger-Campeau,' said Spicer....
Gazette (Montreal) 19 Nov. 1990: A1

(This example illustrates the Quebec English use of *primordial* to mean essential.)

See also -AE-, -OE-, -E-; QUEBEC ENGLISH.

Prince Edward Island   see APPENDIX I

principal, principle   The adjective *principal* means main or most important. The noun *principal* refers to the head of a school or college, to a person playing a key role in an event, or to a sum of money on which interest is charged or paid.
Principle is always a noun and means a fundamental law or a moral standard. 'In principle' means in theory.

BC Stena's principle asset, the passenger-car ferry Vancouver Island Princess, remains tied up in Victoria....
Vancouver Sun 23 Nov. 1990: D10

(The correct spelling here is *principal*.)

The aquarium has been granted approval in principal for a federal fisheries permit to catch beluga whales....
Vancouver Sun 10 July 1990: B4

(The correct spelling here is *principle*.)

prioritize, priorize *Prioritize*, meaning give priority to or arrange in order of priority, is labelled jargon by most usage guides; in fact, the word is usually found in business writing and only rarely in formal prose.

Canadians use *priorize* as an alternative form of this verb fairly frequently. However, since dictionaries have not yet listed this form, it is not recommended.

'We need to identify and prioritize issues.'
Financial Post 28 April 1989: 18

The failure of the trustees ... to give priority to salaries and research funds over 'new buildings and that sort of thing' made it difficult for the university to attract and hold faculty members of high calibre....
Frederick Gibson *Queen's University* 2 (1983): 46

(In academic writing *prioritize* is generally avoided; here 'give priority to' is used instead.)

'This necessity to protect and priorize French in all its forms of expression is ... absolute', wrote Masson....
Gazette (Montreal) 27 July 1989: B3

See also -IZE, -ISE.

pristine Originally *pristine* meant belonging to earliest times, before civilization. The word later came to mean uncorrupted by civilization, and was used as a synonym for *unspoiled, uncorrupted,* or *unpolluted*. The use of *pristine* to mean spotlessly clean, tidy, or like new dates from around 1940 and is common in both North America and Britain. Some dictionaries do not list this meaning at all, however, and others label it disputed. To avoid the criticism of those who do not accept these newer meanings of *pristine*, you may want to use another word, such as *immaculate* or *unsoiled*, instead.

... Comet Kohoutek probably had a surface layer of frozen hydrogen, a pristine remnant from the solar system's formation.
Terence Dickinson *Halley's Comet* 1985: 37

The land appeared pristine, deserted, but for hundreds of years Inuit camped here in season to intercept caribou migrations and fish in the rapids.
Uphere Jan.–Feb. 1990: 42

'Environmental disasters such as ... the giant Exxon tanker spill in Valdez, Alaska, illustrate the impossibility of returning an area to its formerly pristine state, the difficulty of cleaning up after an accident, and the extreme hazards inherent in operating in such climates.'
Irving M. Zeitlin and Robert J. Brym *The Social Condition of Humanity* 1991: 377

At dinnertime one night there are 17 pairs of men's rubbers cluttering the otherwise pristine glass foyer.
Globe and Mail (Toronto) 23 Feb. 1985: M9

(Some commentators would prefer *spotless* or *immaculate* here.)

The machine would go up the block, turn and, snuffling and grousing like some large impatient animal, would charge back over the territory, leaving the street in a near pristine condition.
Dogs in Canada Special Issue 1986: 78

(Some commentators would prefer *spotless* or *immaculate* here.)

See also IMPECCABLE, IMMACULATE.

pro, pros *Pro* is an informal short form of *professional*, but not all types of professionals are called pros: doctors, lawyers, and accountants, for example, are not. Generally 'the pros' are athletes whose job it is to play a sport; the leagues they play in are also called 'the pros'. The *pro* at a golf or tennis club is a highly skilled player, usually employed by the club to give lessons.

In Britain *pro* is also slang for *prostitute*. This *pro* is probably a short form of *prostitute*, reinforced by a connotation of lost amateur status.

The expression 'to be a pro' simply means to be expert at something.

'Every kid that plays basketball hopes to make it to the pros, and that's my goal.'
Globe and Mail (Toronto) 8 May 1985: S2

Jill Fraser, the pro at Streetsville Glen Golf Club in Brampton, Ont., suggests the following exercises to help golfers relax and limber up before they tee off.
Canadian Living 17 May 1986: 13

No matter how friendly, frisky, and helpful your salesman is, he's a pro who wheels and deals over cars daily.
Canadian Consumer March 1986: 5

proactive The word *proactive*, which has become popular since 1970, is sometimes criticized as a redundant synonym for *active*. However, *proactive* does have a particular meaning as the opposite of *reactive*. The prefix *pro-* in *proactive* means beforehand. The word is used to describe people, policies, or measures that anticipate problems and thus avoid them, or that anticipate new developments in order to take advantage of them. Thus a proactive health-care system would emphasize preventing illness rather than reacting to it.

Proactive should not be used to mean energetic or active. This imprecise use of the word, especially in business writing, has led some commentators to claim it is meaningless.

Proactive is quite often written with a hyphen, *pro-active*, but most dictionaries list the unhyphenated form first.

... Lanskail said council must begin to address the shortage of seniors' housing in a pro-active manner rather than just responding to inadequate proposals.
Vancouver Sun 26 July 1990: C2

'The traditional "reactive" mode of supervision [of banks] must give way to a "proactive" mode.'
Globe and Mail (Toronto) 7 Nov. 1985: A1

A senior executive can teach the manager to recognize the myriad signals that are part of being proactive and anticipating the market.
Globe and Mail (Toronto) 7 Jan. 1985: B5

She also needs to take pro-active measures to placate a disaffected and influential green lobby that feels stonewalled by the Socred government.
Financial Post 23 Sept. 1991: 2

(This is a loose use of *proactive*, since measures to placate a disaffected lobby are necessarily reactive; '*active* measures' would be more accurate.)

The company philosophy is described by Haycock as 'pro-active.' 'We're not interested in sitting on a problem. We want to move on it and resolve it.'
Financial Post 27 Sept. 1991: 18

(Since the speaker is talking about reacting quickly to problems, this use of *proactive* is questionable.)

See also REACTIVE.

proceed   see -CEED, -CEDE, -SEDE

pro-choice   see ABORTION

Procrustes, Procrustean   In Greek legend Procrustes was a celebrated robber who had a macabre way of accommodating his guests. He offered them one of two beds: a very short one or a very long one. If a guest chose the short bed and was too long for it, Procrustes cut off any overhanging body parts to make him fit; if he chose the long bed, Procrustes stretched him until he filled it. Theseus put an end to Procrustes by making him lie on his own bed. Hence *Procrustean* and *Procrustes' bed* have become figures of speech for an arbitrary standard or scheme imposed rigidly or ruthlessly.

The correct pronunciation is *pro KRUH steez*. The adjective *Procrustean* is generally capitalized.

It is perhaps not his fault that he has had to snip and stretch a little to fit the past neatly into his Procrustean structure.
Margaret Atwood *Second Words* 1982: 30

... Americans have become more narrow-mindedly intolerant of unfettered free speech and dissent as they, like Canadians, turn more and more to procrustean censorship laws to ban what is deemed 'offensive.'
Financial Post 29 June 1990: 10

(The adjective *Procrustean* is usually capitalized.)

prodigal   The adjective *prodigal* means recklessly wasteful, as in Jesus' parable of the prodigal son (Luke 15: 11–32) who left home and squandered his money on riotous living. However, today *prodigal* only rarely connotes wastefulness, riotous living, or lavishness. In contemporary Canadian usage, *prodigal* is most often associated with the return of the son, when his father welcomed him home and killed a fatted calf in his honour. While the parable teaches sinners that God will forgive their sins as the prodigal's father forgave his, most current references to someone as 'a prodigal' imply simply that the person has (literally or figuratively) left home, returned, and been welcomed back.

Since the greenhouse effect grew out of a lifestyle built around the automobile and a prodigal waste of energy, more efficient vehicles are being designed....
Vancouver Sun 10 March 1990: A10

(Here *prodigal* does mean reckless.)

When he went upstairs to the office to collect his stack of leaflets, they greeted him like the prodigal son.
Margaret Atwood *Life Before Man* 1979: 281

Yet all those who now pretended to be converted were being accorded preferential treatment. They were welcomed back in the manner of prodigal children returning to the fold.
Canadian Journal of History 14.1 (1989): 32

Ann Ditchburn Dances ... marks the first time she has performed in a professional setting since arriving back in Toronto last year. And, judging by the cheers from the capacity crowd, all are very happy to have the prodigal home again.
Globe and Mail (Toronto) 30 Jan 1985: M7

Dent is a finback that had been identified 16 years before in the water off the Rock. He hadn't been seen in three years. The prodigal had returned.
Gazette (Montreal) 28 April 1990: I12

program, programme *Program* is the usual Canadian spelling, although *programme* (the British spelling) is not uncommon, especially in reference to the works to be performed at a concert or to a plan of action. *Programme* may be more frequent in federal government contexts and in Quebec because it is also the French spelling. Note that in reference to computers, Canadian and British writers use *program*, the spelling used for all meanings in American English.

The usual verb forms in Canada are *programmed* and *programming*, although *programed* and *programing*, alternative American spellings, are also acceptable.

... the regional development program was not designed to handle major structural shifts in the economy.
The Canadian Geographer Spring 1989: 57

Mulroney frankly presented himself to the party not as a man with a programme or a set of ideas but as a potential winner, nothing more.
Saturday Night Feb. 1986: 5

Mr. Lithgow comes to York University from the Ottawa Civic Hospital where he was ... responsible for the Hospital Foundation's fundraising programme.
Globe and Mail (Toronto) 26 Nov. 1985: B5

Next year, if it only takes two analysts to set up a similar program for another customer, the statistician can conclude the computer company's productivity on this task has risen by one-third.
Ottawa Citizen 1 Aug. 1991: A3

... by means of computer programmes, we used the *Survey* results for subsets of this collection of items...
W.C. Lougheed, ed. *In Search of the Standard in Canadian English* 1986: 172

(The spelling *program* is more common when the reference is to computers.)

The number of radio stations cutting back on local news programming in the United States has increased so dramatically that local news may soon become the exception on radio....
Globe and Mail (Toronto) 2 Jan. 1985: B5

They're written in the BASIC programing language and, with a few modifications, can be run on any IBM or IBM-compatible office computer.
Country Guide Nov. 1986: 11–12

Progressive Conservative see CONSERVATIVE

proletariat see BOURGEOIS

pro-life see ABORTION

prone, -prone *Prone* means disposed to or susceptible to, usually with negative implications: 'prone to error', 'prone to headaches'. *Prone* may be followed by either an infinitive or an -*ing* form of a verb: 'He was prone to let in (*or* prone to letting in) easy goals'. Some object to the use of *prone* to indicate a liking or fancy for a particular thing, as in 'prone to chocolate and anchovies'. *Partial* is a better choice in such contexts.

Prone is also commonly used to form hyphenated compounds: *accident-prone*, *erosion-prone*.

At least two chains are basing their prices on two-day rentals. For those of us who are prone to send the movie back unwatched because we've fallen asleep ... this is a worthwhile option.
Province (Vancouver) 9 Oct. 1990: 45

Most doctors now agree that if ASA is taken by a child suffering from a viral illness such as chicken pox ... the child becomes more prone to developing a devastating illness called Reye's Syndrome.
Province (Vancouver) 31 Dec. 1990: 45

She's personally rather prone to cottons and linens ('very crisp') for weddings....
Globe and Mail (Toronto) 8 Jan. 1985: F10

(Here *partial* would be a better choice.)

See also PRONE, SUPINE.

prone, supine, prostrate, recumbent These words for describing how someone is lying down cause confusion. Most of us manage with expressions such as 'face up (*or* down)', 'on his stomach', or 'on her back'. According to dictionaries, *prone* means lying face downwards, while *supine* means lying face upwards. In popular Canadian writing, however, *prone* is used for both positions. Likewise, though *prostrate* means stretched out full-length, face down, it is often used simply to mean lying down. Often this word is used figuratively: 'She was prostrate with grief'. The word *supine* is quite uncommon; however, it is sometimes used figuratively to mean passive, apathetic, or morally slack. *Recumbent* is also uncommon; it means lying down or reclining—in any position—and usually suggests repose.

The biathlon includes cross-country ski sprints of five to 20 kilometres, with up to five standing and prone shooting intervals.
Globe and Mail (Toronto) 18 Feb. 1985: S4

Fortunately she had trained herself to sleep in the supine pose of a marble saint on a sarcophagus lid.
Globe and Mail (Toronto) 24 Sept. 1985: F13

... the former superintendent of financial institutions ... seemed powerless to do much more than plead with the supine board to heed his advice.
Toronto Star 19 Nov. 1994: B2

(Here *supine* is used figuratively to mean morally slack.)

Along Lhasa's Free Market Street, a pair of pilgrims ... prostrate themselves full-length on the street, forehead touching the ground.
Globe and Mail (Toronto) 27 July 1985: T9

Yet, despite taxpayers' prostrate condition, the city of Montreal actually spent 1.8 per cent more money in the fiscal year ending last March than in the previous year.
Gazette (Montreal) 21 Sept. 1994: B3

(Here *prostrate* is used figuratively to mean overcome or weakened.)

I rounded the rear bumper and saw an old woman prone on a padded bench, straining beneath a barbell.
Canadian Fiction Magazine 64 (1988): 38

(Technically, since this woman must be lying on her back, the correct word would be *supine*; however, *supine* has connotations—slack, apathetic—that are inappropriate here; simply 'lying on a padded bench' would be better.)

He gave her a wheedling look from his almost prone position in the armchair with the broken springs.
Constance Beresford-Howe *Night Studies* 1985: 67

(Here 'almost *supine*' or 'almost *recumbent*' would fit the context better.)

The hired man tried to sit up, holding onto his shoulder. With a groan, he fell back onto the dirt floor. 'This guy is nuts,' said Rick, pointing to the prostrate man.
Canadian Fiction Magazine 64 (1988): 69

(This man is *supine*, or lying on his back.)

See also PRONE, -PRONE; PROSTATE, PROSTRATE.

pronoun agreement   see AGREEMENT, GRAMMATICAL

pronoun reference   see THAT, WHICH

pronoun with possessive antecedent   A few contemporary language commentators state that the antecedent of a pronoun cannot be in the possessive case. They would consider the sentence 'I took Jim's calls while he was out' ungrammatical,
because the antecedent of the pronoun *he* is *Jim*, and the word *Jim* does not appear in the sentence except as the possessive *Jim's*.

When a pronoun has a possessive antecedent, certainly there may be doubt about whether the pronoun refers to the possessive noun or to the noun that the possessive modifies: for example, 'We toned down the committee's remarks. They were quite angry.' Here *they* could refer to either the committee members or their remarks. Nevertheless, possessive antecedents should not be considered ungrammatical simply because it is possible to construct ambiguous examples around them. As the citations below show, pronouns with possessive antecedents are very common in English, even in formal writing, and the construction is usually readable and clear.

Maryon Pearson's displeasure increased by several notches the following morning when she was confronted with breakfast.
George Ignatieff *The Making of a Peacemonger* 1987: 129

In some of the interviews, Davis's distaste for the whole affair is almost palpable, and the information he surrenders is largely opaque....
Jack Chambers *Milestones* 1983: ix

The educator's fourth responsibility is to get fully involved in the society around him.
W.C. Lougheed, ed. *In Search of the Standard in Canadian English* 1986: 74

Mackworth's political views were subject to considerable comment, for he had expressed himself on all the major issues of the day.
J.A.W. Gunn *Beyond Liberty and Property* 1983: 129

Shirley's job requirements were many and complex: 'she uses her judgement as well as her clerical skills.'
Carl J. Cuneo *Pay Equity* 1990: 1

... are there still immutable principles of justice that ought to be used to judge people's conduct, no matter where they find themselves?
J.E. Smyth et al. *The Law and Business Administration in Canada* 1987: 7

(Although *they* is not technically ambiguous in this example, since 'immutable principles of justice' do not travel, the antecedent of *they* is momentarily unclear. Here it might be better to replace 'no matter where *they* find themselves' with 'anywhere'.)

See also POSSESSIVE.

pronunciation Unlike *pronounce, pronunciation* contains only one *o*. It is often misspelled and sometimes mispronounced: *pruh NUN see AY shun,* not *pruh NOUN see AY shun.*

> Incidentally, the rhyme also indicates the correct pronounciation of 'Halley.'
> *Queen's Quarterly* 92.2 (1985): 284

(The correct spelling is *pronunciation.*)

See also MISPRONUNCIATION AND PRONUNCIATION SHIFTS.

proof see EVIDENCE

prophecy, prophesy, [prophesize] Canadians most often spell the noun *prophecy* (pronounced *PROF eh see*; plural *PROF eh sees*) with a *c*, as do the British. Americans use either spelling for the noun. In all three countries it is standard to spell the verb *prophesy* (*PROF eh sigh*). Verb forms are *prophesies* (pronounced *PROF eh sighs*), *prophesied* (*PROF eh sighed*), and *prophesying* ((*PROF eh sighing*). Sometimes non-standard forms such as *prophesize, prophesized,* and *prophesizing* appear both in speech and in writing.

> The quotation from Ezekiel is part of a biblical story—many would call it a prophesy—about an evil place called 'Gog, the land of Magog.'
> *Globe and Mail* (Toronto) 12 Jan 1985: P10

(The more common spelling of the noun is *prophecy.*)

> ... living as an Asian man in the East End of London, England, is the one awaited by all religions and prophecied to come at the end of the age.
> *Globe and Mail* (Toronto) 20 April 1985: P7

(The verb is correctly spelled with an *s: prophesied.*)

> 'He may have lost this one, but he'll win a stakes race before the season is through,' prophesized Mark Zimmer....
> *Canadian Thoroughbred* Aug. 1989: 33

(The correct spelling is *prophesied.*)

> ... Mr. Speaker not only confirmed he is a Reform member but prophesized that the Reform would win all 26 Alberta seats in the next federal election.
> *Financial Post* 10 Dec. 1991: 11

(The correct spelling is *prophesied.*)

propitious *Propitious,* meaning favourable or suitable, may simply modify a noun, as in 'a propitious time', or it may be followed by *for* and a noun or a gerund, as in 'The weather was propitious for running'. *Propitious* also may appear with *to* and an infinitive: 'It was propitious to announce her plan'. Canadian writers use the last structure infrequently.

> The visit did not start off on a propitious note.
> George Ignatieff *The Making of a Peacemonger* 1987: 65

> ... Heylin was a friend to Stuart government, and the times were not propitious for accounts of tyranny by stealth.
> J.A.W. Gunn *Beyond Liberty and Property* 1983: 15

> Mr. Crow's approach has been to hold off inflation with high interest rates until the time is propitious to lower them.
> *Vancouver Sun* 2 Feb. 1990: A16

proscribe see PRESCRIBE

prostate, prostrate The *prostate* gland, situated at the base of the bladder in men, is susceptible to medical problems. *Prostate* is sometimes mispronounced and misspelled with an *r*, as if it were *prostrate,* which means lying face-down.

> The area has 20 per cent more low-weight births than normal and a significantly higher incidence of liver and prostrate cancer in men.
> *Ottawa Citizen* 22 Nov. 1994: A4

(The correct spelling is *prostate.*)

See also PRONE, SUPINE, PROSTRATE, RECUMBENT.

protagonist see ANTAGONIST

prothesis see MISPRONUNCIATION AND PRONUNCIATION SHIFTS

protocol A *protocol* is the first draft of a diplomatic agreement, or an amendment to, or clarification of, an existing treaty. *Protocol* (no article) is the code of etiquette observed by the diplomatic corps on formal occasions.

More generally, a *protocol* is any established set of procedures. For example, a professional group may develop a protocol to be used in certain circumstances for the sake of consistency, safety, or fairness: a dental association might establish a protocol for dealing with HIV-positive patients, or the police might have a protocol for dealing with wife assault.

In computing, a *protocol* is a set of instructions for transmitting data between the parts of a computer system or between remote computer systems that are not directly linked.

> Under a protocol known as the Cullen-Couture Agreement, Quebec obtained the right to select its own immigrants.
> *Vancouver Sun* 15 May 1990: A9

> The tribal police force now has a protocol agreement

that covers contracts with five Indian bands in the Lillooet area....
Vancouver Sun 14 July 1990: A5

And Shea said that protocol dictates that no royal engagement can be announced while the Queen is out of the country.
Maclean's 24 Feb. 1986: 37

Meanwhile, a delicate protocol problem over speaking order was resolved last week.
Maclean's 24 Feb. 1986: 24

'We need the Criminal Code to reflect this ... ,' said Ald. Bev Longstaff, spokeswoman for the city's prostitution policy, procedure, protocol and research committee.
Calgary Herald 24 Nov. 1994: B3

prototype   see ARCHETYPE

provenance, provenience, providence   *Provenance* means place of origin and is often used to refer to the ownership history of a work of art. *Provenience* is a synonym, used mainly in the United States.

Providence, meaning God's protective care, is usually capitalized. Without a capital, *providence* may mean destiny, luck, or, occasionally, good management.

... in the impressive notes which detail the provenance of each song, the editor emphasizes the difficulties involved with treating the songs of the Indians as texts.
Queen's Quarterly 92.1 (1985): 177

Part of the coronation service instituted for William and Mary referred to the role of divine Providence in placing the king over his people....
J.A.W. Gunn *Beyond Liberty and Property* 1983: 156

provinces and territories   see APPENDIX I;
NAMES OF RESIDENTS

provost   In Canada a *provost* is usually a senior administrator in a college, university, or cathedral. In this sense the word is usually pronounced *PRO voast* or *PRAW vuhst*.

Provost (or *provost marshal*) is also a term designating the head of a military police unit or other police officer. In this sense it is generally pronounced *PRO vo*; both syllables rhyme with *go*.

... I got a phone call asking whether I would allow my name to go forward as a candidate for the position of provost of Trinity College at the University of Toronto.
George Ignatieff *The Making of a Peacemonger* 1987: 254

He won the position of civilian provost in November 1984—a key position in charge of the jail guards and matrons—which is run by the district for the RCMP.
Vancouver Sun 24 July 1990: B2

pseudonym, pen-name, nom de plume, nom de guerre, alias, a.k.a.   All these terms refer to assumed names. *Pseudonym*, from the Greek for 'false name', is the most general, and may be used for any assumed name. *Pen-name* is a direct translation of the nineteenth-century pseudo-French expression *nom de plume* (plural *noms de plume*); both terms refer to a fictitious name used by an author.

The expression actually used in France is *nom de guerre* (plural *noms de guerre*); literally it means war name, but it is used to refer to a name assumed in pursuit of any profession or goal. In formal writing *nom de guerre* should be italicized as a foreign phrase.

An *alias* is a false name often, but not necessarily, associated with criminal activity. The term *a.k.a.* (or *aka*), pronounced as three letters, is police jargon for 'also known as'.

Miss Duncan wrote for The Globe under the pseudonym Garth Grafton....
Globe and Mail (Toronto) 5 Jan. 1985: P7

They mark the birth on Nov. 30, 1835, of Samuel Langhorne Clemens [Mark Twain], the satirical writer who took his pen-name from the two-fathom depth marker call of the Mississippi River pilots.
Globe and Mail (Toronto) 8 June 1985: T11

Mr. Abbas, known under the noms de guerre of Abul Abbas or Abu Khaled, is a tall, powerfully built 38-year-old....
Globe and Mail (Toronto) 14 Oct. 1985: A9

'I'm not a daredevil,' said Mr. Fitzgerald, who used the alias Nathan Boya when he rode his rubber ball over the Horseshoe Falls on July 15, 1961.
Globe and Mail (Toronto) 2 Feb. 1985: M1

Henri Charriere, aka Papillon, a petty criminal condemned for a murder he didn't commit, did escape on his ninth attempt.
Toronto Star 22 Oct. 1994: L23

'I don't know all the tunes, but Richard (Newell, AKA Biscuit) knows 'em all ...'
Spectator (Hamilton) 14 dec. 1995: 10

(Because *a.k.a.* is an abbreviation for a phrase that would not be capitalized, *a.k.a.* or *aka* is preferable.)

psychiatrist, psychologist   see DOCTOR

pub   see BEER PARLOUR

publicly Adjectives of more than one syllable ending in *-ic* form adverbs by adding *-ally*: *basic, basically; fantastic, fantastically; holistic, holistically; realistic, realistically. Publicly*, the only common exception to this rule, is often misspelled *publically*.

> Lloyd Quantz, 45, is the first candidate from outside the provincial cabinet to publically express an interest.
> *Calgary Herald* 18 Oct. 1992: A2

(The correct spelling is *publicly*.)

pun A pun is a joke that plays on words that sound alike but have different meanings.

> ... a chance encounter between your dog and the back end of [a skunk] can 'reek' havoc in your life.
> *Gazette* (Montreal) 1 Oct. 1990: B7

(Here the pun is on *reek*, 'smell' and *wreak havoc*, 'reduce to chaos.')

> 'She criticized my apartment so I knocked her flat.'
> Richard Davies and Glen Kirkland, eds. *Dimensions* 1986: 55

(Here a double pun turns on the two senses of *knock*, 'punch' and 'criticize', and the two senses of *flat*, 'horizontal' and 'apartment'.)

See also DOUBLE ENTENDRE; HOMOPHONE.

punctilious, punctual see METICULOUS

punctuation see APOSTROPHE; COLON; COMMA; DASH; EXCLAMATION MARK; PARENTHESES, BRACKETS; QUESTION MARK; QUOTATION, QUOTATION MARKS; SEMICOLON; SENTENCES, SENTENCE FRAGMENT, RUN-ON SENTENCE.

purebred, thoroughbred, pedigree In North America *purebred* and *thoroughbred* can be used interchangeably for any domestic animal that has been carefully bred through several generations. For horse breeders, however, *thoroughbred* (often capitalized) refers to a specific type of race horse developed in the seventeenth and eighteenth centuries by crossing English mares with Arabian stallions. *Thoroughbred* is sometimes used metaphorically to describe someone who is refined, or 'of good breeding'.

The noun *pedigree* means the recorded line of descent of a purebred animal. The adjective form *pedigreed* describes such an animal. *Genealogy* and *family tree* are more often used of records of human descent, but *pedigree* can also apply to people and, figuratively, to ideas or products.

> ... if she had been fertile her value as a purebred breeding cow would have been ten times the beef price.
> J.E. Smyth et al. *The Law and Business Administration in Canada* 1987: 215

> Standardbreds will often jog or 'brush' (sprint) five or six miles before a race: sturdier than their thoroughbred cousins, they need the distance to loosen up.
> *Saturday Night* July 1986: 32

> Breeders love to rattle off pedigrees—generation after generation after generation.
> *Dogs in Canada* Aug. 1986: 30

> His first act is to stock it with prize cattle and pedigreed sheep.
> *Harrowsmith* Aug.–Sept. 1985: 52

> In Paul Martin, they have a bilingual, high-profile candidate with ... an impeccable Liberal pedigree—and, as a bonus, he's from Quebec.
> *Vancouver Sun* 30 Jan. 1990: A9

purple prose, blue language, yellow journalism In *De arte poetica*, the Roman poet Horace refers to overly flowery passages in a literary work as 'purple patches sewn on to make a fine display in the distance'. The expression *purple prose* thus describes ornate writing in which style is emphasized over substance. It is often confused with *blue language*, a term for profane or sexually explicit writing; in fact, *Random House Webster's College Dictionary* now lists *risqué* as one of the definitions of *purple*.

Yellow journalism is sensational or unscrupulous newspaper writing: it may exploit human suffering to sell copy, or dispense with fairness and objectivity to advance a certain point of view.

> But the temptation to wallow and disport myself in the purple prose of the doting collector is strong, and it will need all my vigilance to resist it.
> Robertson Davies *A Voice from the Attic* 1960: 252

> Otherwise, information takes precedence over fine writing, which is as it should be, especially in a field long beset by purple prose and indifference to hard fact.
> *Globe and Mail* (Toronto) 23 Jan. 1985: SB1

> ... the writer's dirty, purple prose [is] giggled, moaned, bitched and sighed by Ms Burroughs.
> *Performing Arts in Canada* July 1988: 10

(Here *purple* is used to mean *risqué* rather than *ornate*.)

> Evidently, those purple novels—peopled with doe-eyed virgins whose hearts thump thrillingly 'neath straining bodices until both heart and bodice threaten to burst, are going to be somewhat greyer in future.
> *Globe and Mail* (Toronto) 19 Jan. 1985: E22

(Here *purple* is used to mean *risqué* rather than *ornate*.)

The headline, some callers said, inappropriately attached political meaning to a story of personal tragedy and suffering. . . . 'I was offended, I found it totally incredible. The Citizen is isolated on this one. It's yellow journalism.'
Ottawa Citizen 3 Dec. 1994: A2

purposely, purposefully *Purposely* means on purpose, and is the opposite of *accidentally. Purposefully* means with a sense of purpose, with determination to accomplish a goal, and is the opposite of *aimlessly.* To avoid ambiguity and possible criticism, *purposefully* should be reserved for contexts in which the action described is performed with determination, or with a definite goal in mind. Used in this sense, *purposefully* generally follows the verb, while *purposely,* meaning on purpose, usually precedes it. In some contexts either word makes sense.

So she purposely kept news of the grant a secret.
The Beaver Feb.–Mar. 1990: 35

Even then, assuming that no conscientious banker purposely makes a bad loan, there is plenty of room for error.
Queen's Quarterly 94.4 (1987): 954

. . . his prominent jaw thrust ahead of him as both lance and shield, he strides purposefully to a small blue chalkboard.
Ken Dryden *The Game* 1983: 166

During Moure's reading, another local poet sat with his back to her at the bar, chin in hand, purposefully disinterested.
Gazette (Montreal) 10 Dec. 1994: I1

(Here *purposefully* means resolutely.)

Dressed in . . . a silk smoking jacket turned purposefully inside out, his famed mustache a little limper now but still curled up, Dali was seated for the interview in a white-draped armchair.
Globe and Mail (Toronto) 23 March 1985: E6

(Here *purposely* would be better: Dali put the jacket on inside out on purpose.)

I have purposefully omitted the names of the companies, for all were said to have 'good names' in the community. But alas, what's in a name?
Ottawa Citizen 14 Oct. 1994: A12

(Here *purposely* would be better.)

In this collection of blurred and purposefully poorly lighted photos, we have a musty sensation of secrecy and loss.
Province (Vancouver) 24 April 1990: 45

(Here *purposefully* means to achieve a certain effect, but *purposely* would also make sense.)

purposes see INTENTS AND PURPOSES.

pyjamas, pajamas Canadians use both spellings with about equal frequency. British dictionaries list *pyjamas* first, American dictionaries *pajamas.*

The premier, clad only in pyjamas and dress shoes, suffered minor injuries to his hand and knee when he chased a thief outside his Fantasy Gardens home. . . .
Ottawa Citizen 25 July 1990: A5

I used to wear in the winters two pairs of flannel pajamas, a pair of woollen socks, and a red beret.
Richard Davies and Glen Kirkland, eds. *Dimensions* 1986: 117

pyrohy see PEROGY

Pyrrhic A *Pyrrhic victory* is won at too great a cost. The phrase originated when Pyrrhus, king of Epirus, was victorious in a battle against the Romans, but was said to have claimed that another such battle would ruin him. In contemporary use the phrase sometimes denotes a hollow victory. While paying too dearly can make a victory seem empty, sometimes a victory seems hollow only because it was attained too easily; in such cases, the adjective *Pyrrhic* is inappropriate.

The pronunciation is *PEER ik.* Dictionaries capitalize *Pyrrhic,* although many writers do not. Many words derived from proper names, such as *philistine* and *maverick,* lose their capital letters as they are integrated into everyday speech, but *Pyrrhic* appears to be only part of the way along in this process. In formal writing it's probably best to retain the capital *P.*

[The strike] was a Pyrrhic victory for the steelworkers, many of whom aren't being recalled to work.
Gazette (Montreal) 23 Nov. 1990: D1

Instead, the government pressed on, apparently supported by public opinion, and paid a pyrrhic price.
Toronto Star 13 June 1987: B3

Surely it is a pyrrhic victory if the library is unchallenged merely because it is unchallenging.
Globe and Mail (Toronto) 5 Oct. 1985: D19

(This victory was hollow because it was obtained without effort, not because it was won at great cost: *pyrrhic* is inappropriate here.)

Q

q-, qu- English words containing *q* without a *u* immediately following are almost always transliterated from other languages, such as Arabic (the emirate of *Qatar*), Chinese (the *Qing* dynasty), or Inuktitut (*Qikirtrjuak*, formerly known as Broughton Island).

Qantas *Qantas*, the name of the national airline of Australia, is spelled without a *u* after the *Q*. *Qantas* is an acronym derived from 'Queensland and Northern Territories aerial service'.

See also ABBREVIATION.

qu- see Q-

qua *Qua*, meaning 'as', is best restricted to literary, academic, and legal writing, because it is slightly ponderous in tone and most people are not sure what it means. In most contexts *as* will do.

The most common construction with *qua* is one in which the same noun or noun phrase is used before and after *qua*. The meaning of this construction varies. For example, 'Art *qua* art has no dollar value' means 'Art in itself has no dollar value'. 'It is not a matter of efficiency; he is enamoured of routine *qua* routine' means '... routine for the sake of routine'. 'Animals *qua* animals cannot legislate their own safety' means 'Animals being animals ...'. Sometimes *qua* is used merely to provide a rhetorical flourish, as in 'I don't dislike sports *qua* sports—I just think they are a waste of time'. Here, the phrase '*qua* sports' does not refine the meaning of *sports* in any way. In cases like this *qua* should be avoided.

Qua also means in the capacity or role of: 'He was a superb surgeon *qua* technician, but his dealings with the unanaesthetized left something to be desired'; 'Is the university overvaluing the professor *qua* researcher and undervaluing the professor *qua* teacher?' In this construction different nouns are used before and after *qua*, the second naming one aspect of the first. Some critics consider this the only usage of *qua* that is appropriate. However, neither common practice nor dictionaries support this restriction of the meaning.

> The novelist *qua* novelist, as opposed to the utopian romancer, takes what is there as a point of departure.
> Margaret Atwood *Second Words* 1982: 428

> The one kind of criticism that the poet himself, *qua* poet, engages in—the technical self-criticism which leads to revision and improvement—is a criticism with which the reviewer has nothing to do.
> Northrop Frye *The Bush Garden* 1971: 124

> ... the complainant ... was seeking relief qua bidder, not qua shareholder.
> *Canadian Bar Review* 66.3 (1987): 633

See also LATIN PHRASES.

Quaker The formal name of the religious group commonly known as Quakers is 'The Society of Friends'. Members of the faith refer to one another as 'Friends'. But *Quaker* is an acceptable term for most references to the religion or one of its adherents. The name *Quaker* may allude to an admonition of the group's founder, George Fox, that they should 'tremble at the word of the Lord'.

> ... the Empress Alexandra of Russia, prompted both by Tolstoy's importunings and by those of the Society of Friends of England, had persuaded the Czar that the Doukhobors might leave Russia....
> Pierre Berton *The Promised Land* 1984: 69

> She was raised a Quaker, and Quakers, from what he'd seen of them, were smilers rather than laughers.
> Margaret Atwood *Life Before Man* 1979: 116–17

quality Many commentators criticize the use of *quality* as an adjective meaning 'of high quality' ('a quality product'), but all the major dictionaries list this meaning without remark. Note, however, that the adjective *quality* has become clichéd in combination with certain nouns ('quality education', 'quality time'), and that *quality* as an adjective usually appears in fairly informal writing. In formal writing *quality* is more likely to be used as a neutral term requiring a modifier: 'high-quality product', 'work of poor quality'.

> ... they simply cannot keep giving quality education without more money.
> *United Church Observer* June 1986: 33

> ... they have found that the consumer is definitely interested in new flavours and quality products.
> *Western Grocer* May–Jun. 1990: 48

See also FUNCTIONAL SHIFT.

quandary *Quandary* is occasionally misspelled *quandry*, probably because it is often pronounced with only two syllables, like *laundry*. Dictionaries list the pronunciation with an optional middle syllable: *KWON d(uh) ree*.

> This approach to Canada's ... constitutional quandary was initiated by the Chambre in the wake of last summer's scuttling of the Meech Lake Accord.
> *Gazette* (Montreal) 29 Sept. 1990: D2

(The correct spelling is *quandary*.)

quantum, quantum leap Some usage commentators object to the use of *quantum* to mean 'large', pointing out that its Latin meaning is simply 'amount'. They also note that the expression *quantum leap* as it is commonly used distorts the meaning of this term in physics.

In physics a *quantum* is the minimum amount of energy capable of existing independently, and a *quantum leap* (the abrupt transition of an electron between one energy level and another), though an extremely significant event, is one of subatomic—infinitesimally small—proportions. Thus some commentators will allow *quantum* to be used in figurative contexts where it means 'significant', but draw the line at its use to mean 'giant'. Nevertheless, despite the inaccuracy, most major dictionaries now list 'large' as a meaning of *quantum*. It's best to avoid this sense when writing for physicists.

> In 1984 ... the national debt had just taken a quantum leap, courtesy of the deep recession of 1980-81.
> *Vancouver Sun* 30 Jan. 1990: A9

> Since that time there has been a quantum acceleration of forest management in the form of planting, tending, nursery capacity. ...
> *Queen's Quarterly* 94.3 (1987): 610-11

quash, squash *Quash* has a special legal sense: to nullify, revoke, or set aside a decision, licence, action, etc. Either *quash* or *squash* can be used to mean suppress or quell.

> Last month a Federal Court of Canada judge said he would quash the project's federal licence if Bouchard did not set up an independent review by the end of January.
> *Gazette* (Montreal) 27 Jan. 1990: A14

> Canada's premiers, who constitutionally have enough power over trade to squash or seal the deal, recognize that fact.
> *Ottawa Citizen* 14 June 1986: H1

(Here *squash* might be defended because it alliterates with 'seal'; however, given the context of formal negotiations, *quash* is recommended.)

> When Torvill and Dean moved on after the 1984 Winter Olympics, the order came from the International Skating Union that ... the precise laws of ice dancing would be enforced strongly and all show business routines would be squashed.
> *Today's Skater* 1991: 26

(Here, given the context of laws and regulations, *quashed* might be better.)

> Popular music routinely finds ways to quash the oddballs, eccentrics and outlaws who provide its flavor.
> *Gazette* (Montreal) 6 June 1990: B4

(Here *squash* would also be possible.)

> 'The membership is a lot more militant than the leadership at this point and the leadership tries to squash the militancy.'
> *Ottawa Citizen* 28 Sept. 1988: A11

(Here *quash* would also be possible.)

> But Martin notes that his father stuck with Pearson, trying to squash attempts to challenge Pearson's leadership during the five years in Opposition.
> *Vancouver Sun* 24 March 1990: A10

(Here *quash* would also be possible.)

quasi Borrowed from the Latin meaning 'as if', *quasi* is used as a prefix before nouns, adjectives, or adverbs to suggest a substitute for the real thing. When used before a noun, *quasi* can mean part-, near- or pseudo-. When it qualifies an adjective or adverb, it can convey a range of meanings, such as nearly, partly, sort of, somewhat, or virtually. Although context usually makes the meaning clear, the tone of *quasi* can be difficult to discern: in some cases it is neutral and in others it is pejorative.

Compounds formed with *quasi* are usually hyphenated. *Quasi* is pronounced to rhyme with *Ozzie* or *day's eye*.

Historians of the *longue durée*, he holds, seem to find themselves compelled to delineate quasi-events, structured by quasi-plots, which recount the fortunes of quasi-agents.
Queen's Quarterly 92.2 (1985): 414

The cast of characters usually includes quasi-historical figures (King Arthur, for instance), along with supernatural beings.
Performing Arts in Canada March 1988: 14

What I wanted to hear was ... a symphony of tolling bells, at times quasi-human in character, speaking of jubilation and also of tears.
Queen's Quarterly 92.1 (1985): 102

quay, key, cay *Quay*, *key*, and *cay* are all usually pronounced *KEE*. A *quay* is a landing platform or wharf. *Key* and *cay* are both terms for a small low island or emergent reef. All three words are derived from the French word *quai*, meaning 'wharf'.

The quay was already empty of passengers from Sweden.
David Williams *Eye of the Father* 1985: 24

The Florida Keys is actually a collection of dozens of small coral islands that separate the Atlantic from the Gulf of Mexico.
Gazette (Montreal) 24 Nov. 1990: 16

The two most isolated islands ... are Long Cay and North East Cay, off Belize.
Vancouver Sun 10 Nov. 1990: E3

Quebec, Québec Most English-speaking Canadians say *kwuh BECK* or *kuh BECK*; *KWEE beck* is dialectal. The French pronunciation *KAY BECK* is rare outside Quebec. Although the English spelling conventionally omits the accent, writers sometimes include it, especially if they are discussing French-language issues.

See also APPENDIX I; QUEBEC ENGLISH; QUE-BECKER, QUEBECER.

Quebec English Anglophones in Quebec—that is, those who speak English as a first language—are concentrated in Montreal, and since the mid-1970s they have been increasingly exposed to the influence of French, especially in the workplace. Francophone Quebeckers are also increasingly exposed to English, both at work (especially in the service industry or the federal government) and

through the media. With increasing contact between the two languages, more and more French words—particularly those connected to provincial institutions, linguistic politics, and local life—have been assimilated into English, resulting in a new Canadian regional dialect: Quebec English.

Some words borrowed from Quebec French, such as *anglophone*, are now used across Canada, while others are restricted to Quebec: for example, *allophone* (someone whose first language is neither English nor French), *dépanneur* (corner store), and *caisse populaire* (credit union). Most of these borrowings, although they may not appear in any English dictionary, cause no more difficulty than any other word that is localized in a particular region or province. However, there are some 'look-alike' words in the two languages that do cause usage problems because they have different connotations, different levels of formality, or different meanings. The examples given below all come from the *Gazette*, Montreal's daily English-language newspaper.

Ameliorate is a rather formal word in world English, but in Quebec English it is used as a general synonym for *improve*.

Animator is restricted to film cartoonists in English, but in French an *animateur* is someone who organizes a workshop, conference, or similar event; *animator* has taken on the French sense in Quebec English.

Conference exists in both English and French, but in English it means a meeting of a group of people to discuss common interests, usually political, professional, or academic, whereas in French a *conférence* is a lecture. A Quebec English-speaker might cause confusion by saying 'I'm giving a conference at a congress', instead of 'I'm giving a paper at a conference'.

Determinant is perfectly acceptable in English as a noun meaning 'determining factor'. However, in Quebec English is it occasionally used as if it were an adjective meaning determining or decisive:

For those Quebecers trying to define a country, Gravel said, it was vital to involve allophones who could have a determinant effect on their plans.

Global is ordinarily used in English to mean worldwide, international, or multinational, in phrases like 'global trade', 'global environment', and 'global village'. In French *global* more often occurs in phrases where it means comprehensive, overall, or far-reaching. In Quebec English, then, one finds it used in contexts such as this:

I have no mandate to take positions on what is a global debate for all Quebecers.

Population, which Canadian English-speakers usually reserve for demographic contexts, is often used in Quebec English where English-speakers would use the noun *public*:

They are admitting to the population that the supply of nursing care can no longer meet the demand for it.

Primordial in Canadian English means originating in the distant past, but often appears in Quebec English in its French sense of essential or fundamental:

Mind you, the quality and the freshness of the fish are primordial.

Professor, used only of university faculty outside Quebec, is frequently applied to secondary school or community college teachers in Quebec English, because the French term *professeur* is used of these teachers as well as of university faculty.

Security, for Canadian English-speakers, refers to protection from intruders, vandals, crowds, etc., while in French *sécurité* includes protection from a far wider range of hazards (for which English-speakers use the word *safety*). The wider sense of the French word has affected the use of *security* in Quebec English:

The left-turn ban was part of a plan between Roxboro, Canadian National and Transport Canada to improve security at the rail crossing.

Verify in English means to check, but is usually applied only to checking such things as references, documents, facts, or words. In Quebec English, again because of the wider application of the verb *vérifier* in Quebec French, people sometimes talk about verifying the brakes on the car.

These are just a few examples of the shifts that are occurring in English in Quebec. These usages may in time become standard within the region. At the moment, however, they exist in an uneasy territory between English and French, and may well cause difficulty for audiences outside Quebec.

Quebecker, Quebecer, Québécois(e), Franco-, French Canadian Neither *Quebecker* nor *Quebecer* is clearly preferred; either is acceptable. *Quebecer* predominates in English-Canadian newspapers, probably because it is recommended by the *Canadian Press Stylebook*. *Quebecker* is preferred by the authors of *Editing Canadian English*. Some people think *Quebecer* looks odd because most English words that end in *c* add *k* before a suffix (as in *trafficker*, or *panicked*).

The French words *Québécois* and *Québécoise* (feminine) are also frequently used in English, but generally only to refer to the French-speaking residents of Quebec. Since English keyboards and word processing programs do not always offer French accents, it's futile to insist on their use. However, if you can produce them, note that *Québécois(e)* requires either two accents or none. Often anglophone writers omit the second accent in *Québécois*, probably because *Québec* has only one accent and because in English *Québécois* is usually pronounced *KAY beck wah*, not *KAY BAY kwah*. Sometimes English writers use *Québécois*, without a final *e*, to refer to a woman; in French this *e* would be required. While it is common for words assimilated into English to lose their inflections as well as their accents, in this case it's worth making the effort to retain them.

Approximately 1.2 million francophone Canadians live outside Quebec: they are known as *Franco-Ontarians*, *Franco-Manitobans*, *Fransaskois* (singular and plural; French-speaking residents of Saskatchewan), *Franco-Albertans*, and *Franco-Columbians* (sometimes spelled as in French, *Franco-Colombiens*). Francophones living in the Atlantic provinces are generally called *Acadians*. *Franco-Americans* are francophone citizens of the United States, most of whom are of Canadian descent.

Francophone Canadians inside and outside Quebec have traditionally been referred to as *French Canadians* (the adjective form is hyphenated: 'French-Canadian writers'.) While some francophones value this designation, others reject it, either because they identify themselves only as Québécois or because the label *French Canadian* implies that anglophone Canadians are the norm. Since both English and French are official languages of Canada, *French Canadian* and *English Canadian* should be used in a parallel fashion.

... Quebecers can hardly deny that the New Brunswick Acadians (40% of the province) and Franco-Ontarians are chiefly distinctive because of their language and culture, a heritage they share with their Quebec cousins. *Financial Post* 13 Sept. 1991: 11

In Wasyk's ... movie, two junkies who are also lovers— a blond anglophone man named Snake and a darkly beautiful Quebecoise named Michele—are locked in an underground apartment in a final attempt to drop their heroin habit.
Ottawa Citizen 17 Sept. 1990: C9

(English-language newspapers don't normally use accents; in a magazine or book, this would be *Québecoise*.)

Chloe Gilbert, a Quebecois who has been in B.C. since 1981, married a unilingual anglophone and is now the mother of two children.
Vancouver Sun 17 Feb. 1990: A8

(Here French would require *Québecoise*.)

Lavoie, a Franco-Manitoban, has chosen to build his career in Montreal as has Roch Voisine, the New Brunswick Acadian who was the big winner at this year's awards gala.
Financial Post 20 Oct. 1989: 12

It is distressing to see Saskatchewan shirking its clear constitutional duty by dropping the school reform plan it had worked out so carefully with the Fransaskois.
Gazette (Montreal) 25 April 1990: B2

Marie Bourgeois, president of the Federation of Franco-Columbians, said ... the vote 'was akin to thumbing your nose at what Canada stands for.'
Vancouver Sun 28 Oct. 1989: A1

See also ACADIA; FRANCOPHONE, ANGLOPHONE, ALLOPHONE.

question see LEADING QUESTION, LOADED QUESTION; RHETORICAL QUESTION

question mark Question marks are placed at the end of direct questions:

Is there any way to fix this?

How did it end?

Direct questions include tag questions, which are separated from the main sentence by a comma, and questions in declarative word order:

Sue already did that, didn't she?

You're not putting that on your credit card?

A period, not a question mark, is used at the end of an indirect question:

He asked if there was any way to fix this.

They wondered if she'd already done that.

Polite requests for action are often framed as questions, and some commentators state that they do not need question marks:

Will you turn off that light, please.

Can I squeeze in here.

However, it is unlikely that anyone will complain if you follow such requests with a question mark. In letters concerning employment, or official letters of invitation or inquiry, a request phrased as a question should be punctuated with a question mark to indicate that compliance is not being taken for granted:

Could you please respond to our proposal as soon as possible?

When a direct question is an element within a sentence, it is followed by a question mark:

Why me? is a typical first response.

The question on all our minds was why did we wait?

For some people Who can I blame? is a mantra.

When the question element begins in the middle of the sentence, you may capitalize the first word if that makes the sentence more readable.

When one sentence conflates a series of separate questions, use a series of question marks:

Have you ever had rubella? red measles? mumps? chicken pox?

Use only one question mark if a question is not complete till the end of a series:

Do you prefer milk, cream, or an edible oil product in your coffee?

A question mark goes inside the quotation marks if the quotation is a question and outside them if the main sentence is a question. If both are questions, only one question mark, inside the quotation marks, is needed:

We asked, 'Can we come?'

Did she really say, 'Ask Nana, my cat'?

Do they routinely say, 'And how will you be paying?'

Notice that there is no period after the question marks above, and that no comma follows the question mark in sentences like the following:

'Shall we dance?' he whispered.

A question mark in parentheses (?) indicates uncertainty about the accuracy of a date or fact, or about whether something should be included in a final draft. A question mark in parentheses may also be shorthand for incredulity–a graphic sign of disbelief in, or shock at, the information being passed along. This use of the question mark should be reserved for letters to friends or other semi-private writing. For a wider audience, which cannot be depended upon to share the writer's assumptions, some explanation is required.

questionnaire *Questionnaire* is sometimes misspelled with only one *n*. The term was borrowed from French around the turn of the century, and is pronounced *KWES chu NAIR* or, less commonly, *KES chu NAIR*.

> Ideally questionnaire studies ... should be paired with descriptive studies to see to what extent those answering the questionnaire actually reveal the same preferences in their practice.
> W.C. Lougheed, ed. *In Search of the Standard in Canadian English* 1986: 32

> Ministry spokesman David Baker said yesterday stress questionaires were being circulated to all staff.
> *Province* (Vancouver) 12 Sept. 1990: 15

(The correct spelling is *questionnaires*.)

quick, quickly *Quick* can be used as both an adjective ('They made a quick decision') and an adverb ('Come quick'). However, *quick* is rarely used as an adverb in formal writing; it most commonly appears in reported or fictional speech, or in fixed expressions such as 'get rich quick'. Most usage guides, while acknowledging the legitimacy of *quick* as an adverb, are quick to note that writers prefer *quickly*. Certainly this is the case in Canadian English.

> 'Mommy, come quick,' Sarah screams again....
> Ken Dryden *The Game* 1983: 17

> ... the idea has taken off in Montreal and the promoter expects it to catch on quickly in the Quebec City region too.
> *Chronicle-Telegraph* (Quebec) 3 April 1991: 2

> He knew he must act quickly.
> Pierre Berton *The Promised Land* 1984: 72

See also SLOW, SLOWLY; ZERO ADVERBS.

quid pro quo *Quid pro quo* is a Latin expression meaning 'this in return for that'. A *quid pro quo* may be an exchange, a trade-off, a covert deal, or, less commonly, an act of retaliation.

> ... when the government imposed capital gains taxation, it removed the tax on inherited wealth in Canada as a quid pro quo for the wealthy.
> *Globe and Mail* (Toronto) 30 May 1985: P5

> Canadian officials have strongly denied recent reports that Reagan wants any sort of quid pro quo on defence spending by Canada ... for his announcement on acid rain.
> *Toronto Star* 28 March 1987: B1

See also LATIN PHRASES.

quiet, quieten *Quiet* and *quieten* are both accepted as verbs meaning to make quiet or to become quiet. Either may be followed by *down*.

> The talk has localized and quieted.
> Ken Dryden *The Game* 1983: 166

> Things quietened down near midnight and I decided to go back to the office.
> *Gazette* (Montreal) 17 Jan. 1990: A4

> What followed was his standard-issue speech, warning that the deficit must be cut to quieten the fires of inflation, to calm international markets and to improve the financial legacy left to future generations.
> *Ottawa Citizen* 2 March 1990: A4

quip Usage commentators discourage the use of the verb *quip* on the grounds that it is unnecessary: a remark witty enough to qualify as a quip should not have to be identified, and a trite or dull remark cannot be made humorous with a label. However, *quip* often serves an important function by letting the reader know that a quotation that could be taken seriously was delivered facetiously.

> 'Before I had a child, I had no identity,' quipped Copps, who also pointed out that sexism in the media isn't the sole preserve of men.
> *Province* (Vancouver) 25 Nov. 1990: 36

(Here *quipped* identifies the ironic tone of the remark.)

> 'He's my new idol,' Hayward quipped.
> *Gazette* (Montreal) 2 Oct. 1990: F5

(Here again *quipped* conveys the ironic tone of the remark.)

quisling   see COLLABORATION

quit *Quit* is not only the present tense but also the past tense and past participle; *quitted* is also correct for the past tense and past participle, but it is extremely rare.

The basic meaning of the verb *quit* in contemporary Canadian English is to stop in a progression through time. The significance of that action varies, and thus *quit* has a range of synonyms, including *cease* ('Have you quit smoking?'), *desist* ('Quit complaining!'), *break off* ('We quit because we were getting nowhere'), *give up* ('Don't quit now!'), and *withdraw from* ('She quit Girl Guides and band'). One can stop and start an activity without giving the matter any thought, but *quit* implies that a conscious decision was made.

Older senses of *quit* have been preserved only in literary writing. These include leave ('They quit London'); be rid of ('We'll be quit of them soon'); and let go of or give up ('She knew she could never quit her creature comforts').

> I realized that I'd better quit studying fast or I might ruin myself with too much education.
> Max Braithwaite *The Night We Stole the Mountie's Car* 1971: 49

> Her name was Maureen and she made me quit hockey for my teeth.
> *Canadian Fiction Magazine* 64 (1988): 39

> ... they quit their jobs to move when their husbands, with a primary commitment to their own careers, are relocated.
> Carl J. Cuneo *Pay Equity* 1990: 140

> Yet tens of thousands of sturdy men, women, and children, who quit their tiny Carpathian farms to make a new life in a world of strangers, endured it all....
> Pierre Berton *The Promised Land* 1984: 49

> So I told him ... that he was making an ass of himself, that he was well quit of Gates Ajar Honeypot, and that he must positively stop trying to be Charles Dickens.
> Robertson Davies *One Half of Robertson Davies* 1978: 112

> She refuses to quit the conjugal apartment ... because, as she says, 'I live here.'
> Janice Kulyk Keefer *Reading Mavis Gallant* 1989: 144

quite *Quite* has two meanings: entirely, as in 'quite dead', and to an extent, as in 'quite funny'. The first meaning dates from the fourteenth century, the second from the nineteenth. Many usage commentators have remarked on the potential ambiguity of *quite*, and many have labelled the more recent meaning informal. However, *quite* troubles language commentators far more than it does language users.

The possibility for ambiguity is certainly present in Britain. In British English 'I was quite happy' may mean either 'I was utterly happy' or 'I was fairly happy'. 'This tea is quite cold' may mean 'This tea is stone cold', or simply 'This tea is rather cold'. Stress and intonation differentiate these meanings in British speech, and context may do the same in writing.

In contemporary Canadian English these sentences would rarely be ambiguous: only the second interpretations are likely. In Canadian English there are only two contexts in which *quite* is taken to mean entirely, exactly, or absolutely. The first is after *not*: 'I'm not quite ready'; 'That isn't quite full'. The second is before 'all-or-nothing' adjectives or adverbs (words that *fairly* could not modify): 'quite dead', 'quite alone', 'quite unsolicited', 'quite genuine'. In any other context *quite* means to a certain extent. The meaning fairly or moderately, as in 'quite good' or 'quite quickly', shades into the meaning noticeably or significantly, as in 'His ears turned quite red'; 'It's quite far away'; 'We waited quite some time'. The 'to an extent' meaning of *quite* is certainly not restricted to informal writing in Canadian English and need not be avoided.

The idiom *quite a*, as in 'quite a nice place' or 'quite a light colour', is conversational in tone and acceptable in most contexts. However, in very formal writing the order of the two words should be reversed: 'a quite light colour'. When *quite a* precedes a bare noun (without an adjective), it is sometimes appropriate to formal writing and sometimes not. When it means notable or considerable, as in 'quite a contrast' or 'quite a reduction', it is staid enough for formal writing. When it means 'an impressive specimen of a', as in 'quite a man', it is slang.

> For what we witness ... is the laceration of young lives: wounds severe enough to maim, if not quite kill.
> Janice Kulyk Keefer *Reading Mavis Gallant* 1989: 90

> Although difficult to define, post-modernism exhibits one quite unmistakable trait: it revises and disputes agreed-upon notions of progress and modernity....
> *The Canadian Geographer* Spring 1989: 70

> Much to his astonishment, he found it quite interesting.
> Irving M. Zeitlin and Robert J. Brym *The Social Condition of Humanity* 1991: 236

> Tattoos are quite popular on the men....
> *Maclean's* 16 Dec. 1991: A72

I find the music of composers of French background ... to be frequently quite dense in texture compared to that of their Anglo-Canadian colleagues.
Queen's Quarterly 94.1 (1987): 185

I make no pretense to owning an impressive collection, but I have quite an assembly of folios, quartos, octavos, and duodecimos....
Robertson Davies *A Voice from the Attic* 1960: 161

'The night Cissy took a snootful? That was quite a night.'
Howard Engel *Murder Sees the Light* 1984: 210

(Here *quite a* is slang.)

Quixote, quixotic *Don Quixote,* the name of the hero of Cervantes' satiric novel, is usually pronounced *DON kee HO tee.* The adjective *quixotic,* meaning romantically idealistic or foolishly impractical, is pronounced *kwik ZOT ic.*

quiz To *quiz* someone is to ask him or her a lot of questions, usually in a teasing manner or simply to satisfy one's own curiosity. A *quiz* may be a short test at school, a not-so-serious self-directed test in a magazine, or a series of questions on a television game show. Some usage guides contend that *quiz* should be used only in popular writing. In fact, although *quiz* often describes an informal activity, the word itself is not slang or even informal, and is appropriate for any level of writing.

Also disputed is whether *quiz* (noun or verb) should be used for highly formal interrogations and inquiries, such as those conducted by police and government committees. This usage is rare except in newspaper writing, where the brevity of *quiz* appeals to those writing headlines. In formal writing, words with more serious connotations, such as *interrogate* and *investigate,* are preferable.

The *z* is doubled in the plural of the noun (*quizzes*) and in the verb forms (*quizzes, quizzed, quizzing*).

Mistaken by everyone for a nurse ... I quizzed and eavesdropped my way through the evening.
Margaret Atwood *Second Words* 1982: 88

Sunday afternoons were given over to a record review programme ... that was made 'entertaining' by quizzes, contests and spoofs by Alan MacFee.
Queen's Quarterly 92.1 (1985): 25

COUPLE QUIZZED IN ATTACK ON SHIP: A French-speaking couple has been detained for questioning in connection with last week's bombing of the Greenpeace flagship Rainbow Warrior....
Globe and Mail (Toronto): 16 July 1985: P1

(Here *quizzed* replaces the more appropriate verb *questioned* in a headline.)

The opposition also quizzed Miss Fish about high lead levels in the blood of children in east-end Toronto....
Globe and Mail (Toronto): 8 June 1985: P11

(Here *questioned* or *interrogated* would convey the seriousness of the investigation more clearly than *quizzed.*)

quotation, quotation marks British publishers use single quotation marks (' ') for a first quotation and double quotation marks (" ") for a quotation within a quotation. American publishers prefer double quotation marks first, and single within. Both styles are used in Canada and either is correct—though switching back and forth is not. This book uses single quotation marks first:

'Did you memorize "In Flanders Fields" in school?'

punctuating quotations of speech Quotation marks are placed around a direct quotation, but not around indirect speech (a report of what someone said):

She said, 'I'll see you there.'

She said she would see us there.

The clause that identifies a speaker is set off from a quotation by commas:

'I don't know what I think,' he said, 'until I start to write.'

A quoted sentence that is integrated into another sentence and is not reported speech is not set off by commas:

'Live free' is very appealing, but I don't like 'Live free or die' quite as much.

A sentence break can be contained within a pair of quotation marks:

'I'll get it. You got it last time,' she said.

Question marks and exclamation marks are placed inside the quotation marks if they belong to the quotation and outside if they belong to the main sentence:

She said, 'What can I do?'

They actually used the word 'antiquated'!

He said, 'That's ridiculous!'

If the quotation and the main sentence are both questions, only one question mark is needed, inside the quotation marks:

Did you hear Larry say, 'Don't you hate that kind of thing?'

Note that a question or exclamation mark at the end of a quotation replaces the usual comma or period:

'Oh, no!' he said.

Colons and semicolons are always placed outside quotation marks:

He is always disparaging 'the junk they sell today'; meanwhile, he buys every new gadget that comes on the market.

Most Canadian publishers follow the American convention of putting all periods and commas inside closing quotation marks. This book follows the British style: periods and commas are placed outside closing quotation marks unless the punctuation is part of the passage being quoted.

He was a 'remittance man', which means he was being paid to stay away from home.

The comma after *visit* in the example below is placed inside the closing quotation mark because it takes the place of an understood period.

'My brother is coming for a visit,' she said.

punctuating quotations from written sources A quotation of prose longer than four lines is usually indented in a block rather than enclosed in quotation marks:

> Indent the whole passage five spaces from the normal left margin; the right margin does not have to be changed. Block quotations do not begin with a further indentation, even if you are quoting the beginning of a paragraph. However, if the quotation has a paragraph break *within* it, begin this paragraph on a new line and indent it five spaces from the margin of the block quotation. In a book, the block containing the quotation is often set in reduced type.

Newspapers and magazines set in columns cannot mark long quotations of speech or writing by indenting. Instead, the beginning of each paragraph in a long quotation is marked with opening quotation marks. The quotation marks are closed only at the end of the final quoted paragraph.

One or two lines of poetry may be quoted within a text in quotation marks (line breaks should be indicated by a slash), but more than two lines of poetry are set off from the text in an indented block that preserves the original format of the poem.

The spelling and punctuation of the original should be retained in a quotation. If there is an error in what you are quoting and you want to signal to your reader that you are merely reproducing what was in the original, insert *sic* (a Latin word meaning 'thus'; usually italicized) right after the error, in square brackets:

'Toronto, the capital of Canada [sic], is located on the shore of Lake Ontario.'

'We have asked for full cooperation from the medias [sic].'

If you are forced to change a verb tense or pronoun in a quotation so that it will fit into your sentence, enclose what you have changed in square brackets. For example:

In *Apartment Seven* (1989: 32) Waddington describes F.R. Scott as 'shin[ing] with an icy composure that always made [her] feel like a pre-World War I Russian immigrant fresh off the boat'.

An omission of words within a quotation should be marked with ellipsis points (. . .), although what is obviously only a fragment of a sentence may be quoted without them. In formal writing three ellipsis points are used to indicate an omission within a sentence and four to indicate an omission between sentences. The first of the four is considered to be the sentence period, so it does not need a space in front of it. It and the following three points each have one space between them. The ellipsis points between sentences can indicate that you have dropped the end of the first sentence or the beginning of the next (or both), or that you have omitted one or more sentences between these sentences. Commas, dashes, semicolons, and colons before or after ellipsis points may be dropped or preserved, depending on whether they clarify the structure of the altered sentence. Here are two versions of the same text—the first complete, the second compressed—illustrating various uses of ellipsis points:

> The pages of Mayhew are a huge peepshow of Victorian London as it really was, and not as the novelists of the day were compelled by convention to represent it. It is not too much to say that the general reader who delights in Dickens, Thackeray, Surtees, Trollope, Cockton, Lever—yes, and perhaps also George Eliot—cannot squeeze the fullest flavour from his favorites unless he has some knowledge of Mayhew. He primes the pump of

our imagination. To him, therefore, our homage and our thanks. He was not a novelist, but a sociological journalist. Yet after a perusal of his masterly pages, we come to the novelists who were his contemporaries fresher, better informed, and capable of a deeper understanding, a richer enjoyment.

Robertson Davies *A Voice from the Attic* 1960: 127

Here is the compressed version:

The pages of Mayhew are a huge peepshow of Victorian London as it really was, and not as the novelists of the day were compelled by convention to represent it.... The general reader who delights in Dickens, Thackeray, Surtees, Trollope ... cannot squeeze the fullest flavor from his favorites unless he [sic] has some knowledge of Mayhew.... He was not a novelist, but a sociological journalist. Yet after a perusal of his masterly pages, we come to the novelists who were his contemporaries ... capable of a deeper understanding....

Notice that after the first ellipsis, where the beginning of a sentence has been dropped, the first letter of the resulting sentence has been capitalized. In scholarly or legal writing, where even such a slight alteration might be considered important to the interpretation of the text, this capital letter would be enclosed in square brackets.

The *sic* in the compressed version of the passage above is optional: a contemporary writer might insert it to indicate that conventions of gender-neutral language used today might support the use of *he or she* here, rather than *he* alone, to stand for the general reader.

When a quoted sentence ends with an ellipsis and then is followed by a page number or other reference in parentheses, the sentence period migrates to follow the last parenthesis: 'Yet after a perusal of his masterly pages, we come to the novelists ... capable of a deeper understanding...' (127).

In academic writing, the sources of all quotations are documented (i.e., recorded) either in parentheses in the body of the text or in footnotes or endnotes. Documentation allows the reader to verify or follow up on any material quoted. For the proper format of documentation, consult a style guide currently in use in your field.

quotation marks for titles Quotation marks are conventionally placed around the titles of chapters, articles, essays, short poems, songs, episodes in television series, or anything else that is part of a larger work. The titles of self-contained works, such as books, newspapers, magazines, journals, compact discs, movies, and television programs, are italicized (or underlined). The title of a work that has never been published, such as a lecture or dissertation, is usually put in quotation marks. For a more thorough discussion of these conventions, see ITALICS AND QUOTATION MARKS.

referring to words Either quotation marks or italics are used to indicate words that are being referred to as words:

'Cygnet' and 'signet' are pronounced the same way.

Quoth is an archaism.

A translation of an italicized foreign word usually appears in quotation marks:

The name derives from Latin *rufus*, 'redheaded'.

Quotation marks around a word may signal that it is likely to be unfamiliar to the reader:

Mark Jones is a 'Pakeha', a Maori word used widely in New Zealand for non-Maoris.

Once the word has been explained, the quotation marks should be dropped.

Indicating irony Quotation marks may also signal irony—a quarrel with a word that others use straightforwardly:

My 'rehabilitation' consisted of being beaten up and tutored in crime.

Unless the irony is very obvious, this shorthand method of signalling dissatisfaction with a word may simply confuse the reader.

Fowler, in his 'Superiority' article, chastises writers who are eager to use vogue words or slang phrases but at the same time put them in quotation marks to signal disdain of such expressions. He recommends that they have the courage of their convictions and either use an expression straight or avoid it altogether.

See also QUOTE, QUOTATION.

quote, quotation   According to many usage commentators, *quote* is only a verb. It should not be used as a short form for the noun *quotation* ('quotable quotes'); nor should *quotes* be used as a short form for *quotation marks* ('Should this sentence be in quotes?'). This advice is often ignored.

The noun *quote* is fairly common in published academic writing, and in journalism and business writing the noun *quote* is used far more frequently than *quotation*. *Quotes* appears in the discussion of single and double quotation marks in some very conservative style guides. In short, the nouns *quote* and *quotes* are too common in writing at every level to be considered incorrect, though it is true that *quotation* and *quotation marks* are preferred in formal and academic writing.

... all translated quotations from both previously translated and untranslated texts are my own.
Ben-Z. Shek *French-Canadian & Québécois Novels* 1991: vii

Any archivist or historiographer ... will be disturbed further by the mistakes that appear in quotations from the archival record.
Arctic 41.1 (1988): 76

The word 'sovereign', in this quote from 1969, has a very contemporary ring in 1990....
Ben-Z. Shek *French-Canadian & Québécois Novels* 1991: 62

To appreciate the centrality of language in the production of meaning and of self (and incidentally to make sense of the language postmodernists typically employ, as in this Kristeva quote) it is useful to recall the traditions upon which postmodernism has been built.
Queen's Quarterly 97.3 (1990): 405

Malcolm's work is now the subject of a libel action by Masson, who claims that some quotes ascribed to him were fabricated.
Maclean's 24 Feb. 1986: 8-9

'Socialism'—my quotes this time—turned out to be alien and uncivilized in Russia.
Vancouver Sun 17 Feb. 1990: A4

See also QUOTATION, QUOTATION MARKS.

quoth   *Quoth* is an archaism. When it appears in contemporary prose it is invariably facetious, signalling a mock elevation of style. Several commentators think *quoth* is never funny, but of course this is a matter of taste.

Quoth means 'said' and is used to identify the speaker of a direct quotation. It is the past tense form of the verb *quethe*, 'to say', which (unlike its derivative *bequeath*) did not survive to become a regular verb in contemporary English. *Quoth* takes a first- or third-person subject (never *you*), and the subject always follows the verb: 'quoth he', not 'he quoth'. Note that *quoth* does not end in *e*.

Check out the projected $420 million 1976 Montreal Olympics, which, quoth mayor Jean Drapeau, 'could no more lose money than man could have a baby.'
Province (Vancouver) 17 May 1990: 85

See also ARCHAISMS.

Qur'an   see ISLAM

q.v.   The Latin abbreviation *q.v.* stands for *quod vide*, 'which see', and alerts the reader to a reference or cross-reference. Though *q.v.* (plural *qq.v.*) is common in older works, more recent reference publications tend to use either the English word *see* or a special typeface to direct the reader to related items.

See also LATIN PHRASES.

R

race   *Race* is a term weighed down by the history of European imperialism and the pseudo-scientific hierarchization of people of different skin colours that was used to rationalize it. *Race* is unquestionably an imprecise concept, and arguably an irrelevant one. At the same time, the political ramifications of visible differences among people are so real that discussions of the concept of *race* cannot be avoided. The African-American literary theorist Henry Louis Gates Jr. has suggested putting the word *race* in quotation marks to remind readers that the whole concept of racial categorization is

questionable. Some newspaper style guides now recommend avoiding racial categories wherever possible and using country of origin, when necessary, to indicate a person's background.

See also BLACK; CAPITAL LETTERS; INDIAN; -ISM; VISIBLE MINORITY.

rack, wrack   A *rack* is a type of framework. One notorious rack was an instrument of torture; as a result, *rack* has connotations of extreme suffering, as in the expressions 'nerve-racking' and 'racked with pain'. *Wrack* is related to wreckage, and now is most often found in the expression 'wrack and ruin', which suggests a state of utter destruction. *Rack* and *wrack* are confused so frequently that most dictionaries now list both spellings for the verb meaning torment and the noun meaning destruction.

… breeders rack their brains to come up with suitable, original, memorable names for each pup.
Dogs in Canada Aug. 1986: 8

Yes, Flora sold the place, and these new people picked it up real reasonable. Old Wayne'd let it go to wrack and ruin.
Howard Engel *Murder Sees the Light* 1984: 192

The short story which he was writing wracked him with tension.
Canadian Fiction Magazine 63 (1988): 66

(The traditional spelling of the verb meaning torment is *rack*.)

The luxury of studying such abundant wildlife has its own problems. For example, getting the information without disrupting your subjects can be nerve-wracking.
Beautiful British Columbia Spring 1990: 37

(The traditional spelling is *nerve-racking*.)

In fact, he had to wrack his brain to remember his toughest saves.
Vancouver Sun 17 Jan. 1990: D1

(The traditional spelling in the expression meaning to strain one's brain is *rack*.)

They were warned year after year that building a country by credit card would lead to rack and ruin.
Calgary Herald 18 Oct. 1993: A4

(Here the traditional spelling is *wrack*.)

See also WREAK.

racquet, racket   In Canadian English *racquet* is the more common spelling for the item of sporting equipment and the game of *racquetball*, but *racket* is not considered incorrect. *Racket* is used for all other meanings of the word, such as an uproar or a fraudulent scheme. *Raquet*, without the *c*, is a misspelling.

… until the end of September, buyers get a free membership in a golf and raquet club.
Vancouver Sun 17 Sept. 1990: B8

(Both spellings require a *c*: either *racquet* or *racket*.)

radiator   The pronunciation of *radiator* as *RAD ee ay ter* is quite common in Canada, perhaps influenced by the pronunciation of *rad*, the short

form for *radiator*. Dictionaries give the pronunciation as *RAID ee ay ter* (matching that of *radiate*), and this is the pronunciation preferred by the CBC. If you need to use this word outside the confines of your local garage, you may want to use the *RAID* pronunciation.

Radio-Canada, Radio Canada   *La Société Radio-Canada*, or *Radio-Canada*, is the French-language network of the Canadian Broadcasting Corporation (CBC) and the name by which the entire corporation is known in French. Like the anglophone division, *Radio-Canada* broadcasts on both radio and television. *Radio-Canada* is not to be confused with *Radio Canada International*, Canada's international short-wave radio service.

raft   see ARMADA

railway, railroad   Canadians say both *railway* and *railroad*, but *railway* is much more common, as in the company name Canadian National Railways. *Railway* is also preferred in Britain. *Railroad* is more common in the United States.

Perhaps because of the American connection, the nineteenth-century escape route into Canada for slaves is usually known as the Underground Railroad.

Railroad has several informal senses that are not shared with *railway*. If the government forces a measure hastily through the legislature, it is said to have *railroaded* it through. To be *railroaded* is to be coerced into doing something, or to be falsely convicted of a crime.

Because of its proximity to Detroit, [Windsor] was a terminal on the Underground Railroad.
The Beaver Feb.–Mar. 1990: 34

Once again, the people of Ontario were railroaded into something they did not want. …
Maclean's 1 Oct. 1990: A4

raise, rise   In Canada and the U.S. an increase in salary is a *raise*; in Britain it is usually a *rise*. Some dictionaries also list *raise* as a noun meaning an increase in price, a higher bet, or a raised place. Other authorities insist that only *rise* is correct in these contexts.

When it functions as a verb, *raise* takes an object: 'Don't raise her hopes'; 'The landlord will raise our rent'. The verb *rise* does not take an object: 'The dough will rise'; 'The temperature rose last night'.

The past tense and past participle of *raise* are both *raised*: 'The cheers raised the roof'; 'They had raised the bridge'. The past tense and past participle of *rise* are *rose* and *risen*: 'The temperature rose yesterday'; 'The sun has risen'.

> But there it was for all to see: our senators voting themselves a raise....
> *Ottawa Citizen* 8 June 1990: A2

> But when there is more money than there are goods, money loses its value. For some time this was taken into consideration by a raise in prices.
> *Our Times* April 1990: 20

(Here *rise* would be more widely accepted.)

raising, negative-　see DON'T THINK

RAM, ROM　RAM and ROM are computer terms. *RAM* is an acronym for 'random-access memory', the type of information-storing capacity built into a computer to hold programs, databases, and working files. What is stored in RAM can be retrieved (i.e., called into use or viewed), or erased, or replaced. In computer jargon, you can 'read from' or 'write to' RAM.

ROM is an acronym for 'read-only memory'. Once information is stored in ROM, it can be accessed but not altered or replaced. The basic instructions that operate a computer mechanically are stored in ROM by the manufacturer. CD-ROMs (ROM in the form of compact discs) are used to hold large reference databases as well as music, games, and movies. On CD-ROM a database is safe from accidental erasure and can be searched by computer in complicated ways and at high speeds.

rancour, rancor　*Rancour* rhymes with *banker*. It means spite or festering ill will. *Rancor* is an alternative American spelling, uncommon in Canada. The adjective has only one spelling: *rancorous*.

See also -OUR, -OR.

rarefy, [rarify]　The correct spelling is *rarefy*. *Merriam-Webster's* is the only dictionary to list *rarify* as an acceptable variant spelling. *Rarify* is a common mistake, perhaps because of the influence of the words *rarity* and *verify*.

> Vancouver Sun columnist Nicole Parton has abandoned the rarified atmosphere of her media bubble to enter the secular world of Social Credit politics.
> *Province* (Vancouver) 5 June 1990: 6

(The correct spelling is *rarefied*.)

rarely ever　Some critics object to *rarely ever*, preferring *rarely if ever* or *rarely* alone. However, *rarely ever* was used as early as 1694 and is found at all levels of Canadian writing.

> Supplies rarely ever meet demand.
> *Dogs in Canada* Aug. 1996: 29

See also EVER.

[rarify]　see RAREFY

rates　see TAX

rationalize, rationalization　The original meaning of *rationalize*, to make something conform to reason, or to explain it in rational terms, still appears occasionally in academic writing. In popular usage, however, this meaning has been almost completely supplanted by a psychological meaning that first became current in the 1920s: to *rationalize* is to offer excuses to oneself and others for behaviour that one is not proud of. In the context of business and administration, Canadians also use *rationalize* to mean reorganize to operate more efficiently. This use is often euphemistic, since rationalizing usually entails eliminating jobs.

> Lengthy and learned treatises were written in attempts to digest and rationalize the cases into a logical pattern. J.E. Smyth et al. *The Law and Business Administration in Canada* 1987: 374

> ... he rationalizes his obsession by pretending that he gambles only to secure a fortune and future safety for his granddaughter, Nell.
> Robertson Davies *One Half of Robertson Davies* 1978: 218

> For a Christian husband to use chain-of-command thinking to rationalize the physical and psychological abuse of his wife is abominable.
> *Mennonite Brethren Herald* 7 March 1986: 15

> The hospitals have agreed to more rationalization of clinical services—a turn of events that's remarkable to those who remember the turf wars between doctors protecting their departments....
> *Whig-Standard* (Kingston) 5 June 1992: 1

ravage, ravish To *ravage* means to destroy or cause severe damage to. The related noun is most often used in the plural to refer to the destructive effects of something, as in 'the ravages of war'. The countryside is ravaged, not ravished, by war. To *ravish* means either to rape or abduct, or to transport with emotion and fill with pleasure and delight. *Ravish* is a literary word, and it is rarely used nowadays to mean actual rape. To find someone *ravishing* usually means to find that person attractive.

During late summer, the same hurricanes that ravage the Caribbean can blow themselves out weak as pussycats on the final leg through Atlantic Canada with a day or two of rain.
Alan Tucker, ed. The Penguin Guide to Canada 1991: 32

Apollo attempted to ravish a maiden named Daphne.
Vancouver Sun 12 May 1990: R8

(In this reference to Greek myth, *ravish* means rape.)

She was ravishingly beautiful, to begin with. His first impulse was to bring her home and feed her a good meal, but his wife would never put up with that.
Canadian Fiction Magazine 63 (1988): 11

The ravishes of drugs, broken homes, crime, suicide and a thousand other blights on our society all tell us the same message....
Canadian Baptist Feb. 1986: 55

(The word required here is *ravages*.)

ravel, unravel Both *ravel* and *unravel* mean to fray or come unknit: 'The flag was ravelled'; 'My cuffs were unravelling'. Both words also mean disentangle or elucidate ('unravel the mystery'), though *ravel* is rare in this sense.

Either verb is correctly spelled with a single or a double *l* before *-ed* or *-ing*; Canadians prefer the double-*l* spellings.

Paint the cord ends with FrayCheck or clear nail polish against ravelling....
Toronto Star 16 Dec. 1993: FA7

She steals scenes without even trying, just by lurking about forlornly in her unravelling sweater and muttering to herself.
Calgary Herald 4 March 1994: E1

Police now are trying to unravel a sophisticated money-laundering scheme that involved drug profits being sent overseas....
Vancouver Sun 30 June 1994: B1

See also DOUBLING THE FINAL CONSONANT.

ravish see RAVAGE

raze The current meaning of *raze* is to demolish or level a structure. Thus the expression 'raze to the ground' is redundant. However, it is idiomatic and sometimes used for emphasis.

Under Pretoria's long-range plan, black villages located in areas now designated for whites are to be razed and their residents moved to tribal homelands....
Globe and Mail (Toronto) 8 Jan. 1985: P11

... a fire razed the Lower Town in 1845.
Chronicle-Telegraph (Quebec City) 7 Aug. 1991: 5

The scene is usually set in an older, upscale neighborhood. A small bungalow on a large lot is sold. Its new owner has it razed to the ground.
Ottawa Citizen 9 April 1990: D1

re *Re* is a Latin word meaning 'in the matter of' or 'regarding'. It is not generally italicized, nor is it followed by a period, since it is not an abbreviation. Typically *re* is used in naming legal cases or at the head of business letters and memoranda to introduce the subject. In general use it is considered informal and thus appropriate to journalism but not to academic essays, where *in regard to, concerning,* and *about* are better choices.

According to the court, the correct question was identified in the American case of Re Guardianship of Eberhardy....
Canadian Bar Review 66.3 (1987): 643

Re your question: In my opinion Prozac will continue to be available.
Ottawa Citizen 31 Dec. 1990: C5

Re: Diane Francis's column.... I am 72, retired, but born and raised in Alberta and a fifth-generation Canadian.
Financial Post 30 Dec. 1991: 5

See also LATIN PHRASES.

re- The prefix *re-* has two basic senses: 'back', as in *rebel* (fight back), *recall* (call back), *reject* (throw back), and 'again', as in *refill, rekindle,* and *remake. Re-* in the sense of 'again' is a productive prefix, which means it is used freely to create new words such as *reborrow, refreeze,* and *reinvestigate.* Though many writers use hyphens in such words, style guides consistently advise against hyphenating unless the base word begins with an *e* (*re-elect, re-enter*), or the absence of a hyphen would lead to confusion with a homonym: for example: *re-cover*

('I'm going to have that chair re-covered') and *recover* ('They won't recover a penny of their investment'); *re-sign* ('The American Sign Language interpeter re-signed the lawyer's question') and *resign* ('He refuses to resign'); *re-form* ('Twenty years later the group re-formed and went on tour') and *reform* ('He will never reform').

Repay back is redundant because *repay* means pay back.

It is possible that maintaining a response set from original learning to relearning is necessary to find savings in a recognition test.
Canadian Journal of Psychology 44.3 (1990): 415

The historical vineyards were re-worked to show that 'significant differences' existed, and could be traced to variations in founding traditions.
Neil Nevitte and Roger Gibbins *New Elites in Old States* 1990: 2

(The hyphen in *re-worked* is unnecessary.)

... the Goetz who re-entered the school system was not the same man who had taken leave the year before.
Canadian Journal of History 14.1 (1989): 69

... the wilfully imaginative and subjective re-creation of Vancouver's voyage to the west coast of Canada undermines the echoing of the cliché of 'objective' historiography.
Linda Hutcheon *Splitting Images* 1991: 22

(The hyphen in the word *re-creation* distinguishes it from *recreation*.)

See also REFER BACK; REVERT.

-re, -er Canadian writers overwhelmingly prefer the *-re* (i.e., British) spellings of the words *fibre*, *lustre*, *meagre*, *metre* (for the metric unit; the measuring device is always spelled *meter*), *sombre*, *spectre*, and *theatre*. However, the preferred American spellings (*fiber*, *luster*, *meager*, *meter*, *somber*, *specter*, and *theater*) are also found in Canadian writing and dictionaries, and are perfectly acceptable. Most style guides recommend the consistent use of either *-re* or *-er* spellings.

See also CENTRE, CENTER; MACABRE; SPELLING, CANADIAN; TIMBER, TIMBRE.

reactive, reactionary Anything that reacts to or is a reaction to something else may be called *reactive*. For example, unstable chemicals are highly reactive; a psychological depression triggered by some particular event is called a 'reactive depression'.

Reactionary is less broadly applicable; it is usually restricted to the sphere of politics, where it refers to extreme conservatism. A person who strongly resists (reacts against) social and political change may be called 'a reactionary'. This label, the opposite of 'a radical', is usually pejorative.

'I work on a very reactive basis. It is crisis management.'
Maclean's 18 July 1988: A42

Still, it was in keeping with the kind of advice that Decima has been giving Peres: to try to set the campaign agenda and avoid a strictly reactive posture.
Macleans's 31 Oct. 1988: A28

'The Court is a reactionary bastion standing in the way of badly needed reform.'
J. E. Smyth et al. *The Law and Business Administration in Canada* 1987: 23

'We always seem to be reactionary,' [Social Services Minister John] Efford told a news conference. 'We need emphasis on prevention.'
Vancouver Sun 1 Nov. 1990: A14

(Here *reactive* would be better. The minister is deploring the timing, not the conservatism, of social programs.)

'We're thinking about the future, when in the past, especially after [the steroid scandal in] Seoul, we were in a reactionary role.'
Province (Vancouver) 18 June 1990: 24

(Here *reactive* would be better.)

See also PROACTIVE.

real estate agent see REALTOR

really, real *Really* can mean 'in truth' or 'unquestionably' ('He didn't really want to go'; 'We really hit it off'), or *very* ('I was really tired'). In the phrase 'really sick', *really* is thus open to two interpretations: either 'genuinely' or 'extremely'. In context, this potential ambiguity is quickly dispelled and rarely causes confusion.

In principle, only adverbs modify adjectives or other adverbs. Yet sometimes *real* replaces *really* and functions as an adverb meaning *very*: 'It's a real nice car; it goes real fast'. This adverbial use of *real*, which has been noted with disapproval for over a century, is common in North American but not in British English. Even in Canada and the United States the usage is generally a spoken form, signalling a high degree of informality, and carried into published writing only as an imitation of relaxed talk.

Real and *really* have also come under attack as filler words. Some commentators claim that, in phrases such as 'real facts', 'real life', 'real dairy products', and 'real danger', the adjective *real* actually weakens the sense of the noun. Some also claim that the adverb *really* could be cut from almost any sentence with no change in meaning. In fact, whether *real* or *really* is redundant cannot be determined out of context. The phrase 'real facts' may seem irredeemable, yet it might be used to differentiate the truth from the 'facts' contained in a falsified résumé. And someone who urges you to 'really have a holiday' may be thinking of your tendency to take work along on vacation. Often *real* and *really* are used to signal a contrast, explicit or implied. On the other hand, for some speakers *real* and *really* are simply verbal tics. If *real* and *really* crop up frequently in your writing, it may be time to start cutting.

I told my parents I intended staying out until it got really cold.
Richard Davies and Glen Kirkland, eds. *Dimensions* 1986: 116

'And if we don't get some real cold weather, it could be later than that.'
Globe and Mail (Toronto) 3 Jan. 1985: M9

(The use of *real* is informal.)

'We played real well in the third period'.
Globe and Mail (Toronto) 8 Jan. 1985: S3

(The use of *real* is informal.)

But not many reasonable people today would deny that the poet is entitled to change whatever he likes when he uses a theme from history or real life.
Northrop Frye *The Educated Imagination* 1963: 24

(Here *real life* contrasts with life as a novelist or poet constructs it.)

See also ADJECTIVES AND ADVERBS.

Realtor, real estate agent   Though the Canadian Real Estate Association and its American counterpart are trying to stop it, *Realtor* seems to be going the way of *Kleenex*: today it often appears without the capital indicating that it is a trademark. *Realtor* was specially coined to distinguish real estate agents belonging to member companies from those in companies that did not belong to the association. However, *realtor*, without a capital, has come to refer to anyone making a living in the real estate business. This generic use of *realtor* to mean real

estate agent or salesperson is now found in all types of published writing, including newspapers, even though the style books of several Canadian newspapers instruct their writers to avoid *realtor*, or to use it only with a capital letter in reference to companies belonging to the Canadian Real Estate Association.

In Britain the term *Realtor* is not used; real estate agents are called 'estate agents'.

Clerks, barbers, motormen, storekeepers all became instant realtors.
Pierre Berton *The Promised Land* 1984: 323

Homeowners, realtors and renovation experts we consulted said you should renovate to improve your enjoyment of a house....
Canadian Consumer Feb. 1986: 11

Leung, a Vancouver realtor, flew to Taiwan last spring and laid the groundwork for the sale.
Ottawa Citizen 10 Sept. 90: A5

Mr. James R. Gairdner, President and Chairman of Johnston & Daniel Limited, Realtor, is pleased to announce the appointment of Ms. Judith Rucinski as Vice-President....
Globe and Mail (Toronto) 22 March 1985: B2

(Here *Realtor* is used as a proprietary term in the manner approved by the Canadian Real Estate Association.)

See also TRADEMARKS, BRAND NAMES.

reason is because, reason why   Objections have been made to both these phrases on the grounds that they are redundant. *Because* is usually defined as meaning 'for the reason that', in which case writing *the reason is because* is the same as writing 'the reason is for the reason that'. Any sentence using the phrase can be rewritten to drop either *because* or *the reason*. For example, 'The reason he agreed is because he is her friend' can be rewritten 'He agreed because he is her friend', or 'The reason he agreed is that he is her friend'. Although examples of *the reason is because* can be found in the work of eminent writers since the seventeenth century, editors and teachers often find it objectionable; thus the safest course is to avoid it.

The reason why is similarly redundant, since *why* in this context means 'for that reason'. Nonetheless, *the reason why* is viewed more tolerantly, perhaps because, if *why* is replaced by the unobjectionable *that*, the resulting sentence may appear to have too many *that*s: 'The reason *that* he agreed was simply *that* he was in a hurry'. For whatever reason, most authorities defend *the reason why* as an idiom, and Canadian literary writers are certainly not averse to using it. Be aware, however, that some people will criticize the usage.

> Freed figures the reason for the rash of listings headaches is because of increased competition.
> *London Free Press* 28 April 1988: C3

(Here *because of* could be deleted or the sentence could be rewritten: 'Freed figures the rash of listings headaches results from increased competition.')

> Johnston said one reason why Fraser Surrey Dock got into difficulties three years ago was because Pacific Australia Direct Line moved to Lynnterm....
> *Vancouver Sun* 7 Dec. 1990: D7

(This sentence could be rewritten: 'Johnston said one reason for Fraser Surrey Dock's difficulties was that Pacific Australia Direct Line moved to Lynnterm....')

> But not many reasonable people today would deny that the poet is entitled to change whatever he likes when he uses a theme from history or real life. The reason why was explained long ago by Aristotle.
> Northrop Frye *The Educated Imagination* 1963: 24

> What stories does my culture have to tell me about such [self-directed] women? Not very many at the public school level, which is probably the reason why I can remember nothing at all about Dick and Jane....
> Margaret Atwood *Second Words* 1982: 223

See also SIMPLE REASON; THAT, OMISSION OF

rebellion, revolution, revolt In history a *rebellion* is a widespread and usually armed uprising against an established ruler or government. Rebellions are usually unsuccessful; a rebellion that succeeds is called a *revolution*. A *revolution* is the actual overthrow of the government and results in significant change to the social organization. *Revolution* is often used figuratively to refer to a major change in social practice: 'sexual revolution', 'computer revolution', 'communication revolution'. A *revolt* is an uprising or an act of protest against authority that may be quickly contained, but that in retrospect is often seen as marking the beginning of a period of significant social change.

> In December 1837 authorities in Upper Canada put down an attempted rebellion.
> *The Beaver* Feb.–Mar. 1990: 28

> [Nelson Mandela] was further charged with sabotage and conspiracy to overthrow the government by revolution.
> *Chatelaine* Jun.–Jul. 1986: 103

> A national tax revolt is on the horizon unless the federal government moves quickly to ease the tax burden on Canadians....
> *Calgary Herald* 15 June 1994: A8

rebound, redound *Rebound* means spring back, as in 'The puck rebounded off the boards', and in this sense is usually followed by *off* or *from*. To *rebound* is also used metaphorically in Canadian English to mean to recoil or to adversely affect the originator, and in this sense it is followed by *on* or *upon*: 'Our neglect of the car rebounded on us'. In British English, the sense 'to recoil on' is filled by *redound* followed by *on* or *upon*: 'Their malicious comments redounded on them'. In Canadian use, *redound* is usually followed by *to* and then a word such as 'credit', 'advantage', or 'dishonour'. It means add or accrue to, as in 'Your children's behaviour redounds to your credit'. *Redound* is also used in this way in British English.

> Name-calling also has a way of rebounding on the perpetrator.
> *Engineering Dimensions* May–Jun. 1988: 25

> ... the critic who feels free to avoid evaluation ignores an important reality, which may one day rebound on his own freedom.
> *Queen's Quarterly* 92.2 (1985): 374

> 'In all humility, we suggest a few amendments which will redound to your credit should you adopt them.'
> *Globe and Mail* (Toronto) 14 Feb. 1985: P7

> In many cases, takeovers redound to the benefit of both the purchaser and the company purchased.
> *Financial Post* 15 Jan. 1990: 10

recant, recount Heresies are *recanted*; stories are *recounted*. To *recant* is to formally retract statements one has made or disavow beliefs one has held. To *recount* means to tell or narrate.

> ... the Roman Catholic Church admitted that it had erred in its dealings with astronomer Galileo when they arrested him and forced him to recant his teachings as heresy or be burned at the stake.
> *Toronto Star* 26 Dec. 1992: J26

> R—— recounted for the court the final few minutes of P——'s life.
> *Toronto Star* 12 Dec. 1992: A6

recapitulate, recap To *recapitulate* means to briefly go over the main points of something, usually a speech or discussion. It does not refer to wholesale repetition, as some writers mistakenly believe. The clipped form *recap* has come into use as both a verb and a noun. Most dictionaries label *recap* informal. Its use is largely restricted to speech, newspaper and magazine writing, and sports and news commentaries on radio and television.

And yet when it came time for the presiding judge to instruct the jury, he had recapitulated the evidence and the arguments in only a few words....
Jack Batten *Robinette* 1984: 134

Of course, the press of the early 1770s was given to presenting shabby copy; only the intrusion of unprecedented events seems to have spared readers a wholesale recapitulation of essays penned seventy years before.
J.A.W. Gunn *Beyond Liberty and Property* 1983: 28

(A *recapitulation* is a summary; 'wholesale repetition' would be better here.)

As I look forward to my 1985 forays into the marketplace, I can't help but recap—nay, rehash—last year's triumphs and failures.
Canadian Consumer Jan. 1985: 2

reciprocal see MUTUAL

reckon *Reckon* meaning suppose, expect, or guess is informal. Mainly restricted to speech or reported speech, it is more common in Britain, the U.S., and Australia than in Canada.
Reckon in the sense of calculate or judge is standard in formal writing.

Monte Vines reckoned he couldn't win the case, so he struck a deal with Moses.
Saturday Night April 1986: 35

(This use is informal.)

I don't know where they went ... but I reckon she was finding more comfort in Max's mature arms than she did in Minty's big ones.
Canadian Fiction Magazine 64 (1988): 100

(This use is informal.)

... the social bonds that we know derive from the society we know and from the feelings that Platonists and vulgar moralists reckon to be 'lower.'
Queen's Quarterly 95.3 (1988): 598

(The use of *reckon* meaning deem or judge is accepted in any type of writing.)

Municipal police forces generally are reckoned to cost more than those contracted to the RCMP.
Vancouver Sun 25 Aug. 1990: B2

(The use of *reckon* meaning calculate is accepted in any type of writing.)

reconnaissance, reconnoitre *Reconnaissance* (pronounced *reh CON uh sunse*) is a military term referring to an exploratory survey of enemy territory—a look at the lay of the land—preceding a military operation. The word is often used figuratively. A related word is *reconnoitre* (*reh con NOY ter*), which is used as both a verb and a noun. *Reconnoiter* is an alternative, chiefly American, spelling.
Note that *reconnaissance* is spelled with a double *n* and a double *s*.

He had the mannerisms of a rodent on trap reconnaissance.
Vancouver Sun 6 Dec. 1994: B1

Maj.-Gen. (Air Vice-Marshal) Richard Rohmer was a Mustang fighter-reconnaisance pilot in the Second World War.
Globe and Mail (Toronto) 16 Nov. 1985: E9

(The correct spelling is *reconnaissance*.)

The shooter had apparently reconnoitered the area and picked a spot in the lane from which he could see the doctor through a patio window.
Vancouver Sun 15 Nov. 1994: A3

It was déjà vu all over again for Pyette, who was here for a pretty serious reconnoitre in the late 1980s.
Vancouver Sun 28 June 1994: A13

recount see RECANT

rector, vicar In the most general terms, a *rector* is a person in charge and a *vicar* is a deputy.
In the Anglican Church of Canada a *rector* is a priest in charge of a parish or ministry; a *vicar* is a priest who ministers in a parish or within a ministry, but is not officially in charge of it. A vicar may also be an assistant to a bishop.
In the Roman Catholic Church a *rector* is a priest in charge of a parish, or at the head of a seminary, college, or university. A *vicar* is a priest serving as an administrative assistant, official delegate, or missionary for a bishop. *Vicar of Christ* is one of the pope's titles.
In the Church of England a *rector* is a priest in charge of a parish where, historically, the priest received the tithes of the parish. A *vicar* is the priest

in charge of a parish where, historically, the priest was paid a stipend by the layperson, cleric, or religious house that received the tithes.

Not all rectors are clerics. At certain secular universities, colleges, and schools, the head or principal is called the rector. In a tradition that originated in Scotland, a university official elected by the student body is also called the rector.

The preacher was Canon Robert Greene, rector of St. Bartholomew, Toronto.
Canadian Churchman April 1986: 5

There are complete plans of the building itself, a list of vicars since 1514 and chronological and scholarly research by archeological and theological experts.
Canadian Churchman April 1986: 11

Ottawa's Archbishop Marcel Gervais has named Rev. Pat Powers as episcopal vicar for administration.
Ottawa Citizen 16 May 1992: F6

The Health Department has asked Denis Gagnon, vice-rector of research at Laval University, to study new drug review and drug monitoring procedures....
Toronto Star 26 June 1992: C8

[He] announced that Norman Rogers, ... who had been elected rector by the students, had accepted appointment for the customary three-year term.
Frederick Gibson *Queen's University* 2 (1983): 146

See also MANSE, PARSONAGE, RECTORY; RELIGIOUS TITLES.

rectory   see MANSE; RECTOR

recumbent   see PRONE, SUPINE

recur, recurrence, reoccur, reoccurrence
Recur and *recurrence* are the established and recommended forms. *Reoccur* rarely appears in Canadian writing, and is not found in most desk dictionaries, although it is listed in the *OED* with citations from the nineteenth century. Both words mean to happen again or repeatedly.

... an analysis of recurring metaphors held considerable potential for penetrating the unstated or obscure ways in which a teacher constructs a professional world.
Perspectives: Profiles of Research at Queen's University 1986: 45

... Canada's war effort would be one of limited liability ... aimed at avoiding a recurrence of the dread conscription crisis of 1917.
Frederick Gibson *Queen's University* 2 (1983): 179

This is playing havoc with our federal finances as budget deficits reoccur from one year to the next....
Financial Post 10 April 1989: 17

(The more widely accepted form is *recur*.)

The NAJC [National Association of Japanese Canadians] wanted acknowledgement, a compensatory sum of money it has not decided upon and legislative amendments ... to preclude any reoccurrence of the Japanese experience.
Globe and Mail (Toronto) 4 Feb. 1985: P7

(The more widely accepted form is *recurrence*.)

See also OCCURRENCE.

redolent   *Redolent* is used with the prepositions *with* and *of*. When *redolent* is used in its literal sense, 'exuding a certain smell', it is usually followed by *with*. Figuratively, *redolent* means suggestive and is usually followed by *of*, but this is not a rule. Both prepositions are used in both senses.

A sugar refinery worker spent an hour leading us through the cobwebbed, Dickensian factory redolent with the sweet smell of molasses.
Vancouver Sun 8 Dec. 1990: E1

... Purdy recounts an incident in which he's told his poems aren't 'romantic' but are instead 'hard-boiled:' a slightly archaic adjective, redolent of rock-jowled, mush-hearted 'thirties newspapermen and Humphrey Bogart private detectives.
Margaret Atwood *Second Words* 1982: 98

redound   see REBOUND

Red Tory   see CONSERVATIVE

redundancy   see WORDINESS

reeve   In Ontario, Manitoba, Saskatchewan, Alberta, and British Columbia, a *reeve* is the chair of a rural municipal council whose duties are similar to those of the mayor of an urban community. This meaning is a Canadianism. Historically, in British English, a *reeve* was a magistrate or the manager of a landowner's estate. *Reeve* should be capitalized only when used as a title before a name.

The man ... was a local contractor, William Brewer, who later became the first reeve of South Vancouver.
Province (Vancouver) 20 June 1990: 2

Westminster Reeve Dave Murray said ... the proposal was made in the spirit of co-operation.
London Free Press 28 April 1988: B1

refer back In this phrase *back* is not always necessary, but neither is it always redundant. Sometimes it can help to clarify the meaning, especially in cases where *back* means again or indicates a reference to the past.

> But Morgentaler admitted he's not optimistic about the defeat of Bill C-43, which a House of Commons committee referred back to parliament this week. . . .
> *Vancouver Sun* 7 April 1990: A8

(Here *back* means again.)

> When I saw that the Opposition was likely to persist, I . . . asked that the report of the committee be referred back for further study.
> *Queen's Quarterly* 97.3 (1990): 468

(Here *back* means again.)

> 'In referring to those painters, I was referring back to my own education, and to when I made those Mao paintings with all this hope and idealism.'
> *Maclean's* 22 July 1991: A39

(Here *back* means back in time.)

See also RE-.

referendum, referendums, referenda During the constitutional debates in 1991–92 on the Charlottetown Accord, major Canadian newspapers overwhelmingly preferred the regular plural *referendums* to the Latin plural *referenda*. Either is correct.

> It took two referendums before a majority of only 7,000 Newfoundlanders voted to become Canadians on July 22, 1948.
> *Toronto Star* 18 Dec. 1991: A1

> Referenda should be held on important issues such as abortion, capital punishment and key constitutional questions.
> *Ottawa Citizen* 30 March 1991: B2

See also PLURALS, REGULAR, IRREGULAR, FOREIGN.

reflexive pronouns see -SELF, -SELVES

refugee see ÉMIGRÉ

refute, confute, dispute The verbs *refute* and *confute* both mean to disprove, while to *dispute* means to question or argue against.

Refute usually implies that evidence or a developed argument has proved something or someone wrong. *Refute* is sometimes used simply to mean deny or dispute. This extended sense is not widely accepted and should be avoided.

Confute is an uncommon word implying the application of overwhelming proof against a person or case: 'Security videos confuted his claim that he had never set foot in the building'. Note that to *confute* does not mean to mix up or confuse.

> Herder's primary object was to refute this thesis by submitting evidence and argument to show that language was invented and gradually perfected by man as the natural means of developing his own reason.
> R. A. Wilson *The Birth of Language* 1937: 21

> 'I seriously refute the observations of some senior police management who are saying the increase in injuries is a direct result of our work to rule.'
> *Globe and Mail* (Toronto) 11 June 1985: M1

(Here *dispute* would be better.)

> And here is a new Mitchell novel, *Ladybug, Ladybug*. . . . The man who accused him of goofing off [and wasting his talent as a writer] is confuted by the fact that the novel was written at all.
> *Ottawa Citizen* 14 Jan. 1989: C3

> The confuted logic by which they justify the irrational policy is that the others are 'rogue' states. . . .
> *Toronto Star* 23 June 1994: A27

(The word required here is *confused*.)

regarding see IN REGARD[S] TO

regardless, irrespective, [irregardless] *Regardless* means without regard to: 'regardless of ability to pay'. *Irrespective* is a slightly more formal synonym. *Irrespective* is always followed by *of*, whereas *regardless* may appear alone, without anything after it: 'We loved her regardless'. In this position *regardless* means nonetheless.

Irregardless, presumably a blend of these two words, is heavily stigmatized as uneducated. Because it contains two negative affixes, *ir-* and *-less*, it is considered a double negative. Although it is heard in speech and occasionally appears in writing, it should be avoided in both.

> Guralnick and Marcus agree Johnson's recordings would have made him a crucial figure regardless.
> *Vancouver Sun* 18 Oct. 1990: A18

> Who should have access to technologies such as test tube fertilization? Couples only? Single women irregardless of their sexual inclinations?
> *Gazette* (Montreal) 22 Nov. 1990: A6

(Here either *irrespective* or *regardless* is required.)

Logic would dictate that those intractable fellows must have carefully quantified and considered the cost implications of their actions to their constituents, choosing to go ahead irregardless.
Financial Post 30 Oct. 1990: 14

(The word required here is *regardless*.)

See also DOUBLE NEGATIVE.

regard(s)   see IN REGARD[S] TO

Registered Indian   see ABORIGINAL PEOPLE(S)

regretful, regrettable   *Regretful* is usually applied to people; it means feeling sorry or distressed: 'Now it was too late and she was regretful'. *Regrettable* usually describes events or circumstances, or other people's behaviour, and means causing or likely to cause regret (as in 'a regrettable move'); *unfortunate* and *ill-judged* are synonyms. *Regretful* is often used where *regrettable* is appropriate. The same confusion occurs with the adverbs *regretfully* and *regrettably*.

Jean-Pierre Beaudry was laid off after 23 years with Shell Canada, but he's neither bitter nor regretful.
Ottawa Citizen 15 Jan. 1994: E4

It was an ill-timed, regrettable decision.
Daily News (Halifax) 30 June 1994: 20

'It's really regretful the whole thing is off,' she said. 'It's going to disappoint a lot of people.'
Province (Vancouver) 4 July 1990: 5

(The word required here is *regrettable*, meaning unfortunate.)

'They have a regretful attitude that lawyers interfere with the normal immigration process.'
Globe and Mail (Toronto) 24 April 1985: M3

(The word required here is *regrettable*; 'they' are not feeling regret.)

'The response from the Bulgarians has been, regretfully, insults.'
Globe and Mail (Toronto) 22 May, 1985: P5

(The word required here is *regrettably*.)

rein   see FREE REIN

reindeer   see MOOSE

reiterate, iterate   Something that is *reiterated* is said or done again or repeatedly. *Iterate* means the same thing, but for some reason the apparently redundant *reiterate* is the more common form. Some usage commentators have attempted to distinguish between the two words, claiming that *iterate* (meaning simply repeat) is properly used when something is done or said again, whereas *reiterate* (meaning repeat again) should apply to something that has been stated or done three times or more. This is pure pedantry and has nothing to do with actual usage. In fact, *iterate* appears very rarely in Canadian writing.

... Wordsworth reiterates in poem after poem the invitation: Come forth, and bring with you a heart / That watches and receives.
R.A. Wilson *The Birth of Language* 1937: 69

Already, Quebec voices are iterating their deep misgivings about the vortex of nationalism.
Gazette (Montreal) 9 March 1991: H8

relatively, comparatively   *Relatively* and *comparatively* both mean in relation to something else. They are also commonly used in all types of writing to mean fairly or somewhat. Although this use is standard, words such as *fairly*, *somewhat*, or *nearly* are better choices in contexts where no specific comparison is being made.

To Gassy Jack, a sailor and saloon-keeper of the early days, [urban pollution] represents a perversion of life far more sinister than his own relatively healthy vulgarity and vice.
Northrop Frye *The Bush Garden* 1971: 15

(Here an explicit comparison is being made between pollution and vulgarity.)

From a precarious, nomadic existence they now enjoy a comparatively secure, permanent base equipped with medical facilities, government housing, electricity and television.
Arctic 41.1 (1988): 75

(Here an explicit comparison is being made between a nomadic and a settled life.)

The trend to increasing off-farm income, even for families considered to be farming relatively full-time, is consistent with observations made elsewhere....
The Canadian Geographer Spring 1989: 39

(Here *almost* would be a better choice.)

Macdonald—previously relatively unknown to the British public—became infamous now as a Machiavellian, cunning politician....

William Teatero *John Anderson: Fugitive Slave* 1986: 114

(Here too *almost* would be a better choice.)

relatives, omitted   see THAT, OMISSION OF

relevant   *Relevant*, meaning pertinent or bearing on the matter at hand, is often mispronounced and misspelled *revelant*.

'In our minds, we're champions,' he declared, 'because we beat all the amateurs entered here.'... Right or wrong, the quote becomes revelant now because Brasseur and Eisler will defend their 1993 world championships in Japan next Tuesday....
Toronto Star 18 March 1994: E4

(The correct spelling is *relevant*.)

See also MISPRONUNCIATION AND PRONUNCIATION SHIFTS, METATHESIS.

religion, spirituality, spiritualism   *Religions* are moral codes and traditions of worship, believed to be divinely inspired, and the social institutions that their adherents form. The word *spirituality* sometimes refers to supernatural beliefs or rituals that are not endorsed by institutionalized religions, as in 'new age spirituality'. *Spirituality* also refers to matters of the spirit, as opposed to physical nature, or an emphasis on the spiritual over the worldly. *Spiritualism*, which is often used mistakenly for *spirituality*, is the belief that the spirits of the dead can communicate with the living, usually through mediums.

They clung tenaciously to their religion; indeed, the presence of Roman Catholic and Greek Orthodox churches in the rural Prairies acted as a spur to the retention of language and culture.
Pierre Berton *The Promised Land* 1984: 62

In the delicate balance he sought between sensuality and spirituality, Coltrane became a touchstone for the artistic temper of the time.
Jack Chambers *Milestones* 1983: 273

Relatives of the victims said they had previously attended healing rites in the house that were a mixture of Christianity and spiritualism, calling the spirits of the dead for consultation.
Vancouver Sun 14 Dec. 1990: A3

Judaism provides me with the faith and power to see and realize a purer spiritualism, a closer look at God and humanity than I've ever experienced before.
Vancouver Sun 11 Dec. 1990: B3

(The word required here is *spirituality*.)

See also GOD, GODS; RELIGIOUS TITLES.

religious titles   Titles for clergy vary from denomination to denomination. The Roman Catholic title *Cardinal* is placed between the first name and the last: 'Joseph Cardinal Ratzinger'. In subsequent references the first name is omitted: 'Cardinal Ratzinger'. In both the Roman Catholic and Anglican churches, *Archbishop* and *Bishop* are placed before the full name: 'Archbishop Desmond Tutu'. *Archbishop* with the surname is used in subsequent references: 'Archbishop Tutu'. Catholic priests are called *Father*. Catholic *Monsignors* are so titled only in the first reference: 'Monsignor Boyle'. Subsequent references use *Father*: 'Father Boyle'. Though a Catholic priest may be referred to as Reverend So-and-so, Catholics don't use 'the Reverend' as a noun, as in 'The Reverend dropped in for a visit'; many Protestant denominations also discourage this usage. *Reverend* is never abbreviated when used with *the*, whether as a noun or with the full name: 'the Reverend John Smith'.

In the Anglican Church deans are referred to as *Very Reverend* (which may be abbreviated *Very Rev.*), and then *Dean*. Archdeacons are called *Venerable* (*Ven.*) and then *Archdeacon*. Canons are called *Reverend* and then *Canon*. Lesser Anglican clergy are referred to as *Reverend* and in subsequent references as *Mr.*, *Mrs.*, *Miss*, *Ms.*, or *Dr.* Note that the honorifics *Very Reverend*, *Venerable*, and *Reverend* should always be followed by the first and last name.

A United Church moderator, if ordained, is *Right Reverend* on the first reference and then *Mr.*, *Mrs.*, *Ms.*, *Miss*, or *Dr.* Former moderators are *Very Reverend*. A lay moderator is called simply *Moderator*: 'Moderator Anne Squires'. All United Church ministers are called *Reverend* and, in second references, *Mr.*, *Mrs.*, *Ms.*, *Miss*, or *Dr.* Presbyterian ordained moderators and all ministers are *Reverend* in the first reference and then *Mr.*, *Mrs.*, *Miss*, *Ms.*, or *Dr.* Most other Protestant ministers can be referred to in the same way, though some denominations do not use the honorific *Reverend*; among them are the Christian Scientists, the Jehovah's Witnesses, the Mormons, and the Seventh-day Adventists.

The title *Rabbi* is used before the full name in the first reference; *Mr.*, *Mrs.*, *Miss*, *Ms.* or *Dr.* is used in subsequent references.

Imam is the title of various religious leaders in Islam, including those who lead prayers in mosques.

reluctant

See also RECTOR, VICAR; TITLES OF PEOPLE.

reluctant   see RETICENT

renown, renowned   *Renown*, which rhymes with *crown*, is a noun meaning fame. *Renowned* is the corresponding adjective and means famous. Sometimes *renown* is incorrectly used as the adjective; dictionaries do not recognize this usage.

Reknown and *reknowned* sometimes find their way into print (presumably writers are thinking of *well-known*), but these spellings are considered errors.

Rigoletto, an operatic singer of great renown, was engaged to give a concert in Montréal.
J.E. Smyth et al. *The Law and Business Administration in Canada* 1987: 304

The view that the numerical size of a group is highly significant in determining its forms of interaction was first systematically stated by the renowned sociologist Georg Simmel.
Irving M. Zeitlin and Robert J. Brym *The Social Condition of Humanity* 1991: 60

Renown Canadian pianist Louis Lortie will join the orchestra for the tour, which will feature a number of Canadian compositions.
Vancouver Sun 11 Jan. 1990: F6

(The correct spelling of the adjective is *renowned*.)

He put himself in position for a promotion by gaining some reknown as the tutor of the Flames....
Province (Vancouver) 26 Jan. 1990: 59

(The correct spelling is *renown*.)

'Canadian manufacturers are reknowned worldwide for the quality of their work.'
Financial Post 11 Jan. 1989: 15

(The correct spelling is *renowned*.)

reoccur, reoccurrence   see RECUR

repairable, unrepairable, reparable, irreparable
Generally, *repairable* and *unrepairable* describe machines ('The toaster is repairable'), while *reparable* and its negative *irreparable* are used to describe such things as damage (e.g., to reputations), harm, or loss.

Repairable is pronounced *reh PAIR uh bul*, and *reparable* is pronounced *REP er uh bul*.

... in his address to the recycling conference, Anderson revealed that only one in 12 appliances is repairable.
Gazette (Montreal) 22 Oct. 1990: D2

Business should ask questions such as those posed in a submission to the Brundtland Commission.... 'Is this the best design ... built to last ... easily reparable or recyclable'?
Financial Post 22 May 1989: 18

(This use of *reparable* to describe an object is unusual in Canadian writing.)

All we could expect to accomplish would be to ... cause irreparable damage to our friendship with Nigeria.
George Ignatieff *The Making of a Peacemonger* 1987: 237

repatriate   see PATRIATE

repel   see REPULSE

repertoire, repertory   *Repertoire* and *repertory* are interchangeable when they refer to the inventory of pieces that an artist, band, theatre company, etc., is prepared to perform, or, by figurative extension, the range of behaviours that a person or animal is capable of. *Repertoire* is the more common choice.

Repertory is also used as an adjective to describe a type of theatre in which a company performs short runs of many different plays, or a type of cinema presenting short runs of many previously released films rather than long runs of new films.

He had but a small repertoire: pieces by Bach, Kreisler and a handful of others.
Queen's Quarterly 92.1 (1985): 98

... the nightly repertory of the quintet includes surprisingly few of the compositions recorded for Dial and Savoy the previous year.
Jack Chambers *Milestones* 1983: 78

Animals possess a small repertory of sounds and gestures by which they communicate danger and the like to one another.
Irving M. Zeitlin and Robert J. Brym *The Social Condition of Humanity* 1991: 13

It had one repertory theatre, no ballet company, and hardly any decent brie.
Margaret Atwood *Second Words* 1982: 402

replace   see SUBSTITUTE

replacement worker, scab, strikebreaker   Of the terms commonly used for someone who takes over the work of a striking worker, *replacement worker* is the most neutral. In the eighteenth century, *scab* was first used to refer to someone who refused to join a trade union. Around the turn of that century it took on its contemporary meaning of *replacement worker*; it can also refer to a worker who refuses to join a strike. Because *scab* is highly partisan and pro-union, it often appears in quotation marks in print. The slightly less partisan term *strikebreaker* was in use as early as 1904 for workers brought in to do the work of strikers.

> The proposals, unveiled last week, would make union-organizing easier and limit the use of replacement workers during a strike.
> *Ottawa Citizen* 12 Nov. 1991: A4

> Bousquet ... received at least one call from a part-time employee who claimed he had been harassed and treated 'like a scab' by the unionized workers.
> *Gazette* (Montreal) 23 Feb. 1990: A1

> He joined the majors as a 'scab' during the 1979 umpires' strike....
> *Ottawa Citizen* 30 June 1990: E5

> In Ottawa, an orthopedic surgeon ... suffered a concussion after picketers, apparently mistaking him for a strikebreaker, knocked him from his bicycle.
> *Maclean's* 23 Sept. 1991: A32

replete, complete   *Replete* in most uses means filled to abundance with something, whereas *complete* means whole, full, lacking nothing. In some contexts, either word may be used; if the writer wishes to stress abundance, *replete* is the best choice. *Replete* is often used in connection with food, meaning that the eater's appetite is satisfied, or even sated.

> Thus, while the book is replete with facts and figures, it is further enhanced by direct quotes....
> Harry M. Rosenthal and S. Cathy Berson, eds. *Canadian Jewish Outlook Anthology* 1988: 115

(Here *replete* means abundantly filled with; *complete* would not work.)

> Burlington's produced an 'Avengers' show, complete with catsuits, tattoos, bouffants, mid-parts, guns and glitter.
> *Gazette* (Montreal) 30 Dec. 1990: F3

(Here *replete* would also fit, if the writer wished to suggest abundance.)

> Andrew and Gordievsky have produced a big book, replete with a full scholarly apparatus.
> *Gazette* (Montreal) 29 Dec. 1990: I2

(Here *complete* would be better, since presumably a scholarly apparatus is not improved by abundance.)

> 'When replete, the eaters washed their hands....'
> *Gazette* (Montreal) 31 March 1990: B2

replica   In fine arts a *replica* is a reproduction of a work made by, or supervised by, the original artist. Although some critics insist on preserving this specialized sense, *replica* is used generally to mean a copy or reproduction, and is now more often applied to artifacts than to works of art. The phrase 'replica copy' is redundant.

> Perdue, dressed in a miniature replica of the same suit, stood beside him.
> Geoffrey Ursell *Perdue: And How the West Was Lost* 1984: 41

> The fisherperson is allowed one trophy-size fish to take back home: however, a replica can be made by the taxidermist and you will not be able to tell the difference.
> *Uphere* Jan.–Feb. 1990: 55

> [They] have created an exact replica of the century-old Ontario Georgian house where Mr. MacRobbie spent his childhood and early years.
> *Globe and Mail* (Toronto) 18 May 1985: H1

repulse, repel   Both *repulse* and *repel* mean to ward off or drive back. To *repel* also means to evoke a feeling of repulsion or disgust. Some usage guides argue that *repulse* should not be used in this way. However, since *repulse* is so close in form to *repulsion* (disgust) and *repulsive* (disgusting), this advice seems rather pedantic. According to dictionaries, to *repulse* meaning to cause a feeling of repulsion is standard.

> In fact, the very opposite was happening as hundreds joined their local militias to repulse this invasion.
> *The Beaver* Feb.–Mar. 1990: 29

(This is the undisputed meaning of *repulse*.)

> War has a peculiar power to rivet and repel, to engage the mind even as it tears at the heart.
> *Maclean's* 28 Jan. 1991: A19

> [A horror movie] should shock, terrify, repulse, and quite possibly offend.
> *Ottawa Citizen* 28 Oct. 1990: F5

(Here *repulse* means disgust.)

> 'A man's clothes can either repulse or intrigue me,' says Heather Hinsdale....
> *Ottawa Citizen* 1 March 1990: D1

(Here *repulse* means disgust.)

reputation   see CHARACTER

reserve, reservation, rez, res   Aboriginal peoples in Canada who signed treaties were settled on *reserves*. In the United States these areas are called *reservations*, and objections are often raised to the use of *reservation* to refer to a Canadian reserve. *Rez* (sometimes *res*) is slang for *reserve*, as in Tomson Highway's play *The Rez Sisters*.

A group of Mohawks snarled traffic yesterday on part of a highway on the Kahnawake reserve to show solidarity with Indian demonstrators in Toronto.
Gazette (Montreal) 18 Dec. 1994: A3

A particularly senseless and counterproductive policy was the official opposition to the use of farm machinery on Indian reserves.
NeWest Review Dec.–Jan. 1990: 33

Speaking for the Native Council of Canada, the central organization for off-reservation Indians, Viola Robinson proposed a permanent forum....
Ottawa Citizen 27 Aug. 1991: A4

(Here *reservation* should be replaced by *reserve*.)

Tomson's father, Joe Highway, was originally from the Pelican Narrows Indian Reserve in northeastern Saskatchewan and his ancestors came from this 'rez' and from Cumberland House, Saskatchewan.
Tomson Highway The Rez Sisters 1988: vi

resident   see CITIZEN

resin, rosin   *Resin* is the general term for the sticky liquids and gums exuded by plants, and for similar synthetic substances such as epoxy. *Rosin* is a solid residue obtained by boiling off the turpentine contained in the resin of pine trees. *Rosin* is rubbed on violin bows to increase friction and is used by baseball players to keep the ball from slipping out of their hands. *Rosin* is also a verb meaning to rub rosin on something, as in 'Rosin the dance floor so that no one falls'.

The tang of pine resin reminded me of my new teacher—clean, strong, healthy.
Room of One's Own June 1990: 75

With the help of geneticists and chemists, Wool has developed a resin for the manufacture of plastic garbage bags....
Engineering Dimensions May–Jun. 1988: 27

The playing commences unevenly as half a dozen late kids ... rosin their bows, etc.
Gazette (Montreal) 15 Feb. 1990: A2

respective, respectively   *Respective* and *respectively* are by far most common in academic writing. Often these words have no real function in the sentence, in which case they are both wordy and pretentious. *Respective* or *respectively* should be used only when one series of particulars must be matched with another in the same sentence—and even then the sentence can often be unambiguously worded without them.

If, respectively, geographers and anthropologists elaborate in this way, historians have any number of temporal, topical, or biographical lacunae to which they can channel their attention.
Queen's Quarterly 97.4 1990: 567

(Here *respectively* could be omitted.)

Thus Malinowski delineated the respective spheres of magic, science, and religion and their effects on both the individual and society.
Irving M. Zeitlin and Robert J. Brym *The Social Condition of Humanity* 1991: 210

(Here *respective* could be omitted.)

The causes of the conflict between them are to be found not in their biological makeup but in their respective social organizations.
Irving M. Zeitlin and Robert J. Brym *The Social Condition of Humanity* 1991: 31

(Here *respective* could be omitted.)

The APR reputed for temperate crop plants such as tomato, wheat and peas amounts to 17, 45 and 2% of total respiration respectively.
Arctic 41.1 (1988): 1

(In this sentence *respectively* is useful.)

New and used implements are interest-deferred until November 1 and May 1 next year, respectively.
Country Guide Dec. 1986: 20

(Here too *respectively* is useful.)

respite   *Respite* means reprieve or temporary relief from a stressful situation. Sometimes it is preceded by an article ('grant a respite') and sometimes it is not ('find respite'). The standard pronunciation in Canada and the United States is *RESS pit*. Canadians also say *reh SPITE*, but this pronunciation is criticized.

... it is a place where visitors find a friendly welcome in idyllic surroundings, relaxation and a wonderful respite from city life.
Leisure Life 1988: 49

responsible, responsibility The correct spellings are *responsible* (ending in *-ible*), *responsibility*, and *responsibilities*. These words are frequently misspelled in various ways.

The Canadian Radio-Television and Telecommunications Commission would close up shop in Quebec or be responsable for a few marginal technical matters.
Gazette (Montreal) 7 Sept. 1991: B3

(The correct spelling is *responsible*. Since *responsable* is French for *responsible*, this misspelling probably reflects the influence of Quebec French.)

The Canadian-U.S. agency is responsibile for waterways along the international border.
Globe and Mail (Toronto) 12 Dec. 1985: A30

(The correct spelling is *responsible*.)

See also -ABLE, -IBLE.

restaurateur The owner of a restaurant is a *restaurateur*, spelled without an *n* and pronounced *RES tuh ruh TER*. However, *restauranteur* is common enough that one dictionary, *Merriam-Webster's*, lists it as a variant spelling.

The Polar Bear Swim Club and the yearly dip were founded in 1920 by the late Vancouver restaurateur Peter Pantages.
Province (Vancouver) 29 Dec. 1994: A2

Food service professionals, in particular—whether chefs, caterers, ... or restauranteurs—are realizing the specialty food industry supplies quality foods to help business.
Western Grocer Aug. 1990: 26

(The accepted spelling is *restaurateur*.)

restive, restless Both words may mean fidgety or agitated, but *restive* usually implies impatience or rebelliousness in the face of restraint or authority, while *restless* is not necessarily associated with restraint. *Restive*, which comes from the Middle French *rester*, 'to remain', was once commonly applied to horses that were balky and obstinate.

The students ... could grow restive on bitter winter days when compelled to accompany the professor and his instruments out onto the windswept and frozen lake for what must have seemed interminable lectures.
Hilda Neatby *Queen's University* 1 (1978): 9–10

One of the cows is restive, shifting her weight from back hoof to back hoof as Cinnamon ... prepares her for the milker.
Canadian Heritage Magazine Aug.-Sept. 1986: 14

[Kim Campbell] alone was in a position to keep restive Quebecers and disaffected westerners from turning to regional parties.
Toronto Star 23 Oct. 1993: A1

If you need a break from the restless, all-day scampering between live jazz sites, pop into Metro Reference Library....
Toronto Star 29 June 1994: D2

restrictive and non-restrictive clauses see COMMA; THAT, WHICH

résumé, resumé, resume A *résumé* is any summary, though in Canadian English the word most often refers to a summary of someone's work experience written as part of a job application. In French *résumé* is pronounced *ray ZOO may*. The usual English pronunciation is *REH zoo may*. This difference in pronunciation—in English the first *e* is not given a long *a* sound—may account for the tendency to drop the first accent: in Canadian writing, the most widely used form is *resumé*. Note, however, that not all dictionaries list this form. Some dictionaries list *resume* with no accents at all as a standard form but reject *resumé* as a hybrid of English and French. Other dictionaries list *résumé*, presumably because it reflects the English pronunciation and distinguishes the noun from the verb *resume*, but do not list the accentless *resume*. In formal writing *résumé* with two accents is the safest spelling. All three spellings are defensible, however, and if your word processor doesn't produce accents you may be stuck with *resume*.

His exotic résumé included a B.A. in Asian studies ... and a stint with U.S. Airforce intelligence.
Saturday Night July 1986: 40

Some professionals ... estimate that personnel specialists spend approximately 30 seconds reviewing a resumé.
Queen's Quarterly 94.4 (1987): 852

Philip's relationship to Janie Burroughs was something Elizabeth had forgotten during her witty, lighthearted resumé of her domestic situation at the lunch table....
Margaret Atwood *Life Before Man* 1979: 198

(Here *resumé* means a brief account, or vignette.)

You may apply in confidence by forwarding a complete resume naming the position for which you are applying....
Engineering Dimensions Jul.–Aug. 1988: 52

See also CURRICULUM VITAE.

reticent, reluctant   *Reticent*, in its most common and widely accepted sense, is the opposite of *talkative* or *forthcoming*. Sometimes *reticent* means restrained, especially with respect to artistic productions.

In addition, *reticent* is frequently used as a synonym for *reluctant* or *hesitant*. This usage, however, is acknowledged by only a few dictionaries and is disputed by language commentators; it should be avoided in writing. *Reticent* is pronounced *RET ih sent*.

But the normally reticent ... developer happily discusses the episode now as one that has set a precedent....
Vancouver Sun 23 Aug. 1990: D12

On the subject of Shaw's unconsummated and mostly unhappy marriage ... Holroyd is fairly reticent.
Vancouver Sun 3 Feb. 1990: C4

Hammer, reticent in the slow introduction, achieved his customary virtuoso form in the main part....
Globe and Mail (Toronto) 23 Sept. 1985: S12

... many ventured reasons why the church seemed reticent to engage, at a local level, the pain of the economy.
United Church Observer May 1986: 37

(In this example *hesitant* or *reluctant* would be preferable.)

Consumers are 'a bit more reticent' to spend, he adds.
Province (Vancouver) 5 Dec. 1995: A24

(In this example *hesitant* or *reluctant* would be preferable.)

revenge   see AVENGE

reverend   see RELIGIOUS TITLES

revert   To *revert* is to go back or return to a former condition, belief, or subject. In law, money or property that *reverts* to former owners (or their heirs) is returned to them. The common usage *revert back* is redundant.

No one wants to revert to the feudal systems our ancestors tried to escape.
Country Guide Nov. 1986: 42

Shares in these corporations may then be sold to whites, and ownership of land will revert back to them.
Irving M. Zeitlin and Robert J. Brym *The Social Condition of Humanity* 1991: 165

(The word *back* is unnecessary here.)

He claims 90 per cent of people who try vegetarianism revert back to eating beef.
Vancouver Sun 17 July 1990: D6

(The word *back* is unnecessary here.)

review, revue   A *review* is a critical report, a periodical publication, a military inspection, a general survey of the literature in a scholarly field, or a revue. *Revue* has only one meaning: a stage show featuring sketches, dancing, and songs that parody current events and fads. Revues were a popular form of entertainment in nineteenth-century France, and the English borrowed both the idea and the word from the French. While the English spelling *review* can be used for the stage show, *revue* is not an accepted spelling variant for the other meanings of *review*.

Since Elias does not offer his readers a review of the literature, appropriate questions need to be raised about the place of this research within the existing knowledge.
NeWest Review Dec.–Jan. 1990: 33

Hosted by comedians Roger Abbott and Don Ferguson of CBC's *Royal Canadian Air Farce*, the 'Against Free Trade Revue' poked fun at Prime Minister Brian Mulroney's plans for a free trade agreement with the United States.
United Church Observer May 1986: 51

But there's more—theatrical comedy six nights a week ... and noon-time musical reviews.
Canadian Living 17 May 1986: 3

Other highlights of the Sarnia Games are the colourful opening ceremonies ... and the Ceilidh Tent featuring 'Fraser's Highlanders', a local group gaining great revues from the visitors....
Leisure Life May 1988: 24

(The correct spelling here is *reviews*.)

revolt, revolution   see REBELLION

revue   see REVIEW

rez   see RESERVE

rhetorical question In oratory a rhetorical question is one posed purely for effect, not to get information. The question is phrased in such a way that there is only one possible answer, which the listeners are expected to supply for themselves. Some humorous rhetorical questions are 'Are we men or are we mice?' and 'Do fish swim?' A rhetorical question has the effect of a forceful statement and is usually delivered in a persuasive tone. However, such questions can lead to unexpected results in writing, where the readers' reactions cannot be gauged. Writers should make sure that their readers will answer a rhetorical question correctly—even if that means supplying the answer themselves.

rhinoceros, rhinoceroses The usual plural form is *rhinoceroses*. The singular form, *rhinoceros*, can also be used as a plural: 'The rhinoceros are under the trees'. *Rhinoceri* is listed in some dictionaries, but this form is considered incorrect by some commentators because it is based on the false assumption that *rhinoceros* is a Latin noun forming its plural in *-i*. In fact, the correct Latin plural of this originally Greek word is *rhinocerotes*, a form that had some currency in the nineteenth century but is now obsolete. Many writers avoid the problem of selecting the correct plural by using the informal short forms *rhino* and *rhinos*.

Just as rhinoceroses in Africa are killed for their horns, so sheep in Quebec might be killed for their stomachs.
Gazette (Montreal) 13 Dec. 1990: B2

The vintage prints speak eloquently, filling the Special Exhibitions Hall with images of ... rhinoceri and elephants, circus performers, an hermaphrodite, jazz musicians, statues in Rome.
Ottawa Citizen 6 Oct. 1990: G3

(Either *rhinoceroses* or *rhinoceros* is recommended.)

See also PLURALS, REGULAR, IRREGULAR, FOREIGN.

rhyme, rime The earliest spelling, *rime*, was displaced by *rhyme* in the fifteenth century because scholars mistakenly believed that the word was derived from *rhythm*. *Rhyme* refers to words with similar terminal sounds, or to simple verse, as in 'nursery rhymes'. *Rime* usually means frost, although it can still be used as a variant spelling of *rhyme* (Coleridge used this spelling to create an archaic effect in *The Rime of the Ancient Mariner*). *Rhyme off* is an informal expression meaning to list or name a series of things.

'It works for me too, except for the place where he rhymes "spastic" with "plastic."'
Margaret Atwood *Second Words* 1982: 338

His fingers dance over the listings and he rhymes off case quantities for all the good vintages of Chateau Lafite as far back as 1868 ... and scads more.
Bon Vivant Aug.–Sept. 1982: 14

rid, ridded The past tense and past participle (the form used after *have*) can be either *rid* or *ridded*.
Occasionally *ridded* is mistakenly substituted for *ridden* meaning infested or afflicted, as in 'flea-ridden'.

'With its use of "free" verse, Imagism rid a lame poetry of a musty Georgian Romanticism.'
Queen's Quarterly 92.2 (1985): 310

'We've rid him of the habit,' says veteran 86ers trainer Lou Moro.
Vancouver Sun 27 April 1990: E3

... the Rockets ridded themselves of the Utah Jazz with a 94-83 victory in their best-of-seven Western Conference championship series.
Gazette (Montreal) 1 June 1994: F5

With slump-ridded Leo Gomez out for at least a month following wrist surgery, Baltimore Orioles are considering signing third baseman Kevin Seitzer....
Toronto Star 24 July 1993: C3

(Gomez was *slump-ridden*.)

riding In Canada, and only in Canada, a *riding* is an electoral district or constituency. The term was borrowed into English from the Old Norse word *thrithjungr*, later spelled *triding*, which meant a third part. Originally, in England, *triding* was particular to the county of Yorkshire, which was divided into three administrative divisions. Over time, *triding* lost its initial *t*, and *riding* was the form that was brought to Canada. Although the ridings in Yorkshire were abolished by the British government in 1974, and the term is now seldom used in Britain, it is an integral part of Canadian political vocabulary.

Provincial Liberals ... nominated him as their candidate in the riding of West York in 1948.
Jack Batten *Robinette* 1984: 156

riff, rift Sometimes *riff* is mistakenly used in place of *rift*. In jazz a *riff* is a repeated musical phrase, especially one used as background for a soloist or improvisation; the term is probably a shortened form of *refrain*. A *rift* is a split or break.

But they have handed the opposition Parti Québécois an array of problems to use as ammunition during the daily question period: the handling of the Mohawk crisis, ... the public riff between Environment Minister Pierre Paradis and Energy Minister Lise Bacon over future James Bay development....
Gazette (Montreal) 13 Oct. 1990: B5

(The word required here is *rift*.)

'Our opposition to it created a huge storm,' d'Aquino recalls. 'It caused a major riff between the Mulroney government and ourselves.'
Toronto Star 30 June 1991: F1

(The word required here is *rift*.)

rifle, riffle   The verb *rifle* means to ransack, rob, or steal; to *rifle through* a purse, drawer, etc., is to search it hurriedly. The verb *riffle* means to leaf through pages, or to shuffle a deck of cards.

'You're not getting off so easily,' she breathes, and rifles his pockets for change.
Canadian Fiction Magazine 63 (1988): 17

'The reporter was wrong to rifle [the file] and the editor showed a conspicuous lack of morals in printing the story.'
Saturday Night March 1986: 26

One of the great joys in life ... is a fashion bargain, so you may see me rifling through the racks at the great Canadian designer clearance sale.
Toronto Star 19 May 1994: D5

He scooped out his pigeonhole of mail and riffled through it.
Constance Beresford-Howe *Night Studies* 1985: 85

The premier smiled and riffled through his papers.
Ottawa Citizen 30 Nov. 1994: A10

Mr. Keegstra ... rifled through a small pamphlet as he listened to the prosecutor.
Globe and Mail (Toronto) 17 July 1985: 3

(If Keegstra was leafing through a pamphlet, the word required is *riffled*.)

rift   see RIFF

rime   see RHYME

ring   The past tense is *rang*: 'Before the war, the bells rang every Sunday for an hour'. The past participle (the form that follows *have*) is *rung*: 'She has rung your doorbell twice'. The use of *rung* as the past tense is considered dialectal: 'She *rung* that bell as if she wanted to break it'.

'I rang the handbell at 9 sharp.'
Gazette (Montreal) 2 Sept. 1990: A2

Through the centuries, church bells have rung in celebration and in warning, in victory and in defeat.
Province (Vancouver) 29 June 1990: 22

'The last World Cup rung the alarm bells.'
Vancouver Sun 2 Oct. 1990: C7

(The standard past tense is *rang*.)

See also PHONE.

rise   see RAISE

road, concession road, side road, street, highway, parkway, expressway, freeway, autoroute, trail, motorway, turnpike, toll road, thruway   *Road* is the most general of these words. In the past *road* referred to the main route between towns or cities, and often the road took its name from a destination. (In Kingston, for example, Bath Road leads to Bath, Sydenham Road to Sydenham, and Montreal Road to Montreal.) Now *road* may designate anything from a paved highway to a dirt track, depending on the context. A *concession road* is a rural road, especially in Ontario and Quebec. In these provinces the land for settlers was subdivided into parcels called concessions, and concession roads generally run east–west along the boundaries between them. *Side roads* are north–south rural roads. *Streets* are usually urban.

Highway has, at least since 1859, meant the most direct and least time-consuming route from one place to another and is still used figuratively in this sense: 'the highway to riches', 'the information highway'. Now, in North America, a *highway* is a road designed to carry fast-moving traffic. In Canada *highway* generally refers to a two-lane road connecting two major centres. *Expressway* is the common term for a multi-laned, limited access road. *Freeway*, which originated in the United States in the 1930s, is widely used in western Canada. *Highway*, *expressway*, and *freeway* are used interchangeably by many Canadians.

The French word *autoroute* sometimes finds its way into Canadian English in reference to highways in Quebec. *Trail* is often used in the names of historic scenic highways in various parts of Canada. A *parkway* is an expressway bordered by beautiful scenery or well-tended trees and grass.

In Britain *motorway* is the only term for a limited access highway with at least two lanes in each direction. A *turnpike* was originally a *toll road* (which motorists paid a toll for using); now *turnpike* is used in the United States like *thruway* (an accepted spelling in the U.S.) for any major highway, whether or not tolls are charged.

> [Hunters] had set up at the edge of a wheat field earlier that morning and had already taken a couple of [Canada geese] when they saw yet another car stop along the concession road about three quarters of a mile away.
> *Gazette* (Montreal) 20 Oct. 1990: 65

> Seferis purchased the property . . . and two months later learned that the highway on which it was located would be superseded by the new freeway. . . .
> J.E. Smyth et al. *The Law and Business Administration in Canada* 1987: 223

> The 'new' city [of Quebec], beyond the 18th-century bastions, reaches out . . . to the shopping malls of suburbia, the provincial autoroute (highway) network, and the airport at nearby Sainte-Foy.
> Alan Tucker, ed. *The Penguin Guide to Canada* 1991: 272

> Drive the Cabot Trail, too, . . . and also try the Lighthouse Route south from Halifax along a coast that's furrowed and rocky.
> Alan Tucker, ed. *The Penguin Guide to Canada* 1991: 9

See also SKID ROAD; THRU.

rob, steal, robbery Generally speaking, people and places are *robbed* ('The bank was robbed'; 'I was robbed'), while objects are *stolen* ('My wallet was stolen'). 'Our jewels were robbed' is considered archaic or dialectal. Some commentators disapprove of 'Their house was robbed while they slept', insisting on 'Their house was burglarized', because the legal definition of *robbery* includes a face-to-face encounter and violence or intimidation.

See also BURGLARY.

rococo see BAROQUE

ROM see RAM

romance, Romance languages, Romanticism, romantic, romancer The word *romance* was first used to distinguish the vernacular Latin dialects used in the Roman provinces from the Latin spoken in Rome. Modern *Romance languages* include French, Spanish, Portuguese, Italian, and Romanian. The first *romances* were fanciful adventure tales written in these dialects (Latin was reserved for scholarly and official writings), and it is to them that one modern meaning of *romance*—a

fictional tale of extraordinary events, a fabrication—refers. Thus the original romances were stories told in poetry and prose dealing with the exotic, the heroic, and the passionate as opposed to the everyday or the real. Gradually, however, *romance* took on the meaning that is more common today: a passionate love story.

Romanticism refers to an artistic movement of the late eighteenth and early nineteenth centuries that celebrated freedom of individual expression and creativity. The adjective *Romantic*, when capitalized, refers to this movement ('Keats was a Romantic poet').

Some usage guides object to the verb *romance* meaning to woo or court, but most dictionaries accept this usage. Note, however, that the noun *romancer* usually refers to a storyteller or liar, not one who seeks romantic love.

> In romance we have a simplified and idealized world, of brave heroes, pure and beautiful heroines, and very bad villains.
> Northrop Frye *The Educated Imagination* 1963: 48

(Here *romance* means the early adventure-story genre.)

> In a survey of 48 women, those who regularly read romance novels reported making love twice as often as women who said they didn't enjoy this genre.
> *Chatelaine* April 1986: 32

(Here *romance novels* are love stories.)

> John's romancing of Lois was wholesome, orderly and single-minded.
> Jack Batten *Robinette* 1984: 28

(Here *romancing*, from the verb *romance*, means courtship.)

Roman nose see AQUILINE NOSE

romantic, Romanticism see ROMANCE

rosin see RESIN

rostrum see DAIS

rouge see BLEU

round see AROUND

route, rout Most Canadians pronounce *route* like *root*, but a strong minority rhyme it with *pout*. Both pronunciations are accepted. British dictionaries list the *root* pronunciation first, but note that the *pout* pronunciation is frequently used by the military. Americans, like Canadians, are divided: some use the pronunciation that rhymes with *pout* for a paper route and the one that rhymes with *root* for a highway.

The pronunciation that rhymes with *pout* was popular in Britain until the nineteenth century. Early British colonists carried the older pronunciation to Canada and the United States, where it survived, while in Standard British (non-military) English it faded from use.

Rout in all its various senses ('put to rout', 'rout out', etc.) is always pronounced to rhyme with *pout*.

royal anthem   see O CANADA, GOD SAVE THE QUEEN

rubric   *Rubric* is derived from the Latin for 'red ochre', a pigment used by the Romans for the titles of legal documents. Hence a *rubric* is the title of a law. It is also any title, heading, or note that is printed either in red or in some distinctive typeface. Figuratively, a *rubric* is a topic or theme: 'They discussed the embargoes under the rubric of economic development'.

Rubrics are the directions for conducting a religious service, which originally appeared in red type in prayer books. A *rubrician* (rhymes with *magician*) is an expert on ecclesiastical rites. By extension of the liturgical meaning, a *rubric* is any established rule of procedure or conduct.

> The mayor and council draw up some impressive arguments in their manifesto ... under the compelling rubric: 'Toward a New Generation of Government.'
> *Vancouver Sun* 5 Sept. 1991: A16

> It is a dereliction of responsibility ... to defend bad scholarship under the rubric of academic freedom.
> *Maclean's* 6 March 1989: A5

> One cannot forge a nation by encouraging separateness under the rubric of multiculturalism.
> *Maclean's* 10 Sept. 1990: A11

running shoes, tennis shoes, gym shoes, trainers, runners, tennies, sneakers   Many Canadians call the rubber-soled shoes they use for sports *running shoes*; Americans tend to call them *tennis shoes* or *gym shoes*. In Britain the parallel term is *trainers* (which might puzzle those of us who think of trainers as absorbent underpants for toddlers undergoing toilet training). The informal term for these shoes in Canada is usually *runners*; in the U.S., *tennies*, *sneakers*, or *sneaks*.

run-on sentence   see SENTENCE

rye   see WHISKY, WHISKEY

S

-'s, -s'   see APOSTROPHE; POSSESSIVE; POSSESSIVE AFTER GERUND

saccharin, saccharine   The artificial sweetener is *saccharin* (*SACK a rin*). The adjective meaning sickeningly sweet is *saccharine* (the last syllable of the adjective rhymes with *sin*, *seen*, or *sign*).

sacred writings   Names of sacred texts, such as the Bible, the Koran, the Talmud, the Torah, the Upanishads, and the Vedas, are capitalized; unlike the titles of other books, however, they are not italicized. Names of books and sections of the Bible (Genesis, Ezekiel, the New Testament) are capital-ized but neither italicized nor put in quotation marks. The word *bible* is not capitalized when it is used metaphorically to refer to an indispensable guide: 'the birdwatcher's bible'.

The adjective *biblical* is never capitalized, and some editors recommend not capitalizing the adjectives derived from the names of other sacred texts. But this seems to be a cry in the wilderness: *Vedic* and *Koranic* are always capitalized, and *Talmudic* more often than not. Dictionaries consistently capitalize such adjectives; *biblical* remains the exception.

> According to the Bible, ... King Herod ordered the massacre of all children two years old and under.
> *Ottawa Citizen* 29 Dec. 1992: B1

Rao ... recites passages from the Vedas and the Bhaga-vad-Gita, ancient Hindu texts.
Calgary Herald 24 Oct. 1992: G8

It is further believed that this will mark the beginning of a thousand years of peace, which was spoken of in the biblical Book of Revelation.
Toronto Star 26 Dec. 1992: J21

The women ... chant, perform healing rituals, discuss social justice and read from *Dreaming the Dark* by American witch Starhawk—the bible to many of this kind of group.
Calgary Herald 26 Dec. 1992: H7

As regards religion, most of my friends remember Biblical stories from Sunday school and that's about it.
Ottawa Citizen 28 Dec. 1992: B8

(The adjective *biblical* should not be capitalized.)

Segal is a professor of Talmudic studies at the University of Calgary.
Calgary Herald 9 July 1992: B3

Ali Abdulah Mohamed, who ran a private Koranic school before the war, has saved at least 570 abandoned children and orphans from the streets of Mogadishu.
Toronto Star 17 Feb. 1992: A13

sacrilegious *Sacrilegious* is sometimes misspelled *sacreligious*, probably because of the influence of *religious*, but the two words are not etymologically related. *Sacrilegious*, which refers to the disrespect-ful treatment of something sacred, is derived from the Latin *sacr-*, meaning 'sacred', and *legere*, 'to steal'. *Religious* is derived from the Latin *religio*, 'reverence'.

> The apparent shortcomings of his defensive personnel notwithstanding, it seemed sacreligious to ask Wayne Gretzky to backcheck.
> *Province* (Vancouver) 24 Oct. 1990: 76

(The correct spelling is *sacrilegious*.)

Sahara *Sahara* is the Arabic word for desert. Some commentators object to *Sahara desert* as re-dundant, and prefer *Sahara* alone. Canadian writers use both forms. Since most Canadians are not fa-miliar with Arabic, *Sahara desert* is not recognized as a redundant usage and is perfectly acceptable.
Many Canadian place names are similarly derived from non-English words. For example, although *Ontario* is probably derived from an Iroquoian word meaning 'beautiful lake', the name *Lake Ontario* is not considered redundant. And *Yukon* comes from *yu-kun-ah*, 'great river', but few English-speakers are aware that *Yukon River* means 'great river river'.

Experts claim those areas are drier than the Sahara desert.
Uphere Mar.–Apr. 1990: 42

He is also planning a grand-scale movie in the Sahara.
Globe and Mail (Toronto) 20 Feb. 1985: M9

said   see AFOREMENTIONED

Saint(e)   see ST., STE.

Saint John, St. John's Saint John is the largest city in New Brunswick. *Saint* is usually spelled out, and abbreviating it may annoy New Brunswickers.
St. John's is the capital and largest city of Newfoundland.

> In the 1930s, Messer organized the New Brunswick Lumberjacks who played dances and a Saint John radio show.
> *Queen's Quarterly* 95.2 (1988): 296

> Incidentally, St. is not a standard spelling for the city of 'Saint' John, although it is used for the name of the river and the county.
> W.C. Lougheed, ed. *In Search of the Standard in Canadian English* 1986: 18

> Air Canada flight 663 left St. John, New Brunswick, on March 31, 1980, for a 23-minute flight to Fredericton.
> *Canadian Consumer* Feb. 1986: 31

(The usual spelling is *Saint John*.)

> A graduate of Memorial University in St. John's [Nfld.], Murphy is a Rhodes Scholar.
> *Daily News* (Halifax) 29 June 1994: 27

See also ST., STE.

sake Canadian writers use possessive forms in phrases such as *for old time's sake* or *for Pete's sake*. In expressions such as *for goodness' sake* or *for conve-nience' sake*, where the possessive noun ends with an *s* sound, most commentators consider the apostro-phe optional.
However, shifting the possessive *s* to the end of *sake* (*for god sakes* instead of *for god's sake*, or *for heaven sakes* instead of *for heaven's sake*) is consid-ered dialectal.

> For goodness' sake, even a selection of cantaloupe, strawberry and watermelon ices is underlaid with a tricolor sauce for a total of six contrasting flavors.
> *Globe and Mail* (Toronto) 14 Dec. 1985: D17

> The sales were good, for goodness sake.
> *Globe and Mail* (Toronto) 21 Dec. 1985: D1

(This spelling is accepted, but *goodness'* is more common.)

Photographers are even following Jennifer into the ladies' room, for goodness sakes.
Vancouver Sun 31 Aug. 1990: D2

(The final *s* in *sakes* is dialectal unless preceded by a plural, as in 'for their sakes'.)

salad days   see HEYDAY

salvo   see BARRAGE

sanatorium, sanitarium, [sanitorium]   Canadian writers use both *sanatorium* and *sanitarium* to refer to a place of treatment for the physically or mentally ill or a place of rest and relaxation. Some usage guides have tried to distinguish these words on the basis of etymology. *Sanatorium*, they argue, is derived from the Latin root *sanatorius* meaning 'health-restoring', and should therefore refer to a place that treats the sick. *Sanitarium*, which is derived from the Latin *sanitas* meaning 'health', should be reserved for the 'health resort' sense. This tenuous distinction is certainly not reflected in usage.
  Canadian writers use both words with equal frequency. *Sanatorium*, the older form, is preferred in Britain. *Sanitarium* is an American variant spelling that is now fully established in North America. Many Canadian writers use a hybrid spelling, *sanitorium*, but few dictionaries acknowledge this variant, and it should be avoided.

Should one Table Officer miss his bus while the other is holidaying at a sanatorium, Parliament could well stall in want of a name for a face.
Globe and Mail (Toronto) 3 April 1985: 6

(Here *sanatorium* means health resort.)

In 1876, John Harvey Kellogg tried to develop a nutritious food that feeble and often toothless patients in a sanitarium could eat.
Ottawa Citizen 14 Feb. 1990: C1

(Here *sanitarium* means place of treatment.)

Most telling perhaps was his encounter in Volgograd (formerly Stalingrad) with eight veterans of the city's defence in the Great Patriotic War, out for the day from their sanitorium.
Financial Post 16 Sept. 1991: 39

(Most dictionaries do not recognize the spelling *sanitorium*.)

sanction   To *sanction* something always means to approve of it, but as a noun *sanction* has two contradictory meanings. Sometimes a *sanction* is a sign of approval and sometimes it's a sign of disapproval (i.e., a penalty). In the negative sense *sanction* is often plural: 'economic sanctions'. When using this word, writers should ensure that the context makes it clear whether the positive or the negative sense is intended.

If political authority has sanctioned nuclear-generated power, should the individual researcher avoid involvement with it on the grounds of personal disapproval?
Perspectives: Profiles of Research at Queen's University 1986: 34

Short of a papal confirmation ... a cardinal's blessing and encouragement is about the highest sanction Descartes could have hoped for to confirm his vocation.
Canadian Journal of Philosophy 19 (1989): 216

(Here *sanction* is used positively.)

Anthropologists have found that sanctions for criminal behaviour exist in the most primitive societies.
Richard Davies and Glen Kirkland, eds. *Dimensions* 1986: 66

(Here *sanction* is used negatively.)

sang   see SING

sanguine, sanguinary   *Sanguine* (pronounced SANG gwin) means cheerful, optimistic, or rosy. *Sanguinary* means bloody or delighting in violence.

Unfortunately, there are two factors which make this conclusion too sanguine.
Queen's Quarterly 94.4 (1987): 801

'Naturally of a bold and sanguine temperament, when occasion demanded he could display the tenacity and patience of the man of routine.'
Hilda Neatby *Queen's University* 1 (1978): 172

There are many ironies in this discussion, which takes place at the approach of the 50th anniversary of history's most sanguinary war, unleashed by Nazi Germany....
Financial Post 8 March 1989: 12

Anne Parillaud portrays a woman [a vampire] with sanguine taste in Innocent Blood.
Vancouver Sun 25 Sept. 1992: C6

(Here *sanguinary* would be more appropriate.)

sanitarium, [sanitorium]   see SANATORIUM

sank   see SINK

sans   From the French meaning 'without', *sans* is found primarily in speech and in the breezy journalistic prose of entertainment, travel, and gossip columnists. It is pronounced as in French: like *song* without the *g*.

> ... to accuse a middle class couple of eating at McDonald's, sans children, is akin to accusing them of putting plastic slipcovers on the couch.
> *Globe and Mail* (Toronto) 14 March 1985: CL3

Sansei   see ISSEI

Sarcee, Tsuu T'ina   Members of the Alberta First Nation formerly called *Sarcee* now refer to themselves as *Tsuu T'ina* (singular and plural). *Sarcee*, their language, which has fewer than 100 speakers, is a member of the Athapaskan family.

> ... Roy Whitney, chief of the Tsuu T'ina Nation west of Calgary, formerly known as the Sarcee reserve, became the first Native appointed to the board.
> *Calgary Herald* 26 Nov. 1992: B1

> The [Treaty 7 Tribal Council] represents the Tsuu T'ina, Siksika, Peigan, Blood and Stoney Nations.
> *Calgary Herald* 3 Sept 1992: A3

sartorial   The adjective *sartorial*, from the Latin *sartor*, 'tailor', means having to do with tailors or fashions in clothing. Some usage experts call *sartorial* pretentious, but it is almost always used with humour or irony.

> Maggie and George were suddenly in the room, she in one of her voluminous caftans, and George in yellow boots and his usual sartorial indifference.
> Howard Engel *Murder Sees the Light* 1984: 80

> The journalist also thinks the long shorts look ridiculous but ... is wearing Dockers and cannot afford to be sartorially smug.
> *Toronto Star* 2 April 1993: C1

Saskatchewan   see APPENDIX I

Sasquatch, Bigfoot, Abominable Snowman, yeti   According to folklore, a hairy, man-like creature inhabits the mountainous regions of the Pacific Northwest and of Tibet. In British Columbia and Alberta it is called *Sasquatch*, from the Salish word for 'hairy man'. Arguments for its existence are based on Native legend, reported sightings begin-ning in 1850, and large footprints found in the snow and earth, which gave rise to its name in the United States, *Bigfoot*.

Abominable Snowman is the name given to the Sasquatch-like creature in the Himalayas. The Abominable Snowman is also called the *yeti*, a Tibetan term for this man-like creature.

> The most controversial presentation ... will be evidence that the so-called 'wildman,' or Bigfoot or Sasquatch, observed in the Canadian and U.S. Rockies, could actually be a species of giant ape which supposedly became extinct more than 600,000 years ago.
> *Globe and Mail* (Toronto) 13 April 1985: P10

> Fully garbed for winter, you resemble Bigfoot or an overloaded coat-tree.
> *Uphere* Jan.–Feb. 1990: 78

> If this giant ape is still alive, it could also explain persistent reports of Asian man-like creatures, known as the Yeti (the Abominable Snowman) in the Himalayas....
> *Globe and Mail* (Toronto) 13 April 1985: P10

> But the Shenzhen paper was insistent—not only was the yeti reposing comfortably in the Wuhan walk-up, it was drinking from a ladle, eating from a rice bowl and 'making sounds like an old man.'
> *Globe and Mail* (Toronto) 12 Feb. 1985: P11

sault, the Soo   *Sault* (pronounced *SOO*) is a Canadian English word dating from the seventeenth century and borrowed from the French of the early explorers. As a noun it means waterfall or rapids. In the expression 'sault the rapids', it is a verb meaning shoot. In contemporary English *sault* is rare, though it has found its way into place names such as Long Sault and Sault Ste. Marie. In French the *l* has been dropped and *saut* is pronounced *so*.

The Soo is the nickname of the city of Sault Ste. Marie and the canal system there; it should be used only in informal writing.

> Sault Ste. Marie, affectionately known as the 'Soo,' is the navigational gateway between Lake Superior and Lake Huron; the International Bridge across the St. Marys River connects the city to its Michigan sister of the same name.
> Alan Tucker, ed. *The Penguin Guide to Canada* 1991: 444

> 'A few [freighters] always run until freeze-up. Sometimes they get caught in the ice-pack through the Soo.'
> David Williams *Eye of the Father* 1985: 46

> Lindros said he didn't want to play in the Soo because it didn't have a university and there was increased travel.
> *Ottawa Citizen* 1 Sept. 1990: C1

savant, idiot savant A *savant* (pronounced *sa VONT*) is a learned person, especially a distinguished scholar. Sometimes the word is used sarcastically.

Idiot savant is a medical term, now considered outdated, for someone with mental deficiencies who nonetheless possesses an astonishing aptitude in areas such as music or mathematics. In current medical usage *savant* alone is used for this group as well.

> And so it came to pass that … Andrew Petter, law professor, constitutional savant and resident authority on the infamous Meech Lake accord, was acclaimed the new champion of virtue in Saanich South.
> *Vancouver Sun* 6 Feb. 1990: B1

> [Sociologists] Jim and Mary Maxwell, garage sale savants at Queen's University in Kingston, say it was the tight economy of the early seventies that first impelled us to turn our houses inside out for the neighbors' amusement.
> *Globe and Mail* (Toronto) 27 April 1985: H1

> Fortunately I do not waste valuable mental space on foolish things like sports statistics. I specialize in telephone numbers, a field in which I am practically an idiot savant.
> *Gazette* (Montreal) 24 Nov. 1990: A2

savvy The noun *savvy* means know-how or street smarts; the adjective means knowing or shrewd; and the verb means understand ('Do you savvy?'). All these uses are informal; the verb form is the least common and the least acceptable in writing. *Savvy* is derived from Portuguese via pidgin English.

> The president was in many ways like … Eisenhower, but the former actor lacked the general's intelligence, savvy, and realistic sense of limitations.
> *Queen's Quarterly* 95.4 (1988): 811

> … it was clear to all who knew him that he had extraordinary ambition, tenacity, and savvy.
> *Saturday Night* July 1986: 20

> The savvy nightlife purveyor knows that the surest path to a person's wallet is not through the head but through the crotch.
> *Saturday Night* Feb. 1986: 52

saw, seen The past tense of *see* is *saw* ('I saw her leave for work'); the past participle is *seen* ('I have seen her leave every morning this week'). *Seen* as the past tense ('I seen her leave for work') is a common but stigmatized usage, considered unacceptable in both speech and writing. Examples of *I seen* usually appear in print only in transcribed speech or fictional dialogue.

> 'I seen he was going crazy and saw my chance to get away.'
> *Vancouver Sun* 6 Dec. 1990: A20

(Here, in quoted speech, a newspaper editor has let the non-standard 'I *seen*' stand.)

> I seen you looking at the snake and dagger on my forearm.
> *Canadian Fiction Magazine* 64 (1988): 94

(Here the non-standard 'I *seen*' is put in the mouth of a fictional character.)

say Writers often use words such as *admit, advise, allege, assert, claim, contend, declare,* and *disclose* to avoid repeating *say* and *said* when recording direct speech or attributing statements to their sources. But these substitutes for *say* have drawbacks: they can distract readers, and they can also convey connotations unintended by the writer. For example, *according to* may suggest lack of credibility; *admit* may seem to imply confession, *affirm* to support a statement as fact, *allege* to imply accusation, *claim* to suggest that the statement is not fact, *concede* to admit defeat, *disclose* and *reveal* to suggest a prior attempt at concealment, and so on. Journalists should be especially careful to accurately record not only speakers' words but also the manner in which they are presented. Although *said* is not an exciting word, it is often the most accurate one.

See also GO, SAY; WORDINESS, VARIATION.

say for   see LIKE FOR

scab   see REPLACEMENT WORKER

Scandinavian, Nordic, Alpine Scandinavia is a region in northwestern Europe that includes Sweden, Norway, Denmark, and parts of Finland. Culturally, Greenland, Iceland and the Faroe Islands can also be considered part of Scandinavia, while some parts of Finland are culturally and linguistically distinct.

Nordic is an anthropological term used to describe the physical characteristics of the Scandinavian and Finnish peoples. It is now also used more generally as a synonym for *Scandinavian*. In the sporting world *Nordic* refers to cross-country skiing and ski jumping, while *Alpine*, which means 'from the mountains', refers to downhill skiing. *Nordic* and *Alpine* are usually capitalized.

> Parliament made beer legal in May, but gave the island country of 251,000 until March 1 to prepare for the change that ended Iceland's isolation from its ale-loving Scandinavian cousins.
> *Gazette* (Montreal) 2 March 1989: A10

> A group including Canada, the United States, the Nordic nations, Switzerland and Australia have already started. . . .
> *Globe and Mail* (Toronto) 23 March 1985: P1

> The 22-year-old started out in Nordic skiing, which he called 'our country's most popular sport,' but after five years, he switched to Alpine skiing. . . .
> *Gazette* (Montreal) 6 March 1989: C5

scapegoat A *scapegoat* is sacrificed for the sins of others. This biblical noun was made into a verb in psychological writing in the 1940s; since then the verb has spread into Standard Canadian English. To *scapegoat* a person or a group of people is to blame them, or attack them, for problems they did not cause.

> There is no justification for scapegoating the 18-to-21-year-olds because . . . the higher age groups are just as guilty.
> *Globe and Mail* (Toronto) 5 March 1985: P7

> . . . opinion polls point to significant anti-foreigner sentiment throughout the population, showing itself in a swing toward right-wing political parties which scapegoat minorities for the problems of unification.
> *Financial Post* 23 Oct. 1991: 10

See also FUNCTIONAL SHIFT.

scarcely see HARDLY

scared of Some authorities maintain that the idiom is either *scared by* or *afraid of*. Canadian writers avoid *scared of* in academic and serious writing, but use it freely in journalism and fiction.

> It's enough to make you scared of flying. . . .
> *Gazette* (Montreal) 4 March 1989: K3

> The police said we were heroes, but we were more scared of what the editor would say if we came back without our story.
> *Province* (Vancouver) 6 Dec. 1990: 3

scarify, scarey, scarification *Scarify* has two senses, one related to *scar* and one related to *scare*. To *scarify* someone may mean to scar them physically, to lacerate their feelings, or to frighten them. Whereas *scarey* has childish overtones, *scarifying* has horrifying overtones. *Scarification* is the practice of scarring the body for aesthetic or ritual purposes, or of scoring seeds to assist in germination.

> In African cultures, they have things like tattoos and scarification, where you go from boyhood to manhood.
> *Ottawa Citizen* 22 July 1990: E1

> His preoccupation with video intervention in private lives is scarifying, and all too true.
> *Gazette* (Montreal) 1 Sept. 1990: T48

> Scarification means scraping a hard seed, nicking it or treating it with heat or boiling water—making germination easier by physically changing the seed.
> *Harrowsmith* Aug.–Sept. 1986: 63

scenario A *scenario* is the outline of a play, film, or television program. Over the last few decades the theatrical meaning has been extended so that a situation unfolding in real life or a hypothetical situation can be called a *scenario*. *Scenario* can also refer to a proposal, a plan, or a setting. Although several critics call the extended uses of *scenario* trite, they are standard in all types of writing.
Scenario is sometimes misspelled *scenerio*.

> With . . . a rough scenario in his head, he then set to work with the dancers and musicians.
> *Performing Arts in Canada* March 1988: 9

> Consider the following scenario, recently sketched by one Harvard economist.
> Irving M. Zeitlin and Robert J. Brym *The Social Condition of Humanity* 1991: 252

> In Quebec . . . a much more disturbing scenario was unfolding.
> Janine Brodie, Shelley A. M. Gavigan, and Jane Jenson *The Politics of Abortion* 1992: 93

> Miller's WEFA Group . . . has developed a scenerio in which the deficit could be reduced by $9 billion by the end of 1992 without unduly harming the economy.
> *Financial Post* 17 April 1989: 8

(The correct spelling is *scenario*.)

sceptic see SKEPTIC

schedule   The competing pronunciations for this word are *SKEH jool*, *SKEH joo ul* (favoured by Americans) and *SHEH jool* (favoured by the British). Sociolinguistic studies indicate that the *sk* pronunciations are by far preferred by Canadian speakers of all ages and backgrounds, and that *SHEH jool* is on the decline.

scientific English   The level of technicality in a given piece of writing should reflect the background knowledge of the likely reader, not the expertise of the author. Because technical terms and phrasings defeat communication if a reader doesn't fully understand them, it is preferable to use non-scientific terms for non-specialist readers (e.g., *bruises* rather than *contusions*). When it is necessary to use a technical term, a concise explanation can be worked into the sentence in which the term first appears. Writing can clearly communicate scientific information to general readers without being technically daunting. Even a scientist writing for other scientists should try to keep scientific jargon to a minimum.

It is possible that individual variations in the three-dimensional context resulting from positionings of to-be-detected target lines within the context are more dissimilar than is the case when the same target lines appear within unconnected contexts or alone.
Canadian Journal of Psychology 44.3 (1990): 389

(Here even a research psychologist would probably appreciate less complicated phrasing.)

See also COLLOQUIAL, INFORMAL, SLANG, JARGON; SPECIES, GENUS.

score   In one of its senses *score* means twenty or a set of twenty. For example, the phrase 'threescore and ten' means seventy: three times twenty, plus ten. The plural form *scores* is often used loosely to mean many, but usually implies less than a hundred.

... I found myself scribbling lists of words and idioms ranging from a dozen to a score or more of items I wanted to remind myself of for one reason or another....
W.C. Lougheed, ed. *In Search of the Standard in Canadian English* 1986: 49

The loneliness of the long-distance runner is nothing compared with the loneliness of working at home, especially if you once worked among scores of people.
Toronto Star 21 June 1993: B3

Scottish, Scots, Scotch   The *OED* describes the use of the adjectives *Scotch*, *Scots*, and *Scottish* as 'somewhat unsettled'. *Scottish* is the original adjective, which was contracted to *Scots* in Scotland and to *Scotch* in England. The Scottish writers Robert Burns (1759–96) and Walter Scott (1771–1832) often used the 'English' form, *Scotch*. Since their time, however, the adjective *Scotch* has fallen out of favour in Scotland, and *Scots* has also become less common. In contemporary Scotland the preferred adjective form is *Scottish*. Canadians tend to use *Scottish* or *Scots*, reserving *Scotch* for certain fixed expressions including 'Scotch whisky', 'Scotch pine', 'Scotch plaid', 'Scotch broth', and 'Scotch egg'.

The people are *Scots* or *the Scottish*. The dialect of English spoken in Scotland (particularly in the Lowlands) is called *Scots*.

Mrs. Marchenko maintained ... a genuine Scottish reserve....
Canadian Fiction Magazine 63 (1988): 84

[Alice] Munro, counterpointing the story with an ancient Scots ballad about faeries and an enchanted boy, weaves in and out of the past with confidence.
Vancouver Sun 14 April 1990: C4

'If it weren't for the Irish and the French and the Scottish in Canada, there would be no folklore here.'
Performing Arts March 1988: 15

The two men were ... rivals for the leadership of the Kingston Scots community.
William Teatero *John Anderson: Fugitive Slave* 1986: 174

We referred to ourselves as Scotch and not Scots. When, years later, I learned that the usage in Scotland was different it seemed to me rather an affectation.
John Kenneth Galbraith *The Scotch* 1966: 12

scrupulous   see METICULOUS

sculpture, sculpt   The verb forms *sculpture* and *sculpt* are found in most Canadian, British, and American dictionaries. Some critics prefer the older verb *sculpture* to the back-formation *sculpt*, but Canadian writers use *sculpt* more often.

More consideration is being given to sculpturing of interiors, Riley says....
Vancouver Sun 24 March 1990: G4

... there is virtually no form of expression in the visual arts that she can't master, whether it be printmaking, installations, sculpting or her mainstay—drawing.
Gazette (Montreal) 5 May 1990: I5

See also BACK-FORMATION.

Scylla and Charybdis   To be *between Scylla and Charybdis* means to be faced with two choices, each of which involves hardship. The phrase comes from Homer's epic *The Odyssey*, in which Odysseus must sail between two rocky shores. On one side is a multi-headed monster named Scylla (*SILL uh*) and on the other is a violent whirlpool named Charybdis (*kuh RIB dis*). Avoiding one peril means moving closer to the other. To 'steer a mid-course between Scylla and Charybdis' means to find a way of avoiding both difficulties.

Between a rock and a hard place is a more common metaphor for the same situation, but it is not appropriate in formal writing.

> Guiding the screw through the channel, with only 1.5-millimetre clearance on either side, Tredwell felt as if he were navigating between Scylla and Charybdis.... 'If we put the screw too far to the left, we'll put it through his spinal cord and he'll be paralysed. If we put it too far to the right, it'll go into one of his arteries and he might bleed to death.'
> *Vancouver Sun* 11 Sept. 1992: A1

> [Unions] know they have farmers and other shippers caught between a rock and a hard place.
> *Country Guide* Nov. 1986: 12

-se   see -CE

sear, sere   To *sear* is to scorch, cauterize, or brand. A *sear* is the mark that results from being burned. The adjective *sere* means dried up or withered. Shakespeare's character Macbeth compares old age to 'the sere and yellow leaf' (*Macbeth* 5.3.23).

> When the pan is very hot, place the steaks in it and sear the meat for 4 minutes.
> *Globe and Mail* (Toronto) 9 Jan. 1985: SB2

> Both plays deal with the crises of middle-aged protagonists beginning to glimpse the sere leaf of old age beyond the fading dreams and glories of youth.
> *NeWest Review* Oct.–Nov. 1989: 46

> In no time, the sere forest floor was sodden and silent.
> *Gazette* (Montreal) 13 Nov. 1990: D16

seasonable, seasonal   *Seasonable* means appropriate to the time of year, or timely: 'seasonable advice'. *Seasonable* weather is normal for the season. *Seasonal* means controlled by the season of the year or limited to a season. *Seasonal* employment (for example, fruit picking) occurs only during a particular season.

> Temperatures soared to 11.6 Thursday and Friday. Early next week, however, they will plummet to more seasonable lows of -8 to -11....
> *Ottawa Citizen* 17 March 1990: A20

> In the factory ... the women are lucky to be working, and live in fear of seasonal layoffs.
> Henry M. Rosenthal and S. Cathy Berson, eds. *Canadian Jewish Outlook Anthology* 1988: 294

> Granted, the loch was covered with heavy haze, for it was still morning and unseasonally mild for early May.
> *Globe and Mail* (Toronto) 27 April 1985: T7

(The word required here is *unseasonably*.)

second   When it means next after the first, or is used as a verb meaning to support and endorse, *second* is pronounced with the stress on the first syllable: *SECK und*.

A military sense of *second*, to shift someone temporarily to another unit, has moved into general usage, particularly in business. This verb is stressed on the second syllable: *se KOND*.

> The motion was duly seconded and unanimously approved by the meeting....
> J.E. Smyth et al. *The Law and Business Administration in Canada* 1987: 172

> Lunan, an officer in the Canadian Army, had been seconded in 1944 to the Wartime Information Board where he was employed as editor of a military journal, Canadian Affairs.
> Frederick Gibson *Queen's University* 2 (1983): 278

> Through the Inspector General of Banks, that peer review took the form of 25 officials seconded from Canada's six major banks who spent ... eight days examining 80 per cent of Continental's loan portfolio.
> *Globe and Mail* (Toronto) 2 Nov. 1985: A6

secondary colour   see COLOUR

Second World War   see FIRST WORLD WAR

secrete   *Secrete* (pronounced *suh CREET*) has two meanings: to hide something and to ooze fluid.

> ... today's penitentiaries are secreted away in the boonies in the hope of swinging the votes of the rural unemployed the government's way.
> *Globe and Mail* (Toronto) 20 July 1985: E17

> ... under optimal growing conditions, with an ample force of foraging bees to gather all of the nectar secreted, an acre of fireweed bloom could yield as much as 450 pounds of honey.
> *Harrowsmith* Oct.–Nov. 1985: 51

secular, sectarian *Secular* means having to do with this world rather than the next, worldly or temporal as opposed to religious or spiritual. In the Catholic Church a secular priest is one who does not belong to a religious order. *Sectarian* means having to do with religious or political sects.

> ... the division of reality into secular and sacred worlds that was at the very centre of this culture provided the justification for separating women from men and assigning distinct roles to each sex.
> *Queen's Quarterly* 98.1 (1991): 284

> For many years a feature of the Winnipeg bonspiel was its annual church service; but, in an increasingly secular society, the church service has been done away with along with the one-time reverence for Sunday.
> *The Beaver* Dec. 1989–Jan. 1990: 52

> Vancouver school board ended a 25-year tradition last year because the School Act says schools must be conducted on strictly 'secular and non-sectarian principles.'
> *Province* (Vancouver) 24 Dec. 1990: 5

> The conflict in Northern Ireland is 'sectarian,' while here in Canada we call our rivalries 'regional.'
> *Vancouver Sun* 9 Oct. 1990: A13

Secwepemc see SHUSWAP

-sede see -CEED

see see SAW, SEEN

seeing as, seeing as how When *seeing* is used to mean 'in view of the fact', it is usually followed by *that*: 'Seeing that I had the day off, I slept in'. *Seeing as* and *seeing as how* are constructions that, to some, have a quaint or rural flavour, and are rarely found in formal writing.

> That requires a tremendous leap of imagination as well as faith, seeing that the halcyon days come only at this time of year and last only for a couple of weeks.
> *Vancouver Sun* 17 Dec. 1990: A10

> But the people of the hamlet were polite at first, seeing as they hadn't had a visitor of Rambo's species before.
> *Uphere* Jan.–Feb. 1990: 14

See also BEING AS.

Seeing Eye Dog see GUIDE DOG

seen see SAW

see where Constructions that use *where* to mean *that* ('I see where it's time to go'; 'I read where they are going to take down the steeple') are now considered unsuitable for writing and informal in speech. This use of *where* is rare in Canadian writing.

> 'I can see where it will take more of my time ... but not more than I figured before I agreed to run for the office.'
> *Canadian Rodeo News* March 1990: 15

Sekani see CARRIER

seldom ever, seldom if ever *Seldom ever* is sometimes criticized as redundant because 'We seldom ever go out' can be written 'We seldom go out' without changing the sense. But *seldom ever* is a respectable idiom with a long history in English. Today it is mainly restricted to informal writing, such as journalism. In formal writing the more logical version of the expression, *seldom if ever*, is strongly preferred.

> In Britain, the government seldom ever changes and the underlings are so unhappy they travel thousands of miles abroad to smash up other people.
> *Maclean's* 23 July 1990: A44

> The vast majority of people who call themselves skiers will seldom ever venture beyond the security of the ski area boundaries....
> *Vancouver Sun* 2 Jan. 1992: B10

> Myths are seldom if ever actual hypotheses that can be verified or refuted; that is not their function: they are co-ordinating or integrating ideas.
> Northrop Frye *The Modern Century* 1990: 115

See also EVER.

-self, -selves The pronouns that end with *-self* or *-selves* are called reflexive pronouns because they normally refer back to the subject of the sentence or clause in which they appear: 'I will do it myself'; 'Henry thinks for himself'; 'They take themselves very seriously'. If the pronoun form is singular, it is followed by *-self*: 'Did you do that by yourself?' If plural, it is followed by *-selves*: 'You were squabbling among yourselves'. Since *we* and *they* are plural pronouns, the corresponding reflexive pronouns are also plural: *ourselves* and *themselves*, not *ourself* and *themself*.

Occasionally, especially in speech, people use the non-standard form *themself* when it is clear that the pronoun, though plural in form, actually refers to a single person: 'Someone could really hurt themself'. Similarly, writers sometimes use the non-standard form *ourself* when they are referring to themselves formally as 'we': 'We satisfied ourself that indeed these exquisite desserts were made on the premises'. However, both these usages are considered unacceptable and should be avoided. *Ourselves* should be used even when the reference is to only one person. Sentences such as 'Everyone must look out for him- or herself' may sound awkward, but (apart from *themselves*) this construction is the only alternative to *himself*, because English has no indefinite reflexive form corresponding to the gender-neutral indefinite pronouns. *Oneself* won't do, not only because it is regarded as extremely formal, but also because conventionally it is linked only to *one*: 'One must look out for oneself', not 'Everyone must look out for oneself'. Although some commentators think that the time has come to legitimize the use of *they* to mean 'he or she' and *themself* to mean 'himself or herself', using *themself* in formal writing will almost surely elicit strong criticism.

We can't separate ourself completely from our past.
Daily News (Halifax) 3 Feb. 1993: 20

(The accepted form is *ourselves*.)

We can appreciate what they're doing ... but we'd just as soon do it ourself.
Ottawa Citizen 6 June 1990: E11

(The accepted form is *ourselves*.)

'I just hope the person who did this has the decency to give themself up.'
Vancouver Sun 9 March 1990: A8

(In formal writing *themself* should be replaced with *himself or herself*.)

See also EVERYONE; [HISSELF], [THEIRSELVES]; MY-SELF; SEXIST LANGUAGE; YOU, ONE.

self-deprecating, self-depreciating   see DEPRE-CIATE

semi-, demi-, hemi-   All three of these prefixes mean half: *semi-monthly, demitasse, hemisphere. Semi-* is derived from Latin, *demi-* from French, and *hemi-* from Greek. Often the sense of the prefix is 'partly', as in *semi-automatic* and *demigod*. Only *semi-* is used freely to form new combinations (which are usually hyphenated until they become familiar words): *semi-retired, semi-detached, semi-serious.*

semicolon   Semicolons are used to link closely related independent clauses. Sometimes the semicolon takes the place of a coordinating conjunction (e.g., *and, but, for*) or a conjunctive adverb (e.g., *instead*):

Nobody talked about it on the street; they just shook their heads and bit their lips.
Max Braithwaite *The Night We Stole the Mountie's Car* 1971: 57

Personally, I mistrust the notion of thinking on one's feet; I have known many speakers who prided themselves on that ability, and I am sorry to say that many of them were blatherers; they did not know when to stop.
Robertson Davies *One Half of Robertson Davies* 1978: 9

A sentence introduced by a conjunctive adverb, such as *however, nevertheless,* or *thus,* may be joined to the previous sentence using a semicolon:

Rock outcrops in the study area are oriented along a northwest-southeast axis; consequently, cliff faces most often face either southwest or northeast.
Arctic 41.1 (1988): 27

It is a common error to use a comma rather than a semicolon to make the linkages described above, resulting in a run-on sentence (see SENTENCES, SENTENCE FRAGMENT, RUN-ON SENTENCE).

Usually a comma separates items listed in a text, but when the elements listed are complex, or contain commas, semicolons are used to separate them:

The proposed cut-offs by the CHRC were as follows: fewer than 100 employees, 70 per cent; 100 to 500 employees, 60 per cent; and more than 500 employees, 55 per cent.
Carl J. Cuneo *Pay Equity* 1990: 30

Note that semicolons are always placed outside any quotation marks:

However, this did not mean 'simply the transfer of title of large enterprises to the state'; rather, it called for 'decentralized ownership and control'.
Alan Whitehorn *Canadian Socialism* 1992: 63

senior   see SENIOR CITIZEN; SUPERIOR

senior citizen, senior, aged, elderly, pensioner, oldster   Some commentators, particularly British ones, consider the North American expressions *senior citizen* and *senior* euphemistic. They argue that *old people, the aged, the elderly,* and *pensioners* are perfectly good terms to describe people who are old or retired. However, it is difficult to imagine a North American journalist who would replace

'Martha is a senior, active in several community organizations' with 'Martha is an old person, active in ...'. Though they should be neutral terms, *old*, *elderly*, and *aged* often carry negative connotations of frailty, dependence, and diminished capability. *Senior* and *senior citizen*, on the other hand, are terms of respect; there seems to be no good reason to avoid using them.

Oldster is a humorous coinage modelled on *youngster*; it should be used only in a lighthearted context.

sensational In contemporary writing, *sensational* tends to be used in one of two ways: to describe something that piques in the general public an intense, often prurient, curiosity ('sensational evidence at the murder trial') or to describe something felt to be excellent or superb ('The movie was sensational'). Some critics object to the second sense, but it is widespread in informal use and standard in informal writing. *Sensational* originally meant pertaining to the senses, a meaning now conveyed by the word *sensory*.

Increased supplies of newsprint accentuate an emphasis on sensational news.
Wallace Clement and Glen Williams, eds. *The New Canadian Political Economy* 1989: 120

Tourism has been a mainstay, with some fluctuations, since the mid-1940s, but this past year was sensational.
Beautiful British Columbia Spring 1990: 38

'He's a sensational father,' she says.
Margaret Atwood *Life Before Man* 1979: 132

Sensational rookie goaltender Troy Gamble yesterday flew from Winnipeg to Vancouver. ...
Province (Vancouver) 4 Dec. 1990: 37

sensible, sensibleness, sensibility, sensitive, sensitivity, sensitiveness The most common meaning of *sensible* is having sound judgment. The related noun is *sensibleness*. An old-fashioned, now literary, meaning of the phrase *sensible of* is aware of: 'I am sensible of your predicament'. This older meaning of *sensible* is related to the noun *sensibility*, meaning the capacity for subtle feeling. A person of 'delicate sensibility' has subtle emotional, aesthetic, or intellectual responses. When a particular sensibility is ascribed to a sex, a nationality, an occupation, a period, a place, etc., the term refers to a set of ideas, attitudes, and preferences believed to characterize that group, occupation, etc.

The adjective *sensitive* and its related noun forms, *sensitivity* and *sensitiveness*, have to do with the capacity to respond to stimuli: 'The human ear is not sensitive to these frequencies'. *Sensitive* can mean finely tuned or accurate ('a sensitive measure') attuned to others ('a sensitive listener'), or easily hurt ('sensitive about his hairline'). To be *sensitive to* something means to be aware of and concerned about it; the sense is similar to that of the old-fashioned expression *sensible of*.

In a political context, a 'sensitive issue' is one that could cause a strong public reaction. Thus it is one that is handled carefully, often evasively.

Sensible planning also demands that you reserve your accommodations in advance.
Dogs in Canada Special Issue 1986: 14

The sensibleness of his judgments gave readers everywhere much of what they needed to know about opera in general in order to appreciate other productions of other works in their own towns. ...
Queen's Quarterly 94.2 (1987): 352

'We are, at the same time, sensible of the inconvenience that may result from the exercise of such a jurisdiction.'
William Teatero *John Anderson: Fugitive Slave* 1986: 127

(This quotation dates from 1861, when *sensible* was commonly used to mean *aware*.)

As a critical approach to works of art, [psychoanalysis] has been productive of much that is interesting and revealing, though it is by no means a substitute for a cultured mind, or for delicate sensibility and intuition. ...
Robertson Davies *A Voice from the Attic* 1960: 68–9

The title of the book has been pilfered from Margaret Atwood's *Journals of Susanna Moodie*, a book unusually rich in suggestive phrases defining a Canadian sensibility.
Northrop Frye *The Bush Garden* 1971: x

Despite his stern demeanour Draper was a sensitive man, patient, humane and with a warm sense of humour.
William Teatero *John Anderson: Fugitive Slave* 1986: 162

After years of ignoring time, I have become sensitive to it.
Ken Dryden *The Game* 1983: 13

'This is a very sensitive matter that unfortunately has already received unduly extensive publicity.'
Maclean's 24 Feb. 1986: 21

sensory, sensual, sensuous *Sensory*, *sensual*, and *sensuous* all refer to what we apprehend through our five senses. *Sensory* is neutral, referring to the senses in a purely physical way: 'Sensory input is relayed to the brain'. *Sensual* usually refers to the indulgence or gratification of carnal desires. *Sensuous* was apparently coined by Milton in 1641 to avoid any hint of the lewdness implied by *sensual*. *Sensuous* is the broader term, applied to any type of aesthetic, intellectual, or physical pleasure derived from the senses. However, many writers use *sensual* and *sensuous* interchangeably.

> The sensory processes include visual, auditory, olfactory, and tactile.
> *Queen's Quarterly* 92.2 (1985): 419

> The cult of the Maenads ... worshipped Dionysus ... in a ritualized frenzied celebration of sensual and sexual existence. ...
> *NeWest Review* Oct.–Nov. 1990: 44

> ... poetry, according to Milton, who ought to have known, is 'more simple, sensuous and passionate' than philosophy or science.
> Northrop Frye *The Educated Imagination* 1963: 9

> When given colour, the sensual quality of her art form increased dramatically.
> *Arctic* 41.1 (1988): 74

(Here some commentators would recommend *sensuous*.)

> There was tremendous pressure ... to have a really hot, sensuous, passionate scene between Daisy and Max. ...
> *NeWest Review* Feb.–Mar. 1990: 18

(Here some commentators would recommend *sensual*.)

sentence adverbs   A sentence adverb differs from a simple adverb in that it relates to the whole sentence, or to a whole clause within a sentence, rather than to a single word or phrase: 'Fortunately, they got home before their guests arrived'. This construction, meaning 'It is fortunate that ...', is not disputed. However, the use of certain words as sentence adverbs is often criticized. An example is *hopefully*. In the sentence 'They waited hopefully for the surgeon's report', *hopefully* acts as a simple adverb describing the manner in which they waited: 'full of hope'. By contrast, in the sentence 'Hopefully, he won't need an operation' *hopefully* does not modify a particular word or phrase but the sentence as a whole; it's a sentence adverb meaning 'It is to be hoped that ...'. Those who object to this use of *hopefully* maintain that, since the same word can also be used as a simple manner adverb, it may be ambiguous. Other dual-purpose adverbs, such as *thankfully* and *mercifully*, have also been criticized as sentence adverbs, though not so vociferously.

There is no justification for condemning the use of these words as sentence adverbs on the grounds of usage or grammar; nevertheless, writing that uses them, particularly *hopefully*, is liable to attract criticism.

The sentence adverb flourishes despite critics' objections because it is a concise way of expressing an attitude towards a statement. In the sentence 'Thankfully, she escaped without injury', the single word *thankfully* conveys the sense of the phrase 'it is fortunate that'; in 'Bluntly, they are not up to the task', the sentence adverb *bluntly* condenses the sense of 'If I may be blunt', or 'Bluntly speaking'.

Sentence adverbs can appear in a number of positions in a sentence, though the most common position is at the beginning of a sentence. Common sentence adverbs include *bluntly*, *briefly*, *candidly*, *confidentially*, *frankly*, *generally*, *honestly*, *personally*, and *seriously*. Note the placement of the sentence adverbs in the following examples: 'They are probably out for the evening'; 'You may join us, certainly'; 'Despite their unappetizing appearance, surprisingly, they are quite delicious'. Because many adverbs function as both manner adverbs and sentence adverbs, writers need to be careful to avoid using them in ambiguous contexts: for example, 'Thankfully they left' could mean 'They left with a feeling of gratitude' or 'Thank goodness they're gone'. When a sentence adverb is the first word in the sentence, many writers put a comma after it to avoid this ambiguity.

> He then thankfully accepted a gift of $2,000 from the grateful trustees. ...
> Hilda Neatby *Queen's University* 1 (1978): 167

(Here *thankfully* is a regular adverb modifying the verb *accepted*.)

> Copy protection is thankfully not a problem in the CD-ROM arena and that alone should spur development.
> *Computer Dealer News* 21 March 1991: 51

(Here *thankfully* is a sentence adverb.)

> Mercifully the hall chime announced the end of the hour.
> Constance Beresford-Howe *Night Studies* 1985: 24

(Here *mercifully* is a sentence adverb.)

> Hopefully she looked up for their elevator to arrive.
> Constance Beresford-Howe *Night Studies* 1985: 35

(Here *hopefully* is a regular adverb modifying the verb *looked*.)

Hopefully Albert Einstein's views will help to … restore the cynics to a more healthy view of the need to continue the campaign for human rights.…
Henry M. Rosenthal and S. Cathy Berson, eds. *Canadian Jewish Outlook Anthology* 1988: 330

(Here *hopefully* is a sentence adverb; this is the disputed usage.)

Hopefully, the resources available to the group will be increased for next year's festival so that this regrettable situation will not be repeated.
Fuse Magazine 13.4 (1990): 11

(Here *hopefully* is a sentence adverb; this is the disputed usage.)

sentences, sentence fragment, run-on sentence, comma splice The boundaries of a sentence in writing are the capital letter of the first word and the period, exclamation mark, or question mark that follows the last word. To be complete in grammatical terms, a sentence must have a subject and a predicate. Inexperienced writers occasionally produce sentence fragments: strings of words that lack a subject or a predicate, even though they are punctuated as if they were sentences. Sentence fragments are common and accepted in speech, or in writing that represents speech, and skilled writers occasionally use them for effect. Some types of fragments, however, are not acceptable. Examples of the most common types of fragments follow.

A complete sentence, such as 'The issues were different', has a subject ('The issues') and a predicate ('were different'). However, when *because* (or any other subordinate conjunction, such as *although* or *when*) is placed in front of such a sentence it is transformed into a subordinate clause, which, as its name suggests, requires something to complete it. 'Because the issues were different' is a sentence fragment. To make a complete sentence, the fragment must be attached to an independent clause: 'I didn't agree with you then, because the issues were different'.

Similarly, relative clauses beginning with *who(m)*, *which*, *whose*, or *that* are not sentences; as their name suggests, they relate to something else in the same sentence. 'Which I don't like' is a fragment; 'He came in late, which I don't like' is a complete sentence.

Being cannot be used as a predicate, nor can other *-ing* verb form. Thus 'My candidate being of the same party as Pierre Trudeau' is a fragment: simply substituting *was* for *being* would produce a sentence.

Run-on sentences (sometimes called run-together sentences) are not just long sentences but two sentences punctuated as one. Usually such sentences are closely connected in meaning. Sometimes the writer puts a comma between the two sentences, an error called a comma splice or a comma fault. Often adverbs such will as *however* or *therefore* will trigger a comma splice because writers assume that these words have the force of conjunctions when in fact they do not. Usually the simplest way to correct a run-on sentence or a comma splice is to insert a semicolon between the sentences (see SEMICOLON).

Only if sentences are very short and parallel in structure can they be connected with commas in formal writing. Julius Caesar's comment on the conquest of Britain—'I came, I saw, I conquered'—needs only commas (although semicolons would also be acceptable).

He doesn't know what 'love' means between them any more, though they always say it. For the sake of the children.
Margaret Atwood *Life Before Man* 1979: 6

(Here the fragment 'For the sake of the children' is punctuated as a sentence, although it has neither subject nor verb and could have been attached to the preceding sentence. Atwood has purposely used a sentence fragment to highlight the cliché.)

Few will ever see this timeless land. Its rivers go unnamed, its animals roam without fear.
Uphere Mar.–Apr. (1990): 27

(Although the second sentence in this passage is actually two sentences joined with a comma, this is acceptable because they are short and parallel in structure.)

But while the place isn't perfect, I can work to make this the co-op I want. I can lobby, I have a vote.
Women and Environments Spring (1990): 5

(Although the second sentence in this passage is actually two sentences joined with a comma, this is acceptable because they are short and parallel in structure.)

See also COMMA.

separate *Separate, separately,* and *separation* are often misspelled with *-per-* instead of *-par-*.

It should not matter whether GST is already included in your shelf prices or calculated seperately at the time of sale.
Financial Post 23 Nov. 1989: 18

(The correct spelling is *separately*.)

separatist, sovereignist, independantiste, sovereigntist, independentist All these terms describe supporters of an independent Quebec. *Separatist* is the term commonly used by those who dislike the idea of Quebec's breaking away. *Sovereignist* and *independantiste* are favoured by those who espouse a sovereign Quebec. *Sovereignist* and *independantiste* are Canadianisms (you won't find them listed in British or American dictionaries) adapted from the French words *souverainiste* and *indépendantiste*. The variants *sovereigntist* and *independentist* also appear in Canadian journalism, but much less frequently.

He was whisked into cabinet by Brian Mulroney, only to turn on the Tories and found the separatist Bloc Quebecois two years later.
Ottawa Citizen 24 Dec. 1994: A4

To understand why Quebec will never give up its sovereignist aspiration, one will have to take a look at history.
Gazette (Montreal) 14 Dec. 1994: B2

Although independantiste sentiment was much in evidence, some who joined in the parade described themselves as federalist.
Gazette (Montreal) 25 June 1993: A1

Dumont, straddling the fence as both a sovereigntist and a confederalist, needs platforms from which to promote his views.
Ottawa Citizen 27 Dec. 1994: A12

... he was sure Quebecers would re-elect the Liberal government instead of an independentist Parti Quebecois.
Gazette (Montreal) 13 May 1994: B2

See also NATIONAL ASSEMBLY; QUEBEC ENGLISH; QUEBECKER.

seppuku see HARA-KIRI

sepsis, septicemia, septic, aseptic, antiseptic *Sepsis* is infection of the body by toxin-producing bacteria. *Septicemia* (occasionally spelled *septicaemia*) is sepsis of the blood, commonly known as blood poisoning. *Septic* usually means causing infection or infected; however, a *septic tank* is a disposal system in which waste is decomposed and purified by bacterial activity. *Aseptic* (the *a* is stressed and rhymes with *pay*) means free from bacteria and viruses—a desirable state for a wound or an operating room, but not for a septic tank. *Antiseptics* are substances that kill germs; in metaphorical contexts *antiseptic* means sterile.

All these words are derived from the Greek root *sep-*, meaning rot. People sometimes mistakenly insert a *c* into that root, writing *sceptic*, for example, instead of *septic*.

In newborn care, for example, about eight in a thousand babies get an infection called neonatal sepsis....
Calgary Herald 28 Dec. 1992: B1

The [germ] creates a condition called septicemia, which causes the breakdown of all internal organs....
Calgary Herald 3 June 1992: A1

But if all doctors were hacking off legs with septic instruments in barber shops and losing sponges inside people's lungs because they're drunk during the operation, we would not think of medicine as an honourable profession....
Margaret Atwood *Second Words* 1982: 347

... a regulation septic system [was] installed where there had been only a holding tank before.
Harrowsmith Oct.–Nov. 1985: 62

Using aseptic techniques in handling the milk, I thought we were safe.
Harrowsmith Oct.–Nov. 1985: 10

It has antiseptic properties that will keep the disease organisms at bay until the seedling has time to harden off.
TLC ... for plants Spring 1991: 14

But there's a balance to be found between too much reality and an antiseptic museum with fish photos on the wall.
Vancouver Sun 30 June 1992: B1

Cottagers are being forced to check their sceptic tanks for leaks.
Ottawa Citizen 19 Sept. 1992: F1

(The correct spelling is *septic*.)

Showing more convenience than invention is a new, small, ascceptic package of shelf-stable 2 per cent milk labelled Caf-O-Lait.
Gazette (Montreal) 27 May 1992: C6

(The correct spelling is *aseptic*.)

See also -AE-, -OE-, -E-; SKEPTIC, SCEPTIC.

sere see SEAR

serve see SERVICE

server see WAITER

service, serve Many usage commentators have objected to the use of *service* as a verb, as in 'This hospital services a population of 100,000'. Most of these commentators explicitly endorse only one meaning of the verb *service*: to do maintenance and repair work on cars or other machines. Their advice is to avoid *service* where the older and perfectly adequate verb *serve* is possible.

But there are now many contexts where *service* has acquired a special meaning and *serve* is not possible. For example, to service land is to provide it with utilities such as electricity and sewers. To service a debt is to make periodic payments on it. To service a region is to provide a specific service within it. Male animals service female animals; sex-trade workers service their clients. The real point of contention is whether people are properly said to *be serviced* in contexts other than the sex trade. In business and administration this usage is extremely common; outside that sphere, however, it should be avoided.

The municipalities must pass on the costs of buying and servicing industrial land to end users.
Financial Post 2 Dec. 1991: U3

... many African countries find themselves forced to borrow not for development purposes but to service their debts.
Globe and Mail (Toronto) 15 July 1985: B12

The Rusholmes' house was serviced by gas.
J.E. Smyth et al. *The Law and Business Administration in Canada* 1987: 97

... the plane Federal Express normally uses to service Calgary, an F-27 turbo-prop, has been replaced by a much larger 727.
Calgary Herald 14 Feb. 1988: OA14

Izvestia's former stablemate With Approval ... was servicing 'as good a book [selection] of mares in relation to his stud fee as any freshman stallion in North America this year.'
Financial Post 24 Oct. 1991: 51

The customers [include] a prostitute and several electricians who are servicing nearby hotels, each in their own way.
Financial Post 9 Aug. 1991: 7

Granada Canada now operates 55 stores and service centres, servicing about 200,000 customers.
Financial Post 16 Oct. 1991: 17

(Here *serve* would also work.)

Trailer fees are annual service fees paid by fund managers to brokers for initiating the relationship and servicing the client over time.
Financial Post 13 Aug 1991: 15

(Here *serve* would also work.)

'We're not servicing that 13-17 age group,' says Morena Mazzara, community recreation co-ordinator....
Province (Vancouver) 23 Oct. 1990: 57

(Here *serve* would also work.)

serviette see NAPKIN

settee, settle see CHESTERFIELD

sew, sewed, sewn The past tense of the verb is *sewed*: 'Leo sewed the buttons on his coat yesterday'. The past participle is either *sewn* or *sewed*.

I had sewn since I was 6—for my dolls.
Gazette (Montreal) 28 Aug. 1990: D2

'The doctors told my husband ... that they had just sewed me up with sponges and were expecting me to die.'
Province (Vancouver) 28 June 1990: 65

sex see GENDER

sexism, chauvinism *Sexism* is the attitude, or a manifestation of the attitude, that one sex is superior to or more important than the other. Usually *sexism* refers to a bias against women, but logically the term can also refer to discrimination against or stereotyping of men.

Chauvinism is not the same thing as *sexism*. *Chauvinist* is derived from the name of Nicolas Chauvin, a French soldier who served under Napoleon and who became famous for his aggressive loyalty to the Empire and his devotion to his leader. *Chauvinism* originally referred to unreasoning devotion to one's country; then its meaning was broadened to include proud and blinkered partiality to any place, group, or cause. *Male chauvinism*, a phrase that became popular in the 1970s, means overweening pride in the male gender. Thus in the phrase *male chauvinist* the adjective *male* identifies not the sex of the biased person but the nature of the bias. It's best to avoid using *chauvinism* by itself to mean *male chauvinism* unless the context makes the meaning clear.

> Finally, we should actively support those feminists struggling to combat sexism and inequality in sport.
> *Queen's Quarterly* 94.1 (1987): 129

> ... Devor's women have an intense resistance to the cultural trappings of femininity, view femininity as a variety of 'consensual sexism,' and display a real impatience, sometimes contempt, for women who adopt 'feminine' ways.
> *Rites* March 1990: 14

> ... we were going to hear a fine concert and—this was what gave a special edge to the occasion—we were going to hear a Canadian, one of our own, who had beyond all question achieved world celebrity. There was a spice of chauvinism in our enthusiasm, and who would say that we were unjustified, or wrong?
> Robertson Davies *One Half of Robertson Davies* 1978: 23

> Huck, it is claimed, is a white chauvinist and Jim is a stereotyped, chuckleheaded Black.
> Henry M. Rosenthal and S. Cathy Berson, eds. *Canadian Jewish Outlook Anthology* 1988: 259

> The more chauvinistic Vancouver gourmets claim flatly that their city has the finest Chinese food this side of the Pacific.
> Alan Tucker, ed. *The Penguin Guide to Canada* 1991: 551

> A suicide pact by four girls who took rat poison so their parents could lavish everything on their brother has shocked South Koreans and raised questions about male chauvinism and the plight of the poor.
> *Gazette* (Montreal) 6 March 1989: E7

> 'Dad,' Wilson jokes, 'was responsible for the men, who all turned out to be chauvinists, and Mom was responsible for the women, who all turned out independent.'
> *Chatelaine* June 1986: 97

(Here the context makes it clear that these *chauvinists* are sexist rather than nationalist.)

See also -ISM; SEXIST LANGUAGE.

sexist language   Most writers' handbooks, style guides, and composition texts now contain a section on sexist language. Avoiding sexist language means describing women and men in ways that do not stereotype them on the basis of their sex and omitting irrelevant references to such things as appearance and marital status. The terms used to describe the two sexes should be parallel (e.g., not 'man and wife' but 'husband and wife') and gender-neutral (e.g., 'police officer', not 'policeman').

In the past *man* and *mankind* were used as 'generic' terms to refer to both sexes; now *people*, *individuals*, *humankind*, and *human beings* are all considered better alternatives. Similarly, the 'generic' pronoun *he* is replaced in several ways: by rewriting the sentence to avoid pronouns altogether; by using plural forms; or, when no alternative is available, by using *his or her*, *he or she*, or *her and him*. Some writers alternate between masculine and feminine pronouns; others routinely use *she* where *he* was used in the past, and still others use *s/he*; however, these choices are less conventional than those above, and are quite likely to distract the reader.

Following the indefinite pronouns (*anyone*, *none*, *one*, *each*, *either*, *everyone*, *someone*, etc.), most usage guides accept the common use of the plural pronoun *they* in speech: 'Anyone who hasn't handed in their assignment should see the teacher'. Many commentators feel that the use of the plural pronoun should now also be accepted in writing; for a detailed discussion of this point, see EVERYONE.

Non-sexist usage guides also recommend avoiding the verbs *master*, meaning learn thoroughly (as in 'master French'), and *man*, meaning staff (as in 'man the booth'). Words in which *man* is a prefix or suffix, such as *manpower*, *manmade*, *foreman*, and *cameraman*, are eschewed in favour of phrases like *work force*, *synthetic*, *supervisor*, and *camera operator*. However, many words with the letters *man* in them do not in fact derive from *man*, but from the Latin root *man(u)*, 'hand', as in *manufacture*, *manipulate*, and *manuscript*. To go to extremes in attempting to eradicate every trace of possible sexism in language may actually be counterproductive, leading readers to feel that the project is either ridiculous or impossible.

See also ALUMNUS; BLOND; BRUNETTE; CHAIRMAN; CO-ED; JOB TITLES; MASTERFUL; MOTHER NATURE; SEXISM; WAITER.

sexual harassment   see HARASS

sexual minorities   Sexual minorities are groups that do not share the heterosexual orientation of the majority of the population: *lesbians*, *gay men*, *bisexuals*, *transsexuals*, and *transgendered people* (those who do not identify themselves as belonging to one gender or the other).

> Like judges and all links in the justice system, they should always be rigorously neutral—not just to the

media but to ethnic groups, political groups, sexual minorities and everyone else.
Gazette (Montreal) 25 Oct. 1990: B2

... it is no longer possible to make jokes about disempowered groups such as ethnic or religious minorities, and it is becoming increasingly unacceptable to joke about sexual minorities....
Queen's Quarterly 96.2 (1989): 232

See also GAY; SEXUAL ORIENTATION; VISIBLE MINORITY.

sexual orientation, sexual preference Both terms are in common use and considered inoffensive except by people who think that having a sexual orientation at all is in poor taste. However, those heterosexuals, bisexuals, lesbians, and gays who don't feel that they 'chose' their sexuality may prefer the term *sexual orientation* to *sexual preference*.

For some time, groups have been lobbying to have the Human Rights Act amended to include protection against discrimination on the basis of age, family status and sexual orientation.
Vancouver Sun 26 July 1990: A15

Customs officers can ask visitors to the U.S. what their sexual orientation is.
Rites Feb. 1990: 6

'Why do people feel it necessary to tell you they've come out of the closet? I don't go around telling the world my sexual preference.'
Canadian Churchman April 1986: 14

See also GAY; SEXUAL MINORITIES.

shade see COLOUR

shall, will Many Canadians have been taught a rule for *shall* and *will* that they do not use in speech and ignore in all but the most formal writing. The first part of the rule requires one to express the simple future in the first person with *shall* ('I/we shall') and in the second or third person with *will* ('you will'; 'he/she/they will'). Canadians usually express the simple future in the first person with *will* ('I will come tomorrow'), as do most speakers of Scottish, Irish, and American English.

The second part of the rule requires the use of *will* with the first person to indicate a clear intention or resolve on the part of the speaker(s): 'I (*or* we) will do it' amounts to a promise, whereas 'I (*or* we) shall do it' simply indicates what is expected to happen.

Shall with the second and third persons, according to this rule, indicates necessity: 'They shall be captured'; 'Britons never shall be slaves'.

This 'rule', which was derived from the practice of educated speakers in southern England, is no longer reflected in usage even in that variety of English. H.W. Fowler and F.G. Fowler's *The King's English* (3rd ed. 1931) comments: 'It is unfortunate that the idiomatic use [of the shall-will distinction], while it comes by nature to southern Englishmen ... is so complicated that those who are not to the manner born can hardly acquire it' (142). *Fowler's* (1965) notes that the idiom of North America, Scotland, and Ireland 'has made formidable inroads; and insistence on the rules laid down in the OED ... may before long have to be classed as insular pedantry'.

In Canadian English *shall* is now reserved mainly for asking polite questions with the first person: 'Shall we play cards now?'; 'Shall we meet tomorrow?'; 'Where shall I put my coat?' In academic prose *shall* persists with the first person to indicate the simple future in fixed expressions like 'as we shall see'. In Canadian legal English *shall* is still often used with the second and third persons to emphasize the binding nature of an agreement.

Perhaps you would like to know about the day John wakes up and notices that Mary has turned into a great white shark, in which case we will quickly realize that we are in the middle of a modern psychological novel and change the subject at once.
Margaret Atwood *Second Words* 1982: 335

(Here *will* is used with the first person to indicate the simple future.)

If the price of oil and gas skyrockets in the future ... we shall have to continue to supply the U.S. at the same price charged to Canadians.
Engineering Dimensions 1988: 34

(Here *shall* is used to indicate the simple future; a promise or resolve would have required the phrasing 'we *will* have to continue'.)

We shall see that political language at the election of 1734 already included a number of terms for the voice of the people on political matters....
J.A.W. Gunn *Beyond Liberty and Property* 1983: 262

(Here *shall* indicates the simple future; 'we *shall* see' is a fixed expression in academic contexts.)

But he is a veritable gourmet compared to his friend, who shall remain nameless for the sake of his mother. The friend opens a can of Duncan Hines vanilla icing when he's hungry, and eats it off his index finger.
Globe and Mail (Toronto) 21 March 1985: CL3

(Although here the context is informal, 'who *shall* remain nameless' is a fixed expression.)

'Canada is and shall remain a haven for those fleeing oppression and we want that clearly understood,' Miss Macdonald said. . . .
Globe and Mail (Toronto) 12 Jan. 1985: P3

(Here *shall* is used with the force of *must*.)

Company's auditors shall prepare and deliver a statement of operating profits to you and to us as promptly as possible after 31st December each year, which statement shall be binding upon the company and you.
J.E. Smyth et al. *The Law and Business Administration in Canada* 1987: 281

See also SHAN'T.

shambles   The most common sense of *shambles* is general confusion or mess. Originally, a *shambles* was a butcher's slaughterhouse. This sense was subsequently extended to refer to any scene of destruction and bloodshed. A few usage commentators still dispute the legitimacy of a *shambles* without blood, but Canadian writers use the word in all types of writing simply to mean great disorder; a writer trying to preserve the older sense of *shambles* would almost certainly be misunderstood.

So the discipline of the school was a shambles. Big kids bullied little kids. At noon they played rugby in the halls or set up folding chairs and had hurdle races.
Max Braithwaite *The Night We Stole the Mountie's Car* 1971: 60

shammy   see CHAMOIS

shan't   *Shan't* is the contraction of *shall not*: 'I shan't be attending'. It is seldom used in Canadian or American writing, since *shall* is not used commonly. *Won't*, the contraction of *will not*, is used much more often: 'I won't be attending'.

Stephen Stills was, with Neil Young (whom we shan't discuss any longer in this piece), a founding member of Buffalo Springfield.
Vancouver Sun 30 Aug. 1990: F2

And even if I live to be a very old person, I shan't know the answer.
Robertson Davies *One Half of Robertson Davies* 1978: 60

See also CONTRACTIONS; SHALL, WILL.

share   Some critics disapprove of using the verb *share* to mean express, reveal, exchange, or tell about thoughts, experiences, hopes, fears, and so on. According to the *OED*, this use of *share* began in the 1930s with the Moral Rearmament movement, which favoured the open confession of sins. The meaning became secularized and popularized when it was adopted by encounter groups in the 1960s and support groups in the 1980s, where 'sharing and caring' were de rigueur. Though *share* meaning bare your soul is undoubtedly standard, and the practice may be good for your mental health, many language commentators consider the usage cloying in general prose. It's important to know your audience.

We sincerely hope that you will find the book's themes and topics to be relevant and appealing, and that the essays themselves will move you to share your own views with others.
Richard Davies and Glen Kirkland, eds. *Dimensions* 1986: 1

she, her   see CASE; GENDER

shear, sheared, shorn, shears, sheer, sheers   To *shear* means to cut. The past tense is *sheared*. The past participle (the form used after *have* or as an adjective) is either *sheared* or *shorn*. *Shears* are used to shear sheep, clip hedges, cut heavy cloth, and so on.

Sheer means nearly transparent. Very thin fabric is *sheer*, and curtains made of such fabric are *sheers*. *Sheer* also means steep ('a sheer drop') and utter or complete ('sheer luck'). The verb to *sheer*, meaning to swerve, is rarely used in Canadian writing.

The fire and explosion sheared off the top two floors of both buildings.
Gazette (Montreal) 20 March 1990: A1

'Grass can't grow well if it's underfed, but the bizarre American syndrome of force-feeding it only to sheer off all its luxuriant locks contributes nothing to its health and is wasteful to boot'.
Province (Vancouver) 14 June 1990: 112

(The correct spelling is *shear*.)

Coats have been made of virtually every fur. Mouton—sheepskin sheared and dyed to resemble beaver—no longer makes the grade.
Globe and Mail (Toronto) 14 March 1985: CL1

RCMP Const. J.C. Degrace said investigators couldn't find a single hair from the shorn mane.
Ottawa Citizen 9 Oct. 1990: A4

I would recommend that you use as little as possible for your window treatments. A sheer fabric that will filter

natural light will be sufficient as long as privacy is not a factor.
Vancouver Sun 26 Oct. 1990: E4

Curtains may be as simple as light tinted sheers that are pulled to one side, framing the view out of the picture window.
Vancouver Sun 20 July 1990: H3

On one side the cliff crowds the bridge. On the other, inches away, a sheer drop—from higher than the tallest building in Vancouver.
Vancouver Sun 7 Feb. 1990: A15

By this time, through sheer hard work, she had risen to the top of the pile in the only job she knew, stenography.
Province (Vancouver) 11 May 1990: 80

sherbet, sherbert, sorbet   The usual and most widely accepted spelling is *sherbet*, but *sherbert* reflects a common pronunciation and appears in several recently published American dictionaries. The word is derived from the Turkish *serbet*, and has recently been reborrowed in its French form: *sorbet*, pronounced either *SOR bet* or as in French, *sor BAY*.

Give yourself extra points if you wear designer running shoes ... and order cassis sherbet for dessert.
Chatelaine April 1986: 2

For festive but light desserts on individual serving dishes, consider ... citrus-berry sherbert.
Province (Vancouver) 6 June 1990: 49

(The usual spelling is *sherbet*.)

Between the salmon and venison courses, Stadtlander plans to serve a prune, plum and apple sorbet.
Ottawa Citizen 19 Oct. 1994: E5

sheriff   *Sheriff* is often misspelled *sherrif*. In Canada a sheriff executes orders of the court, serving writs, seizing chattels, evicting tenants, escorting people to jail, and so on. Assistants to the sheriff are called sheriff's officers or bailiffs. In the United States a sheriff is the chief law-enforcement officer of a county.

At the courthouse, the sheriff addresses potential jurors to determine if any changes have occurred since they filled out the form, such as financial disability or illness.
Toronto Star 23 June 1992: A1

Some became emotional as he was led away between two sheriff's officers.
Daily News (Halifax): 22 Dec. 1992: 3

The family of the boy ... has filed a $5-million US lawsuit alleging that he was wrongfully killed by a deputy in the Los Angeles County Sheriff's Department....
Vancouver Sun 17 June 1992: A17

The other day he turned up in Dodge City, Kan., where they gave him an honorary sherrif's badge.
Gazette (Montreal) 2 July 1992: C9

(The correct spelling is *sheriff*.)

shibboleth   *Shibboleth* is most often used to mean a firmly established but mistaken belief, especially one connected to ethnic difference. A shibboleth is also a peculiarity of speech, dress, or behaviour that identifies someone as part of a particular group, race, or social class. In the biblical story (Judges 12: 4–6) the word *shibboleth* was used by Jephthah to distinguish his own Gileadite men from the defeated Ephraimites, who could not pronounce the *sh* sound. All men were asked to pronounce *shibboleth*, and anyone replying *sibboleth* was executed.

I was dismayed to see The Globe and Mail repeating the old shibboleth that whites 'have lived on the tip of the continent for three centuries, longer than the Bantu people, who migrated south after the Cape Dutch settlers arrived'.
Globe and Mail (Toronto) 4 March 1985: 6

His 78 years have not slowed him down exactly: indeed, instead of being a firecracker trying to explode every social shibboleth within range, he has become a cannon, aiming big shots at big targets.
Maclean's 19 Nov. 1990: A45

For them *joual* is a shibboleth: those who speak it pass, those who don't fail.
Margaret Atwood *Second Words* 1982: 265

shine, shined, shone   In Canada *shone* (rhymes with *gone*) is the usual past tense and past participle of *shine* except in the 'polish' sense, where *shined* is the usual choice: 'The sun shone while we shined our shoes'. Speakers of British English also tend to maintain this distinction, but in the United States usage is more mixed. There *shined* often refers to light: 'They shined the light in his face'.

The balance of the soloists performed to the standard that was expected, though none shone with exceptional sparkle.
Province (Vancouver) 2 April 1990: 42

During the course of the trip he has his suit pressed and shoes shined.
Financial Post 10 July 1991: 12

'It was dark and when my lights suddenly shined on it, I ... tried to swerve out of the way,' says Efford, who wasn't injured when the huge animal collapsed on his left front fender.
Province (Vancouver) 9 Nov. 1990: 64

(The more common form is *shone*, but *shined* is correct.)

The grey upholstery silks shined in the dim light from the streetlamp.
NeWest Review Oct.–Nov. 1989: 26

(The more common form is *shone*.)

ship   see BOAT

shire   see GLOUCESTER

shone   see SHINE

shorn   see SHEAR

shortfall, shortcoming   A *shortfall* is a situation in which—or the amount by which—actual income falls short of anticipated income, or what one has falls short of what one needs. *Shortfall* has strong economic connotations. A better choice for human failings and defects of design is *shortcoming*.

In 1985 the conference received only 94.4% of expected congregational donations, a shortfall of $127,000.
Mennonite Brethren Herald 7 March 1986: 25

In 1986, the crop shortfall is predicted to be between 900,000 and 1.2 million tonnes, with 5.8 million [people] continuing to need assistance.
Canadian Baptist Feb. 1986: 6

The main shortcoming of Durkheim's theory is its one-sidedness.
Irving M. Zeitlin and Robert J. Brym *The Social Condition of Humanity* 1991: 207

They did admit to some minor shortcomings, such as gossiping, cheating on diets and being lazy about cleaning up.
Chatelaine June 1986: 28

The sports centre, which offers activities ranging from gymnastics to roller blading, is Galperin's way of addressing what he believes is a serious shortfall in the Canadian sports system.
Toronto Star 1 Oct. 1992: NY6

(Here *shortcoming* would be more appropriate.)

Despite its shortfalls, however, the encyclopedia offers much new information that would not otherwise be readily available.
Canadian Heritage Magazine Feb.–Mar. 1986: 43

(Here *shortcomings* would be more appropriate.)

short shrift   To give someone *short shrift* means to pay little or insufficient attention to him or her. On the crowded scaffolds of Elizabethan England, busy executioners often limited Roman Catholic priests to a shortened version of the Catholic sacrament known then as *shriving*, in which a penitent confesses sins and receives absolution. This practice became known as giving *short shrift*. Now occasionally the expression is mistakenly rendered as *short shift*. The confusion of *shift* and *shrift* probably reflects the infrequent use of the archaic word *shrift* in modern English.

A common error in dealing with prescribed topics is to emphasize one portion while giving short shrift to another.
Margot Northey and David B. Knight *Making Sense in Geography and Environmental Studies* 1992: 66

Fireworks fans in the Lower Mainland are short-changed compared to fans in Montreal, where the symphony [of fireworks] goes on for 10 nights....The reason for the short shift [4 nights] in Vancouver is that here...[the] sponsor has to pay the costs associated with the event....
Vancouver Sun 11 Aug. 1994: A16

(Here *short shift* could actually be argued to work; however, to use the expression in the accepted way would require rephrasing: 'The reason Vancouver is being given such short shrift....')

See also FOLK ETYMOLOGY.

short-sighted   see NEAR-SIGHTED

shot   see GUN

[should of]   see [COULD OF]

show, showed, shown   The past tense is *showed*: 'She showed me her pictures of Iceland'. The past participle can be either *shown* or *showed*: 'She had shown the pictures to the class'; 'The cinema has showed this film before'. However, *shown* is the usual choice.

Experience has shown, though, that class actions can reduce court congestion and costs by allowing similar suits to be combined.
Ottawa Citizen 20 Dec. 1990: A14

None of the horses in the Daffodil had showed the slightest inclination to set the pace in an earlier race.
Province (Vancouver) 27 May 1990: 68

show up Some usage guides consider *show up* informal in the sense of arrive or appear: 'They finally showed up two hours late'. However, in its senses of expose, discredit, reveal, or outdo, *show up* is agreed to be standard: 'Her questions showed Jane up as an insincere fraud'.

> Injuries, which ripped apart Canada's bull riding contingent last season, have already begun to show up again this year.
> *Canadian Rodeo News* March 1990: 6

> Show up in jeans if you want to convey a more casual image.
> *Vancouver Sun* 14 Feb. 1990: C3

> 'You fear that the guy is going to make you look bad. Show him up.'
> *Province* (Vancouver) 27 July 1990: 57

shrift see SHORT SHRIFT

shrink, shrank, shrunk, shrunken Although the usual past tense of *shrink* is *shrank*, some authorities also allow *shrunk*: 'My T-shirt shrank (*or* shrunk) in the dryer'. *Shrunk* is more common in speech, but is never used in formal writing. The past participle is either *shrunk* or *shrunken*. *Shrunk* is more common when the past participle is part of a verb ('The market has shrunk'), *shrunken* when it functions as an adjective ('shrunken hopes').

> Herman shrank into the seat of his cutter like a turtle withdrawing its exposed, vulnerable skin into the cavern of its shell.
> *Queen's Quarterly* 92.3 (1985): 493

> Yet on the subject of academic freedom, as on all others, he shrank from professions of piety.
> Frederick Gibson *Queen's University* 2 (1983): 343

> The Canadian Football League shrunk its distinctive ball a few years ago, the result, some say, of complaints from transplanted American quarterbacks.
> *Vancouver Sun* 1 Dec. 1990: D6

> While economies have become global, the world has also shrunk in other ways.
> Neil Nevitte and Roger Gibbins *New Elites in Old States* 1990: 15

> She looks surprisingly old, like a woman shrunken by age to the size of a ten-year-old. . . .
> Margaret Atwood *Life Before Man* 1979: 30

shuck see HUSK

Shuswap, Secwepemc Both *Shuswap* (*SHOO swop*) and *Secwepemc* (*SHWEP muh*; singular and plural) are in use to refer to this Aboriginal group whose traditional territory is in southern British Columbia. Their language belongs to the Salishan family. *Shuswap* is occasionally misspelled *Shushwap*.

> The Shuswap have lived in the Thompson Valley for at least 4,000 years.
> *Vancouver Sun* 9 Aug. 1994: B4

> Now when English fails her she comes alive . . . speaking Shuswap.
> *Vancouver Sun* 29 July 1994: A3

> About 60 natives, from the Chilcotin, Shushwap, Nuxalk, and Carrier peoples, gathered for the opening of the judicial hearings . . . at the Ulkatcho reserve, 330 km west of Williams Lake.
> *Vancouver Sun* 8 Dec. 1992: A4

> (The correct spelling is *Shuswap*. Note that *Native(s)* should be capitalized when it refers to Aboriginal people; note too that this word is more acceptable when used as an adjective, as in *Native people*.)

> He challenged the Reform MP to take a program at the Secwepemc Cultural Education Society for a year.
> *Gazette* (Montreal) 12 June 1994: A6

See also NATIVE.

shut see CLOSE

SI see APPENDIX II

sibyl, Sybil, sibylline Legend has it that the Romans often consulted a female prophet named *Sibyl* (the name is also spelled *Sybil*) for her wisdom about the future. There were later said to be ten *sibyls* in the ancient world, and their writings were described as *sibylline*. Since the 1600s *sibyl* has been used more generally to mean female fortune-teller, prophet, or witch, and *sibylline* to mean prophetic or mysterious.

> It involved the 14 arched panels . . . depicting Old Testament prophets and heathen sibyls.
> *Globe and Mail* (Toronto) 29 April 1989: M9

> There is also something sibylline about these round-ups—the critics look into the past as if they were scanning the future, and try to tell us through their readings in what direction our literature is headed.
> *Ottawa Citizen* 4 Aug. 1990: B11

sic see PARENTHESES; QUOTATION

sick, ill, vomit In Canadian English the expression *to be sick* covers a wide range of meaning, including most forms of ill health as well as nausea, so that *to be sick* and *to be ill* are very nearly synonyms. In Standard Southern British English, however, *to be sick* usually means to vomit, as it does in Australian English. In Britain someone is *ill*, not *sick*, with a bad cold. When the adjective *sick* is used before a noun, as in 'a sick child' or 'sick time', the meaning is the same in North American and British English.

In Canadian English, to be nauseated or vomiting is to be 'sick to (*or* at) one's stomach'. Newfoundlanders say 'stomach-sick'. Of the dozens of informal expressions meaning to vomit, *to throw up* is perhaps the most widespread.

See also NAUSEOUS, NAUSEATING, NAUSEATED.

sideroad   see ROAD

sight   see CITE

significant other   see SPOUSE

Sikh   The Hindi word *sikh* means disciple and is traditionally pronounced *SICK*. Because this pronunciation is an unfortunate homophone of the English word *sick*, *Sikh* is commonly pronounced *SEEK* in Canada and the United States, even though Sikh Canadians prefer the *SICK* pronunciation. British dictionaries list both pronunciations. *Sikh* should always be capitalized; Sikhs, like Jews, are distinguished as both an ethnic and a religious group.

The Sikh religion emerged in the Punjab region of the Indian subcontinent in the sixteenth century. Sikhism requires that all Sikh men vow to observe what are called the 'five K's': to carry a ceremonial dagger (*kirpan*), to wear a beard and not cut their hair (*kes*), and to wear a comb (*kanga*), soldier's shorts (*kach*), and an iron bracelet (*kara*). The common titles *Singh* ('Lion') and *Kaur* ('Princess') are often adopted by male and female Sikhs respectively, usually as last names. To avoid confusion, it is best to write Sikh names out in full. Note that not all those with the last name Singh are Sikh.

> Richard Popplewell tells the fascinating ... history of British efforts to monitor the Sikh diaspora before World War I, especially on the West coast of Canada.
> *Canadian Journal of History* 14.1 (1989): 87

silicon, silicone, silica   *Silicon* and *silicone* are different substances; these terms are not interchangeable. *Silicon*, the earth's second most abundant element, is widely used in electronic devices in the form of 'chips' of pure silicon. *Silicones*, a group of compounds containing silicon, carbon, hydrogen, and oxygen, are resistant to water, heat, and electric currents; they are used in plastic surgery and the manufacture of lubricants and waterproof polishes and sealants.

Silicon combines with oxygen to make *silica*, which occurs as quartz, mica, opal, and clay, and is the main component of sand.

> Other cultures offer decorative tattooing ... while ours offers silicon injections....
> *Globe and Mail* (Toronto) 16 Feb. 1985: E17

(Plastic surgeons inject *silicone*, not *silicon*.)

similar   see ANALOGOUS

simple, simplistic   *Simple* means plain, easy, straightforward, or uncomplicated: a simple solution to a problem is a good one. *Simplistic* is a negative word, usually applied to ideas and arguments, that means lacking in depth, complexity, or subtlety. *Simplistic* should not be used as a high-flown substitute for *simple*.

> Of all the ... gifts sent to the students, one very simple present made the biggest impression: A maple tree from Acton.
> *Calgary Herald* 2 July 1992: N1

> Good intentions notwithstanding, Spindler's analyses of literary works ... are too simplistic, too pat.
> *Queen's Quarterly* 92.1 (1985): 169

> While ... the mind can be seen as analogous to a computer ... to regard ourselves as nothing more than sophisticated computers is simplistic and dangerous.
> *Saturday Night* Jan. 1986: 10

> 'Units are becoming more complicated rather than more simplistic,' admits Orla Johnston, assistant marketing manager for Panasonic's personal communications division....
> *Canadian Living* Nov. 1990: 208

(Here *simpler* should replace *more simplistic*.)

simple reason   A number of usage commentators object strongly to the expression *for the simple reason that*, since the reason given may not seem as simple to the reader as it does to the writer; instead they recommend *because*. However, the tone of *for* *the simple reason* is not always patronizing. Often *simple* means something like sole, and substituting *because* would eliminate a nuance of the meaning.

> Despite finishing last or near last in most of her races, she usually wins the masters women [title] for the simple reason that she is the only masters woman.
> *Daily News* (Halifax) 22 Dec. 1994: 48

> He could find no fault with the legislation for the simple reason that he authored it. . . .
> *Toronto Star* 24 Oct. 1994: A16

simulacrum   Usually an image or shadowy representation of something, a *simulacrum* may also be a deceptive substitute, a sham. *Simulacra* is the preferred plural form, but *simulacrums* is also correct. *Simulacrum* is pronounced *sim uh LAY crum*.

> . . . the Mexican actress Ofelia Medina is an eerie simulacrum of Frida—she appears on screen next to the real self-portraits, and the feeling that she is Frida intensifies.
> *Globe and Mail* (Toronto) 2 Sept. 1985: S11

> . . . tourists impose their own reality on that place, a 'simulacrum' that approximates the past but distorts the very reality they seek.
> *Vancouver Sun* 26 May 1990: D1

See also PLURALS, REGULAR, IRREGULAR, FOREIGN.

simultaneous, simultaneously   The adjective *simultaneous* ('simultaneous translation') is quite often used mistakenly in place of the adverb *simultaneously* ('The two will run simultaneously').

> Ferchat said the Koreans would get the next two at a better price, as construction would take place simultaneous with last year's sale.
> *Financial Post* (Toronto) 14 Nov. 1991: 4

(Here the adverb *simultaneously* is required.)

See also ADJECTIVES AND ADVERBS; SYNCHRONOUS.

sine qua non, ne plus ultra   In Latin *sine qua non* means 'without which not'. In English the phrase is used as a noun for a thing or condition that is essential or indispensable. The usual pronunciation is *SIN eh KWA NAWN*. Several usage guides suggest using a more familiar phrase, such as 'indispensable condition', 'absolute prerequisite', or 'essential ingredient', because *sine qua non* may not be widely understood. This concern is legitimate. In

fact, *sine qua non* is sometimes confused with another Latin phrase, *ne plus ultra*, meaning the acme, the ultimate.

> Restoring faith in the political process is the sine qua non of solving our economic and social problems.
> *Daily News* (Halifax) 2 Jan. 1994: n.p.

> Apricot nectar, the sine qua non of the recipe, is not always available on grocery store shelves.
> *Daily News* (Halifax) 3 March 1993: 23

> The networks can count on an audience [for the 1986 Grey Cup game] of upwards of five million. By comparison, the National Football League's Super Bowl, supposedly the ne plus ultra of professional football, has never pulled an audience that big in Canada.
> *Gazette* (Montreal) 29 Nov. 1986: D1

> The psychologists . . . should explore what dark side of the human psyche posits aging mothers as either disgusting or funny while aging fathers are regarded as the sine qua non of virility.
> *Ottawa Citizen* 9 Jan. 1994: B2

(The phrase required here is *ne plus ultra*, referring to 'the height' of virility.)

See also EPITOME; LATIN PHRASES.

sing, sang, sung   The usual past tense of *sing* is *sang*: 'We sang happily'. The past participle is *sung*: 'We have sung carols every year'. In the nineteenth century *sung* was commonly used as the past tense, but this form is now considered dialectal.

> At 25, he sung We Are the World—doing each of the song's 18 distinct voices. . . .
> *Vancouver Sun* 11 Oct. 1990: F5

(The standard past tense is *sang*.)

sink, sank, sunk, sunken   The usual past tense of *sink* is *sank* and the past participle is *sunk*: 'The ship sank'; 'The ship has sunk'. *Sunk* is sometimes used as the past tense, but rarely in writing. *Sunken* is usually an adjective: 'sunken treasure', 'sunken eyes', 'a sunken living room'. *Sunken* is obsolescent in Canadian writing as a variant of the past participle.

> In 1991, drilling activity in Canada sunk to its lowest level since 1975.
> *Financial Post* 23 Dec. 1991: 28

(The past tense *sunk* is not wrong, but *sank* is far more common in Canadian writing.)

> . . . it is still too early to know whether Bourassa's proposal will present Mulroney with a plank on which to

walk out of the political hole in which his party has sunken following the failure of the Meech Lake talks. . . . *Gazette* (Montreal) 2 Feb. 1991: B4

(The usual past participle is *sunk*.)

sirup   see SYRUP

sister-in-law   see MOTHER-IN-LAW

site   see CITE

situation   *Situation* is criticized as redundant in phrases such as 'emergency situation', 'crisis situation', and 'classroom situation'. The words *emergency*, *crisis*, and *classroom* alone are more direct and effective.

The phrase *no-win situation* has been criticized on the same grounds, but in fact it is not redundant. It is an economical way to describe a situation that precludes a clear victory for either side, or in which a single person or group is doomed to failure.

The media have an important role to play in any crisis situation but it is imperative that they do not jeopardize a safe resolution.
Ottawa Citizen 3 Dec. 1990: A9

(Here *crisis* alone would convey the nature of the situation.)

The Anti-lock Braking System (ABS) allows any driver to handle emergency situations like a professional.
Canadian Consumer March 1986: 10

(The single word *emergencies* would describe the situation adequately.)

The Social Credit party is in a possible no-win situation.
Province (Vancouver) 24 Dec. 1990: 81

Six Nations   see IROQUOIS

skeptic, sceptic   Canadian newspapers overwhelmingly use *skeptic* and its related forms, but *sceptic* and *skeptic* are used with equal frequency in other types of writing. British dictionaries list *sceptic* first, American dictionaries *skeptic*. Both spellings are pronounced *SKEP tic*. Many authorities argue that the *sk* spelling more accurately reflects this pronunciation and avoids confusion with *septic*. They may have a point: see SEPSIS, SEPTICEMIA, SEPTIC.

skewer, skew   Writers sometimes use *skewer* when they mean *skew*. To *skew* means to twist or distort, while to *skewer* means to pierce, as with a skewer. *Skewer* is also used figuratively at all levels of writing to mean ridicule or satirize.

Don't run with the stick in your mouth, he'd tell the kids, already seeing them fall, seeing the pointed stick skewering up through the roof of the mouth.
Margaret Atwood *Life Before Man* 1979: 24

The police have managed to skew the law in ways that produce the results they want, namely, a relatively certain conviction against certain kinds of individuals.
Globe and Mail (Toronto) 23 March 1985: 10

(Here *skew* means distort.)

There's a deliciously tangy literary spat abrewing, pitting ... Margaret Atwood against portly Robert Fulford, a sort of high priest of Canadian arts and letters who says he was skewered in a recent Atwood work.
Ottawa Citizen 30 June 1990: C12

(Here *skewer* means ridicule.)

One may also wonder whether ... her insistent skewering of our expectations that anything European must be superior ... has been influenced by her sense of what Americans wish to hear about themselves.
Janice Kulyk Keefer *Reading Mavis Gallant* 1989: 34

(Here *skewer* means ridicule.)

But one thing [drugs] all do the same is to skewer the way things normally work inside your head.
Gazette (Montreal) 29 April 1990: C4

(The word required here is *skew*.)

The Phillipses are big on Do's and Don'ts lists—and they're guaranteed to induce major chuckles from folks with a skewered sense of reality.
Gazette (Montreal) 1 Oct. 1990: B11

(The word required here is *skewed*.)

A lingering drought ... could end up making our mortgages cost more, along with many food items. It may skewer the world economy and stock markets. . . .
Maclean's 18 July 1988: A9

(Although *skewer* is possible here, *skew* might make more sense.)

skid road, skid row   Some critics prefer *skid road* on the grounds of historical accuracy; however, most Canadian writers use *skid row*. Dictionaries list both forms.

Skid road was originally a logging term for a road made of greased logs, or skids, over which lumber was dragged by teams of mules or oxen. The term was first applied to a slum area—the loggers' part of town—in Seattle, Washington, in 1852, and it had become common in Vancouver well before 1900. Gradually the term *skid row* came into use as well to refer to a slum or an area frequented by drifters and alcoholics, even in cities with no lumber industry.

Both terms should be capitalized only when they name a specific place.

> The street's off at an angle, a curious little hiccup in the orderly progression of arrow-straight thoroughfares on either side.... That odd lean to Gore is a reminder that it was once a 'skid road,' the genuine article, a wide swath cut through the forest down which loggers skidded their trees with the assistance of yoked oxen.
> *Province* (Vancouver) 19 Aug. 1990: 27

> Mere decades ago, Hastings Street, around Main—today's Skid Road, home to the poor and socially disenfranchised—was Vancouver's bustling downtown.
> *Vancouver Sun* 12 Jan. 1990: B6

> By ... 1974, the longtime working class neighborhood had deteriorated into flophouses and a Skid Road.
> *Toronto Star* 23 Aug. 1987: E1

(The capitals are unnecessary: 'a *skid road*'.)

> Maj. David Perry, a Salvation Army spokesman in Calgary, said that the average age level of his city's skid row inhabitants has markedly decreased....
> *Maclean's* 12 Feb. 1990: A58

> One was a fortified wine ... which came under fire because of its Skid Row popularity.
> *Financial Post* 17 Sept. 1990: 14

(The capitals are unnecessary.)

skim milk, skimmed milk, whip cream, whipped cream, whipping cream The form *skim milk* is more common in Canadian English than *skimmed milk*, except in the phrase 'partly skimmed milk'. *Whip cream* is common in speech but almost never appears in writing. In writing, *whipped cream* and *whipping cream* are used to distinguish the beaten dessert topping from the heavy cream from which it is made.

See also ICE CREAM.

slain see SLAY

slang see COLLOQUIAL

slant see SLASH

slash, slash mark, virgule, slant, diagonal, solidus A *slash* or *slash mark*, also called a *virgule*, a *slant*, a *diagonal*, or a *solidus*, is used to separate alternatives ('a strictly objective/quantified research method', 'a German industrialist/playboy'), the elements of a date ('98/7/14'), and the numerator and denominator of a fraction ('5/8'). It is also used to replace *per* in measurements ('100 km/h') and *to* in ratios ('new/returning customers'; 'male/female parity'). A slash is sometimes used instead of a hyphen to indicate a period spanning two calendar years ('1962/63'). Note that there is no space before or after the slash in any of these uses.

A slash is also used to separate lines of poetry run on in a prose text; in this use, a space should be inserted before and after the slash.

> The law, however, 'oldest of the hierarchs / Composed of electronic sparks', ... ultimately denies the significance of man in the scheme of things.
> *Queen's Quarterly* 97.3 (1990): 423

See also AND/OR; DATES; HYPHENATION; QUOTATION.

slate In Canada and the United States, to *be slated* means to be scheduled or designated, as in 'slated for surgery' or 'slated for publication'. In British English, to *slate* is a colloquialism meaning to criticize severely. The two expressions have different roots. The North American verb *slate* is related to the noun *slate* meaning chalkboard and its figurative extension meaning a list of candidates proposed for election or nomination. The British verb *slate* is thought to be a modern variation on the verb *slat*, which dates from the thirteenth century and means to slap or to knock down. *Slate* meaning criticize is unfamiliar in North America, as is a political *slate* in Britain.

> They were slated to arrive in mid-January.
> Pierre Berton *The Promised Land* 1984: 75

> Alderman John Bannister ... took pains to deny rumours that property on Barrie Street, one block east of the university, 'was slated for expropriation'.
> Frederick Gibson *Queen's University* 2 (1983): 386

> An alliance of about 800 artists, artist-run centres and art critics ... have proposed a slate of 11 candidates to stand for election at the VAG annual general meeting on March 28.
> *Globe and Mail* (Toronto) 28 Feb. 1985: E1

slaughter   see MASSACRE

Slavey, Dene-Tha(h)   Both names, *Slavey* and *Dene-Tha* or *Dene-Thah* (pronounced *DEN ay THAH*), are in use for this Aboriginal group, whose language, Slavey, is a member of the Athapaskan language family (sometimes called Na-Dene). They occasionally identify themselves as *Slavey Dene*. Most of their traditional territory is in the Northwest Territories, although it extends into northern British Columbia and Alberta. Both names can be used as singular and plural.

Characters [on the television program *North of 60*] will sometimes speak the Slavey language, and a Northwest Territories cultural advisor is on hand to help keep things authentic.
Calgary Herald 6 Oct. 1992: D1

'I don't think we can resurrect anything before the next election,' [Western Arctic MP Ethel] Blondin, a Slavey Dene and strong Yes campaigner, said as the reality of Monday's referendum results began to sink in.
Calgary Herald 28 Oct. 1992: A8

With the abuse finally surfacing, the Dene Tha band is starting a time of healing and recovery....
Calgary Herald 21 Dec. 1992: A15

See also ATHABASKAN; DENE.

slay, slew, slain, slayed   The past tense of *slay* meaning kill is *slew* and the past participle is *slain*. *Slay* has a second, informal sense: an act or performer that slays an audience is a huge hit. In this sense the past tense can be *slayed*.

Brian Mulroney climbed Parliament Hill looking grim and talking cheeky, as Clyde Wells slew the Meech Lake behemoth.
Toronto Star 5 Jan. 1991: G4

... legend says that demigod Maui chased and slayed the dragon Moo Kuna for trying to drown his mother, the goddess Hina.
Vancouver Sun 8 Dec. 1990: E1

(The usual past tense for this sense is *slew*.)

In a recent five-week period in Quebec, 13 women were slain by a husband or lover.
Province (Vancouver) 11 Oct. 1990: 38

Monday night, before a near-capacity house at the Centrepointe Theatre, Crowell ... slayed the audience with a high-energy, two-hour set.
Ottawa Citizen 1 May 1990: D5

McDonald ... is auteur of Roadkill, the fab rock 'n roll road movie that slayed 'em at the Toronto and Vancouver film festivals.
Vancouver Sun 27 July 1990: C1

See also SLOUGH, SLOUGH OF DESPOND, SLEW.

sled, sleigh, toboggan, cutter, sledge, cariole, carryall   In Canada the children's toy on runners used for coasting down snowy hills is called either a *sled* or a *sleigh*. A *toboggan*, used for the same purpose, is curved up at one end and has no runners. Larger sleighs, now primarily used for winter parties, are pulled by horses. *Cutter* is a Canadianism for a light horse-drawn sleigh. The small, low cargo vehicle used in the north, pulled by dog teams and occasionally by people, is called a *sled* or a *sledge*. *Cariole* is a Canadianism derived from Canadian French; it refers to a light sleigh pulled by horses or occasionally dogs. In English Canada *carryall* was once a common spelling, influenced by folk etymology.

Parents pulled their children on sleds past the Pantheon and skiers glided through the Spanish Steps area.
Globe and Mail (Toronto) 7 Jan. 1985: C10

Off he went on a tour of all the villages, seated in a six-horse sleigh, with a choir of maidens chanting psalms.
Pierre Berton The Promised Land 1984: 95

Outside the door the sleigh and horses awaited. No, not prancing steeds pulling a fancy cutter. Just a large farm sleigh piled high with fragrant hay....
Vancouver Sun 24 Dec. 1993: A3

So when Doug Hannah hooked the harness onto the sled, the big Malamute was howling and leaping with the rest of the sled team.
Globe and Mail (Toronto) 4 Dec. 1985: C4

Bring your camera to capture the age-old arts of travelling by dog team and sledge and of traditional Inuit seal hunting.
Uphere Mar.–Apr. 1990: 38

In temperatures of -52C, the men travelled an average of 14 kilometres daily, each carrying 60 kilograms ... of supplies divided between a backpack and sledge each man pulled behind.
Province (Vancouver) 4 Oct. 1990: 19

... these shaggy ponies hauled logs out of the bush and pulled the family to Sunday mass; released from their labours, they drew daredevil carioles over frozen rivers.
Saturday Night July 1986: 33

See also FOLK ETYMOLOGY.

slew   see SLAY; SLOUGH

slips of the tongue   A slip of the tongue is an unintentional error in speech, either in pronunciation or in word choice. Such verbal gaffes often provide amusement; they are also of particular interest in the field of psycholinguistics because they shed some light on language is produced in the brain.

Slips of the tongue fall into a number of patterns. One of the most frequent errors is the transposition of initial letters between two terms, as in 'You have hissed my mystery lecture'. William Archibald Spooner, an Oxford don, produced so many funny examples of such slips that they are now called 'spoonerisms'. English-speakers often transpose sounds within particular words, a phenomenon known as *metathesis*: for example, saying *intregal* instead of *integral*. A consonant may be shifted from one word to another: *pinch hit* comes out as *pitch hint*. Or an initial or final consonant may carry over to another word, as in this slip in a commentary by Don Cherry (on *Hockey Night in Canada*, 24 Oct. 1992): 'Cream rises to the crop' (instead of 'to the top'; or perhaps Cherry was thinking of the phrase 'cream of the crop').

Words are sometimes unintentionally blended in speech, producing 'boibbling' instead of *boiling and bubbling*. Sometimes words that are 'close' are introduced into phrases that sound plausible but don't quite make sense: 'a *reclining* hairline', '*unravelling* a plaque', 'the basic *tenants* of an argument'. This sort of slip of the tongue, choosing the wrong word, is commonly called a *malapropism*. The celebrated *Freudian slip*, technically a *parapraxis*, is the unintentional substitution of a word in speech or writing that supposedly reveals an unconscious thought or desire, usually construed as sexual: 'She bakes the breast bed I've ever had'.

See also MALAPROPISM; MISPRONUNCIATION; SPOONERISM.

slough, slough of despond, slew   The definition of *slough* varies across Canada: on the Pacific coast it is a shallow saltwater estuary or a backwater channel of a river; in the interior of British Columbia it is a marsh; and across the prairies it is a hollow that fills with water in the wet season and often produces good-quality hay called 'slough grass'. Some prairie sloughs are round areas of sinking soil also known as potholes. In this sense, Canadians usually pronounce *slough* to rhyme with *slew* (which is also an alternative, though uncommon, spelling). However, in the expression *slough of despond*, meaning a fit of depression and despair, they often use the British pronunciation, which rhymes *slough* with *cow*; the phrase comes from the name of a bog that blocks the path of the hero of John Bunyan's *Pilgrim's Progress* (1678).

Slough (pronounced SLUFF) is the old, shed skin of a snake or other animal. To *slough* (usually followed by *off*) is to shed something or to cast it off: 'He sloughed off their critical comments'.

Slew is the past tense of *slay*. The noun *slew* is an informal term for a large number or amount. Less commonly, *slew* is used as a verb meaning to turn or swing as if on a pivot, or to skid or turn sharply.

> The sun shone, the snow melted, the frogs sang in the sloughs.
> Max Braithwaite *The Night We Stole the Mountie's Car* 1971: 182

> John Turner admits to no dark night of doubt during his slog through the slough of Liberal despond.
> *Saturday Night* March 1986: 17

> The same tendency to slough over the consequences was present in efforts by Mandeville and others to identify luxury with happier circumstances.
> J.A.W. Gunn *Beyond Liberty and Property* 1983: 98

> (Here the writer seems to have confused two idiomatic expressions: *slough off* and *gloss over*.)

> I looked at my watch at the side of the bed, where I'd left it behind as I sloughed all my city clothes nearly a week ago.
> Howard Engel *Murder Sees the Light* 1984: 150

> However tempting it may be . . . to try to slough responsibility off on the provinces, abortion law is not traffic law.
> *Vancouver Sun* 21 July 1989: A14

> They killed and ate several of the Emperor's pedigree Australian sheep, and also slew two horses.
> *Globe and Mail* (Toronto) 26 Sept. 1985: P20

> The car slewed on a patch of ice.
> David Williams *Eye of the Father* 1985: 148

See also SLAY; SWAMP.

slow, slowly   The use of *slow* as an adverb, as in 'go slow', 'driving too slow', and 'talk slower', has often been subjected to criticism on the grounds that *slowly* is the correct adverb form. However, there are a few adverbs in English, called 'flat adverbs' or 'zero adverbs', that have the same form as the corresponding adjective. These include *fast, slow, quick, wide,* and *deep*: 'Come quick'; 'Turn wide'. Most zero adverbs also have an adverb form that ends in *-ly*. Often these forms are used in different contexts. For example, *slow* is used directly after a verb, while *slowly* can be placed elsewhere in the sentence: 'Slowly he opened his mouth to speak'.

See also ZERO ADVERBS.

small arms   see GUN

smite   To *smite* means to strike. The past tense, *smote*, is archaic or poetic. Sometimes its connotations of biblical justice and dragon-slaying are exploited facetiously.
   The past participle is *smitten*. This form does not have an archaic ring, but in contemporary English it is used only in the figurative senses of love-struck or awe-struck.

The air smote his cheeks like the flat of an axe.
David Williams *Eye of the Father* 1985: 151

Since the age of 14, Fontaine has been smitten with the theatre.
Vancouver Sun 28 Sept. 1990: TV52

In prison, [she] continued to enlist the help of smitten admirers.
Ottawa Citizen 2 Nov. 1990: A1

smoulder, smolder   Both spellings are common in Canadian writing. The British use *smoulder*; Americans strongly prefer *smolder*.

A lit cigarette or spark carelessly dropped can cause upholstery or carpeting to smoulder through the night.
Vancouver Sun 16 Oct. 1990: B6

Economists have been looking for a surge in consumer spending as a key to reignite the smoldering recovery, but there was little sign of that in July's numbers.
Edmonton Journal 22 Sept. 1992: n.p.

See also SPELLING, CANADIAN.

sneaked, snuck   In Canadian writing the usual past tense or past participle of *sneak* is *sneaked*. The form *snuck* is sometimes used in fiction and journalism, and is very common in speech. *Snuck* was first recorded in the dialect of the American South at the end of the nineteenth century. This form has made rapid progress towards acceptability in the United States and Canada; it may even sneak into formal Canadian writing in the next few years.

While George took care of family business, somebody sneaked into his backyard and made off with two prize boars.
Vancouver Sun 9 April 1990: A9

'He'd been hoping for a crime that at best would be apprehended, snuck up on, come across.'
Howard Engel *Murder Sees the Light* 1984: 219

[Hospital] user fees are being snuck in by the back door—as an example, the delicately called 'co-payments,' now of some $1,000 a month, being charged to chronic care patients in Ontario.
Toronto Star 3 Dec. 1993: A29

sneakers   see RUNNING SHOES

snicker, snigger   Both *snicker* and *snigger* describe a half-suppressed laugh. Americans prefer *snicker*, but the English consider the word obsolete and use only *snigger*. For Canadians, *snigger* may imply more malice than *snicker*, but they use both words with about equal frequency.

The very computer I have used for the past 8 years now has an antiquated look about it. My own children snicker when I defend it.
Daily News (Halifax) 4 Aug. 1994: n.p.

She thought the man would be offended—she was intending to be offensive—but she was almost sure she heard a snicker at the other end of the line.
Margaret Atwood *Life Before Man* 1979: 274

Spiteful, sniggering, conceited, infantine Mozart!
Queen's Quarterly 92.2 (1985): 331

I have never thought of myself as a satirist: I do not sit down to my work sniggering with malice and muttering, 'Here goes with the acid!'
Robertson Davies *One Half of Robertson Davies* 1978: 281

snuck   see SNEAKED

so ... as   see AS ... AS

so-called   The expression *so-called* signals irony. Its use indicates the writer's skepticism about the accuracy of a title, name, or label, as in 'this so-called expert'. *So-called* should not be used simply to give the usual name for something, as in 'these so-called home pages'.

Most language guides recommend that what follows *so-called* not be put in quotation marks, on the grounds that a double indication of irony is unnecessary.

> [Wollstonecraft] believed that physical exercise was essential and that doll-playing and other so-called feminine games would quickly be relegated to rainy afternoons if girls were allowed to romp in the fields along with their brothers.
> Miriam Waddington *Apartment Seven* 1989: 173

> 'Women are already flooding the so-called traditional jobs by the millions.'
> Carl J. Cuneo *Pay Equity* 1990: 115

> Clearly Englishmen had long been familiar with the notion that individual liberty did not necessarily flourish in a so-called 'free-state.'
> J.A.W. Gunn *Beyond Liberty and Property* 1983: 239

(Some editors would remove the quotation marks around 'free-state'.)

> As they began their power struggle to wrest hegemony from their so-called 'betters,' they staked out a new moral high ground from which to look down on men like Chesterfield.
> Katherine M.J. McKenna *A Life of Propriety* 1994: 5

(Some editors would remove the quotation marks around 'betters'.)

> Associated with the Urban Revolution is the introduction of copper and bronze—the so-called Bronze Age.
> Irving M. Zeitlin and Robert J. Brym *The Social Condition of Humanity* 1991: 303

(Here *so-called* is not necessary unless the writer has an objection to the term *Bronze Age*.)

See also QUOTATION, QUOTATION MARKS.

soccer, football   What Canadians and Americans call *soccer* is what the rest of the English-speaking world calls *football*. Canadians and Americans reserve the term *football* for the contact sport, developed in the United States, in which heavily padded players throw, kick, or run with an oval ball. Internationally, this game is known as American football. Most North American sports fans know that Americans and Canadians play the game by slightly different rules, and call the Canadian version 'Canadian football'.

> Strangely, Quinn, a native of Quebec City, has never played a game of soccer in his life. 'Football was always my game,' said Quinn....
> *Gazette* (Montreal) 18 June 1992: H1

> 'If we don't grant clubs a license, they can play their football—but without spectators.'
> *Gazette* (Montreal) 20 Jan. 1992: C5

(Here a British speaker is referring to the game known in Canada as *soccer*.)

> [In] American or Canadian football ... a team must advance the ball 10 yards to get a first down.
> *Vancouver Sun* 20 June 1992: D3

Social Credit Party, funny money, Créditiste, Socred   Social Credit principles were developed in the 1920s by an English engineer named C.H. Douglas. Douglas believed that a strong economy depended on the purchasing power of the people, and that the government should distribute 'credit' to consumers. His ideas were seized upon by an evangelist named William Aberhart, who led the Social Credit Party to victory in Alberta in 1935. The Aberhart government's monetary reforms and issuing of scrip known as *funny money* gave rise to the nickname *funny-money party*.

However, over the next few decades Social Credit policy diverged significantly from Douglas's original ideas, and the party gained prominence in several provinces by following conservative financial policies and promoting development. Social Credit members in Quebec formed their own group in 1963 and adopted the name *Ralliement des Créditistes*, or simply *Créditistes*. Members of the Social Credit Party or the Ralliement des Créditistes held seats in the House of Commons between 1935 and 1980. By the end of the 1980s the Social Credit Party was active only in British Columbia. Members of the Social Credit Party are informally known as *Socreds*.

> Similarly, even today, in Western Canadian elections, a protest vote may go Social Credit or NDP without much regard to the difference in political philosophy between these parties.
> Northrop Frye *The Bush Garden* 1971: 229

> ... Mr. Bourassa's Liberals thrashed the Union Nationale, the Créditistes and the Parti Quebecois at the polls, and Mr. Bourassa became the youngest premier in Quebec's history.
> *Globe and Mail* (Toronto) 28 Nov. 1985: A4

> The Socred government had been plagued by a series of mini-scandals ranging from vote juggling to cabinet ministers guzzling expensive French wine on the taxpayers' tab.
> Henry M. Rosenthal and S. Cathy Berson, eds. *Canadian Jewish Outlook Anthology* 1988: 316

soda see SOFT DRINK

sofa see CHESTERFIELD

soft drink, pop, soda All these words refer to a drink of sweetened, carbonated water. *Soft drink* is the term that most Canadians use in writing and formal speech. In casual speech Canadians, like the British, often say *pop*; but in writing *pop* is considered slang. The compound *soda pop* is now rare. While some Americans use *soda* instead of *pop*, in Canada *soda* usually means club soda; however, a *soda* may also be a float, a drink made with ice cream in a soft drink.

> ... he stood at the soft drink and hot-dog stand, hands in his pockets fingering pennies, keys, feeling out of place, a scavenger.
> Margaret Atwood *Life Before Man* 1979: 288

> Since 1980, the $3-billion soft drink market has been growing at around five percent per year.
> *Western Grocer Magazine* May–Jun. 1990: 20

> The Grade 8 students left the chamber and paced the foyer outside the meeting, listlessly sipping pop while the fights continued.
> *Globe and Mail* (Toronto) 16 Jan. 1985: M4

solder In Canadian and American English *solder* (both the noun meaning the metal alloy and the verb meaning to fuse) rhymes with *fodder*. In British English the *l* is pronounced.

solicitor see LAWYER

solid, stolid *Solid* things are heavy, firm, sturdy, or strong; *solid* people are physically strong and big or figuratively staunch or reliable (as in the cliché 'a solid citizen'). *Stolid* people are phlegmatic, slow, unemotional, and undemonstrative. Once applied only to people, *stolid* is now occasionally used to describe places and institutions, apparently with the sense of solid or staid and conservative. This new sense—if that is what it is—is far from established.

> He was dignified, a devout Presbyterian, true to its puritanical tradition of stolid self-development and public duty....
> William Teatero *John Anderson: Fugitive Slave* 1986: 78

> The first black American expert in modern dance to work with one of Europe's most stolid cultural institutions, he spent three years as assistant director of the Opera Ballet's experimental arm.
> *Globe and Mail* (Toronto) 16 Feb. 1985: E9

> (Here *stolid* appears to mean *conservative* or *traditional*, in contrast to 'experimental'.)

> Two institutions played on the same stage at stolid and splendid Roy Thomson Hall Tuesday night....
> *Globe and Mail* (Toronto) 19 June 1985: S10

> (Here the writer may have meant *solid*, or perhaps *staid*.)

> The stolid, comforting structures of today's workplace will fall away, washed away by a startling new fluidity.
> *Vancouver Sun* 11 May 1995: A20

> Dr. Savage's popularity will get its truest test only when his candidate faces the electorate in one of the traditional swing seats, or a stolid Liberal riding.
> *Daily News* (Halifax) 4 No. 1993: 20

> (Here *stolid* could be argued to apply to a personified riding, meaning one that is unlikely to prove volatile or to change its loyalties. However, *solid* would convey the same meaning without puzzling readers.)

solidus see SLASH

solstice see EQUINOX

soluble, solvable, insoluble, unsolvable, dissolvable A problem for which a solution can be found is *soluble* or *solvable*; a problem that cannot be solved is *insoluble* or *unsolvable*. Substances that can be dissolved in a liquid are *soluble* or *dissolvable*; those that do not dissolve are *insoluble*.

> This seems to indicate that the problem is soluble.
> *Globe and Mail* (Toronto) 7 Feb. 1985: M12

> The Canadian Institute for Advanced Research [is] setting its sights on the kinds of big questions not normally solvable in Canada.
> *Globe and Mail* (Toronto) 28 Jan. 1985: P13

> Spokesmen for the Ottawa and Carleton boards of education asked a provincial education commission ... to help them find solutions to problems that they feel are insolvable without provincial guidelines or arbitration.
> *Globe and Mail* (Toronto) 15 Feb. 1985: M3

> (The word required here is either *insoluble* or *unsolvable*.)

> A cleanup was not possible ... because the chemicals are water soluble and were dispersed in the river.
> *Globe and Mail* (Toronto) 23 Dec. 1985: A17

someplace, somewhere see -WHERE, -PLACE

something, somewhat *Something* and *somewhat* are sometimes used interchangeably as adverbs: 'Nova Scotia is something/somewhat like her home in Maine'; 'The visit was something/somewhat less than perfect'. In these phrases either word suggests an undetermined portion or extent. Some commentators prefer *somewhat* to *something* in descriptions of people ('She is somewhat—*not* something—like her mother') but allow that *something* and *somewhat* are both acceptable in the fixed expression 'something/somewhat of a': 'He's something/somewhat of a snob'.

More often in speech than in writing, *something* intensifies an adjective, creating an adverb phrase: 'The dog howled something terrible'; 'She smokes something fierce when she's working'. This construction is listed in dictionaries as informal, and in writing it is appropriate only for representations of very casual speech. The more widely accepted construction replaces the *something* phrase with an adverb: 'The dog howled terribly'. Also considered inappropriate for formal writing is the use of *something* to describe a remarkable person, event, or thing, as in 'That storm was really something!' or 'She's something else!'

The somewhat rigid but manifestly decent Clyde Wells remains immensely popular....
Province (Vancouver) 31 Dec. 1990: 20

He was a young, handsome farm-implement dealer in a windbreaker, whose interest in school matters was somewhat less than nothing.
Max Braithwaite *The Night We Stole the Mountie's Car* 1971: 20

Isn't he somewhat of a bohemian?
NeWest Review Dec. 1989–Jan. 1990: 29

This makes Inga and Gertrude something less than friends and something more than strangers.
Queen's Quarterly 92.1 (1985): 51

Productivity in these cattle ranches is ridiculously low, something like 30 to 50 kilograms per hectare, annually.
Irving M. Zeitlin and Robert J. Brym *The Social Condition of Humanity* 1991: 366

The process is something of a vicious circle.
J.E. Smyth et al. *The Law and Business Administration in Canada* 1987: 100

'Cat's panting something terrible!'
Queen's Quarterly 95.3 (1988): 612

(This use is acceptable only in informal dialogue.)

someway   *Someway* is a variant of *somehow* or *in some way* ('I'll do it someway'; 'Someway he got out'). *Someway* is less formal than *somehow* and

rarely appears in Canadian writing except in transcribed speech. It is listed in American but not English dictionaries.

'I find when people are really getting serious about something, whether it's a union or whether it's dying, they want God involved someway or somehow.'
Ottawa Citizen 18 Nov. 1990: F3

'We're going to have to look for runs someway.'
Ottawa Citizen 31 July 1994: E1

somewhat   see SOMETHING

Soo, the   see SAULT

sophist, sophistry, sophistication   In the fifth century B.C., in ancient Greece, *sophists* were men admired for their wisdom and knowledge. A century later a group of travelling teachers in Greece called themselves the *Sophists*. They received payment for providing an education designed to enhance success in public life. Because they were criticized for valuing success in debates more than truth and knowledge, the Greek root *sophos*, 'wise', took on connotations of cleverness and deceit. Thus *sophistry* became a term for subtle but deceptive argumentation.

Sophistication, which originally meant the use of sophistries, or disingenuousness, by 1850 was beginning to mean worldliness, or a lessening of naturalness or simplicity. The word's connotations have since changed from negative to positive, or at least neutral. Now sophistication is often something to be admired: for example, 'sophisticated new technology' is complex and highly evolved.

That the ethical point of view need not be accepted by the individual as overriding was the message of the Sophist.
Canadian Journal of Philosophy 19 (1989): 298

(Here *Sophist* is capitalized because the reference is to the historical Sophists.)

What is a good book, says the sophist, smiling like a wolf trap. Any book is a good book which feeds the mind something which may enlarge it, or move it to action. A book is good in relation to its reader.
Robertson Davies *A Voice from the Attic* 1960: 293

(Here 'the *sophist*' represents any tricky debater.)

Our national antipathy to mental skill may be due in part to religious and literary traditions that often equate such

accomplishment with sophistry and the devil, in contrast with the simpler virtues of plain, honest folk.
Globe and Mail (Toronto) 7 Sept. 1985: P6

I longed for the wit and sophistication of New York City.
Max Braithwaite *The Night We Stole the Mountie's Car* 1971: 11

(Unlike *sophistry*, *sophistication* often has positive connotations.)

... improvement in the quality of medical records and the sophistication of medical diagnosis has facilitated the connecting of certain diseases with certain occupations.
J.E. Smyth et al. *The Law and Business Administration in Canada* 1987: 513

sorbet   see SHERBET

sort of   see KIND OF

sound out   According to most dictionaries and usage guides, *sound out* is now an accepted idiom referring to questioning carried out in order to discover someone's opinion or attitude. At election time, for example, politicians sound out voters. The verb *sound* by itself used to have this meaning; in fact, some commentators maintain that it still should, and that *out* is redundant. In contemporary Canadian English, however, only depths are *sounded*: people are *sounded out*.

Munro attracted support from several trustees and especially from J.M. Macdonnell who went to Halifax to sound him out.
Frederick Gibson *Queen's University* 2 (1983): 85

H.R. Halpin, the Moose Mountain farm instructor, was told to sound out the Indians.
Pierre Berton *The Promised Land* 1984: 246

source   see INFORMER

south   see EAST

South Asian   see INDIAN

Southeast Asia, South Asia   see ASIA

sovereignist, sovereigntist   see SEPARATIST

sow, sowed, sown   The past tense is *sowed*: 'The president sowed the seeds of her own downfall'. The past participle is either *sown* or *sowed*: 'The farmer has sown the field'; 'The mistake has sowed suspicion'. *Sown* is far more common.

But it won't be too many years before you're going to reap what you've sown.
Toronto Star 12 Nov. 1994: K9

The scandal of Christian missionary outreach has been competing denominations. Introducing Jesus Christ from different perspectives has sowed confusion....
Ottawa Citizen 20 Jan. 1990: C12

span   see SPIN

spat   see SPIT

spay   see NEUTER

Speaker, deputy speaker   Some editors capitalize *Speaker* when it refers to the presiding officer of a legislative assembly; others don't. However, since legislatures are full of small-*s* speakers, capitalization is recommended to avoid ambiguity. Since *deputy speaker* is not ambiguous, the name of this position is often not capitalized. The name of either position is capitalized if it's used as a title directly before a person's name.

He soon became a leading Manitoba politician, rising to Speaker of the legislature.
Pierre Berton *The Promised Land* 1984: 21-22

Still, Mulroney succeeded in winning a prediction from Thomas (Tip) O'Neill, the powerful speaker of the House of Representatives, that Congress was unlikely to stall trade negotiations.
Maclean's 31 March 1986: 23

(Here a capital *S* would make *speaker* unambiguous.)

Steve Paproski speaks English, as well as Ukrainian and Polish, and is now struggling with a fourth tongue—French—for his role as deputy speaker of the House of Commons.
Saturday Night Feb. 1986: 17

Charbonneau remained out of the chamber yesterday, leaving Deputy Speaker Nathan Nurgitz to handle his duties.
Gazette (Montreal) 6 Oct. 1990: A1

See also CAPITAL LETTERS.

special, specially, especial, especially   Some critics would reserve *special* and *specially* for things that are exceptional in that they are meant for a specific purpose: 'She is a special agent working overseas'; 'I made dinner specially for him'. *Especial* and *especially* then would be used to describe things that are exceptional by virtue of degree: 'There's an especial closeness between them'; 'The dinner was especially tasty'. However, in contemporary Canadian writing *special* has largely replaced the rarely used adjective *especial*, while the adverb *especially* is used far more often than *specially*. *Especial* and *specially* are uncommon and may strike some readers as formal or even literary. *Specially* is still recommended in expressions where it means for a specific purpose: 'These cases were made specially for his antique camera equipment'.

Some commentators feel that *special* is becoming less special with overuse.

He ... is convinced that French needs special protection to survive in Quebec.
Gazette (Montreal) 1 March 1989: A4

Among the issues on the Paris summit agenda, two took on a special urgency.
Maclean's 24 Feb. 1986: 26

While most new managers assume positions of responsibility with little or no formal preparation ... women are often at an especial disadvantage as new managers.
Ottawa Citizen 4 Nov. 1990: C7

(This use is uncommon.)

Blowing snow limited visibility along the Coquihalla, where holiday travellers made traffic especially heavy.
Province (Vancouver) 27 Dec. 1990: 5

The Hague is home to what's billed as the world's largest panoramic painting, in a building erected especially to house the huge work.
Calgary Herald 2 July 1994: B12

(Here some commentators would prefer *specially*.)

Regrettably, it is perfectly possible to be an effective writer and a boob as well; writers are not, by definition, intellectual or even specially literate.
Robertson Davies *A Voice from the Attic* 1960: 345

(Some commentators would prefer *especially* here.)

specialty, speciality Canadians are far more likely to use *specialty* than the chiefly British form *speciality*, but either form is acceptable.

specie, species *Specie* (pronounced *SPEE shee*) is a rare word for money in the form of coins. *Species* is both singular and plural for a biological category of plants and animals: 'a rare species of plant'; 'many endangered species of wildlife'. By extension, in general writing *species* is used to mean sort or kind: 'That species of politician is unaware of these issues'.

The *c* in *species* is usually pronounced as *sh* outside Canada, but *SPEE seez* is a common and accepted Canadian pronunciation.

... Beck provides considerable detail as to the manner in which Howe, as a believer in specie, tried to stem the flow of paper money....
Queen's Quarterly 92.2 (1985): 386

In order to ensure the survival of a species, its natural habitat must be preserved.
Chronicle-Herald (Halifax) 14 May 1988: 3

... gulls are taking over nesting areas previously used by other species, especially the common tern.
Globe and Mail (Toronto) 4 Jan. 1985: M1

Dream a Little Dream, latest of this tired species, stars heavyweight actor Jason Robards....
Gazette (Montreal) 5 March 1989: F6

She keeps a record of every specie she encounters in a given year by placing a check mark beside 'Peterson's Systematic Checklist' in the handy book just described.
Ottawa Citizen 9 June 1990: B7

(The correct spelling is *species*, even in the singular.)

See also SPECIES, GENUS.

species, genus, family, order, class, phylum, division, kingdom *Species* is at the bottom of the hierarchy used by biologists to categorize living beings: species, genus, family, order, class, phylum, division, kingdom. Members of the same species can interbreed; those of different species cannot. The system of binomial (two-term) nomenclature followed in biology uses the species and genus designation together to distinguish particular plants, animals, and micro-organisms from one another.

Robin, for example, is a sufficiently accurate term to use when a large red-breasted bird shows up on your lawn or your child has a project about spring. In Britain, however, *robin* names a much different, smaller bird. Both have red breasts and both belong to the family Turdidae, but that's where the similarity ends. The North American robin's scientific name is *Turdus migratorius*, while the European robin is *Erithacus rubecula*.

The first term in these Latin names designates the genus and is capitalized; the second designates the species and is not capitalized. Both terms are italicized. Often a popular name is given first, with the scientific name following in parentheses. By convention, categories above the rank of genus are printed in roman rather than italic type.

See also SCIENTIFIC ENGLISH; SPECIE, SPECIES.

spectators see AUDIENCE

spectrum see COLOUR

spelling, Canadian Spelling, like punctuation, is ultimately governed by convention. In contemporary English, creative, freestyle spelling is not tolerated. Accepted spellings are codified in dictionaries, and spelling difficulties are generally the same for all writers of English, wherever in the English-speaking world they may live. Established variants do exist, however, especially between British and American conventions, and it is here that Canadian writers tend to show a distinctive pattern of preferences.

British and American spelling initially diverged because of the influence of Samuel Johnson's dictionary (1755) in Britain and of Noah Webster's (1828) in the United States. Canadian spelling preferences have varied over time, and vary today from region to region, as the result of settlement history; the choice of spellers, dictionaries, and textbooks by school boards; and the influence of newspaper spelling. Generally, Ontarians are the most British in their spelling choices, with British Columbians and Newfoundlanders close behind, while Albertans, followed by other Prairie Canadians, are the most American.

Most Canadians, whatever they think or say they do, use a mixture of British and American spellings. The major Canadian newspapers carry stories from both British and American wire services; these may or may not be rewritten to conform with the local style before publication. Thus Canadian readers take in variant spellings every day, often without really thinking about it. And if they do think about it, they may think they are using the British spelling when they are using the American, or vice versa. Further, Canadians never use the British spellings for some words (like *gaol*, *kerb*, and *tyre*) and very rarely use the American spellings for others (like *check* for bank draft, or *maneuver*). Although Canadians do not use either British or American spelling consistently, they tend to be consistent within some major categories. For example, most Canadians choose the *ize/yze* endings (also favoured by Americans) over the *-ise/yse* endings preferred by the British. Like the British, Canadians tend to double the *l* at the ends of words when adding suffixes: *equalled*, *modelling*, *traveller*. Canadians, like the British, prefer *-ce* endings on nouns like *defence* and *offence*. Most Canadians choose the British spellings of *axe*, *catalogue*, *centre*, *cheque*, *fulfil*, *grey*, and *manoeuvre*, but follow American spelling with *analyze*, *carburetor*, *criticize*, *encyclopedia*, *judgment*, *medieval*, *movable*, *peddler*, *plow*, *program*, *raccoon*, and *woollen*. Canadians are divided over whether to use *our* or *-or* endings. The authors of *Editing Canadian English* conclude that although it makes sense to advise against mixing spellings within the major categories (such as *-our*, *-or*), 'mixing *between* categories not only is acceptable, but may well constitute the "Canadian style." '

See also -ABLE, -EABLE; -ABLE, -IBLE; -AE-, -OE-, -E-; AQ-, ACQ-; -C, -CK; CAPITAL LETTERS; -CE, -SE; -CEED, -CEDE, -SEDE; CENTRE, CENTER; DOUBLING THE FINAL CONSONANT; -E; EXH-, EX-; -IE-, -EI-; -IZE, -ISE, -YZE, -YSE; -L, -LL; -LOG, -LOGUE; -OUR, -OR; PLURALS; Q-, QU-; QUEBEC ENGLISH; -RE, -ER.

spendthrift Since *thrift* now means good money management, one might think a *spendthrift* a frugal sort. In fact, a spendthrift is a person who spends money recklessly and wastefully. An early meaning of *thrift* was accumulated wealth or, more specifically, an inheritance: thus a spendthrift was someone who squandered an inheritance.

A hard drinker and spendthrift, he borrowed heavily to supplement the small amounts that he earned....
Maclean's 24 Feb. 1986: 60

spigot see TAP

spin, span For the verb *spin*, the past tense and the past participle (the form used after *have*) are both *spun*. *Span* in this sense is an archaic past tense. To *span*, meaning to extend over, is a regular verb with the past tense and past participle *spanned*.

Knitters spun the hair of various animals for yarn....
Vancouver Sun 13 Dec. 1990: F10

A success in Calgary's 1988 Winter Olympics has spun off some extra gold—in the form of a contract for a city firm to work on the 1994 edition of the Games in Norway.
Province (Vancouver) 14 Nov. 1990: 42

Langley ... focuses his inquiry on US foreign policy in Central America and the Caribbean during the three decades spanned by the two Roosevelts.
Queen's Quarterly 92.2 (1985): 397

spiral The verb *spiral* means to move upwards or downwards in a circular motion. Some critics object when the direction of the spiral is not specified, but normally the context makes the direction clear.

> Davis's artistic course in the last half of the 1950s has the appearance of a steady upward spiral at the head of the cohesive quintet....
> Jack Chambers *Milestones* 1983: 216

> In public housing especially, the maxim 'everybody's property is nobody's property' [helps explain] the all too frequent downward spiral of neglect.
> *Queen's Quarterly* 94.4 (1987): 979

> Professionalization, specialization, inflation, and the rapid growth of an elderly Jewish population will spiral service costs over the next decade.
> Henry M. Rosenthal and S. Cathy Berson, eds. *Canadian Jewish Outlook Anthology* 1988: 45

(Clearly costs are expected to *spiral upward*.)

spiritualism, spirituality see RELIGION

spit, spat, spitted The past tense and past participle of *spit* can be either *spat* or *spit*. *Spat* is the preferred past tense and past participle in Canada and Britain, but in the United States *spit* is preferred for both forms.

Spitted is the past tense and past participle of the verb *spit* meaning to pierce with a stick.

> [He] cursed and struggled with the arresting officer, then spat at him....
> *Vancouver Sun* 15 Nov. 1990: A8

> My salmon turned down river, went over the bar and into the rapids, leaped and spit out the tiny fly all in a matter of seconds.
> *Atlantic Salmon Journal* Summer (1990): 28

> ... Brian started thumping on Stephen. Ordered to stop, he said: 'Somebody spitted on me.'
> *Ottawa Citizen* 23 April 1990: B1

(The standard past tense is either *spit* or *spat*.)

> She was impatient ... with these stories which were so foreign and which, like their endless stories about wars and suffering and horror, children spitted on swords, had nothing to do with her.
> Margaret Atwood *Life Before Man* 1979: 249

(Here *spitted* is the past tense of the verb meaning to impale.)

See also SPITTING IMAGE, SPIT.

spitting image, spit The phrase *spitting image* is now considered standard, but it is actually a distortion of the original expression, *spit and image*. A *spit* is an exact likeness.

> Consecon, a 3-year-old Boomer Drummond colt who is the spitting image of his sire, looms as the horse to beat this year....
> *Gazette* (Montreal) 4 June 1990: C7

> Wasn't it interesting, wagged all the Ottawa tongues, how her son was the spitting image of the prime minister?
> *Toronto Star* 20 Jan. 1990: J1

> 'In September of '44,' she said ... 'I gave birth to a baby boy, the spit of Bohozuk.'
> Jack Batten *Robinette* 1984: 64

See also FOLK ETYMOLOGY; SPIT, SPAT, SPITTED.

split infinitive The infinitive form of the English verb is preceded by *to*: 'to run', 'to think', 'to write', and so on. It is one form of the verb that can be used like a noun: 'To err is human'. Some usage experts have argued that the two-word infinitive phrase should be treated as a unit; thus, if a word is inserted between *to* and the base verb, they name the structure that results a 'split infinitive'. A well-known example of a split infinitive is the motto from *Star Trek*: 'To boldly go where no man has gone before' (*boldly* 'splits' the infinitive). Split infinitives are very common in speech and quite common in writing. They are least common in scholarly writing in the humanities. Because of a widespread prejudice against split infinitives, it might be best to avoid them in letters of application or academic essays, even if you find the argument for avoiding them unconvincing.

The rule against splitting the infinitive is one of the few that are more firmly adhered to by teachers than by usage guides. Most guides admit, with varying degrees of reluctance, that in the interests of clarity or smoothness it is sometimes better to split the infinitive than to avoid doing so.

English writers started splitting the infinitive at least as early as 1380; condemnation of such constructions did not begin until the nineteenth century. And certainly it seems rather arbitrary that the split infinitive in the sentence 'To carefully revise this will take time' is vehemently opposed when no one objects to the interjection of the adverb in quite similar structures, such as 'This needs to be carefully revised' or 'This appears to have been carefully revised'. Fowler notes that the rule against the split infinitive (which prohibits 'to really understand') has led some people to overcorrect (see HYPER-CORRECTION) and pluck adverbs out of all verb phrases, producing structures like 'really to be understood' or 'to be understood really', even though no authority objects to 'to *be* really understood'.

Various structures in English suggest that there is no indissoluble bond between the *to* and the base verb in an infinitive. In the sentence 'We were going to but we decided not to', the base verb has been dropped altogether. In the informal expression 'Gotta go', the *to* of the infinitive has been assimilated to the preceding word, *got*.

Theoretical arguments aside, it is not difficult to produce examples of sentences that require a split infinitive: 'They gave her enough to *more than* satisfy her needs'; 'They gave her enough to *all but* satisfy her needs'; 'His key failure was to *not* require an estimate in advance'. In this last example, if *not* were placed in front of *to*, readers might assume that the key failure was something other than not insisting upon an estimate.

Trying to avoid a split infinitive can also lead to ambiguous or awkward writing. If 'She wanted to really help him' is rewritten 'She wanted really to help him', the reader may wonder whether *really* modifies *want* or *help*. If it is rewritten 'She wanted to help him really', the implication is that her intentions were good, but she didn't succeed. Neither revision is equivalent to the sentence with the split infinitive. To avoid splitting an infinitive, then, simply shifting the adverb will not always work; frequently the entire sentence must be reworked.

> Only the moon and a handful of asteroids are known to ever approach closer.
> Terence Dickinson *Halley's Comet* 1985: 2

> ... the university was prepared to ask a professional editor to teach their [students] how to deal with written material, how to correctly cite references, and to do general copy editing.
> W.C. Lougheed, ed. *In Search of the Standard in Canadian English* 1986: 133

> ... recent political liberation makes it possible for women to publicly discuss their dissatisfactions.
> *Canadian Journal of History* 14.1 (1989): 153

> It is indeed difficult to systematically plan and implement legal and social reforms.
> J.E. Smyth et al. *The Law and Business Administration in Canada* 1987: 18

> The Association resolved ... to strongly encourage all airlines licensed in Canada to voluntarily ban smoking on all flights of three hours or less scheduled flying time.
> *Canadian Consumer* Jan. 1985: 49

spoonerism   Reverend William Archibald Spooner was warden of New College at Oxford from 1903 to 1924. Spooner had a habit of transposing the initial sounds of words in a sentence. Although he certainly did not produce all the slips of the tongue that are attributed to him, he is known to have said 'in a dark glassly' and to have told a nervous bridegroom that 'It is kisstomery to cuss the bride'. He is also reported to have once called Queen Victoria 'our queer old dean'. In honour of Spooner, funny slips of this sort came to be called *spoonerisms*.

See also MISPRONUNCIATION; SLIPS OF THE TONGUE.

spoonful   see -FUL

spouse, partner, significant other   Because the percentage of the population in legal marriages has dropped dramatically, the traditional terms *husband* and *wife* have become less useful. Today *spouse* is starting to be used for partners of either sex who live together in a long-term relationship without marrying. Indeed, the expression 'same-sex spouse' has some currency in references to people living in homosexual relationships. However, some continue to reserve *spouse* for legally married heterosexual couples. The term *partner* is broader, as it applies to either sex and can describe married couples or unmarried couples, opposite-sex or same-sex couples, impassioned or weary couples, couples co-habiting or couples maintaining separate residences. Outside its original sociological context, the term *significant other* has not really caught on except in informal contexts, where it is often used facetiously.

> It's worse yet if you are no longer living with your spouse and have no control over his or her financial habits.
> *Canadian Consumer* Jan. 1985: 42

> You get back in the car and head home to talk with your significant other about onerous mortgage payments.
> *Vancouver Sun* 27 Dec. 1990: D1

> 'Some years ago I had occasion to spend my partner's sabbatical leave in the United States....'
> W.C. Lougheed, ed. *In Search of the Standard in Canadian English* 1986: 133

But Ontario can't provide survivor-pension benefits to gay partners because it must register that change with the federal government, which doesn't recognize such partners as spouses under the Public Service Pension Plan.
Province (Vancouver) 21 Dec. 1990: 139

See also COMMON LAW.

spring, sprang, sprung The usual past tense is *sprang*: 'The cat sprang after the bird'. *Sprung* is less common but not wrong. The past participle is always *sprung*: 'The cat had sprung after the bird'.

Some school boards decided to bend the rules for the year, but many didn't and a coalition of anti-dual-entry parents sprang into being.
Vancouver Sun 15 Nov. 1990: C2

The Toronto offence, dormant in the opening 15 minutes, sprung to life for 13 second-quarter points....
Province (Vancouver) 23 Aug. 1990: 75

(The usual past tense is *sprang*, but *sprung* is not wrong.)

square brackets see PARENTHESES, BRACKETS; QUOTATION

squash see QUASH

St., Ste., Saint(e) In English Canada, abbreviations of the title *Saint* (or its French feminine form, *Sainte*) usually take a period (*St., Ste.*; plurals *Sts., Stes.*), although a no-period style is also acceptable (see ABBREVIATION). In Quebec, place names with *Saint(e)* always include a hyphen ('Saint-Ambroise'); when the title is abbreviated it does not take a period ('St-Ambroise', 'Ste-Agathe'). The French style is also used for many Canadian place names outside Quebec. All these abbreviations are normally alphabetized under *sa-* rather than *st-*.

stadium, stadiums, stadia Both plural forms of *stadium* are in use in Canadian writing, though the Latin plural *stadia* is much less common than the English plural *stadiums*.

There are domed stadiums in Montreal, Toronto and Vancouver.
Vancouver Sun 14 Sept 1990: D4

Additionally, Canada now is equipped with two of the most magnificent indoor stadia on the entire continent.
Province (Vancouver) 29 Jan. 1990: 29

See also PLURALS, REGULAR, IRREGULAR, FOREIGN.

stalactite, stalagmite Both are mineral formations found in caves: *stalactites* point down and *stalagmites* point up. Some people avoid confusion of these terms by thinking of the *c* in *stalactite* as standing for the ceiling from which stalactites hang and the *g* in *stalagmite* as standing for the ground from which they rise. Others think of stalac*tites* as hanging on tight.

Tiny dribbles of water often form icicle-like stalactites that hang from the ceiling, or stalagmites that rise up from the floor like graceful pillars.
Globe and Mail (Toronto) 12 Dec. 1985: A2

stamp, stomp *Stomp* is a variant of *stamp* meaning bring one's foot down heavily. A few sources label *stomp* dialectal, but it is standard in Canadian English.

The Indian government and the World Health Organization are both predicting the plague will be stomped out by mid-October.
Gazette (Montreal) 8 Oct. 1994: H8

See also CHOMP, CHAMP AT THE BIT.

stanch, staunch In Canadian journalism, the verb meaning to stop the flow (of blood, tears, etc.) is more often spelled *stanch* than *staunch*; however, it is more often pronounced to rhyme with *paunch* than *ranch*. The adjective meaning firm, strong, or steadfast is almost always spelled *staunch* and pronounced to rhyme with *paunch*. Canadian, British, and American dictionaries give both spellings for both the verb and the adjective.

They also wanted to stanch the losses at the government's landholding corporation, B.C. Place, which was so debt-ridden that it was borrowing money just to pay interest on previous borrowings.
Vancouver Sun 6 March 1990: A16

The best that can be hoped for if Meech Lake does pass is relief—relief that the present ordeal is over, the flood of words stanched for a time.
Gazette (Montreal) 21 June 1990: B3

It is true that Via Rail was costing taxpayers more than $600 million a year, and that the drain had to be staunched.
Gazette (Montreal) 12 Jan. 1990: B2

He was a staunch supporter of his patron and former employer, John A. Macdonald.
William Teatero *John Anderson: Fugitive Slave* 1986: 172

stand   see FOREST

Standard English, standard   Standard English is used in the media, taught in the education system, and understood from region to region. Broadly speaking, it is the English spoken by educated people in cities.

A particular word, meaning, spelling, pronunciation, or grammatical construction is called standard if it is widely used by educated people, and non-standard if it is not. Non-standard usages fall into two categories: regionalisms, which are confined to a particular area within a country ('I'm after doing that' means 'I've just done that' in Newfoundland dialect but not in the rest of Canada) and usages that are considered uneducated, such as the double negative ('Nobody said nothing').

Usage commentators do not always agree on whether particular usages are standard. One reason is that the usages they tend to discuss are in transition. As individuals, we judge the acceptability of usage on the basis of our knowledge and experience of the language. For example, if we think people are starting to confuse two words, we resist the change. Ultimately, though, Standard English is defined collectively and socially. Once enough influential people have made a mistake, the 'mistake' becomes standard. For example, over the course of the sixteenth century, 'a napron' became 'an apron' because most people thought the initial *n* of *napron* (which is related to the word *napkin*) belonged to the indefinite article. While Standard English is conservative—which contributes to its intelligibility over long periods of time—it is not unchanging.

As well as evolving over time, Standard English varies from country to country in the English-speaking world. 'I am having a cat [I own a cat]' is a standard construction in Indian English, but non-standard in Canadian, British, and American English. 'I could have done' is a standard sentence in British English, but it would need to be either shortened or lengthened to conform to the rules of Canadian English. One distinctive aspect of Standard Canadian English is its pattern of blending British and American pronunciations and spellings (see SPELLING, CANADIAN); another is its uniformity across a great geographic expanse. Unlike the British, the French, or even Americans, Canadians often cannot tell by their accents what region or city their fellow Canadians hail from.

In many cases, the recommendations made in this book do not hinge on whether a particular usage is standard: instead, they have to do with its formality or informality. The word *booze*, for example, is used by most educated speakers and appears frequently in newspapers. It is undoubtedly a standard word, and yet it would be out of place in the title of an article in a medical journal. For a discussion of levels of formality, see FORMAL, INFORMAL WRITING.

See also ACCENT, DIALECT; COLLOQUIAL; VERNACULAR.

standard time, daylight time, daylight saving(s) time, summer time   There are six time zones in Canada: Newfoundland, Atlantic, Eastern, Central, Mountain and Pacific.

name	abbreviation	time variance
Newfoundland Standard Time	NST	12:30 p.m.
Atlantic Standard Time	AST	12 noon
Eastern Standard Time	EST	11:00 a.m.
Central Standard Time	CST	10:00 a.m.
Mountain Standard Time	MST	9:00 a.m.
Pacific Standard Time	PST	8:00 a.m.

Abbreviations for the time zones should be used only with specific times: '8 a.m. NST'.

Both the *Globe and Mail Style Book* and the *Canadian Press Stylebook* recommend *daylight time* rather than *daylight saving time*: 'Pacific Daylight Time', 'Eastern Daylight Time', '8 a.m. NDT'. However, most Canadians refer to the general phenomenon as either *daylight saving time* or *daylight savings time*. The British refer to daylight saving time as British Summer Time, or BST.

Daylight saving time for all of Canada except Saskatchewan, which remains on standard time year round, runs from 2 a.m. on the first Sunday in April to 2 a.m. on the last Sunday in October. In April the clock is put ahead one hour, and in October it is put back, as in the popular saying 'Spring forward, fall back'. The names of specific zones are capitalized ('Eastern Standard Time'), but general references ('switch from standard time to daylight time') are not.

Trapping, education spending, sex education, daylight saving time, metric, free trade—name the cause and you can find someone organized against it.
Ottawa Citizen 8 April 1990: A9

It contains most of the same features as the original, but adds slow-motion playback ... and a world clock on-screen menu with a Daylight Savings Time feature that automatically changes the time.
Toronto Star 21 July 1994: G2

(The capital letters are unnecessary.)

See also TIME.

stank   see STINK

starboard   see PORT

state, head of   see HEAD OF STATE

States, the   see AMERICAN

stationary, stationery   *Stationary* meaning standing still ends in *-ary*. One way to remember this is to think of the *a* in 'stand'. *Stationery* meaning writing materials (paper, cards, envelopes, etc.) ends in *-ery*. *Stationary* is often misused for *stationery*; the opposite error is seldom made.

While the Ticats' play last season suggested the need for some housecleaning, Beckman said he isn't ready to order pink slips from the local stationary store.
Vancouver Sun 19 Dec. 1990: D12

(The word required here is *stationery*.)

Status Indian   see ABORIGINAL PEOPLE(S)

staunch   see STANCH

stave, stave off   The verb *stave* is rare except in the phrase *stave off*, which means to fend off. The past tense and past participle of this phrase are the same: *staved off*. The variant past tense and past participle *stove* is usually used in reference to boats. In this context, *stove* means smashed, with either an active or a passive sense.

Dartmouth staved off elimination by defeating Smith Falls in Hardy Cup Eastern Canadian final play....
Ottawa Citizen 17 April 1990: C6

... they were almost swamped in a tangle of jammed driftwood, almost stove in on a snag....
Robert Kroetsch *Badlands* 1975: 121

steal   see ROB

step-, half-   You acquire a *stepsister* or *stepbrother* if your father or mother marries someone who already has a son or daughter. A *half-sister* or *half-brother* is related to you by blood ties: you share the same biological father or mother. The *step-* prefix is usually used without a hyphen: *stepmother, stepfather, stepchild*; however, the hyphen is preferred in *step-parent*. Most commonly *half* is combined with a hyphen, but it may also appear simply as an adjective: *half brother*.

'Does that mean Mum could get married again, too, and we'd have a stepfather?'
Constance Bereford-Howe *Night Studies* 1985: 130

The group will focus on problems and concerns that step-parents face on a daily basis.
Gazette (Montreal) 13 April 1990: B8

Her half-sister Micki tells how ... Christiane would lower peanut-butter sandwiches on a string from the balcony.
Ann Davis *Somewhere Waiting* 1991: 218

But she worried about how her boyfriend would react if he realized that one of the Fab Four up on the screen was her half brother.
Maclean's 17 Oct. 1988: A40

stereotype   see ARCHETYPE

sterilize   see NEUTER

stifling   see STULTIFYING

stigma, stigmatize, stigmata   A *stigma* was the owner's mark burned into the skin of a slave in ancient Rome. *Stigma* later came to be used figuratively to mean disgrace or shame. To *stigmatize* is to reproach or to set a mark of disgrace upon. *Stigmata*, the marks left on the hands and feet of Christ by the crucifixion, are also said to occur on the bodies of certain holy people by divine favour. The plural of *stigma* is usually *stigmas*, but the Greek plural *stigmata* is favoured for this religious sense.

Coal also faces the stigma of being the most environmentally unfriendly of the fossil fuels.
Financial Post 14 June 1990: 18

Western culture tends to over-value high intelligence and stigmatize low intelligence.
Globe and Mail (Toronto) 29 July 1985: P7

Only 20 kilometres distant is St. Giovanni Rotondo, site of the Capuchin monastery where Padre Pio is said to have received the Stigmata—the wounds of crucifixion.
Globe and Mail (Toronto) 24 Aug. 1985: T9

(Here *Stigmata* is capitalized to indicate reverence.)

See also PLURALS, REGULAR, IRREGULAR, FOR-EIGN.

stimulant, stimulus, stimuli In scientific writing a *stimulant* is a drug or other agent that temporarily increases the activity in a part of the body, while a *stimulus* is any agent causing a psychological or bodily change: 'Caffeine and nicotine are common stimulants'; 'The stimulus of hot, humid weather causes an overheated body to perspire'. Dictionaries list both terms as standard for 'an incentive to action or thought'. In Canadian writing *stimulus* (plural *stimuli*) is more often chosen for this general sense: 'Money was insufficient stimulus; she would not work overtime'.

Caffeine acts as a stimulant, and sugar causes the blood sugar level to shoot up. . . .
Chatelaine April 1986: 30

The truly dedicated, omnivorous reader is almost physically sick when deprived of his innocent stimulant.
Ottawa Citizen 15 March 1986: B3

(Here books are humorously compared to a *stimulant* such as caffeine.)

The past three decades have seen a flowering and variegated enrichment of the novel as both an echo of, and a stimulus for, the changes of the Quiet Revolution.
Ben-Z. Shek *French-Canadian & Québécois Novels* 1991: 45

The press had absorbed the political functions of the pulpit and, as the necessary stimulant to public opinion and vehicle of it, increasingly dominated the political system.
J.A.W. Gunn *Beyond Liberty and Property* 1983: 287

(In this sense *stimulus* is more common.)

We should care because the bombardment of visual stimuli (including the average viewer's annual exposure to 32,000 TV commercials) is transforming the way we learn, speak and interact.
Gazette (Montreal) 8 Nov. 1989: C1

See also PLURALS, REGULAR, IRREGULAR, FOR-EIGN.

stink, stank, stunk *Stank* and *stunk* are both accepted for the past tense of *stink*. Generally, writers prefer *stank*, but *stunk* is common in speech.

Stunk is the only accepted past participle: 'It has stunk in here for days'.

The cities stank of horse manure.
Pierre Berton *The Promised Land* 1984: 293

The place stunk and occasionally someone would get their arm or hand pecked.
Canadian Fiction Magazine 64 (1988): 63

St. Jean Baptiste Day see NEW YEAR'S DAY

St. John's see SAINT JOHN

Stl'atl'imx see LILLOOET

stoic, stoical *Stoic* and *stoical* both mean unmoved by emotions or indifferent to pain. Capitalized, *Stoic* refers to a school of Greek philosophers or their intellectual heirs. Zeno founded this school around 300 B.C.; it got its name from the portico, or *stoa*, where he taught in Athens. Stoic philosophy held that it was virtuous to be wise and wise to be unmoved by the vicissitudes of fortune, whether they brought pleasure or pain.

Some usage guides suggest that *stoic* should be reserved for this school of philosophy: however, *stoic* is used more often than *stoical* to mean impassive or uncomplaining. This general use is widespread and accepted.

Some writers use *stoic* where *steadfast, determined,* or *restrained* would be more precise.

. . . the waning days of the pagan Roman Empire . . . saw a swing to the anti-sex Stoic philosophy that also called into question all non-procreative sexual acts.
Edmonton Journal 24 July 1994: D8

She was independent, self-sufficient, stoic, and imbued with the Protestant work ethic.
Edmonton Journal 10 Jan. 1994: B3

Most of the women wept, the men were stoical.
Vancouver Sun 9 Nov. 1992: A1

On the other side are the stoic royalist faithful. The Royal Family, they insist, has been in tight places before. . . .
Spectator (Hamilton) 22 Dec. 1994: A9

(Here *steadfast* might be better than *stoic*, since these royalists clearly demonstrate passion for the monarchy.)

Artworks don't get much more austere or stoic than those of Ryoji Ikeda.
Edmonton Journal 3 Dec. 1994: D2

(Here *restrained* might be better.)

Asia is a market where contacts, family links, personal attention and, above all, stoic long-term commitment are essential for success.
Edmonton Journal 20 Nov. 1994: A7

(Here *determined* might be better.)

stolid   see SOLID

stomach   see BELLY

stomp   see STAMP

stone   A *stone* (plural *stone*) is a British measure of weight equivalent to 6.35 kilograms, or 14 pounds. *Stone* is generally used to give the weights of people or hefty pets: 'He weighed 12 stone'.

stoop   see PORCH

store-bought   see [BOUGHTEN]

story, storey, floor   The word meaning a narrative is always spelled *story*, and its plural is *stories*. In Canada and in Britain, the floor of a building is usually spelled *storey* (plural *storeys*). *Story* and *stories* are less common variant spellings for this sense, favoured in the United States.
In North America, the ground level of a building is the first floor or the first storey; a building of ten floors has ten storeys. In Britain the ground level (the first storey) is called the ground floor and the next level up (the second storey) is called the first floor, the level after that the second floor, and so on.

By 1910, Eaton's had completed an eight-storey building and was planning to go to twelve storeys.
Pierre Berton *The Promised Land* 1984: 322

The building's upper story was completely gutted and the ground floor suffered extensive smoke and water damage.
News North 19 Feb. 1990: 2

straight-, strait-, straightened, straitened
Straight- is used in combinations to mean directly, as in *straightaway* or *straightforward*. *Strait-* is used in combinations to mean restricting or rigid, as in *straitjacket*, a device that restricts the arms, or *strait-laced*, describing someone whose conduct is restricted by prudish morals.

Something that has been *straightened*, such as a bent nail, has been made straight; someone in *straitened* circumstances is restricted by poverty and hardship.

I remember watching a TV movie where Houdini is in a straitjacket immersed upside down in a tank of water.
Room of One's Own March 1990: 97

But if the Canadian mining industry has had little to cheer about during the past three or four years, it has shown a capacity to adapt to more straitened circumstances.
Globe and Mail (Toronto) 14 March 1985: B2

There's nothing mysterious about the way our [pulp and paper] industry reacts to straightened circumstances.
Vancouver Sun 27 March 1990: C1

(The correct spelling is *straitened*.)

[The] Social Services Minister ... wants to be a 66-year-old Socred sex symbol—not a straight-laced prude.
Province (Vancouver) 15 March 1990: 3

(The correct spelling is *strait-laced*.)

Jim Mills looked about as uncomfortable as any 6'8", 280-pound free spirit could tucked into a tuxedo that felt like a black straightjacket.
Vancouver Sun 23 Nov. 1990: D1

(The correct spelling is *straitjacket*.)

stratum, strata   *Stratum* is the singular form, *strata* the plural. Though American and Canadian dictionaries accept *stratums* as an alternative English plural, it rarely appears in Canadian writing. Sometimes *strata* is mistakenly used as if it were singular to refer to a single layer of something; this use is uncommon and is not accepted. Usage commentators flatly condemn the double plural *stratas*. Pronunciation varies: *STRAY tum*, *STRA tum*, or *STRAW tum*.

The Mounted Police subscribed to the commonly held belief that criminality was a phenomenon largely confined to inferior people at the lowest stratum of the social order.
Pierre Berton *The Promised Land* 1984: 221

He tries to burrow under its blacktop and find out what really makes it beat by talking to people from all strata of society, and exploring the areas the city tourist bureaus would rather he didn't see.
Vancouver Sun 4 Aug. 1990: D13

It is brought back up to its 'natural' level by adding carbon dioxide pumped out of the ground from below the pocket, or strata of water.
Ottawa Citizen 26 April 1990: D15

(Here *strata* is mistakenly used as a singular noun.)

No social strata eludes the broad expanse of her gaze, from the humble lives of superstitious Swiss peasants, to the structured culture of Chinese mandarins, or the tragic intransigence of Thai emperors.
Globe and Mail (Toronto) 15 June 1985: B9

(Here again *strata* is mistakenly used as a singular noun.)

A minimum of an hour is required to view the complex didactic materials that build layer upon layer, association upon association like stratas of a rich, multinational archeological dig.
Vancouver Sun 21 April 1990: E9

(*Strata* is already plural; here either *strata* or *stratums* would be correct.)

See also PLURALS, REGULAR, IRREGULAR, FOREIGN.

street   see ROAD

strike, struck, stricken   *Struck* is the usual past participle of the verb *strike* ('struck by a car', 'struck by the resemblance'); *stricken* is an archaic past participle that survives in the expression 'stricken from the record' and is used in figurative contexts to mean afflicted ('drought-stricken', 'panic-stricken').

... should a player compete in five consecutive games without having a major for fighting or roughing, one of his prior offences shall be stricken from the record.
Daily News (Halifax) 7 Sept. 1994: 37

Could the medical profession do more for Terry if he were alive today than they were able to do when he was first stricken with cancer?
Queen's Quarterly 97.2 (1990): 253

Last Sunday we had a rolled-rib roast that looked like a sausage stricken with bloat.
Richard Davies and Glen Kirkland, eds. *Dimensions* 1986: 53

I remember how stricken she looked that morning Mother was asleep in her chair by the wood-stove.
David Williams *Eye of the Father* 1985: 110

strikebreaker   see REPLACEMENT WORKER

string, strung, stringed   The past tense and past participle of the verb *string* are both *strung*. *Stringed* is an adjective used of musical instruments.

[They] painstakingly strung garlands of purple, pink and green cellophane-wrapped candy and hung them on a six-foot blue cascade fir.
Ottawa Citizen 1 Dec. 1990: E1

The Warriors had strung a large sheet of nylon across the entrance to the compound to shield their eyes from the glare of the powerful spotlights the soldiers use.
Ottawa Citizen 11 Sept. 1990: A2

strive, strove, strived, striven   The past tense is either *strove* or *strived*. The past participle (the form used after *have*) is either *strived* or *striven*.

Both strove to upgrade playing standards.
Gazette (Montreal) 22 Dec. 1990: F2

Here we strived to put on a show that we hoped would impress our neighbors and all who came to visit.
Vancouver Sun 21 July 1990: F4

Branch, who has strived to rid junior hockey of its blood-and-guts image, said the public perception of the OHL will suffer.
Province (Vancouver) 7 Feb. 1990: 64

Such an outcome could destroy everything the two reformers have striven to achieve in foreign and domestic policy.
Gazette (Montreal) 21 Dec. 1990: A10

struck   see STRIKE

strung   see STRING

stultifying, stifling   *Stultifying* originally meant making foolish, and *stifling* originally meant smothering. Both words are now used to describe things that have an oppressive or dulling effect on people. Note, however, that only *stifling* means uncomfortably hot and humid.

And, worst of all, it has been saddled with stultifying union contracts which lead to ridiculous work practices, excessive overtime and featherbedding.
Globe and Mail (Toronto) 6 Feb. 1985: P6

To the youngsters of stable, manicured and socially stifling England, the magazines fired dreams of freedom, wealth and mobility.
Globe and Mail (Toronto) 11 May 1985: T6

stunk   see STINK

subject   see CASE; CITIZEN

subject–verb agreement   see AGREEMENT, GRAMMATICAL

subjunctive The English verb is described in traditional grammar as being in one of three moods (or modes): the imperative, the indicative, or the subjunctive. A verb in the imperative mood is an order: 'Slow down!' A verb in the indicative mood describes a real action (or a fictional action intended to imitate a real one) in the past, present, or future. A verb in the subjunctive mood refers to an action hoped for, thought probable, recommended, imagined, and so on, as opposed to one being reported as fact. In contemporary English the subjunctive mood is usually indicated by special auxiliary verbs, such as *should, may, might*, and *would*, which are called modals:

It might be serious.

I wish he would see the doctor.

Though the modal auxiliaries serve a subjunctive function in contemporary English, they are not what is traditionally called the subjunctive, which is marked by distinctive verb forms that predate the modal auxiliaries. These forms survive in contemporary English in a few situations. First, phrases that use the subjunctive to express a wish persist as 'fossils' or fixed expressions: 'God save the Queen'; 'God bless you'; 'Heaven forbid'. Today sentences like these are often interpreted as orders because their verbs lack the *-(e)s* ending they would have in statements. But to issue orders to God would be presumptuous; in fact, these sentences express wishes: 'May God bless you', etc. Sometimes these phrases invert the subject and verb: "perish the thought', 'suffice it to say', 'be that as it may', 'far be it from me'. People do not make new sentences of this type. We do not say, for example, 'Last my new car until it is paid for'. Instead we use *may* or *let*: 'May you do well' or 'Let the best candidate win'.

In North America, the subjunctive is also regularly used in *that*-clauses expressing a recommendation, intention, demand, etc.:

They insist that she *study* piano.

We thought it best that he *take* a holiday.

My recommendation will be that it *stay*.

The subjunctive in these phrases is easy to spot because it is used with third-person singular subjects (*he, she, it*) where the indicative form of regular verbs would end in *s*. This subjunctive can be replaced either by *should* ('They insist that she should study piano') or by the indicative ('They insist that she studies piano').

Finally, the subjunctive is commonly used in clauses expressing conditions in the present or future that are impossible, improbable, or hypothetical; these clauses are usually introduced by *if, as if, though*, or *as though*, or triggered by verbs like *wish* or *suppose* in the main clause. In this form, the subjunctive is usually marked by the use of the verb *were* instead of the usual indicative *was*:

'He talks as if he were the boss.'

'I wish he were here.'

'Suppose he were able to go after all.'

Again, the subjunctive in these sorts of sentences may be replaced by the indicative.

Standard Canadian English does require the subjunctive in the common phrase 'if I were you', even though the indicative 'if I was you' is common in Standard British English. (British and Australian writers usually avoid the subjunctive in all but the most formal prose.) In all other hypothetical *if*-clauses in the present or future, including those referring to conditions that are clearly impossible, either the subjunctive or the indicative mood is grammatically correct.

Because the use of this subjunctive structure has become optional, language commentators have been speculating for over a century that it will disappear. In fact, it is still quite common, especially in formal usage. The subjunctive mood is now a stylistic choice. For example, it can make a suggestion seem more polite—purely hypothetical rather than directive:

If you came to our next meeting ... (*indicative*)

If you were to come to our next meeting ... (*subjunctive*)

Or it can be a sign of cynicism, the equivalent of adding the disclaimer 'not that that would ever happen' to a hypothetical clause:

If the government was serious about reform ... (*indicative*)

If the government were serious about reform ... (*subjunctive*)

If I lost twenty pounds ... (*indicative*)

If I were to lose twenty pounds ... (*subjunctive*)

Even in formal writing, however, the subjunctive is not an option in every *if*-clause. Where *if* means 'whether', it should not be followed by the subjunctive: 'He wondered if it was (*not* were) time to go'. Nor should the subjunctive be used in references to real or hypothetical possibility in the past: 'The driver swerved as if he was (*not* were) falling asleep'; 'If I had been (*not* were) there, surely I would remember'.

Our pilot program was successful and independent evaluators recommended that it be continued.
Province (Vancouver) 30 Dec. 1990: 24

(Canadians use the subjunctive—*be*, in this case—in *that*-clauses containing recommendations or demands.)

There, Bourassa quickly came under heavy pressure to insist that Quebec receive an expanded constitutional veto....
Maclean's 7 Oct. 1991: A22

(Here *receive* is a subjunctive used in the context of a demand.)

Furthermore, I also suggest that Mr. Cote accept complete medical, ethical and legal responsibility for those who suffer increased morbidity and mortality from delayed attention.
Gazette (Montreal) 27 Dec. 1990: B2

(Here *accept* is a subjunctive used in the context of a recommendation.)

All the while she hummed or sang and moved slowly and gently as if she were warming up for a dance instead of a drawing session.
Arctic 41.1 (1988): 74

(Here the subjunctive is used in an *if*-clause presenting an imagined condition.)

I am quite sure that if it were available in an inexpensive but rugged paperback edition, English-language newspapers across the nation would buy it.
W.C. Lougheed, ed. *In Search of the Standard in Canadian English* 1986: 124

Also, a government would have no choice but to resign or call an election if it were defeated on an issue it had previously declared to be a matter of confidence.
Andrew Heard *Canadian Constitutional Conventions* 1991: 69–70

(The subjunctive mood is most common in formal writing.)

'If I were you I wouldn't put up with me.'
Howard Engel *Murder Sees the Light* 1984: 157

'Only if I was you, miss, I'd keep a sharp eye on my belongings.'
Constance Beresford-Howe *Night Studies* 1985: 72

(Standard Canadian English requires 'if I *were* you'. The fictional speaker here is a British immigrant.)

At that moment, without warning, the elevator gave a sudden lurch as if it was about to drop.
Constance Beresford-Howe *Night Studies* 1985: 210

(The indicative mood is used in this hypothetical *if*-clause. The subjunctive *were* would also be correct.)

Anyone, they claimed, stood to gain if he was willing to apply himself.
NeWest Review Oct.–Nov. 1989: 12

(The subjunctive *were* would also be correct in this hypothetical *if*-clause.)

... indeed, he wondered if it were really desirable.
W.C. Lougheed, ed. *In Search of the Standard in Canadian English* 1986: 39

(When *if* means whether, it should not be followed by the subjunctive. The form required here is the indicative *was*.)

Perhaps you are reminded of the story of the traveller in Ireland who stopped a native on a country road and asked him if he were going in the right direction for Ballyragget.
Robertson Davies *One Half of Robertson Davies* 1978: 199

(When *if* means whether, it should not be followed by the subjunctive. The form required here is the indicative *was*.)

See also COME; IF I WERE YOU; LEST.

subpoena, summons A *subpoena* and a *summons* are both calls to appear in court, but their legal applications differ. *Subpoenas* are usually issued to witnesses or to obtain records; *summonses* are issued to people accused of minor offences, requiring them to appear in court and answer the charges.

Subpoena, from the Latin for 'under penalty' (in other words, appear or else), is pronounced *sub PEE na*. Verb forms include *subpoenaed* and *subpoenaing*, and the plural *subpoenas* is more common than the Latin plural *subpoenae*. A variation in spelling found occasionally in American usage is *subpena*.

A judge has issued a subpoena for Washington Post reporter Bob Woodward to testify at a preliminary hearing....
Globe and Mail (Toronto) 9 April 1985: P13

A police officer arrived on the scene and presented her with a summons for dangerous driving.
J.E. Smyth et. al *The Law and Business Administration in Canada* 1987: 2

Police officials said it is hard to determine how many parking tickets and summonses police in Toronto issue every day.
Globe and Mail (Toronto) 19 Feb. 1985: P1

She is going to try to have the child subpoenaed as a witness.
Ottawa Citizen 5 Oct. 1994: B3

See also -AE-, -OE-, -E-.

subsist, exist   *Subsist* shares with *exist* the idea of continuing to have life, being, or animation. However, *subsist* suggests that life is barely maintained; it is often used in the context of inadequate nourishment.

Most Nepalese subsist by eking out a living on farms in the valleys and terraced hillsides south of the Himalayan range, areas accessible only by foot.
Globe and Mail (Toronto) 17 May 1985: B6

Nutrition is culturally determined and poor people are likely to subsist on what comes in packages; fast-food outlets cluster like scavengers in low-income areas.
Globe and Mail (Toronto) 18 Dec. 1985: A2

Plant life has been found to exist on the sea floor at much greater depths than previously predicted.
Globe and Mail (Toronto) 7 Jan. 1985: M6

substantial, substantive   Both words mean 'of substance'. However, *substantial* usually refers to things of real physical substance ('a substantial meal', 'substantial holdings; 'a substantial piece of furniture'). *Substantive* usually refers to matters of intellectual, theoretical, or political significance. A *substantive* is a noun.

The profits that will be generated when this is reversed will be substantial.
Calgary Herald 31 Dec. 1994: C3

Doubtless we owe an immense intellectual debt to those extraordinary thinkers, for we have acquired from them a large body of substantive knowledge about a wide range of human societies and cultures.
Irving M. Zeitlin and Robert J. Brym *The Social Condition of Humanity* 1991: 328

Although Twigg offers a self-deprecating assessment of B.C. Bookworld as an 'intentionally superficial publication,' ... its pages nonetheless carry some substantial content.
Vancouver Sun 29 Sept. 1990: D2

(Here *substantive* would work as well or better, since the reference is to intellectual content.)

substitute, replace   No one will object if you say or write 'I substituted margarine for butter', or 'I replaced the butter with margarine'. But many commentators do object to the use of *substitute* to mean replace or make do, as in 'I substituted butter with margarine', or 'I had no currants so I substituted with raisins'. The disputed structures are not new; they have been used in informal English for about 300 years. Nevertheless, some people find them confusing, and they are rarely found in edited writing.

Brian Topp, forest products analyst ... , said the down-time strategy has forced customers to substitute with lower quality pulps, such as U.S.-produced southern softwood, where price drops have been substantial.
Financial Post 31 Oct. 1990: 19

(Here 'make do with' or *substitute* alone, without *with*, would be better.)

'You don't eat excessive amounts of protein and fat, but they could be lowered,' she says, adding that I can substitute with more carbohydrates.
Vancouver Sun 23 Jan. 1990: B3

(The word *with* should be dropped.)

subtle   The *b* is silent. *Subtle* rhymes with *shuttle*.

subway   see METRO

succeed   One succeeds *in doing* something or *at* something. One succeeds *to* a position. The construction *succeed* plus the infinitive (e.g., 'succeed to do') is unidiomatic.

At the last U.S. Open ... a microcomputer succeeded in defeating several players rated higher than 2000, which would put it into the Expert category.
Globe and Mail (Toronto) 12 Jan. 1985: H6

'I am convinced that we will succeed to emerge from this deep crisis.'
Gazette (Montreal) 19 Nov. 1990: B1

(Here 'succeed to emerge' is unidiomatic; 'succeed in emerging' would be better.)

See also PREDECESSOR, SUCCESSOR.

successor   see PREDECESSOR

succinct   see CONCISE

such as   see LIKE, SUCH AS

Sudbury   see BURY

suite, apartment, flat A *suite* is a set of connecting rooms. For most Canadians the term suggests commercial space or rooms in a hotel, but some, particularly British Columbians, use *suite* as a synonym for *apartment*. The equivalent British term, used occasionally in Canadian English, is *flat*.

> Within each triplex are two three-level suites and one single-level suite, each with two bedrooms and two bathrooms.
> *Vancouver Sun* 17 Feb. 1990: C4

> Me, I fled for a while to one of Vancouver's few Women's Shelters; then found a basement suite and a job.
> *Room of One's Own* June 1990: 8

> ... Tony Bradbury packed up his family and boarded a plane back to England where they'll live in a one-bedroom flat with relatives.
> *Vancouver Sun* 12 Dec. 1990: A13

sulphur, sulfur Canadian writers prefer the spelling *sulphur* (*sulphate, sulphuric*, etc.) to *sulfur*. The British use *sulphur*, while Americans use both spellings, but *sulfur* more frequently.

> Since sulphur is heavier than air and the unit was located in the man's basement, high levels of sulphur gas leaking from the fridge remained in the area.
> *Canadian Consumer* Feb. 1986: 7

> The town's location was determined by the discovery of hot sulfur springs in 1887, which led to the creation of a European-type spa.
> Alan Tucker, ed. *The Penguin Guide to Canada* 1991: 520

summary offence   see INDICTABLE OFFENCE

summer time   see STANDARD TIME

summons   see SUBPOENA

sung   see SING

sunk, sunken   see SINK

[supercede]   see SUPERSEDE

superior, senior, inferior, junior, major, minor
Superior and *senior* are comparative adjectives borrowed from Latin. In comparisons, *superior* means higher or better, and *senior* means more advanced or older. In explicit comparisons it is generally considered unacceptable to precede these words with *more*, for the same reason that one would not precede an English comparative like *higher* with *more*. *Superior* and *senior* and their opposites *inferior* and *junior* are followed by *to* rather than *than*: 'John's work is superior to (*not* superior than) Jane's'; 'Jill is senior to (*not* senior than) Jack.'

Superior and *senior* have also developed non-comparative senses. *Superior* means high-quality, and *senior* means high-ranking or experienced, as in 'superior artistry' or 'senior academics'. Strictly speaking, if these non-comparative senses are admitted, it should be possible to write 'His artistry was more superior than mine', but such constructions are still unacceptable. *Senior* and *junior*, however, are so widely used in their non-comparative senses that some commentators do accept structures like 'Gail is more senior than Jack'. Similarly, the phrase 'our more senior managers' is accepted because it means 'our more experienced managers'.

Major and *minor* have gone further along the path from Latin comparative to English adjective, in that they are not used in comparisons with *to*. However, commentators still argue that they are comparative, meaning greater and lesser. Thus these critics condemn the use of *major* and *minor* as ordinary adjectives. They would change 'My operation was more major than yours' to 'My operation was more serious than yours', and amend 'It's not as minor a problem as you think' by substituting *trivial* or *insignificant* for *minor*. Eventually, *major* and *minor* may lose any connotation of comparison, but for now it is safest to treat these words as if they meant 'relatively large or important' and 'relatively small or unimportant'.

> We feel superior to him, but we do not scorn him.
> Robertson Davies *A Voice from the Attic* 1960: 231

> It is more superior to anything likely to be concocted in the constitutional pressure cooker this month.
> *Gazette* (Montreal) 7 Aug. 1992: B3

> (Here *more* should be dropped.)

> Not only was this very much more than any previous Queen's principal had received, it was also three times the salary of the most senior professor.
> Frederick Gibson *Queen's University* 2 (1983): 88–9

> (Here *senior* is used as a non-comparative adjective meaning highly ranked. Thus 'the *most senior* professor' is the most highly ranked.)

> The bacteria is not as major a problem in Nova Scotia as it is in Alberta, said Sullivan....
> *Cape Breton Post* (Sydney, N.S.) 27 June 1990: 17

(Here *major* should be replaced with *serious*; 'as major as' is non-standard because *major* means *relatively* important.)

United, which had made previous repairs to the plane's plumbing system, made a more major repair before putting the plane back in service.
Gazette (Montreal) 6 Nov. 1992: E7

(Since *major* is already comparative, *more major* is non-standard. The sentence could be rewritten: 'United, which previously had made minor repairs … made a major repair before putting the plane back in service.')

See also INFERIOR TO.

supersede, [supercede] *Supersede* is the only spelling recognized by Canadian, British, and American dictionaries with the exception of *Merriam-Webster's*, which has begun to list the very common misspelling *supercede* as a variant. The word is often misspelled because it deviates from the common spelling pattern in *precede, recede, intercede,* and so on.

… the Supreme Court decided that the provinces may no longer supercede the priorities set out in the Federal Bankruptcy Act.
Financial Post 9 Oct. 1989: 15

(The most widely accepted spelling is *supersede*.)

See also -CEED, -CEDE, -SEDE.

supine   see PRONE

supper   see DINNER

supplement   see COMPLIMENT

suppose   see SUSPECT, SUPPOSE

supposed to   The expression *supposed to* meaning 'expected to' or 'should' is sometimes misspelled *suppose to*, probably because the *d* is not always clearly pronounced.

So, it is different from other forms of communication in that it is not suppose to have a purpose or aim apart from the success of the sociable moment. …
City Magazine Spring 1988: 19

(The correct spelling is *supposed*.)

See also USED TO.

surmise   see SUSPECT, SUPPOSE

surrounded   Some consider the phrases 'completely surrounded' and 'surrounded on all sides' redundant, since *surrounded* alone means encircled or enclosed on all sides. The same critics find 'surrounded on three sides' illogical. However, these phrases are idiomatic and seem perfectly natural to most people. In formal writing, to avoid what some consider to be a misuse of *surrounded*, words such as *bordered, bounded,* or *flanked* may be used to describe an object or person that is not completely encircled.

The fortress is completely surrounded by water.
Globe and Mail (Toronto) 2 Feb. 1985: T3

Surrounded by thick woods on all sides, it is composed only of a private (pay) beach and restaurant.
Vancouver Sun 10 Feb. 1990: A10

To Torontonians, Ontario is a wealthy, self-assured metropolis, surrounded on three sides by a hinterland of farms and towns, and beyond, wilderness.
Ottawa Citizen 23 Sept. 1989: B3

The reconstructed City of Refuge is bounded on three sides by sea and on the fourth by a high wall, so a fugitive faced a marathon swim to reach the safety of its confines.
Globe and Mail (Toronto) 17 April 1985: M7

suspect, suppose, surmise   All three of these verbs mean to think something is likely. To *suspect* often—though not always—implies wrongdoing. To *suppose* means to assume an imaginary situation for the sake of argument or investigation. To *surmise* (sometimes misspelled *surmize*) means to form an opinion from inconclusive evidence, to speculate.

Police said they suspect the death is a slaying and have told area residents the section of ravine will be cordoned off for two days while officers examine the body and the site.
Vancouver Sun 6 Dec. 1990: A13

Just suppose we had to get by with less.
Province (Vancouver) 25 Nov. 1990: 35

Not having enough fundamental numbers on Tokyo stocks, Healy can only surmise about the stock-price insolvency effect there.
Financial Post 10 April 1990: 20

(The correct spelling is *surmise*. Further, *about* does not normally follow *surmise* and should be omitted here.)

See also SUPPOSED TO; SUSPECT, SUSPICIOUS; SUSPECTED.

suspect, suspicious Both words are regularly used to describe something that is viewed with suspicion, or that arouses suspicion. However, *suspect* is a better choice in contexts where *suspicious* could also mean 'feeling suspicion'. For example, 'The neighbours are rather suspicious' is ambiguous, since it could mean either that they act as if they suspect something odd is going on or that they are up to something odd themselves. To make it clear, one could write either 'The neighbours are getting suspicious' or 'The neighbours are rather suspect', depending on which meaning is intended.

> ... cast and crew eat lunch, joking about the take-out sandwiches filled with meat of highly suspect origin.
> *Globe and Mail* (Toronto) 4 Jan. 1985: E3

> Biopsies of suspicious areas are taken and analyzed.
> *Globe and Mail* (Toronto) 3 Jan. 1985: P18

> ... if, in order to attain such a result, a court has to go to the lengths of overturning settled principles, the methodology and policy of the court become even more suspect and open to criticism.
> *Canadian Bar Review* 66.3 (1987): 610

(Here *suspicious* would be confusing.)

See also SUSPECT, SUPPOSE; SUSPECTED.

suspected Many commentators object to phrases like 'the suspected murderer' because the person referred to is being given the label *murderer* before this has been established by a court of law. Phrases like 'the murder suspect', 'the suspect', or 'the man suspected of murder' are more considerate and more accurate.

See also ALLEGED.

suspension see ABBREVIATION

suspicious see SUSPECT

sustain To *sustain* can mean to support ('sustain life') or to suffer ('sustain injuries'). Some commentators have criticized its use in the second sense on the grounds that it is logically inconsistent with the first. Critics of the second sense usually regard it as a recent corruption. In fact, the verb *sustain* has had these two meanings since the 1400s and both are accepted.

> ... the Cree and Inuit appear determined to defend the values that have helped to sustain them in their harsh environment over thousands of years.
> *Maclean's* 12 Aug. 1991: A10

> And in January, his wife ... died as a result of injuries sustained in a car accident.
> *Maclean's* 8 July 1991: A42

> The producer sued the owner for damages to compensate for losses sustained in having to cancel the concert and festivities planned.
> J.E. Smyth et al. *The Law and Business Administration in Canada* 1987: 316

swale see SWAMP

swam see SWIM

swamp, marsh, bog, muskeg, slough, pothole, coulee, swale, wetlands *Swamp* and *marsh* are both used to describe an area of wet, spongy land periodically or permanently covered with water. The vegetation of marshes differs from that of swamps: a *marsh* contains mostly grasses and sedges, whereas a *swamp* also has trees and shrubs. A *bog* is an area of wet, spongy, usually peaty ground that forms over thousands of years as vegetation slowly invades a lake. In Canada, bogs cover large areas in the northern parts of the Prairie provinces and consist of acidic water covered by a deep mat of vegetation that includes moss and black spruce trees. This terrain is called *muskeg*.

Slough is pronounced to rhyme with *slew* or sometimes, in Atlantic Canada, with *cow*. The definition of a slough varies across Canada (see SLOUGH). Prairie sloughs are hollows that fill with water in the wet season and often produce good hay called 'slough grass'. Some prairie sloughs are round areas of sinking soil also known as *potholes*. A *coulee* is a deep ravine or gully that is usually dry in the summer. A *swale* is a shallow depression in the land that often collects water. *Wetlands* is a general term for areas that are wet for much or all of the year.

> The entire country in spring was a heaving bog, dotted by sloughs, little streams, and ponds left by the rapidly melting snow.
> Pierre Berton *The Promised Land* 1984: 129

> Each had to find his own way, work out his own salvation in slough or muskeg, and care for his family at nightfall.
> Pierre Berton *The Promised Land* 1984: 128

> Perhaps it came from the grassy banks of old melt-water coulees and stream valleys, Willow Creek and the Oldman River, that we explored as children.
> *NeWest Review* Dec. 1989–Jan. 1990: 15

Grass that had been 10 inches high the year before went up to 20, and in the swales where it had been high to begin with, it looked something like a bamboo grove.
Harrowsmith Aug.–Sept. 1985: 56

The Waterfowl Gardens depict eight different wetland habitats in Manitoba, ranging from prairie potholes to the tundra of the far north....
Alan Tucker, ed. *The Penguin Guide to Canada* 1991: 476

See also TUNDRA.

swap, swop *Swap*, meaning exchange, functions as both a noun and a verb. It's an informal word, largely restricted to magazine and newspaper writing. *Swop* is a British spelling variant, rarely used by Canadians.

... participants enjoyed an afternoon of rodeo games, followed by a ... great evening of tunes, with tall tales being swapped around the campfire till the wee hours.
Canadian Biker Magazine Feb. 1990: 10

... the city attained ownership of most of the land there through a series of land swaps in the 1960s with a railway and the B.C. government.
Gazette (Montreal) 5 March 1989: I4

swell, swelled, swollen The past tense of *swell* is *swelled*: 'Her ankles swelled in the heat'. The past participle may be *swollen* ('The wood had swollen after the rainstorm') or *swelled* ('The river had swelled after the thaw'). Both forms are used as adjectives: 'swollen head' *or* 'swelled head'.

My heart had swollen to three times normal size from the strain of working too hard.
Ottawa Citizen 12 Oct. 1990: F1

... by the time police had searched all the cars and the convoy reached LaSalle, the crowd in LaSalle had swelled to 400.
Gazette (Montreal) 8 Nov. 1990: A3

They sought refuge in the tree overnight to escape the freezing waters of a swollen creek below.
Ottawa Citizen 2 May 1990: B6

'We can't afford to go into the game with swelled heads because we're unbeaten and ranked second in the country.'
Gazette (Montreal) 5 Oct. 1990: B6

(Here *swelled* is an adjective.)

swim, swam, swum The past tense of *swim* is *swam*. The past participle is *swum*: 'She has swum it before'.

'We've never swam a big meet like this before in January.'
Province (Vancouver) 26 Jan. 1990: 60

(The past participle *swum* is required here.)

swollen   see SWELL

swop   see SWAP

Sybil   see SIBYL

sympathy   see EMPATHY

synchronous, simultaneous, coincident, concurrent These adjectives all mean existing or occurring at the same time. *Synchronous* is common only in technical and scientific writing. *Simultaneous* usually refers to activities proceeding at the same time. Literally, *coincident* means occupying the same time or space, but it is also applied metaphorically to people or things that are in exact agreement. *Concurrent* often refers to prison terms, especially life sentences, to be served simultaneously rather than consecutively (since the power of human justice does not extend beyond the grave).

Alternatively, climatic change may have been synchronous across the southern Canadian Cordillera....
Canadian Journal of Earth Sciences 26 (1989): 263

The provincial government is considering allowing off-track wagering in 'teletheatres,' where simultaneous telecasts of live horse races are played.
Vancouver Sun 18 Oct. 1990: A17

Their coincident time in office spanned only 27 months, from Kennedy's inauguration on Jan. 20, 1961, until Diefenbaker's departure on April 22, 1963.
Maclean's 10 Dec. 1990: T6

For at the end of this intellectual trail is the reality that B.C.'s real interests are coincident with Quebec's real interests.
Vancouver Sun 9 Nov. 1991: B5

Running on a $1.5 million Stratus mainframe computer, SUZY can currently handle up to 200 concurrent users....
Vancouver Sun 9 May 1990: D1

He was sentenced to 11 concurrent life terms with no eligibility for parole for at least 25 years.
Vancouver Sun 7 Dec. 1990: A14

syndrome In medicine, *syndrome* refers to a set of distinct symptoms that usually appear together and indicate a disease or condition. Most authorities now accept the figurative, often jocular, use of *syndrome* to refer to a characteristic attitude or pattern of behaviour, but many consider the word to be overused in this sense.

> When I was five years old we didn't know what DNA did ... or the causes of Down's syndrome.
> *Queen's Quarterly* 93.1 (1986): 86–7

> To avoid the deluge-and-dearth harvest syndrome—having too much of one vegetable at one time and none at another—plan before you plant.
> *Canadian Living* 17 May 1986: 98

> Today, he says, we've succumbed to the MCS Syndrome—Mindless, Compulsive Scurrying. We rush about all year, to work, to self-improvement classes, to the gym, to committee meetings or whatever....
> *Toronto Star* 23 Dec. 1994: A25

synecdoche   see METONYMY

synonym, antonym, thesaurus, synonym finder *Synonyms* are words with similar meanings (e.g., *thin*, *svelte*, *slim*, and *skinny*), while *antonyms* have opposite meanings (*hot* and *cold*, *tall* and *short*, *high* and *low*). While they are similar, synonyms can't always be used interchangeably. For example, water can be called either *clear* or *colourless*, but a *clear* red liquid could not be called *colourless*. Because of the connotations of the words, most people would rather be called *slim* or *slender* than *skinny*.

Peter Mark Roget published the first book-length collection of words categorized according to meaning in 1852. *Roget's Thesaurus*, or word treasury, was modelled on the scientific classification of plant and animal species. It gathers and groups all the words that convey a certain general meaning, but offers no definitions. Roget's book has been followed by a succession of *synonym finders*. These books are useful tools for the writer struggling to find the *mot juste* or to recall a word that has slipped the memory, but they can have a very peculiar effect on the style of writers hoping to inject some elegance and variety into their vocabularies. Because synonyms aren't equivalent words, a thesaurus should be used only in conjunction with a good dictionary. Even better, perhaps, is to write in your own idiom and to avoid words you haven't encountered before.

See also CONNOTATION(S); HOMOPHONE, HOMO-GRAPH, HOMONYM.

synthetic   see ARTIFICIAL

syrup, sirup   Canadian, British, and American dictionaries all list *syrup* first. *Sirup* is an American variant, rare in Canadian usage.

systematize, systemize   Both forms of this verb entered the language in the late 1700s, and both are listed in many current dictionaries. However, *systematize* dominates in contemporary English and is the only form found in formal Canadian writing.

> Atwood seems compelled to classify and systematize, to make patterns, in one part of her mind, while an alternative self glimpses a more fluid reality, a creative surreality.
> *Saturday Night* Jan. 1986: 41

systemic, systematic   *Systemic* was originally a medical term describing a condition that affected a whole organism or biological system. A virus that wreaks havoc with your whole body is having a *systemic* effect. Now *systemic* is often used metaphorically to describe problems infecting or pervading social systems and institutions. This is the sense of *systemic* in the common phrases 'systemic racism' and 'systemic discrimination'. 'Systemic discrimination' has to do with inequities and prejudices within the operation of a system (the education system, etc.) that are not overt or easy to locate, but that are present nonetheless. For example, a requirement that all firefighters be over six feet tall could be seen as evidence of systemic discrimination against most women and, in some minority groups, most men as well. (Today, most such physical requirements have been replaced by standards of strength and fitness, so that no one is automatically excluded.)

The phrase 'systemic discrimination' is quite often confused with 'systematic discrimination'. To be *systematic* in your approach to a task is to make a plan and carry it out in a thorough and orderly way. Thus 'systematic discrimination' and 'systematic racism' involve not unconscious prejudice but deliberate acts of repression. The Nazis' treatment of the Jews during the Second World War was an extreme example of 'systematic racism'. Apartheid in South Africa—an explicit government policy of exclusion on the basis of race—was another.

> Employers do not have to work at discriminating against these groups; it comes naturally. This massive and systemic discrimination cannot be eradicated by dealing with its manifestations on a one by one, case by case basis, as our human rights system demands.
> *Maclean's* 15 Oct. 1990: A44

Communist China invaded its tiny neighbor in 1950 and began a process of systematic repression, torture and—according to Tibetans—genocide.
Maclean's 15 Oct. 1990: A44

Contrary to the claims by the immigration ministry, the facts seem to indicate that delay is caused by a policy of systemic discrimination against visible minorities.
Gazette (Montreal) 13 Dec. 1990: B2

(A policy of deliberate exclusion of visible minorities would be 'systematic discrimination'. Given the sense of the sentence, either 'caused by a policy of discrimina-

tion' or 'caused by *systematic* discrimination' would be better.)

The Quebec government, which had always denied practising any systemic discrimination against women, allocated $240 million in special funds to redress discrimination against its employees.
Gazette (Montreal) 15 Sept. 1990: B5

(Any form of discrimination that is deliberately 'practised' is *systematic*. Perhaps what the writer meant to say was something along these lines: '... which has always denied a systemic discrimination against women in its hiring and promoting practices ...'.)

T

-t, -ed *Leant, learnt, smelt, spelt, spilt,* and *spoilt* are chiefly British forms of the past tense and past participle forms. Canadians, like Americans, are far more likely to use the *-ed* forms of these verbs. However, Canadians do use *burnt, dreamt, knelt,* and *leapt* quite often.

See also BEREAVED, BEREFT; CLEAVE; -ED.

table In Britain, to *table* a resolution, motion, or bill is to put it on the table, to bring it forward for consideration. In the United States, the opposite is meant: to *table* an item on the agenda is to postpone it. In Parliament, Canadians employ the British meaning. However, confusion may arise in other settings, where Canadians use the same word for both meanings.

The legislation must be tabled and passed in the House of Commons before January 1, 1989, when the agreement comes into effect.
Engineering Dimensions Mar.–Apr. 1988: 31

(Here *table* means bring forward.)

'If it's not settled by Monday, we will have to make a decision, whether we table legislation or we give more time to negotiate.'
Gazette (Montreal) 26 April 1990: A7

(The speaker here is wondering whether or not a strike should be ended immediately by bringing forward legislation.)

Burnaby council tabled the report until next week, and North Vancouver district council's vote remains confidential.
Vancouver Sun 2 October 1990: A1

(Here *table* means postpone.)

table d'hôte see À LA CARTE

tack, take a different tack, tact, track The expression *take a different* (or *another*) *tack* comes from sailing. A boat sailing against the wind must run at an oblique angle, zig-zagging to make headway. It is time to take another tack (sail at a different angle to the wind) when the boat has gone as far upwind as possible without getting too far off course. Figuratively, the phrase means to take another approach.

Since not everyone is a sailor, and taking a different tack often involves exercising *tact*, some people confuse *tack* and *tact* in this expression. Others have made sense of an unfamiliar metaphor by substituting rail for sail: 'taking a different track'.

However, Canadair is taking its competition seriously, and officials have decided to take a new tack in marketing the CL-215T.
Maclean's 12 Sept. 1988: A26

Elizabeth Anderson of the B.C. Green Party took a slightly different tact in her presentation, lashing out at the very roots of representative democracy.
Vancouver Sun 18 April 1990: NS3

(The idiom calls for *tack*.)

The Odyssey, an imaginative series that spent its first two seasons following a 12-year-old coma victim's imaginary struggles in a fantasy world, has taken a different track this third season.
Vancouver Sun 21 Nov. 1994: C1

(The idiom calls for *tack*.)

See also FOLK ETYMOLOGY.

taiga   see TUNDRA

take   see BRING

Talmud   see SACRED WRITINGS

tantamount   see PARAMOUNT

tap, faucet, valve, spigot   Canadians use *tap* more frequently than *faucet*, though many use either word. *Tap* is the usual term in Britain, while *faucet* is common in the United States. Some Canadians make a distinction of sense, reserving *faucet* for the fixture that uses one tap to control the flow of both hot and cold water. While kitchens and bathrooms have either faucets or taps, *tap* is the broader term. Only *tap* is used in industrial settings for devices controlling the flow of liquids. A British-style pub may be called a 'taproom', while many bars sell 'beer on tap' or 'draft beer'. Water that is piped into homes is called 'tap water', never 'faucet water' (even in the United States).

Some Canadians, especially in Newfoundland and Quebec, distinguish between indoor taps and outdoor *valves* used for hoses and sprinklers. *Spigot* is an uncommon word in Canadian English, most often used figuratively.

I took the hand and ran it under the cold tap.
Howard Engel *Murder Sees the Light* 1984: 92

When a bathroom hot water faucet is quickly turned off, sometimes a 'bang' is heard in the pipes behind the wall.
Toronto Star 16 Dec. 1994: A1

A pipeline that supplies the Ontario Hockey League with high-octane talent is slowly having its spigot closed.
Daily News (Halifax) 24 Oct. 1994: 30

Tapirisat   see INUIT

taps   see LAST POST

target   The use of *target* to mean quota, objective, or goal has been criticized because, according to some, a target is something 'aimed at', 'hit', or 'missed', not something 'reached', 'achieved', or 'exceeded'. Nonetheless, many writers do use *target* as a synonym for *objective* or *goal*, and dictionaries record this meaning.

Critics of the metaphorical use of *target* could just as well take aim at the word *goal*, but no one suggests that the literal sense of *goal* (winning post or net) should govern the verbs with which it can be used. This is probably because *goal* has been used as a metaphor since the early seventeenth century, while the figurative sense of *target* dates only from the 1940s.

But Drew was as determined as any Soviet commissar to fulfil his self-imposed export quota, and the fuse to his temper began smouldering whenever anyone suggested the fifteen per cent target might be overly ambitious.
George Ignatieff *The Making of a Peacemonger* 1987: 177

Initially, industry participation will be voluntary but if the first target of reduction ... is not met, the federal government intends to enforce the guidelines with legislation.
Western Grocer May–Jun. 1990: 94

tartan, plaid   In Scotland, *tartan* is the distinctive design on the fabric used to make kilts and other garments. Specific tartans are traditionally associated with specific clans. A *plaid* is a length of woollen cloth worn over one shoulder as part of traditional Scottish Highland dress. However, Canadians generally use *plaid* for the pattern ('a plaid shirt'), and occasionally refer to the garment that the Scots call a *plaid* as a *tartan*.

Hanging on the walls are tartans and Scottish memorabilia.
Saturday Night April 1986: 60

[The man] was last seen wearing a green cotton plaid shirt, beige pants and plaid bedroom slippers.
Globe and Mail (Toronto) 4 June 1985: M4

(The Scots would say *tartan*.)

He was ... strikingly attired in winter in the Royal Stuart tartan which he preferred to an overcoat, and apparently occasionally substituting a highland bonnet for the conventional mortarboard.
Hilda Neatby *Queen's University* 1 (1978): 89

(The Scots would call the garment a *plaid*.)

tautology   see WORDINESS

tax, excise, duty, customs, rates   *Tax* is a general word for a compulsory payment levied by government to support state expenditures. *Excise* is tax paid on goods manufactured or produced within the country. *Duty*, or *customs*, is tax paid on goods brought into Canada from another country. In Canada and the United States, local taxes paid on the assessed value of property are called *property taxes*; the equivalent British term is *rates*. In Canada a *ratepayers' association* is a municipal taxpayers' group.

> The municipalities don't think their ratepayers should pay higher taxes for Victoria's decision to buy the most expensive technology available.
> *Globe and Mail* (Toronto) 9 March 1985: 6

See also AD VALOREM; EXCISE.

tea   see DINNER

team, teem   *Team* is certainly the more common word, but some people mistakenly use it for all meanings of these two homophones.

A group of people working or playing together is a *team*; animals harnessed together are a *team*. To *team up* means to join forces.

To *teem* is to be plentiful, to swarm. If something is *teeming* with something, it abounds in it. In reference to rain, to *teem* means to pour.

> Anybody out there interested in teaming up with me to open a consulting firm?
> *Ottawa Citizen* 24 May 1992: A6

> Paris in the 1960s was teeming with Quebec students, virtually all of them ardent separatists.
> George Ignatieff *The Making of a Peacemonger* 1987: 215

> I am 77 and walk a mile and a half to the store to pick up my Gazette, unless there is teeming rain or a blizzard, at which time I take the car.
> *Gazette* (Montreal) 27 Jan. 1990: A7

> Montreal's Old Port ... is teaming with activity this summer.
> *Gazette* (Montreal) 13 June 1992: K4

(The correct spelling is *teeming*.)

> The difference is that this is not the teaming streets of Manhattan, but the home of Michelangelo, the precious cultural centre of Italy.
> *Financial Post* 22 March 1990: 15

(The correct spelling is *teeming*.)

teaspoonful   see -FUL

technical illustrator   see DRAFTSMAN

teem   see TEAM

telecast, televise   These verbs are now used interchangeably: to broadcast a television program is to *telecast* or to *televise* it. In the past some people distinguished between these words, using *telecast* to mean transmit or broadcast a program, and *televise* to mean record it with television equipment. (Now we use *videotape* for the latter meaning.) The spelling *televize*, with a *z*, is incorrect. Like *broadcast*, *telecast* also functions as a noun meaning television program.

> Using satellite technology, the Canadian Information Processing Society ... achieved a first last month with a symposium telecast to 12 cities across Canada.
> *Computing Canada* 1 March 1991: 4

> The Toronto-based network will televise 41 of the World Cup's 52 games live and the remaining 11 matches on a same-day, tape-delayed basis.
> *Vancouver Sun* 15 May 1990: C7

> Within a week of Terry's return home to his family, the CTV network had organized a five-hour telecast as a tribute to his achievement.
> *Queen's Quarterly* 97.2 (1990): 256

> Mrs. Thatcher had recently indicated support at least for televizing major debates....
> *Globe and Mail* (Toronto) 21 Nov. 1985: A14

(The correct spelling is *televising*.)

temblor   see TREMOR

temperature, fever   *Temperature* is sometimes used to mean fever, as in 'She stayed home from school because she had a temperature'. This use is considered imprecise by those who point out that everyone (and everything) has a temperature, the normal temperature of the human body being 37 degrees Celsius. Some usage guides criticize this loose use of *temperature*; others defend it as idiomatic. To avoid criticism, substitute *high temperature* or *fever*.

> I was running a temperature, and my shadow, Georgi Alexandrovich, was all for wiring ahead to have a doctor meet me when we reached Leningrad.

George Ignatieff *The Making of a Peacemonger* 1987: 133

temporize   see EXTEMPORIZE

tenant, tenet   A *tenant* is a renter. A *tenet* is a fundamental principle or belief. *Tenent* is a common misspelling for both these words.

... when a unit is vacated, the doorknobs are changed and new keys are issued to the new tenant.
Calgary Herald 3 June 1992: B1

It is a basic tenet of business that you profit from your competitor's misfortune.
Calgary Herald 29 Dec. 1992: A7

Many of the tenets of Mao's brand of communism have been abandoned since his death in 1976.
Gazette (Montreal) 27 Dec. 1992: B5

'Irving (Ace) Bailey, Toronto hockey star, who by all the tenents of medical science, should have been dead days ago, is definitely on the road to recovery.'
Toronto Star 8 April 1992: C4

(The word required here is *tenets*.)

This week, it was one of football's basic tenents—hang onto the ball.
Vancouver Sun 19 July 1990: C1

(Again, the word required is *tenets*.)

tendinitis, tendonitis   The term for inflammation of a tendon is spelled either *tendinitis* or *tendonitis*. Both spellings are common and accepted; *tendinitis* is more common in Canadian writing.

Valdez [suffered] a broken thumb and tendinitis in his shoulder....
Gazette (Montreal) 7 March 1989: B4

Chouinard quietly learned to deal with a tendonitis problem that surfaced last year and kept her from doing triple toe jumps in practice.
Today's Skater 1991: 34

tenet   see TENANT

tennies, tennis shoes   see RUNNING SHOES

terminate   Critics find this word pretentious and overused: anything today—from marriages, to people, to conversations—may be said to be terminated. While *terminate* is common and appropriate in legal and quasi-legal contexts, there are many preferable synonyms for general use, including *end*, *stop*, *bring to an end*, and *fire*.

A buyer may terminate the contract during this period by giving written notice to the seller.
J.E. Smyth et al. *The Law and Business Administration in Canada* 1987: 411

Unhappy marriages were usually tolerated in previous generations; today they are usually terminated.
Irving M. Zeitlin and Robert J. Brym *The Social Condition of Humanity* 1991: 195

(Here *terminated* fits the context, since marriage is being discussed as an economic arrangement.)

Again, at this point the conversation was terminated.
City Magazine Spring 1988: 19

(Here *ended abruptly* or *ceased* would be preferable.)

Michael had discussed terminating Brian with the President of the Company and the Director of Human Resources a number of times....
Queen's Quarterly 94.4 (1987): 843

(Simply *firing* him would be kinder.)

terrorist   see GUERRILLA

testimony   see EVIDENCE

Tex-Mex   see HISPANIC

than   For centuries, language commentators have debated whether the pronouns that follow *than* should be subjective (*I, she, he, we,* and *they*) or objective (*me, her, him, us,* and *them*). At present, usage varies with the level of formality. In informal speech and writing, the objective pronouns are used: 'She is taller than *him*'; 'He trusted Michael more than *me*'. In formal speech and writing, either subjective or objective pronouns are used, depending on which would be appropriate if the verb were repeated after *than*: 'She is taller than he [is]'; 'He trusted Michael more than [he trusted] me'. 'He trusted Michael more than I' would mean 'more than I did'. Note that this distinction can't be made in informal usage.

Many people balk at using a subjective pronoun after *than* ('They were more fortunate than we') because they think it sounds pedantic. The pedantic ring can always be avoided by repeating the verb: 'They were more fortunate than we were'.

A comparison that starts with *as* must be completed with *as* ('It's *as* good *as* new'), never with *than* (as in 'There were twice *as* many *than* before').

Than is often misspelled *then*, though the error is more likely to reflect haste than genuine confusion.

... there were younger men around the clubs, men such as Sonny Rollins, a tenor saxophonist from Harlem who was three years younger than he.
Jack Chambers *Milestones* 1983: 122

I don't think they know any better than me.
Canadian Fiction Magazine 64 (1988): 106

(Here *than me* is appropriate, since the tone is conversational; *than I* would be required in a formal context.)

... I learned inadvertently that a male hired later than I was being paid significantly more than me.
Women and Environments 12.2 (1989–90): 26

(Given the formal tone of the sentence, *me* should be replaced by *I*.)

And twice as many civilians were hurt in those chases than in 1987.
Gazette (Montreal) 3 March 1989: A3

(Here *than* should be changed to *as*.)

See also CASE; DIFFERENT FROM; INFERIOR TO, SUPERIOR TO.

thankfully   see SENTENCE ADVERBS

Thanksgiving Day   see NEW YEAR'S DAY

that, omission of   Especially in spoken English, *that* is often omitted: 'the gloves [that] you thought [that] I'd left behind'. The *that*-less construction is referred to by grammarians as a 'contact clause' or an 'omitted relative'. In the eighteenth century, usage writers condemned the omission of the relative pronoun *that* in written English. Now some usage guides maintain just the opposite, that it is better to omit *that* whenever possible. Since both structures are grammatically correct, rhythm and clarity should guide your choice. The omission of *that* is more common in informal writing than in formal prose.

See also REASON IS BECAUSE; THAT, WHICH; THAT, WHO, WHOM.

that, which   Most writers use *that* and *which* without any difficulty. However, they may well be troubled by a sense that there is some rule about these words that they are breaking. Even Robertson Davies felt this unease: 'To this day I cannot be sure when I should use "that" and when I should use "which", but my secretary knows, and between us we keep up some sort of pretence' (*One Half of Robertson Davies*, 1978: 13). In fact, the problem is with the 'rule', not the writers. It can be traced to Fowler, who suggested that 'if writers would agree to regard *that* as the defining [restrictive] relative pronoun, and *which* as the non-defining, there would be much gain in both lucidity and ease.' Most book editors follow Fowler's advice, particularly in scholarly and reference books. Yet even Fowler admitted 'it would be idle to pretend that it is the practice either of most or of the best writers.'

Later usage guides elevated this suggestion to a rule. Now, however, most writers ignore it, and literary writers are the most likely to use both *which* and *that* to introduce restrictive clauses.

If you are still interested in knowing the 'rule', you need to understand the difference between a restrictive and a non-restrictive clause. A restrictive clause is one that is essential to the meaning of the word it modifies; it defines or restricts it. In the sentence 'The book that (*or* which) John lent me last week is fascinating', the clause preceded by *that* or *which* is required to make it clear which book we are talking about. Writers sometimes use *that* to begin restrictive clauses and sometimes *which*, and either is acceptable, although it is possible that one might sound better than the other in certain sentences. To change the sentence above so that it contains a non-restrictive clause is easy: '*Wuthering Heights*, which John lent me last week, is fascinating'. Now, the clause that begins with *which* is not needed to specify which book we are discussing, but simply adds more information. Writers rarely use *that* with non-restrictive clauses ('*Wuthering Heights*, that you say is your favourite novel, is on the reading list')—nor should they.

The use of *which* to refer not to one noun (as in the examples above) but to a whole preceding sentence or idea ('Robin chews gum almost constantly, which I don't like') has been condemned as an incorrect pronoun reference, as has the similar use of *this*. However, both usages are common in standard English, and even usage guides have begun to relent.

But no means did the Tory Creed consist only of ideas that had outlived their time.
J.A.W. Gunn *Beyond Liberty and Property* 1983: 136

(Here *that* is used with a restrictive clause.)

Death occurs today on the same general principle which governed it a century ago; for every living creature there is a death apiece.
Robertson Davies *A Voice from the Attic* 1960: 129

(Here *which* is used with a restrictive clause.)

Sam Pollock, then general manager of the Canadiens, offered me a generous extension to my contract, which had one year left to run.
Ken Dryden *The Game* 1983: 13

(Here *which* is used with a non-restrictive clause.)

... Guangzhou's White Swan, located on Shamian Island that was once headquarters for the opium trade, remains one of the most opulent.
Vancouver Sun 1 Jun. 1990: G1

(Since Shamian Island is clearly identified by name, the information provided in the restrictive *that* clause is not essential: *which*—preceded by a comma—should replace *that*.)

See also COMMA; THAT, OMISSION OF; THAT, WHO, WHOM.

that, who, whom Some people think it inappropriate to use the relative pronoun *that* to refer to a person, as in 'the man that just spoke to me'. They think only *who* (or *whom*) should refer to people: 'the man who spoke to me'. But dictionaries and usage guides do not support this idea: they agree unanimously that *that* can refer to people.

However, *that* and *who* or *whom* are not freely interchangeable. When *that* refers to a person, the clause it introduces is almost always restrictive. In other words, the *that*-clause identifies the person, or the type of person, being referred to: 'the girl that just jogged by', 'anybody that thinks so'. *That* is not acceptable in formal writing when it links a non-restrictive clause to a person: in other words, when it introduces a clause adding information about a person whose identity has already been specified: 'The previous owner, who (*not* that) told us the roof was new, must have been mistaken'.

But now she found herself sitting with the very man that Lastivka had just talked about.
Canadian Fiction Magazine 63 (1988): 73

'Do you have anybody that you consider to be your poetic father?'
Bruce Meyer and Brian O'Riordan, eds. *In Their Words* 1984: 109

There are many disturbing examples of this, from the continued gender gap in wages to the growing proportion of households headed by women that are poor.
Women and Environments 12.1 (1990): 15

'And what about the night watchman that uses this—'
Constance Beresford-Howe *Night Studies* 1985: 214

(Since the phrase 'the night watchman' identifies a particular person, formal English would require *who* instead of *that*.)

My friend that helped me manoeuvre about the big city wouldn't even buy into the magazine for a 50% ownership.
Canadian Biker Magazine Feb. 1990: 4

(Either '*The* friend *that* helped me ...' or '*My* friend, *who* helped me...' would be required in formal writing.)

See also COMMA; THAT, WHICH; WHO, WHOM.

that is *That is* is used in formal prose as a connecting phrase to introduce a rewording or explanation of what has just been said. Such constructions are often punctuated as two separate sentences: 'These pigments are photosensitive. That is, they will fade if exposed to strong light.' Punctuation problems can arise, however, when sentences such as these are linked to form a single unit. *That is*, unlike *and*, *but*, etc., is not a coordinate conjunction; it cannot form the link itself. Either a semicolon or a colon is required: 'These pigments are photosensitive; that is, they will fade. ...' If the elements equated by *that is* are not complete sentences, *that is* should be preceded by a comma: 'Photosensitive pigments, that is, pigments that fade when exposed to strong light, are not recommended'.

... in the early years of North American economic development, Canada's frontier was 'harder' than that of the United States. That is, Canada was a vast and inhospitable country compared to the U.S., and its natural resources were less accessible.
Canadian Journal of Sociology 14.2 (1989): 164

The four greatest historians of the post-Roman period are often thought of as national historians; that is, there is a general assumption that Jordanes was concerned to record the history of the Goths, Gregory of Tours that of the Franks, Bede the history of the English Church, and Paul the Deacon the deeds of the Lombards.
Canadian Journal of History 14.1 (1989): 92

The other reason is based on precedence: that is, a writer has to write something before a critic can criticize it.
Margaret Atwood *Second Words* 1982: 11

If the term is broken, that is, if the seller delivers a substantially different quantity, the buyer is free to reject the goods.
J.E. Smyth et al. *The Law and Business Administration in Canada* 1987: 383

the, a, an An initial definite or indefinite article (*the*, *a*, or *an*) is ignored in the alphabetizing of titles in indexes or library catalogues. In other words, *The Progress of Love* can be found under *P*, not *T*.

When a title beginning with *the*, *a*, or *an* is mentioned in a text, the initial article is normally retained, with a capital and in italics. But there are exceptions. When the title of a book is preceded by a possessive or an adjective, the initial article may be omitted: 'We read Dickens' *Christmas Carol* every year' (*A Christmas Carol*); 'The much-maligned *Fire-Dwellers* depicted an extramarital affair in a sympathetic light' (*The Fire-Dwellers*). The word *the* at the beginning of the title of a handbook, almanac, atlas, encyclopedia, or dictionary is rarely capitalized and italicized except in scholarly writing: 'There is a picture of Howie Morenz in the *Canadian Encyclopedia*' (*The Canadian Encyclopedia*). Scholars, however, often refer to a title exactly as it appears on its title page. According to the practice of many editors, the word *the* before the name of a newspaper is never capitalized and italicized, regardless of whether *The* appears on the newspaper's masthead. But again, scholars may make a point of reproducing the exact title of the newspaper as it appears on the masthead of the issue(s) they are citing. The French definite article is never dropped from the name of French-language newspapers such as *Le Soleil* and *Le Devoir*.

The should not be capitalized before the name of a company, a publisher, or an organization—the Hudson's Bay Company, the University of Toronto Press, the Institute for Research on Public Policy—unless *the* is part of the legal name of the organization and the context requires the legal name.

When *The* is part of a place name (as it would appear on a map), it is capitalized: 'The Hague', 'The Pas', but 'the South', 'the Northwest Territories', 'the Soo' (the nickname of Sault Ste. Marie).

Not even the *Canada Year Book* or Mel Hurtig's *Canadian Encyclopedia* had room for it.
United Church Observer May 1986: 43

It is attested to by an average of one letter per week in the correspondence columns of *The Globe and Mail*.
W.C. Lougheed, ed. *In Search of the Standard in Canadian English* 1986: 26

Why should the Hudson's Bay Company publish a history magazine? Most Canadians already know the answer to that question. . . . it is also The Governor and

Company of Adventurers of England Trading Into Hudson's Bay.
The Beaver Feb.–Mar. 1990: 4

'French-English battle creeps into the N.W.T.,' declared the weekend Globe and Mail, wrapping us neatly up with a story on the Soo, a column from Quebec and an editorial.
North News (Yellowknife) 19 Feb. 1990: 6

theft see BURGLARY

their, they're, there Occasionally people mix up *their* ('their things'), *they're* ('They're here'), and *there* ('There aren't any'). These substitutions usually result from inattention rather than genuine confusion.

Some tried their luck at the wheel.
Daily News (Halifax) 1 July 1992: 5

They're still on their feet, and in all likelihood, winning every battle.
Business Journal June 1991: 20

There is a middle way.
Bon Vivant Feb.–Mar. 1983: 10

'All their doing is putting out our records.'
Gazette (Montreal) 3 Dec. 1992: F1

(The correct spelling here is *they're*.)

. . . his reading rewarded his solitude and extended it, for their were few children his own age who could match his devotion to the printed word.
Calgary Herald 8 Aug. 1992: B9

(The correct spelling here is *there*.)

Big projects can acquire a life force of there own.
Queen's Quarterly 92.2 (1985): 368

(The correct spelling here is *their*.)

theirs *Theirs* is a possessive pronoun like *mine*, *ours*, *yours*, *his*, *hers*, and *its*. Like them, it has no apostrophe. However, because in many other contexts possession is indicated with an apostrophe, sometimes *theirs* is incorrectly written *their's*.

For Canadians who want a united country, the best strategy is to stay cool, optimistic and flexible, and support those leaders who keep their heads while many about them are losing their's.
Ottawa Citizen 3 Jan. 1991: A13

(The correct spelling is *theirs*.)

See also ITS, IT'S; POSSESSIVE.

[theirselves] see [HISSELF]

them, those 'Do you like them?' is Standard English, but 'Do you like them shoes?' is not. In Standard English, *them* never functions as an adjective. The accepted adjective form is *those*: 'Do you like those shoes?' The use of *them* as an adjective, though not uncommon, is stigmatized as an uneducated usage.

'Tell them kids to keep the hell outa the furnace room.'
Max Braithwaite *The Night We Stole the Mountie's Car* 1971: 69

(The standard form is *those*.)

... I even wrote the President, I scrawled out them words and took the letters to Miss Payne, my old school teacher and asked her would she fix the grammar.
Queen's Quarterly 94.1 (1987): 92

(The standard form is *those*.)

there   see THEIR

therefor   Once a variant of *therefore*, *therefor* now has a distinct meaning and pronunciation. Pronounced with the emphasis on the last syllable, the word means 'for that (*or* those)'. *Therefor* is rare; some dictionaries label it archaic, and its use is now confined mostly to legal and business writing.

The frigate program will be abandoned and replaced with icebreaker building, designs therefor having already been completed.
Ottawa Citizen 22 March 1986: B3

Sections 40 to 42 of the Constitution Act, 1982, are repealed and the following substituted therefor....
Province (Vancouver) 10 June 1990: 40

The Inter-Church Committee for Refugees, a group comprised of representatives of most Canadian faiths, charged that the bill violates Canada's human rights guarantees and is therefor illegal.
Toronto Star 6 May 1987: A1

(The intended meaning here is 'as a result'; the correct spelling is *therefore*.)

there is, there are   *There is* or *there's* before a plural, as in 'There's more glasses somewhere,' is very informal. In writing, *there are* is required before a plural noun.

Before a collective noun, either *there is* or *there are* is correct: 'There is a whole group of people on your porch' or 'There are a host of options'. *There is* is more common.

A list of two or more things that begins with a singular noun is usually introduced by *there is*: 'There is time and money at stake'. *There are* is also correct.

'The day is gone when the league can rely on its hard-core fans—there's not enough hard-core fans to pay the bills.'
Leader-Post (Regina) 27 Feb. 1988: C5

(This is a quotation of informal speech. Even in semi-formal writing, *there are* should replace *there's*.)

'If there's problems with residence life we'll just have to look at it and see if we can fix it.'
News North (Yellowknife) 26 Feb. 1990: 2

(To agree with the plural noun 'problems', *there's* should be *there are* and both *it*'s should be *them*.)

We're talking travel accessories, of which there is a mind-boggling assortment available.
Chronicle-Herald (Halifax) 14 May 1988: 9

And where there are fitness programs, there is also above-average productivity, morale, motivation and loyalty among workers....
London Free Press 28 April 1988: B8

(Here *there is* introduces a list that begins with a singular noun; *there are* would also be correct, but rarely introduces a list unless the first item mentioned is plural.)

See also AGREEMENT, GRAMMATICAL; COLLECTIVE NOUNS.

thesaurus   see SYNONYM

they   see EVERYONE

they're   see THEIR

think   see DON'T THINK

this week   see NEXT, THIS

this writer   see PRESENT WRITER

thither   see HITHER

Thompson, Nlaka'pamux   The Aboriginal group formerly known as the *Thompson Indians* are now usually called the *Nlaka'pamux* (pronounced *un tla KAP mooh*); this is the most common spelling and is both singular and plural. Their traditional territory is in the Stein Valley in south-central British Columbia. Their language, Nlaka'pamux, belongs to the Salishan family.

> ... land claims have been made on the Stein by the Nlaka'pamux ... and the Lil'wat ... peoples.
> *Vancouver Sun* 15 July 1994: B4

> As in many Native North American societies, dreams and visions were considered important among the Nlaka'pamux—particularly those visions which came after days of living shelterless in the wild while fasting.
> *Toronto Star* 30 July 1994: G13

thoroughbred   see PUREBRED

those   see ONE OF THOSE THINGS; THEM, THOSE

though   see ALTHOUGH

thrash, thresh   In rural Canada, the verb *thrash* is commonly used as a variant of *thresh*, meaning to separate grain from husks and stems. However, in standard urban dialects the two words are usually distinguished. *Thresh* refers to the farm operation (*threshing*), while *thrash* is almost always reserved for other meanings: to administer a beating, to flail one's limbs, to go over something repeatedly. To 'thrash something out' is to discuss it thoroughly in the hope of reaching a resolution or consensus.

> His triumph as he tracks down each part of his trouble has the quality of a man who has chased a burglar and given him a sound thrashing.
> Robertson Davies *A Voice from the Attic* 1960: 64

> He thrashes, moans; his elbow flails the window.
> Margaret Atwood *Life Before Man* 1979: 209

> The purpose of the conference was to bring all the left-wing elements of the party together to thrash out a common programme....
> *Canadian Journal of History* 14.1 (1989): 24

> Fava beans can be shelled by hand or threshed by foot in a box or on a tarp.
> *TLC ... for plants* Spring 1991: 57

> She does not want to line up and learn to throw grenades, she doesn't want to work a threshing machine....
> Margaret Atwood *Life Before Man* 1979: 291

thru, thro', thruway   *Thru* is a chiefly American spelling variant of *through*. In Canada it is mainly restricted to journalism (usually in entertainment notices, etc., giving dates: 'Monday thru Thursday'). *Thru* was introduced by the American spel-

ling-reform movement of the late nineteenth and early twentieth centuries. Though Canadian and British dictionaries list it as an established American spelling, the *American Heritage Dictionary* labels *thru* informal, and it should be avoided in formal writing. The poetic short form of *through* is *thro'* or *thro*.

Thruway, a common word for an expressway or toll highway in the United States, is fully established.

> ... Thursday thru Sunday, seniors pay $6.99 for dinner.
> *Vancouver Sun* 22 Sept. 1990: A6

> It runs Tuesday thru Saturday for the next three weeks.
> *Province* (Vancouver) 10 July 1990: 2

> The easiest way is via Interstate 81 and the New York Thruway to the Massachusetts Turnpike.
> *Ottawa Citizen* 9 June 1990: G2

See also ROAD.

thunderous   see DISASTROUS

thus, [thusly]   Some people are tempted to add *-ly* to *thus* in order to make it an adverb (as *quick* is turned into *quickly*). In fact, *thus* is itself an adverb and hence does not require an *-ly* ending. Though *thusly* is listed in some dictionaries, many people consider it pompous or even ridiculous.

> She dedicates the novel thusly: 'To my Ryerson colleagues, not one of whom is depicted in these pages.'
> *Globe and Mail* 28 Nov. 1985: D1

(Here *as follows*, *in this way*, or *thus* would be a better choice.)

tidal wave, tsunami   Strictly speaking, *tidal waves* are not tidal. These enormous, destructive ocean waves are usually caused by seismic activity. Geographers and oceanographers use the borrowed Japanese term *tsunami* (from *tsu*, 'harbour', and *nami*, 'wave'). In technical use, *tsunami* (pronounced *tsoo NAM ee*) is the appropriate term; however, *tidal wave* is well-established and unobjectionable in general use.

> Underwater seismic activity off Mexico's southern coast produced a tidal wave that swept away 300 homes in the fishing village of Cuajinicuilapa.
> *Vancouver Sun* 30 June 1990: B7

> The Japanese have discovered that low-lying bushes or hedges dissipate the effects of tsunamis—the giant

waves which are generated by undersea earthquakes and volcanic eruptions.
Globe and Mail (Toronto) 29 May 1985: P13

Even before Los Angeles rapper Ice-T opened his mouth Wednesday night at the Commodore, the anticipation of what he might say had already sent out enough tsunamis of outrage....
Vancouver Sun 16 Aug. 1990: B7

(Here *tsunamis* is used figuratively.)

'til, till see UNTIL

timber, lumber Many Canadian and American writers distinguish between *timber*, wood to be cut, and *lumber*, the processed product ready for use in building. Thus Canadians refer to a 'stand of timber' but a 'lumberyard', though they may refer to a single piece of finished wood, such as a beam in a house, as a *timber*.

The primary meaning of *lumber* in British English is what North Americans call *junk*: useless and cumbersome objects. The North American *lumberyard* is a *timberyard* in Britain.

Peeking his head out from the branches more than 25 metres above ground, Victoria resident Paul Winstanley said he took up residence in the tree to protest logging old-growth timber.
Province (Vancouver) 9 Dec. 1990: 14

Hazelwood said Northwood's sawmills can produce 680 million board feet of lumber annually.
Province (Vancouver) 30 Nov. 1990: 64

... here was a crudely squared-off four-inch by four-inch timber almost six feet long, exactly like the kind used to shore up a mine shaft.
Atlantic Salmon Journal Autumn (1990): 28

See also TIMBER, TIMBRE.

timber, timbre *Timber* is wood. *Timbre* is a musical term for the tonal quality that identifies a particular musical instrument or singing voice. Both words can be pronounced to rhyme with *limber*. *Timbre*, in an approximation of its original French pronunciation, can also be pronounced *TAM ber* or *TAM bruh*.

Her rich, strong voice has the timbre that characterizes great Strauss interpreters....
Globe and Mail (Toronto) 28 Feb. 1985: E6

See also -RE, -ER; TIMBER, LUMBER.

time, a.m., p.m., midnight, noon A colon separates the hours and minutes of the time of day in Canadian and American English ('8:15'), while in British English a period is used ('8.15'). The abbreviations *a.m.* and *p.m.*—also correctly but less commonly written without periods, with capital letters, etc.—stand for the Latin words *ante meridiem* and *post meridiem*, 'before noon' and 'after noon'.

'Five in the afternoon', 'five o'clock in the afternoon', '5:00 in the afternoon', '5:00 p.m.', and '5 p.m.' are all acceptable ways of writing the time. However, '5 p.m. in the afternoon' is redundant, and style guides also reject 'five p.m.', on the grounds that *a.m* and *p.m.* should be used only with figures.

A.m. and *p.m.* should not be used to distinguish midnight from noon. Even usage guides do not agree on which abbreviation belongs to which twelve o'clock. It's best to write '12 midnight' or '12 noon'.

The twenty-four-hour clock eliminates the confusion inherent in having a twelve-hour cycle occur twice each day: noon is 12:00; midnight is 24:00 or 00:00; 12:45 a.m. is 00:45; 6 p.m. is 18:00, and so on. This system is used internationally and is familiar to francophone Canadians. Most English Canadians, on the other hand, grapple with it only in bus and train schedules and do not have an idiom ('Come about 19:30') to use the system conversationally.

The convention for presenting an elapsed time, such as the winning time in a race, is to separate the hours, minutes, and seconds by colons and to separate the seconds from the tenths or hundredths of a second by a decimal point. Thus '2:18:49.89' means 'two hours, eighteen minutes, and 49.89 seconds'.

We had been warned that we had to be on board before 4.00 p.m....
George Ignatieff *The Making of a Peacemonger* 1987: 26

(The use of a period instead of a colon in the time is not common in Canada.)

In Ottawa he had the reputation of staying all night at his desk, leaving behind a pile of work for his clerks at 6 a.m. and returning at ten o'clock looking as fresh as ever.
Pierre Berton *The Promised Land* 1984: 19

Then, a minute or two before 12 noon, Lemaire moves.
Ken Dryden *The Game* 1983: 108

Summerland's Linda Stenseth topped the women in 2:55.17.
Vancouver Sun 9 Oct. 1990: C4

(This race was a marathon. The winning time was nearly three hours—2:55:17, with two colons—not two minutes and 55.17 seconds.)

See also STANDARD TIME.

time period   see PERIOD OF TIME

times less, times more   Many language commentators maintain that the phrase *times less* ('costs five times less') is illogical because 'times' suggests multiplication, not division. They prefer 'One-tenth as much rain this summer' to 'Ten times less rain this summer'. On the other hand, these expressions are idiomatic, and many reputable writers have used them.

Commentators also prefer '*x* times as many/much' to '*x* times more' in comparisons, because '*x* times more' is ambiguous. If Sanjay has three apples, to say that Lee has 'five times more' could mean either that Lee has three apples and then fifteen *more* on top of that, or simply that Lee has fifteen apples. In contexts where precision matters, it is clearer to say '*x* times as many' or '*x* times as much'.

> ... worse still, she does not perform the function parents insistently demand of their children: extending their egos ... making them feel authoritative and important to someone, even if that someone is six times smaller than he or she.
> Janice Kulyk Keefer *Reading Mavis Gallant* 1989: 114

> Keep the engine in tune because a badly tuned car may emit ten times more pollution than one that's well maintained.
> *Vancouver Sun* 9 Oct. 1990: 13

(In a scientific context, 'ten times *as much* pollution *as* one ...' would be more precise.)

time zones   see STANDARD TIME

tint   see COLOUR

titillate, titivate   To *titillate*, derived from the Latin word for 'tickle', means to amuse or excite. *Titivate* is an old-fashioned, humorous word meaning to spruce up or adorn something, often oneself. Sometimes *titillate* is misspelled *titilate*, and sometimes it is confused with *titivate*.

> It's a judgment call, but one based on the highest sense of professionalism, not on prurient curiosity intended to titillate.
> Richard Davies and Glen Kirkland, eds. *Dimensions* 1986: 147

> A driver applies mascara to her eyelashes in the rear-view mirror as she zips along in the passing lane of the 401.... Surely these movers and sprucers worry about safety. 'Definitely,' states one traffic light titivator, 'but beauty comes first.'
> *Toronto Star* 21 Nov. 1992: H1

> It would be the easiest thing in the world for me to write a rhapsodic tribute that would titivate the jaded taste-buds of Stratford or Charlottetown....
> *Globe and Mail* (Toronto) 13 April 1986: E1

(The word required here is *titillate*.)

title   see ENTITLE

titles of people   A good general Canadian reference to titles, honours, and forms of address is the *Canadian Almanac and Directory*, published annually (Toronto: Canadian Almanac & Directory Publishing Co.). The *Canadian Press Stylebook* contains a useful section on military ranks, titles, and abbreviations.

See also ATTRIBUTIVE NOUNS, FALSE TITLES; DOCTOR; HONOURABLE; MISS, MRS., MR.; MS.; RELIGIOUS TITLES.

titles of works   see ITALICS AND QUOTATION MARKS; THE, A, AN

toboggan   see SLED

toe the line, toe the mark   The first word in this idiom is *toe*, not *tow*. This expression, meaning to do what is expected of one, to conform to the rules, is a figurative use of a term once used literally in sports such as foot racing and boxing, where contestants began the event by positioning themselves with a toe touching a line or mark. Contemporary writers often appear to have a tug-of-war, rather than a foot race, in mind.

> Lolita makes him toe the mark by threats of exposure and prison; Humbert keeps her somewhat in check by counterthreats that if he goes to jail, she goes to reform school.
> Robertson Davies *A Voice from the Attic* 1960: 244

> One recent and small example is the Labour Party's Stalinist directive to Lesbian and Gay Socialists to tow the Party line....
> *Rites* Feb. 1990: 13

(The correct spelling is *toe*.)

A review of the membership indicates three definable groups: seven pro-federalist, 15 separatists, and the remainder expected to tow the Quebec Liberal party line.
Ottawa Citizen 6 Nov. 1990: A15

(The correct spelling is *toe*.)

See also FOLK ETYMOLOGY.

together   The adverb *together* is often criticized as redundant after the verbs *assemble, connect, join,* and *gather*; yet usage guides do not suggest that *together* should never follow these verbs. Sometimes it is used effectively for emphasis or balance: 'For where two or three are gathered together in my name, I am there in the midst of them' (Matthew 18: 20).

It says legislation should gather all these provisions together under one law that is simpler and easier to understand.
Globe and Mail (Toronto) 22 March 1985: P5

(Here 'under one law' suffices; *together* isn't necessary.)

Customers were tied to their manufacturer by the high cost of switching to other systems and by the difficulty of connecting together alien equipment.
Financial Post (Toronto) 10 June 1991: 6

(Here again, *together* could be dropped.)

See also ALL TOGETHER; TOGETHER WITH.

together with, as well as, in addition to   *Together with, in addition to,* and *as well as* are compound prepositions introducing phrases that—at least in grammatical terms—are parenthetical, and thus do not affect the verb. When *together with, as well as,* or *in addition to* is used to link a singular noun to another noun, the verb that follows must be singular: 'A strong theoretical background, together with some practical experience, is what we are looking for'. All these expressions are different from the linking word *and*. *And* links two singular nouns to create a compound subject requiring a plural verb: 'A college diploma *and* some practical experience *are* what we are looking for'. Overall, Canadian writers follow the recommended usage.

The other, Arsino de las Casas, together with his wife Elena, provides me with a link to the outside world.
Canadian Fiction Magazine 63 (1988): 122

The modest increase, together with Thursday's report of a 0.6-per-cent drop in retail sales in April, was likely to allay some of the fears in financial markets....
Chronicle-Herald (Halifax) 14 May 1988: 31

See also AGREEMENT, GRAMMATICAL; TOGETHER.

tome   Although it originally referred to a volume in a set, *tome* can now refer to any large, heavy book. *Tome* is often used facetiously in light writing and journalism.

This tome was a monumental contribution to law and became known as Justinian's Code.
J.E. Smyth et al. *The Law and Business Administration in Canada* 1987: 46

... [Middlemarch] will be serialized on PBS over the next six weeks.... The sound you hear is the mass exhalation of students with this weighty tome on their reading list.
Ottawa Citizen 9 April 1994: F5

tone   see COLOUR

too   see NOT TOO

toonie   see LOONIE

toothsome, toothy   *Toothsome* means pleasant to the taste or palatable, as in 'a toothsome piece of cheesecake'. It is also used figuratively and often jocularly to mean sexually attractive. *Toothsome* does not mean *toothy*, as in 'He flashed a toothy grin'.

A plateful of the obscure wild vegetable purslane—cooked or raw—is surprisingly toothsome....
Province (Vancouver) 1 June 1990: 52

Like Playboy of 30 years ago, Scope Magazine surrounds its essential content, pictures of toothsome girls, with heavy articles on issues of the day.
Ottawa Citizen 10 May 1990: I1

As a stage personality, he has a distinct affinity with our national animal; like the beaver, he's toothy, genial and insanely busy....
Globe and Mail (Toronto) 18 Sept. 1985: T10

toque   see TUQUE

Torah   see SACRED WRITINGS

tornado   see CYCLONE

tortuous, torturous *Tortuous* means full of twists and turns, circuitous, as in 'tortuous roads' or 'tortuous conversation'. It can also mean devious: 'a tortuous mind'. *Torturous* means excruciatingly painful: 'torturous medical tests'. The senses of these words often overlap: for example, a 'tortuous negotiation' can also be 'torturous' to the participants.

The tortuous streets narrowed and climbed in steps, but cobbles had been replaced like missing teeth, and the centuries sand-blasted from the rough stone exteriors of houses.
Queen's Quarterly 96.2 (1989): 354

During a decade of tortuous negotiations ... the Crees managed, if not to stop the project, to exact a multi-million dollar price.
Gazette (Montreal) 12 May 1990: K3

For almost half a century, efforts to develop a less archaic and torturous method of trapping animals have been made by assorted interests. . . .
Gazette (Montreal) 18 June 1990: B2

McRuer examined each statement in detail, dwelling on them at torturous length, but in the end he decided that, like it or not, he was bound by Robertson's judgement.
Jack Batten *Robinette* 1984: 82

Unfortunately for everyone concerned, Alec does not die with the rapidity his English doctor had guaranteed: he lingers in a pale limbo, a situation as tortuous to his children as it is inconvenient to his wife. . . .
Janice Kulyk Keefer *Reading Mavis Gallant* 1989: 89–90

(Here the word needed is *torturous*).

'Repeatedly beating and mutilating someone else can only be described as tortuous conduct.'
Calgary Herald 30 June 1994: A24

(Here the word needed is *torturous*.)

Tory see CONSERVATIVE

total, totally *Total* and *totally* are overused modifiers that can often be omitted with no loss of meaning or emphasis. In fact, phrases such as 'total fiasco', 'totally annihilated', and 'totally eradicated' are probably more emphatic without the modifiers.

tow see TOE THE LINE

to wit *To wit* is criticized as an old-fashioned and legalistic phrase meaning namely or that is (to say). It is rare in contemporary Canadian usage and is most often used humorously.

Back in 1066, a chap by the name of William the Conqueror invaded England and, as conquerors will, demanded that his new subjects speak his language—to wit: Norman French.
Province (Vancouver) 1 Nov. 1990: 40

townie, bayman *Townie* and *bayman* are Newfoundland terms. A townie lives in St. John's, the capital, while a bayman is from an outport or a coastal fishing village.

Definitely try fish and chips in St. John's. Ask around and you'll find there's a running debate amongst 'townies' there as to which institution is best.
Ottawa Citizen 12 Aug. 1992: E1

Every Newfoundlander knows that the right word for a fellow from an outport, as opposed to St. John's, is bayman.
Gazette (Montreal) 8 Sept. 1990: K2

toxic, toxin see POISON

track see TACK

trademarks, brand names A *trademark* is a distinctive name or logo, registered in law, that identifies products or services in the marketplace as those of a particular company. A company can lose exclusive rights to a registered name if it can be proven that the name is no longer associated with a particular brand in people's minds. Brand names for new products, especially products for which there is no established term, are often used generically. In addition, brand names are sometimes used figuratively to suggest something quite different from the original sense (as in the phrase 'a Band-Aid solution', where 'Band-Aid' means inadequate). In both these cases, brand names sometimes appear in writing without the capital letters that distinguish them as trademarks. This usage is strongly discouraged by trademark-owners who risk losing sole rights to brand names they have marketed. Sometimes, when a usage that infringes on a trademark appears in a publication that is widely circulated and influential, such as a dictionary or large-circulation newspaper, the owners of the trademark take legal action against the publisher. For this reason it is standard practice in certain kinds of writing, particularly journalism, to capitalize all trademarks ('Kleenex', 'Aspirin', 'Band-Aid') or to use their generic equivalents ('tissue', 'painkiller', 'adhesive bandage').

British and American dictionaries indicate which trademarks are registered in Britain and the United States, but they do not give information for Canada. Consumer and Corporate Affairs Canada maintains a database of trademarks registered in Canada, and the *Canadian Trade Index*, found in reference libraries, also lists trademarks. A long list of generic equivalents for common trademarks can be found in the *Canadian Press Stylebook*.

Note that the common-noun elements in brand names are usually not capitalized: 'Bic pen'.

'They also used to have a trademark on the term "jumbo" but they lost too many legal battles and it became accepted as part of the vernacular.'
Calgary Herald 7 Nov. 1993: C1

Royal Bank's trademark lion is now migrating to Royal Trust's logo, a discreet symbol of its $1.6 billion takeover that combines the country's biggest bank with its second-biggest trust company.
Vancouver Sun 27 Dec. 1993: D9

Ticket prices are kept low, shows are usually benefits, and promotion consists of cheaply Xeroxed posters plastered all over town.
Ottawa Citizen 25 Sept. 1993: F1

tragedy   In literature a *tragedy* is the story of the downfall of a heroic figure; a modern tragedy may feature a more ordinary figure who suffers (and usually dies) as a result of psychological or social conflicts. These literary definitions have led some critics to object to the use of *tragedy* to describe minor misfortunes and mishaps. To avoid being accused of lacking a sense of proportion, it's probably best to reserve *tragedy* for events that involve loss of human life or potential.

The death of seven American astronauts was a tragedy.
Maclean's 24 Feb. 1986: 2

It would be a tragedy to do away with the zoo altogether.
Vancouver Sun 9 Nov. 1990: B6

(Here *tragedy* is rather strong; *regrettable* might be better.)

The tragedy is that to most youngsters in primary school, science is perceived as a formal, mechanistic, passionless activity.
Queen's Quarterly 93.1 (1986): 89

(That science is perceived in this way is a sad fact, but not irreversible, not a *tragedy*.)

trail   see ROAD

trainers   see RUNNING SHOES

traipse, trapes   *Traipse* is an informal verb of unknown origin meaning to walk, wander, or trudge. *Trapes* is a rare alternative spelling.

Mary Had a Little Lamb ... was based on Mary Sawyer, whose lamb would traipse after her like a pet dog.
Vancouver Sun 3 July 1990: 20

My partner is ... a charming and professional go-getter who interviews everyone who moves as I traipse lamely behind with my notebook.
Ottawa Citizen 13 Dec. 1990: E1

Community groups traipse down to City Hall to battle developers rummaging around in their neighborhoods.
Globe and Mail (Toronto) 2 Jan. 1985: M1

transparent, opaque, translucent, luminous, clear, colourless   Ordinary window glass is *transparent*: you can see everything through it. Wood is *opaque*: you can't see through it. Most white paper is *translucent*, or semi-transparent: only shadowy forms can be seen through it. *Transparent* and *opaque* are also used figuratively, the first to mean easily seen through and the second to mean obscure or difficult to understand.

A *translucent* material does not emit light; it only lets light through. The word *luminous* refers to something that emits light. Nevertheless, these words are used interchangeably in figurative contexts, especially in reference to skin or complexions.

Transparent and *clear* are synonyms; note, however, that these terms do not necessarily mean colourless. A piece of stained glass or a tinted lens can be described as transparent or clear.

... they realized that translucent glass doors would admit light into a dark entry from a windowed kitchen.
Globe and Mail (Toronto) 7 Dec. 1985: G3

This week's tour by senior federal cabinet ministers in Alberta is a transparent effort to win back Tory party supporters, opposition MPs said....
Ottawa Citizen 6 Sept. 1990: A5

She is opaque as a rock.
Margaret Atwood *Life Before Man* 1979: 199

The same features that can make Pfeiffer look gorgeous in another movie—the translucent skin, the large lop-

sided mouth—make her look interesting in Frankie & Johnny.
Maclean's 21 Oct. 1991: A98

While her latest heroine is obsessed with the physical ravages of middle age, Atwood seems to be holding up well: she is physically striking, with luminous skin and penetrating blue eyes.
Maclean's 3 Oct. 1988: A56

Glass on all windows facing the Cardinal's house would be opaque.
Globe and Mail (Toronto) 15 May 1985: M4

(Presumably windows let in some light: perhaps *translucent* was intended here.)

'I think it's a translucent opera. You can see the motives clearly.'
Globe and Mail (Toronto) 5 Oct. 1985: D5

(The word required here is *transparent*: *translucent* suggests that things can't be seen clearly.)

Another tapered-waist vase in rich red, emerald green, blue and clear glass, fetched a little less—$1,840.
Canadian Collector 21.4 (1986): 30

(Here *clear* means colourless.)

The filigrana technique embeds threads of glass in opaque white or colours within clear glass of another colour.
Canadian Collector 21.4 (1986): 30

(Here *clear* glass is coloured.)

See also IRIDESCENT.

transpire   Plants *transpire*, which means that they release water vapour. More generally, *transpire* means to leak out or to be emitted. In the eighteenth century *transpire* began to be used figuratively of secrets that had leaked out or become known. Used in this figurative way, sometimes 'It transpired that . . .' seemed to mean 'It came about that . . .', and by the early 1800s *transpire* was being used as a synonym for *happen* or *occur*.

Because this newest sense of *transpire* was based on a misunderstanding, it has been bitterly disputed. Some people still regard it as incorrect, even though reputable writers have used *transpire* in this sense for well over a century. Most dictionaries now list 'happen' as a standard meaning, and Canadian writers commonly use the word in this way. However, if you are sensitive to criticism you may want to restrict *transpire* to contexts where 'come to be known' would also fit.

. . . trees transpire—that is, they breathe in dry, carbon-dioxide-laden air and breathe out moisture and oxygen.
Harrowsmith Jun.–Jul. 1985: 27

If events at Queen's Park transpire as expected, Ontario's Lieutenant-Governor faces a difficult decision.
Globe and Mail (Toronto) 4 June 1985: P7

(This is the disputed use.)

Richardson therefore addressed a long and exceedingly tactful letter to McNeill, giving him a full account of what had transpired in Edmonton. . . .
Frederick Gibson *Queen's University* 2 (1983): 141

(This is the disputed use.)

trapes   see TRAIPSE

trawler, troller   *Trawler* and *troller* (pronounced *TRAW ler* or *TROLE er*) both refer to a boat that drags a fish-catching contraption through the water, or to a person who fishes from such a boat. *Trawling* is a type of commercial fishing: a *trawler* is a large boat equipped to catch fish, either by dragging a bag-shaped net (trawl net) along the ocean floor or by trailing a long buoyed line (trawl line) to which are attached short lines with baited hooks. *Trolling* generally refers to a type of sport fishing in which a fishing line, often rotating, is dragged behind a slowly moving boat.

In British Columbia, a distinction is made in the commercial fishery between *trollers*, which fish with baited hooks, and *trawlers*, which fish with a trawl net.

. . . a small dock sheltered a beamy rowboat with a small battery-powered motor for trolling. . . .
Howard Engel *Murder Sees the Light* 1984: 67

They were trolling with downriggers and using a Cisco Kid red-and-white artificial bait when the trophy fish struck.
Whig-Standard (Kingston) 14 Oct. 1986: n.p.

Maritime National Fish Ltd. operated five trawlers, each of which was fitted with an otter trawl for catching fish. . . .
J.E. Smyth et al. *The Law and Business Administration in Canada* 1987: 327

Mr. Fraser offered last week to allocate 35,000 chinook . . . to commercial trollers, with the rest for anglers.
Globe and Mail (Toronto) 19 April 1985: P8

(In British Columbia *trollers* are commercial vessels.)

tread, trod, trodden *Tread* is an irregular verb, with the past tense *trod* and the past participle *trod* or *trodden*:

Don't tread any more mud into the living room.

Yesterday, the whole soccer team trod mud into the carpet.

You've trod(den) on my petunias.

Occasionally, in Canadian and American English, *tread* is treated as a regular verb with the past tense and past participle *treaded*: 'He treaded water for thirty minutes'. *Treaded* is unlikely to arouse much controversy if it is limited to this one aquatic context.

However, a surprisingly large number of writers treat *trod* as the present tense of the verb ('Every time I tango, I trod on my partner's feet'), with the past tense and past participle *trod* or *tread*. This usage is definitely non-standard.

But if judicial attention were turned to the operation of the legislative branch of government, it would have to tread lightly.
Andrew Heard *Canadian Constitutional Conventions* 1991: 99

On their first date, the St. Andrew's Ball, Wilson wore a kilt and trod on her feet on the dance floor.
Saturday Night March 1986: 23

The way ahead led through the bush on a path that had been well trodden at one time, but which was beginning to allow new growth through the packed earth.
Howard Engel *Murder Sees the Light* 1984: 115

He looked at the crystal-dark heavens and treaded water slowly, throbbing up and down as his head circled the sky.
Queen's Quarterly 93.2 (1989): 320

Football observers have long thought that the CFL has treaded on the NFL's toes by expanding into the U.S. with four franchises.
Province (Vancouver) 25 July 1994: A36

(The usual past participle is *trod* or *trodden*.)

Fillion learned to trod the boards here starting with high school plays. . . .
Edmonton Journal 28 April 1994: D3

(The correct form here is *to tread*.)

It's not news that the traditional family is trodding down the dinosaur path.
Vancouver Sun 20 Nov. 1990: B3

(Either 'treading the dinosaur path' or 'trotting down the dinosaur path' would do here.)

. . . Amos continues along the path a growing community of women who emerged in the early '90s have tread, steadily re-inventing the music scene as they go.
Ottawa Citizen 3 Nov. 1994: F1

(The past participle is *trod* or *trodden*.)

Treaty Indian see ABORIGINAL PEOPLE(S)

treble see TRIPLE

trek A *trek* is a long, slow journey, especially one made over land. English borrowed *trek* from the Afrikaans verb *trekken*, meaning to travel or make an organized migration. The word was used to describe the northward migrations of the Boers of South Africa during the eighteenth and nineteenth centuries. Even when it is used humorously, *trek* should connote an arduous journey.

He and the other Klondikers faced a 64 kilometre trek over the notoriously steep White Pass.
Uphere Jan.–Feb. 1990: 33

. . . there was the long journey across Europe from their home villages, then the stormy ocean voyage in the holds of immigrant ships, and finally the trek first by rail and then by ox cart to their prairie homesteads.
Pierre Berton *The Promised Land* 1984: 45

It was a Saturday night near the end of my first rickshaw season when a co-runner and I were making our usual trek back from Hull.
Ottawa Citizen 10 Dec. 1993: C5

tremor, earth tremor, temblor Canadians use *tremor* and *earth tremor* as synonyms for *earthquake*. Americans also use *temblor*, a word borrowed from Spanish. *Tremblor* is a misspelling of the Spanish borrowing; some authorities also consider *trembler* a misspelling, but others accept it as a colloquial term for an earthquake, derived from the verb *tremble*. In formal writing *tremor* is a better choice.

Every few months, many residents of Victoria hear dishes rattling because of barely perceptible earth tremors.
Maclean's 1 May 1989: A59

Meanwhile, the U.S. National Earthquake Information Centre . . . said in a news release that the official magnitude for the first temblor on the Richter scale of earthquake intensity had been revised up to 8.1.
Globe and Mail (Toronto) 26 Sept. 1985: P14

(This report is from an American press agency.)

... the Arctic trembler was nearly as strong as the horrifying San Francisco quake last October.
Uphere Mar.–Apr. 1990: 11

(This usage is informal; in formal writing *tremor* is preferred.)

trigger Commentators accept the use of *trigger* as a verb meaning to set off a process or series of events. However, many complain that it is overused; depending on the context, a word such as *activate*, *initiate*, or *precipitate* may be more appropriate.

> The Norstad statement triggered a chain reaction which was to lead within a few weeks to the demise of the Diefenbaker government.
> George Ignatieff *The Making of a Peacemonger* 1987: 209

See also ACTIVATE, ACTUATE.

trillion see BILLION

triple, treble *Triple* and *treble* are interchangeable both as verbs meaning to make or become three times greater and as adjectives meaning threefold or three-part. *Triple* has also acquired specific associations having to do with sports: 'triples' in baseball, the 'Triple Crown' in horse racing, the 'triple axel' in skating, and the 'triple jump' in track and field, to name but a few. In addition, *treble* has a special musical sense: high-pitched or above middle C. In Canadian English *treble* is used far less commonly than *triple*, but it is sometimes favoured by business writers.

> To root them out, the Montreal immigration office plans to more than triple its inspectors to 20.
> *Gazette* (Montreal) 4 March 1988: B1

> The company will treble Canadian purchases and plans to build a $25-million parts plant north of Toronto.
> *Globe and Mail* (Toronto) 31 May 1985: B6

triumphant, triumphal *Triumphant* refers to people—specifically, those who are victorious and exultant. Objects that commemorate a victory and activities contingent on victory or success are *triumphal*: 'triumphal arch', 'triumphal parade', 'triumphal tour'. People are never *triumphal*, though a mood can be either *triumphant* or *triumphal*.

> But the Soviet leader has emerged triumphant—if battered—from a fight to steer the party toward reform.
> *Ottawa Citizen* 14 July 1990: B4

> We reached London in July 1919 just in time to see a triumphant Lord Haig ride through the city at the head of a parade which marked the victory of British forces over their World War I enemies.
> George Ignatieff *The Making of a Peacemonger* 1987: 31

The triumphal gates were typical of exhibition architecture while the statue was modelled on the Winged Goddess of Samothrace in the Louvre.
Toronto Star 17 June 1987: A6

> With almost triumphal confidence, the PQ will use this weekend to commemorate the 10th anniversary of the referendum and to announce plans for a membership and fundraising drive.
> *Gazette* (Montreal) 17 May 1990: B3

> Their first engagement was at the Three Deuces, the setting for many of Parker's past successes and a fitting site for his triumphal return.
> Jack Chambers *Milestones* 1983: 58

> Conductor Rafael Kubelik made a triumphant return to his native Czechoslovakia after a 42-year absence to open the 45th annual Prague spring music festival.
> *Ottawa Citizen* 14 May 1990: E5

> No, in this Academy Award-winning performance, she came off sounding triumphal, lecturing, like a younger, blonder version of Margaret Thatcher.
> *Province* (Vancouver) 19 July 1995: A22

(Here, in reference to a person, *triumphant* would be better.)

trivial, trivia *Trivial* means insignificant or trifling. The noun form *trivia* is derived from a Latin plural meaning 'unimportant matters'. In English *trivia* is usually treated as a plural form, but few object to its use as a singular.

> In a free society the dull stuff of politics is often the important stuff, but the exciting trivia command the most attention.
> *Vancouver Sun* 23 June 1990: B4

(Here *trivia* is treated as a plural noun.)

> In the end, such trivia is about all we have to work with.
> *Province* (Vancouver) 10 Oct. 1990: 63

(Here *trivia* is treated as a singular noun.)

See also COLLECTIVE NOUNS.

trod, trodden see TREAD

troller see TRAWLER

troop, troupe, trooper, trouper, troops Both *troop* and *troupe* come from the Middle French word *troupe*, 'group' or 'herd'. In modern English *troop* and its variants usually refer to military or uniformed groups of some kind, while *troupe* is reserved for groups of actors or entertainers. Thus a *trouper* is a cavalry soldier or an American state police officer, while a *trouper* is an actor, usually an experienced one who can be counted on to perform well under difficult circumstances. It is this kind of theatrical trouper that the expression *old* (or *real*) *trouper* refers to—someone who carries on through good and bad. Traditionally associated with *troopers* is an aptitude for swearing: 'swears like a trooper'.

Although a *troop* is a military unit, the plural form *troops* usually refers to individuals: for example, '10,000 troops' means 10,000 soldiers, not 10,000 groups of soldiers.

> That ... is what the old trooper hopes as he prepares to play one of his most important roles.
> *Globe and Mail* (Toronto) 27 May 1985: P12

(The correct spelling is *trouper*.)

truculent, truculence The first meaning of *truculent* (pronounced *TRUK yu lunt*) was fierce or savage, as in 'truculent wars', but now *truculent* means defiant or belligerent. The noun form is *truculence* or, rarely, *truculency*.

> The view of public spirit promoted by Thomas Gordon in *Cato's Letters* suggested a more active and truculent citizenship than had been advocated by many others.
> J.A.W. Gunn *Beyond Liberty and Property* 1983: 269

> 'He was quiet, reflective, a little drunk, maybe, a little truculent, but nothing wild.'
> Howard Engel *Murder Sees the Light* 1984: 103

> Tiger was a fighter but his public truculence has been over-emphasized.
> *Province* (Vancouver) 26 Feb. 1990: 27

true facts Facts are true by definition. The phrase *true facts* is redundant except where there is an explicit contrast between alleged facts and true ones.

> Upon learning the true facts, Matheson sued for rescission of the contract and for damages.
> J.E. Smyth et al. *The Law and Business Administration in Canada* 1987: 239

> I watched this episode and was in no way offended, but rather glad that at last the true facts of this campaign were being openly aired.
> *Ottawa Citizen* 14 Nov. 1992: A11

> Once a false idea is in place considerable effort may be needed before the true facts are known.
> William Norton *Human Geography* 1992: 19

> The people of Ontario and York [had] better face the true facts.
> *Toronto Star* 5 Nov. 1992: NY10

(Here *true* is redundant.)

> If George Bush wanted to help his old friend Brian Mulroney, he might direct his ambassador in Ottawa to make a few pointed remarks about these true facts of American political life.
> *Financial Post* 16 April 1991: 13

(Here *true* is redundant.)

> The Romantic poet Clemens Brentano wrote about her extensively, but the Church still seeks the true facts from his writings and others.
> *Catholic Register* 16 Aug. 1986: 5

(Here too, *true* is redundant, but simply dropping the word would not improve the sentence. The intended meaning seems to be 'the Church is still evaluating the testimony of Brentano and others'.)

trust company see BANK

trustee, trusty A *trustee* (pronounced *trus TEE*) is a member of a board that administers a corporation or institution, or a person appointed to administer property in trust. A *trusty* (pronounced *TRUS tee*; plural *trusties*) is a prison inmate who has been granted special privileges in recognition of good behaviour. The adjective *trusty* is an old-fashioned word meaning trustworthy; it may have a slightly comic effect in modern usage.

> Since she requires someone to administer the fund and to pay the money out for his care, she appoints a trustee.
> J. E. Smyth et al. *The Law and Business Administration in Canada* 1987: 288

> He said he initially asked for the assignment ... because he knew it carried with it a highly prized trusty status within the prison system.
> *Winnipeg Free Press* 17 Nov. 1990: 20

try and, try to The expression *try and*, as in 'I'll try and get there soon', is used less in writing and is somewhat less formal than *try to*, as in 'I'll try to get there soon'. Some commentators argue that the construction with *and* is ungrammatical, but it is not an error. Although some critics prefer the infinitive construction (*try to*), *try and* was used as early as 1686 (*OED*)—far earlier than *try to*. Fowler comments that *try and* is 'an idiom that should not be discountenanced'.

> 'I think that we try to do two things,' Professor Wittke concludes. 'We try and look at fundamental problems ... but then we try to do things that are of interest to government agencies and industry as well.'

Perspectives: Profiles of Research at Queen's University 1986: 14

(This speaker uses both constructions.)

Usishkin's brother was among them, but Mike remained behind to try and save some money.
Miriam Waddington *Apartment Seven* 1989: 76

Tsilhqot'in   see CARRIER

tsunami   see TIDAL WAVE

Tsuu T'ina   see SARCEE

tuff, tuft   *Tuff* is a porous rock formed from volcanic ash. A *tuft* is a bunch of hair, feathers, threads, or the like, joined together at one end.

Molokini has Maui's only 'tuff' volcano cone, formed when molten rock superheats water inside the lava, exploding it into ash and dust. When cooled, it hardens into 'tuff,' a spongy, buff-colored rock.
Vancouver Sun 3 Nov. 1990: E6

Another guide [to distinguish the male panda from the female] ... is the tuffs of fur, which are almost like whiskers, on Qing Qing's face.
Globe and Mail (Toronto) 18 July 1985: M1

(The correct spelling is *tufts*. See the example that follows.)

'Tuffs'? Poor little Qing Qing. Imagine having to lug around chunks of volcanic detritus on his whiskers.
Globe and Mail (Toronto) 29 July 1985: P6

(A reader caught the mistake.)

tummy   see BELLY

tundra, Barrens, Barrenlands, taiga   The *tundra*, in Canada also called the *Barrens*, the *Barrenlands*, or the *Barren Grounds*, is a huge region of the northern hemisphere characterized by permafrost, low-lying vegetation, muskeg, low annual precipitation, long dark winters, and short summers of almost continuous sunlight. In Canada the tundra extends from the Mackenzie Delta to James Bay and east to Labrador.
  The Canadian *taiga* is the arc of forest just south of the tundra, consisting of spruce, fir, pine, and tamarack trees, as well as birch and poplar in the more southerly areas.

You can revel in the colorful mosses, lichens and tiny wildflowers of the tundra, the stunted spruce and tamarack forest of the taiga....
Globe and Mail (Toronto) 15 June 1985: T7

But fall is a time of abundance on the Barrens, so we feast on the profusion of ripe berries at our feet.
Uphere Mar.–Apr. 1990: 26

All my reading had not prepared me for one strange thing about the Barrenlands: you always have the feeling that the land is somehow sentient, watching you.
Uphere Jan.–Feb. 1990: 43

And now the provincial government has just opened the Parc des Grand Jardins, a tract of mountains, forest and taiga that supports a caribou herd and is home to dozens of rare species of plants and flowers.
Gazette (Montreal) 14 July 1990: I3

See also SWAMP, MARSH, BOG, MUSKEG.

tuque, toque   *Tuque* (the vowel pronounced as in *too* or *few*) is a Quebec French variant of the French word *toque*; originally it referred specifically to the long knitted hat worn by voyageurs and habitants. Adopted into English, it came to refer not only to these hats but also to any plain knitted woollen winter hat. Some writers spell this word *toque*, but *toque* (pronounced *TOKE*) has several other senses, including a chef's hat and a close-fitting brimless woman's hat.

Grab your tuque and head to the Experimental Farm's arboretum to see some of Canada's best young cross-country skiers.
Ottawa Citizen 4 March 1990: A3

An ordinary toque and small earmuffs have been adequate when I am moving.
Uphere Mar.–Apr. 1990: 16

[The] chef, Shamash Brooks, is a Rastafarian. (His toque has an extra big balloon top to hold the dreadlocks.)
Calgary Herald 3 Aug. 1994: B7

turgid, turbid, limpid, pellucid   *Turgid* means swollen or distended; it is generally used figuratively to describe writing that is pompous or bombastic. *Turbid* means muddy or cloudy; it is a less common word than *turgid* and is most often used literally. The two words can appear in similar contexts, literal and figurative. A river in flood can be both turbid (muddy-coloured) and turgid (swollen beyond its banks). A poor piece of prose may be both turbid (unclear or obscure) and turgid (stuffy and overwritten). However, these words are not synonyms.

Both *limpid* and *pellucid* mean clear (the opposite of *turbid*), and are used of liquid, eyes, literary style, etc.

> We all know of refereed journals that publish articles of inferior quality, that are dry as dust, turgid and predictable, and of unrefereed journals that are outstanding and have sparkle.
> *Queen's Quarterly* 92.2 (1985): 442

> Water in the Capilano and Seymour reservoirs is also turbid, which means Vancouverites will see cloudy water coming from their taps for the next while.
> *Vancouver Sun* 27 Nov. 1990: A1

turn off, turn out   see CLOSE

turnpike   see ROAD

twister   see CYCLONE

tycoon   *Tycoon* was the honorific used by foreigners in the mid-nineteenth century to refer to the powerful Japanese shoguns. In English it became a popular term for describing any powerful leader. Since the 1920s *tycoon* has usually referred to a business magnate, and this meaning is standard.

At the end of the decade a gift of $50,000 from Samuel Insull, the Chicago utilities tycoon, helped to make possible the establishment of a department of preventive medicine and public health....
Frederick Gibson *Queen's University* 2 1983: 33

typhoid fever   see TYPHUS

typhoon   see CYCLONE

typhus, typhoid fever   *Typhus* and *typhoid fever* are sometimes confused. In fact, typhoid fever was once thought to be a form of typhus, but now it is understood that the two diseases are caused by completely different micro-organisms.

Typhus is caused by various bacteria of the genus *Rickettsia* and spread by three kinds of insects: lice, fleas, and ticks. Ticks spread the variety of typhus known as Rocky Mountain Spotted Fever.

Typhoid fever, also known as enteric fever, is caused by the bacterium *Salmonella typhi*. It is spread by infected food, water, or food-preparation workers; the most notorious of the latter was 'Typhoid Mary', a cook who was the source of an outbreak of typhoid in the U.S. in the 1930s. *Typhoid fever* can now be prevented by immunization.

Both diseases are characterized by fever and red spots on the skin (hence the initial confusion), and if untreated may lead to delirium and death. Typhoid fever also causes diarrhea and intestinal hemorrhaging.

U

Ukrainian, Ukraine   *Ukrainian* is often misspelled *Ukranian*. *Ukraine* has been preferred to *the Ukraine* since the country became independent, in 1990, because the definite article suggests a geographic area ('the Caribbean', 'the Arctic', 'the Maritimes') rather than a political entity ('Scotland', 'Angola').

> Independence has also created a burst of self-confidence that has spurred Ukranian officials to challenge Moscow on the most fundamental issues.
> *Calgary Herald* 28 Jan. 1992: A4

(The correct spelling is *Ukrainian*.)

Russian separatists in the Crimean peninsula of Ukraine have said delineation of the border with Russia could trigger armed resistance.
Vancouver Sun 24 June 1992: A8

In the spring of 1944, the Red Army came crashing into the Ukraine and the lands bordering the Black Sea.
Canadian Journal of History 14.1 (1989): 79

(In this historical reference *the Ukraine* is appropriate.)

See also YUKON.

Ulster   see IRELAND

ultimate see PENULTIMATE

ultimatum, ultimatums, ultimata The usual plural of *ultimatum* is *ultimatums*. *Ultimata*, the Latin plural, is also correct but rare.

> He said no ultimatums had been presented to Prime Minister Brian Mulroney.
> *Province* (Vancouver) 16 Feb. 1990: 31

> ... the forthcoming campaign ... would, after all, have been launched with or without ultimata by the Liberal Senate.
> *Toronto Star* 31 July 1988: B3

See also PLURALS, REGULAR, IRREGULAR, FOREIGN.

unaffected see DISAFFECTED

unaware, unawares *Unaware* and *unawares* both date from the sixteenth century, and used to function interchangeably as both adjectives and adverbs. Now *unaware* is usually an adjective, and is often followed by *of* or *that*: 'She is unaware of our visit'; 'He is unaware that she is here'. *Unaware* now rarely functions as an adverb. *Unawares* is obsolete as an adjective, but is the usual choice for adverbial use, as in 'stumble on something unawares' or 'be caught unawares'.

> ... three different specialists had been prescribing drugs for her, each unaware of what the other was doing.
> *Gazette* (Montreal) 4 March 1989: A1

> Many companies are developing policies on sexual harassment and those who aren't may find they are caught unawares.
> *Province* (Vancouver) 22 May 1990: 49

> But in less than a week Magnus came home in the forenoon, catching me unawares.
> David Williams *Eye of the Father* 1985: 88

unbeknownst, unbeknown Usage commentators variously maintain that these words are dialectal, slang, humorous, or pretentious. Since *unbeknownst* and *unbeknown* are widely used in neutral contexts, you may ignore the controversy.

> The trade can also be revoked if the player is seriously ill or injured, unbeknownst to the team acquiring him.
> *Financial Post* 19 Oct. 1989: 51

> Unbeknownst to you, the plant could harbour such scourges as scale or mealy bugs.
> *Canadian Consumer* Jan. 1986: 14

> Unbeknown to me, Peggy had persuaded mother that having one child so totally dependent on someone who was not part of the family was unhealthy....
> George Ignatieff *The Making of a Peacemonger* 1987: 22

> They ... couldn't care a fig for any of the four outsiders that each has, unbeknown to the others in the family, invited down for the weekend.
> *Vancouver Sun* 8 March 1990: D6

uncharted, unchartered *Uncharted* means unmapped, unknown. *Unchartered* is a rare word meaning not furnished with a charter, unauthorized. People often mistakenly substitute *unchartered* for *uncharted* in such expressions as 'uncharted territory' and 'uncharted waters'.

> ... the American ship of state drifted irrevocably toward the rocks and threatened to drag other nations into the uncharted waters of political uncertainty.
> William Teatero *John Anderson: Fugitive Slave* 1986: 111

> Long before [the charter was issued], however, the board of the still unchartered university at Kingston had been constituted under the Act of Incorporation.
> Hilda Neatby *Queen's University* 1 (1978): 28

> Those are unchartered waters for the Blue Jays, their fans and Canada.
> *Daily News* (Halifax) 5 Oct. 1992: 44

(The word required here is *uncharted*.)

> When they get really old and ready to die, they wander off to a secret site in some unchartered jungle wilderness.
> *Gazette* (Montreal) 2 Sept. 1992: A2

(The word required here is *uncharted*.)

underbar see E-MAIL ADDRESSES

under way, underway Canadians write *under way* and *underway* for the adverb with about equal frequency: 'We got under way/underway at about noon'. Since the two-word form is older, it might be a better choice in formal writing.

> ... at a time when the survival of Britain was in serious doubt and negotiations were under way for the possible transfer of the government to Canada, Mr Massey insisted on absolute perfection of style and tone in all his utterances.
> George Ignatieff *The Making of a Peacemonger* 1987: 62

> A big new project underway in Winnipeg is *The Forks*, a development in the historic area at the juncture of the Red and Assiniboine rivers.
> Alan Tucker, ed. *The Penguin Guide to Canada* 1991: 466

undiscriminating see INDISCRIMINATE

undoubtedly, undoubtably *Undoubtedly* is an idiomatic expression meaning certainly or very likely. *Undoubtably* is a rare word meaning in a way that precludes doubt ('tests showed undoubtably . . .'). Sometimes *undoubtably* is used where idiom calls for *undoubtedly*.

> . . . Dryden was arguably hockey's greatest goalie and undoubtedly its greatest pontificator.
> *Vancouver Sun* 29 June 1993: D8

> Other great greys include Spectacular Bid, undoubtably one of the best race horses of all time. . . .
> *Canadian Thoroughbred* Aug. 1989: 15

(The word required here is *undoubtedly*.)

> A tax of $100 for every tonne of carbon dioxide released into the atmosphere would undoubtably hit hard in Alberta. . . .
> *Vancouver Sun* 23 March 1990: B2

(The word required here is *undoubtedly*.)

unemployment insurance see POGEY

unequivocal, unequivocally, [unequivocable], [unequivocably] *Unequivocal* means unmistakable, unambiguous. The adverb form is *unequivocally*. *Unequivocable* and *unequivocably* are nonstandard variant forms of these words.

> A resolution will go before the UN Security Council in the next few weeks, but it is still unclear whether it gives an unequivocable green light to the use of force against Iraq.
> *Ottawa Citizen* 21 Nov. 1991: A1

(The standard spelling is *unequivocal*.)

> But if some companies or sectors are unequivocably shown to be taking advantage of the tax changes to gouge the public, they could be named as doing so.
> *Financial Post* 29 June 1990: 13

(The standard spelling is *unequivocally*.)

> Despite a recent court decision that struck down a comparable bylaw in Toronto, the committee states unequivocably: 'Municipalities do have the right to regulate the display of pornography . . .
> *Gazette* (Montreal) 29 April 1985: B2

(The standard spelling is *unequivocally*.)

See also AMBIGUOUS, AMBIVALENT, EQUIVOCAL.

unexceptionable, unexceptional, exceptionable *Unexceptionable* means not open to criticism or objection; *unexceptional* means ordinary. An unexceptionable speech is irreproachable, while an unexceptional speech is lacklustre. The rare word *exceptionable* means giving cause for objection.

> Although the cleaning of the Sistine Chapel ceiling is complete, controversy still goes on about the project. . . . By now, most art historians and conservators have found the restoration procedures unexceptionable. . . .
> *Vancouver Sun* 11 Jan. 1992: D10

> The Bootle Freemans were similarly unremarkable, leading lives as unexceptional as those of any of their neighbors.
> *Calgary Herald* 13 Feb. 1994: B7

> The statement that an exotic dancer's 'profession is to promote lust' is not, on its own, exceptionable; that is indeed why such dancers are hired.
> *Globe and Mail* (Toronto) 13 Feb. 1985: P6

> Manning's support for free-market economics is unexceptional; his preference for balanced budgets is an admirable goal, difficult for any government to accomplish.
> *Financial Post* 26 June 1991: 11

(The intended sense appears to be *unexceptionable*, beyond reproach.)

unhuman see HUMAN

unilateral, bilateral, multilateral An action that is undertaken by one party is *unilateral*; by two parties, *bilateral*; and by three or more, *multilateral*. Generally these terms are applied to the acts of institutions or states rather than of people: 'unilateral declaration of independence', 'bilateral agreement'. But lately people as well as institutions have been accused of making 'unilateral (i.e., unnegotiated) decisions'.

> We should deal with the United States more often in multilateral forums to 'blunt (American) unilateral policies,' the foreign policy report recommends.
> *Toronto Star* 15 Nov. 1994: A1

uninterested see DISINTERESTED

unique *Unique* means one of a kind or different from all others. Hence some critics maintain that it should not be used with modifiers such as *very*, *most*, or *more*, since nothing can be 'very' or 'more' one of a kind. Note, however, that something or someone can be almost or nearly one of a kind, and that *unique* has also been used as a synonym for terms such as *unusual, distinctive, exceptional, outstanding*, and *remarkable* since the early seventeenth century (*OED*). In this sense it can be modified. Although Canadian writers use *unique* in both ways, in formal writing the safest course is to use it only in the first sense.

> The rate at which these coastal, old-growth trees are being cut means that this unique forest is disappearing just as the tropical forests are.
> Irving M. Zeitlin and Robert J. Brym *The Social Condition of Humanity* 1991: 369

(Here *unique* means one of a kind.)

> She is almost unique among Quebec writers in that her work has been translated into twelve languages.
> Margaret Atwood *Second Words* 1982: 259

(Here *unique* means one of a kind.)

> Perhaps the most unique attribute of this volume is the coverage given to the history of Japanese intelligence by Ian Nish and John Chapman.
> *Canadian Journal of History* 14.1 (1989): 87

(Here *remarkable* or *outstanding* would be a better choice.)

> Everywhere you look there is a very unique use of textured plaster, brick and hewn beams.
> *Leisure Life* 1988: 88

(In formal writing *very* should be omitted.)

See also COMPLETE; PERFECT.

United Church The United Church is Canada's largest Protestant denomination. It was formed in 1925 through the union of the country's Methodists and Congregationalists with most of its Presbyterians. This denomination exists only in Canada. *United* (or *United Church*) is often used as an adjective: 'We're United; they're Catholic'.

> In worship, Sunday-school classes and conferences, United Church members will soon be dissecting television and newspapers while exploring the church's 1990-91 mission theme: Gospel, Culture & Media: Where Do We Get Our Values?
> *Vancouver Sun* 14 July 1990: A11

> '[My mother] was United Church.'
> Bruce Meyer and Brian O'Riordan, eds. *In Their Words* 1984: 138

See also MANSE.

United Empire Loyalist   see CONSERVATIVE

United Kingdom   see BRITAIN

United States   see AMERICAN

university, school, faculty, college, collegiate, community college, CEGEP   A *university* provides post-secondary education leading to degrees in a range of subjects; at the core of the university curriculum are the liberal arts and general sciences. Most Canadian universities grant graduate degrees and carry out advanced research. Within a university, a *school* focuses on a particular area of study: 'school of business', 'school of urban planning'. A *faculty* is a group of departments focused on a particular branch of knowledge: 'faculty of medicine', 'of law', 'of engineering'. The teaching staff of a university is referred to as the *faculty*, or *faculty members*.

In Canada a *college* is either a private high school, part of a university, or a community college. Within a university, a college usually has its own teaching staff, classrooms, and residence. Unlike Americans, Canadians seldom use *college* as a synonym for *university*. Since many high schools in Ontario are called *collegiate institutes*, the term *collegiate* is as likely to refer to secondary as to post-secondary education.

Community colleges, found in all provinces and both territories, were first established in the 1960s to provide post-secondary education, including vocational and technical courses, relevant to the needs of the community. Community college programs usually grant diplomas, but most also offer remedial education and a limited range of first- and second-year university courses. A few offer university degrees. In Quebec a community college is called a *CEGEP* (pronounced *SAY zhep*), an acronym for 'Collège d'enseignement général et professionel'.

unlawful   see ILLEGAL

unmoral   see IMMORAL

unorganized   see DISORGANIZED

unpractical   see IMPRACTICAL

unravel   see RAVEL

unreadable, illegible, indecipherable All three words can refer to a text that cannot be read because the person who wrote it had bad handwriting, the publisher produced it in tiny type, etc. However, only *unreadable* can be used to describe material that is legible but so dull or poorly organized that no one can bear to read it.

The price for a pound is large, the price for a kilogram is small, sometimes so tiny it is almost illegible.
Globe and Mail (Toronto) 24 Oct. 1985: A1

... his plays were performed only in living rooms or read, like the covert samizdat works of banned Russian artists, on secretly-circulated typescripts that became fainter and fainter with every photocopying so that by the sixth or seventh edition of these 'un-books' on onion-skin, the text was practically unreadable.
Vancouver Sun 6 Jan. 1990: E3

Theal and other historians of southern Africa who wrote long and detailed narratives were often unreadable.
Queen's Quarterly 92.1 (1985): 225

(Here *unreadable* means that no one can read these historians with any pleasure.)

unrepairable see REPAIRABLE

unsanitary, insanitary *Unsanitary* is preferred in Canadian English; *insanitary* is rare. Both forms of this word are common in American English. In Britain *insanitary* is the usual form.

unsatisfied, dissatisfied Both terms imply that someone or something is left unfulfilled. *Unsatisfied* is more often applied to things (hunger, debt, curiosity, etc.), to suggest that a demand remains unfulfilled or a condition unappeased. *Dissatisfied* almost always describes people and implies a personal or emotional response of discontent. At a restaurant, John's dinner may leave his hunger unsatisfied (or unappeased), but that does not necessarily mean that he is dissatisfied with his meal. At art school, Mary may be personally dissatisfied with her drawings, even though they do not leave the requirements of her course unsatisfied. *Dissatisfied* is the more common word, and its connotations of disgruntlement are stronger.

The reader cannot help thinking that Sachs could not have been unaware of Violette's painful desire for him, or without pleasure in leaving it unsatisfied.
Miriam Waddington *Apartment Seven* 1989: 185

... the FDA could refuse to allow Canadian blood into the United States for processing if it remains unsatisfied

with the Canadian Red Cross's handling of the blood it collects.
Ottawa Citizen 7 Sept. 1994: A3

Sometimes, then, both parents will be dissatisfied with the psychologist's conclusions.
Ottawa Citizen 18 Nov. 1994: B6

But it was not long before more militant feminists ... became dissatisfied with mere legislative fairness.
Queen's Quarterly 94.1 (1987): 3

'I see a lot of subcontractors who are unsatisfied because they're not going to get the business,' committee chairman Gay Helmsing said, referring to three businesses that have lodged verbal complaints and a stack of written complaints.
Leader-Post (Regina) 27 Feb. 1988: A3

(Discontented people are usually described as *dissatisfied*.)

unsociable see ANTISOCIAL

unsolvable see SOLUBLE

until, till, 'til, up until, until such time In current usage *until* is by far the most common form in all varieties of writing. *Till*, however, is just as respectable, and is not the short form that some people believe it to be; in fact, *till* was the earliest form of the word. *Until* is almost always preferred as the first word in a sentence. An abbreviated form of *until*, the poetic *'til* is sometimes found in advertising copy and breezy, tongue-in-cheek writing. It should not be used in serious contexts. Both *til*, without an apostrophe, and *'till*, with one, are spelling errors.

The phrase *up until* is objected to by some critics who judge the *up* unnecessary. As well, *until such time as* is considered verbiage, since *until* itself means up to the time of. But shorter is not always better; sometimes these longer expressions can improve the rhythm of a sentence.

Until recently, there was reason for cautious optimism.
Business Journal June 1991: 1

Till recently, I too held this myth dear to my heart.
Henry M. Rosenthal and S. Cathy Berson, eds.
Canadian Jewish Outlook Anthology 1988: 282

(*Till* is unusual at the beginning of a sentence.)

So shop 'til you drop; your country's economy is counting on you.
Financial Post 8 Dec. 1989: 9

'If you think sales are bad now, wait 'til you see the beginning of next year because they are going to get a lot worse.'
Vancouver Sun 9 Nov. 1990: C5

We had a lazy lunch and didn't fish again 'till evening.
Atlantic Salmon Journal Autumn 1990: 24

(Since it is not a short form, *till* does not require an apostrophe.)

Up until quite recently, the creative person, say in literature, was typically one who 'wanted to write', and what he wanted to write was usually poetry or fiction.
Northrop Frye *The Modern Century* 1990: 99–100

(Some critics object to *up until*.)

Until such time as we can pluck the fetus from a woman's body and give it life, should we not entrust the destiny of that fetus to the person whose body holds it and allow that person to be responsible to God?
Calgary Herald 21 Feb. 1988: D4

(Some critics object to *until such time as*.)

See also WORDINESS.

unwieldy, [unwieldly] *Unwieldy* is the accepted and common form of the word meaning cumbersome or awkward. *Unwieldly* is sometimes used in speech and newspaper writing, but is not listed in contemporary dictionaries. The *OED* conjectures that *unwieldly* originated as a typographical error.

The tax specialist owes much of his worth to his clients to the enormous complexity of tax laws; the lawyer is similarly indebted to a cumbersome and unwieldly legal system as is the accountant to an equally cumbersome and unwieldly set of accounting rules....
Financial Post 4 Jan. 1990: 9

(The accepted spelling is *unwieldy*.)

up Some usage guides object to the use of *up* as a verb meaning increase ('They upped their prices overnight'), but dictionaries list this sense without comment. It is more common in newspapers and magazines than in formal or academic prose. The expression *up and* ('They just up and left') is very informal and rare in print.

Pete also autographed the photo, upping its value.
Gazette (Montreal) 13 May 1990: D3

When Louis Riel touched off the Saskatchewan rebellion in 1885, White began to churn out extras, hiring gangs of boys to turn the press and upping the price to a quarter.
Pierre Berton *The Promised Land* 1984: 171

See also UNTIL.

Upanishads see SACRED WRITINGS

up until see UNTIL

upward(s) see -WARD(S)

urban, urbane *Urban* means having to do with cities or towns. *Urbane* describes manners that are smooth, refined, and courteous—manners that were once associated with city-dwellers.

I was urbane, witty, cocky, capable of the greatest heights.
Max Braithwaite *The Night We Stole the Mountie's Car* 1971: 13

Urdu see HINDU

-us Some people mistakenly assume that all nouns borrowed from Latin that end with *-us* should form their plurals with *-i*, along the pattern of *stimulus, stimuli* (see also PLURALS, REGULAR, IRREGULAR, FOREIGN). In fact, the Latin words *apparatus, census, conspectus, hiatus, impetus, nexus, plexus, prospectus, sinus*, and *status* do not change to form their plurals. Thus the Latin plural of *impetus* is simply *impetus* (not *impeti*); the English plural is *impetuses*. All these words are best pluralized with *-es*: 'My sinuses are killing me'.

Another group of Latin nouns ending in *-us* form their plurals by changing a vowel and adding *-ra*: *corpus, corpora*; *genus, genera*; and *opus, opera*. These words can also be made plural by adding *-es*: *corpuses, genuses, opuses*.

A third group of nouns with the *-us* ending are either pseudo-Latin or Latin expressions other than nouns in their base form. The only way these words can be made plural is by adding *-es*: *ignoramus, ignoramuses*; *minus, minuses*; *omnibus, omnibuses*; *rebus, rebuses*.

A fourth group of nouns derived from Latin simply never take Latin plurals: *bonus, bonuses*; *chorus, choruses*; *campus, campuses*; *circus, circuses*; *virus, viruses*.

Finally, some *-us* nouns are late Latin renderings of Greek words and are made plural by adding *-es*: *hippopotamus, hippopotamuses*; *octopus, octopuses*; *platypus, platypuses*; *rhinoceros, rhinoceroses*.

use, usage The definitions of the nouns *use* and *usage* overlap to some extent, but *use* applies to any act of using or being used, whereas *usage* suggests a pattern of habitual use by a number of people. To use *usage* when *use* will do ('his usage of my driveway') is to risk sounding pompous. With respect to language, *usage* refers to established or customary patterns of language use; in law a *usage* is a customary practice—for example, a standard business practice—that may be taken into consideration in a judicial decision.

> Lum Bim yesterday became the latest and the biggest name among China's record-setting women swimmers to be suspended for drug use.
> *Toronto Star* 8 Dec. 1994: D6

> In 1989 and 1992, the Seniors Drug Action Program studied drug-usage patterns of 2,000 B.C. long-term care residents....
> *Vancouver Sun* 1 Nov. 1994: A12

> So the word has been turned on its head in American usage and now a 'liberal' is regarded by many Americans as being close to socialist, if not communist.
> *Ottawa Citizen* 30 Dec. 1994: A8

> ... the traditional distinctions between usage, binding convention, and positive law may seem over-simplified and inadequate to describe the many informal rules that give substance to constitutional structures and processes.
> Andrew Heard *Canadian Constitutional Conventions* 1991: 15

> [The book's] herculean usage of primary sources and relevant statistics is truly impressive.
> *Canadian Journal of History* 14.1: 122

(Here *use* would be a better choice than *usage*, since no group behaviour is implied.)

See also UTILIZE, USE.

used to In speech it is difficult to distinguish between *used to* and *use to* in expressions such as 'The water level used to be higher' and 'She used to walk to work' because the *d* is not pronounced. Consequently, the *d* is sometimes forgotten in writing.

Complications arise when *used* is combined with *did* or *didn't*. In these cases some usage guides prefer *use to*, noting that just as we would write 'She didn't want to swim', and not 'She didn't wanted to swim', so we should write 'She didn't use to swim' rather than 'She didn't used to swim'. Others argue that *used to* is now an invariant form. *Webster's Dictionary of English Usage* suggests that *didn't use to* is the more common form in American writing. The British *Longman Guide to English Usage* suggests

that *didn't used to* is preferable. In Canadian writing *didn't used to* appears to be more common than *didn't use to*, but neither form of the expression is common in writing except in representations of speech. *Never used to* is always an acceptable way of sidestepping the controversy.

> She used to recall with nostalgia the natural beauty which surrounded her during her happy childhood.
> George Ignatieff *The Making of a Peacemonger* 1987: 9

> 'I use to pretend I was Canadian skater Lynne Nightengale.'
> *Gazette* (Montreal) 4 March 1989: T10

(Only *used to* is standard.)

> The record-breaking point was a special moment for the east Vancouver kid, who use to sneak into Empire Stadium to watch Lion kickers.
> *Vancouver Sun* 21 Aug. 1990: C1

(Only *used to* is standard.)

> Senators didn't used to be embarrassed by their office.
> *Ottawa Citizen* 3 Oct. 1990: A2

> She didn't used to get bored.
> Margaret Atwood *Life Before Man* 1979: 240

> Fort Washington, Penn., didn't use to be a household name but through the magic of television advertising it is becoming well known, too much so.
> *Ottawa Citizen* 11 May 1990: C16

> [Writing essays is] all too much like homework, which I never used to get done on time either....
> Margaret Atwood *Second Words* 1982: 11

See also SUPPOSED TO.

UTC see GREENWICH MEAN TIME

utilize, use The verb *utilize* usually suggests an especially clever or effective use of something. Where the meaning is merely 'make use of', *use* is recommended.

Utilise is a British spelling seldom seen in Canadian writing.

> The upgraded ground station will utilize remote sensing technology to improve management of natural resources and monitoring of the environment.
> *Province* (Vancouver) 22 Nov. 1990: 51

> Foot traffic utilizes pathways through rank growth.
> *Vancouver Sun* 7 July 1990: E1

(Here a simple 'walkers *use*' or 'pedestrians *use*' might be clearer than 'foot traffic *utilizes*'.)

See also -IZE, -ISE.

V

vacation   see HOLIDAY

vaccination   see IMMUNIZATION

vacillation   see AMBIVALENCE

vacuity, vacuousness   Both forms of this noun, which means emptiness or stupidity, are standard. Some commentators suggest using *vacuousness* only to refer to a vacant facial expression, but Canadian writers do not appear to observe this distinction, using either term in any context.

A truly happy ending (and a more mythically Canadian one as well) would have had them acknowledging the vacuity of Montana as a goal ... and confronting their real fates in Winnipeg.
NeWest Review Oct.–Nov. 1989: 49

The most frightening portrait is Cole's, whose face and, especially, eyes are like a mask—rather, not a mask at all, because there's nothing in all that scary vacuity to hide.
Vancouver Sun 3 May 1990: D8

The minute the great unwashed did what until recently only movie stars and marquesas could enjoy, the utter vulgarity and vacuousness of that lifestyle hit home.
Maclean's 28 Aug. 1989: A9

vagary, vagaries   A *vagary* (the plural form, *vagaries*, is more common) is an unpredictable action or an eccentric whim. The usual pronunciation in Canada and Britain is *VAY guh ree*; *va GAIR ee* is common in the United States.

... it was at least as hard a century ago as it is now for people of conventional mind to recognize that a man can be interested in the vagaries of sexual behavior without wishing to practise them himself.
Robertson Davies *A Voice from the Attic* 1960: 270

vale, veil   A *vale* is a valley, although this old-fashioned term is now seldom used except in place names such as 'River Vale'. 'Vale of tears' is a poetic reference to the world as a place of sorrow and trouble.

Something that conceals or obscures, like the gauzy fabric that may hang from a woman's hat, is a *veil*. To 'take the veil' is to become a nun.

valorous   see -OUR, -OR

value-added tax   see AD VALOREM

valve   see TAP

vanguard   see AVANT-GARDE

variation   see WORDINESS

various   Some usage commentators object to the use of *various* as a pronoun, as in 'I spoke with various of the delegates'. They argue that *various* is an adjective and should not be used as a pronoun. While comparable terms such as *several*, *some*, *many*, and *few* have shifted to pronoun use and are now undisputed in that capacity, *various* is still rarely used as a pronoun in Canadian writing, and most dictionaries do not list it as one.

Meanwhile he called on various of his friends in Toronto who were also friends of Queen's....
Hilda Neatby *Queen's University* 1 (1978): 273

(Some would omit the *of his* and use *various* as an adjective: 'He called on *various* friends'.)

See also FUNCTIONAL SHIFT; VARIOUS DIFFERENT.

various different   *Various different* is an idiom meaning 'several different'. However, the phrase grates on many people's ears because the primary meaning of *various* is different or diverse. In formal writing *several different*, or *various* or *different* alone, is recommended.

The view is consistent with treating the various different correct descriptions of reality as complementary rather than competitive.
Canadian Journal of Philosophy 19 (1989): 307

(Here *several different*, or *various* alone, would be better.)

See also WORDINESS.

vase Canadians pronounce this word *VAHZ*, *VAYZ*, or *VACE*. The first is the usual British pronunciation; the second is primarily Canadian; and the third is chiefly American.

Vedas see SACRED WRITINGS

vegetarian, ovolactovegetarian, lactovegetarian, vegan *Vegetarian* is the broadest term for a person who does not eat meat. Vegetarians who do eat eggs and dairy products are sometimes called *ovolactovegetarians*. *Lactovegetarians* drink milk but will not eat eggs. Someone who refuses to eat or use any animal products (including leather and fur clothing) is called a *vegan* (pronounced *VEJ un* or *VEE gun*).

veil see VALE

venal, venial A *venal* person can be bribed; a *venal* system is corrupt. *Venial* faults are trivial and easily excused; *venial* sins—unlike mortal sins—are not punishable by damnation. Unlike *venal*, *venial* is never applied to people.

> ... anyone who wanted to get rid of a tiresome relative (perhaps to gain access to his money) had but to bribe a couple of venal apothecaries, and the deed was done....
> Robertson Davies *A Voice From the Attic* 1960: 116–17

> ... most of the faux pas are the venial sins of omission.
> *Globe and Mail* (Toronto) 7 Dec. 1985: D3

venue *Venue* (pronounced *VEN yoo*) has been used for centuries in legal parlance to refer to a location. A judge may order a change of venue for a trial, fearing the defendant cannot be fairly tried in the locale where the crime was committed; or *venue* may refer to the scene of a crime. Only in this century has the use of the term broadened so that concerts, special events, and public meetings can be said to take place in a certain venue. Some commentators disapprove of this use, probably because it is new. Interestingly, though *venue* is borrowed from French, in that language it doesn't refer to a location; rather, it means arrival or coming.

> An Ontario Supreme Court judge has ordered a change of venue for the trial of two youths who were charged as juveniles in October, 1982, with first-degree murder....
> *Globe and Mail* (Toronto) 30 Jan. 1985: M3

(This is an example of common legal usage.)

> When city people buy an old farm, not just as a venue for lawn parties but because they're converts to country life, they usually get carried away.
> *Harrowsmith* Aug.–Sept. 1985: 52

> The bottom has dropped out of Nova Scotia's only arts centre, the province's sole full-time venue for entertainment of a national or international calibre.
> *Gazette* (Montreal) 1 March 1989: C11

veranda(h) see PORCH

verbal, oral *Verbal* usually means spoken, as in the legal expressions 'verbal contract' and 'verbal order'. But *verbal* does have another meaning, which can sometimes cause confusion. Any communication in words—whether it is spoken or written—can be described as *verbal*. In this sense *verbal* can be contrasted to *physical, spatial,* or *mathematical*. To eliminate the ambiguity, some editors insist that only *oral* be used to distinguish spoken from written communication, and that *verbal* be used to mean 'in words'. Although this recommendation isn't widely followed, it does make sense, in literary criticism or in discussions of language itself, to refrain from using *verbal* to mean *oral*.

Oral, besides meaning spoken, as in 'oral examination', can refer to anything to do with the mouth: 'oral surgery', 'oral hygiene'.

> Verbal proposals were permissible, but a letter was much to be preferred because it could be kept for future reference.
> Robertson Davies *A Voice from the Attic* 1960: 85

> Yet nowhere in all of the correspondence or in the contractual agreements ... was a pledge of secrecy asked for or given. Preston insisted he'd made a verbal commitment to the directors....
> Pierre Berton *The Promised Land* 1984: 233

> Reality, in this fifteen-chapter novel, becomes a species of verbal confetti.
> Janice Kulyk Keefer *Reading Mavis Gallant* 1989: 83

(Here *verbal* means having to do with words, in this case written.)

> Nabokov writes with style, and style—as distinguished from verbal and syntactical foppery, which is sometimes mistaken for it—gives a dimension to a book which can be disquieting when exercised on such a theme as this.
> Robertson Davies *A Voice from the Attic* 1960: 245

(Here *verbal* means having to do with words, in this case written.)

The written prose ... doesn't have the excitement of the verbal version, and so, it is argued, the journalist, particularly if he is writing for TV or radio, should try for more of that, by using the patterns of ordinary speech.
W.C. Lougheed, ed. *In Search of the Standard in Canadian English* 1986: 91

(Here *spoken* or *oral* might be more precise than *verbal*.)

verbal phrases, verbs with prepositions see PHRASAL VERBS

verb–subject agreement see AGREEMENT, GRAMMATICAL

veritable Although *veritable* literally means real or true, it usually modifies metaphors rather than statements of literal fact. Its function is to assure readers that no matter how exaggerated the metaphor may seem, it is appropriate.

We ... were soon clawing our way through veritable dunes of gold dust.... There was gold here by the bagful.
Atlantic Salmon Journal Autumn (1990): 28

The explosion of literary output in Quebec in the 1960s was followed by a veritable flood of translations.
Ben-Z. Shek *French-Canadian & Québécois Novels* 1991: 136

One had a raffia bag on her lap, a veritable cornucopia from which she drew mandarins, biscuits, and candy to bribe her two small boys on the seat behind.
Queen's Quarterly 96.2 (1989): 353

See also LITERALLY, FIGURATIVELY.

vermin *Vermin* is a collective noun for offensive or injurious insects, animals, or, figuratively, persons. Occasionally it refers to a single creature.

In the backyard of this same building, a deserted mother and two children shared a woodshed with rats and other vermin.
Pierre Berton *The Promised Land* 1981: 294

It seems [he] found a rat in his garden and dispatched the vermin with a broom handle.
Toronto Star 16 Nov. 1994: E6

See also COLLECTIVE NOUNS.

vernacular The *vernacular* is everyday language as it is spoken in a particular place, as opposed to formal, literary usage. To use the vernacular, therefore, means to use natural, unstuffy, conversational language. Perhaps because a good deal of slang

makes its way into everyday language, writers sometimes use a phrase such as 'in the vernacular', or 'to use the vernacular', to apologize for introducing slang into their writing.

In the Renaissance the term *vernacular* referred to the language spoken in a particular country—English, French, German, etc.—as opposed to Latin, the universal language of scholars and the church.

In the stories in this issue of CFM, I see the vernacular is still alive. The colloquial voice which speaks for the human condition is loud in Saskatchewan.
Canadian Fiction Magazine 64 (1988): 6

In their early years they had been sodbusters, to use the vernacular, and she had hated it.
Pierre Berton *The Promised Land* 1984: 161

Marcel's paranoid ravings about being chased by policemen (dogs, in the Quebec vernacular) ... are far more dramatic....
Gazette (Montreal) 13 June 1992: D10

'In the vernacular, cut the crap in future issues.'
Catholic Register 23 Aug. 1986: 4

Yiddish has always been the vernacular, everyday language spoken by the Jews of Eastern Europe. Hebrew was the language of learning, prayer, and ritual.
Miriam Waddington *Apartment Seven* 1989: 74

See also COLLOQUIAL; FORMAL, INFORMAL; STANDARD.

vertigo, vertiginous *Vertigo* is pronounced with the stress on the first syllable (*VER ti go*) and refers either to physical dizziness or to a dizzy, confused state of mind. The adjective *vertiginous* (pronounced *ver TIJ in us*) means suffering from dizziness, or dizzying: 'vertiginous cliffs'.

very, much Most adjectives can be intensified with *very* ('very pretty', 'very large', etc.), but often past participles cannot. The past participle is the verb form that follows *has*, *have*, and *had*, as in 'has teased', 'have eaten', or 'had discussed'. Often these forms are used as adjectives ('the teased puppy', 'the half-eaten cookie'). Many of these participial adjectives, including such common words as *excited*, *interested*, *pleased*, *surprised*, and *tired*, have become fully established and are regularly modified by *very*. Others, though, retain some of their verbal quality and are customarily modified by a different adverb, such as *much*, *greatly*, *highly*, or *thoroughly*: 'much debated', 'much loved', 'much travelled', 'greatly appreciated', 'highly admired', 'thoroughly disliked'. If you think that *very* sounds odd in front of a particular participial adjective, try substituting one of these adverbs; if it fits, it is almost certainly a better choice.

vest   To *vest* means to confer on or charge with. Financial control, authority, property rights, etc., are vested *in* a person or group. For example, the chancellor of a university awards degrees by virtue of the authority vested *in* him or her. A person or group is vested *with* these rights or powers: 'The government is vested with budgetary control'. A 'vested interest' is the legal right to the present or future enjoyment of a property or benefit, or, metaphorically, a personal stake or selfish interest in a particular arrangement or system.

> Thus the Lieutenant Governor is vested with the prerogatives of the Crown for all aspects relevant to the governing of the province.
> Andrew Heard *Canadian Constitutional Conventions* 1991: 17

> The fact is, present politicians have such an enormous vested interest in the status quo it is ridiculous to expect them to even consider fundamental change.
> *Financial Post* 13 May 1991: 11

viable   The primary meaning of *viable* is capable of living and developing. Thus living thing such as infants and plants, and by extension businesses and nations, may be described as *viable*. Some critics disapprove of describing inanimate things, such as plans, alternatives, and products, as *viable*; however, dictionaries now list economically sound, workable, practicable, and reasonable as standard meanings of the word. A few commentators recommend giving *viable* a rest and instead choosing among these alternatives.

> ... it appears that the human infant is born when it is because its head size has attained the limit compatible with viable birth.
> Irving M. Zeitlin and Robert J. Brym *The Social Condition of Humanity* 1991: 12

> The company said it will consider resuming production when the price of gold returns to an economically viable level.
> *Globe and Mail* (Toronto) 8 Jan. 1985: B18

vial, phial   These are variants of the same term for a small bottle, often used to contain medicine or perfume. *Phial* is pronounced with an initial f

sound. Both words are standard in Canadian, American, and British dictionaries, but Canadian writers prefer *vial*.

> The doctor also gave a vial of blood to a policeman.
> *Gazette* (Montreal) 19 July 1990: B5

> ... a phial of white powder and a syringe are part of the library display.
> *Globe and Mail* (Toronto) 7 March 1985: CL4

vicar   see RECTOR

vicarage   see MANSE

vice, vise   *Vice* and *vise* both rhyme with *mice*. Most North American writers distinguish between depravity, *vice*, and a clamp, *vise*, but the British use *vice* for both meanings.

> Truly, this is an instance where vice loses half its evil by losing all its grossness.
> Robertson Davies *A Voice From the Attic* 1960: 281–2

> She gripped my arm as if in a vise and led me to the bus stop.
> *Canadian Fiction Magazine* 63 (1988): 92

> ... he held us off with one hand while the other clamped a vice around our pet's muzzle, twisting it upside down....
> *Room of One's Own* June 1990: 4

(Most Canadians use *vise* for this sense.)

vicious circle, vicious cycle, vicious spiral   One meaning of *vicious circle* is a fault of logic in which a proposition is used to establish a conclusion, which is in turn used to prove the original proposition (see also BEG THE QUESTION, another term for circular reasoning). Since the early nineteenth century, *vicious circle* has also been used to describe situations in which the short-term solutions to problems only aggravate the original problems. *Vicious cycle* is also used to describe this pattern of self-perpetuating ill effects. *Vicious spiral* often describes an inflationary economy.

> Awards of damages for professional negligence have led to extensive use of liability insurance; because of uncertainty concerning liability and the risk of heavy damages, insurance premiums are steadily increasing. Professional fees, in turn, must increase to cover insurance costs. As fees increase, clients expect more for their money, and when they are disappointed are much more likely to sue. The process is something of a vicious circle.

J.E. Smyth et al. *The Law and Business Administration in Canada* 1987: 99–100

'I have no appetite in the morning.' It's a vicious circle. A person who has long abandoned the breakfast habit isn't going to be hungry in the morning.
Chatelaine April 1986: 30

Once out of prison, a heroin addict had to begin the vicious cycle of crime all over again to feed his or her habit. . . .
Province (Vancouver) 6 July 1990: 3

. . . the inflationary impact of currency declines could lead to a vicious spiral of depreciation and inflation.
Globe and Mail (Toronto) 17 Jan. 1985: B7

victuals, vittles *Victuals*—the term is almost always pluralized—means food and provisions. It is pronounced *VIT uls*, which accounts for the non-standard variant spelling *vittles*. The discrepancy between the standard spelling and the pronunciation dates from the sixteenth century, when scholars altered the Old French borrowing *vitaille* to make it resemble its Latin root, *victualia*. The new spelling included a *c*, but the pronunciation remained unchanged.

Infrequently, *victual* functions as a verb: 'The army was victualled for a long expedition'.

Records at Moose Factory show that on Christmas Day, 1705, each four-man mess had been doled out enough victuals to make the York Factory rations look like a snack.
Globe and Mail (Toronto) 19 Oct. 1985: A10

On the way out, patrons can purchase vittles they just can't live without from a food boutique.
Globe and Mail (Toronto) 26 Sept. 1985: E9

(This spelling is supposed to have a humorous effect.)

. . . clerks in the victualling office were ordered to burn Byng in effigy. . . .
J.A.W. Gunn *Beyond Liberty and Property* 1983: 274

villain, villein A *villain* is a scoundrel, someone of depraved or criminal character. *Villein* is a historical term for a peasant in medieval England. Villeins were bound in servitude to their feudal lords but were free in their relations with all others. *Villain* is sometimes misspelled *villian*, perhaps because of the influence of *ruffian*, or perhaps because -*ian* is such a common word ending ('Kantian', 'Canadian'). *Villain* is pronounced *VILL un*; *villein* may be pronounced *VILL un*, *VILL ane*, or *vill ANE*.

violin see FIDDLE

virago *Virago* (pronounced *vi RAH go* or *vi RAY go*) is derived from a Latin word meaning 'warrior maid' and was first used in English in a complimentary sense, referring to a heroic woman. By 1387, however, *virago* had acquired derogatory connotations, and Chaucer used it to mean a loud-mouthed and bad-tempered woman. Feminists, such as those who run Virago Press in England, are attempting to revive the original connotations of *virago*. The plural is *viragos* or *viragoes*.

Eugenie turned out to be a frigid virago who hated sex yet who gained enough influence over her husband to goad him into his most disastrous foreign policy adventure, in Mexico.
Maclean's 3 Oct. 1988: A51

Virago Press, the feminist publishing house from London, England, is marching into its second decade with an impressive list of books that intend to 'illuminate and celebrate all aspects of women's lives.'
Globe and Mail (Toronto) 26 Jan. 1985: E17

See also -OS, -OES.

virgin birth see IMMACULATE CONCEPTION

virgule see SLASH

virtu *Virtu*, also spelled *vertu* (pronounced *vir TOO*), is the love and knowledge of rare, beautifully crafted artistic objects, or the quality of excellence distinguishing such articles, or the collectible articles themselves.

Esther Shipman requests our attendance at Virtu, an exhibition of furniture and fittings by a mixed bag of young industrial designers, architects, artists and craftspeople. . . .
Globe and Mail (Toronto) 12 Jan. 1985: E11

virtuoso, virtuosic, virtuosity *Virtuoso* is a term that has always teetered between high praise and disparagement. From the seventeenth century to the nineteenth, *virtuoso* meant both scholar and dilettante, connoisseur of the fine arts and frivolous collector of arty objects. The meaning most familiar today dates from the eighteenth century: someone with outstanding technical skill in playing a musical instrument or singing. This meaning is equivocal, however, because technical excellence may be considered either the basis of the highest achievement in music or the prop of a sterile performance. The domain of the word *virtuoso* has broadened in the twentieth century: a contemporary Canadian virtuoso is as likely to wield a hockey stick as a violin bow.

The plural of *virtuoso* is either *virtuosos* or *virtuosi*. The adjective form of the noun, *virtuosic*, is uncommon; more often writers use the noun as an adjective: 'virtuoso performance'.

Virtuosity is the talent of the virtuoso, not moral goodness or virtue.

'Everybody tried to be a virtuoso. The drummer who played the fastest, the trumpeter who blew the highest—they were the best.'
Jack Chambers *Milestones* 1983: 131

The musicians who earn Davis's highest praise are always those who articulate melodies by a few carefully placed notes rather than by virtuoso runs at great speed.
Jack Chambers *Milestones* 1983: 33

Without virtuoso individual skills, team play becomes both virtue and necessity, and what others understand as unselfishness is really cold-eyed realism.
Ken Dryden *The Game* 1983: 85

From the first flirtatious encounters to the final, rapturous pas de deux, they gave one of the virtuoso performances that have made them the company's most popular new partnership.
Saturday Night May 1986: 61

There is no self-preening here, no virtuosic critical warbling.
Queen's Quarterly 92.1 (1985): 146

He has consistently been overlooked by critics because he lacks the virtuosity of his contemporaries.
Jack Chambers *Milestones* 1983: 66–7

virus   see FLU

vis-à-vis   *Vis-à-vis* is pronounced *VEEZ a VEE*. The accent over the *a* is sometimes omitted from English-language texts, but the hyphens should be used. Literally, this French borrowing means 'face to face with', but in contemporary use it more often means in relation to, in comparison with, or concerning.

The intensity of the sectarian divisiveness in Canadian towns, both religious and political, is an example: what such groups represent, of course, vis-à-vis one another, is 'two solitudes,' the death of communication and dialogue.
Northrop Frye *The Bush Garden* 1971: 226

The Great Ape Project is controversial largely because it demands a huge leap in our thinking about ourselves vis-a-vis the rest of the living world.
Toronto Star 6 Nov. 1994: C8

... your staff should get a copy of Halifax's ineffectual and unenforced legislation vis-a-vis restaurants.
Daily News (Halifax) 18 Sept. 1994: 28

vise   see VICE

visible minority, people of colour, non-white
Some writers use the term *visible minority* very broadly to include any group whose appearance may be used as a basis for discrimination, including people with disabilities, members of racial minorities, and women. Others use the term only for those who do not belong to the majority racial group. However, *minority* is a misleading and unsatisfactory term, for it implies that the group it designates matters less than the majority. Further, many populations who are labelled in this way are in fact the majority. For example, First Nations peoples constitute the majority of the population in the north. However, those belonging to such groups are treated as if they were a 'minority', so the term has a certain metaphorical aptness.

People of colour refers to those who do not fall into the category *white*, and is preferred to *non-white*, which implies that white is the norm. *Women of colour* is a term used by feminists in particular to characterize women struggling against both racism and patriarchal authority.

Another striking limitation in the university system is its accessibility for people of colour.
Rites March 1990: 9

Canadian employers feel 'quite free' to discriminate against non-white people, a federal New Democratic Party task force was told....
Globe and Mail (Toronto) 7 March 1985: M5

(Here *non-white* should be replaced with *people of colour*.)

I think that many women today, including poor women, and women of colour, poor or not, are able to tap into a collective reclamation of at least some of the components that make home.
Room of One's Own June 1990: 36

See also BLACK; INDIAN; RACE; SEXUAL MINORITIES.

visionary In Canadian English *visionary* is most often used as a complimentary term for someone far-sighted and imaginative. Yet most dictionaries and usage guides define a *visionary* negatively as a dreamer whose plans and ideas are unrealistic and impractical; and commentators suggest that a person with unusual foresight be called 'a person of vision' rather than 'a visionary'. Nevertheless, *visionary* and 'person of vision' are often used interchangeably. Similarly, while the dictionary definition of the adjective *visionary* is 'impractical and unrealistic' or 'seen in a vision', the adjective too is now most often used to mean far-sighted and imaginative.

Bruce Firestone was called a visionary and a maverick, an impulsive dreamer with out-of-this-world ideas.
Province (Vancouver) 11 Dec. 1990: 37

(Here *visionary* is used in a negative sense.)

Throughout the dismal autumn of 1864, through hours of suspicion-tinged clashes, they carefully narrowed the focus of their talks from the visionary to the pragmatic.
Maclean's 1 July 1991: A70

(Here *visionary* is somewhat negative.)

Kristin, born during an eclipse of the moon, is a visionary who can see things that aren't there.
Margaret Atwood *Second Words* 1982: 238

(Here *visionary* is nearly neutral.)

I have said nothing of William Blake, a very great visionary poet who seemed mad to many of his contemporaries.
Robertson Davies *One Half of Robertson Davies* 1978: 175

(Here *visionary* has favourable connotations.)

Elsewhere the author shows him as a visionary, 'a pioneer of invention,' whose influence far exceeded the number of works he produced.
Queen's Quarterly 92.2 (1985): 399

(Here *visionary* has favourable connotations.)

There is a need for people who are visionary, energetic, outgoing and who are willing to knock on doors.
Canadian Baptist Feb. 1986: 9

(Here *visionary* has favourable connotations.)

Visionaries in the computer field ... are setting new goals for machines that challenge some of the highest of human capabilities.
Globe and Mail (Toronto) 28 Nov. 1985: B2

(Here *visionary* has favourable connotations.)

visit, visit with British usage guides criticize the phrase *visit with* as a wordy variant of *visit*. However, in North America the phrase *visit with* has a slightly different meaning from *visit*. It means to chat or talk with, and is occasionally used even in reference to telephone conversations.

They've visited all 10 dealerships in town, searching for the best price.
Calgary Herald 31 Dec. 1994: E3

Current club and federation leaders should visit with their predecessors, to delve into the historical perspective....
Snowmobile Canada 1991 Buyer's Guide: 4

(Here *visit with* means 'talk to'.)

See also VISITATION.

visitation, visit *Visitation* is a formal word for a formal visit. It may be used in reference to pastoral calls made by members of the clergy, to official visits such as ship inspections, or to the visits made to a funeral home to pay last respects to a deceased person. In North America 'visitation rights' are court orders allowing parents without custody to visit their children.
The Visitation (capitalized) refers to the visit that the Virgin Mary paid to Elizabeth before the birth of Jesus (Luke 1: 39-56). A *visitation* can also be an affliction 'visited' upon someone by God, or a divine inspiration.
Visitation should not be used as a fancy synonym of *visit*, though it is sometimes used humorously to describe an unwelcome visit.

U.S. courts are coming up with tortured solutions like awarding divorced parents 'joint custody' of their frozen embryos (nothing so far about visitation rights).
Winnipeg Free Press 17 Nov. 1990: 58

Will its purported visitation from the Holy Spirit manifest itself in ways other than ecstatic physical surrender?
Toronto Star 4 Dec. 1994: A1

'Maybe we will [move] one day, but we like our Oxfordshire home so much, and would miss terribly the perpetual visitations from our sons and their wives and the grandchildren.'
Globe and Mail (Toronto) 16 Nov. 1985: E6

(Here *visits* would be more appropriate—unless the writer is being humorous about these 'perpetual' visits.)

visual arts   see ARTS

vittles   see VICTUALS

vocal, voluble   *Vocal* means produced by the voice, as in 'vocal music'. It also means expressive, unguarded in speech, or outspoken. *Voluble*, from the Latin for 'rolling', means characterized by a rapid or steady flow of speech. Although *voluble* can overlap with *vocal* in this sense, it does not necessarily suggest outspokenness, nor does it mean loud.

> The most vocal conservatives were the Fascist parties of Italy, Germany, Spain, France, and England.
> *Queen's Quarterly* 96.3 (1989): 601

> Roosevelt had made enemies and his critics were vocal.
> *Gazette* (Montreal) 31 Dec. 1994: H3

> Galley, affable as well as voluble, has had a lot to talk and yip and be high-tempo about this season. . . .
> *Ottawa Citizen* 19 May 1990: E1

> On issue after issue the government's critics . . . are voluble on what they are against but silent or vague about what they are for.
> *Gazette* (Montreal) 18 Oct. 1990: C1

> (Here *vocal* or *outspoken about* would be better.)

vocation, avocation   Taken from the Latin for 'calling', a *vocation* is a primary occupation, job, or profession. The prefix *a-* means 'away from' in Latin; thus an *avocation* is a diversion from one's calling—an occupation pursued for enjoyment, or a hobby.

> His introduction to law (his vocation) and politics (his avocation) came in the legal offices of John Sandfield Macdonald, Ontario's first premier.
> *Globe and Mail* (Toronto) 16 Nov. 1985: E17

> I should like to think of myself as a writer in a country where a writer is recognized as a man with a vocation and not merely as a man with a hobby.
> Robertson Davies *One Half of Robertson Davies* 1978: 138

> . . . gardening is one of the few careers where it's possible to combine an avocation with a vocation.
> *Globe and Mail* (Toronto) 22 June 1985: H7

vociferous   see VORACIOUS

volley   see BARRAGE

voluble   see VOCAL

vomit   see SICK

voracious, vociferous   *Voracious* means gluttonous, insatiable, or very eager about some activity. It comes from the Latin verb *vorare*, 'to devour'. *Vociferous* means noisy, clamorous, or forceful in expressing one's views. It derives from the Latin verb *vociferari*, 'to cry out'.

> Although a struggling reader is unlikely to become a voracious bookworm, you can help him improve by reading to him. . . .
> *Chatelaine* June 1986: 32

> The combination of fear, rain, mud and voracious mosquitoes in the black of night had its effect: the next year, we purchased a more reliable truck.
> *Harrowsmith* Oct.–Nov. 1985: 54

> This [season] is ideal for field trips, preferably in the early morning when bird song is most vociferous. . . .
> *Chronicle-Herald* (Halifax) 14 May 1988: 11

> . . . the unanimous and vociferous condemnation of this proposal by the provincial justice ministers caused the initiative to die an unpublicized death.
> Andrew Heard *Canadian Constitutional Conventions* 1991: 113

vouch, avow, vouchsafe   To *vouch* for a statement is to stand behind its truth. To *vouch* for a person is to confirm his or her integrity. To *avow* means to admit, acknowledge, or declare openly. Thus to *avow* that someone is honest and true is to *vouch* for that person's character.

Vouchsafe is a formal word meaning to give or to grant, as one would a favour. Sometimes it is misused to mean say, attest, or confirm.

> The books mentioned . . . are vouched for by Miss Hackett as having attained this sale, though in some cases their success was not immediate.
> Robertson Davies *A Voice from the Attic* 1960: 360

> Hoadly was quite conspicuous as a Whig who clearly and frankly avowed that the king and the two houses of Parliament were 'co-ordinate.'
> J.A.W. Gunn *Beyond Life and Property* 1983: 133

> Such truth as we are vouchsafed is a truth of disconnections and lacunae.
> Janice Kulyk Keefer *Reading Mavis Gallant* 1989: 160

To read *Hurly-Burly* is to be vouchsafed an entry into the otherwise closed universe of big-league journalism.
Gazette (Montreal) 17 Feb. 1990: K2

What these ideas were, Peres would not vouchsafe—although they appeared to involve the composition of the Palestinian delegation to peace talks.
Vancouver Sun 25 Jan. 1990: A3

(Here *vouchsafe* is misused to mean divulge.)

... the people who are victims of long lenses, bugging and taped telephone calls are rarely ordinary citizens asleep in small flats. As Diana, Charles et al. can vouchsafe.
Maclean's 1 Feb. 1993: 13

(Here *attest* or *confirm* would be more appropriate.)

voyageur   see COUREUR DE BOIS

vulnerable   The standard pronunciation is *VUL nur a bul*—with an audible *l* in the first syllable.

W

Wade-Giles   see PINYIN

waffle   see LIE

waiter, waitress, server, wait staff   Restaurants today are making less use of the gender-marked terms *waiter* and *waitress*, perhaps because they are required to use a gender-neutral term when they advertise such positions (see JOB TITLES). The preferred term for food-service staff in major Canadian restaurant and hotel chains is *server*. *Wait staff* is also used as a collective noun. *Waiter* is only very occasionally applied to female staff.

Francine Lachapelle, a server in a tiny coffee shop in Old Montreal, said women are discriminated against even in some of their more traditional jobs....
Gazette (Montreal) 11 June 1990: A9

Part of it is the genuine friendliness of the wait-staff, the apparently unforced delight that they take in the fact that of all restaurants, you have chosen this one.
Vancouver Sun 11 Oct. 1990: F21

Caesar's Palace and Restaurant manager ... wanted only female waiters.
Province (Vancouver) 25 May 1990: 21

See also COLLECTIVE NOUNS; JOB TITLES; SEXIST LANGUAGE.

wait on, wait for   To most Canadians the verb *wait on* means to serve, but in some dialects *wait on* also means wait for. This second sense of *wait on* appears in Canadian writing only in fictional representations of speech and should probably be avoided in formal writing. Curiously, there is a highly formal use of *wait on* meaning 'wait for' that has escaped censure: to wait on a board or governing body is to await its official decision or action.

An obsolescent meaning of *wait on* is to call on or pay a respectful visit to.

I'm waiting on UIC benefits and keep hoping Orville, who owns this place, will get an opening so he can give me a job.
Canadian Fiction Magazine 64 (1988): 106

... three separate and independent agencies ... had to wait on the unpredictable movements by the benevolent but often apparently somnolent monster at Whitehall.
Hilda Neatby *Queen's University* 1 (1978): 33

(This is the formal use of *wait on*.)

In 1881, when there were only two women undergraduates, one Mr. Anderson was appointed 'a committee' to wait on the ladies and ask them to attend the meetings of the society.
Hilda Neatby *Queen's University* 1 (1978): 209

(This is the obsolescent meaning of *wait on*.)

waitress, wait staff   see WAITER

wait up   To *wait up*, meaning to slow down or stop so that someone can catch up, is a colloquialism common in Canadian but not in British English. In British English the usual meaning of *wait up* is to delay going to bed until someone returns; Canadians tend to say *stay up*.

waive, wave, waivers To *waive* means to relinquish ('waived our right to sue') or to refrain from enforcing ('waived the dress code for the day'). To *wave* something aside is to dismiss it, as with a wave of the hand. In professional sports, to be *waived* or put on *waivers* is to have your contract offered to other clubs.

Lourdes hospitals offer food and lodging for the sick, who are charged 60 francs a day, although the fee is waived for those too poor to afford it.
Catholic Register 16 Aug. 1986: 9

But Judge McFarlane waved aside his objections, saying that 'he was listening and noting carefully' what was taking place.
Globe and Mail (Toronto) 31 May 1985: P13

(Here *waved aside* means dismissed perfunctorily.)

Parrott didn't say so in the House, but the project would also be waived past the Environmental Protection Act, which meant that it would be built with virtually no legislative or public scrutiny.
Harrowsmith Aug.–Sept. 1985: 32

(Here *waived past* appears to be a confusion with *waved past*. Alternatively, the author could have written that proper procedures would be *waived*—put aside or not enforced.)

He picked up winger Martin Gelinas on waivers from the Quebec Nordiques. . . .
Vancouver Sun 16 June 1994: F3

wangle   see WRANGLE

want for   see LIKE FOR

wapiti   see MOOSE

-ward(s) When directional words such as *downward(s)*, *inward(s)*, *outward(s)*, *toward(s)* and *upward(s)* function as adjectives, they do not end in *s*: 'a downward glance'. When they function as adverbs, they may or may not end in *s*: 'She looked downward(s)'. Canadians do not strongly favour one form of the adverb over the other. The British generally prefer the *-s* adverbs, Americans the shorter forms.
   Backward(s) is a special case. Canadians use both *backward* and *backwards* as adjectives. *Backward* means shy ('a backward child'), or slow to develop, or towards the back ('a backward pass'). The adjective *backwards* means back-to-front: 'I think that's backwards'; 'He went about it in his usual backwards way'.

Wind shear is a sudden shift in wind speed and direction due to a rapid downward rush of cooled air.
Calgary Herald 30 Dec. 1992: B1

(Here *downward* is an adjective.)

Over the last few weeks rates across the board have trickled downward—again.
Toronto Star 26 Dec. 1992: F1

(Here *downward* is an adverb; *downwards* would be equally acceptable.)

According to the Conference Board survey, increases to base pay are moving downwards.
Ottawa Citizen 12 Dec. 1992: J1

(Here *downwards* is an adverb; *downward* would be equally acceptable.)

Where she used to be backward and shy, she now asserts herself as a full shareholder in the collaboration with Eisler.
Toronto Star 7 Feb. 1992: C5

Well, time for another of our backwards critiques. (This column was always slightly cockeyed.)
Gazette (Montreal) 25 June 1992: D1

Old Backwards Knees [the ostrich] isn't the most attractive of God's creatures.
Gazette (Montreal) 28 June 1992: B6

See also AFTERWARD(S).

warp, weft, woof On a loom, the *warp* threads are the ones that run lengthwise and are repeatedly crossed by the *weft* (or *woof*) threads. *Warp and weft* (or *warp and woof*) is often used figuratively with the same sense as *fabric*.

Bias garments are cut ... with the grain arrows aligned to the fabric's true bias, the 45-degree angle mid-way between warp and weft.
Toronto Star 24 March 1994: C4

'Canadian Pacific is part of the warp and woof of Canadian history.'
Maclean's 24 Feb. 1986: 47

warranty   see GUARANTEE

WASP *WASP* is an acronym for 'White Anglo-Saxon Protestant' and is often used as a shorthand reference to the Canadian elite. Some have objected that it is inaccurate when applied to white Canadians in general or the elite in particular, since many are neither Anglo-Saxon nor Protestant. Although it is frequently found in contexts where it cannot be read as derogatory, some consider the term slighting; therefore it should be used with care. Normally *WASP* is written in capitals to avoid confusion with the insect.

It is about WASP migrants almost exclusively, virtually ignoring the large number of ethnic pioneers. . . .
The Beaver Dec. 1989–Jan. 1990: 44

(Here *WASP* is used fairly neutrally.)

I soon deduce that I'm not the only wasp at the table.
Globe and Mail (Toronto) 26 Sept. 1985: E9

(Here, in a story about the insect, the writer is using the word humorously.)

William Wasp, she used to call him, fondly enough, before she realized that he found it a racial slur.
Margaret Atwood *Life Before Man* 1979: 20

Would the editors of The Gazette kindly consider a moratorium on the use of the term 'WASP'—especially in the context of the 'anglo-Canadian business establishment'. . . ?
Gazette (Montreal) 2 Sept. 1990: B3

See also ABBREVIATION; CELT, ANGLO-CELTIC.

wastage, waste   *Wastage* is loss caused by wear and tear, leakage, evaporation, decay, illness, and so on. The word does not imply human mismanagement and should not be used as a fancy synonym for *waste*—which is the reckless use of resources.

The result is that MAP packaged products have a much longer shelf life resulting in less food wastage and easier inventory control.
Daily News (Halifax) 7 March 1994: 15

(Here *wastage* means spoilage.)

Britain's poor health performance and its poor economic performance 'have common roots in the social divisions and wastage of human skills and abilities among a substantial proportion of the population,' Wilkinson maintains.
Toronto Star 14 May 1994: B2

(Here *waste* would be better: poor use is being made of people's skills.)

watershed, divide   Canadians use *watershed* to refer to the region drained by a single river system, or to a slope that drains in one direction. In this they differ from Fowler, who maintained that a watershed is the line of high land from which water flows into two different river systems or oceans. Canadians, like Americans, usually call this line of high land a *divide*. However, Canadians use *watershed*

figuratively in all kinds of writing to mean a turning point or critical turn of events, a sense derived from the one that Fowler preferred.

The focus could shift almost immediately to the Stein watershed, an 1,160-square-kilometre wilderness region the province has slated for development.
Globe and Mail (Toronto) 4 Nov. 1985: N4

Just north of Sunwapta Pass lie the Columbia Icefields, a continental divide that separates waters heading to the Pacific and Arctic Oceans from those heading to Hudson Bay.
Gazette (Montreal) 5 May 1990: J1

The Franklin expedition of 1845 was the watershed of Britain's arctic epic.
Arctic 41.1 (1988): 46

It was a watershed in the child-welfare system, and a victory for the native people of Manitoba.
Saturday Night April 1986: 35

waterspout   see CYCLONE

wave   see WAIVE

wax   One sense of the verb *wax* is to grow or become. Things that 'wax and wane' grow and shrink. Perhaps because the phrases 'to wax poetic' and 'to wax eloquent' are common, some people incorrectly assume that to *wax* means to speak; this assumption is made obvious when they modify the word with an adverb such as *eloquently*, even though no one would write 'become eloquently' or 'grow eloquently'.

Attendance in the public galleries, mostly senatorial aides, waxed and waned. . . .
Province (Vancouver) 6 Dec. 1990: 13

Our consumer panelists didn't wax poetic, though, as they ran the five stirrers through their paces.
Canadian Consumer Jan. 1986: 21

. . . foreign residents wax eloquently about having to pay $13 for a bunch of asparagus at one of the currency grocery stores.
Ottawa Citizen 21 Oct. 1990: W3

(The word required here is the adjective *eloquent*.)

It is true that many *philosophes* . . . waxed enthusiastically about the virtues of the Chinese empire which they perceived to be a rationally disciplined and ordered society run by mandarin intellectuals.
Canadian Journal of Sociology 14.2 (1989): 263–4

(The word required here is the adjective *enthusiastic*.)

we, us, our   see CASE

wean   To *wean* means to accustom a young mammal to food other than its mother's milk. *Wean* is also used figuratively to refer the process of detachment from any habit, dependence, etc. The usual prepositions for both these uses are *from*, *away from*, and *off*. A new, non-standard meaning of *wean* has established itself in journalism and informal writing. In this use, *wean* is usually followed by *on*.

Many reformers ... tried to wean women from superficial criteria of beauty and to promote health and exercise....
Queen's Quarterly 92.2 (1985): 426

It is never easy to wean the secretive away from their bad habits, but it is worth all the effort we can put into it.
Globe and Mail (Toronto) 2 Jan. 1985: P6

The Canadian game of hockey was weaned on long northern winters uncluttered by things to do.
Ken Dryden *The Game* 1983: 134

(Here 'born of' might be better.)

Question is, can a generation weaned on kiwi learn to love Brussels sprouts?
Chatelaine April 1986: 2

(In formal writing *raised* would be better.)

Growing up in the postwar era of unprecedented prosperity, boomers were weaned on the promise that if they were smart and willing to work, opportunities would abound....
Financial Post 21 Oct. 1991: 11

(In formal writing 'raised with the idea that' would be better.)

See also OVERWEENING.

wear, wore, worn   The past tense of *wear* is *wore* and the past participle is *worn*. The use of *wore* as a past participle, as in 'She has wore it ever since', is dialectal, as is the construction 'to wear something on somebody', meaning to dress someone (usually a child) in something: 'I wore his little vest on him'.

He wore a black patch over his right eye.
Robert Kroetsch *Badlands* 1975: 114

He hasn't worn a raincoat.
Margaret Atwood *Life Before Man* 1979: 23

weft   see WARP

weird   *Weird* means supernatural or unearthly, or, by extension, unusual or strange. Some critics object to the extended sense, but it is now standard. *Weird* is derived from the Old English noun *wyrd*, meaning 'fate' or 'destiny'. In *Macbeth* Shakespeare used the noun as an adjective, calling the three witches the 'weird sisters'; hence the modern use of *weird*. *Weird* is commonly misspelled *wierd*, because it does not follow the *i* before *e* spelling rule.

The blaze began in earnest then, with flickering fingers of flame lighting up the room and throwing weird, dancing shadows on the wall.
Dogs in Canada Special Issue 1986: 90

Honey Harbour to the south and Go Home Bay (weird names but great country) to the north also have summer churches.
United Church Observer June 1986: 22

... *Weather Watch* is loaded with wierd and fascinating facts and trivia like the true story of how a group of glider pilots turned into human hailstones!
Province (Vancouver) 13 May 1990: 96

(The correct spelling is *weird*.)

See also -IE-, -EI-.

Welsh, Welch   The current spelling for someone or something from Wales is *Welsh*; the older spelling *Welch* now survives in the name of the Royal Welch Fusiliers. The slang verb *welsh* or *welch*, meaning to fail to pay a debt or to go back on a promise, is now considered a slur against people of Welsh descent.

Opera lovers may see the Welsh National Opera Company perform Bellini's Norma....
Globe and Mail (Toronto) 5 Jan. 1985: T2

... Mr. Graves went to France to fight as an infantry captain with the Royal Welch Fusiliers during the First World War.
Globe and Mail (Toronto) 9 Dec. 1985: D14

He accused the federal Government of trying to 'fuzzify and welsh out' on the negotiation roles that it agreed to at the first ministers' meeting in Halifax last week.
Globe and Mail (Toronto) 5 Dec. 1985: A3

Edwards was 'a four flusher,' 'a tin horn,' and 'a welcher on poker debts.'
Pierre Berton *The Promised Land* 1984: 271

went   see GO

were   see IF I WERE YOU; SUBJUNCTIVE

west   see EAST, WEST, NORTH, SOUTH

West Indian   see INDIAN; WEST INDIES

West Indies, Caribbean   There is no established distinction between the terms 'the West Indies' and 'the Caribbean'. In the strict geographical sense, they refer only to those islands within or bordering on the Caribbean Sea, namely the Greater Antilles—Cuba, Jamaica, and Hispaniola, containing Haiti and the Dominican Republic—and the Lesser Antilles, the chain of islands extending from the Virgin Islands to Curaçao.

However, cultural and political discussions of the West Indies or the Caribbean, particularly those associated with the British colonial heritage, sometimes include the Bahamas and Bermuda and the mainland countries of Belize (formerly British Honduras) and Guyana (formerly British Guiana).

Caribbean is frequently misspelled; remembering that it is derived from the name of the Carib Indians, who inhabited the West Indies when Columbus arrived, may help with the spelling. The usual pronunciation of *Caribbean* is *kair i BEE un*, but *kuh RIB ee un* is equally acceptable.

> But the two young men were basking in an unmistakably Caribbean atmosphere. The town house was filled with the pungent smell of a West Indian fish fry. . . .
> *Maclean's* 29 April 1991: T8

> The meeting was aimed at strengthening century-old trade ties between Canada and Caribbean nations such as Barbados, Belize, Guyana, Trinidad and Tobago, Jamaica and Grenada.
> *Financial Post* 20 March 1990: 3

> (Here Belize and Guyana are included in the Caribbean.)

> Although Florida, Bermuda, Mexico and Venezuela are not technically part of the Caribbean, they are considered as Caribbean destinations by many travel agents and tour operators.
> *Gazette* (Montreal) 19 Dec. 1992: C1

> The Commonwealth Best First Book award, worth $4,000, went to Bahamian author Robert Antoni, also from the Carribean and Canada region.
> *Toronto Star* 5 Nov. 1992: A2

> (The correct spelling is *Caribbean*.)

wetlands   see SWAMP

Wet'suwet'en   see CARRIER

when   see IS WHEN

where   see IS WHEN, IS WHERE; SEE WHERE

-where, -place   The adverbs *anywhere*, *everywhere*, *somewhere*, and *nowhere* are used on both sides of the Atlantic, but the variants *anyplace* and *someplace* (especially 'someplace else', 'anyplace else') are common only in Canada and the United States. British authorities label the *-place* variants unacceptable, while the Americans defend them. In Canada *anyplace* and *someplace* are common in speech, but they are decidedly less formal than *anywhere* and *somewhere*, the only forms to appear in formal writing. *Anyplace* and *someplace* appear occasionally in fiction and the press. *Noplace* and *everyplace* are rarely used.

> You're not going to find this much entertainment value anyplace else.
> *Toronto Star* 13 June 1994: A2

> I hear sirens far away urgently going someplace.
> *Queen's Quarterly* 93 (1986): 70

> And it will happen again next year, someplace else, for the same reasons. . . .
> *Daily News* (Halifax) 18 June 1994: 19

whereas   The conjunction *whereas* has two different meanings. In the preamble of a formal proclamation or resolution it means 'in view of the fact that'. The Canadian Constitution Act, 1982, begins 'Whereas Canada is founded upon principles that recognize the supremacy of God and the rule of law' and goes on to list the freedoms and rights that every Canadian is entitled to. Much more commonly *whereas* is used like *while* to suggest contrast, and it is particularly useful in contexts where *while* might simply mean 'during the time'. Consider the difference between 'She went to chef school while he did an MBA' and 'She went to chef school, whereas he did an MBA'.

> WHEREAS $900,000 of a $1.4 million fund for the elimination of wage discrimination is being shuffled into the mill rate stabilization fund; and WHEREAS the remaining $500,000 allotted to pay equity will only be disbursed after union negotiations with the city have been completed; therefore BE IT RESOLVED that the female members of city council . . . accept an annual

salary of $30,276.18, which is calculated as 66 per cent of what the male members of city council....
Calgary Herald 6 Feb. 1994: A6

(In this pseudo-proclamation, *whereas* means 'in view of the fact that'.)

... the bands were trained to the new lively tempo of the piece, whereas the crowds, though full of fervor, leaned toward the old dirge-like version.
Ottawa Citizen 23 June 1994: A11

whet the appetite   *Whet* derives from an Old English word meaning sharpen. To *whet the appetite* is to sharpen or stimulate it—not, as some writers think, to satiate it. Occasionally *whet* is misspelled *wet*, perhaps by writers who plan on whetting their appetites with an aperitif, or perhaps through confusion with the expression *wet one's whistle*, meaning take a drink.

Anne of Green Gables, a 1985 mini-series ... whetted viewer appetites for more Montgomery.
Gazette (Montreal) 7 Jan. 1990: F1

Even success in the replacement market, however, isn't really enough to whet the appetites of TV manufacturers. Nor will it satisfy PC makers.
Computer Dealer News 21 March 1991: 32

(Given the context and the parallel second sentence, it appears that this writer is mistakenly using *whet* to mean satisfy.)

Domestic accounts appear now to have fully whetted their appetite with new supply.
Financial Post 22 Nov. 1990: 27

(Here again it appears that the writer is mistakenly using *whetted* to mean satisfied.)

... you may only find a few tantalizing details to wet your appetite in the book's 246 pages.
Edmonton Journal 13 Sept. 1992: np

(The correct word is *whet*.)

See also FOLK ETYMOLOGY.

whether   see IF; WHETHER OR NOT

whether or not   Many usage guides recommend omitting *or not* after *whether*. However, there are contexts where this is not possible: 'We are going ahead whether they like it or not'. It is possible to omit the *or not* when the sense of the phrase is roughly equivalent to 'if'. For example, 'I don't know whether or not I did the right thing' may be rewritten 'I don't know whether I did the right thing', which is more concise. In formal writing, where conciseness is highly valued, an optional *or not* is usually omitted. In fiction and journalism, where the writing is usually more idiomatic, *or not* is often retained. This is a point of style. Sometimes *whether* alone is more elegant; sometimes including *or not* is more rhetorically effective. Let your ear guide your choice, keeping in mind the level of formality required.

Whether is often misspelled *wether* (which, incidentally, is the term for a castrated ram).

... fifty-seven per cent favoured it whether it created jobs or not.
Saturday Night Jan. 1986: 13

(Here it is not possible to omit *or not*.)

As a result there is some debate about whether the Charter of Rights applies to the internal workings of the legislatures and to the operation of political parties.
Andrew Heard *Canadian Constitutional Conventions* 1991: 84–5

(In formal writing, *or not* is usually omitted if possible.)

Those who have made this argument have questioned whether a distinctively Japanese pattern actually exists.
Irving M. Zeitlin and Robert J. Brym *The Social Condition of Humanity* 1991: 360

(In formal writing, *or not* is usually omitted if possible.)

The real question is: Does she care whether the human race survives or not?
Margaret Atwood *Life Before Man* 1979: 19

(In fiction and journalism, an optional *or not* is often retained.)

... her client will also await the RCMP's conclusions before deciding whether or not to pursue charges.
Maclean's 11 Nov. 1991: A29

(In fiction and journalism, an optional *or not* is often retained.)

'I don't know yet—in the minds of the committee—wether we should be there in more than observer status.'
Financial Post 13 Aug 1990: 3

(The correct spelling is *whether*.)

See also IF, WHETHER.

which   see THAT, WHICH

Whig   see GRIT

while   see AS, WHILE, BECAUSE; AWHILE; WHEREAS

whip cream, whipped cream   see SKIM MILK

whisky, whiskey   Almost all dictionaries and usage guides suggest that *whisky* is the British and Canadian spelling, while *whiskey* is the Irish and American spelling. However, some Canadian writers maintain the distinction between Scotch *whisky* and Irish *whiskey*, and in general Canadians use the two variants about equally. What Canadians refer to as *rye* or *rye whisk(e)y* is called 'Canadian whisky' outside the country. The usual plural of *whisky* is *whiskies*; of *whiskey*, *whiskeys*.

> Harry invited me out to his car for a drink of fairly good rye whiskey.
> Max Braithwaite *The Night We Stole the Mountie's Car* 1971: 108

> We even tried, God help us, to sell rye whisky to the Scots.
> George Ignatieff *The Making of a Peacemonger* 1987: 177

white   see BLACK

white paper   see GREEN PAPER

whither   see HITHER

who, whom   Traditionally, *who* is used as the subject of a sentence or clause and *whom* is used as the object of a verb or preposition. In spoken Canadian English, however, *who* has largely displaced *whom*—which is not to say that *whom* is moribund. The same people who find *whom* overly fastidious in casual conversation take pains to use it correctly in their formal writing.

informal usage In informal spoken Canadian English, *who* tends to be the form of the interrogative pronoun at the beginning of a sentence, whether it is a subject or an object:

> 'Who is asking?'
> (subject)

> 'Who are they interviewing?'
> (object)

> 'Who do I send it to?'
> (object)

Whom is used consistently only in constructions such as 'some of whom', 'none of whom', or 'seven of whom'.

formal usage In formal writing 'Whom are they interviewing?' and 'To whom do I send it?' are still required. When *who* or *whom* is used as a relative pronoun, the correct form is determined by its function *within* the relative clause:

> 'She chose someone whom they knew.'
> ('they knew him'—object of the relative clause)

> 'She chose someone who would entertain them.'
> ('he would entertain them'—subject of the relative clause)

The objective form is always required directly after a preposition: 'by whom she had a child', 'with whom they had much in common'.

overuse of whom Because *whom* sounds more refined than *who*, it tends to be overused in formal speech and writing. People sometimes insert it in sentences where *who* is the appropriate form: 'Whom do you think you are?'; 'I cannot say whom it will be' (see also HYPERCORRECTION). This erroneous substitution is particularly common when *who* is a relative pronoun directly followed by a parenthetical phrase such as 'I think' or 'we imagine':

> 'Chris is someone whom we think will go far.'
> ('who will go far'—*who* is correct)

> 'Here at last was someone whom he hoped could love him.'
> ('who could love him'—*who* is correct)

> 'Whom shall I say is calling?'
> ('who is calling?'—*who* is correct)

This error is very common in literary writing and has been since the Renaissance—so common, in fact, that some commentators refuse to regard it as an error at all. They label the whole structure grammatically ambiguous and accept either *who* or *whom* in the context. While these commentators may be more realistic about English grammar, they also tend to be less adamant than those who consider *whom* wrong in the examples above. It's probably best, therefore, to avoid *whom* in such contexts.

> ... in order to get the coveted degrees or (real baseness, this) to gain favor with people whom I temporarily believed knew better about such things than myself, I have pretended to love the drama only.
> Robertson Davies *A Voice from the Attic* 1960: 158

> (Some editors would correct '*whom* I temporarily believed knew better' to '*who* I temporarily...'.)

See also CASE; THAT, WHO, WHOM; WHO'S, WHOSE.

who's, whose   *Who's* is a contraction of *who is* or *who has*: 'Guess who's here!'; 'Who's been using my computer?' *Whose* is the possessive form of *who*: 'Whose coat is that?'; 'Whose are these?' Because *who's* ends with an apostrophe followed by *s*, it looks like a possessive form, and people mistakenly substitute it for *whose*: 'Who's card is this?' And occasionally people make the opposite mistake, using *whose* where the contraction is required: 'Whose on the phone?'

Whose is also a possessive adjective: 'the woman whose house we bought'. Some people are ill at ease using *whose* with things: 'a car whose wheels are out of alignment'. They feel obliged to write 'a car the wheels of which are out of alignment', even though that sounds stiff. Grammarians in the late eighteenth century invented the rule that the relative pronoun *whose* should be reserved for people. At that time the rule was a departure from established usage, and it never did catch on in either popular or literary writing. However, the rule has been a bugbear for generations of conscientious writers. Happily for the contemporary writer, usage guides are now unanimous in approving the use of *whose* with a non-human antecedent. In fact, many guides express a preference for *whose* as less clumsy than *of which*.

They meet at a reception attended by everybody who's anybody in Hong Kong.
Financial Post 16 Dec. 1990: 7

'I'm a big guy whose going to work the corners, drive for the net and help my teammates.'
Daily News (Halifax) 18 March 1992: 43

(Here *who's*, the contraction of *who is*, is required.)

For weeks he talked about the little girl he'd played with all day and who's name sounded something like 'Maggie.'
Province (Vancouver) 7 Oct. 1990: 6

(Here *whose* is required.)

The mosses include species whose distribution is widespread in Canada.
Canadian Journal of Earth Sciences 26 (1989): 261

(Often *whose* is more readable than *of which*.)

He also assumes ... that we are in the midst of a profound ... environmental crisis whose solution might require a theory of its origins.
Queen's Quarterly 92.1 (1985): 208–9

See also CONTRACTIONS; THEIRS.

why   see REASON IS BECAUSE

widow, widower   *Widow* is perhaps the only word in the English language that is feminine in its basic form and adds a suffix to form a masculine: *widower*.

In figurative use, a *widow* is a hand of cards dealt to the table, or, in printing, a single line of type carried over to the top of a new page.

Many commentators object to the phrase 'widow of the late', since if a woman is a widow, her husband must be dead. 'Widow of so-and-so' and 'wife of the late' are both unobjectionable.

Chamorro was chosen because of her symbolic status, being the widow of Pedro Chamorro, ... who was assassinated for his opposition to the Somoza dictatorship.
Briarpatch April 1990: 27

We read ... of the growing affection of Mina for Angéline's father, the widower M. de Montbrun.
Ben-Z. Shek *French-Canadian & Québécois Novels* 1991: 10

See also LATE, THE.

will   see SHALL

-wise   The suffix *-wise* is standard in compounds such as *streetwise* and *travelwise*, where it means knowledgeable about. It is also long established as meaning in the position or direction of, as in *crosswise* and *clockwise*. Since the 1930s *-wise* has also come to be used to mean 'in terms of', or 'with regard to'. This sense is common in business jargon (*careerwise, marketwise, profitwise, salarywise, saleswise*) and has begun to proliferate, but there is still strong resistance to it in serious general writing. New words formed with *-wise* are usually considered slangy or inelegant.

What a religious attitude will not give you is a shrewd, worldly-wise novel by Trollope or Thackeray.
Robertson Davies *One Half of Robertson Davies* 1978: 207

'The focus that our social conditioning places upon us (and I say even from before we're born—class-wise, gender-wise, race-wise, culturally) fragments everything.'
Room of One's Own June 1990: 37

(The phrase after the dash could be rewritten: 'with respect to class, gender, race and culture'.)

'We have a great board. Everybody on there is easy to talk to and they're all level-headed. And there's a good mix personality-wise.'
Canadian Rodeo News March 1990: 15

(The *-wise* suffix is unnecessary: 'And there's a good mix of personalities' would do.)

See also HYPHENATION.

wish it was, wish it were   see SUBJUNCTIVE

wit   see TO WIT

withdrawal   *Withdrawal* is widely misspelled *withdrawl*, perhaps because it is often pronounced with only two syllables, and because *drawl* is a recognizable (albeit unrelated) word. Both the three- and two-syllable pronunciations are standard: *with DRAW ul* or *with DRAWL*.

The decision ... has since led to the dismissal or withdrawl of about 50,000 charges....
Financial Post 9 July 1991: F7

(The correct spelling is *withdrawal*.)

with regard[s] to   see IN REGARD[S] TO

witness box, witness stand   In Canadian and British courtrooms, witnesses testify from a *witness box*. Because American legal dramas are common fare on Canadian television, American legal terminology creeps into Canadian usage. American courtrooms have a *witness stand*, and witnesses 'take the stand'. Some Canadians strongly object to the use of American terminology in Canadian contexts.

As the mother sobbed, her son leaned forward in the witness box and began to weep quietly, causing Judge Gove to order a brief adjournment.
Vancouver Sun 13 Oct. 1990: A1

... she kept checking the clock as though preparing for the next session in a witness box.
Globe and Mail (Toronto) 11 Jan. 1985: P1

But when Jackson took the witness stand, he was giving in to waves of belligerence.
Jack Batten *Robinette* 1984: 16

wonder   To state that one is wondering something is not to ask a question, and thus no question mark is required:

I wonder when they'll finish.

She wondered why they did that.

On the other hand, if the word *wonder* introduces a direct question, a question mark is required:

I wonder, 'Will they ever finish?'

Why did they do that? she wondered.

Some writers put the direct question (Will they ever finish? or Why did they do that?) in quotation marks, while others reserve quotation marks for things that are actually spoken, not merely thought. Either style is acceptable.

It makes one wonder if the Newfoundlanders will seek the same kind of status.
W.C. Lougheed, ed. *In Search of the Standard in Canadian English* 1986: 70

I often wondered what he was doing, where he was going.
Jack Chambers *Milestones* 1983: 124

'What will wicked boys do now?' he wondered.
Queen's Quarterly 92.3 (1985): 494

Why didn't he know that? Adam wondered.
Canadian Fiction Magazine 64 (1988): 56

(This writer does not use quotation marks around thoughts.)

I wonder what my uncle would recommend?
Queen's Quarterly 96.1 (1989): 44

(This is a statement and should end with a period, not a question mark.)

What part did she play in her mother's life, I wondered.
Max Braithwaite *The Night We Stole the Mountie's Car* 1971: 165

(The first part of this sentence is a direct question: a question mark should replace the comma after 'life'.)

See also QUOTATION, QUOTATION MARKS.

wondrous   see DISASTROUS

wont, wonted   *Wont* is used as a adjective after the verb *be* to mean apt, or likely, or accustomed: 'They are wont to complain'. The noun *wont* normally occurs in the expression 'as is my (your, his, etc.) wont', where *wont* means habit or custom. The adjective *wonted* is placed before the noun it modifies and means usual or customary. Pronunciation of *wont* varies: it may rhyme with *won't*, *want*, or, occasionally, *punt*.

... the Coliseum crowds are wont to boo the Rangers....
Globe and Mail (Toronto) 28 Nov. 1985: C5

Instead, as has been his wont for almost 30 years, Dylan weathered the storm and delivered the ultimate in idiosyncratic performances....
Gazette (Montreal) 30 May 1990: E9

... the Montreal Symphony Orchestra's 1990-91 season begins next Tuesday, when Charles Dutoit takes his wonted place on the podium....
Gazette (Montreal) 12 Sept. 1990: C5

wood, woods   see FOREST

woof   see WARP

Worcester, Worcestershire   see GLOUCESTER

wordiness, variation   The rallying cry of William F. Strunk Jr. and E.B. White in their widely known *Elements of Style* was 'omit needless words'. Attempting to cut the number of words in a piece of writing is certainly a good way to focus revision. However, not everyone likes a consistently plain style. The point of cutting words is not to reduce all prose to sameness, but to ensure that the writer's points are made engagingly and convincingly by cutting out trite, boring, or unnecessary phrases.

In many cases, repeating a key phrase helps to remind the reader of the main point. Some writers, however, strive to avoid repeating themselves so earnestly that they fall into the trap that Fowler calls 'elegant variation'. He points out that if we vary a key word, readers may well wonder if the varied term should be read as equivalent to the key word or different from it. Here is one of his many examples: 'There are 466 cases; they consist of 366 matrimonial suits, 56 Admiralty actions, and 44 Probate cases'. He recommends omitting *suits* and *actions* so that the reader will not have to wonder how a suit, an action, and a case might differ.

One of the most annoying forms of elegant variation is the attempt to avoid repeating *say* by using words such as *admit, advise, affirm, allege, argue, assert, claim, concede, contend, declare, disclose, opine, reveal*, and *state*. These words all have different connotations, if not different meanings, and should not be used simply to avoid repeating *say* (see also SAY).

Sometimes writers repeat an idea in different words without clarifying or amplifying the original idea: 'Shakespeare's historically inaccurate picture of Richard III is no longer believed to be true to the facts of the monarch's life'. This sort of repetition is sometimes called *tautology*. Some usage guides make fine distinctions between various kinds of wordiness, such as redundancy, tautology, and circumlocution, but these distinctions are less important than being able to distinguish between useful and unnecessary repetition.

Experienced writers and editors know that certain phrases and structures that are common and defensible in speech can often be dropped in writing. Sentences that begin with the indefinite 'it' (that is, an *it* that does not refer to a noun) can often be rewritten to better effect, so that 'It is significant that he failed to inform us' becomes 'Significantly, he failed to inform us'. Similarly, sentences that begin with 'there' can often be shortened: thus 'There are many students who want to take the course' becomes 'Many students want to take the course'.

Some abstract nouns should be replaced or omitted wherever possible. Here are a few of the most common: *aspect, basis, case, circumstances, connection, facet, fact, factor, function, instance, problem, situation, thing, type*.

Some wordy phrases are hardly ever defensible in writing. Here are some of the most common ones, with suggested alternatives.

wordy	*alternative*
as far as *x* is concerned	concerning *x*, with respect to *x*
at this point in time	now, today
by means of	by
due to the fact that	because
during the course of	during
in the event that	if
in the near future	soon
in spite of the fact that	although
on a temporary basis	temporarily
until such time as	until
with the exception of	except

The passive voice, although common and acceptable in much scientific and legal writing, is more wordy and less direct than the active voice. 'A committee has been established by the board of trustees to consider the question' is better rewritten 'The board of trustees has established a committee to consider the question'. However, the passive voice can be used to rhetorical effect: 'The world watched the case on television' is not an improvement on the passive sentence 'The case was televised worldwide'.

A pleonasm is a phrase in which one or more words are superfluous because they express a meaning already expressed in another word. Some pleonasms have entered the language. The phrase 'I saw it with my own eyes' was perhaps first used for comic emphasis, but now it is an idiom. Others in the same category are 'gather together', 'mental telepathy', and 'the reason why'. Among the pleonasms commonly criticized by the experts are these:

audible to the ear	most favourite
combine together	necessary prerequisite
consecutive days in a row	predict in advance
free gift	revert back
general consensus	subject area
limited to only	weather conditions

Speech is often more redundant than writing—and it should be, because, unlike readers, listeners have no chance to go back and reread something they didn't understand the first time. Even in writing, the discussion of complex or unfamiliar concepts may also require a somewhat repetitive style.

However, no cure has been found for writing that is produced to fill a page rather than to pursue an argument or entertain or inform. Sometimes writers are expected to produce prose that sounds impressive while conveying little in the way of detail. Advertising copywriters and bureaucrats often fall victim to the demand for prose that does not commit them (or their employers) to anything specific. Here is an example (from *Background Paper on Regional Planning and Development in Ontario*, Ontario Regional Trilevel Conference, 1973):

In our modern society a government cannot govern effectively without planning ahead. The great and often competing demands made upon all levels of government today mean that government must have a clear and realistic idea of how these demands can be met. To do this is to plan. Any other approach is irresponsible.

The act of planning and developing policies for program implementation can take many forms and operate at many levels. Within the framework of provincial responsibilities the process of planning covers a multitude of programs and interests. For example, as part of our continuing concern for individual wellbeing the province has developed a coherent set of policies and implementation programs in the field of social development.

Apart from conveying the vague sense that the government has plans intended to promote 'individual wellbeing', this passage is filler—which may well have been all it was intended to be.

It was in Oxford in 1981, during the course of a sabbatical, that Dewdney had the idea of adding a new instalment to the Flatlandian saga.
Saturday Night Jan. 1986: 11

(The single word *during* could replace 'during the course of'.)

If the IOC can't secure its own drug testing sites, then it should halt testing until such time as the tests can be conducted fairly.
Gazette (Montreal) 7 March 1989: B4

(The phrase 'until such time as' is a long-winded way of saying *until*.)

The burden of evidence is the greater yet for the reason that the party seeking to avoid the contract must show not only that he was incapable of a rational decision at the time of the agreement, but also that the other party was aware of his condition.
J.E. Smyth et al. *The Law and Business Administration in Canada* 1987: 178

(Here 'for the reason that' could be replaced by *because*.)

As far as weather is concerned, fall can come as early as mid-September, with alternatively wet and cold days followed by brilliant sunshine, crisp, clean air, and cloudless blue skies.
Alan Tucker, ed. *The Penguin Guide to Canada* 1991: 175

(Here 'As for the weather' could replace 'As far as weather is concerned'.)

Too few motorcycle shops are willing to take on another brand at this point in time.
Canadian Biker Magazine Feb. 1990: 13

(Here *today* or *nowadays* or *now* could replace 'at this point in time', or the phrase could simply be dropped.)

See also BEAR, PANDA, KOALA; BEING AS; COMPARISONS; CONSENSUS; DESPITE; FOR FREE; GOES WITHOUT SAYING; IN REGARD(S) TO; INTENTS AND PURPOSES; INVITED GUEST; PAST HISTORY; PERSONAL; RE-; REASON IS BECAUSE; REFER BACK; REVERT; TOGETHER; TOTAL; UNTIL.

wore   see WEAR

worked   see WROUGHT

workman   see JOB TITLES

World War I, World War II   see FIRST WORLD WAR

worn   see WEAR

worse   *Worser* is non-standard. *Worse* is correct as an adjective ('a worse result'), an adverb ('We played worse than the beginners'), and a noun ('definitely the worse of the two'). Until the eighteenth century, *worser* and *worse* were both common in literary writing, but today *worser* is considered uneducated.

> Worser still, it was utterly delicious and, in our weakened state, irresistible.
> *Gazette* (Montreal) 23 Feb. 1990: B7

(The correct word is *worse*.)

See also COMPARISONS.

worth   'Twenty dollars' worth' means the worth of twenty dollars in kind. It is a possessive construction that has traditionally required an apostrophe. However, usage on this point is shifting. Where other dictionaries list 'two cents' worth', *Merriam-Webster's* now lists 'two cents worth'. Increasingly, the apostrophe is being dropped from plural possessives that specify amounts: 'two million dollars worth of business', 'three weeks holidays'. Books and scholarly journals tend to retain the apostrophe in these expressions, and this book is no exception. However, either style—with or without the apostrophe—is acceptable, as long as it is used consistently. Note that the apostrophe is always required when the amount is singular: 'a day's pay'.

> If the stairs are well proportioned, a few dollars' worth of paint may be all that's needed to brighten them.
> *Chatelaine* April 1986: 114

> Robinette gave Eagleson an appointment and thirty minutes' worth of advice.
> Jack Batten *Robinette* 1984: 222

> ... while the proceedings cost him forty thousand dollars in lost work, he gained a million dollars worth of publicity for his cause....
> *Queen's Quarterly* 95.4 (1988): 838

> But, as a scattering of words to buttress the display of 15 seconds worth of film, it is effective, and even laudable.
> W.C. Lougheed, ed. *In Search of the Standard in Canadian English* 1986: 96

> The Michigan Press Association was so eager that it offered to give two or three dollars worth of ads for

> every dollar Canada expended.... Factoria, it was said, would attract a million dollars' worth of industries and would have a population of two hundred in its first year.
> Pierre Berton *The Promised Land* 1984: 172–3, 340

(For the sake of consistency, an apostrophe should follow *dollars* in both of these sentences or in neither.)

> That means you have to put 1,000 snow crystals in a row to get one centimetre's worth.
> *Toronto Star* 3 May 1992: G6

(When the possessive is singular, the apostrophe is required.)

See also POSSESSIVE.

would have   see [HAD HAVE]

[would of]   see [COULD OF]

wrack   see RACK

wrangle, wangle   To *wrangle* means to bicker or quarrel over something: 'They wrangled over expenses'. In North American English, *wrangle* can also mean to get something by arguing or quarrelling: 'He wrangled his expenses out of payroll'. Although this sense was listed as obsolete or rare by the *OED* in 1982, it is still current in North America (*Webster's Dictionary of English Usage*). To *wangle* means to get something by scheming or fawning.

> The ship sat in harbor for two months while officials wrangled over the passengers' fate.
> *Vancouver Sun* 14 Feb. 1990: B8

> He [Michael Wilson] has lashed out at the United States for trying to wangle concessions from Canada....
> *Toronto Star* 24 July 1991: A11

> Both the Defence Agency and the Foreign Ministry successfully wrangled more money out of the tight-fisted Finance Ministry in negotiations....
> *Financial Post* 24 Jan. 1989: 9

> Selby, who calls Reagan 'a Messiah figure,' would like to wangle an introduction to meet his hero....
> *Globe and Mail* (Toronto) 9 March 1985: E14

wrath, wrathful, wroth   *Wrath* is intense anger or great indignation. *Wrathful* is the adjective form meaning deeply angry or moved to vengeance. *Wroth*, an archaic variant of *wrathful*, is used only as a predicate adjective, as in 'God was wroth'. Generally, Canadians pronounce *wrath* to rhyme with *path* and *wroth* to rhyme with *moth*. For some British speakers, *wrath* rhymes with *moth* and *wroth* with *both*.

> 'While I would not give vent to my wrath so overtly, I understand his point.'
> *Queen's Quarterly* 92.2 (1985): 442

> It made you think of Church words like the wrath of God. . . .
> Constance Beresford-Howe *Night Studies* 1985: 142–3

> . . . Chunky, in a wrathful temper reminiscent of his grandfather, quit after 25 years as a director of the Royal Bank of Canada.
> *Globe and Mail* (Toronto) 29 Nov. 1985: P68

wreak *Wreak* (pronounced *REEK*) is used most often in the expression *wreak havoc*, meaning to cause destruction. But one can also wreak (i.e., inflict) such things as mayhem, evil, anger, and vengeance. 'Wreck havoc' is a mistaken form of 'wreak havoc', influenced no doubt by the fact that wreaking havoc amounts to wrecking things.

The past tense of *wreak* is *wreaked*: 'wreaked havoc'. 'Wrought havoc' is often seen but, strictly speaking, is not idiomatic. *Wrought* is an archaic past form of the verb *work* ('What hath God wrought?'). The confusion is hardly surprising, given that both *wreaked* and *wrought* are nearly obsolete and mostly confined to fixed expressions.

> But when men took it upon themselves to wreak the wrath of God on transgressors, they assumed the right to wreak some of their own wrath in the process.
> Richard Davies and Glen Kirkland, eds. *Dimensions* 1986: 66

> Equally absent is . . . any mention of the havoc wreaked on the urban landscape by the freeway.
> *Canadian Heritage Magazine* Feb.–Mar. 1986: 43

> In other matches, the eerily unpopulated SkyDome continued to wreck havoc on seeded players.
> *Ottawa Citizen* 14 Feb. 1990: F2

> (The idiom is *wreak havoc.*)

> As in the ill-fated Meech Lake amendment, changes in provincial governments could again wreck havoc by reversing ratifications.
> *Ottawa Citizen* 2 Feb. 1991: A3

> (The idiom is *wreak havoc.*)

> The greenish-yellow cloud wrought havoc among unprotected Canadian and French North African troops huddled in their trenches.
> *Maclean's* 18 Feb. 1991: A34

> (The idiom is *wreaked havoc.*)

See also WROUGHT, WORKED.

wreck see WREAK

writer, present see PRESENT WRITER

wroth see WRATH

wrought, worked In Early Modern English, *wrought* was the usual past tense and past participle of *work*. Although *worked* is the past participle used generally today, *wrought* is preserved in several distinct usages. For example, things that are well crafted are often called 'finely wrought'. A person whose emotions are all worked up may be described as 'overwrought'. *Wrought* is sometimes used to mean brought about, as in 'changes wrought by revolution'. Finally, *wrought iron* is decorative iron-work often used for furnishings and railings.

> They appreciate the beauty of top-quality turquoise beads and the intrinsic worth of . . . a finely wrought silver bracelet.
> *Globe and Mail* (Toronto) 5 March 1985: F9

> In 1844, inventor Samuel Morse sent the first public message—'What God hath wrought'—over his electric telegraph between Washington, D.C., and Baltimore.
> *Globe and Mail* (Toronto) 24 May 1985: M2

> So one should acknowledge that improvements have taken place, . . . but I am not sure Davis can be said to have wrought them himself.
> *Queen's Quarterly* 94.2 (1987): 347

> The commemorative cairn is enclosed by a knee-high, wrought-iron fence.
> *Canadian Fiction Magazine* 63 (1988): 31

See also WREAK.

X

X When X-rays were discovered in 1895, their nature was a mystery: hence the name *X-rays*. In every domain from mathematics to game shows, *x* represents something or someone unknown or unidentified.

Apart from *X-ray*, almost every one of the handful of English words beginning with *x* is derived from Greek, and the initial *x* is usually pronounced as if it were a *z*.

Unlike the British, Canadians seldom call an X-shaped mark a 'cross'.

> Mr. X is a lawyer and the nexus of a $400-million merchandising fortune.
> *Globe and Mail* (Toronto) 21 Dec. 1985: A10

Xmas *Xmas* (pronounced *KRIS mus* or, more in-formally, *EX mus*) is not another deplorable mani-festation of the commercialization of Christmas. However, since that is what this abbreviation is widely believed to be, it is best reserved for advertis-ing copy and informal writing. In fact, *Xmas* has been in use since the 1500s, and *Xianity* was used before 1100. The *X* represents *chi*, the first letter of the Greek word for Christ; thus *X* is an abbreviation of *Christ*.

> The toys are distributed at Xmas by the Salvation Army to needy children in the area.
> *Canadian Biker Magazine* Feb. 1990: 12

> ... the Websters' annual Xmas bash is usually held at their home in Westmount....
> *Gazette* (Montreal) 27 Jan. 1990: K3

Y

-y, -ies Nouns that end in *-y* preceded by a conso-nant form their plurals by changing the *y* to *i* and adding *-es*: *lady*, *ladies*; *spy*, *spies*; *sty*, *sties*. Nouns that end in *-quy*, like *colloquy*, *obloquy*, and *soliloquy*, are pluralized the same way: *colloquies*, *obloquies*, *soliloquies*. Most nouns that end in *-ey* are pluralized *-eys*, but some have an alternative *-ies* plural: *moneys* or *monies*. Proper names retain the *y* when made plural: 'three Marys'.

See also PLURALS; MONEY.

yacht *Yacht* (pronounced *YOT*) is often mis-spelled *yatch*, on the pattern of more familiar words such as *catch* and *hatch*.

> The Aga Khan ... knew Pierre Trudeau and had hosted him on his yatch in the Mediterranean....
> *Toronto Star* 15 Oct. 1992: E14

(The correct spelling is *yacht*.)

yang see YIN

Yankee, Yank Today *Yankee* and the short form *Yank* can refer to any inhabitant of the United States, but originally only inhabitants of New En-gland were called *Yankees*. Thus these terms are still sometimes used to refer specifically to New Eng-landers or, especially in the American South, to inhabitants of the states that fought against the Confederacy in the American Civil War. *Yankee* or *Yank* is sometimes used to convey a stereotype of Americans as brash, egocentric, and materialistic, but these words are not necessarily pejorative. Americans themselves have used *Yankee* with pride: 'Yankee ingenuity', 'New York Yankees'.

The Canadian likes to be objective about Americans, and likes to feel that he can see a bit of Sam Slick in every Yankee: as a North American, therefore, he has a good seat on the revolutionary sidelines. . . .
Northrop Frye *The Bush Garden* 1971: 137

Along came Noah Webster, a Yankee individualist on whom Old-World precedent sat uneasily.
W.C. Lougheed, ed. *In Search of the Standard in Canadian English* 1986: 5

(Here *Yankee* means New Englander.)

Every other head in the place turns slowly, sizing him up, with wordless malevolence, as yet another Yank with too much money.
Globe and Mail (Toronto) 5 Jan. 1985: M7

The Brits and the Yanks are part of a contingent of some 75 aircraft currently in Cold Lake for . . . tactical air exercises.
Globe and Mail (Toronto) 1 June 1985: P10

See also CANUCK.

yay see YEA

ye *Ye* is an archaic or dialectal form of *you*. In Middle English it was the plural of *thou*, and in some current dialects it can replace *you* as either subject or object, singular or plural.

Ye is also an archaic spelling of *the*—now always facetious or intentionally quaint. Authorities are divided over whether *ye*, as in 'Ye Olde Gifte Shoppe', should be pronounced *YEE* or *the*. Certainly the historically correct pronunciation is the same as *the*. In Middle English writing, the symbol δ represented the sound *th*, and *the* was spelt δe. Early printers, who had only the Roman alphabet at their disposal, could not reproduce δe, so they substituted the letter *y* for it. However, this printer's convention was never intended to reflect pronunciation. In reading historical documents, therefore, the definite article *ye* should be pronounced *the*. Contemporary usage is another matter. In contemporary contexts the 'mispronunciation' *YEE* is actually preferable, because it cues the listener to the quaint spelling and the mock-archaic style.

'Be ye salmon fishermen?'
Atlantic Salmon Journal Autumn 1990: 23

'Well, Mr Shaw, I'll tell ye: Latin is the only language that myshtifies [sic] the Devil.'
Eugene Forsey *A Life on the Fringe* 1990: 5

'This Philosophy is not of that kind which tendeth to vanity & deceipt but rather to profit & to edification inducing first ye knowledge of God & secondly ye way to find out true medicines in ye creaters. . . .'
Queen's Quarterly 95.1 (1988): 34

(In this historical quotation, the definite article *ye* should be pronounced as *the*.)

Model versions of the British originals, local snuggeries are springing up all over town, purveying imported ales and Ye Olde England conviviality. . . .
Alan Tucker, ed. *The Penguin Guide to Canada* 1991: 292

(Here the pronunciation *YEE* is acceptable, even preferable.)

See also ARCHAISMS.

yea, yay, yeah A vote of approval may be called a *yea*; a dissenting vote is a *nay*. Both words rhyme with *say*.

Yea means 'indeed' in constructions such as 'difficult, yea impossible'. It means 'so' in the slang expression *yea big*, which is usually accompanied by a hand gesture. The cheer is spelled *yea*, or *yay*, or, occasionally, *yeah*; all these words rhyme with *say*.

The casual pronunciation of *yes* (*YA*) is almost always spelled *yeah*.

[The] new council . . . will want to hear the results of a two-year environmental study . . . before saying yea or nay to residential development on the property.
Vancouver Sun 10 May 1990: B1

What is false, what is legitimate, what is right, yea, what is moral in a free society can be determined only by the constant play of unfettered debate.
Globe and Mail 27 March 1985: P6

'Yea,' shouted a covey of school kids, spotting Mr. Buzzer and waving.
Vancouver Sun 28 June 1990: B1

'Yay, yay, yay, yay!!!' Everyone cheered, jumping up and down.
Gazette (Montreal) 23 Dec. 1990: D1

Curious onlookers cheered, shouting 'Yeah!' at every sound of shattered glass as cars sped through.
Gazette (Montreal) 29 Aug. 1990: A1

'Yeah, I guess.'
Queen's Quarterly 95.2 (1988): 403

yellow journalism see PURPLE PROSE

yeti see SASQUATCH

Yiddish   see JEW

yin, yang   In Chinese Taoist philosophy, *yin* and *yang* are the two opposite but complementary principles of the universe, thought to coexist in most things and to operate cyclically to produce change. *Yin* is the passive principle; *yang* is the active principle. The spread of Eastern philosophy to North America has brought these words into popular use here. Allusions to *yin* and *yang* in Canadian writing usually suggest a harmonious blending of opposites.

Sometimes writers take the principle of complementarity too far, spelling *yin* incorrectly as *ying*. The expression *yin-yang* is slang.

> It also means we can experience, in one, the yin and the yang of New York live entertainment from the bright lights of Broadway to the basements of Greenwich Village.
> *Globe and Mail* 18 May 1985: T2

> But there is a yang to the ying of this celestial cruise.
> *Gazette* (Montreal) 23 July 1990: A1

(The correct spelling is *yin*.)

> As choreographer, he is well aware of the yin-yang balance of his creative energy—the need to alternate very theatrical pieces with more straightforward but equally challenging dance invention.
> *Performing Arts in Canada* March 1988: 7

> 'I had yin-yang feelings for my new son. I loved him dearly. But then I would wonder if I made a real mistake having him.'
> *Vancouver Sun* 27 Dec. 1990: B3

> 'Every year we have this yin-yang on the abortion issue. The only reason these people run (for election) is because of abortion.'
> *Vancouver Sun* 19 Feb. 1990: A1

yogurt, yogourt, yoghurt, yoghourt   *Yogurt* is the most common Canadian spelling. *Yogourt*, *yoghurt*, and *yoghourt* are also found, though infrequently. *Yogourt* is the French spelling, used in English only in Canada. In North America the first syllable, *yog-*, is pronounced to rhyme with *vogue*; in Britain it rhymes with *log*.

> ... frozen yogurt is healthier than ice cream because it has less cholesterol, less fat and fewer calories.
> *Province* (Vancouver) 29 July 1990: 69

> ... her small stationwagon is so filled with yogurt containers, clattering cans and plastic bottles, it looks like a travelling depot.
> *Gazette* (Montreal) 22 April 1990: A1

> Nichol stocks ... yoghurt and cheese.
> *Province* (Vancouver) 7 Feb. 1990: 45

> Smoked salmon and avocado roulade with cucumber and yoghourt salad.
> *Bon Vivant* Aug. 1981: 7

yoke, yolk   A *yoke* is a wooden crosspiece fastened over the necks of a pair of draft animals to allow them to pull together. *Yoke* has many other senses that are extensions of this literal sense.

A *yolk* is the yellow part of an egg. People often misspell the egg *yolk*, probably because *yoke* and *yolk* sound the same and *yoke* appears more often in print.

> A wooden yoke that fits loosely around the neck permits him to carry (precariously) two pails at a time to the more remote planted areas.
> *The Beaver* Dec. 1989–Jan. 1990: 7

> [The Canadian West] was like an emerging nation that has shaken off the Imperial yoke and is determined to rally under one united political force.
> Pierre Berton *The Promised Land* 1984: 276

> ... sometimes the birds would actually lay an egg while being lifted. These would land on the floor, their yokes bleeding into the mud.
> *Canadian Fiction Magazine* 64 (1988): 63

(The correct spelling is *yolks*.)

Yonsei   see ISSEI

you, one   In all but the most formal styles of writing, the pronoun *you* is now commonly used both in direct address to the reader ('You can avoid this problem by ...') and as an indefinite pronoun ('You can't balance the budget without cuts to services'). In the past, usage guides suggested that *one* replace these uses of *you* in writing. However, *one* is not common in Canadian English, and can sound stilted unless the whole passage is quite formal. Slightly more informal than *you* but less stuffy than *one* are constructions with *those who, anyone, everyone, people,* etc.: 'Those who insist on lower taxes should expect reduced services'. Ultimately, this is a question of style and tone, and the writer must decide which pronoun is most appropriate in a particular context. Switching back and forth between *you* and *one* in the same passage is considered a stylistic fault.

See also FORMAL, INFORMAL WRITING; PRESENT WRITER; -SELF; [YOUS].

your, you're, yours   *Your* is a possessive adjective: 'Bring your bathing suit'. *You're* is a contraction of *you* and *are* that is common in speech but rare in writing except in representations of speech: 'If you're not here by nine, we won't expect you'.

Yours is a possessive pronoun like *mine*, *hers*, *his*, and *theirs*: 'I forgot my copy. Did you bring yours?' Though it is a possessive form, *yours* is never written with an apostrophe.

'You need ATMs if your going to attract young people.'
Daily News (Halifax) 7 April 1994: 28

(Here the correct spelling is *you're*—a contraction of *you are*.)

See also CONTRACTIONS; POSSESSIVE; THEIRS.

[yous], [youse], you all, you guys   In Standard English *you* is both singular and plural. The use of *yous* (also spelled *youse*) to refer to more than one person is considered uneducated or dialectal. (In some dialects *youse* has been generalized so that it also applies to an individual.) *Youse* is common in Ireland and in areas of Irish settlement in Canada, the United States, and Australia. In the American South, *you all* or *y'all* functions similarly. Many Canadians use *you guys* in informal speech to address a group, regardless of gender. These informal variants of *you* never appear in writing, except in representations of speech.

'Why doan youse come and sit with me?'
Canadian Fiction Magazine 64 (1988): 129

'At this rate it'll take you guys a week.'
Canadian Fiction Magazine 64 (1988): 63

-yse   see -IZE

Yukon   Though other Canadians often say *the Yukon*, residents of this territory prefer that the definite article be dropped, indicating that Yukon is not just a geographic area like 'the North', but a political entity like Alberta or Canada.

He has worked as a high school teacher in Ontario, British Columbia, Yukon and Northwest Territories.
Ottawa Citizen 28 Aug. 1990: E3

See also APPENDIX I; NORTHWEST TERRITORIES; UKRAINE.

-yze   see -IZE

Z

zed, zee   Canadians usually pronounce the name of the last letter of the alphabet *ZED*, as do the British. Although most Canadians are aware of the American pronunciation, *ZEE*, few use it—except in Newfoundland, where *ZEE* is more common. There has been some speculation that the American children's television program *Sesame Street* would make inroads on the *ZED* pronunciation in Canada. Surveys in southern Ontario indicate that very young children there do say *ZEE*, but later (perhaps reflecting the influence of formal education) shift to *ZED*.

zenith   see APOGEE

zero, oh   Canadians often say *oh* for *zero* when giving telephone numbers; however, *zero* should not be read as *oh* in any context that combines letters and numbers, such as a postal code. The Canadian postal code K0H 1M0, for example, should be read aloud as 'kay zero aitch one em zero'.

In some typefaces zero is marked with a slash (∅) to distinguish it from the letter *O*.

zero adverbs   Most adverbs end in *-ly*: *coarsely*, *foolishly*, *happily*, *jauntily*, *rudely*, etc. However, there are some English adverbs—many of them common words that have been in the language for a long time—that have a form identical to the adjective, including *cheap*, *clean*, *clear*, *close*, *deep*, *flat*, *high*, *quick*, *right*, *slow*, and *wrong*. These adverbs are called either 'zero adverbs' or 'flat adverbs'. Most zero adverbs also have an *-ly* form.

The zero form is often found in common idioms: 'get rich quick', 'come clean', 'see my way clear', 'come close', 'turn wide', 'flying high', 'go wrong', 'live right'. The *-ly* form is more likely to appear in formal contexts: 'resolved the issue quickly', 'was wrongly accused', 'propagated widely'. This may explain why some usage guides recommend against using the zero forms where an *-ly* form exists. However in many of these idiomatic expressions the *-ly* form either sounds odd ('took the turn widely') or changes the sense ('He's always turning up late/lately').

See also CHEAP; SLOW.

zoology According to some authorities, the only acceptable pronunciation of *zoology* is *zoh ALL uh jee* (the first syllable rhyming with *go*), but most Canadians, including zoologists, say *zoo ALL uh jee*, influenced, no doubt, by the word *zoo*. Recent dictionaries give both pronunciations.

Appendix I

province or territory	abbreviations		legislature	legislative member
	common	postal		
Newfoundland and Labrador	Nfld.	NF	House of Assembly	MHA
Nova Scotia	N.S.	NS	House of Assembly	MLA
Prince Edward Island	P.E.I.	PE	Legislative Assembly	MLA
New Brunswick	N.B.	NB	Legislative Assembly	MLA
Quebec	P.Q. *or* Que.	PQ *or* QC	National Assembly	MNA *or* deputy
Ontario	Ont.	ON	Legislative Assembly	MPP
Manitoba	Man.	MB	Legislative Assembly	MLA
Saskatchewan	Sask.	SK	Legislative Assembly	MLA
Alberta	Alta.	AB	Legislative Assembly	MLA
British Columbia	B.C.	BC	Legislative Assembly	MLA
Yukon	Y.T.	YT	Legislative Assembly	MLA
Northwest Territories	N.W.T.	NT	Legislative Assembly	MLA

See also NAMES OF RESIDENTS.

Appendix II

measurement, SI, metric system   The Canadian government switched from the Imperial system of units (feet, yards, miles, pounds, gallon, acres, etc.) used in Great Britain and the United States to SI units in 1971. SI is short for Système international d'unités; in English Canada this system is usually referred to as the metric system. The system has clear conventions for how measurements should be written. For detailed guidance see the *Canadian Metric Practice Guide* and other publications of the Canadian Standards Association.

The base units of SI are *metre*, m, for length; *kilogram*, kg, for mass; *second*, s, for time; *ampere*, A, for electric current; *kelvin*, K, for thermodynamic temperature; *candela*, cd, for intensity of light; and *mole*, mol, the base unit of pure substance. All other SI units are derived from these. The following non-SI units relating to time are used in the system: *day*, d; *hour*, h; *minute*, min; and *year*, a; the last symbol is derived from Latin word for year, *annum*. Some other non-SI units that have been approved for use with SI are the *revolution* (r), the *hectare* (h), the *metric ton* or *tonne* (t), the *litre* (L), and the *millilitre* (mL). (The letter symbol for *litre* is capitalized to avoid confusion with the numeral *1*.)

The symbols for the SI units are called letter symbols, not abbreviations; they are not italicized, followed by periods or made plural: 'a distance of 17 km'. A space is left between the number of units and the letter symbol—'The dog is 2 kg overweight'—except when writing temperatures: '15°C' (fifteen degrees Celsius). In SI the numbers and the unit names are either both spelled out ('fifteen kilograms') or given as numeral and symbol ('15 kg').

Some common expressions are abbreviated as follows:

kilometres per hour: km/h
grams per millilitre: g/mL
kilowatt-hours: kwh
revolutions per minute: r/pm

Some of the names for units are derived from proper names. With the exception of *Celsius*, these units are written out without capital letters, although their letter symbols are capitalized: *ampere*, A; *joule*, J; *kelvin*, K; *newton*, N; *watt*, W. The letter symbols for prefixes up to *kilo-* are also written without capital letters, while those above, such as *mega* (10^6) and *giga* (10^9), are capitalized when written as symbols: 'The output is 10 MW (megawatts)'.

The pronunciation of *kilometre* varies: both *KILL o mee ter* and *kill AW muh ter* are accepted. See also CELSIUS.

Glossary

article   The definite article (*the*) and the indefinite article (*a/an*) both precede nouns; the former usually indicates that the noun to come has been mentioned before, while the latter indicates either that the noun is being introduced into the discourse or that the reference is not specific ('indefinite'). (See A, AN.)

Canadianism   A Canadianism is a word or expression that is used only in Canada (*Mountie, EI*) or a sense of a word that is exclusively or nearly exclusively restricted to Canada (*acclamation, allophone, dépanneur, loonie, pogey*).

clause   A clause contains, as a minimum, a subject and a predicate: 'Birds sing'. An independent clause can stand alone as a complete sentence. Independent clauses can also be joined by coordinate conjunctions: 'Birds sing, fish swim, and we dance the tango'. (See **conjunctions** below.)

A subordinate clause cannot stand alone as a sentence. It is preceded by a subordinate conjunction, which links the clause to the main clause in the sentence: 'Because I like singing, I joined the choir'. Noun clauses ('I didn't like *what I saw*'), adjective clauses ('The book, *which was shoved under the couch*, finally turned up'), and adverb clauses ('His eyes rolled *as if he were going to faint*') perform the same functions in sentences as nouns, adjectives, and adverbs.

Adjective clauses are also called 'relative clauses'. A relative clause may be introduced by a relative pronoun (*who, whom, which*, or *that*): 'She looked around for the umbrella *that he had lent her*'. A relative pronoun acts both as a pronoun, in that it refers to a noun, and as a subordinate conjunction, in that it heads a clause that is dependent on a main clause. Relative clauses may also be introduced by relative adverbs such as *where, why*, and *when*: 'The locker *where he stored*

his clothes is empty'. For restrictive and non-restrictive clauses, see THAT, WHICH.

coin   To coin a word is to make it up: 'The residents of Banff coined the term *go-bys* to refer to the tourists'.

comparative   The comparative form of an adjective or adverb—used in making comparisons—is usually marked by an *-er* ending (*taller, further*) or by the use of *more* (*more beautiful; more wildly*). (See COMPARISONS.)

compound subject   A compound subject is a subject formed from two nouns or noun equivalents joined by a coordinate conjunction: '*Boys* and *girls* come out to play'; '*What I like* and *what I get* are two different things'.

conditional   A conditional clause expresses the idea that one thing will happen on condition that another one happens; conditional clauses usually begin with *if, unless*, or *provided that*: 'If he comes, we can get started'. (See [HAD HAVE].)

conjunction   A conjunction is a word that joins other words, phrases, or clauses. The main coordinate conjunctions—*and, but, or, nor*—join items that are considered equal in importance or parallel. Correlative conjunctions come in pairs: *either … or; neither … nor; both … and; not only … but also*. Subordinate conjunctions, such as *because, while, even though*, and *as soon as*, join items that are considered unequal in importance.

conjunctive adverbs   These words form links between sentences. Some common conjunctive adverbs are *however, therefore, nevertheless, further*, and *for example*. (See SENTENCES.)

convention   In the field of language study, a convention is a writing practice that has been worked out or evolved over time by editors, lexicographers, and educators. Most conventions relate to matters of spelling, punctuation, and style.

countable noun, uncountable noun   A countable noun (sometimes called a count noun) refers to things that can be counted and thus can be singular or plural (*word, words*), whereas an uncountable noun (sonetimes called a mass noun) refers to things without clear boundaries and is generally found in the singular (*flour, wine*). Note that when an uncountable noun is pluralized, it means 'kinds of': *flours* (e.g., whole wheat, graham, rice); *wines* (e.g., red, white, sparkling). When an uncountable noun is treated as a countable noun ('I'll have a coffee'), the reference is to some understood quantity: 'a (cup of) coffee'. (See FEWER, LESS.)

figure of speech   A figure of speech at its most general is a use of language that departs from the ordinary in structure, sound, rhythm, or content to achieve a special effect. For example, metaphors and similes (see below) are figures of speech, as are puns. Figures of speech sometimes include what are usually called rhetorical figures, such as the rhetorical question (see RHETORICAL QUESTION).

gerund verbal noun   see **verbals** below

infinitive   An infinitive is the base form of the verb preceded by *to*: *to run, to be*. It can be used as a noun ('To err is human'), an adjective ('I need something to read'), or an adverb ('They were anxious to see me'). In some formulations, the *to* can be dropped, as in 'The children helped us (to) carry the packages', or does not occur, as in 'They made him do it' (*to* is not possible before *made*). In other formulations, the *to* may be expanded: 'He came *in order to* help me'; 'They laid out their clothes *so as to* be ready in the morning'.

inflection, inflected form   Nouns, pronouns, adjectives, adverbs, and verbs have inflections (suffixes), or inflected forms marked by changes in vowels, etc. (e.g., *him, went*) that indicate such things as number (*cat, cats*), gender (*she, he*), case

(*his, him*), degree of comparison (*big, bigger, biggest*), tense (*do, did*), mood (see below), and so on.

intensifier, intensify   An intenifier is an adverb that either heightens or tones down the impact of the meaning of an adjective or adverb: '*very* good', '*somewhat* badly', '*highly* motivated', '*slightly* interested'.

intonation   This term refers to the patterns of falling and rising pitch that indicate sentence types. Usually, in English, intonation rises at the end of a question and falls at the end of a statement.

metaphor   A metaphor is a figure of speech that draws an analogy between two things by equating them: 'He is a rock'. (See DEAD METAPHOR; MIXED METAPHOR.)

modifier, modify   Words and phrases that modify the meaning of other words, phrases, or clauses are called modifiers. For example, adjectives modify nouns and sentence adverbs modify whole sentences. (See ADJECTIVES AND ADVERBS; MISPLACED MODIFIER; SENTENCE ADVERB.)

mood   English has three moods: indicative (a factual statement, such as 'He runs daily'), imperative (an order, such as 'Run for your lives!'), and subjunctive (a wish or hypothetical statement, such as 'God be praised!'; 'If I were you...'; see SUBJUNCTIVE).

noun   Nouns name persons, places, things, or ideas. Proper nouns are the names of specific people, institutions, places, etc., and are capitalized; common nouns—all the others—are not capitalized. Abstract nouns (*liberty, democracy, insight*, etc.) are contrasted with concrete ones (*wood, applesauce*). Individual nouns (*cow, insight*) are contrasted with collective nouns (*team, herd*). (See COLLECTIVE NOUNS; and **countable nouns**, above.)

object   The person or thing that receives the action of the verb is its object. Any sentence that contains a transitive verb has a direct object: 'The truck crashed into the *pillar*'. Some verbs (for example, *give, offer, pay, send*) routinely take both a direct and an indirect object: 'The government paid my cousin a pension'. Here *cousin* is the indirect object, that is, the person or thing indirectly affected by the action. In most sentences of this kind, the indirect object can also appear in a phrase beginning with *to* or *for*: 'The government paid a pension to my cousin'.

Prepositions also take objects: 'on the *desk*'. Pronouns that are objects of verbs or of prepositions are in the objective case: 'I love *him*'; 'Between you and *me*, he's lovable'. (See CASE.)

object complement The object complement is an adjective or noun that identifies, locates, or describes the direct object: 'They painted the kitchen *green*'; 'We thought him *a fool*'. The verbs *believe, call, consider, choose, find,* and *think* often precede this structure.

parenthetical elements These are elements that are not essential to the meaning of a sentence. To set them off from the main body of the sentence, they are often enclosed in commas, parentheses, or dashes: 'My nephew, *who is nine*, loves baseball'; 'We had a great deal of trouble at Customs (*don't even ask*), but finally we found our way outside to the sunlight again'.

parts of speech The parts of speech are the different classes, or types, of words. The traditional parts of speech are noun, pronoun, verb, adverb, adjective, preposition, interjection ('Oh!'), and conjunction.

participle This is the general term for two verb forms: the present participle, formed with *-ing*, and the past participle, formed in various ways—most often with *-ed*, and occasionally with *-t* (*knelt,) -en* (*proven*), or *-n* (*known*), or irregularly (*sung, thought*). The present participle is used to form the present and past continuous tenses ('He is running for mayor'; 'They were hoping for victory'), as a noun (here a gerund, or verbal noun: 'Running is my life'), as an adjective ('running water'), or as an adjectival or adverbial participial phrase ('Running desperately, they caught the train'). The past participle is used to form the present or past perfect tense with forms of *have*

(*have lived, had run*) and the passive voice with forms of *be* (*has been depressed, was stolen*). It is also used in adjectival or adverbial participial phrases ('Aged five, he entered kindergarten'). (See **verbals**, below.)

phrase A phrase is a sequence of grammatically related words that can be distinguished from a clause in that it has no finite verb (i.e., no verb that is marked for tense; see **tense**, below). Phrases often include verbals (see **verbals**, below), but these act as nouns, adjectives, or adverbs, rather than verbs.

predicate In traditional grammar, the predicate is one of the two major constituents of a sentence: the other is the subject. The predicate contains a verb (i.e., a verb marked for tense; see **tense**, below) and can be thought of as asserting something about the subject.

prefix, suffix A prefix is an element such as *dis-, non-, over-,* and *re-* that when added to the beginning of a word changes its meaning (e.g., *non-* added to a word makes it negative: *non-smoker*). A suffix is an element attached to the end of a word that changes its grammatical or lexical meaning or function. For example, the suffix *-s* indicates that a noun is plural, and *-ed* marks the past tense of regular verbs, while the suffixes *-ness* and *-ity* are used to make nouns from adjectives: *goodness, generosity*. The addition of prefixes or suffixes often raises questions of spelling (e.g., *likeable* vs. *likable*) or hyphenation (*non-profit* vs. *nonprofit*).

preposition A preposition is a word that is placed before a noun or noun equivalent to show the relation between that noun and something elsewhere in the sentence: 'I put the book *on* the desk'; 'She ran *towards* the entrance'. Some common prepositions are *about, above, at, below, down, during, except, past,* and *within*. The preposition with its noun object is called a prepositional phrase.

pronoun A pronoun is a word that is used instead of a noun. Normally, it refers to a particular noun or noun equivalent that has already been mentioned; this noun is called its antecedent. Some pronouns do not have antecedents (for example, the *it* in 'It is raining') and others use the speech situation to form the link ('Which book?' '*That* one'.) The eight kinds of pronoun are personal (e.g., *I, you, them*), reflexive (e.g., *himself, themselves*), indefinite (e.g., *some, each, any*), reciprocal (e.g., *one another, each other*), demonstrative (e.g., *this, that, these, those*), interrogative (e.g., *who, which, what*), relative (e.g., *who, which, that*), and intensive (e.g., I *myself*, they *themselves*).

rhetoric This term is often used to refer to wordy or ideologically charged speech ('empty rhetoric', 'right-wing rhetoric'). However, rhetoric is also the art and study of persuasion. Courses that are called composition courses in Canada are often called rhetoric courses in the United States. (See RHETORICAL QUESTION.)

semantic drift Over time, many word senses shift, sometimes slowly, sometimes quickly. For example, *Canadian* first referred to Aboriginal peoples, then to French-speaking settlers, then to inhabitants of Upper and Lower Canada, and now often is used to refer to English-speaking Canadians only. (See EFFETE.)

simile A simile is a figure of speech that draws attention to a comparison by using *like* or *as*: 'She sings like a bird'.

stress In English, some syllables are emphasized more strongly than others. Stress can differentiate meaning. For example, the verb *permit* is stressed on the second syllable ('Do *per MIT* me to come'), while the noun is stressed on the first ('I need a building *PER mit*'). Most contemporary dictionaries indicate the stress with a mark preceding the stressed syllable, so that the verb is written *per'mit*, and the noun *'permit*. Every word spoken in isolation has at least one stressed syllable, but in sentences only certain words are stressed.

subject Grammar conventionally divides the sentence into the subject and the predicate. The subject in a statement—a noun phrase—usually precedes the verb: 'The cat chased the mouse'. Pronouns that are in subject position take the subjective case: 'I am going'. (See CASE.)

subject complement see **verb**, below

superlative The superlative form of adjectives and adverbs is typically formed by adding *-est* (*biggest, fastest*) or *most* (*most beautiful, most efficiently*). (See COMPARISONS.)

syllable A syllable in English is either a vowel alone or a vowel with one or more consonants before or after it. Words are made up of one or more syllables. Dictionaries often mark syllable breaks.

tense Verbs that are marked for tense indicate the time at which something took place. The present and past tenses are marked by inflections of the verb (I *walk*, he *walks*; I *walked*, he *walked*), while the future is formed most often by combining *will* with the infinitive (I will *walk*). Other tenses are formed by combining *be* and *have* with the infinitive, present participle, or past participle (I am *walking*; I have *walked*; I had *walked*). Sometimes verbs that are marked for tense are called finite verbs, to distinguish them from verb forms such as infinitives and verbals, which are not marked for tense and are called non-finite.

uneducated Although few people in Canada have no education, there are forms of speech that are associated with a lack of education. These are usually criticized when they appear in writing and often elicit disapproval when they appear in speech. Thus the label 'uneducated' marks stigmatized usages and pronunciations.

variant Often there are two (or more) ways of spelling or pronouncing a word, or of combining words in structures, that are acceptable. These forms are called variants.

verbals This is the collective term for gerunds (sometimes called verbal nouns) and participles, past and present. They do not have tense, and act as nouns, adjectives, and adverbs rather than as verbs. (See DANGLING MODIFIER and POSSESSIVE WITH GERUND.)

verb   A verb describes an action (*run, scrub*), a happening (*fall, flow*), or a state of being (*be, exist, feel*). Verbs that describe actions are classified as transitive (those that require a direct object) or intransitive (those that don't). Some verbs can be either transitive or intransitive. For example, in 'I hurried the children out the door', *hurried* is transitive, with *children* as the object. In 'We hurried', the verb is intransitive.

Copula or linking verbs describe a state of being; they link the subject to its complement: 'I am bored'; 'She seems an excellent speaker'; 'He remained Dean'. This complement—the subject complement—describes or identifies the subject. The most common copula verb is *be*; others are *appear, feel, remain, seem*, and *sound*. Some regular verbs are also used as copula verbs: *go* (*bad*), *get* (*married*), *run* (*wild*), *turn* (*bitter*).

voice   Sentences with transitive verbs can be in the active voice or the passive voice: 'I ate the cake'; 'The cake was eaten by me'. In an active sentence, the subject is the agent of the action; in a passive sentence, the subject is the object of the action. Some argue that the passive voice is wordier and more formal than the active, but often it is useful (when the agent is not known, for example) or conventional (in scientific and legal writing, for example). (See WORDINESS, VARIATION.)

Index

PLEASE NOTE: This index lists only items that do not appear as headwords or cross-references in the text.

AARTC, 2
able-bodyism, 282
abridgement, abridgment, 172
accede, 100
according to, 436
achieve, 260
acknowledgement, acknowledgment, 172
acreage, 172
actor, 289
addendum, addenda, 381
admit, 167, 436
adult books/movies, 193
advance agent, advance man, 289
advertise, 286
advise, 436
aeon, 18
aesthetic, 18
affirm, 436
African American, African-American, 257
ageism, 282
agriculturalist, agriculturist, 283
AIDS, Aids, 1, 2
Albertan, 335
all but, 467
allege, 436
allocable, 3
already, 15
although, 444
altos, 356
am, see *be*
amazement, 172
ameba, 18
ameliorate, 404

amoeba, 18
ampere, 535
anaemia, 18
analyse, analyze, 286
anchor, anchorman, 289
and, 118
anemia, 18
anemone, 99
Anglo-Irish, Anglophile, 219
animator, 201, 404
antebellum, 41
antechamber, 41
antedate, 41
antenatal, 41
anteroom, 41
anti-American, 41
anticlimax, 41
antihero, 41
anti-intellectual, 41
antipasto, 41
antithesis, antitheses, 381
anybody else, 179-80
apostrophe, 99
appal, appall, appalling, 295
apparatus, 506
appear, 171
appendix, appendices, 381
Archbishop, 423
Archdeacon, 423
are, see *be*
aren't, 133
argue, 525; *argument*, 172
as . . . as, 121
as far as x is concerned, 525
aspect, 525
assert, 436
audible to the ear, 526

audit, 224
automate, 63
axis, axes, 381

B.A., 2
babysit, 63
Bach, 229
bacillus, bacilli, 381
back up, back-up, 376
banjos, 380
basically, 400
basis, 525
bathroom, 193
battery, 115
Bauhaus, 229
B.C., 2; *BCer*, 335
be, 15, 23, 24
bear hug, bear-hug, 257
because, 444
become, 15
Beethoven, 229
begin, 167
begrudgement, 186
behavior, behaviour, 357
beliefs, 201
believe, 166, 260
benches, 380
between a rock and a hard place, 439
bias, 167
big shot, 116
bike, 2
bisexual, 447
Bishop, 423
blind pig, 70
bluntly, 443
BMW, 1

board, 115
bonuses, 506
bookkeeping, 257
boomers, 111
botanic, botanical, 258
both . . . and, 121, 362
BQ, 2
brain drain, 111
bravo, 356
break-in, 376
break up, break-up, breakup, 376
brethren, 380
briefly, 443
British Columbian, 335
Brooklynese, 191
buffaloes, 356
bummer, 116
bureau, bureaux, 381
bureaucrat, 66; *bureaucratese*, 191
burnout, 376
burnt, 482
bushed, 216
but, 118
butter (someone) up, 259
by means of, 525
bypass, 224

café, 70
caffeine, 260
calculable, 3
calves, 201
cameos, 356
cameraman, camera operator, 447
Canada goose, 91, 95
candela, 535
candidly, 443
canoeing, 172
Canon, 423
can't, 2
carafes, 201
carburetor, 465
Cardinal, 423
career-minded, 325; *careerwise*, 523

carful, 222
cargo, 356
carrier, 289
carry on, 260; *carry-on*, 376
carry out, 260
carryover, 376
case, 525
catalyse, catalyze, 286
cave-in, 376
caveat emptor, 297
CBC, 2
ceiling, 260
cellos, 356
census, 506
CEO, 2
certainly, 443
certainness, 338
CFB, 2
changeable, 3
château, châteaux, 381
cheat, 116
chief, 260; *chiefs*, 201
choruses, 506
Churchilliana, 258
CIDA, 2
circumstances, 525
circuses, 506
civilize, civilization, 286
claim, 436
clean, 532, 533
cleaner, cleaning lady, 289
clear, 532, 533
cleft, 110
clerk, 289
close, 532, 533
closed-minded, 325
cloven, 110
cloverleaf, 201
club, 70
clump, 216
CN, 2
CNIB, 2
co., 1
co-op, 257
coals to Newcastle, 111
cocktail lounge, 70
cod, 380

codeine, 260
colicky, 89
collateral damage, 193
colloquies, 529
coloration, 357
combine together, 526
comfort station, 193
committed, committing, 122
committee, 115
communicable, [communicatable], 3
compendium, compendia, 381
computerese, 191
concede, 100, 436
conceit, 260
concerto grosso, concerti grossi, 381
confer, 167; *conference*, 404
confidentially, 443
connection, 525
conscience, 260
consecutive days in a row, 526
consensus, general, 526
conspectus, 506
contact, 224
contend, 436
conveyer, conveyor, 190
cooperate, 257
coordinate, 257
copse, 216
corpus, corpora, 381, 506; *corpuses*, 506
cortex, cortices, 381
council, 115; *councillor*, 289
counterfeit, 260
courageous, 172
course of, during the, 525
courtly, 221
couth, 63
cover-up, 376
covetousness, 186
CP, 3
cranium, crania, 381
crazy, 172
crematorium, crematoria, 381
cricketana, 258
crisis, crises, 381

criticize, 465
crocus, croci, 381
CRTC, 3
cruising, 193
CSA, 3
CUPE, 2
cupful, 222
cursed, 175, 176
cutthroat, 257

dachshund, 95, 229
daughters-in-law, 380
day, 535
debatable, 3
declare, 436
declassification, 144
decriminalize, 144
de-emphasize, 144
de-energize, 144
deep, 459, 532; *deepness*, 338
defence, defense, defensible,
  defensive, 100
defer, 167
dehire, 144
de-ink, 144
delouse, 144
demagogue, 259
demigod, 441
demitasse, 441
demonstrable, [demonstratable],
  3
demonym, 335
demoralize, 286
dépanneur, 404
desegregate, 144
desk-bound, 82
destabilize, 193
determinant, 404
Deutschmark, 229
diarrhea, diarrhoea, 18
dictatable, 3
didn't, 2
Diefenbaker, 229
diesel, 229
differ, 167
difficultness, 338
disclose, 436

disillusionment, 144
distil, distill, 295
DNA, 1
dogged, 175
domino, 356
don't, 133
dreadful, 61
dreamt, 482
dud, 116
due to the fact that, 525
duly, 172
during the course of, 525
Dutch oven, 95
dwarf, 201
dyke, 227

eastbound, 82
easy, 15
eavesdrop, 168
echoes, 356
economize, 286
Edinburgh, 86
Edmontonian, 335
educable, [educatable], 3
EI, 3
either . . . or, 121
electric, electrical, 258
electrocution, 66
ellipsis, ellipses, 381
elves, 201
enrol, enroll, enrolment, 295
enthral, enthrall, enthralled,
  295
eon, 18
equal, 168
escalate, 63
esophagus, 18
esprit de corps, 221
EST, 3
esthetic, 18
estrogen, 18
event that, in the, 525
ever, 15
exceed, 100
excellent, 370
exception of, with the, 525
executor, 190

expect, 166
expel, expell, 162
extreme, 370; *extremely,*
  extremism, 172

fabliau, fabliaux, 381
faceable, 3
facet, 525
facsimile, 99
factor, 525
faculty, 115
faeces, 18
fairly, 14
Fallopian tubes, 95
family, 115
fanatic, fanatical, 258
fantastically, 400
fast, 459
favorite, favourite, 357; *most*
  favourite, 526
feces, 18
feign, 260
fetid, 18
fetus, 18
fiber, fibre, 416
fiddler, 208
Filipinos, 356
fill in, 260
finalize, 286
flashback, 223
flat, 532
fleet, 115
floral, 213
flourish, 213
focus, 167; *foci*, 381
foetid, 18
foetus, 18
follow-through, 376
for, 118
foreign, 260
foreman, 447
forfeit, 260
format, 223
formula, formulae, 381
foxes, 380
Franco-Prussian, 219
frankly, 443

Frau, 229
Fräulein, 229
free gift, 526
freight, 260
Freud, 229; *Freudian slip*, 458
friend, 260
frolicking, 89
function, 525
fungus, fungi, 381
future, near, 525

Gaspé, 95
gather together, 526
Gay Nineties, 95
Gaza Strip, 95
genera, 381, 506
generally, 443
genus, 381; *genuses*, 506
geographic, geographical, 258
gerbil, 95
get by, 260
gift, free, 526
gift horse, 111
giga, 535
glamorous, 357
global, 404-5
Gold Coast, 95
good for nothing, 110
go on about, 260
go out (with), 376
government, 115
governor-elect, 179
graffito, graffiti, 381
grantor, 190
graveness, 338
green, 224
grovel, 63
gruntled, 63
GST, 3

habitual, 1
haemophilia, 18
hallucination, 1
halves, 201
Hambletonian, 335
handicap, 168
handkerchiefs, 201

handoff, 223
handout, 376
harmonious, 1
Hatter, 335
have, 24; *have the heart to*, 259
health-minded, 325
heart to, have the, 259
hectare, 535
height, 260
Heinz, 229
heir, 1
hemisphere, 441
hemophilia, 18
here, 15
heroes, 356
heterosexism, 282
hiatus, 506
high, 532, 533; *high-minded*, 325
hippo, 2; *hippos*, 356
hippopotamuses, 506
historical, 1
HMCS, 3
hoeing, 172
holistic, 1; *holistically*, 400
Holstein, 95
homely, 221
honestly, 443
honorarium, 357
honorary, 357
honorific, 357
honour, 1; *honour-bound*, 82
hoof, 201
horrible, 61
horticulturalist, horticulturist, 283
hostess, 253
hour, 1; *hour*, 535
housebound, 82
housecleaner, 289
however, 444
human beings, humankind, 447
humorist, 357
humorous, 357
hush, 353
hyperthermic, hypothermic, 256
hypothesis, hypotheses, 381

hysterical, 1

I'm, 133
ignoramuses, 506
illegible, 4
Imam, 423
imitable, 3
impetus, 506
implausible, 4
in fact, 119
in spite of the fact that, 525
inaccessible, 4
inbound, 82
include, 125
incomprehensible, 4
indeed, 119
index, 224; *indices*, 381
individuals, 447
Indo-Caribbean, 271
inedible, 176
ineducable, 4
inexcusable, 4
infeasible, 206
infernos, 356
inflatable, 3
inimitable, 4
innocuous, 265
instance, 525
instil, instill, 295
integral, 327
intenseness, 338
intercede, 100
inveigle, 260
inward(s), 517
Irish coffee, 95
ironic, ironical, 258
irreparable, 4
irresponsible, 4
is, see *be*
ISBN, 3

jaeger, 229
jaywalk, 116
jockdom, 165
Johann, 229
joule, 535
journalese, 191

junior (student), 210
Jurassic period, 95

kangaroos, 356
keep your shirt on, 259
keister, 88
kelvin, 535
kerb, 465
kibitz, 287
kilogram, 535
kilometre, 535
kindly, 221
kitsch, 229
klutz, 286
knelt, 482
knives, 201

Labradorian, 335
Labrador retriever, 95
lady doctor, 289
larva, larvae, 381
lashes, 380
late, 15
laze, 63
leant, 482
leapt, 482
learned, 175; *learnt*, 482
leaves, 201
legalese, 191
leisure, 260
lemma, lemmata, 381
letter carrier, 289
licence, license, 100; *licensed premises*, 70
likable, likeable, 4
limited to only, 526
linage, 172
lineage, 172
litre, 535
livable, liveable, 4
loaves, 201
local, 224
look, 15; *look out, look up*, 260
lookism, 282
lounge, 70
lovable, loveable, 172
lovely, 15

low-lifes, 201
loyalness, 338
luster, lustre, 416

M.A., 2
Mach, 219
Madame, 2
Mademoiselle, 2
maestro, maestri, 381
mail carrier, 289
makeover, 376
male nurse, 289
manageable, 3
mango, 356
manipulate, 447; *manipulable*, 3
Manitoban, 335
manmade, 447
manpower, 447
manufacture, 447
manuscript, 447
marketwise, 523
Marxism, 282
matrix, matrices, 381
maverick, 401
Me Decade, 95
meager, meagre, 416
mega, 535
mercifully, 443
metamorphosis, metamorphoses, 381
meter, 416
methinks, 48
metre, meter, 416, 535
metric ton (tonne), 535
mgr., 1
microwavable, 4
Middle Ages, 95
Midwest, 95
mileage, 172
milieu, milieux, 381
millilitre, 535
mimicked, 89
minuses, 506
minute, 535
mischief, 260
mission statement, 111
MLA, 3

Mlle, 2
Mme, 2
model, 168
Moderator, 423
mole, 535
molly, 227
Monctonian, 335
Monsignor, 423
mont, 221
Montréalais(e), 335
Montrealer, 335
moose, 380
Moose Javian, Moose Jawanian, 335
more than, 467; *more ... than*, 121
Mormonism, 282
mosquito, 356
movable, moveable, 4
moviedom, 165
Mozart, 229
MP, 2
MPP, 3
muck-a-muck, muckety-muck, muckymuck, 377
multi-entry, 257
murmur, 353
muscle-bound, 82
musickal, 89
mythic, mythical, 258

namely, 116
narcissus, narcissi, 381
NATO, Nato, 2, 30
natural, 224; *naturally*, 119
Nazi, 229
near future, in the, 525
necessary prerequisite, 526
neighbour, 260
neither ... nor, 121
nevertheless, 119
New Brunswicker, New Brunswickian, 335
Newburgh, 86
Newcastle, coals to, 111
Newfoundlander, 335
newly-wed, newlywed, 257

newton, 535
nexus, 506
NFB, 3
NHL, 2
nighttime, 257
ninth, 172
no, 194; *no smoke without fire*, 110
nobody, 194; *nobody else('s)*, 179-80
noes, 356
non-profit, nonprofit, 257
non-stick, 257
noplace, 520
nor, 118
NORAD, 2
not only . . . but also, 362
nucleus, nuclei, 381
nurse, 289

oasis, oases, 381
obloquies, 529
OC, 3
odor, odour, odoriferous, 357
oesophagus, 18
oestrogen, 18
of course, 119
offence, offense, offensive, 100
offer, 167
officialdom, 165
often, 15
oh, 119
ongoing, 169
Ontario, 433; *Ontarian*, 335
opera, 381, 506
opus, 381; *opuses*, 506
or, 23, 39
organize, organisation, organization, 286
Ottawan, 335
Ottawa Valley, 95
[ourself], 440, 441
outbound, 82
outward(s), 517
oxen, 380

p., 1

Pacific Rim, 95
palomino, 95
Panhandle, the, 95
papyrus, papyri, 381
parachute, 361
paraglider, 361
paralyse, paralyze, 286
paramedic, 361
paramilitary, 361
paranormal, 361
parapraxis, 458
parasailing, 361
parasol, 361
paratrooper, 361
parent, 223
pass away, 193
passers-by, 380
PCBs, 3
peccadillo, 265
Pegger, 335
Pekinese, 95
people, 447
per diem, 298
perhaps, 119
permafrost, 2
personally, 443
Peterborough, Peterboro, 86
photos, 356
piano, 116
picnicker, 89
piercèd, 154
Pittsburgh, 86
placable, 3
plateau, plateaux, 381
Platonism, 282
platypuses, 506
play-off, playoff, 376
plexus, 506
plop, 353
PMO, 1
poets laureate, 380
point in time, at this, 525
ponies, 380
population, 405
potatoes, 356
PQ, 3
practice, practise, 100

Precambrian era, 95
precede, 100
predate, pre-date, 257
predict in advance, 526
prefer, 167
pre-issue, 257
prepackaged, 41
prerequisite, necessary, 526
preseason, 41
president-elect, 179
pretence, pretense, 100
pre-trip, 257
Prince Edward Islander, 335
princely, 221
prioritize, 286
prison, 286
probably, 443
problem, 525
proceed, 100
professor, 405
profitwise, 523
proofs, 201
prospectus, 506
protein, 260
PST, 3
pushoff, 376
put up with, 260

quantum, quanta, 381
queen, 96, 227
queer, 227
Quiet Revolution, 95
quixotic, 95

Rabbi, 423
raccoon, 465
racist, 283
radios, 356
radius, radii, 381
range, 115
rascally, 221
ratios, 356
RCMP, 2
realistically, 400
realize, realization, 286
reason being, the, 116
rebel, 415

reborrow, 415
rebuses, 506
recall, 415
recede, 100
receive, 260
recognize, 286
recover, 416; *re-cover*, 257, 416
recyclable, 4
re-elect, 415
re-enter, 415
re-examine, 257
refer, 167
refill, 415
reform, re-form, 416
refreeze, 415
Reich, 229
reign, 260
rein, 260
reinvestigate, 415
reject, 415
rekindle, 415
relieve, 260
remake, 415
remarkably, 14
Renaissance, 95
repay, 416
resign, re-sign, 416
resister, resistor, 190
reveal, 436
Reverend, 423
revision, 62
revolution, 535
right, 532, 533; *right-minded*, 325
rigorous, 357
RMC, 3
roadhouse, 70
robin, 95, 464
roman type, 95
roofs, 201
root-bound, 82
RRSP, 3
RSC, 3
runneth, 48

safes, 201
Saint Johner, 335

salable, saleable, 4
salarywise, 523
salesgirl, saleslady, sales representative, 289
saleswise, 523
salmon, 380
saloon, 70
saltchuck, 377
same, 197
sans, 221
SASE, 3
Saskatchewaner, Saskatchewanian, 335
Scarborough, 86
scarf, 201
schema, schemata, 381
Schiller, 229
schnapps, 229
schnitzel, 229
scholarly, 15, 221
science, 260
secede, 100
second, 535
security, 405
seem, 15, 166, 171
seize, 260
selves, 201
semi-automatic, 441
semi-detached, 441
semi-monthly, 441
semi-retired, 441
semi-serious, 441
senior (student), 210
seriously, 443
setup, 376
sexist, 283
Shakespeareana, Shakespeariana, 258
sheaves, 201
sheep, 380
sheik, 260
shelves, 201
shocking, 61
shoeing, 172
short, 224
should've, 133
shut-in, 376

Siamese cat, 95
sidle, 63
signal, 168
simile, 99
SIN, 3
sincereness, 338
singeing, 172
single-minded, 325
sinus, 506
situation, 525
sizable, sizeable, 4
sizzle, 353
skiffs, 201
slave driver, slave-driver, 257
slip-on, 376
smelt, 482
smoke without fire, no, 110
snowbound, 82
so, 118; *so . . . that*, 121
soliloquies, 529
somber, sombre, 416
somebody, someone, 194; *somebody else('s)*, 180
sophomore, 210
sound, 15
sour grapes, 111
southbound, 82
sovereign, 260
speakeasy, 70
specialize, specialization, 286
species, 260; *speciesism*, 282
specter, spectre, 416
spectrum, spectra, 381
speedometer, 66
spellbound, 82
spies, 380
spilt, 482
spinney, 216
spiral, 223
spoilt, 482
squish, 353
SSHRCC, 2
St. Johnsian, 335
staffs, 201
state, 525
stately, 15
stationary engineer, 289

status, 506; *status quo*, 298
stein, 229
stiff upper lip, 111
still lifes, 201
stormbound, 82
streak, 223
streetwise, 523
streptococcus, streptococci, 381
strophe, 99
stylus, styli, 381
subject area, 526
succeed, 100
successes, 380
such as, 116
sufficient, 260
Sunshine Coast, 95
supervise, 286; *supervisor*, 447
suppose, 166
surprise, 286; *surprisingly*, 443
surveil, 63
swinging, 193
syllabus, syllabi, 381
synopsis, synopses, 381
synthetic, 447

tableau, tableaux, 381
take off, 260; *takeoff*, 376
takeout, 376
takeover, 223
tap (telephone), 86
taproom, 70
tavern, 70
team, 115
telepathy, mental, 526
televise, 62; *television*, 66
temporary, 224; *on a temporary basis*, 525
temps, 221
tempus fugit, 297
terminus, termini, 381
terrible, 61
terrorize, 286
thankfully, 443
Thatcherism, 282
that is, 116
theater, theatre, 416
thee, 48

[themself], 440-1
therefore, 444
there's, 133
thesis, theses, 381
they're, 133
thieves, 201
thing, 525
though, 119
tip of the iceberg, 110-11
together, 15
toilet, 193
tomatoes, 356
ton, tonne (metric), 535
too, 14
top of, be on, 259
Torontonian, 335
torpedoes, 356
total, 168
toward(s), 517
traceable, 3
trafficking, 89
transgendered people, 447
translatable, 3
transsexual, 447
travel, 168; *travelwise*, 523
truly, 172
TSE, 3
Turkish bath, 95
turn-on, 376
'twas, 48
type, 525
tyre, 465

ugly, 15
UI, 3
umlaut, 153
UN, 2
un-Canadian, 257
uncomfortable, 4
uneatable, 176
unfeasible, 206
unfriendly, 224
UNICEF, Unicef, 2, 30
unpresentable, 4
unworkable, 4
upcoming, 169
U.S., 2

USC, 3
uterus, uteri, 381

valorize, 357
Vancouverite, 335
vehicular, 240
veil, 260
vein, 260
Venerable, 423
venetian blinds, 95
verify, 405
verily, 48
very, 15
vetoes, 356
Victoriana, 258
vigorous, 357
viruses, 506
volcanoes, 356
VON, 3
VSE, 3

Wagner, 229
walk-on, 376
Walpoliana, 258
warmness, 338
washroom, 193
watt, 535
WCB, 3
weather conditions, 526
weathergirl, weatherman, weather reporter, 289
we'd, 133
weigh, 260
well, 14, 15
Weltanschauung, 229
wharf, 201
whisky jack, whisky-john, 214
whisper, 353
whiteness, 172
whizz, 353
WHO, 3
who else('s), 180
wholly, 172
whosoever, 48
wide, 15, 459
wifedom, 165
wind-up, 223

Winnipegger, 335
wives, 201
wolves, 201
woman doctor, 289
woollen, 465
worker, 289
work force, 447

worship, 168
wouldn't, 133
wright, 379
wrong, 532, 533

year, 535
yet, 118

younger, 178
Yukon, 433; *Yukoner*, 335
yuppiedom, 165

zero, 356
zigzag, 168
zoom, 353

THE CANADIAN
OXFORD DICTIONARY

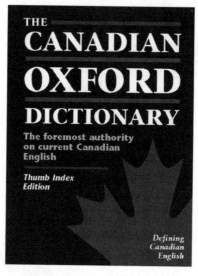

The *Canadian Oxford Dictionary* establishes a new authoritative standard for dictionaries in Canada. This book serves Canadians like no other dictionary, answering their basic questions about the language by giving them advice on Canadian spelling and usage, and defining more Canadian words and senses (almost 2000) than any other dictionary. With about 140,000 words, it combines in one reference book information on English as it is used worldwide and as it is used particularly in Canada. Definitions, worded for ease of comprehension, are presented within entries in order of their familiarity or frequency in Canadian usage, making the dictionary easy to consult.

The dictionary is exceptionally reliable in its description of Canadian English because it is based on thorough research into the language. It represents five years of work by five professionally trained Canadian lexicographers examining almost 20 million words of Canadian text, and another 20 million words of American, British, Australian, and other international English sources. These databases represent over 8000 different Canadian sources. Favoured Canadian pronunciations have been determined by surveying a nationwide group of respondents.

An added feature of this dictionary is its encyclopedic element. It includes short biographies of over 1000 Canadians and 4000 individuals and mythical figures of international significance, and over 5000 place names, more than 1200 of them Canadian.

With the publication of the *Canadian Oxford Dictionary*, Oxford University Press adds another work to its highly respected range of dictionaries.

Publication date: June 1998

ISBN: 0-19-541120-X